WILLIAM MORRIS

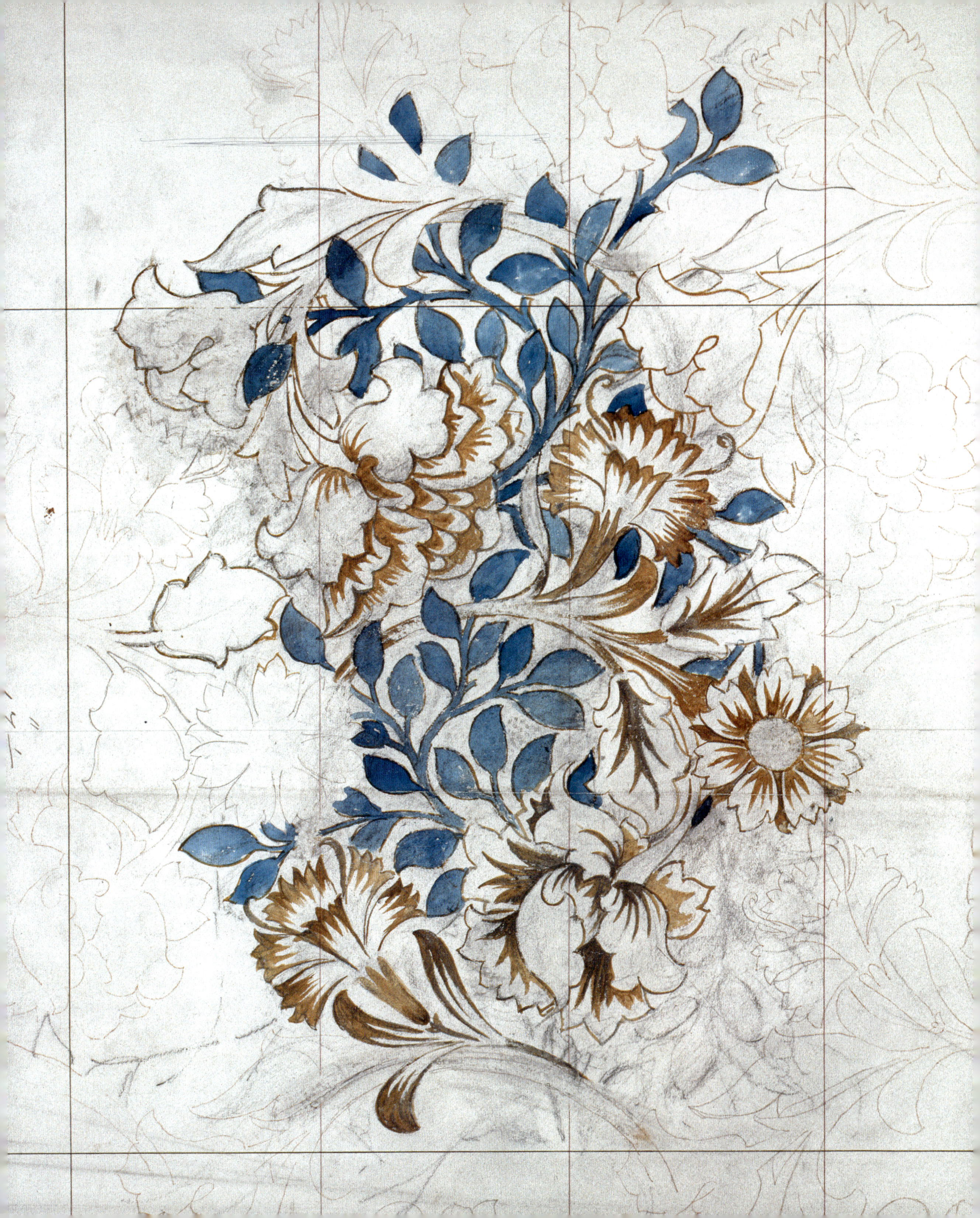

WILLIAM MORRIS

Edited by Anna Mason

Thames & Hudson | V&A

Publisher's Note
This volume is a completely revised, updated and expanded edition of *William Morris*, edited by Linda Parry, published by Philip Wilson Publishers to coincide with the exhibition *William Morris 1834–1896* held at the Victoria and Albert Museum, London, in 1996.

The editor of this edition, Anna Mason, has also revised and updated the texts for Chapters IV, IX, X and XIV from the 1996 publication. Where applicable, other chapters have been revised by the original authors.

Note on Object Descriptions
All entries are written by authors of individual chapters unless denoted by initials:

SA	Stephen Astley
MB	Mary Bennett
LP	Linda Parry
ET	Eric Turner

Measurements are in centimetres, height then width then depth.

Frontispiece: Design for *Poppy*, also known as *Pink and Poppy*, William Morris, April 1880 (see XI.20a). William Morris Society, Kelmscott House, London

This edition first published in the United Kingdom in 2021 by
Thames & Hudson Ltd, 181A High Holborn, London WC1V 7QX
in association with the Victoria and Albert Museum, London

This edition first published in the United States of America in 2021 by
Thames & Hudson Inc., 500 Fifth Avenue, New York, New York 10110

Reprinted 2022

Designed by Ocky Murray

British Library Cataloguing-in-Publication Data
A catalogue record for this book is available from the British Library

Library of Congress Control Number 2021933964

ISBN 978-0-500-48050-2

Printed and bound in China by RR Donnelley

FSC www.fsc.org MIX Paper from responsible sources FSC® C144853

CONTENTS

PREFACE

Anna Mason

'History (so called) has remembered the kings and warriors, because they destroyed; Art has remembered the people, because they created.'

William Morris, 'The Art of the People', 1879

This book, published to mark the 125th anniversary of William Morris's death, explores the art, life and ideas of one of Britain's most extraordinary cultural figures. Morris was both a visionary and a man of action, working determinedly to democratize art and bring about a radical new social equality. For Morris, these two things were inseparable – art could only thrive in a world where everyone could live alongside nature in self-respect and dignity with the opportunity to participate in creative activity. His rage at the damage caused to the environment by industrialization and over-consumption drove his life's work. As he argued in his lecture 'Art and the Beauty of the Earth' (1881), 'surely there is no square mile of earth's inhabitable surface that is not beautiful in its own way, if we men will only abstain from wilfully destroying that beauty'. All human endeavour, he argued, including art, should enhance the natural world, not detract from it. His ideas about how to live, and what constitutes a meaningful life, remain as vital and inspiring as ever.

First published in 1996, this book accompanied the V&A's landmark exhibition, *William Morris 1834–1896*, held on the occasion of Morris's centenary year. The most comprehensive and ambitious exhibition ever mounted on his life and work inspired a new wave of scholarship and generated enormous public interest. Conceived and curated by Linda Parry, former Deputy Keeper of the Department of Furniture, Textiles and Fashion at the V&A, it was a watershed moment in Morris studies and the book has remained indispensable for anyone interested in his work ever since. It is also far more than a monograph on a single artist. The collaborative way in which Morris worked means that this book is additionally an important study of his decorating business, Morris & Co., and the many artists and craftspeople with whom he co-operated.

This revised, updated and substantially expanded edition incorporates new discoveries and research, generated in part by the excitement and momentum that followed the centenary exhibition. Significant developments have included the National Trust's acquisition of Red House, Morris's first marital home, in 2003. A meticulous decade-long programme of conservation and investigation at the property has transformed understanding of what the interiors looked like in Morris's day, revealing just how radical and unusual they were. Other material in private hands has since entered public institutions and thus become more accessible for study. Most notable in this category is the rich collection assembled by Sanford and Helen Berger that was acquired in 1999 by the Huntington Library and Art Museum, San Marino, California. Unique objects, such as the spectacular hand-knotted carpet with a design of peacocks and birds (see XII.96), have also come to light in the intervening years and are presented here. Just as this volume was going to press, the V&A acquired one of the medals of commendation awarded to Morris's newly founded firm at the 1862 International Exhibition, the first public display of its wares and a prelude to the success that was to follow.

Research into Morris's collaborators has expanded exponentially over the last two and half decades. This is particularly true for the designer and architect Philip Webb and Thomas Wardle, dyer and printer of Leek in Staffordshire. Edward Burne-Jones, Ford Madox Brown and Dante Gabriel Rossetti have all been the subject of major exhibitions and monographs that have brought new information and perspectives to bear. Research into the women connected with Morris and the firm, particularly his wife, Jane, and daughter May Morris, has enabled a much fuller picture of their achievements and personalities to emerge. Studies of many of the leading architects of the era, not least George Frederick Bodley, whose patronage was so important to the firm, have also proved invaluable. We extend our warmest appreciation to all those scholars, many of whom are thanked in the acknowledgments, whose work has enriched this project in so many ways.

As well as research into individual artists and designers, there have been numerous important studies that help set Morris's ideas and achievements in wider contexts. As one example, the conservation movement in Britain and internationally has been the focus of much new scholarship since the late 1990s and brings fresh perspectives to Morris's work in this field. Similarly, art historians have approached the Victorian interior from different angles, with a greater concentration on the role and preoccupations of the consumer or client. Even in a book of this length it is only possible to touch on some of these developments, but it is hoped that it will play a role in stimulating further investigation. It is, for example, a mine of information on many of the clients for whom Morris & Co. worked, and the properties that were furnished. Many of these projects would repay further exploration and help to establish patterns of patronage and consumer tastes.

The institutions and societies that care for, present and debate Morris's legacy today deserve special mention. It is very appropriate that the V&A, a museum that Morris delighted in and used his expertise to support, should lead this project. Crucial encouragement has also come from the William Morris Gallery in Walthamstow, the William Morris Societies in the UK and the US, Kelmscott Manor owned by the Society of Antiquaries of London, the National Trust and the Society for the Protection of Ancient Buildings. Many individuals are thanked in the acknowledgments, but here we also pay tribute to all the staff, volunteers, artists and creative practitioners, past and present, who work to create vibrant, exciting opportunities for the public to engage with his legacy. In addition, we are grateful to all those who have provided new photography.

If this publication conveys the complexity, originality and radical spirit of Morris and his co-workers it will have succeeded. Morris knew how lucky he was to have stimulating work that brought him joy and creative fulfilment and his hope was to build a society in which this would be possible for everyone.

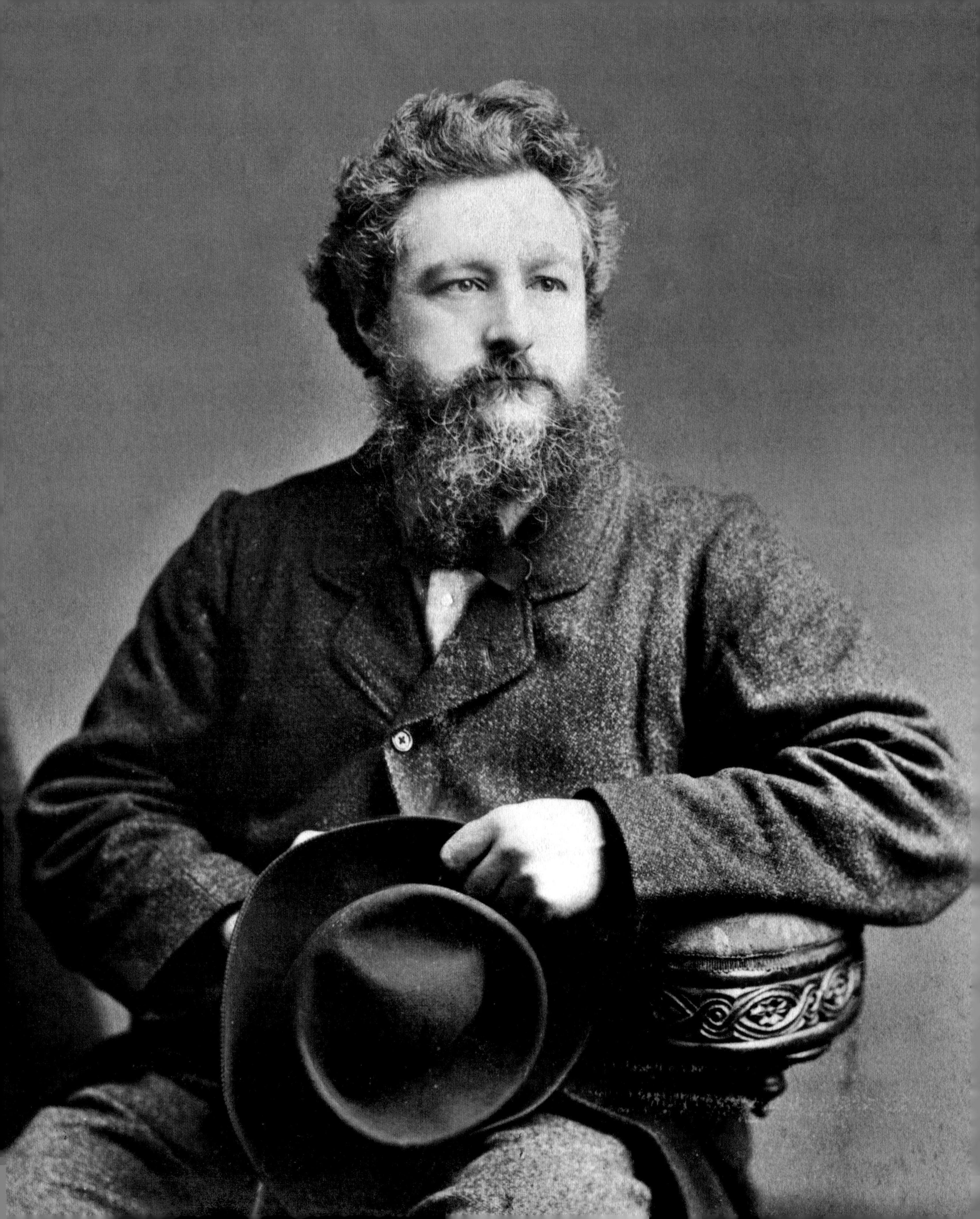

INTRODUCTION

Anna Mason

'What business have we with art at all unless all can share it?'

William Morris to the editor of *The Manchester Examiner*, March 1883

Fig.1 **William Morris, photographed by Elliott & Fry, 21 March 1877.**
William Morris Gallery

The versatility of William Morris (1834–1896) is legendary. Known to his contemporaries as a designer, craftsman, decorator and successful man of business, he was also a best-selling poet and storyteller. The most high-profile artist to embrace socialism, through his campaigning activities, journalism and creative writing he offered both a devastating critique of the inequalities of Victorian society and a positive and hopeful vision of what a fairer, and greener, future might look like.

Morris's love and sympathy for nature, immediately apparent from his designs, was a strong unifying thread through his life's work. Equally important was his passion for medieval buildings of all shapes and sizes, from the soaring Gothic cathedrals of northern France to the tithe barns, cottages and dovecots of rural England. For Morris, these buildings were as much a natural part of the landscape as the hedgerows and the songbirds. He imbued them with human qualities and these structures epitomized what he defined as a truly 'popular art', built by people who were sensitive to the beauty of their surroundings, understood their materials and took pleasure in their work.

The idea that art reflects the condition of the society in which it is made, as well as helping to shape that society, was very current in the 1850s when Morris came of age. Its most famous exponent was the art critic John Ruskin, whose influence on Morris is explored throughout this book and cannot be overstated. Other pioneering designers and architects, including A.W.N. Pugin and one of Morris's most important early mentors, George Edmund Street, not only shared this belief, but also sought to reunite architecture with the decorative arts through their work and practical example. In their view, the exterior form and interior detail of a building went hand in hand; both should be treated as part of one harmonious whole and were equally deserving of serious artistic consideration.

Even among the strongest supporters of Britain's industrial 'progress', it was recognized from the 1830s that design standards needed to improve to compete successfully in global markets. Various initiatives, including new government-sponsored design schools, were established to meet this need. Narratives of Morris's life and work frequently begin with his refusal to visit the Great Exhibition of 1851; apparently even as a 17-year-old he set himself in opposition to that hugely popular wonder of the industrial age. While this episode is revealing of his rebellious teenage spirit, not everyone took such a dim view of the exhibits. Some design reformers saw signs of progress, and out of this project came the Museum of Ornamental Art, later renamed the South Kensington Museum (today the V&A), a lifelong source of inspiration and delight for Morris.

Morris was not a lone genius in a single-handed crusade against the age. The objects, interiors, works of literature and hard-fought campaigns described in this book tell a very different story. Morris's talent for collaboration, for recognizing ability in others and creating opportunities for men and women to combine their skills to create something greater than the sum of their parts is one of his most compelling legacies. His voracious appetite for work, exacting standards of craftsmanship and the challenges he continually set himself undoubtedly inspired those around him, as did his personal integrity. The various strands of his activities – artistic, literary and political – were all powered by his anger at the damage wrecked by unchecked industrialization and his conviction that there must be better, less wasteful and more beautiful ways to live.

In this publication leading scholars introduce different aspects of Morris's life and work. Divided into three sections, part one investigates his life through the lens of his principal occupations – as a designer and maker, writer, entrepreneur, political activist and conservationist. Part two explores in detail the artworks, furnishings, interiors and books created by Morris and his collaborators. Experts in different media place these achievements in context, combining close analysis of individual objects with a wider consideration of how they were originally used, both in public settings and in the home. The careful attention that Morris himself paid to materials and techniques makes it essential to engage closely with the intricacies of each medium, be it stained glass, tiles, wallpaper or the huge variety of textiles that he created. At the same time, each contributor is attuned to the high degree of cross-fertilization in his work, the way that one activity spurred on another. A chapter on interior decoration considers how furnishings were used in combination and the exciting new ways that Morris and his decorating company responded to the specifics of client, location and function.

In part three, Morris's relationship with the V&A is fruitfully examined as a microcosm of his ideas about art, equality and education. An essay on Morris and the Arts and Crafts Movement explores some of the ways that his ideas were taken up and expanded upon, both across the British Isles and internationally, signposting readers to the rich scholarship on this subject. Since his death in 1896, interest in Morris has remained intense and each generation has found different things to admire. In recent decades there has been a strong and welcome move to engage with Morris the polymath. Rather than treating his diverse pursuits in isolation from one another, writers

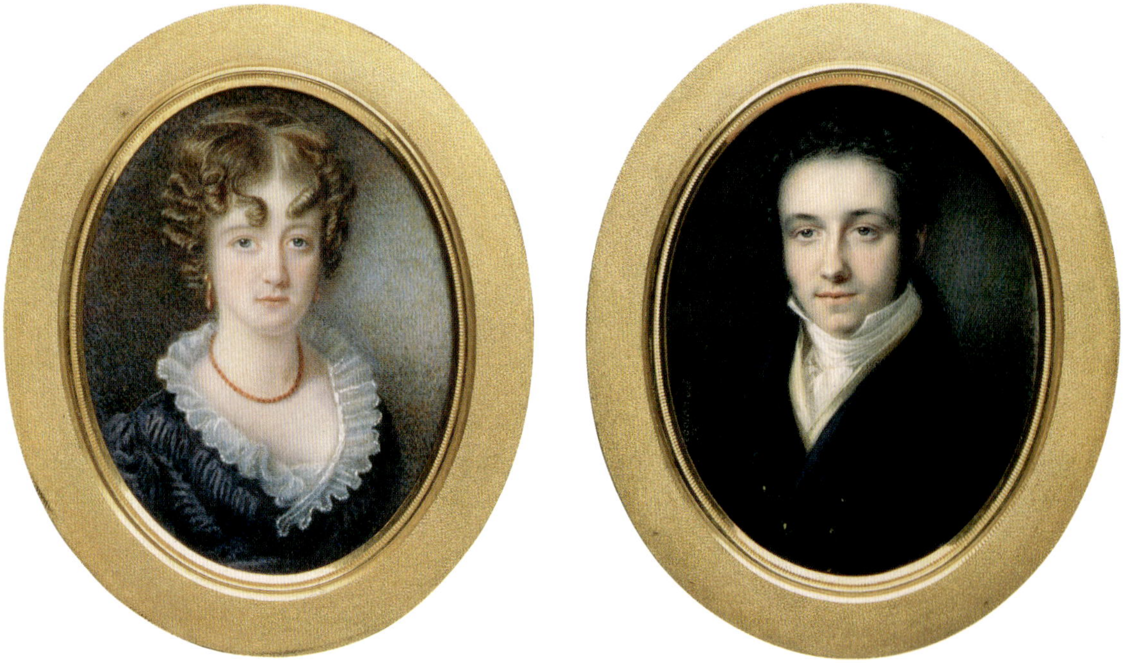

Fig.2 **Portrait miniatures of Emma Shelton Morris and William Morris Senior, probably commissioned to mark their engagement in 1824.**
William Morris Gallery

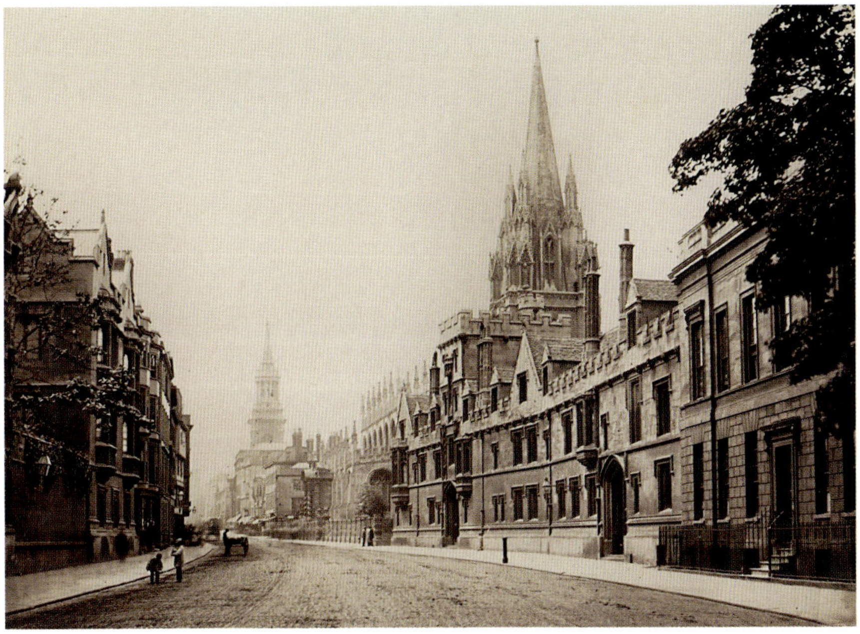

Fig.3 **High Street, Oxford, 1860.**

and researchers have taken an increasingly cross-disciplinary approach, teasing out the common themes and motivations driving all his work. To set the scene for what follows, this introduction combines a biographical overview of his life with a sense of his ideas as they evolved.

William Morris was born Walthamstow in 1834, the third child and eldest surviving son of William Morris Senior and Emma Shelton Morris (fig.2). His father was a city broker and the area, then part of Essex, was conveniently close to London while retaining its rural character. The family prospered, particularly after Morris Senior invested in a new copper-mining enterprise, Devon Great Consols. In its heyday in the 1850s it was the largest copper producer in Europe. After Morris Senior's unexpected death in 1847, on the eve of a financial disaster that caused his bill-broking firm to collapse, it was income from the mine that secured his family's future and later gave Morris the financial independence to pursue a career in art.

The flat marshy Essex countryside, and particularly Epping Forest, was the young boy's playground, he knew it 'yard by yard'. Between 1840 and 1848, the family lived at Woodford Hall, a Palladian-style mansion with extensive parkland and well-stocked kitchen gardens. After Morris Senior's death, his widow and nine children moved to Water House, a comfortable but more modest dwelling, now the William Morris Gallery. Emma Shelton Morris, eager that her son should pursue a career in the Church, invested in his education. His father had already secured him a place at Marlborough College in Wiltshire, then a recently founded boarding school, popular with clergymen's sons. Though Morris later claimed he learnt 'next to nothing there', he had access to its fine library and acquired a thorough grounding in Latin and Greek. The surrounding countryside scattered with ancient woodlands and prehistoric monuments captured his imagination.

Morris was fortunate in his next instructor. Withdrawn from Marlborough at the end of 1851, his mother engaged the Reverend Frederick Guy to prepare him to sit his Oxford entrance exams. Guy was a member of the Oxford Architectural Society in the 1840s and seems to have shared and encouraged his pupil's visual tastes. It was to Guy that Morris appealed when nearly a decade later he was seeking business and contacts for his new decorating venture.

The ancient buildings of Oxford were among the most powerful influences on Morris's developing artistic consciousness (fig.3). When he arrived at Exeter College in 1853 the city was still largely fifteenth century in character, built predominantly of grey limestone. Although a few collegiate buildings had been constructed in the Baroque style in the seventeenth and eighteenth centuries, the medieval townscape was legible. As his biographer Fiona MacCarthy describes with such skill, Morris's sensitivity to his environment was acute. The small, intimate scale of the city, surrounded by meadows and orchards, enthralled him. In later years, as the pace of redevelopment accelerated, Morris defended the historic fabric of Oxford with the same loyalty and passion that he brought to his closest friendships.

At university he met Edward Burne-Jones (then just plain Ned Jones) and so began one of the most creative partnerships of his life. Initially fired up with religious zeal and plans to establish a monastic order, the friends soon found their energies were absorbed by art and literature, inspired in large part by Ruskin's *The Stones of Venice* (1851–3). As Julia Griffin explores in Chapter VI, Ruskin's advocacy of the Pre-Raphaelites and first-hand encounters with their work changed the direction of their lives. Burne-Jones, the son of a Birmingham framer and gilder, introduced Morris to a group of talented friends from his native city, including Cormell (Crom) Price, Charles Faulkner and Richard Watson Dixon. Through them he became more aware of the industrial realities and inequalities of Victorian Britain. He lost his religious belief but in its place discovered a new faith in the transformative power of art and fellowship.

Morris's travels in France and Belgium during the long vacations deepened his admiration for medieval art and architecture. Some of his earliest responses are recorded in his contributions to *The Oxford and Cambridge Magazine* (fig.4), a literary and cultural periodical that he founded in 1856 with his university friends, inspired by the short-lived Pre-Raphaelite journal *The Germ*. His essays in particular explore the strong emotional connection he felt to the anonymous craftsmen who built, carved and decorated the Gothic cathedrals of northern France. For Morris, their work was so skilled, so full of individuality and character, it allowed them to communicate across time, 'those same builders, still surely living, still real men, and capable of receiving love, I love no less … than my breathing friends whom I can see looking kindly on me now' ('Shadows of Amiens', February 1856). The sight of the cathedrals against the backdrop of the verdant French countryside filled him with joy. However, there was already a keen sense in his letters that all this beauty, natural and man-made, was under threat from modern society. He vented his anger at insensitive restoration and the 'nasty, brimstone, noisy, shrieking railway train that cares not twopence for hill or valley'.

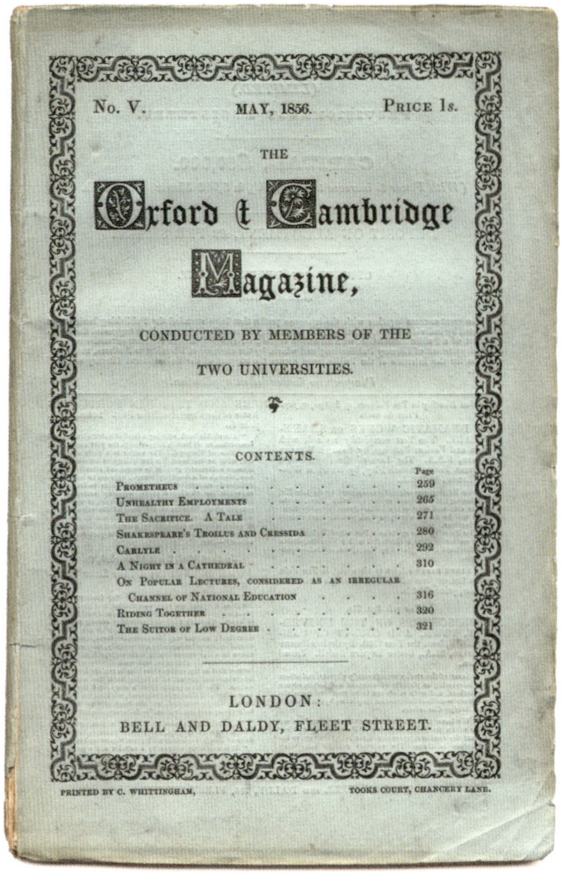
No. V. MAY, 1856. Price 1s.

THE

Oxford & Cambridge

Magazine,

CONDUCTED BY MEMBERS OF THE

TWO UNIVERSITIES.

CONTENTS.

	Page
Prometheus	259
Unhealthy Employments	265
The Sacrifice. A Tale	271
Shakespeare's Troilus and Cressida	280
Carlyle	292
A Night in a Cathedral	310
On Popular Lectures, considered as an irregular Channel of National Education	316
Riding Together	320
The Suitor of Low Degree	321

LONDON:

BELL AND DALDY, FLEET STREET.

PRINTED BY C. WHITTINGHAM, TOOKS COURT, CHANCERY LANE.

Fig.4 ***The Oxford and Cambridge Magazine*, May 1856.**
William Morris Gallery

Fired up by his experiences in France, Morris decided to become an architect. In January 1856 he signed his articles with Street, diocesan architect for Oxford and a leading exponent of the Gothic Revival. Though this apprenticeship lasted only nine months, it exposed Morris to new possibilities in the decorative arts. Street held craftsmanship in high regard and was particularly knowledgeable about embroidery. He encouraged his protégés to gain hands-on experience of different craft disciplines in their spare time, a challenge that Morris took up with enthusiasm. In his churches and domestic buildings, Street was adept at exploiting the natural qualities of his materials and creating bold harmonies of pattern, colour and texture. His working methods, in which he personally controlled every aspect of the design process, may have been frustrating for those working under him but it was fertile training ground.

Morris was supervised by Street's chief assistant, Philip Webb, and they quickly discovered their shared love of vernacular buildings and the English countryside. A few years older than Morris, Webb grew up in Oxford where his father practised as a doctor. He went straight from school into his architectural training and so had considerably more practical experience when they met. In different but equally significant ways, this lasting friendship was to prove as productive as Morris's relationship with Burne-Jones. Their personalities were complementary. Morris was boisterous, subject to sudden enthusiasms and occasional fits of explosive rage. Webb by contrast was self-controlled and modest, with an extreme aversion to any kind of self-publicity. Beneath these differences in temperament, their values and outlook were very closely aligned. Both were to become socialists and together they played a leading role in the conservation movement. Webb's contribution to the success of Morris's decorating business is a recurring theme throughout this book.

In the late 1850s Morris threw himself into an astonishing range of creative activities. Inspired by a new friendship with the Pre-Raphaelite painter and poet Dante Gabriel Rossetti he took up life-drawing and painting. Towards the end of 1856 he left Street's office to pursue this full time but even then he continued to experiment with multiple disciplines including calligraphy and embroidery. Together with Burne-Jones, Rossetti and most probably Webb, he designed and decorated furnishings for the lodgings he shared with Burne-Jones in Red Lion Square, Bloomsbury (fig.156). The surviving painted furniture and textiles, discussed in detail in Chapters VI, IX and XII, are vitally important evidence of their developing tastes and collaborative way of working. A sense of Morris's ideal interior in this period can be gleaned from his oil painting *La Belle Iseult* (see VI.12). In its sophisticated layering of different patterns and textures, colour palette of deep blues and reds, and the careful selection of found objects, Morris was feeling his way as a designer.

Having declared his hand for art, his first foray into the public arena was his contribution to the decoration of the Oxford Union debating hall. A group of artists, led by Rossetti, undertook to paint the upper walls of the chamber with scenes from Arthurian legend (fig.21). It was a brave, even foolhardy, experiment. With no experience of mural painting or working on such a vast scale, they nevertheless attacked the challenge with great spirit. The results, discussed in detail in this volume, were mixed but the project was formative. For the rest of his life, Morris took on seemingly impossible challenges, learning through the process of doing. Each artist worked on their own mural but Morris also designed a patterned ceiling, an early instance of his impulse to tie together or unify the contributions of others. This is an important skill in its own right, one he was to develop especially in regard to stained glass. His ability to harmonize the work of different artists while retaining their individual character would prove to be a major factor in his success.

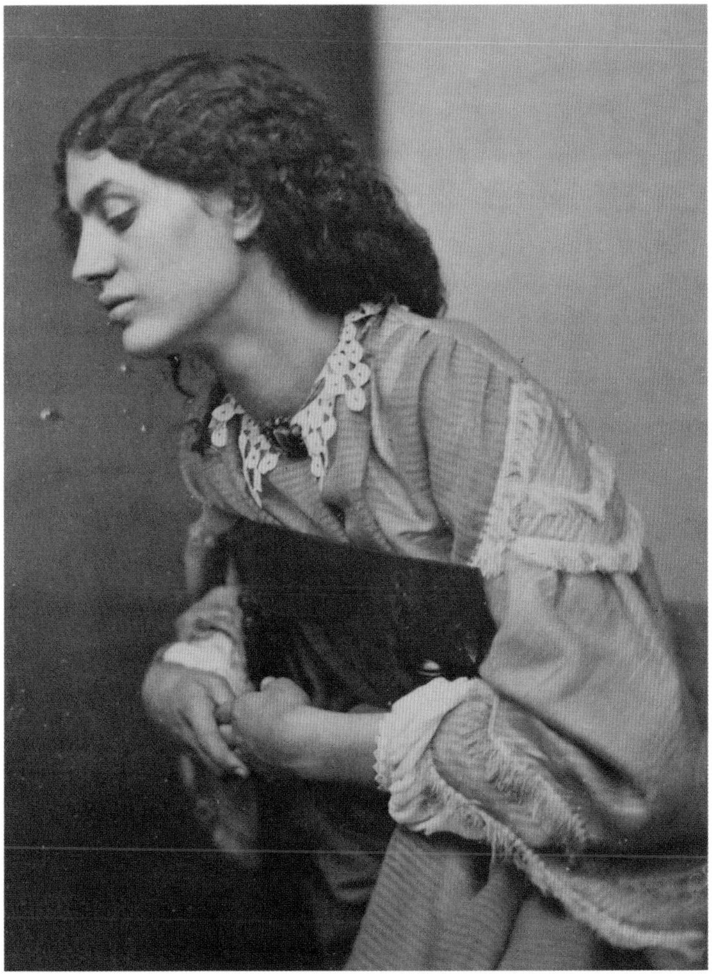

Fig.5 **Jane Burden, unknown photographer, 1858.**
V&A (1735–1939)
Presented by Dr Robert Steele

In the autumn of 1857, when work on the murals was well underway, Rossetti and Burne-Jones approached Jane Burden at a performance of the Drury Lane Theatre Company in Oxford. Attracted by her striking, yet unconventional, looks they persuaded her to model for them and thus Morris was introduced to his future wife (fig.5). Like Webb, Jane grew up in Oxford but in very different circumstances. Her father, Robert Burden, worked as a stablehand and her mother, Ann Maizey, who was illiterate, probably came to Oxford to seek employment as a domestic servant. Jane had only a rudimentary education and was most likely already in service when they met. A vast class divide separated them but Morris cared little for convention. He had the financial freedom to make his own decisions and proposed. Jane embraced the opportunity to raise herself and her family out of poverty and expand her own cultural horizons. Her surviving correspondence, edited by Jan Marsh and Frank Sharp (2012), reveals her lively and inquisitive mind. Though their marriage was to face many challenges, Morris had found a partner who was fundamentally sympathetic to his outlook on life and willing and able to participate in many of his creative endeavours. His new-found experience of romantic love fed into his first volume of poetry, *The Defence of Guenevere*, published in 1858. These early poems, discussed further in Chapter II, are deeply sensuous, evoking a medieval world full of colour, violence and complex female characters.

Soon after their engagement, Morris enlisted Webb to design the couple a house 'very mediaeval in spirit'. Red House was Webb's first independent commission (fig.6). The site was chosen with care, a modest one-acre orchard plot in Bexleyheath, Kent, close to the ancient pilgrim route to Canterbury.

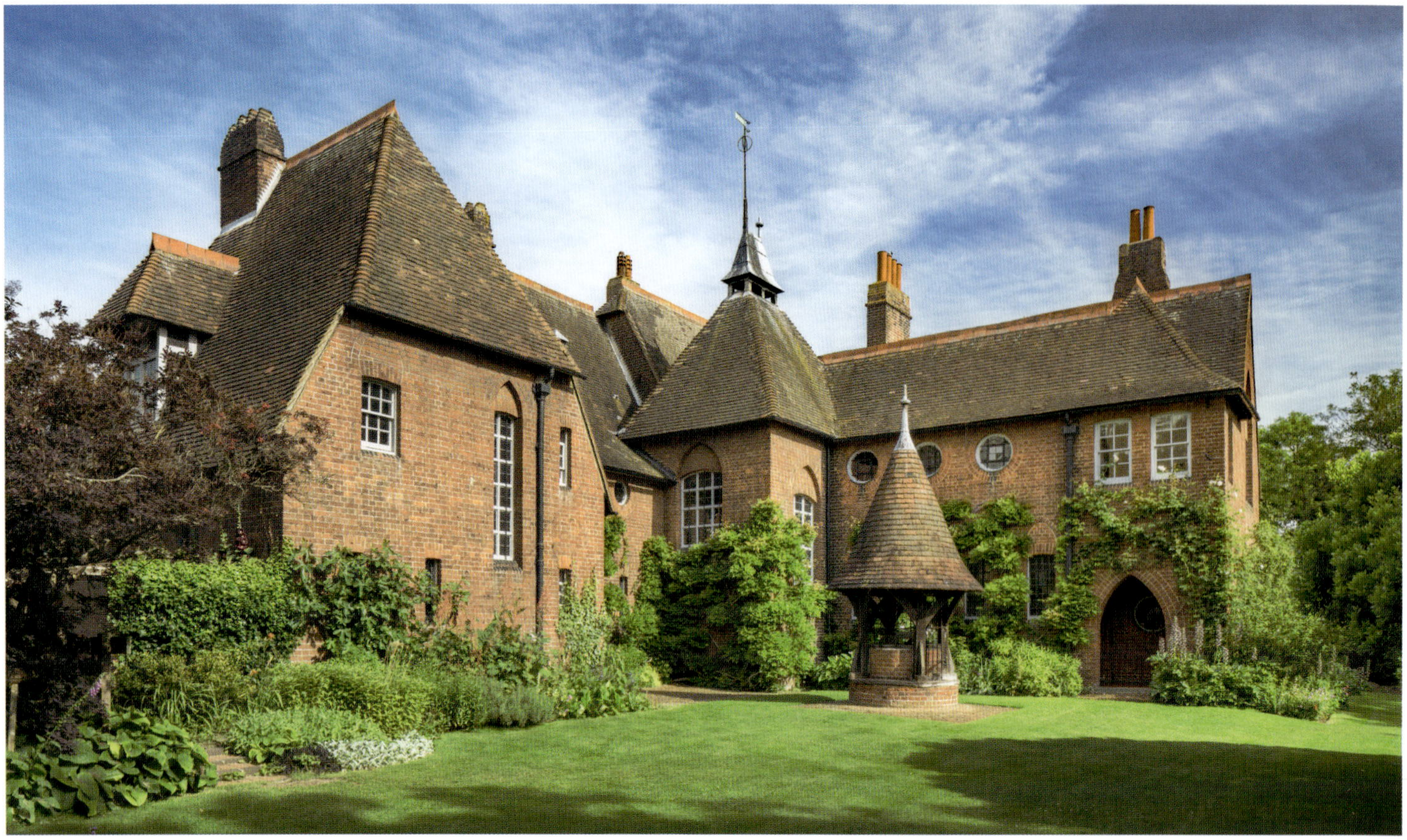

Fig.6 **Red House, Bexleyheath, from the south. The two open sides of the 'well court' were enclosed by wattle fences in Morris's day.**
National Trust

The house, garden and interiors were conceived as one entity, a series of interflowing spaces in which boundaries between indoors and outdoors were deliberately blurred. Partly inspired by the parsonages and school buildings of Street and William Butterfield, Webb also carefully referenced the materials and techniques of local buildings. The brand-new house was designed to fit snugly into the existing landscape, providing a sense of continuity with the past and relying for its beauty on the colour and texture of its materials and careful massing of form.

The garden and interiors, masterminded by Morris in close collaboration with his architect, were radically new and deeply personal. Research by Tessa Wild and the National Trust has transformed our understanding of their appearance and coherence in Morris's day. Walls and ceilings were once hand-painted in a dazzling array of patterns and colours, set off by Webb's exposed red brick hearths. The iconographic scheme and furnishings are explored in Chapters VI, VIII and IX. Both intellectually and physically, it was a collective effort, as Morris, Jane and their closest circle of friends spent long weekends and holidays creating a 'Palace of Art' that reflected their shared interests in medieval art, literature and heraldry.

The garden was divided into a series of trellised enclosures or 'outdoor rooms', intimate spaces that only slowly revealed themselves. As Dinah Roe has argued, the Pre-Raphaelites were drawn to the motif of the enclosed garden as a sensuous space that intensifies our relationship with nature. This idea was echoed in Morris's poetry. In *The Defence of Guenevere*, his heroine recalled her first kiss with Lancelot, 'In a quiet garden walled round every way; I was right joyful of that wall of stone, That shut the flowers and trees up with the sky, And trebled all the beauty: to the bone'. He had Red House in mind when he later articulated some of his ideas on successful garden design in his lecture 'Making the Best of It' in 1879: 'Large, or small, it should look both orderly and rich ... It should by no means imitate either the wilfulness or the wildness of Nature, but should look like a thing never to be seen except near a house. It should, in fact, look like a part of the house.' Morris approached laying out a garden in the same way as he approached pattern-making.

It was during the excitement and adventure of decorating Red House that Morris, Marshall, Faulkner & Co. was founded in April 1861. Described in their first prospectus as 'Fine Art Workmen', the seven partners were William Morris, Edward Burne-Jones, Philip Webb, Dante Gabriel Rossetti, Ford Madox Brown, Charles Faulkner and Peter Paul Marshall. They set out to offer an ambitiously wide range of decorating services, from painted murals to stained glass, metalwork, furniture and embroidery. There was certainly strong competition from other firms but the breadth of what they wanted to achieve in both domestic and ecclesiastical furnishing was distinctive. As with many new ventures, their marketing materials somewhat overstated the case. It would take years to hone their technical skills and offer full product ranges. Nevertheless, their pluckiness and bold claims attracted attention. Both Webb and Rossetti played a critical role in securing commissions, the former's architectural expertise no doubt reassuring clients, especially when it came to the installation of complex schemes of stained glass. As Chapter VII explores, they were particularly fortunate in winning the patronage of the architect George Frederick Bodley. From the start, Morris was the organizing spirit, galvanizing his friends and driving the enterprise forwards. In 1862 the firm made its debut in the Medieval Court of the International Exhibition.

The early 1860s were busy in other ways too. Red House was soon home to a young family. The Morrises' two daughters, Jenny and May, were born just over a year apart in 1861 and 1862. William and Jane were affectionate, loving parents and the girls flourished, surrounded by and later sharing in their creative occupations. They were christened in the local church, presumably as a concession to Morris's mother, but otherwise brought up without religion. As well as caring for her family, Jane contributed to the success of the business, executing embroideries and overseeing the female outworkers who were employed as the volume of orders increased. The firm was relatively unusual at the time in providing opportunities for women to participate in its activities, albeit mainly the wives and sisters of the partners. This publication discusses the contributions made by Jane's sister Elizabeth (Bessie) Burden, Kate and Lucy Faulkner and Catherine Holiday, who all worked in a freelance capacity and pursued other projects independently.

By 1864, the business was outgrowing its first premises at Red Lion Square in Bloomsbury. Morris's daily commute from Bexleyheath was exhausting and Jane and the girls were isolated during the week. He seriously contemplated moving the workshops out of London, close to Red House, which was to be enlarged to accommodate the Burne-Jones family. Webb designed a sensitive extension that would have provided separate living quarters with the garden shared in common. It was the closest Morris ever came to realizing his dream of an artistic community living and working in the countryside. In the event, personal tragedy intervened. Edward and Georgiana Burne-Jones withdrew, shattered by the death of their second son Christopher at just a few weeks old and anxious that the new build would overstretch their finances. There was also a part of Morris that needed London and the stimulus it provided, as he later wrote, 'I fear I am a London bird; its soot has been rubbed into me, and even these autumn mornings can't wash me clean of restlessness.'

The firm leased a large townhouse at 26 Queen Square, Bloomsbury, in 1865 and Morris moved his family to live above the showroom. Red House, its interior decoration only partially realized, was put on the market. Morris bore the loss with his characteristic resilience, throwing himself into new creative projects. George Wardle, who later worked as the firm's general manager, left a tantalizing description of the family's new living quarters:

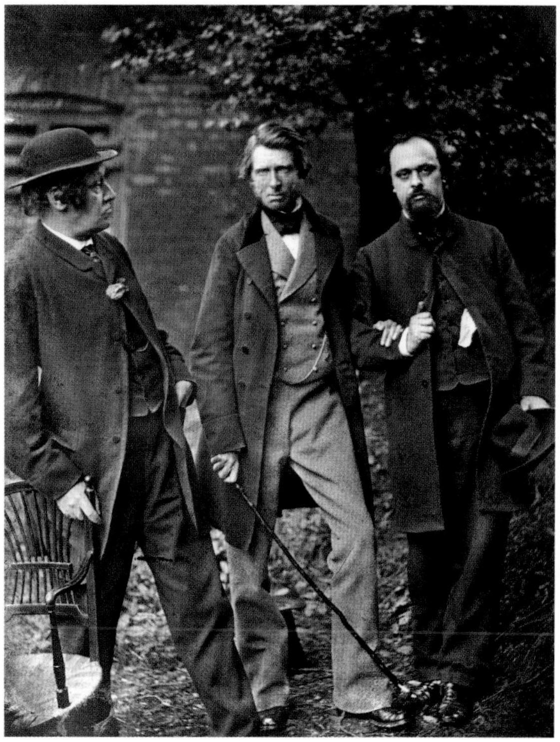

Fig.7 **Dante Gabriel Rossetti (right), John Ruskin (centre) and the painter William Bell Scott in Rossetti's garden at Cheyne Walk, Chelsea. Photographed by W. & D. Downey, June 1863.**

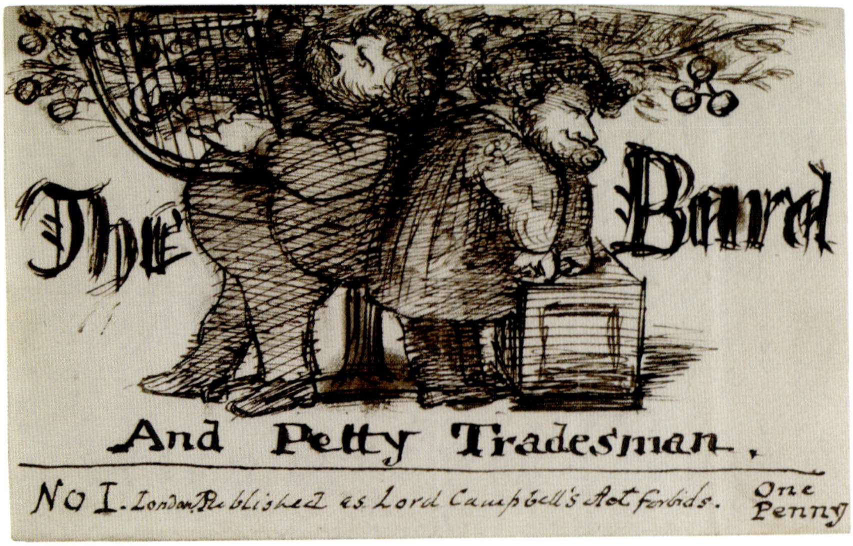

Fig.8 ***The Bard and Petty Tradesman*, Dante Gabriel Rossetti, 1868.**
British Museum

'The decoration of the drawing rooms in Queen Square in which both Mr Morris and Webb had part was original & though extremely simple, very beautiful.' There are no visual representations of this 'lost' interior but it would be fascinating to know more about this space, created so soon after the rich medieval idiom of Red House. As Wardle rightly surmised, it was a showpiece for the firm, and given Morris's sensitivity to external surroundings, no doubt reflective of its urban setting.

Poetry was one of his major occupations in the second half of the 1860s, culminating with the publication of his epic cycle of narrative poems, *The Earthly Paradise* (1868–70). Conceived in homage to Chaucer's *Canterbury Tales*, Morris's retelling of 24 stories from classical and medieval sources captured the public's imagination and catapulted him to fame. From then on he was known first and foremost as 'the author of *The Earthly Paradise*'. Rossetti's caricature, *The Bard and Petty Tradesman* (fig.8), captures something of the bemusement with which the public greeted the idea of a 'man of letters' who was also a decorator and retailer. It was an unusual combination but, as explored in Chapter II, Morris's storytelling instinct was fundamental to his character. He was only half in jest when he remarked, 'If a chap can't compose an epic poem while he's weaving tapestry … he'll never do any good at all.' His lifelong habit of throwing himself into multiple projects simultaneously fed his creativity.

Work also provided solace and purpose at times of emotional stress. In the summer of 1865 Jane, accompanied by her husband, posed for a series of photographs in Rossetti's garden at Cheyne Walk, Chelsea (fig.9). These were to be used as studies for future compositions. After the family's return to London, Jane became Rossetti's principal model for over a decade and he drew and painted her obsessively. She was cast as a series of mythological heroines and their artist–model partnership yielded some of the most iconic works of Pre-Raphaelite art. Although the date is debated, their relationship became romantic and Morris suffered a double blow, betrayed by both his wife and one-time close friend and artistic mentor. Critics have detected signs of grief in his poetry from the late 1860s onwards but whatever his private feelings, he continued to treat Jane with kindness and respect. There was no public separation or scandal. In 1871 Morris and Rossetti jointly leased Kelmscott Manor, a seventeenth-century yeoman's farmhouse in Oxfordshire (fig.10). Away from prying eyes, though accompanied by Jenny and May who were not privy to the affair, Rossetti and Jane spent the summer there together.

Morris meanwhile was off in pursuit of one of his own obsessions. In July 1871 he travelled to Iceland to experience for himself the land of the sagas, what he called 'the most romantic of all deserts'. He made two journeys, the second in 1873, each lasting for around two months (fig.11). On both occasions he kept a journal filled with his

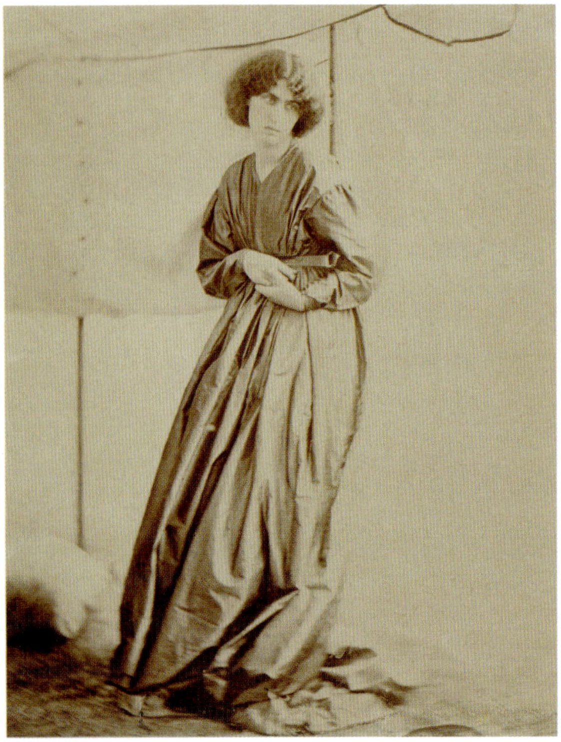

Fig.9 **Jane Morris at Cheyne Walk, photographed by John Robert Parsons, 1865.**
V&A (1740–1939)
Presented by Dr Robert Steele

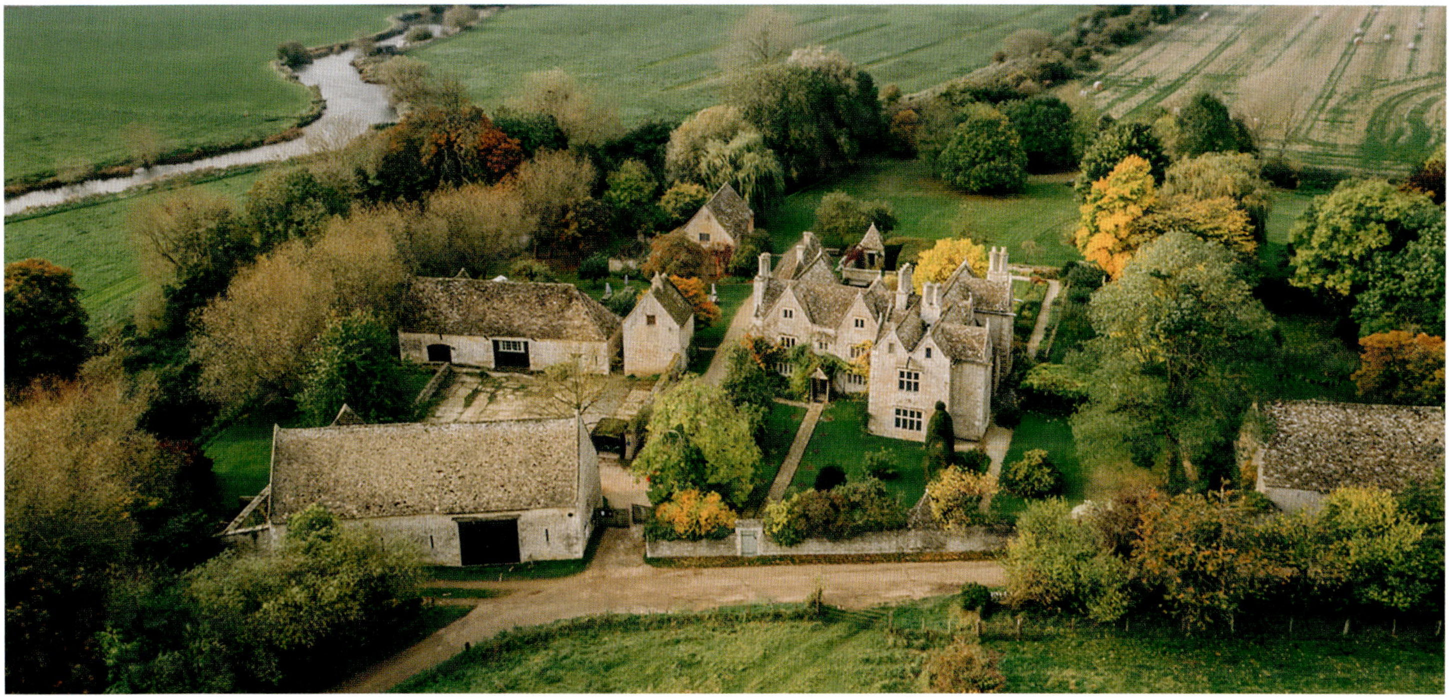

Fig.10 **Kelmscott Manor, barns and garden, Oxfordshire. The Thames landscape inspired Morris's design and literary works.**
The Society of Antiquaries of London

impressions of the landscape. As an undergraduate Morris had read Benjamin Thorpe's *Northern Mythology* (1851) and his interest in Old Norse and Icelandic literature was shared by many other Victorians. What made him unusual was his decision to master the Icelandic language and, with his collaborator Eiríkr Magnússon, translate and publish many of the sagas into English. They met in 1868 and Morris was soon fitting regular three-hour translation sessions around his other commitments. May Morris described his engagement with the language as 'a poet's entering into possession of a new world, only partly his till now.'

Icelanders welcomed Morris, aware of his reputation as a poet and translator. Both trips were physically arduous; the party trekked across the landscape on ponies and mostly camped, occasionally staying in farmsteads enjoying warm but basic hospitality. Morris was in charge of the cooking (fig.12). He was deeply affected by the way of life he encountered and the contrast with industrial Britain. Weaving and other crafts were widely practised and the ancient sagas were still part of the popular consciousness, 'while over the greater part of Europe at least, all knowledge of their *historical* past has faded from the memory of the people ... in Iceland every homestead, one may almost say every field, has its well-remembered history'. Life was challenging but dignified, lived in close proximity to a harsh but unspoilt natural landscape. As Morris himself was to recognize, Iceland played a critical role in his own increasingly radical rejection of the Victorian status quo. In 1883 he expressed this bluntly to a socialist comrade, 'I learned one lesson there, thoroughly I hope, that the most grinding poverty is a trifling evil compared with the inequality of classes.'

Morris's Icelandic diaries were written for Georgiana Burne-Jones (fig.13), wife of Edward and a close and much-loved friend in her own right. His relationships with women could be as sustaining as the brotherhood. Georgiana was also the principal beneficiary of his renewed and intense engagement with calligraphy in the first half of the 1870s. As explored in Chapter XIII, for six years Morris worked hard to give the literary works he admired fitting physical embodiment. As well as the sagas, he wrote out classical and Persian texts, experimenting with scripts, page layouts and gilding and illumination techniques. Just as with his approach to interiors, he was interested in how to combine all these different elements to create a coherent whole. This activity, mainly carried out on Sunday mornings, was quite separate from his commercial work for the firm but no less serious in its intent. Several of his manuscripts were given as gifts to Georgiana who, as a younger woman, had also experimented with book design and illustration. There is something extremely tender

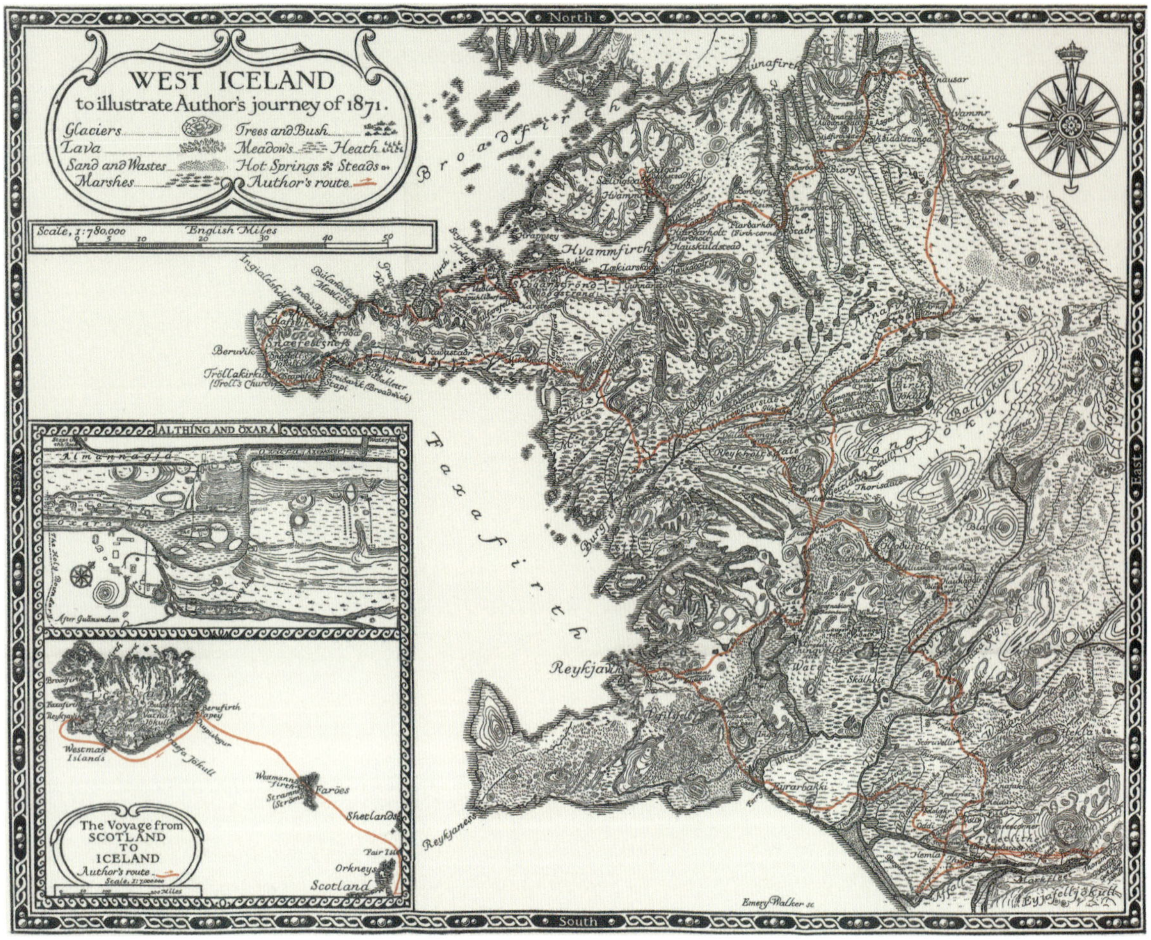

Fig.11 **Map of Morris's journey around Iceland in 1871. Published in *The Collected Works of William Morris*, Volume VIII, 1911.**
William Morris Gallery

and endearing about these tokens of friendship, created at a time when both were silently suffering the fall-out of their partners' infidelities (in the late 1860s Edward had a very public affair with the sculptor Maria Zambaco).

By the early 1870s Morris had a pressing need to secure his family's financial stability. His once enviable private income from mining shares had fallen dramatically; by the middle of the decade it was negligible. He understood that in order to flourish the firm needed to end its heavy reliance on the stained-glass market and introduce a wider range of products for the home. Morris was the partner constantly on the premises, creating new designs, liaising with manufacturers and clients. As he told another close friend, Aglaia Coronio, 'I should very much like to make the business quite a success, and it can't be unless I work at it myself.' In 1874 he began negotiations with the other partners to reconstitute the firm under his sole control. Webb, Burne-Jones and Faulkner supported his decision; Rossetti, Madox Brown and Marshall took legal advice. The process was painful and protracted but Morris held his nerve and in March 1875 the firm began trading as Morris & Co. under his exclusive direction.

Morris became one of the world's most innovative manufacturers by necessity rather than design. From its foundation the firm had turned to outside companies to make many of its products. The

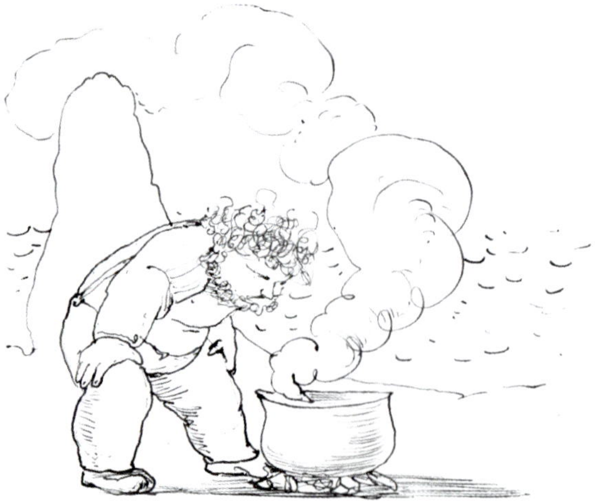

Fig.12 **Morris cooking in Iceland, caricature by Edward Burne-Jones, *c*.1871.**
British Museum

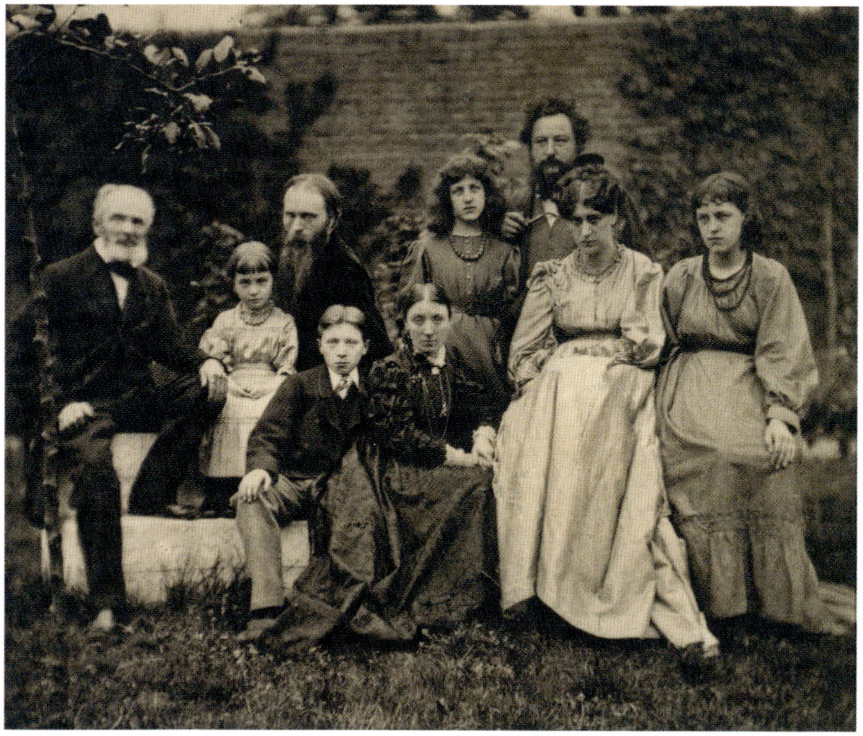

Fig.13 **The Burne-Jones and Morris families in the garden at The Grange, the Burne-Joneses' house in Fulham. Photographed by Frederick Hollyer, 1874.**

From left to right: Burne-Jones's father, Edward Jones, Margaret, Edward, Philip and Georgiana Burne-Jones, May, William, Jane and Jenny Morris.

V&A (1813–1939)
Presented by Dr Robert Steele

raw materials for stained glass were provided by James Powell & Sons of Whitefriars, who also executed Webb's elegant designs for glass tableware. Wallpapers were hand-printed by Jeffrey & Co., an established firm that interpreted Morris's designs with sensitivity and skill. However, in other areas, particularly textiles, he struggled to find manufacturers with the expertise or interest to create the effects he was seeking. Emboldened by the reorganization of the firm, he spent the next decade learning new techniques and expanding the range of wares produced in-house.

Morris's intimate engagement with his materials and the way things were made was unusual but not unique. At Leek, in Staffordshire, the pioneering dye chemist Thomas Wardle had a considerable reputation for his work with natural dyes when Morris sought him out in the mid-1870s. Together they revived the use of vegetable dyes to create rich lasting colours that offered an alternative to the fugitive chemical dyes that then dominated the textile industry. They were both risk takers, investing heavily in time and money to get the results they desired and to prove that there was a market for beautiful, handmade goods created with skill and care.

With almost manic energy, Morris graduated from one craft to the next, mastering dyeing, hand-block printing, weaving, carpet knotting and finally his 'bright dream', high-warp tapestry. Success was not achieved overnight. It was an iterative process, advancing slowly through trial and error. Design and making went hand in hand, feeding off one another as Morris teased out the unique potential of each new technique. Buoyed up by his growing confidence as a maker, he entered his most productive period as a pattern designer. The garden and landscape around Kelmscott Manor, where he had begun to spend more time after Rossetti gave up his share of the lease in 1874, were a vital source of inspiration in this period. Native plants and flowers appear in endlessly inventive combinations, their forms abstracted and simplified but always retaining a sense of growth and movement. Ornament, he argued in his lecture 'Some Hints on Pattern-Designing' (1881), should remind us of 'the outward face of the earth'.

He also drew stimulation from an increasingly wide range of global craft traditions. Unsurprisingly he owned a copy of Owen Jones's famous *Grammar of Ornament* (1856), a visual encyclopaedia of patterns from around the world. But the real magic happened when Morris was physically in touch with his source material. He needed to feel the texture and weight, examine the colours in different lights, experience the pattern in the context of the object or surface it adorned. Thomas Wardle shared his own deep knowledge and enthusiasm for Indian textiles and Morris was particularly drawn to the carpets of Safavid Iran. He had moments of epiphany, such as in April 1877 when he wrote to Wardle, 'I saw yesterday a piece of *ancient* Persian time of Shah Abbas (our Elizabeth's time) that fairly threw me on my back: I had no idea that such wonders could be done in carpets.' As Linda Parry and Tristram Hunt explore in this book, his growing expertise in historic European and Middle Eastern textiles was recognized by the staff of the South Kensington Museum, who sought his advice when building its collection. His respect for what had been achieved in the pre-industrial past motivated and fueled his determination to create work as original and well-crafted for his own time.

Despite immersing himself in the minutiae of different craft disciplines, Morris never lost sight of the bigger picture. The expansion of Morris & Co.'s product range was driven by his desire to provide all the necessary elements of household decoration. In 1877 he opened a new showroom on Oxford Street where furnishings could be viewed side by side, giving customers a better sense of how they worked together. As Harvey and Press explain in Chapter III, the retail offering was increasingly sophisticated and designed to appeal to different levels of the market with both off-the-shelf and bespoke options available.

The firm also provided a complete decorating service, with Morris in the role of interior designer. This is one of the most important but challenging aspects of his work to assess. Interiors are, by their nature, dynamic inhabited spaces subject to constant change and evolution. Moreover, none of the domestic schemes that Morris *personally* supervised for clients have survived. In George Wardle's reminiscences, he singled out Old Swan House in Chelsea, designed for the solicitor Wickham Flower, and two properties decorated for the banker Edward Baring, Coombe Cottage in Surrey and Membland Hall near Plymouth in Devon. Of the Baring commissions very little is known, though there is a tantalizing glimpse in the survival of some splendid tile panels intended for one of the bathrooms (see X.21). Old Swan House, like other high-profile schemes, is recorded in a series of black-and-white photographs taken by the celebrated architectural photographers Bedford Lemere & Co. Such images are rich sources of information but, as many scholars have noted, have their limitations. People rarely feature; the rooms, devoid of their inhabitants, are frozen in a moment of time. They cannot communicate the interplay of colour, light and texture or the relationship between the indoors and the outdoors. Yet, as Linda Parry demonstrates in Chapter VIII, by combining sensitive reading of the photographic evidence, close analysis of objects and contemporary descriptions, we can get closer to experiencing Morris & Co.'s mature house style and the different approaches adopted for city and country living.

Morris's company catered to the high-end of the market. The products he sold were extremely labour intensive and therefore expensive. While their impeccable quality and longevity may have represented good value for money, they were not accessible. Morris himself was the first to recognize this fact. His own practical, hands-on experience as a manufacturer, employer and retailer was absolutely fundamental to his growing radicalization. It threw into relief the wastefulness of industrial capitalism that produced shoddy, inferior goods at terrible cost to people's lives and the environment. It also confirmed that the alternative – a lightly mechanized, design and craft-driven enterprise – could never be anything but an elite concern in the context of Victorian Britain. In the late 1870s, Morris embarked on a new phase in his life as a cultural and political activist. Though he had a reputation as a poet and decorator, he had yet played no part in public life. It is no coincidence that that this leap into action was taken at the time when he was most heavily engaged with reviving traditional craft skills; handicrafts, he believed, had the potential to transform society.

Morris started campaigning on several fronts simultaneously. In 1876 Ottoman troops massacred thousands of Bulgarian Christians following their demands for increased autonomy. The Conservative government, fearful that a weakened Ottoman Empire would lead to increased Russian influence in the region, refused to condemn the massacres. At one point it looked as if Britain might even go to war to defend Turkey's interests. Morris joined the anti-war movement, aligning himself with the radical wing of the Liberal Party and speaking out against Britain's imperial self-interest. At the same time as he was becoming involved with political causes, in March 1877 he set up a pressure group to defend historic buildings against reckless restoration practices. Co-founded with Webb (fig.14), the Society for the Protection of Ancient Buildings brought together like-minded individuals from across the political spectrum to advocate for a gentler, more sensitive approach to repair that protected the integrity of the historic fabric. As Chris Miele demonstrates in Chapter V, sections of the architectural community were already moving in this direction but Morris and his fellow campaigners turned the issue into a public debate. Ancient buildings, they argued, were part of a shared architectural inheritance, belonging in a sense to everyone, future generations included. They were too precious to be left to the whims of private owners or the discretion of individual architects. At the time, many perceived the Society's actions as meddlesome interference, an unwarranted attack on the rights of private property. Now these ideas are widely accepted and enshrined in law.

The feelings and ideas that drove Morris's participation in these varied campaigns were not new; they can be traced back to his undergraduate days at Oxford. However, he felt an increasing sense of personal responsibility, an urgent need to act. He started to give talks to students of design and those working in industry. His first formal public lecture, 'The Decorative Arts' (later published as 'The Lesser Arts') was delivered to the Trades Guild of Learning in December 1877. At this stage Morris still believed that society could be reformed from within and that those working in the decorative arts had a critical role to play. This might sound implausible but it stemmed from the importance he attached to the material conditions of everyday life. Our living environments, he argued, affect the way we feel and behave. The *things* we surround ourselves with and the conditions under which they are made matter; they have the power to rejuvenate or oppress. From the very start of his lecturing career, a recurrent theme is the interdependence of human society and the natural environment. They thrive or perish together: 'at the root of the whole matter, everything made by man's hands has a form, which must be either beautiful or ugly; beautiful if it is in accord with Nature, and helps her; ugly if it is discordant with Nature, and thwarts her; it cannot be indifferent.'

In 1881 Morris began to hunt for new workshop premises with the space and facilities to expand his production, especially of hand-knotted carpets and tapestries. He still toyed with the idea of abandoning London for a rural setting, going to view a deserted silk mill at Blockley in Gloucestershire. However, pragmatism prevailed and he settled on a former print-works at Merton Abbey near Wimbledon. The river Wandle provided the necessary supply of fresh water for dyeing and printing textiles, and the existing low-rise, weather-boarded buildings could be repurposed to meet his needs. Though Morris found the surrounding suburbs 'woeful beyond conception', the 7-acre site was once part of a medieval priory, which lent it an air of romance and history. There was also a long tradition of textile production in the area, providing a welcome sense of continuity with the past. Morris restored the gardens, reviving their 'ancient gaiety', and planted new poplar trees. There was a dormitory for apprentices, who were recruited locally, and the former kitchen gardens were divided into plots and let to some of the workmen.

Merton Abbey was not paradise, but the conditions were a far cry from those experienced by workers in large industrial factories. Apprentices were encouraged to develop their artistic skills by attending art classes in the evenings and the practical training they received was thorough. As research by Linda Parry and David Saxby has demonstrated, their expertise was in demand. Some of the tapestry weavers in particular went on to have distinguished careers outside the firm. The success of the apprenticeship system at Merton, which did not involve any kind of selection process, confirmed in practice Morris's intuitive belief that under the right conditions everyone has the artistic impulse. Labour was still divided; the craftsmen and women at Merton had no input into the design process. However, the nature of the techniques that Morris used meant that the work was creatively demanding. Operating the dye vats, for example, was a sensitive task requiring intuition and experience. For the glass painters and tapestry weavers especially, the process of successfully translating designs on paper into finished objects required their own imaginative input. As Morris explained in 1894 when he was interviewed about his revival of tapestry weaving, 'considerable latitude in the choice and arrangements of tints in shading, &c., is allowed to the executants themselves, who are in fact, both by nature and training, artists, not merely animated machines.' Wages were as high as market conditions would allow.

Outwardly at least, by the early 1880s things were going well for Morris. His investment in manufacturing was paying off and the firm was acquiring an international reputation for the artistry and quality of its wares. His work for the Society for the Protection of Ancient Buildings, his lecturing and political activism had given him a public platform through which to share his views. He could (had it been in his nature) have

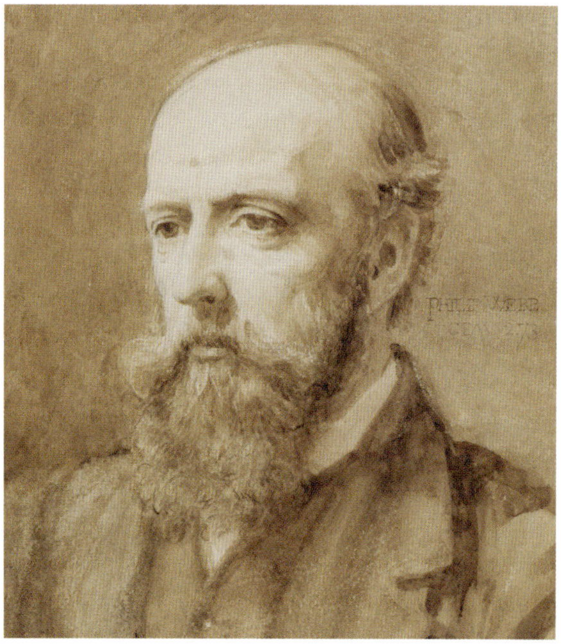

Fig.14 **Philip Webb by Charles Fairfax Murray, 1873.**
National Portrait Gallery

congratulated himself on being an enlightened employer. Instead, the opposite happened. He entered one of the most anguished and soul-searching periods of his life. As Nicholas Salmon explains in Chapter IV, he lost all faith in parliamentary politics. The Liberal Party's failure to implement a programme of radical reform was a bitter blow, heightened by the fact he had worked so energetically in its cause. The harsh policies of coercion pursued in Ireland and British military intervention in Egypt in 1882 disturbed him greatly. He gradually came to the conclusion that whichever party was in power, it would only ever govern in its own self-interest at the expense of the working classes. In order for art and nature – the two great passions of his life – to thrive, there needed to be a clean slate, a totally new kind of society. In 1883 he joined the fledging socialist movement and abandoned reform for revolution.

Some friends were shocked, others supportive, but for Morris the decision once made brought a huge sense of relief. He now had a clear goal, nothing less than 'the destruction of the system which seems to me mere oppression and obstruction'. His leadership role, first in the Democratic Federation and then in the Socialist League, is explored in detail in Chapter IV. While his socialist comrades were united in their desire to uproot capitalism, tactics were hotly debated. Morris was uncompromising in his rejection of parliamentary politics. Change, he believed, had to come from those most oppressed by the current system. Every effort should be directed towards educating the workers in socialism, everything else was a distraction. His faith in the working classes to set society on a new path and his anti-paternalistic approach were distinctive. He did not have to look far for inspiration. As Jan Marsh and Frank Sharp have suggested, it is likely that Jane Morris had a profound influence on her husband's socialism. Raised in poverty, given access to education she had transformed herself into a widely read, multilingual, politically engaged and culturally sophisticated individual.

The Morrises' marriage had survived Jane's affair, which petered out when Rossetti succumbed to a nervous breakdown. Their shared anxiety over their elder daughter Jenny may well have brought them closer together. As a young woman Jenny showed academic promise and her parents hoped to send her to Girton College, Cambridge, but in 1876 she started to experience violent seizures. Usually diagnosed as epilepsy, there was no effective treatment for managing her illness and she required lifelong care. Morris's letters to Jenny are among the most open and affectionate he ever wrote. For her part, she took a great interest in his conservation work and joined the Socialist League, though her health prevented her from taking an active part. Morris remained close to both his daughters as they entered adulthood, describing them as 'very sympathetic with me as to my aims in life.' May Morris was his disciple in art and politics. Stimulated by a childhood immersed in her parents' craft practices, May enrolled at the National Art Training School in South Kensington in 1878. Specializing in embroidery, she took over the supervision of Morris & Co.'s embroidery department in 1885 and was responsible for many of the firm's most successful designs in this medium. With her father's encouragement she studied 'the gospel of Socialism' and became a committed activist.

The Morris family home in Hammersmith became a centre for political debate and agitation. In 1878 Morris had taken out a lease on a large Georgian property fronting the river Thames (see fig.222). He named it Kelmscott House in honour of his country retreat, delighting in the fact that both were situated near the banks of the same river. The house was in a poor state of repair but he could see its potential. The garden, generously sized for London, was a major draw and included a small orchard and kitchen garden at the rear. Georgiana Burne-Jones recalled that he divided it up into separate spaces, just as he had done at Red House. The first-floor drawing room ran the full width of the property with views out over the river. Morris transformed this space, replacing the red flock wallpaper with woven hangings of his own *Bird* design, hung in gently undulating folds against the walls (fig.15). The furniture and furnishings were an eclectic mix of the firm's own products combined with antique tiles, metalware and rugs collected on his travels or purchased in London. Painted furniture from Red Lion Square and Red House provided a tangible link to the earliest creative endeavours of his circle of friends. The layering of different textures and patterns, the juxtaposition of diverse traditions – carved horns from Iceland, inlaid tables from India, rugs from Turkey, to name just a few – created an interior that was rich but not ostentatious. George Bernard Shaw called it a 'magical house'.

After Morris founded the Socialist League, the coach house, initially used for hand-knotting

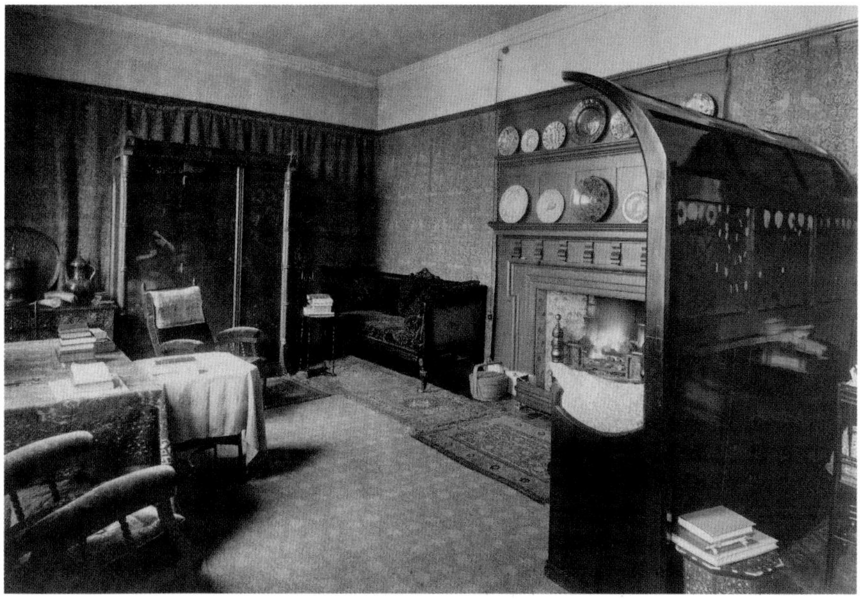

Fig.15 **The drawing room at Kelmscott House, Hammersmith. Photographed by Emery Walker, *c.*1896.**
V&A (2–1973)
Given by Wilfrid Scawen Blunt

carpets, was converted into a meeting place for the Hammersmith branch. Weekly lectures were held from 1884 until 1896, the year of Morris's death, and virtually every leading socialist thinker spoke there at some point. There was a strong international flavour to these gatherings. Political exiles from across Europe gravitated to London in the 1880s and many found their way to Hammersmith. Speakers included the Russian anarchist Peter Kropotkin and the Austrian furniture designer Andreas Scheu. Morris's home became one of the most important venues in London for exploring and debating the full spectrum of socialist opinion, despite his own strongly held views on how to achieve the desired revolution. After these Sunday gatherings, speakers and close comrades joined the family for dinner, where the discussion continued. As always, Morris's activities, be it his design work or his activism, permeated his living environment. Unlike the couple's daughters, Jane never converted to socialism; her sympathies lay with the radical wing of the Liberal Party and she was a passionate supporter of Irish Home Rule (the latter cause closely linked to her mid-life affair with the poet Wilfrid Scawen Blunt). Nevertheless, she played an important supporting role in the 1880s, hosting Morris's socialist comrades and respecting his decision to throw all his time, money and energy behind the cause.

There were two sides to Morris's activism. On the one hand, he sought to expose the inequalities and hypocrisies of nineteenth-century capitalist society by engaging with specific issues of the day. He spoke out against the suppression of free speech, police brutality, class bias in the judicial system, the sexual exploitation of women and girls and the wanton destruction of the environment. The root cause of these evils, he argued, was a system driven by profit. As he outlined in his lecture 'How We Live and How We Might Live' in 1884: 'It is profit which draws men into enormous unmanageable aggregations called towns ... profit which crowds them up ... into quarters without gardens or open spaces; profit which won't take the most ordinary precautions against wrapping a whole district in a cloud of sulphurous smoke; which turns beautiful rivers into filthy sewers'. He used the Socialist League's newspaper, *Commonweal*, to condemn British imperialism, accusing the government of acts of aggression designed solely to expand the market for British goods. Like many of his comrades in the Socialist League, his outlook was international. Social equality could not exist in a vacuum. 'Wage-workers of all countries' must unite to ensure their collective freedom and end the system whereby they were pitted against one another. In the same speech, Morris argued,

> so far-reaching is this curse of commercial war that no country is safe from its ravages; the traditions of a thousand years fall before it in a month ... the Indian or Javanese craftsman may no longer ply his craft leisurely ... producing a maze of strange beauty on a piece of cloth: a steam-engine is set a-going in Manchester ... and the Asiatic worker, if he is not starved to death outright, as plentifully happens, is driven himself into a factory to lower the wages of his Manchester brother worker ...

However, the savagery of his attack on contemporary society and the class system was always balanced by an optimistic and inspiring vision of what a better future might look like. Morris's new society was a bountiful, sensuous one in which people would take 'a pleasurable interest in all the details of daily life'. When he wrote to *The Manchester Examiner* in 1883, 'What business have we with art at all unless all can share it?', he was not thinking of widening access to art galleries or other philanthropic schemes to improve the lot of working people. What use were fleeting glimpses of paintings and sculptures to men and women forced to live in overcrowded, degrading conditions, 'houses for whose wretchedness there is no name'? He even spoke of museums as places of sadness, home to 'treasured scraps', a reminder of a popular art now lost. For Morris the human impulse to ornament his or her surroundings was natural. His idea of democratizing art was to work towards a world where everyone would have the opportunity to pursue creative work, exercising their brains and their hands and with time and space to enjoy the fruits of their labour. He expanded on this in one of his most popular lectures, 'Useful Work versus Useless Toil', first delivered in 1884. 'To compel a man to do day after day the same task, without any hope of escape or change, means nothing short of turning his life into a prison-torment.' Instead, work should offer 'hope of rest, hope of product, hope of pleasure in the work itself'. All work done with pleasure, he argued, is art.

These ideas found their fullest expression in his utopian fiction, *News from Nowhere* (1890), a work discussed by many of the contributors to this book as it ties together so many strands of Morris's thinking. In his imaginary society of the future, set after the revolution, people live in small, largely self-sufficient communities. 'No longer hurried' and freed from fear of poverty, they can examine their true needs and desires. London is a green and pleasant place, with salmon swimming in the Thames and houses interspersed with meadows, woods and orchards. The inhabitants of Nowhere enjoy varied, interesting work, each according to their own individual inclinations. Producing only what they need, waste has been eliminated. It is unapologetically personal, a land filled with the things that brought Morris joy – good food and wine, handsome buildings, beautiful crafts, resplendent countryside, clothes reminiscent of the fourteenth century. Work has become so enjoyable and fulfilling that the only anxiety is that it may one day run out.

In the 1880s a younger generation of architects, designers and makers started to develop the ideas of Ruskin and Morris in exciting new ways. As Karen Livingstone explores in Chapter XVI, Morris was a figurehead for what became known as the Arts and Crafts Movement. This is not a role he actively sought and his ambivalence to new ventures, such as the Arts and Crafts Exhibition Society, is on the face of it difficult to understand. However, seen against the context of his revolutionary politics, it makes sense. Morris had come to believe that only the rebirth of society could bring about a true revival in art. He was pleasantly surprised by the warmth and interest with which sections of (largely middle-class) society greeted the revival in craft practice, but he was also aware that on its own this was not enough to bring about the transformation and equality for which he yearned.

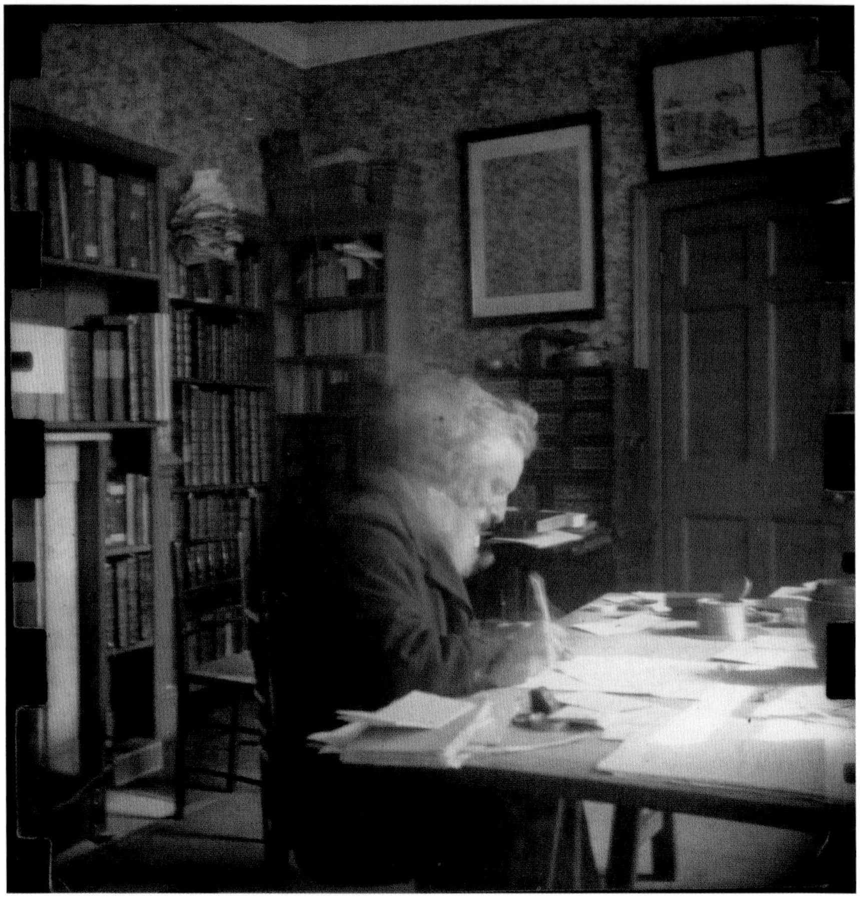

Fig.16 **William Morris in his study at Kelmscott House, Hammersmith. Photographed by Henry Halliday Sparling, early 1890s.**
National Portrait Gallery

The last decade of Morris's life was one of his most creative. By 1890 the Socialist League had fallen apart and while he remained a highly respected figure within the movement, his direct influence declined. He never abandoned his belief in the need for revolution but he had to find new ways to inspire change and express his ideas. Since the 1860s and his aborted attempt to produce an illustrated edition of *The Earthly Paradise*, he had long held an ambition to design and print his own books. His calligraphic experiments had taught him a great deal about letter form and book design. Characteristically, the catalyst that unlocked the potential of these stored-up experiences was finding a talented collaborator. Morris always needed a creative community. Webb had fulfilled this role in interior design and conservation, Magnússon

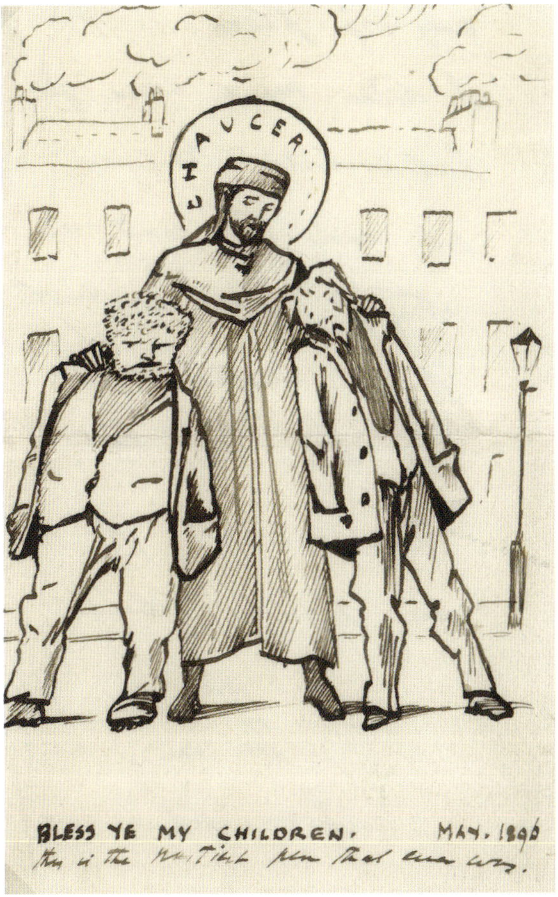

Fig.17 ***Bless Ye My Children*, caricature by Edward Burne-Jones, May 1896.**
Bridwell Library Special Collections, Southern Methodist University, Dallas

in translation, Thomas Wardle in dyeing and printing, Burne-Jones in stained glass and tapestry. For books, the printer and photo-engraver Emery Walker was his ally. Morris's new venture, the Kelmscott Press, set up in 1891, owed its existence to their combined efforts, though Walker declined to become an official partner.

To appreciate the full impact of a Kelmscott Press book there is no substitute for leafing through the pages. As John Dreyfus explores in Chapter XIV, Morris paid meticulous attention to his materials – the ink, handmade paper and vellum were carefully selected for their quality. The design was approached like a piece of architecture in which the type, illustrations and ornament were the building blocks. The whole enterprise encapsulated Morris's design philosophy. He reformulated and reimagined past traditions (the 1890s were his most frenzied period as a book and manuscript collector) to create something new for his own age. Just as he brought nature into the home, the leaf and flower forms that often frame the pages are not merely incidental, they remind us of the beauty of the earth and what we have to lose if we destroy it. As objects, they could have come straight out of *News from Nowhere*.

In the final few years of his life Morris aged visibly (fig.16). He had always suffered from gout but kidney problems and diabetes meant that by the summer of 1895 he was very weak. Despite his physical frailty, he never lost his sense of purpose or creative energy. In the 1890s, alongside the Kelmscott Press, he wrote and published a series of fantasy novels and defended his favourite buildings and landscapes with a new intensity. Protesting against the felling of trees in his native Epping Forest was one of his last acts. Though he stepped back from the day-to-day management of Morris & Co., there were projects he found irresistible. Under his guidance and in collaboration with Burne-Jones, the firm produced extraordinary figurative tapestries, revitalizing a medium that had long appeared obsolete.

In December 1895 Morris caught a chill giving his last open-air speech at the funeral of the Russian revolutionary Sergius Stepniak. A month later his final public address was made in support of the Society for Checking Abuses in Public Advertising. In the summer, on the advice of his doctors, he took a holiday at Folkestone in Kent. It was here that he received the first sample bound copy of the Kelmscott Press edition of *The Works of Geoffrey Chaucer*, a project many years in the making (fig.17). A cruise to Norway, also undertaken for health reasons, could not reverse his steady decline. Though there were moments when he appeared to rally, congestion of the lungs had set in. He died at home in Hammersmith on 3 October, aged 62, and was buried in a simple ceremony at Kelmscott Church three days later. A fellow socialist remembered him saying shortly before his death, 'This has been a jolly world to me and I find plenty to do in it.'

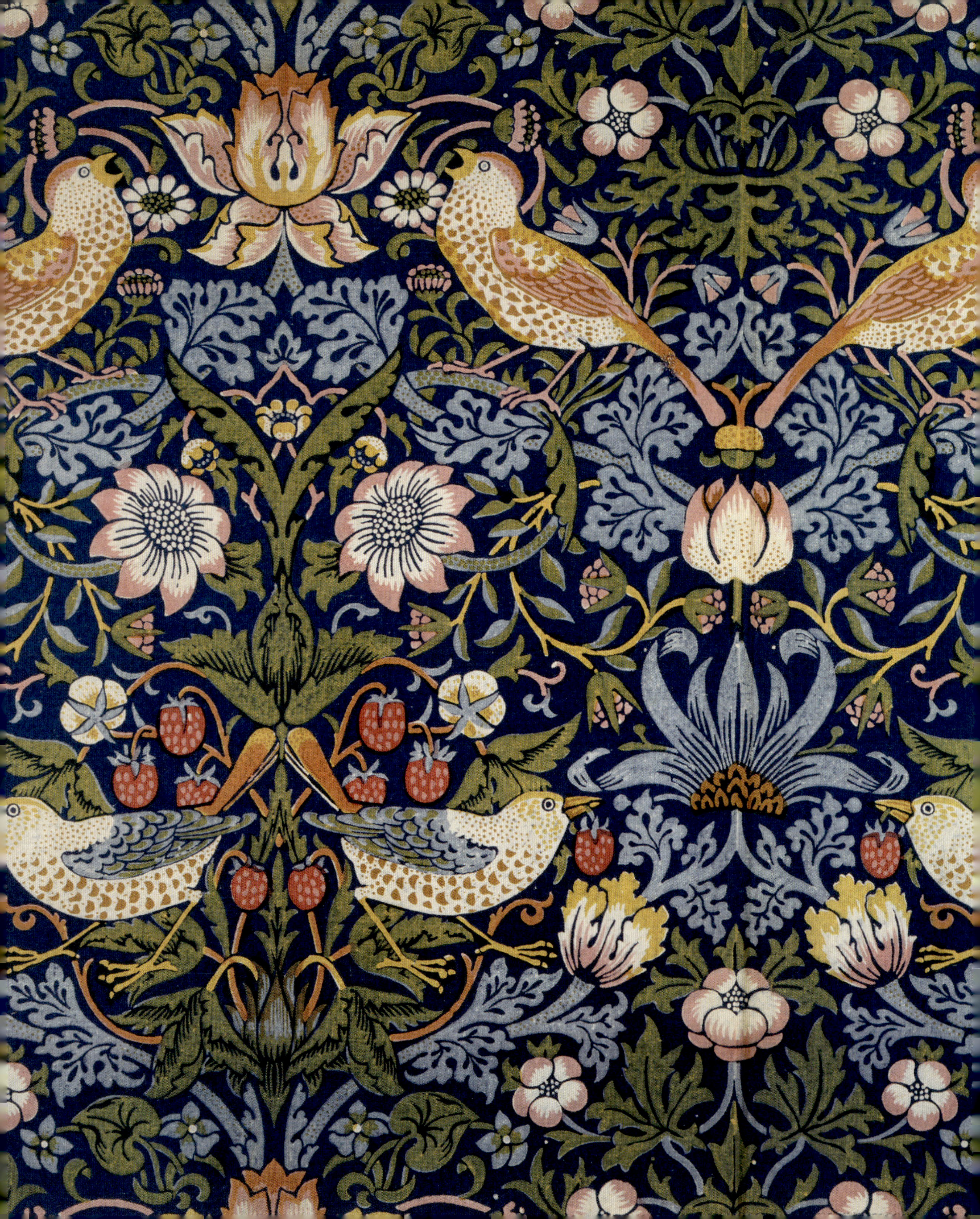

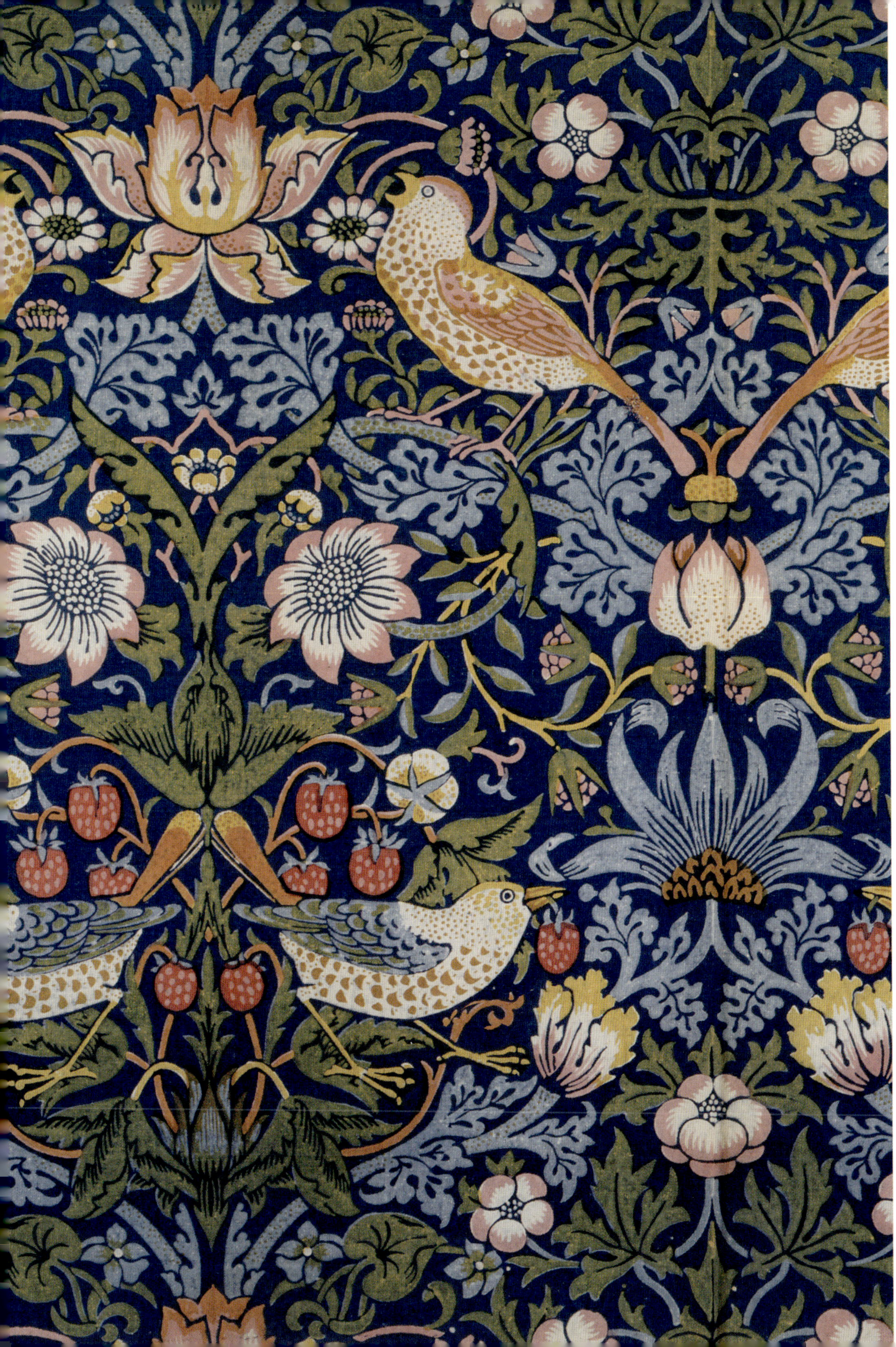

THE MAN

I

THE DESIGNER

Fiona MacCarthy

In the late spring of 1878 Morris was in Venice with his wife and his two daughters. All four went, like other tourists, on a day trip to Murano and stopped at one of the smaller glass-blowing workshops, a dark shack which gave out a sudden, dull red glow as the furnace door was opened. Outside was the glittering sunlight and a fig tree and the scent of the sea, 'all so primitive and pleasant', as recollected in the memoir of her father by Morris's younger daughter May. Morris swept aside the standard Murano glass the craftsman proffered and, picking up his stick (he suffered painfully from gout), he drew the outline of a tumbler on the dusty workshop floor. The 'bright-eyed friendly glass-blower' used this design to produce a simple glass, slightly coloured, slightly bubbly in its texture, which pleased Morris greatly, although to his frustration he could not make the craftsman understand that he wanted to place a quantity order for his shop in Oxford Street.

That brief scene tells us a lot about Morris the designer: his high-speed assessment of technical parameters; his almost instinctive understanding of the potential of material and craftsman; his pragmatic efficiency in conveying his instructions; the way the design process permeated all his thinking, at home or abroad, on holiday or not. Morris never stopped designing, redesigning and improving. The encounter shows his grand impetuosity in action: Morris fertile, forthright, comically optimistic. It would make the perfect subject for a Burne-Jones cartoon.

William Morris was many kinds of man: visual artist, poet, political activist, Marxist theoretician. He was also many kinds of designer. Morris designed numerous special one-off objects that he either made himself, the design often evolving through the processes of making, or collaborated on with his craftworkers and friends. He designed for one-off and small batch production in his early workshops and for relatively large-scale production runs in later days at his factory at Merton Abbey. To an extent that few people are aware of he designed other products to be made by subcontractors and sold through his firm's showrooms. He acted as designer–buyer for his shops in the sense of searching out and commissioning new ranges to be sold alongside Morris, Marshall, Faulkner & Co.'s own products. On an earlier visit to Italy his travelling companion Edward Burne-Jones complained about Morris's obsessive 'merchandizing for the firm'.

As chief designer and overall controller of the firm's visual and technical standards, Morris

Fig.18 ***Brother Rabbit* printed cotton, designed by William Morris, before June 1881 (see XII.46).**
V&A (T.648–1919)

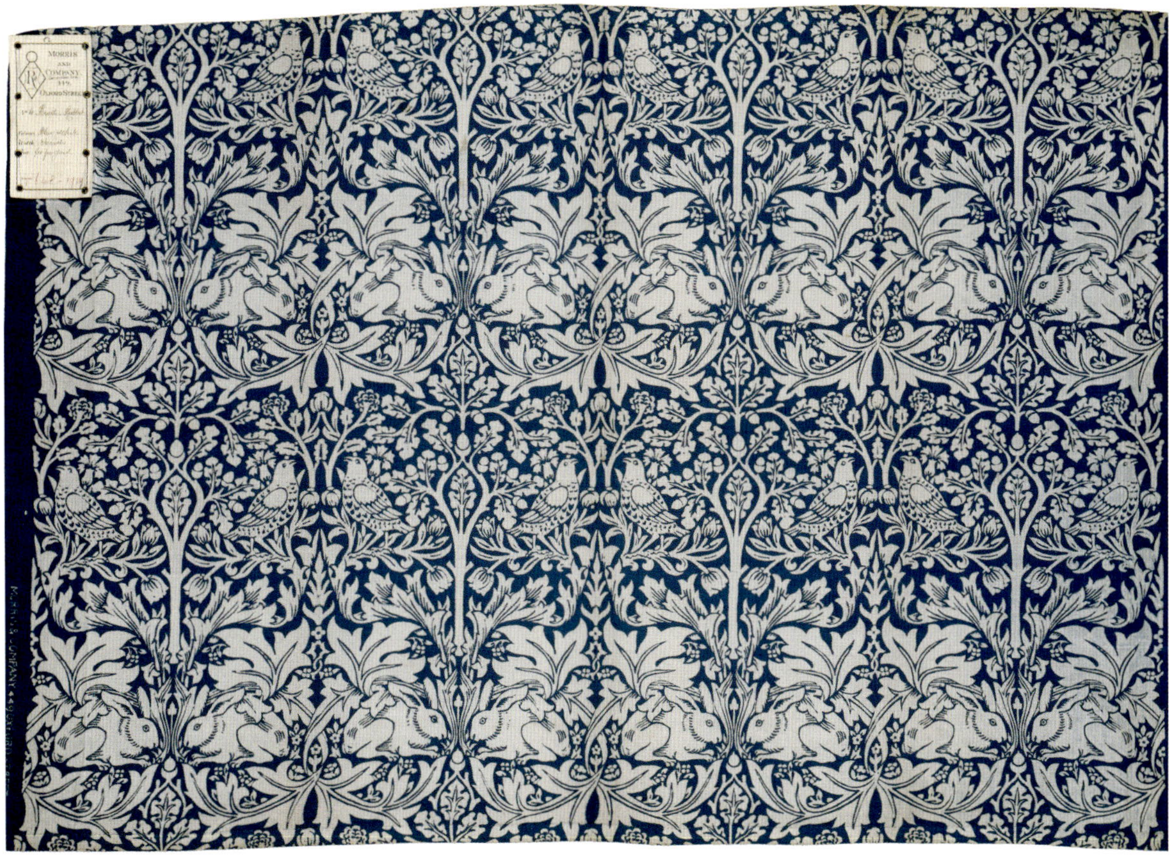

covered a stupendous range. In his neurotically energetic lifetime his interests and technical knowledge burgeoned outwards to include embroidery, furniture, stained glass, wallpapers and mural decorations; wood engravings, illumination and calligraphy; printed and woven textiles, and high-warp tapestry. At the end of his life there was the final challenge of book design and type design at his own Kelmscott Press. William Morris saw things whole. His view of design was rich, complex and dominated by his reverence for buildings as repositories of history and keepers of the soul. The point of Morris's acutely detailed knowledge of individual processes and products was his passion for the total architectural *mise-en-scène*. He liked the completeness of designing for a church or domestic interior. He was as interested in gardens as in houses and, as we see at his own Red House, Morris had great feeling for interflowing spaces. His generous concept of the role of the designer would eventually lead him to envisage whole communities, networks of productive and sociable semi-self-sufficient small country towns, precursors of the early twentieth-century garden cities. As expounded so sturdily in a famous lecture, 'Art under Plutocracy' (1883), his view of art encompassed what we would now think of as total environmental planning: design for 'all the externals of our life'.

Morris argued that art was not merely a matter of painting and sculpture, architecture, 'the shapes and colours of all household goods', it also took in 'the arrangement of the fields for tillage and pasture, the management of towns and of our highways of all kinds'. He saw visual alertness as a basic human function and the shared appreciation of beauty and design in everyday surroundings and ordinary objects as the means of reconciling the artist with society. In his utopian novel *News from Nowhere*, art has become so deeply embedded in the life of the community of Morris's new England that it has no name.

Morris's strengths as a designer spring from the exactness of his observation. Even as a child exploring gentle, quirky rural Essex, and his later expeditions as a disaffected schoolboy into the countryside around Marlborough College, his sense of landscape was almost uncannily acute. In a letter written after Morris's death, his daughter Jenny commented on his facility for grasping the essentials: 'in half a dozen words Father could make one see a place exactly'. The details of known landscapes stayed in his mind forever and he drew on what became almost a library of riverscapes and tree forms, flowers, fruits and the little living creatures of the meadows and the woodlands: starlings squawking, robins hopping, kingfishers swooping, sleek and amiable rabbits (fig.18). They recur in his design work as vividly as they do in his poetry and prose. Morris was often caustic about the vapid, fashionable decorative designs of his contemporaries, citing Lawrence Alma-Tadema's with particular venom: 'they appear to me too much made up of goose giblets and umbrellas.' His own idea of pattern embraced memory and nature, a theme he followed through in his 1881 lecture, 'Some Hints on Pattern-Designing'. Morris's ideal pattern held 'unmistakable suggestions of gardens and fields'.

He reached out for solidity, the real, the unmistakable. Again, back in his childhood, he glorified the tactile, clinging to a rag at bedtime, recalling with precision a picture of Abraham and Isaac worked in worsted, a carved ivory junk with painted, gilded puppet figures, a particular Dutch toy town spread out satisfactorily upon the floor. Gradually, as a designer and a design theorist, he evolved a whole philosophy of things, arguing the strengths of well-printed books and splendid tapestries, beautiful and functional kitchens as a bulwark against social alienation and decay. What is fascinating is the scope of his intelligence. His great originality, a facet of his genius, is the way that Morris moves, apparently without self-consciousness, between the solid, 'manly' worlds of furniture and buildings and the soft, traditionally female textile crafts.

At a very early stage Morris had begun drawing. It was almost a compulsion, like his spurts of fluent writing. At Oxford in the middle 1850s his fellow undergraduates watched him pouring out his sketches of windows, arches and gables. A sketchbook of the Red House period, now in the British Library (fig.106), contains rapidly made drawings of knights in armour, flowers, medieval maidens and architectural detailing, suggesting the way in which Morris used these sketches to arrive at design concepts. Late in life he was still doodling, covering the notes for his lectures, adorning the sheets of his agendas for committees, with an endless profusion of patterns. Morris was his own best exemplar of the power of pattern to soothe and civilize. He would argue for drawing, and in particular for drawing from the human figure (hard as he himself always claimed to find it), as the central, essential discipline in a training for design. Morris recommended accurate drawing as the antidote to the 'sloppiness or vagueness' he so much disliked in the visual arts, as indeed in politics. The thousands of Morris's remaining working drawings, mostly for wallpapers and textiles, show his characteristic linear exactness reining in the deep sweep of his imaginative surge.

Morris absorbed colours with the poet's eye that made him the supreme colourist of the Victorian period. His precocious reading of Gothic stories and medieval mysteries taught him to see colour in terms of panoramic history. He would always be enraptured by the colours of banners, the insignia of battle, the dazzle of the novels of Sir Walter Scott. Morris's sense of history was creative and dynamic. He was immensely knowledgeable and was also adept, with the fanatic's sure-fire intuition, at recapturing the details and the atmosphere of medieval life: 'When I think of this', he said in his lecture 'The Hopes of Civilization', 'it quickens my hope of what may be'. Morris took the colours of the past – the red of the knights, the purple of the emperors, the stern grey stonework of old village churches, the shrill blue that was the colour of ancient holidays – and gathered them into his own decorative palette. His use of colour is intensely reminiscent; it reminds one inevitably

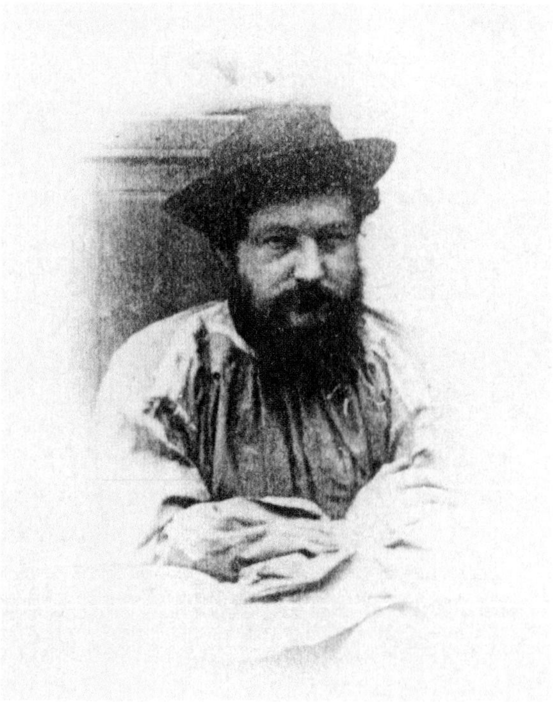

Fig.19 **William Morris in working smock, unknown photographer, *c.*1876.**
V&A (1808–1939)

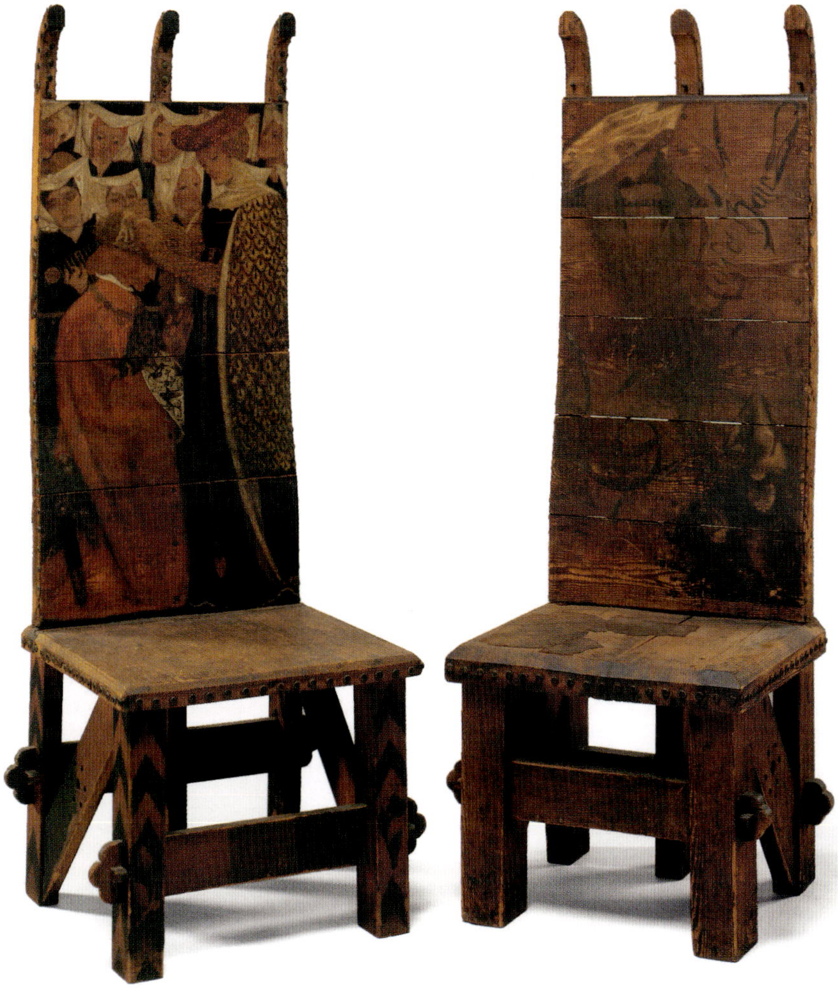

Fig.20 ***Glorious Guendolen's Golden Hair*** **(right) and** ***The Arming of a Knight*** **(left), designed by William Morris and decorated in collaboration with Dante Gabriel Rossetti for Red Lion Square, 1856 and** ***c.*****1857–8 (see IX.3).**
Delaware Art Museum, Wilmington

of the luminosity of colour in Morris's early poetry, the vivid violent narratives of *The Defence of Guenevere*. As so marvellously described by his disciple William Richard Lethaby, 'Morris's colour-work glows from within'.

As a designer his most radical departure was in his approach to materials and processes. He confessed in his lecture 'The Aims of Art' that he was never truly happy unless either making something or making believe to make it; and he developed a passionate attachment to the properties and potential of materials. Addressing some art students in Burslem in 1881 he entreated them to 'try to get the most out of your material, but always in such a way as honours it most.' Morris's views on right-making became the received wisdom of the (very gentlemanly) Arts and Crafts Movement. But in its day it was defiantly eccentric. As John William Mackail, Morris's first official biographer, explains so valuably from his closer vantage-point, 'a poet who chose to exercise a handicraft, not as a gentleman amateur, but under the ordinary conditions of handcraftsmen, was a figure so unique as to be all but unintelligible.' Mackail also made the comment, which was true, that the secret of the excellence of Morris's designs was that he never designed anything that he did not know how to produce with his own hands (fig.19). Morris needed handwork psychologically. From the time he was at Marlborough, observed by his schoolfellows making nets for catching fish or trapping birds, with one end of the net fixed to the classroom desk, he relied on the rhythms of repetitive manual activity to control his inherent restlessness and edginess. Morris needed to feel himself literally in touch.

Handwork also brought a theoretical solution to the intellectual problems assailing him since Oxford, where Morris first read John Ruskin's essay on art and workmanship in *The Stones of Venice*. Morris perceived that handwork could be a way of ending the deadly separation between the operative and the designer, and a means of challenging that vaster, more iniquitous divide between the labourer and the non-labouring employer. By the middle 1850s, still in his early twenties, Morris had embarked on stone carving, clay modelling, illuminating, mural decoration and painted furniture. He had a frame made for embroidery, based on an old example, and supervised the special dyeing of his worsteds. His practical involvement in the techniques of production justified the detail of his glowering criticisms.

It was once he moved to London in 1856 that Morris began to find himself as a designer. Sharing rooms in Red Lion Square with Edward Burne-Jones, he evolved his ideal of the interior as a place that was tidy but not too tidy (indeed, Red Lion Square had its elements of chaos, with its clutter of old armour, draperies, tapestry, and sketchbooks) and his concept of the home as spiritual space. As Morris would expound in a later lecture, houses had to be fit for the 'noble creatures, tall, wide-shouldered, and well-knit, with their bright eyes and well moulded features, these men full of courage, capacity and energy' who inhabit them. Already at Red Lion Square one detects the beginnings of the risky combination of the homely and heroic that became his mature decorative style.

This was the period of the 'Barbarossa' furniture (fig.20). Morris had commissioned for Red Lion Square the series of large-scale, rough-hewn pieces

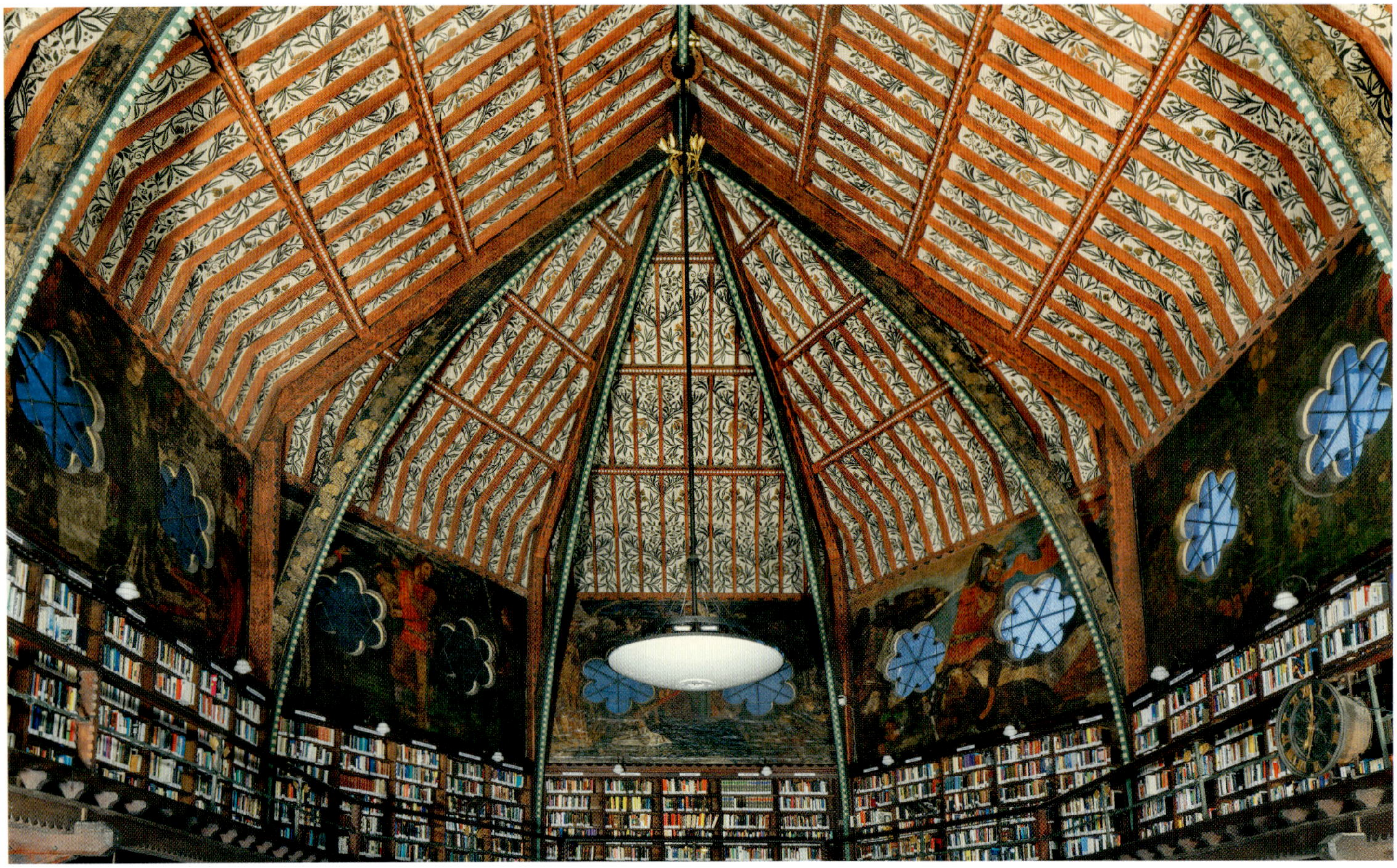

described by Dante Gabriel Rossetti as 'intensely mediæval ... tables and chairs like incubi and succubi.' Morris, Burne-Jones and Rossetti painted the big bare panels with decorative scenes. This was the kind of co-operative venture Morris hymned in his later lectures on design. The Barbarossa furniture was hardly functional. There were other things at issue beyond mere practicality. Morris believed in resonance, the mystic, the spectacular. As a designer of furniture he had a sweeping arrogance: 'If you want to be comfortable go to bed.'

In the development of Morris the designer two early episodes were absolutely central. The first was the decorating of the Oxford Union through the summer of 1857 (fig.21). The second was the building two years later of Red House at Bexleyheath (fig.6), the home designed by Philip Webb for Morris on his marriage to Jane Burden, with Morris in the role of ultimate creative client. Both these architecturally distinguished brand-new buildings were important in giving Morris his first real experience of practical design work: the building up of pattern, the layerings of colour, the controlled but exuberant approach to the interior that Morris was to perfect in his professional practice on a much more lavish scale. Both episodes confirmed his faith in the romantic concept of male creative teamwork, the band of brother artists, experts in different disciplines, that surfaced so hopefully (and ended so tragically) with Morris, Marshall, Faulkner & Co. Most crucially, Morris's own intense enjoyment of these working holidays gave a new conviction to his views on joy in labour. His heartfelt thesis that creative work gives pleasure and that life without pleasurable work is mere endurance can be traced back to the Oxford Union, the popping of the soda-water corks and Morris ebulliently pressing his thumb into the wet paintwork, leaving traces on the sandwiches the artists ate while they were working: 'This is mine and this and this.'

Morris, Marshall, Faulkner & Co., established in 1861, provided Morris with a framework for design activity that lasted, more or less unaltered, until his death. 'The firm', as it was called informally and jokily, consisted originally of seven partners, but much of the creative impetus was Morris's. The firm had been financed largely

Fig.21 **Oxford Union debating hall, showing a section of the murals with Morris's contribution on the far right (see VI.7).**
The Oxford Union Society

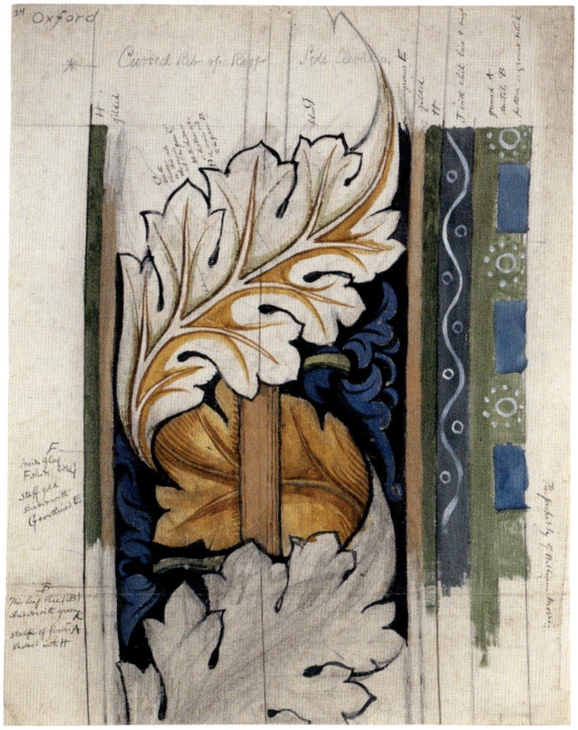

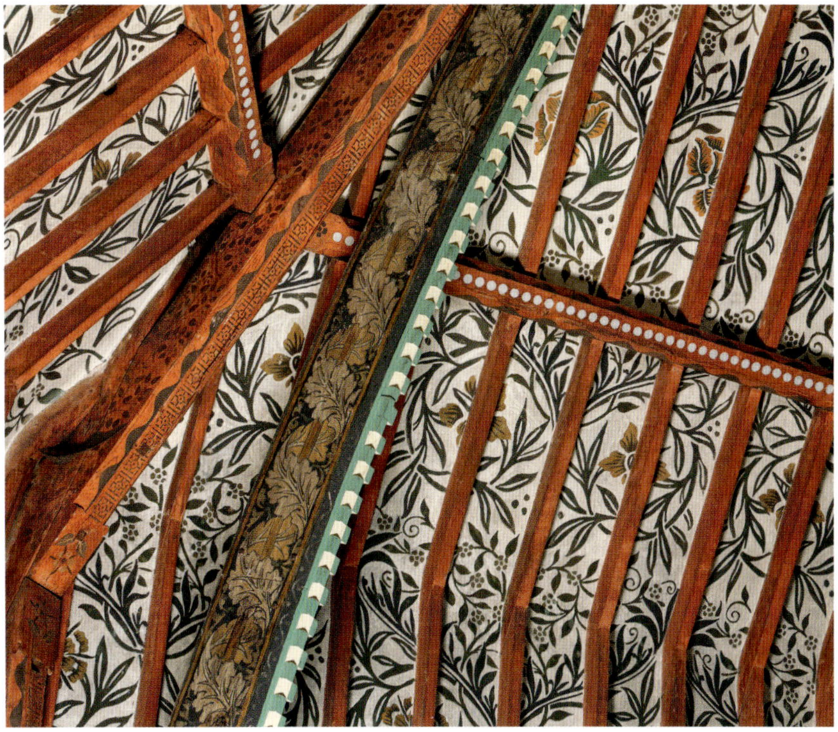

Fig.22 **Design for the curved ribs of the roof of the Oxford Union, created by Morris *c*.1874–5 during a later phase of decoration and annotated with detailed notes for the painter-decorators.**
William Morris Society

Fig.23 **Detail of the painted ceiling with its profusion of pattern.**
The Oxford Union Society

by himself and with loans from his mother, and from very early days Morris was paid a salary as business manager. He was the partner permanently on the premises, fulfilling the role we would now call the art director's. Morris was responsible for overall design decisions and quality control. He became the designer who was also delegator over a wide spectrum. His daughter May, who later worked as Morris's assistant, described the degree of his involvement.

> He was in direct relation with silk-weavers and carpet-weavers, dyers and blockers, with pattern-makers and block-cutters, with cabinet-makers and carvers in wood; with glass-painters, kiln-men and labourers and with his wall-paper printers; and it was not as if he sat in an office and received reports from managers of different departments with the technical details of which he was unfamiliar: he had grasped the nature of all this industry of which he was the pivot and with it the nature of those whom he employed – understanding their limitations as well as their capabilities.

For Morris designing was an exercise in fellowship.

From the early 1860s William Morris was also in direct relation with the public, in the form of the firm's professional and private clients and random visitors to the shop and showroom attached to the firm's workshops, first in Red Lion Square, then in Queen Square, Bloomsbury. Morris liked the idea of shopkeeping, imbuing with romance the discreet exchanges of small specialist traders. The expertise of London food merchants had intrigued him when he visited his father in the City as a boy. He saw shopkeeping as part of the whole cycle of designing, the personal fulfilment of the contract between the creator and end-user of the product. A visitor to the shop at Red Lion Square was at first a little startled to be shown around by the tousle-headed proprietor himself. When she chose two tumblers, Morris and his friend Val Prinsep wrapped them up in paper. The customer, Mrs Richmond Ritchie, went away 'very much amused and interested, with a general impression of sympathetic shyness and shadows and dim green glass.'

By 1862, when the firm made its official debut at the International Exhibition at South Kensington, Morris was already immersed in the first and longest lasting of his great design enthusiasms, the revival of stained glass. This was partly pragmatism: the refitting of old churches and the building of new ones in the onsurge of ritual revival made it a commercially sensible development (fig.24). But, as always with Morris, there was more to it than that. On his tours of northern France as an undergraduate he had seen

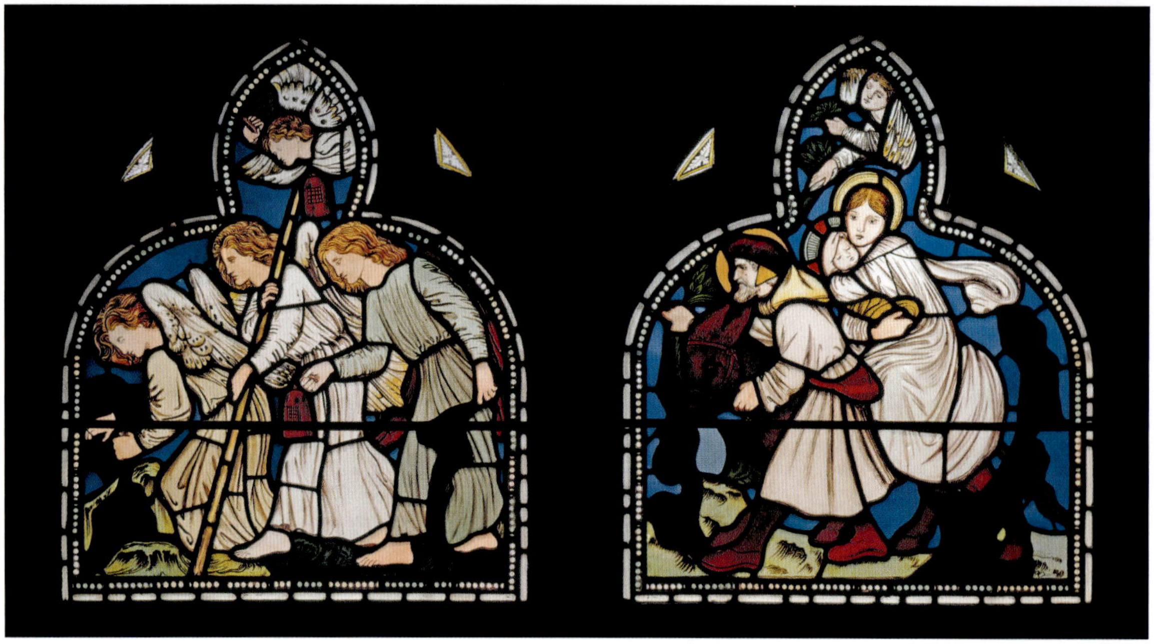

Fig.24 ***The Flight into Egypt*, designed by Edward Burne-Jones, St Michael and All Angels, Brighton, 1862.**

the medieval stained glass in the Gothic cathedrals. Its possibilities lay deep in his imagination. Stained glass appears in several of his stories of that time. He responded not just to the sparkle and the glamour but to the narrative qualities. Stained glass conveyed its message even to the illiterate. Morris felt he had discovered a truly populist art.

His contribution to the firm's stained glass was less that of designer of individual windows, though some of his own glass had a great clarity and sweetness. His chief role was to keep overall control over the colour and, in later years, also the leading of each window. The artists submitted their designs in cartoon form for the men in the workshop to 'glassify' as Morris directed them. His serious and selfless involvement in the project can be gauged by William De Morgan's description of Morris at Red Lion Square dressed in vestments and posed as if playing on a regal 'to illustrate certain points in connexion [*sic*] with stained glass'.

Morris's sympathies were always with the recondite. His brilliance was in rescuing apparently lost causes, pulling forgotten processes out of their obscurity to give them a highly personal contemporary significance. In the mid-1860s it was wood engraving. Burne-Jones and Morris were working on a series of illustrations for Morris's 'Big Book of Stories in Verse', his *Earthly Paradise*. They based their style on Italian Renaissance woodcuts, particularly those of the *Hypnerotomachia Poliphili*, printed in Venice in 1499. Morris attacked the task with an almost manic vigour, cutting at least 35 blocks himself. Burne-Jones drew a famous cartoon of him in action, with his graver's tools around him, hunched up with energy (fig.221). By 1869 Morris was reviving lost techniques first of calligraphy and then illumination, laboriously learning the rudiments of Roman and italic scripts, rediscovering the ancient art of gilding. May remembered her father's study for years after, strewn around with his experimental squares of gilding as Morris tried out ancient recipes given by Theophilus. He could not regard design work as a separate activity. Its cyclic concentrations dominated Morris's personal life and eddied through his homes.

Fig.25 **The textile printing shed at Merton Abbey. Published in Lewis F. Day's *The Art of William Morris*, 1899.**
V&A

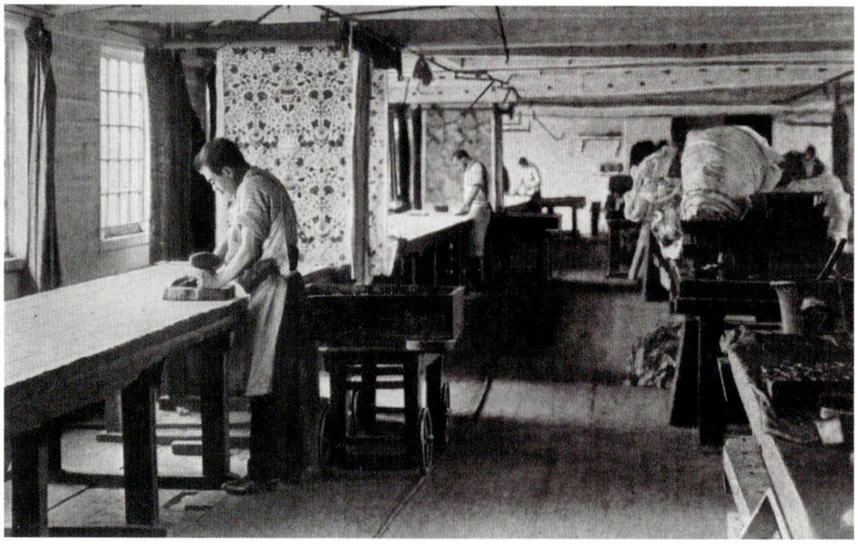

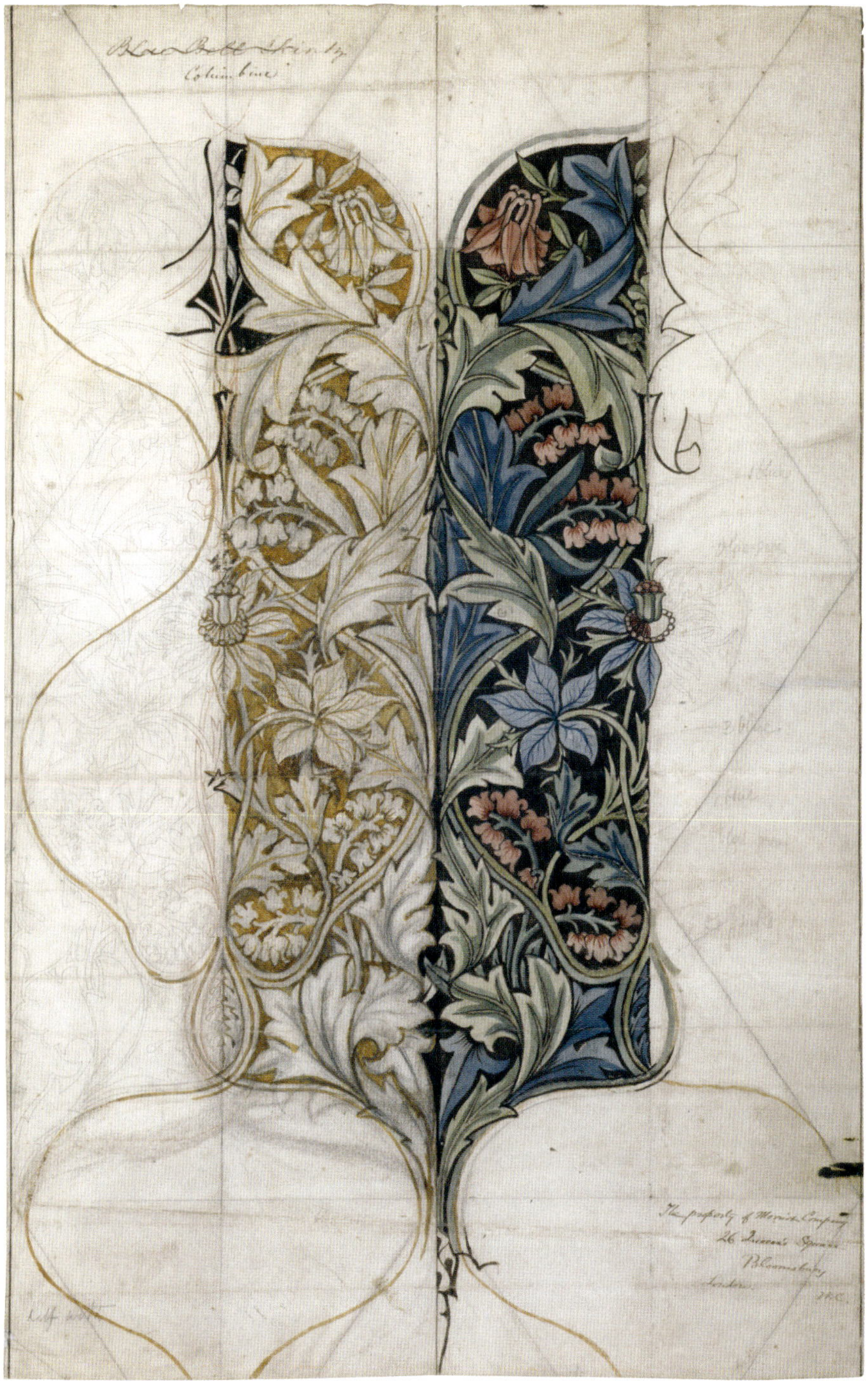

Fig.26 **Design for *Bluebell* or *Columbine* printed cotton by William Morris, 1876 (XII.42).**
V&A (E.44–1940)
Bequeathed by May Morris

The main thrust of Morris's life was integration. He worked passionately for an end to class divisions, both as a political thinker and as a practical socialist. As an early environmentalist he attempted to reconcile the country and the city. As a writer William Morris shifts conventional boundaries: his political polemic is poetic, in his poetry and novels the inventiveness masks hard political statement. He is always a great deal more complex than he seems. The importance of Morris the designer in his period, and indeed in any period, is the degree of integration he achieved between the visual design processes and the productive. The extent to which Morris designed through making, proposing and retracting, developing and adapting according to the progress of his technical experiments is clear from his extensive, detailed, often agitated correspondence with his collaborator Thomas Wardle, the textile dyer and printer of Leek.

For the whole decade from the mid-1870s Morris's energies were focused upon textiles. It is fascinating to watch his dogged progress as he masters the techniques in one area after another, gradually drawing in production under his own control. First, we find him investigating vegetable dyeing, working in Leek with Wardle, his arms plunged in the dye vats, 'taking in dyeing at every pore'. Next, he turns his formidable attention to weaving. Morris rising in the dawn through the summer of 1879 to work on the experimental loom set up in his bedroom at Kelmscott House in Hammersmith is as heroic a Victorian as Charles Darwin, driven by the same necessity to know. By the time Morris's workshops transferred to Merton Abbey in 1881, they were increasingly self-sufficient in dyeing, in weaving silk and woollen fabrics, in hand-knotting rugs and carpets, and were at the early stages of making the high-warp tapestry that had for so long been Morris's 'bright dream' (fig.25). His technical confidence gave Morris's design work a new urgency, huge buoyancy. He produced at least 32 designs for printed fabrics (fig.26), 23 for woven fabrics, 21 designs for wallpapers as well as designs for carpets and rugs, embroideries and tapestries between 1875 and 1885. At this period his productivity approached frenzy. He wrote to his friend Aglaia Coronio: 'I am drawing patterns so fast that last night I dreamed I had to draw a sausage; somehow I had to eat it first, which made me anxious about my digestion: however I have just done quite a pretty pattern for printed work.'

Morris's test of a successful pattern was that it provoked thought and concentrated feeling. It spoke of shared human experience and 'ancientness'. It gave an intimation of things beyond itself. Perhaps one explanation for the increasing depths in Morris's magnificent patterns of this later middle period is the growing despair of his political analysis. Design was his own life blood. In one of his lectures, 'The Prospects of

Architecture', Morris admitted he would die if deprived of what he called his 'ordinary daily work', by which he meant his routine production and supervision of designs. How to equate his own necessary quest for perfectionist excellence with his perception of civilization on a collision course, his bleak belief that art must go under in the end? Morris in the 1880s has been misrepresented. He could never be complacent about his continuing to manufacture luxury goods for the sophisticated bourgeoisie while so actively embroiled in the socialist cause. If Morris was much goaded he was his own chief goader: 'Am I doing nothing but make-believe then, something like Louis XVI's lock-making?' was his anguished question to Georgiana Burne-Jones. In the socialist turmoil Morris from time to time neglected his design work. But inevitably, and with poignant joy, he would return to it. Some of his designs of that period – for example the extraordinary *Woodpecker* tapestry (fig.27) – have the dignity of imperfectibility.

In January 1891 Morris was once again beaming with activity. He had rented a cottage at 16 Upper Mall in Hammersmith, where he was installing the Kelmscott Press. The Press, his last great opus in practical designing, has been interpreted as an old man's aberration, a softening, almost a reneging on his socialist fervour. In fact it should be seen as a triumphant culmination, a drawing together of many of the threads that had fascinated Morris throughout his life in the politics of art. Morris, so endlessly, productively resilient, had recast his long experience as bibliophile and collector, with his immersion in the book crafts of illumination and calligraphy, and his own history as a reader avaricious for knowledge and for narrative. Morris began his Press with a very clear idea of what a book could do. Most of all it was the final illustration of his theory that 'Nothing should be made by man's labour which is not worth making, or which must be made by labour degrading to the makers.' The Press was not a revolutionary workshop: it was almost paternalistic in its structure. But it was the final expression of Morris's belief in community endeavour, his sense of the importance not just of what we make but of how we relate to one another while we make it. Its coherence and integrity of purpose and of product were to be influential in the whole development of twentieth-century European and American typographic and book design.

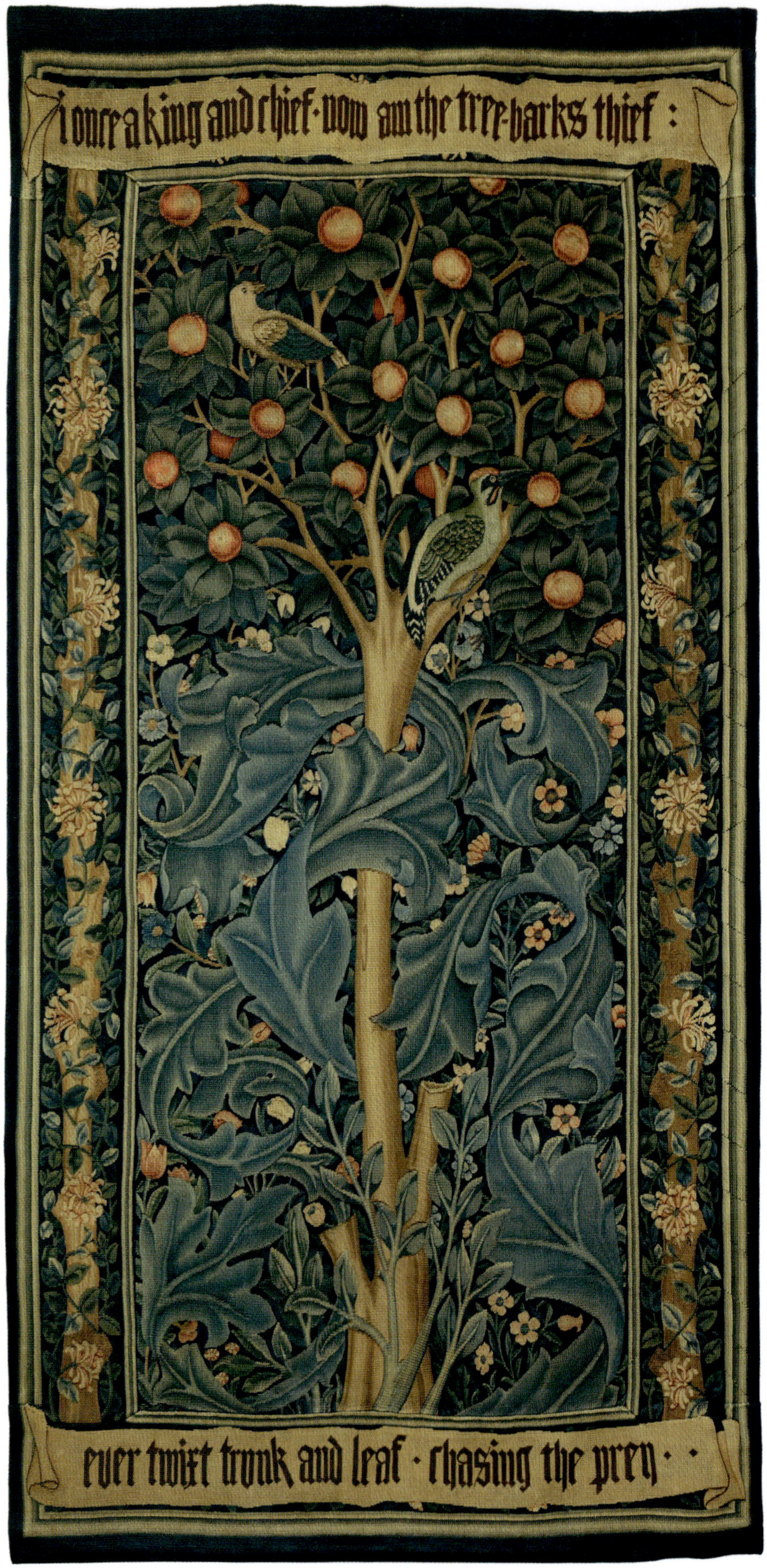

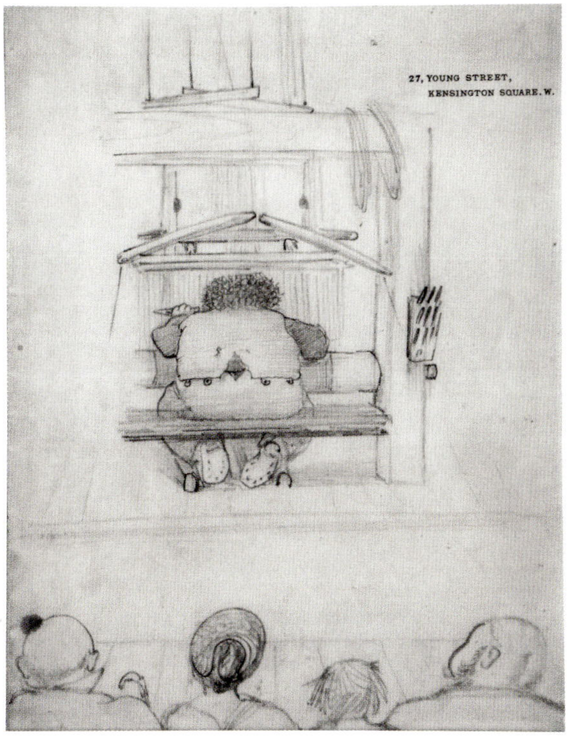

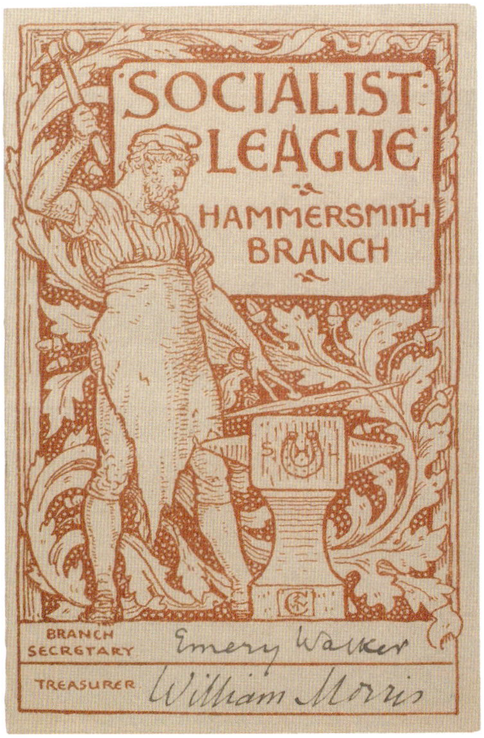

Fig.27 (opposite) ***Woodpecker* tapestry, designed by Morris, 1885.**
William Morris Gallery

Fig.28 (right) **Morris giving a weaving demonstration at the Arts and Crafts Exhibition, caricature by Edward Burne-Jones, November 1888.**
William Morris Gallery

Fig.29 (far right) **Membership card for the Hammersmith branch of the Socialist League, designed by Walter Crane, 1885.**
William Morris Society

Reminiscing in the 1890s Morris's friend and chief collaborator Edward Burne-Jones summed up his career with exasperated fondness:

> When I first knew Morris nothing would content him but being a monk, and getting to Rome, and then he must be an architect, and apprenticed himself to Street, and worked for two years, but when I came to London and began to paint he threw it all up, and must paint too, and then he must give it up and make poems, and then he must give it up and make window hangings and pretty things, and when he had achieved that, he must be a poet again, and then after two or three years of Earthly Paradise time, he must learn dyeing, and lived in a vat, and learned weaving, and knew all about looms, and then made more books, and learned tapestry, and then wanted to smash everything up and begin the world anew, and now it is printing he cares for, and to make wonderful rich-looking books and all things he does splendidly – and if he lives the printing will have an end – but not I hope, before Chaucer and the Morte d'Arthur are done; and then he'll do I don't know what, but every minute will be alive.

It is tempting to wonder what Morris would have turned to had he lived a few years longer. Metalwork is the prime candidate. There is only one isolated example of the Arthurian armour he commissioned from a forge near Oxford Castle, the helmet of which trapped him inside it, 'dancing with rage and roaring' (fig.108). Yet Morris's writings, in particular those late fantasy novels, show just how attuned he was to metalwork: they clatter with drinking cups and breastplates, swords and ankle clasps and hauberks. He admired the antique silverwork when he was in Iceland and brought back decorative girdles for his daughters. Morris's robust physique and confrontational character appeared to his contemporaries the model metalworker's: both in *King René's Honeymoon* cabinet of the 1860s (fig.230) and Walter Crane's membership card for the Socialist League Hammersmith branch of the 1880s (fig.29) Morris is depicted as a smith. George Bernard Shaw bemoaned the fact that there was never a Kelmscott Theatre. It is more to the point to regret that there was never a Kelmscott forge or Kelmscott silversmithing workshop. Morris with his strength and grace could have made admirable metalwork. But very shortly after Burne-Jones spoke those words he died.

II

THE WRITER

Peter Faulkner

Amid all his other activities and commitments, Morris was a prolific writer. *The Collected Works*, splendidly edited by his daughter May between 1910 and 1915, run to 24 volumes and she added two further bulky volumes in 1936. Subsequently there have been editions of his other writings, including letters, journals, diaries, lectures, journalistic articles and a play: and there is plenty more, especially in the form of uncollected political material. His writings cover an enormous range but their favoured form is the story, whether in verse or prose. Morris was already a storyteller when he was a schoolboy at Marlborough – the captain of his dormitory apparently found him 'an inexhaustible source' of the stories he wanted to hear – and on his death-bed Morris was correcting the proofs of his last story, *The Sundering Flood*, having enjoyed the completion of his Kelmscott edition of the works of Chaucer, the greatest of English storytellers.

By the time he entered Oxford in 1853, Morris was already widely read, with the works of Sir Walter Scott early favourites for their combination of exciting narrative and attention to the earlier history of Britain. At Oxford he read Keats and Tennyson, together with such social critics as Thomas Carlyle and John Ruskin, and socially responsible novelists such as the Christian Socialist Charles Kingsley and the High Church Charlotte Yonge. His friends, knowing him as a rather boisterous young man with a wide range of enthusiasms, particularly for medieval history and architecture, were surprised by his presenting himself as a poet, suddenly in the autumn term of 1854. Much later Richard Watson Dixon was to recall, vividly, listening to Morris reading 'The Willow and the Red Cliff' to Burne-Jones and himself and thinking the poem astoundingly original and impressive. When congratulated, however, Morris is said merely to have remarked, 'Well, if this is poetry, it is very easy to write'. This story, though it may have been simplified in memory and lends itself to presenting a Morris more naive than he actually was, does suggest something of his undoubted fluency and, more importantly, his eager and energetic imagination. His was a naturally creative sensibility, and one way in which this expressed itself was in telling a great proliferation of stories.

Almost all these stories are set in the past. Morris's imagination, guided by his wide reading, ranged freely back into history and found its home there. He was, of course, not unaware of the condition of the country in which he was living

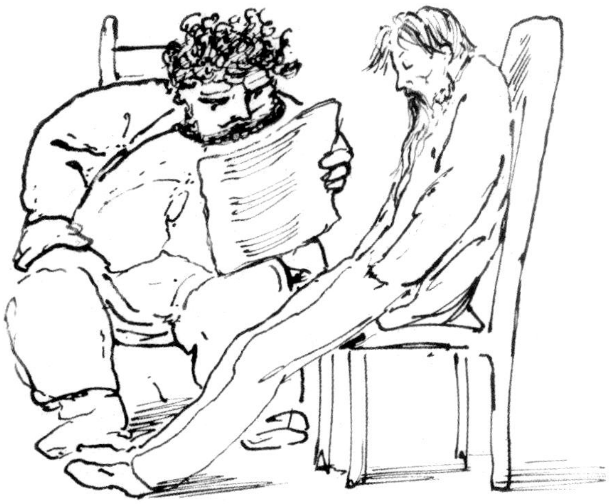

Fig.30 **Morris reading poetry to Burne-Jones, caricature by Edward Burne-Jones, *c*.1870.**
V&A (E.450–1976)

and became more so as his experience expanded, but he discussed such matters largely in lectures and non-fictional prose. In his poetry and fiction the past provided him with a distance through which he could focus more readily on his subject matter: human behaviour and society as revealed to an imaginative and historically informed mind. In *News from Nowhere* in 1890 he was to criticize, through the intelligent observations of the vivacious Ellen, the realist literature of his own day as having done nothing to liberate its readers from their social oppression – for having been, as recent critics have suggested, in collusion, however unconscious, with that oppression.

However that may be, Morris consistently rejected the present as the setting for his stories. There seem to be only two exceptions. In *The Oxford and Cambridge Magazine* (which was produced with the aid of Morris's inheritance, an income of £741 in 1855), there is only one story out of eight with a contemporary setting, 'Frank's Sealed Letter'. Later, in 1872, Morris was to start writing a novel in a modern setting, but he abandoned it as 'abortive'. 'Frank's Sealed Letter' is highly melodramatic and cannot compare in quality with the other stories in the magazine with their dreamlike or vaguely medieval settings, and names such as 'The Hollow Land' and 'Gertha's Lovers'. The most disturbing of them is 'Lindenborg Pool', adapted from a story called 'The Sunken Mansion' in Benjamin Thorpe's *Northern Mythology* (1851). The narrator's experience is that of nightmare as he finds himself riding, in the costume of a thirteenth-century priest, to a great house, where he is taken to what he expects to be a dying man to whom he can minister – but who turns out to be a pig. The revelation is received with grotesque laughter by the hundreds of people present, while the narrator escapes, horrified. As he turns back, however, he sees that the castle has disappeared, and all that is left is a cloud of lime dust and a deep black lake. The reader has been taken into a Gothic world like that of Edgar Allan Poe. It is an astounding story for the young Morris to have written, as indeed are the others, though none is so succinctly powerful and all are shot through with more positive qualities of hope, love and beauty.

However, the world of Morris's early writings is, for whatever reasons – largely psychological we must suppose, since at this stage he was not deeply concerned with social issues – a sombre world of conflict and violence. Ingrid Hanson gives an illuminating account of this aspect of Morris's writings in *William Morris and the Uses of Violence, 1856–1890* (2013). Violence plays an important part in Morris's early poems, published as *The Defence of Guenevere and Other Poems* in 1858, when Morris was only 24. The 30 poems in the volume show Morris employing a remarkable variety of poetic forms, adapted to the varying subject matter. The title poem and the following three are taken from the Arthurian legends, which were one of the Victorians' favourite sources of material for both literature and painting. Tennyson's *Idylls of the King* (of which the first group was to appear in the following year, 1859) constitute the most elaborate handling of this material, always inflected by the Poet Laureate with a sense of duty and of morality. Morris's handling is very different. Guenevere is shown defying her accusers, offering her physical beauty as its own justification, and referring to her marriage to Arthur in dismissive terms. Everywhere in these poems Morris is interested principally in vivid and dramatic scenes or characters. By contrast with most other Victorian writers, he seems disinclined to moralize. The violence and suffering are vividly shown, both in the world of Sir Thomas Malory and that of Jean Froissart, who described the wars between England and France in the fourteenth century. A poem such as 'The Haystack in the Floods' gives a powerful picture of the failure of the loving Robert to save his beloved Jehane from the evil Godmar. Godmar's killing of Robert is chillingly described, as is Jehane's response, while the haystacks remain amid the rain and mud, as dreary as the human experience conveyed. There is also a group of more mysterious poems, with titles such as 'The Wind', 'The Blue Closet' and 'The

Tune of Seven Towers' (the last two derived from watercolours by Dante Gabriel Rossetti, which Morris had bought). They evoke a mysterious world of ghostly presences and threatening supernatural forces. The volume also includes 'Praise of My Lady', a love poem to Jane Burden, whom he was soon to marry, seeing her with as much awe as confidence, and as a lady of romance.

The Defence of Guenevere was the first book of Pre-Raphaelite poetry to be published – neither Rossetti nor Algernon Swinburne had yet done so. It accordingly drew scorn from a critical establishment still uneasy about the influence of the Brotherhood founded ten years previously. *The Spectator* was representative in speaking of the 'faults of affectation and bad taste' in the poems, although there were a few favourable responses. What seemed affectation to conventional minds was what attracted younger readers to poems that carry the Romantic impulse strongly forward in the narrative form which, as we have seen, held the strongest appeal to Morris. These are some of the most powerful poems of the mid-century; but Morris was never to write in the same mode again. There is no direct evidence that he was affected by the reviews – few letters survive from the period and it was a busy one in other ways, and so he may well have had less time for writing. He did start writing some poems on the fall of Troy, but they came to nothing. At all events, he was to publish nothing further until 1867, the longest gap in his writing career. However, during this period he married Jane Burden, moved into Red House, established Morris, Marshall, Faulkner & Co., began his career as a designer, and fathered two daughters. His next poem was to be on a classical theme. *The Life and Death of Jason*, published with great success in 1867, tells the story of Jason and the Golden Fleece, devoting a good deal of attention to the heroine-enchantress Medea – as we have already seen, Morris was inclined to give female characters a good deal of attention in his poetry. *Jason* is a very long poem, in 17 books, which is little read today, but it appealed to Victorian taste. The young Henry James reviewed it, praising its appeal 'to the jaded intellects of the present moment' as offering a world 'where they will be called upon neither to choose, to criticise, nor to believe, but simply to feel, to look, and to listen.' These may now seem odd grounds for praise, but they suggest that the appeal of the poem lay in its remoteness from the social and political issues of the age. Morris had found a subject matter which he could handle with confidence and fluency, and which appealed to the large and growing middle-class reading public.

Jason had originally been intended, before it grew so long, for inclusion in a larger poem, to be called *The Earthly Paradise*. The structure of this was based on such poems as Chaucer's *Canterbury Tales*, where a number of stories are brought together within a single work. In *The Earthly Paradise*, published in four volumes from 1868 to 1870, there were to be as many as 24 stories, told alternately each month by a group of Northern Wanderers in the fourteenth century and their hosts in 'some Western land', where they settle in old age after lives spent vainly seeking an earthly paradise. The stories are taken from a variety of sources, classical, medieval, Persian and Icelandic, from 'Cupid and Psyche' to 'The Lovers of Gudrun' (fig.31). Morris took pleasure in retelling these stories for the benefit of contemporary readers who might be unable to read them in the original languages, and the public received them with pleasure. Morris's later books were often published with the inscription, 'By the author of *The Earthly Paradise*'. The poem is structured around the months of the year, and each narrative poem is introduced by a brief lyrical poem. Some of these, particularly that for November, express a deeply personal sense of suffering and doubt, as do other lyrical poems written at the time, reflecting the failure of Morris's marriage, as Jane turned towards the charismatic Rossetti. It seems extraordinary that a man so emotionally reticent as Morris should publish in *The Atlantic Monthly* in May 1870 a poem like 'May Grown A-Cold', which concludes: 'Thy love is gone, poor wretch, thou art alone.' However, it was not for such private poetry that Morris was admired, but rather for his narrative works.

Morris published another ambitious – but not well received – poem in 1872, entitled *Love is Enough*. It is his most complex poetic structure; at its centre is a morality play about a king seeking love, which is performed before a newly married emperor and empress; the performance is framed between two peasant lovers and the royal couple, and there are a number of lyrical passages entitled 'The Music', which assert the theme of the centrality of love. However, the poem seems unsure of its own direction, and the Love (with a capital letter) that it celebrates hangs uncertainly between the divine and the human. *Love is Enough* shows unusual formal

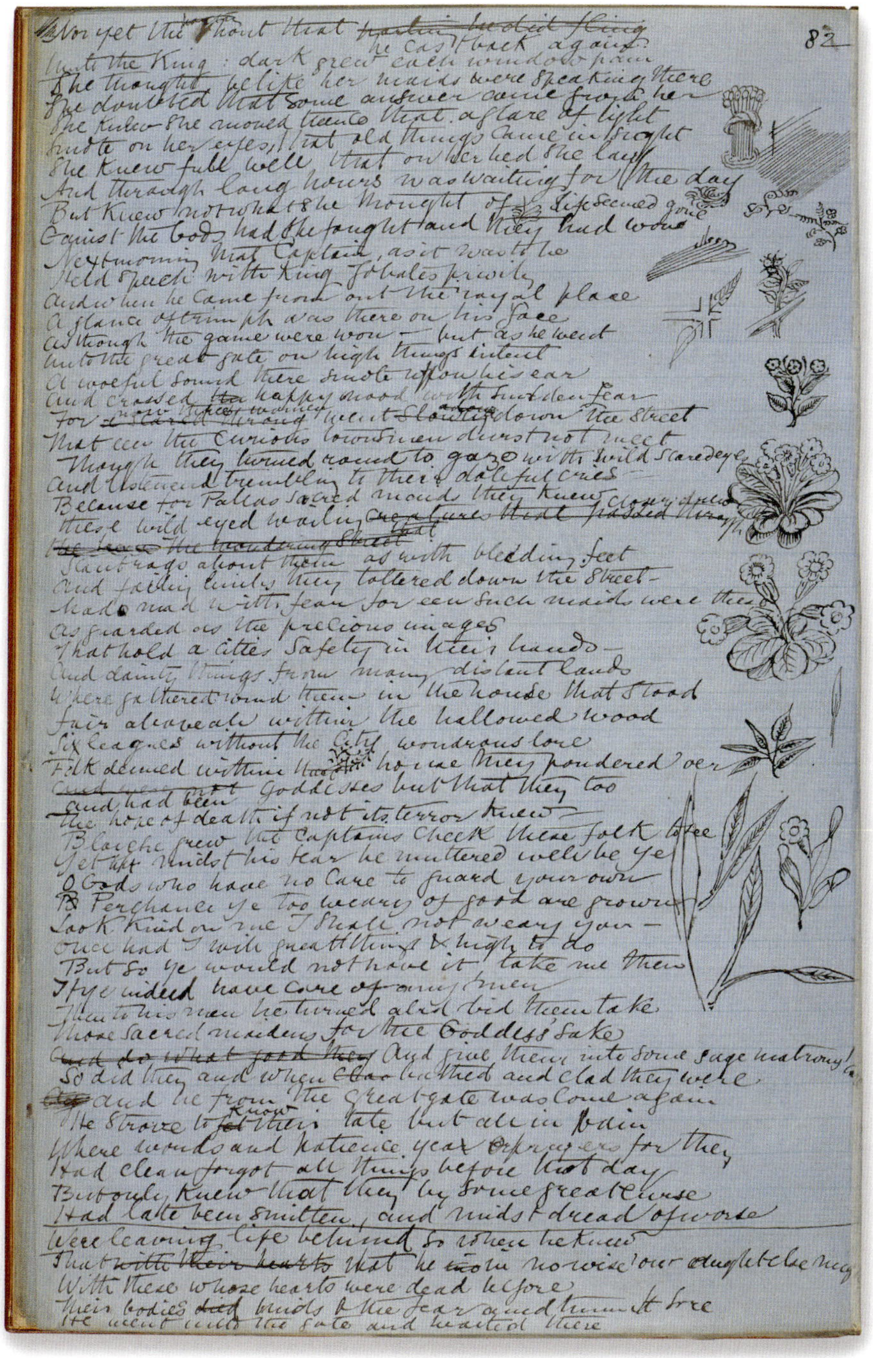

Fig.31 **Page from the manuscript 'Bellerophon in Lycia', a tale from *The Earthly Paradise*, 1869.**
British Library

ingenuity on Morris's part, but perhaps this was a way of avoiding the difficult personal questions that the title suggests. Morris wrote nothing like it subsequently. In later life, according to Henry Halliday Sparling in his 1924 book *The Kelmscott Press and William Morris Master-Craftsman,* Morris repudiated the title of the poem:

> On one occasion, he electrified those present by snatching down the volume from his bookshelves, rapping upon it with a paper-knife, pointing to its title, and exclaiming: 'There's a lie for you, though 'twas I that told it! Love isn't enough in itself; love *and work*, yes! *Work* and love, that's the life of a man! Why, a fellow can't even love decently unless he's got work to do, and pulls his weight in the boat!'

Reference has already been made to 'The Lovers of Gudrun', a poem in the third part of *The Earthly Paradise* and often considered the most dramatic and powerful of all its stories. The subject matter is taken from the Icelandic *Laxdaela Saga*, and this is evidence of the important turn Morris took at this stage towards the literature and culture of the North. In 1868 Morris met the Icelander Eiríkr Magnússon, with whose help he set about learning the language. Soon Iceland was to become vitally important to him, and to lead to the publication of a number of translations, including *The Saga of Gunnlaug Worm-Tongue* and *The Grettis Saga* in 1869 and *The Story of the Volsungs and Niblungs* in 1870. Icelandic culture inspired Morris as he sought for positive values in a mid-Victorian world in which *laissez-faire* industrialism was eating up the countryside and creating hideous towns. Iceland was first known to Morris through the sagas, but he visited the country in both 1871 and 1873. His journal of 1871, though not intended for publication, contains some of Morris's most vigorous writing, as do the poems which commemorate his visits, especially 'Iceland First Seen'. The *Three Northern Love Stories* of 1875 show his continuing enthusiasm, which culminated, as far as literature is concerned, in *Sigurd the Volsung* in 1876. Morris wanted to make 'the great story of the North' available to English readers, believing it was as important as the classical tale of Troy so widely accepted in Victorian culture. The result was his most energetic long narrative poem, told in hexameter lines which rhyme in couplets, with a good deal of alliteration. The story is that of the hero whom Wagner, employing the German account, was celebrating at the same time in *The Ring* (Morris did not like opera or consider it dignified enough to do justice to this material). Morris's poem is in four books, 'Sigmund' (the father of Sigurd), 'Regin' (the early life of Sigurd), 'Brynhild' (in which Sigurd is tricked into forgetting Brynhild, whom he loves, and into marrying Gudrun, and is killed by Guttorm, driving Brynhild also to her death), and finally 'Gudrun' (with Atli's destruction of the Niblungs). Morris manages to convey the uncompromising

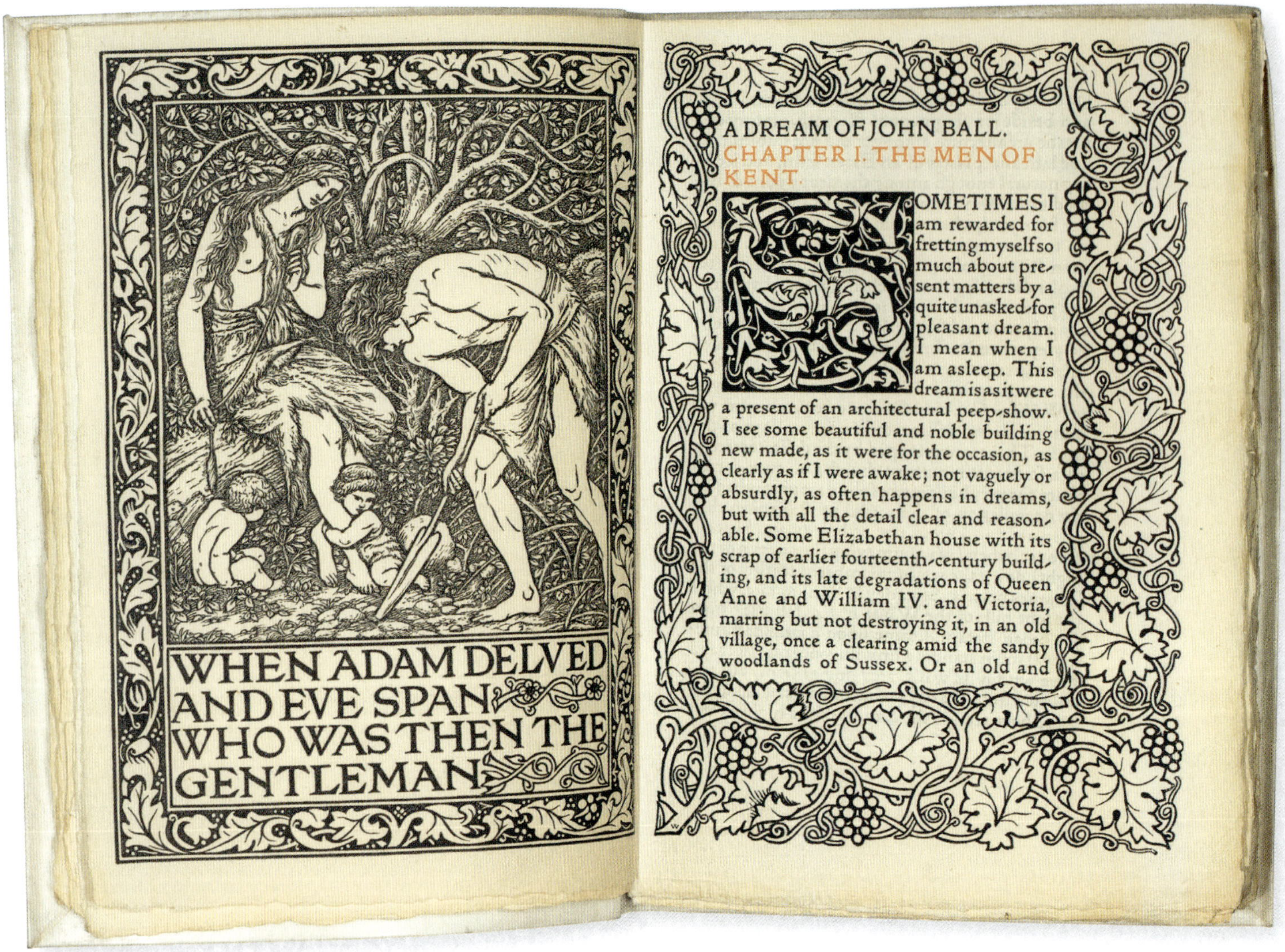

Fig.32 **Kelmscott Press edition of *A Dream of John Ball*, designed by William Morris and Edward Burne-Jones, 1892.**
William Morris Gallery

spirit of the saga with great success; but it is a spirit that did not appeal to the Victorian public. The critics praised the poem, but the public did not buy it; there was no second edition until 1887. Whether as a direct result of this or not, Morris turned more to prose in his later years.

But Morris's poetic energy did not altogether subside; it expressed itself in the form of translations, notably *The Aeneids of Virgil* in 1876, *The Odyssey of Homer* in 1887–8, *The Tale of Beowulf* (with A.J. Wyatt) in 1895 and *Old French Romances* in 1896. The range of Morris's ability and enthusiasms is remarkable, especially when we bear in mind his continuing work with Magnússon for the five volumes of the Saga Library, published between 1891 and 1895 (the sixth was published in 1905, after Morris's death). *The Odyssey* now reads most effectively: among the reviewers who praised it was Oscar Wilde, a good classical scholar, who saw it as expressing 'the fine loyalty of poet to poet'. However, by 1889 Morris was being criticized for the diction of his translations. R.Y. Tyrrell accused his version of Virgil of possessing an inappropriate 'olde-world tone' because of its 'Wardour-Street English' – a reference to a street noted for its production of sham-antique furniture. Morris did deliberately employ a special vocabulary in his later work, aimed to take the reader away from the contemporary world into that of the historical text. Some have regarded this as a positive imaginative feat, especially in the later prose romances. Norman Talbot celebrates it in his introductions to the Thoemmes Press editions of *The Water of the Wondrous Isles* (1994) and *The Story of the Glittering Plain & Child Christopher* (1996).

In the 1880s, however, much of Morris's formidable energy went into lecturing and political activity. Although he continued to write as much as ever, because of the subject matter of these writings they are discussed in other sections of this book. But, unsurprisingly, his remarkable literary ability contributed significantly to the success of his socialist writings, including the fictions *A Dream of John Ball* in 1886–7 and the masterpiece *News from Nowhere* in 1890. The former was illustrated by Burne-Jones with what became one of his best-known designs, based on the medieval couplet 'When Adam delved and Eve span, Who was then the gentleman?' (fig.32). Throughout his final decade – and alongside the creation of the Kelmscott Press – Morris continued to create works of imaginative fiction, usually referred to as the 'late prose romances' because of their avoidance of contemporary subject matter and of a realist mode of writing. A fine account is given by Phillippa Bennett in *Wonderlands* (2015). The first of these is *A Tale of the House of the Wolfings* (1888), which dramatizes (in a mixture of prose and verse) the conflict between the Romans and a Germanic tribe, or between commercial imperialism and the idea of community. *The Roots of the Mountains* (1889) deals with another Germanic tribal community under threat, this time from the Huns, some centuries later. Morris now wrote at greater length, and uniformly in prose, a carefully constructed prose whose diction is appropriate to the culture described. By the end, the Men of Burgdale have defeated the Dusky Men; these late romances contrast with the prose stories Morris had written as a young man at Oxford in their happy endings in which society and its leaders come together in a healthy unity. The optimism contrasts strongly with the tone of the realist fiction of the era, that of Thomas Hardy and George Gissing.

As the years passed, the romances became less historical and more purely symbolic, as their titles suggest. In *The Story of the Glittering Plain* (1890) the hero finds himself in a sterile world, a nightmare version of an earthly paradise. He exclaims, 'I seek no dream, but the end of dreams'. In so far as he speaks for Morris, we may interpret this not as meaning that there will be a turn towards realism; rather it may suggest that he now felt able to look directly at reality because of his political hopes for transforming it. At all events, the late romances all culminate in success for their attractive central characters, both male and female (the latter in particular being endowed with an independence and vitality very unusual in Victorian fiction), and for the societies in which they exist and to which they contribute their abilities as leaders. The same qualities are celebrated in some of Morris's later poems, included in the 1891 volume *Poems by the Way*, such as 'The Folk-Mote by the River' or 'Mine and Thine'. The movement towards something like fairytale can be seen in a poem such as 'Goldilocks and Goldilocks', but this again culminates in an attractive social unity.

That Morris did not want his romances to be interpreted too crudely is made clear by his letter to *The Spectator* in 1895, telling its readers that in the volume that had been reviewed, *The Wood Beyond the World*, he had intended no political allegory: 'it is meant for a tale pure and simple, with nothing didactic about it.' But of course, stories have implications, even if the intention is not didactic, and the defeat of the evil Dwarf and his deceptively beautiful Lady by Golden Walter and the Maid must prove heartening to the reader who has sympathized with the latter pair throughout. More powerfully in *The Well at the World's End* (1896) the eventual triumph of Ralph and Ursula is welcome to the reader because they have endeared themselves by their exemplary courage and humanity; again, it is notable that Ursula is as important a character as her partner. The symbolic world of the Dry Tree and the Well where the lovers drink together is finely rendered, as is their choice not to linger by the Well but to return together to their social responsibilities. In *Child Christopher and Goldilind the Fair* (1895) Morris produced a version of the fourteenth-century English poem *Havelock the Dane*, with a similar structure to his other romances. *The Water of the Wondrous Isles* (1897) is notable for having a female hero in a genre in which women are traditionally relegated (though not by Morris) to the roles of reward-for-male-courage or danger-to-be-avoided. Finally, in *The Sundering Flood* (of which Morris did not live to complete the final revision) the movement is again towards unity, as the river fails to prevent the lovers from coming together and creating a new society through their heroic efforts. When, towards the end, the heroic Steelhead responds to a hermit's valedictory 'Go in peace, and God and Allhallows keep thee', with the words, 'we will not contend about it, but I look to it to keep myself', the reader feels close to Morris's humanism, with its note of Icelandic stoicism. The Steelhead, who 'therewith strode off into the night', speaks to us of and for Morris, whose writings constitute an important part of his extraordinary all-round achievement.

III

THE BUSINESSMAN

Charles Harvey and Jon Press

William Morris was from a commercial background and he became familiar at an early age with both the rewards and tribulations of business life. He also acquired during his childhood a profound love of art, architecture and literature, especially that of the medieval period. In his youth he studied classics and theology, was articled to George Edmund Street, one of the leading architects of the Gothic Revival, and tried his hand at painting at Rossetti's insistence. All of these experiences were to have a profound influence upon his subsequent career in the decorative arts.

The prestige of the decorative arts grew rapidly in the 1850s. Street insisted that decoration was integral to architecture and that architects should seize the potential of crafts such as stained glass, metalwork and embroidery. John Ruskin likewise emphasized that every aspect of a building should form 'a great and harmonious whole', and his belief that the designer should be 'entirely familiar' with decorative techniques and materials made a great impression on Morris. The ideas of men such as Street and Ruskin struck a chord with a wide cross-section of Victorian society and Morris was not unusual in responding to them. What made him unique was the immense effort he made during his lifetime to give their ideas practical expression, and to extend them in important ways. This process began with the building and decoration of Red House, Morris's home at Bexleyheath, Upton, Kent, and led in turn to the formation of Morris, Marshall, Faulkner & Co. in April 1861.

There were six other partners in the firm: Dante Gabriel Rossetti and Ford Madox Brown were already famous; Philip Webb was an architect and Edward Burne-Jones had just begun a career in painting; Charles Faulkner was a mathematics don and Peter Paul Marshall an engineer and amateur painter. With supreme self-confidence, these young men set out on a commercial venture, the ultimate purpose of which was to transform the British public's appreciation of the decorative arts. The task was harder than they expected. It was as though they had gone out to start a revolution, only to find that it had already begun. From the outset, they faced strong competition from established firms such as Lavers & Barraud, Clayton & Bell, and Heaton, Butler & Bayne in stained glass, and Skidmore's of Coventry and Hardman's of Birmingham in ecclesiastical furnishings.

Clearly, the firm could only be successful by dint of much hard work. The view later put about by Rossetti that Morris, Marshall, Faulkner & Co.

Fig.33 (opposite above)
Minute book for Morris, Marshall, Faulkner & Co., 10 December 1862 to 4 November 1874.
The Huntington Library, Art Museum and Botanical Gardens

Fig.34 (opposite below)
Philip Webb's account book for Morris, Marshall, Faulkner & Co. and the early years of Morris & Co., *c.*1861–78. The left page records his work for the firm and his fees, the right his purchases including wine glasses and tumblers.
Archive of Art and Design, V&A (AAD/2014/5/3/5)

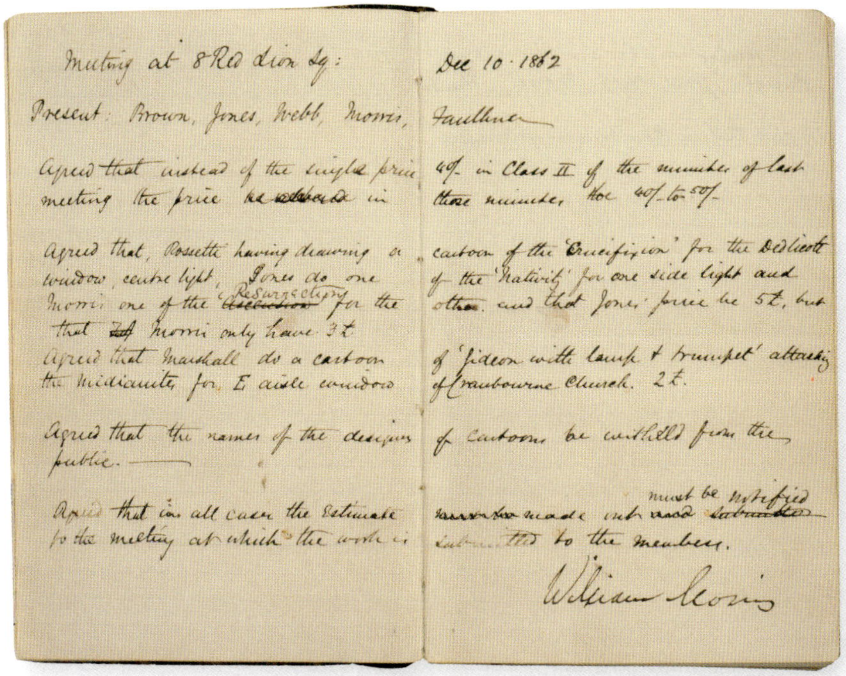

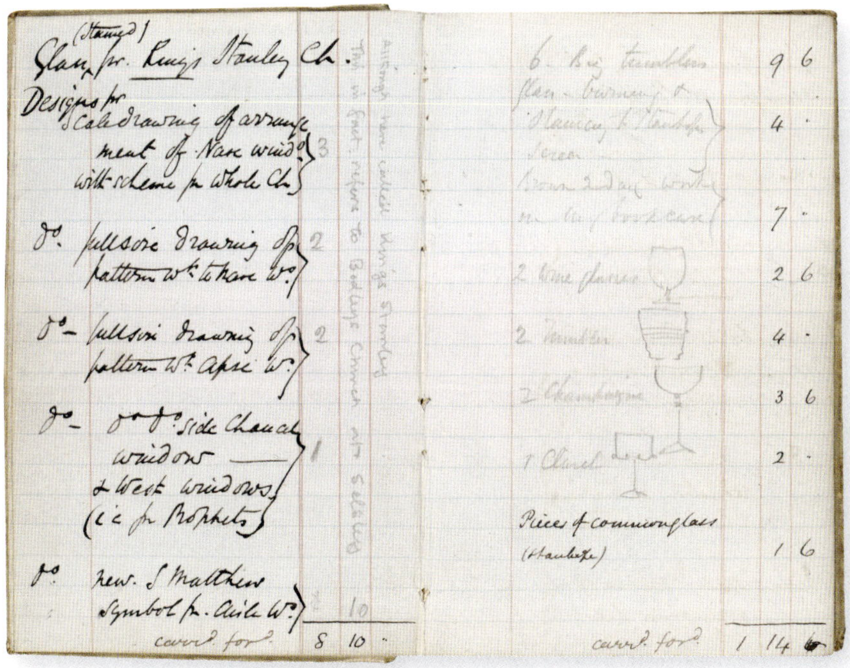

was 'mere playing at business' might well reflect his own attitude, but tells us little about the other members. Marshall was probably no great asset; but Morris, though blessed with a substantial private income, had a voracious appetite for work. Burne-Jones suffered all his life from anxieties about money and was keener than anyone that the firm should be a paying proposition. He needed work and income, not membership of a pleasant, civilized, unremunerative club. Nor is it likely that the practically minded Madox Brown would have given much time to the sort of casual business concern so airily described by Rossetti.

There was nothing casual or light-hearted in the thinking that caused the partners to band together. The firm's operations and finances were planned and worked out in detail (fig.33). Morris was made business manager at a salary of £150 a year. Commissions were shared out according to the actual contributions made by individual members. This did not merely apply to the quantity of work done: the greater skills of Rossetti, Burne-Jones and Madox Brown were rewarded with higher fees than those of Morris and Marshall. The partners were well aware of the advantages that this type of association could confer: a group of artists working together could offer a much more complete service than they could possibly do as individuals – a point emphasized in the firm's prospectus.

The establishment and development of the firm was based upon the partners' appreciation of the rapidly growing market for ecclesiastical products. During the early decades of Queen Victoria's reign there was an upsurge of church building on a scale unknown since the thirteenth century. Between 1840 and 1876, the Church of England built 1,727 new churches and rebuilt or extensively restored 7,144, at a total cost in excess of £25 million. As the years passed, churches became more elaborate, decoration more lavish and costly. All kinds of furnishings were in demand and stained glass for windows was particularly favoured. Morris and his friends made effective use of personal contacts in securing commissions and efforts of this type were crucial to establishing the reputation of the company. Morris and Webb (fig.34) got work from Street, George Frederick Bodley and other architects of their acquaintance. Rossetti, with his wide social circle and ready charm, also managed to win numerous contracts.

Within a few years of its formation, however, the firm ran into difficulties. It had become too dependent upon the stained-glass market, which declined sharply in the general depression of the late 1860s. Fashions changed, too, and several potential customers expressed a preference for more straightforward Gothic Revival work. The firm undertook some large secular projects in the mid-1860s, notably the St James's Palace commission and the decoration of the Green Dining Room at the South Kensington Museum between 1866 and 1869 (figs 35 and 140). But while these projects

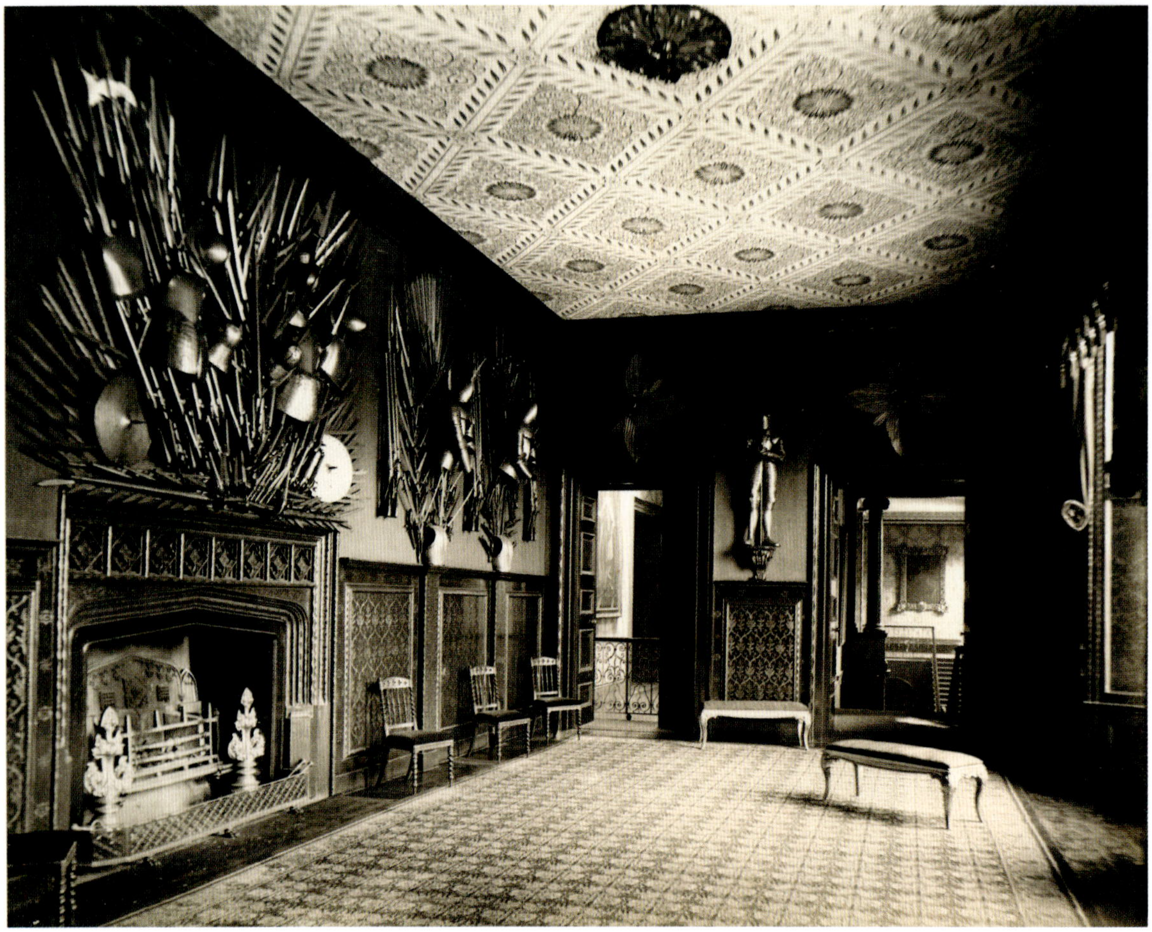

Fig.35 **The Armoury at St James's Palace, decorated by Morris, Marshall, Faulkner & Co., 1866–7. The machine-woven carpet was added in the 1880s. Photographed by Bedford Lemere & Co., 1887.**
Historic England Archive

were prestigious and very profitable, the market was necessarily small and unpredictable.

It was clear by the late 1860s that the business, in its existing form, could never provide large incomes for the partners. For some, this hardly mattered. Faulkner had returned to academic life at Oxford. Marshall, who always had to be chased for designs, had not given up his career in surveying. For Rossetti, the firm was never more than a sideline. It was Morris who was most affected by the changing fortunes of the firm. Just as sales began to slump, his once substantial unearned income from mining shares entered a terminal decline. It was through necessity that he became a committed man of business, intent on expanding trade and acquiring an income that would safeguard his financial future.

The principal lesson learned by Morris during his early years in business was that if the firm was to prosper, it would have to enter new markets and establish its reputation with the general public. This was easier said than done. A complete interior decorating service called for a whole new range of products of good quality and design. In the early 1870s Morris worked long and hard to produce fresh designs for wallpapers and chintzes and get suppliers to meet his needs. He was often disappointed with the results, but still managed to impart a characteristic style to his interiors.

Growing recognition and financial success, however, brought new problems in their wake. Morris, Marshall, Faulkner & Co. remained a partnership and each partner was legally entitled to an equal share of the profits, but Morris was no longer prepared to devote his life to generating profits for sleeping partners. In August 1874, he announced his intention to reconstitute the firm under his sole ownership. The result was a prolonged and acrimonious dispute with Madox Brown, Rossetti and Marshall. As risk-sharers, they felt entitled to an equal share of the profits and assets of the firm, just as they accepted 'joint and several' liability for its debts. They had a point, and it is possible that a court would have upheld their claims to substantial compensation.

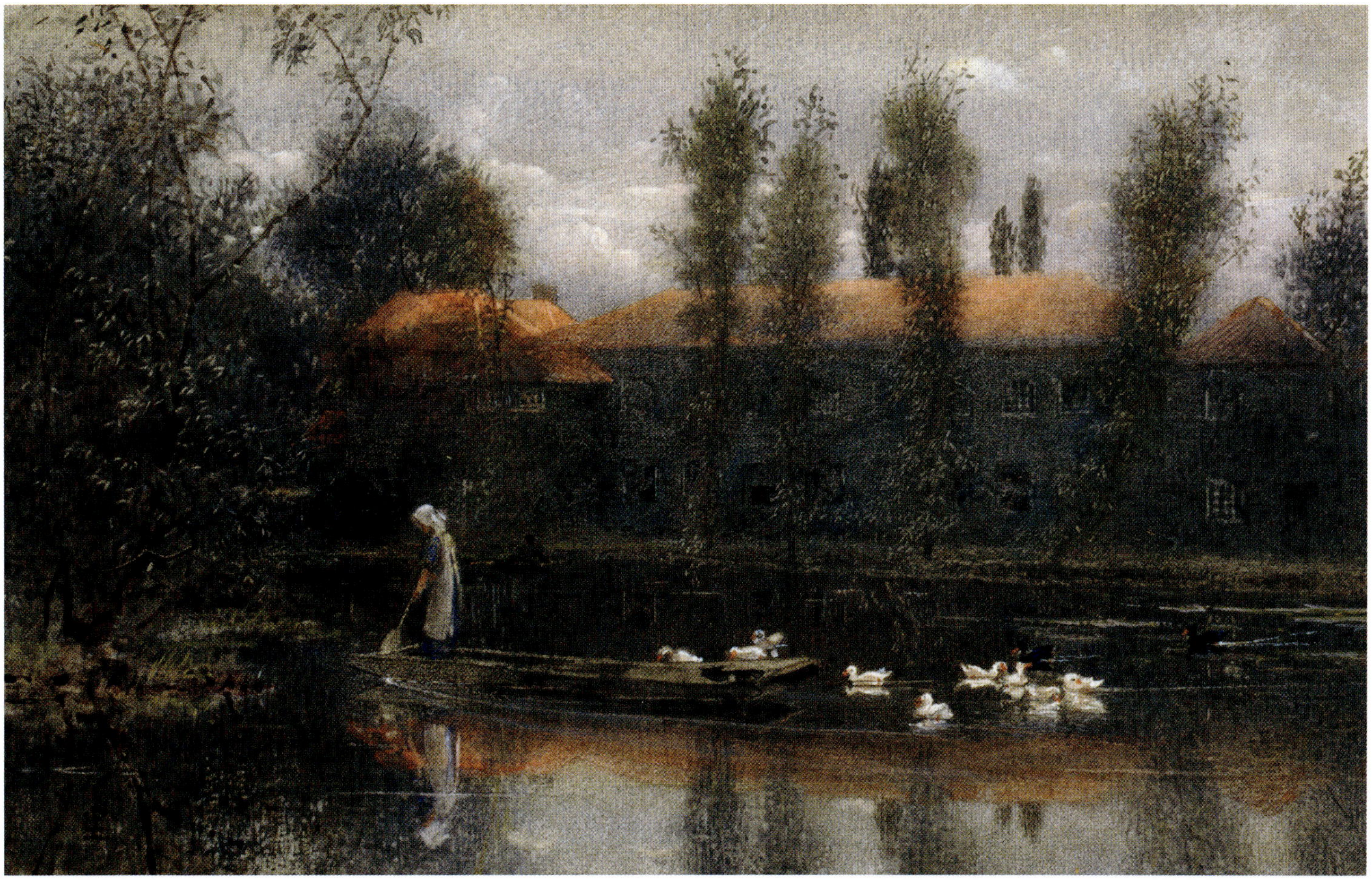

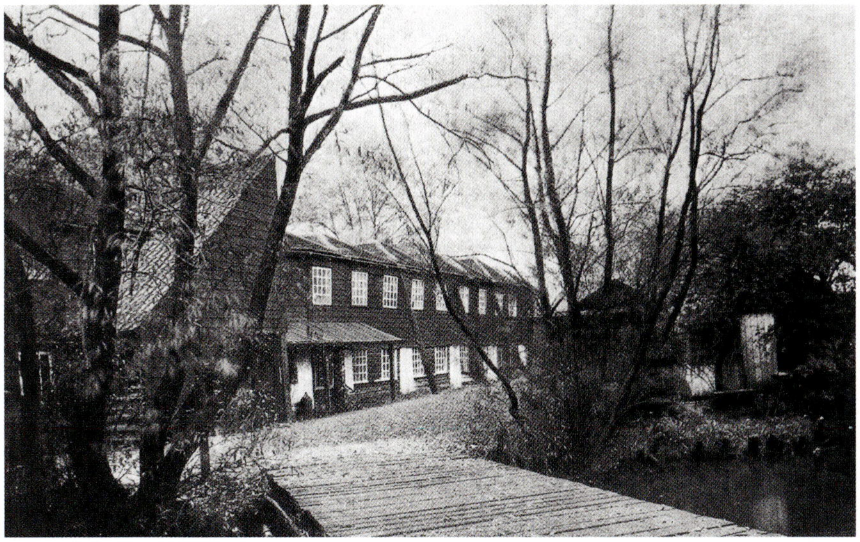

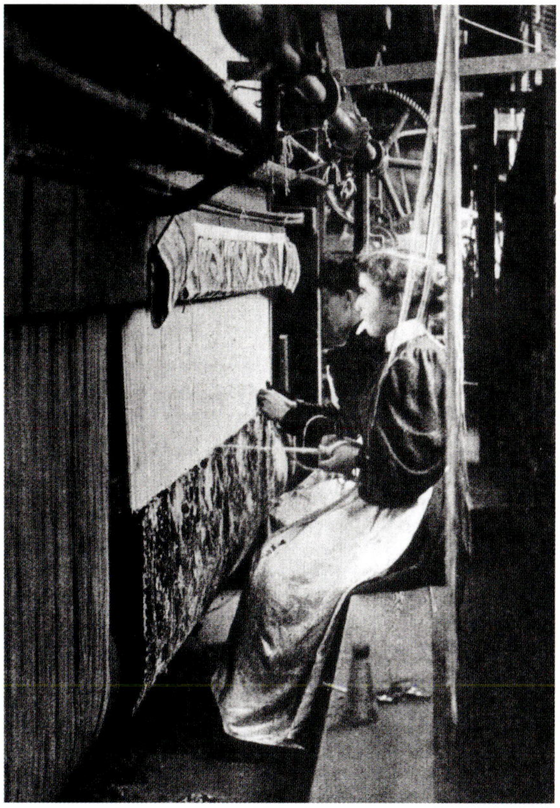

Fig.36 (top) ***The Pond at William Morris's Works at Merton***, **Lexden Lewis Pocock, after 1881. An idealized watercolour of the site of Morris's factory.**
V&A (P.34–1924)

Fig.37 (above) **Exterior view of the Merton Abbey Works looking across the bridge spanning the river Wandle. Published in Lewis F. Day's *The Art of William Morris*, 1899.**
V&A

Fig.38 (right) **Carpet knotters at work at Merton Abbey. A design on point paper can be seen attached to the top of the loom. Published in Lewis F. Day's *The Art of William Morris*, 1899.**
V&A

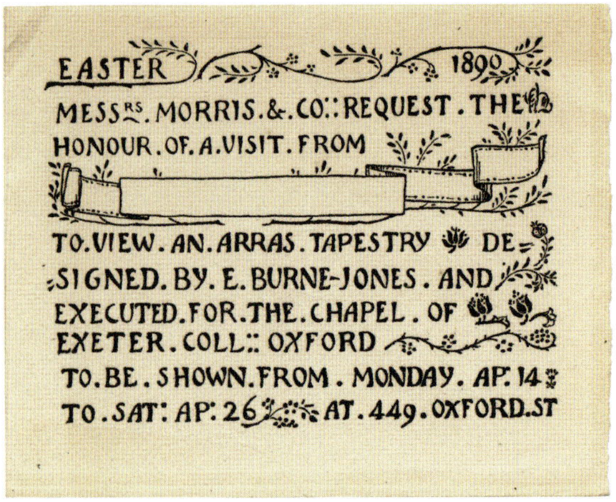
EASTER 1890
MESSRS. MORRIS. & CO.: REQUEST. THE
HONOUR. OF. A. VISIT. FROM
TO. VIEW. AN. ARRAS. TAPESTRY DE-
SIGNED. BY. E. BURNE-JONES. AND
EXECUTED. FOR. THE. CHAPEL. OF
EXETER. COLL: OXFORD
TO. BE. SHOWN. FROM. MONDAY. AP. 14th
TO. SAT: AP. 26th AT. 449. OXFORD. ST

Fig.39 **Invitation to view *The Adoration* tapestry woven for Exeter College at the Morris & Co. Oxford Street showroom. The firm exhibited prestigious works in London to encourage further commissions.**
The Huntington Library, Art Museum and Botanical Gardens

Yet, even if one accepts the logic of their argument, it is hard to resist the conclusion that they got more out of the firm than they had put into it. Morris made the mistake of not acting sooner, before the furnishing and decorating business had really taken off. Even so, the balance of sympathy must lie with him, for while the others had been building their own careers, he had devoted much of his time to reviving the company's fortunes. In the end, fearing the damage an all-out legal battle might cause, Morris agreed to pay each partner £1,000, although Burne-Jones, Faulkner and Webb decided not to take their share. On 31 March 1875 it was announced that the partnership had been dissolved. Thenceforth the business traded as Morris & Company, with Morris as sole owner.

The years that followed were the most creative of Morris's career in business. Within a decade, his designs and products were admired throughout the western world. The strenuous efforts that he made to master such techniques as dyeing, fabric printing, weaving, tapestry making, and the high quality of the resulting products, are justly celebrated. The reasons for Morris's exceptional productivity deserve consideration. In the first place, he was powerfully motivated by the need to safeguard financial security; the freedom to work creatively was for him 'a dear delight'. The wellbeing of his family was also an important factor. Secondly, Morris's appetite for work was fundamental to his character. He derived tremendous pleasure from the anticipation of reaching a goal. Once a thing was done, it was quickly set aside in favour of the next challenge. It should not be thought, however, that Morris's appetite for new projects caused him to cut corners. He was dedicated to perfection. Only after the most meticulous research and testing would he begin the manufacture of a new range of products. The thoroughness of his approach ultimately made for a high level of personal efficiency. He was capable of carrying out many tasks in parallel while giving of his best to each.

The need for commercial success became even more pressing with the move to Merton Abbey in June 1881 (figs 36–8). It was essential to take full advantage of Morris's years of experimentation, but it represented a substantial capital investment for a relatively small company. The old buildings had to be thoroughly overhauled and modified, and new tools and equipment acquired. Many months were to pass before the works were fully operational; block printing, for example, did not begin in earnest until late 1882.

Of course, the commercial success of Morris & Co. did not depend simply upon the energy of its owner and excellence of its designs and products. Morris was acutely aware of the importance of marketing and did not intend to leave matters to chance. He made a big effort to win favour with the public. The firm's brochures developed the theme that beautiful design, colouring and originality, though expensive, represented good value for money, and that product quality was assured by first-rate materials and high standards

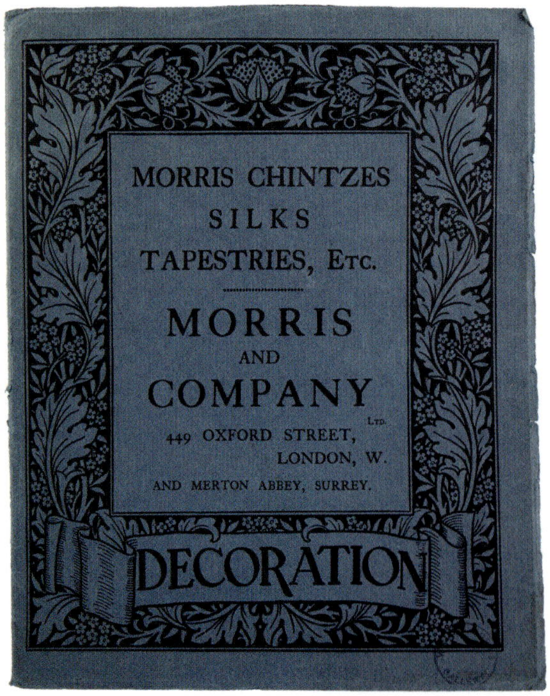

Fig.40 **Cover of one of Morris & Co.'s catalogues, *c*.1912.**
William Morris Gallery

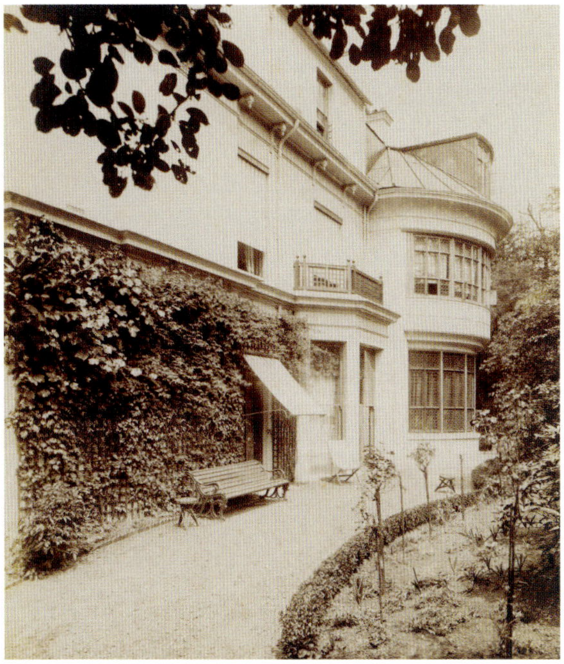

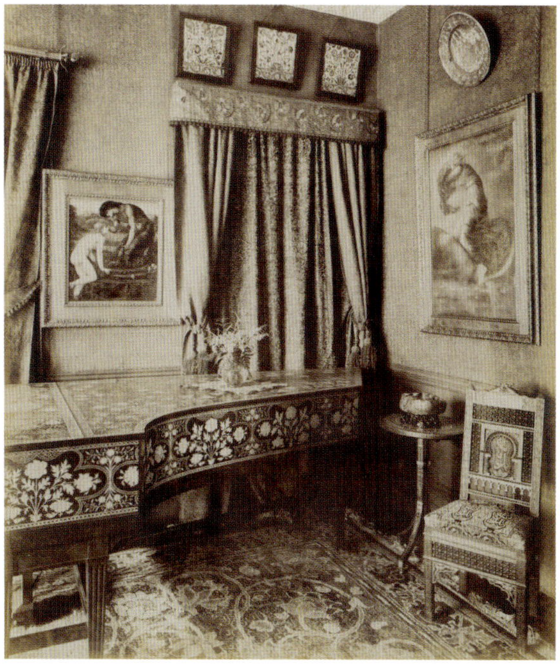

Fig.41 **An exterior view of 1 Holland Park from the garden. Photographed by Bedford Lemere & Co., 1889.**
V&A (E.1:2–1995)

Fig.42 **The second drawing room at 1 Holland Park. Broadwood piano case designed by Edward Burne-Jones, with gesso work conceived and executed by Kate Faulkner (IX.28). The walls are covered with *Flower Garden* woven silk and a handwoven carpet adorns the floor (XII.70 and XII.98).**
V&A (E.1:12–1995)

of manufacture. The emphasis on 'the luxury of taste' rather than 'the luxury of costliness', first set out in the firm's prospectus of 1861, remained a characteristic theme of its publicity in the 1880s and 1890s (figs 39–40).

The wealthy responded with some enthusiasm. Webb introduced important clients, such as the fashionable George and Rosalind Howard, later Earl and Countess of Carlisle, and friends such as the Ionides family, wealthy members of the Greek merchant community in London, gave their social blessing to the Morris venture. Their house at 1 Holland Park became one of the great showcases for Morris & Co. The firm's letters to Alexander Ionides (known as Aleco) are preserved in the V&A and elsewhere, and provide the most detailed correspondence to survive between Morris & Co. and one of its major customers. In describing the decorative work undertaken at 1 Holland Park, they tell us much about Morris's business practices. Additionally, the house was the subject of several contemporary articles, notably in *The Art Journal* and *The Architectural Review*, and was photographed by the celebrated architectural photographer Harry Bedford Lemere. It provides invaluable evidence of the domestic environment preferred by members of London's commercial elite (figs 41–2).

Another feature of the firm's marketing strategy in this period was the expansion of its range to include goods of varying grades and prices. Handmade Hammersmith carpets were extremely costly (£113 for a 16 × 13 foot example), but by the late 1870s Morris designs were available for Wilton, Axminster, Brussels and Kidderminster carpets at a range of prices. This placed more of the firm's products within the reach of the middle classes. Most customers had relatively modest incomes and bought wallpapers, fabrics and carpets for inclusion in their own decorative schemes. Likewise, throughout the 1880s and 1890s, Morris & Co. sold a limited number of large, high-quality pieces of embroidery at high prices; but such small items as cushion covers, work bags and fire screens were increasingly important, most being sold for 15*s*. to £1 10*s*. Embroidery was a popular and respectable occupation for middle-class women and many of the firm's designs were available as kits, with the pattern already inked or painted on to fabric ready to embroider.

In 1877, Morris & Co. opened an elegant showroom at 264 Oxford Street (fig.43). After the establishment of the Merton workshops it was extended to provide more display space, and Morris took steps to reach a wider clientele beyond the metropolis. In January 1883 he opened a showroom in Manchester, a wealthy city with a reputation for patronage of the applied arts, although this was short-lived and the firm subsequently used Kendal, Milne & Co. as its local agent. Agents were also appointed in North America and Europe. In the United States, for example, Elliot & Bulkley of New York acted as the firm's general agents, while in Boston A.H. Davenport sold Morris wallpapers, cretonnes, damasks, dress-silks, embroidery-silks and crewels; J.F. Bumstead & Co. sold wallpapers and Joel Goldthwait & Co. carpets. The firm exhibited at the Boston Foreign Fair of 1883. George Wardle's Boston brochure has survived and provides fascinating insights into the firm's approach to design and production. Morris was exasperated by the generally high level of import duties, often complaining of 'almost prohibitory' tariffs, but was not put off, recognizing that wealthy overseas customers were willing to pay premium prices for goods of the highest quality and originality. In Montreal, W. Scott & Sons advertised themselves as 'the Canadian agents for Morris & Co., the leading silk and tapestry merchants in London', and by the turn of the century Morris products could be found in Toronto and western Canadian cities as well. In Europe, as Linda Parry has noted, they were taken up by 'influential commercial establishments such as Siegfried Bing's Maison de l'Art Nouveau in Paris and Hirschwald's gallery in Berlin, and shops owned by Walther in Frankfurt-am-Main and Robert Furtwangler in Zurich'.

Morris often looked to past ages for technology and artistic inspiration, yet the commercial side of his business was very much of the present. He knew his markets, and he knew how to attract those who could afford his goods. The shop in Oxford Street, not the Merton Abbey factory, was the strategic hub of his operations. It was here that his creations were displayed in a tastefully fashionable setting. The business, moreover, was managed in a prudent and professional manner. Due attention was paid to costs, prices and profit margins. If an estimate exceeded £500, advances were required as the work progressed to ease the problem of cash flow. Additional charges were made 'for attendance to view such buildings or rooms as are proposed for us to decorate'. Morris & Co. never sold at discount prices and prompt payment was demanded of all customers, whatever their rank or social standing. Prices were 'for ready-money payments', and the warning was issued that 'all sums unpaid after one month from the delivery of the account will be charged with interest at the rate of 5 per cent per annum'. This was a distinctly modern feature; the better-off were accustomed to long periods of credit. Another break with convention was that names, dimensions and prices were marked on all items. It was still the normal practice in high-class shops to avoid labelling, although the Morris approach was shared by newer types of retailers such as department stores.

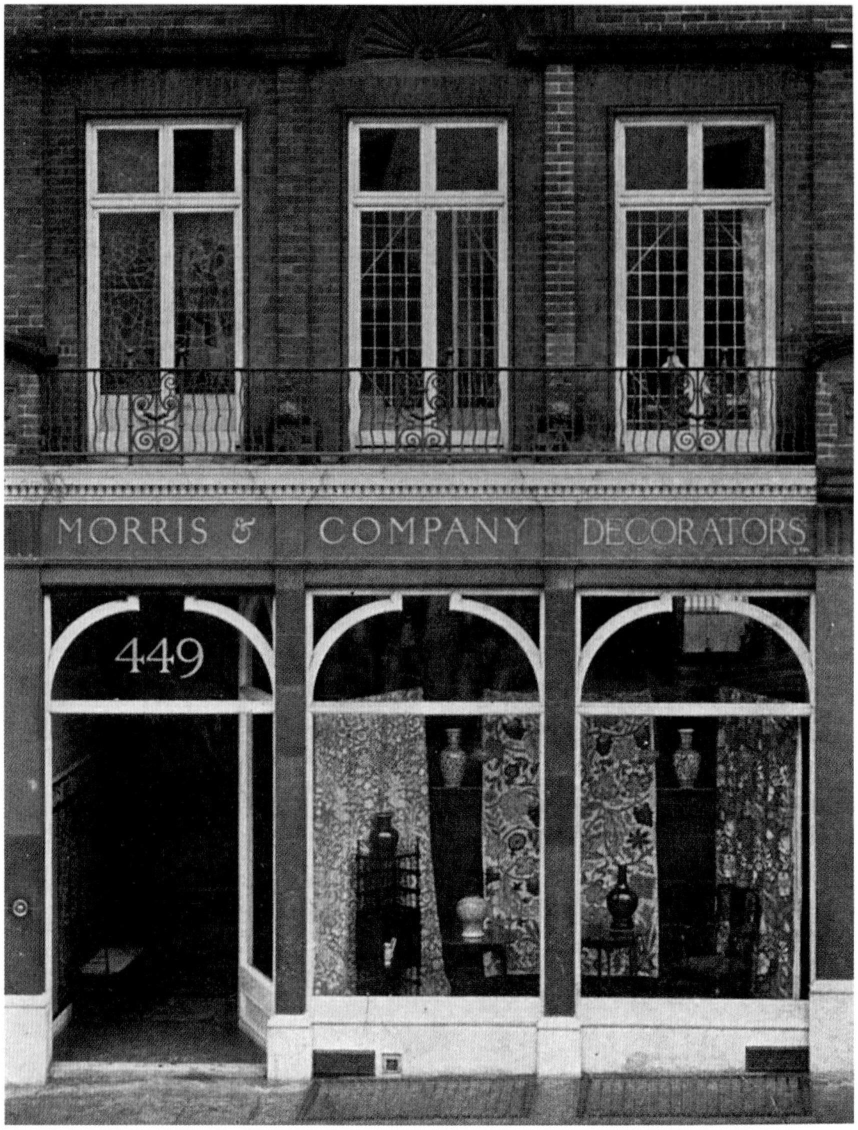

Fig.43 **Exterior of the showroom at Oxford Street, London. Originally 264, it was renumbered 449 in February 1882.**
V&A

Costs were carefully controlled. Subcontractors' charges were monitored and, although Morris had the reputation of being a good employer who paid somewhat above the market rate, he always ensured that the wage bills did not drive up the price of goods to unsaleable levels. This was important, for while its leadership of the market may have allowed Morris & Co. some flexibility in setting prices, it could not completely ignore those of its rivals.

Morris & Co. demonstrated considerable shrewdness in combatting the competition. This was manifested in the way it exploited the reputation of its principal designers, Burne-Jones and Morris. To establish the identity of the firm, the partners had originally agreed to keep the names of individual designers secret. This policy was reversed in the 1880s and early 1890s when Burne-Jones's reputation was at its peak and his work commanded high prices. It was with some pride that Morris & Co. announced in 1882 that 'Mr Burne Jones entrusts us alone with the execution of his Cartoons for Painted Glass'. Even more important was the reputation of Morris himself. He was by now a famous figure and his very name drew fashionable people to take an interest in his art, whether or not they agreed with his political ideas. His conversion to socialism appears to have done little to deter customers. Nor did his lofty attitude and forthright opinions. The firm was not slow to exploit the celebrity of its owner, announcing that he would 'personally advise Customers as to the best method and style of Decoration to be used in each case'. By the late 1880s, indeed, as Morris's personal reputation soared, he felt obliged to ration his time by charging fees for visiting clients – five guineas in London, and £20 elsewhere. He made it clear to his managers, however, that the charges did not apply to 'well known and useful customers ... but only to stop fools and impertinents'.

Morris was quick to recognize the firm's methods of design and manufacturing as a source of competitive advantage. Merton Abbey in particular attracted a steady stream of visitors who, directly or indirectly, helped spread the reputation of the firm. Yet, while many of his admirers believed him to combine high principles with business acumen, Morris himself was becoming more and more critical of his achievements. His disillusionment is summed up in the oft-quoted statement that 'art cannot have a real life and growth under the present system of commercialism and profit-mongering'.

Morris's commitment to socialism, deep and passionate though it was, did not release him from the need to earn his living. He continued during the 1880s to visit Merton two or three times a week, and his enthusiasm for work continued unabated. However, his role in the business was now less intensive, and he delegated day-to-day responsibility to others. Throughout his career, Morris had the knack of getting the best out of senior colleagues and workpeople. He appointed managers who combined enthusiasm, shrewdness and integrity, and allowed them considerable freedom of action. Most notable was George Wardle, general manager from 1870 to 1890,

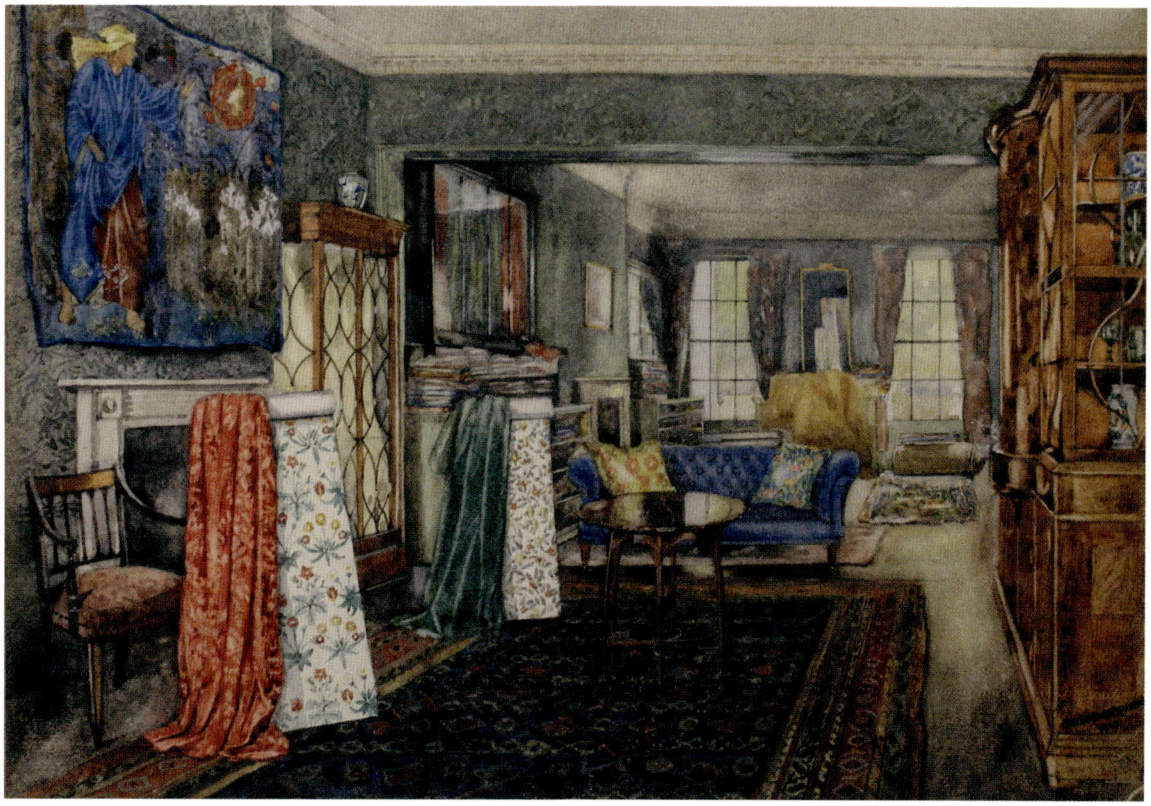

Fig.44 **During the First World War the company relocated the showroom to George Street, Hanover Square. This watercolour by Dulce Wornum confirms the lasting popularity of Morris's early designs, *Daisy* and *Fruit* wallpapers can both be seen on display.**
William Morris Gallery

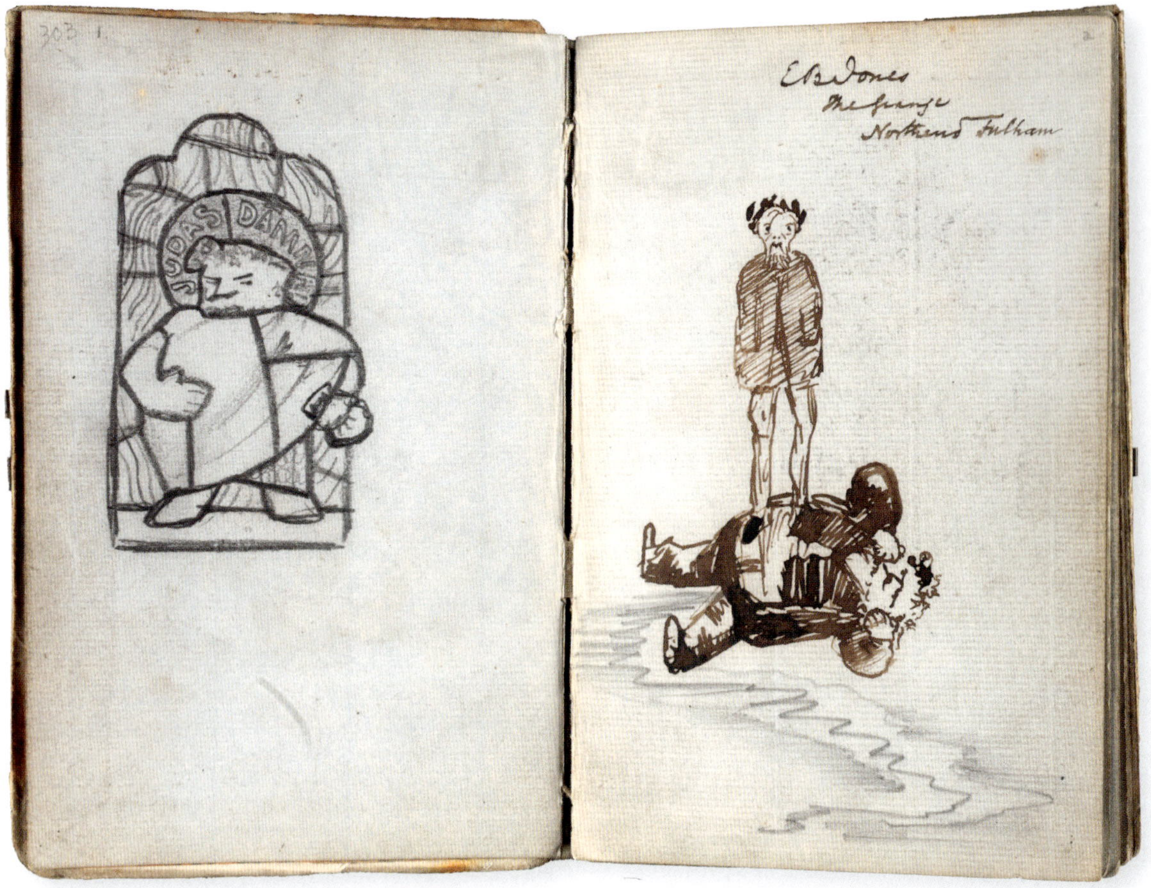

Fig.45 **One of Edward Burne-Jones's account books with the firm, 1861–82, providing evidence of the authorship and dating of designs. Notes and caricatures reveal much about his relationship with Morris.**
Fitzwilliam Museum, University of Cambridge

who took overall control of operations at Merton. He fully concurred with Morris's views on design and manufacture, and his contribution to the success of the firm has not received due recognition. John Henry Dearle supervised the tapestry, weaving and fabric-printing departments. His best designs are often mistaken for those of Morris, and he became the firm's principal designer after the death of Morris in 1896. Frank and Robert Smith also made a major contribution to the mature firm. They had worked for Morris on the commercial side of the business since the mid-1870s, and they were later appointed joint commercial managers. Morris obviously had a great deal of respect for their business acumen, and this was recognized in the late 1880s when he made them partners. His aim was to maintain his income while progressively withdrawing from active participation in the business. The deed of partnership (now at The National Archives, Kew, IR 59/173) signed by Morris and the Smiths on 19 March 1890 allowed the brothers to buy into the business on very favourable terms, and the firm continued to develop in the 1890s under their leadership, despite Morris's almost complete withdrawal from active management.

The overall picture revealed by our research into Morris & Co. is of a financially healthy and well-managed business with considerable scope to charge premium prices. But there were always limits; Morris operated in a highly competitive environment and succeeded because he understood it very well. The truth is that William Morris was a practical, hard-working, hard-headed, imaginative and original man of affairs. The success of Morris & Co. owed much less to good fortune than it did to Morris himself.

IV

THE POLITICAL ACTIVIST

Nicholas Salmon

In the 1880s Morris joined the fledgling socialist movement intent on destroying capitalism, eradicating class difference and ending the despoliation of the natural environment. He wanted nothing less than the total transformation of society, a new way of life in which everyone could enjoy the dignity of meaningful and creative work, and for nature to thrive and art flourish as an integral part of everyday life. As he wrote in 1883, 'the contrasts of rich and poor are unendurable and ought not to be endured by either rich or poor ... feeling this, I am bound to act for the destruction of the system which seems to me mere oppression'. Morris's commitment to activism and to appealing directly to the working classes marked him out from other social critics and reformers at the time and shocked many of his middle-class contemporaries.

One of his first tastes of public campaigning came in 1877, when he founded the Society for the Protection of Ancient Buildings in protest against reckless restoration practices. He also lent his support to environmental protection, speaking out against the lack of town planning, uncontrolled pollution of town and countryside, litter and advertising. In his own field, the decorative arts, he began giving lectures to art students and societies, using his public profile as a decorator and poet to urge for a less wasteful and more considered approach to design and manufacture. However, his experiences during these early campaigning years convinced him that piecemeal reform and philanthropy were insufficient to tackle the scale of the problem that society was facing. More than that, they were potentially a harmful distraction, masking deep inequalities and encouraging working people to aspire to nothing more than benign subjugation rather than genuine freedom. He became a committed revolutionary and as his fellow activist Walter Crane later wrote, in his dedication to the cause, 'it is certain that William Morris spent some of the best years of life, he gave his time, his voice, his thought, his pen, and much money to put Socialism before his countrymen.'

William Morris's early life gave little indication of the important role he was to play in the British socialist movement. The son of a wealthy city businessman, he entered Exeter College, Oxford, in 1853 with the intention of taking holy orders. At that time his views were High Church and he spent his first few terms immersed in such religious works as Henry Hart Milman's *History of Latin Christianity* and Kenelm Digby's *Mores Catholici: or, Ages of Faith*. At one point he and Edward

Burne-Jones even considered founding a monastic order and becoming Roman Catholics.

This phase of Anglo-Catholicism was short-lived. Burne-Jones soon introduced him to a group of his Birmingham friends at Pembroke College, which included William Fulford, Richard Watson Dixon and Charles Faulkner. Their interests extended beyond religion to the discussion of secularism, modern literature and social reform, influenced in part by their exposure to the industrial realities of the city in which they grew up. It was through this group of freethinking students that Morris became acquainted with the criticisms of nineteenth-century capitalism made by Thomas Carlyle and the controversial academic and Christian Socialist Charles Kingsley. In return, Morris energetically championed the work of John Ruskin within the group, particularly the recently published second volume of *The Stones of Venice*. Ruskin's attack on the dehumanizing effects of industrialization and his insistence that art is a reflection of the society in which it is created, had a profound and lasting impact on Morris. Along with his reading of French and German philosophy, these influences led him to renounce religion and devote his life to art. Morris's subsequent friendship with Dante Gabriel Rossetti, whose family were revolutionary refugees from Italy, also played a part in his political development. Rossetti introduced him to a number of continental radicals and encouraged him to support the nationalistic aspirations of the occupied states in Europe.

It was appropriate, therefore, that it was the Turkish suppression of a series of uprisings in the Balkan states that led Morris to enter national politics. In 1875 revolts against Turkish rule had broken out in Bosnia, Montenegro and Serbia. The following year these spread to Bulgaria where the rebellion was supported by Russia. During the suppression of this uprising, Turkish mercenaries committed a number of atrocities, details of which were published in the *Daily News* on 23 June 1876. This report led to a wave of opposition to the pro-Turkish foreign policy of the Prime Minister, Benjamin Disraeli.

At first this protest was orchestrated by radical clubs and working-class organizations. It only became a national issue when William Gladstone, seizing the opportunity of attacking the Conservative government, published his famous pamphlet *Bulgarian Horrors and the Question of the East* in September 1876. In this he demanded an immediate Turkish withdrawal from Bulgaria. Morris, enraged by the 'Bulgarian Atrocities', pledged his support to the campaign the following month in a letter published in the *Daily News* under the title 'England and the Turks'. Following Gladstone's intervention, a conference was held at St James's Hall on 8 December 1876 at which the Eastern Question Association was formed with A.J. Mundella, the Liberal MP for Sheffield, as chairman and Morris as treasurer.

Morris became one of the most active of the Association's campaigners. On 11 May 1877 he issued his first political manifesto 'To the working-men of England', in which he bitterly condemned the Tories for defending their own class interests and urged the workers to speak out against Disraeli's 'unjust war' (fig.47). Written shortly after Russia had declared war on Turkey on 24 April, its anti-war message is presented in straightforward class terms: 'Who are they that are leading us into war? ... Greedy gamblers on the Stock Exchange, idle officers of the army and navy (poor fellows!), worn-out mockers of the Clubs, desperate purveyors of exciting war-news for the comfortable breakfast tables of those who have nothing to lose by war'. Thereafter, he devoted all his energy to the cause – making speeches, organizing petitions and attending committee meetings.

The agitation reached its climax when Russian troops began to advance on Constantinople in early January 1878. For a time British intervention on the

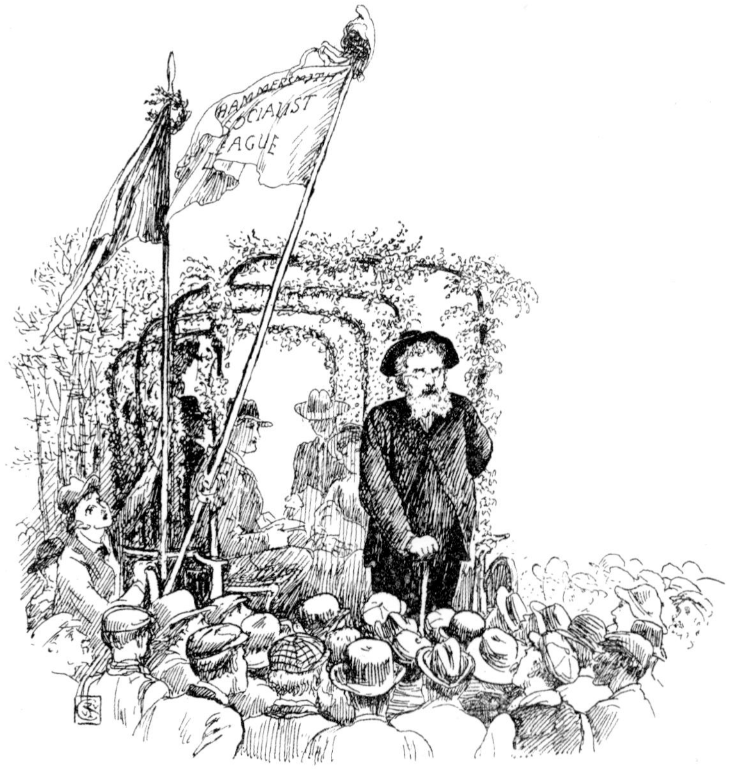

Fig.46 **Morris speaking at a May Day rally in Hyde Park, sketch by Walter Crane, 1894. Published in *William Morris to Whistler* (1911).**
National Art Library, V&A

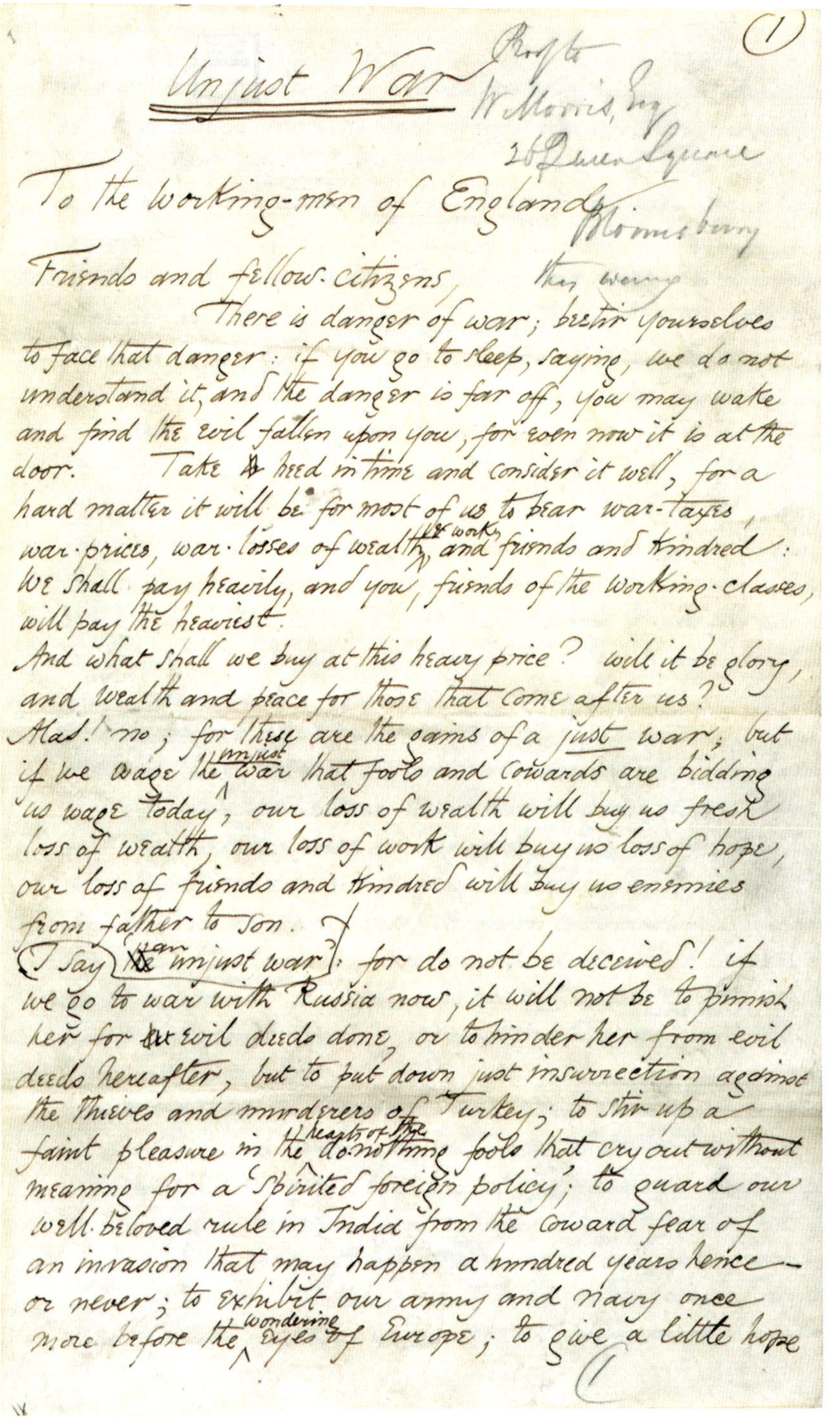

(1)

Unjust War

W Morris, Esq
26 Queen Square
Bloomsbury

To the working-men of England

Friends and fellow-citizens,

There is danger of war; bestir yourselves to face that danger: if you go to sleep, saying, we do not understand it, and the danger is far off, you may wake and find the evil fallen upon you, for even now it is at the door. Take heed in time and consider it well, for a hard matter it will be for most of us to bear war-taxes, war-prices, war-losses of wealth, of work, and friends and kindred: we shall pay heavily, and you, friends of the working-classes, will pay the heaviest.

And what shall we buy at this heavy price? will it be glory, and wealth and peace for those that come after us? Alas! no; for these are the gains of a just war; but if we wage the unjust war that fools and cowards are bidding us wage today, our loss of wealth will buy us fresh loss of wealth, our loss of work will buy us loss of hope, our loss of friends and kindred will buy us enemies from father to son.

I say an unjust war: for do not be deceived! if we go to war with Russia now, it will not be to punish her for evil deeds done, or to hinder her from evil deeds hereafter, but to put down just insurrection against the thieves and murderers of Turkey; to stir up a faint pleasure in the hearts of the do-nothing fools that cry out without meaning for a 'spirited foreign policy'; to guard our well-beloved rule in India from the coward fear of an invasion that may happen a hundred years hence or never; to exhibit our army and navy once more before the wondering eyes of Europe; to give a little hope

Fig.47 **Manuscript for Morris's first political manifesto, *Unjust War*, addressed 'To the working-men of England' and signed 'A Lover of Justice', 1877.**
William Morris Gallery

Turkish side appeared imminent. The Association responded by calling a large anti-war meeting at Exeter Hall on the Strand for 16 January 1878. This was opened by a lusty rendition of 'Wake, London Lads', a song specially written for the occasion by Morris, led by a choir from Henry Broadhurst's Stonemasons' Union and set to the well-known tune of 'The Hardy Norseman's Home of Yore'. The first of Morris's poems written for an explicitly political purpose, its positive reception at the packed meeting helped convince him of the power of song in mobilizing popular support. He later quoted Ruskin's remark that 'a cause which cannot be sung of is not worth following'. In his own speech Morris condemned the 'war-at-any-price' party and annoyed some of the audience by criticizing Queen Victoria for her support of Disraeli.

This was to be the Association's last success, as the country was soon gripped by anti-Russian jingoism. Morris, along with friends such as Burne-Jones, desperately tried to keep the agitation going by attempting to organize another huge meeting at the Agricultural Hall in Islington for 25 February 1878. However, this never materialized as Gladstone, who had originally agreed to speak, decided it was politically expedient to withdraw. Without the support of the parliamentary Liberals the Eastern Question Association effectively collapsed. Morris was appalled by what he perceived as the cowardice of the 'so-called Liberal party' and the experience was critical to his growing despair with Parliament as an agent of change.

Despite the failure of the Association, Morris did not withdraw from politics. In contrast to Burne-Jones's resolution never again to leave his studio for 'causes I can scarcely help', this was just the start of Morris's active engagement in public life. As his faith in the parliamentary system waned it was replaced by a growing respect for the working classes. In 1879 he was elected treasurer of the National Liberal League, a largely working-class organization formed from the groups who had opposed Disraeli's pro-Turkish foreign policy. Its initial aim was to help Gladstone win the general election of 1880. In this it was successful. However, its subsequent attempt to persuade the new government to implement a programme of radical reform proved a complete failure. The government instead pursued imperialistic policies in Africa and went on to pass the notorious Irish Coercion Bill, which gave it sweeping powers to enforce order in the province and imprison Irish National League sympathizers without trial. Completely disillusioned with the Liberals, Morris resigned from the League early in 1882. As he wrote the following year, he was now convinced 'that Radicalism is on the wrong line ... and will never develope [*sic*] into anything more than Radicalism: in fact that it is made for and by the middle classes and will always be under the control of rich capitalists'.

Having firmly rejected parliamentary politics, Morris was now ready to consider socialism. During 1882 he read a great deal of proto-socialist literature, including Henry George's *Progress and Poverty* and Alfred Wallace's *Land Nationalisation*. However, he was to claim later that the crucial event in his conversion to socialism was his reading of John Stuart Mill's critique of François Fourier's utopian socialism. Paradoxically, Mill's fairness in presenting Fourier's arguments convinced Morris 'that Socialism was a necessary change, and that it was possible to bring it about in our own days'. By the summer of 1882 he declared himself ready 'to join any body who distinctly called themselves Socialists'.

The only socialist organization in England at this time was the Democratic Federation. This had been formed in 1881 as an amalgamation of radical clubs. However, it soon came under the leadership of the socialist Henry Mayers Hyndman, who abandoned its original reformist programme in the summer of 1882. During the winter of 1882–3 Hyndman held a number of meetings, which Morris attended, to discuss a series of provisional reforms to be pursued on the way to the ultimate goal of social revolution. These included free education, public health improvements and land nationalization. Impressed by the earnestness of these discussions, Morris joined the Federation in January 1883. Socialism in Britain at this time was a small and almost unknown movement. Although the Democratic Federation had not yet publicly declared for socialism, Morris joined on the assumption that it would.

Hyndman was delighted to have secured the services of the famous author of *The Earthly Paradise*, and Morris was duly elected to the executive of the Federation in May 1883. His position as treasurer was especially appropriate as he was soon subsidizing the campaign liberally from his own pocket. In the autumn of 1883 he designed a distinctive membership card bearing the French revolutionary epithet 'Liberty, Equality, Fraternity' along with the Federation's propaganda slogan 'Educate, Agitate, Organise' (fig.48). As Morris wrote in his lecture 'Art and the People' (1883): 'Educate, Agitate, Organise; these words the motto of our Federation do most completely express what is necessary to be done by those who have any hope in the future of the People.' The central design of a spreading oak tree, with a pattern of stylized acorns and leaves, symbolizes the aspirations of the Democratic Federation.

As part of his education in theoretical socialism Morris read Karl Marx's *Das Kapital* in French during the early months of 1883. He thoroughly enjoyed the 'great work' and made annotations in his copy, which became a treasured possession and was later specially bound by Thomas James Cobden-Sanderson (fig.49). Morris probably purchased the book during the early months of 1883, shortly after he joined the Democratic Federation. His friend Crom Price noted in his unpublished diary on 22 April 1883 that he had visited the Burne-Joneses and found Morris 'full of Karl Marx, which he had begun to read in tr[anslation].' Cobden-Sanderson recorded that when it was brought to him a year later it 'had been worn to loose sections by his own constant study of it'.

Morris threw himself wholeheartedly into the propaganda work. He gave many lectures, regularly attended the weekly meetings of the executive and composed a series of 'chants' to be sung at meetings. He also contributed articles to *Justice*, the Federation's journal, and sold the paper on street corners in the West End. The vigour of the Federation's early propaganda attracted such valuable recruits as Edward Aveling, Henry Hyde Champion and John Burns, and Morris was to write enthusiastically in 1884 that 'the *hope* is spreading, and even far more speedily than some of us would have thought possible a little time ago; and it is clear that when the hope is once received into the hearts of the mass of our people, the beginning of the new day is at hand'.

However, it was not long before disagreements began to arise over aims and tactics. The central issue was whether the Federation should continue to support ameliorative reform or reject parliamentary

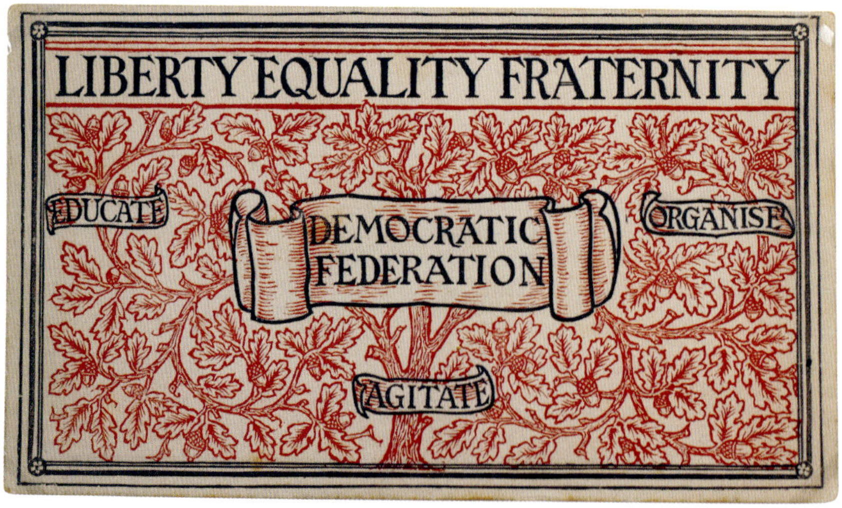

Fig.48 **Morris's own membership card for the Democratic Federation, designed by him in 1883.**
William Morris Society

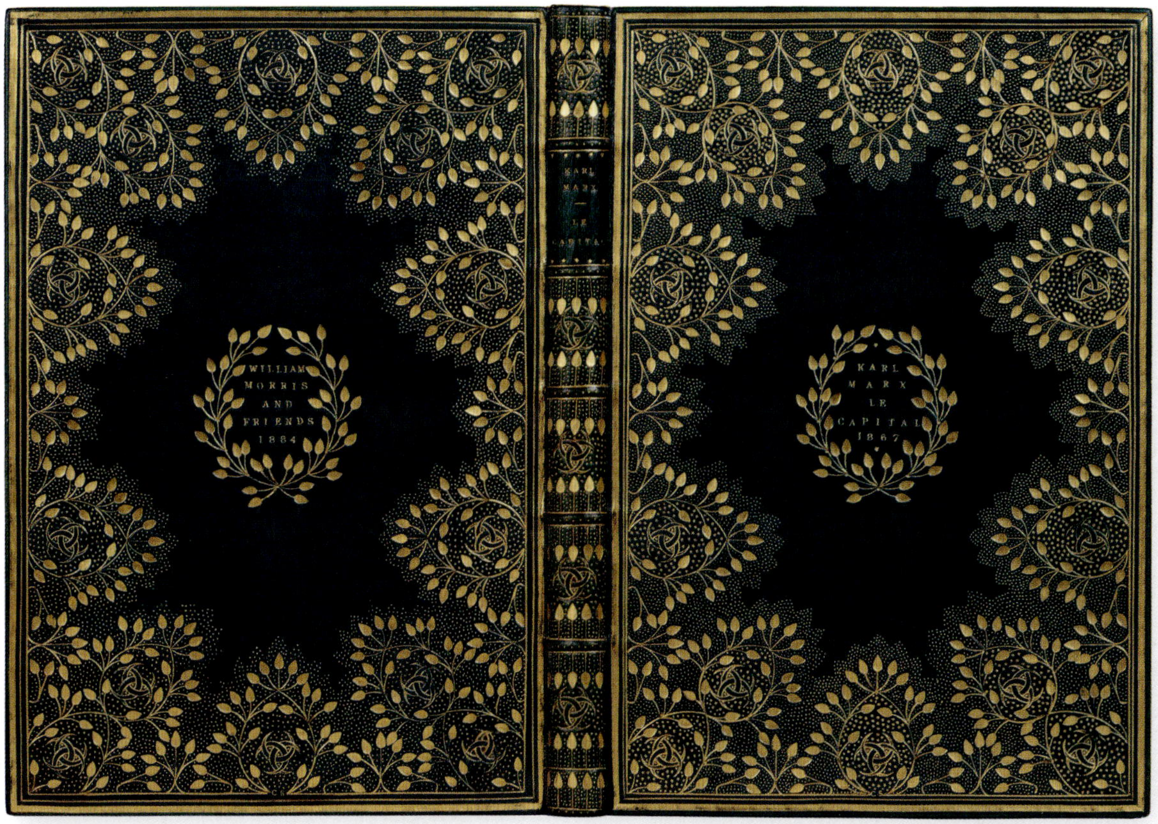

Fig.49 **Morris's copy of *Le Capital* by Karl Marx, bound by Thomas James Cobden-Sanderson in 1884.**
The Wormsley Library

methods in favour of educating the workers in socialism. A split appeared in the executive between those such as Hyndman, Champion and Aveling, who believed that legislative reforms should serve as the basis of the agitation, and those, like Morris, Joseph Lane (the working-class anarchist activist) and Andreas Scheu, who saw them as deflecting attention away from the real aim of social revolution. This dissent was accompanied by growing suspicion of Hyndman's autocratic role on the executive and his editorial control of *Justice*.

These differences emerged at the Federation's annual conference in 1884, when the opposition group succeeded in having Hyndman replaced as president by a rotating chairman elected by the executive. Despite this defeat, Hyndman refused to relinquish power and continued to present his own case through the editorship of *Justice*. When the executive attempted to gain control of the paper he refused to co-operate. Morris, who found Hyndman's intransigence increasingly frustrating, soon assumed the leadership of the opposition on the executive.

Things came to a head when Morris was on a socialist lecture tour of Scotland. While he was visiting the Glasgow branch on 14 December 1884, a letter was read out from Hyndman denouncing Scheu as an anarchist. Morris was then heckled for his alleged ignorance of Marxist economics. Infuriated by this attempt to undermine his credibility, Morris returned to London determined to bring the dispute with Hyndman out into the open. Two weeks later, on 27 December 1884, a vote was forced on Hyndman's leadership. This was won by Morris and his supporters by ten votes to eight. They immediately resigned *en masse* to found the Socialist League on 30 December 1884.

The rebels had won a hollow victory. Hyndman retained the majority of the 400 members of the Federation, which had been renamed the Social Democratic Federation at the annual conference in 1884, and had the benefit of an established organization with branches throughout the country. More serious was the lack of unity among the rebels themselves; while there had been a common distrust of Hyndman's autocratic leadership, some of them still broadly agreed with his aims. Among this group were Eleanor Marx and Aveling who were both in close contact with Friedrich Engels.

These differences were apparent from the start. Morris was determined that the League should adopt an anti-parliamentary stance and confine itself to educating and organizing the

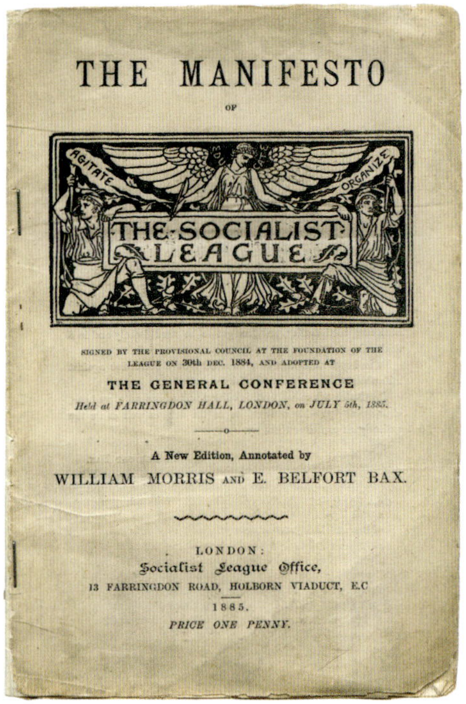

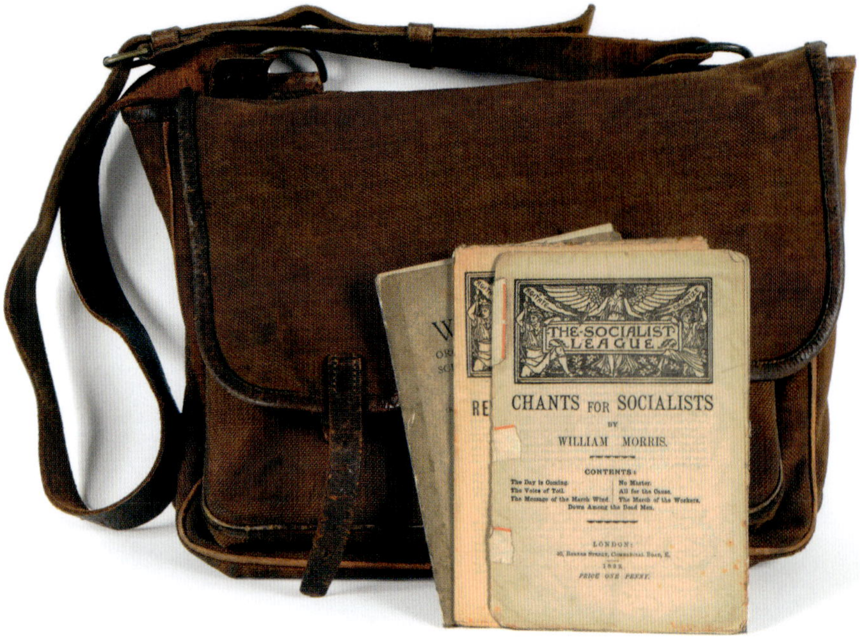

workers. On New Year's Day 1885, Price visited Kelmscott House and found Morris and Ernest Belfort Bax hard at work drafting a manifesto for the new organization (fig.50). This described the League as a body 'advocating the principles of Revolutionary International Socialism' and seeking to end all distinctions of class and nationality. Based on Marxist theory, the manifesto committed the League to extra-parliamentary propaganda. However, Aveling drafted a constitution that was pro-parliamentary and recommended that the League should work towards the formation of a Socialist Labour Party. Although this was rejected, at Morris's insistence, at the first annual conference in 1885, it marked the beginning of a serious difference of opinion in the council of the League.

At first these divisions were hidden by the enthusiasm with which the League set about its task. Nobody worked harder than Morris, who conscientiously attended committee meetings, spoke regularly at the open-air stands the League set up in the East End of London and travelled the country on extended lecture tours. Between 1883 and 1890 it is estimated that he addressed over a thousand meetings and was heard by around a quarter of a million people. Public speaking did not come naturally to Morris; it was something that he worked hard at, believing that the only way to effect a total transformation of society was by appealing directly to working people. He was painfully aware of the deep class divide that separated him from his audiences and often felt frustrated by the sense that he was not communicating the message of socialism clearly enough. Rosemary Taylor's study, '"The City of Dreadful Delight" William Morris in the East End of London' (2009), has revealed just how frequently Morris was to be found speaking in working men's clubs, coffee houses and in Victoria Park, where open-air speakers had to compete with the sounds of Salvation Army bands, hecklers and numerous other distractions.

Morris's experience as an active propagandist convinced him that for socialism to win hearts and minds, people had to be persuaded that a better future was possible. Economic theory could be learnt later but first an appeal had to be made to the imagination, helping potential converts visualize a society free from capitalist exploitation. One of his most important contributions to the movement was to create, almost single-handedly, a body of revolutionary socialist literature. This included a long narrative poem based on the events of the Paris Commune called *The Pilgrims of Hope* (1885–6), a topical play entitled *The Tables Turned; or Nupkins Awakened* (1887) (fig.52) and two socialist prose romances: *A Dream of John Ball* (1886–7) and *News from Nowhere* (1890). In these last two works, Morris turned to the past and the future respectively to educate and inspire hope. *A Dream*

Fig.50 (above left) ***The Manifesto of the Socialist League*** **with a cover designed by Walter Crane. First issued as a pamphlet in January 1885, this second, annotated edition was printed in October.**
William Morris Gallery

Fig.51 (above right) **Morris's brown canvas satchel and a copy of his popular pamphlet** ***Chants for Socialists*****, which ran into several editions and was sold to raise money for the 'Cause'.**
William Morris Gallery

Fig.52 (right) **The original cast list for *The Tables Turned; or Nupkins Awakened*, with Morris as the Archbishop of Canterbury, 1887.**
V&A

Fig.53 (below) **Design for a leaflet to promote *Commonweal*, c.1886.**
International Institute of Social History, Amsterdam

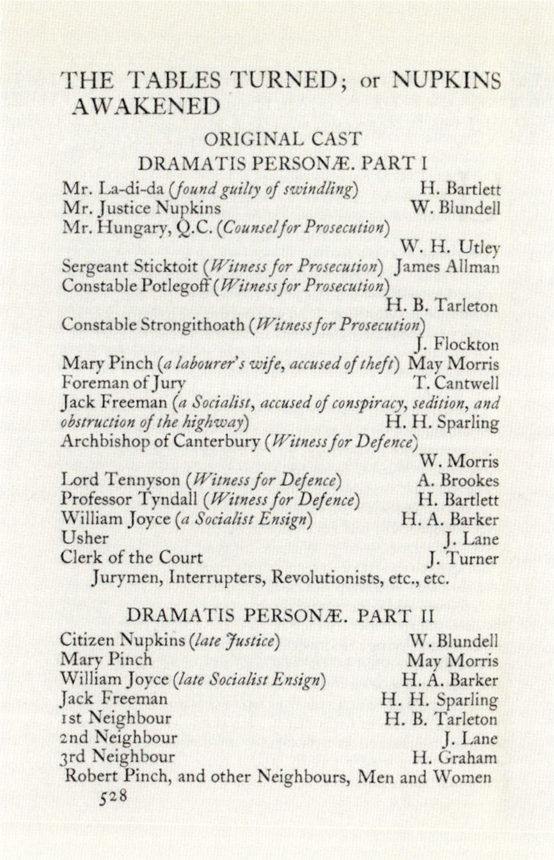

THE TABLES TURNED; or NUPKINS AWAKENED

ORIGINAL CAST

DRAMATIS PERSONÆ. PART I

Mr. La-di-da (*found guilty of swindling*)	H. Bartlett
Mr. Justice Nupkins	W. Blundell
Mr. Hungary, Q.C. (*Counsel for Prosecution*)	W. H. Utley
Sergeant Sticktoit (*Witness for Prosecution*)	James Allman
Constable Potlegoff (*Witness for Prosecution*)	H. B. Tarleton
Constable Strongithoath (*Witness for Prosecution*)	J. Flockton
Mary Pinch (*a labourer's wife, accused of theft*)	May Morris
Foreman of Jury	T. Cantwell
Jack Freeman (*a Socialist, accused of conspiracy, sedition, and obstruction of the highway*)	H. H. Sparling
Archbishop of Canterbury (*Witness for Defence*)	W. Morris
Lord Tennyson (*Witness for Defence*)	A. Brookes
Professor Tyndall (*Witness for Defence*)	H. Bartlett
William Joyce (*a Socialist Ensign*)	H. A. Barker
Usher	J. Lane
Clerk of the Court	J. Turner

Jurymen, Interrupters, Revolutionists, etc., etc.

DRAMATIS PERSONÆ. PART II

Citizen Nupkins (*late Justice*)	W. Blundell
Mary Pinch	May Morris
William Joyce (*late Socialist Ensign*)	H. A. Barker
Jack Freeman	H. H. Sparling
1st Neighbour	H. B. Tarleton
2nd Neighbour	J. Lane
3rd Neighbour	H. Graham

Robert Pinch, and other Neighbours, Men and Women

528

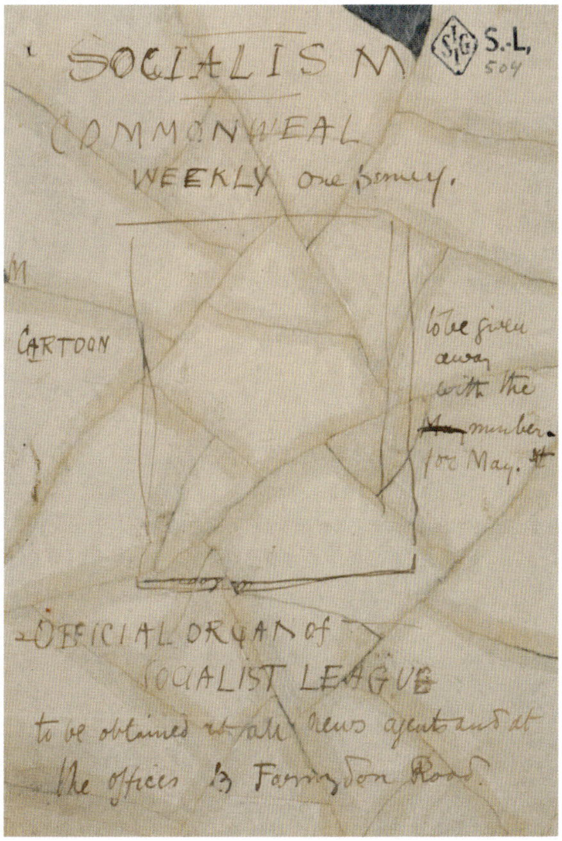

of John Ball is a moving fictional account of the last days of the revolutionary priest who helped organize popular resistance to Richard II and his nobles in the so-called Peasants' Revolt of 1381. Morris was aware of recent historiography that reinterpreted this event as a watershed moment in the consciousness and organization of ordinary people and he saw its potential, as a powerful revolutionary precedent, to motivate his comrades. *News from Nowhere*, his most widely read literary work, is an inspired vision of a decentralized egalitarian society following the revolution. As he said in an interview in 1885, 'The discontented must know what they are aiming at when they overthrow the old order of things ... a life in which every human being should find unrestricted scope for his best powers and faculties.'

Some of these works were published in serial form in the League's paper, *Commonweal*, which first appeared in February 1885. Morris's work for the paper, which quickly established itself as the foremost socialist journal in Britain, is probably his most underestimated achievement. He served as editor from its inception until 1890 when the anarchists on the League's council succeeded in having him replaced by David Nicoll. First appearing monthly, from 1 May 1886 it became an eight-page weekly. Between 1885 and 1890 Morris made more than 400 contributions, including reviews, numerous essays and a remarkable series of articles on contemporary events entitled 'Notes on News'. In this column he tried to show would-be recruits how Parliament always governed in its own middle-class interest, regardless of which party was in power. His articles constitute one of the most powerful and sustained attacks ever made on the nineteenth-century capitalist system. He also published essays by the most influential socialist thinkers of the age, including Engels, George Bernard Shaw and the Russian revolutionary Sergius Stepniak.

When Morris founded *Commonweal* it was one of only a handful of journals promoting revolutionary socialism. Financing the paper was a continual source of anxiety for him. Although the first edition had sold 5,000 copies, sales soon stabilized at around 2,000–3,000 during its most successful period between 1886 and 1888. At this level the paper made a loss and its publication was only possible because Morris subsidized its weekly deficit of £4 and guaranteed the wages of the staff who printed it at the League's offices at 13 Farringdon Road in Clerkenwell. The crude

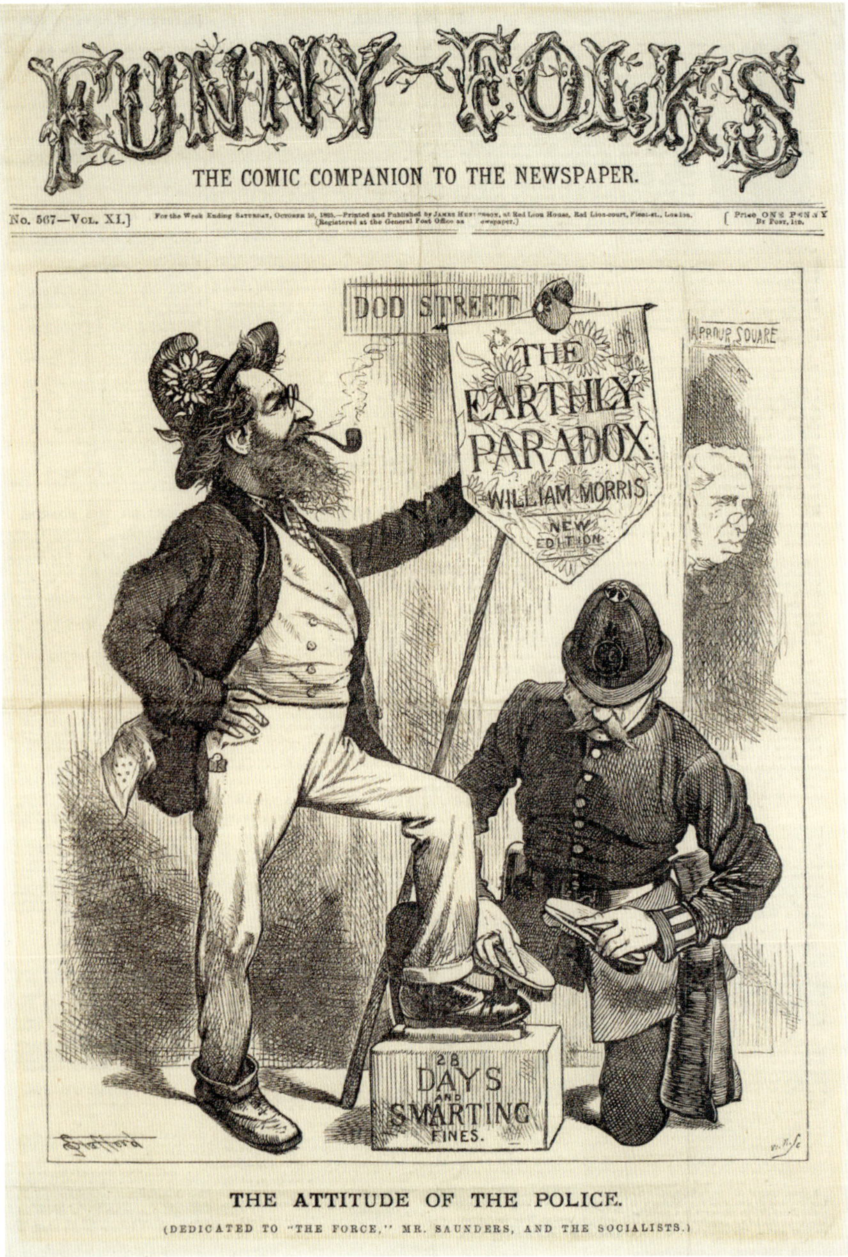

FUNNY FOLKS

THE COMIC COMPANION TO THE NEWSPAPER.

No. 567—Vol. XI.]

THE ATTITUDE OF THE POLICE.

(DEDICATED TO "THE FORCE," MR. SAUNDERS, AND THE SOCIALISTS.)

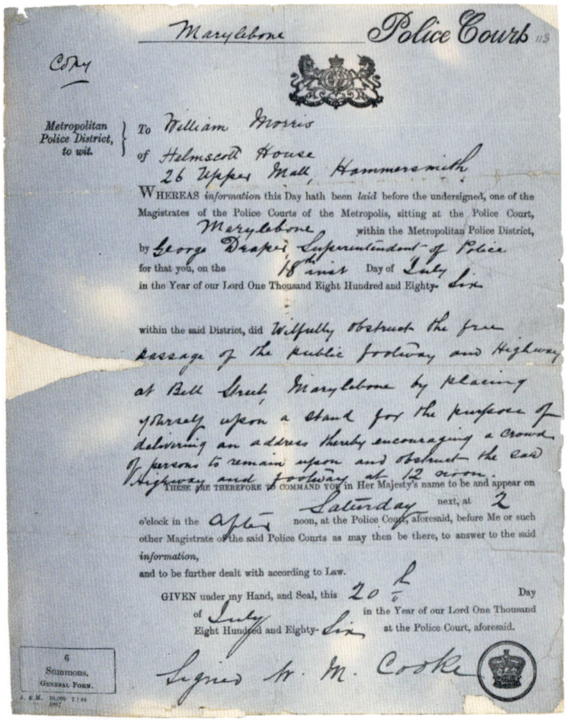

Marylebone Police Court

Copy

Metropolitan Police District, to wit. } To William Morris of Helmscott House 26 Upper Mall, Hammersmith

WHEREAS *information* this Day hath been *laid* before the undersigned, one of the Magistrates of the Police Courts of the Metropolis, sitting at the Police Court, Marylebone, within the Metropolitan Police District, by George Draper, Superintendent of Police for that you, on the 18th inst Day of July in the Year of our Lord One Thousand Eight Hundred and Eighty-Six

within the said District, did Wilfully obstruct the free passage of the public footway and Highway at Bell Street, Marylebone by placing yourself upon a stand for the purpose of delivering an address thereby encouraging a crowd of persons to remain upon and obstruct the said Highway and footway at 12 noon.

THESE ARE THEREFORE TO COMMAND YOU in Her Majesty's name to be and appear on Saturday next, at 2 o'clock in the after noon, at the Police Court, aforesaid, before Me or such other Magistrate of the said Police Courts as may then be there, to answer to the said *information*, and to be further dealt with according to Law.

GIVEN under my Hand, and Seal, this 20th Day of July in the Year of our Lord One Thousand Eight Hundred and Eighty-Six at the Police Court, aforesaid.

Signed W. M. Cooke

6 Summons, General Form.

Fig.54 **'The Attitude of the Police', from the magazine *Funny Folks*, caricature by J.P. Stafford, October 1885. Dod Street in Limehouse was the scene of many meetings by the Social Democratic Federation.**

William Morris Gallery

Fig.55 **Police summons for wilful obstruction, issued to Morris on 20 July 1886.**

British Library

design illustrated here (fig.53), which has obviously been screwed up and discarded, was for one of a number of leaflets produced to promote sales. It probably dates from the early months of 1886, just before the paper was relaunched as a weekly. Distribution was extremely challenging, especially as local newsagents often refused to stock it. Morris personally co-ordinated the distribution of the paper from London to provincial branches of the League but, despite these efforts, there was always a shortfall of funds.

At first the propaganda work of the League was helped by the prevailing economic conditions. A recession during the early 1880s had led to many unemployed men sleeping rough in London. In 1885 the Social Democratic Federation succeeded in organizing these discontented workers and began to hold weekly marches of the unemployed. This campaign culminated in a riot on 8 February 1886, when a large crowd ran amok looting and smashing windows along Pall Mall and Piccadilly. *The Times* described London as gripped by 'something little short of panic'. Although Morris was not present on this occasion, his daughter May, also an active member of the Socialist League, watched from the sidelines. Later in the day, the looting spread to Oxford Street and Morris & Co.'s shop windows only narrowly missed being smashed.

The authorities responded by attempting to curb the activities of the socialists. What became known as the 'free speech' campaign began when the police broke up a meeting of the Social Democratic Federation and arrested two of its speakers. Thereafter, frequent attacks were made on the outdoor meetings of both the Federation and the League and a number of speakers were sentenced to imprisonment for 'obstruction'. Morris, aware that his presence on the streets greatly embarrassed the police, made a point of speaking at the meetings they most frequently disrupted. He was even summoned and fined a shilling for addressing a crowd in Bell Street, Marylebone, in July 1886 (fig.55). In persecuting the socialists in this way the authorities made a tactical mistake. Both the League and the Federation gained valuable publicity from the heavy-handed actions of the police and the harsh sentences of the courts. In his journalism and speeches, Morris sought to expose the inherent class bias in the judicial system, pointing out that his own lenient treatment in court was very different from the heavy sentences and fines given to his working-class comrades. These double standards were caricatured in the press (fig.54) and explored in Morris's socialist farce *The Tables Turned* (1887).

By 1886 the League had succeeded in establishing a solid base for its agitation. Of its 20 branches, 11 were in provincial towns outside London including Morris's former university city, Oxford. It had a particularly strong presence in the north with active branches in Leeds, Bradford, Glasgow and Edinburgh. Morris's own Hammersmith branch had over a hundred members and held regular outdoor meetings which attracted audiences in excess of two hundred people. In 1887 membership of the League peaked at about a thousand. It was during the most successful period of agitation that Morris began his short-lived 'Socialist Diary' (fig.56). His original intention was that the diary might one day be published to give future generations some idea of the League's day-to-day propaganda activities, 'a kind of view of the Socialist movement seen from the inside, Jonah's view of the Whale', as he described it to his daughter Jenny. In the event, the sheer volume of his lecture engagements, correspondence and political journalism forced him to abandon the project after just three months. The last entry, on 27 April 1887, began with the apology, 'I have been busy about many things and so unable to fill up this book.'

However, there were already indications that the tactics of the League were failing. While it gained some radical recruits from its support of the agitation over Irish coercion, it failed to exploit the rise in trade unionism and the associated industrial unrest. This was because Morris refused to allow the League to become involved with issues that interfered with its main task of educating the workers in revolutionary socialism.

Two events contributed to the subsequent disintegration of the League. The first was what became known as 'Bloody Sunday'. As part of its programme of unemployment agitation the Federation had continued to hold meetings in Trafalgar Square. During October and early November 1887 these meetings were regularly

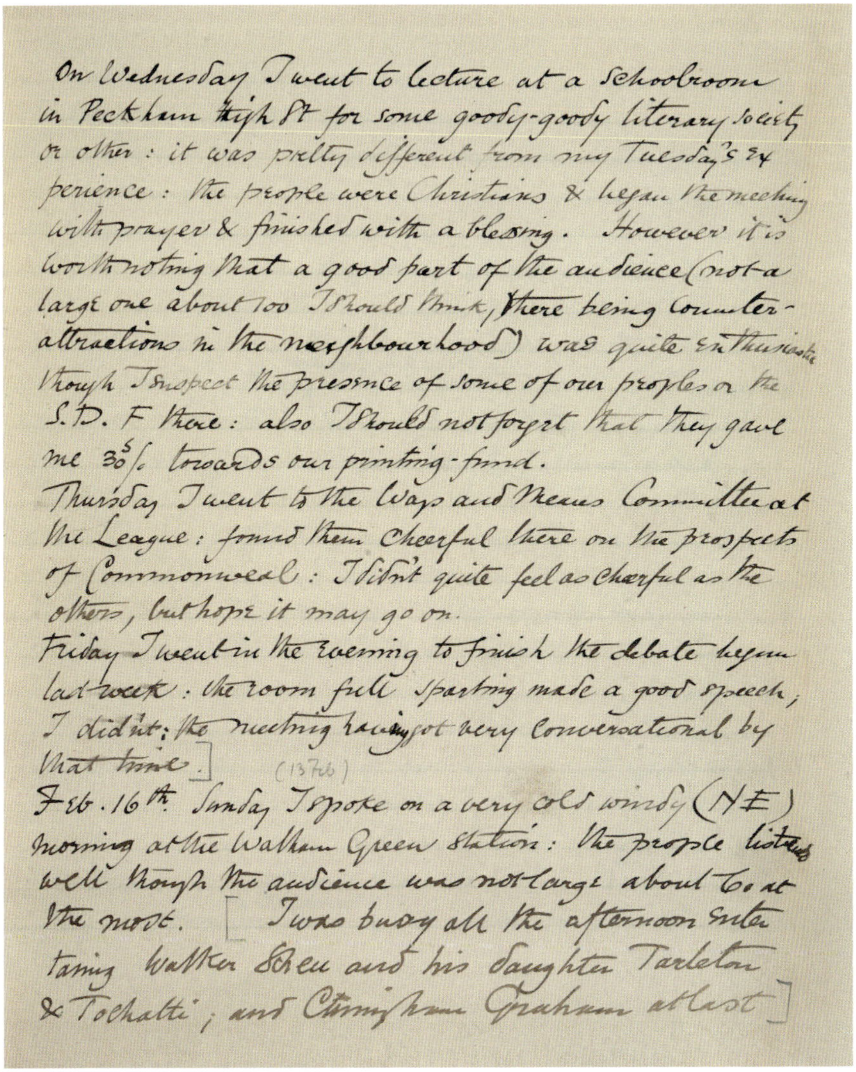
On Wednesday I went to lecture at a Schoolroom in Peckham High St for some goody-goody literary society or other: it was pretty different from my Tuesday's experience: the people were Christians & began the meeting with prayer & finished with a blessing. However it is worth noting that a good part of the audience (not a large one about 100 I should think, there being counter-attractions in the neighbourhood) was quite enthusiastic though I suspect the presence of some of our people or the S.D.F there: also I should not forget that they gave me 30s/. towards our printing-fund.
Thursday I went to the Ways and Means Committee at the League: found them cheerful there on the prospects of Commonweal: I didn't quite feel as cheerful as the others, but hope it may go on.
Friday I went in the evening to finish the debate begun last week: the room full Sparling made a good speech; I didn't: the meeting having got very conversational by that time.]
Feb. 16th. Sunday I spoke on a very cold windy (NE) morning at the Walham Green station: the people listened well though the audience was not large about 60 at the most. [I was busy all the afternoon entertaining Walter Crane and his daughter Tarleton & Tochatti; and Cunninghame Graham at last]

Fig.56 **Morris's 'Socialist Diary', 25 January–27 April 1887. The entries illustrated here provide a glimpse of his punishing schedule at the height of the agitation.**
British Library

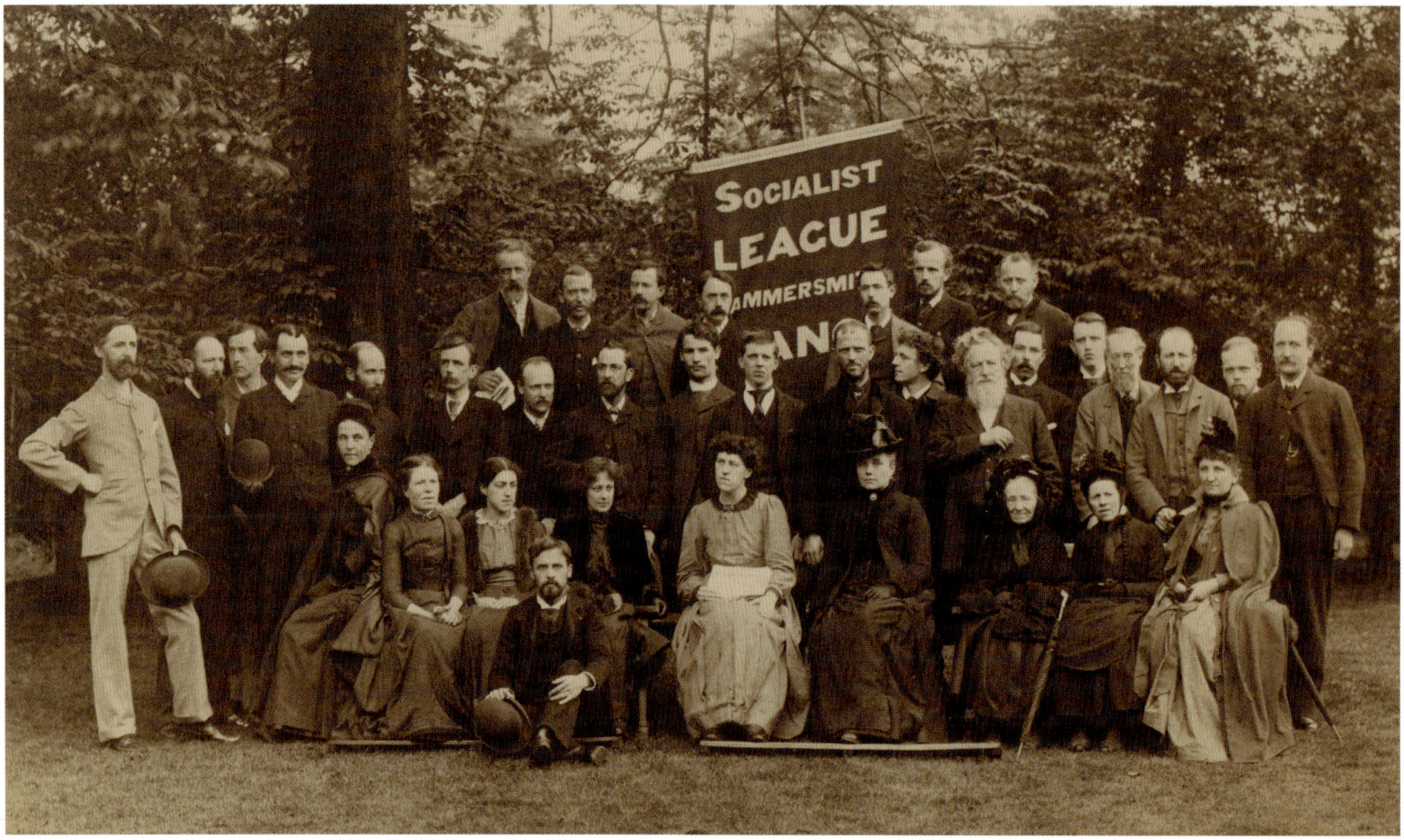

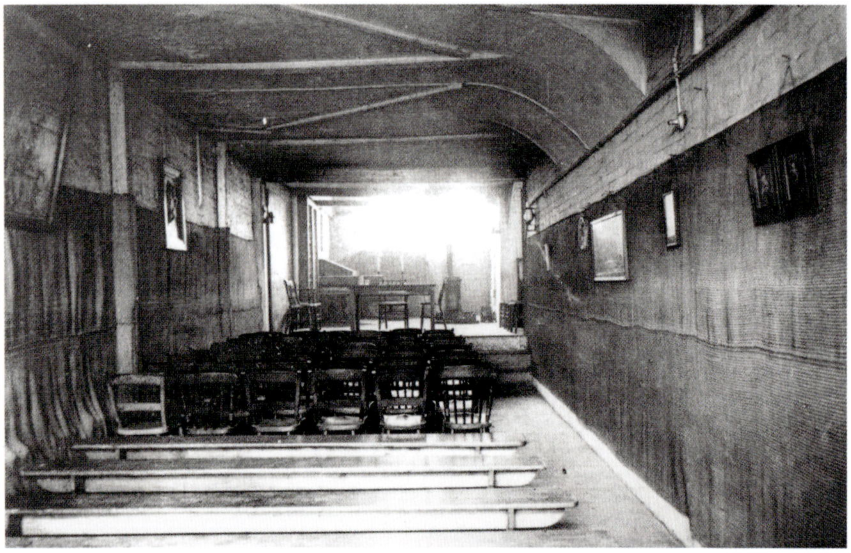

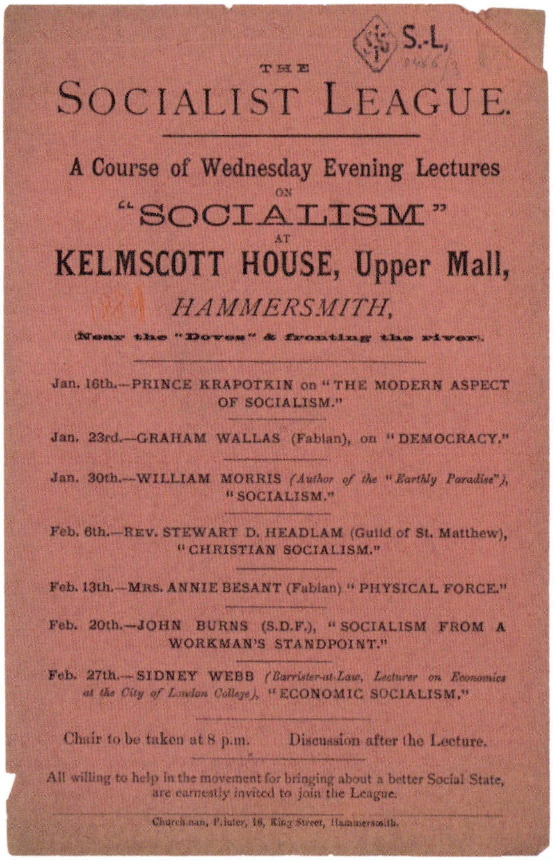
S.-L,

THE

SOCIALIST LEAGUE.

A Course of Wednesday Evening Lectures

ON

"SOCIALISM"

AT

KELMSCOTT HOUSE, Upper Mall,

HAMMERSMITH,

(Near the "Doves" & fronting the river).

Jan. 16th.—PRINCE KRAPOTKIN on "THE MODERN ASPECT OF SOCIALISM."

Jan. 23rd.—GRAHAM WALLAS (Fabian), on "DEMOCRACY."

Jan. 30th.—WILLIAM MORRIS *(Author of the "Earthly Paradise")*, "SOCIALISM."

Feb. 6th.—Rev. STEWART D. HEADLAM (Guild of St. Matthew), "CHRISTIAN SOCIALISM."

Feb. 13th.—Mrs. ANNIE BESANT (Fabian) "PHYSICAL FORCE."

Feb. 20th.—JOHN BURNS (S.D.F.), "SOCIALISM FROM A WORKMAN'S STANDPOINT."

Feb. 27th.—SIDNEY WEBB *(Barrister-at-Law, Lecturer on Economics at the City of London College)*, "ECONOMIC SOCIALISM."

Chair to be taken at 8 p.m. Discussion after the Lecture.

All willing to help in the movement for bringing about a better Social State, are earnestly invited to join the League.

Churchman, Printer, 16, King Street, Hammersmith.

Fig.57 (top) **The Hammersmith branch of the Socialist League at Kelmscott House, probably photographed by Frank Pellatt with Emery Walker's assistance, July 1888. May and Jenny Morris sit in the front row, third and fifth from the left, William stands behind to the right.**
V&A (1817–1939)

Fig.58 (above) **The coach house at Kelmscott House, used for socialist meetings and debates, photographed in 1896.**
William Morris Gallery

Fig.59 (right) **Socialist League flyer for a course of evening lectures at Kelmscott House, 1889. The line-up reveals the diversity of ideas debated in the Morris family's coach house.**
International Institute of Social History, Amsterdam

dispersed by the police. On 8 November Sir Charles Warren, the Metropolitan Commissioner of Police, took the provocative step of banning any further meetings in the Square on the dubious grounds that it was Crown property. To protest against this attack on 'free speech' – and the government's policy of coercion in Ireland – a combined radical, Irish and socialist demonstration was called for Sunday 13 November 1887. The plan was that several columns of marchers would converge on Trafalgar Square where a massive meeting would be held in defiance of the authorities.

Morris's experiences on 'Bloody Sunday' were similar to those of the other marchers. The Hammersmith branch of the League formed part of a contingent of 5,000 demonstrators who assembled on Clerkenwell Green. Here Morris and Annie Besant (secularist, Fabian and later theosophist and supporter of Indian independence) addressed the crowd, urging them to march to the Square in a dignified and orderly fashion. However, shortly after the marchers crossed Shaftesbury Avenue they were charged by the police and dispersed in complete disarray. 'It was all over in a few minutes,' Morris was to write later in *Commonweal*, 'our comrades fought valiantly, but they had not learned how to stand and turn their column into a line, or to march on to the front.' Morris managed to reach Trafalgar Square in time to see the Riot Act read and the Square cleared by a regiment of Guardsmen with fixed bayonets (fig.60).

A week later on Sunday 20 November, a second demonstration was held to protest against the Trafalgar Square outrages. In Northumberland Avenue, just off the Square, mounted police knocked down a young radical law-writer, Alfred Linnell, who subsequently died from his injuries. Morris wrote 'A Death Song' for his funeral on 18 December which was issued as a penny pamphlet to raise money for Linnell's orphans (fig.61). The funeral was both a spectacle and a protest. Mourners gathered in Soho and followed the coffin to the cemetery in Bow near Linnell's home. Morris and Besant were among the six pallbearers and by the time it reached Mile End Road the procession was nearly a mile long with many flag bearers. Morris gave a rousing speech at the graveside and a choir led the crowd in singing his revolutionary refrain, 'Not one, not one, nor thousands must they slay, But one and all if they would dusk the day.'

'Bloody Sunday' had a significant psychological effect on the British socialist movement. The ease with which the police achieved their victory destroyed many activists' faith in direct action and encouraged the movement towards parliamentary methods and the more gradual approach to achieving socialist goals advocated by the Fabian Society (formed in 1884). Within the League this tendency had already been apparent at the third annual conference, when a resolution proposed by John Lincoln Mahon in favour of supporting

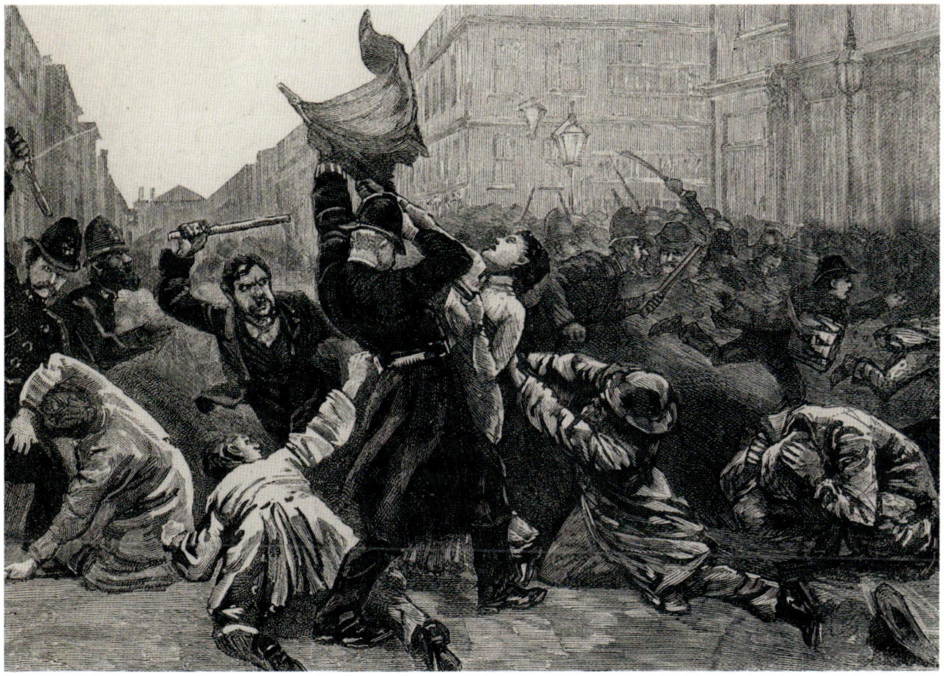

Fig.60 (below left) **Police dispersing the Clerkenwell contingent of the marchers on 'Bloody Sunday', engraving in *The Graphic*, 19 November 1887.**

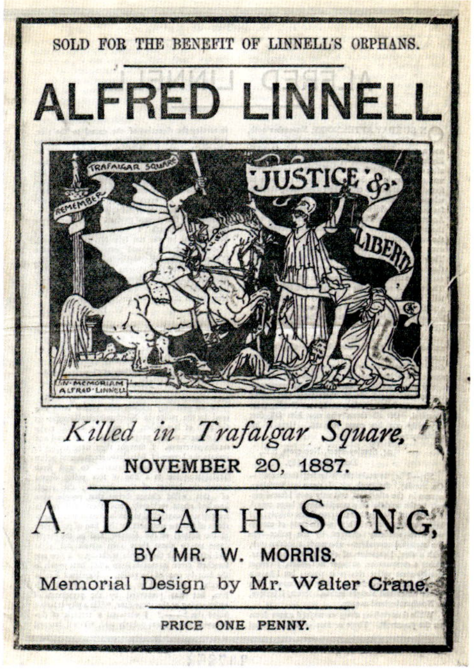

Fig.61 (below right) **'A Death Song' written by William Morris for Alfred Linnell's funeral, 1887. Walter Crane's design shows a policeman clubbing the unfortunate Linnell.**
Manchester Metropolitan University Special Collections

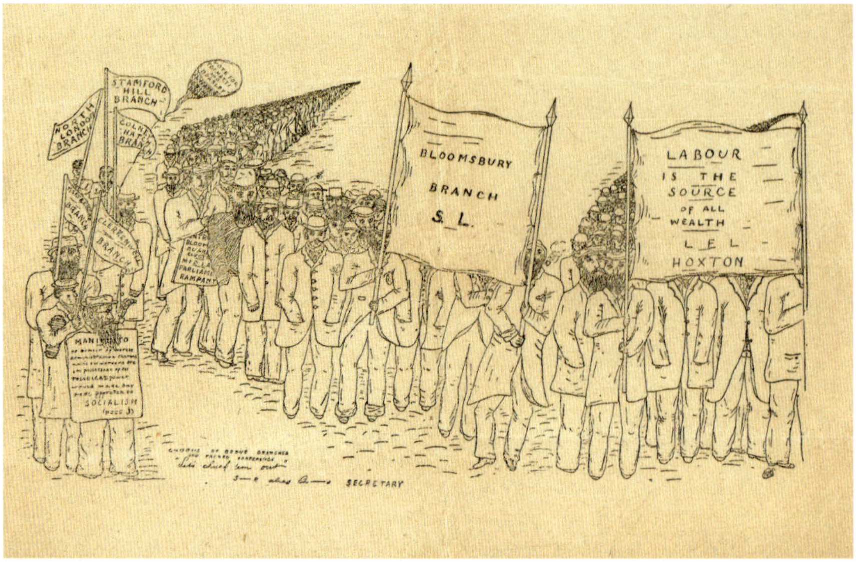

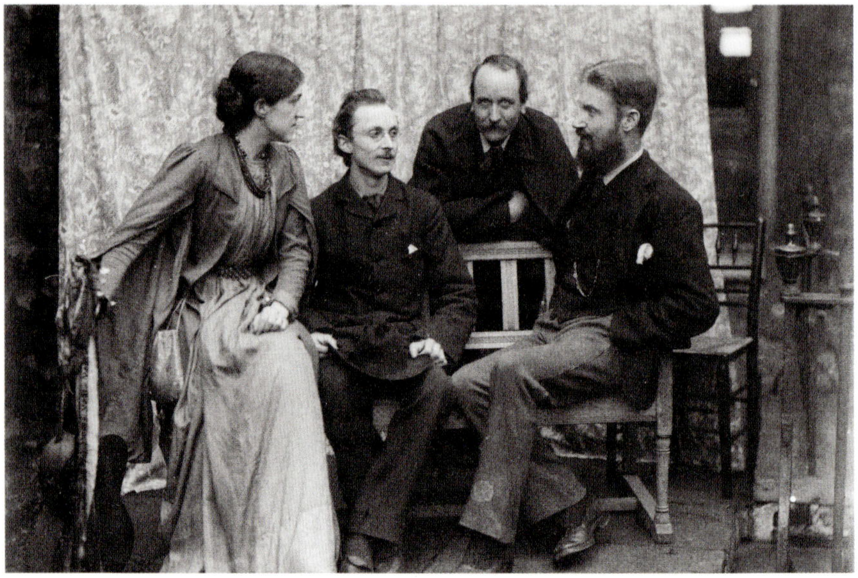

parliamentary candidates was defeated by only 17 votes to 11. Following 'Bloody Sunday', Mahon withdrew from the League taking with him much of the support he had built up in the north. He was followed by Bax and the Bloomsbury branch after another pro-parliamentary resolution was defeated at the fourth annual conference in May 1888 (fig.62).

The divisions within the League were deepened by the case of the Chicago Anarchists. In May 1886 a fight had broken out between strikers and strike breakers at the McCormick Harvesting Machine Co. in Chicago. When the police arrived, they fired at a group of strikers running away from the scene, causing numerous injuries and four deaths. The American anarchists subsequently arranged a meeting in Haymarket Square in Chicago to protest at the police action. During the police attempt to disperse the crowd a bomb was thrown that killed seven police officers. The police then opened fire on the crowd wounding over 200 and causing a number of fatalities. Unable to identify the bomb thrower, the authorities arrested eight Chicago anarchist leaders, only one of whom had actually been present at the Haymarket meeting. Despite this all of the men were found guilty. Long sentences were passed on three of them, while four were hanged on 11 November 1887. Another, Louis Lingg, cheated the gallows by committing suicide in his cell.

Morris was among those who had protested against the treatment of the Chicago Anarchists and condemned their 'judicial murder'. The fact that the anarchists had been prosecuted for their beliefs rather than their actions immediately elevated them to the status of martyrs. Many socialists were impressed by the way they conducted their defence and faced the prospect of death. Such influential figures within the League as Joseph Lane, Frank Kitz and Charles Mowbray began to listen with respect to the anarchists' case. By the early months of 1888 this group, along with James Tochatti, had assumed a prominent position in the leadership of the League. Morris inadvertently strengthened their position at the fourth annual conference when he relied on their support in order to maintain the League's anti-parliamentary stance.

In fact, the fourth annual conference marked the end of the League as an effective organization. Membership soon fell into decline and the remaining provincial branches became isolated and outside the control of the leadership in London. At the annual conference in May 1890 the anarchists succeeded in gaining control of the council and ousted Morris from the editorship of *Commonweal*. Disheartened by this defeat, Morris and the Hammersmith branch eventually withdrew from the League in November.

One of Morris's last activities before his departure was the publication of *News from Nowhere* in *Commonweal*. It appeared in 39 instalments between 11 January and 4 October 1890. By this point his subsidies of the paper were around £500 per year, roughly the same amount as the firm was paid for *The Adoration* tapestry, a commission that took four years to complete (XII.119). Despite being ousted from the editorship in May, he probably continued his substantial funding until the end of the year to

Fig.62 (top) **Flyleaf satirizing Morris and the anti-parliamentary branches distributed by the Bloomsbury branch of the Socialist League, 1888.**
International Institute of Social History, Amsterdam

Fig.63 (above) **May Morris, Henry Halliday Sparling, Emery Walker and George Bernard Shaw rehearsing for a Socialist League entertainment, 3 February 1889.**
The Wilson Art Gallery and Museum, Cheltenham

see through the publication of his utopian fiction. The *Commonweal* text was almost immediately appropriated by Roberts Brothers of Boston – apparently without Morris's permission – and issued as an *editio princeps* in the United States. Morris revised the book in the autumn of 1890 and made a number of significant additions and alterations. The revised edition of *News from Nowhere* was published by Reeves & Turner in the spring of 1891 and a one shilling paperback edition was also issued (fig.66).

Without Morris's financial support and mediative influence the League disintegrated into a series of uncoordinated revolutionary groups. *Commonweal* continued erratically in various guises and eventually ceased publication. While his break with the League did not shake Morris's belief in revolutionary socialism, it did restrict his influence on the wider movement. In November 1890 the Hammersmith branch was renamed the Hammersmith Socialist Society (figs 64–5). Although its 'Statement of Principles' reaffirmed Morris's purist views, it was never to pursue a fixed policy and soon became an anachronism within the wider movement. From October 1891 it published a modest four-page monthly paper, the *Hammersmith Socialist Record*, in which Morris occasionally recorded his views on the general progress of socialism but it was no substitute for *Commonweal*. Morris's deteriorating health prevented him from undertaking the gruelling schedule of outdoor speaking he pursued in the 1880s, however the Society's weekly lectures and monthly discussions at Kelmscott House did provide a platform for a host of divergent views. This reflected Morris's growing conviction that the internal squabbles within the movement had been detrimental to the wider propaganda campaign. In 1894 he was to write that 'our business at present seems to me to preach Socialism to non-Socialists, and to preach unity of action to Socialists'.

In an attempt to foster unity within the movement the Hammersmith Socialist Society held a debate in December 1892 on the subject: 'Is it now desirable to form a Socialist Federation?' The question was answered in the affirmative and a sub-committee, including Morris, was formed 'to promote the alliance of Socialist organisations in Great Britain'. This sub-committee then approached the Fabians and the Social Democratic Federation and a joint committee of the three organizations was formed in February 1893, with Morris as chairman. There appeared to be real signs that the joint committee might succeed in May 1893 when it issued *The Manifesto of English Socialists*, a collaborative work written by Morris with input from Hyndman and Edward Pease, representing the Fabians.

However, this initiative was to be overtaken by events. During 1892 a number of northern socialist and radical organizations had amalgamated to form the Independent Labour Party. This had immediate success in the general election of 1892, when three of its candidates were elected to Parliament. At its first conference, held in Bradford in January 1893, some of the ex-Leaguers, including Mahon and Alexander Karley Donald played a prominent role. Such was

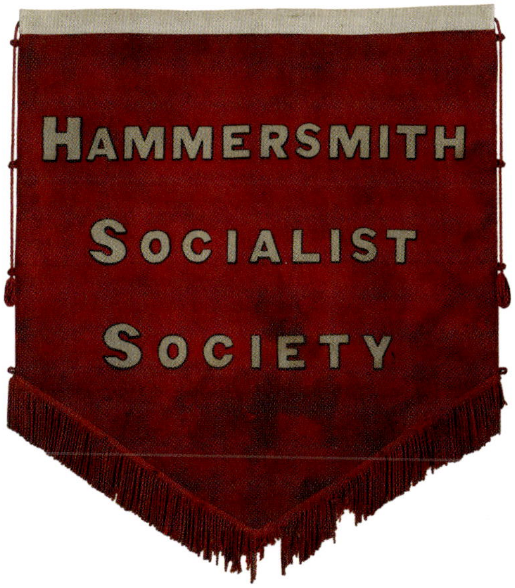

Fig.64 (below left) **Banner for the Hammersmith Socialist Society with painted inscription, unknown maker, *c.*1890–1.**
Marx Memorial Library & Workers' School, London

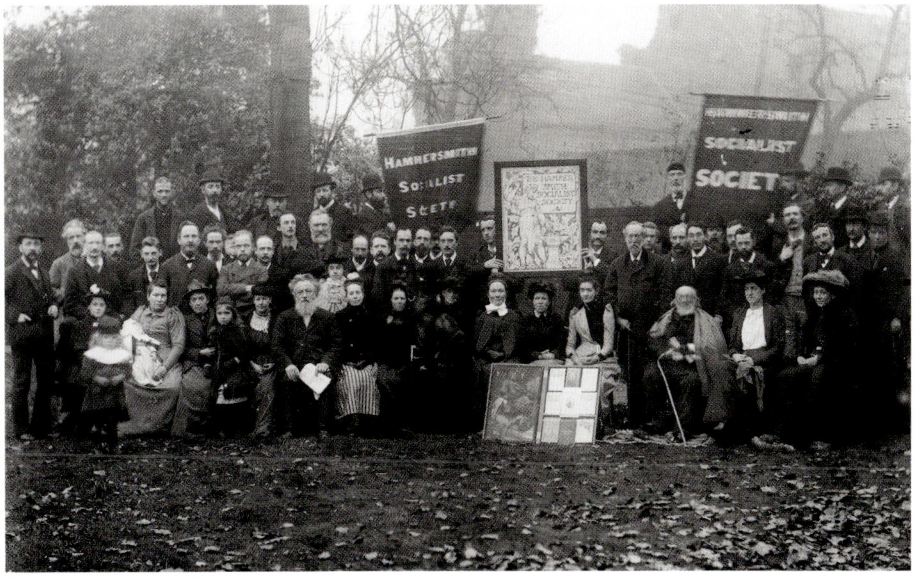

Fig.65 (below right) **Hammersmith Socialist Society, possibly photographed by Emery Walker. The framed sign was adapted from Walter Crane's design and painted by Comrade 'Cosmo' Rowe to hang outside the meeting room at Kelmscott House in 1892.**
National Portrait Gallery

Morris's standing in the movement that Robert Blatchford, in the *Clarion*, urged him to take his rightful place among the leadership of the new organization.

For a few months it appeared that the Independent Labour Party might join the joint committee. In February 1893 the Hammersmith Socialist Society invited two prominent figures within the Party, Keir Hardie and Shaw Maxwell, to speak at Kelmscott House. Indeed, Shaw Maxwell returned the following month to lecture on the 'Aims and Objects of the Labour Party'. Morris wanted to call a united conference to include the Party but he once more came into conflict with Hyndman who considered the new organization not to be a truly socialistic body. Faced with Hyndman's intransigence – and the withdrawal of the Fabians in July 1893 – the joint committee collapsed.

During his last few years in the movement a subtle shift can be detected in Morris's views. Although he was never to lose his belief in the need for revolutionary change, he began to regard industrial action and specific reform – like the eight-hour day and the minimum wage – more favourably. He came to the conclusion that the working classes could learn valuable lessons in organization in pursuing such aims and that a transitional stage of state socialism might be inevitable before the revolution itself could be achieved. This change in attitude caused him to reconcile himself with the Social Democratic Federation in 1894, although he never rejoined the organization, preferring to retain his independence while there was still a chance of uniting the various socialist bodies.

One of Morris's new occupations in the 1890s was the founding of the Kelmscott Press, motivated by his desire to produce books with a 'definitive claim to beauty'. A lovingly crafted edition of *News from Nowhere* was issued on 24 March 1893 (though printed bearing the date 22 November 1892), with 300 copies on paper and ten on vellum (fig.67). The 'old house by the Thames' in the frontispiece is a wood engraving of his country home, Kelmscott Manor, from a drawing by Charles March Gere. It has been suggested that the Kelmscott Press symbolizes Morris's retreat from active political work and that by creating a luxurious and expensive edition of his utopian fiction he was betraying his socialist ideals. Yet, as Rowan Williams has eloquently argued,

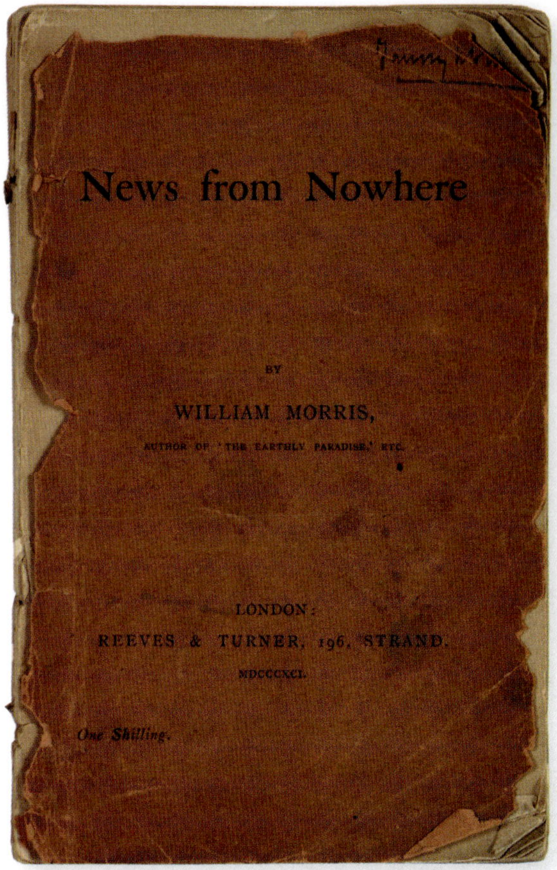

Fig.66 **One shilling paperback edition of *News from Nowhere*, 1891.**
William Morris Gallery

> this is to miss the point. Morris imagines a future in which items such as this, the product of first-rate craftsmanship, would be routinely produced ... the Kelmscott Press printing [of *News from Nowhere*] is not a cynical contradiction of Morris's principles but a defiant statement of them: the communist future is emphatically not one of functional bareness ... but one of abundance, and the book shows what that might literally look like.

Equally persuasively, Elizabeth Miller, in her study of the Victorian radical press, *Slow Print* (2013), identifies important continuities between Morris's two printing and publishing endeavours. In her view, both *Commonweal* and the Press were attempts by Morris to reinvent print to counter the damaging effects of a mass print culture, which, driven by profits, could never produce anything but 'apologies for capitalism'.

Some idea of the immense impact that Morris had on the socialist movement can be gained from the tributes paid to him after his death in October 1896. Blatchford summed up the sorrow

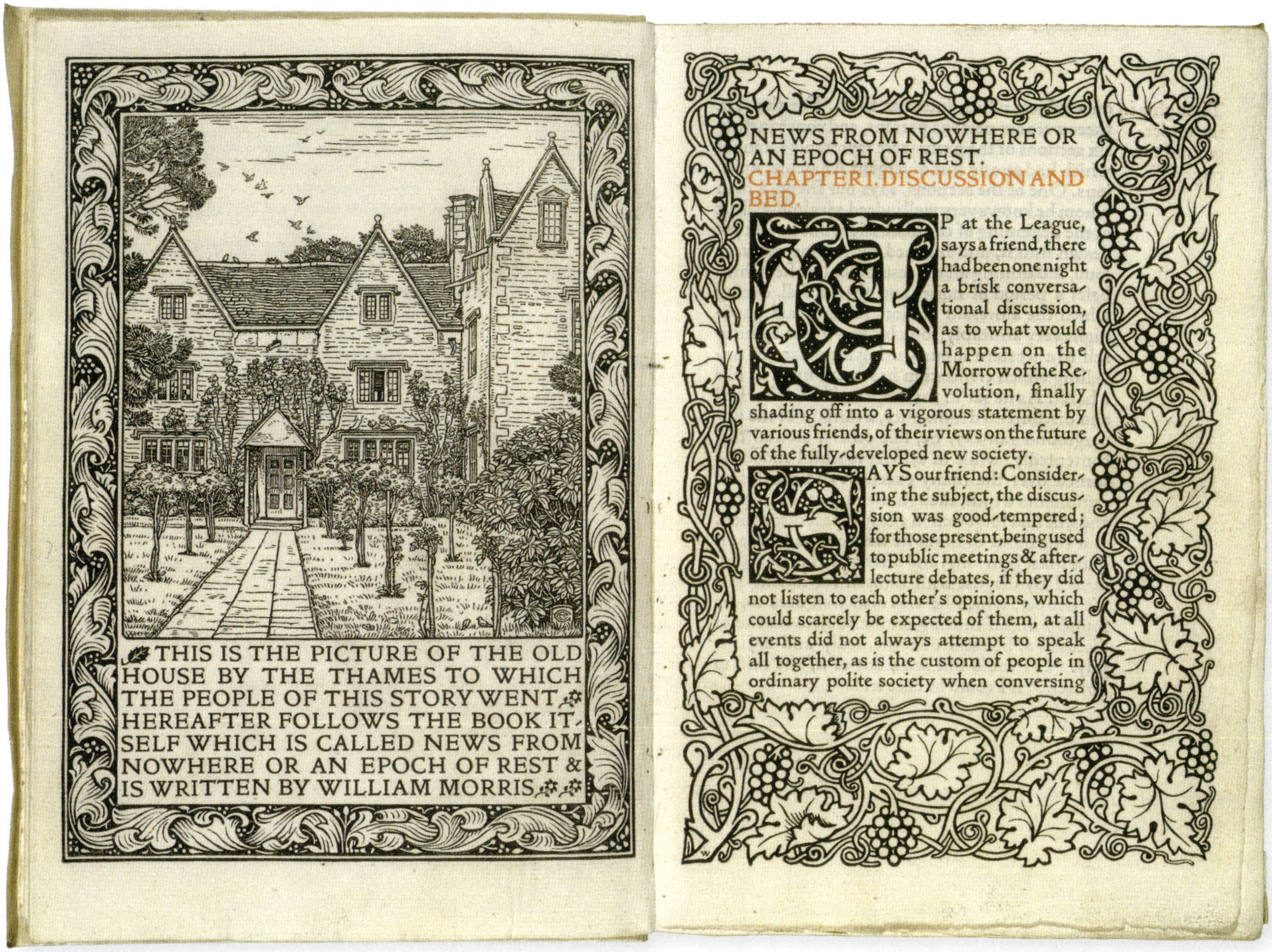
THIS IS THE PICTURE OF THE OLD HOUSE BY THE THAMES TO WHICH THE PEOPLE OF THIS STORY WENT. HEREAFTER FOLLOWS THE BOOK IT-SELF WHICH IS CALLED NEWS FROM NOWHERE OR AN EPOCH OF REST & IS WRITTEN BY WILLIAM MORRIS

NEWS FROM NOWHERE OR AN EPOCH OF REST.

CHAPTER I. DISCUSSION AND BED.

UP at the League, says a friend, there had been one night a brisk conversational discussion, as to what would happen on the Morrow of the Revolution, finally shading off into a vigorous statement by various friends, of their views on the future of the fully-developed new society.

SAYS our friend: Considering the subject, the discussion was good-tempered; for those present, being used to public meetings & after-lecture debates, if they did not listen to each other's opinions, which could scarcely be expected of them, at all events did not always attempt to speak all together, as is the custom of people in ordinary polite society when conversing

Fig.67 ***News from Nowhere*** **by William Morris, Kelmscott Press edition, issued 24 March 1893.**
National Art Library, V&A

of his comrades when he wrote: 'I cannot help thinking that it does not matter what goes into the *Clarion* this week, because William Morris is dead … he was our best man, and he is dead.' Another moving tribute came from a Lancashire branch of the Federation: 'Comrade Morris is not dead there is not a Socialist living would believe him dead for he lives in the heart of all true men and women still and will do so to the end of time.' Such was the affection in which he was held that his name soon adorned socialist halls and Labour churches. His portrait was even hung alongside that of Marx in the clubrooms of the Federation. These were fitting tributes to a man who was one of the pivotal figures in the history of modern socialism.

V

THE CONSERVATIONIST

Chris Miele

'The love of the Middle Ages was born in him.' This was how John William Mackail, his first official biographer, described the young Morris's passion for the past. The source of these strong feelings was, Mackail reported, 'the old Essex churches within reach of Woodford', the location of Morris's childhood home, now part of Greater London. Mackail also recorded a visit Morris, aged eight, took with his father to Canterbury where he saw the cathedral, which 'left on his mind an ineffaceable impression of the glory of Gothic architecture.' The first primary evidence we have for Morris's interest in ancient buildings and monuments is a letter he wrote to his sister, Emma, from Marlborough College on 13 April 1849 recounting a trip to two nearby prehistoric sites, Silbury Hill (fig.68) and the henge monument at Avebury village. Morris returned the next day, intrigued by the massive stones and the pretty parish church with its Norman doorway. He also climbed Silbury Hill, 'not very high', he noted, 'but yet I should think it must have taken an immense long time to have got it together.'

This letter does not provide much insight into his thinking about historic sites. For that evidence we have to look to his time at Oxford, in particular in articles written for the short-lived journal he funded, *The Oxford and Cambridge Magazine*. His essay on Amiens Cathedral (fig.69) is effusive, 'I think I felt inclined to shout when I first entered ... it is so free and vast and noble'. The artistic achievement of the building inspires passionate longing in the narrator whose description has an erotic character that goes beyond anything the young Morris would have taken from John Ruskin's writings. The strength of feeling we find here and in a handful of letters from the period look forward to the intensity of feeling that would characterize Morris's involvement with building conservation more than 20 years later.

That interest led Morris to pursue a career in architecture and, so, in January 1856 he entered into articles in the Oxford office of George Edmund Street. Street was one of the most accomplished Gothic Revival architects of his generation and by far the larger part of his output was the repair of ancient churches and the design of new ones for an Anglican clientele. When Morris joined, Street was pioneering a new approach to colourism in architecture. His All Saints, Boyne Hill in Maidenhead (consecrated in 1857) and St James the Less in Pimlico, London (1858–61), combined colourful materials and strong forms influenced by the Italian Gothic to create powerful

Fig.68 **Silbury Hill, the largest prehistoric mound in Europe, photographed in 1911.**
Historic England Archive

Fig.69 **Cathedral of Nôtre Dame, Amiens, photographed by Henri Le Secq in 1851 as part of a government initiative to determine the urgency of restoration work at historic sites across France.**
National Galleries Scotland

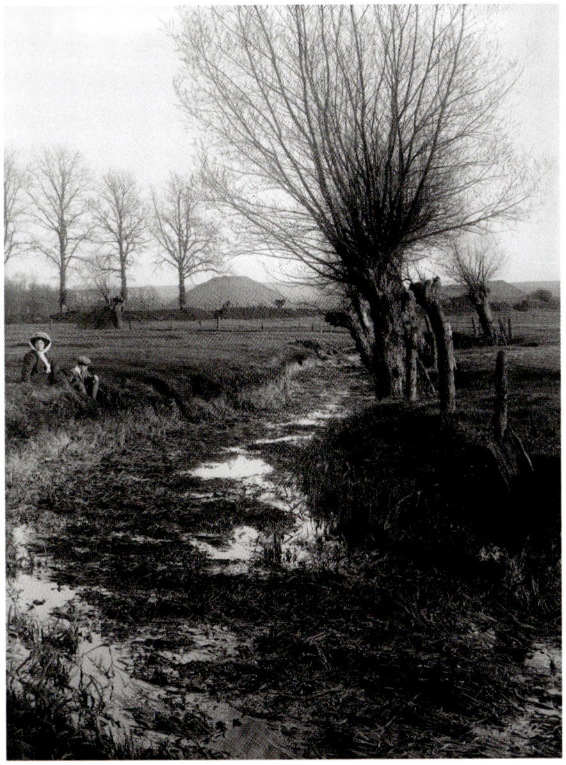

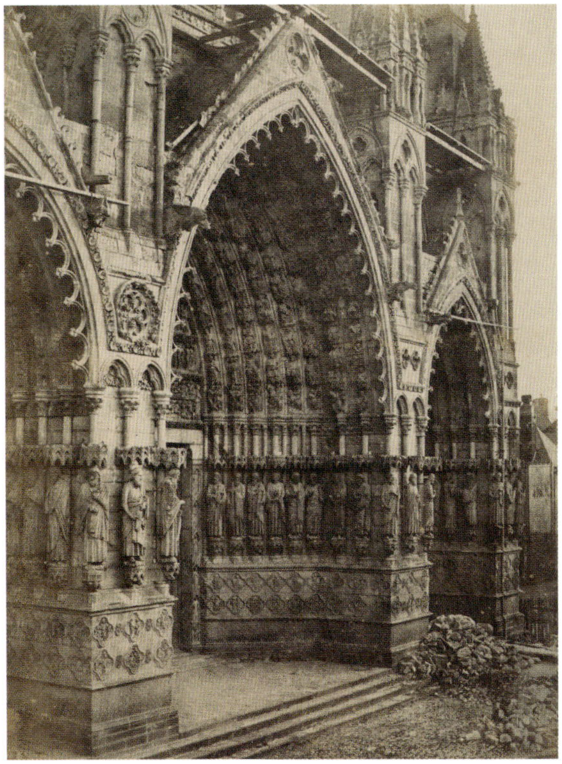

buildings (fig.70). Street also took great care over the design of ornament and furnishings, which helped stimulate Morris's interest in different craft disciplines and strongly coloured and patterned interior decoration. Morris moved to London when Street's office relocated there in August 1856, but soon abandoned architecture for painting under the influence of Dante Gabriel Rossetti. Yet he took one more important and lasting thing from Street's office: an acquaintance, later friendship, with his chief assistant, Philip Webb.

Critically, Morris and Webb (with help from others as we shall see) worked closely together from 1877 to establish and run the Society for the Protection of Ancient Buildings (SPAB). Webb's contribution to this endeavour, one of the most important of Morris's later activities, has always been acknowledged, however, the depth of his involvement has only recently been documented through John Aplin's excellent collection of the architect's correspondence. This essay begins with the ideas Morris promoted through the SPAB because these represent a solid, lasting legacy of relevance to modern thinking. The Society's origins and working methods are then explored in more depth.

The ideas behind the new society were clearly set out in its manifesto, written by Morris (with some encouragement from Webb and the firm's general manager, George Wardle) shortly after its first meeting on 22 March 1877. The SPAB manifesto is probably one of the most widely read statements of conservation philosophy in the world, and familiar to any professional who works seriously in the business of caring for, adapting or modernizing historic buildings. It is a short document, about 1,000 words or so, and in it Morris explains the sort of approach this new kind of organization would promote. As defined in the manifesto, 'protection' has four dimensions or themes. These remain relevant, to an extent at least, and capable of wider application notwithstanding that the bulk of the SPAB's casework in Morris's time was devoted to the medieval places of worship serving the Church of England.

The first theme was curatorial or aesthetic. Morris believed that if historic buildings needed to be adapted, repaired or extended to sustain them in use or maintain their fabric or structure, then new work should be recognizably of its time and not a pastiche of older or original work. This idea was indebted to Ruskin's *Seven Lamps of Architecture* (1849), and in particular the chapter titled 'The Lamp of Memory', which expressly attacked then current approaches to building 'restoration' that sought to replicate old work by rebuilding, reconstructing or extending in a matching style. According to Ruskin and Morris, trying to recreate the style or character of an old building produced a false historical narrative and undermined its authenticity. Heavily patinated surfaces and irregular settlement, weathered stonework, and so on, all communicated the passage of centuries and were a source of beauty in themselves. We apply this approach today and recognize too the idea that new work serving a modern purpose should be visibly of its time, and in fact this commonly takes the form of extensions that deliberately contrast with older buildings.

However, this clash of contrasting styles was not at all what Morris had in mind. The sort of additions the SPAB promoted had a complementary form, using similar and traditional materials, so that from a distance the old and new would form a seamless whole. The window repairs William Samuel Weatherley, working with the approval of the SPAB, specified at St James's Church, Shere, in Surrey in the mid-1890s are a good example of this approach. Here, the detailing of new features is simplified but complementary so that, from a distance, the character of the church as a historic artefact, evolved slowly over time, is not disrupted. The new materials match the old and were constructed using similar techniques but without any unnecessary elaboration.

The manifesto also stressed that only fabric that was beyond repair should be removed. A good example of this is the careful work that the office of George Gilbert Scott specified at Godalming Church between 1876 and 1881. Here, masons were directed to cut away only the outer face of failing window tracery. The repair techniques Webb himself specified, using the young Detmar Blow, at St Mary's Church, East Knoyle, in Wiltshire consolidated the failing structural masonry of the tower effectively from within, and in stages, so that the external surface of the building was undisturbed (figs 72–3). A large part of the practical advice the SPAB gave relied on technique, an understanding of materials and refined craftsmanship. The Society today continues this tradition and is renowned for its technical expertise, which it promotes through educational initiatives. Here, in its practical advice, we see Webb's contribution most clearly.

The manifesto also grappled with those not unusual cases where, to meet reasonable modern requirements, an original building had to be so altered as to change its character fundamentally. This was quite a common approach in the period and understandable in areas where population densities were increasing beyond the capacity of the old parish church and where the Church of England was in competition with Nonconformist denominations. Morris's suggestion was to leave the old building untouched as a historical document and build a new one in a more convenient location. This might sound impractical, since it required the promoter of the scheme to find new land and then to maintain the old building without any regular use beyond its value as a monument. Yet it was not unknown and a good example was

Fig.70 **Interior of All Saints, Boyne Hill, designed by George Edmund Street. This church was under construction when Morris entered Street's office in January 1856.**

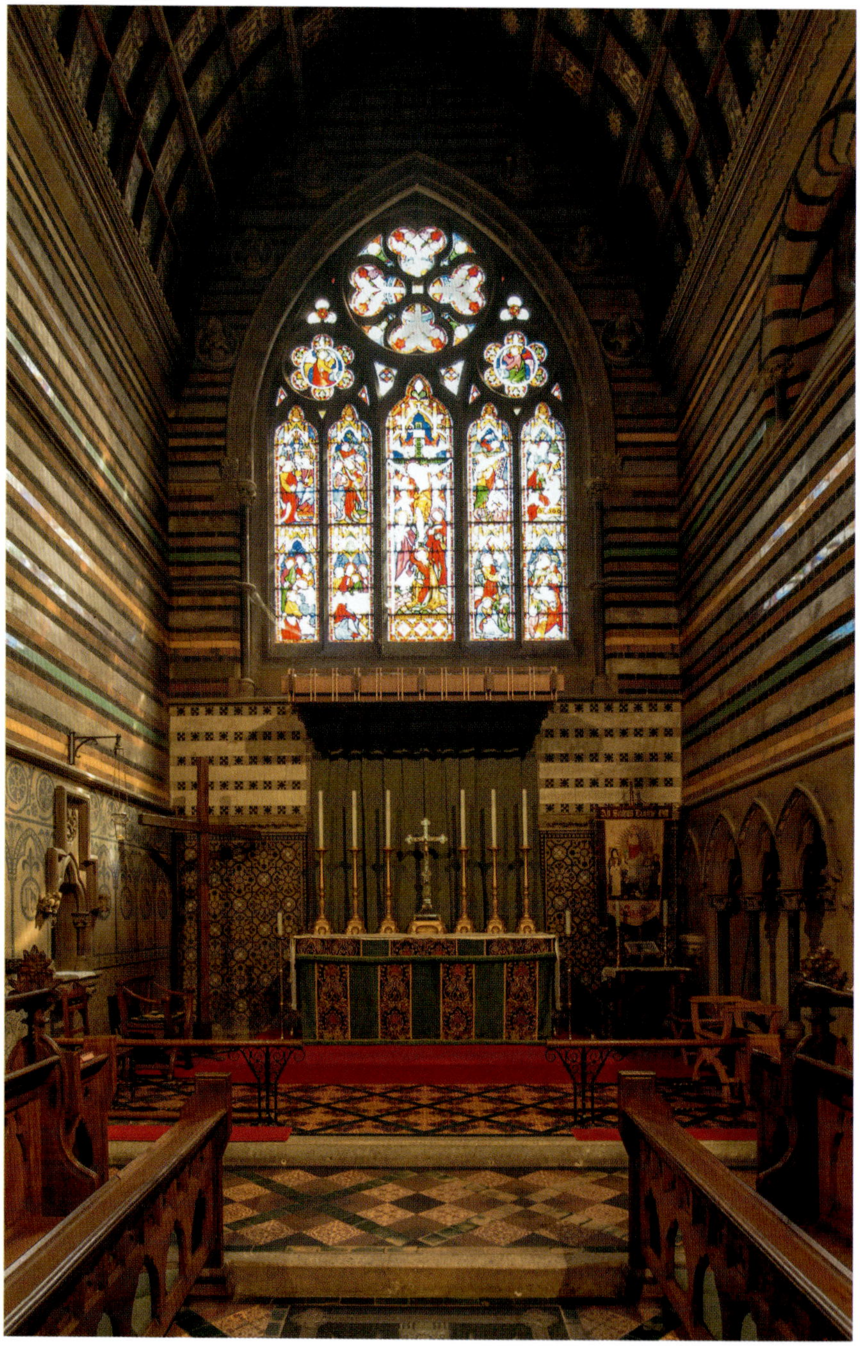

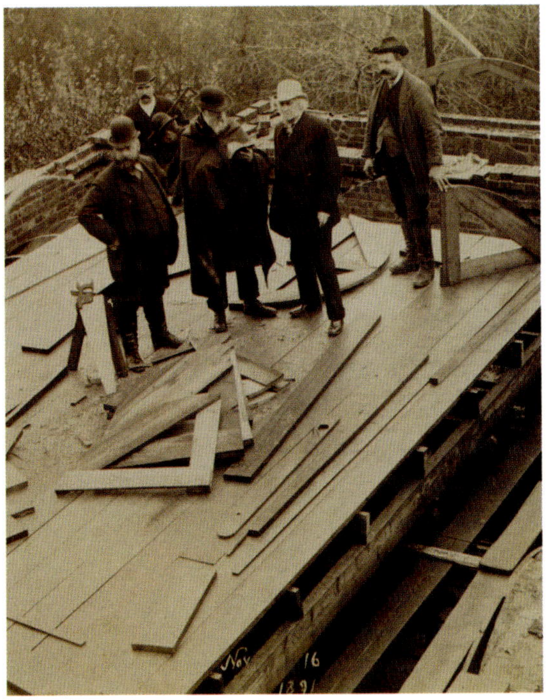

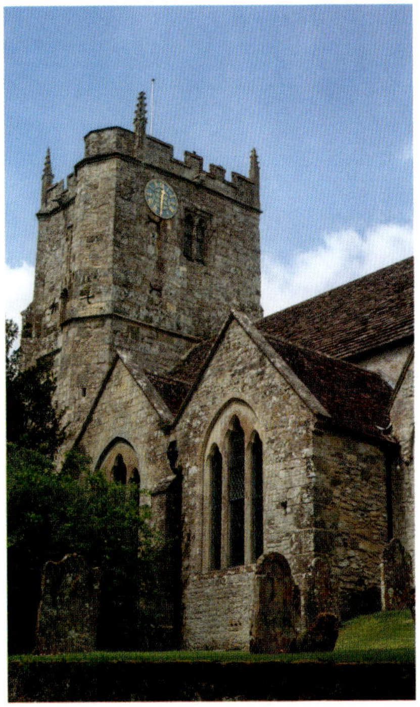

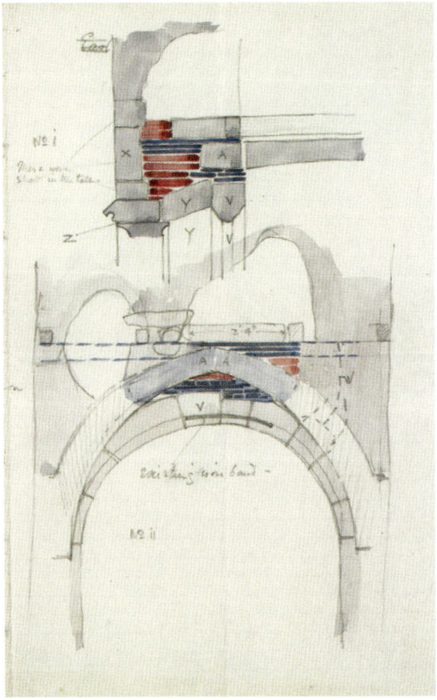

Fig.71 (above left) **A rare photograph of Philip Webb (wearing a black cape) on a site visit to Joldwynds, Surrey, 16 November 1891.**
RIBA

Fig.72 (above centre) **The exterior of the tower, St Mary's, East Knoyle, Wiltshire.**

Fig.73 (above right) **Diagram in a letter from Detmar Blow to Philip Webb showing planned repairs to the tower of St Mary's, East Knoyle, 14 January 1893.**
V&A (E.367–2014)

the decision of the vicar of Stoke Newington in London to maintain the old Elizabethan parish church for smaller services on one side of the high street, while commissioning George Gilbert Scott to design and oversee the construction of a very large town church, St Mary's, opposite. Consecrated in 1858, it could accommodate more than a thousand people. The pair of buildings sit across from one another still to this day.

It was more common either to replace the ancient church entirely or, in some circumstances, to retain the original building as an aisle of a much larger one. That was what happened to the superb late Saxon church at Kirk Hammerton in Yorkshire in 1892 (fig.74). From the south, across the churchyard, it retains the character of a tiny eleventh-century building that would have served the needs of a dispersed rural parish, similar to a number in this part of England. Walk into it, however, and you appreciate the whole of the north wall of the old building has been demolished and replaced with an arcade opening onto a large new nave with beautiful late Victorian murals. We enjoy these contrasts today but, of course, achieving permission for them is impossible to contemplate, not least as a consequence of the paradigm change Morris and the SPAB initiated. The Society, incidentally, objected to this work.

The idea that one might create a monument by not using it likely reflects the circumstances of the day. There was a great depression in agricultural land values from 1872 and a consequent acceleration in the depopulation of rural parishes in England and Wales, a process that continued for decades. As a result, anyone travelling to more remote areas would realize that there was no pressure to modernize country churches at all. Many of the churches the Victorians forgot (to quote the title of Mark Chatfield's evocative survey of 1989) came to be vested in the Redundant Churches Fund, now the Churches Conservation Trust, as consecrated buildings retained for their historical interest and beauty, available only for occasional and special events. The Trust works off an endowment and relies on grants and donations for particular projects. It achieves, then, the sort of enlightened stewardship that Morris encouraged in 1877.

The second theme we meet within the manifesto, and the one that actually forms the backbone of it, is a rejection of the Gothic Revival in architecture. The consequence of the Revival was, Morris wrote, to leave 'the civilised world of the nineteenth century' with no real or genuine 'style' it could call its own. This idea derived from the so-called 'Battle of the Styles', the question of what was the most suitable style (classical or medievalizing or some blend of the two) for modern buildings. This debate defined architectural culture in Europe during the middle decades of the nineteenth century. Morris's response was not to side with one camp or another but instead to reject the idea that any historical style could possibly create a genuine and vital modern architecture. This sounds a lot like Modernist rhetoric from the 1920s, explaining why Nikolaus Pevsner's famous *Pioneers of Modern Design* (1936) is subtitled 'From William Morris to Walter Gropius'.

The SPAB manifesto foreshadows, then, Le Corbusier's 1923 *Vers une architecture*, which asserts 'Architecture has nothing to do with the various "styles"'. His solution was to base a new architecture on the aesthetics of the engineer and the machine. It may not be good history to imagine what Morris might have thought of the Villa Savoye (though it is a diverting thought problem). Fortunately, in his 1888 lecture, 'The Revival of Architecture', Morris identified several contemporary buildings that he believed were nearest to achieving the vital architectural culture he imagined. The list included Street's Royal Courts of Justice in the Strand, a masterpiece of thirteenth-century revivalism, completed in 1882. Morris also admired the work of George Frederick Bodley and Thomas Garner at St Swithun's Building, Magdalen College, Oxford, a new accommodation block that was taller than nearby historic ranges but in all other respects redolent of the sixteenth century (fig.75). He singled out the school buildings designed for the new London School Board, by John James Stevenson, who was active in the SPAB as we shall see, and Edward Robert Robson, who became its lead architect. The choice of the Law Courts is puzzling; it is arguably the high point of the Revival. We get closer to Morris's architectural vision with Bodley and Garner's Oxford work, which shows a real sensitivity to the qualities of the natural stone facing. The new houses and mansion flats built in Chelsea and Kensington at this time, for example in Lowther Gardens by Stevenson (fig.76), exploiting the natural properties of brick, are carefully massed and rely on architectural details that are creative interpretations of not one but several periods. Stevenson referred to his designs in this manner as 'homely', 'simple and manly', comparing them to 'colloquial speech'. He favoured the term 'Free Classic'.

The SPAB manifesto paints an ugly picture of what too much historical knowledge does to architecture. At its worst, it created an over-familiarity with the past. Architects felt able to match their knowledge against the ancients' and on that basis did not scruple to interfere with old buildings, 'improving', reconstructing, even reimagining them. The most

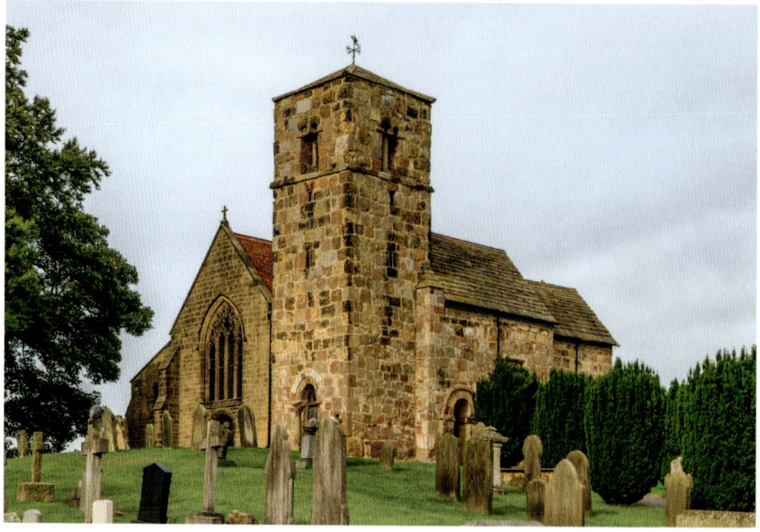

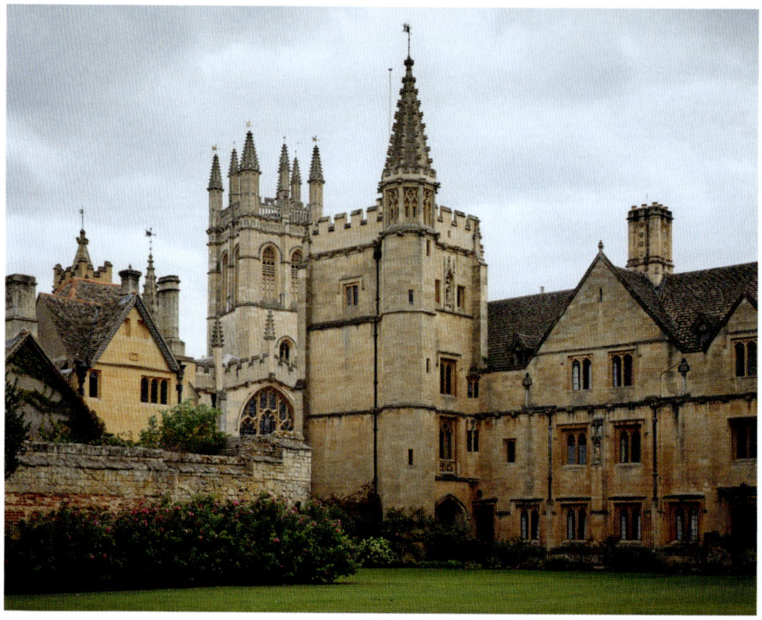

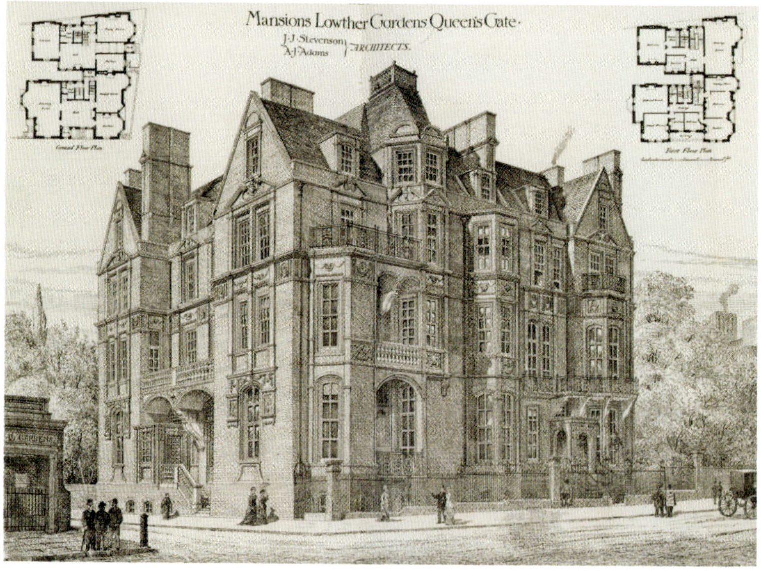

Fig.74 (opposite above) **Exterior of St John the Baptist, Kirk Hammerton, Yorkshire.**

Fig.75 (opposite centre) **St Swithun's Building, Magdalen College, Oxford, designed by Bodley and Garner.**

Fig.76 (opposite below) **Mansions in Lowther Gardens, Kensington, designed by John James Stevenson, published in *The Building News*, 20 September 1878.** V&A

important architectural and decorative arts innovation of Morris's lifetime, the Gothic Revival, the movement which had nurtured his aesthetics and supported his business, was in his considered view not just outmoded – it was institutionalized cultural vandalism.

Manifestos written by artists are rhetorical. Their dramatic narrative requires a straw man to act the part of the villain. The Revival played that role. In fairness to Morris, the changes worked on some ancient buildings were indeed dramatic. A textbook example is the programme of work the young George Gilbert Scott supervised at St Mary's, Stafford between 1841 and 1845. The before-and-after comparison is surprising (figs 77–8). Scott removed a late medieval clerestory to reinstate an earlier roof form, rebuilt the south transept to match, embellished the tower and replaced late Gothic tracery with designs based on an earlier style. There were countless such transformations, many thousands in fact, and in their end state the buildings are often unrecognizable to what they were previously.

The manifesto's third theme flows from the second, and it anticipates the direction of our own legislative system. Morris wrote that those vicars and patrons who had legal responsibilities for ancient buildings were not in fact the best people to respect their historic interest. Neither, for that matter, were the architects in charge of them, like Scott (who had the largest restoration practice in Europe at the time). Essentially, these parties could not act in the national interest, mindful of the future, because they each were pursuing their own narrow professional aims and client instructions. Vicars wanted to modernize their churches to make them more attractive and suitable for modern worship, to increase their capacity to meet the needs of a growing population, and to project a confident image at a time when the Church of England's traditional privilege and authority was fast being undermined by modern legislation and the proliferation of so-called Nonconformist denominations. Architects were prospering by meeting the needs of their clients and had no professional incentive to counsel less intervention over more since they generally earned fees as a percentage of the capital cost of construction.

The alternative offered up in the manifesto was those 'educated, artistic people' who had no interest beyond a generalized public one that extended to future generations, whose right to enjoy historic buildings should be protected. It is too easy to see this as elitist but in fact many late Victorians who fit that bill, including Morris himself, were involved in promoting socially progressive initiatives in the public interest. All Morris was doing, in the terms of his own social context, was inviting that cohort to open another front in an established battle of ideas. Today, we see that role as performed by the state mainly, assisted by charities. But in 1877 there was no legal locus or mechanism for such people to secure historic buildings for future generations. The prospect that the state might do this was *almost* inconceivable in 1877. 'Almost' because there was at that very time the first legislation in the UK intended to protect historic sites (prehistoric monuments primarily). After a long, tortuous process, the Ancient Monuments Act 1882 received the Royal Assent, creating the first Inspectorate of Ancient Monuments. There is today, in every country

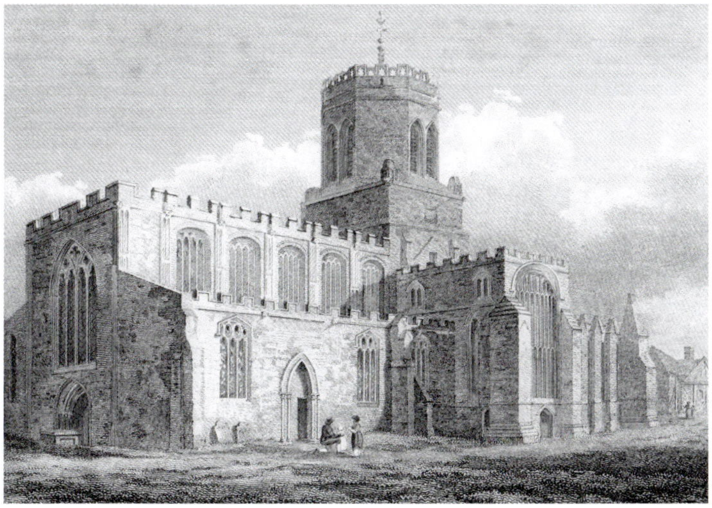

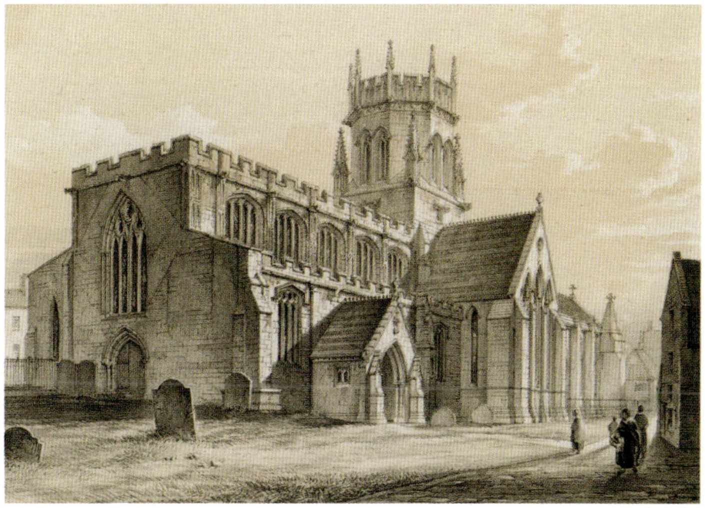

Figs 77–8 **Engravings of St Mary's, Stafford, before and after restoration by George Gilbert Scott in the 1840s.**

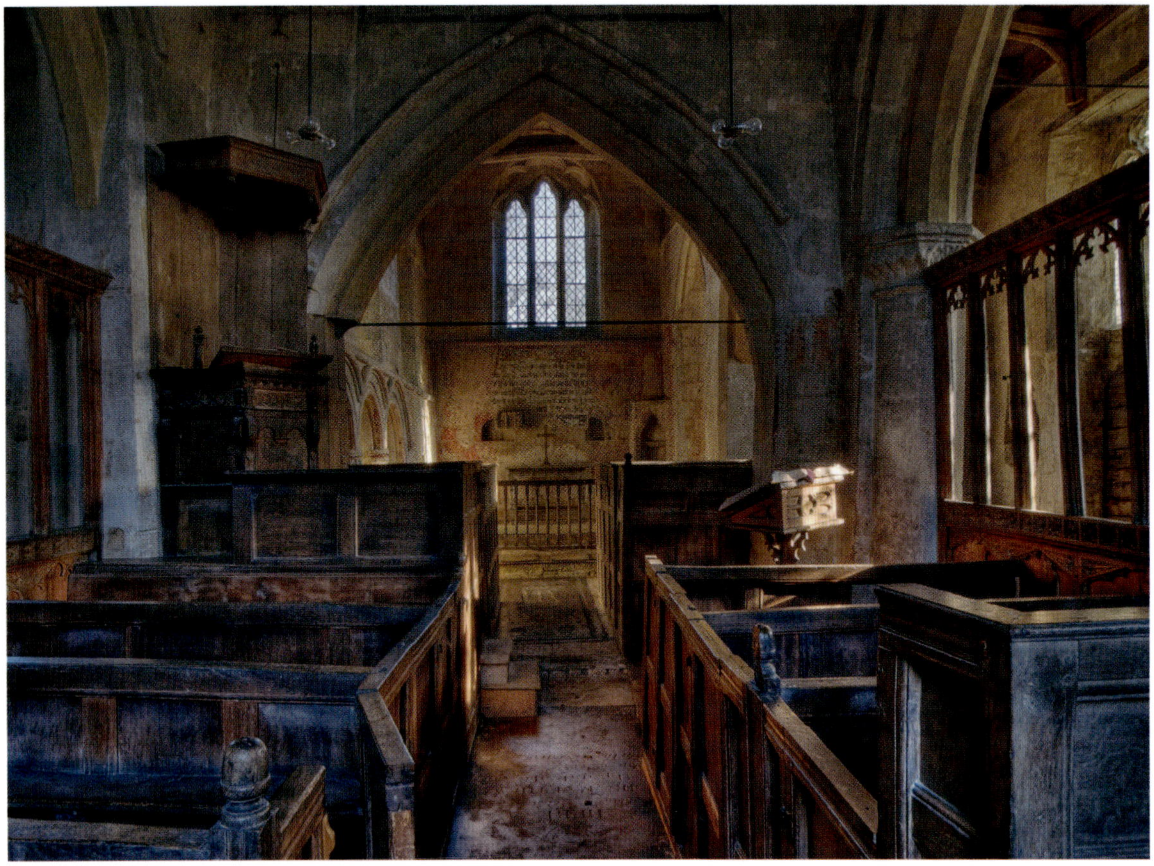

Fig.79 **Interior of St John the Baptist, Inglesham, Wiltshire.**

where conservation is managed by the state, a cadre of professionals whose job description fits the objectives Morris outlined in 1877, working in local and national governments to administer and manage the historic environment.

As Astrid Swenson's excellent comparative work has shown, many European countries had by Morris's time already legislated to protect that same public interest. But in the United Kingdom, the right to enjoy one's property free from the intervention of the state was a bedrock of the political settlement. Ancient churches were effectively held in trust for Her Majesty's subjects, but they were not public property. They were, however, the nearest thing to being historic public property that could be conceived of at that time, and it is for this reason that Morris and his colleagues concentrated the Society's work on them. Even a William Morris, shortly to set himself in opposition to the property-owning establishment, either did not dare or think it expedient (or both) to criticize publicly what private householders chose to do with the ancient houses in their ownership. A man's home in England was, as the saying goes, his castle.

The fourth and final theme is perhaps the most interesting and is defined in answer to a rhetorical question: how does one decide what should be conserved for the future? Morris wrote that if pressed for a definition of 'what kind of amount of art, style, or other interest in a building, makes it worth protecting, we answer anything which can be looked on as artistic, picturesque, historical, antique, or substantial'. He continued, 'any work, in short, over which educated, artistic people would think it worthwhile to argue at all.' This was prescient. Across the world, the buildings and structures identified for conservation are increasingly more varied and more recent. The UK has in fact led the way in this area of practice through its formal 'listing' process, whether the Lloyd's building of 1986 in the City of London or a 1960s bus station and multi-storey car park in Preston. Conservation practice has become diverse to reflect our own society's diversity. The concept of what the historic comprises is today an open textured one.

The SPAB manifesto turns out to be quite like the manifestos we associate with innovative art forms (painting and architecture particularly) and like these it was ultimately an avant-garde gambit. We should allow its authors a very wide berth when it comes to facts and figures, not least because the SPAB manifesto, like most of the others we know, was drafted very quickly. Morris wrote it in one go in the offices of Morris & Co., after hours, with Webb and the firm's business manager at his side. It was not diplomatically worded or persuasive.

It is surprising, then, that the Society relied on the manifesto in its practical day-to-day work. It included a copy in almost all its correspondence with the promoters of restorations, most commonly vicars but also architects and those funding schemes, in other words, the very people the manifesto criticizes for being short-sighted and self-interested. Did this in itself explain why the Society had almost no success in persuading those to whom it wrote to change their approach? Possibly. But in the end, Morris and his colleagues knew they were trying to insinuate themselves into a well-established practice and habit. The chances of success were always going to be slim and so nothing was lost by taking a deliberately controversial line. The Society's object was to change public opinion, to move the terms of a debate. Morris was clear about this in his addresses to the first and second Annual General Meetings of the Society. Reflecting on all the evidence, I conclude he had no real expectation of practical success.

This is not to say the Society had no influence on projects in Morris's lifetime. It did, but usually in those cases where a scheme's promoter or his architect was already in sympathy with the Society's ideals. Three good examples of this are easy to visit as part of any Cotswold tour around Morris's house, Kelmscott Manor. There is, notably, Kelmscott Church itself where Morris's grave is marked by a slab designed by Webb. There is also Burford Church, and, best of all, Inglesham Church (fig.79). Morris contributed anonymously to the repairs at Inglesham and wrote an architectural appreciation of it for a fundraising pamphlet.

Inglesham was conserved from 1887 through collaboration between the local vicar and the Society, using a SPAB recommended architect, John Thomas Micklethwaite. It is a gorgeous building, beautiful as a collage of historic finishes on a structure that has settled seamlessly into the land. It only avoided modernization because its congregation had dwindled, the result in part of that rural depopulation noted earlier. In fact, many of the Society's successes were achieved in locations suffering the same fate, where the parish church, conserved 'as found' according to SPAB principles, became a kind of elegy reflecting the Church in decline. It is no surprise that many Church of England clerics of the time were uncomfortable with the SPAB's approach, which has a secular, modern cast to it. Or possibly not? Inglesham is still a place of worship, after all, and looked at in one way is profoundly spiritual, creating a sense of continuous Christian worship and faith over centuries. Looked at in another way, it becomes no more than an artefact or a work of art whose aesthetic is Romantic in nature, a rumination on the end of the age of faith.

Not all of the ideas Morris put into the manifesto were new. Ruskin's influence and in particular 'The Lamp of Memory', has already been cited: 'Do not let us talk then of restoration. The thing is a Lie from beginning to end ... Accept it as such, pull the building down, throw its stones into neglected corners, make ballast of them, or mortar, if you will; but do it honestly, and do not set up a Lie in their place.' Ruskin was here responding to an established critical tradition in Britain, one that had developed since the late eighteenth century, when Romanticism, religious revival and the anxiety prompted by the French Revolution prepared the ground for the Gothic Revival. In particular, and increasingly from the 1820s and 1830s, the Church of England began to modernize itself and the way it delivered its ministry to a growing and increasingly urban population, and in a context where progressive legislation was incrementally undermining the Church's own ancient privileges. That process had a clear architectural programme: to build new churches in a genuine Gothic style and to restore ancient ones in an authentic way. 'Authentic' in this context meant 'in the appropriate style', communicating the venerability of the institution and its relevance by modernizing its existing churches. Some ancient buildings were in a terrible state, physically, and many churchmen saw their run-down condition as an affront to the Church-by-Law Established. Church interiors crowded with private pews undermined the Church's ministry by catering to the rich at the expense of the poor, an image that finds its way back to the early eighteenth century (fig.80).

Morris's ideal of 'protection' was formed against this background, a process of institutional modernization, theological development and corresponding physical renewal. The architectural programme turned on building new churches and restoring ancient ones. The term 'restoration' was a portmanteau. It could mean structural repair and rebuilding or just the replacement of worn window tracery. A 'programme of restoration' might include the construction of a new nave aisle to increase seating capacity or the wholesale 'reconstruction' of lost features (transepts, chancels and roofs were not uncommon) for aesthetic reasons. Almost universally, 'restorations' included schemes of redecoration too, the installation of new tile floors, say, or stained-glass windows, as well as the introduction of central heating (commonly hot water systems) and gas lighting. It is no small irony that more Morris glass went into ancient restored interiors than modern ones until 1877, when Morris & Co. announced it would no longer supply stained glass to medieval buildings.

As noted earlier, Morris's portrayal was not always unfair. But the sort of work Scott specified at St Mary's, Stafford, in the 1840s had by 1877 become a thing of the past, at least among the more talented cohort of Revival architects (including Scott himself). An important early instance of a more cautious approach is William Burges's restoration of Waltham Abbey, which was underway in 1859. In completing the new east wall of the nave, Burges used a deliberately contrasting modern form of Gothic and stabilized large areas of decaying fabric. This project is also significant for featuring early stained-glass windows designed by Edward Burne-Jones for Powell's of Whitefriars (VII.3). In 1860 Street specified careful repairs at the fine thirteenth-century church of St Mary at Stone near Dartford, including new tile flooring in a muted tonality, avoiding the brightly coloured tiling schemes that were then favoured. He reconstructed stone vaulting in the chancel (an antiquarian approach of a kind that Morris and Webb would later condemn) but re-roofed the nave with simple, unadorned oak framing having a character that anticipates the work of later Arts and Crafts architects. William White's repairs of Newland Church in Gloucestershire between 1861 and 1863 were particularly sensitive and the architect promoted them as a model of practice in lectures and a pamphlet. White was keen to draw attention to the absence of any strong, strident colours in the restored interior and to the careful repair of existing masonry.

The years 1857 to 1864 also saw a series of debates on prevailing practices in England, Wales and on the Continent. In 1863 there was a petition from nine of the most active restoration architects to the Royal Institute of British Architects (RIBA) to set up a formal board of inquiry or standing committee to investigate bad practice. This bore fruit in 1864 when the RIBA lodged a formal complaint against the proposed restoration of Heckington Church in Lincolnshire, a masterpiece of late Decorated architecture. In November the Institute founded the Committee on the Conservation of Ancient Architectural Monuments and Remains and published a pamphlet advocating practices which look forward to what the SPAB would advise. This was sent to all associates, fellows and affiliated societies as well as offered to the public. Over the next six years the Committee took up 16 cases under the chairmanship of George Gilbert Scott.

Though few in number, each intervention achieved a practical improvement to proposed works and that may be explained by the fact that the Committee was staffed by practising architects, speaking with the authority of their professional body, to other professionals who were, mostly, members too. New personnel reinvigorated the Committee in 1870, and they included George Godwin, an architect who exercised considerable influence through the widely read professional journal, *The Builder*. In the next few years he used the trade paper as a platform to press for higher professional standards, promoting practices that, again, anticipated the SPAB's approach.

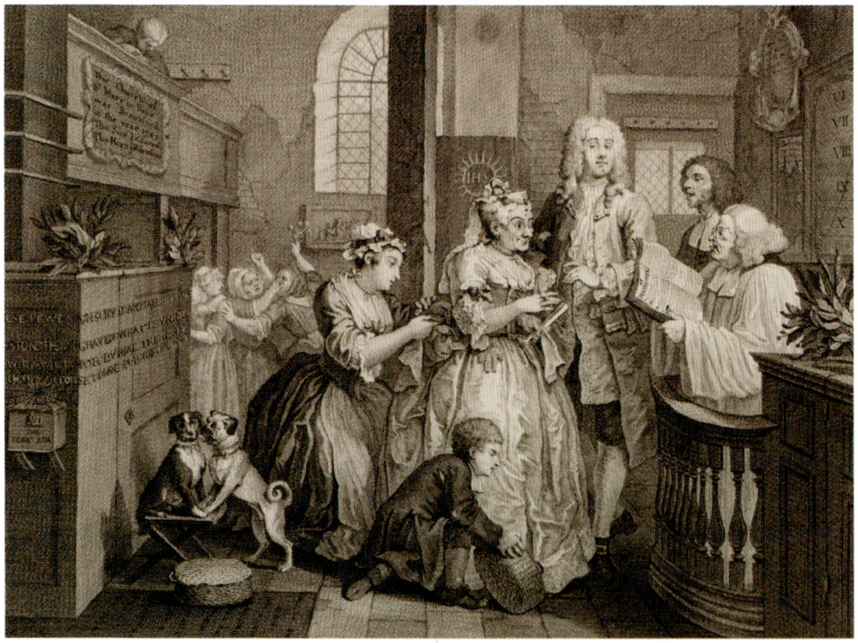

Fig.80 **Plate 5, *A Rake's Progress*, by William Hogarth. A satire of corrupt practices in a dilapidated church interior, 1735.**
V&A (E.1269–1990)

The most high-profile campaign from this period came in 1874 and was in response to the proposed auction of the splendid medieval chapel of the former Bishop of Ely's Palace near Farringdon in central London. Scott, then RIBA president, devoted part of his annual address to it. Between 1874 and 1876, the Committee pressed 20 separate cases.

These two years saw a sea change to restoration in architectural and critical circles and so prepared the ground for the SPAB. The event was the publication of a Parliamentary statistical return, the national *Survey of Church Building and Restoration 1840 to 1874* (issued in stages from March 1874 and in full in 1875). The data showed that over that period more than 7,000 medieval parish churches, abbeys and cathedrals in England and Wales had been restored to some extent, out of a total of about 9,000 buildings. This was over three times the number of new churches built in the same period, and the total bill was also higher in absolute terms than for new constructions.

The *Survey* (which has never been properly analysed) had been ordered in response to a long-standing dispute over the church rate, a tax levied in parishes in England and Ireland to maintain the parish church and meet the costs of services and salaries for various officials. Nonconformists and Catholics were subject to this compulsory tax until it was abolished in 1868. The rate remained, however, as a voluntary one and those who refused to pay had no right to approve or even enquire into how the funds were being spent. Some alleged that rates, including those raised by Nonconformists, had fuelled an Anglican church building boom. The results of the *Survey* proved that this enormous amount of architectural work had, in fact, been grant-funded from the Church of England's Ecclesiastical Commission or from church building societies, but more significantly by private donations raised locally and entirely voluntarily. The *Survey* also demonstrated that the pace of restoration had picked up markedly since 1855, outstripping new church construction.

In April 1874, shortly after the first results from the *Survey* were published, Scott, as RIBA President, wrote to Ruskin to see whether he would accept the Institute's prestigious Gold Medal, which would have made him the first ever non-architect to be honoured in this way. Ruskin declined to accept specifically in protest against the profession's treatment of ancient buildings, pointing out that the scale of church restoration had generated considerable fees, which were charged commonly as a flat rate of 5 per cent on the capital cost of any project. Thus, architects had every incentive to increase the scale of restoration work. It was, he alleged, a corrupt practice. He would happily accept the honour, he concluded in ringing Evangelical terms, if Scott could produce even one architect who was blameless.

The same conclusions had been reached by the editor of the influential journal of art and criticism, *The Athenaeum*. Frederic George Stephens, an original member of the Pre-Raphaelite Brotherhood, mounted a campaign against architects whom he accused of pillaging ancient buildings to line their pockets. And so was born the phrase 'Mr 5%', a term of rebuke repeated in critical literature during the summer of 1874, when Ruskin's rejection of the RIBA Gold Medal became public. Scott could not simply overlook this unprecedented outcome, and so had to comment on it, delicately, in his presidential address that November.

And it was exactly at this time, when Morris was engaged in the painful process of reorganizing the firm under his sole control, that he took part in his first organized protest against a restoration by adding his name to a petition which appeared in *The Times* on 8 August 1874. The lead campaigner was an architect, Basil Champneys, acting on behalf of the self-styled Committee for the Preservation of the Tower of Hampstead Parish Church, a pressure group of like-minded individuals. This petition was very likely composed with the help of George Gilbert Scott Junior, who promoted Morris's decorative work and would later be a strong supporter of the SPAB despite its public opposition to his father. The point at issue was the ailing Georgian tower to the parish church (fig.81). The architect appointed to advise the vestry concluded it had to be rebuilt and proposed a larger Gothic one for an otherwise classical building. The opponents argued that the tower was a kind of public property because it was well known in the local area. This obliged, the campaigners asserted, the church authorities to consult with local residents and interested parties before proposing any changes. There was no legal requirement to do this, of course, but in Hampstead, thickly populated with architects and artists, the protest had the necessary effect, drying up public subscriptions to the restoration. The scheme was abandoned in July 1876. This triumph furnished Morris with the practical example he needed and at exactly the right moment, providing a template for how such a society might operate nationally. Just two months later Morris was incensed on a visit to Burford Church, witnessing what he considered harmful works underway. May Morris's later observation that the idea for a society to oppose restoration first occurred to her father in summer of 1876 fits the historical record pretty closely.

The exactly contemporary efforts of the Commons Preservation Society would also have been influential on Morris's thinking. It was formed to conserve for public use and enjoyment the remnants of the once vast Royal Forest of Epping. The enclosure of the forest was successfully opposed in the courts in March 1874, a decision confirmed by Royal Commission in 1875. Morris grew up in Walthamstow on the edge of the forest and Mackail's biography records that he 'never ceased to love Epping Forest, and to uphold the scenery of his native county as beautifully and characteristically English. The dense hornbeam thickets,' he continued, '... reappear again and again in his poetry and his prose romances.' Mackail then quotes a letter Morris wrote in support of objections to the treatment of those unusual pollarded trees: 'Nothing could be more interesting and romantic than the effect of the l ong poles of the hornbeams rising from the trunks and seen against the mass of the wood behind.' The image calls to mind the dense and enclosed landscapes one finds in Morris & Co. tapestries or the paintings of Burne-Jones.

The SPAB had no formal interest in landscape conservation but in the mid-1880s it did correspond with the Commons Preservation Society (which turned its attention to other green spaces) and the Metropolitan Public Gardens Association (which had a similar object, particularly in overcrowded urban areas). Many of the nation's municipal parks were formed as a consequence of this and similar activism in this period, the larger part created, however, by municipal authorities. It was a case of campaigning zeal stimulating public action through the purchase of land for public parks. Significantly, the SPAB would be instrumental in persuading the newly founded National Trust to purchase its first property in 1896, the Clergy House at Alfriston in Sussex (fig.82). The Society also gave practical advice on its repair.

In the event, the stimulus that led Morris, Webb and Wardle to found the SPAB was an advertisement in *The Times* in early March 1877 soliciting public donations to complete the restoration of the ancient abbey of Tewkesbury in Gloucestershire, a superb Romanesque building with fine late Gothic vaulting and other additions. This led Morris to write to *The Athenaeum*, where his letter was published on 10 March: 'My eye just now caught the word "restoration" in the morning paper, and, on looking closer, I saw that this time it is nothing less than the Minster of Tewkesbury that is to be destroyed by Sir Gilbert Scott.' Surely, he continues, it is time

> that an association should be set on foot to keep a watch on old monuments, to protest against all 'restoration' that means more than keeping out wind and weather, and, by all means, literary and other, to awaken a feeling that our ancient buildings are not mere ecclesiastical toys, but sacred monuments of the nation's growth and hope.

On 22 March a meeting was held at Morris & Co.'s Queen Square premises to do just that, and so the Society came into being.

The obstacles facing the SPAB were far higher than those facing the Commons Preservation Society. 'Commons' comprised land belonging already to a local community as a whole by some specific grant or historic right. Thus, the Commons Preservation Society could use the

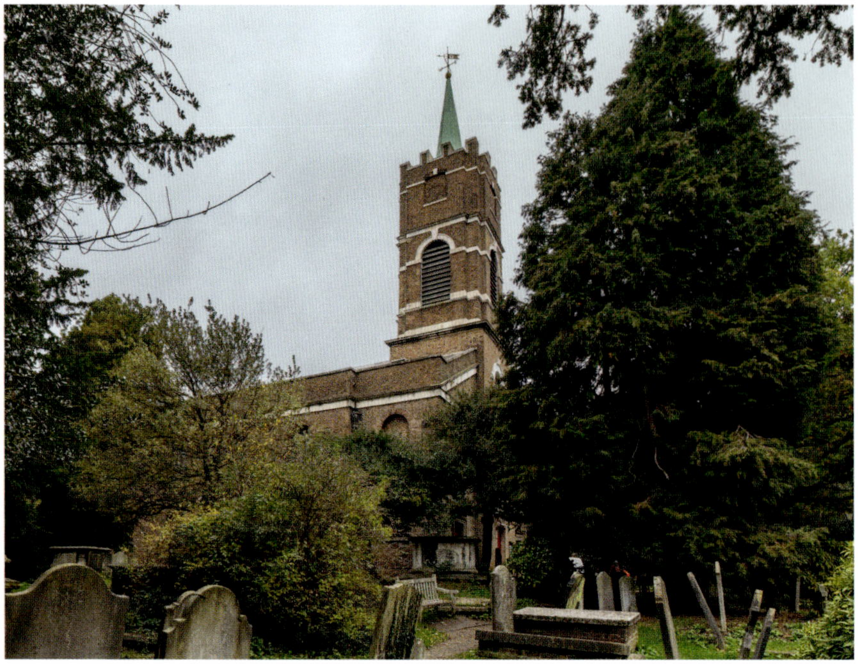

Fig.81 **Hampstead Parish Church, from the south-east corner of the churchyard.**

Fig.82 **Clergy House at Alfriston, Sussex, photographed in the early 1890s before its conservation according to SPAB principles.**
The Society for the Protection of Ancient Buildings

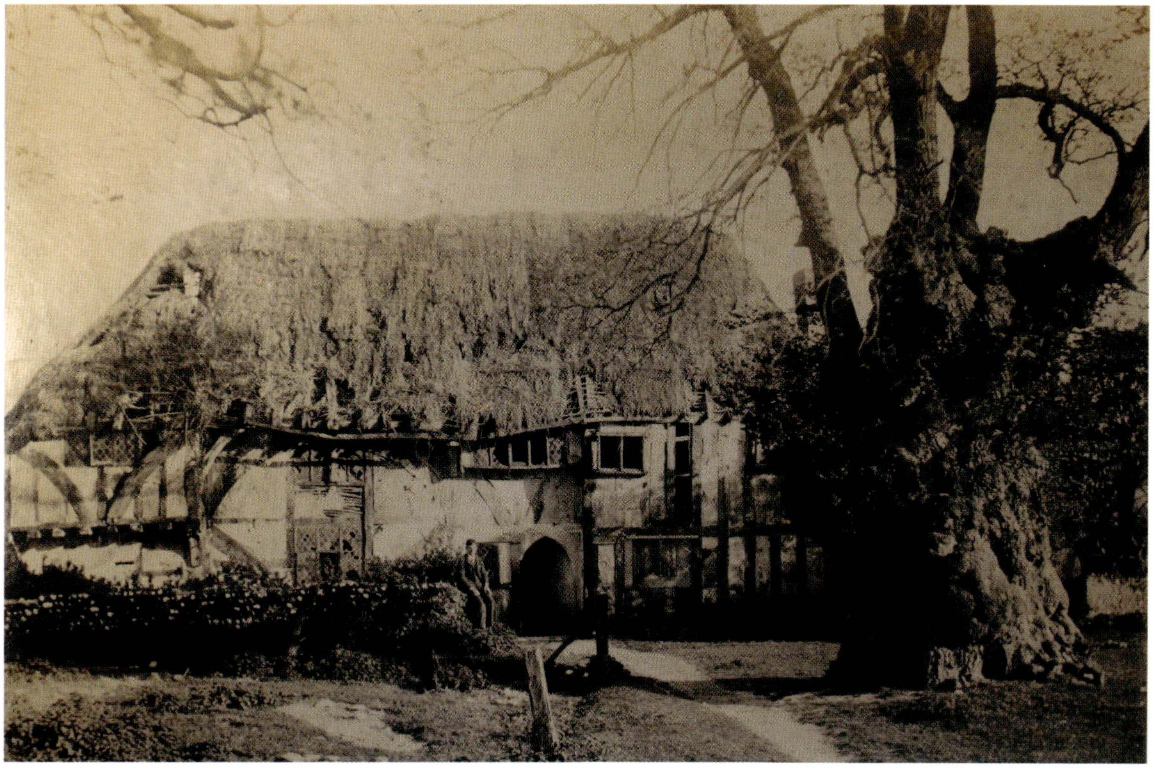

courts to stop the development of land without title, which as a matter of fact had been used for communal activities historically, typically pig grazing, wood collecting or turf cutting. There was no corresponding principle in respect of ancient buildings, even parish churches are held, essentially, in trust for the nation as the property of the National Church.

The Society's founding was covered in the specialist press and in *The Times*. The summer of 1877 saw the delivery and publication of several addresses, articles and pamphlets from sympathizers and members seeking to provoke public debate, building on the work that Godwin and Stephens had begun at *The Builder* and *The Athenaeum*. First was the paper Stevenson delivered to the RIBA on 28 May 1877, expressly promoting the SPAB's objectives. Later that year he published an expanded version in pamphlet form. Stevenson was a very active early member, attending many meetings. He was a Glaswegian who had trained in Edinburgh and then moved to London, and in the late 1850s he worked in the office of Gilbert Scott. Stevenson specialized in domestic architecture associated with the Queen Anne revival. His own house in Chelsea, designed in 1870–71, is an important example of that style. He named it 'Red House' in homage to Morris and Webb.

There followed William John Loftie's article 'Thorough Restoration' in the June number of *Macmillan's Magazine*. He was Irish and an ordained Anglican minister remembered today as a travel writer and historian. Shortly after was George Aitchison's 'The Principles of Restoration', read before the National Association for the Promotion of Social Sciences at Aberdeen in September. Aitchison was another architect, associated with the Aesthetic Movement (he designed Lord Leighton's house in Kensington in phases between 1865 and 1896). In October Sidney Colvin, an art historian and later director of the Fitzwilliam Museum, published another promotional piece, 'Restoration and Anti-Restoration' in *The Nineteenth Century*. The debate was now being aired among the chattering classes, to the point where a popular satirical journal, *Fun*, picked it up. Its June 1877 edition published a caricature that captured the Society's criticisms perfectly (fig.83).

From the start Morris worked with great determination to promote the Society. There were regular meetings, visits and much correspondence pursuing what he called 'casework', frontline engagement with one scheme promoter after another. Perhaps he hoped to repeat Champneys' success at Hampstead Church in 1876, but that really was a very special case of highly motivated local residents, all of a similar cast of mind. Morris was instead engaged in a kind of cold calling, starting with the abbey at Tewkesbury, which had provided the impetus.

In the spring and summer of 1877 Morris wrote to the chair of the Abbey Restoration Committee, Sir Edmund Lechmere. Without asking permission, he later handed the exchange over to Stephens, who published it in *The Athenaeum*. This first case came quietly to a close, though, when it emerged that Morris did not know what exactly was proposed. It turned out that the whole Abbey had been worked over several years before by a local architect. Morris would not have been a good propagandist if he let facts stand in the way of a public relations opportunity. Scott had built his career on church work and restoration and was a past president of the RIBA, an ideal publicity target. So when the chance to attack him again presented itself in May 1877 Morris took it. This time the building was Canterbury Cathedral, where Scott was proposing works that included the removal of choir stalls said to be the work of Grinling Gibbons.

Private protests had been made to the Dean and Bishop in February of the previous year. In 1877 Loftie wrote critically of the scheme in *The Times* but did not admit his connection with the SPAB (conservation groups today work in the same way). Alexander Beresford Hope, a Conservative MP and outspoken champion of the Gothic Revival, rose to Scott's defence, leaving the way clear for Morris to write in on behalf of the Society. His letter, published in *The Times* on 4 June, was trenchant and emotive. All the Cathedral Dean would get in the end was the 'usual mass of ecclesiastical trumpery and coarse daubing'. This might have pleased supporters, but it was unlikely to persuade the Dean and Chapter who pursued their original plans.

To judge from the evidence of early casework files and agendas, Morris did little else that first summer. When the SPAB committee reconvened at the end of August to start what would become

Fig.83 (below left) **'The Art of Restoring', published in *Fun*, 27 June 1877.**
George A. Smathers Libraries, University of Florida

Fig.84 (below right) **Famous for its striking Art Nouveau-style title-page, *Wren's City Churches* made the case for the preservation of buildings then being declared redundant, and thus threatened with demolition, 1883.**
National Art Library, V&A

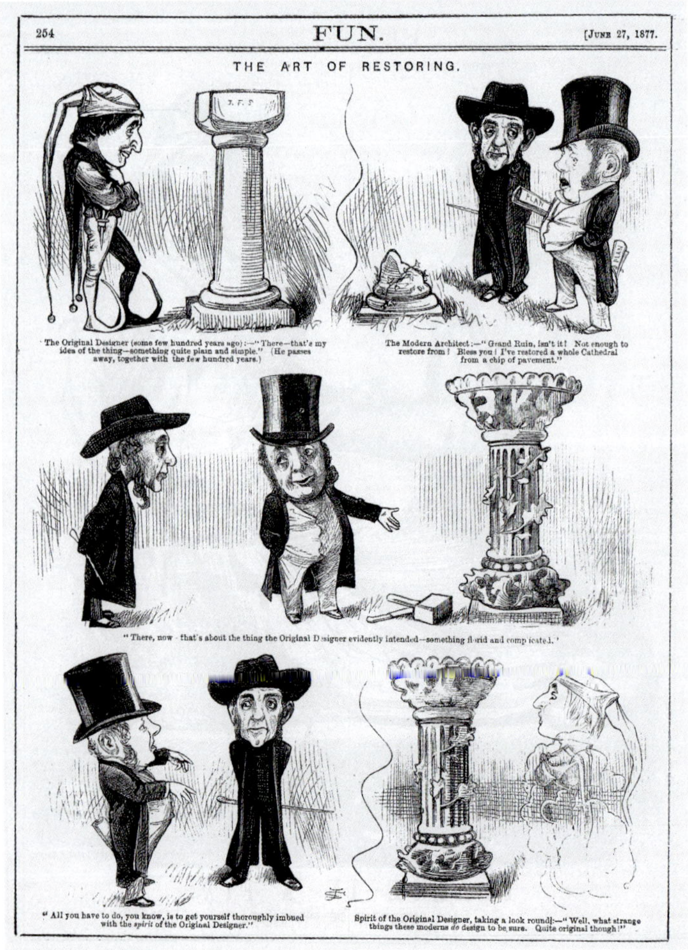

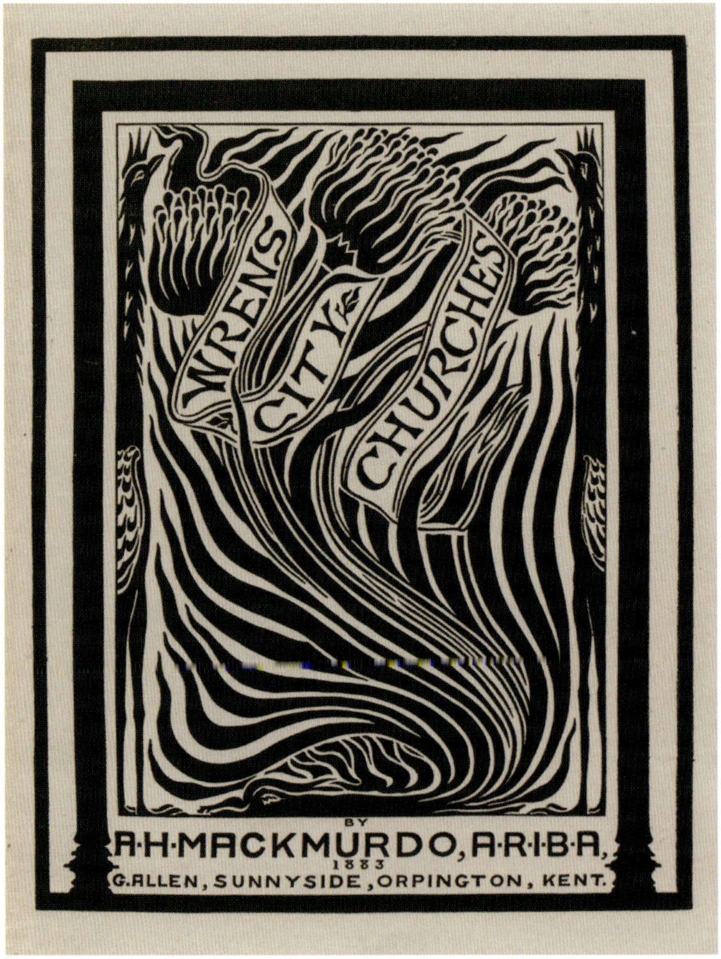

Fig.85 **Completed reporting form for St Andrew's, Mells, Somerset, 1879.**
The Society for the Protection of Ancient Buildings

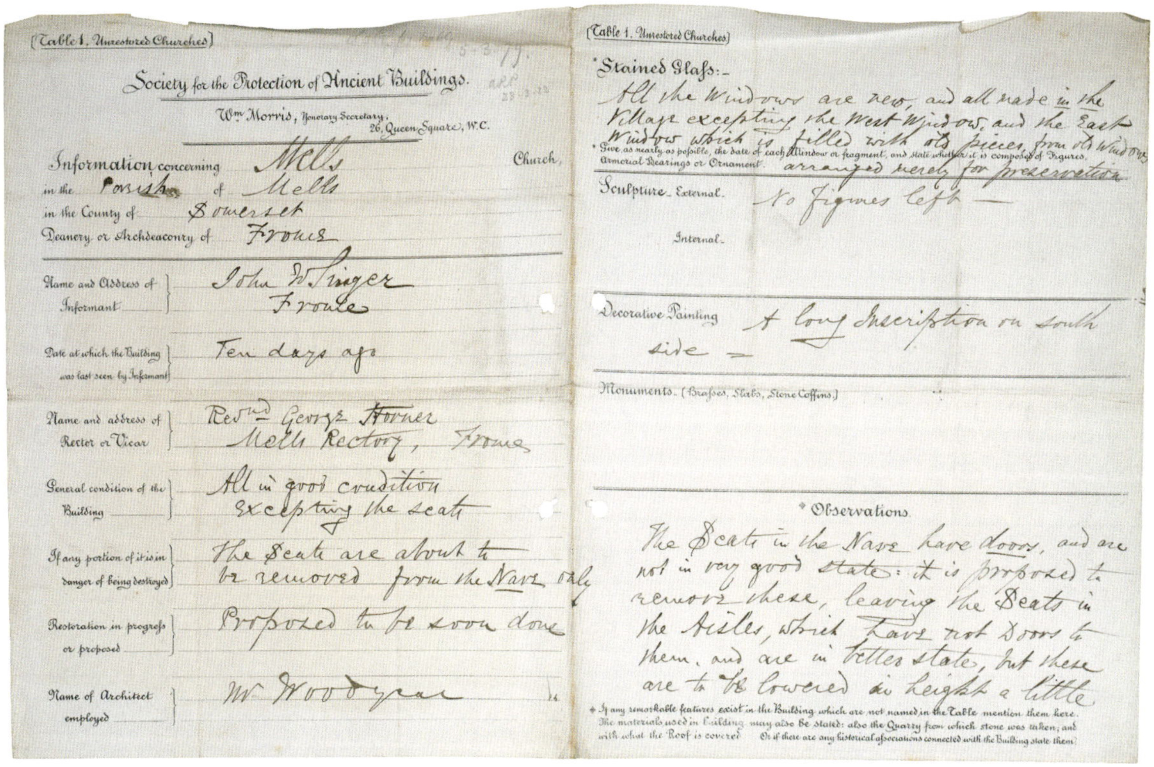

[Table 1. Unrestored Churches]

Society for the Protection of Ancient Buildings.

Wm. Morris, Honorary Secretary, 26, Queen Square, W.C.

Information concerning Mells Church, in the Parish of Mells in the County of Somerset Deanery or Archdeaconry of Frome

Name and Address of Informant: John W. Singer Frome

Date at which the Building was last seen by Informant: Ten days ago

Name and address of Rector or Vicar: Revd. George Horner Mells Rectory, Frome

General condition of the Building: All in good condition excepting the seats

If any portion of it is in danger of being destroyed: The Seats are about to be removed from the Nave only

Restoration in progress or proposed: Proposed to be soon done

Name of Architect employed: Mr Woodyear

[Table 1. Unrestored Churches]

*Stained Glass:– All the Windows are new, and all made in the Village excepting the West Window, and the East Window which is filled with old pieces, from old Windows arranged merely for preservation

* Give, as nearly as possible, the date of each Window or fragment, and state whether it is composed of Figures, Armorial Bearings or Ornament.

Sculpture. External. No Figures left –

Internal.

Decorative Painting: A long Inscription on south side –

Monuments. (Brasses, Slabs, Stone Coffins.)

* Observations.

The Seats in the Nave have doors, and are not in very good state: it is proposed to remove these, leaving the Seats in the Aisles, which have not Doors to them, and are in better state, but these are to be lowered in height a little

* If any remarkable features exist in the Building which are not named in the Table mention them here. The materials used in Building may also be stated: also the Quarry from which stone was taken; and with what the Roof is covered. Or if there are any historical associations connected with the Building state them.

its regular cycle of fortnightly meetings, the members, led by Morris and Webb, began to consider a more comprehensive strategy. Henry Brewer, an architectural draughtsman who was involved in virtually every one of the SPAB's early cases, persuaded the committee to sponsor the compiling of a national schedule of unrestored churches, starting with Norfolk churches. Local vigilance committees would be formed to watch these buildings and report proposed threats to the London committee. A similar project to catalogue ancient buildings in the City of London was discussed and then scaled back to include only the churches of Wren and the Wren school. This led to the formation of the City Church and Churchyards Protection Society in the winter of 1878–9 and the splendid memorial publication on Wren's churches of 1883 by Arthur Heygate Mackmurdo (fig.84). To promote the idea of a national schedule, the Society printed a standard reporting form which it distributed to local supporters (fig.85). This closely resembled pro forma reports that architectural societies keen to promote church restoration had been using since the early 1840s. Many of the ones completed by SPAB members survive in the archives of early cases but they soon fell out of use and the Society gave up on the idea of a comprehensive survey. The reasons are not recorded but it is easy to see that a national survey required a considerable investment of time and had no real public relations value. Volunteer time was necessarily limited, and casework was by far the most efficient way to use that time.

Morris and his colleagues were also running a membership organization, charging subscription fees to support its work rather than relying on larger, private donations. The national architectural amenity societies active today are run broadly in this way, albeit with grant funding from central government. In exchange for their 10*s.* 6*d.* members expected to be able to mobilize the Society against proposals that affected buildings near where they lived or worked. In September 1877 a 'gentleman' wrote in to ask the Society to stop the destruction of two churches near Duxford. Later that month four members demanded the Society object to four different church restorations. Before the year's end, members in the shires had notified roughly 36 cases to the London committee. Within five years the annual casework figure had reached 150; a level it sustained through to 1914, in some years exceeding that number. The overwhelming proportion of cases treated medieval churches but gradually the number of secular buildings increased, so that by the turn of the century some 10 to 15 per cent of the Society's casework focused on small private houses, bridges and farm buildings.

Initially, Morris was secretary and he worked frenetically from October to December 1877 on the day-to-day business of the Society. However, the volume of work was too much even for a William Morris. Late in 1877 Wardle suggested that the Society retain Newman Marks as part-time corresponding secretary at a monthly salary of £10. The bulk of his time would be spent investigating the details of cases by personal inspection or correspondence. Without first-hand knowledge and accurate reporting, the Society would simply appear foolish and ill-informed, reducing the public relations value of any campaign. The object of the casework committee was to ensure accurate information could be collected efficiently.

Knowing the right person also helped. The Society's archives evidence this again and again. The first instance comes in the form of correspondence from October 1877. Eustace Balfour, then serving his articles with Champneys, alerted the SPAB to the proposed restoration of the church at Cherry Hinton, a village just outside Cambridge. Morris called at the office of the architect in charge, George Gilbert Scott Junior, who assured him that although earlier works by his father had been somewhat harsh, only routine maintenance was at present contemplated. The church was in the patronage of Peterhouse, where a few years before Morris, Marshall, Faulkner & Co. had decorated the Old Hall after its rebuilding by the younger Scott. In 1883, when works at Cherry Hinton were contemplated in earnest, a carefully worded letter from the Society to the College led to the appointment of Micklethwaite, the SPAB's preferred architect.

Unfortunately, most of the Society's casework concerned churches in remote rural parishes where it had little or no influence and often incomplete information. At about the same time that Morris was communicating with Scott about Cherry Hinton, the Society received a fundraising circular for the church at North Frodingham in Yorkshire (fig.86). This little pamphlet featured thumbnail-sized sketches of the building before and after the proposed restoration. On the basis of this evidence alone Morris sent off a hot-headed letter to the vicar, calling the plans an 'act of vandalism'. The vicar duly passed this communication to his architect, Hugh R. Gough, who sent back a long testy letter reminding Morris that interfering in the architect–client relationship in these terms left the Society open to the charge of libel, a possibility no one in the Society appears to have contemplated. The letter back from Morris was carefully worded, suggesting the committee took the allegation seriously and had taken legal advice. The Society's objections, Morris wrote to Gough, were not intended to call his professional skills into question. The criticism was rather of a common professional practice. Gough yielded but reminded Morris that not all architects would take such a tolerant view of this sort of approach. In future the SPAB's letters were always careful to put criticisms in those terms.

The first year or so of casework taught Morris and his colleagues the importance of establishing strict protocol. In October 1878 he, the ever-faithful Wardle and John Hebb (a draughtsman in the Metropolitan Board of Works and another unstinting supporter of the SPAB in its early years) formed a subcommittee to report on the best means of transacting the Society's business. Their recommendations established the SPAB working methods for the next 40 years. Above all else, the Society needed reliable evidence of what was proposed and an understanding of the building in question, usually from an eyewitness account. From this point on, the secretary or a member of the committee generally visited sites in London and the Home Counties, producing a detailed report. For more distant places a network of local reporters or correspondents was established. All cases began

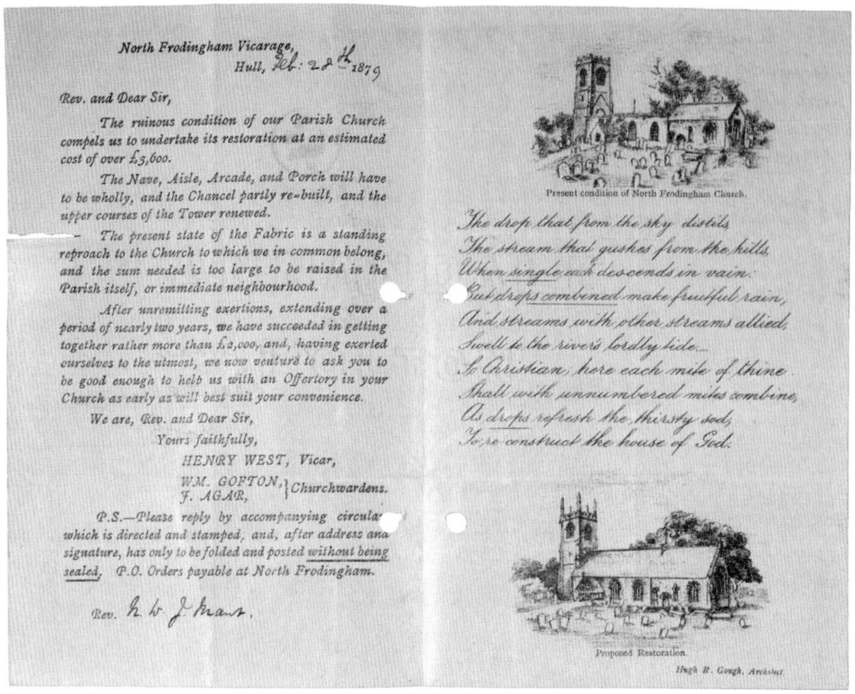
North Frodingham Vicarage,
Hull, Feb: 28th 1879

Rev. and Dear Sir,

The ruinous condition of our Parish Church compels us to undertake its restoration at an estimated cost of over £3,600.

The Nave, Aisle, Arcade, and Porch will have to be wholly, and the Chancel partly re-built, and the upper courses of the Tower renewed.

The present state of the Fabric is a standing reproach to the Church to which we in common belong, and the sum needed is too large to be raised in the Parish itself, or immediate neighbourhood.

After unremitting exertions, extending over a period of nearly two years, we have succeeded in getting together rather more than £2,000, and, having exerted ourselves to the utmost, we now venture to ask you to be good enough to help us with an Offertory in your Church as early as will best suit your convenience.

We are, Rev. and Dear Sir,
Yours faithfully,
HENRY WEST, Vicar,
WM. GOFTON, J. AGAR, Churchwardens.

P.S.—Please reply by accompanying circular which is directed and stamped, and, after address and signature, has only to be folded and posted without being sealed. P.O. Orders payable at North Frodingham.

Rev. [illegible]

Present condition of North Frodingham Church.

The drop that from the sky distils,
The stream that gushes from the hills,
When single each descends in vain:
But drops combined make fruitful rain,
And streams with other streams allied,
Swell to the river's lordly tide.–
So Christian, here each mite of thine
Shall with unnumbered mites combine,
As drops refresh the thirsty sod,
To re-construct the house of God.

Proposed Restoration.

Hugh R. Gough, Architect.

Fig.86 **Fundraising circular for North Frodingham Church, Yorkshire, 1879.**
The Society for the Protection of Ancient Buildings

with an initial letter of inquiry accompanied by a copy of the manifesto to the person in charge of the fabric. When negotiations reached a deadlock, the Society threatened to bring the matter before the public. If the case was serious enough, involving a very prominent, or particularly contentious, building, then the Society would mount a public campaign. A limited number (15 or 20 per cent at most) played themselves out in the local press. A smaller percentage still escalated to national campaigns. As a consequence of all this work, the committee agendas were full, and on any one Thursday evening a dozen or more cases might be discussed. The really significant campaigns were pursued by formally constituted subcommittees, which included one or more of the dedicated committeemen (and they were all men).

The Society was not content simply to have cases reported to it by members. Early in its history, it subscribed to a press clipping service (the first in the world had been founded in London in 1853). This scanned national and major regional papers for articles featuring the word 'restoration'. The network of local correspondents, which steadily expanded to a total of 30 or so at any one time, were tasked to investigate these, and also reported items that came to their attention. Each one had to agree a code of conduct. The most active correspondents in the Morris period were three Anglican vicars, Newton Mant of Sledmere in the East Riding of Yorkshire, Thomas Norwood of Nantwich in Cheshire, and Oswald Birchall of Buscot in Oxfordshire. Birchall is a particularly interesting figure, a friend of Morris's who shared his socialist beliefs. From time to time he would come down to London to address the committee on a particular case. He oversaw the installation of a superb stained-glass window by Burne-Jones in 1892. This might seem to have violated the firm's stated policy, but exceptions were made when churches were being carefully conserved, as Buscot Church was. Birchall was also instrumental in promoting the conservation of Inglesham Church, noted earlier. The involvement of ordained ministers demonstrates that the elegiac mood achieved through careful conservation was not simply an attempt to turn ancient churches into modern monuments of past belief.

The archives of the Society record payments to obtain photographs of many buildings which were the subject of casework. Very few, however, survive in the files. Some may have entered the private collections of committee members. It is worth noting a group of photographic albums in the National Library of Wales, bequeathed by Mary Frances Vivian Lobb, May Morris's partner in later life. The collection includes many photographs of historic parish churches that were also SPAB cases, for example, Edington Church in Wiltshire (fig.87). While the precise history of these albums is still under investigation, several clearly have a Morris family provenance and these

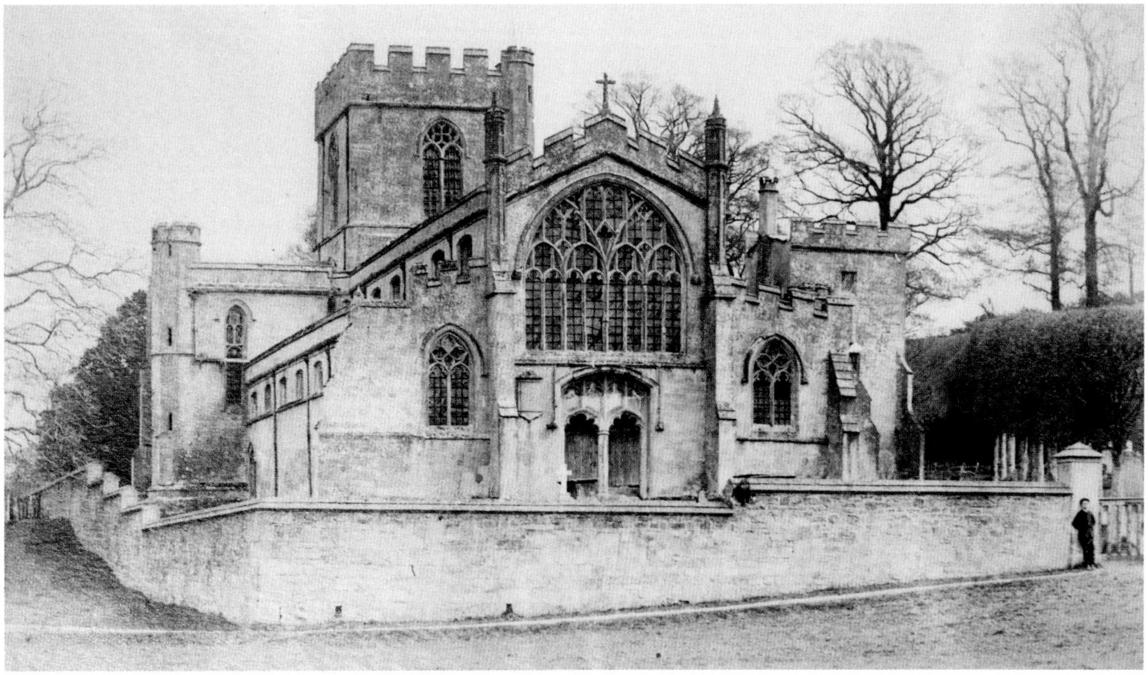

Fig.87 **The fourteenth-century church at Edington in Wiltshire was one of the Society's early successes.**
National Library of Wales

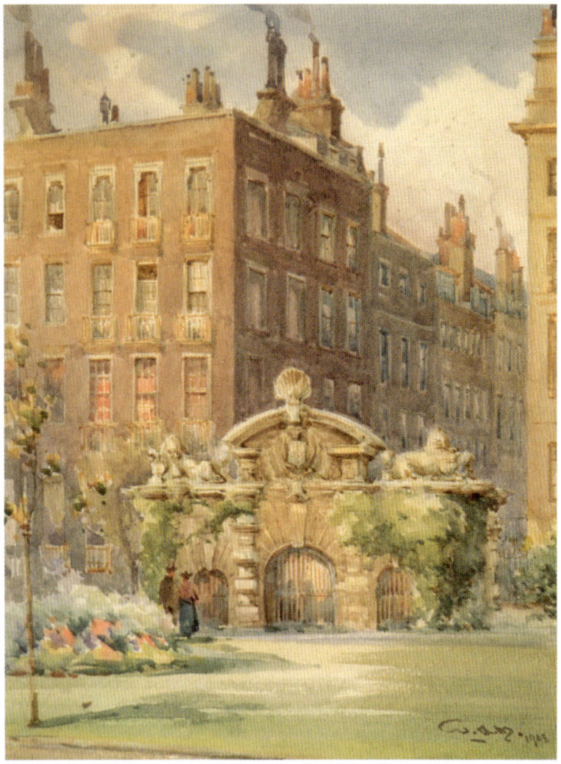

Fig.88 ***York Water Gate, Embankment Gardens***, **William Alister Macdonald, 1903.**
Guildhall Art Gallery

photographs may relate to cases Morris himself had something to do with. Equally, they may have been photographs sent to the Society from local correspondents. In any event, the collection is an important one warranting close study.

The strategy the SPAB pursued was, in short, to seek to influence and to educate, one parish, one vicar and one architect at a time. And if that sounds at first unworkable, we should bear in mind that the number of medieval churches that remained unrestored and authentic was finite and limited. Thus, an annual caseload of 150 would in a decade engage the Society in correspondence with the vicars in charge of 1,500 churches, out of a total of some 9,000 parish churches of medieval origins. A large number of those had already been restored and so did not concern the Society. Morris had devised a kind of targeted public relations campaign, an effective strategy considering the number of vicars was in fact limited.

The Society's papers from the period 1877 to 1879 show that its main activists at this time were Morris, Wardle, Webb, Hebb, Brewer, Stevenson and George Price Boyce (a late Romantic landscape painter). Record keeping appears to have been irregular, as one might expect given the number of correspondents. From 1879, records survive in better condition and for more cases. In October of that year the Society took permanent premises at 9 Buckingham Street, London, its office for many years to come. The building survives. It is a fine late Georgian terraced house in a street running down from the Strand beside Charing Cross Station to the newly formed Embankment with its underground station. This was a very well connected and convenient location. The offices are also close to one of the Society's early secular cases, the fine, early seventeenth-century river gate to the demolished York House. This was relocated to the new Embankment Gardens in 1863 but it had fallen into disrepair by the early 1890s. The Society highlighted its plight and the newly formed London County Council undertook its conservation (fig.88).

In January 1883, a young architect, Hugh Thackeray Turner, who had trained in the elder Scott's office, took over as secretary. To make the poorly paid post more attractive, the Society allowed Turner to conduct a portion of his private practice from Buckingham Street. Turner later entered practice with Colonel Eustace Balfour who secured the lucrative appointment as surveyor to the Duke of Westminster's London estate, including most of Mayfair. In this way, Turner, a talented designer, came to be architect of many townhouses and commercial properties on the Duke's land. He developed an eclectic style of architecture that Morris admired, and one today termed 'Arts and Crafts'. Many of

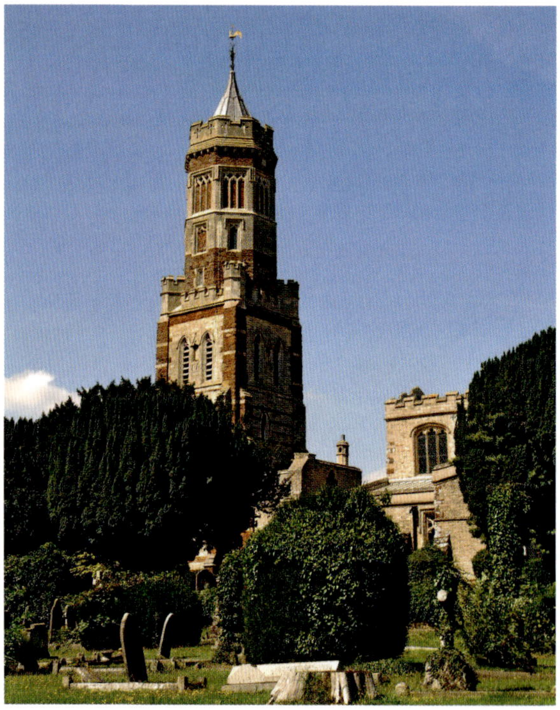

Fig.89 **St Peter's, Irthlingborough, Northamptonshire, visited by Philip Webb in 1883.**

Turner's finest buildings in this manner are to be seen on Grosvenor land today. Turner also had a large country house practice in Surrey, producing Lutyens-esque buildings of great interest. He did all this while devoting about half of his working week to SPAB business through to 1911. Prior to that he published *Notes on the Repair of Ancient Buildings* (1903), a kind of digest of repair techniques that the Society had influenced in one way or another.

Early Society casework committees became social occasions. According to Webb's biographer, William Richard Lethaby, meetings started at five finishing about seven when 'a group consisting usually of Webb, frequently of Morris, and of some younger members, Walker, Cockerell, Gimson, and others, would go across the Strand to Gatti's for a simple meal … Here talk flowed.' As did the claret, of which Webb was reputed to be particularly fond. Over time, younger men were drawn to the Society's activities not least because they provided access to Morris and, in particular, to Webb, who had a small practice and limited office assistants but a considerable reputation among advanced architects who are today associated with the Arts and Crafts Movement. Casework visits out of London would likely have had a social side to them too, creating friendships that sustained a sense of shared purpose and values.

From the beginning and for decades to come, SPAB committee members undertook site views alongside their committee work, often in the company of local correspondents. In Morris's time, the committee's architect members were particularly active and visited to assess the condition of buildings for themselves, to review the works proposed in context and so to write technical reports. Stevenson undertook a number of these along with Hebb and of course Turner himself. Webb appears to have been most active in this respect, and one of the earliest documented examples dates to 1883, when the Society was alerted to proposals to rebuild in facsimile the unusual, two-stage west tower at St Peter's, Irthlingborough, in Northamptonshire. His detailed report survives in the Society's archives and his advice formed the basis of the Society's correspondence with the vicar, most of which was conducted by Morris himself. The works here appear to have been set aside at that point, albeit largely for reasons of cost. Between 1889 and 1893 the tower was pulled down and rebuilt despite the campaign for its careful repair (fig.89).

Even after the Society appointed a casework secretary, Morris continued to be active, perhaps aware that his celebrity offered some advantage. In addition to the early cases already mentioned, he was directly involved in the attempt to prevent the part demolition of the parish church of Truro (which became an adjunct to the massive new cathedral), St Albans Cathedral, Southwell Minster, Blundell's School in Tiverton (an unusual early instance of a secular building), Norwich Cathedral, Higham Gobion Church (fig.90), St Andrew's in Mells, St Peter Mancroft in Norwich and Wimborne Minster. If more of the early casework files of the Society had survived, it is likely the list would be much longer, and there are doubtless many Morris letters waiting to be discovered in parish archives held by county record offices. Morris also delivered many of the lectures that

Fig.90 **Drawings of St Margaret's, Higham Gobion, Bedfordshire, by Henry Brewer, 1878.**
The Society for the Protection of Ancient Buildings

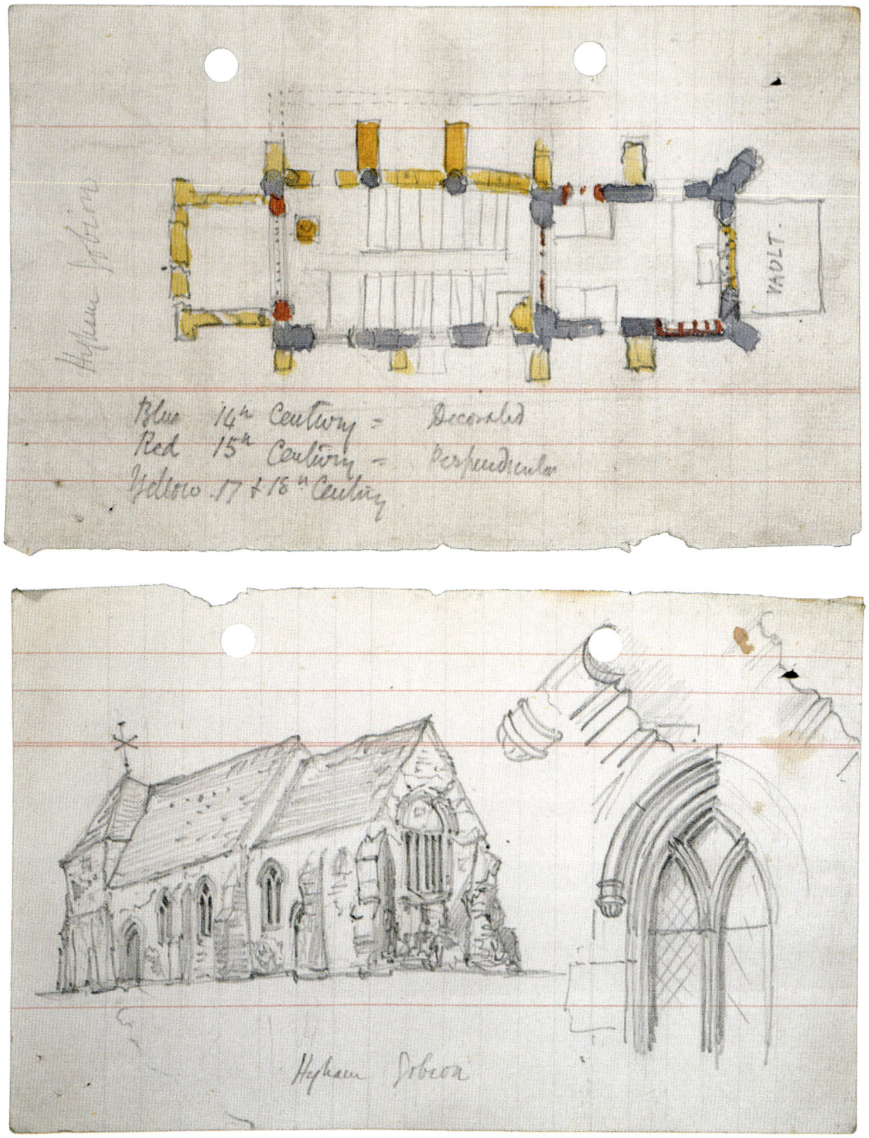

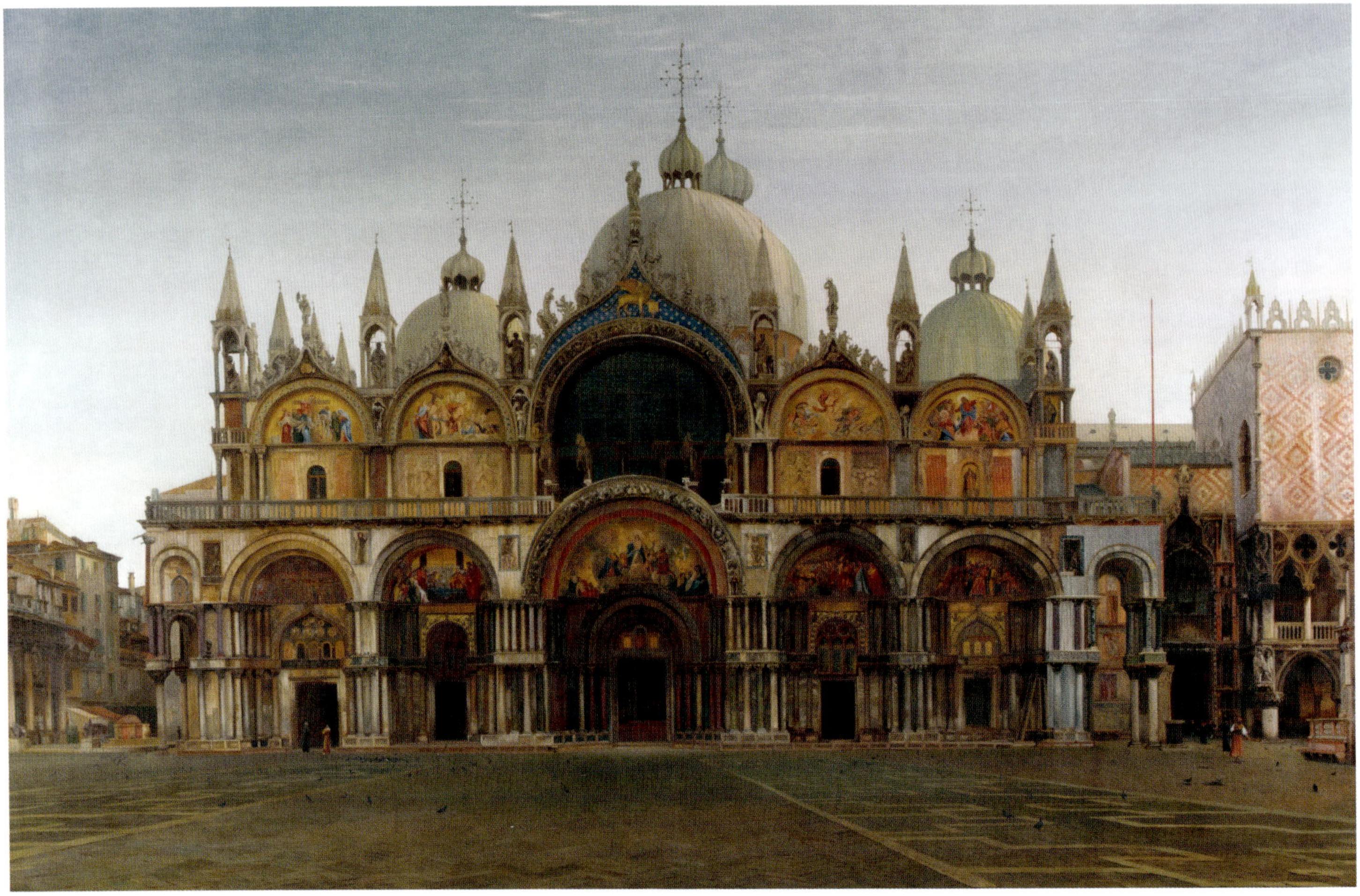

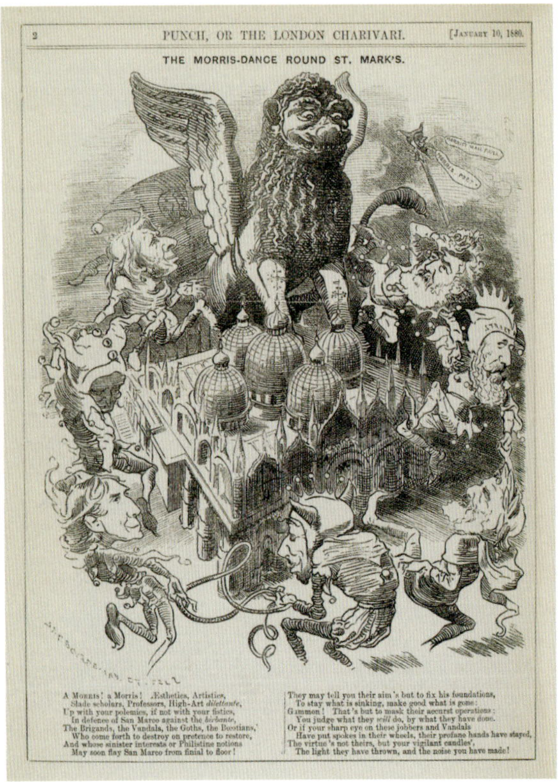

2 PUNCH, OR THE LONDON CHARIVARI. [JANUARY 10, 1880.

THE MORRIS-DANCE ROUND ST. MARK'S.

A MORRIS! a Morris! Æsthetics, Artistics,
Slade scholars, Professors, High-Art *dilettante*,
Up with your polemics, if not with your fistics,
In defence of San Marco against the *birbante*,
The Brigands, the Vandals, the Goths, the Bœotians,
Who come forth to destroy on pretence to restore,
And whose sinister interests or Philistine notions
May soon flay San Marco from finial to floor!

They may tell you their aim's but to fix his foundations,
To stay what is sinking, make good what is gone:
Gammon! That's but to mask their accurst operations;
You judge what they *will* do, by what they have done.
Or if your sharp eye on these jobbers and Vandals
Have put spokes in their wheels, their profane hands have stayed,
The virtue's not theirs, but your vigilant candles',
The light they have thrown, and the noise you have made!

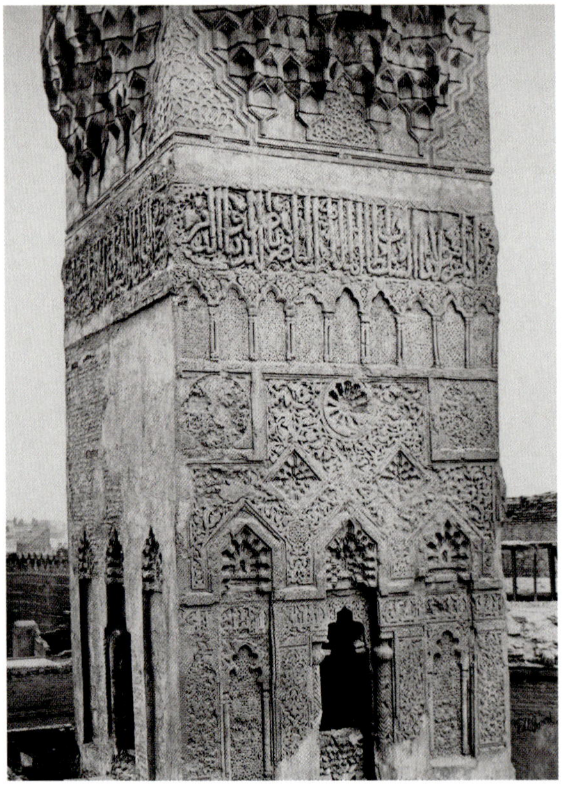

Fig.91 (above) ***The West Front of St Mark's, Venice*, John Wharlton Bunney, 1877–82, showing the building under restoration.**
Ruskin Gallery, Collection of the Guild of St George, Sheffield

Fig.92 (far left) **'The Morris-Dance Round St Mark's', this *Punch* cartoon satirizing the SPAB's campaign shows what a high profile it had in England, 10 January 1880.**
National Art Library, V&A

Fig.93 (left) **Detail of the Mosque of the Sultan Kaloun, Cairo.**
National Library of Wales

became fixtures of the Society's Annual General Meetings and which are reprinted in its Annual Reports. The paper he delivered to the 1884 meeting, titled 'Architecture and History', was one of his most important essays on historic buildings and it had a polemical cast to it, reflecting his recent reading of Marx. What those attending thought of it is unclear, though the meeting ended promptly without any questions from the floor.

It was Morris's idea to expand the Society's activities outside the United Kingdom. It seems to have originated in the spring of 1878 when he joined his wife Jane and their daughters who were travelling in Italy. In Venice he saw mosaics being removed from St Mark's Cathedral for restoration. On his return to England, he encouraged the committee to extend its activities across Europe. A 'foreign' casework committee was constituted in March 1879, its members comprising Morris, Webb and notable painters, Burne-Jones, Boyce, Charles Fairfax Murray as well as Colvin and George Howard, later Earl of Carlisle, a close friend and patron of Morris. The manifesto was translated into French, Italian, Dutch and German. The painter John Bunney, who assisted Ruskin and was many years resident in Venice, became the Society's Venice correspondent (fig.91). The subsequent campaign the Society ran to oppose the culture ministry's proposals for St Mark's was the most widely covered one in its early history. There was extensive correspondence in British and Italian newspapers and public meetings held throughout Britain. Morris himself spoke at gatherings in Birmingham and Oxford. Letters from him and Ruskin were read to the Manchester meeting that was chaired by the local MP. There is no doubt that the exposure arising from this did more to promote the Society in Britain than any other early campaign and in entirely positive terms. In the event, as Frank Sharp has argued, the confrontational tactics Morris pursued with the Italian government and the absence of any real support from Italians backfired, creating indignation locally (fig.92).

Later foreign casework was conducted more sensitively, through appropriate channels. Italy continued to be the main focus of work, with forays into Germany, Spain, Greece, the Middle East and India, and the Society could legitimately claim some success in this area. In 1881 William

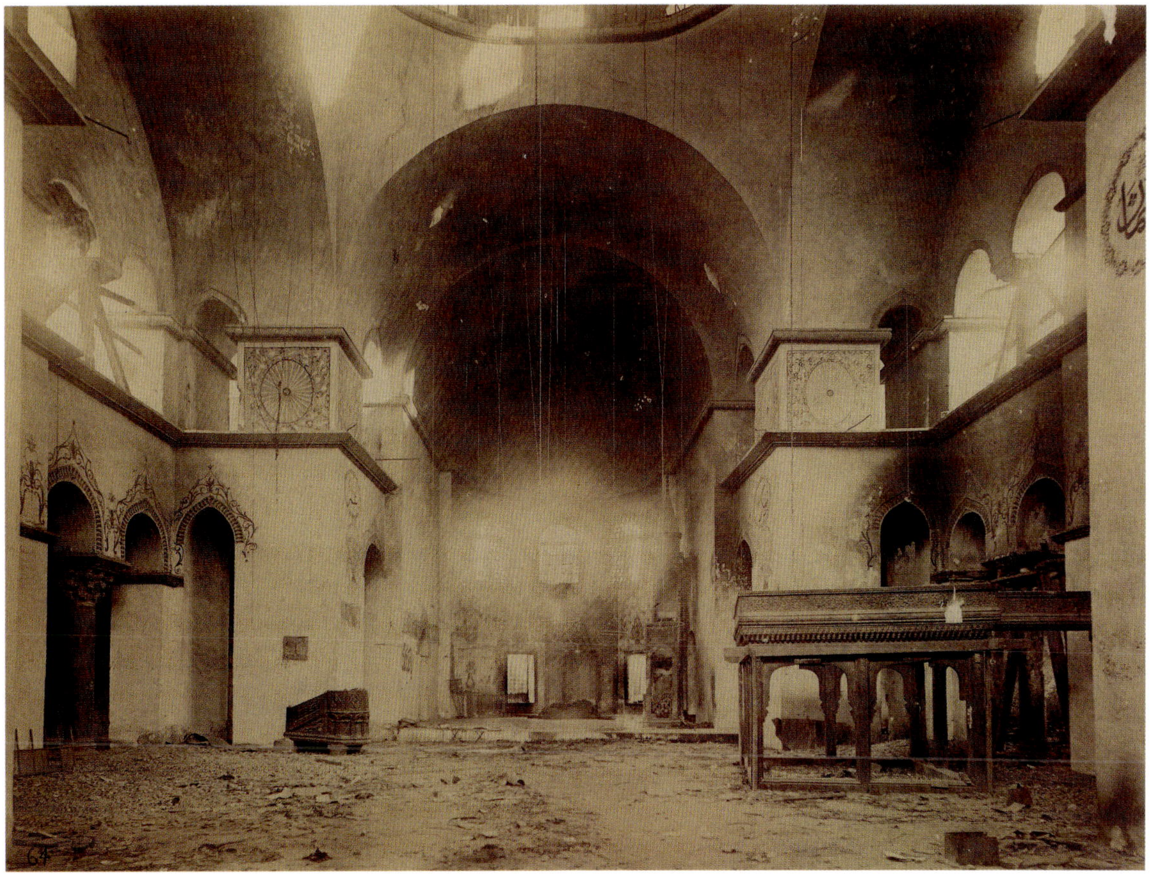

Fig.94 **Interior of St Sophia, Thessaloniki.**
Conway Library, The Courtauld Institute of Art, London

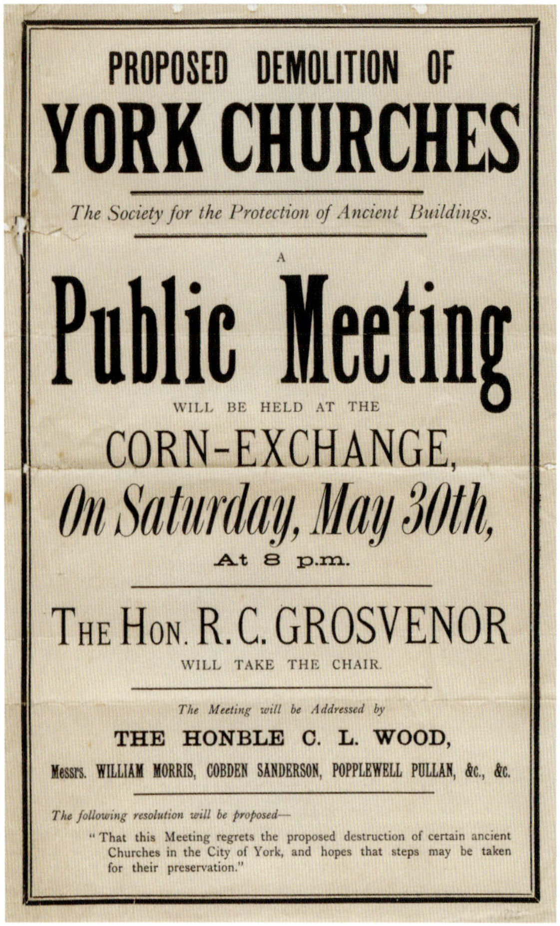

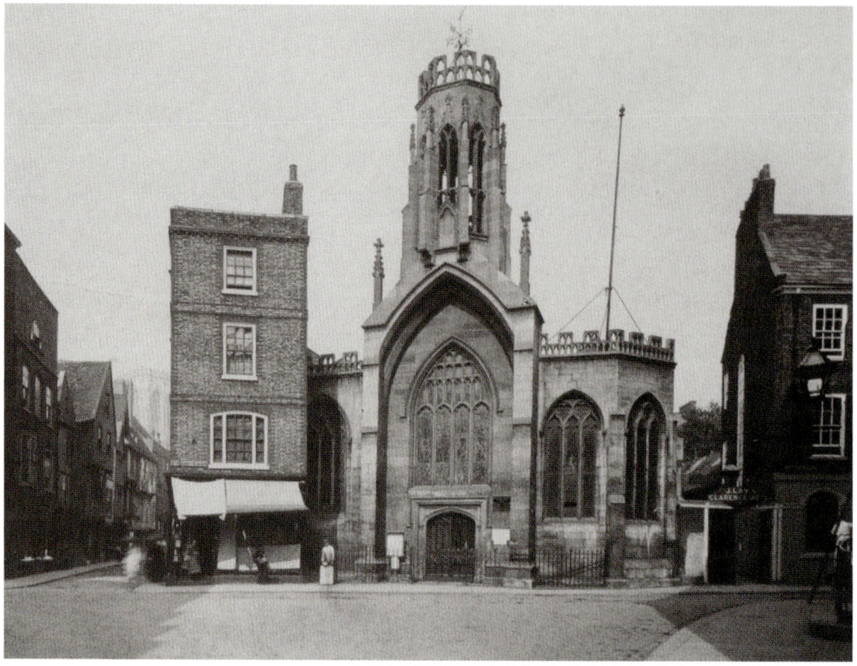

Figs 95–6 **Poster advertising the public meeting in York at which Morris spoke in 1885, and a photograph of St Helen's, one of the churches under threat.**
The Society for the Protection of Ancient Buildings

Holman Hunt asked the SPAB to get involved in proposals for the restoration of the Dome of the Rock in Jerusalem, then being promoted by the Ottoman government. The Society, led by Morris, submitted a joint petition with the RIBA, a rare instance of the two organizations collaborating. In 1891 the SPAB used Sir Evelyn Baring, the British Resident in Egypt, to deliver letters urging more careful conservation of the Mosque of the Sultan Kaloun in Cairo. Images of both these sites appear in the photographic albums at the National Library of Wales (fig.93). In 1895 Webb contacted the Greek authorities through his friend Aglaia Coronio, a member of the Greek community in London, on behalf of St Sophia in Thessaloniki (fig.94). The Society's approach was careful and polite, avoiding the public relations trouble that arose from its early campaign against the Italian government's proposals for St Mark's in Venice.

At home, Morris also took a leading role in a small number of high-profile campaigns. An important early one was the Society's opposition to the closure and sale of many ancient churches in York, appearing at a public meeting there in 1885 (figs 95–6). He was also closely involved in the campaign against proposals for the treatment of Westminster Hall. Sir John Soane's former Law Courts (which Street's replaced) had abutted the Hall on the north, and demolition revealed valuable archaeological evidence of the Norman precursor to the later medieval hall whose hammerbeam roof is a masterpiece of carpentry from the Middle Ages. The Society argued that these remains should be conserved and left open to view as a feature in a new public park beside Parliament (fig.97). Parliament's appointed architect John Loughborough Pearson's proposal was to put a new range of committee rooms along the north side of the Hall, and to re-front it with two towers, tying the building visually to the rest of the Palace. Concern over Irish terrorism also led to proposals for a secure iron fence. The dispute induced Parliament to convene a select committee to hear testimony from experts. In 1885 Morris gave evidence for the Society along with Micklethwaite,

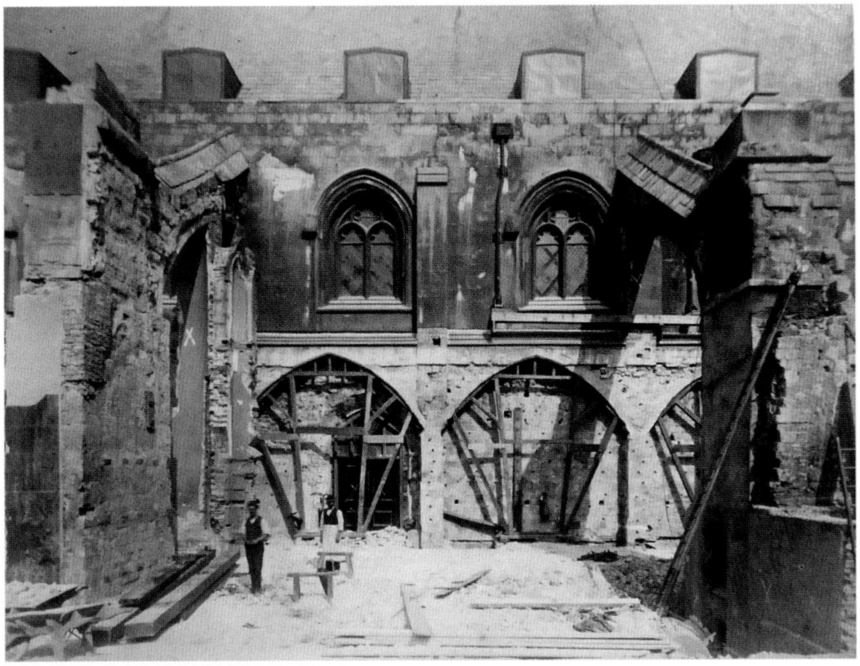

Fig.97 **Detail of twelfth-century masonry on the west flank of Westminster Hall, exposed to view by the demolition of Soane's Law Courts. Photographed by Bedford Lemere & Co., 1883.**
The Society of Antiquaries of London

whom the Society regularly recommended for conservation work. In the end, Parliament found in favour of Pearson and the works survive to this day. The internal corridor to the committee room exposes some of the earlier remains but one has no sense of them as a whole.

The documented list of churches Morris visited in furtherance of the Society's work and in the company of an architect or surveyor includes Lechlade Church (with Stevenson); Minster in Thanet, Nunnington and East Bergholt (with the surveyor Charles G. Vinall); Inglesham Church (with the architect–scholar John Henry Middleton whom Morris met on board the outward journey of his 1873 visit to Iceland) and Fulbrook Church (with Micklethwaite). Morris appears to have visited many more sites on his own consistently through the 1880s: St Crux in York, Chard Church and Blythburgh in 1882; Kirkstall Abbey in Leeds, Bowthorpe and Eastleach Martin in 1884; St Margaret's, Norwich, and Monken Hadley Church, Barnet, in 1886 and Framlingham, Broadwater and Fairford in 1887.

During the mid-1880s, his attendance at meetings became less frequent, doubtless because of his political activities in this period. But from 1888, Morris was once again a regular fixture at the Society's fortnightly meetings. In his last decade he reported less from the field, and then usually in relation to sites that he had the occasion to visit for some business reason (see, for example, his reports on Rye and Orton Churches from 1891 and 1892 respectively).

In early addresses to the Society's Annual General Meetings, Morris had naturally to report to members what had been achieved. This official record of the Society documented very few practical successes among the nearly 1,500 cases pursued in its first ten years. Early on Morris grappled with this difficult fact. His 1879 address argued that the Society's real success could not be measured statistically. The purpose of its huge caseload, promoted through countless hours of time given freely by dozens of people (the committee and local correspondents), was to shift the terms of public debate one step at a time.

The Society might well have achieved more practical success by working through professional channels, the RIBA, say, or the institutional framework of the Church of England. But doing so would inevitably have meant compromise, which Morris, as the Society's founder and guiding spirit, was not able to contemplate. In this respect, we think of his politics, of the decision to reject Parliamentary democracy that separated him from others on the left, for example, the early Fabians. That said, though, the tide did eventually turn Morris's way, albeit he did not live to see it. One of the best measures of that success is the Joint Select Committee Report that Parliament published to consider the terms of three competing Ancient Monuments Bills in 1912. An important feature of this debate was the extension of legislative protection to ancient buildings as distinct from prehistoric monuments. All the professional evidence heard was consistent with the SPAB's practice and ideas. Webb was still alive to have read it. He died in 1915. If he had, or even followed the proceedings in *The Times*, he might well have been pleased to see that the battle of ideas he and Morris joined nearly 40 years before had been won and within the establishment too. His surviving correspondence from this period is, however, silent on the matter.

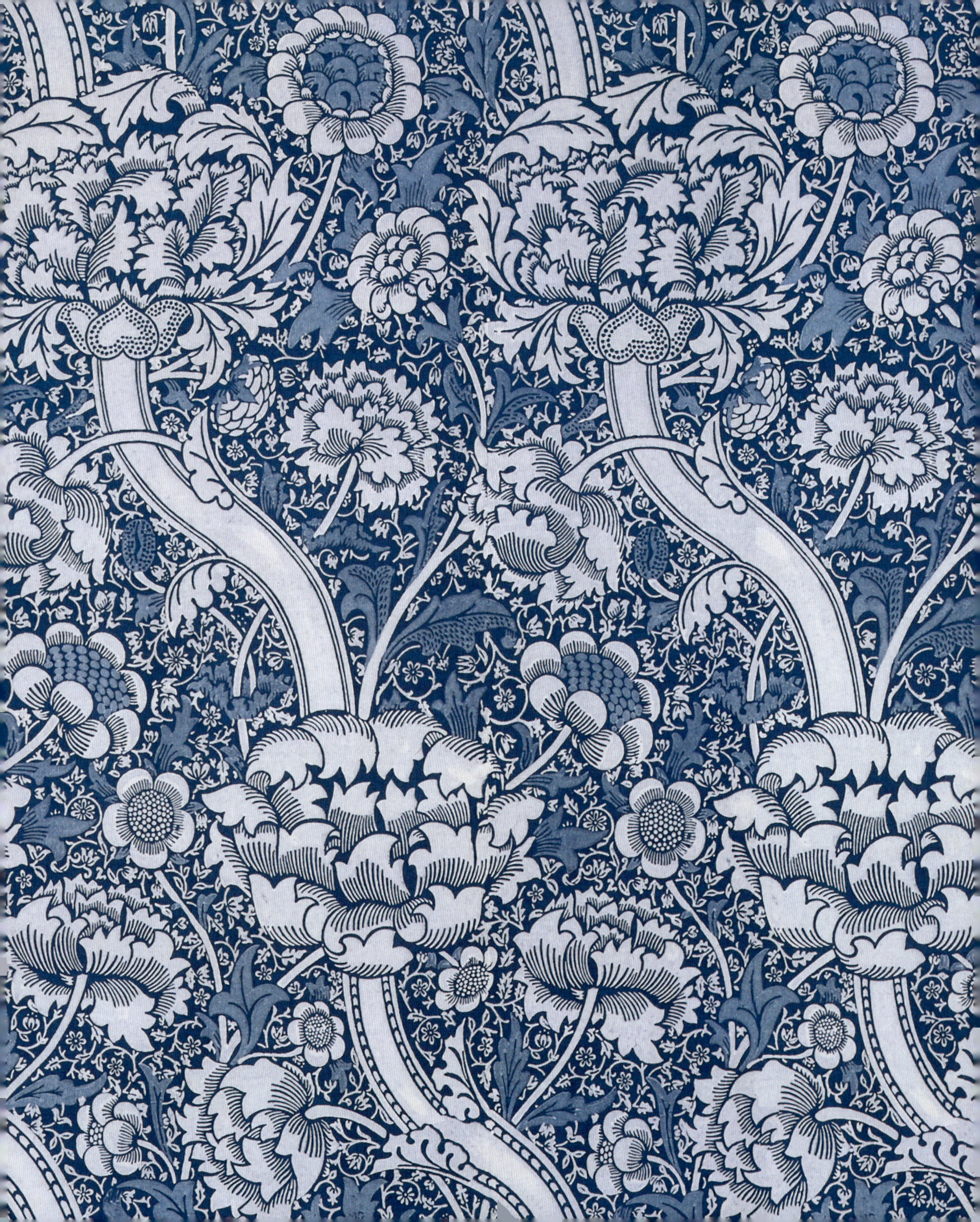

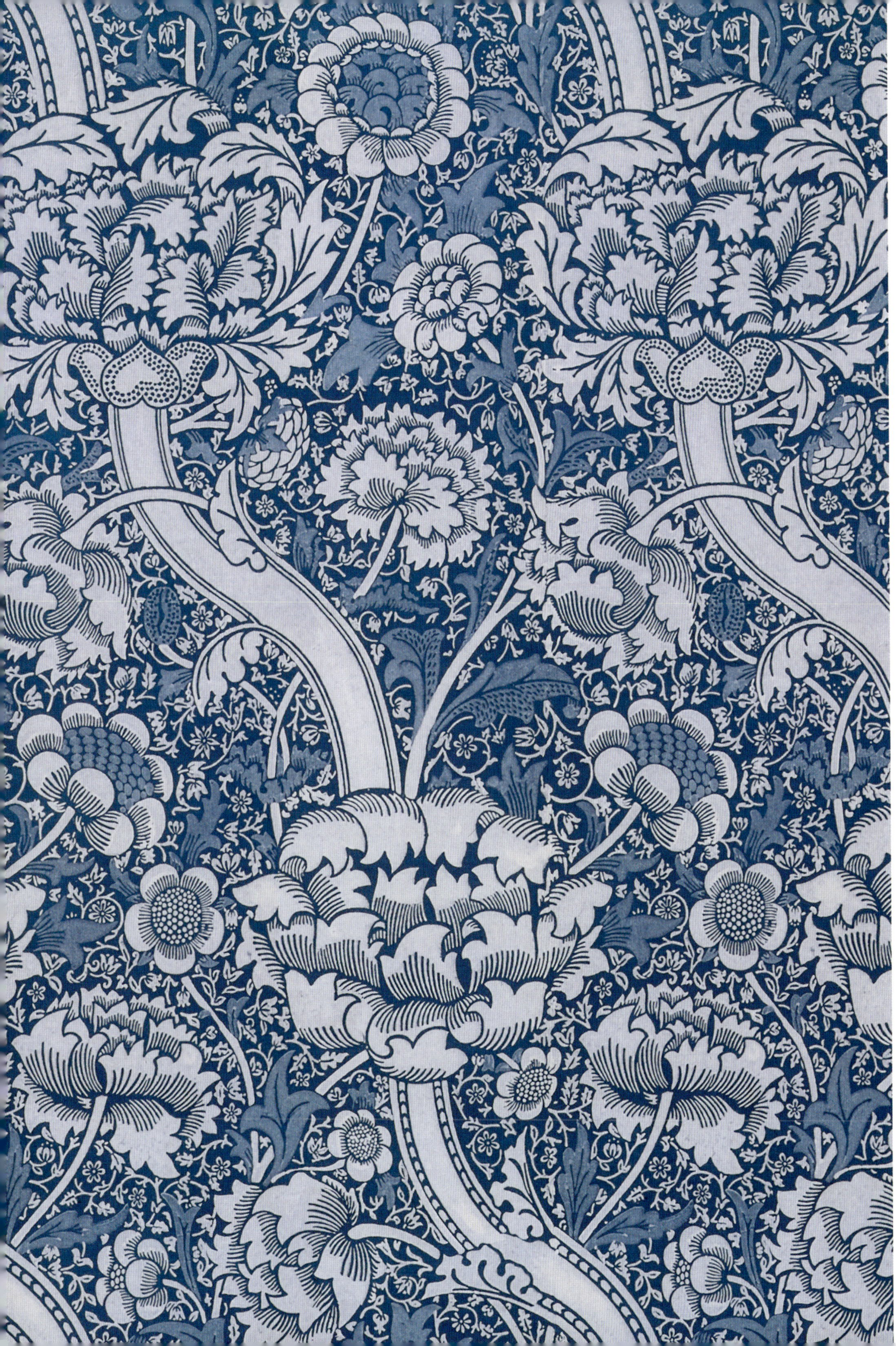

THE ART

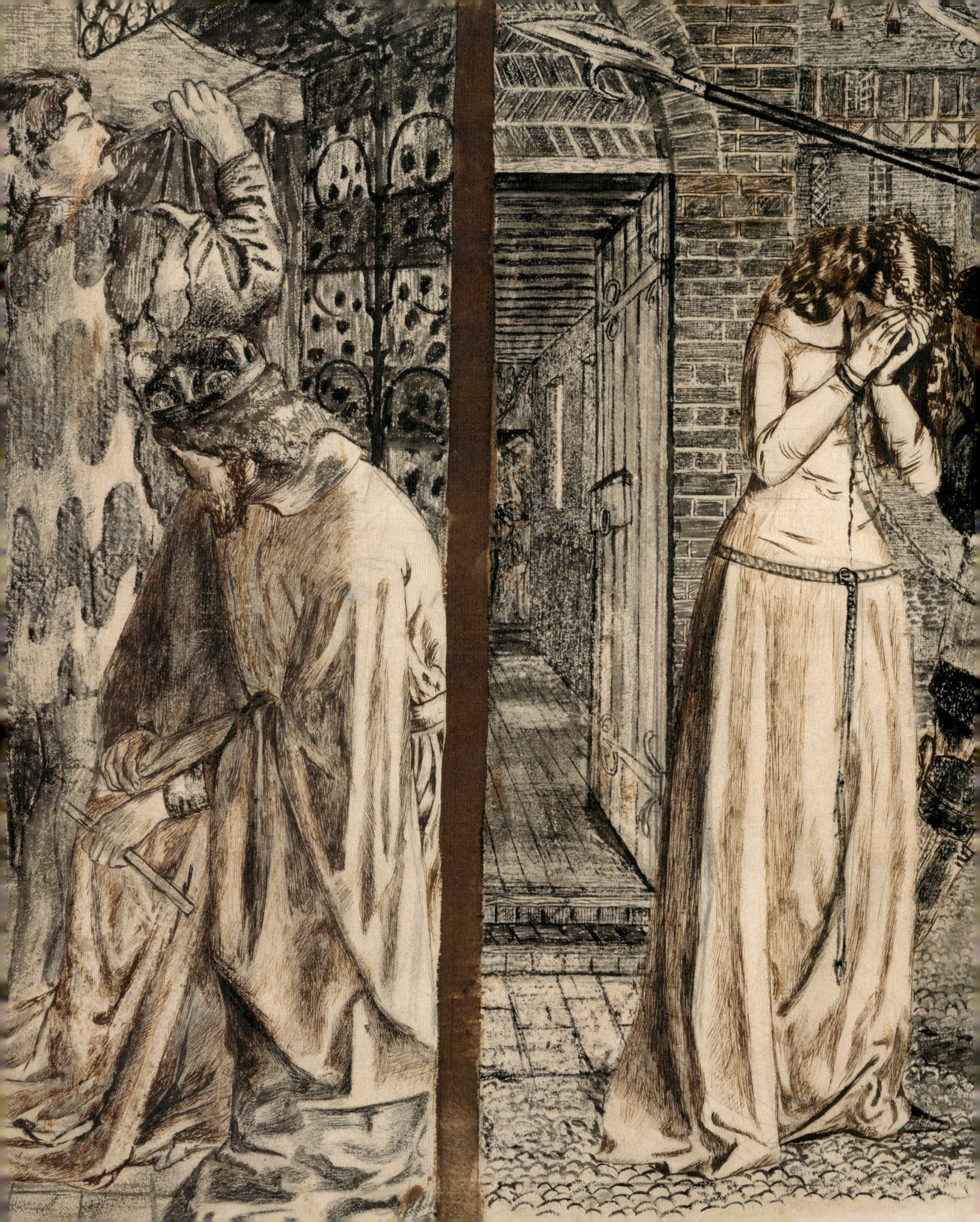

VI

PAINTING AND DRAWING

Julia Griffin

'I shall have enough to do, if I actually master this art of painting ...'
William Morris to Crom Price, July 1856

Morris's engagement with figure drawing and painting has often been portrayed as a short-lived and inconsequential pursuit – an unwelcome distraction from his true vocation for the applied arts. The story goes that in the summer of 1856 he resolved to become a painter under the charismatic influence of the Pre-Raphaelite artist and poet Dante Gabriel Rossetti. The verdict of Morris's first official biographer, John William Mackail, has shaped many subsequent life writings:

> For the two years or so during which he worked hard at painting, he was moody and irritable ... He became not only a pupil but a servant ... How long Rossetti's daily influence might have kept him labouring at what he could not do, when there was work all around that he could do, on the whole, better than any man living, it is needless to inquire.

Mackail described Morris's figure drawings for illuminated manuscripts and stained glass as 'obviously faulty' and stated that in his design work he turned to Philip Webb and Edward Burne-Jones for the depiction of animals and figures respectively. He went as far as to conclude that Rossetti's influence was one of the two 'great disturbing forces' in Morris's life (together with socialism).

In fact, Rossetti's artistic mentorship was, arguably, one of the most significant formative influences on Morris's creative vision. Proclaimed by John Ruskin as the greatest genius of the age and the leader of the Pre-Raphaelites, Rossetti inspired and facilitated the professionalization of Morris's fine as well as decorative arts practice. His experimental engagement with painting, both on canvas, but perhaps more significantly on walls and applied to furniture, was an essential part of Morris's artistic development, honing his natural faculty for pictorial storytelling, ornament and colour. As a university graduate with no formal arts training, the discipline of drawing from life (both from models and from nature) – an activity that Morris took up with Rossetti's support in the late 1850s – was vital preparation for his career as a designer. However challenging he may have found the process, Morris recognized its value. In 'The Lesser Arts', a lecture of 1877, he argued that life-drawing was essential training for the decorative arts designer, 'both because the lines of a man's body are much more subtle than anything else, and because you can more surely be found out and set right if you go wrong.' Above all, the pictorial idiom of Morris's paintings as well as his figurative designs for the firm, was certainly Pre-Raphaelite.

Fig.98 **Detail of a study for the painted doors of the *St George* cabinet, William Morris, 1861 (see VI.24a).**
V&A (E.2787–1927)

Mackail usefully points to key factors, which had first kindled Morris's interest in the visual arts before exposure to Rossetti: 'the combined influence of his delight in architecture, his natural dexterity of hand, and the companionship of Burne-Jones, whose drawings, then chiefly of a fantastic nature, had already made him a reputation among his schoolfellows'. Explored more fully in Chapter V, Morris's early interest in buildings and the material remains of the past – intrinsically connected with his passion for history – is also relevant here because Morris would develop an all-encompassing concept of art, going beyond traditional hierarchies and distinctions between the fine and decorative arts, disciplines or media. Morris's lifelong pastime of brass-rubbing expeditions to historic churches, begun as a boy, was an early manifestation of this outlook. Even before conceiving any artistic career aspirations, he was compelled to sketch details of buildings he admired. According to Mackail 'he was constantly drawing windows, arches, and gables in his books; and even in his letters ... there comes a half unconscious scribble of floriated ornament.' Morris's copy of Horace features one such sketch of an unidentified church with a detail of the spire, a rare early surviving example of this habit (fig.99).

John Ruskin's writings on art (and subsequently on architecture) became another key early influence. Reading the first two volumes of *Modern Painters* (1843, 1846), concerned mainly with J.M.W. Turner and the importance of documentary and symbolic depictions of nature, marked the beginning of Morris's lifelong admiration for the art critic's views. In time, it would lead to his elaborations on, and practical implementation of, Ruskin's doctrines concerning the ennobling power of handicrafts. At university, fired by his reading of 'The Nature of Gothic' (1853), Morris sought first-hand encounters with medieval art, from the built fabric of Oxford itself (Merton College Chapel was a favourite haunt) to the Bodleian Library's superb collection of illuminated manuscripts. The richly illustrated thirteenth-century Douce Apocalypse made a particular impression and its palette of deep reds, blues, greens and gold would later be reflected in Morris's earliest decorative schemes. The manuscript was never finished and the miniatures are in various stages of completion – this may well have added to its appeal, offering Morris insight into the illuminator's process. His newly found friendship with Burne-Jones further fuelled Morris's interest in the visual arts. Burne-Jones was to be consistently more advanced at painting and drawing, and unlike Morris, he would persevere in his determination to be a painter. However, it is important to stress the commonality of the friends' shared experience at the early stages of their artistic journey, recorded in the *Memorials of Edward Burne-Jones* by Georgiana Burne-Jones (1904).

From Priesthood to Pre-Raphaelitism

At the same time as the pair were deepening their familiarity with the art and literature of the medieval past, Ruskin's writings introduced them to the Pre-Raphaelites, a group of young painters who were leading a revolution in contemporary art. The Pre-Raphaelite Brotherhood was founded in 1848 and its leading personalities – Rossetti, William Holman Hunt and John Everett Millais – rebelled against what they considered the dire state of contemporary British art, largely resulting from the formulaic style of teaching practised at the Royal Academy Schools. While the Academy held the idealization brought about by the High Renaissance in the greatest esteem, the Pre-Raphaelites looked to the 'archaic honesty' of earlier Italian and Netherlandish art for inspiration. Their work shocked critics and public alike and was much ridiculed until Ruskin, recognizing their originality, came to their defence in 1851. In his Edinburgh lectures of 1853 (published the following year), he praised the artists' commitment to working

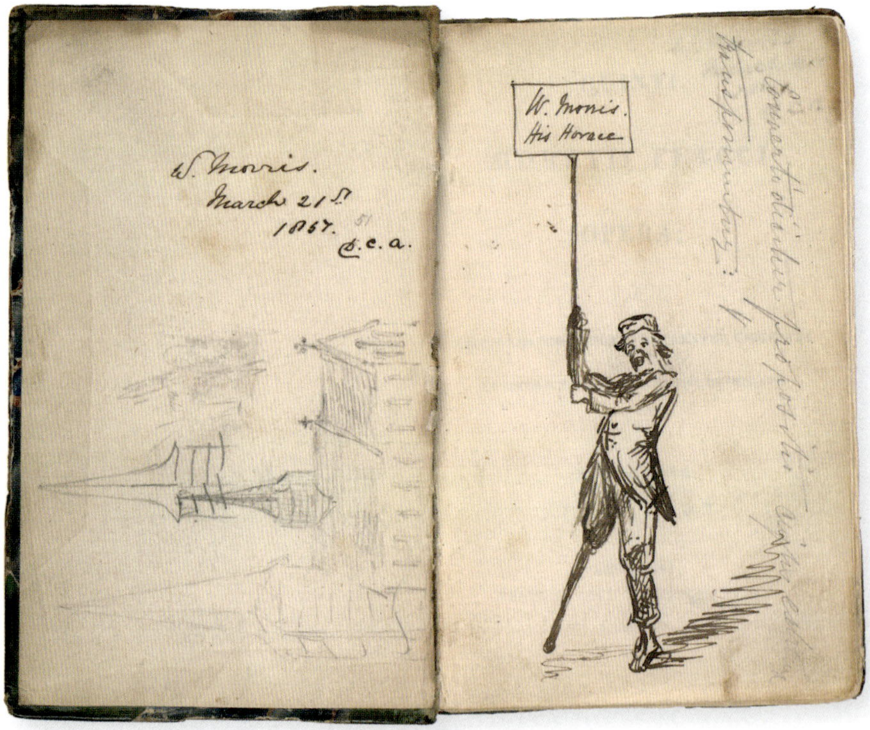

Fig.99 **Architectural sketch by William Morris, inside his copy of *The Odes of Horace*.**
The Huntington Library, Art Museum and Botanical Gardens

Fig.100 (right) ***The Maids of Elfen-Mere***, **Dalziel Brothers after Dante Gabriel Rossetti, wood engraving, 1855.**
V&A (E.2923–1904)
Given by Mr E. Dalziel

Fig.101 (far right) ***Going to the Battle***, **Edward Burne-Jones, pen and ink with grey wash on vellum, 1858.**
Fitzwilliam Museum, University of Cambridge

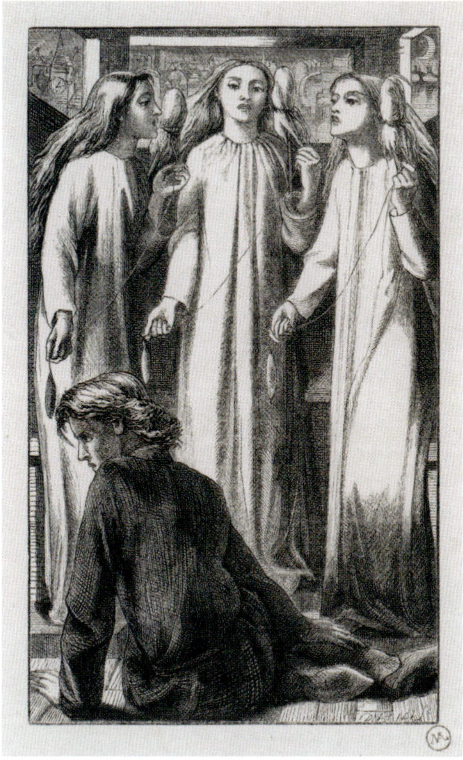

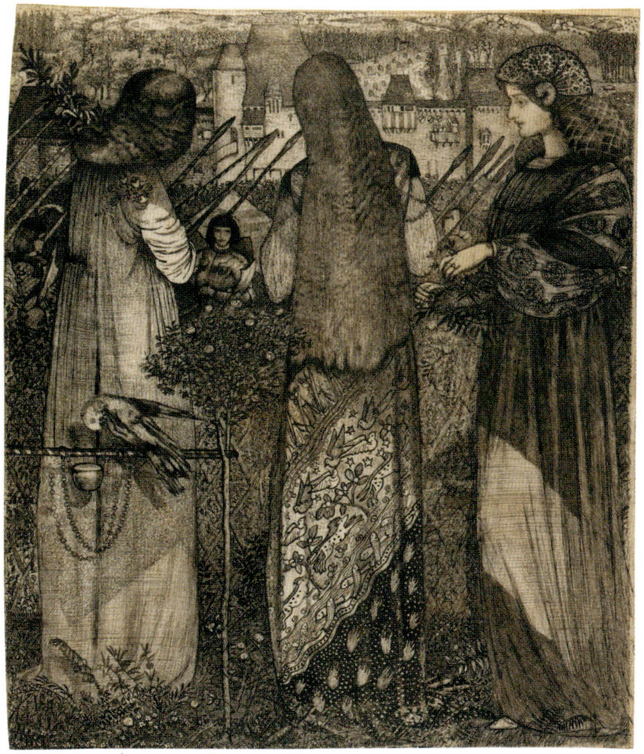

from nature and imbued this aspect of their work with a moral dimension, 'Pre-Raphaelitism has but one principle, that of absolute, uncompromising truth in all that it does'. He singled out the art of Rossetti and Millais as having 'more exhaustless invention' than the works of the Old Masters.

It was through the prism of Ruskin's advocacy in the Edinburgh lectures that Morris and Burne-Jones first learnt of the Pre-Raphaelites. Burne-Jones later described this shared moment of discovery: 'Morris ran in one morning bringing the newly published book … everything was put aside until he read it all through … So for many a day after that we talked of little else but paintings which we had never seen'. Soon afterwards, Millais's *The Return of the Dove to the Ark* was the first Pre-Raphaelite work they saw when it went on display in the shop of the Oxford art dealer James Wyatt. Then, Burne-Jones said, 'we knew' – marking the beginning of a powerful conversion from priesthood to Pre-Raphaelitism. In the summer of 1854 Morris took his first trip abroad, a tour of Belgium and northern France with his sister Henrietta. Their itinerary was a dual tribute to Ruskin and the Pre-Raphaelites. They visited French Gothic cathedrals, the collections of medieval art at the Louvre and Musée Cluny in Paris, and in Ghent and Bruges Morris had his first introduction to the fifteenth-century painters Jan van Eyck and Hans Memling 'who remained to him ever after absolute and unapproached masters of painting'. He came back to England with souvenirs including photographs of Albrecht Dürer's prints.

In the spring of 1855 the friends got hold of early issues of the Pre-Raphaelite journal, *The Germ*. They were deeply impressed by Rossetti's poem 'The Blessed Damozel' and his short story 'Hand and Soul', a parable about a fictional medieval painter who discovered that art only has meaning if the artist is true to his own soul. Over the following months, though still unacquainted with the artists themselves, they sought out more Pre-Raphaelite pictures, visiting the private collections of Benjamin Windus in Tottenham and Thomas Combe, director of the Clarendon Press, in Oxford. The latter had recently acquired Rossetti's intensely medieval watercolour, *The First Anniversary of the Death of Beatrice* (1853, Ashmolean), which, according to Burne-Jones, met with their 'greatest wonder and delight … and at once he seemed to us the chief figure in the Pre-Raphaelite Brotherhood.'

It was, however, Rossetti's first published book illustration, *The Maids of Elfen-Mere*, which had the greatest impact on their artistic sensibilities (fig.100). It was made to accompany William

Allingham's eponymous ballad included in *The Music Master, A Love Story. And Two Series of Day and Night Songs*, published in June 1855. The poem tells the tragic story of three mystical damsels, who appear every night to spin and sing, invariably departing at eleven o'clock. The pastor's son, infatuated by them, turns back the village clock in a desperate attempt to delay their departure, triggering a curse that brings about their death. Burne-Jones pronounced it: 'the most beautiful drawing for an illustration that I have ever seen; the weirdness of the Maids of Elfenmere, the musical timed movement of their arms together as they sing, the face of the man, above all'. One of Burne-Jones's most accomplished early works, *Going to the Battle* (fig.101), echoes the composition, with three symmetrically placed damsels, this time shown from behind, the rhythm of the yarns and distaffs recalled by the diagonal lines of the soldiers' raised lances. The illustration also sparked Morris's creativity, inspiring him to make wood engravings.

From 19 July until 13 August 1855, Morris and Burne-Jones toured northern France visiting medieval cathedrals. Their itinerary included Amiens, Beauvais, Chartres, Rouen, Bayeux and Mont Saint Michel. Against Morris's wishes (on his last trip the parlous state of Notre-Dame had upset him), they made a quick stop at Paris so that Burne-Jones could see medieval paintings in the Louvre. The year before Morris had delighted in Fra Angelico's *Coronation of the Virgin* (*c.*1430–2), and he would now lead his friend to see it in the flesh. They were also thrilled to come across works by the Pre-Raphaelites in the Fine Art section of the Exposition Universelle. At Rouen, Morris bought a copy of William Thackeray's novel *The Newcomes* (1854–5). The plot echoed the struggle the friends were undergoing at the time as they contemplated giving up a 'respectable career' in the church for a life dedicated to art. The trip proved decisive in their determination to pursue a change of vocation. Walking on the quay at Le Havre at night, Burne-Jones recalled, 'we resolved definitely that we would begin a life of art, and put off our decision no longer – he [Morris] should be an architect and I a painter. It was a resolve only needing final conclusion; we were bent on that road for the whole past year'.

Morris began his architectural training with the leading Gothic Revival architect, George Edmund Street, in January 1856. He was supervised by Webb, Street's chief assistant, who would become a mentor, lifelong friend and a creative associate. Under Webb's watchful eye, Morris practised architectural drawing and also drew *in situ*. In February, for example, they sketched churches at Bloxham, King's Sutton and Adderbury. He seems to have struggled with the discipline of architectural training. Webb later suggested that he gave it up because, 'he found he could not get into contact with it; it had to be done at second hand'. Though Morris worked diligently at his new profession, over the course of the year a developing friendship with Rossetti would play a decisive role in yet another change of direction.

Entering Rossetti's orbit

Burne-Jones described 1856 as, 'a year in which I think it never rained nor clouded, but was blue summer from Christmas to Christmas'. While Morris was working for Street in Oxford, Burne-Jones determined to 'see the face of Rossetti', attending a meeting at the Working Men's College in Great Ormond Street, where his idol taught evening classes. By February he had an invitation to his studio at Chatham Place, near Blackfriars Bridge. There he saw him working on the watercolour *Fra Pace*, a picture of a monk painting a mouse from life in an illuminated manuscript (fig.102). This ultra-medieval subject can be read as a dual

Fig.102 ***Fra Pace***, Dante Gabriel Rossetti, watercolour on paper, 1856. Photogravure published in *Dante Gabriel Rossetti: An Illustrated Memorial of His Art and Life* by H.C. Marillier (1899).

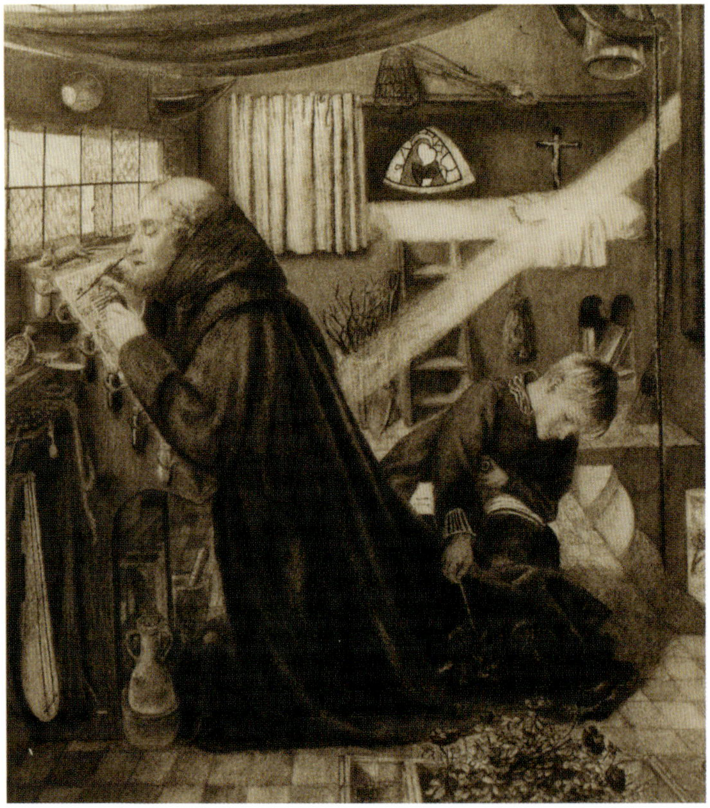

metaphor of a life dedicated to art and of the creative process itself, namely the importance of working from nature. Morris would later acquire *Fra Pace*. Through Burne-Jones, Morris too would soon meet Rossetti, who had already read and admired some of his poetry. From late May, Morris would typically spend his weekends in London, the three of them looking at paintings, going to the theatre, roaming the streets and talking and reading at Rossetti's until the early hours.

Although Rossetti was only around six years older than Morris and Burne-Jones, at first he took on the role of their mentor. Through Rossetti, they met many leading cultural figures including their hero Ruskin, Ford Madox Brown and the poet Robert Browning. In July 1856 they were spending the day in Rossetti's studio, Burne-Jones painting and Morris making drawings, when they were introduced to another Pre-Raphaelite legend, William Holman Hunt. According to Burne-Jones it was 'a glorious day, one to be remembered by the side of the most notable ones in my life ... And all evening through Rossetti talked most gloriously, such talk as I do not believe any man could talk beside him.' Their excitement at being thrown into a world that they had admired from afar since 1854 is palpable. It was on this occasion that Rossetti urged Morris to take up painting and he resolved to try, not giving up architecture, but combining the two pursuits. A letter to his friend Crom Price, written a few days later, is a mixture of apprehension and excitement, with the word 'try' appearing no fewer than five times:

> Rossetti says I ought to paint, he says I shall be able; now as he is a very great man, and speaks with authority ... I *must* try. I don't hope much ... yet will try my best – he gave me practical advice on the subject ... So I am going to try, not giving up the architecture, but trying if it is possible to get six hours a day for drawing besides office work ... I dare scarcely think failure possible at times, and yet I know in my mind that my chances are slender; I am glad that I am compelled to try anyhow; I was slipping off into a kind of small (very small) Palace of Art ...

The resolve to take up painting was brought about by Rossetti's external influence rather than an impulse within Morris. He could nevertheless see that creating pictures, and the disciplined study of drawing this would entail, could help give his life purpose. Conscious that his private income gave him considerable freedom, he was anxious not to fall into the trap of merely playing at art.

It is tempting to speculate that Morris's pencil self-portrait in a suit could have been one of the drawings produced at Rossetti's studio on that memorable occasion; this was certainly a standard exercise for an aspiring painter (VI.1). Recorded by May Morris as simply 'William Morris. From an early drawing by himself', the self-portrait is somewhat clumsy and unfinished, yet full of expression and a good likeness. The iconography and artistic merits of Morris's only other surviving self-portrait imply it is later in date, projecting his artistic identity with more confidence and complete with a Pre-Raphaelite style monogram (VI.2). His friends recognized his determination to succeed, Burne-Jones reporting, 'Topsy will be a painter, he works hard, is prepared to wait twenty years, loves art more and more every day.' Even Mackail had to admit that Morris 'became an ardent pupil ... of the Pre-Raphaelite school ... and painting rose for a time almost ... to the first place in his interest.'

Rossetti's mentorship helped fire Morris with an enthusiasm for collecting Pre-Raphaelite paintings. In May 1856 he had already purchased Arthur Hughes's *April Love* after seeing it at the Royal Academy (fig.103). Praised by Ruskin for its exquisite colour and expression, it shows young lovers after a quarrel in a minutely observed ivy-clad arbour. In August Rossetti took Morris on a visit to Madox Brown's studio, where he bought his small vividly coloured landscape, *The Hayfield*, for 40 guineas (fig.104). Painted almost entirely on the spot in twilight conditions, it shows the effect of the moonlight on a rural landscape as seen through the eyes of the artist, depicted among his equipment – a visual testament to the Pre-Raphaelites' commitment to 'truth to nature'. The bold and unusual palettes of both these paintings reveal Morris's interest in colour.

Morris also began to collect Rossetti's pictures, presumably introducing a new dynamic to their relationship. At this time Rossetti was producing intricate pen and ink drawings and small-scale jewel-like watercolours. The watercolours evoked the aesthetic of illuminated manuscripts with bright and saturated colour schemes of red, blue and green. Their intensity was heightened by their highly decorative quality and the depiction of figures within constricted spaces. Rossetti is known to have studied manuscripts in the British Museum, including the Psalter of Queen Philippa (England, c.1328–40), Christine de Pizan's The Book of the Queen (Paris, c.1410–14) and Jean Froissart's Chronicles (Bruges, c.1470–2). He first sought permission to consult this collection in August 1856 (Burne-Jones and Morris got their letters of recommendation the following February). Rossetti's literary sources included Dante's *Divine Comedy*, the Bible, Shakespeare, Keats and Browning. In 1855 he became involved with the famous project to illustrate Edward Moxon's edition of Tennyson's poems, marking the beginning of his preoccupation with Arthurian subjects. His conviction that the Bible and Sir Thomas Malory's *Morte d'Arthur* were the world's greatest books, struck a chord with Morris and Burne-Jones, who had been developing an independent fascination with Malory since 1855.

The iconography of Rossetti's pictures from the mid- to late 1850s revolved around themes of love, art making, religion and chivalry. The underlying subject in the great majority of works was the interaction of the forces of love and fate, or as Oswald Doughty perceptively observed: 'the inexorable will of destiny threatening the ... flame of love'. This would also become Morris's chief iconographic preoccupation for easel and mural paintings, the overall scheme for Red House and many of the firm's figurative subjects. Over the next few years, Morris would acquire seven of Rossetti's watercolours: the above-mentioned *Fra Pace*, *Paolo and Francesca da Rimini* (1855, Tate, originally owned by Ruskin), two medieval fantastical compositions with uncertain sources and meanings – *The Blue Closet* (1856–7, Tate) and *The Tune of Seven Towers* (fig.105) – as well as three Arthurian pictures: *The Damsel of the Sanct Grael* (1857, Tate), *The Death of Breuse sans Pitié* (1857, British Museum) and *The Chapel before the Lists* (1857–64, Tate). Although Morris parted with these works within a few years, his early collection of paintings is important evidence of his tastes and preoccupations at the start of his artistic journey. Daily exposure to them in his living quarters would no doubt have shaped his artistic sensibilities, while also offering insights into contemporary artists' techniques.

A Pre-Raphaelite apprenticeship

Morris's endeavours to be a painter, under Rossetti's guidance, were based on studying the life. This was the legacy of the Pre-Raphaelites' rebellion against the method of teaching practised by the Royal Academy Schools, which prioritized the copying of antique sculpture and casts. According to Ruskin, even when students were eventually admitted to life-drawing classes, their professors advised that for painting, 'the antique is the best, and they mustn't copy the life'. The *Memorials* are the best source of information for the type of guidance that Rossetti offered his protégés. Burne-Jones recollected that while he received a few mornings' tuition in Rossetti's studio, his chief legacy was instilling a strong sense of self-belief and individuality in his followers,

> He taught me to have no fear or shame of my own ideas, to design perpetually, to seek no popularity, to be altogether myself ... So what I chiefly gained from him was not to be afraid of myself, but to do the thing I liked most: but

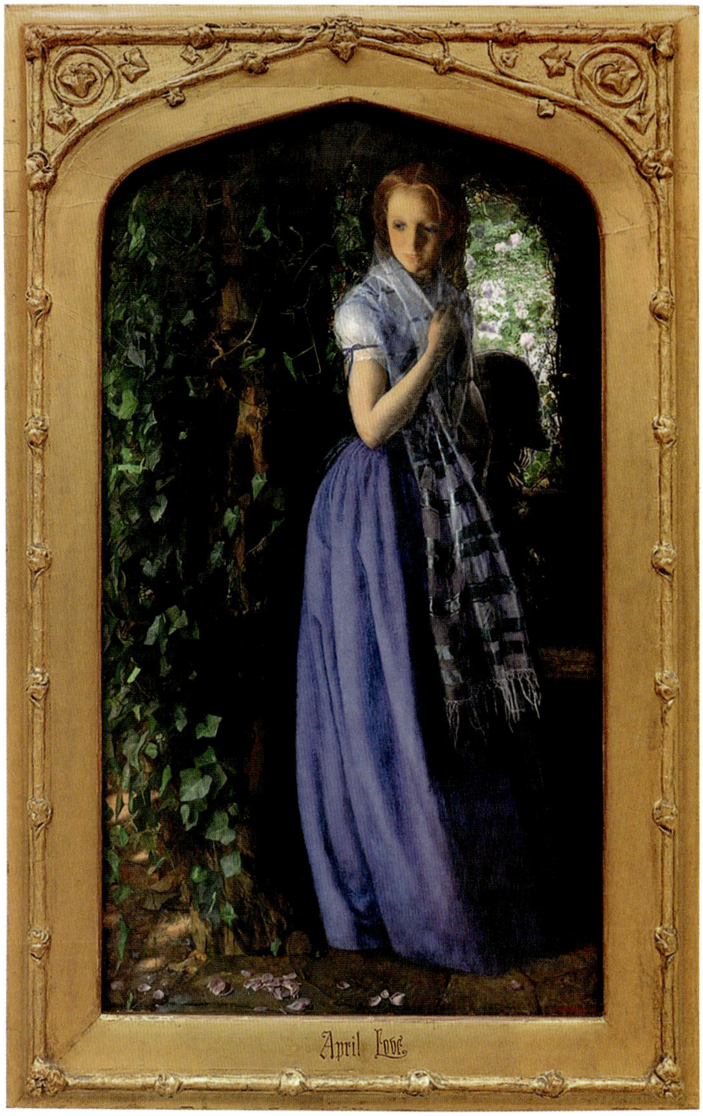

Fig.103 ***April Love*, Arthur Hughes, oil on canvas, 1855–6.**
Tate

in those first years I never wanted to think but as he thought, and all he did and said fitted me through and through.

Like Burne-Jones, Morris also initially aspired to imitate Rossetti. According to Mackail, when Burne-Jones remarked that the designs 'he made in Rossetti's manner seemed better than his own original work, Morris answered with some vehemence, "I have got beyond that: I want to imitate Gabriel as much as I can."' Georgiana Burne-Jones added that the 'close union of mind between Edward and Morris made Rossetti at this time equally a hero to them both' and they came under his influence in equal measure.

Rossetti's own training had included four years at Sass's, the ultra-traditionalist Drawing Academy, and over two years in the Antique School of the Royal Academy. Eager to develop an understanding of colour and the human figure, he took his education into his own hands and sought instruction from Madox Brown and Hunt. He also attended life-drawing classes at the progressive academy on Maddox Street run by the brothers Robert and Lowes Cato Dickinson.

In January 1855 at Ruskin's invitation, Rossetti began to teach watercolour and figure drawing at the recently founded Working Men's College. He advocated life drawing from fellow students and friends rather than professional models, both to save money but also motivated by a collaborative work ethos. Accordingly, Morris's Pre-Raphaelite apprenticeship extended to sitting for a number of Rossetti's key works, not least as the figure of Sir Lancelot in *The Lady of Shalott* illustration for Moxon's edition of Tennyson's *Poems* (1857) and King David in *The Seed of David* triptych at Llandaff Cathedral (1858–64). This practice of sitting for one another was to continue at the firm.

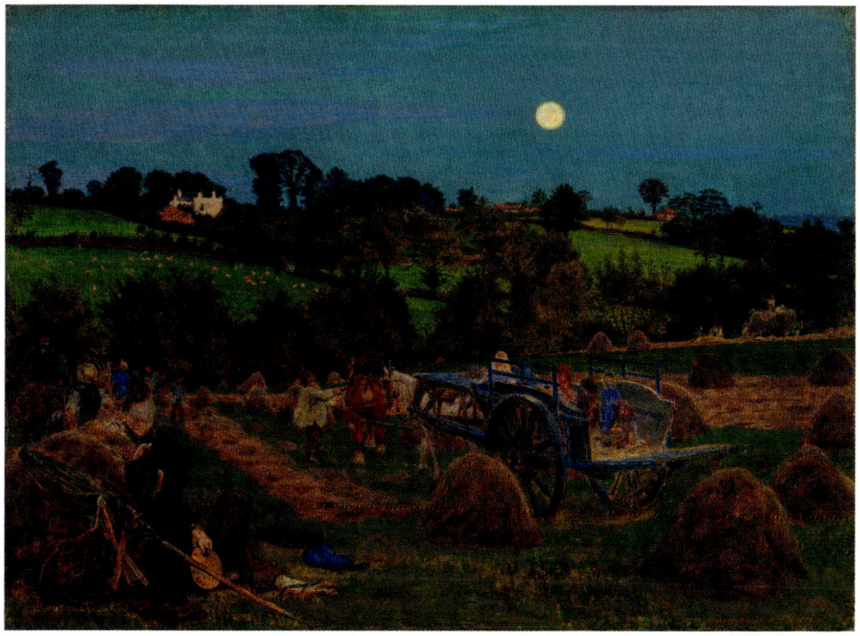

Fig.104 ***The Hayfield*, Ford Madox Brown, oil on panel, 1855–6.** Tate

Rossetti recommended early use of colour, disagreeing with Ruskin's teaching method of monochromatic drawing and modelling. Rossetti believed that design, drawing, expression and colour were the four key 'botherations of a picture', which have to be 'thought of all at once'. His more prosaic logistical considerations included dealing with the elements while working outdoors, procuring and managing models, as well as effective use of lay figures and props. Most importantly, however, Rossetti's approach focused on opening his students' eyes to their own abilities and imagination. As recalled by Val Prinsep, Rossetti considered sentiment, passion and invention as the most important qualities in an artist, far outweighing the mastery of technique.

In August 1856 Morris and Burne-Jones moved into furnished lodgings in Upper Gordon Street, Bloomsbury, coinciding with the relocation of Street's architectural practice to London. According to Mackail, these rooms were rented on account of their proximity to both Street's office in Montague Place and

to the various drawing schools known under the generic name of Gandish's in the neighbourhood of Fitzroy Square ... The double life ... was actually carried on for some time, Morris working at Street's office in the day and going with Burne-Jones to a life school in Newman Street at night.

Gandish's was the fictional art school featured in Thackeray's novel *The Newcomes*. The real-life school attended by Morris and Burne-Jones at 79 Newman Street was Leigh's Academy, set up by the painter James Mathews Leigh in 1848 and later renamed Heatherley's. Leigh's came to rival the well-established Sass's and was more progressive, accepting both male and female students. There were no enrolment requirements. Although copying from the antique was still part of the curriculum, the emphasis was on working from models, encouraging experimentation and peer critique. A number of prominent artists received early training there including Walter Crane, Frederic Leighton and Edward Poynter.

By late November 1856, Morris and Burne-Jones had moved to 17 Red Lion Square. Their unfurnished lodgings consisted of two bedrooms and a north-facing studio-cum-sitting room with 'the middle window cut up to the ceiling for a painting light'. The rooms had been occupied by Rossetti and the painter Walter Deverell just five years earlier. A direct link with Pre-Raphaelitism, this was to be their shared workspace. Burne-Jones's sketch shows two easels – the left-hand one apparently covered in a smock frock, as well as a lay figure, mahl stick, props and other painting paraphernalia (fig.156). Not long after the move, Morris and Burne-Jones had their first proper meeting with Ruskin, who developed the habit of visiting Red Lion Square every Thursday on his way to teach at the Working Men's College. Ruskin would champion their artistic endeavours and had great hopes for both of them.

At the beginning of 1857 Rossetti wrote to his former tutor and now fellow drawing instructor at the Working Men's College, Lowes Cato Dickinson, seeking to admit his protégés to meetings in his studio at Langham Chambers, Langham Place. He vouched for their ability as artists:

> Two friends of mine have already accompanied me thither, and might often like to go when it might not be convenient for me to fetch them; and as they are both stunners as artists and bricks as coves, I venture to make this request: viz: that you will bestow tickets of leave on Edward Jones and William Morris Esqs.

Although documentary evidence is scarce, these meetings, which took place on Saturday evenings, were possibly the private showings of pictures before public exhibition by painters such as Millais and Madox Brown, as well as small displays of lesser-known artists, for fellow artists and collectors, known to have been organized at Langham Place throughout 1856 and 1857.

Following Morris's attendance at Leigh's Academy in the late 1850s, practising life drawing would become his habit over the next decade. A letter to Louisa Baldwin in 1873 implies that he had regularly worked from models until *c.*1867. A large collection of over a hundred figurative drawings spanning the whole period is testimony to both Morris's early training as well as his perseverance in developing the skill (VI.3). Some were clearly created at life-drawing classes; others were executed with specific projects in mind in the 1860s.

In 1856 Morris visited the Low Countries with Street. Mackail wrote that he came back 'fired with a new enthusiasm for painting'. On his return, he adopted Van Eyck's motto, 'Als ich can', which he interpreted as 'If I can' (though it is now translated as 'As I can'). Morris would have been familiar with the artist's exquisite self-portrait, acquired by the National Gallery in 1851, where the motto is prominently emblazoned in Greek letters on the frame. He first incorporated it into crudely worked embroideries that he designed for Red Lion Square (XII.1), and it later appeared in the decorative schemes at Red House (fig.174). It was a way of paying homage to his predecessor and projecting his own artistic identity.

In *Reflections: Van Eyck and the Pre-Raphaelites* (2017), Alison Smith discusses the influence of Van Eyck and particularly his *Arnolfini Portrait* on the development of their radical painting style (fig.107). It was the first early Netherlandish painting acquired by the National Gallery and it caused a sensation when it went on display in 1843. Van Eyck's approach, embodied in this work, was characterized by forensic clarity, microscopic observation and luminous colours. As Smith compellingly argues, it opened up the way for a new modern approach

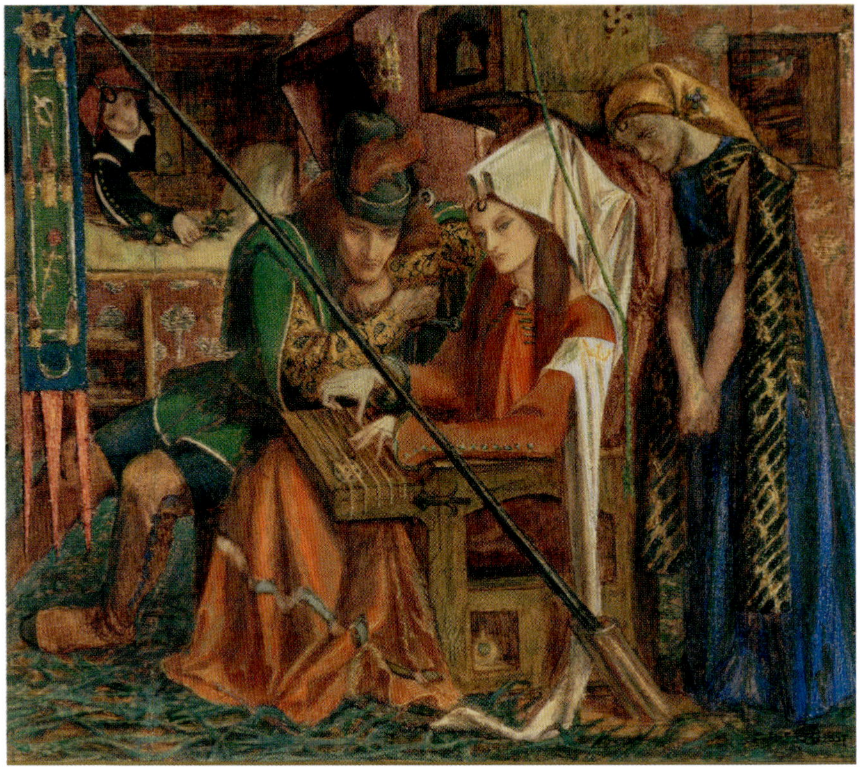

Fig.105 ***The Tune of Seven Towers*, Dante Gabriel Rossetti, watercolour on paper, 1857.**
Tate

to realism as well as symbolism. Pre-Raphaelite artists and subsequent generations of British avant-garde painters would aspire to imitate Van Eyck's mode of painting as well as engage with specific iconographic motifs from his pictures. Elizabeth Prettejohn's *Modern Painters, Old Masters* (2017) has shown that Rossetti had in fact taught himself how to paint in the late 1840s by imitating Van Eyck's technique (as it was then understood). Morris's own ongoing fascination with Van Eyck would manifest itself in multiple ways. In one of his surviving notebooks from the Red House period, he copied the figure of the man (not then identified as Giovanni Arnolfini) (fig.106, British Library Add. MS 45336). His quick sketch and pencil annotations record the fabrics used for his costume. There is no doubt that Morris would have delighted in the technical brilliance with which Van Eyck rendered materials and textures.

The double life of trainee architect by day and artist by night proved difficult to sustain. According to Morris's brief account of his life written for Andreas Scheu in 1883, he gave up Street's practice after just nine months, so by the end of October 1856. In a letter usually dated mid-December 1856, Rossetti wrote to Allingham: 'Morris means to be an architect, & to that end has set about becoming a painter, at which he is making progress.' This interesting comment suggests that Morris and Rossetti saw the two activities as complementary rather than incompatible, a timely idea as the application of colour to architecture was a novelty in the mid-1850s. Following pioneering projects, such as the decoration of the ceiling at Merton College Chapel by John Hungerford Pollen in 1850, practising painting was becoming a new trend among young architects, largely thanks to the influence of the Pre-Raphaelites. However, according to both Mackail and Georgiana Burne-Jones, by the end of 1856 Rossetti had convinced Morris to give up architecture in favour of art.

On 22 April 1857 Morris opened a personal account with the leading artist-materials supplier, Charles Roberson & Co., which he was to retain until his death. The purchase ledgers in the archive of the Hamilton Kerr Institute near Cambridge demonstrate fluidity between Morris and Burne-Jones's accounts with the two men ordering materials for one another. On the very day Morris opened his account, Burne-Jones, who had been a registered customer since January, chose a new easel for Morris. This was probably intended for his first

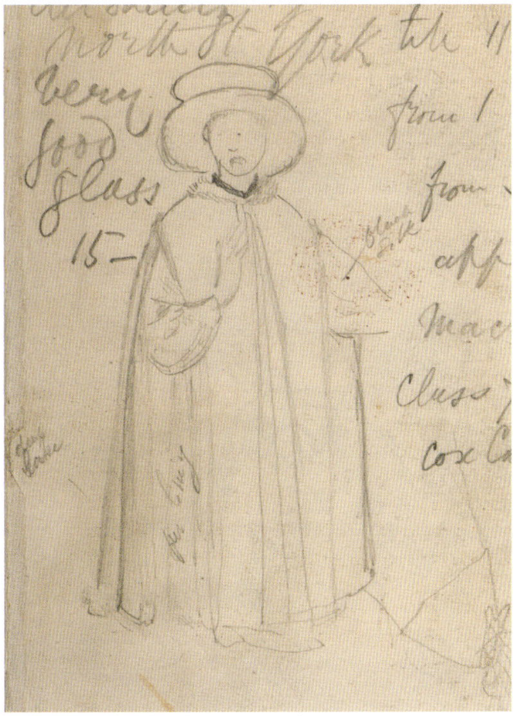

Fig.106 **Pencil sketch of the male figure from the *Arnolfini Portrait* from Morris's notebook, *c.*1859–60.**
British Library

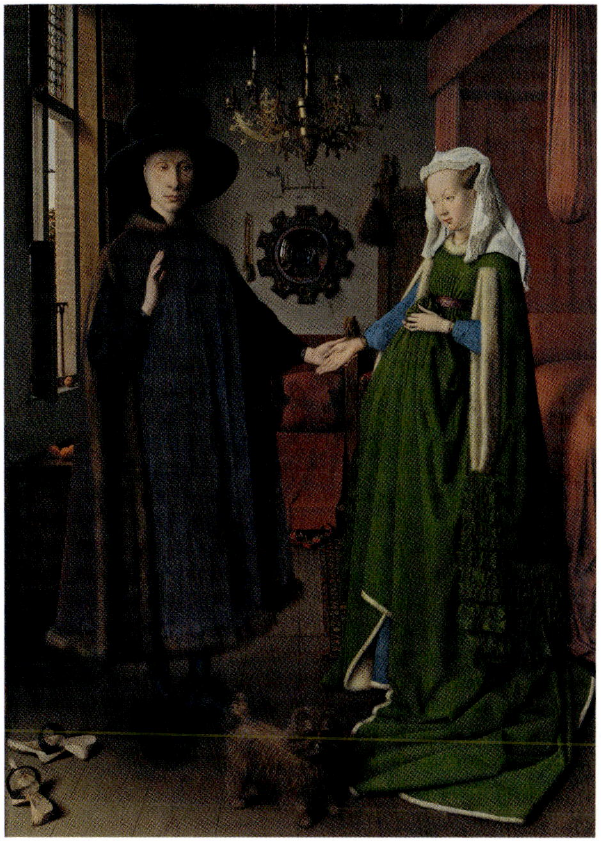

Fig.107 ***Portrait of Giovanni (?) Arnolfini and his Wife*, Jan van Eyck, oil on panel, 1434.**
National Gallery

attempt at oil painting, which was underway by 19 May when Rossetti enquired, 'are you going it still at your picture?' In June, Rossetti included further details in a letter to William Bell Scott:

> Morris has as yet done nothing in art – but is busily painting his first picture at Oxford – the subject from the *Morte d'Arthur* – Sir Tristram after his illness, in the garden of King Mark's palace, recognised by the dog which he had given to Iseult. It is being done all from nature of course, & I believe will turn out capitally.

The same month Morris was seen energetically painting trees in Archibald MacLaren's garden in Summertown, then a small village north of Oxford (returning to resume the work the following summer). MacLaren ran a gymnasium where Burne-Jones and Morris had practised singlestick, boxing and fencing as undergraduates, and a friendship ensued. According to Mackail, 'the holes he dug in the grass by wriggling his chair about as he sat at his easel, and the force of his language when a gust of wind blew the canvas off wet side down, were long remembered'.

The Oxford Union murals (July–November 1857)

Although Morris was yet to complete a single painting, Rossetti invited him to participate in an ambitious collaborative project to decorate the walls of the Oxford Union debating hall in the summer of 1857. Indeed, he used Morris's example to reassure another prospective recruit, Val Prinsep, who was anxious about his own lack of experience, 'That makes no difference – there's one of my friends going to join us who has never painted anything, but you'll see he'll do a stunning thing.' Crucially, it marked Morris's debut both as a painter and a decorator. Though the final results were marred by their lack of technical expertise, the process itself was transformative. Georgiana Burne-Jones claimed that the project 'altered the disposition ... of Morris' whole life.' Even Mackail credited Rossetti for initiating 'the first piece of work which ... began his [Morris's] career as a decorator'. During this time Morris and Burne-Jones lived with Rossetti for four months and received personal tuition from him.

Rossetti was in overall charge and secured the commission from the architect, his friend Benjamin Woodward. According to Burne-Jones, it was Rossetti's idea to base the scheme on Malory's *Morte d'Arthur* and he chose his six collaborators – Morris, Burne-Jones, Hughes, Hungerford Pollen, John Roddam Spencer Stanhope and Prinsep (Hunt and Madox Brown declined invitations). Their task was to paint figurative compositions in the large bays above the gallery that ran around the room. They worked in tempera paints, which were mixed and dispatched to them up the scaffold by a workman. Much has been written about the inadequate preparation of the newly whitewashed brick walls, which caused the originally bright colours to be absorbed into the surface and the rapid deterioration of the designs. This perhaps explains why a contemporaneous caricature made a reference to Morris instructing the workman to add more size to the paints. As has been noted, painted decoration applied to architectural surfaces was a novelty in England at the time – in 1857, the painters William Dyce and George Frederic Watts were both working on ambitious wall paintings in the Houses of Parliament and the Great Hall of Lincoln's Inn respectively. Rossetti described the project as an 'experiment in a style to which I, for one, should like to devote the whole of my time better than to any other branch of the art.'

Morris's mural depicted the lovers Tristram and Iseult embracing, observed by a jealous Sir Palomydes (VI.7). Morris went to great lengths to ensure there would be suitable props available to the artists, who sat to one another according to Pre-Raphaelite custom. To this end, he commissioned a local smith to make a medieval-style suit of armour to his own designs – an ancient

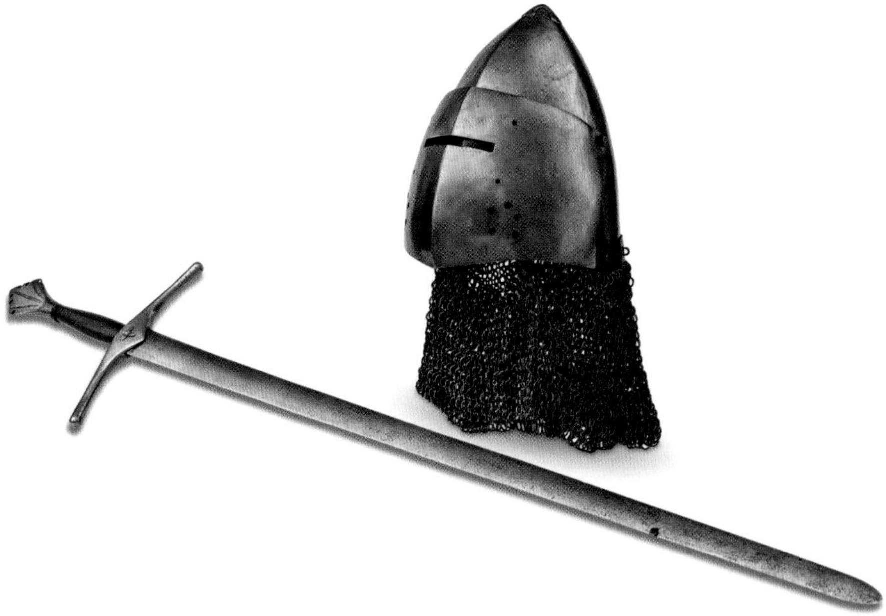

Fig.108 **The helmet and sword Morris commissioned as props for the Oxford Union project, 1857.**
William Morris Gallery

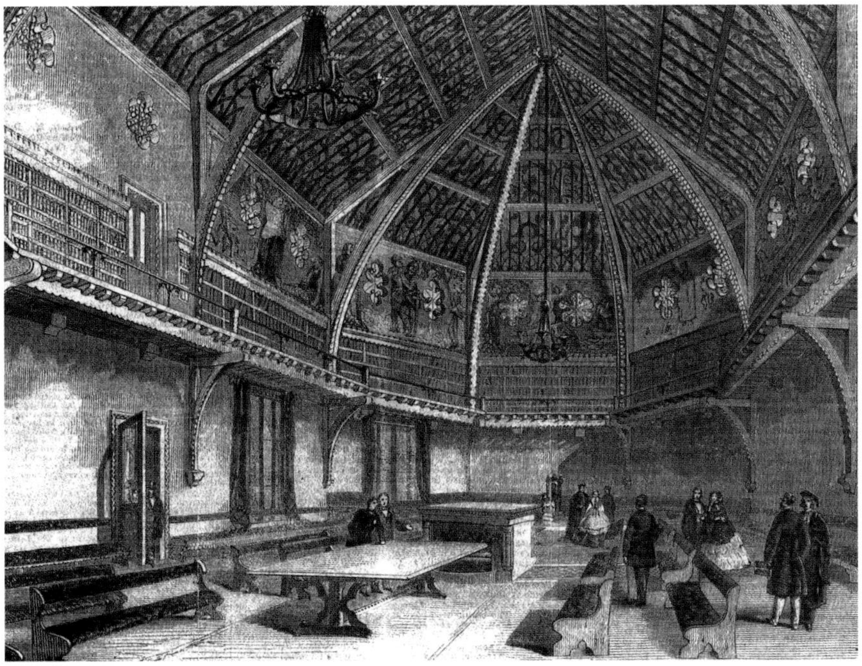

Fig.109 **Oxford Union debating hall, engraving showing the murals still incomplete, *c.*1858.**
The Oxford Union Society

kind of helmet, a great surcoat of ringed mail and a sword (fig.108). Rossetti both encouraged and critiqued his work. According to Prinsep's reminiscences, he ordered Morris to redo the face of Iseult 'from nature', dispatching him to sketch Miss Lipscombe, the daughter of an innkeeper in Godstow. Morris returned crestfallen having failed to persuade her mother to allow her to sit. However, it seems possible that he did eventually repaint Iseult's face from life as her features recall those of Morris's fiancée-to-be Jane Burden, whom he met during the latter months of the project.

As the most conscientious among the painters engaged on the murals, Morris started and finished his wall painting first, subsequently designing a decorative pattern for the ceiling featuring 'quaint beasts and birds' and 'grotesque creatures'. An engraving of *c.*1858 (fig.109) appears to be the only visual record of what this looked like (the ceiling was repainted in 1875 with another design by Morris (figs 22–3)). An enthusiastic account by Coventry Patmore in *The Saturday Review* of 26 December 1857 praised the multisensory effect and luminous colouring of the murals, 'so brilliant as to make the walls look like the margin of a highly-illuminated manuscript.' Owing to the fast deterioration of the murals, it is impossible to determine the effect and impact of Morris's newly finished design. Patmore commended Morris's wall painting and ceiling decoration for 'a real feeling for peculiarly architectural painting', observing that the sunflowers in his picture were a striking example 'of fine artistic power submitting to special material conditions, not only with a good grace, but with delight and profit to itself.' Participating artists gained some distinction, while the ambition of the undertaking seems to have kindled Morris's innate artistic abilities and increased his determination to pursue art.

During his trip to the Manchester Art Treasures Exhibition around this time he produced a watercolour (now untraced) on a subject from *The Arabian Nights*. As recalled by his friend Richard Watson Dixon, Morris 'painted ... at one sitting with the greatest of enthusiasm a picture that he called *The Soldan's Daughter in the Palace of Glass*.' According to Mackail, 'The Soldan's daughter was seated in a heavy wooden armchair, probably studied from one of those at Red Lion Square, and the palace was in all shades of bluish glass.'

The professionalization of Morris's arts practice in 1858

At the beginning of 1858 Morris secured his first paid commission (the Oxford Union murals having been executed for expenses only). Thanks to Rossetti's generous advocacy, his own influential patron, Thomas Plint, purchased Morris's first oil painting, *Sir Tristram in the Garden*, for 75 guineas. The commission, which Rossetti reported to Madox Brown around 21 January, was subject to the picture's completion and Morris continued to work on it throughout that year. Although it remains untraced, its likely composition is known from Morris's later stained-glass design (fig.110) and the actual window, created in 1862 for Harden Grange in Yorkshire, may hint at the original colouring. Plint's commission was an important mark of professional validation as the Leeds-based stockbroker was a notable Pre-Raphaelite art collector. March saw the publication of Morris's first volume of poetry, *The Defence of Guenevere*. Dedicated to Rossetti, it contained a number of poems composed in response to his pictures, including 'The Blue Closet' and 'The Tune of Seven Towers'.

In the spring Morris helped to found the Hogarth Club – a private exhibiting society for artists, collectors and critics. Its significance and operations are discussed in Deborah Cherry's article, 'The Hogarth Club: 1858–1861' (1980). The Club was the culmination of a sustained campaign by Madox Brown, Rossetti and their circle to establish an exhibiting association that would give them independence of the Royal Academy. It was named after William Hogarth, held in high regard by the group as the father of modern art. The first official meeting on 4 May took place at Morris and Burne-Jones's rooms in Red Lion Square, the same occasion at which the artist George Price Boyce noted their 'gorgeously painted' furniture.

Membership of the Hogarth Club provided access to the heart of the avant-garde art world. The social aspect was important and its activities also extended to life-drawing classes. Members included Ruskin, Hunt, Watts, Leighton and architects such as Street and George Frederick Bodley. The Club held 'invitation only' exhibitions at its premises at 178 Piccadilly, and subsequently at 6 Waterloo Place. Although works of fine art constituted the majority of exhibits, after some heated debate designs for the decorative arts, including furniture and stained glass, were also accepted, marking the integration of the arts that Morris was to champion throughout the rest of his career. Unfortunately, printed catalogues do not seem to have been produced, so it is not known if Morris ever exhibited. Burne-Jones showed *The Prioress's Tale* wardrobe in 1860 (IX.5), where it was deemed to emulate the work of Giotto, and it is possible that Morris also exhibited some of his medieval-style painted furniture before the Club was dissolved in December 1861. Despite its short existence and internal wrangling, membership allowed Morris and his future partners in the firm to meet many of the designers and architects with whom they would collaborate in the 1860s.

Morris spent much of 1858 in Oxford for artistic and personal reasons, announcing his engagement to Jane Burden in the spring. He began an ambitious new oil painting modelled from his fiancée, again inspired by Malory's *Morte d'Arthur*. As Jan Marsh has demonstrated in 'William Morris's Painting and Drawing' (1986), the subject was *La Belle Iseult* (VI.12). Accompanied by the little dog given to her by Sir Tristram, Iseult is shown in front of an unmade bed fastening her girdle, confined to her chamber after a suicide attempt (Chapter XX, Book IX, *Morte d'Arthur*). Surviving preparatory studies and a bespoke replica of a medieval dress used by Morris as a prop, offer insights into his creative process (VI.9–11). Conceived as a direct homage to Van Eyck's *Arnolfini Portrait*, according to Webb the picture caused Morris much trouble, but taught him how to paint. It appears he was still busy working on it at the end of the following year and possibly during the early years at Red House; the pattern on Iseult's dress mirrors that on several works from the early 1860s including the canopy in the left-hand panel of the *St George* cabinet (1861–2) (IX.14).

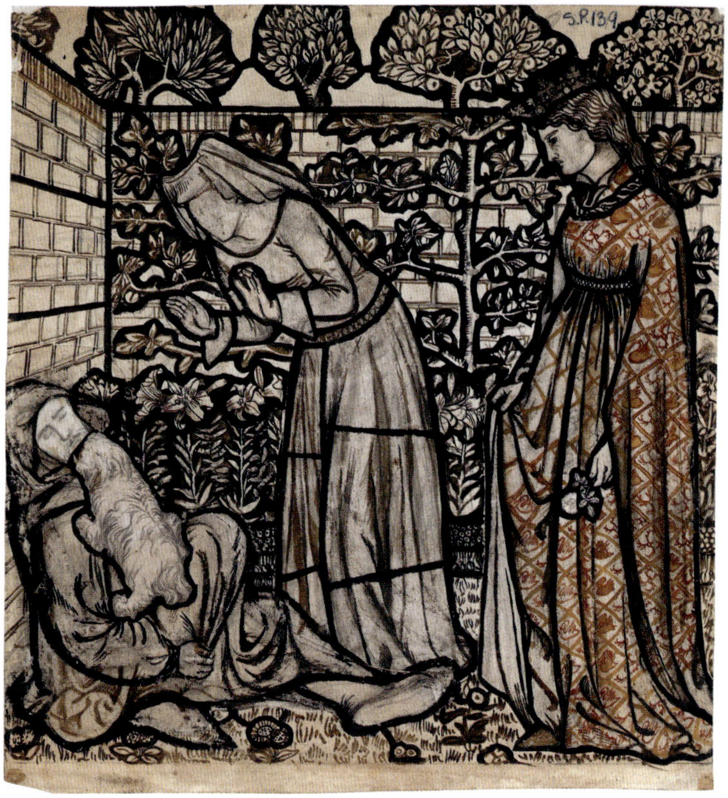

Fig.110 ***Sir Tristram recognized by the dog he has given to Iseult*, cartoon for stained glass, William Morris, pencil, sepia wash and watercolour on paper, 1862.**
V&A (E.572–1940)

Towards the end of June 1858, Rossetti wrote to William Bell Scott that Morris had made 'great advances as an artist' since working on his Oxford Union mural and that he planned to enlist his help to complete the remaining murals over the long vacation. As Rossetti's reputation was at stake, choosing Morris as his collaborator was a mark of confidence in his developing skill. Unfortunately, negotiations with the Union Committee fell through and their estimate was refused. Eventually the Oxford-based artists William and Briton Riviere completed the scheme. Later that summer, Morris returned to northern France, this time in the company of Webb and Charles Faulkner. They made drawings of Gothic cathedrals, but the chief result of the holiday was conceiving the idea for building Red House, Morris's first marital home. The detailed design of Red House, which took shape the following year, included a painter's studio-cum-study.

Though it seems very unlikely that he completed either picture, over the next few years Morris continued to work on *La Belle Iseult* and Plint's commission. Rossetti was probably spurring him on. On 5 September 1859 he wrote to Boyce, 'Top is getting on splendidly (really) with his little picture which promises to be quite surprising.' Two months later he told Bell Scott, 'Morris is very forward with a little picture which promises really to be as good as his poems; & you know that is saying a great deal.' This was probably *La Belle Iseult*, the dimensions of which were modest and others, including Burne-Jones, referred to it as 'that little picture'. On 23 April 1861, in response to an enquiry from Plint, Madox Brown gave an update on Morris's progress on his Tristram subject:

> it is now at my house and at my suggestion he [Morris] has so altered it that it is quite a fresh work ... I take as much interest in Morris's picture turning out good as though it were my own for although it was not commissioned on my recommendation I have repeatedly since told you that Morris is a man of genius.

Plint died shortly afterwards, apparently without ever receiving the picture, which remains untraced. Morris always doubted his pictorial abilities, later claiming that he lacked the '*painters memory* [*sic*] which makes it easy to put down on paper what you think you see; nor indeed can I see any scene with a frame as it were round it'. Nevertheless, the practice of painting and figure drawing, which he developed as an aspiring painter, would prove instrumental for creating his distinctive decorative scheme at Red House and for setting up his interior decoration company.

Red House interiors: a 'House of Love' (1860–5)

In Mackail's words, Morris put 'much of his best thought and work' into decorating Red House, which became his 'canvas to work upon'. Figurative compositions in the form of murals, painted furniture, wall hangings and stained glass were to constitute much of the decoration. Morris's vision for Red House offers a revealing insight into his iconographic preoccupations as an artist and his surviving working designs show skill and invention as a draughtsman (VI.14, 16, 18–21). The project also yielded another oil painting, *Venus* (VI.17). As Julia Dudkiewicz first proposed in the article 'Kelmscott Manor *Venus* and William Morris's idea for a "House of Love" at Red House' (2016), this picture has proven to be the key to unlocking the symbolism of Morris's elaborate decorative scheme.

The decoration of Red House was a collaborative project, both conceptually and practically. Shortly after the Morrises moved into their new home in the summer of 1860, Burne-Jones came over for a working holiday to help Morris plan the details of the scheme. Burne-Jones, Madox Brown, Rossetti, Elizabeth Siddal and possibly Webb all contributed to the figurative decorations. Around 18 September Rossetti reported that Madox Brown had gone to 'join Morris who is out of reach at Upton and with them is married Jones painting the inner walls of the house that Top built.' On 8 December Rossetti himself made his way to Red House 'to paint a panel there'.

With the help of his friends, Morris conceived a pictorial 'House of Love', inviting reflection on different facets and changing fortunes of love. This was a fitting thematic concept as Red House was built as an ideal marital home for Morris and his bride. His notebook from this period contains early ideas for a 'Court of Love', a related unrealized pictorial design. The sketch indicates an enthroned personification of love surrounded by pairs of lovers from Arthurian and mythological sources, including Lancelot and Guenevere, Tristram and Iseult, Paris and Helen and Orpheus and Eurydice. The interconnected forces of love and fate jointly encapsulate the overarching idea for the choice of all the decorative subjects intended for the newlyweds' first home. The *Sir Degrevaunt* murals in the drawing room by Burne-Jones were inspired by the fifteenth-century romance of courtly love that culminates in a wedding. The *Genesis* mural in the master bedroom alludes to three of the Bible's most striking love stories (VI.8). The embroidered wall hangings in the dining room, designed by Morris, invite reflection on different types of love. The unrealized murals envisaged for the hall were to illustrate the Legend of Troy, a war sparked by desire for a woman.

The partially realized dining-room embroidery scheme deserves special attention on account of its complex iconography and the surviving figurative cartoons drawn by Morris (VI.18–21). The series was to include 12 full-length figures of saints, queens and goddesses, representing a wide spectrum of love and relationships. To date ten of the characters have been identified: Venus (Aphrodite), Artemis, Penelope, Guenevere, Lucretia, Hippolyte, Helen of Troy, Catherine of Alexandra, Saint Cecilia and Mary Magdalene. Related to the concept of Chaucer's *Legend of Good Women*, Morris's personal selection of heroines was drawn from a wide range of sources, including Jacobus de Voragine's *The Golden Legend*, Malory's *Morte d'Arthur* and Shakespeare's *Midsummer Night's Dream*. Morris represented each figure with an attribute and headgear, such as a crown or halo, signifying their identity. He also endowed them with the look of Pre-Raphaelite 'stunners' – red hair, pronounced lips and long necks. The characters chosen symbolize different facets of love – from carnal desire through to romantic love and religious devotion. The figures would have invited reflection on themes as diverse as faithfulness and infidelity, desire and abduction, elopement and abandonment, virtue and celibacy, as well as the dangers of extreme love.

The figure of Venus – goddess of love, beauty, desire and fertility – was key to the scheme. Though the embroidery was only partially completed (fig.144), the full intended iconography can be deduced from the oil painting (VI.17) that Morris and Burne-Jones later developed from the now lost cartoon. It follows long-established depictions of the birth of Venus, showing a full-length female nude emerging from the water towards the seashore, with long red hair, a rose wreath, a garland of roses around the figure's hips and foam from the sea. It was likely inspired by Sandro Botticelli's renditions of the topic, both the *Birth of Venus* (1482–5, Uffizi) and *Venus Pudica*, featuring a similar garland, sold at Christie's in London in 1863 (then thought to be an autograph work by the artist though now attributed to his workshop). The painting reflects both friends' lifelong preoccupation with the goddess of love, which they jointly and individually pursued in a number of projects. Its creation may have been triggered by the decision to leave Red House in 1865, and the desire to create a lasting memento of the overall decorative scheme.

Fine Art Workmen: the role of painters and painting in the firm

The founding of Morris, Marshall, Faulkner & Co. in the spring of 1861 took place in parallel with decorating the interiors at Red House. Painting, particularly murals, was one of the principal services offered by the new firm and its early advertising materials made much of the partners' expertise in this area. Described as 'Fine Art Workmen', their first prospectus claimed that as 'Artists of reputation ... they will be able to undertake any species of decoration, mural or otherwise, from pictures, properly so called, down to the consideration of the smallest work susceptible of art beauty.' According to Mackail, 'in this interesting document it is not difficult to trace the slashing hand and imperious accent of Rossetti'. It is notable that four of the partners were painters and that Arthur Hughes was named in the prospectus although he quickly withdrew. Val Prinsep and Simeon Solomon would also contribute designs. As the same document confirms, the intention was never to abandon their individual 'pictorial labours' but to bring these skills to bear on the decorative arts, and by working collaboratively, to enrich both spheres. In January 1862 Rossetti described the aspiration for their burgeoning business to 'have a shop like Giotto! and a sign over the door!!'

In 1858, in a lecture 'On the Future of Art in England', Morris's former employer, the architect George Edmund Street, had praised the revolution that the Pre-Raphaelites had brought about in painting, particularly their treatment of colour. He argued that 'three-fourths of the poetry of a building lies in its minor details', and urged painters to join forces with architects to bring about a similar revival in the decoration of ecclesiastical and secular buildings, specifically by applying their talents to wall painting and stained glass. Singling out the Oxford Union mural scheme (the colours were still vibrant at this date) and Rossetti's commission to paint the reredos at Llandaff Cathedral, he called upon his fellow architects to acknowledge that 'it is necessary to enlist men who are *really* painters to assist in our works.' Through their membership of the Hogarth Club and the contemporaneous Medieval Society, Morris and the firm's future partners had been immersed in debates concerning the interrelationship of different branches of the arts for several years and this would have contributed to the conception of their business venture.

Red House was a crucial laboratory of ideas, but the origins of the firm can be traced further back. In a letter of 19 April 1861 to his former tutor, the Reverend Frederick Guy, Morris stated: 'I have started as a decorator which I have long meant to do when I could get men of reputation to join me, and to this end mainly I have built my fine house.' According to Aymer Vallance, the idea was first mooted in 1859. As Oswald Doughty

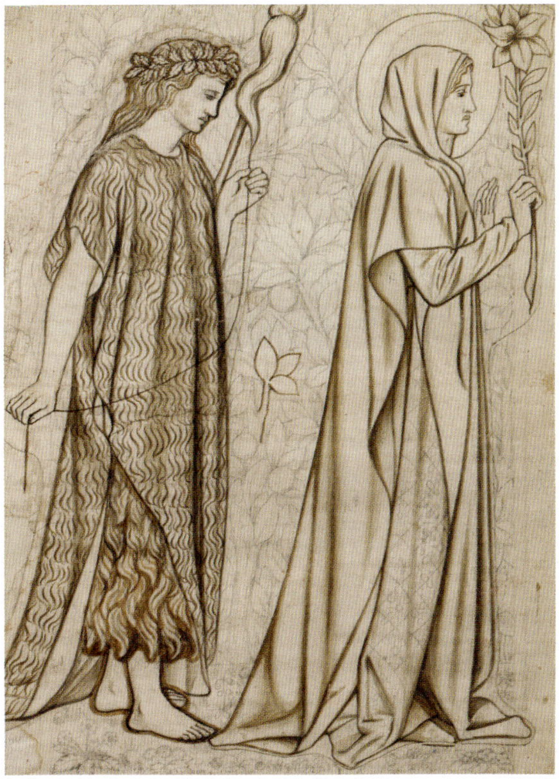

Fig.111 ***Eve and the Virgin*, cartoon for stained glass, William Morris, pencil and sepia wash on paper, 1864.**
William Morris Gallery

demonstrated, ever since the foundation of the Pre-Raphaelite Brotherhood, Rossetti and Hunt had 'discussed the debased state of applied art in Victorian England, the need of a revival of the sense of beauty in architecture, furniture, fabrics and ornaments, as well as in painting. For Hunt, Rossetti and Brown, long before Morris, saw the need which Morris was to meet later.' Morris's apprenticeship in painting brought him into contact with these progressive views, and his early experiments, such as the painted furniture at Red Lion Square, gave them practical expression.

Mackail's unpublished notes, compiled in preparation for writing *The Life of William Morris*, record that according to Burne-Jones the idea for the firm was conceived by Rossetti, 'It was DGR's idea; he saw money in it'. Fiona MacCarthy has argued that Mackail's public narrative in *The Life* was characterized by the omission of uncomfortable truths, describing his practices as a 'conspiracy of memory'. It is therefore more notable that *The Life* did not entirely suppress Burne-Jones's insights about Rossetti's key role: 'The first notion of the firm ... sprang up among the friends in talk, and cannot be assigned to any single author. It was in a large measure due to Madox Brown; but perhaps even more to Rossetti, who, poet and idealist as he was, had business qualities of a high order'. Morris was certainly not the only one fashioning his own interiors. In January 1861, just a few months before the firm launched, Rossetti was designing a striking wallpaper for his drawing room featuring fruit trees, which he planned to have 'printed on common brown packing paper and on blue grocer's paper, to try which is best.' The main partners undoubtedly had a strong sense of shared purpose and identity, which had come about through five years of working collaboratively or in close proximity.

The painted decoration of architectural surfaces was a key component of the firm's early commissions. This aspect of its work tends to be less well known as, where it survives, it remains *in situ* and cannot travel to exhibitions. Morris explicitly stated in his letter to Guy, 'what we are most anxious to get at present is wall-decoration'. At St Michael and All Angels in Brighton, Morris and his associates painted the ceiling of the chancel with their own hands and their work for Bodley at Scarborough featured many painted elements, including a painted pulpit (fig.120). The nave ceiling of Jesus College Chapel, Cambridge, was one of their most splendid achievements in this field, with angels designed by Morris (fig.126). While the execution of this type of painted decoration was increasingly delegated to subcontractors, its origins owed to the partners' own practical experience.

The firm's first public showcase at the International Exhibition of 1862 featured elaborately painted furniture. One of Morris's personal contributions was the decoration of the *St George* cabinet, with a series of narrative paintings to his own designs (IX.14). Morris's pen and ink studies for each of the scenes survive. Despite their technical imperfection and partial state of finish, as a set they count among the most impactful Pre-Raphaelite drawings. They are characterized by remarkable emotive charge as well as storytelling and compositional invention, attesting to Morris's continuing development as a pictorial artist (VI.24). As Douglas E. Schoenherr has argued, 'Drawing was the foundation of William Morris's art and the basis upon which the achievement of Morris & Co. rested. Before there could be a stained-glass window, an embroidery, a wallpaper, a tile, or a font of type, there had to be a drawing.' Schoenherr points out that Morris produced 'an amazing number of designs – 174 cartoons for stained glass, for example ... an achievement as a draughtsman that has scarcely been recognized.'

The majority of his figurative designs for the firm were produced in the 1860s when he continued to practise drawing from life. Some of the most accomplished, for example, his *Eve and the Virgin* for All Saints, Middleton Cheney, Northamptonshire (1864), are dignified and well-formed, showing his instinctive feeling for pattern and appreciation of the requirements of the medium (fig.111). May Morris recognized that these early figurative designs were 'entirely adapted to their purpose, the draperies nobly ... designed.' Some of these cartoons went on display after Morris's death at the New Gallery in 1898. The following year a feature in *The Quarterly Review*, 'William Morris, Poet and Artist', commended them for their 'noble simplicity' and singled out a King Alfred, described as 'bright as an ivory carving', perhaps partly due to its sculptural linearity. The drawing shows the humanity of the king, whose facial expression and knotted eyebrows suggest the weight of his responsibility as a ruler (fig.112).

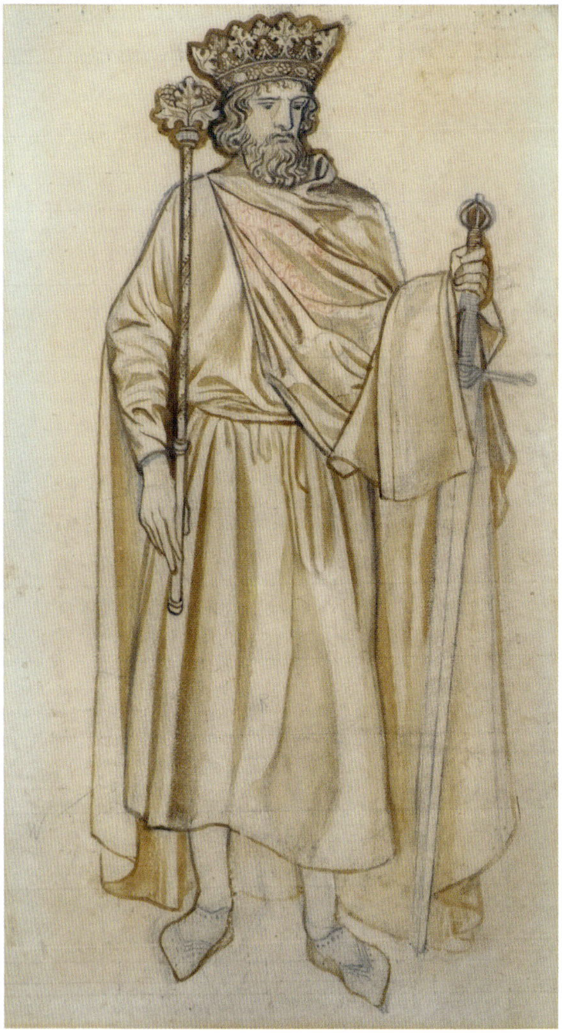

Fig.112 ***King Alfred*, cartoon for stained glass, William Morris, pencil, sepia wash and watercolour on paper, *c.*1865.**
William Morris Gallery

In 1864, when plans to extend and share Red House with the Burne-Joneses fell through, Morris proposed leasing a joint studio in London with Burne-Jones and Spencer Stanhope, hinting at his continuing aspiration to paint. However, from the late 1860s, he grew increasingly despondent concerning his drawing abilities. Having abandoned life drawing around 1867, Morris half-heartedly returned to sketching in the early 1870s. He took watercolours on his first expedition to Iceland in the summer of 1871, though his Icelandic journal confirms he hardly touched them. Visiting Kirkjubøur in the Faroes en route, he wrote, 'I am sorry to say though, that I spoilt it for myself somewhat by making an imbecile sketch of the stead and its surroundings' (fig.113). Despite his own harsh critique, he carefully inscribed it on the reverse with a description and date. When it came to evoking the qualities of a landscape Morris always found this easier in words. The surviving sketch, however, conveys his interest in vernacular architecture and its synergy with the natural landscape.

The pressing need to expand the firm's workshops at Queen Square prompted Morris to relocate his family's living accommodation. In November 1872 he and Jane went to view 7 Theresa Terrace, Hammersmith, the former home of the landscape painter George Heming Mason, which must have had generous studio space as he painted some of his largest works there. Although they eventually moved to Horrington House in Chiswick, Morris's interest in Mason's house hints at an intention to resume fine art. In October 1873 he wrote to Louisa Baldwin (Georgiana's sister) of his decision to take up life drawing again, 'it seems I must needs try to make myself unhappy with doing what I find difficult – or impossible – so I am going to take to drawing from models again, for my soul's health chiefly, for little hope can I have ever to do anything serious in the thing'. Around the end of the year, he engaged the professional Italian model Angelo Colarossi, who sat for many Victorian artists including Watts and Leighton. This was the period of some of Morris's finest illuminated manuscripts, and it seems that he wanted to do more of the figurative illustrations himself. In a letter to his collaborator, Charles Fairfax Murray, on 18 February 1874 he wrote, 'I wish the devil I could do the pictures. A month or two ago I actually began having Colorossi [*sic*]

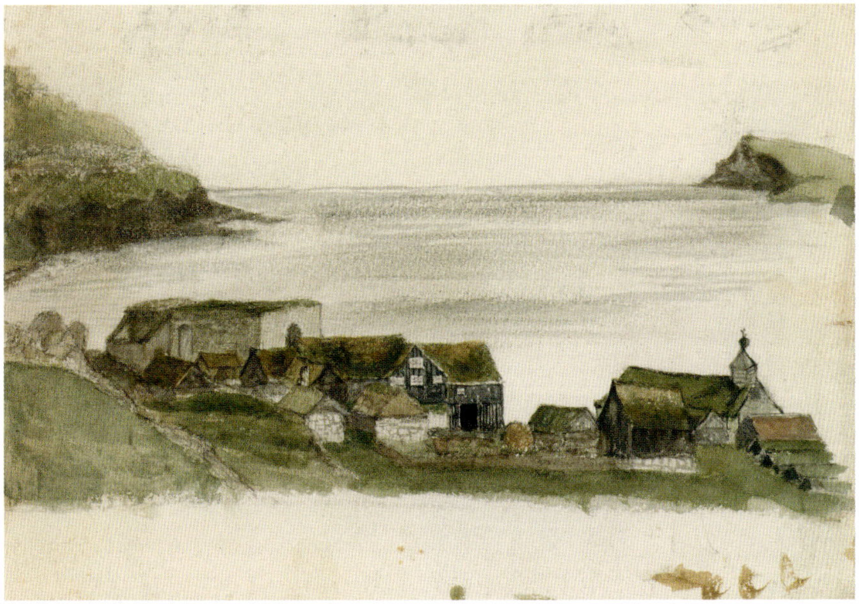

Fig.113 **Sketch of the farmstead at Kirkjubøur, Faroes, William Morris, pencil and watercolour on paper, dated 11 July 1871.** Ashmolean Museum, University of Oxford

here to draw from, & did some very disheartening studies from him, & at last gave it up after making myself a laughing-stock by sending away [*sic*] about every other time.' This is believed to be Morris's final documented effort at figure drawing from life.

In later life Morris did not visit picture galleries often (a review of a Royal Academy exhibition in 1884 was signed 'By a Rare Visitor'). Nevertheless, he continued to surround himself with pictorial art including Pre-Raphaelite portraits of his wife and daughters, such as the large-scale *Mrs Morris* commissioned from Rossetti (1868), German woodcuts, not least Dürer's 'Apocalypse' series (1498), *Melencolia* (1514) and several woodcuts from the monumental sixteenth-century series *The Triumph of Maximilian I*. He also acquired an etching of Botticelli's *Primavera* on vellum made by Feliks Stanisław Jasiński and published by Arthur Tooth in 1892, which hung in his Hammersmith study. Many of these works are now at Kelmscott Manor, alongside Rossetti's collection of Old Masters, which remained at the house throughout Morris's tenure.

Although many discussions of Morris's painting and drawing have revolved around his alleged lack of skill, his efforts in these fields were vitally important to his evolution as a designer and the development of the firm. From the start, and with Rossetti's encouragement, architectural surfaces, furniture, manuscripts and soon stained-glass windows took their place alongside easel painting as 'canvases', requiring skills in draughtsmanship, composition, expression and colour that he was mastering. In a lecture of 1880, 'The Beauty of Life', Morris spoke of the Pre-Raphaelites' ground-breaking artistic revolution,

> I have genuine difficulty of speaking to you of men who are my own personal friends, nay my masters: still ... never in the whole history of art did any set of men come nearer to the feat of making something out of nothing than that little knot of painters who have raised English art from what it was, when as a boy I used to go to the Royal Academy Exhibition, to what it is now.

A decade later, in 1891 he gave an address on 'The Collection of Paintings of the English Pre-Raphaelite School' at Birmingham Museum and Art Gallery, identifying the four defining characteristics of Pre-Raphaelitism as: working from nature, narrative impulse, decorative quality including ornamentation and harmony of colour, and last but not least romance ('rather to be felt than defined'). Looking back at the entirety of Morris's pictorial output – paintings, drawings and figurative designs for the firm – his pictorial idiom was certainly Pre-Raphaelite according to these criteria.

Without Rossetti's formative influence and practical help, the experience of the Oxford Union project, and Morris's 'Pre-Raphaelite apprenticeship', it is inconceivable that the firm would have taken the form that it did – a collective of mostly painters with a focus on murals and painted decoration in its early days. If Rossetti conceived the idea, it was, however, Morris's unique combination of business skills, capital and genius for ornament, together with his tireless energy, which must be credited for bringing the firm to life, shaping it, and branching out into lines of decorative arts not originally envisaged – making a lasting impact on public taste and accomplishing international success. In the penultimate year of his life, Morris paid a tribute to Rossetti by publishing a Kelmscott Press edition of 'Hand and Soul', his former mentor's Pre-Raphaelite manifesto.

VI.1

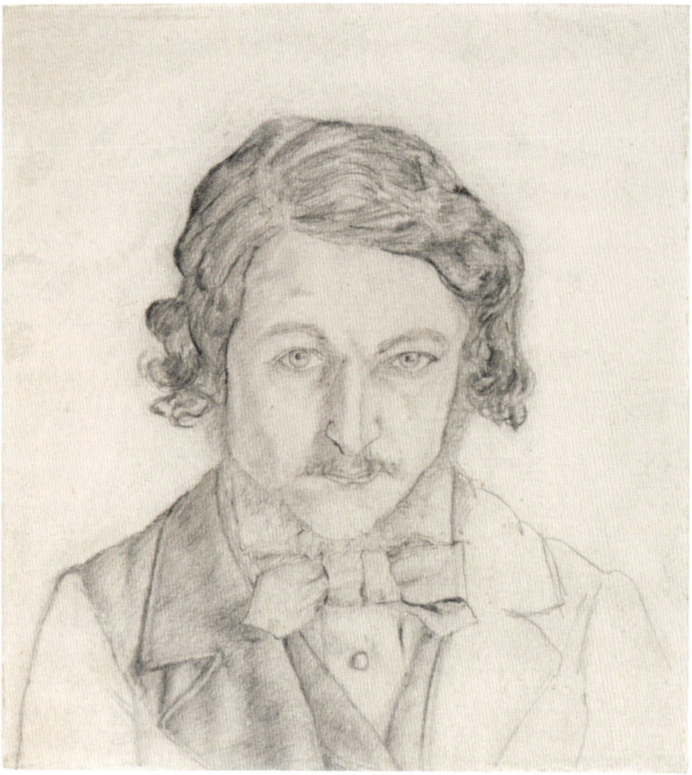

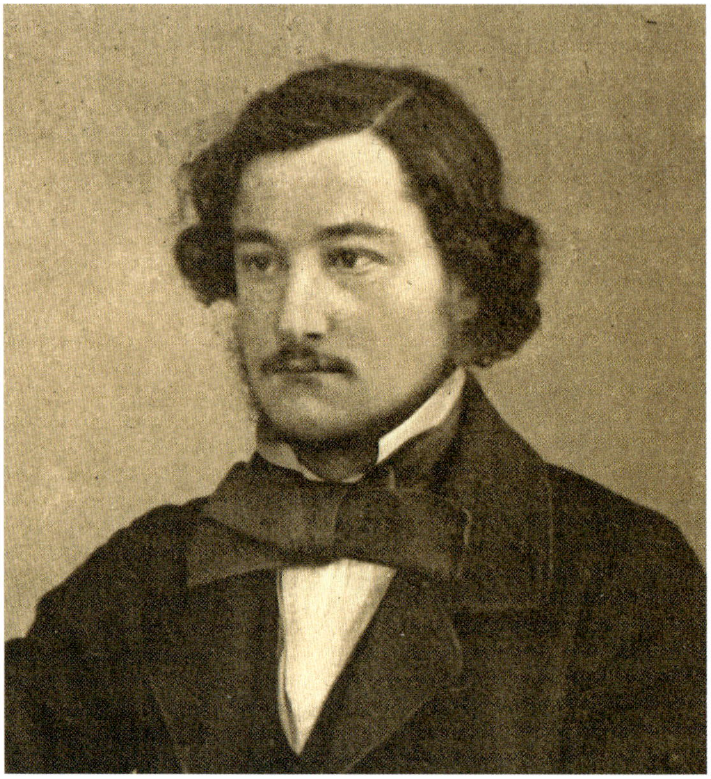

VI.2

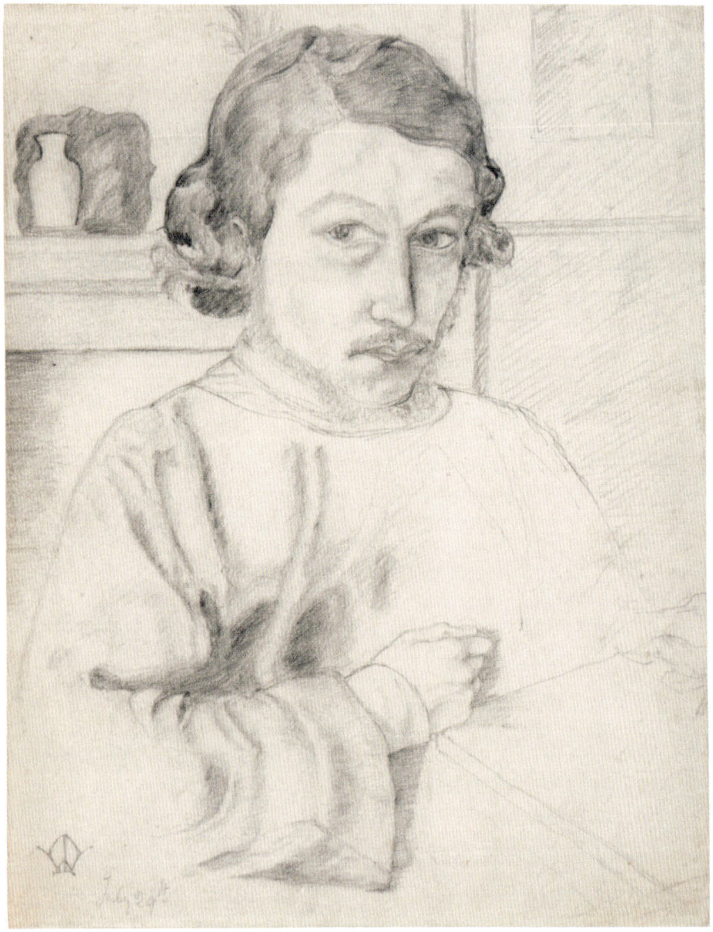

Fig.114 **Studio portrait of Morris aged 23 (detail), unknown photographer, *c.*1857.**
William Morris Gallery

VI.1
Self-portrait
William Morris, *c.*1856
Pencil on paper, 20.8 x 19.3 cm
V&A (E.377–1946)
Given by Dr Reginald Campbell Thompson

The bust-length format and formal dress recall Rossetti's own self-portrait produced almost a decade earlier while a student at the Royal Academy Schools (1847, National Portrait Gallery). Morris's countenance, especially his pursed lips, suggests a mixture of concentration and perhaps frustration as he resolved to master the new skill of drawing. He is shown sporting a moustache and beard, which he grew after graduating from Oxford at the end of 1855.

VI.2
Self-portrait
William Morris, *c.*1857
Pencil on paper, 28.5 x 22.1 cm
Inscribed: 'July 29th'
V&A (E.376–1946)
Given by Dr Reginald Campbell Thompson

Morris consciously projects his artistic identity, depicting himself in a painter's smock in the act of creating his self-portrait. The fact that he added his Pre-Raphaelite style monogram and a date suggests that he was pleased with the result. It may have been completed during the Oxford Union murals project in the summer of 1857 when Morris was 23. According to fellow artist Val Prinsep, while at work Morris 'was duly clad in a smock frock'.

VI.3a

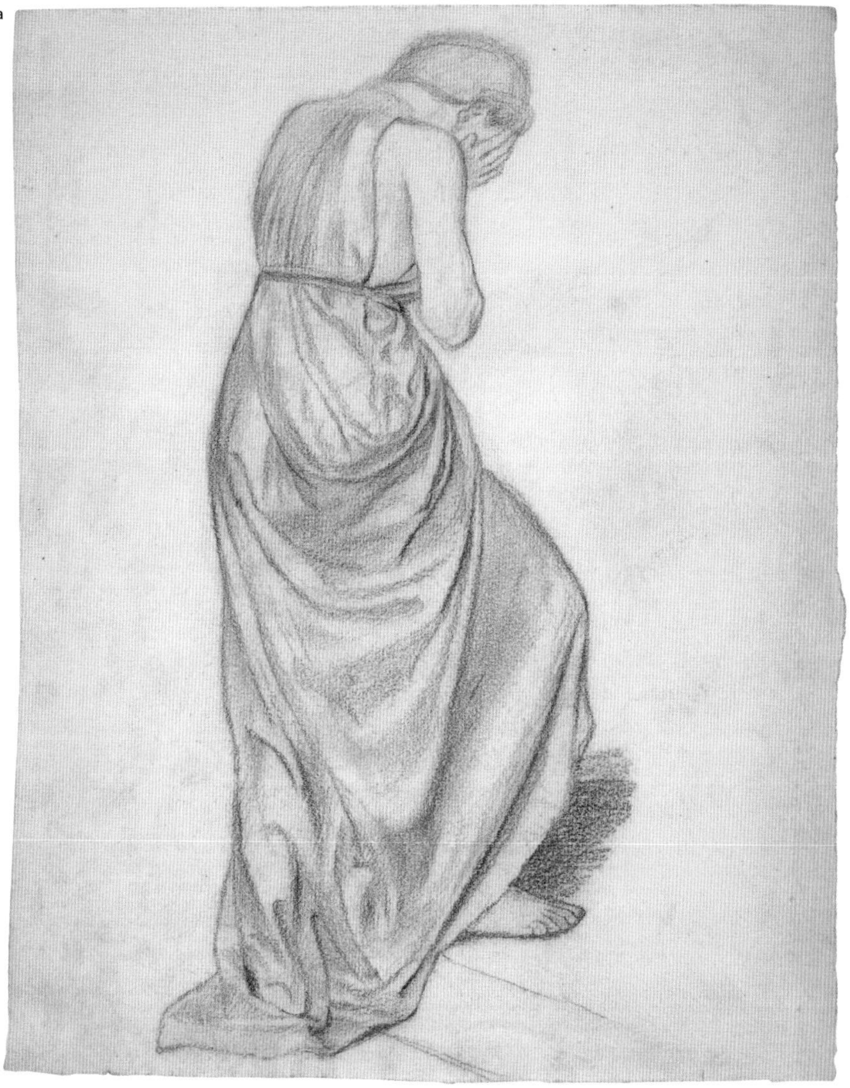

VI.3b

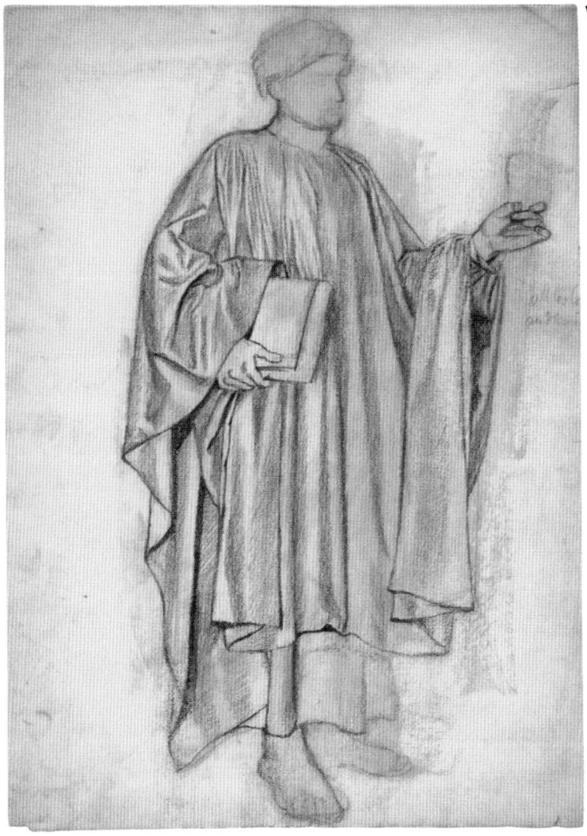

VI.3c

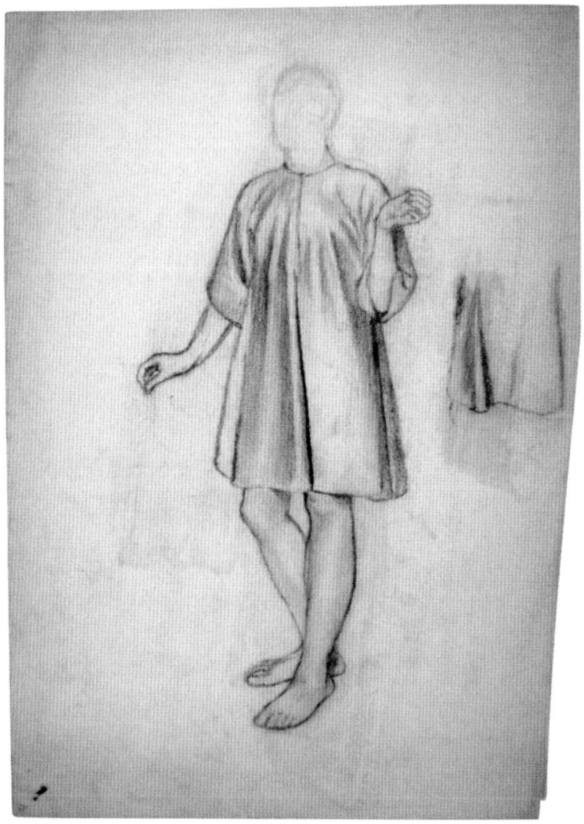

VI.3
Life-drawing studies
William Morris
The Huntington Library, Art Museum and Botanical Gardens

a Standing female figure, *c.*1861
Graphite on paper, 40 x 22.9 cm
(2000.5.16)

b Male figure in a dalmatic, *c.*1857
Graphite and wash on paper, 38.7 x 27.9 cm
(2000.5.285)

c Standing figure in a tunic, *c.*1861
Graphite on paper, 38.7 x 28.3 cm
(2000.5.22)

Morris regularly practised life drawing between 1856 and *c.*1867 and over a hundred of his figurative drawings have survived, the majority in the Huntington's collection. They depict male and female subjects, often with elaborate drapery. The figure in a tunic, in a formal contrapposto pose, may have been made at a life class. Linda Parry has linked the figure in a dalmatic to an entry in Crom Price's diary for 18 October 1857, made during the Oxford Union murals project: 'To Rossetti's ... [Val] Prinsep there; six feet one, 15 stone, not fat, well-built, hair like fine wire, short, curly and seamless – age only 19. Stood for Top for two hours in a dalmatic.' Morris also worked from models to create figurative designs for Red House's decorative schemes and for the firm. The standing female figure may have been an unrealized idea for one of Princess Sabra's poses for the *St George* cabinet (IX.14).

VI.4

Women at their Toilette

Attributed to William Morris in collaboration with Dante Gabriel Rossetti and Edward Burne-Jones, *c.*1857

Oil on deal, clockwise left to right: 69.6 x 48 cm, 69.5 x 43.5 cm, 69.2 x 41 cm x 69.5 x 41 cm (excluding batons)

Ashmolean Museum, University of Oxford

These unfinished paintings of medieval women at their toilette decorate the inside of *The Prioress's Tale* wardrobe doors (IX.5). Technical examination by Jevon Thistlewood in 2019 revealed conclusive physical evidence that the panels were painted prior to being cut down to make the wardrobe doors and pre-date Burne-Jones's painting on the exterior. They appear to have been recycled from another, unrecorded piece of furniture, presumably created for Morris and Burne-Jones's rooms at Red Lion Square.

The women are depicted in outdoor settings putting on a golden slipper, fastening a girdle (in a pose similar to *La Belle Iseult*, VI.12), combing hair and cutting nails. The grassy meads and trees prefigure Morris's later designs for the dining-room embroideries at Red House. Aymer Vallance and May Morris both attributed the panels to Morris, but they were likely a collaborative effort with input from Rossetti and Burne-Jones. A similar grid-like background pattern and grassy mead appear in Rossetti's drawing of a woman in medieval-style dress (*c.*1855, Birmingham Museum and Art Gallery). The figures have been painted directly onto unprimed wood and the extent of underdrawing varies considerably, another indicator that they were a collaborative effort.

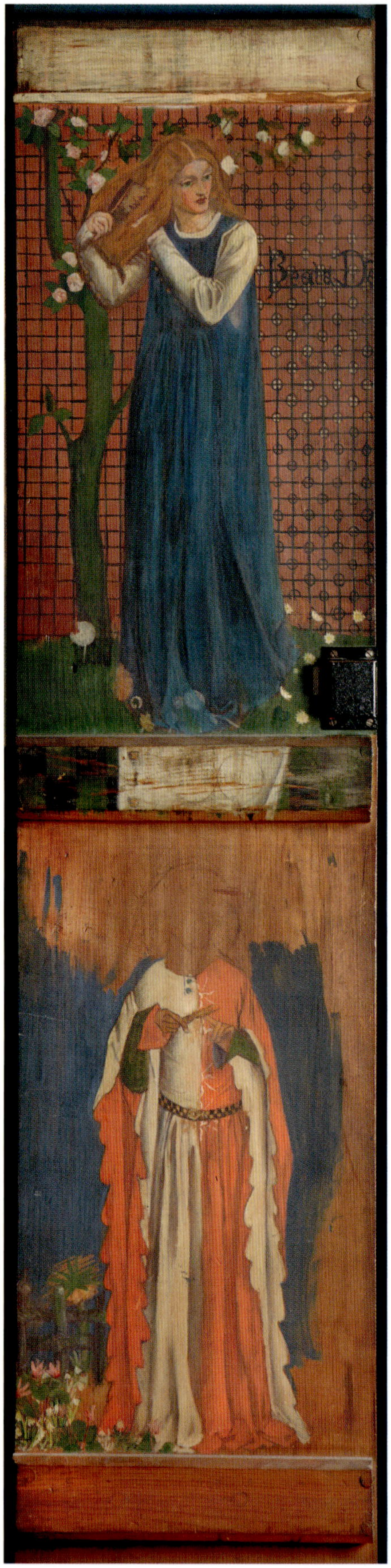

VI.4

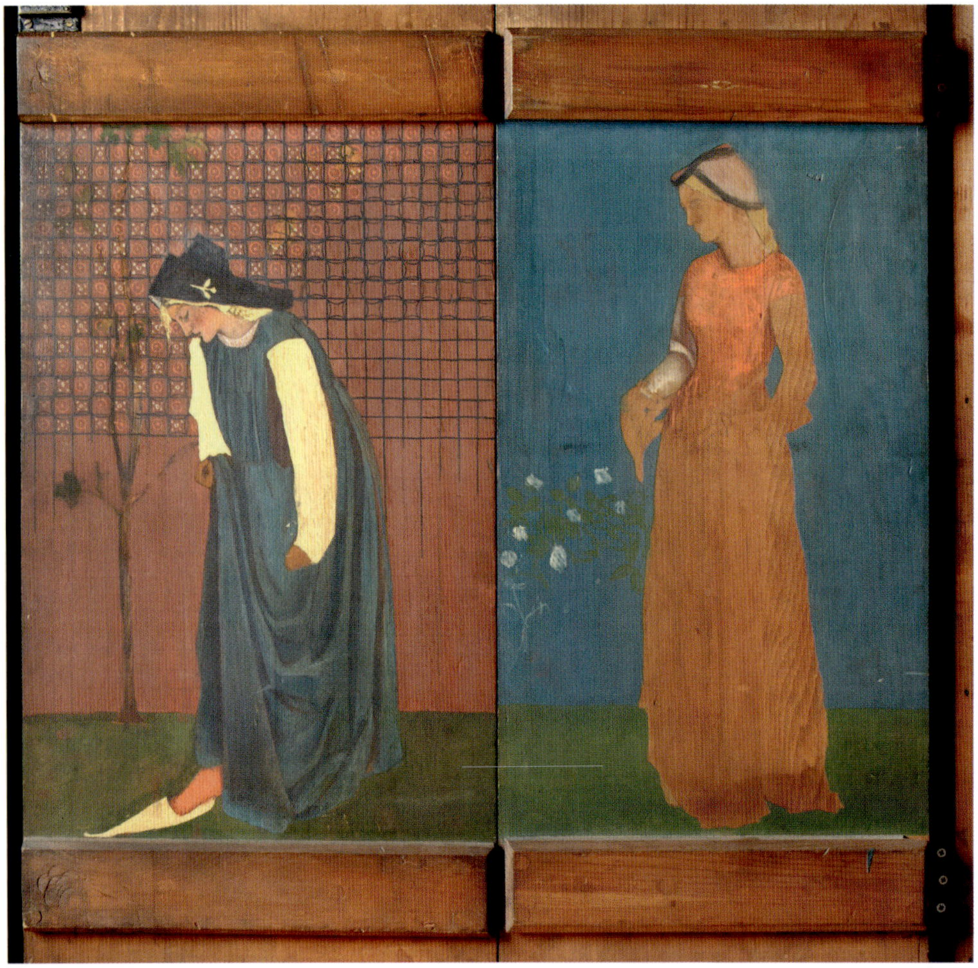

VI.5

Four painted panels

Dante Gabriel Rossetti,
possibly with William Morris and
Edward Burne-Jones, *c.*1860–2
Oil on panel, 61 x 41 x 3.2 cm each
V&A (Circ.310, 311–1960)
Purchased in 1960
V&A (Circ.128, 129–1953)
Given by Christabel Marillier

These panels have often been dated to the Red Lion Square era (*c.*1856–9) and linked stylistically with the interior painted doors of *The Prioress's Tale* wardrobe (VI.4). While there are similarities in size, composition and background, they are more accomplished in design and execution. Two of the panels (below) once belonged to Henry Currie Marillier, Managing Director of Morris & Co. and Rossetti's biographer. The other two (above) were found in Romford market. The women are shown smelling blossom (or possibly tasting fruit), gathering apples, sipping water at a fountain and admiring a nest of young birds, while holding a book. The iconography is ambiguous. The seasons have been suggested, although the senses are another possibility.

Marillier sent Jane Morris photographs of the two panels he owned. On 8 August 1910 she wrote, 'The left hand lady I think is certainly by Rossetti, the other [below right] I can't say – from what you say of the Indian red background with the diaper ... I think it is possible they were the inside of the panels of the bookcase at Red House – which were very thick and may have been divided after they left our ha[nds.]' Jane was possibly referring to the great settle in the drawing room, which could have been used to store books, or another, unrecorded piece of furniture. The panels' construction certainly suggests that they were part of a larger object and technical analysis might yet yield further clues.

All four reflect Rossetti's distinctive style of the early 1860s, demonstrated in works such as the pen and ink study for the title-page of *The Early Italian Poets* (1861, Museum of Fine Arts Boston). The painted frames are similar to the decorative borders on Morris's *St George* cabinet of 1862 (IX.14).

VI.5

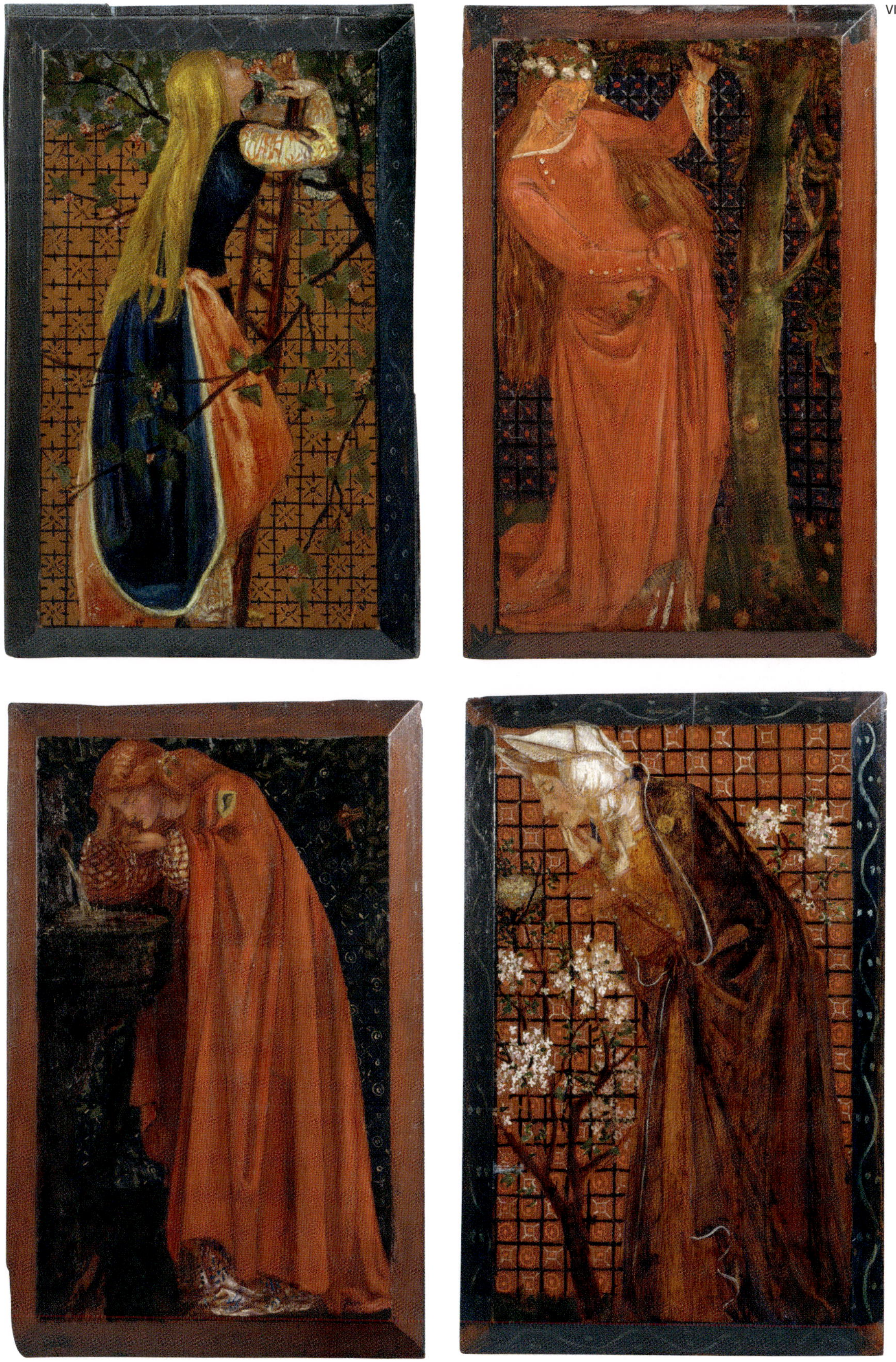

VI.6

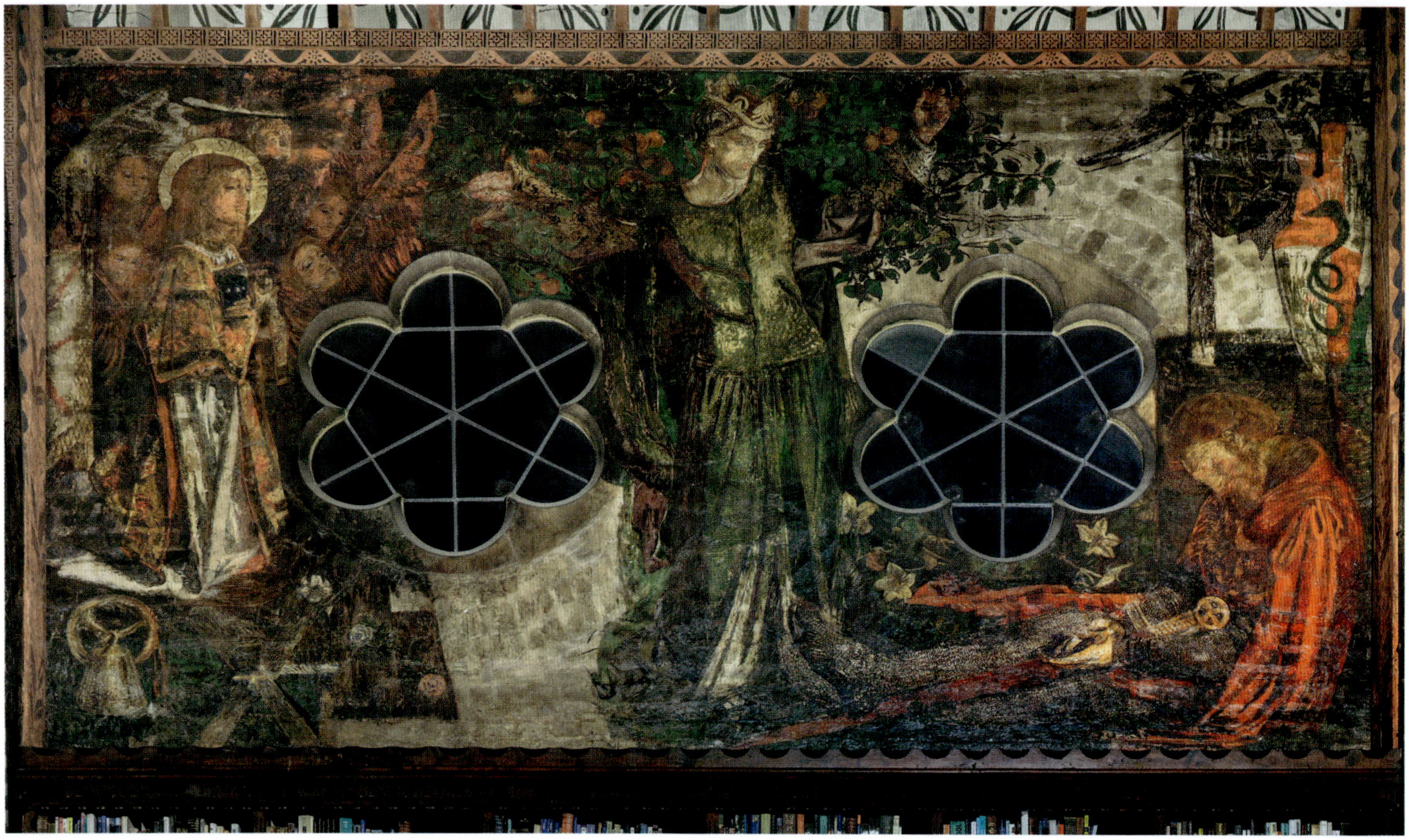

VI.7

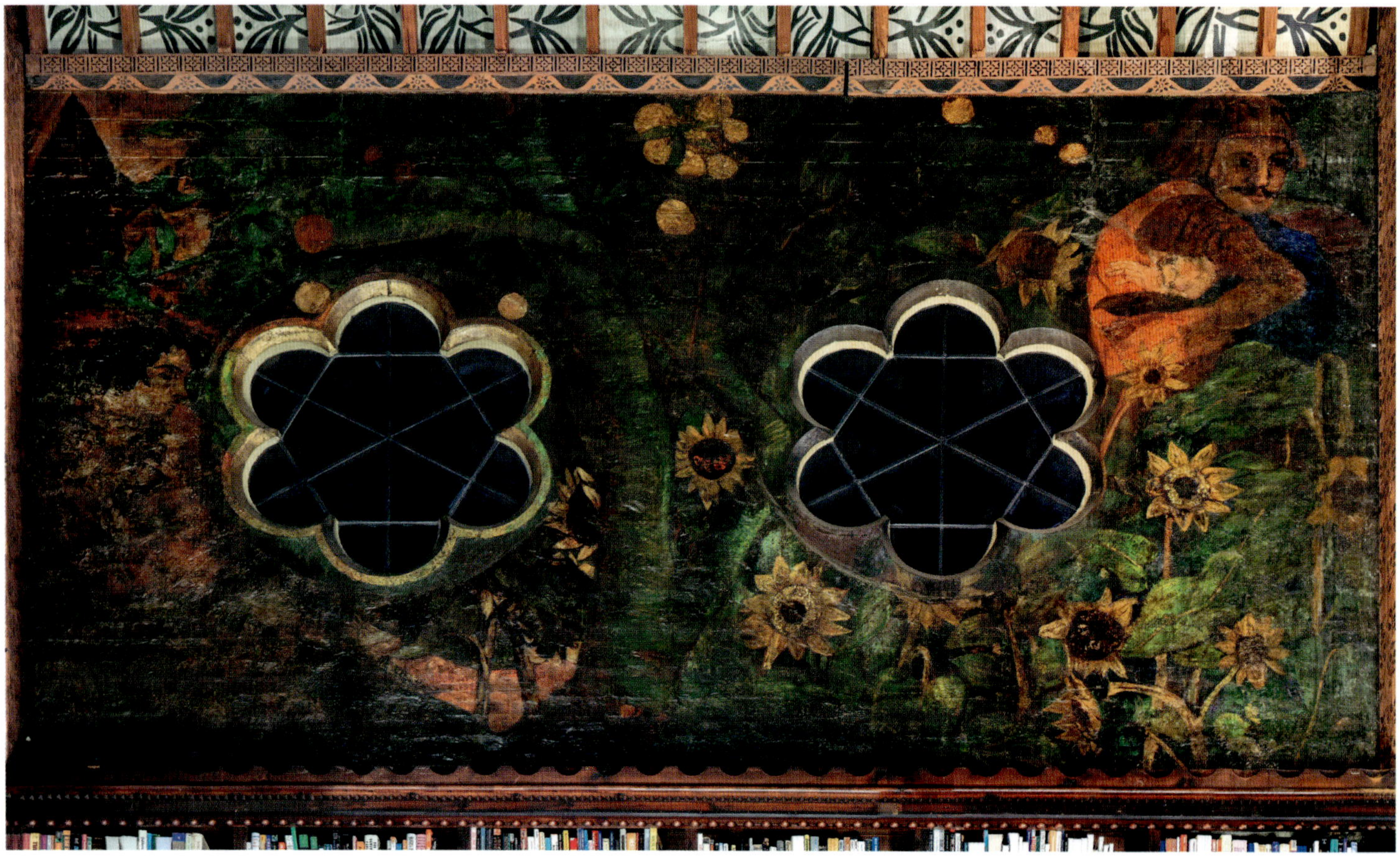

VI.8

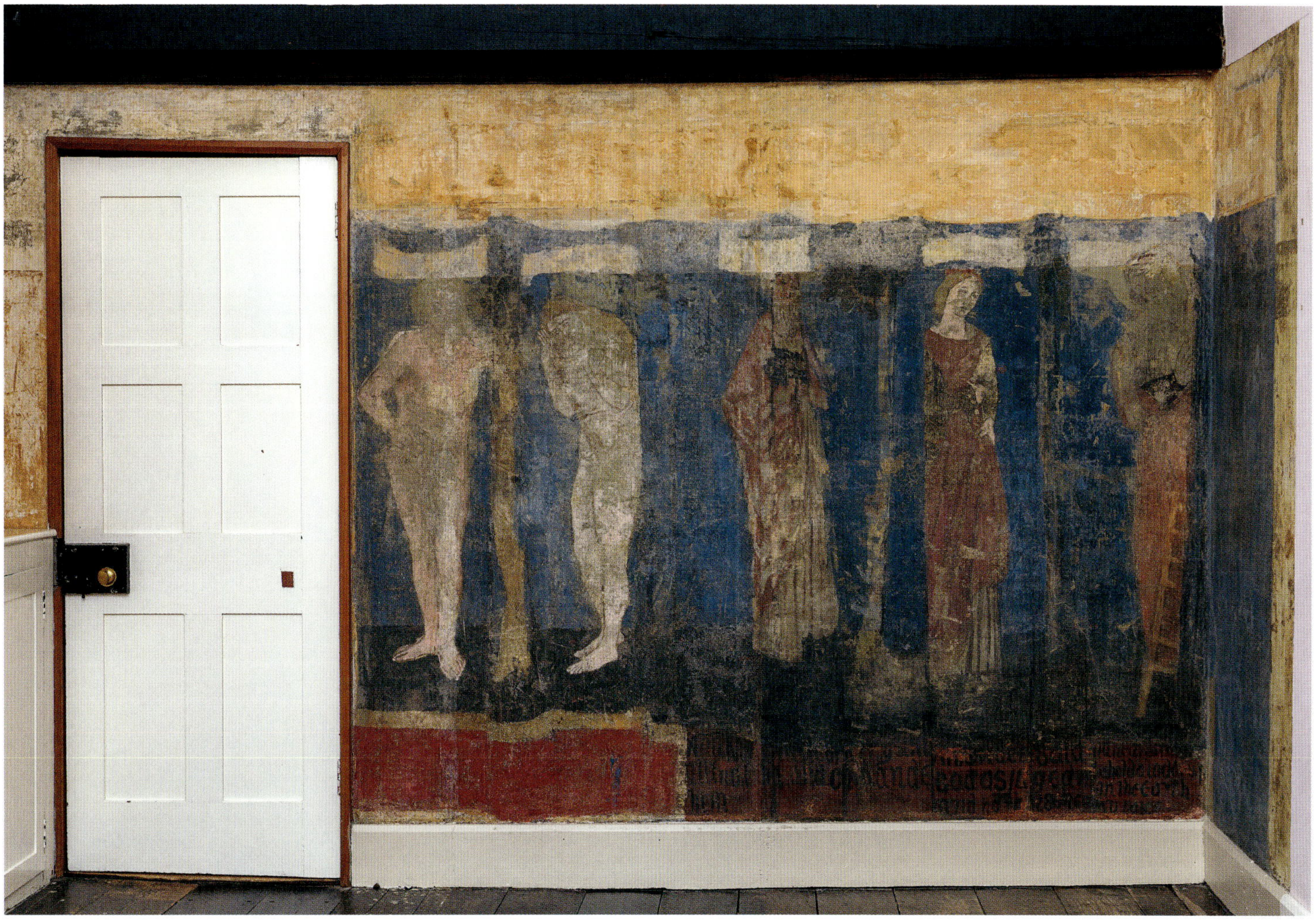

VI.6
Sir Launcelot's Vision of the Sanc Grael
Dante Gabriel Rossetti, 1857
Tempera on plaster, 295 x 508 cm
The Oxford Union Society

Rossetti described the subject of his own contribution to the Oxford Union murals as: 'Sir Lancelot prevented by his sin from entering the chapel of the Sancgrael. He has fallen asleep before the shrine full of angels, & between him & it, rises in his dream the image of Queen Guenevere, the cause of all. She stands gazing at him with her arms extended in the branches of an apple tree.' The apple tree motif was an allusion to Eve's temptation in the Garden of Eden. The composition has been skilfully arranged around the two circular cusped windows that pierce the wall. Burne-Jones sat for the figure of Sir Lancelot and, despite Rossetti leaving the mural unfinished, felt it represented the 'highest character' of his friend's work.

VI.7
How Sir Palomydes loved La Belle Iseult with exceeding great love out of measure, and how she loved not him again, but rather Sir Tristram
William Morris, 1857
Tempera on plaster, 295 x 508 cm
The Oxford Union Society

Morris's Oxford Union mural has deteriorated since completion, however, it is important as it marked his debut as a painter. There are striking parallels with the composition of Rossetti's mural (VI.6). Both feature a centrally positioned tree, figures placed diagonally across from one another and reclining male protagonists. In the lower left corner, Palomydes broods, secretly observing Tristram and Iseult as they embrace. The clumsily painted figures are partly camouflaged by a thick scattering of yellow sunflowers. In a letter of 1869 Morris wrote, 'I believe it *has* some merits as to colour, but I must confess I should feel much more comfortable if it had disappeared from the wall, as I'm conscious of its being extremely ludicrous in many ways.' Comparison with later work reveals how quickly Morris improved.

VI.8
***Book of Genesis* mural**
Attributed to William Morris, Elizabeth Siddal and probably other members of their circle including Dante Gabriel Rossetti, *c.*1860–2
Tempera on plaster, 180 x 400 cm
National Trust, Red House (NT60191)

As Julia Dudkiewicz has demonstrated, the mural uncovered in the Morrises' bedroom at Red House ties in with the overall iconographic scheme of the house. Painted to mimic a draped wall hanging, it depicts five Old Testament figures: Adam and Eve, Noah, Rachel and Jacob. Together they represent different facets of marital as well as divine love – Adam and Eve are expelled from the Garden of Eden to face their fate together, Noah and his family are rescued from a cataclysmic event by God's love, and Rachel and Jacob overcome many struggles, including infertility, through their love for one another. Tessa Wild has suggested that Morris was consciously evoking the splendidly decorated 'chamber of love' inhabited by Melidor in the romance of Sir Degrevaunt. This story was the subject of Burne-Jones's murals in the adjacent drawing room, where Jane modelled for Melidor in *Sir Degrevaunt's Wedding Feast* (fig.145).

While the concept was Morris's, the execution was a collaborative effort. Only Elizabeth Siddal can be named with confidence, though other members of their circle were probably involved. In July 1861 Siddal sent a letter from Red House to Rossetti stating: 'If you can come down here on Saturday evening, I shall be very glad indeed. I want you to do something to the figure I have been trying to paint on the wall.'

VI.9

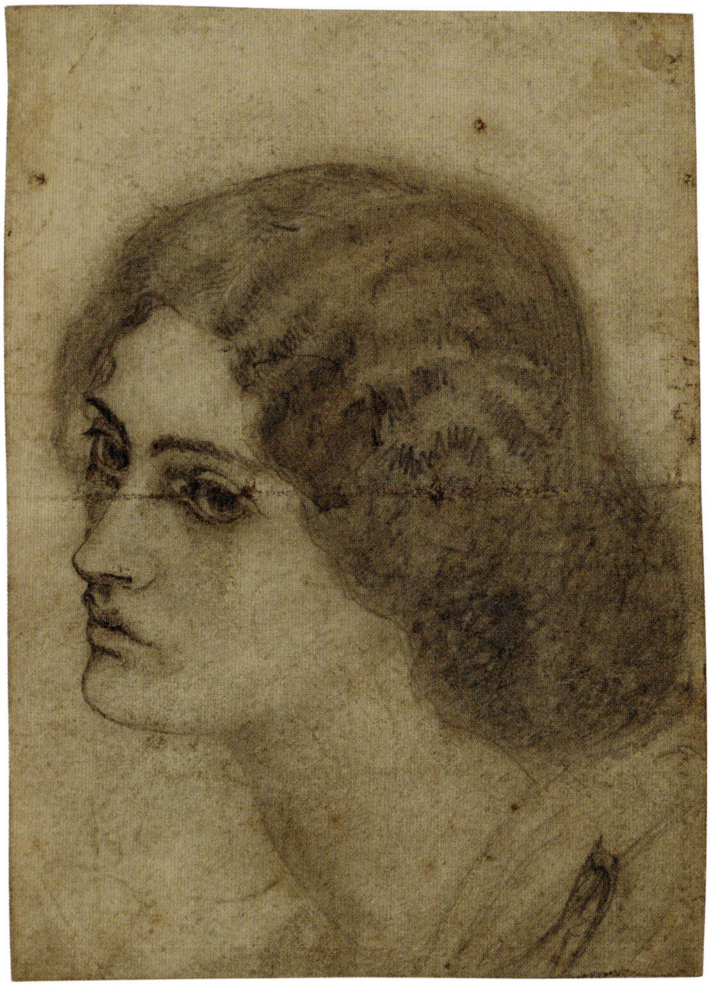

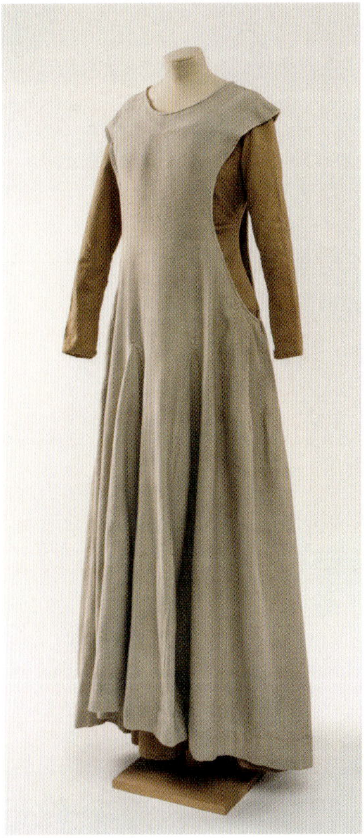

VI.10

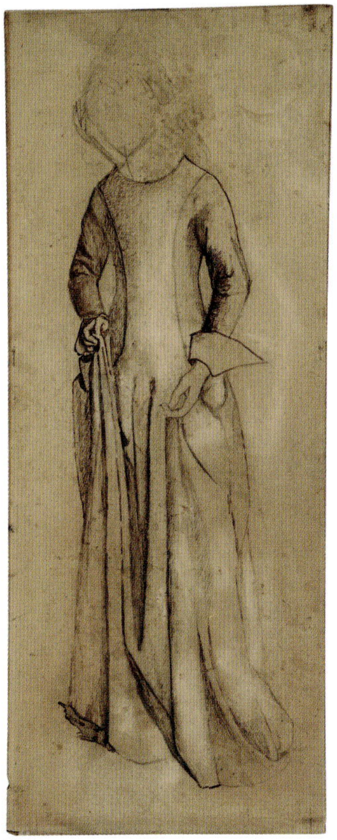

VI.11

VI.9
Jane Burden
William Morris, 1858
Graphite, pen, black ink and grey wash on paper, 10.4 x 7.6 cm
British Museum (1939,0602.1)
Given by Dr Robert Steele

This accurate likeness is Morris's only surviving portrait study of his future wife. It was reproduced as a photogravure in May Morris's introduction to Volume II of *The Collected Works of William Morris* (1910): 'The portrait of my mother is a little pencil drawing done in 1858 – in the Oxford courting days. My mother says it was a study for the picture of "La Belle Iseult" … the original had been lying about, folded in two – across the face – and was altogether in a very unpromising condition.' Although both are three-quarter profiles, the angle of the head differs from the finished oil. Jane's pronounced lips, philtrum and elongated neck, are in keeping with the Pre-Raphaelite ideal of female beauty. Jane later disseminated this likeness – a surviving offprint of the photogravure is inscribed 'With kind regards from Jane Morris. Kelmscott 1910' (William Morris Gallery).

VI.10
Medieval-style dress and gown
Probably designed by William Morris, maker unknown, *c.*1857–8
Wool and cotton, length 140 cm, 135 cm
William Morris Gallery, London Borough of Waltham Forest (H13, H12)

The earliest record of Morris designing costume props dates to the Oxford Union murals project in the summer of 1857 (fig.108). These were valuable resources that were shared among artists: one of Rossetti's letters, for example, refers to borrowing a monk's dress from Lowes Dickinson in 1856, presumably for *Fra Pace*, while G.F. Watts lent props to Burne-Jones. This medieval-style dress and sideless gown appear in the surviving study for *La Belle Iseult* and reflect Morris's commitment to working from life (VI.11). The set also includes a cloak with front-fastening buttons and was acquired from the Central School of Arts and Crafts in 1954.

VI.11
Study for the dress in *La Belle Iseult*
William Morris, *c.*1858
Graphite, pen and ink and wash on paper, 57.8 x 23.2 cm
The Dennis T. Lanigan Collection

This study was probably worked from a lay figure at Red Lion Square, using the dress and gown Morris had acquired. Although the dress in the finished painting is more elaborate, the drawing is clearly related and shows Morris developing his ideas.

VI.12
La Belle Iseult
William Morris, probably with contributions from Dante Gabriel Rossetti and Ford Madox Brown, *c.*1858–early 1860s, retouched and completed before 1882
Oil on canvas, 71.8 x 50.2 cm
Tate, London (N04999)
Bequeathed by May Morris

Modelled from his fiancée Jane Burden, the subject is drawn from Malory's treatment of the Tristram and Iseult legend in *Morte d'Arthur.* The picture shows the emotional aftermath of Iseult's erroneous conviction that her lover is dead. The unmade bed, the presence of Tristram's little dog and the girdle that Iseult fastens around her waist point to her infidelity. As Alison Smith has demonstrated, the picture engages in a visual dialogue with Van Eyck's *Arnolfini Portrait* (fig.107). As well as incorporating many of the same motifs – the bed, carpet, oranges, dog and slippers – Morris has tried to employ a similar head-on box-like perspective with a vanishing point around Iseult's head, accentuating her absorption in grief. The rich colour palette, constricted space and ornamental qualities also recall Rossetti's 'ultra-medieval' watercolours and the illuminated manuscripts that inspired them. The painting is loaded with symbolism, Iseult's crown, for example, is made of rosemary and convolvulus, marks of remembrance and attachment respectively, and both signs of her devotion to Sir Tristram.

The interior, including the bed, is known to have been painted at Red Lion Square and many of the props, such as the brass ewer, would have been owned by Morris. The textiles are particularly interesting and include linen damask, a Turkish rug, a Persian embroidered cover and whitework hangings on the bed. The wall tapestries, inspired by examples depicted in medieval manuscripts, are very similar to the experimental embroideries Morris was creating at the time (XII.1).

Given that the head study was not begun until 1858, the picture itself was most likely commenced that year, possibly inspired by the couple's engagement in the spring. Webb stated that 'after struggling over his picture for months, "hating the brute", [Morris] threw it up. Rossetti took it to finish, and then Madox Brown.' Still unfinished in 1874 when Rossetti acquired it from Oliver Madox Brown, the picture was exhibited in a finished state at the New Gallery in 1898. By inference, Rossetti probably completed it some time before his death in 1882. Tate's technical analysis confirms areas of overpainting.

VI.12

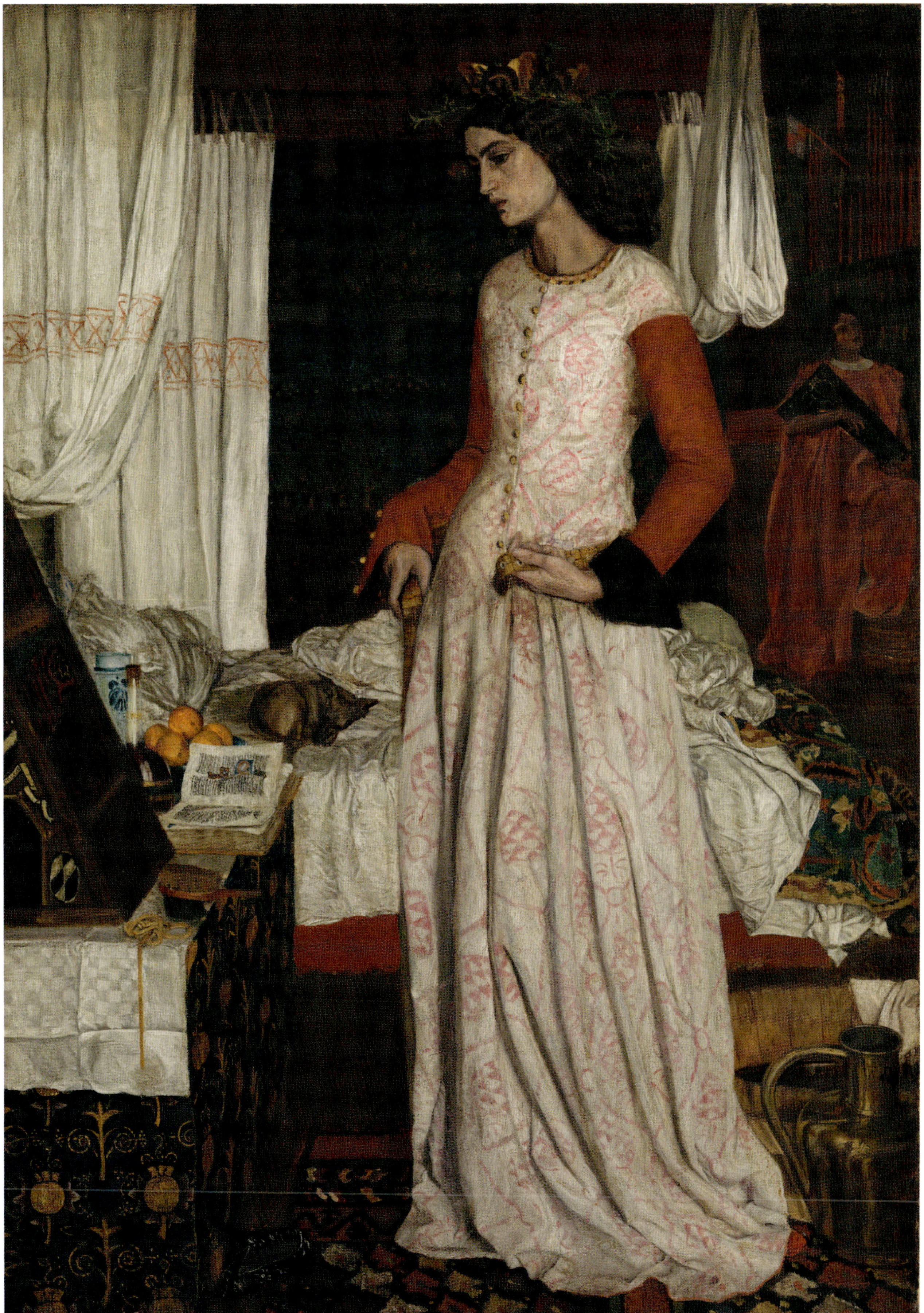

VI.13

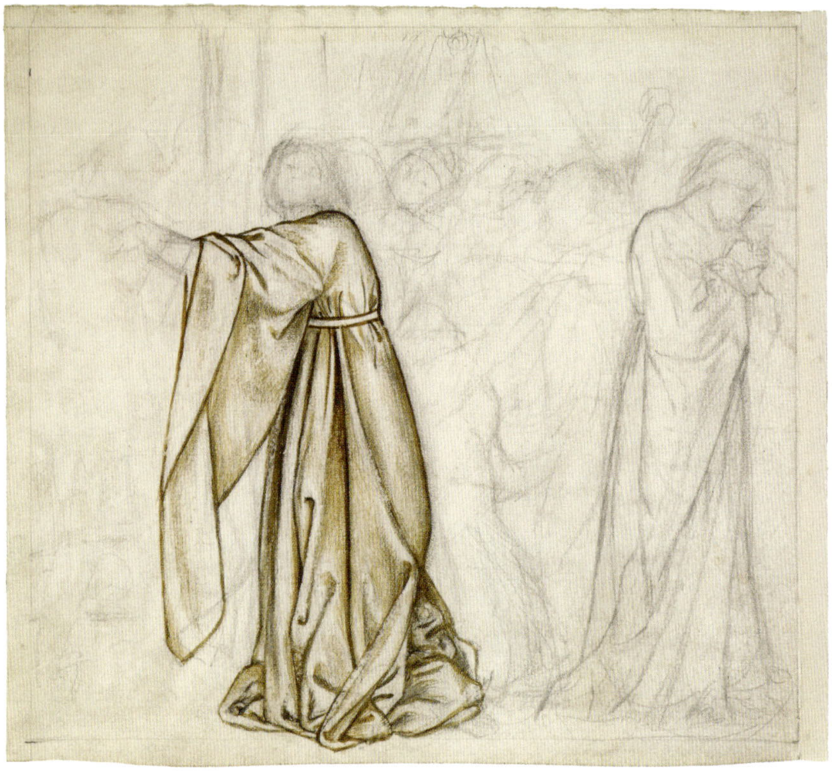

VI.13
Study for unknown figurative subject
William Morris, late 1850s
Pencil and sepia ink on paper,
27 x 30.1 cm
Inscription on the back by Charles Fairfax Murray: 'by William Morris / C. F. M.'
Birmingham Museums Trust (1927P913)

This is a rare example of a compositional study by Morris featuring multiple figures. The unfinished nature of the drawing, faint outlines and lack of archival evidence make it impossible to identify the subject with certainty. Stephen Wildman has proposed that the indication of a mast and rigging suggest Iseult's departure for Cornwall, where she was to marry King Mark.

VI.14

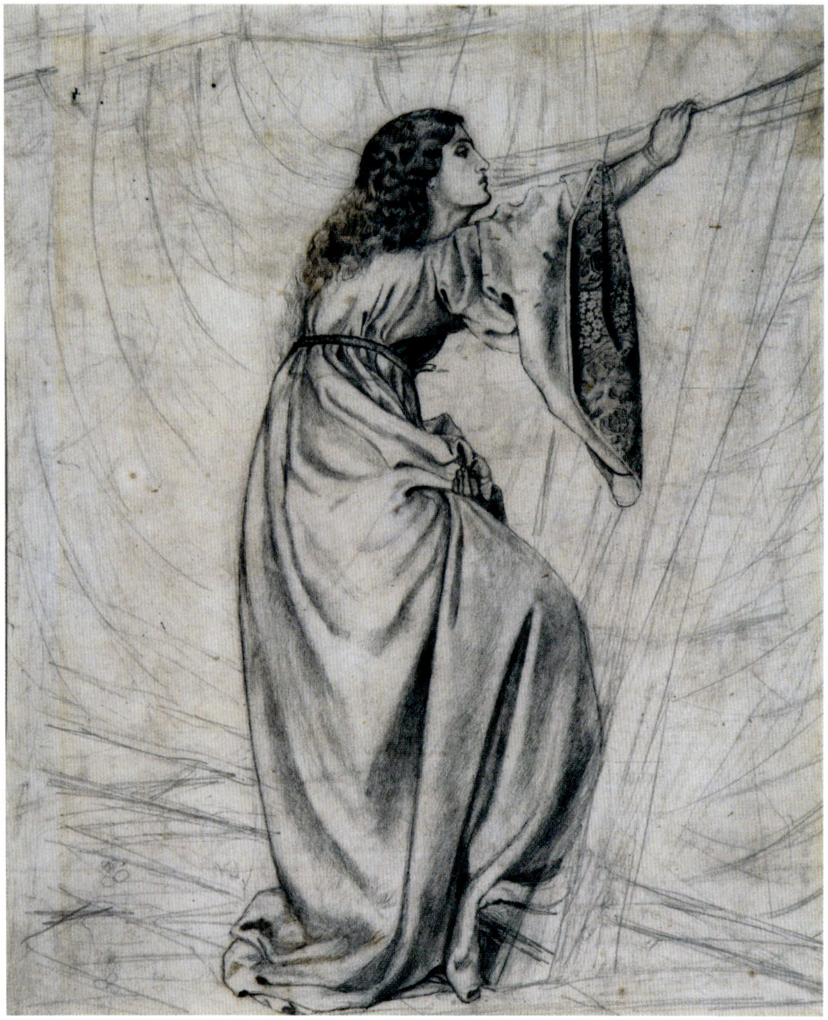

VI.14
Helen of Troy Boarding the Ship
William Morris, *c.*1861
Pencil and ink on watermarked paper 'J. WHATMAN/ 1861', 51 x 41 cm
William Morris Gallery, London Borough of Waltham Forest (D223)

By virtue of the watermark and iconography, this drawing of Jane Morris in a medieval-style dress is probably a study for one of the 'Story of Troy' murals intended for the hall at Red House. Morris's notebook lists possible scenes for this unrealized project: 'Judgment of Paris, Carrying off Helen, A Battle, Death of Hector, [Death of] Achilles, Wooden Horse, Return of Greeks' (British Library Add. MS 45336). The patterned lining of the sleeve reveals his interest in ornament. Although he told a friend that he struggled to 'make his figures move', this composition is a capable treatment of a figure climbing a ladder.

VI.15

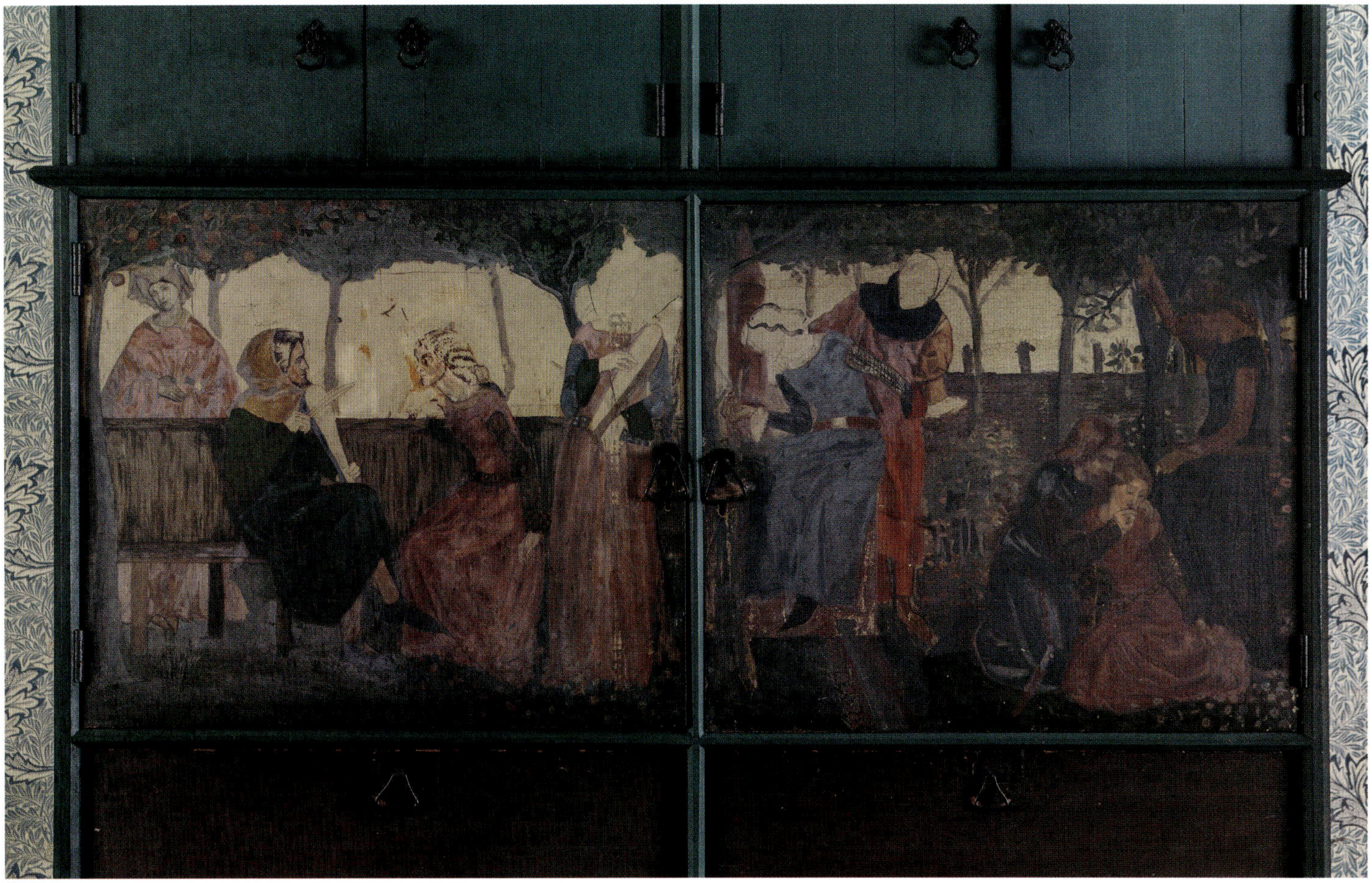

VI.15
Red House hall settle (detail of painted doors)
Settle designed by Philip Webb, figurative paintings attributed to William Morris and Dante Gabriel Rossetti, early 1860s
Oil on mahogany door panels, 65.5 x 76 x 2.1 cm each
National Trust, Red House (NT60108)

The theme of the unfinished painting spanning the cupboard doors of the entrance hall settle is open to debate. In 1988 Ray Watkinson suggested that it was intended to evoke the Arthurian setting of Lancelot's castle, Joyous Gard. It has also been interpreted as a group portrait of Morris's circle of friends. The figures from left to right (excluding those with blank faces) have been identified as: Mary Nicholson, William Morris or Charles Faulkner, Jane Morris, Edward Burne-Jones, Georgiana Burne-Jones and Elizabeth Siddal. The wattle fence, water feature, flowers and fruit trees certainly recall the medieval pleasure gardens that the friends studied in illuminated manuscripts and that inspired the layout of the gardens at Red House. The painting evokes romantic, courtly love, and perhaps also the bonds of fellowship between friends.

Helen Dowding has presented convincing technical evidence that the painting was a collaboration between Morris and Rossetti. The doors were treated like easel paintings, in the sense that they were painted first and then attached to the cupboard (despite their incomplete finish). The areas that Morris worked on have extensive underdrawing, especially of the drapery.

VI.16
Study for Red House hall settle
William Morris, early 1860s
Pencil on paper, dimensions unknown
Reproduced after Crow (subsequently in the collection of Janet Camp Troxell; currently untraced)

This composition of three figures wearing medieval dress is a study for the right-hand door of the hall settle at Red House (see above). The drawing is looser and more confident than some of Morris's earlier sketches and shows him persevering with drawing from life in the 1860s.

VI.16

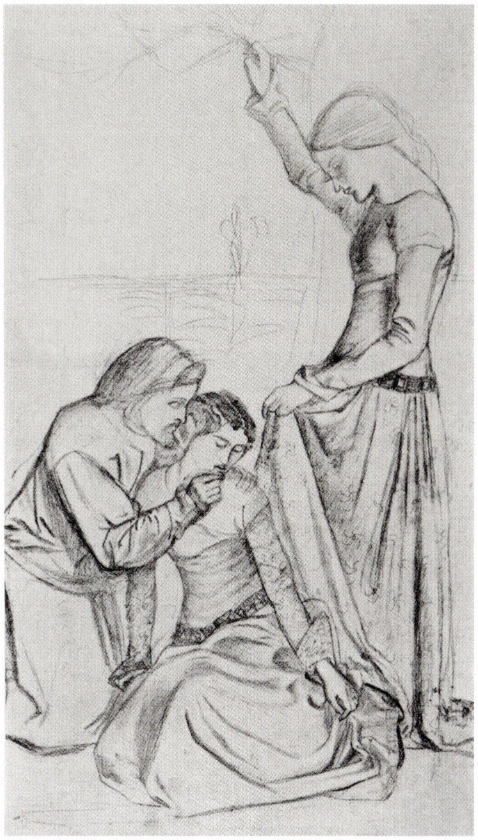

VI.17

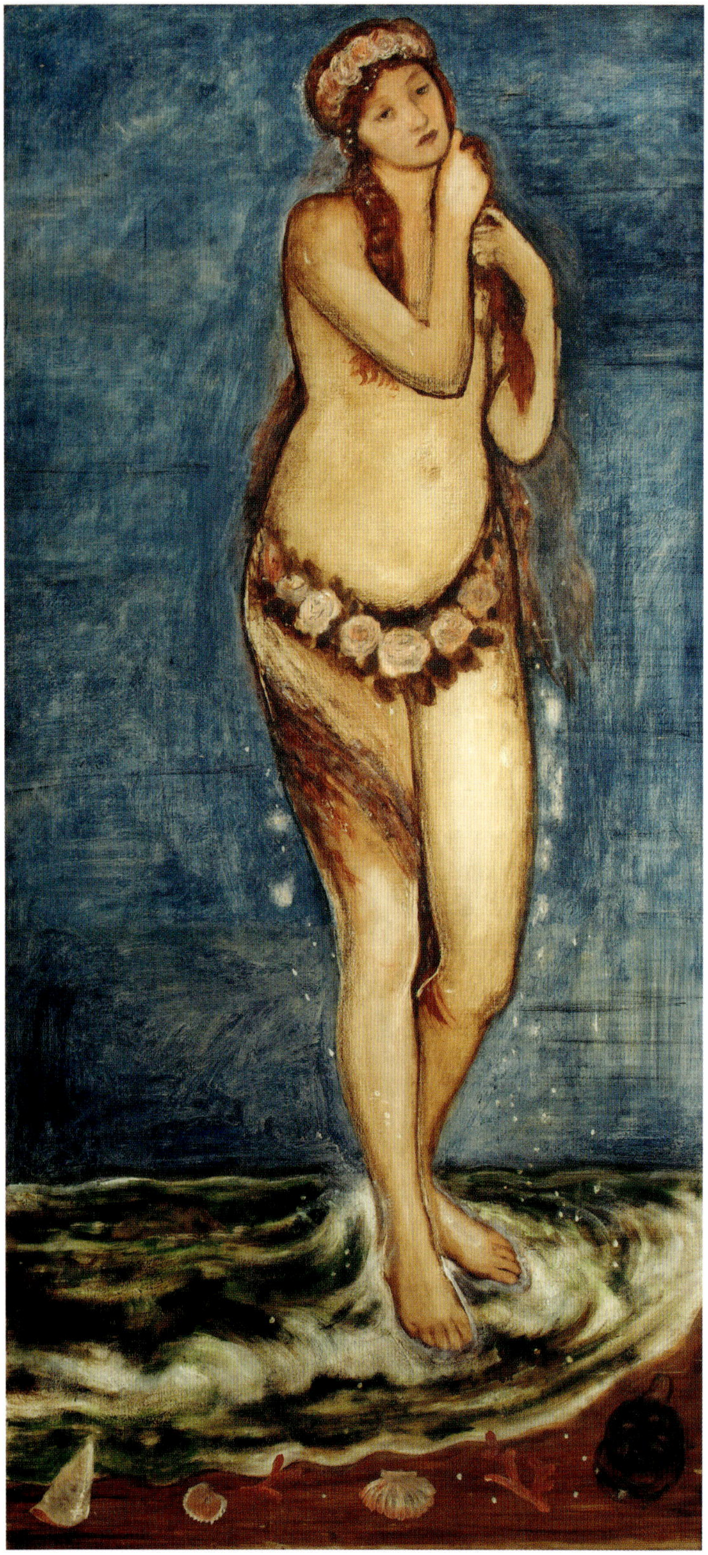

VI.17
Venus (Aphrodite)
William Morris and Edward Burne-Jones, mid-1860s, possibly retouched after 1889
Oil on canvas, 132 x 62.5 cm
The Society of Antiquaries of London, Kelmscott Manor (KM357)

La Belle Iseult is often referred to as Morris's only surviving easel painting, however, he also created this large canvas showing the goddess of love emerging from the sea. It is the only surviving record of his design for the same subject in the Red House embroidery scheme (fig.144), and provides the key for unlocking the latter's iconography. The painting was most probably derived from the (now lost) cartoon. It clearly references the paintings of Botticelli, whose work was little known in England in the 1860s, though Rossetti was an early champion. It is a good example of what Elizabeth Prettejohn has termed 'generous imitation' – the process by which Victorian artists engaged in a visual dialogue with 'forgotten' Old Masters, developing their own practice while contributing to the growing appreciation for their predecessors.

The whole surface of the canvas reveals Burne-Jones's involvement in its execution. Compare, for example, the goddess's face with that of the angel Gabriel in *The Annunciation* and *Fair Rosamund* (both 1863, private collections). The painting is an important example of Morris's continuing engagement with the human form. It was possibly created in the mid-1860s as a memento of the Red House decorative scheme before the family's imminent move to Queen Square. It remained in Morris's possession and was included in May's bequest of treasured objects that were to stay at Kelmscott Manor after her death.

VI.18
***Helen of Troy (Flamma Troiae)* cartoon**
William Morris, early 1860s
Pencil and watercolour on paper, 124.7 x 62.4 cm
V&A (E.571–1940)
Bequeathed by May Morris

The world's most beautiful woman, Helen, Queen of Laconia and wife of King Menelaus, was one of the 12 queens, saints and goddesses that Morris included in his ambitious Red House embroidery series. Helen's abduction sparked the Trojan War. Morris explored this subject in his poetry in the late 1850s and Helen was a natural choice for the Red House embroidery scheme that represented different facets of love. It also tied in with the Trojan murals that Morris and Burne-Jones planned (though never executed) for the adjacent hall (VI.14). Depicted as a 'Pre-Raphaelite stunner', Helen has long flowing red hair and holds an ominous flaming torch, symbolic of the passion that her beauty inspired and the ultimate demise of Troy. The textile was executed by Bessie Burden and is now at Castle Howard (XII.4).

VI.19
***Guenevere* cartoon**
William Morris, early 1860s
Pencil and watercolour on paper, 126.4 x 55.2 cm
Tate, London (N05221)

In Malory's *Morte d'Arthur*, Guenevere has an affair with Sir Lancelot, betraying her husband King Arthur with catastrophic consequences for the Round Table. The title poem of Morris's first published volume of poetry, *The Defence of Guenevere* (1858), is a deeply ambiguous and erotic exploration of her infidelity written from her own perspective. In contrast to the feisty queen in Morris's poem, Guenevere is here depicted as dignified but downcast. The nearly complete embroidery (with a plain rather than patterned dress) survives at Kelmscott Manor, and the design was also adapted for stained glass as the lead lines on the drawing indicate.

VI.18

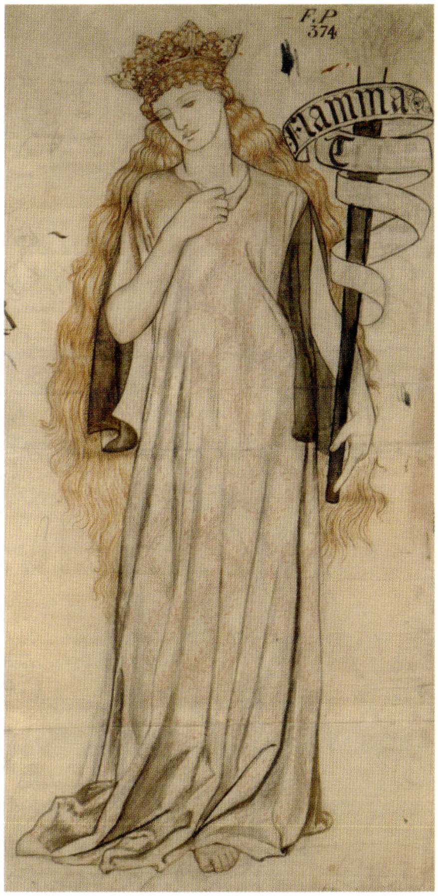

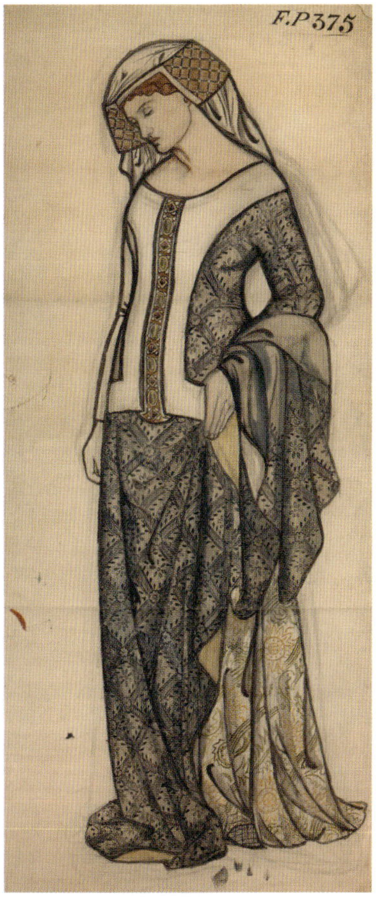

VI.19

VI.20

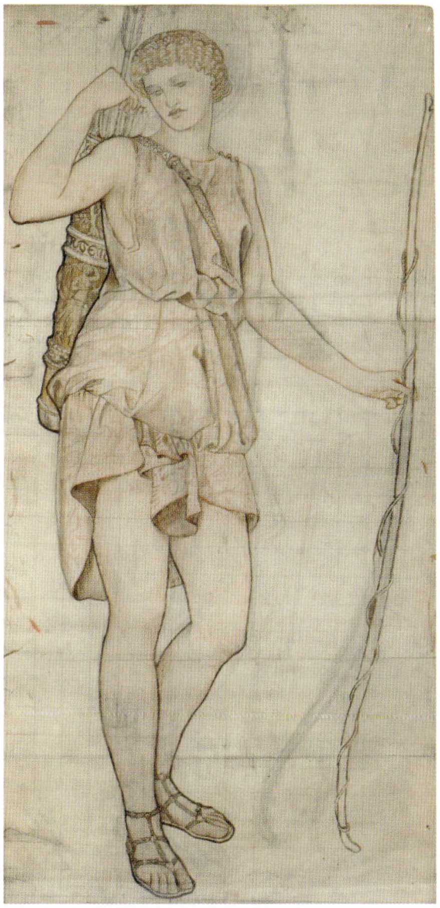

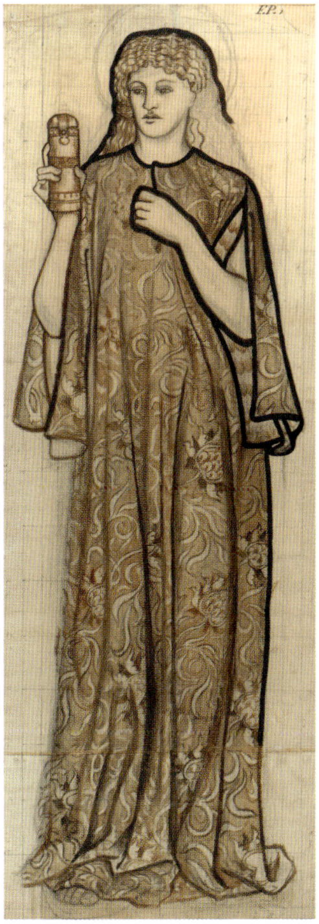

VI.21

VI.20
Artemis **cartoon**
William Morris, early 1860s
Pencil and watercolour on paper, 120 x 58.9 cm
Tullie House Museum and Art Gallery, Carlisle (1949.125.77)

May Morris described this cartoon as a 'design by William Morris for one of the figures in the Red House embroidered hangings' (*The Collected Works of William Morris*, Volume IX, 1911). In this accomplished drawing, Artemis, goddess of chastity and hunting, draws an arrow from a decorative quiver that bears her name. Her bow has been repositioned, and there are other clues that Morris made more than one attempt at the drapery and placing of the feet. The embroidery was never begun and the design later belonged to May's friend, the poet Gordon Bottomley, who acquired it from Morris & Co. with the understanding that it belonged to the Red House scheme.

VI.21
Mary Magdalene **cartoon**
William Morris, early 1860s
Wash, graphite and ink on paper, 121.9 x 43.8 cm
The Huntington Library, Art Museum and Botanical Gardens (2000.5.516)

The style, iconography and size of *Mary Magdalene* all correspond closely to Morris's other designs for the Red House dining-room scheme, suggesting that it was conceived for the same purpose though the project was abandoned before the embroidery could be executed. In particular, the position of the head and neck, the hairstyle and the bare foot protruding from her dress, echo the embroidered figure of *Penelope* (Kelmscott Manor). Mary Magdalene represented both divine and romantic love and is shown with the ointment jar that she used to wash Jesus's feet. The design was also used at an early date for stained glass (All Saints, Langton Green, Kent, *c.*1862), hence the lead lines on the drawing.

VI.22
Nympha Florum
William Morris, early 1860s
Pencil, pen and sepia wash on paper, 28.7 x 18 cm
V&A (E.2792–1927)
Bequeathed by James Richardson Holliday

Nympha Florum is a rare nude figure by Morris, which has iconographic parallels with his *Venus* oil painting, both featuring floral garlands around the figures' hips, long flowing hair falling to their knees and a contrapposto pose. According to Peter Cormack, the technique and scale suggest it was most likely conceived as a design for a tile panel, though stained glass has also been proposed. Studies related to this composition are preserved at the Huntington (2000.5.21) and the V&A (E.2805–1927).

VI.22

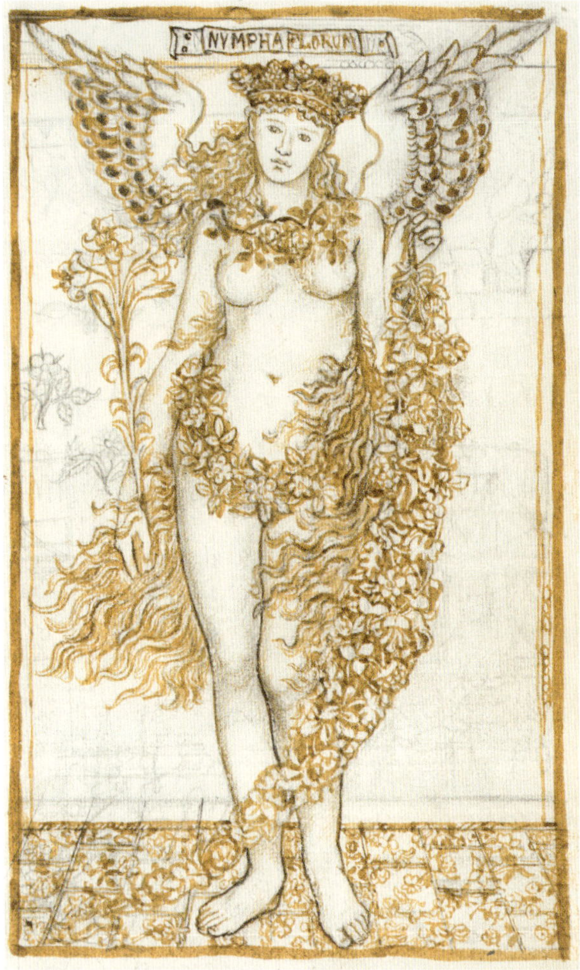

VI.23
Andromeda
William Morris, *c*.1865–8
Pencil and sepia ink on paper, 11 x 8 cm
National Trust, Wightwick Manor (NT1288026)

The drawing's subject matter, composition and size suggest it was intended for the lavishly illustrated edition of *The Earthly Paradise*, which Morris and Burne-Jones planned but never realized (XIV.1). If so, then it is Morris's only surviving illustration for the project; all the other known designs were made by Burne-Jones. The scene depicted comes from 'The Doom of King Acrisius', the classical tale for the month of April. Andromeda, whose mother had boasted that she was more beautiful than the Nereids, was chained naked to the rocks as a sacrifice before being rescued by Perseus.

VI.23

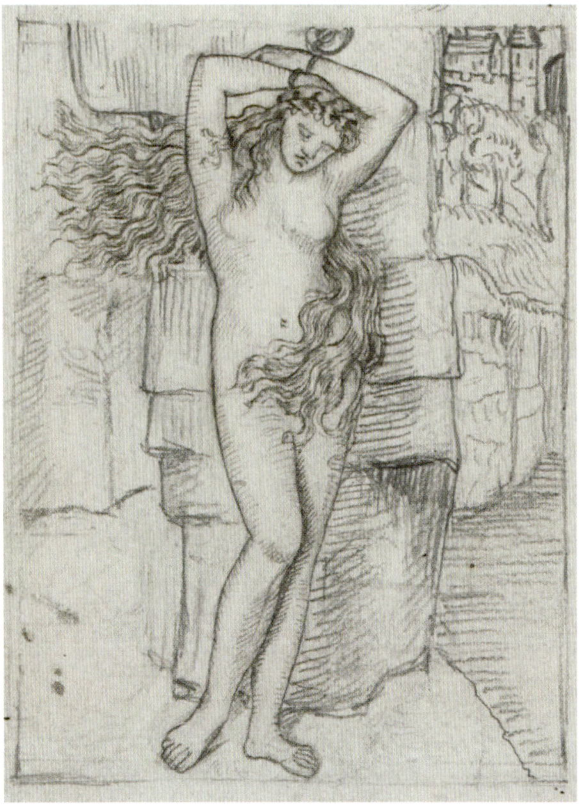

VI.24
Four studies for the painted doors of the *St George* cabinet
William Morris, 1861
Bequeathed by James Richardson Holliday

a Pencil, pen and ink and wash on paper, watermarked 'J Whatman Turkey Mill 1859', 44.2 x 51 cm
V&A (E.2787–1927)

b Pencil, pen and ink and wash on paper, 44.7 x 15.8 cm
V&A (E.2788–1927)

c Pencil, pen and ink and wash on paper, 43.7 x 35.4 cm
V&A (E.2789–1927)

d Pencil, pen and ink, wash and coloured chalk on paper, 43.9 x 50.4 cm
V&A (E.2790–1927)

These are the most complex and moving figurative studies Morris ever produced. Drawn to 1:1 scale, the five narrative scenes were conceived for a cabinet designed by Webb and painted by Morris for the International Exhibition of 1862 (IX.14). The legend was a popular subject in Morris's circle. Rossetti first treated it in 1857 in a watercolour, *The Wedding of St George and Princess Sabra* (Tate), and in 1861 he was working on a series of six stained-glass designs (VII.12). Morris chose to emphasize the despair and grief of the powerless king in the aftermath of his daughter Princess Sabra being led away to be sacrificed, eschewing more physically dramatic moments such as George's slaying of the dragon.

For iconographic details, Morris drew on Thomas Percy's *Reliques of Ancient English Poetry* (1765). The principal figures were modelled from life, with Jane Morris posing for the princess and probably the poet Algernon Swinburne for St George. There are some differences between the drawn and painted versions. For example, in the drawing, the vista through the doorway behind the departing princess closely repeats the first scene, strengthening the focus on her inconsolable father. On the cabinet, Morris altered this compositional device to show a closed door as the princess departs and an open one on her return.

VI.24a

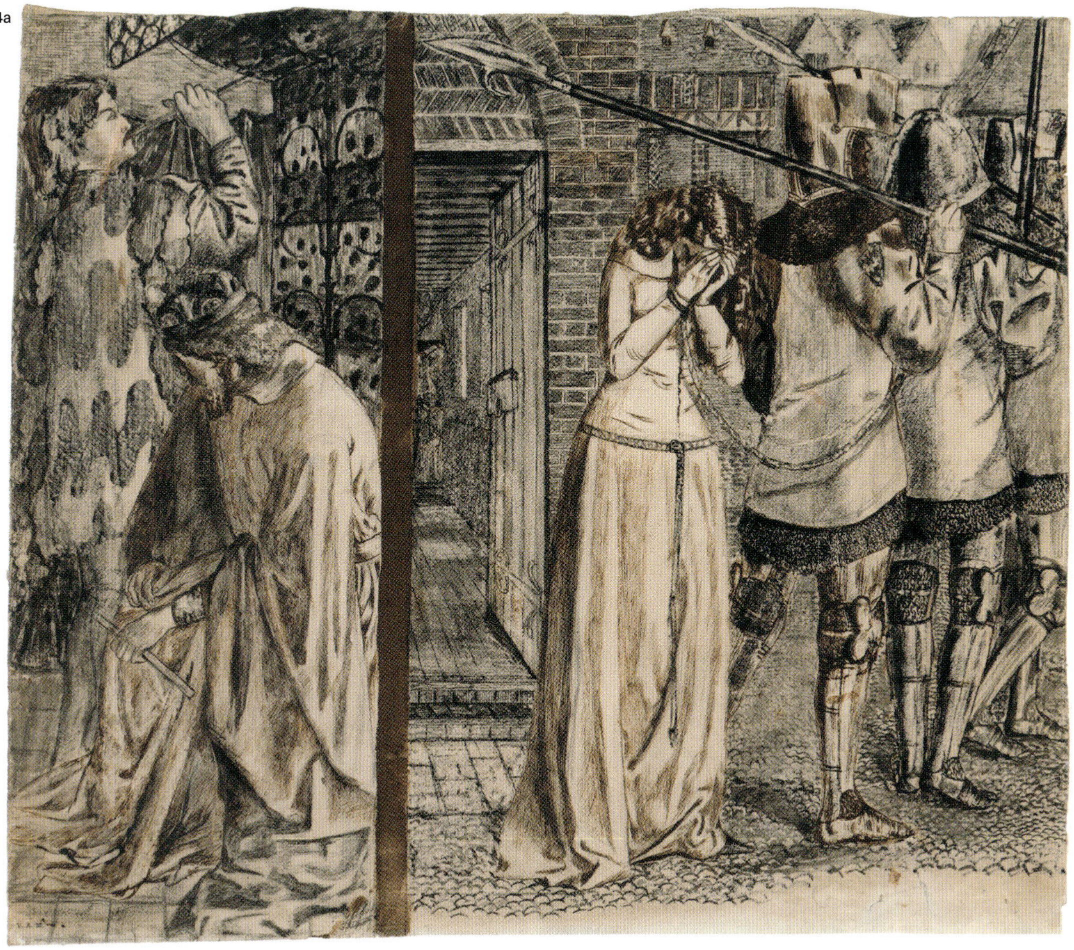

VI.24b

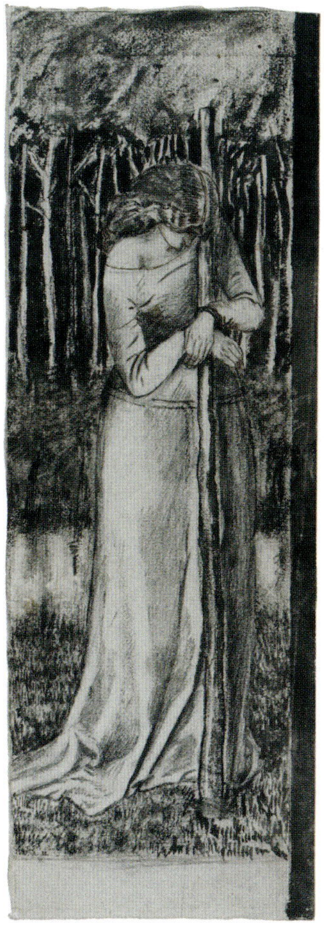

VI.24c

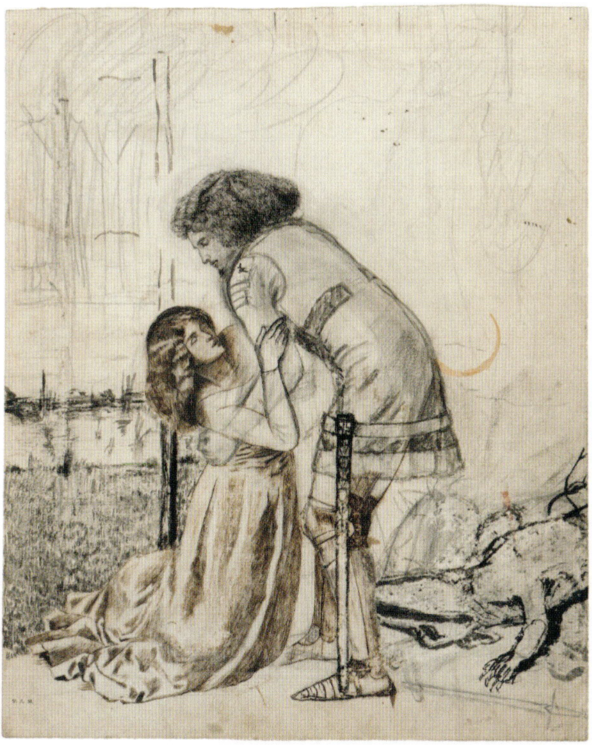

VI.24d

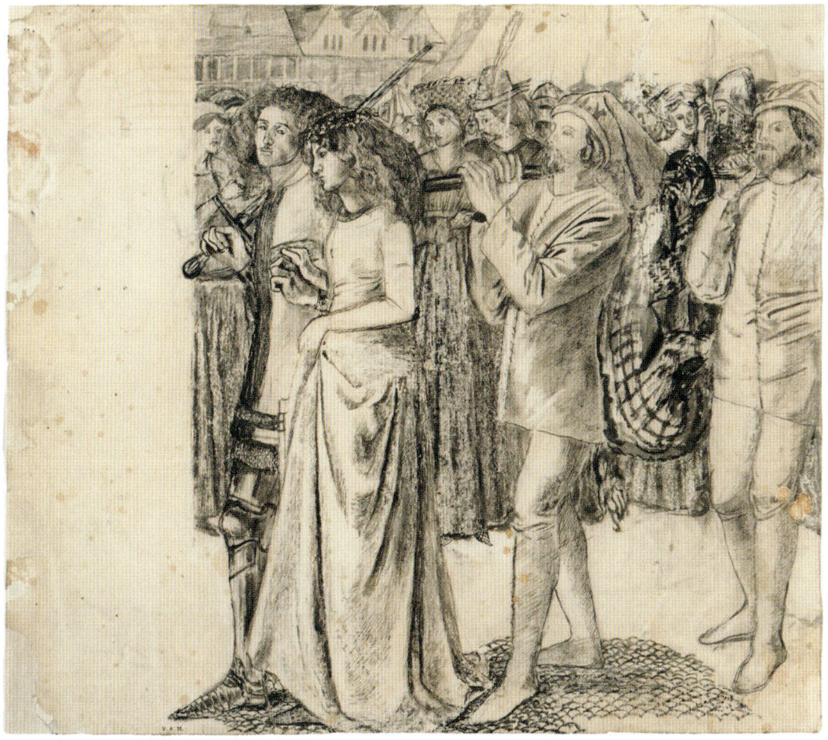

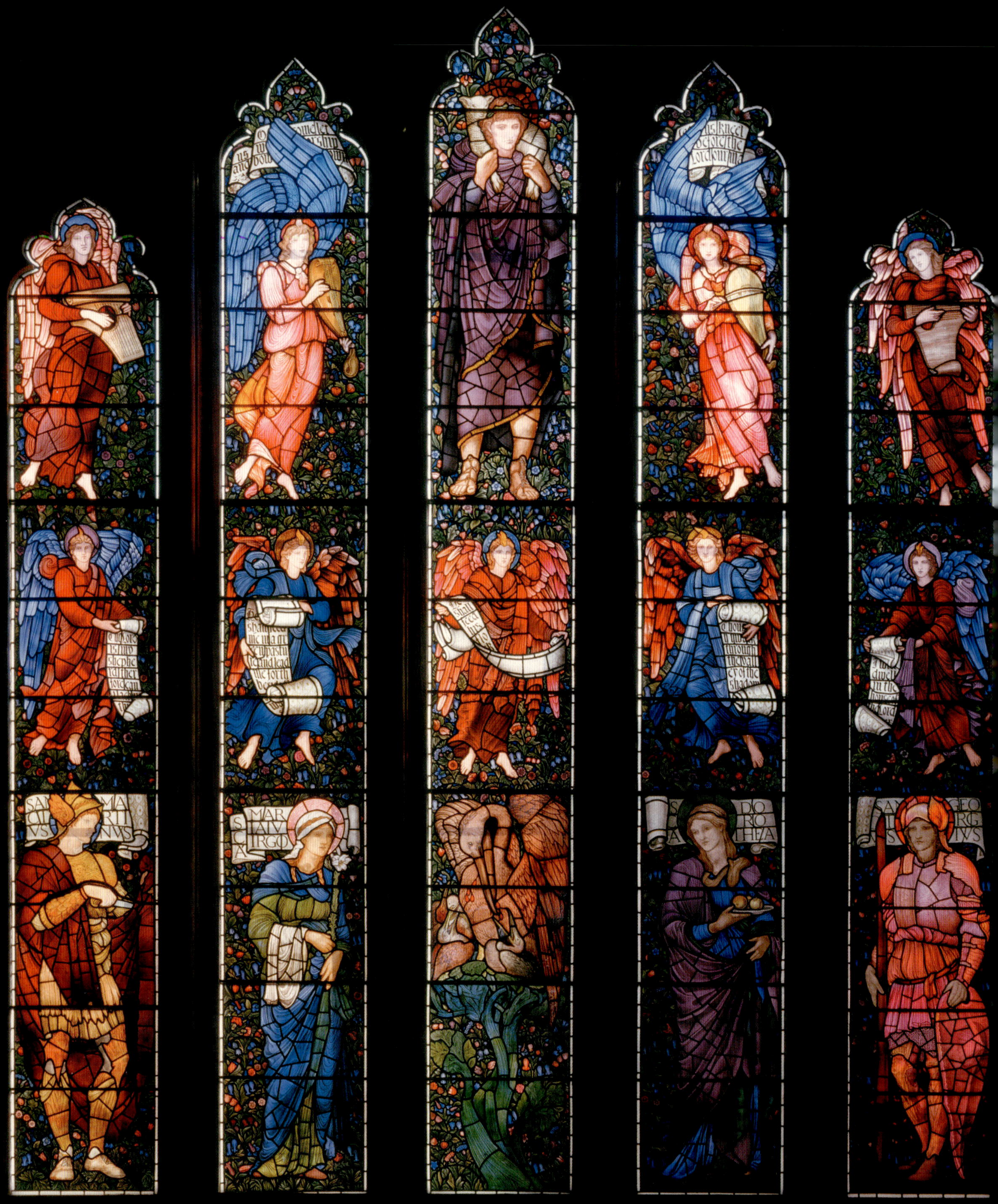

VII

STAINED GLASS AND CHURCH DECORATION

Martin Harrison

'... any departure from the medieval method of production in this art will only lead us astray.'

William Morris, 'Glass, Painted or Stained', 1890

William Morris's rapturous encounter with the cathedrals of Rouen, Chartres, Amiens and Beauvais in 1854 confirmed for him that architecture was 'the foundation of all the arts'. Furthermore, in his essay 'Shadows of Amiens', which romantically evoked 'the apse windows, rich with sweet mellowed stained glass', he embraced the integral role of stained glass in an architectural context. On a tour of northern France in 1855, he and Edward Burne-Jones abandoned their plans to take holy orders; Morris determined to be an architect and Burne-Jones a painter. Burne-Jones had scarcely embarked on his new vocation when he was pitched into the sphere of large-scale public art; early in 1857 Dante Gabriel Rossetti recommended his young protégé to James Powell & Sons as a stained-glass designer. Burne-Jones's designs for the Powells included prestigious commissions for Bradfield College dining hall, Christ Church, Oxford and Waltham Abbey. Morris, who spent most of 1856 in the office of George Edmund Street, may have helped him; he and Burne-Jones shared lodgings from August 1856 until Morris's marriage in April 1859, during which time one of Morris's occupations was 'drawing and colouring designs for stained-glass windows'. The two men would remain the closest of friends throughout their lives, artist and craftsman in a fertile symbiosis.

Fig.115 **East window, Edward Burne-Jones and William Morris, St Martin's, Brampton, Cumbria, 1880.**

A new venture

When Morris, Marshall, Faulkner & Co. was founded in April 1861, the partners' claims to be stained-glass manufacturers were reinforced by Burne-Jones's previous achievements in the medium. Premises were leased at 8 Red Lion Square and a kiln for firing glass and tiles set up in the basement. Two experienced craftsmen were recruited: a glass painter, George Campfield, and a fret lead glazier, Charles Holloway, to cut the glass and fix it into the lead cames. Three apprentices were taken on from the nearby Industrial Home for Destitute Boys, and by 1862 twelve men and boys were employed in the workshop. In line with the firm's experimental origins, Morris familiarized himself with the craft processes and practised by painting glass quarries. Morris was not a technical innovator in this field – the nineteenth-century revival of medieval stained-glass techniques had been accomplished by J.H. Miller, Thomas Willement, A.W.N. Pugin, Charles Winston and others before 1861. Neither, although according to George Wardle it was something Morris 'often regretted', did he manufacture his own coloured or 'pot-metal' glass. However, since 1852 his main suppliers, James Powell & Sons, had been making glass that stood comparison with the medieval material.

Stained glass was the first of the arts at which the firm excelled, and it became the mainstay of its business. All of the partners except Charles Faulkner contributed designs. Rossetti and Peter Paul Marshall provided a limited number until 1863, after which figure cartoons were divided between Burne-Jones, Morris and Ford Madox Brown. Philip Webb had more practical experience of both architecture and stained glass than Morris; it fell to Webb, for example, to test George Campfield's abilities as a glass painter. Webb's contribution was vital and, as William Richard Lethaby remarked, 'the early work of Webb and Morris was so interwoven that we cannot tell in some instances where the work of one man began and the work of another finished.' Webb and Morris planned the architectural arrangements of most of the early windows and Webb designed a majority of their subsidiary elements – symbols of the evangelists, quarries, animals, heraldry, lettering and canopy-work.

Morris, however, was the firm's principal financial investor and its guiding force. His facility for flat-pattern design, fundamental for wallpaper and textiles, crucially enriched the vocabulary of background and drapery motifs in the firm's stained glass. The processes of design and manufacture were strictly separated, and liaison between artists and craftsmen was always through Morris, who supervised all the stages of execution. Above all, Morris addressed the spirit, rather than the letter, of ancient glass. He and his partners grasped that the essence of medieval stained glass was its simplicity, and Morris's concern with process – with craft – enabled him to translate this understanding into practice. His skills as a colourist were paramount: compared to the firm's stained glass, that of their neo-Gothic counterparts tended to be chromatically strident, or inharmonious. Even their most distinguished contemporaries were compromised by archaeology and eclecticism. In 1861 Clayton & Bell, for example, were reworking medieval styles with some originality, but their business expanded exponentially and, lacking the regenerative depth of Morris and his partners, they relied to a greater extent on historical precedent and the recycling of their designs.

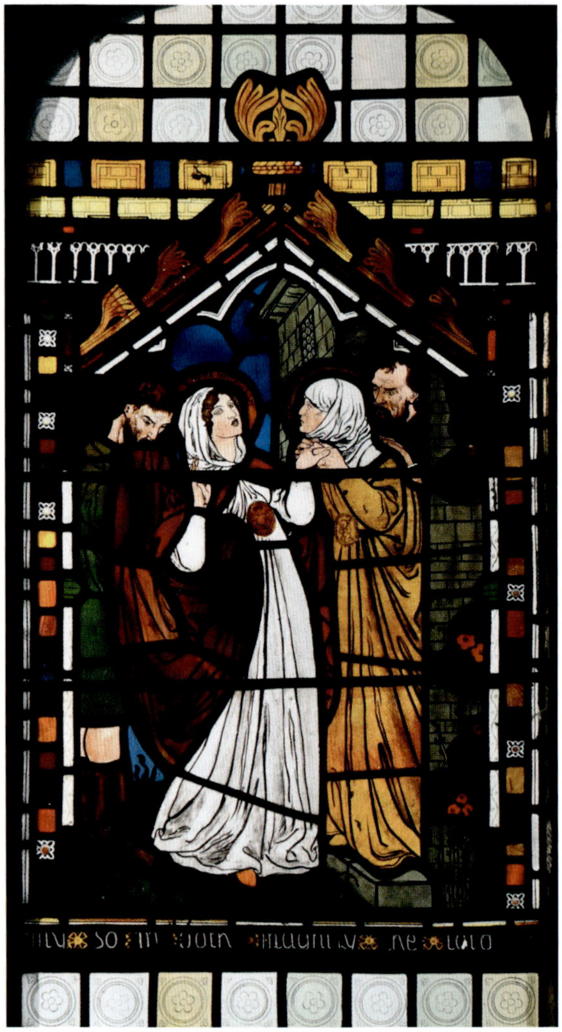

Fig.116 ***The Visitation***, **Dante Gabriel Rossetti, apse window, All Saints, Selsley, Gloucestershire, 1862.**

Yet Morris, too, was obliged to have recourse to the stereotyping of cartoons. At first, all the firm's designs for stained glass were site-specific, but increased demand proved too great for the artists to meet and by 1864 designs were already being repeated. Burne-Jones's *St George* and *St Martin*, designed for Brampton Church, Cumbria, in 1880, were eventually adapted more than 40 times for other churches. The practice was not without its detractors and the decorator John Aldam Heaton, who made stained glass in the 1890s, found it 'really provoking to see the same figures over and over again in Messrs. Morris's windows'. Once Morris had allotted subjects to the individual artists, and provided them with templates of the spaces to be filled, they would produce a sketch design followed by a cartoon (a full-sized drawing) for the glass painters to work from. These were usually drawn in pencil, or pen and ink – Morris was responsible for the colouring of the windows and applying the lead matrix. By 1867 Burne-Jones was employing assistants to scale-up cartoons from his sketches, and from 1874 photographic enlargements were also used to streamline production.

Medieval Modern

As Burne-Jones explained, 'all his life, he [Morris] hated the copying of ancient work as unfair to the old and stupid for the present'. Morris assimilated the palette of blues, rubies, yellows and greens that characterized English fourteenth-century stained glass and redeployed it in distinctive variations; his extensive use of white (clear) glass as a foil to the earth colours he preferred is analogous to the combinations he later obtained with vegetable dyes for fabrics. Without the firm's transformation of the design and colouring of stained glass, the developments of later Gothic revivalists, such as Charles Eamer Kempe and Burlison & Grylls, or 'Aesthetic' designers, such as Henry Holiday and Daniel Cottier, are inconceivable.

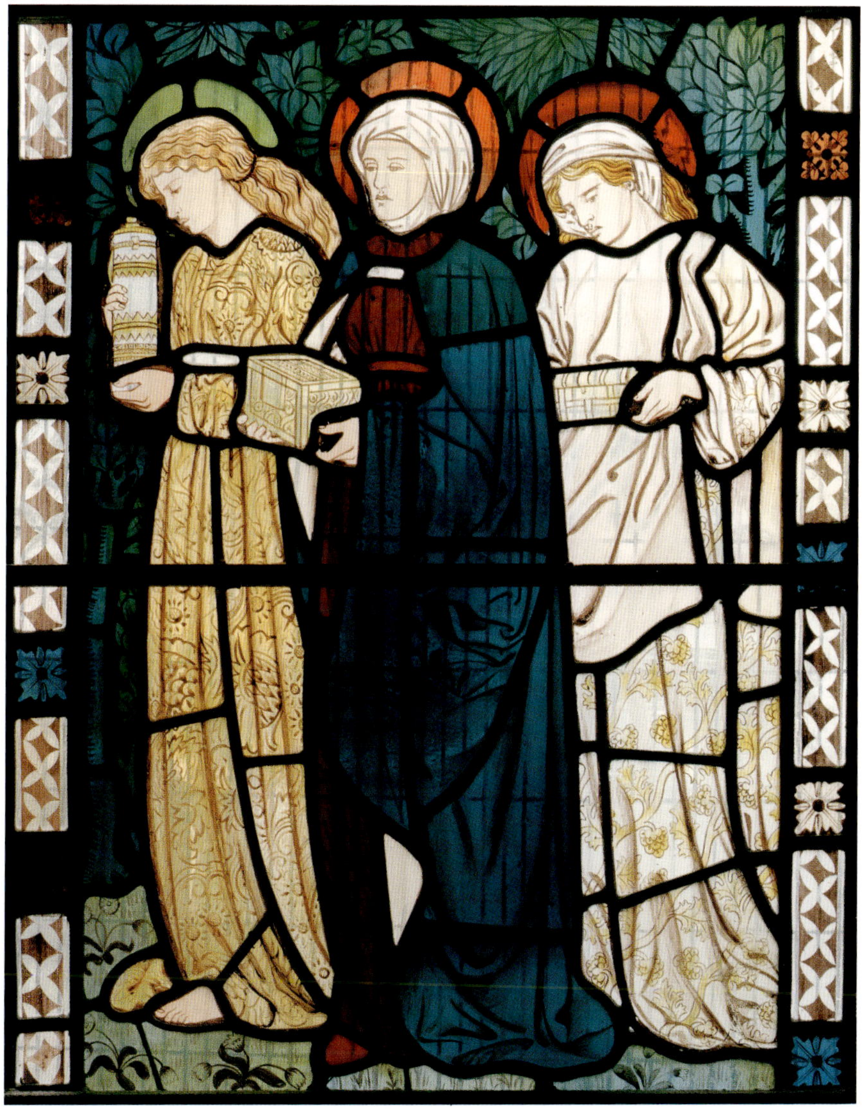

Fig.117 *Three Marys at the Empty Sepulchre*, William Morris, south aisle window, St Michael and All Angels, Brighton, 1862.

Morris and Burne-Jones's anti-pietistic treatment of religious themes was partly a consequence of their youthful disenchantment with the Oxford Movement. The iconography of the firm's stained glass was generally dictated by clients, as the plethora of annunciations and crucifixions attests, but where there was latitude they were inclined to depart from the standard mid-Victorian repertory and select subjects for their humanistic or visual appeal. For Burne-Jones, in particular, the principal attraction of such subjects as St Nicholas or St Ursula lay in the existence of established treatments of those themes within the history of art. Few of the firm's early projects originated outside a coterie of friends and architect patrons. John Hungerford Pollen, Myles Birket Foster and Colonel Gillum all had artistic connections with members of the firm, and Heaton introduced several clients in the Bradford district, which resulted in windows for Bradford Cathedral and the *Tristram and Isolde* series for Harden Grange. However, the bulk of their stained glass in the 1860s was supplied to Gothic Revival architects, the first and most important of whom was George Frederick Bodley.

On completing his pupillage with George Gilbert Scott, Bodley occasionally helped in the office of his friend Street in Oxford, where he would have met Webb, Street's assistant from 1854 to 1859. Bodley knew Morris, Rossetti and Madox Brown by 1857 when they, along with Street, John Ruskin, William Burges, William Holman Hunt, John Pollard Seddon, John Richard Clayton and William White, were among the founder members of the Medieval Society, a short-lived group of enthusiasts for the arts of the early Middle Ages. Early in 1860 he engaged Burne-Jones to paint an altarpiece for St Paul's, Brighton (VII.4). Bodley became, in effect, the firm's eighth partner, responsible for its first three large church schemes and at least 11 further jobs in the 1860s.

The first Morris, Marshall, Faulkner & Co. stained glass, begun in 1861, was for Bodley's new church of All Saints, Selsley, Gloucestershire (fig.116). The nave and apse windows follow the arrangement of the side windows at Merton College Chapel, Oxford, *c.*1310, in which rectangular bands of richly coloured figure panels are set within pale geometric *grisailles*. Merton had been a favourite haunt of Morris and his friends at Oxford and he regarded its glass, with its 'singular elegance and richness', as representing 'the highest point reached by the art'. Philip Webb drew the Merton windows in 1861, doubtless on account of the Selsley job, and he made preliminary sketches of the firm's glazing scheme at Selsley as well as designing all the borders, quarries, canopy-work and lettering. He and Morris integrated the individual styles of the figure cartoonists – Rossetti's vigour, Madox Brown's expressiveness, Burne-Jones's elegant fluency and Morris's own simple, narrative directness – into a coherent entity.

Two further Bodley churches, St Michael and All Angels, Brighton, and St Martin-on-the-Hill, Scarborough, were in progress in 1862. At Brighton, influenced by the theories of Ruskin and the example of Street, Bodley produced one of his most vigorous buildings, its French Gothic outline and Italian brick and stone polychromy thrust audaciously into the resort's polite stuccoed terraces. The glazing at Brighton had already been commenced by Clayton & Bell when Morris was brought in. The chancel roof, the firm's sole contribution to the painted decoration, was applied *in situ* by Morris, Webb and Faulkner; Webb recorded that he spent five days at the task. Of the four windows placed by the firm in 1862, Morris's *Three Marys at the Empty Sepulchre* was the first of his scarce multi-figure compositions (fig.117). In the impressive west window the archangels, designed by Morris and Madox Brown, are appositely formal,

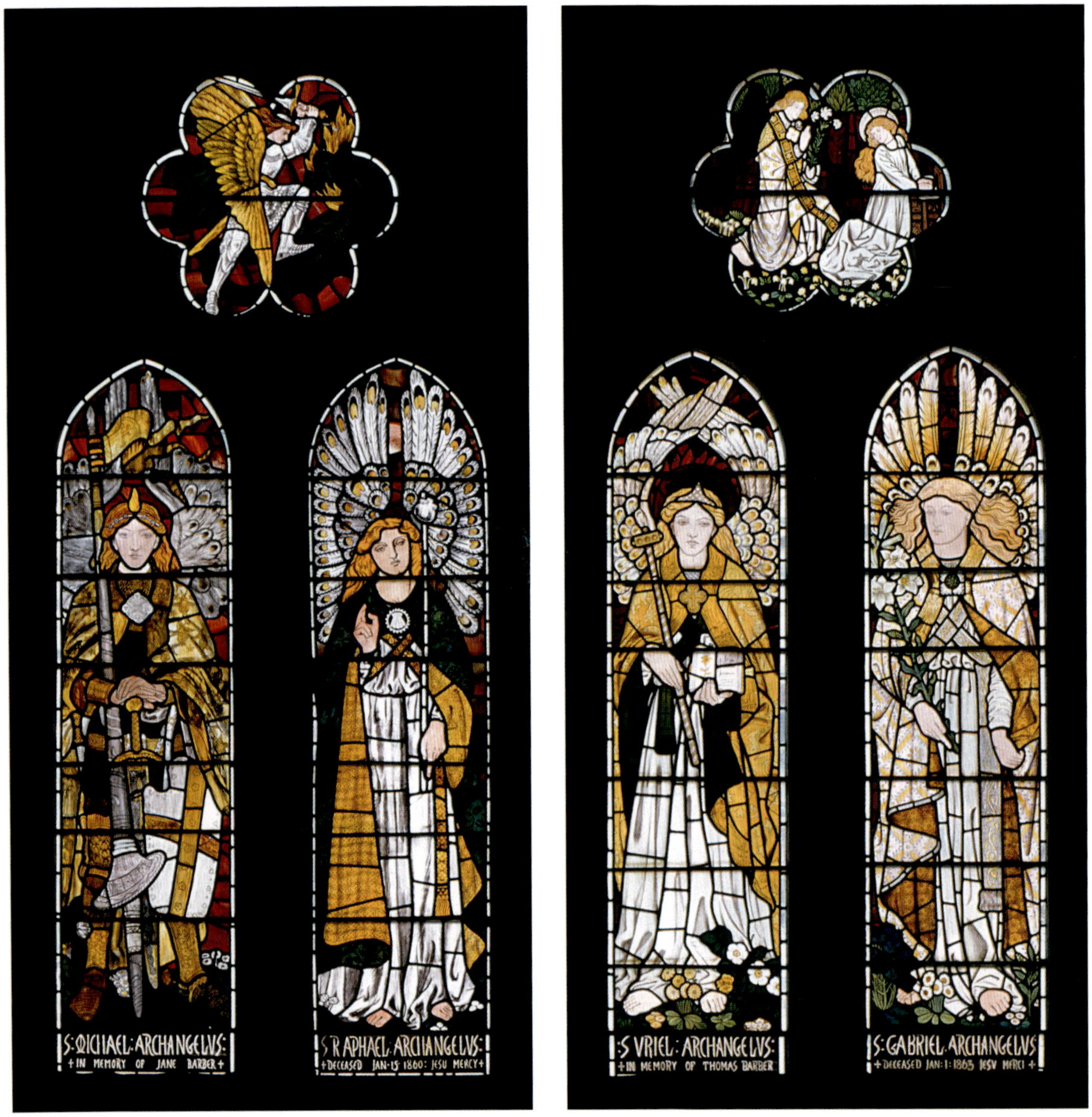

Fig.118 **Details of the west window, St Michael and All Angels, Brighton, 1862. Morris provided the designs for *St Raphael* and *St Gabriel*; Ford Madox Brown *St Michael* and *St Uriel*. The sexfoil *St Michael Slaying the Dragon* is by Peter Paul Marshall, *The Annunciation* by Morris.**

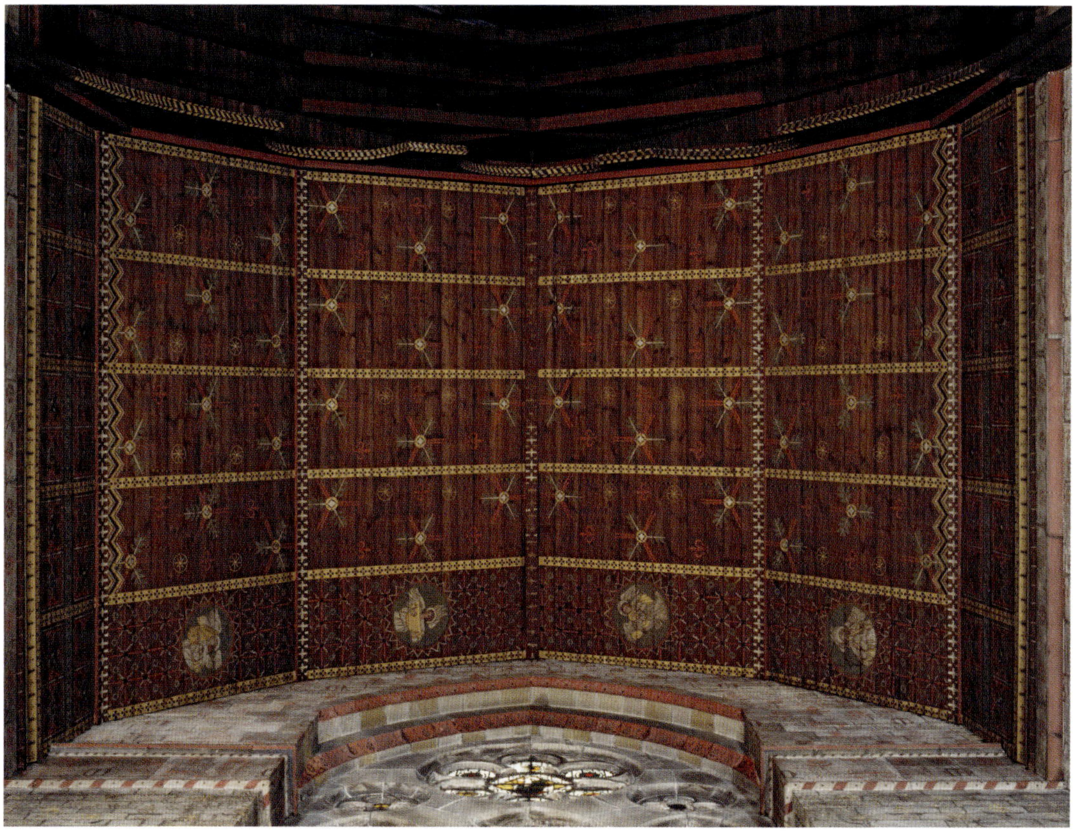

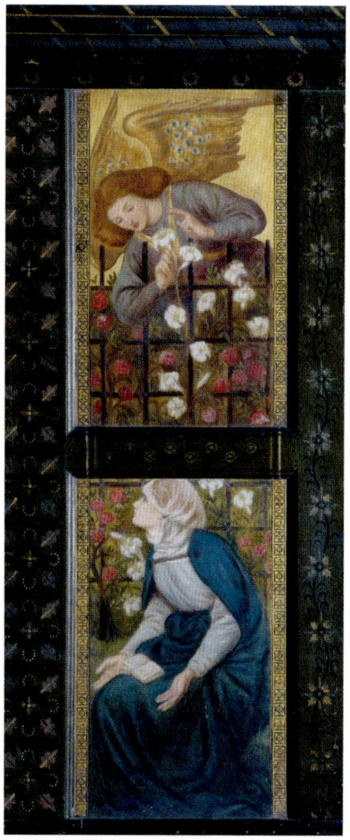

Fig.119 (above left) **Chancel roof, St Martin-on-the-Hill, Scarborough.**

Fig.120 (above right) ***Annunciation*, Dante Gabriel Rossetti, detail of the side of the pulpit, St Martin-on-the-Hill, Scarborough.**

yet their dignity is subtly animated, resembling the *déhanchement* poses of thirteenth-century Gothic sculpture. The seven circles above contain sweet angels playing bells by Burne-Jones, framing his *Virgin and Child*. Colour is introduced sparingly into a composition in which Morris deftly exploited the use of yellow stains on white glass to produce a harmony in silver and gold. Morris translated the frontality of the figures in lead patterns that he arranged in a regular, geometrical rhythm – an astonishingly precocious instance of the 'mosaic system' he advocated but did not return to in this form until the 1880s (fig.118).

The Scarborough church is tough and gaunt, of Whitby stone. Although still in a High Victorian idiom, it foreshadows the churches of Bodley's maturity, in which plain interior surfaces functioned as the foundation for richness in decoration. The painted chancel ceiling at Scarborough was designed by Morris and Webb (fig.119), and beneath the high sill of the east window the blank arcading contains Burne-Jones's painting of the *Adoration of the Magi*, flanked by angels designed by Morris. The pulpit here is a tour de force, painted by George Campfield after designs by Madox Brown, Rossetti and Morris (fig.120). The firm's extensive series of windows at Scarborough was another unified scheme; Madox Brown's languid *Adam* and *Eve* in the west window are particularly effective, in spite of the intrusion of the stanchions (fig.121). His confident handling of these large-scale figures occasions regret that his designs were generally restricted to small narrative panels, although he invested the best of these with considerable emotive power. At least in the Hall and Combination Room windows at Peterhouse, Cambridge, 1871–4, and the *Legend of St Editha* programme at St Editha (fig.122), Tamworth, 1873, Madox Brown had the scope to manifest his gifts as a history painter and ably demonstrated his aptitude for such subject matter.

In the 1860s the firm's ecclesiastical (and most of its secular) stained glass was installed in Gothic Revival buildings, where its 'Anglo-aestheticism' was arguably more 'advanced' than the interiors it adorned. At Brighton, for example, Clayton & Bell's Franco-Italianate east window is more congruous with Bodley's polychrome walls than the reticent Morris window facing it. Morris's principal clients in this period were all Goths – Street, Seddon, George Gilbert Scott, Edward Robert Robson and Thomas Garner. At first the firm's

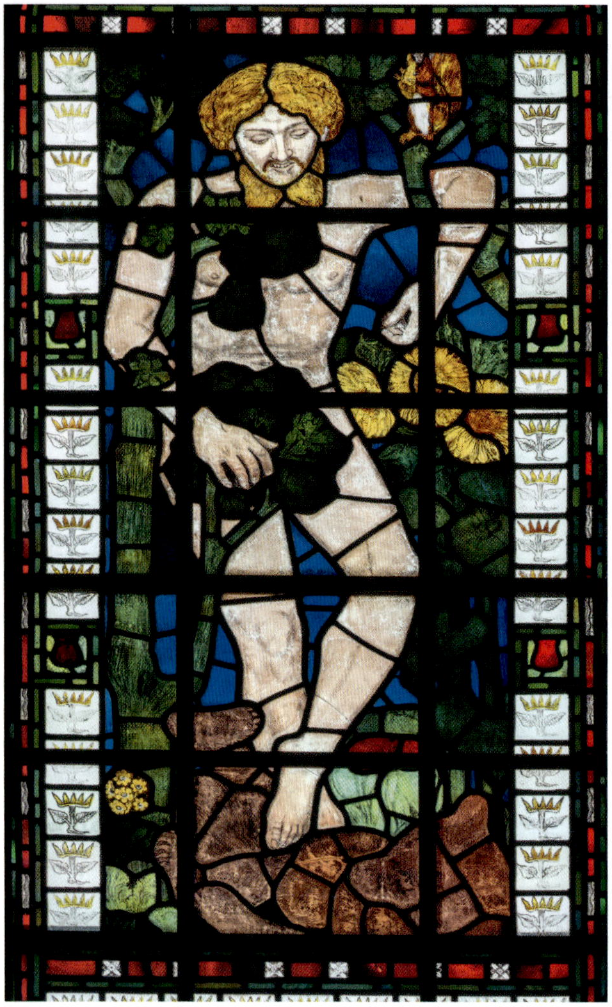

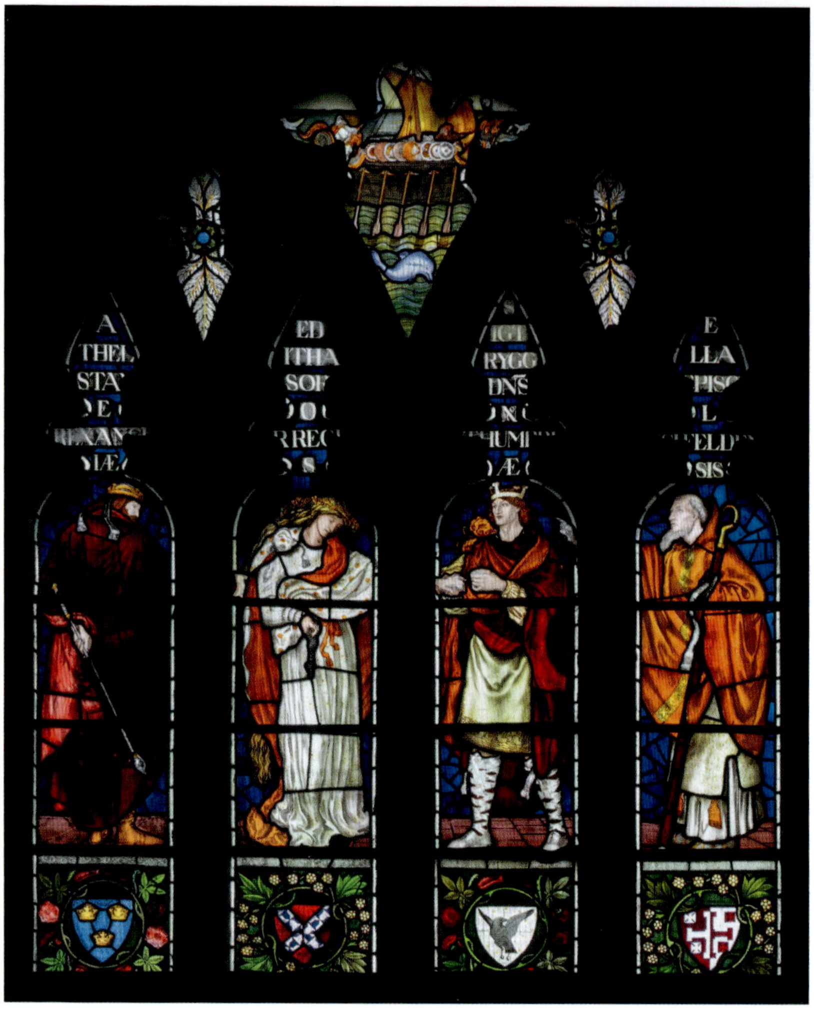

Fig.121 ***Adam*****, Ford Madox Brown, west window, St Martin-on-the-Hill, Scarborough, 1862.**

Fig.122 ***The Marriage of St Editha*****, Ford Madox Brown, chancel south clerestory, St Editha, Tamworth, Staffordshire, 1873.**

modernity was not widely apprehended – as George Wardle observed of Morris, 'so few recognized the real originality and modernness of his art'. The firm's display at the 1862 International Exhibition was, as Morris claimed, 'much ridiculed'; even the generally sympathetic *Building News* noted, oddly, their 'strict adherence to mediæval types'. Eight years later Webb was still at pains to explain to Charles Eastlake that he did not believe his buildings qualified for inclusion in Eastlake's survey, *A History of the Gothic Revival*.

The reaction against the Gothic Revival was partly a rejection of its continental stylistic sources. This is a complex argument – it was, after all, the cathedrals of northern France that had inspired Morris to pursue architecture. There was a political factor: when the firm began, Morris, Burne-Jones, Rossetti and Madox Brown were drilling with the Corps of Artist Volunteers, formed in 1859 when invasion by Napoleon III was perceived as a serious threat. The correspondence of Warington Taylor, with its Francophobic undertones, elucidates further. Taylor was Morris's business manager from 1865 until his early death in 1870, but he had been close to the circle since the early 1860s. As Georgiana Burne-Jones recalled, Taylor 'knew and cared a great deal about the arts', and he became the proxy intellectual spokesman and conscience for the group. In 1862 he wrote to Robson attacking the 'progressive' Goths Burges and Seddon for their 'huge coarse' French Gothic. Instead he advocated Englishness, as 'small as our landscape is small, it is sweet picturesque homely farmyardish, Japanese, social, domestic'. Robson, about to build a muscular, thirteenth-century French Gothic fountain in Durham, may have been startled at such candour. In *The Building News* in 1865 Taylor cited the three architects, William Butterfield, Webb and Bodley, who could be relied upon not to foist 'a small French cathedral' on an English village. Webb saw 'honest building' as the alternative to the syncretic eclecticism that had failed to produce a genuinely modern architecture: 'You don't want any style', agreed Taylor, 'you want something English in character.' Essentially, Taylor and Webb had formulated – and the firm's stained glass of the 1860s is directly analogous – an English vernacular. Webb, however, built only one church, St Martin's, Brampton, Cumbria, and this was not completed until 1878. Robson used Morris glass in the early 1860s at St Oswald's, Durham, and Shotley Hall near Gateshead, Durham, and as Architect and Surveyor to Liverpool Corporation he commissioned a design for a vast lunette window in St George's Hall. However, he adhered to French Gothic until adapting the Queen Anne style for his London School Board buildings in the 1870s.

George Gilbert Scott was nominally a client, although more plausibly it was his son, George Gilbert Scott Junior, who commissioned Morris. Scott Junior was a frequent visitor to 'the shop' in Red Lion Square and an admirer of the firm; evidently his father, who thought their windows 'still more strange than those of any of their predecessors', was not. Some of the earliest stained glass for Scott (at Christ Church, Southgate, Middlesex, and All Saints, Langton Green, Kent) is in a figure-and-canopy idiom close to medieval prototypes, its historicism pointing to Scott Junior's influence. The restoration of the church of St Edward the Confessor, Cheddleton, Staffordshire, is documented as the son's work. Webb's canopy designs for the chancel windows (1864) were modelled on fourteenth-century fragments that survived in the church, an antiquarian conception that anticipated Scott Junior's collaborations with Burlison & Grylls in the 1870s. In two further Scott commissions, Morris's figures of *St Paul* and *St John Baptist* at St Giles, Camberwell, London (1865), and *Ruth* and *Boaz* at Cheddleton (1868), stand under canopies designed by Webb. These were later repudiated by Webb as having been done when he was a 'Gothic man', but his delicately translucent foliated arches effectively develop a traditional formula.

The outstanding Scott–Morris collaboration, the east window of All Saints, Middleton Cheney, Northamptonshire (1865), incorporates figures by Madox Brown, Burne-Jones, Morris, Webb and, uniquely, Simeon Solomon (fig.123). The cartoons for *Abraham and Moses* and *David and Isaiah* were drawn by Solomon, and, in the upper row, the *Tribes of Israel*, who hold aloft banners designed by Webb that stretch into the cusps and link with the tracery lights (apparently, assigning these subjects to Solomon did not, in 1865, register as having anti-Semitic connotations). The subdivision of the main lights into rows of rectangular panels, an arrangement employed in the firm's earlier window at Darley Dale, followed well-known fifteenth-century prototypes, such as those at All Saints, North Street, York, and St Peter Mancroft, Norwich.

Transition

Although Webb's involvement continued beyond 1869, his domed, turreted and battlemented 'Holy City' canopy, designed in that year for the cusps of the main lights in the east window of St Mary's, Bloxham, Oxfordshire, was his last significant contribution of its kind. It signalled the closing of a phase, for Morris, stimulated by his interest in flat-pattern design in other media, had again turned his attention to the backgrounds for windows. Some of these, for example, the south aisle east window of St Michael's, Tilehurst, Berkshire (1869), with its flaming gold stars on a prominent blue wave pattern, are strikingly original reformulations of an ancient symbolic language (fig.124). In the south aisle of Cheddleton Church, Burne-Jones's *Trumpeting Angels* (1869) are a forceful presence; Scott Junior, who thought 'we make a great deal too much of stained glass [which is] essentially an architectural decoration', must have been concerned that their restless contrapposto dominated the interior, and conscious, too, that the gyrating figures had a greater affinity to secular than to devotional art (fig.125). Conversely, in the contemporaneous east window of St Mary's, King's Walden, Hertfordshire, which was designed entirely by Morris, the figures are calmer than Burne-Jones's and do not strain against their architectural framework.

By 1870, however, Burne-Jones was supplying the majority of the firm's figure cartoons, and his artistic passions were no longer directed towards romantic medievalism but to Botticelli, Signorelli and Mantegna. Consequently, Scott Junior, along with many of the leading Gothic Revival architects, switched to more conservative stained-glass makers. Privately donated memorial windows (Morris called them 'gravestones'), which had been an expanding market since the 1840s, would become a substantial alternative source of income for the firm. In 1869, Clement Heaton, founder of a successful stained-glass workshop, Heaton, Butler & Bayne, noted the public relations value to Morris's company of the Green Dining

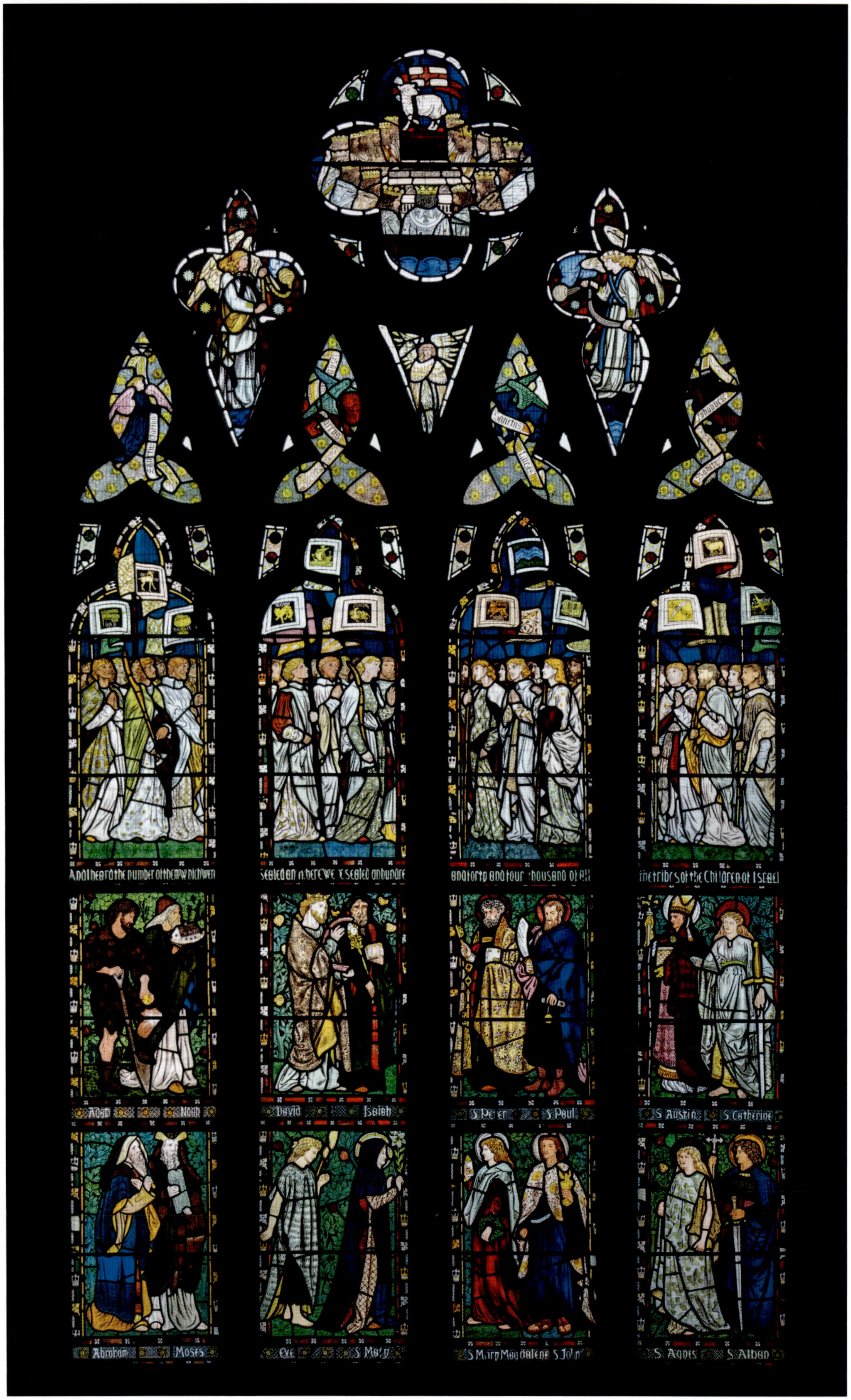

Fig.123 **East window, All Saints, Middleton Cheney, Northamptonshire, 1865.**

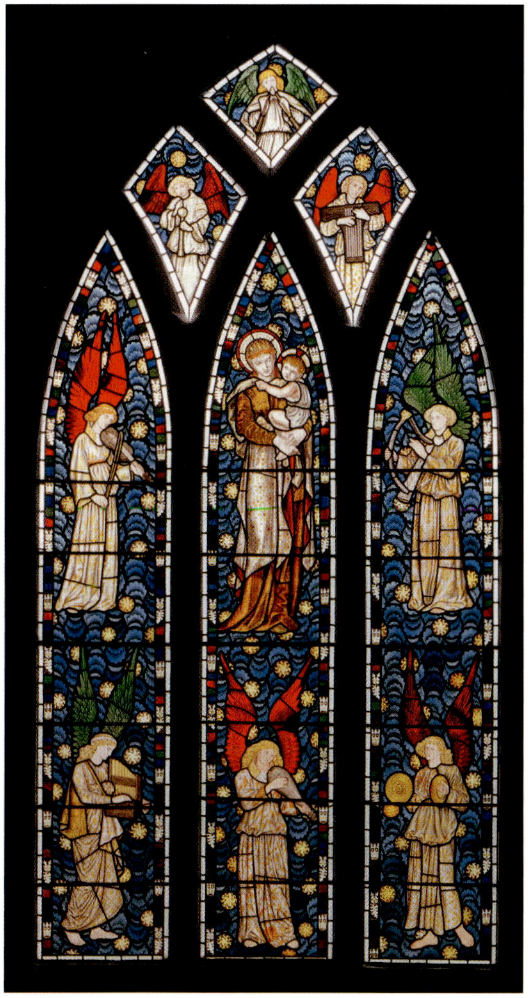

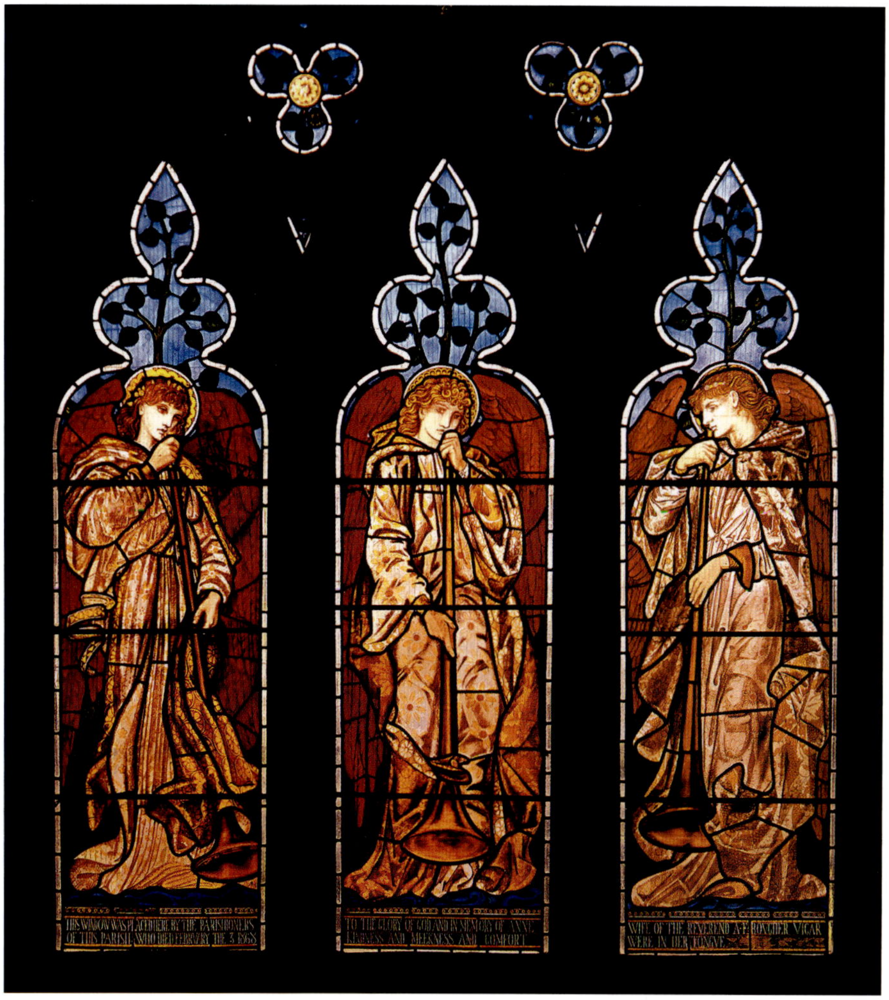

Fig.124 ***Virgin and Child with Angel Musicians*, Edward Burne-Jones and William Morris, south aisle east window, St Michael's, Tilehurst, Berkshire, 1869.**

Fig.125 ***Trumpeting Angels*, Edward Burne-Jones, south aisle, St Edward the Confessor, Cheddleton, Staffordshire, 1869.**

Room at the South Kensington Museum (fig.140) Heaton observed that 'Their works are not always appreciated by the multitude', but that 'their merit is fully seen and acknowledged by art-critics.' After the firm's early success, there was indeed a decline in its stained-glass production between 1866 and 1871, followed by a sustained peak throughout the 1870s; in one year alone, 1875, Burne-Jones supplied 65 full-sized cartoons. But while the production of textiles increased, other forms of church decoration – painted tiles (figs 178–9), furniture and decoration – declined or ceased entirely after 1870.

In 1861 Morris had loftily dismissed the rival firm of Clayton & Bell as 'only glass painters in point of fact'. Although he later conceded that they 'do very fair glass now', this was, he maintained, because 'we have taught them how to colour.' If this imperiousness reflects his awareness, as Lewis F. Day commented, that in technique Morris 'had something to learn from men like Mr John Clayton, who were before him in the field', the sober colouring that Clayton & Bell adopted after 1862 supports the veracity of Morris's claim. Several of the Gothic Revival architects who deserted Morris in the 1870s transferred their patronage to Clayton & Bell and other established workshops such as Ward & Hughes, John Hardman & Co. and William Wailes. The larger firms held certain competitive advantages, as William Eden Nesfield, the architect responsible for Morris's King's Walden window, recognized in warning a client that Morris's glass was liable to be both extremely costly and up to 15 months late in delivery. Among the 'progressive' Goths, neither Burges nor E.W. Godwin patronized the firm. Seddon, who had commissioned Rossetti's painted altarpiece for Llandaff Cathedral (1858–64) and was a regular client for the firm's stained glass, became dissatisfied with what he perceived as its lack of translucency: but this was a criticism Morris had already begun to address.

Against Gothic

In 1867, after Morris had completed the decoration of the nave roof at Jesus College Chapel, Cambridge (figs 126–7), Bodley began to lobby the Dean to commence the glazing of the nave windows. After much prevarication, in 1872 the Dean opted for Morris, but in the interim Bodley had put forward the makers in whose foundation he was instrumental, Burlison & Grylls: 'With Burlison & Grylls', the architect admitted, 'I find I get my own way more than I can with Morris'. Nevertheless, the first Morris windows were in place at Jesus late in 1872. By then, Burlison & Grylls had begun the glazing and decoration of Bodley's church of St Augustine, Pendlebury, Lancashire, and the contrast between these two schemes could not be greater. Bodley thought of medieval glass as 'the story of progress in refinement', and henceforth, like Scott Junior, he found the stained glass of Burlison & Grylls, with its less dynamic gestural language, adherence to late-medieval prototypes and restrained colouring, more congenial.

At Jesus College it is evident that Bodley did not 'get his own way'. The sculptural vigour of the figures reflects Burne-Jones's return, in October 1871, from the third of his four tours of Italy, which confirmed his admiration for Michelangelo, an artist whose 'dark carnality' appalled Ruskin (fig.128). Bodley, who preached 'the avoidance of extravagance of manner', might have concurred with Ruskin. Yet Morris's stunning colour scheme may have unsettled the architect as much as Burne-Jones's figures. Morris had emphasized to the Dean that colour, particularly 'rich blues in the draperies' was his priority, and the chromatic ensemble undeniably dominates the interior. Morris was aware of a dichotomy here, for he advised that stained-glass artists 'should not attempt to design pictures but rather pieces of ornamental glazing ... decorating the buildings of which they form a part'. Yet the glazing of the chapel makes a compelling case for stained glass, on certain occasions, providing a more gratifying aesthetic experience than the masonry. Bodley's vaunted 'refinement' sometimes registers as timidity: Morris's stained glass at Jesus is not timid – cumulatively it is more intense than the architecture. Paradoxically, it was an architect, John James Stevenson, a pioneer of the Queen Anne revival, who posited the most extreme view in support of the artist's autonomy in this respect: 'Dante Rossetti, when designing for a stained-glass window in a church, once asked me if I thought the architect would be offended if he asked him to cut away the cusps, as he could make a better design for his picture if they were away. As Rossetti's picture was a more interesting work of art than the architect's regulation cusps, I said the architect would do well to remove them.'

Morris and Burne-Jones were equally radical at Jesus College. In translating Burne-Jones's designs, Morris wisely kept the broad colour schemes

Fig.126 (below left) **Design of an angel for the nave ceiling, William Morris, Jesus College Chapel, 1866.**

Fig.127 (below right) **Nave ceiling, Jesus College Chapel, Cambridge.**

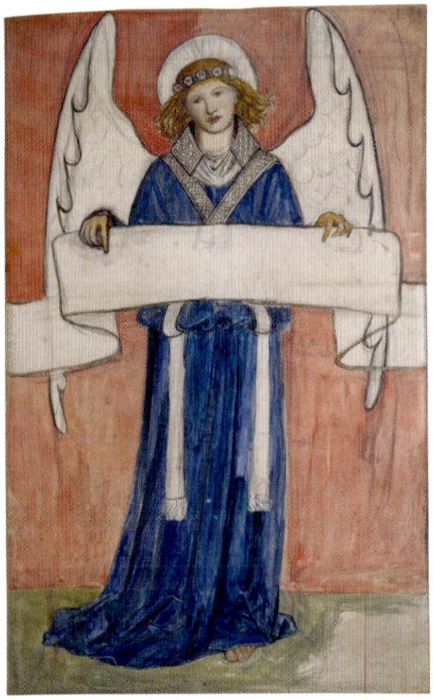

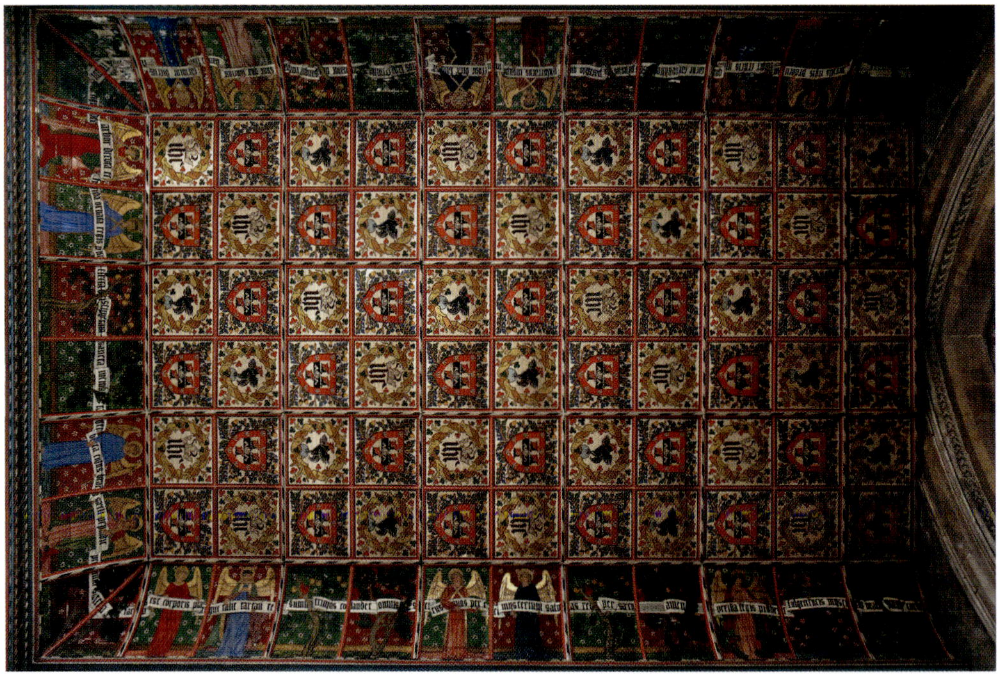

Fig.128 ***Cherubim*, Edward Burne-Jones, detail of south transept window, Jesus College Chapel, Cambridge, 1873.**

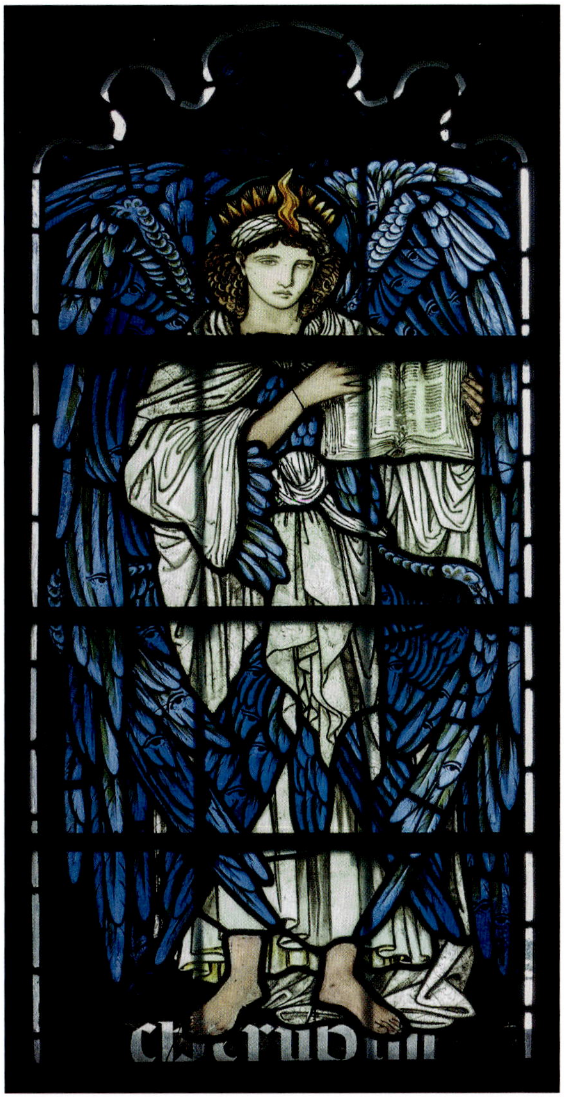

simple: backgrounds were dominated by reds and blues, and verdure was always balanced and harmonious. On close inspection he can be seen to have broken out, within this ordered scheme, into smaller passages in which secondary colours were juxtaposed in unprecedented ways; these effects are mainly confined to the small base panels, designed by both Madox Brown and Burne-Jones. Morris supplied ten windows to the nave and transepts at Jesus, which comprised (excluding the traceries) 38 separate lights. The programme was completed in 1878, but while it was in progress Morris, Marshall, Faulkner & Co., had been reformed as Morris & Company in 1875. Rossetti, Marshall and Madox Brown were unhappy with this arrangement; they split irrevocably from Morris, with the result that subsequently Burne-Jones was responsible for nearly all of the firm's new figure designs.

In 1877 Morris and Webb founded the Society for the Protection of Ancient Buildings, consistent with which Morris announced that he was ceasing to install new windows in medieval churches. In the same year he wrote on behalf of the SPAB to the vicar of Llanbadarn Fawr, Cardiganshire, expressing his concern over the plans to restore this early medieval church and urging only 'judicious repairing'. He must have been aware that Seddon was in charge of the restoration, but tactlessly omitted to refer to him by name. Seddon was incensed, and in the *Ecclesiastical Art Review* he reminded Morris of the debt he owed him, referring to several commissions for Llandaff Cathedral, 1866–74. He redirected his ire at Morris's stained glass: 'though their transparencies (they are no more) stand out in happy relief of sobriety – it is not difficult to be sober if you only deal with mud colours', and when the pseudonymous 'Erwin von Steinbach' replied in defence of Morris, Seddon countered that his windows were 'opacities' and 'not in keeping with architecture'.

Irrespective of Seddon's underlying motives, his taunts may have needled Morris, in whose windows of the late 1860s the colours are sometimes rather muddy, while the use of enamel paints, particularly for the flesh, might be said to approach 'opacity'. But Seddon had elected not to mention, or was not familiar with, the stained glass, such as that at Jesus College, that undermined his argument. Surprisingly, in 1879 – soon after these hostilities – Seddon commissioned Morris to supply a window to his church at Hoarwithy, Herefordshire. Morris's vibrant execution of Burne-Jones's *Trumpeting Angel* at Hoarwithy may have been intended to demonstrate that he could make stained glass with the translucency Seddon desired, and it is possible he purchased innovative raw glass from Seddon's glass-maker, Jesse Rust, in order to achieve this result.

Morris's SPAB stance further cemented his estrangement from Street, but the architect never lost his admiration for Burne-Jones, whom he described as 'an eminent artist who is not above designing for glass in such a way as to make his work absolutely suitable for the material. Some of his windows are equal to any old ones.' Street probably wrote this shortly after the installation, in 1879, of Burne-Jones's monumental *Angeli Ministrantes* and *Angeli Laudantes* at Salisbury Cathedral, to which he had been appointed architect: evidently, Morris had temporarily relaxed his proscription against supplying stained glass to ancient churches. That Burne-Jones's emphatically non-Gothic interventions

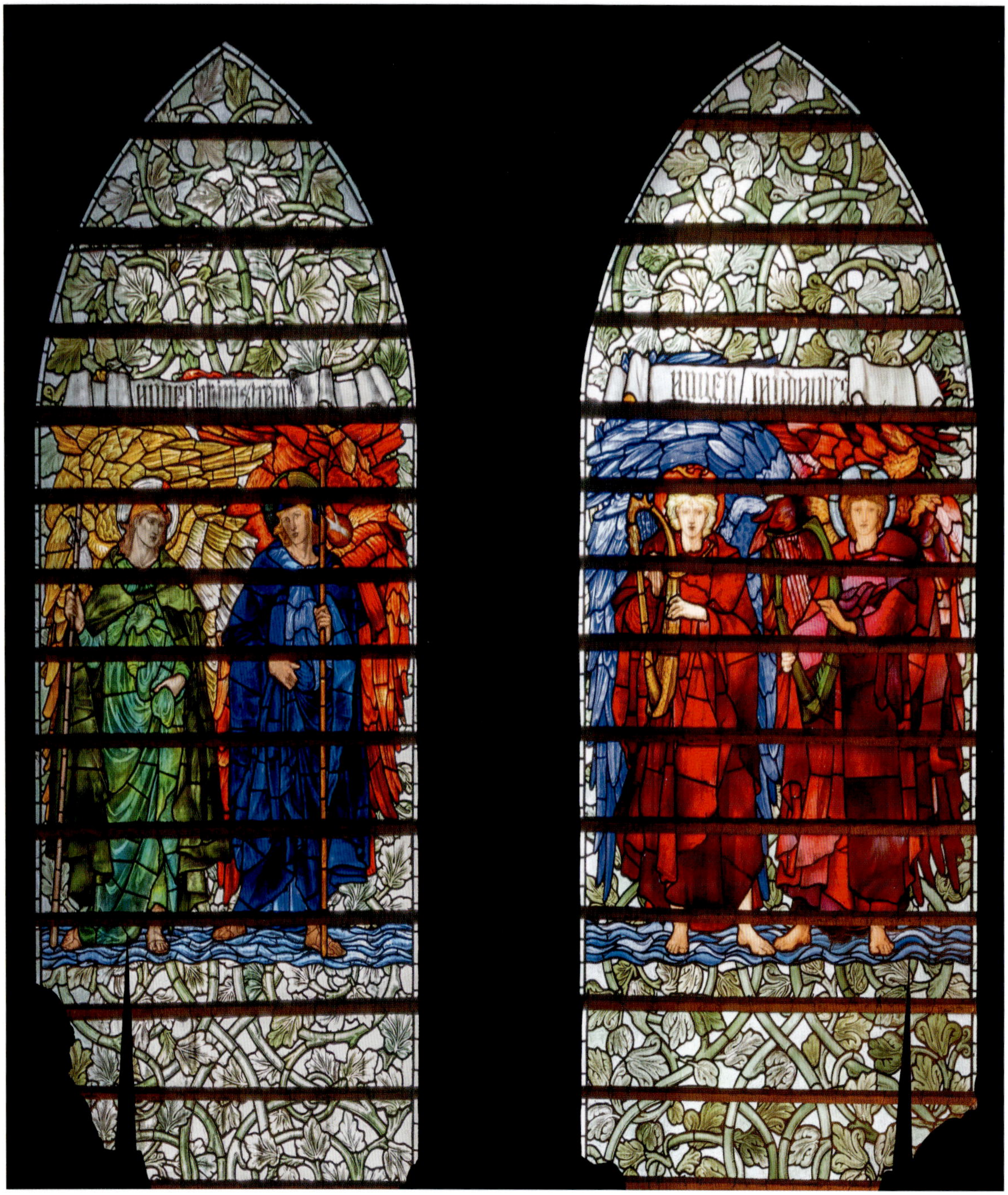

Fig.129 ***Angeli Ministrantes* and *Angeli Laudantes*, Edward Burne-Jones and William Morris, south choir aisle, Salisbury Cathedral, 1879.**

seem appropriate in the context of Salisbury's tall, broad lancets depends to a great extent on Morris's broadly scaled but pale foliate grounds in this imaginative reformulation of the medieval 'banded' format (fig.129). The Venetian grandeur of Burne-Jones's pairs of imposing, standing angels proved very popular, and they were later successfully woven as tapestries (see XII.116).

Burne-Jones drew a clear distinction between 'a picture' and 'a painting'. He placed a premium on draughtsmanship and bestowed infinite care on preliminary drawings; he deplored the lack of finish in the work of J.M.W. Turner, James McNeill Whistler and the Impressionists, and regarded painterliness only as a means to an end – a finished 'picture'. The paintings of the 1870s that sealed his reputation have struck some commentators as overwrought, their protagonists overtaken by dreamy stasis, but such criticisms are less pertinent to his stained glass. In the stained-glass designs the

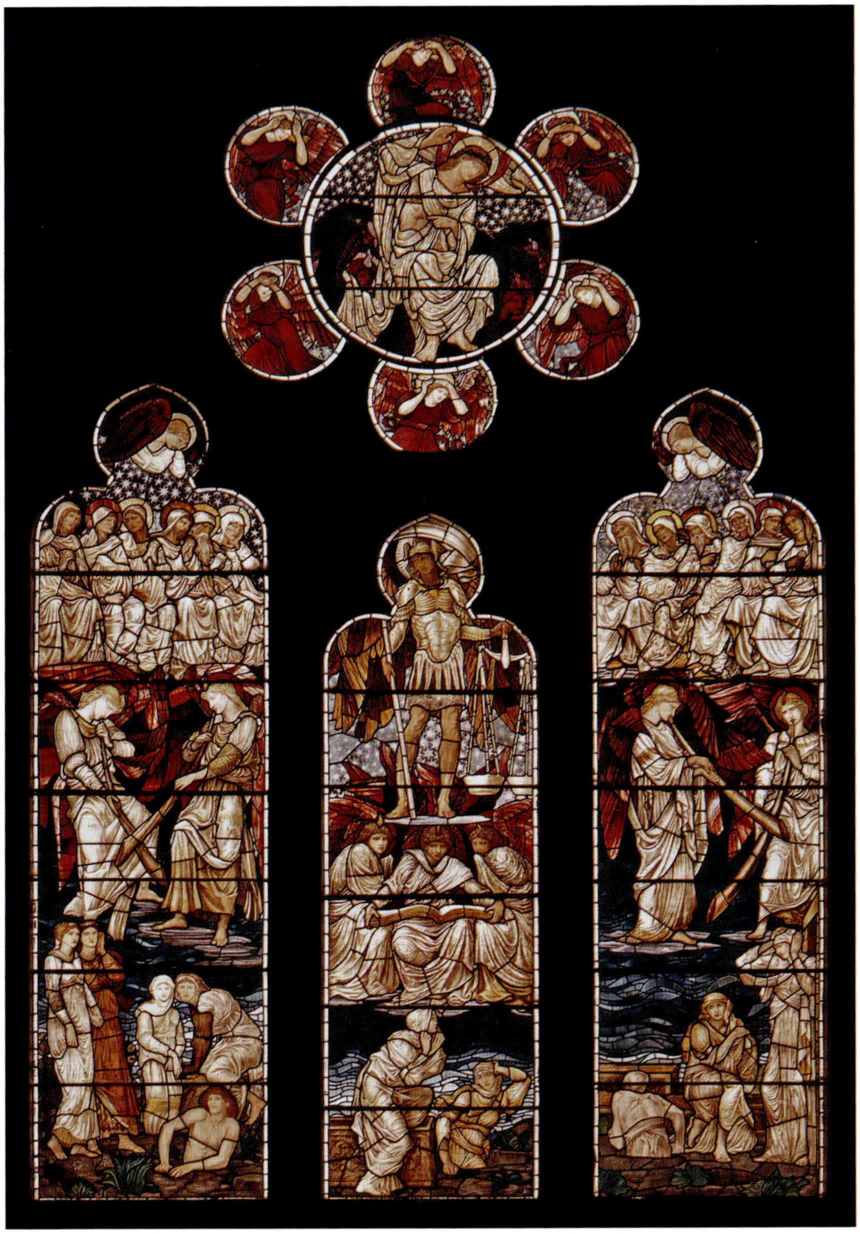

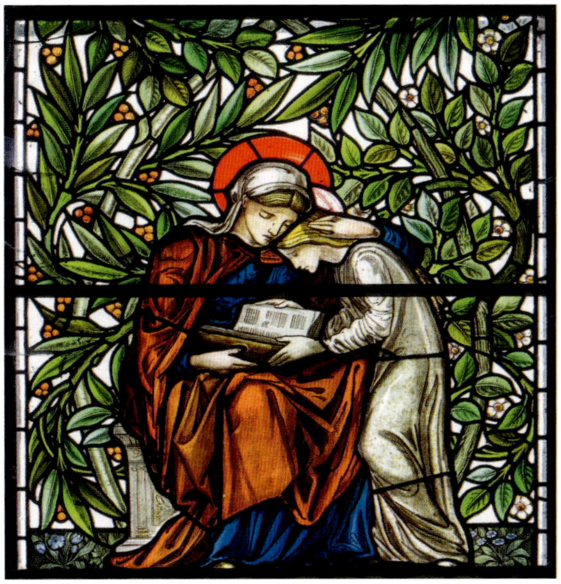

Fig.130 ***Last Judgment*, Edward Burne-Jones and William Morris, chancel east window, St Michael and St Mary Magdalene, Easthampstead, 1876.**

Fig.131 ***The Virgin with St Anne*, Edward Burne-Jones and William Morris, detail of east window, St Mary, Nun Monkton, Yorkshire, 1873.**

psychological and technical extremes were abrogated by his respect for the limits and function of the iconography and the inherent disciplines of the medium, while the linear dynamics and his facility as a designer of figures-in-space remained intact.

The firm's most impressive stained glass of the 1870s falls into two principal categories. In the first Burne-Jones provided a global design to fill a (usually) three- or five-light east window, and in the second Morris, often recycling pre-existing figure cartoons, designed backgrounds that ingeniously harmonized potentially disparate elements. The composition of the *Rivers of Paradise* at All Hallows, Allerton, Liverpool (1875), recalls, in its upward and lateral movement, Burne-Jones's first *Courts of Heaven* design for St Michael and All Angels, Lyndhurst, Hampshire (1862). The focus on the *Agnus Dei* at Allerton is Van Eyckian, but the basic concept, like that at Lyndhurst, derives from Fra Angelico: that is to say, like Burne-Jones's paintings of the time, it is fundamentally Italianate rather than Gothic. The Easthampstead *Last Judgment* (1876) cannot in any meaningful sense be described as Gothic (fig.130). It is Burne-Jones's quintessential homage to Michelangelo, a rationalization of the east wall of the Sistine Chapel that is spectacular on a level seldom achieved in stained glass; the building of the composition from the base of the central panel in ascending cadences of figures is masterly. Morris's contribution to the *Last Judgment* was also considerable, for it was he who provided the beautiful, celestial background details as well as the colour scheme.

Among the mainly Morris-directed windows, those at the east end of two Yorkshire churches, St Mary, Nun Monkton (1873), and St Mary, Tadcaster (1879), are outstanding (figs 131–2). At Nun Monkton appositely Marian figures are supported on stems and leaves of myrtle and olive, finely balanced between naturalism and conventionalism, the sparkling, variegated greens set on white grounds. The three rows of figures at Tadcaster are separated by a device that was unique in Morris's *oeuvre*, a heraldic, sun-ray lambrequin in a dialogue with the atypically prominent scrolls behind the figures; the rich foliage is studded with acorns, quinces, pomegranates, figs, peaches, grapes and roses: as at Nun Monkton, Morris's 'tapestries' are inextricable from, yet in no sense subsidiary to, the figural elements.

In 1881 Morris moved his workshops to Merton Abbey, Surrey. Shortly before this he and William De Morgan had discussed the feasibility of setting up a kiln at Merton in order to experiment with different firing techniques, but local fire regulations prevented it. Merton offered larger workspaces that facilitated the production of not only the woven textiles (and eventually tapestries) to which Morris was devoted but also the ever-larger windows he was called upon to supply. In 1883 Ruskin asked Burne-Jones to design a series of female saints for the chapel at Whitelands Training College for Women, Chelsea, but urged him, 'please, for my sake, the lights mustn't be all brown and grisaille, but as opalescent as glass can be made'. Ruskin also wrote to Morris, requesting him to send specimens of glass. Morris must have been conscious of what Ruskin was implying, for he stressed that in sheets of glass of varied thickness the 'variety is very useful to us in getting a jewel-like quality ... You will understand that we rely almost entirely for our colour on the actual *colour of the glass*; and the more the design will enable us to break up the pieces, and the more mosaic-like it is, the better we like it.'

Morris indulged Ruskin, but he had no cause to be defensive. At St Martin's, Brampton, Webb had insisted that the stained glass be provided by Morris, who evidently attached great importance to the commission. The sumptuous five-light east window of 1880, in memory of George Howard's father, Charles, was conceived in three horizontal tiers, each of the 15 compartments occupied by a standing figure, newly designed by Burne-Jones, within Morris's vibrantly floriated background (fig.115). The variegated rubies, purples and blues are of a radiance and brilliancy that has scarcely been surpassed in stained glass. Glass as vivid as this rendered Ruskin's comments redundant. In the prospectus for the firm's display at the Boston Foreign Fair in 1883, George Wardle stressed Morris's belief that 'Colour, pure and sweet, is the least you should ask for in a stained glass window'. His striving for luminosity is confirmed by his comment following a visit to St Giles' Cathedral, Edinburgh, to inspect the firm's window depicting *Crossing the River Jordan, Jephthah's Daughter, Miriam* and *Ruth* (1886): it 'looks a queer contrast', he remarked, 'with its glittering jewel-like colour to the daubs about it.'

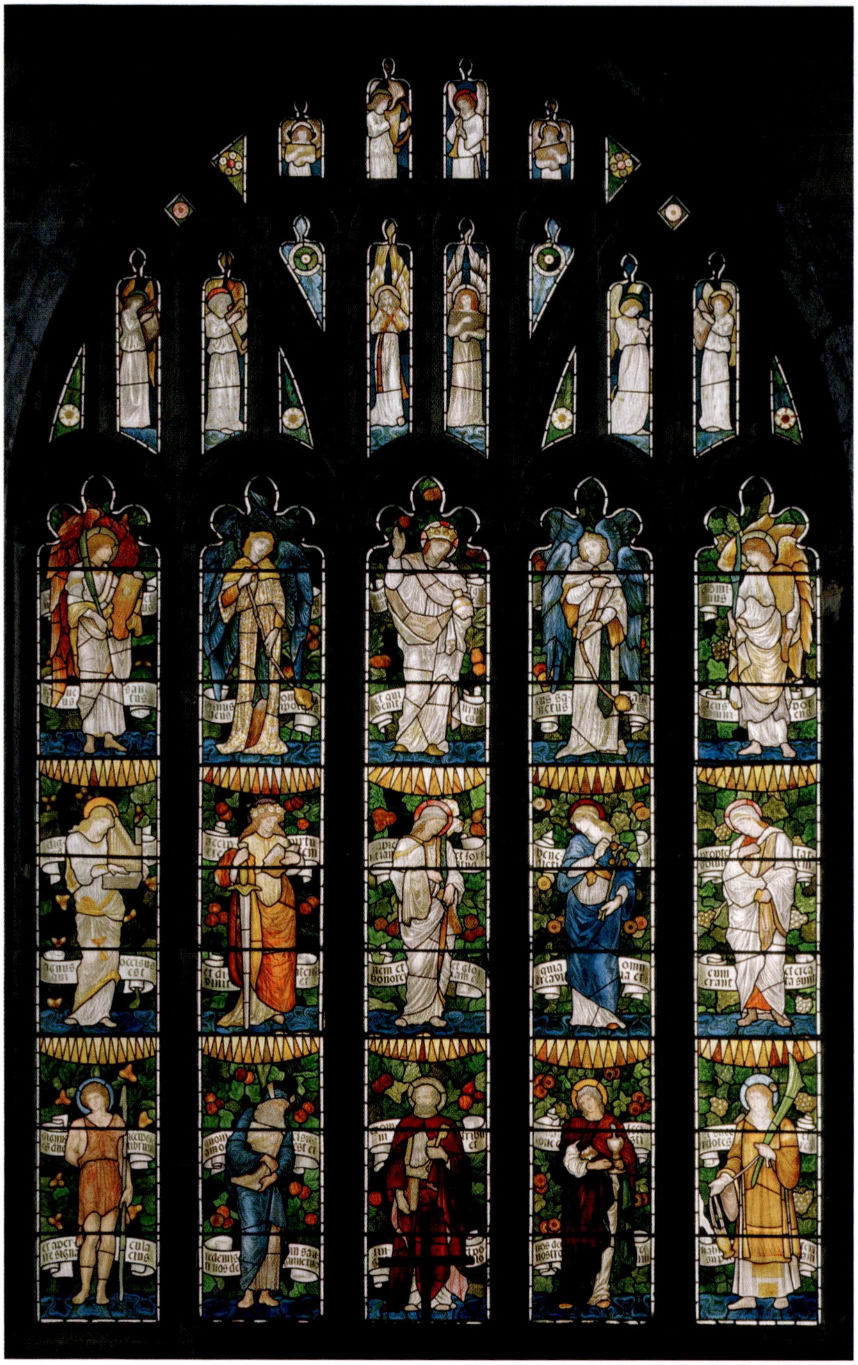

Fig.132 ***Salvator Mundi, the Virgin Mary and St Peter*** **(centre light),** ***surrounded by female and male saints,*** **Edward Burne-Jones and William Morris, east window, St Mary, Tadcaster, Yorkshire, 1879.**

The Byzantine Idiom

In 1881 Burne-Jones was commissioned by Street to design mosaics for the walls of St Paul's American Church in Rome. Burne-Jones had visited Ravenna in 1873, and the ur-schemes of mosaics in the city's early Byzantine churches became the model for his designs for the church in Rome. The mosaics proceeded slowly, but by 1885 Burne-Jones's *Heavenly Jerusalem* design for the apse was installed. Byzantine elements had

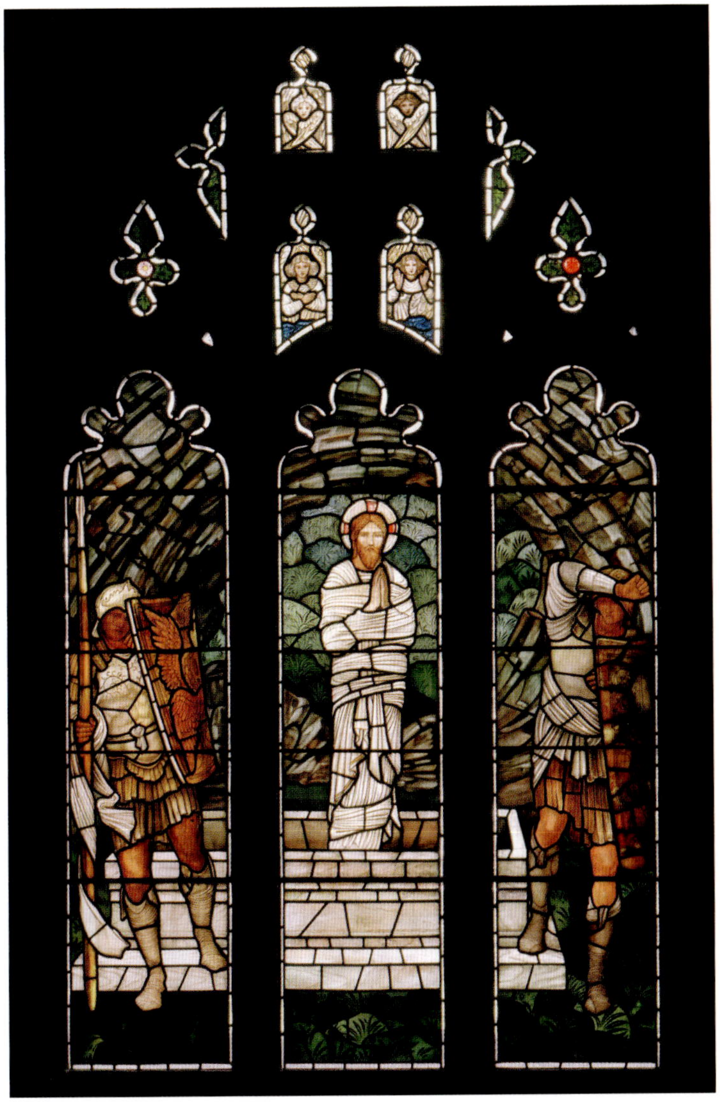

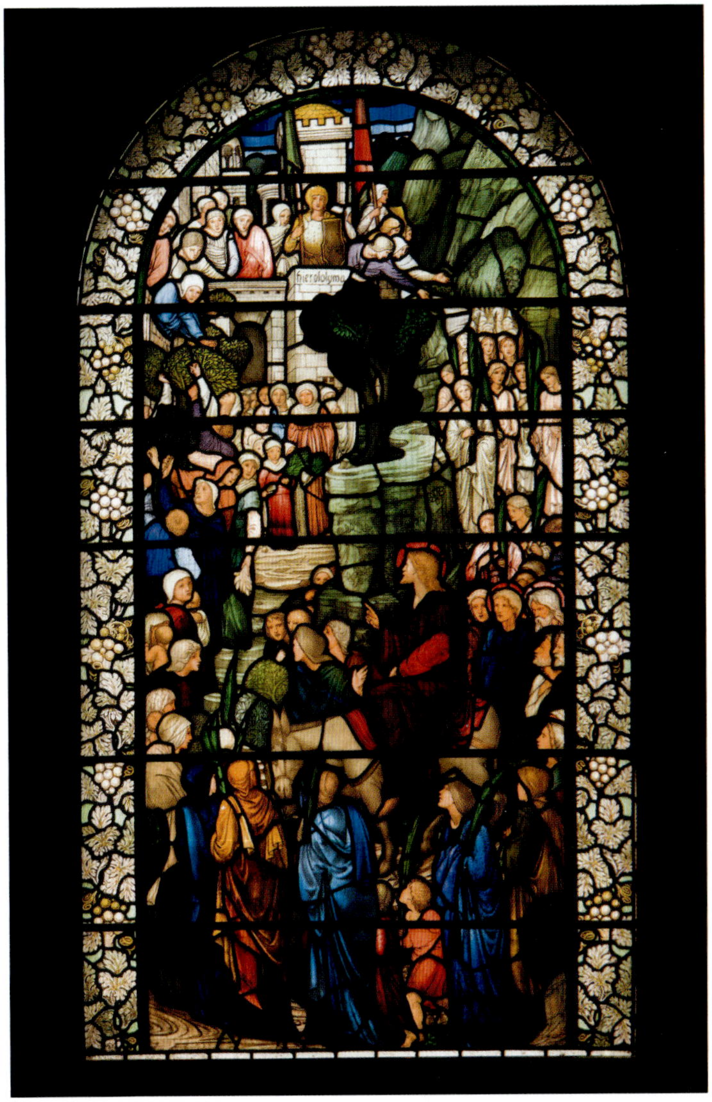

Fig.133 (above left) ***Resurrection*, Edward Burne-Jones, south aisle, All Hallows, Allerton, Liverpool, 1885.**

Fig.134 (above right) ***Christ's Entry into Jerusalem*, Edward Burne-Jones, south window, St Peter's, Vere Street, London, 1883.**

begun to percolate into Burne-Jones's paintings, and by 1885 they were manifested in his stained-glass designs. Consequently, Morris had to develop a mosaic-like system of leading in response to the artist's linear neo-Byzantinism and elongated, frontal and relatively static, or hovering figures. Burne-Jones directed the mosaics from London and was appalled at some of the trial examples he was sent. He was especially anxious that the tesserae be evenly sized, demanding: 'why should the tesserae in the face be seven times as big as those of the wings?' In stained glass, the pieces of glass were, by necessity, larger than mosaic tesserae, but the system Morris devised (probably in consultation with Burne-Jones) invariably adhered to the principle of an all-over grid of leadwork in a regular pattern. In translating Burne-Jones's most overtly neo-Byzantine designs, with their formal, isocephalic rows of heads, this type of matrix was essential. Compared with the firm's stained glass of the 1860s, and the density and compression of Burne-Jones's early compositions, the figures in some of his neo-Byzantine designs occupied the spaces more sparingly – they were unbound, floating. At All Hallows, Allerton, this development, and the corresponding modifications necessitated in the lead matrices, can be followed in detail in eight three-light aisle windows that date from 1882 to 1887 (fig.133).

In Burne-Jones's *Christ's Entry into Jerusalem* (1883), at St Peter's, Vere Street, London (fig.134), the manner in which the procession winds up the picture field through the rocky landscape, with minimal spatial recession, is borrowed from Benozzo Gozzoli's fresco, *Journey of the Magi* (1459–61), in the Palazzo Medici-Riccardi,

Florence. This pictorial conception was suitable for a single, round-headed window in James Gibbs's church, and anticipated Burne-Jones's even larger designs for the similar window forms in Birmingham Cathedral. The device of building a composition in ascending planes, with little or no perspectival depth, recalls Burne-Jones's designs for Bradfield College (1857), and it was a system he revisited intermittently throughout his life; he last employed it for two narrow, single lights depicting *Jacob's Dream* and the *Tree of Jesse* at St Margaret's, Rottingdean, Sussex (1897).

The swirling, stylized wave forms, familiar from Japanese woodblock prints, that Burne-Jones inaugurated emphatically in *Voyage to Vinland the Good* (1884) (fig.135) have been co-opted as precursors of Art Nouveau; the tree that supports the *Pelican in her Piety* design for Brampton Church (1880) was similarly prescient (VII.31). There is also an intriguing precedent for the wave form in a *Baptism of Christ* window of *c.*1250 at the Stiftskirche, Bücken, Lower Saxony, in the depiction of the river Jordan. Burne-Jones utilized variations of this dynamic motif in *Crossing the Red Sea*, Kirkcaldy Old Kirk (1886), and *How Galahad sought the Sangreal* (1886), one of four panels he designed for his house at Rottingdean (fig.136 and VII.32).

Morris's webs of lead are especially conspicuous in the three prodigious, monumental windows in the apse of the Cathedral of St Philip, Birmingham, commencing with the *Ascension*, in 1885; their prominent geometric grids inspired a stanza in Louis MacNeice's poem 'Birmingham' (1934), which evoked 'the Burne-Jones windows in St Philip's broken by crawling leads'. While the illusionism in these soaring, monumental works could be embraced as a response to Thomas Archer's Baroque interior, Burne-Jones found any Baroque church anathema, and he probably accepted the commission only because he had been raised across the street from St Philip's. In 1891 he spurned Bodley's offer to design mosaics of angels for the semi-domes of St Paul's Cathedral in London on the grounds that it was 'nonsense' to attempt any amelioration of the building, 'but let it chill the soul of man and gently prepare him for the next glacial cataclysm.'

Conclusions

In the 1890s Burne-Jones was preoccupied with the completion of existing canvases or the atavistic reworking of old themes. His workload and declining health left fewer opportunities to design stained glass, but those he accepted were an incentive for some of the most original designs of his last years. The *Annunciation to the Shepherds* at Lanercost Priory, Cumbria (1890), the *Stoning of St Stephen* at St Paul, Morton, Lincolnshire (1891) and *Moses and the Burning Bush* and the

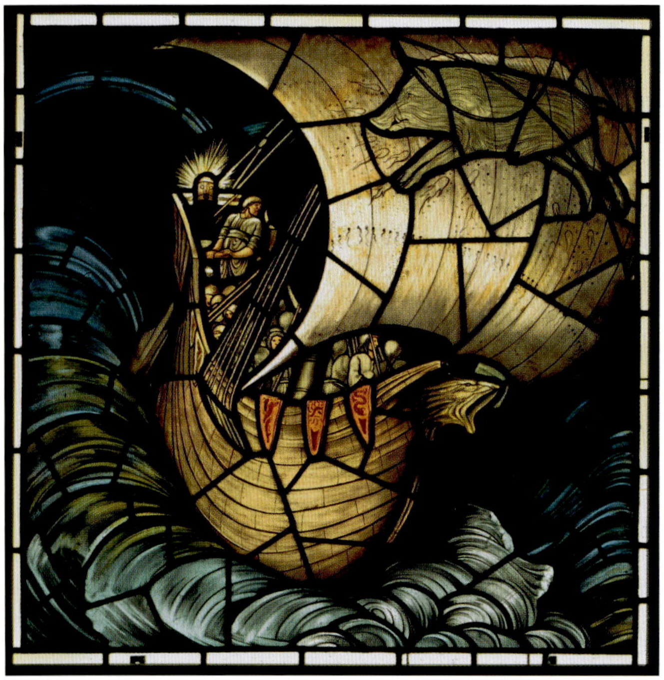

Fig.135 ***Voyage to Vinland the Good*, designed by Edward Burne-Jones for the home of Catharine Lorillard Wolfe, Newport, Rhode Island, 1884.**
Delaware Art Museum, Wilmington

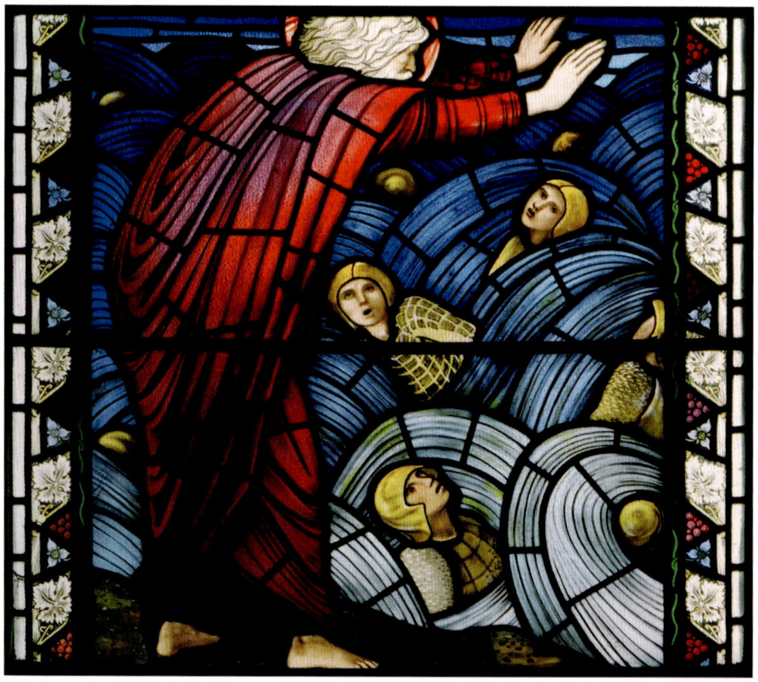

Fig.136 ***Crossing the Red Sea*, Edward Burne-Jones, east window, Kirkcaldy Old Kirk, Scotland, 1886.**

Fig.137 ***Charity* and *Fortitude*, *David Lamenting* and *David Consoled*, Edward Burne-Jones, St Cuthbert's, Newcastle upon Tyne, 1896–7.**
Laing Art Gallery, Newcastle upon Tyne

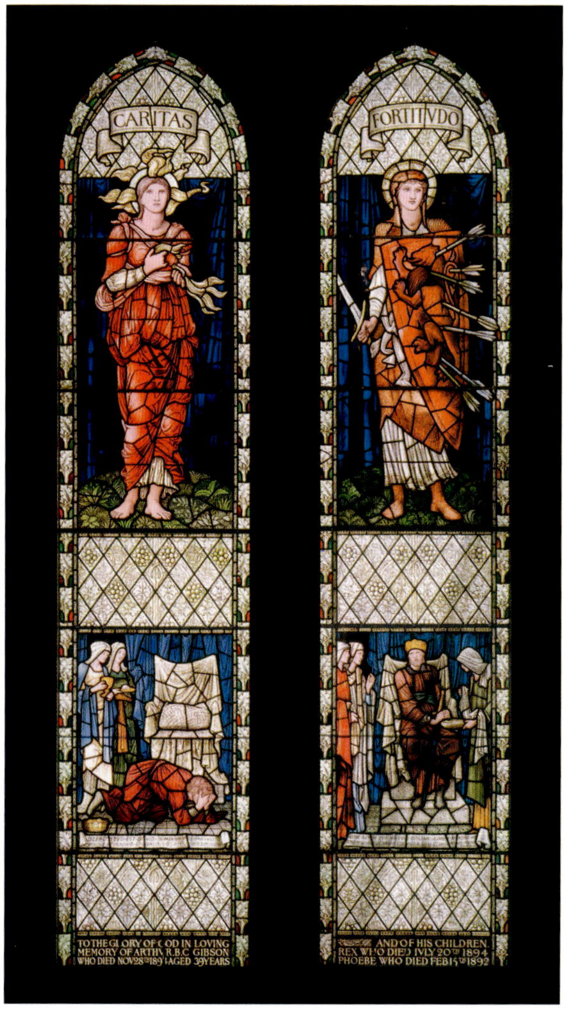

Burial of Moses at St Brycedale, Kirkcaldy, Fife (1892), in which the relatively static, Byzantine elements are punctuated by passages of vigorous movement, were among Burne-Jones's most notable late works. The cartoons for these windows were shown at the Arts and Crafts Exhibition Society in the 1890s, alongside works by many of the younger stained-glass artists of the day, whom they continued to inspire.

Three designs that Burne-Jones made after the death of Morris warrant special mention. First is a two-light window for St Cuthbert's, Newcastle upon Tyne (1896–7), comprising allegorical figures of *Charity* and *Fortitude,* with *David Lamenting* and *David Consoled* beneath them (fig.137). Georgiana Burne-Jones recorded that the cartoons for the two David subjects were the first works Burne-Jones commenced after the death of Morris in 1896. Here, art imitated life, as Burne-Jones reinterpreted the narrative as poignant autobiography. In the *Lament*, the abject King David falls to the ground clutching his head in his hands to hide his grief, Saul's empty throne behind him; without Morris, Burne-Jones was saying, he was bereft: the figure on the throne in *David Consoled* is clearly a self-portrait. The *Last Judgment* that Burne-Jones designed in 1897 for the west window of Birmingham Cathedral stands as a triumphant valediction and a testament to his fluent command of an immense picture field (fig.138). Finally, in 1898, the *Nativity* for St Deiniol, Hawarden, Flintshire, was the last design for stained glass that Burne-Jones completed (fig.139). It was a tribute to William Gladstone who, as Prime Minister, had conferred a baronetcy on Burne-Jones in 1894. The protracted correspondence about the window between Burne-Jones and Mary Drew (Gladstone's daughter and a friend and former model of Burne-Jones), makes it clear that the Gladstone family failed to appreciate the problem of accommodating a nativity scene in a four-light window without crossing the mullions. Burne-Jones pushed for the pragmatic alternative of single figures, but eventually he placed the *Nativity* high up across the two central lights, surrounded by angels, with Magi in the outer left light. He wrote to Mary Drew on 5 June 1898: 'I was really happy making that window – some bits went amiss – one cannot make all come right, but I felt more content than I usually am with work carried out by other hands. They tried very hard at the works, one & all, to make it good.' Gladstone died shortly before the window was unveiled, and Burne-Jones followed him less than a fortnight after writing to Mary Drew: his contentment with his final stained-glass masterpiece was justified.

Of the many craftsmen who passed through Morris's workshops a few achieved minor renown in stained glass, including John W. Brown, who became chief designer for James Powell & Sons, and James Egan, who partnered another Morris protégé, Frederick Fletcher, and made some interesting windows on his own account from the 1880s onwards. More eminent figures, such as Frank Brangwyn, stayed only briefly. The firm's wider influence was by example. Hugh Arthur Kennedy, Seddon's favourite stained-glass designer, wrote a paean to Burne-Jones for the *Contemporary Review*, calling him 'our really god-inspired designer.' 'Beyond his artistic genius', Kennedy added, 'Burne-Jones has a special happiness with regard to art of this nature': Burne-Jones's Easthampstead *Last Judgment* he considered 'perhaps the highest flight in modern art in the direction of imaginative design.' Yet he maintained one reservation: if Burne-Jones had painted the glass himself, Kennedy believed, rather than Morris's craftsmen, it would have been a flawless masterpiece. This qualification, rightly or wrongly, would become axiomatic for the nascent Arts and Crafts Movement. It is true that the streamlined production methods Morris employed, and the division of labour they entailed, were not fundamentally different from those of the large 'trade' workshops. Whereas, according to the Arts and Crafts credo, the artist should carry out, or at least supervise, every stage of a stained-glass window's production. This was a tenable theory, undermined by the lack of artists of the stature of Burne-Jones or craftworkers with Morris's imaginative grasp of the medium. The invention of 'slab' glass, and the firmly graphic painting styles that Christopher Whall and his followers developed in the 1890s to exploit the new material, came too late for Burne-Jones and Morris.

Perhaps surprisingly, Philip Webb arrived at the same conclusion as Kennedy, albeit in hindsight, arguing in a letter of 1904 that the firm's stained glass, 'never could be right good craftsmen's glass, because there were no draughtsmen who could translate the beautiful pictures into effective painting *for* glass.' At the inception of the firm, Morris's six partners had voluntarily agreed to respect a code of anonymity. Ironically, the attention that Morris's stained glass attracted from scholars in the second half of the twentieth century resulted in the identification of the individual artists who designed the stained glass as well as, eventually, many of the craftworkers. It might be inferred from Webb and Kennedy's remarks that Morris's glass-painters were insufficiently skilled, but the draughtsmanship in Morris's stained glass suggests otherwise: indeed, Albert Goodwin and Charles Napier Hemy in the 1860s, and John W. Brown and James Egan in the 1870s, were all artists of considerable technical competence.

Ostensibly 'superior' glass-painting skills were brought to bear on two occasions. The artist and collector Charles Fairfax Murray, who had become Burne-Jones's studio assistant in November 1866, was persuaded to paint the firm's Vyner Memorial window at Christ Church, Oxford in 1872–3. The window is duly signed 'CFM pinx. EBJ inv.' and the draughtsmanship has the slightly agitated linearity that characterizes the cartoons Murray drew up from Burne-Jones's sketches. According to the art historian A.C. Sewter, the tracery lights

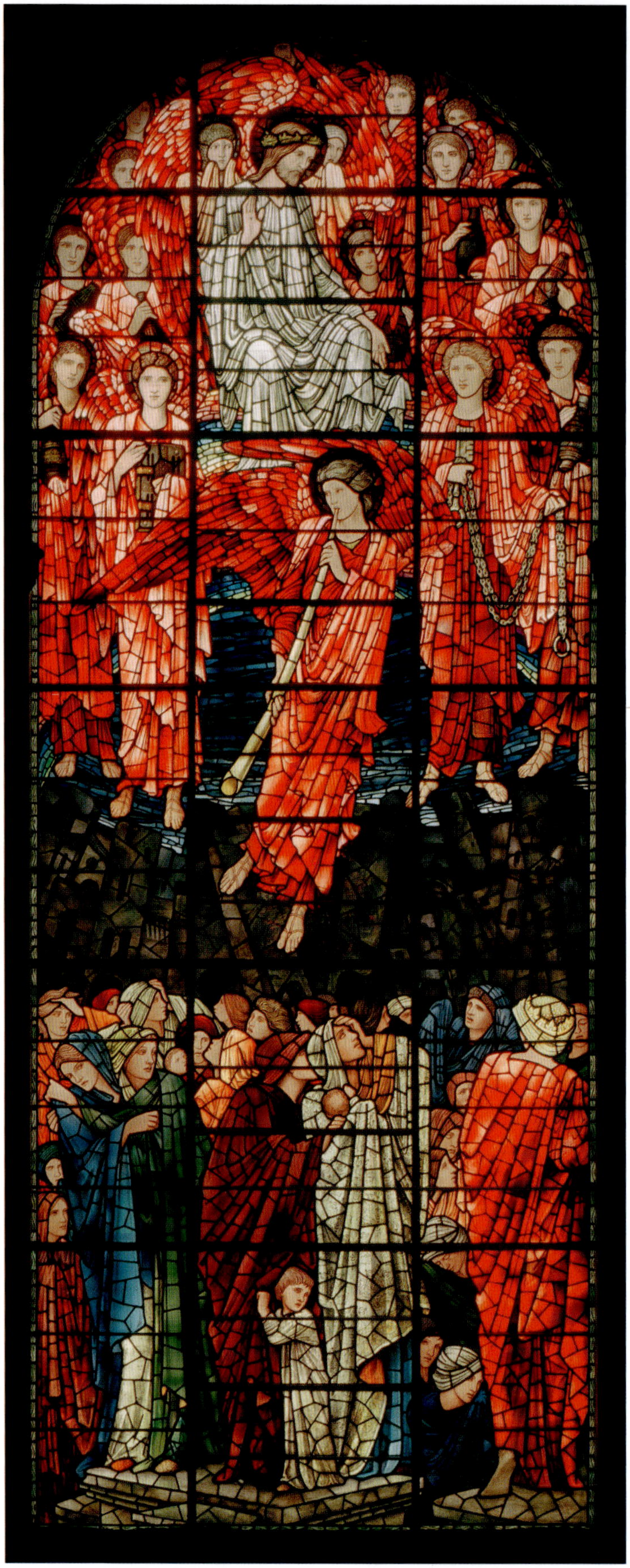

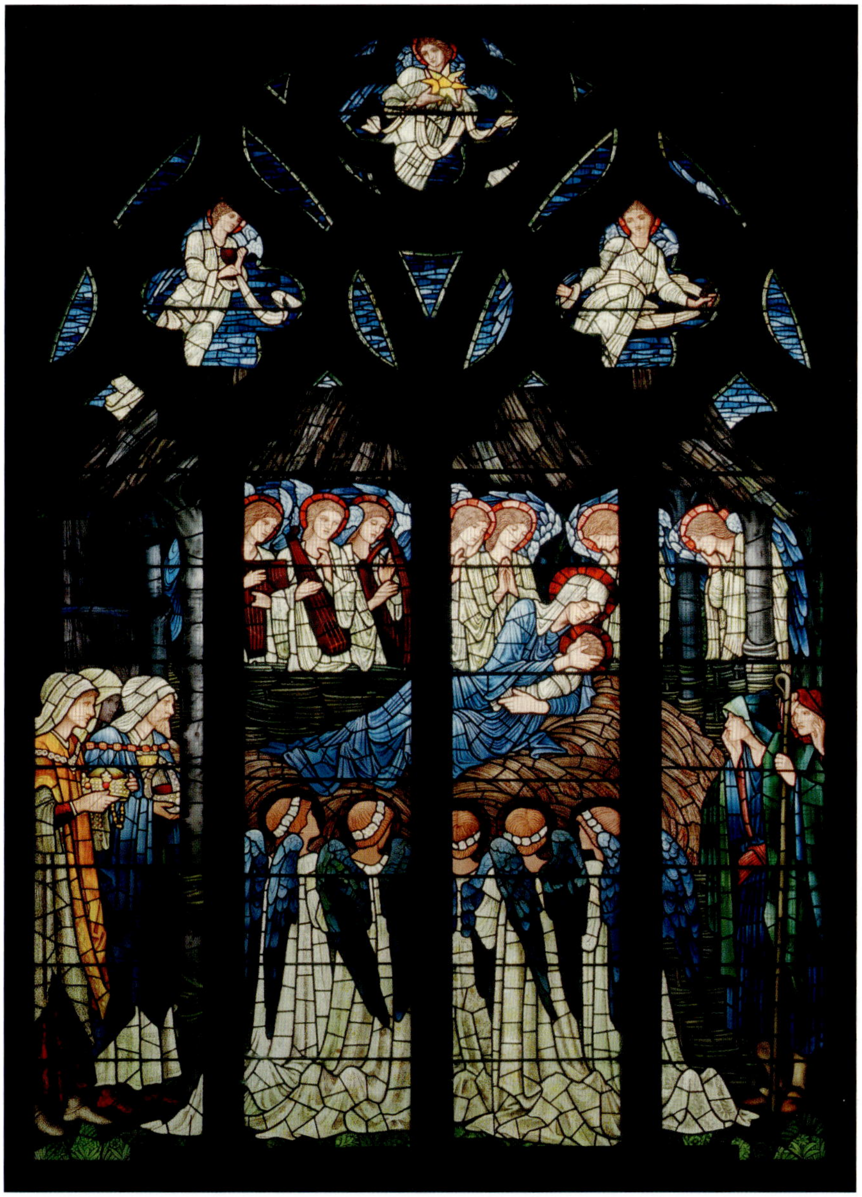

Fig.138 (opposite) ***Last Judgment*, Edward Burne-Jones, west window, Cathedral Church of St Philip, Birmingham, 1897.**

Fig.139 (above) ***Nativity*, Edward Burne-Jones, west window, St Deiniol, Hawarden, Flintshire, Wales, 1898.**

of the *St Catherine* window of 1878, also at Christ Church, Oxford, were, uniquely, painted by Burne-Jones and Morris themselves. Assuming the three angels were painted by Burne-Jones, these, like 'Murray's' window, are ably executed and the flesh enamels subtly graded. But might not the central *St Catherine* also have been painted by Burne-Jones? Her hands are meticulously shaded, the delicate matt washes on the face and hands resembling pencil drawing. Oxford held a special place in Morris and Burne-Jones's affections, and the window was a memorial to Edith Liddell, who had died in 1876 aged 22. It is an impressive performance, yet it could be argued that the glass-painting is *too* subtle for the medium, and superfluous when read from a distance.

Morris's foreman glass-painter, George Campfield (despite having been the target of a Nuremberg Bible, hurled during one his employer's fits of rage), testified to the unfailingly courteous manner in which he had been treated: he was included in a profit-sharing scheme in 1870. But master-and-employee relations were seldom this harmonious: the tenacious myth of the humble medieval craftsman, working contentedly in the service of God, was not so readily transposed to industrialized Britain. In 1896 Morris was succeeded as art director of Morris & Co. by John Henry Dearle, who had joined the firm in 1878, became a glass-painter and designer, and was made a director in 1894. If it was problematic for Morris to reconcile his socialism with his aesthetic ideals, his desire to treat his workmen fairly had some negative repercussions for his products. After Morris's death, Burne-Jones's rare visits to the firm's Merton Abbey workshops were depressing reminders of his late friend's absence, and his unease was exacerbated by Dearle's resistance to criticism. Burne-Jones found Dearle 'competent' but 'peculiar': 'You have to find everything well done. If I give an opinion, I have to be cautious and say "Don't you think" before all my remarks. I can see he wouldn't stand any rebuke. He's extremely sensitive.' By the 1890s only the windows newly designed by Burne-Jones for specific locations generally upheld the firm's high reputation. Otherwise, the over-reliance on recycled and adapted cartoons sometimes betrayed the lack of fresh inspiration. As early as 1874 the architect John Thomas Micklethwaite had complained about the disjunction between single figures placed 'without preparation' on uniform quarry grounds, but it remained a common expedient in the more routine windows of the 1890s.

Although Philip Webb doubted that the devolved workshop system had been compatible with 'right good craftsmen's glass', the legacy of the firm's stained glass was an inspiration to the Arts and Crafts Movement that he and Morris had helped to initiate, and to 'Vernacular Revival' designers across much of Europe. Morris and his circle had been at the centre of a debate that transformed both architecture and the role of the artist–craftsman, and their stained glass had abundantly demonstrated the feasibility of building on a tradition ineluctably associated with the Middle Ages.

VII.1
The Good Shepherd
Edward Burne-Jones for
James Powell & Sons, Whitefriars

a Cartoon, 1857
Watercolour and ink, 128 x 47.7 cm
Inscribed: '18 EBJ 57'
V&A (E.1317–1970)

b Panel, installed 1861
Stained and painted glass, 132 x 51 cm
Birmingham Museums Trust (2001L5)

Approached by James Powell & Sons as a designer for stained glass in 1856 or 1857, Rossetti declined, and instead suggested his friends Madox Brown and Burne-Jones. Madox Brown made only one design, a *Transfiguration* (whereabouts unknown). According to Rossetti, Burne-Jones's *The Good Shepherd*, the first stained-glass cartoon he produced, drove 'Ruskin wild with joy'. The young, untrained artist demonstrated a precocious grasp of the requirements of the medium.

This panel is the first recorded use of the design, which was not fitted into the centre of the five-light east window of the Congregational Church, King Street, Maidstone, until 1861. If the client, the Reverend Henry Hamlet Dobney, specifically selected *The Good Shepherd* at the Powells' glassworks, he may have been attracted by its spontaneity and freshness. Dobney had been prominent in a group of dissenting churchmen considered heretical for preaching the hope of Universal Restoration; he was the first editor of the *Christian Spectator* and an obituary described him as 'an artist of no mean order'. In 1858 Burne-Jones stayed with Arthur Hughes in Marsham Street, Maidstone, and it may not be coincidental that Dobney lived in the same street. The church was demolished in 1974. The cartoon was re-used by James Powell & Sons at St Patrick's, Trim, County Meath, Ireland in 1869.

VII.1a

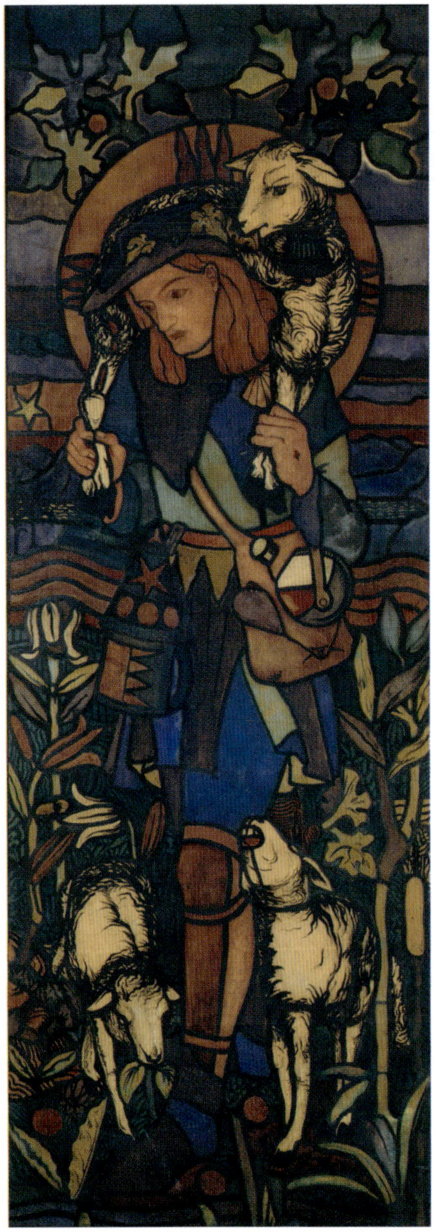

VII.1b

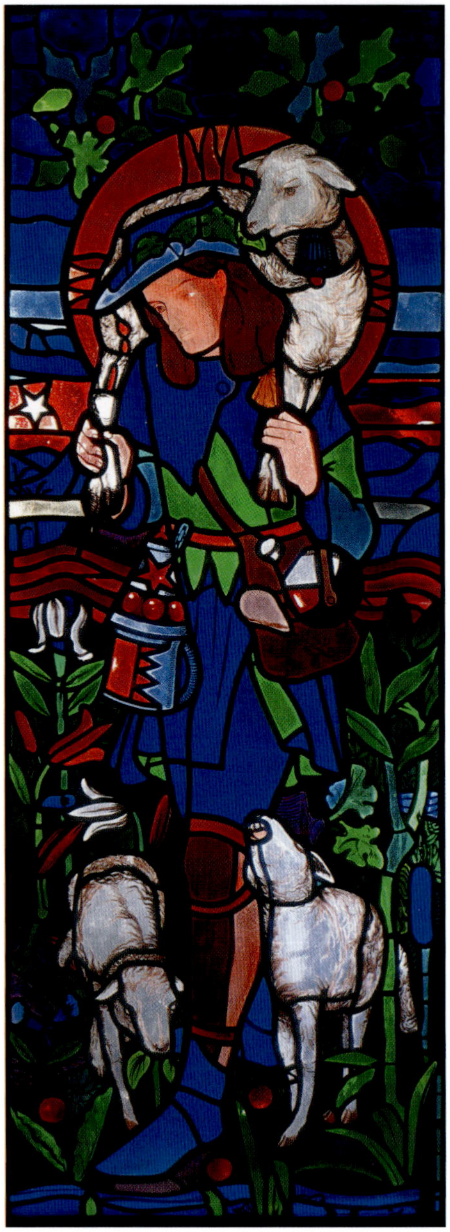

VII.2
Three stained-glass cartoons for the dining hall, St Andrew's College, Bradfield, Berkshire
Edward Burne-Jones for James Powell & Sons, Whitefriars, 1857

a *Adam and Eve after the Fall*
Watercolour and Indian ink,
214.4 x 47.8 cm
Inscribed: 'EBJ 1857', 'No.510'
V&A (E.1319–1970)

b *Building of the Tower of Babel*
Watercolour and Indian ink,
220.4 x 52 cm
Inscribed: 'EBJ 1857', 'No.508'
V&A (E.1318–1970)

c *Solomon and the Queen of Sheba*
Watercolour and Indian ink,
213 x 49.5 cm
Inscribed: 'No.509'
V&A (E.1320–1970)

The archives of James Powell & Sons (Archive of Art and Design, V&A) record that two lights of the Bradfield window were fitted in July 1857. The cartoons were almost certainly among those that Burne-Jones exhibited at the Hogarth Club in January 1859. The artist George Price Boyce, who visited Bradfield in 1858, found the glass 'powerful and glowing' but 'a little glaring and coarse'. In common with all of the Powell/Burne-Jones windows, and in contrast with Powell & Sons' contemporary work, the glass is intense in colour. It is made from the best 'pot metal' or 'muff' glass.

At Bradfield, Burne-Jones introduced a device to which he frequently returned, building up the composition in vertical layers as a means of unfolding a narrative with minimal spatial recession. The disparity in scale between the densely packed *Tower of Babel* and the outer lights of *Adam and Eve* and *Solomon and Sheba* is perhaps a sign that he was still experimenting with the medium. The Old Testament subjects are an unusual, partly typological, conjunction that appositely depict themes of learning.

The window was ordered by the Reverend Thomas Stevens, Warden of the College and a close friend of the hall's architect, G.G. Scott. There are several possibilities for how the commission came about. Arthur Powell, of the eponymous glass firm, was a trustee. The Reverend Frederick Guy, headmaster of Bradfield College from 1850 to 1852, became Morris's private tutor that year when he moved to Forest School, Walthamstow. A tradition at the College says that Morris helped Burne-Jones with the windows; he was certainly the model for Adam. Did Guy, through Morris, introduce Burne-Jones? Thomas Acland was a prominent member of the College Council; in 1857 his son Henry Acland and John Ruskin were building the Oxford Museum. In 1859 their architect, Benjamin Woodward, designed the stonework containing Burne-Jones's *Legend of St Frideswide* window at Christ Church, Oxford. Ruskin often regretted not having become more involved in stained glass; was he wielding his influence on his protégé's behalf in these early commissions?

VII.2a

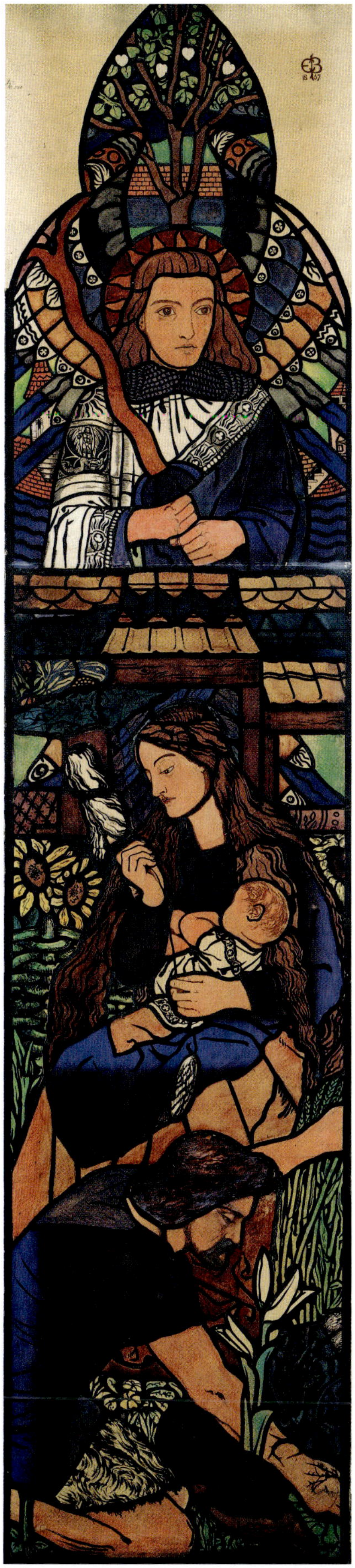

VII.2b

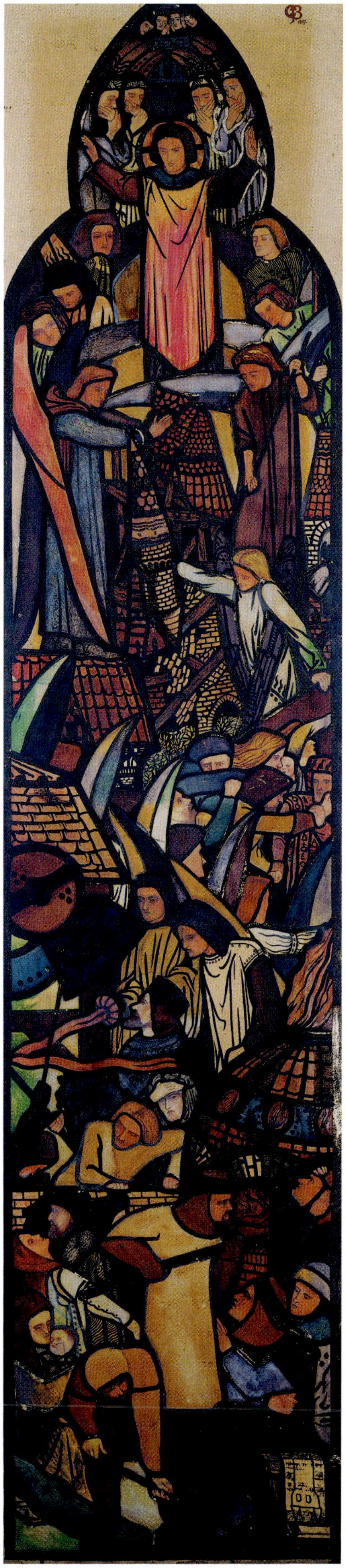

VII.2c

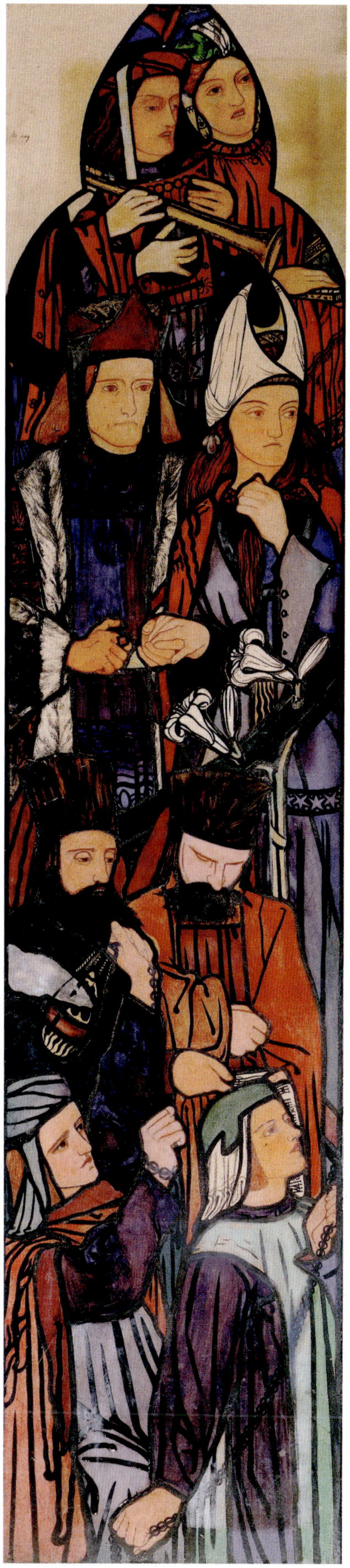

VII.3

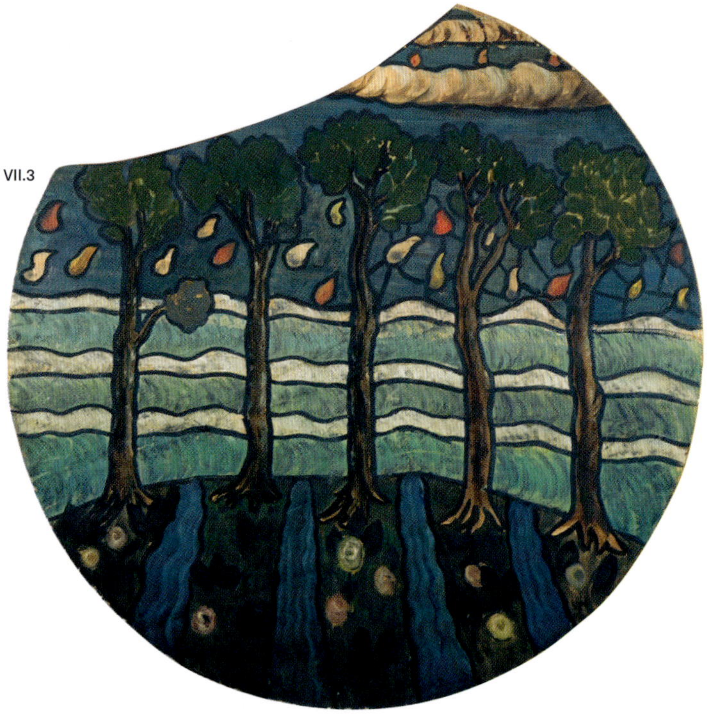

VII.3
***The Third Day of Creation* for Holy Cross and St Lawrence, Waltham Abbey, Essex**
Edward Burne-Jones for James Powell & Sons, Whitefriars, 1860
Gouache, 96 cm diameter
V&A (E.1322–1970)

The designs for the chancel east windows at Waltham Abbey were the last that Burne-Jones made before he became a founding partner in Morris, Marshall, Faulkner & Co. This cartoon, for one of the lobes of the upper rose, is one of only two that have survived, although a preliminary sketch for the three-light *Tree of Jesse* below belongs to Birmingham Museum and Art Gallery. The architect of the restoration, William Burges, may have suggested the fourteenth-century sources – the Gorleston Psalter and Queen Mary Psalter – for the window's iconography, although both Morris and Burne-Jones were familiar with the British Museum's illuminated manuscripts. Nathaniel Westlake, a protégé of Burges, published a volume of drawings based on the Queen Mary Psalter in 1860, but the *Days of Creation* have an equal affinity with the visionary aspect of William Blake.

Burges was a friend of Charles Winston, the antiquarian of stained glass, who instigated the research that resulted in James Powell & Sons's revived manufacture of 'pot metal' glass in 1852. This glass was used in all the windows Burne-Jones designed for them. In *The Builder*, August 1861, Burges stated that the defects of modern stained glass were due to poor quality raw material and the 'lack of adequately coloured cartoons from the artist to guide the workman'. Aware that these criticisms did not apply to the Burne-Jones/Powell *Legend of St Frideswide* window recently placed at Christ Church, Oxford, he opted for the same combination at Waltham Abbey.

VII.4

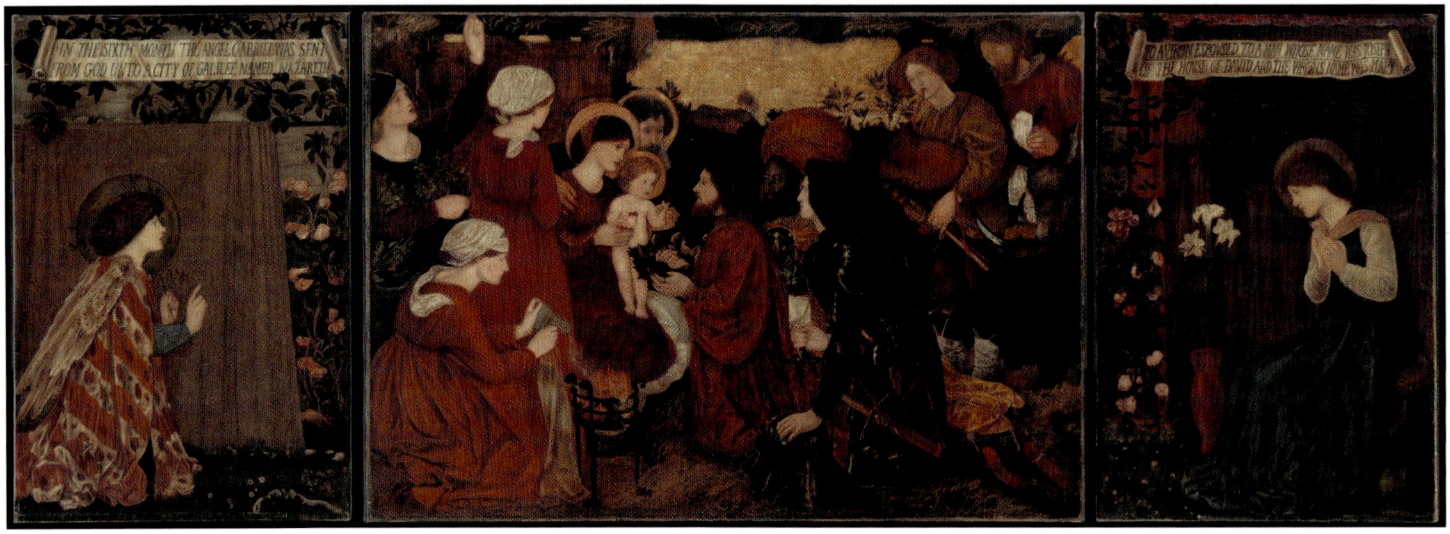

VII.4
***The Annunciation and the Adoration of the Magi* altarpiece for St Paul's, Brighton**
Edward Burne-Jones, 1860
Oil on canvas, centre 109 x 156 cm, wings 109 x 73 cm each
Tate, London (N04743)

The architect of St Paul's, Brighton (1846–8) was Richard Carpenter, but even before Carpenter's death in 1855, Bodley had begun his long association with the church. He was its churchwarden and organist and built the adjacent schoolroom in 1854. About 1860 he commissioned this painted altarpiece from Burne-Jones. The artist's first substantial work in oils, it reflects the studies – instigated by Ruskin – made on his first Italian tour in autumn 1859. His previous experience of working on a large scale was limited to designs for stained glass, his Oxford Union mural of *Merlin and Nimue*, and his painting of *The Prioress's Tale* on the Webb-designed wardrobe (IX.5). Burne-Jones's murals at Red House were also in progress in 1860. Formerly dated 1861, the triptych, too, must have been substantially completed in 1860, for it was recommended by the architect J.P. Seddon to a meeting of the Ecclesiological Society on 11 June 1860.

Installed above the high altar, the composition was too elaborate to be intelligible from a distance, and a second version, in which the shepherds and female attendants were omitted, was substituted in 1861. The original was offered by Burne-Jones in settlement of his debts to the estate of his patron Thomas Plint, who had recently died. In 1867 a dealer sold it to Bodley for £50. Following the death of his son in 1934, it was presented to the Tate. The church sold the second version in 1993.

Several of the models can be identified. The king presenting his gift to Christ is recognizable as Morris, Swinburne is the shepherd playing bagpipes and Burne-Jones himself is behind him. The king in armour in the foreground was painted from an Italian model, Ciamelli; studies for the Virgin were made from Georgiana Burne-Jones, but Henry Currie Marillier claimed that the finished version in oils showed Jane Morris.

VII.5

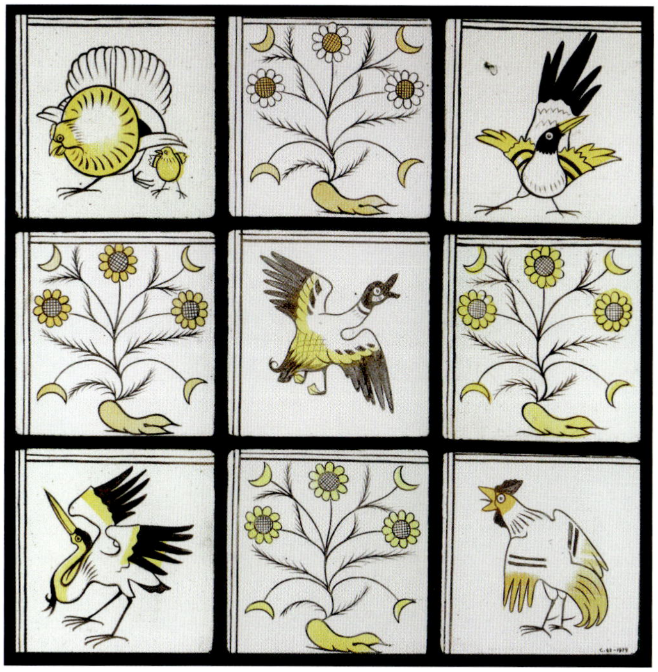

VII.6

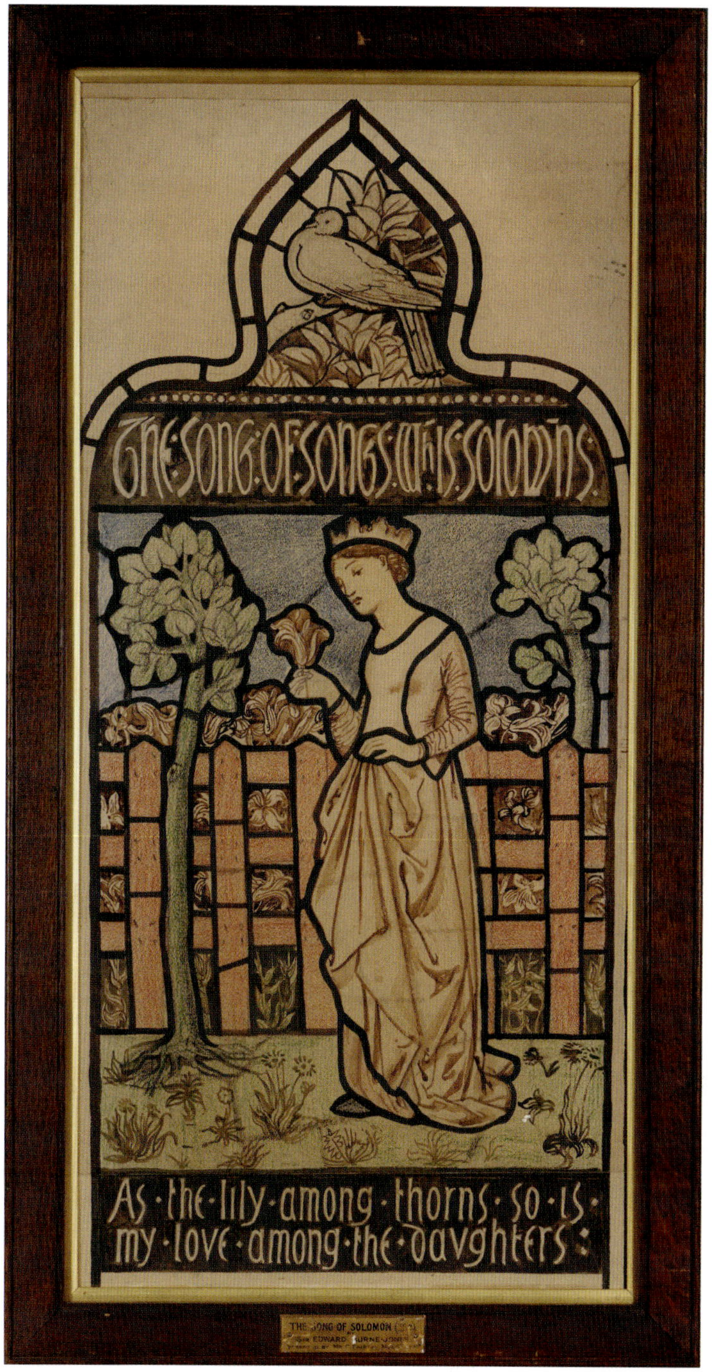

VII.5
Stained-glass panel
Designed by Philip Webb, possibly produced by James Powell & Sons, *c.*1859–60
Stained and painted glass, 50 x 50 cm
V&A (C.63–1979)

This panel was once thought to have come from the nursery at Red House but is not compatible with Webb's sash windows. Tessa Wild plausibly suggests it may have been fitted in one of the windows in the bedroom passage that no longer have their original glazing. Red House was completed – and presumably glazed – before the firm was set up to make stained glass, and it is probable that these quarries were executed by James Powell & Sons. Webb's lively, stylized birds, relieved with silver stain, are closely based on familiar medieval prototypes. They were also adapted for early hand-painted tiles produced by the firm (see X.1).

VII.6
Cartoon from *The Song of Solomon* series for St Helen's, Darley Dale, Derbyshire
Edward Burne-Jones for Morris, Marshall, Faulkner & Co., 1862
Pencil, sepia wash and crayon, 101.5 x 48.2 cm
Birmingham Museums Trust (1900P176)

The Darley Dale window was ordered as a memorial to Dr Raphael Gillum by his great-nephew and principal beneficiary, Colonel William James Gillum. Raphael Gillum, who had lead-mining interests in the district, is buried in the churchyard alongside his wife. Colonel Gillum was an important friend and patron of the firm. He was an amateur artist, a pupil of Madox Brown and member of the Hogarth Club. He sat on the management committee of the Home for Destitute Boys that provided the firm's early apprentices, ordered numerous items of furniture designed by Webb, and bought paintings from Rossetti and Burne-Jones. In 1861 Webb built a row of houses and workshops for him (on land bequeathed by Raphael Gillum) in Worship Street, Finsbury, London. Gillum is the most likely candidate for having suggested the Song of Solomon theme, a paean to earthly love that was unprecedented in stained glass and never repeated by the firm.

The cartoons for all 12 of the principal subjects (one is repeated) have traditionally been assigned to Burne-Jones. *As the lily among thorns ...* was drawn by Burne-Jones but the conception appears to be Morris's. The angle of the woman's head and the position of her left hand, tentatively raising her skirt, are characteristics that recur frequently in Morris's work – for example in his paintings of *La Belle Iseult*, Princess Sabra on the *St George* cabinet, in his cartoons of *Iseult* and of *Ruth*, and in several drawings. In one of the firm's photographic albums an almost identical design is catalogued under Morris; significantly, the alternative version is bordered with Morris's 'Si je puis' motto. The date of Morris's *Trellis* wallpaper, 1862, corresponds exactly with the trellis background in this design.

VII.7

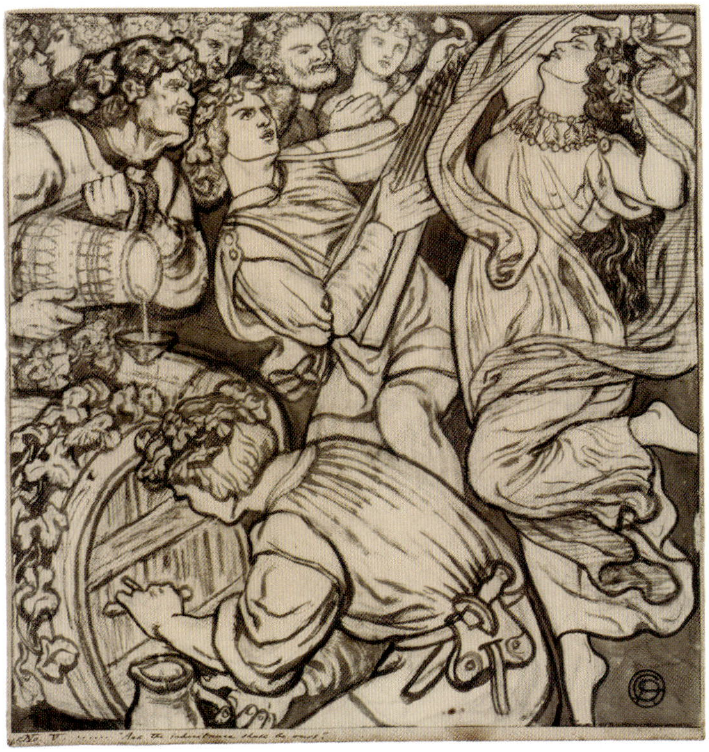

VII.8

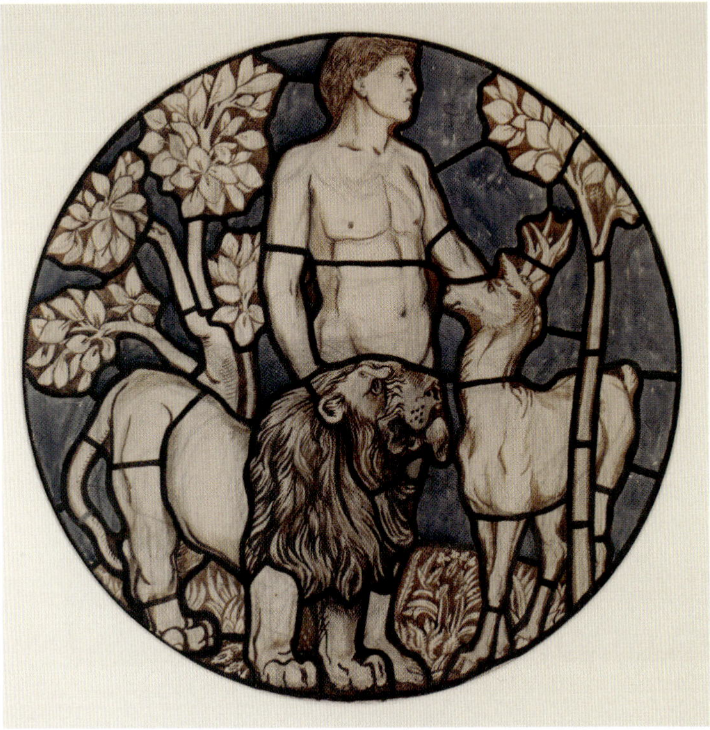

VII.9

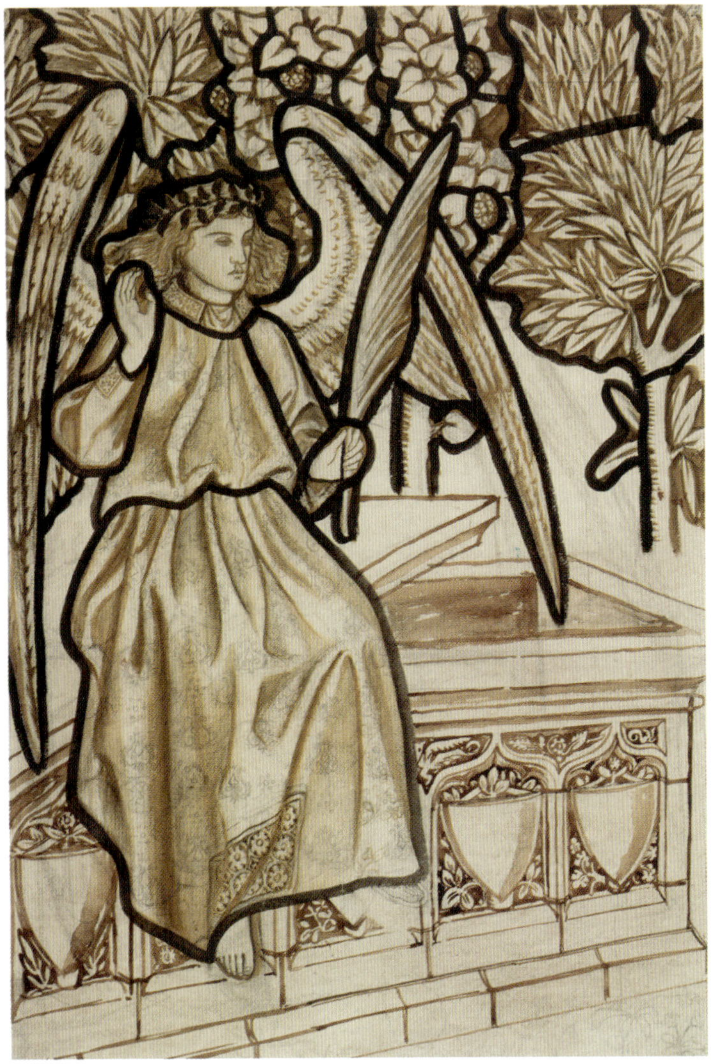

VII.7
***Feast of the Vintage* from**
The Parable of the Vineyard
series, for St Martin-on-the-Hill, Scarborough, Yorkshire
Dante Gabriel Rossetti for Morris, Marshall, Faulkner & Co., 1861–2
Charcoal, black and grey wash, 61.6 x 60.3 cm
William Morris Gallery, London Borough of Waltham Forest (A267)

Designed in 1861, the seven scenes that make up Rossetti's depiction of the *Parable of the Vineyard* are rather awkwardly disposed around Madox Brown's central *Crucifixion* in the east window of Bodley's church of St Martin-on-the-Hill, Scarborough. Some, or all, of the series was displayed in the 1862 International Exhibition. Where this unprecedented treatment of the narrative originated is unknown; the more ribald scenes reflect Rossetti's sensibilities rather than Bodley's and they never recurred in the architect's iconographical schemes. The alcoholic abandon in the *Feast of the Vintage* might conceivably have provoked controversy, had the panels been in a more accessible position. Rossetti wrote to Madox Brown on 24 November 1861 asking if he had a number of the *Pictorial History of England,* which contained an illustration of a Saxon wine press for use in this series, but the idea was evidently discarded.

VII.8
Adam Naming the Animals
for the west window, All Saints, Selsley, Gloucestershire
Philip Webb for Morris, Marshall, Faulkner & Co., *c.*1862
Watercolour, 64.5 cm diameter
V&A (E.1289–1931)

One of the eight outer lobes of the *Creation* rose window at Selsley, designed by Morris and Webb. *Adam* is a rare instance of Webb drawing a figure cartoon for the firm. In some respects the conception for this window borrows from Burne-Jones's *Creation* designs for Waltham Abbey (VII.3), but the indebtedness is more marked in Morris's cartoons than in Webb's. Burges, like Bodley, a friend of the Reverend John Gibson who commissioned the church, designed the altar plate at Selsley and may have suggested repeating the Creation theme here.

VII.9
***Angel of the Resurrection* cartoon for St Michael and All Angels, Brighton**
William Morris for Morris, Marshall, Faulkner & Co., 1862
Watercolour, 68.9 x 47 cm
Tate, London (N05223)

With its companion window (fig.117), this was the first multi-figure design for stained glass that Morris undertook. Unlike its neighbour, Burne-Jones's *Flight into Egypt* (VII.10), the window was arranged in the 'banded' idiom essayed at Selsley, with Webb's quarries above and below and his *Pelican in her Piety* in the circle above.

VII.10

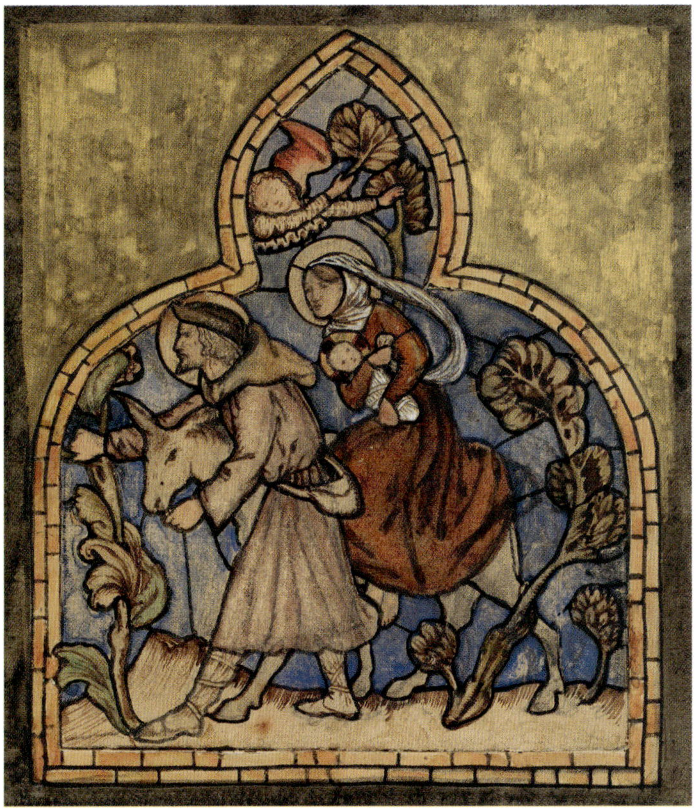

VII.11

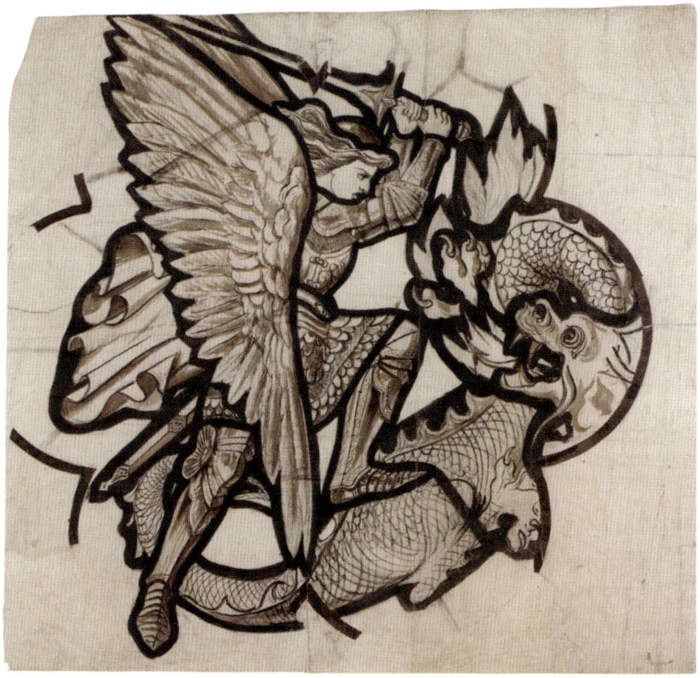

VII.12

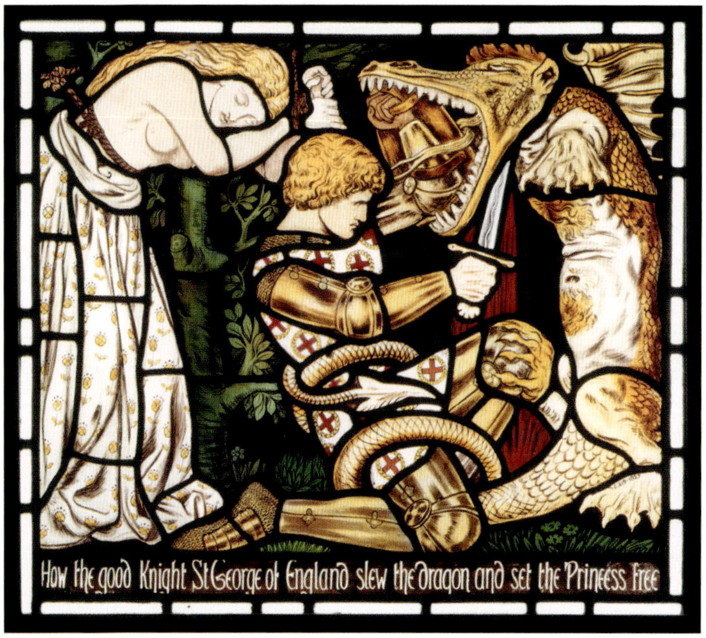

VII.10
***Flight into Egypt* design for St Michael and All Angels, Brighton**
Edward Burne-Jones for Morris, Marshall, Faulkner & Co., 1862
Watercolour and ink over pencil, gold surround to mount, 15.5 x 13.2 cm
Fitzwilliam Museum, University of Cambridge (720)

Burne-Jones's account book with Morris records this design in July 1862; the cartoons were prepared in the following month. It is unusual in the firm's work for Bodley in that it eschews 'Gothic' accessories, such as borders or canopy work. Intended to be read from close quarters, the composition skilfully accommodates the arched tops, as exemplified by the slightly stooping angels in the left-hand light (see fig.24). Burne-Jones revealed his already consummate handling of irregular spaces.

VII.11
***St Michael Slaying the Dragon* cartoon for St Michael and All Angels, Brighton**
Peter Paul Marshall for Morris, Marshall, Faulkner & Co., 1862
Wash, 81.5 x 86.8 cm
V&A (E.1166–1940)

Marshall provided at least ten cartoons for the firm's windows in 1862–3, mostly of single saints, competently drawn in a style close to Rossetti's. But *St Michael Slaying the Dragon*, designed for one of the sexfoil tracery lights in the west window of St Michael and All Angels, Brighton, impressed A.C. Sewter with its 'tremendous dramatic energy' (see fig.118). After 1863 Marshall continued his career as a surveyor and sanitary engineer. When Morris was attempting to dissolve the original firm in 1874, Marshall briefly considered trading under the name Morris, Marshall & Co. Together with Madox Brown and Rossetti, he eventually accepted £1,000 in compensation from Morris in 1875. In 1897 he supplied cartoons for a window in the English Church, Le Havre, to the Exeter glazier Frederick Drake; the window was destroyed by bombing in 1943.

VII.12
Panel from *The Legend of St George* series
Dante Gabriel Rossetti for Morris, Marshall, Faulkner & Co., *c.*1862
Stained and painted glass, 60.5 x 68.8 cm
V&A (C.319–1927)

The vigour and spatial compression of this series is typical of Rossetti's designs for stained glass. There are six panels in total and their history is uncertain. They may have been shown, as Sewter suggested, at the 1862 International Exhibition, while the *Wedding of St George* panel was included in the *Exhibition of Stained Glass, Mosaics, etc.* held at the South Kensington Museum in 1864.

VII.13a

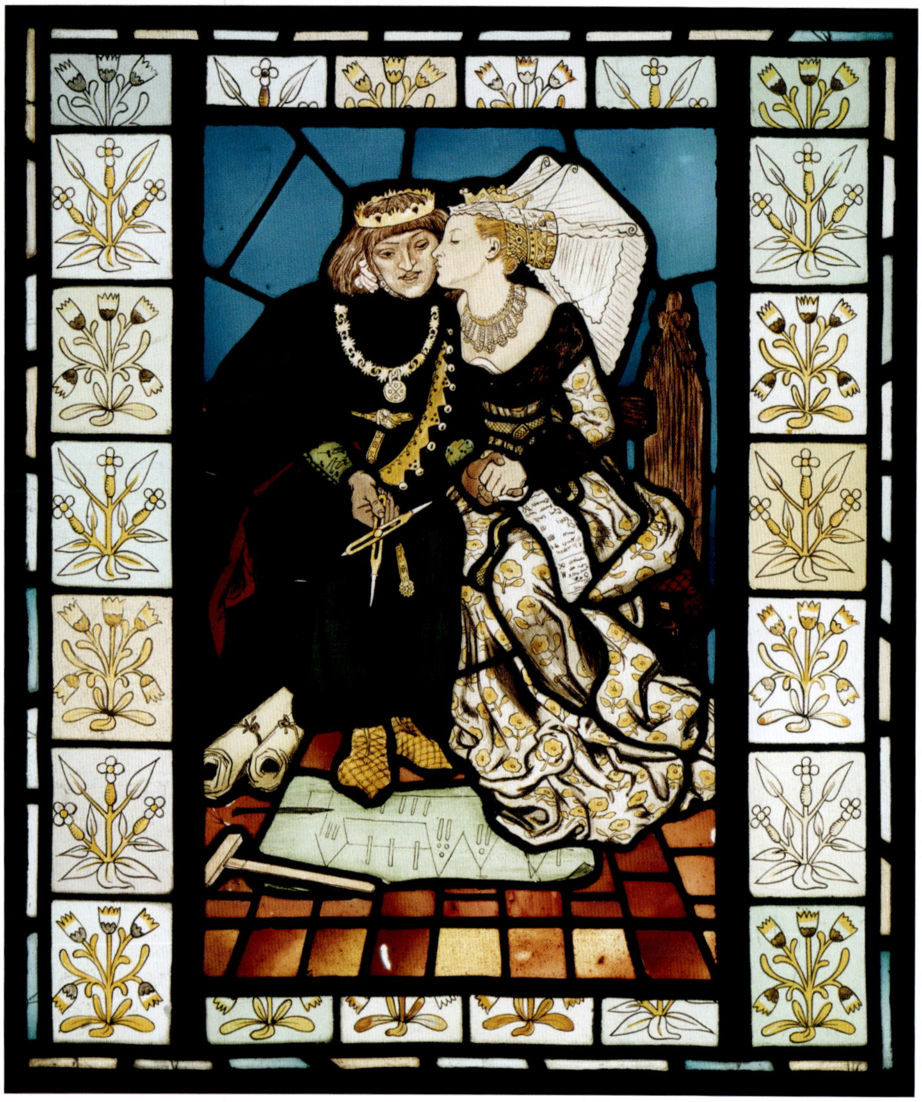

VII.13b

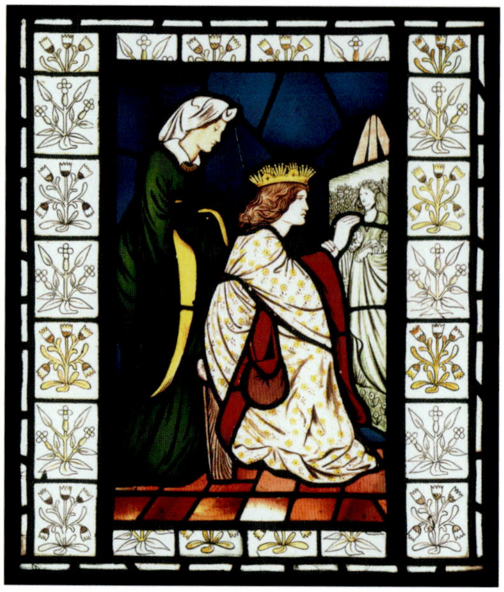

VII.13c

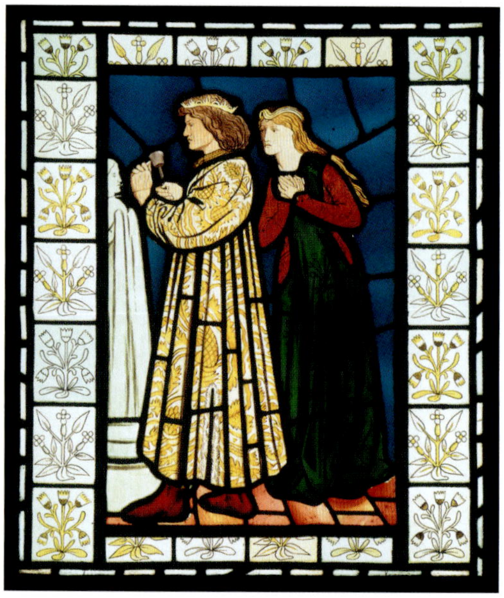

VII.13d

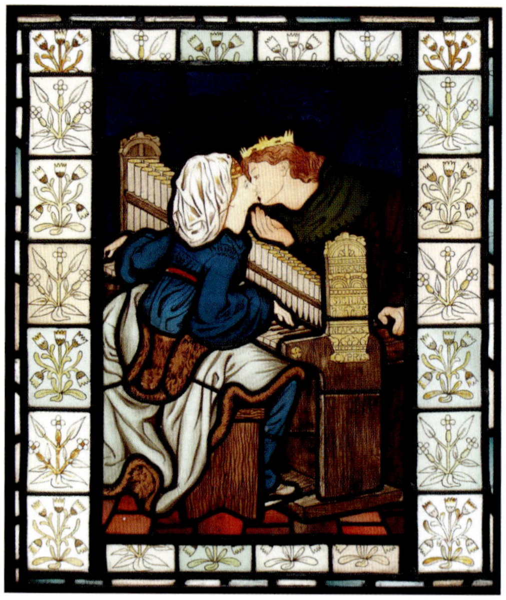

VII.13

Four stained-glass panels depicting scenes from *King René's Honeymoon*

Morris, Marshall, Faulkner & Co., *c.*1863

Stained and painted glass

a *Architecture*
Ford Madox Brown, 63.7 x 54.3 cm
V&A (Circ.516–1953)

b *Painting*
Edward Burne-Jones, 63.7 x 54.3 cm
V&A (Circ.517–1953)

c *Sculpture*
Edward Burne-Jones, 63.5 x 54 cm
V&A (Circ.518–1953)

d *Music*
Dante Gabriel Rossetti, 63.5 x 54 cm
V&A (Circ.519–1953)

The four designs were originally made in 1861–2 for the *King René's Honeymoon* cabinet, designed by Seddon and shown in the Medieval Court of the International Exhibition in 1862 (see IX.13). The panels depict incidents during the honeymoon of King René of Anjou, as related by Sir Walter Scott in *Anne of Geierstein*, who was 'endowed with a love of fine arts'.

The stained-glass versions of the subjects were made about 1863 as part of the firm's extensive interior decoration of The Hill, Witley, Surrey, the house of the painter Myles Birket Foster. Morris's adroit exploitation of variegated depths of flashed ruby glass in the tiled floor foregrounds is noteworthy.

VII.14a

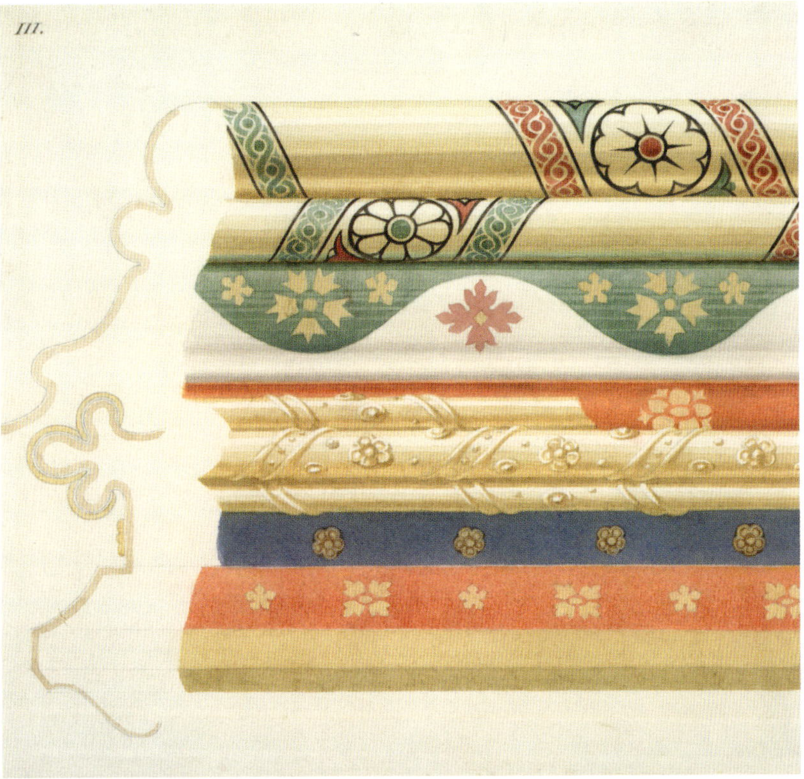

VII.14b

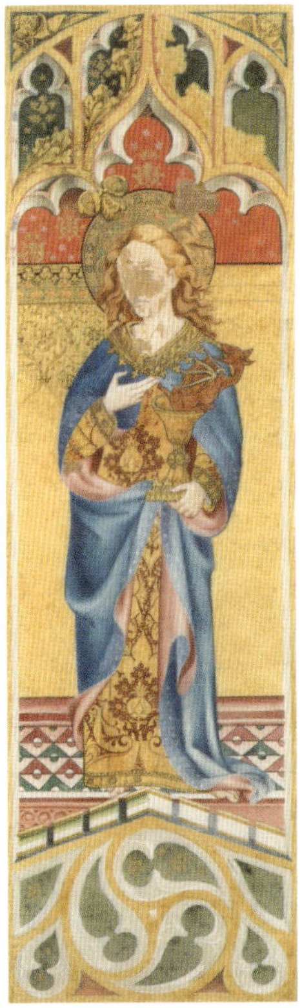

VII.15

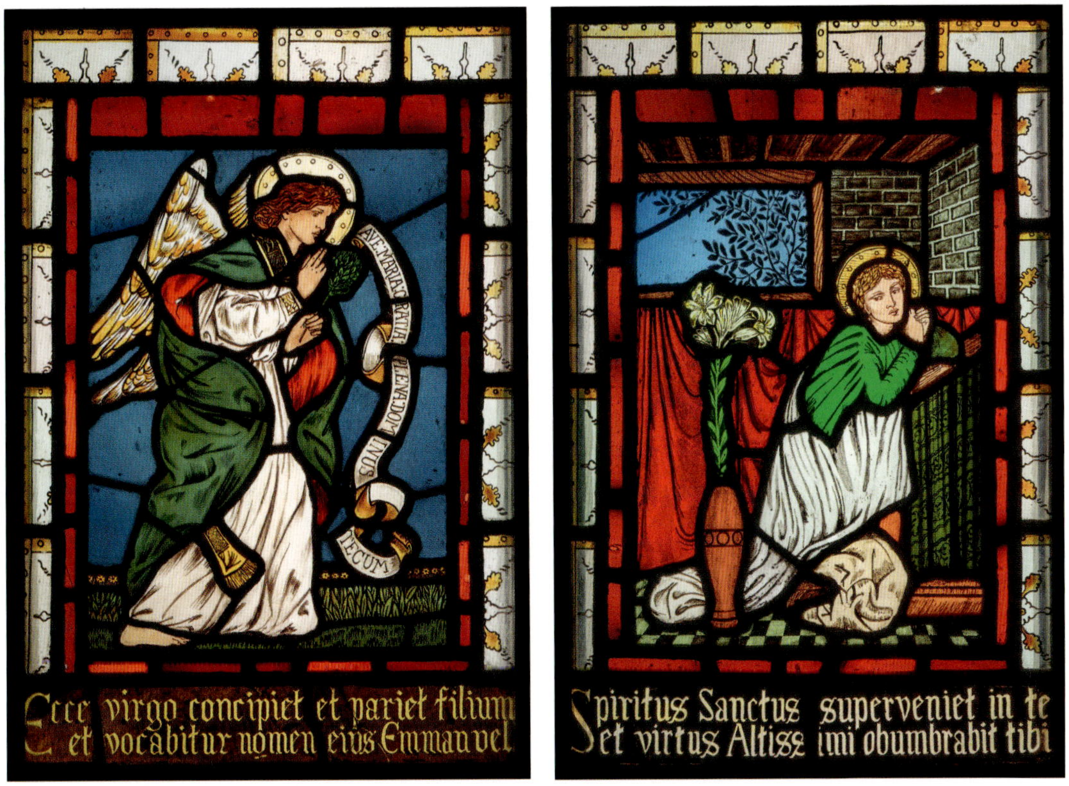

VII.14

Two record drawings of the rood screen, St Edmund's, Southwold, Suffolk

George Wardle

a Part of the rail and a profile of the moulding, 1862–3

Pencil and watercolour, 22.5 x 19.5 cm

V&A (3490)

b *St John the Evangelist*, 1865–6

Pencil and watercolour, 36 x 26 cm

V&A (E.387–1939)

Bequeathed by May Morris

In 1862–3 George Wardle, artist and draughtsman, toured East Anglian churches making meticulous drawings of their medieval fittings and decorations, especially painted decoration. Any restoration of the paintwork was carefully recorded. The South Kensington Museum purchased a set of these drawings in 1864.

St Edmund's is one of the finest of Suffolk's great perpendicular churches. Possibly on the strength of his drawings of the rood screen purchased by the Museum, the firm commissioned Wardle to make further drawings of East Anglian church decoration. These were used as source material for the firm's decorative motifs. They were bequeathed to the V&A in 1939 by May Morris (E.317 to 404–1939). SA/MH

VII.15

***The Annunciation* for All Saints, Dedworth**

Edward Burne-Jones for Morris, Marshall, Faulkner & Co., 1863

Stained and painted glass, 45.5 x 31.5 cm each

All Saints Church, Dedworth, Windsor

Bodley designed Dedworth Church, which opened in 1863. A small, unpretentious brick building, it was demolished in 1971 but the stained glass was re-sited in the new church that replaced it. Nikolaus Pevsner admired its series of Morris windows, describing *The Annunciation* as 'specially lovely'. The design was first made in 1862 for painted tiles, and its translation into stained glass is an early example of the firm's re-use of designs in different media.

Burne-Jones, as the firm's minute book for 18 February 1863 records, was paid 15*s*. to superintend the necessary alterations. He had already painted an Annunciation for Bodley in the wings of the Brighton triptych (VII.4). The architect's fondness for the subject is indicated by its presence, before Dedworth, in the firm's glazing schemes at Selsley, Brighton and Scarborough. By 1865 it was placed even more prominently in the chancel east windows at Malling Abbey, Kent; All Saints, Coddington, Nottinghamshire, and St Stephen's, Guernsey, Channel Islands.

VII.16

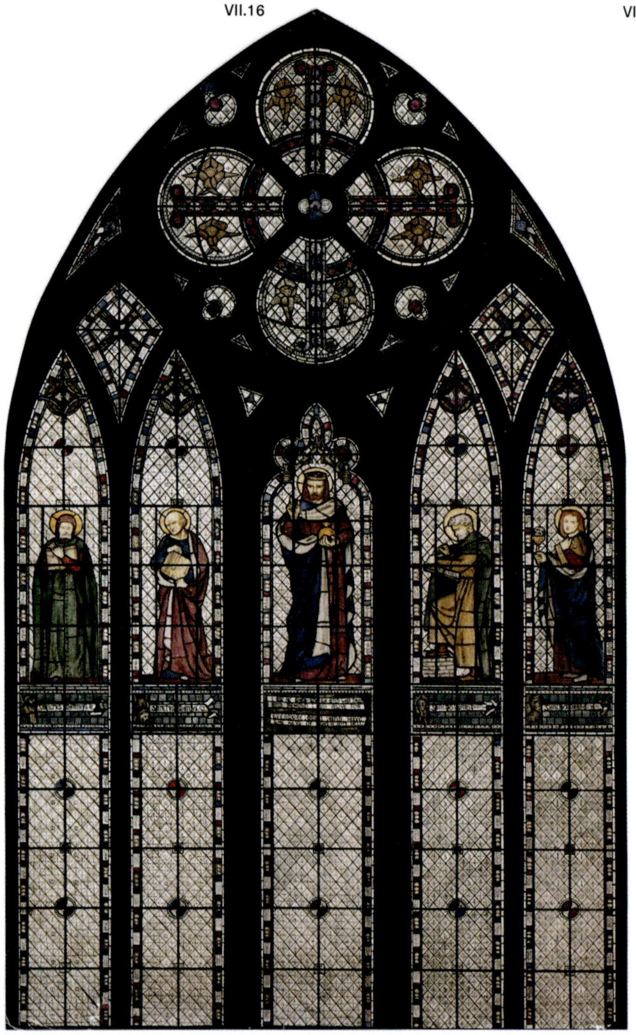

VII.17

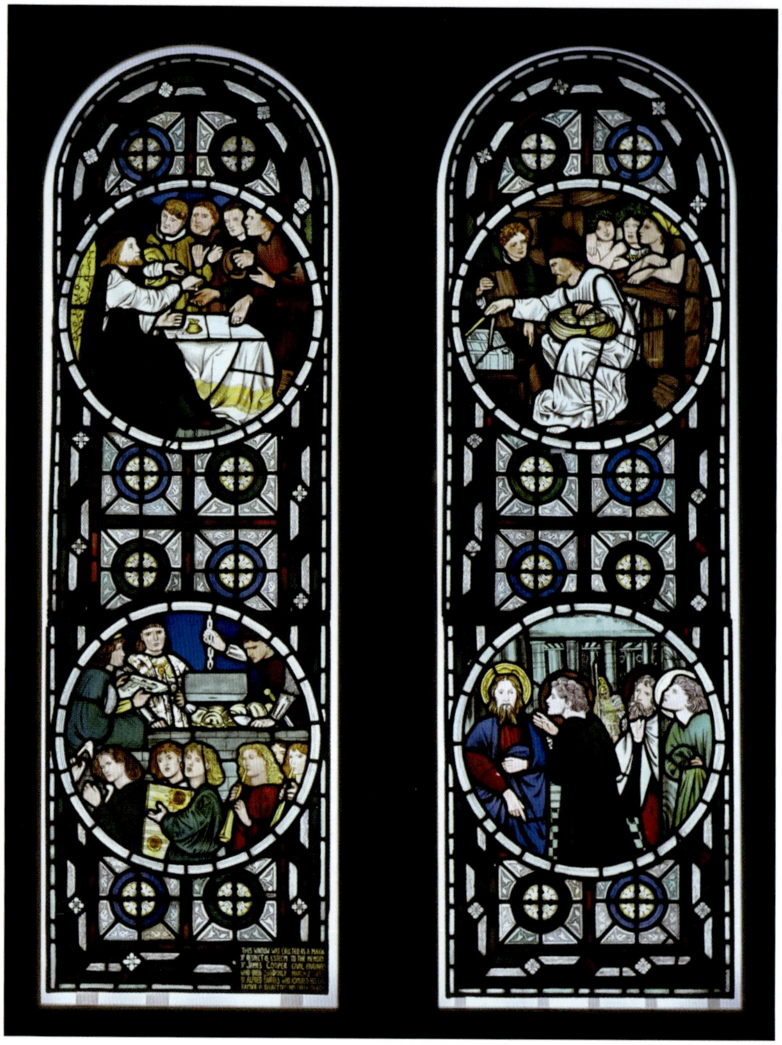

VII.16
One-inch scale drawing for the west window of Holy Trinity, Ossett, Yorkshire
Philip Webb for Morris, Marshall, Faulkner & Co., 1863
Watercolour, 70 x 42.5 cm
The Brian Clarke Collection of Stained Glass

This early design by Webb was drawn on the unusually large scale of one inch to one foot. Webb's account book for October 1862 records designs for the east and west windows at Ossett, charged at £4 10*s*. and £3 10*s*. respectively. The firm's minute book for 25 February 1863 adds, however, that both designs were to be 'considerably simplified', and it is probably one of these simplified versions that survives. The architect of Holy Trinity, William Crossland, had sought tenders from at least two other London firms, James Powell & Sons (Edward Poynter drew their sketch for the east window) and Arthur & William Henry O'Connor. Ultimately, the O'Connors glazed the east and west windows when the church was completed in 1865. Since Morris was intending to charge £400 for each window, cost was probably a factor in Crossland's decision to look elsewhere.

VII.17
Parable of the Labourers in the Vineyard, Solomon Building the Temple, Noah Building the Ark* and *Christ with Three Disciples
Edward Burne-Jones and Philip Webb for Morris, Marshall, Faulkner & Co., 1863
Stained and painted glass, 200 x 60 cm each
Cohen Quad, Exeter College, Oxford

Burne-Jones designed a two-light window for Kentish Town Parish Church in 1862 but drew the full-size cartoons in the following year. The background was designed by Philip Webb. The window was commissioned by Alfred Burges, marine engineer, partner in the highly successful firm Walker & Burges, and father of the architect William Burges. The window was a memorial to James Cooper, a civil engineer, which presumably explains the choice of *Solomon Building the Temple*. The windows were removed when the church was deconsecrated in 1994 and were later purchased by Exeter College.

VII.18

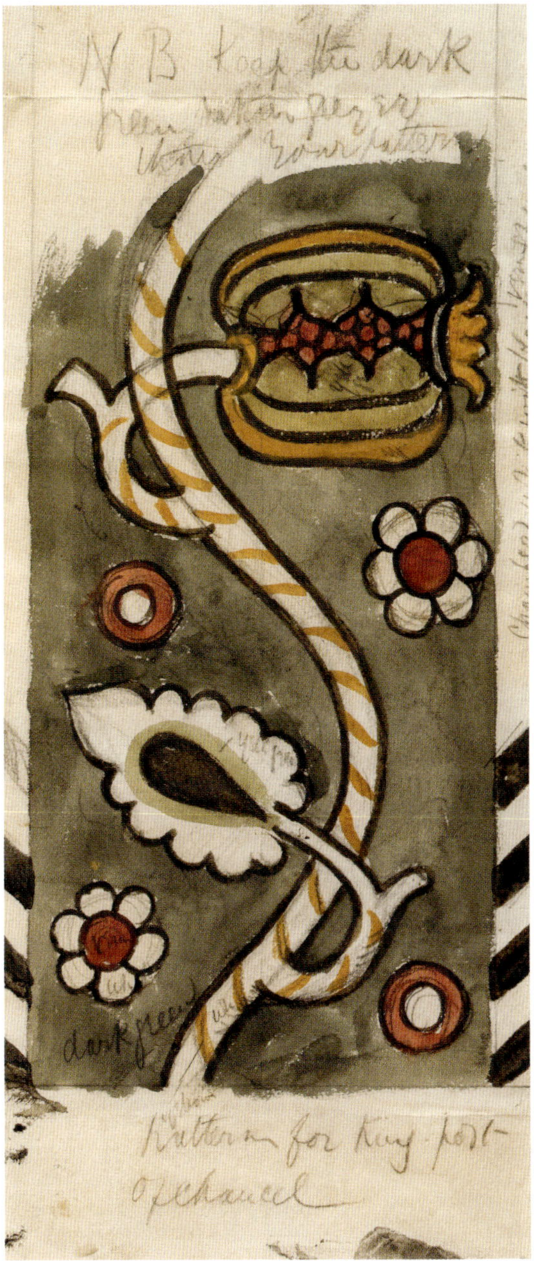

VII.19

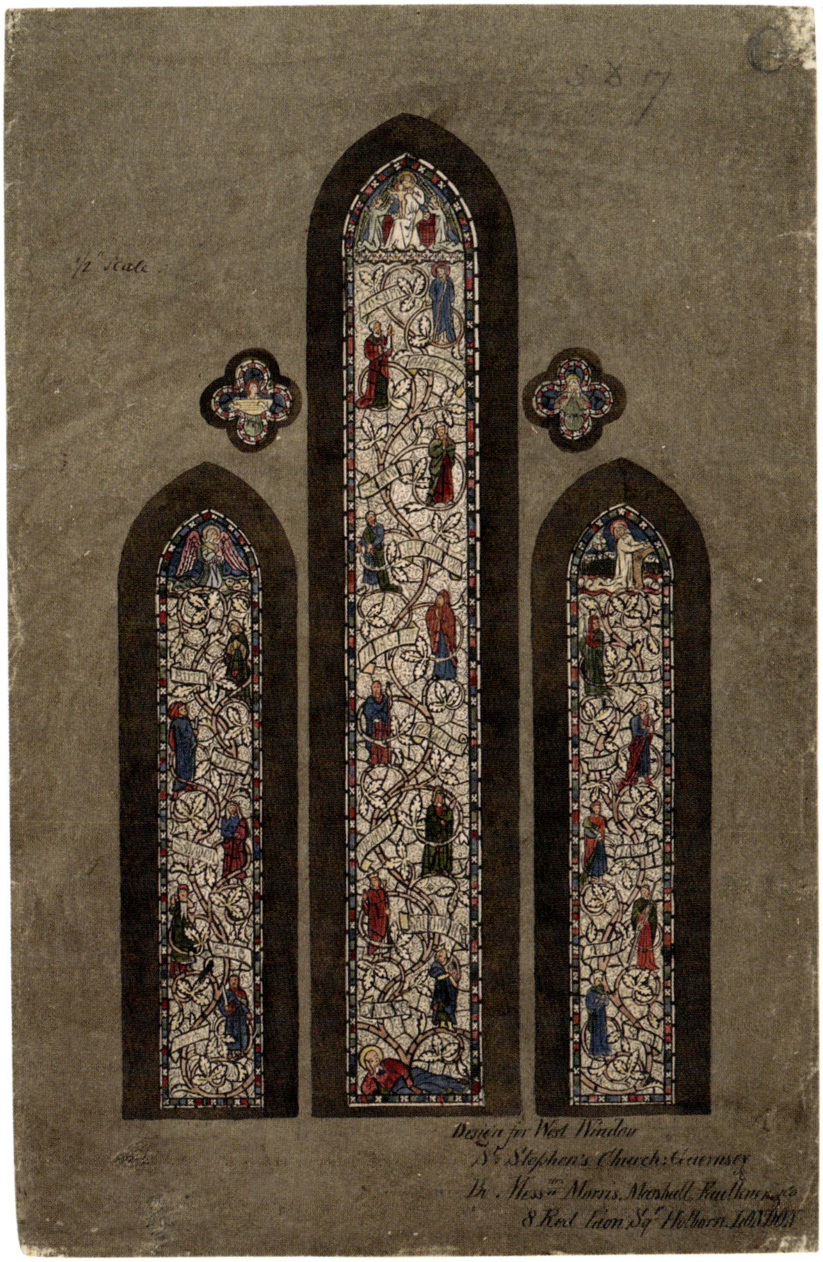

VII.18
Design for roof decoration, All Saints, Middleton Cheney, Northamptonshire
William Morris, 1864–5
Watercolour and pencil, 57 x 21.7 cm
William Morris Gallery, London Borough of Waltham Forest (A27)

The stained glass that Morris, Marshall, Faulkner & Co. supplied to All Saints, Middleton Cheney, made it, in Pevsner's words, 'a place of unforgettable enjoyment'. However, the firm's painted decoration of the nave and chancel roofs, completed in 1865, has been overlooked. Webb's *Lion's Head*, for which Sewter sought in vain in the glass, is gilded on the east and west faces of the nave tie beams. This is one of two surviving designs by Morris for the scheme. The single pomegranate is repeated on each of the king posts of the chancel roof. The pomegranate motif appears in one of Morris's early wallpaper designs (fig.186) and also features in the backgrounds to the main lights of the east window at Middleton Cheney.

Morris added precise instructions to the roof designs because the work was to be carried out by a local contractor, George Cottam of Banbury, who ran an established business as a painter, plumber, glazier and gilder. As the firm's workload increased in the 1860s it was not practicable for a team of painters to be away from the London workshops for extended periods. In engaging a competent local firm – he employed Frederick Leach at Jesus College, Cambridge, in a similar capacity – Morris anticipated what became standard Arts and Crafts/SPAB practice at the end of the century.

VII.19
***Tree of Jesse* for west window, St Stephen's Church, Guernsey**
Philip Webb for Morris, Marshall, Faulkner & Co., 1864
Watercolour, 31.3 x 20.8 cm
The Huntington Library, Art Museum and Botanical Gardens (2000.5.45)

Apart from the single-light *Tree of Jesse* that Burne-Jones designed in 1897 for St Margaret's, Rottingdean, after Morris's death, this was the only version of the subject, popular in the Middle Ages, the firm ever made.

The architect of St Stephen's was Bodley, and the firm also supplied the east window and three windows in the north aisle. Webb's account book confirms that he was responsible for this sketch. In Morris's fine colour scheme, richly draped figures are set against white quarries picked out with yellow stain, while the eponymous tree is in a pale, translucent purple. The 20 principal figures are incompletely documented; seven had previously been used elsewhere and most of the new figures appear to be designed by Morris.

VII.20a

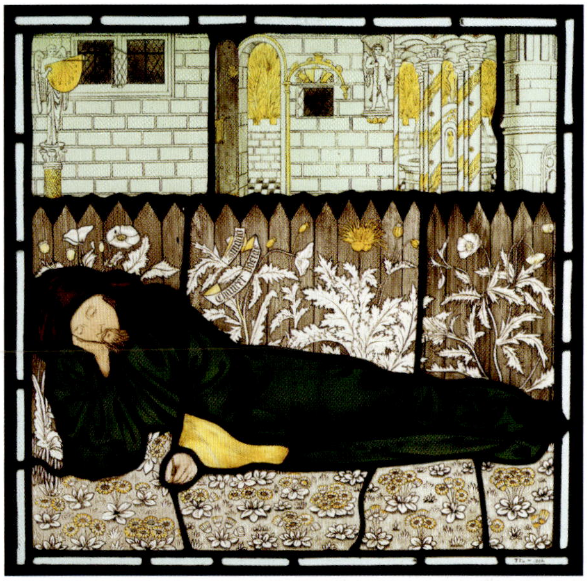

VII.20b

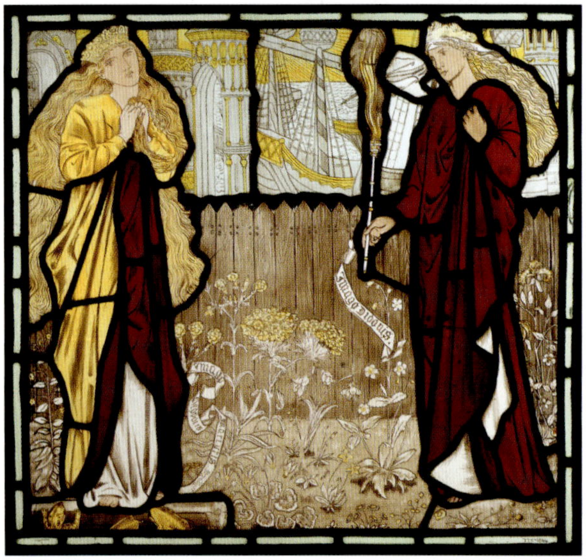

VII.21

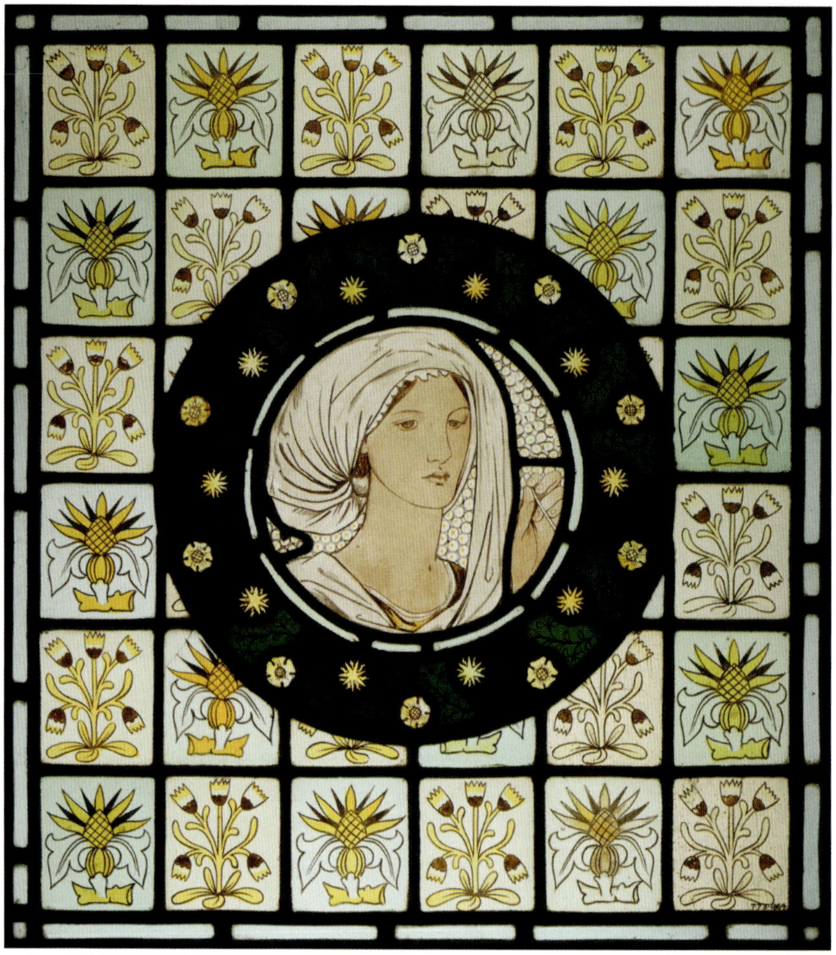

VII.20
Two panels from the series Chaucer's *Legend of Good Women*
Edward Burne-Jones for Morris, Marshall, Faulkner & Co., *c.*1864
Stained and painted glass

a *Chaucer's Dream*, 46.2 x 47.2 cm
V&A (774–1864)

b *Dido and Cleopatra*, 46 x 49.5 cm
V&A (775–1864)

In 1863 Ruskin was threatening to leave England and build a house in his beloved Swiss Alps. Burne-Jones was anxious to persuade him to reconsider. Part of his plan was to encourage Ruskin to settle in the Wye Valley, in a house for which Burne-Jones would design a series of embroideries of Chaucer's *Legend of Good Women* to be worked by the girls of Winnington Hall School, Cheshire, in whom Ruskin took a close interest. Some of the designing was done *in situ*, and Burne-Jones wrote to Ruskin describing how 'damozels such as these at Winnington can't see how Cleopatra and Medea can be good women'. He had already designed a set of *Good Women* tiles in 1862 for Sandroyd, the house at Cobham, Surrey, built by Webb for John Roddam Spencer Stanhope. These designs were substantially modified for the embroidery series, and the embroidery designs became the basis for the stained-glass cartoons.

The full series of seven designs was intended for Birket Foster's house, The Hill, Witley, Surrey, where it formed part of a large collection of both Burne-Jones's paintings and the firm's products (now dispersed). Duplicate versions of three of these were included in the *Exhibition of Stained Glass, Mosaics, etc.* of 1864 and acquired by the South Kensington Museum. They must have been the panels the critic for *The Ecclesiologist* had in mind when he described Morris's glass as 'more nearly a reminiscence of late Dutch or Flemish domestic glass than anything else'. The same writer admired 'their dabs and blots of strong colour in the midst of silvery or creamy white', and their use of flesh tints, which 'applied by them perfectly flat, are in delightful contrast to the treatment of flesh by most other artists'.

The *Good Women* series was repeated in many different versions. The most complete surviving set (it lacks *Chaucer's Dream*) is in the Combination Room at Peterhouse, Cambridge; dating from 1869 it is part of an extensive scheme of tiles, stained glass and painted decoration that the firm carried out there for Scott Junior. A further set of six (again without *Chaucer's Dream*) belongs to the V&A; it was made by Morris & Co. in 1909.

VII.21
Penelope
Edward Burne-Jones for Morris, Marshall, Faulkner & Co., 1864
Stained and painted glass, 57 x 51.5 cm
V&A (773–1864)

This panel was acquired by the South Kensington Museum directly from the 1864 *Exhibition of Stained Glass, Mosaics, etc.* An adaptation in roundel form of the head of *Phyllis* from the *Good Women* series, it proved a popular design for the firm's domestic stained-glass commissions. Penelope, wife of Ulysses, was one of Ovid's heroines, author of the first of his 15 epistolary poems.

VII.22a

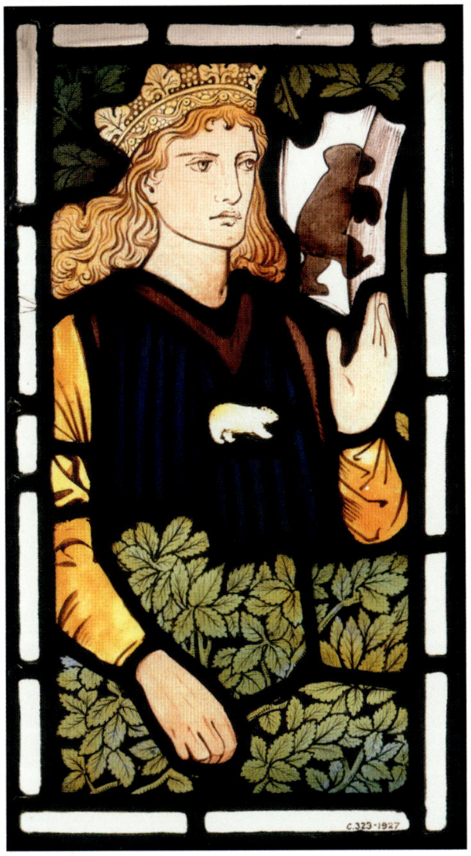

VII.22b

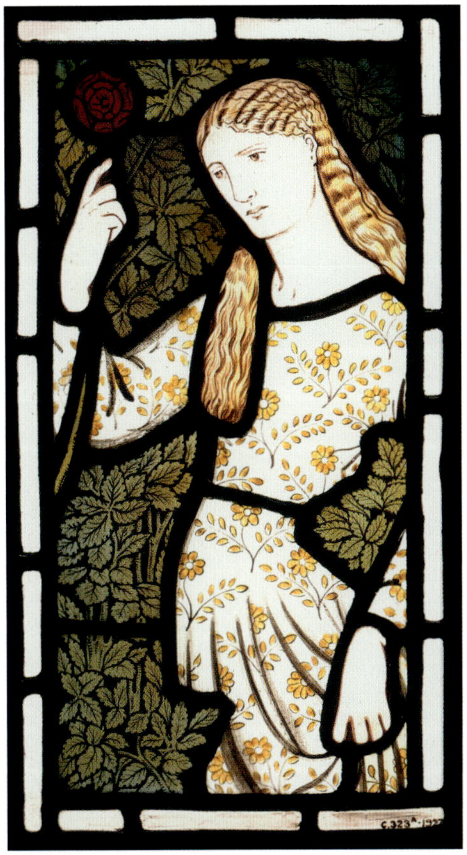

VII.22

Two stained-glass panels
Edward Burne-Jones for Morris, Marshall, Faulkner & Co., *c.*1864
Stained and painted glass
Bequeathed by James Richardson Holliday

a *The Prince*, 33.6 x 18.5 cm
V&A (C.323–1927)

b *Merchant's Daughter*, 33.6 x 18.5 cm
V&A (C.323A–1927)

These panels were made specifically for the 1864 *Exhibition of Stained Glass, Mosaics, etc.* at the South Kensington Museum. The cartoons, as the size of the glass indicates, were adapted from painted tile designs, in this case two of the *Beauty and the Beast* series designed by Burne-Jones for a fireplace in the house of Birket Foster in 1863. No doubt the firm considered the highly attractive panels an effective advertisement for their small-scale domestic glass, but no further versions were made.

VII.23

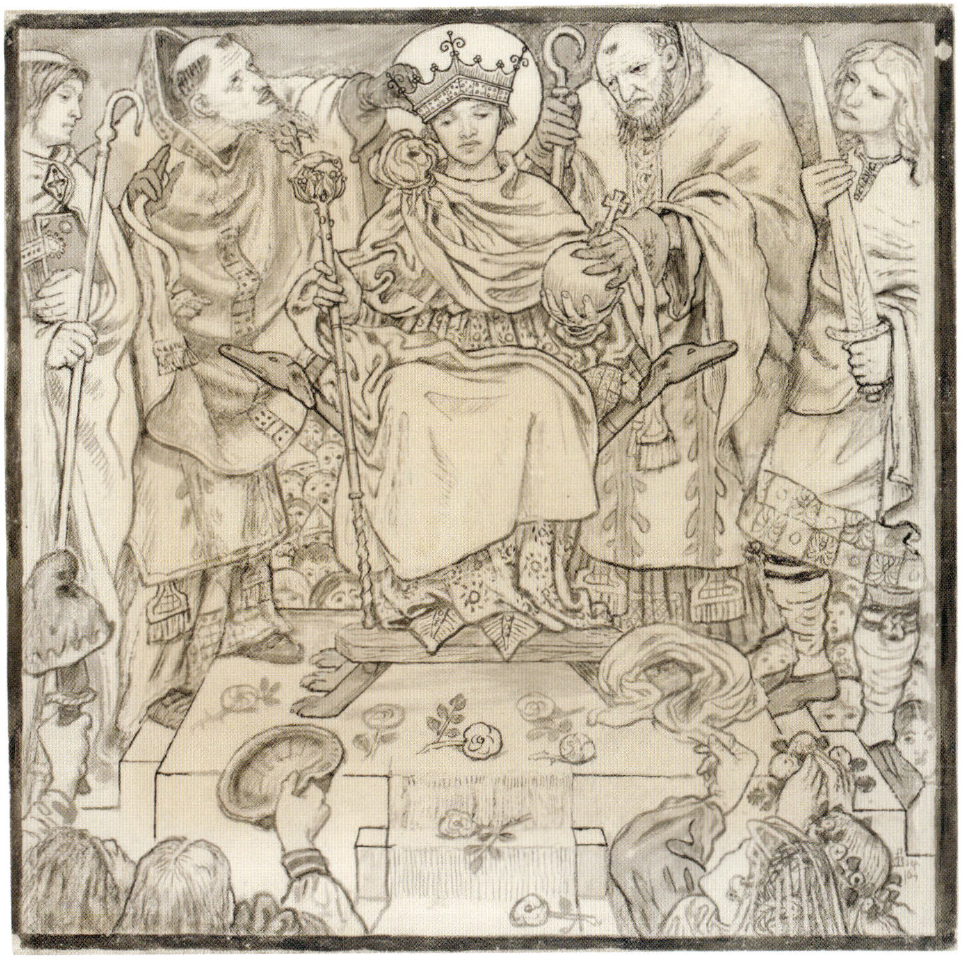

VII.23

***St Oswald Crowned King of Bernicia* from *Scenes from the Life of St Oswald*, for St Oswald's, Durham**
Designed by Ford Madox Brown for Morris, Marshall, Faulkner & Co., 1864–5
Chalk and wash, 49.6 x 50.8 cm
Inscribed: 'FMB Sep. 64'
V&A (E.1853–1910)

One of six cartoons for a three-light window set high at the west end of the medieval church of St Oswald at Durham, executed at intervals during 1864–5. The panels are positioned between shield and decorative work by Webb and roundels of angels by Morris on a field of light quarries.

Full of vigorous line and detail within a limited depth, they characterize Madox Brown's approach to stained-glass design. He considered that 'invention, expression and good dramatic action' should be combined with the imperative of fine colour. He made nearly 130 subject and single figure designs for the firm up to 1874. He retained the copyright, considering them, as a history painter, basic material for his paintings. The *Baptism* in this series was developed much later for part of Madox Brown's first wall painting in Manchester Town Hall, 1878. MB

VII.24

The Lamentation of Christ

Side panels designed by William Morris, painted by Charles Napier Hemy; central panel relief sculpture Franconian, second half of the fifteenth century

Morris, Marshall, Faulkner & Co., 1866

Side panels: oil on oak; centre: polychrome gesso on oak, 152.4 x 193 cm

Even in its present condition – it was partly restored following fire damage in 1957 – this triptych for St Edward the Confessor, Cheddleton, is an instructive example of the firm's church decoration in the 1860s and of the partners' attitudes towards late medieval art. It was made 'under the immediate superintendence' of Scott Junior, who wrote to one of the churchwardens that 'I am greatly pleased with it. It is a great thing to have a good work of art, combining new and old work, and both of them good.' 'The work of these men', he added, 'will have a constantly increasing value, for it is such good work that it cannot be duly appreciated at first.'

Among conflicting accounts of the provenance of the central *Lamentation of Christ*, the most convincing version is that reported in *The Building News*, 13 April 1866, when the triptych was nearing completion, which stated that the reredos was a gift of Edward Wood, of Newbold Revel Hall, Warwickshire. Thomas Wardle, in a paper written in consultation with Morris in 1876, noted that it had been bought 'at an old furniture mart, at the request of the architect'. The Wood family – well-known Staffordshire potters – had Cheddleton ancestors.

The *Lamentation* had been painted a 'dark oak colour' but the polychromy found under this coating was restored under Morris's direction and augmented with his own drapery patterns. The brocade design on the tunic of Joseph of Arimathea is closely related to the pattern on the Southwold rood screen, copied by George Wardle (see VII.14b). The triptych's new oak casing was designed by Scott Junior and made by Rattee & Kett of Cambridge. The wings depicting the *Annunciation* were designed by Morris and painted by Charles Napier Hemy. Hemy, who left soon after to pursue a successful career as a marine painter, had been introduced to the firm by William Bell Scott. Until 1862 he was attached to the Dominican Order and he executed painted decoration for their chapels at Newcastle upon Tyne and Lyons.

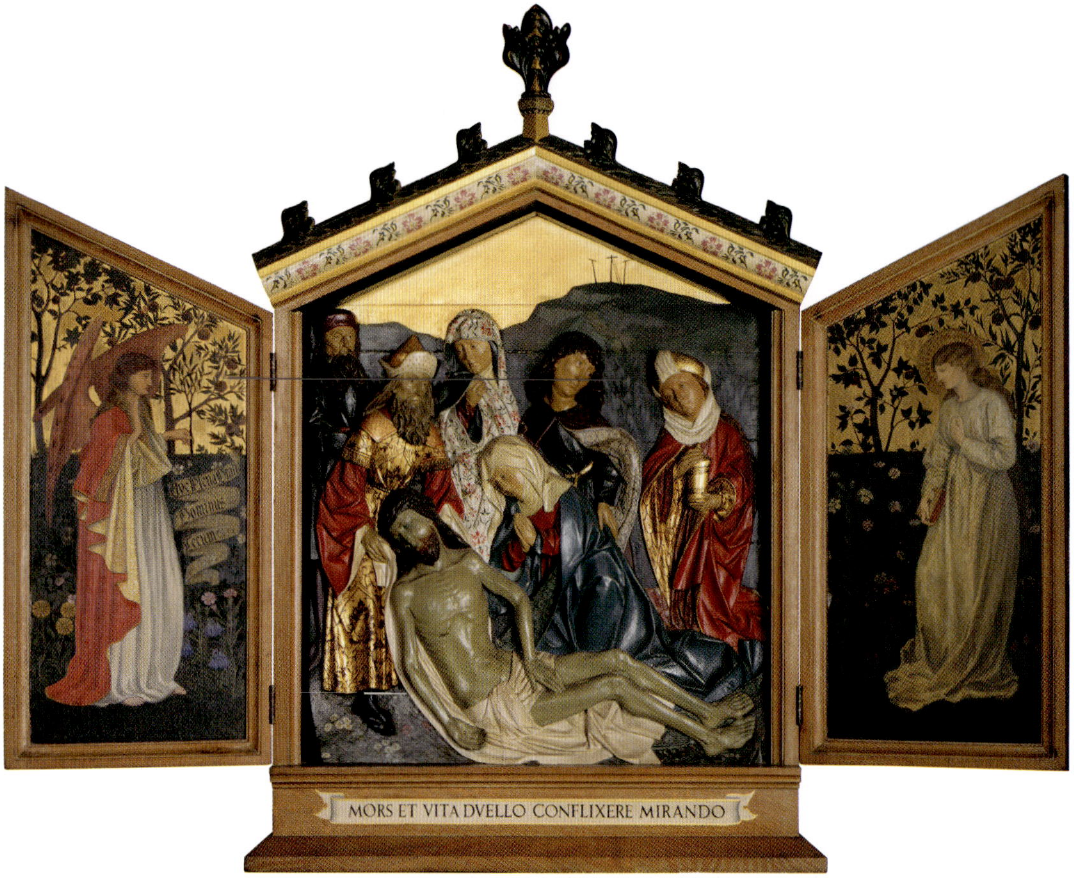

VII.24

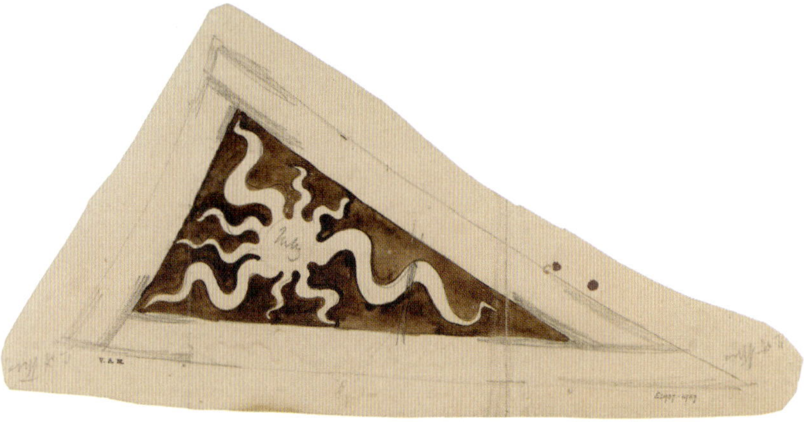

VII.25a

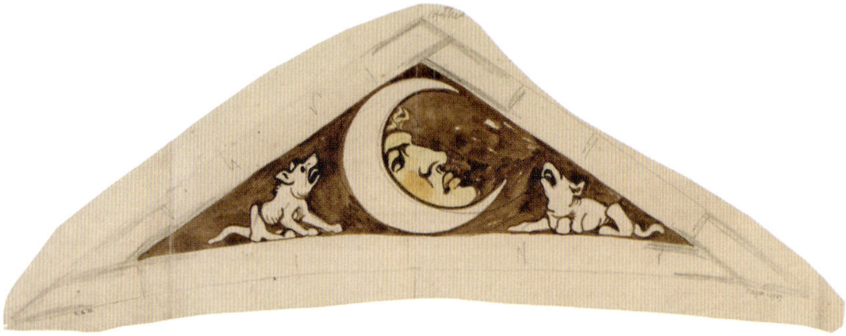

VII.25b

VII.26

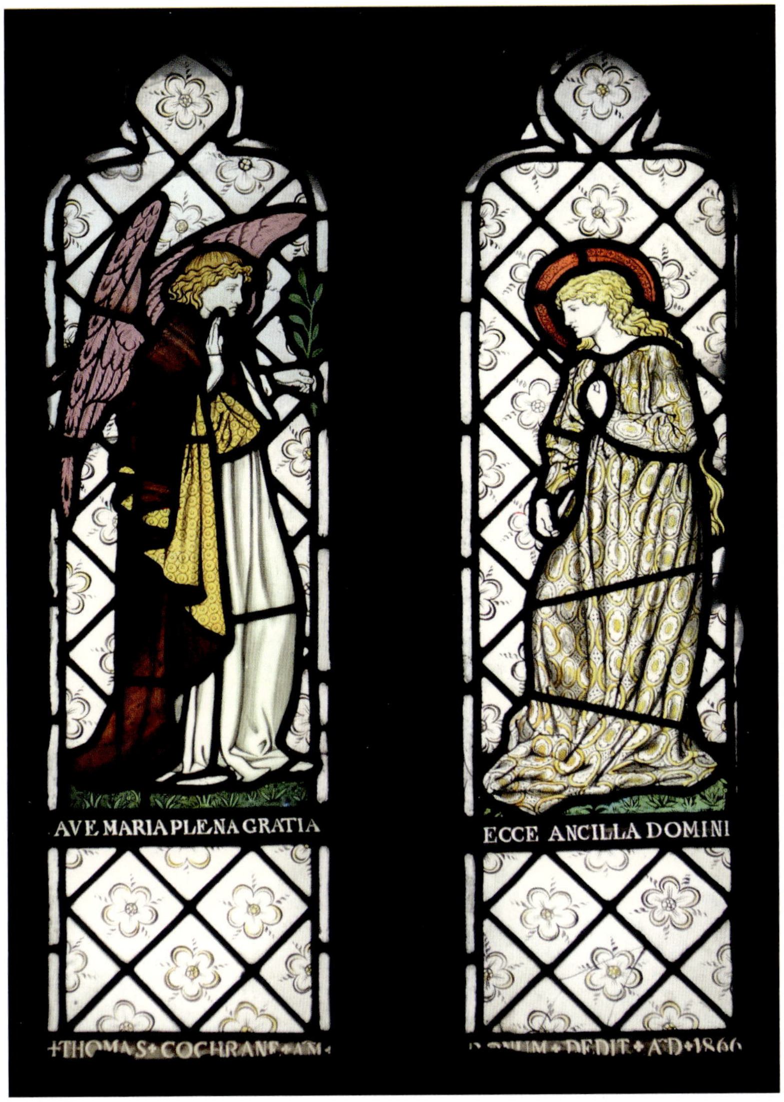

VII.27

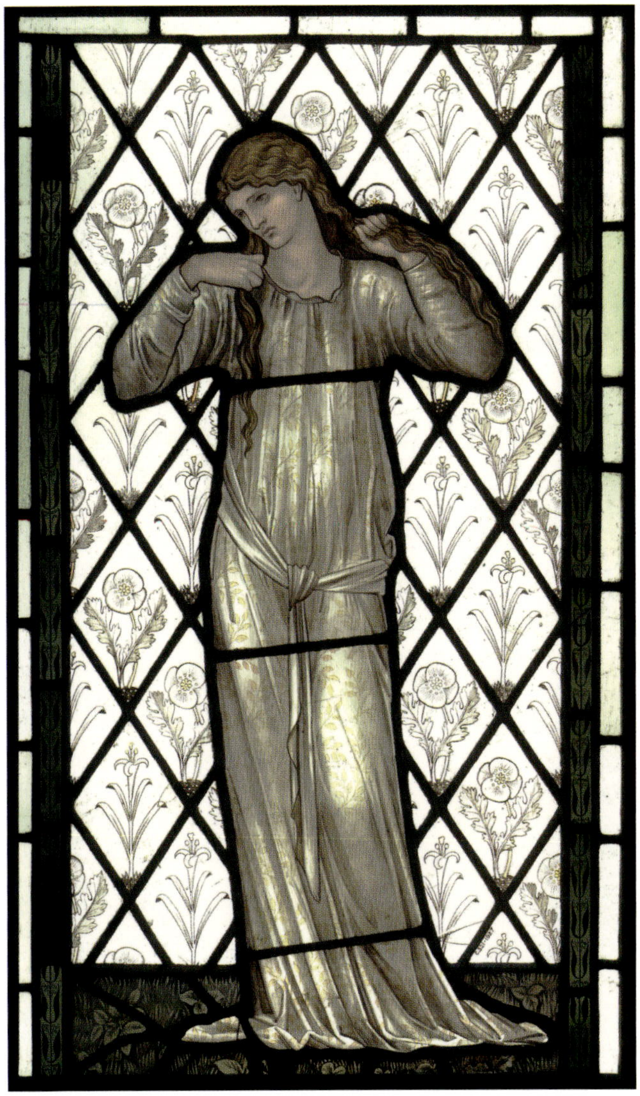

VII.25
Two tracery designs for stained glass from *Signs of the Zodiac* series
Philip Webb, 1865
Pencil, Indian ink and watercolour
Bequeathed by James Richardson Holliday

a *Flaming Star*, 20.3 x 41 cm
V&A (E.2937–1927)

b *Dogs Barking at Moon*, 18.7 x 55.2 cm
V&A (E.2938–1927)

If Webb's designs for tracery lights are under-appreciated, it is probably because they are normally situated in the less accessible parts of windows. These attractive examples can be found in the *Signs of the Zodiac* tracery of the east window in the chapel of the Royal Agricultural College, Cirencester, Gloucestershire. The 'Flaming Star' was a favourite motif of Webb's, and he repeated it in many different forms. It is a common medieval device and A.W.N. Pugin and others had used it earlier in the nineteenth century. In 1863 Webb drew a detail of a flaming star in the fifteenth-century window depicting *St Enoch* at New College Chapel, Oxford, and another possible source was the fourteenth-century glass in the tracery lights of the east window in the chapel of St Lucy, Christ Church, Oxford.

VII.26
***The Annunciation* for Chapel of St James, Lord Leycester Hospital, Warwick**
William Morris for Morris, Marshall, Faulkner & Co., 1866
Stained and painted glass, 78 x 17.5 cm each
The Patron and Governors of the Lord Leycester Hospital, Warwick

The delightful Warwick *Annunciation* is an instructive example of the firm's transposition of designs across different media: Gabriel and the Virgin Mary were adapted from the figures Morris designed for the painted wings of the Cheddleton altarpiece in the same year (VII.24). The architect who restored the Chapel of St James in 1864–6 was Thomas Garner. The figures were repeated on at least five more occasions in stained glass.

VII.27
Elaine
Edward Burne-Jones for Morris, Marshall, Faulkner & Co., designed 1870
Stained and painted glass, 86.3 x 51.4 cm
V&A (C.321–1927)
Bequeathed by James Richardson Holliday

Figures of *Lancelot* and *Elaine* were designed by Burne-Jones in 1870 as part of an extensive stained-glass scheme for Hill Place, Upminster, Essex. The designs were repeated in 1882 for Lunefield, Kirkby Lonsdale, Lancashire. Lunefield was built for Alfred Harris, a Bradford banker; he and John Aldam Heaton were at the centre of the group of industrialists, based around Bradford and Bingley, who were important patrons of the Pre-Raphaelites in the 1860s. Harris's architect was Alfred Waterhouse, whose work Morris detested. The house is now demolished.

Elaine's father, King Pelles, wanted to marry her to Lancelot, whom he tricked into believing Elaine was Guenevere by feeding him a magic potion. When Lancelot awoke to find Elaine in his bed he apologized and took his leave.

The companion figure of *Lancelot* is now lost (although the whole series at Upminster survives; the building there is now the Convent of the Sacred Heart of Mary). *Elaine* is an early example of what became a standard pattern for Morris's windows in the 1870s and later, in which the figure was placed on a plain quarry background.

VII.28

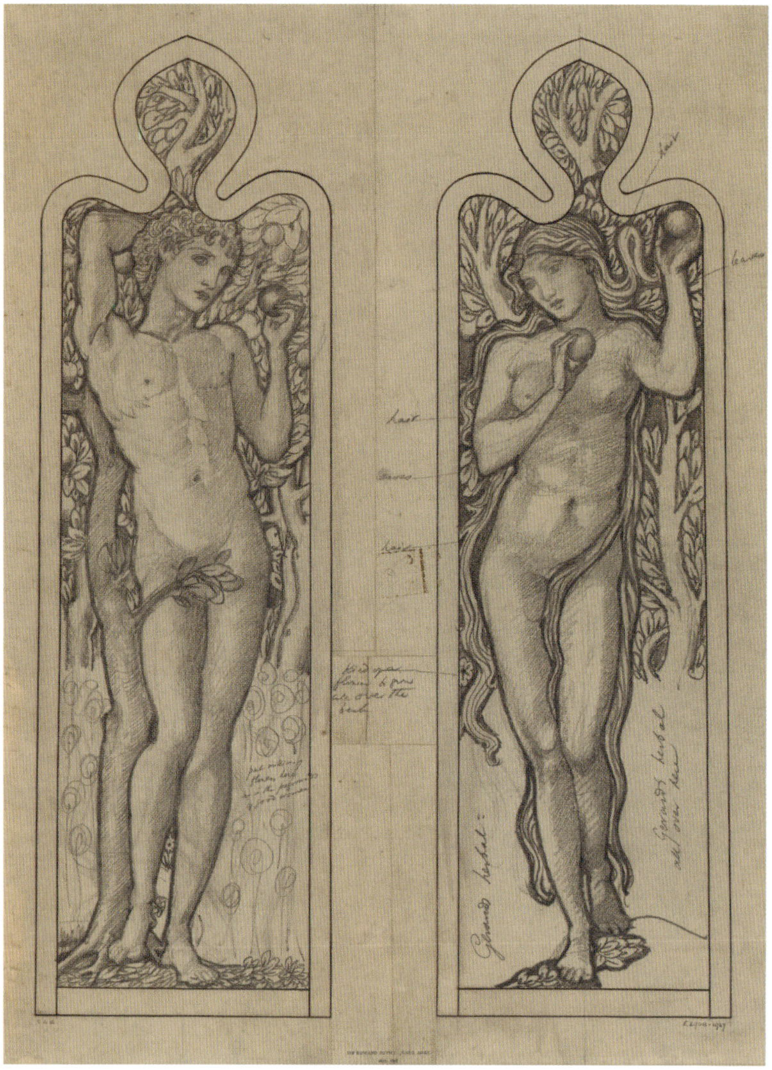

VII.30

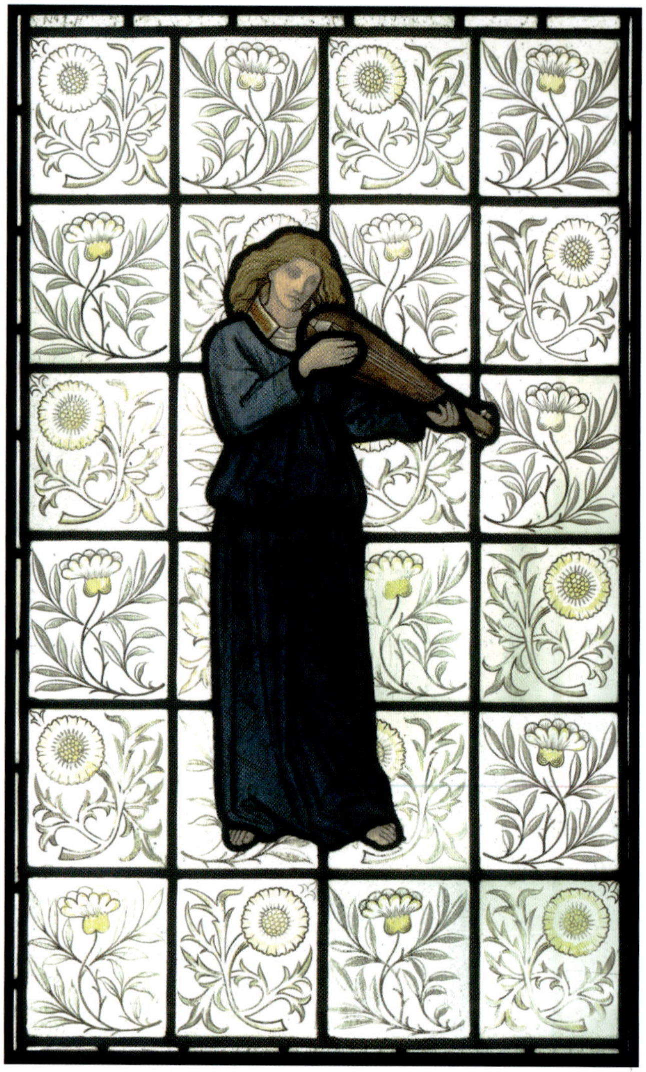

VII.29

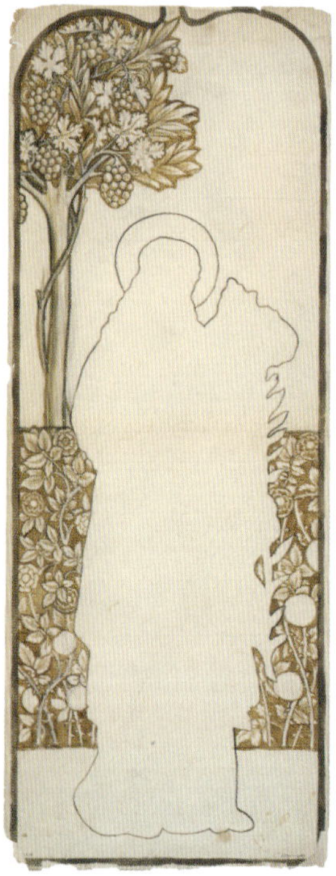

VII.28
***Adam and Eve*, west window, All Saints, Middleton Cheney, Northamptonshire**
Edward Burne-Jones for Morris, Marshall, Faulkner & Co., 1870
Pencil, pen and ink, 83.4 x 64.4 cm
V&A (E.2908–1927)
Bequeathed by James Richardson Holliday

The notes that Burne-Jones appended to this full-sized design for a tracery light provide an insight into the nature of his collaboration with Morris. By Adam's knee he wrote 'put millions of flowers here as in the foregrounds of good women', and alongside Eve, 'Gerard's herbal all over here' – indicating an important source document for such details.

VII.29
Cartoon for background design for St Martin's, Marple, Cheshire
Unattributed designer for Morris, Marshall, Faulkner & Co., 1873
Pencil and wash, 99 x 36.8 cm
V&A (E.2791–1927)
Bequeathed by James Richardson Holliday

The blank space in this cartoon has been left to accommodate a figure of the Virgin Mary designed by Burne-Jones some ten years earlier for the east window of Bradford Cathedral. Adapting the backgrounds enabled figures to be re-used on numerous occasions in windows of different shapes. By this date, the backgrounds were generally drawn not by Morris but by William Emile Pozzi. This meant windows could be designed with Morris merely supervising and without necessitating the direct involvement of Burne-Jones. This streamlining of the company's methods facilitated increased productivity but perhaps also accounts for those windows in which the firm's original inspiration appears diluted.

The restoration of St Martin's Church was completed under the architect John Dando Sedding in 1870, when the firm supplied the east window of the chancel. This was the only occasion on which Sedding commissioned stained glass from Morris: the huge east window of his church of Holy Trinity, Sloane Street, London (the largest the firm ever made), was not fixed until four years after the architect's death.

VII.30
***Minstrel* (*Woman Playing Lute*)**
William Morris for Morris, Marshall, Faulkner & Co., *c.*1874
Stained and painted glass, 75 x 46.5 cm
V&A (C.678–1923)
Given by May Morris

This domestic panel exemplifies the streamlining of Morris's workshop practices to facilitate the re-use of cartoons. Morris's *Minstrel* was one of a series of figures frequently used for secular commissions (both painted tiles and stained glass) and which, with the addition of wings, became minstrel angels for church windows. The backgrounds of simple quarries allowed flexibility in terms of accommodating different window shapes and facilitated homogeneity within sometimes disparate figure styles.

VII.31

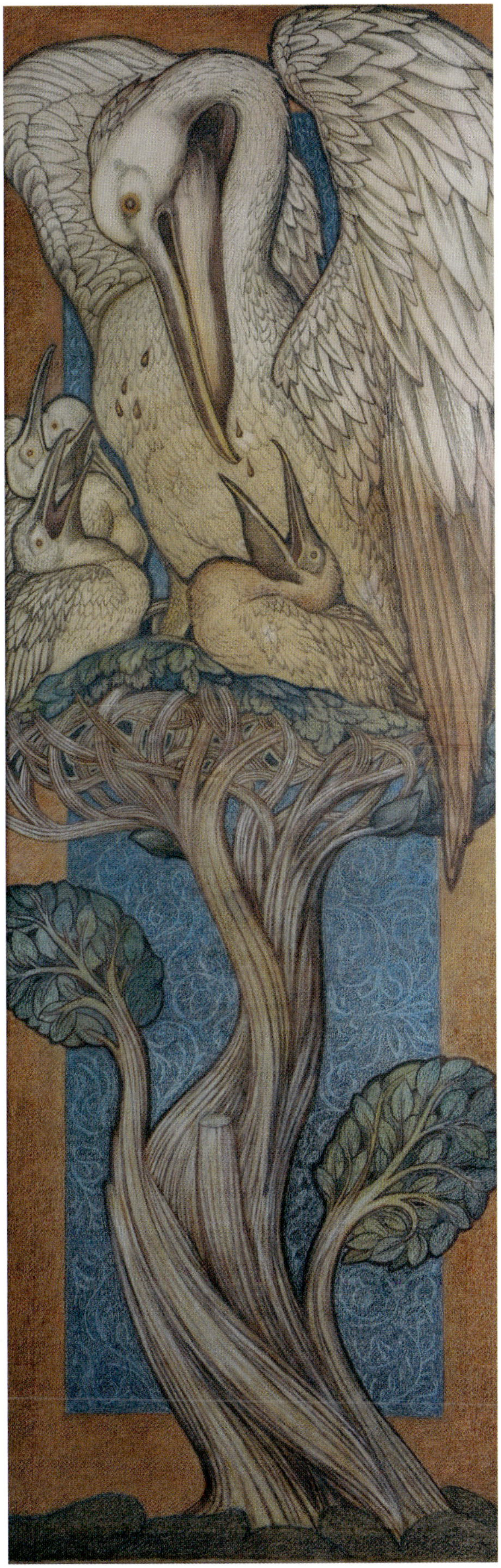

VII.32

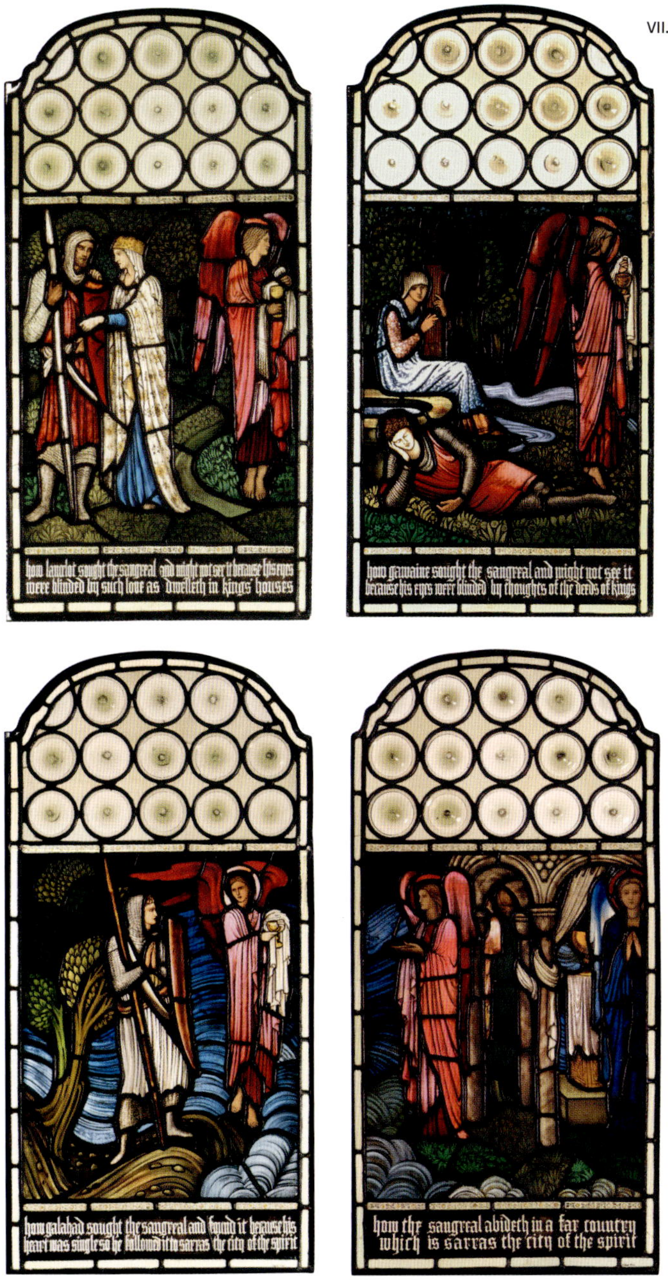

VII.31
***The Pelican in her Piety* for St Martin's, Brampton, Cumbria**
Edward Burne-Jones for Morris & Co., *c.*1880. Coloured chalks and gold, 172.7 x 57.2 cm
William Morris Gallery, London Borough of Waltham Forest (A136)

Burne-Jones worked up this highly finished drawing after the stained-glass cartoon had served its purpose (the design was never repeated in glass elsewhere). The pelican drawing blood from its breast to feed its young was a medieval symbol of Christ's sacrifice. The sinuous curves of the tree that supports the nest are more apparent in this drawing than in the window, where it is set against a background of dense, jewel-like flowers (see fig.115).

VII.32
The Quest for the Sangreal
Edward Burne-Jones, made by Morris & Co., 1886
Stained and painted glass, 46 x 33 cm each
V&A (C.623 to 626–1920)
Given by Sir Philip Burne-Jones, Bart

Burne-Jones returned to the Arthurian legends for these four panels, designed for the family's second home, North End House, Rottingdean. In the first scene Sir Lancelot fails to attain the Grail, thwarted by his adultery with Queen Guenevere. Sir Gawaine is similarly frustrated, this time by worldly ambition. The last two panels are read as a pair, connected by the sinuous swirling waves, which lead the spiritually pure Sir Galahad towards his ultimate reward.

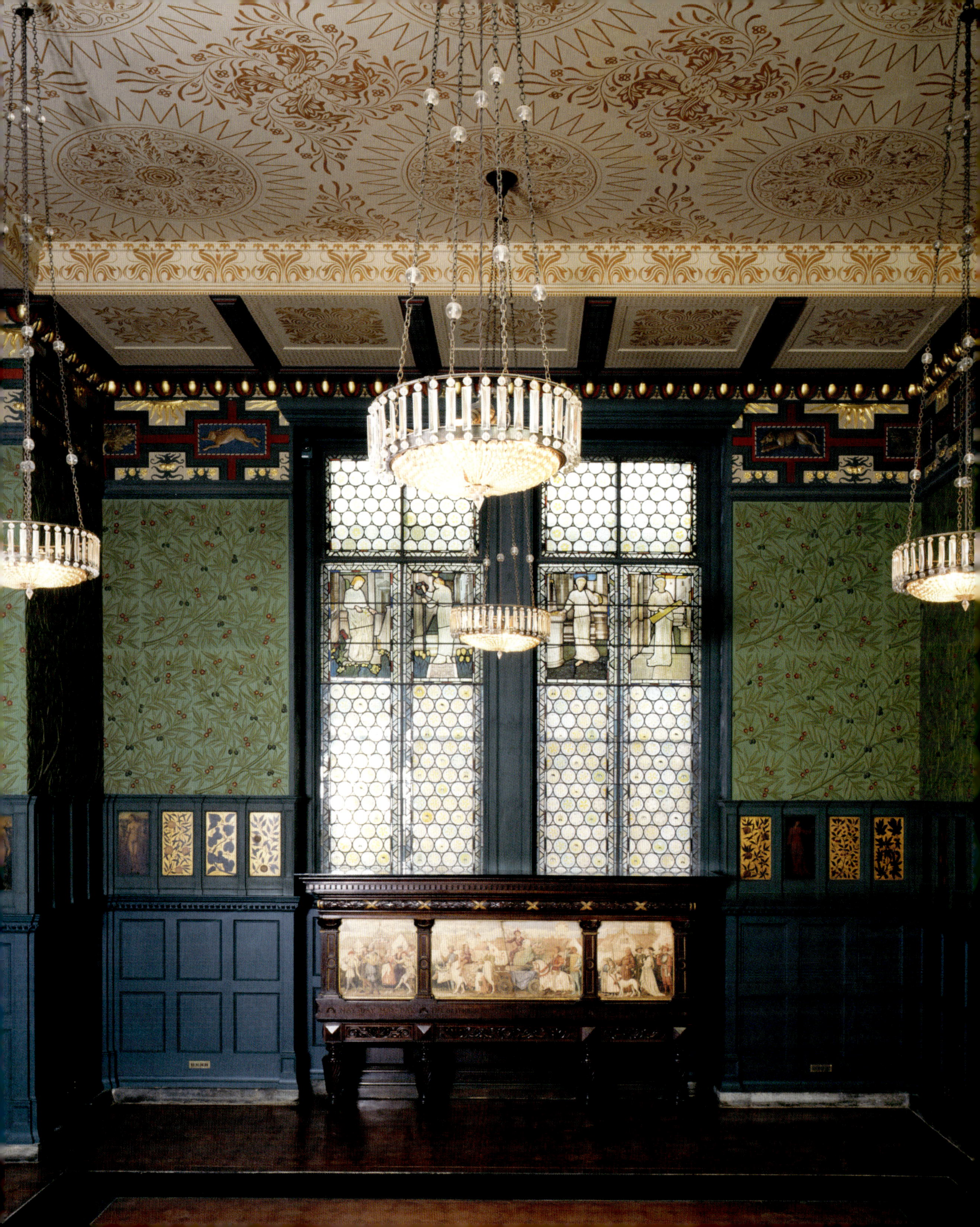

VIII

INTERIOR DECORATION

Linda Parry

'If I were asked to say what is at once the most important production of Art and the thing most to be longed for, I should answer, A beautiful House ...'

William Morris, 'Some Thoughts on the Ornamented Manuscripts of the Middle Ages', *c.*1892

This statement by Morris illustrates his modest aims as designer and retailer. His success in achieving this intent can be judged by his obituaries, many of which remembered him not as a designer, poet, writer or radical socialist, but as a decorator. This was not meant to downgrade his work in other spheres, but simply reflected his popularity in what was then, in 1896, an admired and reputable trade.

All of the decorative patterns and objects that Morris designed or helped to make were purposefully conceived to fit together in room settings and, although beauty was the aim, all were made to be appropriate for their use. This pragmatism is the most overriding characteristic of his work and is a quality that has been seldom recognized in the past, despite it being one of the main reasons why his furnishings are so popular today. It is, therefore, appropriate that a survey of his achievements in various artistic spheres should include a study of his views on the decoration and furnishing of houses and how he actually carried this out in his own commercial practice. As soon as Morris was first able to choose his own surroundings he felt a strong need to decorate and furnish them to his own taste, and he continued to do this for himself and his family and for friends and clients for the rest of his life.

The rooms he rented with Edward Burne-Jones, first at Upper Gordon Street and then from November 1856 at 17 Red Lion Square, London, presented him with his first opportunity for such self-expression. The sheer anticipation of a bohemian life, and the freedom from constraints of home, school, university and Street's office provided Morris with opportunity and confidence, and he began to amass objects and ideas that would later develop into his own personal style of domestic decoration. He had already had some furniture made to his design before moving in and these pieces were painted by Morris, Burne-Jones and their friend and frequent visitor, Dante Gabriel Rossetti. Once installed, Morris designed and embroidered a set of hangings for the walls with the help, volunteered or otherwise, of their servant Mary Nicholson, known as Red Lion Mary. The grouping of these new furnishings (IX.2–4 and XII.1) with the mass of collected items – easels, lay figures, armour, prints and brass-rubbings – that Morris and Burne-Jones acquired for artistic reference or effect, provided a general jumble about which Burne-Jones declared 'all domestic arrangements are of the most limited description'; a fact illustrated by the only existing illustration of the rooms (fig.156).

Fig.140 **The Green Dining Room, South Kensington Museum (now the V&A).**
V&A

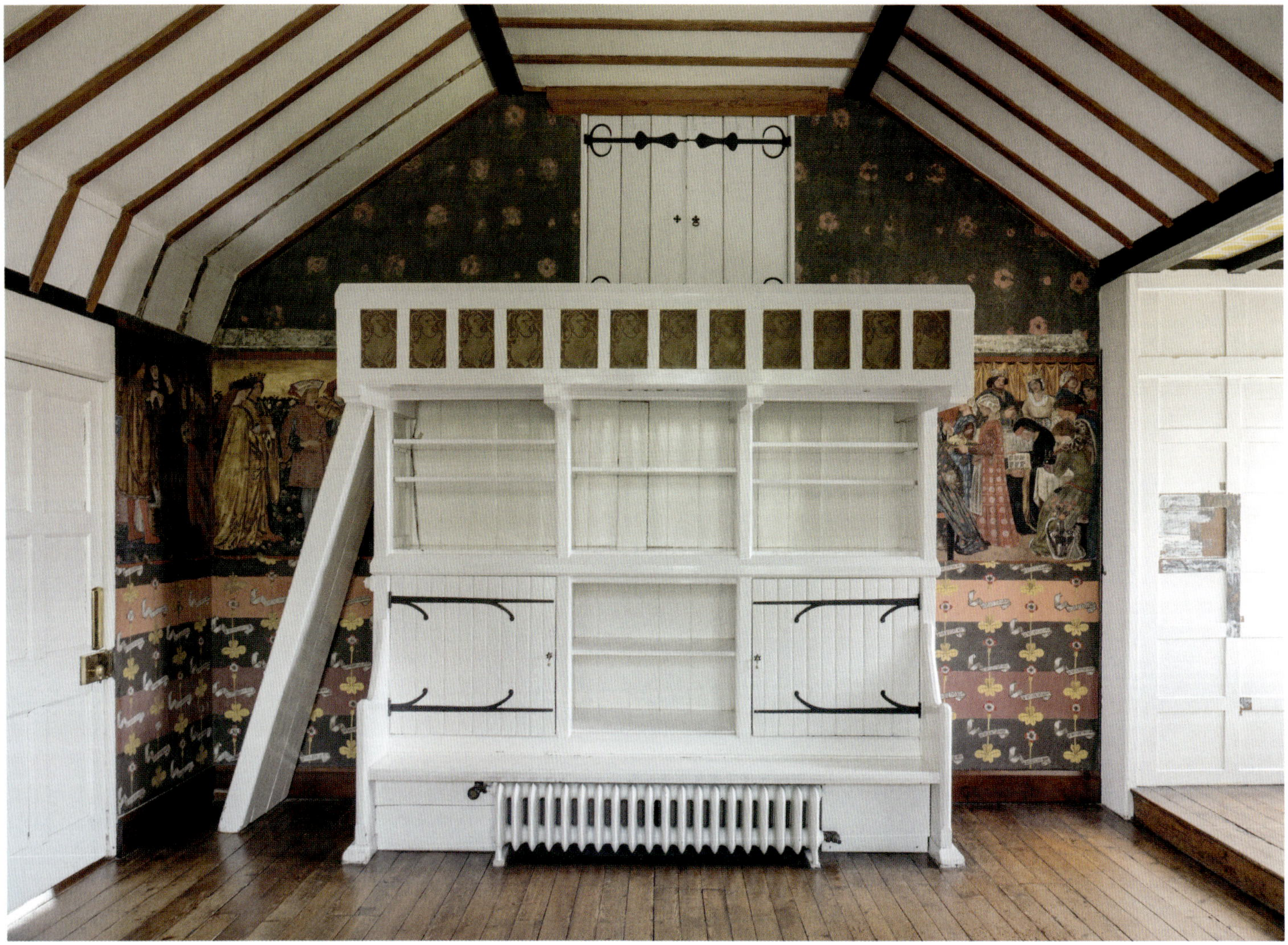

Fig.141 **The drawing room at Red House with richly patterned wall decoration revealed during conservation. The white paint is a twentieth-century addition; the settle was originally painted in shades of red with some pattern work and the ceiling was also highly decorative.**
National Trust, Red House

The first official project that Morris took part in was the decoration of the debating hall of Benjamin Woodward's new Oxford Union building (fig.21), a commission organized initially by Rossetti. After the exuberance of Red Lion Square, this scheme was important to Morris in introducing him to the organization and economics of business life. With his knowledge of Oxford building trades, learned in Street's office, he became responsible for the purchase of materials and the hire and organization of labour. As the Union was only willing to pay for equipment and the food and lodgings of the participants, this must have been an onerous duty. Morris designed a repeating pattern for the roof which, despite being re-painted some years later, was generally approved of, whereas his contribution to the Arthurian themes around the walls, *How Sir Palomydes loved La Belle Iseult with exceeding great love*, has proved to be more of historic than artistic significance (see VI.7).

While painting at the Oxford Union in 1857 Morris first met Jane Burden. They were engaged in the spring of 1858 and married in April 1859, by which time Morris was well advanced with plans for his next decorative project – the biggest so far – the building and decoration of a house for them to live in. He had first broached the subject with Philip Webb while on a boat trip down the Seine from Paris in August 1858. Webb was to design the house and Morris to organize the decoration and furnishing of it; a working partnership that lasted for over 30 years.

As Webb's first building as an independent architect, Morris's commission presented him with an unprecedented opportunity, that of designing a home for a close friend with comparable tastes. His notebooks and delicate, meticulous drawings

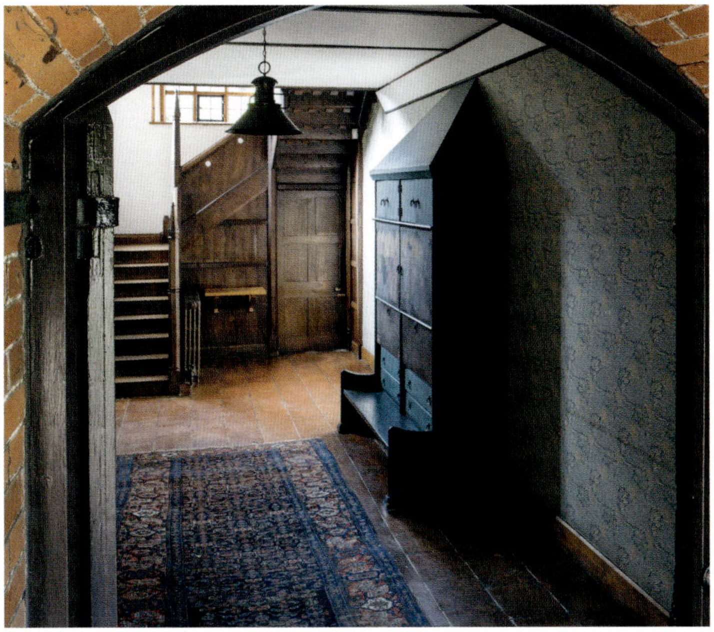 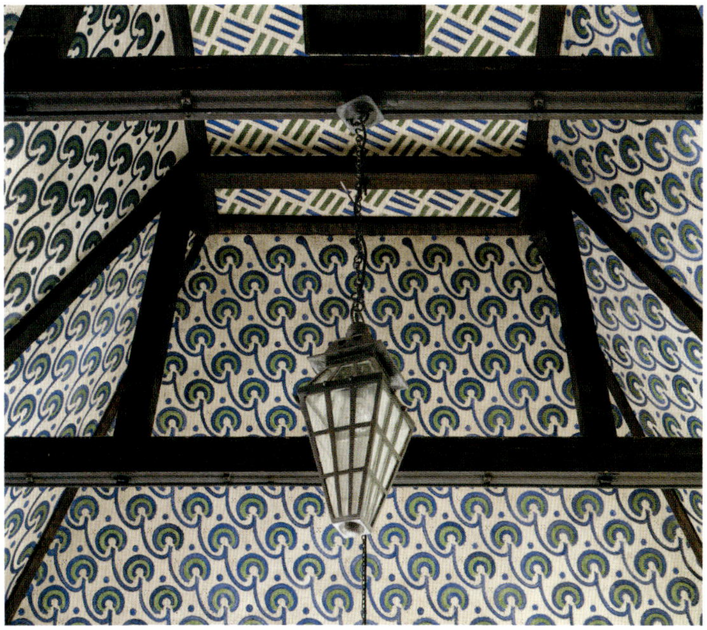

Fig.142 **The generously proportioned hallway at Red House with Webb's built-in settle.**
National Trust, Red House

Fig.143 **The original ceiling decoration above the main staircase at Red House, *c.*1860–1.**
National Trust, Red House

show the care with which he undertook the challenge (VIII.2–4). Morris intended that most of the walls and ceilings of the house should be decorated; either painted with repeating patterns and narrative compositions or covered with embroidered hangings. Many of the original geometric ceiling patterns have survived and, although mostly repainted over time, they still bear the puncture holes made in the wet plaster as a guide for painting. Until extensive paint analysis, commissioned by the National Trust who acquired Red House in 2003, our understanding of Morris's intentions for the rest of the house's decoration had been confined to a few disparate sketches together with reminiscences by friends and other visitors. With the careful investigation of early paint layers, suggestions of pattern and colour have emerged and it is now possible to see the extent of Morris's ambition for the decorative schemes. Throughout the house, walls and ceilings were decorated with strong earthy colours, a rich palette of reds, blues, greens, yellows and browns.

For the hall and staircase, Morris and Burne-Jones planned a series of wall paintings based on the story of Troy (VI.14). These were never attempted, although the painted ceiling of the stairway has survived and shows one of Morris's earliest attempts at pattern-making, which looks both medieval and modern in its use of simple motifs (fig.143). A specially designed and painted cupboard-cum-settle is the only remaining furnishing from the original scheme for the hall (fig.142 and VI.15), though visitors also recalled one of Webb's oak tables in this space.

Morris's plan for the separate formal dining room, running off the hall, was one of his most enterprising. With a paint scheme of deep reds and greens, Philip Webb designed a magnificent dresser for the room and Morris conceived a set of embroidered hangings. Depicting heroines from classical, biblical and Arthurian sources, this project was never completed but many of the separate panels have survived (see XII.4) and one, depicting Aphrodite, was rediscovered at auction in 2007 and has been acquired for the house (fig.144). These embroideries were not the only textiles intended to decorate Red House and for the principal bedroom Morris chose a simpler design of embroidered daisies for a set of hangings on a dark blue ground (XII.3). These hung alongside a wall painting depicting biblical figures (VI.8), uncovered and conserved in 2013, and also designed to create the illusion of a hanging textile.

The most adventurous plans of all were devised for the drawing room on the first floor, a space that extends into the roof and is flooded by light from windows on the north and west (fig.141). A large settle was installed on one wall. Originally part of Morris's furnishings for Red Lion Square, its position was indicated on Webb's detailed drawings of the architectural fittings of the house. Rossetti painted the settle doors with scenes illustrating the Italian poet Dante's enduring love for Beatrice. For the walls,

Burne-Jones planned a series of seven tempera paintings depicting the fifteenth-century romance of Sir Degrevaunt, one of their favourite tales. Only three were completed and survive in the house. These show *The Wedding Ceremony*, *The Wedding Procession* and *The Wedding Feast*, in which William and Jane appear, appropriately, as Sir Degrevaunt and his bride Melidor in the final scene (fig.145). All other sections of the walls and ceiling were painted with a range of brightly coloured patterns, as research by the National Trust has determined. The effect is so busy, so unusual to a modern eye that one can only agree with William Bell Scott's assessment that, 'The adornment had a novel, not to say startling character, but if one had been told it was the South Sea Island style of thing one could have easily believed such to be the case so bizarre was the execution.'

The decoration of Red House, both in terms of original artistic endeavour and the comradeship experienced by Morris and his friends, convinced them to exploit the situation commercially and led to the foundation of Morris, Marshall, Faulkner & Co. in 1861. Their intentions were not solely mercenary for, however the others may have felt about the project, Morris saw it as a crusade. 'All the minor arts were in a state of complete degradation especially in England, and accordingly in 1861 with the conceited courage of a young man I set myself to reforming all that', was how he described it in a letter of 1883.

It is clear that Morris and Webb saw house decoration as one of the main functions of the new company, and at the top of a list of services offered in its initial circular was 'Mural Decoration, either in Pictures or in Pattern Work, or merely in the arrangement of Colours, as applied to dwelling-houses, churches, or public buildings'. The 1862 International Exhibition established the firm in the minds of a section of the fashionable London buying public and a steady flow of work followed over the next few years. By 1865 they were recognized as one of the most exciting new enterprises, even though the business, now moved to Queen Square, was still small and additional financial backing was needed to keep going.

Many more commissions for the decoration of houses were carried out by the firm in its first decade than is now realized. Few of these houses still exist, and the difficulty in identifying which of the clients or locations mentioned in the firm's minute book represent schemes or simply orders for individual objects has added to the confusion. A number of commissions were arranged through contacts within the partners' various artistic circles and those that are known represent a varied and interesting group. These include the decoration of houses for the painters John Roddam Spencer Stanhope (Sandroyd, Cobham), Myles Birket Foster (The Hill, Witley), both in Surrey, and George Price Boyce (Glebe Place, Chelsea); Woodbank and Harden Grange in Bingley, Yorkshire, the homes of the decorator John Aldam Heaton and his neighbour

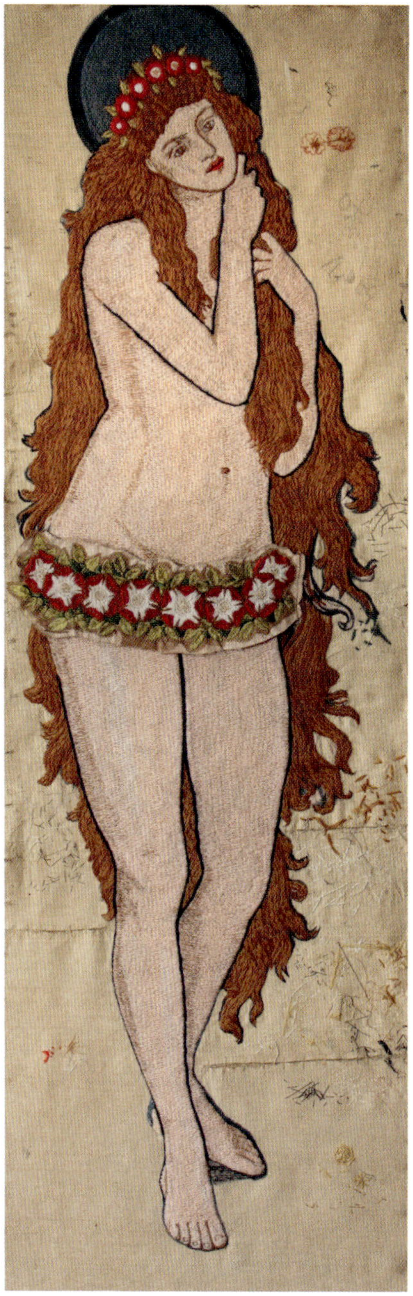

Fig.144 ***Aphrodite* embroidery, designed by William Morris, *c.*1860, and attributed to Jane Morris, *c.*1861.**
National Trust, Red House

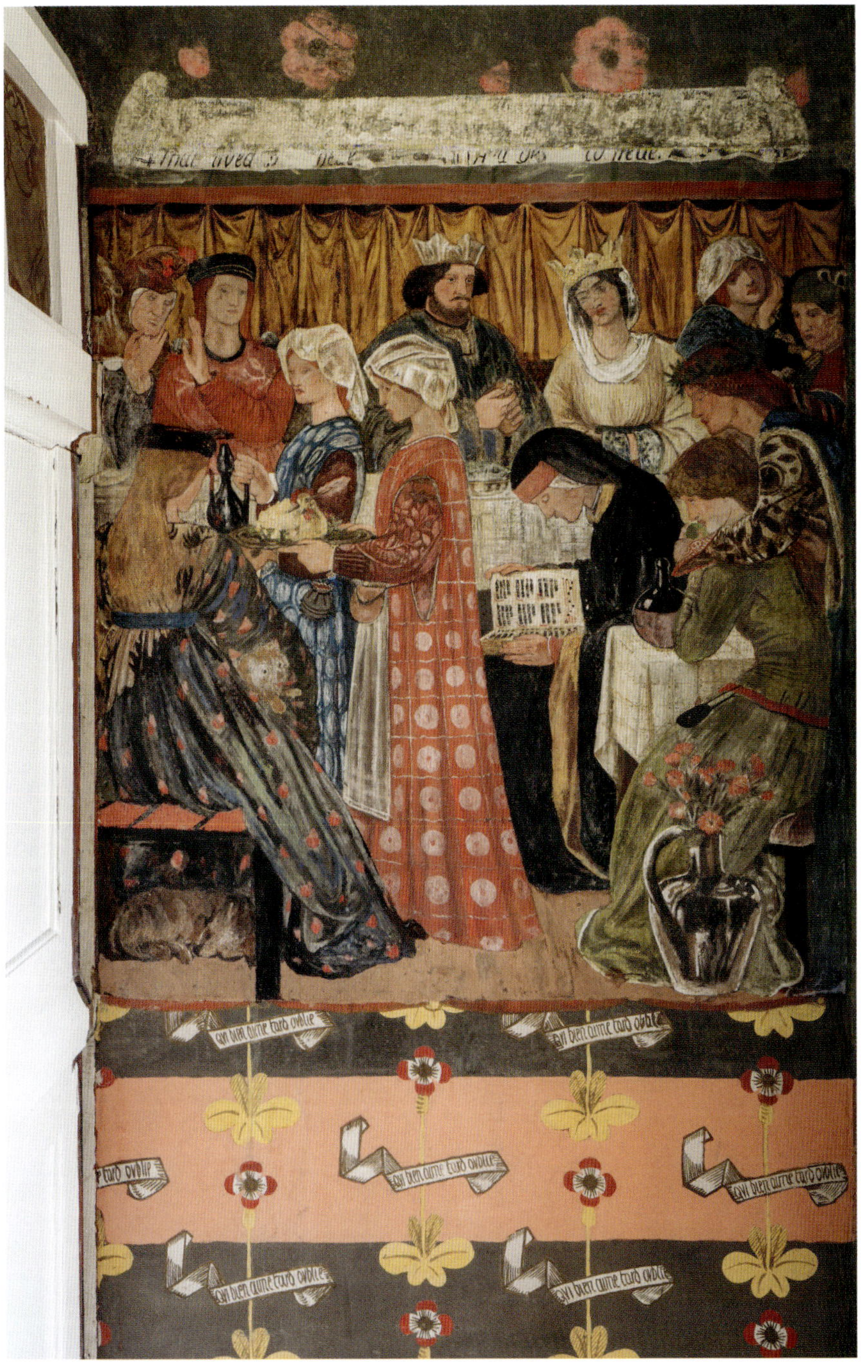

Fig.145 ***Sir Degrevaunt's Wedding Feast*, by Edward Burne-Jones, depicting Jane and William as the bride and groom, 1860.**
National Trust, Red House

Walter Dunlop, and Wensum Lodge in Park Hill, Carshalton, Surrey, for the civil servant and writer William Hale White.

These private commissions can only be evaluated now through a few surviving photographs and from dispersed furnishings such as tiles, stained-glass panels and furniture, so there has been a misleading tendency to judge the firm's early decorative style solely through existing public commissions in Cambridge (Queens' and Jesus Colleges and Peterhouse) and in London at the South Kensington Museum and St James's Palace.

The two prestigious London commissions, conceived and completed between 1866 and 1869, were exceedingly important in establishing the firm. Rossetti had been instrumental in organizing these and one can only marvel at his success in convincing a royal court not known for its love of avant-garde design and a museum that had only moved from temporary headquarters at Marlborough House a few years before, that a new, inexperienced firm of decorators was capable of carrying out work of the quality and standard demanded. Morris and Webb worked on both schemes together, although Webb produced most of the individual designs and supervised the firm's staff and the work of its subcontractors, S. & S. Dunn of 31 Brewer Street, Golden Square. So extensive was Webb's involvement at the time that the firm's minute book records that, at a meeting of the partners on 16 May 1867, Ford Madox Brown proposed and Rossetti seconded a motion that Webb be offered £80 a year 'as consulting manager of the firm to commence from last January'.

Work at South Kensington started a little earlier than the Palace, although the latter took precedence over the next three years. Webb's diaries and account books, and letters between him and the firm's business manager Warington Taylor, provide a near blow-by-blow account of the schemes' developments including visits, measurements, designs, estimates, progress on the work itself and the behaviour of workers. The final costs are not known although S. & S. Dunn charged the firm £602 1*s.* 4*d.* for three years' work at St James's Palace, the largest bill (£465 13*s.* 4*d.*) being for 1866, the first year of their accounts. Warington Taylor humorously referred to the firm 'robbing' the public (a reference to being paid from public funds), but this was far from the truth. Webb, as always, charged little if anything for his designs, so final invoices are unlikely to have reflected the real cost of the work.

The schemes in both the Armoury and Tapestry Room at St James's Palace are eye-catching. Ceilings and cornices, panelled dados, architraves, windows and doors are all painted with repeating patterns of stylized floral decoration intended to complement rather than compete with the existing displays of early tapestries and armour (figs 35 and 146). The unifying colour of the woodwork, gold and brightly coloured highlights on a dark green ground, is regal. The overall effect might at first glance appear to be uncharacteristically dark. However, Webb had already designed a range of ebonized furniture with gilded decoration (IX.17 and 19), and photographs of Birket Foster's house, The Hill, decorated between 1864 and 1865, show a rich dark interior far more in line with contemporary Aesthetic tastes than is now associated with the firm's work.

The Green Dining Room (as it later became known) at the South Kensington Museum was part of a suite of new refreshment rooms, the first to be installed in any museum. Its appearance was quite different from the Palace and, apart from panelled walls (this time plain) and the use of stylized sunflower motifs, there is little else to connect the two contemporary commissions. By choosing a blue-green for the predominating woodwork and plasterwork, it is likely that Morris and Webb intended to provide a restful effect suitable for the domestic purpose of the room. Surface pattern was provided with Webb's repeating design in the plaster filling of the wall and a brightly coloured cornice frieze of a dog chasing a hare (VIII.5). At eye level, a series of painted panels of tree and fruit branches is interspersed with Burne-Jones's figurative designs representing the zodiac or the months (fig.147). The three stained-glass windows show garlanded figures surrounded by quarries of animals and flowers (fig.140).

It is possible to trace the progress of the ceiling and plaster decoration quite closely. Webb charged the firm £7 for the design of repeating olive branches he made for the walls on 26 October 1866, plus £1 3*s*. for one of his many visits to check on the plaster modelling. Once complete, the painting of the plaster took one man one and a half days to finish 'one square of boughs' (one plaster-cast repeat) according to Warington Taylor's notes. The preparation of the ceiling was equally laborious, with one man taking two and a half days to trace, prick and prepare 'two copies of ceiling pattern' (VIII.6), followed by four men working for two days 'To set out pattern on ceiling'. The final painting was completed at a rate of four and a half square feet a day. Taylor added that it was always necessary to have a man employed full time mixing colours, and he estimated that 'The whole work above dado' would take one man 243 days at a cost of £86 16*s*.

The scheme at South Kensington and its efficient completion became a guide for future practice. It taught three important lessons: accurate estimating, efficient organization and the need for a versatile workforce. Before this commission Morris had tended to underprice work, charging an unrealistic five per cent profit. Furthermore, Taylor believed 'Morris is very nervous about work; and he consequently often suddenly takes men off one job and puts them to another'. The partners' lack of experience in handling their workforce presented a number of problems. While work on Jesus College Chapel, Cambridge, was in progress Morris had written to the foreman, George Campfield, complaining that 'The escapades of our men have enraged the dons and they want to get rid of you.' The aftermath of the London commissions was equally worrying: 'What guarantee is there that the men will keep good time when they return to the shop', Warington Taylor wrote to Webb in January

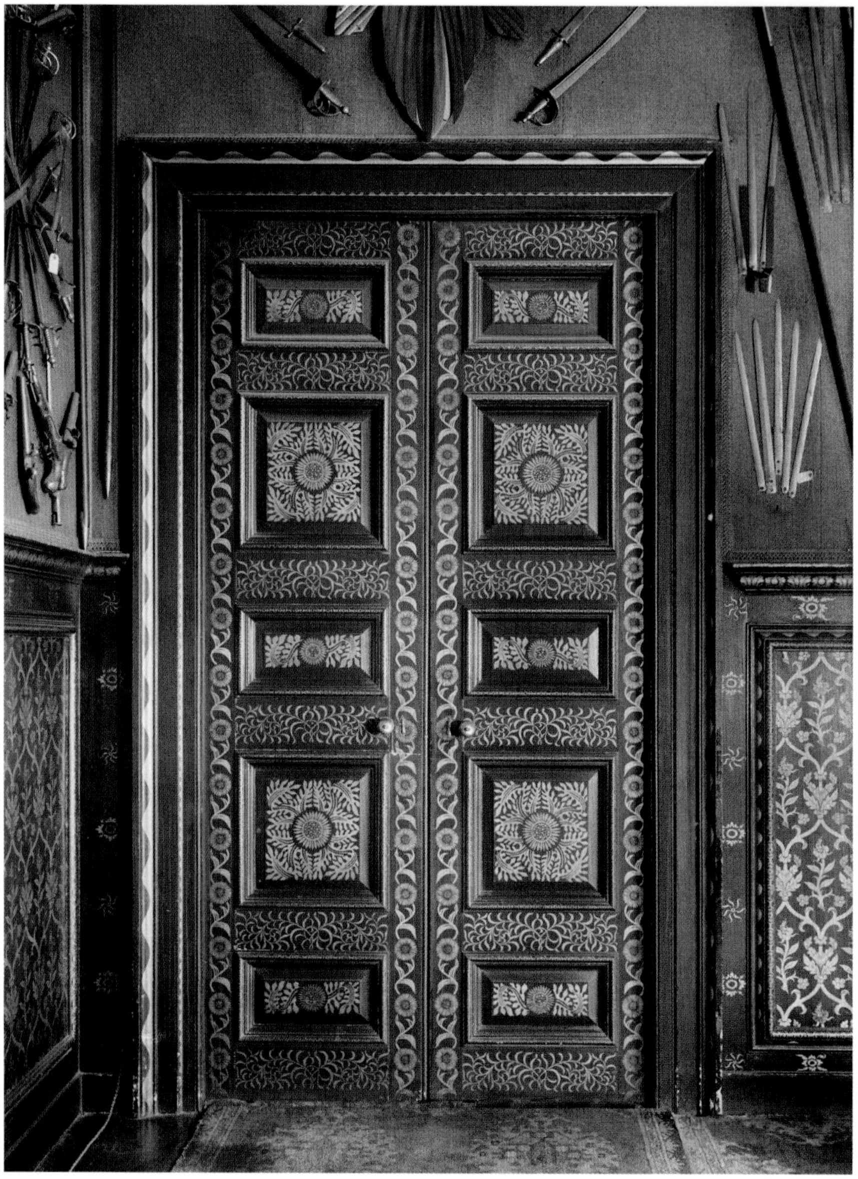

Fig.146 **A painted doorway in the Armoury at St James's Palace.**
Historic England Archive

1869, 'because after 3 months at the Palace their habits will be loose – I know 'em – because about every five weeks they require touching up under ordinary circumstances.'

The project, 'a lesson at being Jack of all trades' according to Taylor, emphasized the need to extend the range and versatility of skills of the firm's workers, and this was greatly helped with the assistance of successful and efficient subcontractors. Alongside the London-based firm of S. & S. Dunn, the Cambridge decorator Frederick Leach was also employed on a number of commissions. Leach had been recommended to Morris by the architect George Frederick Bodley. A letter in the collection of the William Morris Gallery signals the start of their collaboration. Morris asked Leach to undertake preparatory work on the decoration of Jesus College Chapel, including whitening the tower ceiling in preparation for the painting of his designs. The letter also announced their first business meeting in the company of Bodley, the architect of the Chapel, a few days later on 5 July 1866. This letter, together with Dunn's surviving records, proves the early employment of outside contractors by Morris, Marshall, Faulkner & Co.

Further information on Leach's later involvement with the firm can be traced in the work diary of David Parr, one of Frederick Leach's workmen. The diary itemizes projects between May 1871, when Parr first commenced work for Leach, and September 1908, his last work entry. Although the Morris firm is mentioned only once (in 1883 when Parr worked for a month at 449 Oxford Street), the coincidence of many other venues listed with those known to have occupied the company at the same time is too strong to be coincidental. David Parr's surviving sketchbooks also contain clues that he helped to execute Morris's painted schemes and his own intricately patterned home, 186 Gwydir Street, Cambridge, is a testament to his familiarity with the firm's work.

Not only did the two companies work on a great many of the known decorative schemes commissioned from Morris & Co. over a 20-year period but Dunn's accounts show that they were also responsible for supplying many of the necessary accessories of home furnishings, including curtain poles, bronze rings and brackets, canvas and bell balls that the firm needed to carry on this side of its business. Dunn's charges to the firm for four years from 1876 to 1879 (£2,637 5*s*., £2,460 7*s*. 11*d*., £4,520 9*s*. 7*d*. and £2,003 5*s*. 7*d*. respectively) not only show the extent of their work, but actually provide, alongside David Parr's diary, a record of the firm's activities as decorators in one of its most popular periods.

Morris's partners, particularly Webb and Burne-Jones, also chose the firm's products for decorating their homes. Burne-Jones's account books and photographs and watercolours of his house, The Grange, North End Road, Fulham, show how extensive this was (figs 162 and 200). In the autumn of 1867, the year he moved in, he ordered nearly a hundred pieces, or rolls, of Morris wallpaper in five different patterns as well as plain textiles, furniture and tableware (including numerous drinking glasses and crates of wine, the latter ordered presumably in the firm's name). This was not unusual, for his accounts for the years from 1866 to 1870 show a debit account with the firm, despite this being one of his busiest periods for supplying designs.

In 1865 the Morris family moved from Red House to live above the firm's headquarters at Queen Square. William and Jane did their best to provide attractive quarters, and various carpentry and painting works listed by Dunn's for the address may refer to these rooms. George Wardle, the firm's general manager, remembered them as 'extremely simple, very beautiful'. This seems to define Morris's own preference in domestic decoration and both Kelmscott Manor, the family's country retreat from 1871 (fig.10), and Kelmscott House, Hammersmith, where they moved in 1878 (VIII.16, figs 15–16 and 199) displayed a comfort and simplicity of style absent from many of the firm's commercial schemes.

Fig.147 **Detail of the dado frieze in the Green Dining Room, designed by Edward Burne-Jones and William Morris, painted by Charles Fairfax Murray, *c*.1867.**
V&A

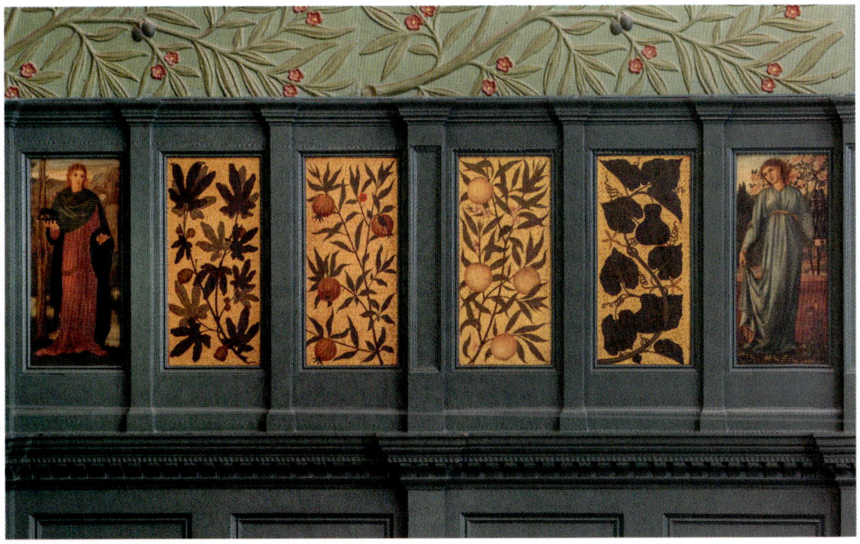

The contrast between countryside and town living became more marked in the firm's interior decoration of the 1870s and 1880s. Contractors' records of work completed for Morris & Co. in 1875 list an extraordinary range of fashionable London addresses – Grosvenor Street, Carlton House Terrace, Belgrave Square, Palace Gate, Stanhope Gardens, Curzon Street, Bryanston Square, Jermyn Street, Princes Gardens and Kensington Palace – to name a few. But the firm was also engaged on projects outside London, from Dorset to Cumbria and Stirlingshire in Scotland to County Offaly in Ireland.

Of the firm's British clients, the Howard and Bell families proved two of the most important. Commissions completed for both in the north of England helped the firm become known further afield. George Howard, Earl of Carlisle, and his wife Rosalind were close family friends of the Morrises, and Rosalind Howard recorded her first visit to 'Morris and Webb's furniture place' at Queen Square in November 1866. The decoration of their London home at 1 Palace Green, built for them by Philip Webb, began in earnest in 1872 and took a decade to complete. Using a similar decorative style to the Green Dining Room, the scheme included elaborately patterned ceilings and wall panelling with, in the dining room, Burne-Jones's early tour de force, a series of paintings of *Cupid and Psyche* from Morris's epic poem *The Earthly Paradise*. Morris also designed a carpet for the Howards' Cumbrian home, Naworth Castle (XII.94), and advised on furnishings for Castle Howard in Yorkshire for which a large quantity of wallpapers and fabrics was bought, with no less than 54 *Sussex* chairs ordered in 1882 for the dining room (see fig.167).

Webb was responsible for introducing Morris & Co.'s work to the Bell family. Isaac Lowthian Bell, the northern ironmaster and chemist, first employed him in the mid-1860s for alterations to Washington Hall, County Durham, and Webb was subsequently commissioned to build his second home, Rounton Grange, as well as Red Barns in Redcar for Bell's son Hugh (XII.92–3) and Smeaton Manor (XII.17) for his daughter Ada Godman.

The decoration of Rounton Grange from about 1874 provided an extensive and varied commission, and despite poor Bell being subject to Morris's confrontational remark that he was sick of 'ministering to the swinish luxury of the rich', photographs show how lucrative this must have been to the firm. For the dining room, painted wooden wainscoting followed the style of earlier work, but instead of a painted frieze, as in South Kensington and Palace Green, Morris and Burne-Jones designed a set of embroideries to be worked by Margaret Bell and her daughters (XII.12). A large carpet was designed for the house (XII.97), ceilings were painted and the walls of most rooms (which were filled with Morris furniture) were either wallpapered or covered in fabric. The overall effect of the furnishings provided an elegant yet comfortable interior (fig.148).

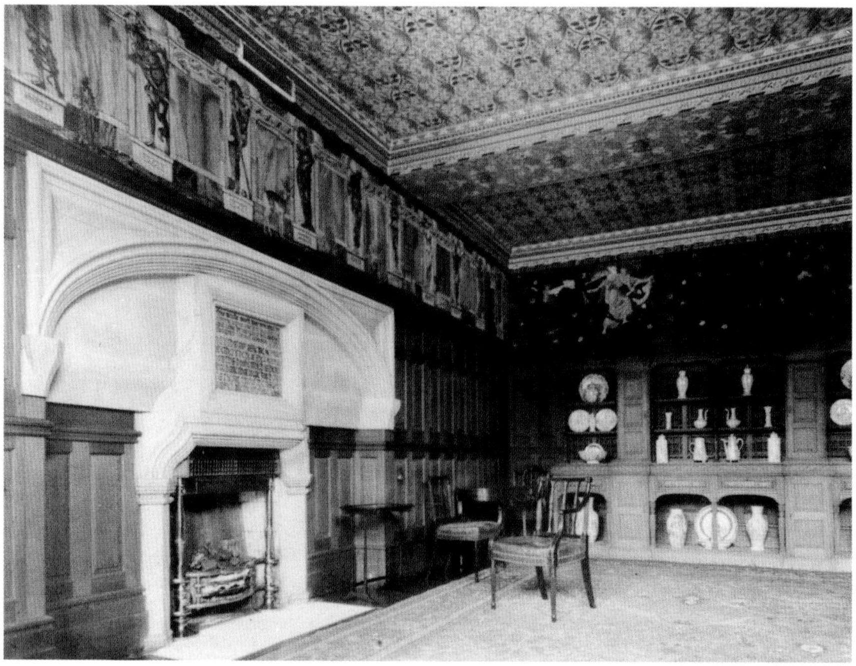

Fig.148 **The dining room at Rounton Grange. An inscription on the fireplace refers to the embroidered frieze above.**
Gertrude Bell Archive, Newcastle University

By the late 1870s, Morris's increasing political awareness began to affect his views on house decoration. Whereas he believed his own duty as a manufacturer and retailer was 'to revive a sense of beauty in home life, to restore the dignity of art to ordinary household decoration', he realized that the high prices charged by Morris & Co. meant his work was not available to all. In 1878, through his membership of the Kyrle Society, he contributed designs for the decoration of the Women's Convalescent Ward in Westminster Hospital, London. Recently founded by Miranda Hill and a group of philanthropic reformers (including her sister Octavia who was later to co-found the National Trust), the Kyrle Society was established 'to supply charity in the form of artistic adornment for those who cannot possibly afford to indulge themselves in such a taste, and perhaps partly in the hope of forming artistic taste and sympathy where it did not already exist.' Morris's scheme comprised pale green walls, a painted frieze and painted ceiling timbers, both decorated with stylized patterns of fruit and foliage. No images have yet been traced, though it would be fascinating to see Morris's work in this public setting. *The Builder* magazine felt the colour scheme was too restrained, arguing that bright colours and naturalistic patterns were more appropriate 'in rooms used by poor and uneducated people'. Some of the designs produced for the Kyrle by other notable artists, including Walter Crane, Lewis F. Day and Henry Holiday, were carried out by middle class (mainly female) volunteers. However, David Parr's diary records him working at Westminster Hospital in June and July of 1878. As a working-class artisan Parr would not have been able to offer his services for free especially when spending periods away from his home in Cambridge, so it is likely that Morris employed him, through the Leach firm, to complete the work.

Morris's second attempt to provide inexpensive ideas for furnishings came with the design of a workman's model 'small house' displayed in the newly opened Art Gallery in Queen's Park, Manchester, in 1884 (fig.149). This was commissioned by Thomas Coglan Horsfall, a Manchester philanthropist for whom Morris had written 'Working Folk and the Future of Art' (1879), a lecture in which he first expounded his now famous advice 'do not have anything in your house that you do not know to be useful or believe to be beautiful.' Although supportive of Horsfall's plans for a new museum, Morris was wary of being involved in a project that 'however good the intention ... to my mind tends to keep up the division of men into classes'. Instead he believed 'what furniture a workman can buy should be *exactly* the same (if his room be big enough) as a lord buys ... If you will alter "workman's cottage" into "small house" I will do what I can'. In his letters to Horsfall he argued that until the class system was destroyed and society organized along more equitable lines, artistic and well-made furnishings could not be manufactured at a cost that made them affordable to all. However, despite these misgivings, he was persuaded to take part in the scheme and co-opted a young associate designer W.A.S. Benson to select items for the exhibition including chairs from the *Sussex* range, a Madox Brown designed washstand (IX.11) and numerous wallpapers and chintzes. Altruism was not Morris's only reason for becoming involved. He had been keen to establish a footing in markets outside London for some years and this provided a means of advertising the work of the firm, which had opened a shop in Manchester the previous year. Unfortunately, this retail adventure was short lived and instead the firm relied on Kendal, Milne & Co., the well-known northern department store, to represent them.

The 1880s saw Morris & Co. complete a number of extensive London commissions, the most important of which was a return to St James's Palace for the decoration of the Throne Room, Blue Room and reception staircases (fig.150). S. & S. Dunn's charges of £1,110 indicate extensive work, all of which was closely monitored by the parsimonious Office of Works. As well as new ceiling, cove and cornice decorations, Morris specially designed a new wallpaper, two silk damasks and embroidered pelmets for the rooms (VIII.8–12 and XI.15–16). It is possible that Morris's first designs were far less conventional than appears from photographs of the finished work. All of the original estimates were cut, and the firm expressed distress that a curtailing of detail would result in a loss of originality. They need not have worried about the effect on the public, however, as this second royal appointment finally established Morris & Co. as one of the most fashionable firms of London decorators, and, as their appeal widened, their bohemian reputation diminished. While Queen Victoria sanctioned the work, there is no further documentary evidence describing how she viewed this later scheme which, although rich in colour and texture, was simpler in style than she was

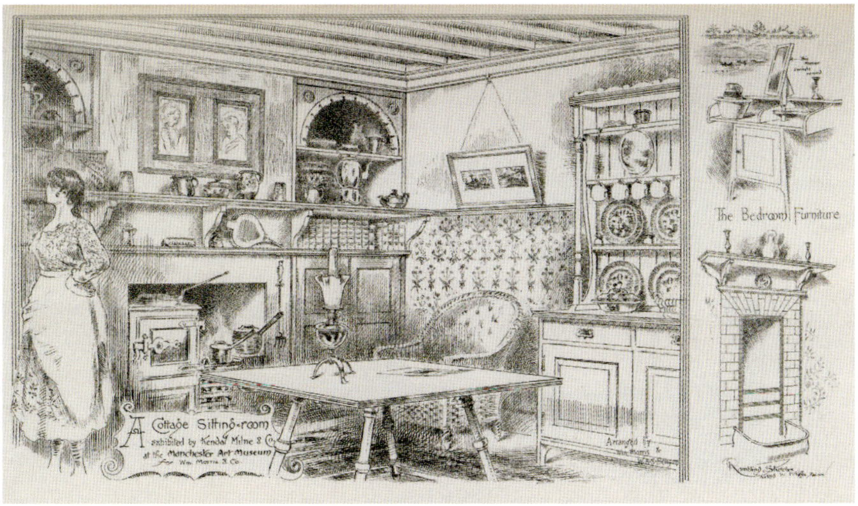

Fig.149 **The model sitting room of a 'small house', devised by Morris and W.A.S. Benson for the newly opened Art Gallery in Queen's Park, Manchester, 1884.**
V&A

used to. However, another member of the royal family was already a follower. As early as 1871 Princess Louise, the fourth daughter of Queen Victoria, an amateur artist and later patron of the Kyrle Society, visited Queen Square in order to select wallpapers for her apartments at Kensington Palace.

The grandest private commission of the period came from the Greek businessman Alexander Ionides (known as Aleco) for the decoration and furnishing of 1 Holland Park. The firm was employed between March 1880 and October 1888 to create interiors that would showcase Aleco's art collection. The house was demolished in 1953 but surviving invoices, bills and photographs provide a unique source of information on the firm's products and costings over this long period (figs 42, 203 and VIII.13–15). Morris closely supervised the work which, as well as a wealth of decorative painting and furnishings, included two Hammersmith carpets (XII.98–9), *The Forest* tapestry (XII.110) and Burne-Jones and Kate Faulkner's extraordinarily ornate piano (IX.28). The rooms were extravagantly decorated with ostentatious use of heavy silk furnishings on walls, windows, across doors and for furniture upholstery. This suggests the client's choice rather than Morris's, but each detail of the work complied with Morris's own views on the rights and wrongs of house decoration. It is difficult to know exactly how much influence Morris wielded over clients. Clearly many were content to accept his advice whereas others were not so tolerant. In 1876 Constance, wife of Lord Leconfield, wrote to her sister-in-law Madeline Wyndham complaining of Morris's 'obstinacy' in insisting on supplying a specific silk for curtains in the Carved Room at Petworth in West Sussex. 'He absolutely refuses to let us have any other ... Poor Henry says meekly that he would not mind if it only were perpendicular, and not branching off in contrary directions.' Morris was to get his way; *Willow* woven silk was used in the Carved Room and *Larkspur* curtains still survive *in situ* in the Red Room.

Comparing the work at St James's Palace and Holland Park with the model room at Manchester and Morris's own homes, one is immediately struck by how versatile Morris could be within the boundaries of his own strongly held views, the details of which were explained by George Wardle in the introduction to the Morris exhibit at the 1883 Boston Foreign Fair. Morris worked hard to end the fashionable mid-nineteenth-century habit of splitting walls in horizontal layers with skirting, dado, chair-rail, filling, cornice and ceiling all receiving different treatment. Instead, he advocated a much simpler and harmonious effect with skirting ignored, dado and filling treated as one and cornice and ceiling united, the look adopted generally from the end of the nineteenth century. He recommended that decoration of the walls should be simple, either painted with plain colours or covered with wallpapers, draped printed cotton or stretched woven damasks for a more decorative effect. The choice of pattern should depend on the character of the room or the colour of woodwork and furniture rather than the popularity of the design. More specific recommendations included the use of metallic papers with walnut or dark-stained ash and textile wallcovering for well-designed (this tended to mean plain) and finished timber.

The environmental setting of houses also played a major role in Morris's attitude towards interior decoration. Kelmscott Manor, the country home he visited for rest and recreation, changed little during his occupancy (Rossetti, as his first co-lessee, initiated most of the alterations that were made), but his London home, Kelmscott House, was decorated and furnished to suit the family's metropolitan lifestyle (VIII.16). Country living, in which gardens and the countryside played an important part, involved quite different requirements from the town and

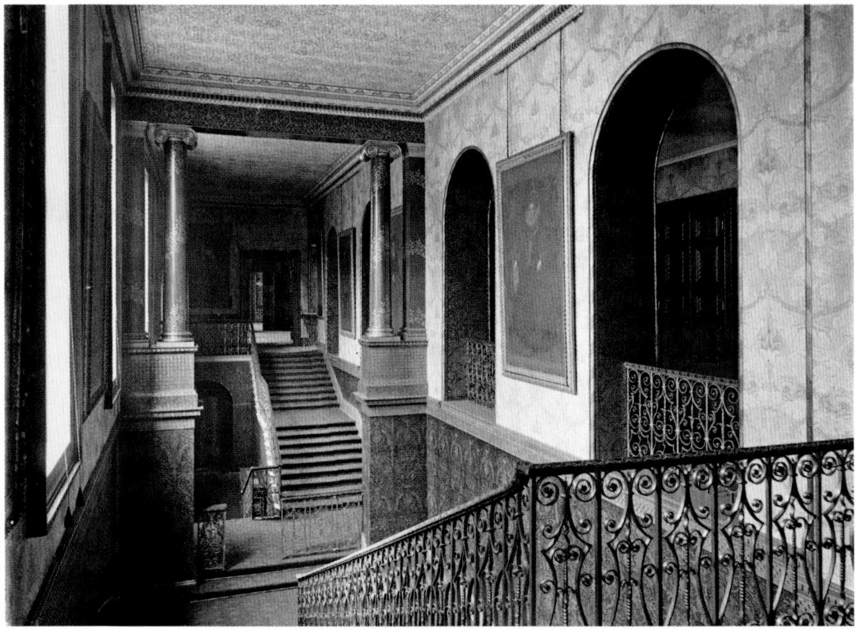

Fig.150 **Grand Staircase at St James's Palace, photographed by Bedford Lemere & Co., 1889.**
Historic England Archive

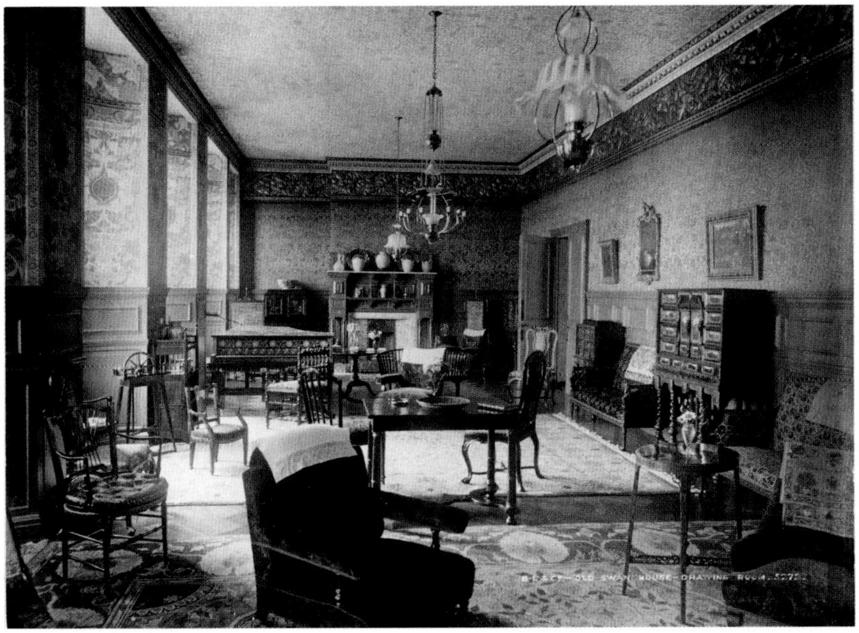

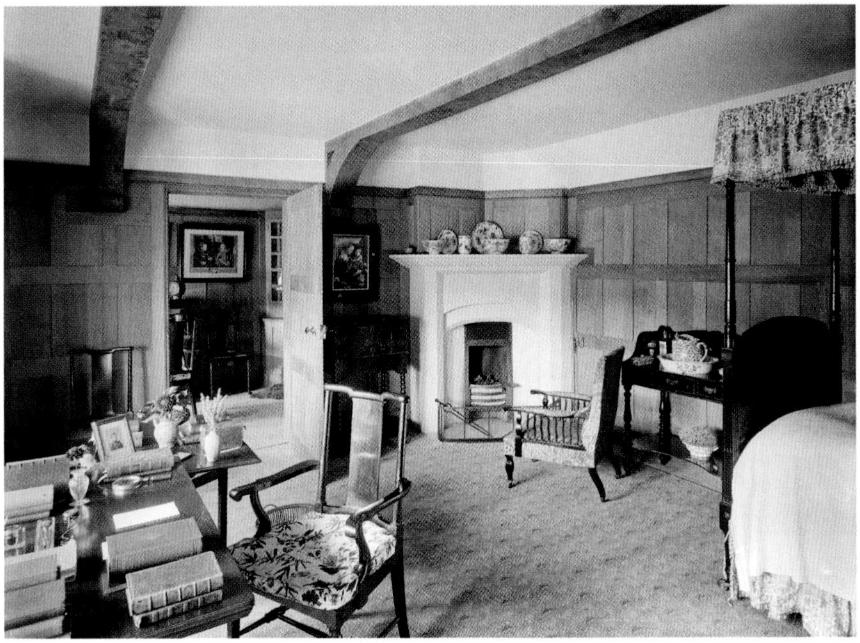

Fig.151 (top) **The drawing room at Old Swan House, Chelsea, photographed by Bedford Lemere & Co., 1884.**
Historic England Archive

Fig.152 (above) **A bedroom at Great Tangley Manor, Surrey, photographed by Bedford Lemere & Co., 1895.**
Historic England Archive

Morris's decorations reflect his own experience. The firm was employed to decorate a number of country houses and Morris developed a much more restrained style for such masterpieces as Clouds, a house outside Salisbury built by Webb between 1881 and 1886, which became famous for fashionable weekend house parties of 'The Souls', a group of aristocratic political, artistic and literary figures, led by the owners, the Hon. Percy and Madeline Wyndham.

The difference between Morris's town and country styles is further emphasized by comparing the decoration of Wickham Flower's two homes, Old Swan House, Chelsea Embankment, and Great Tangley Manor, near Guildford in Surrey, a sixteenth-century country house extended by Philip Webb from 1884 (figs 151–2). The London house, which featured existing extensive architectural detailing, was decorated with an abundance of specially designed ceiling and wall decoration, furniture and carpets, the overall effect of which was luxurious yet conventionally fashionable. Clearly pleased with the project, Morris & Co. was to use a photograph of one room in later printed catalogues. In contrast, the Flowers' country home, though elegant, was decorated very simply, to provide an aura of relaxation and easy living with light coloured woods, plain colours and mass-produced, practical Morris furniture, printed cottons and machine-woven carpeting. Described by Hermann Muthesius in his influential work *Das Englische Haus* (Berlin, 1904) as 'simply a house in which one wants to live ... it is without pomp or decoration, and has the natural decency which ... is so rare in our present culture', this scheme anticipated a style of light, open, airy interiors exemplified in the work of a number of British, European and American architects working at the beginning of the twentieth century.

From the early 1880s Morris & Co.'s reputation abroad had spread not only by taking part in international exhibitions but also through appointing agents in Europe, America and Australia. It was through these representatives that clients were to place some of the firm's most extravagant orders. Several generations of the Barr Smith family in Adelaide, Australia, were among Morris & Co.'s most enthusiastic international clients and furnished a number of houses almost exclusively with Morris & Co. products (fig.153). In Britain the firm was also beginning to attract non-domestic clients, which included providing advice on furnishings for cabins and staterooms for ships of the Orient Line. In 1891 Morris & Co. took part in two theatrical projects; the furnishing of Richard D'Oyly Carte's Royal English Opera House in London (later the Palace Theatre) and in the same year furniture and draperies were produced for a production of Henry Arthur Jones's play *The Crusaders* which opened at the Avenue Theatre (IX.32).

Of the firm's later domestic schemes, Buller's Wood, a house in Chislehurst, Kent, remodelled by Ernest Newton for the Sanderson family, combined Morris's town and country styles.

The ground-floor rooms had plain white walls with pattern-work on cornices and ceilings (fig.213). The bedrooms were equally unfussy, with plain or wallpapered walls and white paintwork. The use of neo-Georgian detailing in the house shows a diversion from Morris's usual style and the commission is likely to have been the last he took an active part in. It also points to the growing involvement of his assistant John Henry Dearle. Similar detailing can be seen in other late projects associated with the firm, including Wightwick Manor and Compton Hall in Wolverhampton, and Standen near East Grinstead in Sussex. At Wightwick and Standen surviving invoices indicate that Morris & Co. were not the only decorators to be involved in the interiors.

Stanmore Hall in Middlesex was the most extensive decoration scheme that Morris & Co. completed and it was also the last commission before Morris's death. The baronial proportions of the house were only eclipsed by the extravagance of the internal decorations. Although Morris visited the wealthy owner of the house, William Knox D'Arcy, at Christmas 1888 to discuss the forthcoming work, it is unlikely that he took any further part in the general decoration, his time being spent on the preparation of a spectacular series of tapestries based on the legend of the Holy Grail for the dining room (XII.120). All of Morris's rules concerning the application of decoration on walls, ceilings and floors so succinctly delineated in the Boston Foreign Fair brochure were followed in the house, yet the effect is unoriginal and typically Victorian (fig.154). Much of this is due to the intervention of Dearle, whose new designs for the house – mosaic floors, wall paintings, woven silks and carpets – compete in scale and style with the overpowering Gothicized architecture of the mid-nineteenth-century building. Through inexperience Dearle included everything he found admirable in Morris's work, neither selecting nor truly understanding the basic principles on which such ideas were based.

After Morris's death in 1896, interior design continued to be an important side of the business, shown by the firm's change of name to Morris & Company Decorators Ltd in 1905. Yet the look adopted in most interiors continued to diversify away from that which Morris had advocated throughout his career, widely embracing reproduction design in an attempt to maintain a place in the fashionable London market. Instead, it was left to followers outside Britain – in America, Canada and across Europe and Scandinavia – to develop Morris's ideas within a modern, forward-looking world.

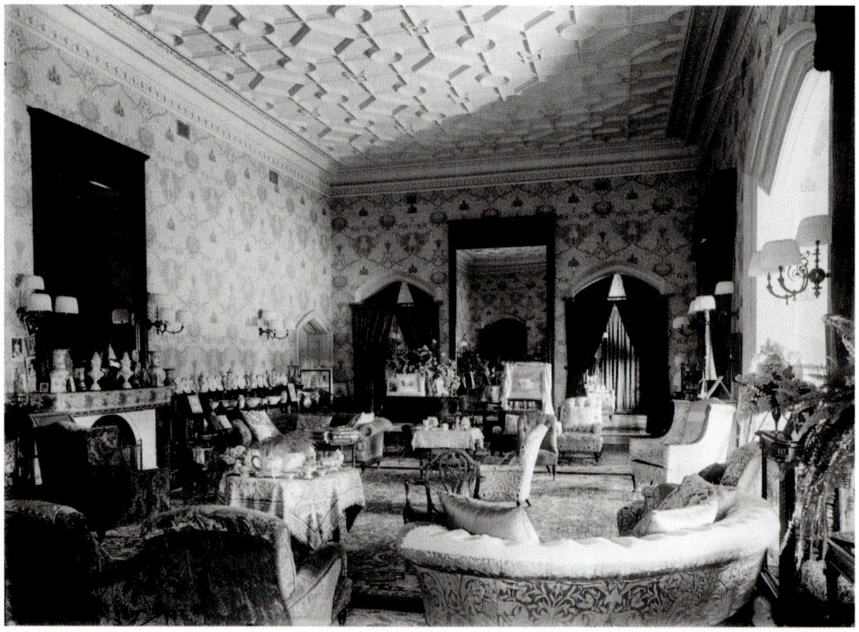

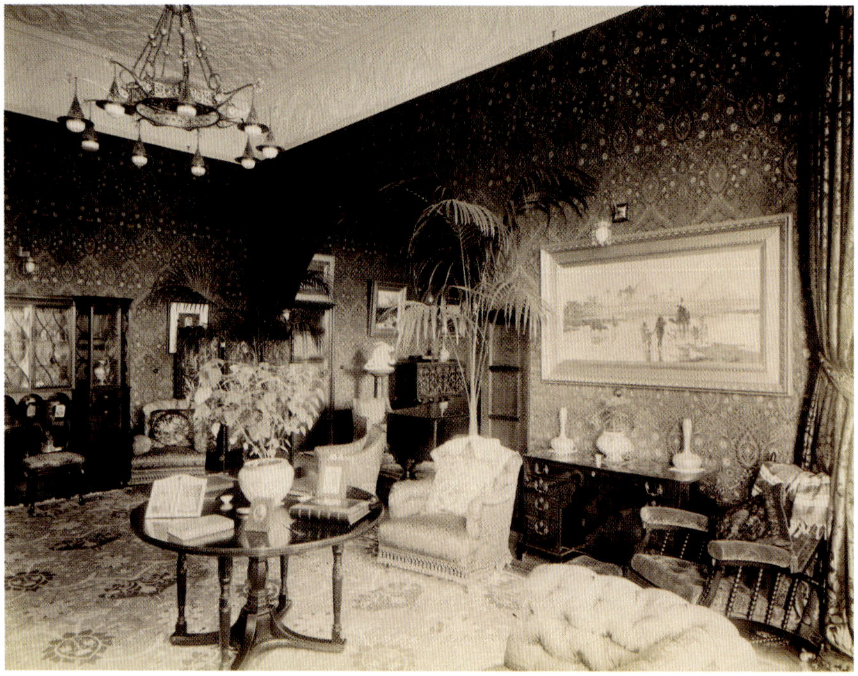

Fig.153 (top) **The large drawing room at Torrens Park, the Barr Smiths' town residence in Adelaide.**
State Library of South Australia, Adelaide

Fig.154 (above) **One of the drawing rooms at Stanmore Hall, Middlesex, photographed by Bedford Lemere & Co., 1891.**
Historic England Archive

VIII.1

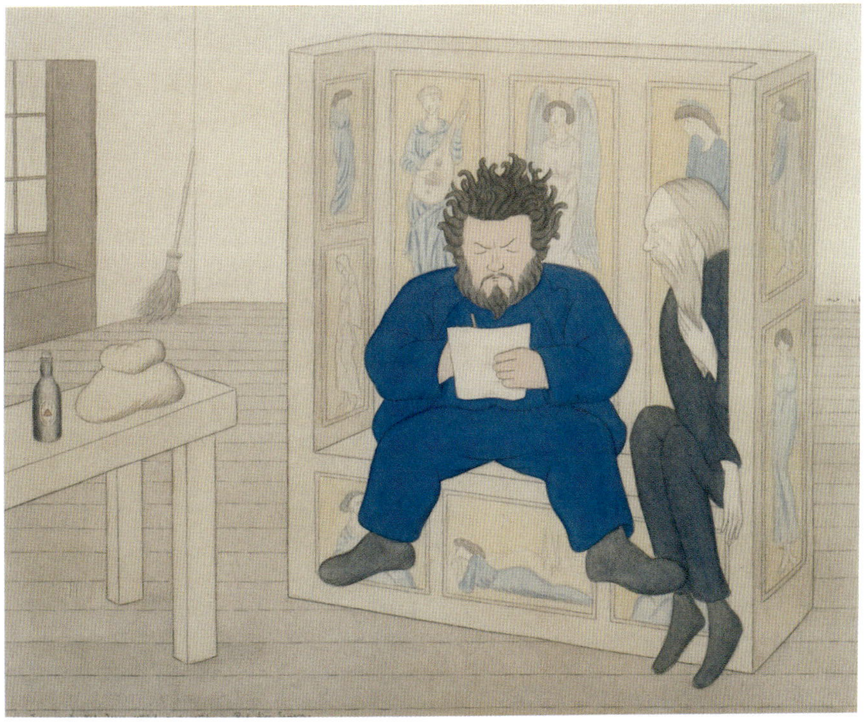

VIII.2

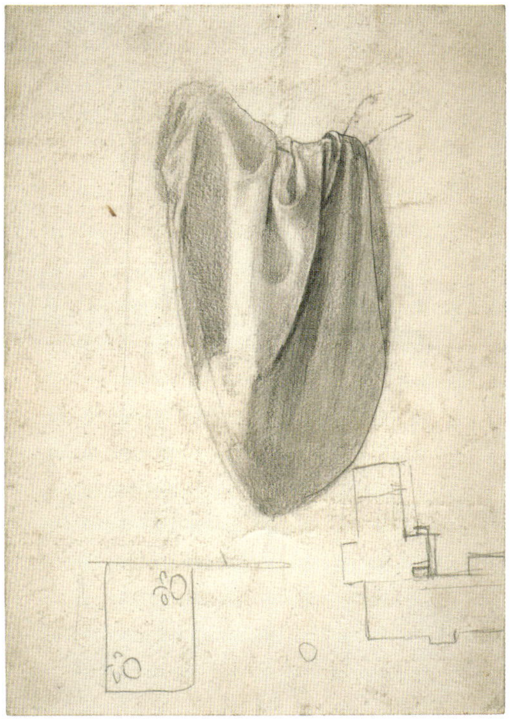

VIII.1
Topsy and Ned Jones Settled on the Settle in Red Lion Square
Max Beerbohm, 1916
Pencil and watercolour, 31.1 x 38.7 cm
Tate, London (A01049)

A fanciful composition drawn by Beerbohm for his volume of caricatures *Rossetti and His Circle*, first published in 1922. The artist based his drawing on J.W. Mackail's description of the sparse furnishings of Morris and Burne-Jones's lodgings at 17 Red Lion Square. Beerbohm has concentrated on the large painted settle made at the time (and subsequently moved to Red House) and although this is quite unlike the actual piece, his imaginary furniture has an uncanny similarity to existing panels painted with female figures about the same time and probably intended for furniture (VI.5).

Beerbohm had little regard for Morris or his work, which he felt was overrated. In a letter to Holbrook Jackson of 1913 he wrote 'He is splendid, certainly, by reason of the bulk and variety of his work, but when it comes to the quality ... I leave a wide margin ... for my necessary injustice' (see N.J. Hall's introduction to a new edition of *Rossetti and His Circle*, 1987).

VIII.2
Drapery sketch with details of Red House
William Morris, *c.*1856–9
Pencil and ink, 31.4 x 22.9 cm
The Huntington Library, Art Museum and Botanical Gardens (2000.5.287)

A large number of Morris's drapery and figure sketches survive from the late 1850s when he was eager to improve his draughtsmanship and take up painting. Drawings like this one must have littered his home and studio at this time. In the lower right-hand corner is a later addition, a rough outline of Red House as designed by Webb and shown in his architectural plan dated April 1859 (VIII.4a). To the side of this, and on the reverse, there are a number of repeating patterns arranged on rectangular grids. These may well be trials or suggestions for the very characteristic wall and ceiling designs used in the house.

VIII.3
Notebook
Philip Webb, *c.*1859
Pencil and pen and ink, 30 x 8 cm (open)
Archive of Art and Design, V&A (AAD/2014/5/6/2)

A notebook with details and rough sketches of Red House. It includes a plan of Morris's wine cellar and a list of 80 trees in the surrounding orchard with apples, plums, cherries, damsons and hawthorns. Mackail claimed that the house 'had been planned with such care that hardly a tree in the orchard had to be cut down; apples fell in at the window as they stood open on hot autumn nights.' The notebook also contains a receipt written out by local tradesman Edward Russell, who supplied wattle fencing for the garden.

VIII.3

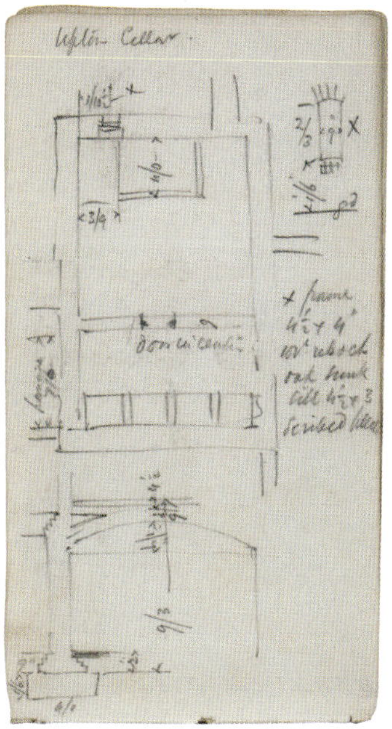

VIII.4a

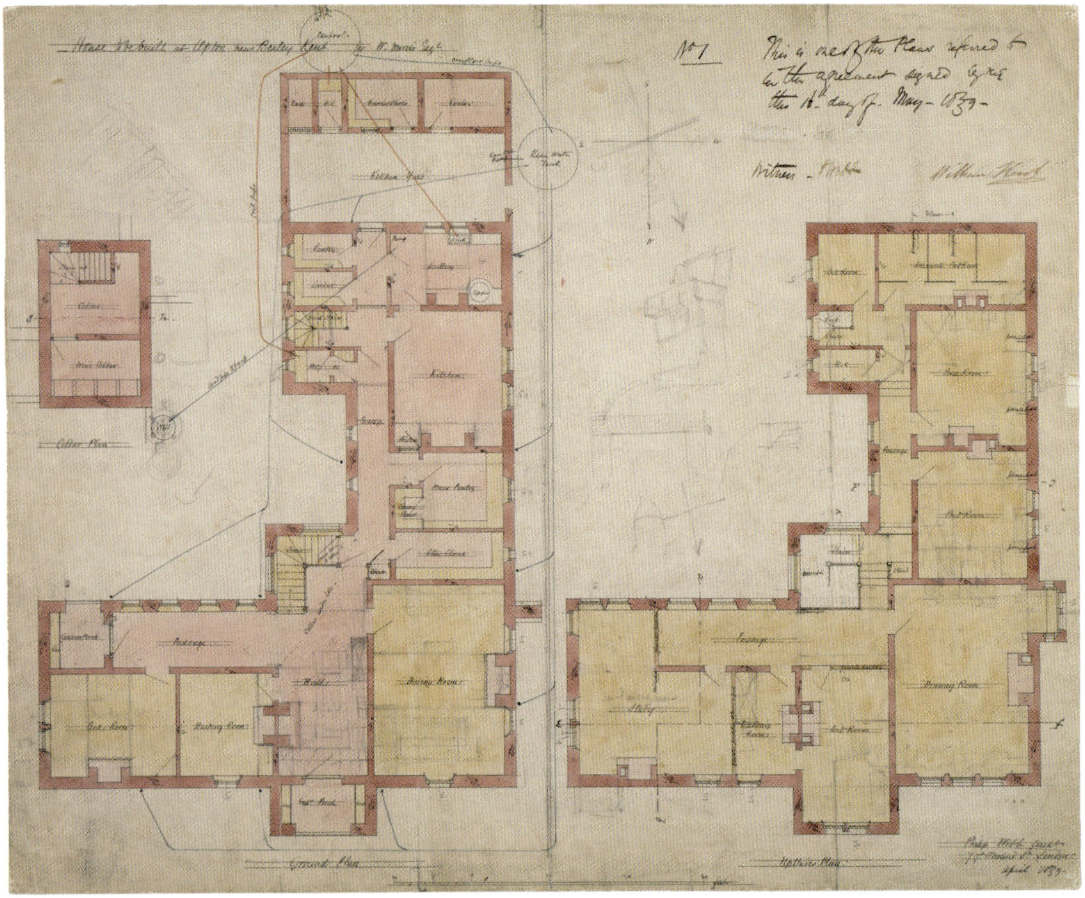

VIII.4b

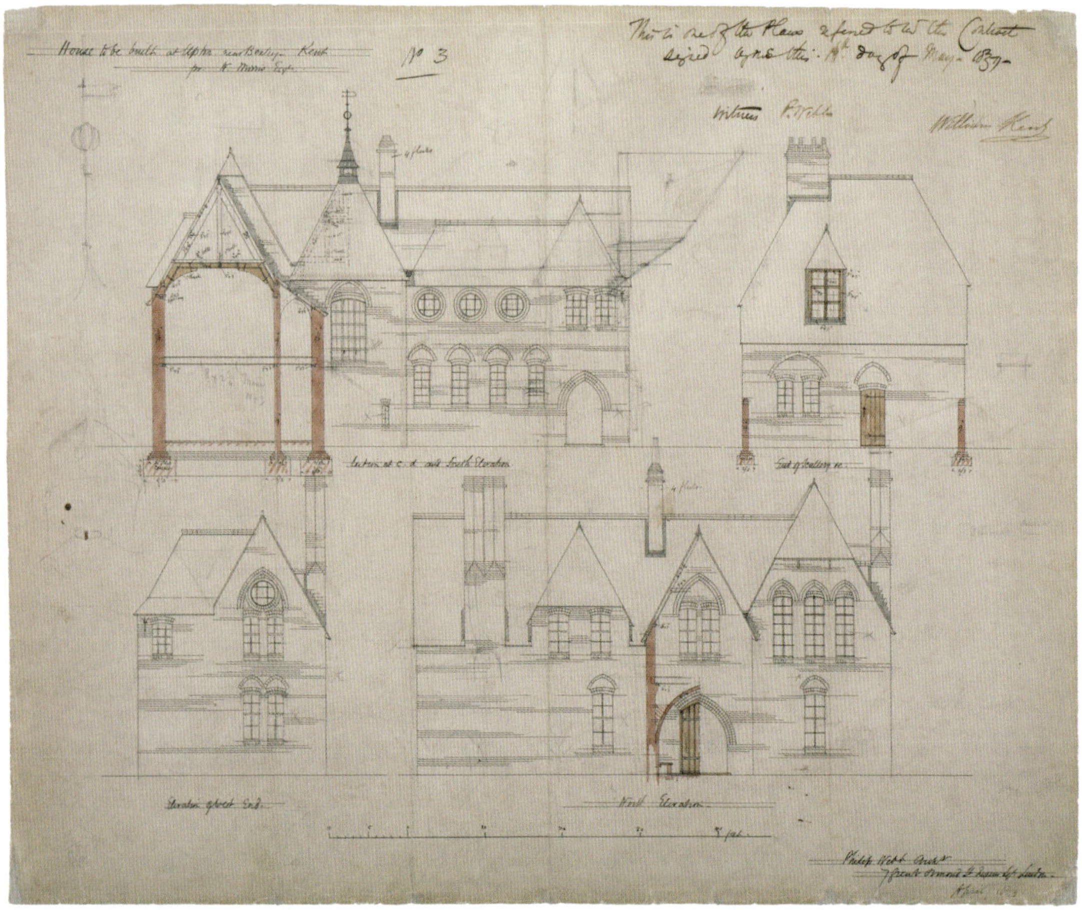

VIII.4
Architectural drawings for Red House, Bexleyheath, Kent
Philip Webb, 1859
Pencil, pen and ink and watercolour
Presented by Lady Burne-Jones

a Ground- and first-floor plans
53.3 x 66 cm
V&A (E.59–1916)

b North and south elevations
52.1 x 63.5 cm
V&A (E.60–1916)

c Entrance gates
(design for stables on reverse)
52.1 x 65.4 cm
V&A (E.63–1916)

d Well-head
53 x 65.8 cm
V&A (E.64–1916)

These drawings formed part of the agreement with the builder, William Kent. The original building contract, dated 16 May 1859, was rediscovered and donated to the National Trust in 2013. Together, the designs and contract reveal Webb's close attention to materials and techniques, with detailed specifications for all the different trades involved. Unusually for contract drawings, the designs have numerous adjustments in pencil, suggesting Webb's determination to achieve the best possible result for his friend, who was also a demanding client. The L-shaped plan shows how the house radiates out from the main staircase and also that the kitchen faces west, receiving full sun while dinner was being prepared. It was practical oversights such as this that prompted Webb, years later, to reflect that houses should only be designed by architects over 40 years of age.
SA/LP

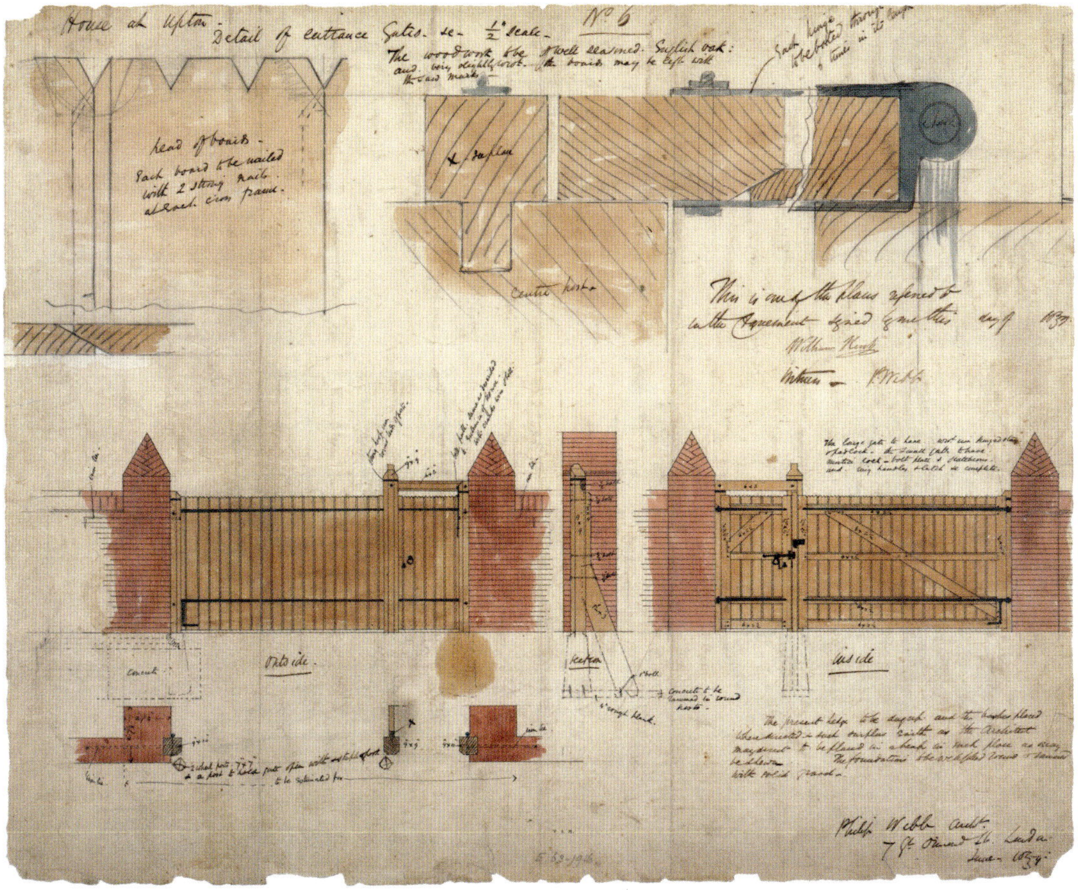

VIII.4c

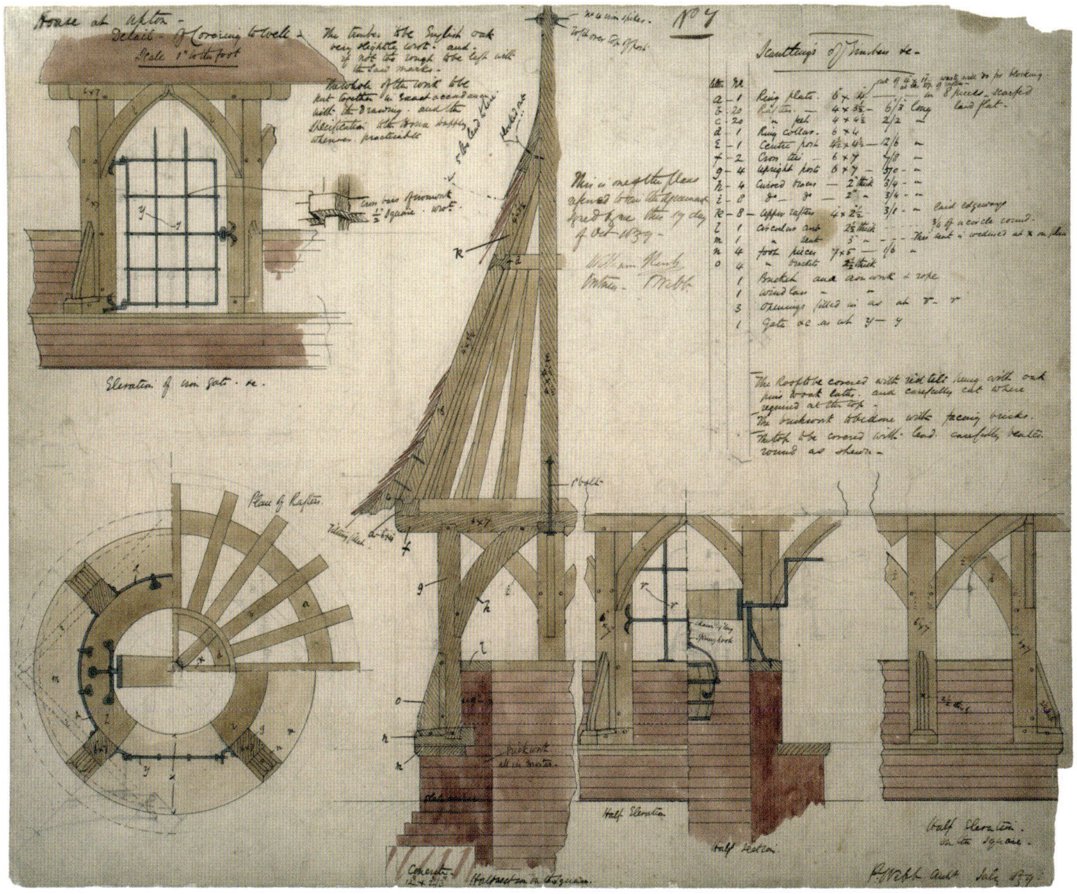

VIII.4d

VIII.5

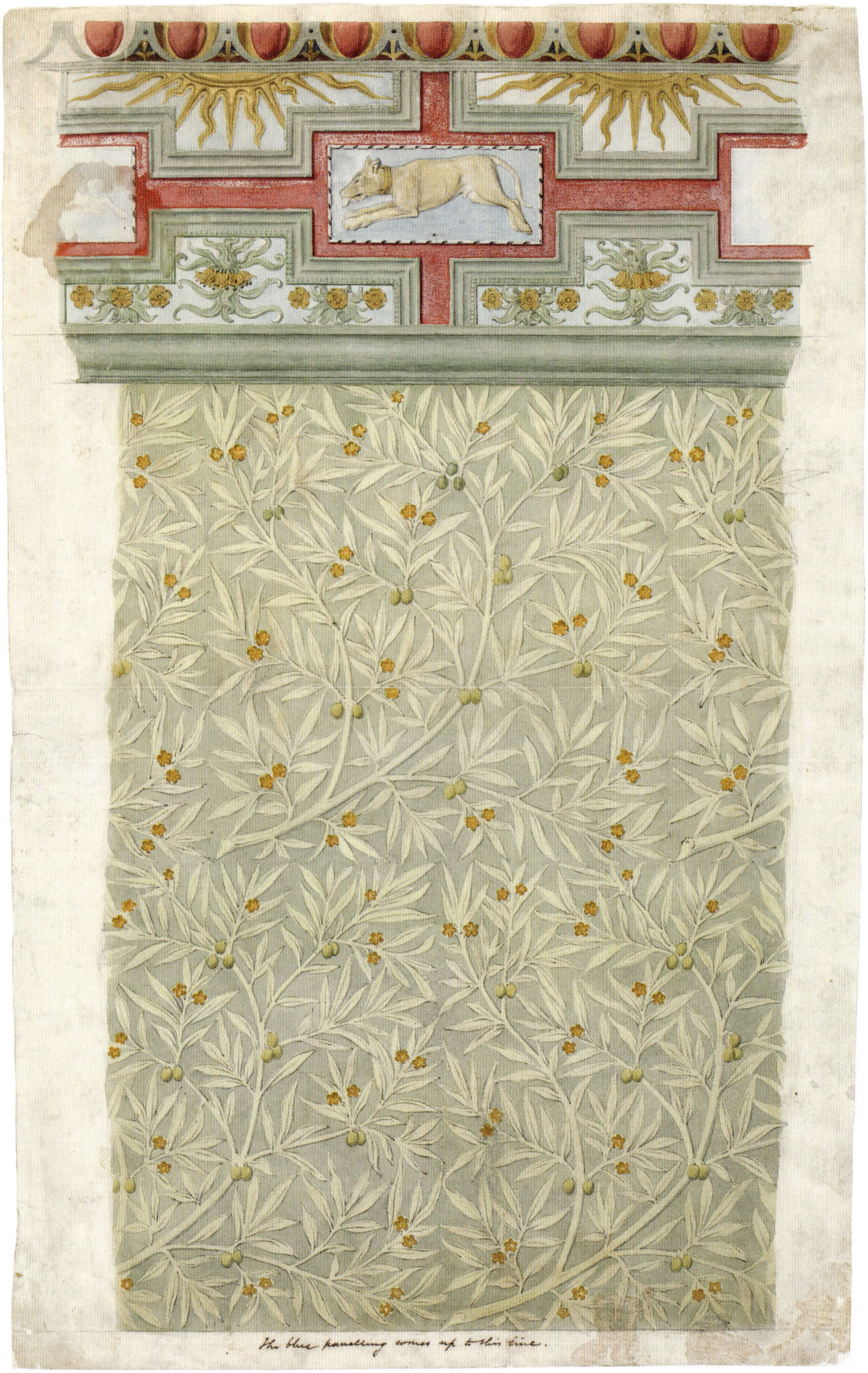

VIII.5

Design for wall decoration and cornice in the Green Dining Room, South Kensington Museum, London

Philip Webb, 1866

Pencil, pen and ink, watercolour, body colour and gold pigment, 49.4 x 31.6 cm

Inscribed: 'The blue panelling comes up to this line'

V&A (E.5096–1960)

Given by Mr H.B. Johnson

This highly finished drawing was presumably prepared for the client, either the Government Department or the South Kensington Museum authorities. It shows a section of the decoration as executed except for changes to the colour scheme. These include the egg and dart cornice, shown here as red but gilded, and the background to the dog that was made much darker in tone. The running hound motif (which alternates with trees and running hares) was derived from the decorations on the fifteenth-century font in Newcastle Cathedral, which Webb had sketched in 1864. Below the frieze, the wall is covered with moulded plaster panels depicting olive branches in low relief. The effect of distributing the pattern evenly over the whole wall is similar to some of Morris's early wallpapers. SA

VIII.6a

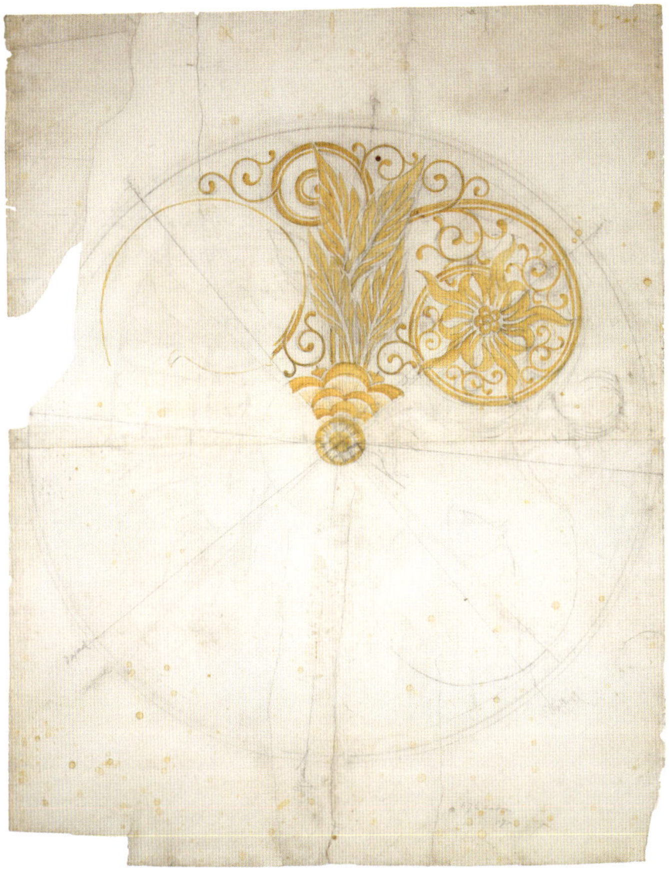

VIII.6b

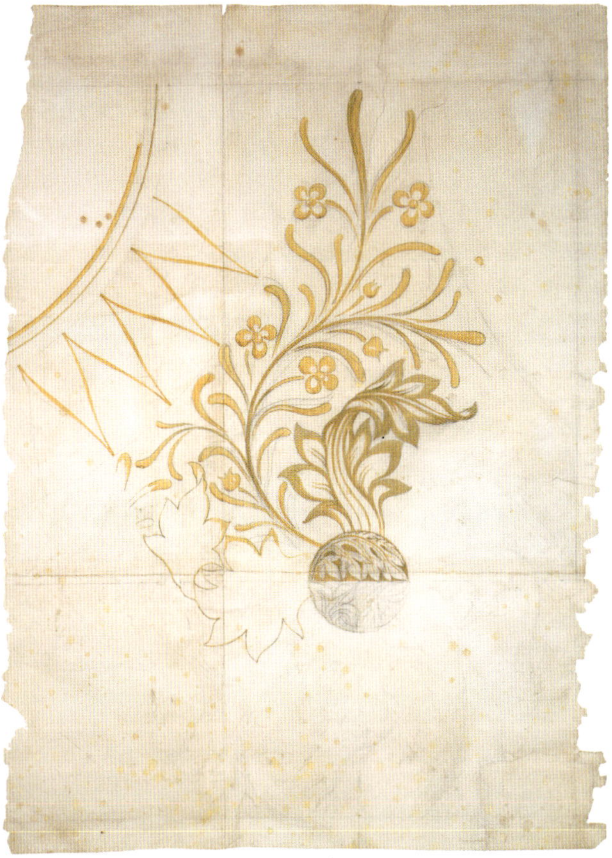

VIII.6
Two designs for the ceiling decoration in the Green Dining Room
Philip Webb and William Morris, 1866–7

a Pencil, charcoal and watercolour, 131 x 101.5 cm
V&A (E.1169–1940)

b Pencil, charcoal and watercolour, 139.8 x 102.5 cm
V&A (E.1170–1940)

Morris and Webb collaborated on the ceiling, as these two designs show. The looser, more organic, and largely ignored charcoal under-drawing is by Morris (VIII.6a). This contrasts with the more carefully drawn and painted arabesques by Webb (VIII.6b), which are more akin to the decorative styles being executed in the rest of the growing museum. Both designs combine stylized foliage with a geometric structure and more organic motifs. They reveal some difficulties in setting out to full scale; Morris seems to have made two attempts at diagonals. Both are splashed with pigment-rich paint, suggesting that they were used when the actual ceiling was being painted with water-based paints on lining paper. SA

VIII.7
Design for painted panels in the Green Dining Room
Edward Burne-Jones, 1866–7
Pencil and chalk, 28 x 13.9 cm
V&A (E.2899–1927)
Bequeathed by James Richardson Holliday

This is one of eight sheets of preliminary designs for the painted panels representing the 12 months of the year or their zodiacal symbols. Burne-Jones's final designs are at Kelmscott Manor and were closely followed in the executed scheme. Although designed by Burne-Jones, the panels were executed in oil by several different hands. Morris felt the result insufficiently uniform in style to give a harmonious decorative scheme, and remedied this by having them repainted by the artist Charles Fairfax Murray. The figurative panels were interspersed with designs of fruits, flowers and foliage in the style of medieval botanical illustrations on gilded backgrounds (fig.147). SA/LP

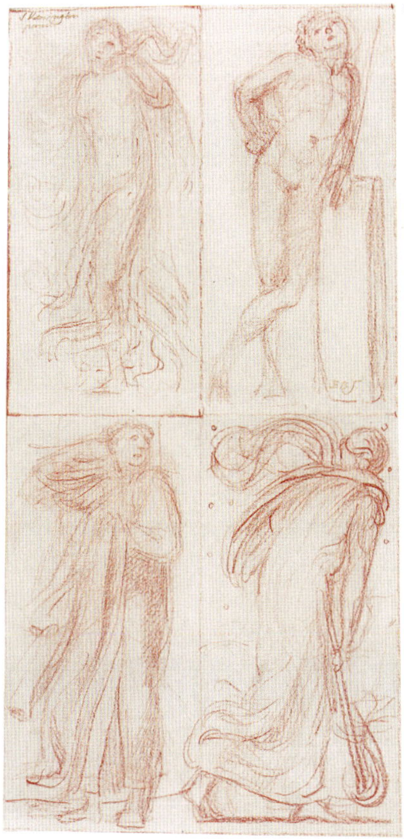

VIII.7

VIII.8
Sketch of the Throne Room window elevation, St James's Palace, London
William Morris, 1881
Pencil and pen and ink, 25.5 x 55.6 cm
V&A (E.53–1940)

This sketch shows the challenges of actually executing a commission. The plan includes details of the windows and pier glass in the Throne Room, with several attempts at measuring and calculating the shaped buckram valances. Notes record how problematic matching the pattern was and, by implication, how important it was to ensure a perfect result. On 13 March 1882 the firm estimated the curtains for the Throne Room at £750 with £360 for the valances. The Office of Works insisted on a less costly proposal – woollen linings were substituted for satin, the quantity of silk lace trimming reduced and the price of the valances revised to £200, presumably having an impact on the embroidered detailing. SA/LP

VIII.9
Design for painted cornice decoration, Blue Room, St James's Palace
William Morris, 1881
Pencil, pen and ink and watercolour, 66.6 x 100.3 cm
Inscribed on reverse by Charles Fairfax Murray: 'Original design by William Morris'
V&A (E.289–1939)
Bequeathed by May Morris

This design shows the richness of effect that Morris was to achieve. Having drawn the cove to scale, he then drew the background pattern of scrolling vegetal decoration in soft pencil. Over this is the final design of acanthus, which in form and density bears a strong relationship to his wallpaper designs at that time. Only a small part of the decoration is shown, the painter presumably being left to extrapolate the pattern to the length of the room. The Blue Room, or Council Room, was painted in yellow and the walls were covered with *St James* silk damask in dark red with matching curtains and embroidered valances. SA/LP

VIII.10
Design for clock case, St James's Palace
William Morris, 1881
Pencil and watercolour, 43.9 x 68 cm
William Morris Society, Kelmscott House, London (D9)

Several entries in Morris's diary for January 1881 record him working on the ornament for a St James's Palace clock case. The decoration is very similar to another design for the same project, illustrated in Lewis F. Day, *The Art of William Morris* (1899), and described as 'Painted Decoration of soffits of arches on staircase in St James's Palace'.

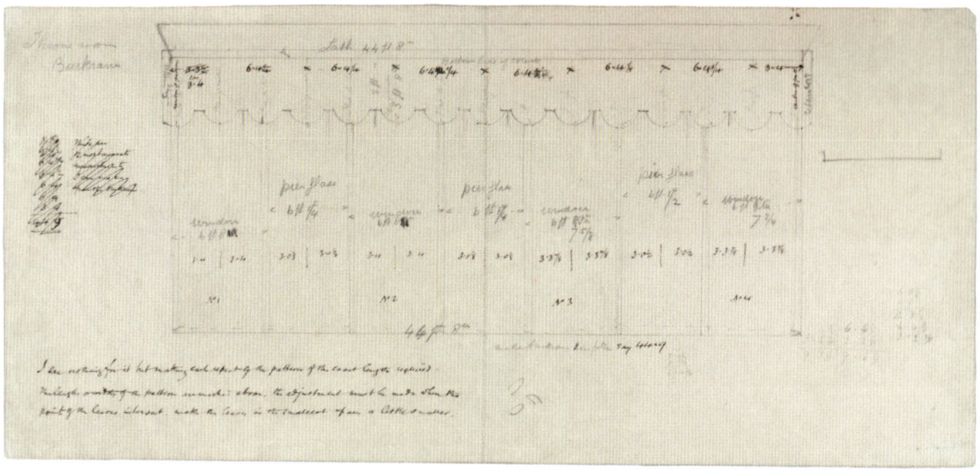

VIII.8

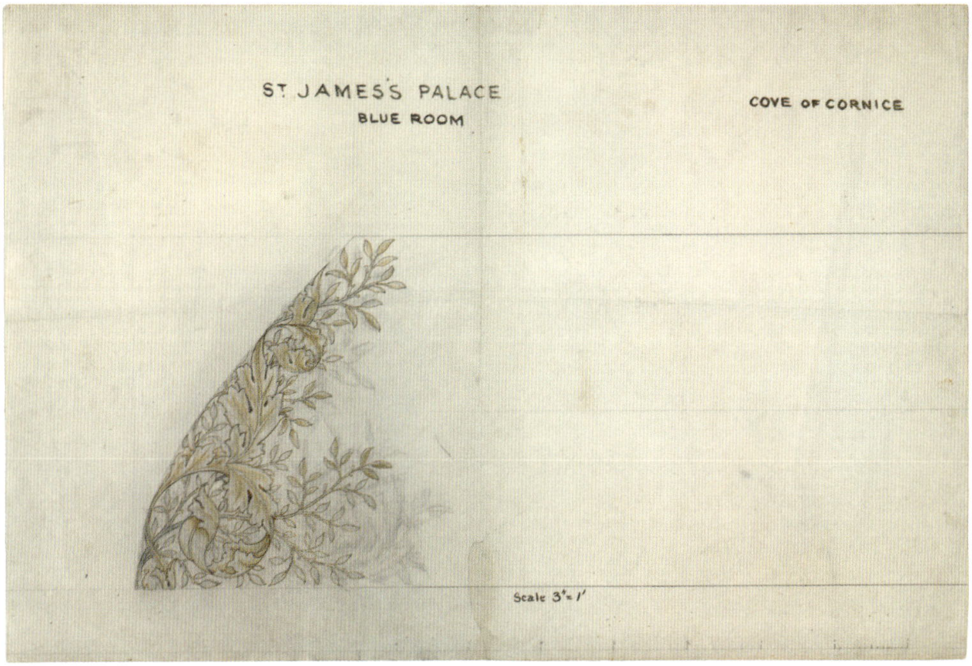

VIII.9

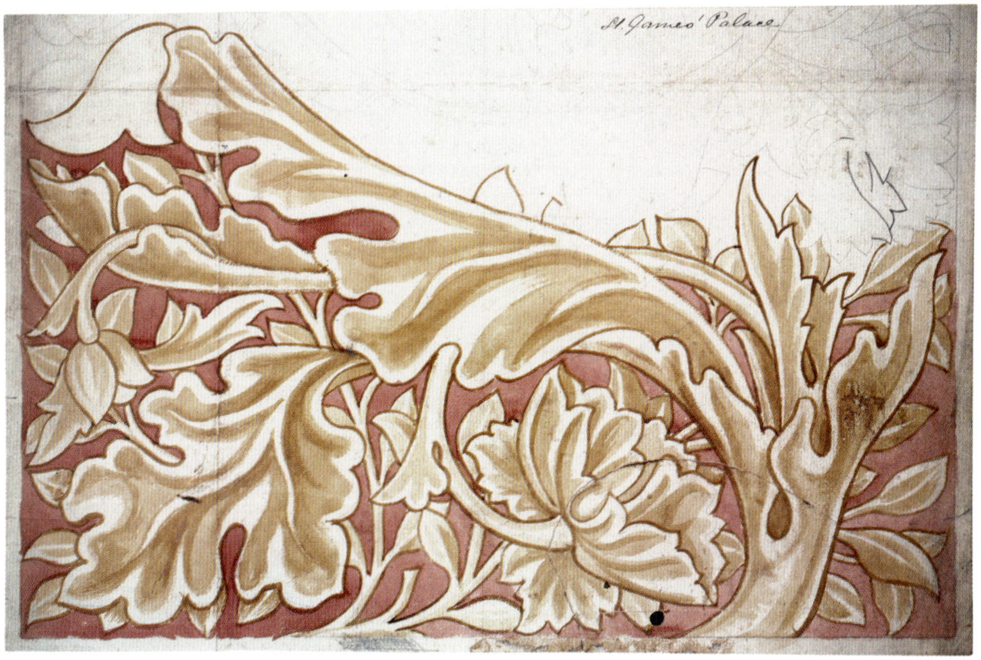

VIII.10

VIII.11

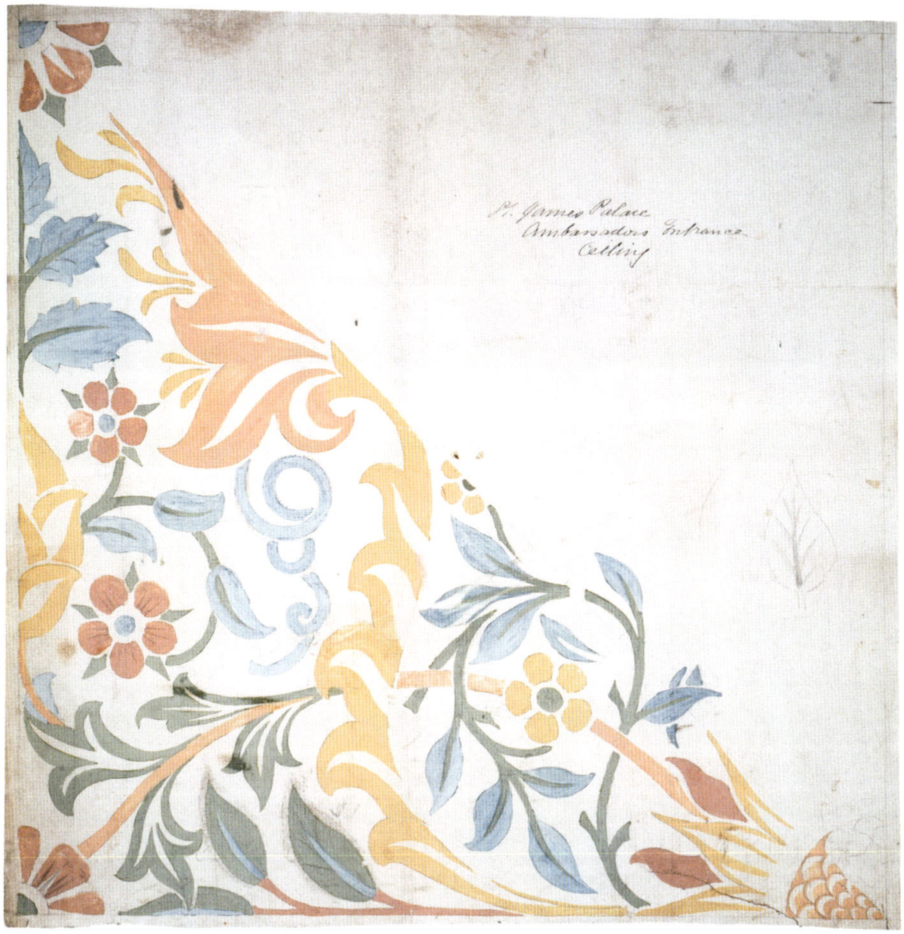

VIII.11
Design for ceiling decoration in the Ambassadors' Entrance, St James's Palace
William Morris or Philip Webb, 1880–1
Pencil and watercolour, 66.9 x 67.1 cm
William Morris Society, Kelmscott House, London (D15)

Morris & Co.'s estimate for the painting and redecoration of the entrances to St James's Palace is dated 20 August 1880. This included £657 for the Ambassadors' Entrance. A new fireplace 'in the recess of oak with panelling all round and seats on either side' was suggested, with a painted ceiling similar in style to that on the Grand Staircase and the Queen's Staircase. The scheme was approved by Queen Victoria on 2 November.

VIII.12

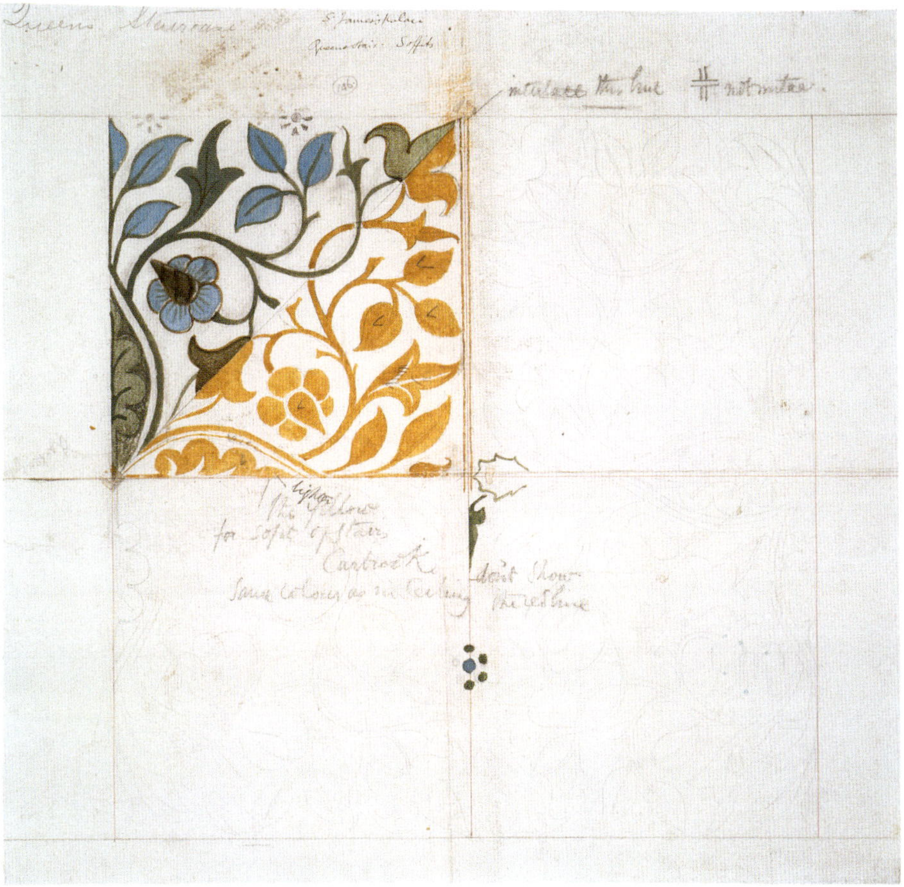

VIII.12
Design for painted decoration for the Queen's Staircase, St James's Palace
William Morris or Philip Webb, 1880–1
Pencil and watercolour, 47.1 x 49.2 cm
William Morris Society, Kelmscott House, London (D18)

The decoration of the Queen's Staircase, which is at the Garden Entrance of St James's Palace, was similar to that of the Grand Staircase and Ambassadors' Entrance. This drawing is inscribed 'the yellow for sofit of stairs same colour as in Carbrook ceiling' referring to a commission at Carbrook House, Larbert, Stirlingshire, Scotland that Morris & Co. was working on at approximately the same time (XII.99).

VIII.13

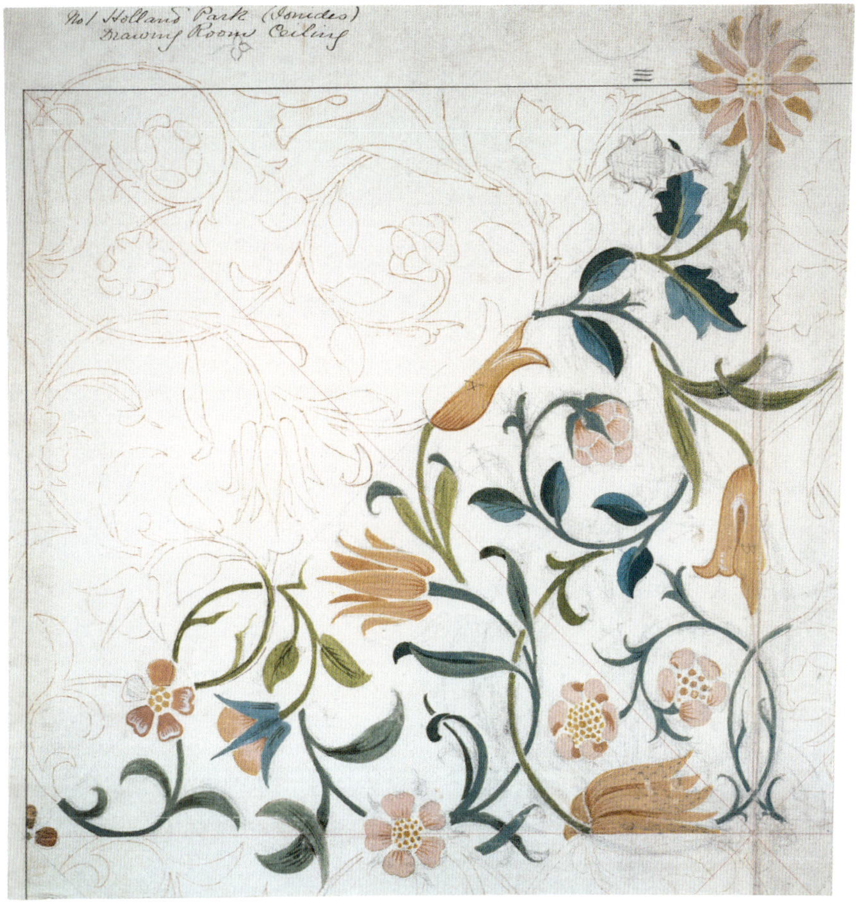

VIII.14

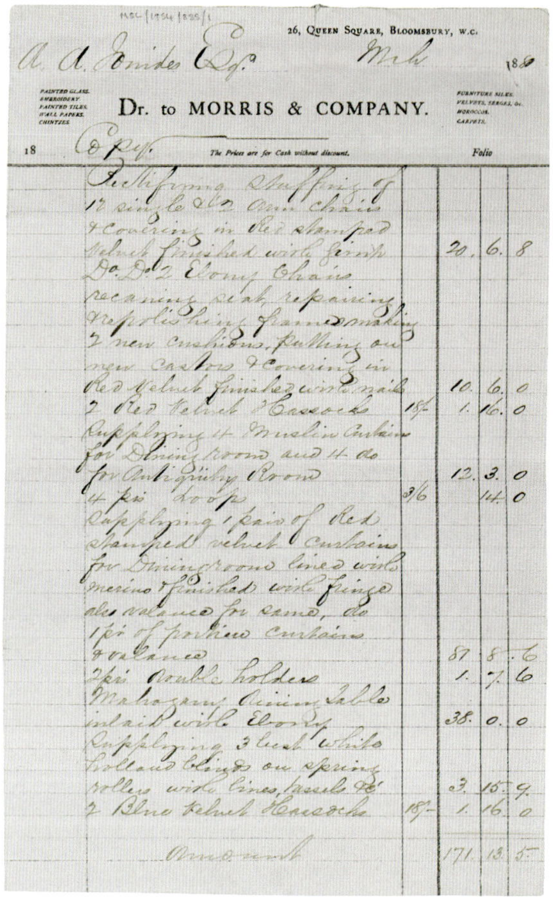

26, Queen Square, Bloomsbury, W.C.

A. A. Ionides Esq. Mch 188

Painted Glass. Embroidery. Painted Tiles. Wall Papers. Chintzes.

Dr. to MORRIS & COMPANY.

Furniture. Silks. Velvets, Serges, &c. Morocco. Carpets.

18 Copy The Prices are for Cash without discount. Folio

Refilling stuffing of 12 single & do Arm chairs & covering in red stamped velvet finished with fringe		20. 6. 8
Do Do 2 Ebony Chairs recaning seat, repairing & repolishing frame, making 2 new cushions, putting on new castors & covering in red velvet finished with nails		10. 6. 0
2 Red velvet Hassocks	18/-	1. 16. 0
Supplying 4 Muslin Curtains for Dining room and 4 do for Antiquity Room		12. 3. 0
4 pr loops	3/6	14. 0
Supplying 1 pair of red stamped velvet curtains for Dining room lined with merino & finished with fringe also valance for same, do 1 pr of portiere curtains & valance		87. 8. 6
2 pr double holders		1. 7. 6
Mahogany dining table inlaid with Ebony		38. 0. 0
Supplying 3 best white holland blinds on spring rollers with lines, tassels &c		3. 15. 9
2 Blue velvet Hassocks	18/-	1. 16. 0
Amount		171. 13. 5

VIII.13
Design for the drawing room ceiling of 1 Holland Park, London
William Morris or Philip Webb, dated May 1883
Pencil and watercolour, 53 x 50.8 cm
William Morris Society, Kelmscott House, London (D29)

The commission from Aleco Ionides to redecorate 1 Holland Park, a house he acquired from his father, Alexander Constantine Ionides, in 1875, lasted from 1880 to 1888. Discussions with the firm began in 1879. Major work in the drawing room and Antiquities Room was estimated by Morris & Co. on 2 May 1883, and included 'Drawing Room – The decoration of the ceiling might cost about £160.0.0d'. The completed scheme was colourful and highly decorative; as well as the painted repeating ceiling design, *Flower Garden* woven fabric was stretched on the walls and used for curtains with embroidered valances (fig.42). The specially designed *Holland Park* carpet (XII.98) and piano (IX.28) also provided part of the furniture for the room.

VIII.14
Estimates and bills for the decoration and furnishing of 1 Holland Park
Morris & Co., 1880–8
32.3 x 22 cm
National Art Library, V&A (MSL/1954/885)

The documentation covers work completed in three stages (1880, 1884 and 1888) and provides the most detailed surviving financial record of any of the firm's major commissions. The estimates and bills (which total £2,360 2*s.* 10*d.*) are not compatible so must reflect changes, nor do they include a number of items known to have been bought for the house (see Harvey and Press, 1994).

VIII.15
Album of photographs of 1 Holland Park
Bedford Lemere & Co., 1889
Albumen prints set into bound album, 31.8 x 40.6 cm (closed)
V&A (E.1–1995)

The album comprises 18 photographs showing exterior and interior views of 1 Holland Park, part of a larger series of images commissioned by Aleco Ionides after the decoration of the house was complete. At least two of these presentation albums are known to exist; the second is in the collection of Stanford University, California.

The project was an important showcase for Morris & Co. and the interiors were illustrated in a number of magazine articles including *The Art Journal* ('A Kensington Interior', May 1893) for which the Bedford Lemere photographs were used, *The Architectural Review* ('On Mr Philip Webb's Town Work', 1897) and *The Studio* ('An Epoch-Making House', 1898).

Harry Bedford Lemere joined his father's photographic business in 1881 working there until his death in 1944. The firm specialized exclusively in architectural and interior photography, producing many thousands of negatives showing the most luxurious and artistic houses, castles and palaces of the period. Many of these negatives were destroyed in the early twentieth century, according to correspondence in the 1950s between the V&A and the firm, which was then based in Croydon. Extant negatives and prints (now owned by Historic England Archive) provide an invaluable source of information on fashionable British interior decoration in the last quarter of the nineteenth century.

VIII.15

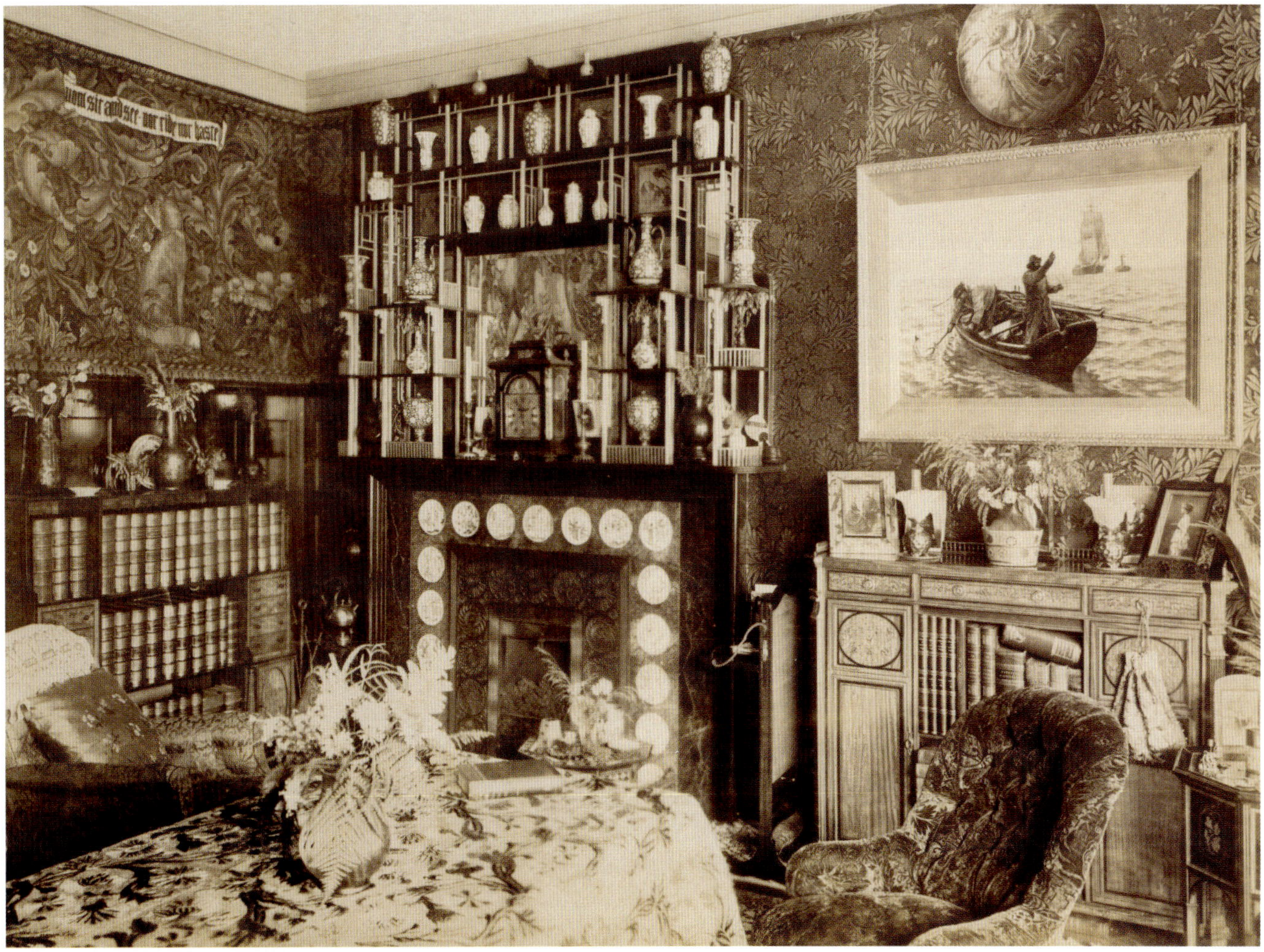

VIII.16

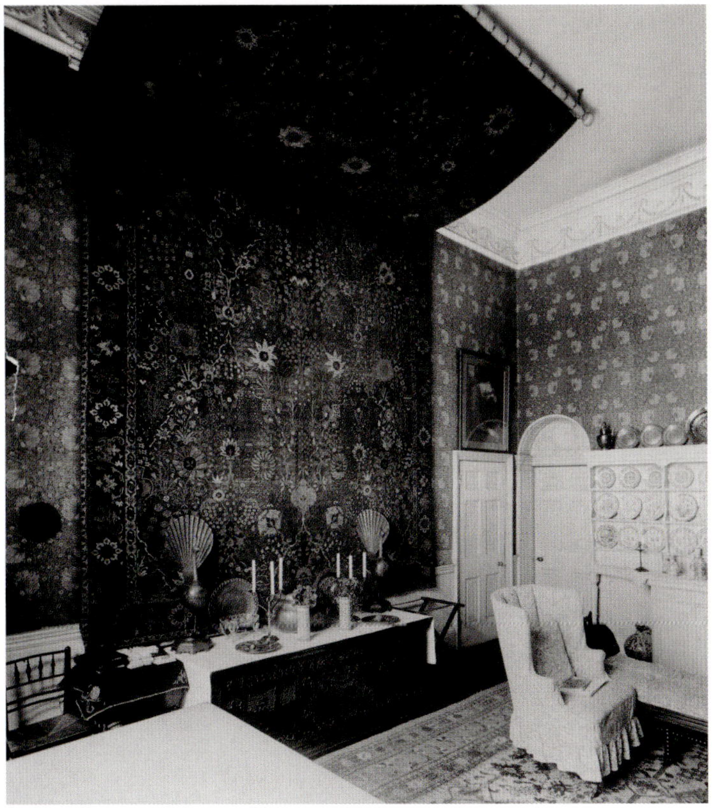

VIII.16

The dining room at Kelmscott House, Hammersmith

Photographed by Emery Walker, *c.*1896

Gelatin silver print, 29.5 x 24.2 cm

V&A (1–1973)

Probably taken soon after Morris's death, this photograph shows the massive seventeenth-century Persian carpet that was sold to the South Kensington Museum in 1897 for £200. The wallpaper is *Pimpernel*, and other Morris & Co. products include a *Sussex* chair and daybed designed by Webb, an embroidered cover and loose cotton chair covers of *Rose and Thistle* and *Brother Rabbit*. The metalwork and china reveal Morris's eclectic taste, with blue and white and traditional pottery, Grès de Flandres ware, and eastern metalwork, including two brass peacocks later described by May Morris as looking 'like guardians of a secret treasure'.

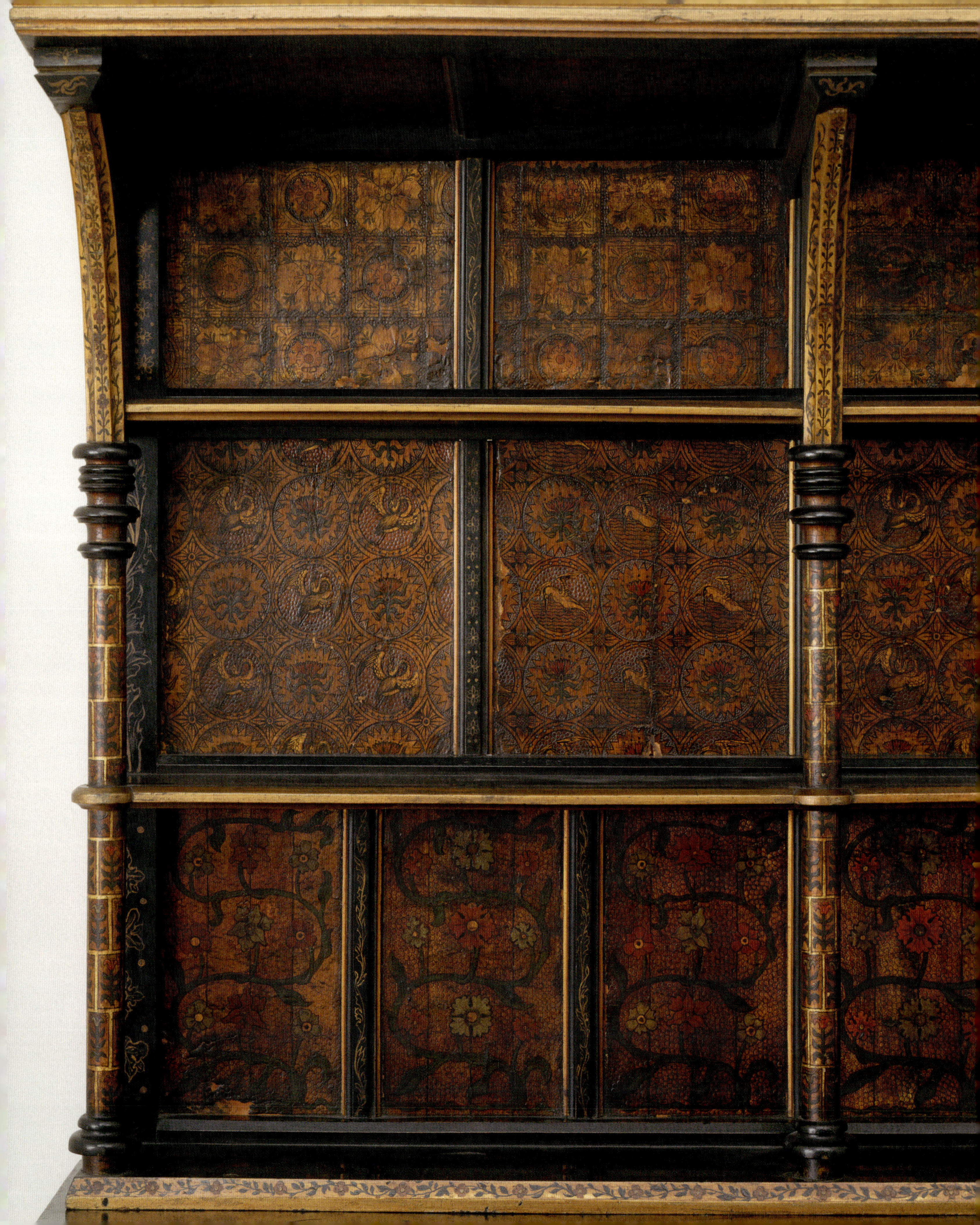

IX

FURNITURE

Frances Collard

'What furniture a workman can buy should be *exactly* the same (if his room be big enough) as a lord buys ...'
William Morris to Thomas Coglan Horsfall, February 1881

Fig.155 **Detail of sideboard, designed by Philip Webb, *c*.1862 (see IX.20).**
V&A (Circ.540–1963)
Given by Ben Weinreb

Morris summarized his theories on the design and construction of furniture in a lecture, 'The Lesser Arts of Life', in 1882. These principles epitomized the furniture associated with Morris and produced by his firm. He advocated 'good citizen's furniture, solid and well made in workmanship, and in design [it] should have nothing about it that is not easily defensible, no monstrosities or extravagances'. While he recognized the practical necessity for certain pieces, such as chairs, to be light and moveable, he preferred furniture 'made of timber rather than walking-sticks'.

For Morris furniture was divided into two categories, 'necessary work-a-day furniture' and 'state-furniture', the latter being elegant and elaborate with carving, inlaying and painting, all of which were 'blossoms of the art of furniture'. These grander pieces, which should be readily available, were recommended for the more prominent positions in important rooms. Furniture for everyday use was to be well made and well proportioned but simple and even crude in execution.

Morris's brief apprenticeship in George Edmund Street's office had stimulated him in various ways, including encouraging him to experiment with woodcarving. Meeting Philip Webb, Street's chief assistant, provided an opportunity to share ideas about architecture, both ecclesiastical and domestic, and design with a friend who had professional skills. Webb later became the main designer of the firm's furniture in the 1860s and 1870s and the originality of his contribution to this field deserves greater recognition.

In 1856 Morris, inspired by compatible companions, and by his studies of medieval architecture and literature, designed his first furniture for the unfurnished rooms he and Burne-Jones rented in Red Lion Square. These pieces were enthusiastically described by Burne-Jones in a letter quoted in the *Memorials*, 'Topsy has had some furniture (chairs and table) made after his own design; they are as beautiful as mediaeval work, and when we have painted designs of knights and ladies upon them they will be perfect marvels.'

The furniture was probably made by Henry Price, a local cabinet maker employed by Tommy Baker of Christopher Street, Hatton Garden. Price's diary, published by Pat Kirkham, records that he was asked to make some 'very old fashioned Furniture in the Mideavel Style', including a 'large Cabinet about 7ft high and as long, a seat forming a bunk, with arms each end Carv to represent Fishes. Three Cupboards The Doors with fantastic

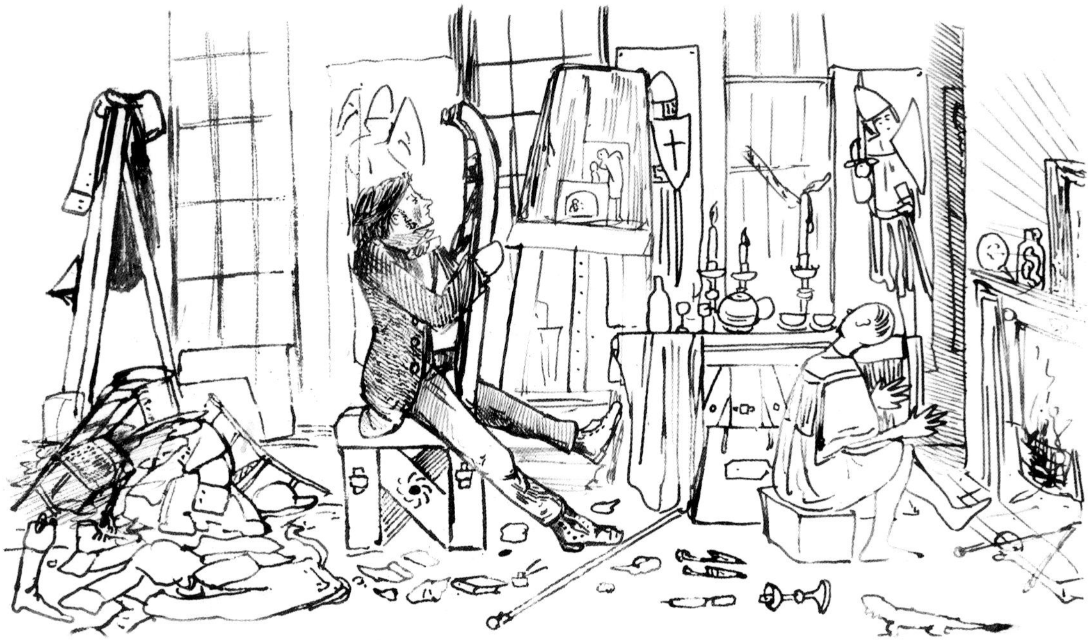

Fig.156 **The young Ned Jones among the debris and new furniture at Red Lion Square, self-caricature, by Edward Burne-Jones, 1856.**
Mark Samuels Lasner Collection, University of Delaware Library, Museums and Press

ironwork hinges, representing Birds, fishes and Flowers Bolted on, and gilt coloured. The hinges cost 14 pounds.'

Price's ambiguous remark that 'He spent a lot of his Leisure in carving the arms and panels' may refer to Morris himself working on the settle with the tools he kept in the folds of a white evening tie nailed to the wall at Red Lion Square. However, Morris's enthusiasm was not always matched by practical skills and when the settle was delivered it was much larger than anticipated. According to Burne-Jones the friends returned home to find that, 'all the passages and the staircase were choked with vast blocks of timber, and there was a scene. I think the measurements had perhaps been given a little wrongly ... but set up it was finally, and our studio was one-third-less in size.' The settle was later adapted and installed in the drawing room at Red House (fig.141). Max Beerbohm's 1916 cartoon, *Topsy and Ned Jones Settled on the Settle in Red Lion Square* (VIII.1), was probably based on Burne-Jones's written descriptions and bears no resemblance to the actual piece.

Other furniture mentioned by Price included 'tables and High backed chairs like what I have seen in Abyes and Cathedrals. A large Oak Table on tressels with a Iron Stretcher twisted and partly burnished.' The high-backed chairs were rediscovered in 1997 after over a century in the hands of the Heathcote family who purchased Red House in 1866 (IX.3). One of them can be seen in Burne-Jones's sketch of Red Lion Square, described by Georgiana Burne-Jones as showing 'Edward himself, in caricature likeness, looking with devouring interest at a picture with which Rossetti had glorified one of the chairs that Morris designed' (fig.156). Morris may have been inspired to experiment with painted furniture following a visit to Lille in the spring of 1856. Street took him to see the exhibition of competition designs for the new cathedral, which included William Burges's drawing for an elaborately painted organ case. He and Rossetti decorated the chairs together, the subjects at least partly inspired by Morris's poetry and their shared interest in medieval art and literature. In their form and decoration they were quite unlike anything else being produced at the time, an early instance of Morris's rebellious instinct and also of the collaborative approach that would define his career.

The oak trestle table described by Price has not been traced, but the description bears a close resemblance to two oak tables designed by Webb for Red House and made towards the end of 1859. The smaller of the two was gifted to the poet Wilfrid Scawen Blunt after Morris's death and has survived in a private collection. According to a letter Webb wrote in 1898, 'Both tables were bound round the edge with scoured iron fixed with clout-headed nails, to keep the impatient from whittling away the edge if victuals lingered on the road.' Although undocumented, it is plausible that Webb played a part in designing the Red Lion Square furniture; certainly Morris is likely to have discussed it with him. A sturdy round table, inspired by Street's example at Cuddesdon College, and a painted tub chair, both date from the Red Lion Square era and help to build a picture of Morris's early tastes (IX.2 and IX.4). Georgiana Burne-Jones recalled another distinctive chair, a 'large one with a box overhead in which Gabriel suggested owls might be kept with advantage.' If it has survived, its whereabouts are unknown but the description is reminiscent of a large canopied chair shown in Rossetti's *The Tune of Seven Towers* of 1857 (fig.105) and such designs were probably inspired by illuminated manuscripts of the fourteenth and fifteenth centuries.

The overall impression of the painted furniture at Red Lion Square was sufficiently gorgeous for the artist George Price Boyce to comment on it in his diary after attending a meeting of the Hogarth Club there on 4 May 1858 (see p.104). Boyce may well have seen the partially completed *Prioress's Tale* wardrobe (IX.5), later described by Jane Morris as a wedding present from Burne-Jones. The most imposing and complex example of 'storytelling' furniture produced by Morris's circle, the wardrobe is frustratingly sparsely documented. J.W. Mackail claimed Burne-Jones painted the scenes from Chaucer's tale in the spring of 1857, but other sources confirm that he actually began it the following year, around the time of Morris and Jane's engagement. In a letter quoted in the *Memorials* Burne-Jones wrote, 'Is Topsy in Oxford? love to him and everyone – tell him not to come up yet till I've done more to the wardrobe.' It was finished in a hurry for exhibition at the Hogarth Club in 1860, and according to Webb, they all worked at getting it done.

This engagement with painted furniture in the late 1850s was not peculiar to Morris and his friends but reflected wider interest among contemporary artists, architects and designers. Chief among these was the architect William Burges, a knowledgeable and enthusiastic champion of medieval furniture who, like Morris, belonged to the Medieval Society and the Hogarth Club. He designed carefully structured cabinets with sophisticated iconographic schemes and was particularly inspired by two French armoires in the cathedrals of Bayeux and Noyon. In 1858 both were illustrated in Eugène Viollet-le-Duc's *Dictionnaire Raisonné du Mobilier Français* (fig.157). Burges also revived a medieval decorative technique, which he had probably found in a recently published translation of Theophilus Presbyter's twelfth-century manuscript, *De diversis artibus* ('On various arts'). This involved using tinted varnishes on silver leaf, and was later employed by Morris, Marshall, Faulkner & Co. on furniture decorated for the International Exhibition of 1862.

Morris and Burges's experiments with medieval-style painted furniture were taking place at roughly the same time but it is striking how different their approaches were. Significant pieces by Burges from this period, including the *Yatman* cabinet

Fig.157 (below left) **The Noyon armoire, published in Eugène Viollet-le-Duc's *Dictionnaire Raisonné du Mobilier Français*, 1858.**
National Art Library, V&A

Fig.158 (below right) ***Wine and Beers* sideboard, designed by William Burges and painted by Edward Poynter, whose monogram it bears with the date 1858.**
V&A (8042–1862)

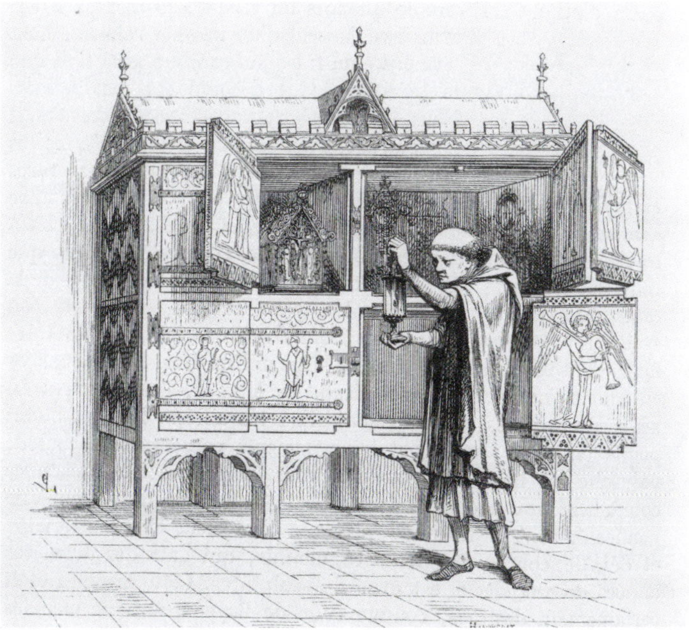

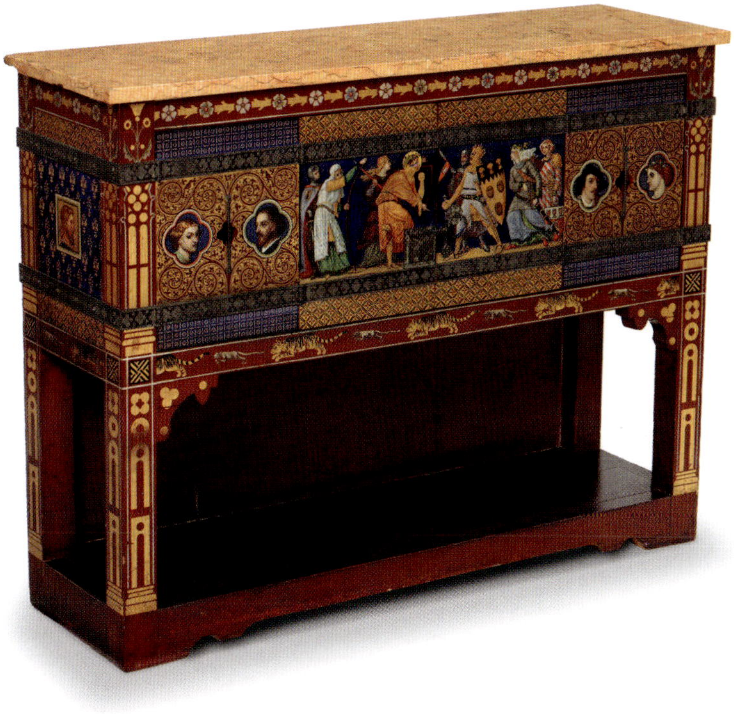

(1858, V&A), the *Wine and Beers* sideboard (fig.158) and the *Great Bookcase* (1859–62, Ashmolean Museum), all have iconographic themes that relate closely to their function. The sideboard, for example, was designed as a drinks cabinet and depicts an imaginary battle between continental wines, led by St Bacchus, and British beers, represented by Sir John Barleycorn. Painted scenes are usually shown against flat, single-colour backgrounds, framed and contained by panels of painted ornament or architectural details. In the early pieces produced by Morris and his circle, particularly *The Prioress's Tale* wardrobe, the painted decoration is not subordinate to the overall structure. Webb incorporated the idea of a folding door (as seen in the Noyon armoire), but in this instance as a vast canvas for Burne-Jones's painting. Rather than showing a lack of understanding of medieval precedents, as is sometimes claimed, this was a conscious aesthetic choice.

Morris and Webb's experience of designing and overseeing the making of furniture proved helpful when planning the furnishing of Red House. The positions of key pieces of furniture were lightly sketched in pencil on Webb's architectural plans (VIII.4a) and the drawing room was designed with the Red Lion Square settle in mind. Various changes were made when it was installed, including the addition of a minstrels' gallery, reached by a ladder. Painted titanium white in the twentieth century, the original colour scheme is still being investigated but traces of red have been found, as well as fragments of polychrome patterns on the sides. In 1859–60 Rossetti painted three doors for the settle with figurative scenes illustrating the enduring love of Dante and Beatrice: *The Salutation of Beatrice on Earth*, *The Salutation of Beatrice in Eden* (both 1859, National Gallery of Canada) and *Dantis Amor* (1860, Tate). For reasons that remain unclear Rossetti had the panels back in his possession by 1863, but while *in situ* they would have been a striking addition to Morris's interior.

As well as adapting furniture from Red Lion Square, Webb designed six built-in pieces specifically for Red House, which through the careful stewardship of later owners have survived *in situ*. The most impressive is the monumental oak dresser in the dining room, painted 'Dragon's blood red' and demonstrating his fluent command of Gothic details (fig.159). The walls and panelling of this room were originally painted in shades of red and green and, together with the tall red-brick fireplace, would have created an impressive setting for the embroidery scheme that Morris planned for this space (XII.4). The dresser's restrained design is enlivened with elegant ironwork fittings (the light is a later addition). For the hallway, Webb conceived another large piece, a cupboard-cum-settle, with figurative paintings attributed to Morris and Rossetti (VI.15) and decorated with pattern work. As Tessa Wild has noted, the form of these sturdy pieces echoes the architecture of the house.

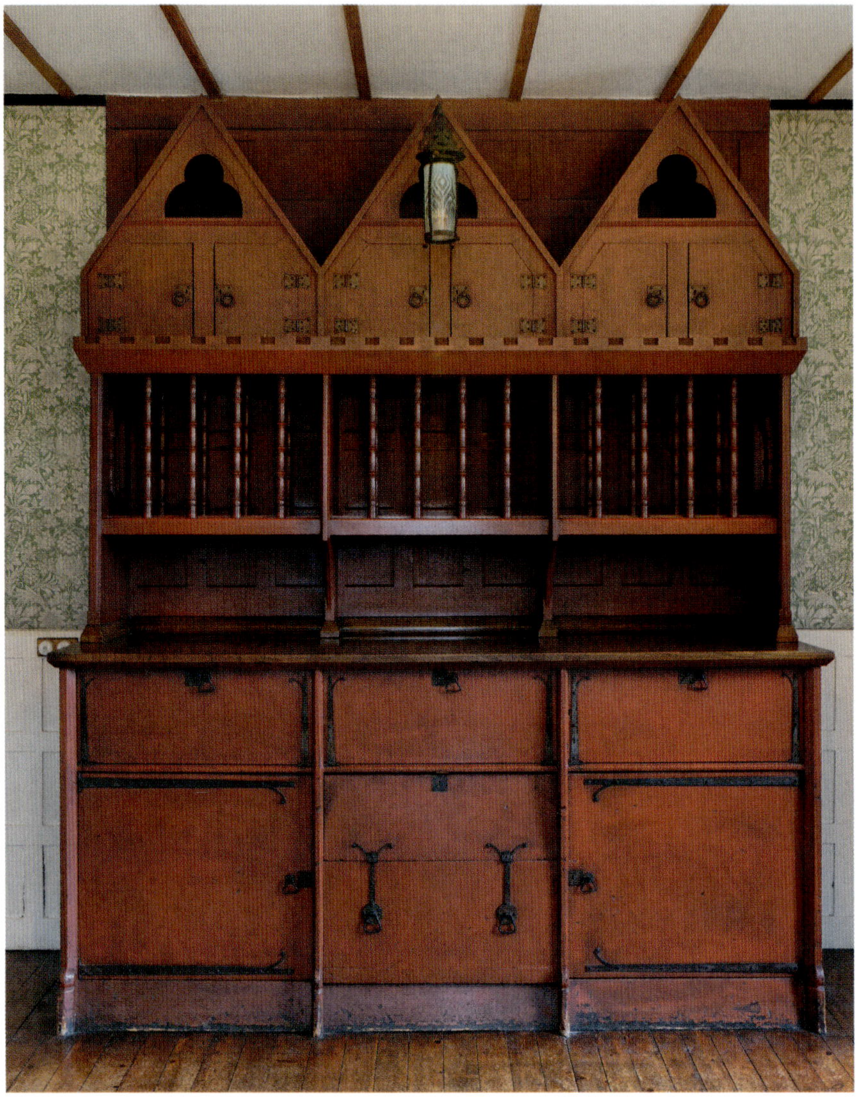

Fig.159 **Dining-room dresser at Red House, designed by Philip Webb, *c.*1859–60.**
National Trust, Red House

Portable furnishings included a jewel casket for Jane, attributed to Webb and painted by Rossetti and Elizabeth Siddal (fig.160). Shaped like a Gothic reliquary, the form loosely recalled the elaborate fifteenth-century *Shrine of Saint Ursula* in Saint John's Hospital, Bruges, with oil paintings by Hans Memling. This object was well known to Morris's circle and would have been seen by Morris and

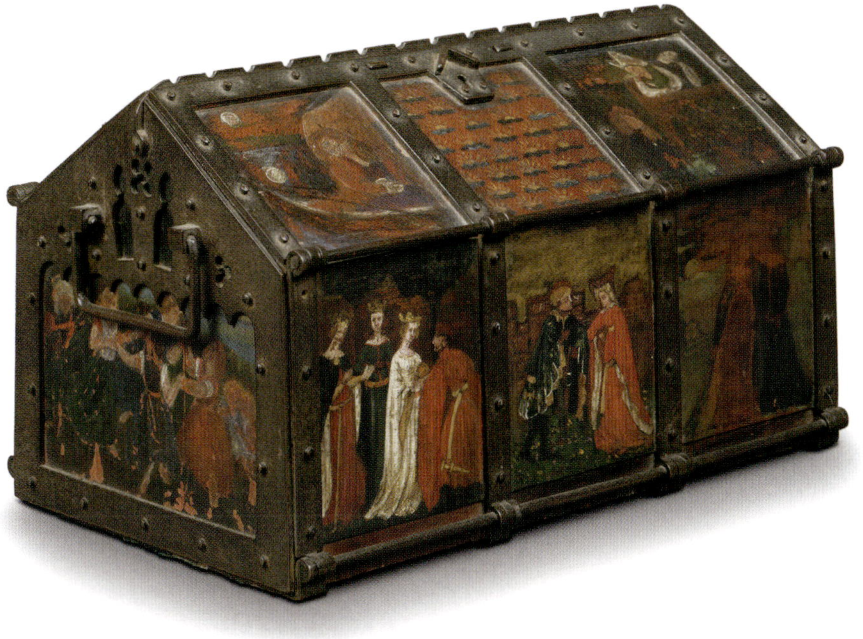

Fig.160 **Jewel casket, design attributed to Philip Webb and decorated by Dante Gabriel Rossetti and Elizabeth Siddal, *c.*1860–2.**
The Society of Antiquaries of London, Kelmscott Manor

Jane on their honeymoon. Ornamented with scenes of medieval romance, two were drawn directly from The Book of the Queen, a fifteenth-century illuminated manuscript in the British Museum (Harley 4431). Other items at Red House included an inventive round table (IX.10) and rush-seated chairs, the latter probably made at the Industrial Home for Destitute Boys on Euston Road where furniture-making was taught. The home was supported by Colonel William Gillum, an important early patron of Webb and later the firm.

Morris was not the only member of the firm who sought to beautify his marital home with painted furniture. When Burne-Jones married Georgiana Macdonald in June 1860 they moved to his spartan bachelor rooms in Russell Place, Fitzroy Square. Unlike Morris at Red House, money was in very limited supply, but Burne-Jones nevertheless created character and interest by decorating a plain deal sideboard (IX.7) and a modest upright piano that they were given as a wedding gift (fig.161). Inside the lid of the piano a figure plays a small portable organ, a composition that later developed into his watercolour *Le Chant d'Amour* (1865, Museum of Fine Arts Boston). On a more sombre note, the painted gesso work beneath the keyboard shows Death, carrying a scythe, and knocking at the door to a garden where a group of youthful yet melancholy women listen to music. The latter was loosely based on the fourteenth-century *Triumph of Death* fresco in the Campo Santo in Pisa that Burne-Jones had seen on his recent trip to Italy. In these one-off, idiosyncratic pieces, painted furniture provided a relatively inexpensive means to stamp his tastes on their living quarters. The couple also had an oak trestle table made to Webb's design by the Industrial Home for Boys and which can be seen in a later watercolour of their dining room at The Grange, Fulham, along with the *Ladies and Animals* sideboard (fig.162).

Furniture was one of the first products advertised by Morris, Marshall, Faulkner & Co. in 1861. The firm's early circular, quoted by Mackail, listed furniture 'either depending for its beauty on its own design, on the application of materials hitherto overlooked, or on its conjunction with Figure and Pattern Painting.' Rossetti's comment, made in a letter to William Allingham in January 1861, that they did not intend to compete with the expensive products of Messrs. Crace but hoped to 'give real good taste at the price as far as possible of ordinary furniture', gives a flavour of their idealistic wish to improve the standards of furniture design. The opportunity to display their work at the International Exhibition of 1862 was taken with speed and energy. The firm showed its wares in the Medieval Court, which was supervised by Burges and the architect William Slater on behalf of the Ecclesiological Society, champions of the Gothic style.

The firm's furniture exhibits included the *St George* and *The Backgammon Players* cabinets, an Egyptian-style sofa designed by Rossetti, Webb's painted chest and black and gold armchair (IX.14–18), as well as a screen with stamped leather panels, a red lacquer music stand, a dressing-table mirror, chairs, a washstand and an iron bedstead. There was also a part-gilt ebonized bookcase with velvet curtains, its sides decorated with scenes showing the life of an English family between 1810 and 1860. Designed by Ford Madox Brown, the bookcase later belonged to one of the firm's founding partners, Peter Paul Marshall, but is currently untraced, though Madox Brown's designs for the decorative panels are in the collection of the Fitzwilliam Museum. Not all the exhibits can be definitely identified since the official catalogue did not give details and reviews in contemporary periodicals are sometimes vague. The firm also contributed to the *King René's Honeymoon* cabinet designed and exhibited by John Pollard Seddon for use in his architectural office (IX.13). The range of furniture was surprisingly varied for such a recently founded enterprise, indicating the talent and imagination of Morris and his friends.

Although the London Stereoscopic & Photographic Company published views of the

Medieval Court, the firm's displays are frustratingly out of shot, with just a glimpse of one of Burne-Jones's designs for stained glass. Max Donnelly, in his article '"Rapture and Ridicule": Furniture in the 1862 Medieval Court', has reconstructed the layout of the entire Court, providing invaluable context for the firm's first public showcase. Painted furniture was the most conspicuous feature of the displays, with examples by Burges, Seddon and Richard Norman Shaw, as well as those pieces exhibited by the firm. The reception of these works was extremely mixed and sparked strong reactions. *The Building News* described the firm's furniture as the 'most thoroughly mediæval of any in the Court. They are consequently the most useless.' The same reviewer thought that 'their hangings, their music stand, their sofa, their chests, would all suit a family which might suddenly be awakened after a sleep of four centuries' (8 August 1862). The expense of the items was also criticized but the partners nevertheless managed to sell £150 worth of goods and received a medal for the good design and workmanship of their 'Decorative furniture'. Although some of the showpieces, including the *St George* cabinet, failed to find buyers, the publicity led to new commissions and helped establish the firm's reputation.

In 1863 the firm issued a new prospectus. In the draft of the accompanying letter Morris specifically mentioned 'the great beauty that can be produced by the ornamentation of cabinets with gilded & lacquered patterns and figures combined with the use of stained & polished woods', and he drew attention to the medal the firm had received the previous year (British Library Add. MS 45336). He also suggested stamped leather panels, coloured and varnished, as suitable for screens, furniture, panelling and for use in ecclesiastical woodwork, confirming that the firm had 'several patterns of great beauty for inspection and are ready to submit designs & prices for any amount.' This is supported by various entries of the early 1860s in Webb's account book and by surviving furniture (IX.20).

Such impressive statements were tempered by modest entries in the firm's minute book in 1863 (fig.33). Webb, Burne-Jones and Morris all provided designs for the decoration of stereoscopic boxes, while Webb supplied a carpenter's drawing of a four-poster bed and Morris discussed a potential furniture commission with Rossetti. Madox Brown's account book with the firm, preserved in the Violet Hunt Papers at Cornell University, records payments in the early 1860s for designing tables and chairs. From the mid-1860s, Webb designed nearly all the firm's furniture and his architectural expertise was also critical to the delivery of many of its interior decorative schemes, including the refreshment room at the South Kensington Museum and work at St James's Palace. To reflect these contributions, and at the urging of the firm's business manager, Warington Taylor, in May 1867 the partners voted Webb a salary of £80 a year as a 'consulting manager'.

The structure and location of the furniture workshops are unclear, although premises in Great Ormond Yard were apparently used. According to Mackail, a local cabinet maker, Mr Curwen, was responsible for some of the early furniture, but few details are known about the individual craftsmen. One cabinet maker employed by the firm was called Stennett, listed in Webb's address book at 23 Wilmot Street, Brunswick Square, who was working on furniture for Burne-Jones in 1865 and 1866. Warington Taylor issued a warning about his prices to Webb, mentioning an estimate for a sideboard, in a letter of 1867 or 1868.

Before joining the firm in 1865, Taylor recorded his impressions of its furniture in a series of letters to the architect Edward Robert Robson in 1862–3, preserved among Burne-Jones's Papers at the Fitzwilliam Museum. He mentioned 'a jolly little round table at Morris' on six legs with trays underneath', which may have been an early example of Webb's circular table (IX.24). He also enthusiastically described another piece,

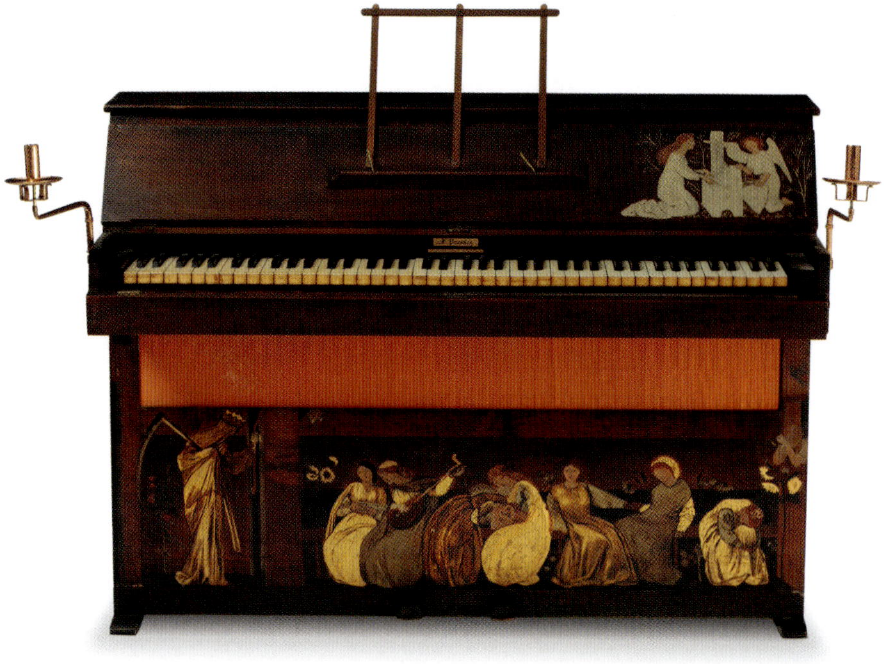

Fig.161 **Piano, manufactured by Frederick Priestley and decorated by Edward Burne-Jones, *c.*1860.**
V&A (W.43–1926)
Given by Margaret Mackail

Fig.162 ***Dining Room, The Grange, North End Road, Fulham*, Thomas Matthews Rooke, 1904.**
National Trust, Bateman's

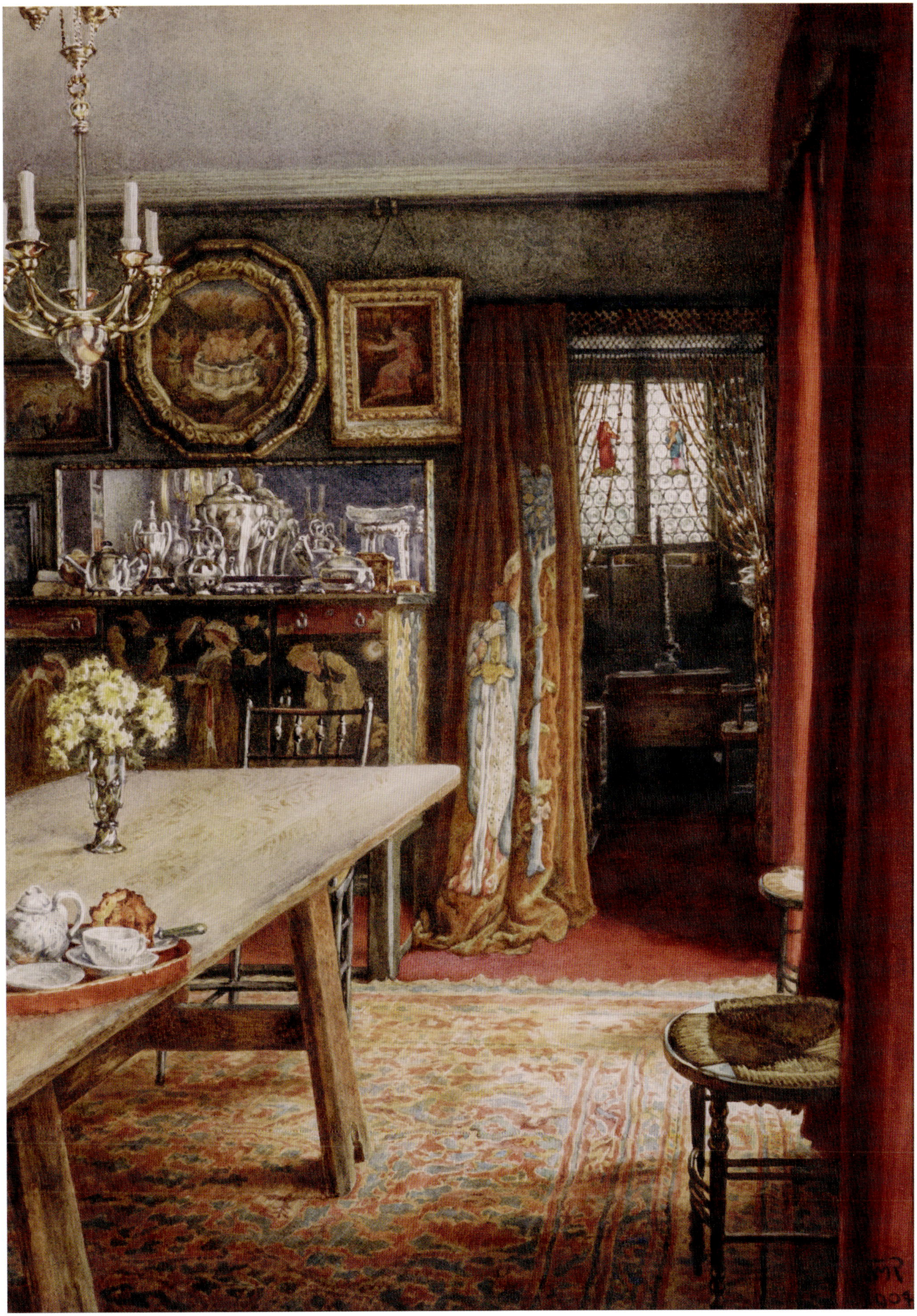

'Anything more beautiful than the turned pillars and mouldings in their new sideboard I have never seen'. This could be a reference to a sideboard designed by Webb (fig.163), several examples of which survive, including narrower two-door versions, one at Kelmscott Manor. The artist Myles Birket Foster ordered one for The Hill, Witley, Surrey, probably during the firm's extensive work at the house in the mid-1860s that included tiles and stained glass. The sideboard was praised by Robert Edis in his *Decoration and Furniture of Town Houses* (1881) and remained available until at least the early twentieth century.

Webb's modest yet subtle use of mouldings in this sideboard, inspired by seventeenth-century architectural woodwork and furniture, was echoed in other pieces produced by the firm in the early 1860s. After the International Exhibition, elaborately painted decoration gave way to more restrained and functional furniture that exploited the inherent qualities of the timber. Both architectural and vernacular sources may have inspired the use of turned details, as in Webb's round table (IX.24). Ebonized finishes, often combined with gilded decoration, such as Webb's 1862 chair (IX.17) or the cheval mirror (IX.19), were inspired by seventeenth-century furniture but also indicate an awareness of Japanese art, particularly the spatial quality of its woodwork that became increasingly influential among contemporary furniture designers, including E.W. Godwin and Christopher Dresser. An oak side table, based on a Japanese altar table, is strikingly abstract and pared down in form and may be one of the pieces commissioned from the firm by Colonel Gillum (fig.164). As Giles Ellwood has shown, a particularly fine serving table designed for Isaac Lowthian Bell's dining room at Rounton Grange has deeply carved fluting on the legs that owes a debt to seventeenth-century Spanish tables (fig.165). Webb drew selectively on a wide range of historical sources to create furniture that was both practical and original.

The introduction of lighter furniture, in complete contrast to the earlier massive medieval painted pieces, was noticed by Taylor: 'Are not the Red Lion people in the right direction in this matter they get gradually lighter, and Rossetti keeps them up to the point'. Certainly Rossetti's documented enthusiasm for antique furniture may have influenced this development. In 1862 he moved to an eighteenth-century house on Cheyne Walk, Chelsea, which he proceeded to fill with an eclectic collection of objects, including Sheraton and Regency furniture. His patronage of Minster of Buckingham Street and other dealers is recorded in his letters and by Allingham and Henry Treffry Dunn. Some of his antique pieces can still be seen at Kelmscott Manor, which he co-leased with Morris in the early 1870s. Interestingly he also undertook painted furniture on his own account, outside his activities for the firm. Shortly after moving to Chelsea, Rossetti painted panels for a bookcase designed by the architect Charles Forster Hayward and acquired by the V&A in 1882. For his own bedroom he decorated a Regency-style sofa with medallions representing Amor, Amans and Amata (Love, the Lover and the Beloved), now in the Fitzwilliam's collection. At the firm, he gave his name to one of the popular rush-seated armchairs, which was based on an early nineteenth-century French country chair (IX.23). A sketch by Frederic Shields shows him painting in the so-called *Rossetti* armchair (fig.166).

The launch of the *Sussex* chair range was an astute commercial move (fig.167), as by this means the firm considerably widened its selection of furniture and was able to offer items at a lower price. The partners, including Morris and

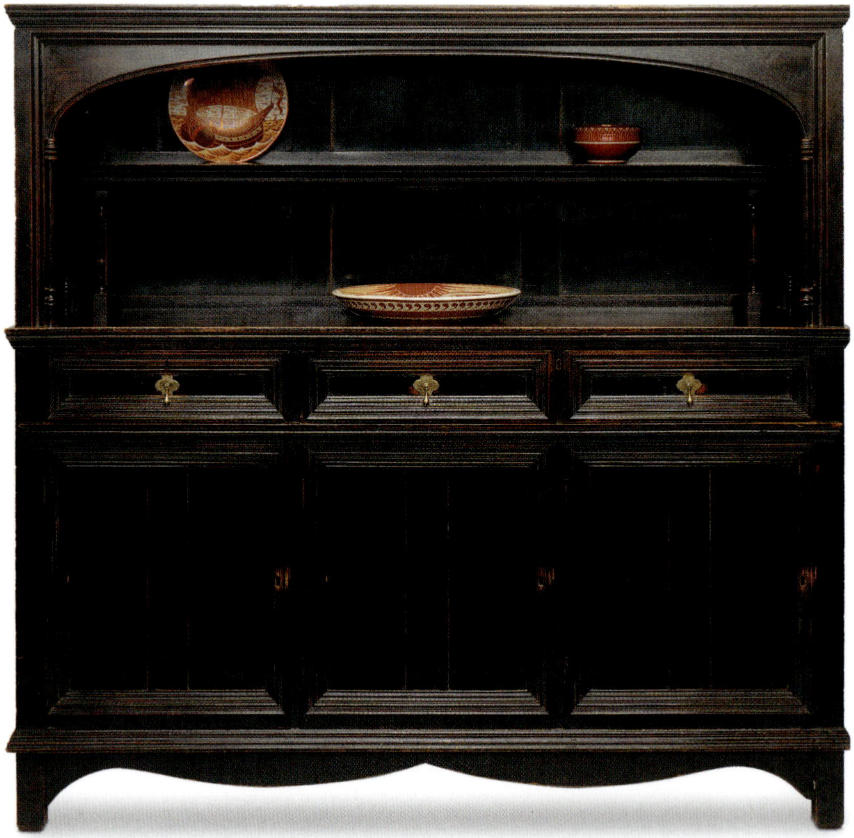

Fig.163 **Stained oak sideboard, designed by Philip Webb *c.*1865, manufactured *c.*1900.**
Art Gallery of South Australia, Adelaide

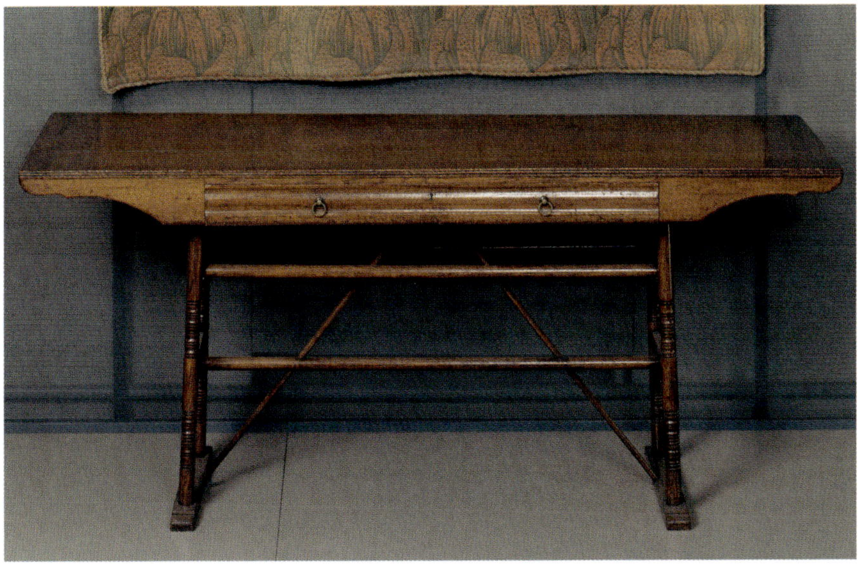

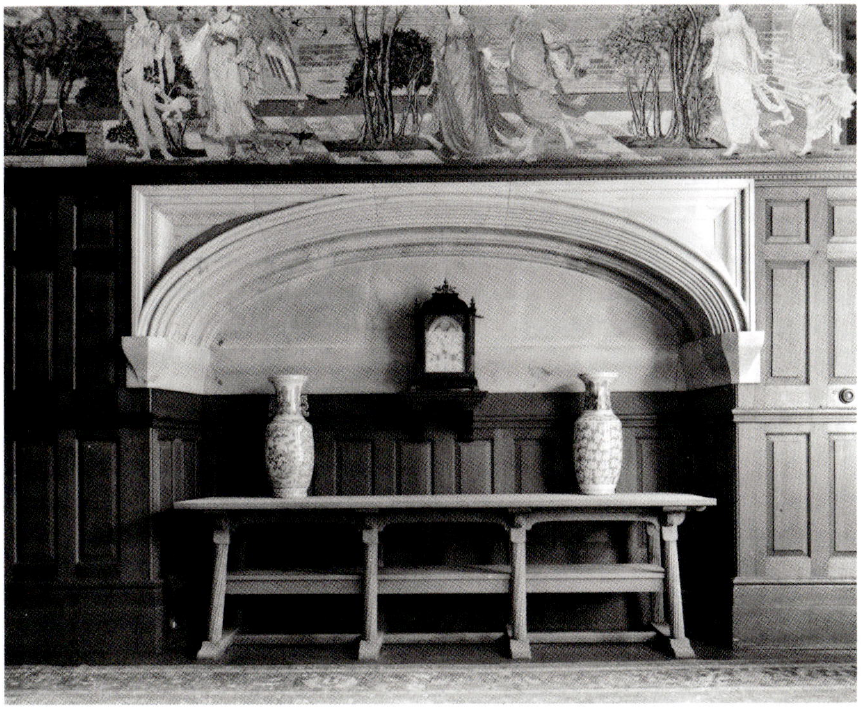

Fig.164 (top) **Oak side table, designed by Philip Webb, early 1860s.**
Musée d'Orsay, Paris

Fig.165 (above) **Oak serving table, designed by Philip Webb for a recess in the dining room at Rounton Grange, Northallerton, *c*.1870–2.**
Country Life

Burne-Jones, furnished their own homes with rush-seated chairs from 1860 onwards and they were retailed from around the mid-1860s. Adapted from Regency prototypes, Webb, Madox Brown and Rossetti have all been linked to their design. The longevity and popularity of the range, which was to be widely copied by other firms, may be explained by Taylor, in another enthusiastic outburst,

> Red Lion Sq. furniture has no style, modern work must only be founded on nature, severity, and true construction. There must be no notion of precedent, fashion, century ... The beauty of Red Lion woodwork I think is that you cannot say it has any style – it is original, it has its own style, it is in fact Victorian.

The interiors at Kelmscott House, Hammersmith – Morris's London home from 1878 – were elegantly furnished with the firm's products. The first-floor drawing room, in particular, was a semi-public showcase for the company's wares (fig.15). The furniture, which included adjustable-back armchairs, chairs from the *Sussex* range and an oak table with strong architectural mouldings designed by Webb, was harmoniously combined with antique pieces, Morris & Co.'s textiles, lustreware, metalwork and eastern rugs. *The Prioress's Tale* wardrobe and Webb's canopied settle, both from Red House, provided continuity with the past and were examples of the elaborate 'state furniture' that Morris advocated for the principal rooms of a house. Other spaces, including Morris's study, were more simply furnished. The latter included an interesting trestle table with ringed legs, probably attributable to Webb. It is now at Kelmscott Manor, along with a second example that Edmund Hort New recorded in a drawing of the Tapestry Room in 1898 (William Morris Gallery).

The mid-1880s marked a shift in the style of furniture retailed by the firm, largely owing to the involvement of the architect and versatile designer–craftsman George Jack. Webb's restraint gave way to a greater emphasis on decoration. Amy Gaimster's research into Jack's career has shed new light on his work for Morris & Co. Jack trained as an architect in Glasgow before moving to London in 1875. By 1882 he had a salaried position in Webb's office as a draughtsman and site architect. He continued working for Webb until the latter's retirement in 1900, when he took over his architectural practice.

Jack's account books, preserved at the William Morris Gallery, show that he began designing furniture for Morris & Co. in 1885. He worked in a freelance capacity, receiving one-off payments for his sketches and working designs but no royalties on sales. His commercial work for the firm was inspired by eighteenth-century traditions (he studied Sheraton and Regency furniture at the South Kensington Museum), in preference to the vernacular and Gothic forms that had informed Webb's earlier designs. Although oak was still used, walnut and mahogany became

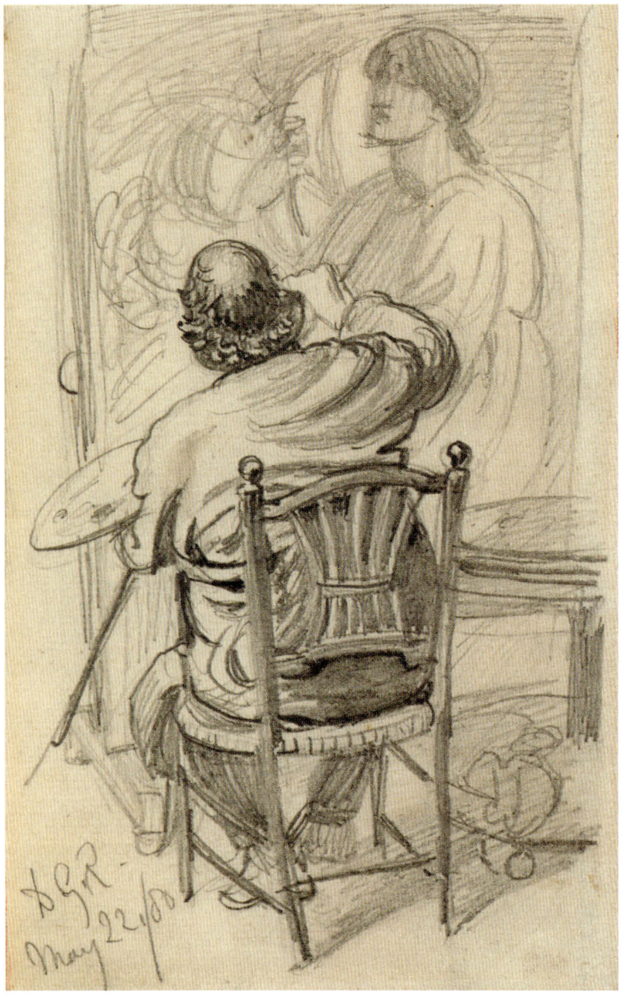

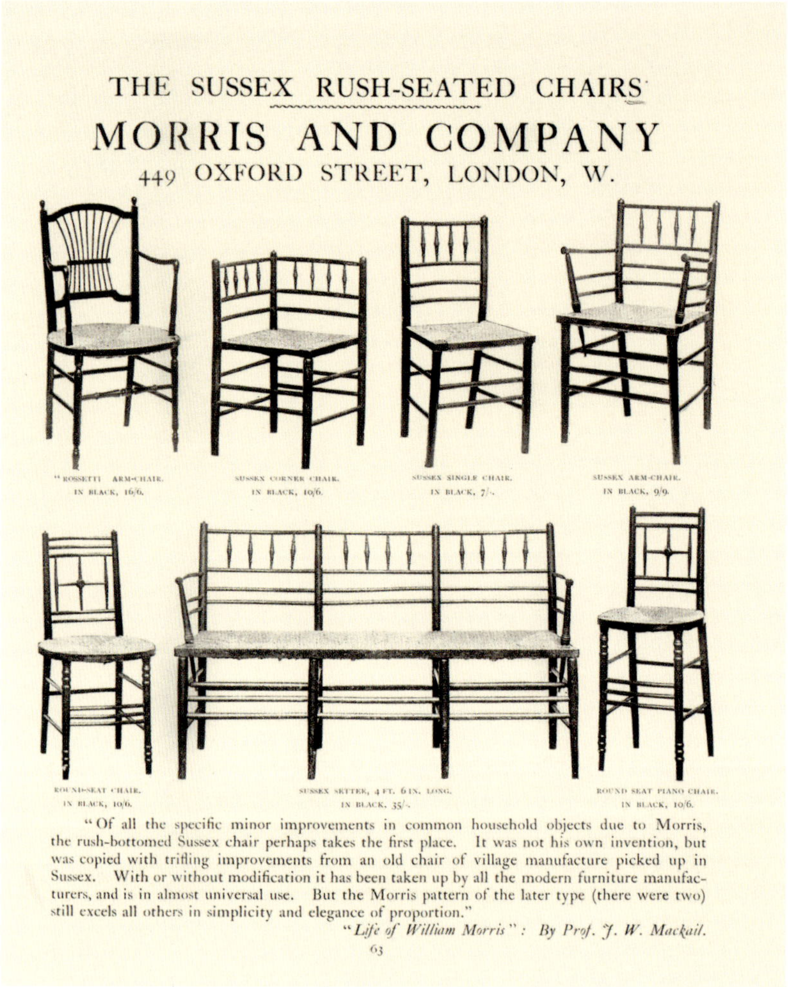

Fig.166 (above left) ***Rossetti at work on 'The Day Dream'*, Frederic Shields, 1880.**
Ashmolean Museum, University of Oxford

Fig.167 (above right) **The *Sussex* rush-seated chair range from Morris & Co.'s catalogue.**
V&A

more common. In 1887 Morris & Co. acquired Holland & Sons' cabinet-making workshops in Pimlico and inherited a skilled team of craftsmen capable of manufacturing Jack's highly finished designs, which often involved delicate inlay and marquetry work. The patterns frequently echoed the style of foliate designs found in Morris's textiles and wallpapers. The firm exhibited Jack's furniture at the Manchester Jubilee Exhibition of 1887 (fig.168) and at the early Arts and Crafts Exhibition Society shows. At the first exhibition in 1888, for example, Morris & Co.'s contribution included an inlaid mahogany cabinet and sideboard made to his designs.

Jack's work for the firm was so different – in materials, technique and style – from Morris's early furniture designs that it has often been argued that by the 1880s Morris took no interest in this side of the firm's business. While he was undoubtedly busy with many other pursuits, it is extremely unlikely that he had no involvement at all. He certainly would not have allowed the firm to retail furniture of which he disapproved. One of Morris's strengths was to recognize talent in others and throughout his career he surrounded himself with like-minded collaborators. The sophistication of Jack's furniture designs for the firm suited the type of interiors that Morris & Co. was designing in the late 1880s and 1890s. Indeed, listed in Jack's account book for 1890–1, are various items of furniture for Buller's Wood, Kent, the house that Morris & Co. was commissioned to decorate for the Sanderson family. As well as furniture, Jack was also entrusted with designing architectural fittings and fixtures including chimneypieces and window and door surrounds. Some of these had carved elements, and as Amy Gaimster has argued, it may well have been Jack's practical understanding of woodcarving that encouraged Morris to employ him. Jack continued to supply Morris & Co. with designs after Morris's death; the last documented instance was in 1907 when he designed a lectern and a carved prie-dieu.

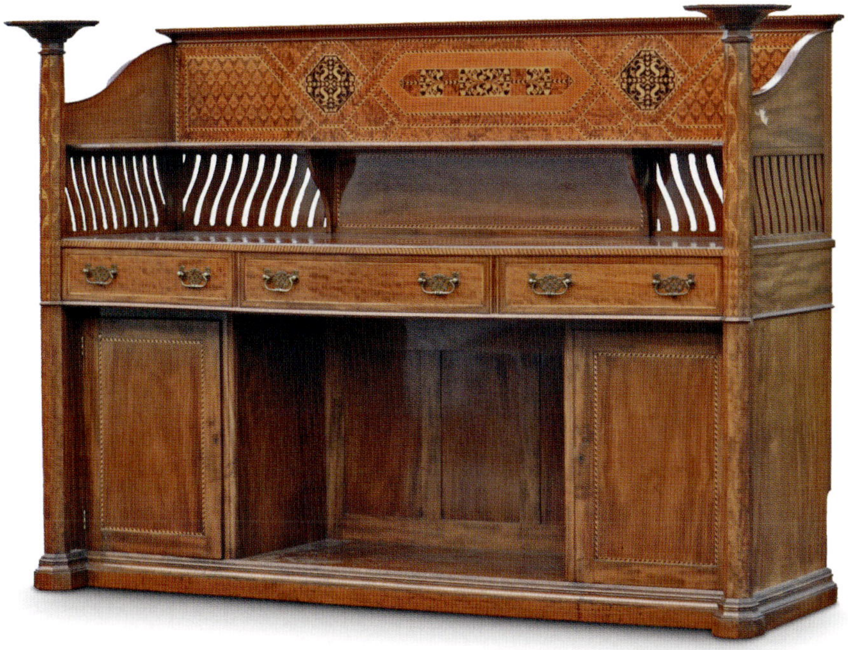

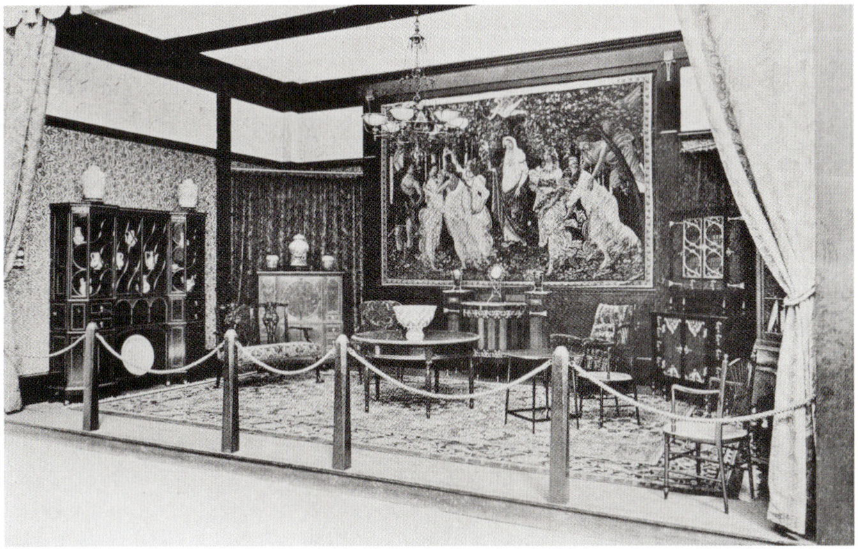

Fig.168 (top) **Sideboard, designed by George Jack and exhibited at the Manchester Jubilee Exhibition in 1887.**
Private collection

Fig.169 (above) **Morris & Co.'s stand at the Franco-British Exhibition of 1908, including furniture designed for the firm by George Jack and W.A.S. Benson.**

It is clear when comparing surviving examples of furniture, contemporary photographs, the firm's catalogues and other information that pieces were made to order from designs kept in the shop, sometimes involving variations on the original.

An article in *The Cabinet Maker* (1 November 1882) claimed, 'Messrs. Morris do not turn out furniture wholesale: they make each article to order, and give it an individual character, and an adaptability to the position which it is intended to occupy.' At some point, possibly around the time the firm acquired Holland & Sons' Pimlico workshops, furniture started to be stamped with the Oxford Street address and a batch number. These numbers have never been systematically studied but so far no corresponding ledgers or documentation have surfaced.

Involvement in furniture manufacture taught Morris that his aspiration to provide good design at an accessible price could not be achieved under the capitalist system. In February 1881 he acknowledged this when asked for advice by the Manchester philanthropist Thomas Coglan Horsfall, Morris wrote,

> The furniture for a workman's cottage? What can be done? If it be well made instead of ill made it will cost not twice as much, but twenty times as much: crede mihi experte. I have made rough furniture, oftenest of the type of what would have been found in a yeoman's stead of old, and I have been aghast at the cost of it.

Despite his personal disappointment, the furniture produced by his firm and under his supervision helped to encourage a radical change in contemporary attitudes to furniture design. After Morris's early experiments with painted furniture, Webb undoubtedly made the most original contribution. In the twentieth century, the firm relied on reusing existing designs and offering a wide range of reproduction furniture. The photograph of its stand at the Franco-British Exhibition of 1908, which included designs by W.A.S. Benson, shows just how conservative its output had become (fig.169). The initiative fell instead to the second generation of Arts and Crafts practitioners, several of whom set up workshops in the Cotswolds, and who, unlike Morris, both designed and made their own furniture.

IX.1

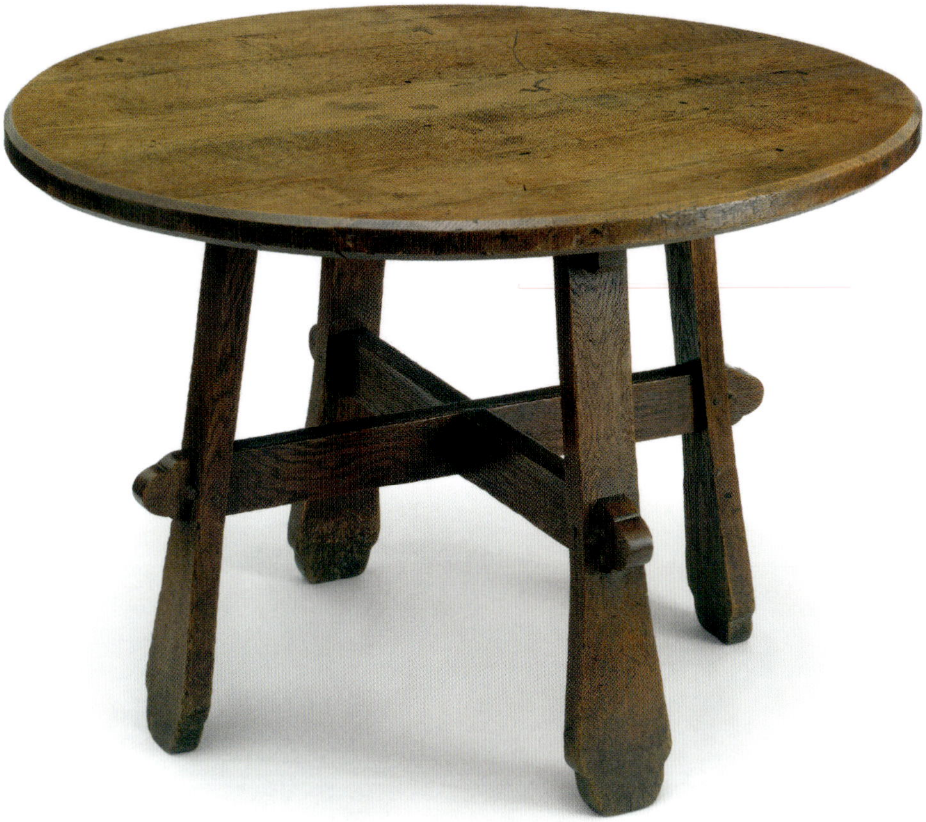

IX.1
Table
Designed by George Edmund Street
Manufactured by George Myers, *c.*1854
Oak, 68 x 102 x 98 cm
V&A (W.88–1975)

Street designed little domestic furniture because his practice was primarily involved in ecclesiastical commissions. However, his furniture for Cuddesdon College, near Oxford, built to his designs between 1852 and 1854, included both large dining tables and these smaller versions for use in the students' rooms.

This table, with its revealed construction and structural honesty, clearly reflects the influence of A.W.N. Pugin, and one of Pugin's designs in the V&A shows a table of similar form (E.1630–1912). George Myers, Pugin's builder, who also worked for Street at Cuddesdon College, is known to have made domestic and ecclesiastical furniture and woodwork, notably the cabinet designed by Pugin for his own dining room at The Grange, Ramsgate. Street's influence on his pupils, Webb and Morris, is illustrated in the very similar table made for Red Lion Square (IX.2).

IX.2

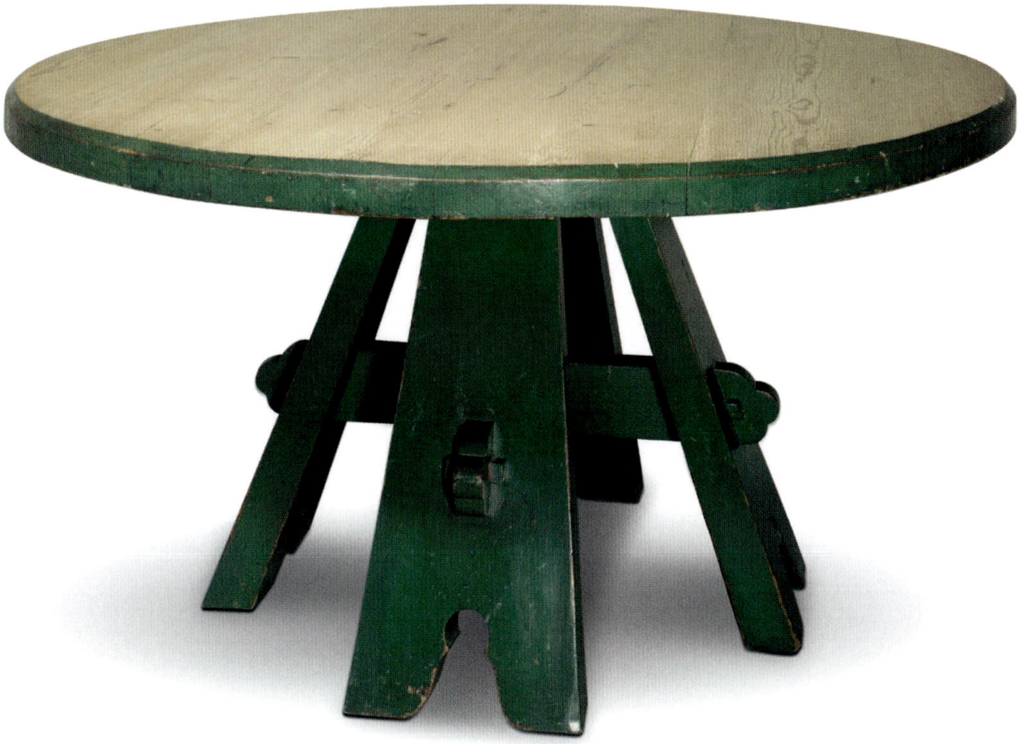

IX.2
Table
Designed by William Morris, *c.*1856
Probably made by Henry Price, Christopher Street, Hatton Garden
Painted deal, 71 x 141 x 138.4 cm
The Wilson Art Gallery and Museum, Cheltenham (1982.1114)
Bought with the assistance of the MGC/V&A Purchase Grant Fund, 1982

As Annette Carruthers first argued, this table was made for Red Lion Square. It closely resembles the table with splayed legs in Burne-Jones's sketch of the cluttered interior (fig.156) and its robustness fits Rossetti's memorable description of a round table 'as firm, and as heavy, as a rock'. Although the simple construction could have been executed by a joiner, tables were listed among the items made for Morris by the cabinet maker Henry Price, who worked for Tommy Baker's 'cabinet factory' in Hatton Garden.

Clearly influenced by Street's Cuddesdon table, the design was possibly a collaboration between Morris and Webb. The plank-like construction and Gothic detail of the legs are similar to Webb's early trestle tables (fig.162). The green paint was added later on May Morris's instructions and beneath it are traces of a red-brown layer. It was photographed in May's Hammersmith home in 1923 and subsequently furnished Kelmscott Village Hall.

IX.3

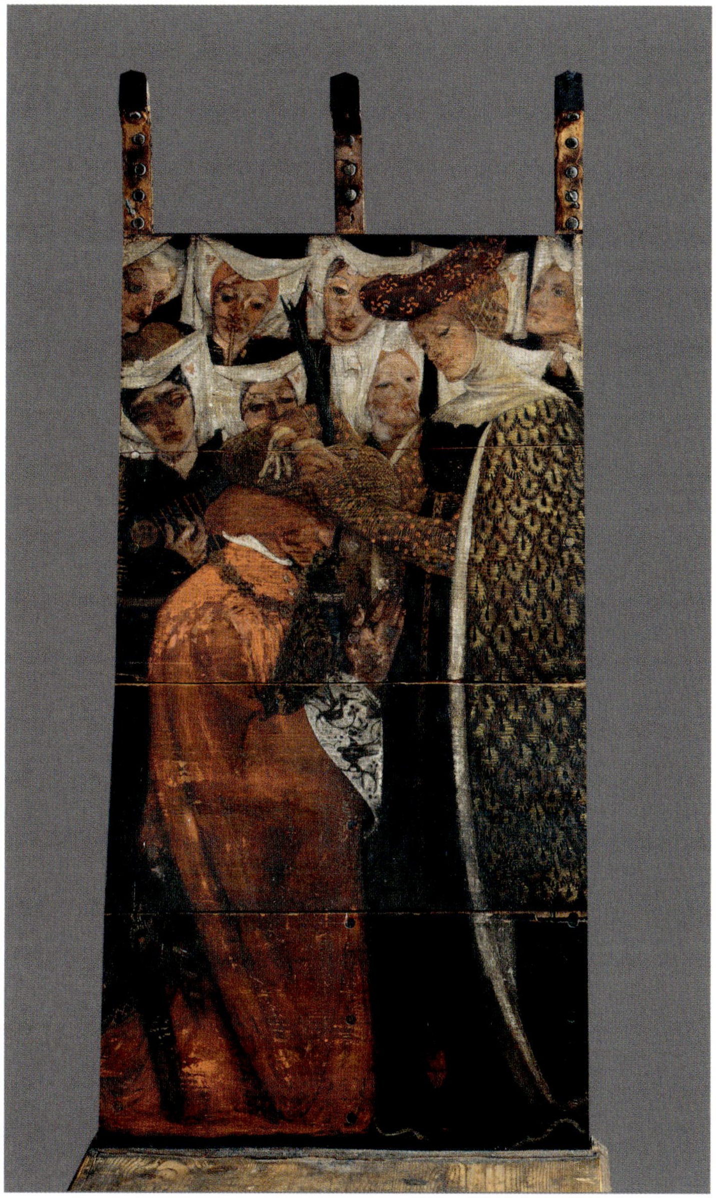

IX.3

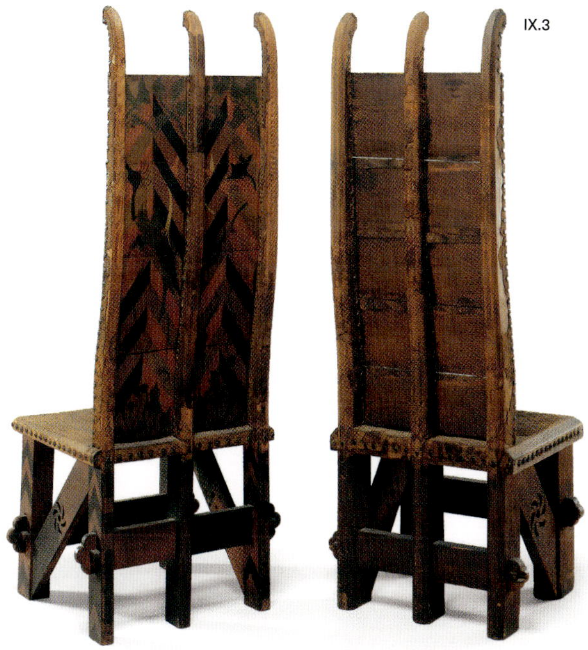

IX.4

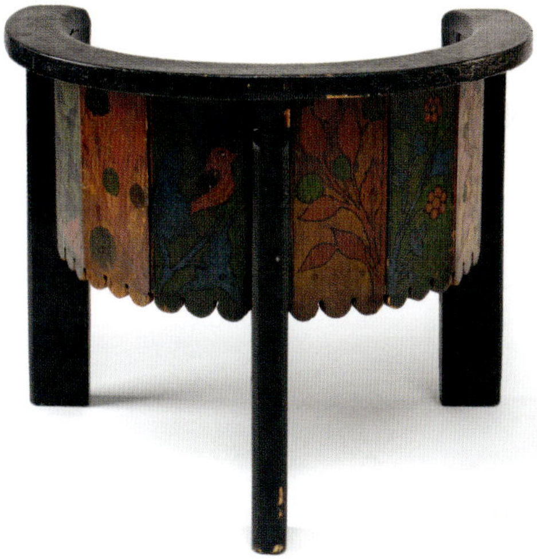

IX.3
Glorious Guendolen's Golden Hair* and *The Arming of a Knight
William Morris and Dante Gabriel Rossetti, 1856 and *c.*1857–8
Made by Henry Price, Christopher Street, Hatton Garden
Painted deal, leather and nails, 141.3 x 43.2 x 43.2 cm, 141.3 x 47.6 x 49.5 cm
Delaware Art Museum, Wilmington, DE (1997–13, 1997–12)
Acquired through the bequest of Doris Wright Anderson and through the F.V. du Pont Acquisition Fund, 1997

These distinctive high-backed chairs were designed by Morris for Red Lion Square and later used at Red House (see also fig.20). Their construction is similar, though not identical. As Jan Marsh has observed, the design combines crude block-like elements, such as the seat and front legs, with chamfered and sinuously shaped uprights forming an unusual trio of back legs. The trefoil-shaped tenons echo those on Morris's round table (IX.2). Leather once covered the seats and uprights but has virtually disappeared. It was thought that the pierced spiral motif on the diagonal stretchers was adapted from a stool in Rossetti's *Hesterna Rosa* (1853, Tate), but Alastair Grieve has shown that Rossetti later reworked this element, presumably inspired by Morris's chairs. It also appears on furniture in several of his medieval watercolours including *The Blue Closet* (1856–7, Tate) and *The Tune of Seven Towers* (fig.105).

Rossetti and Morris collaborated on the decoration, painting directly onto the wood. Morris is credited with the lettering (he was experimenting with calligraphy around this time) and the pattern work. Rossetti's correspondence suggests that *Guendolen*, inscribed with a line from Morris's poem 'Rapunzel', was largely complete by December 1856. The diagonal composition shows Guendolen leaning from her tower, her long hair tumbling down towards Prince Sebald, and was ideally suited to the vertical format of the chairs. The subject matter of the second, more highly finished chair, remains ambiguous but it shows a courtly scene with a medieval lady bestowing her favour on a kneeling knight (without armour). The costumes were adapted from Camille Bonnard's *Costumes Historiques*, a sourcebook of medieval dress.

IX.4
Chair
Designed by William Morris, *c.*1856
Painted deal, 63 x 75 x 51.5 cm
William Morris Gallery, London Borough of Waltham Forest (H26)
Given by Dr Charles Edward Newman

This tub chair was almost certainly part of the suite of furniture that Morris designed for Red Lion Square. The painted decoration on the scallop-edged panels is very similar to the back of *The Arming of a Knight* (IX.3), particularly the treatment of the leaves and the colour palette. It was later taken to Red House and was probably one of two semi-circular chairs that passed to the Heathcote family, who purchased the property from Morris in 1866. The second chair has never been traced.

IX.5

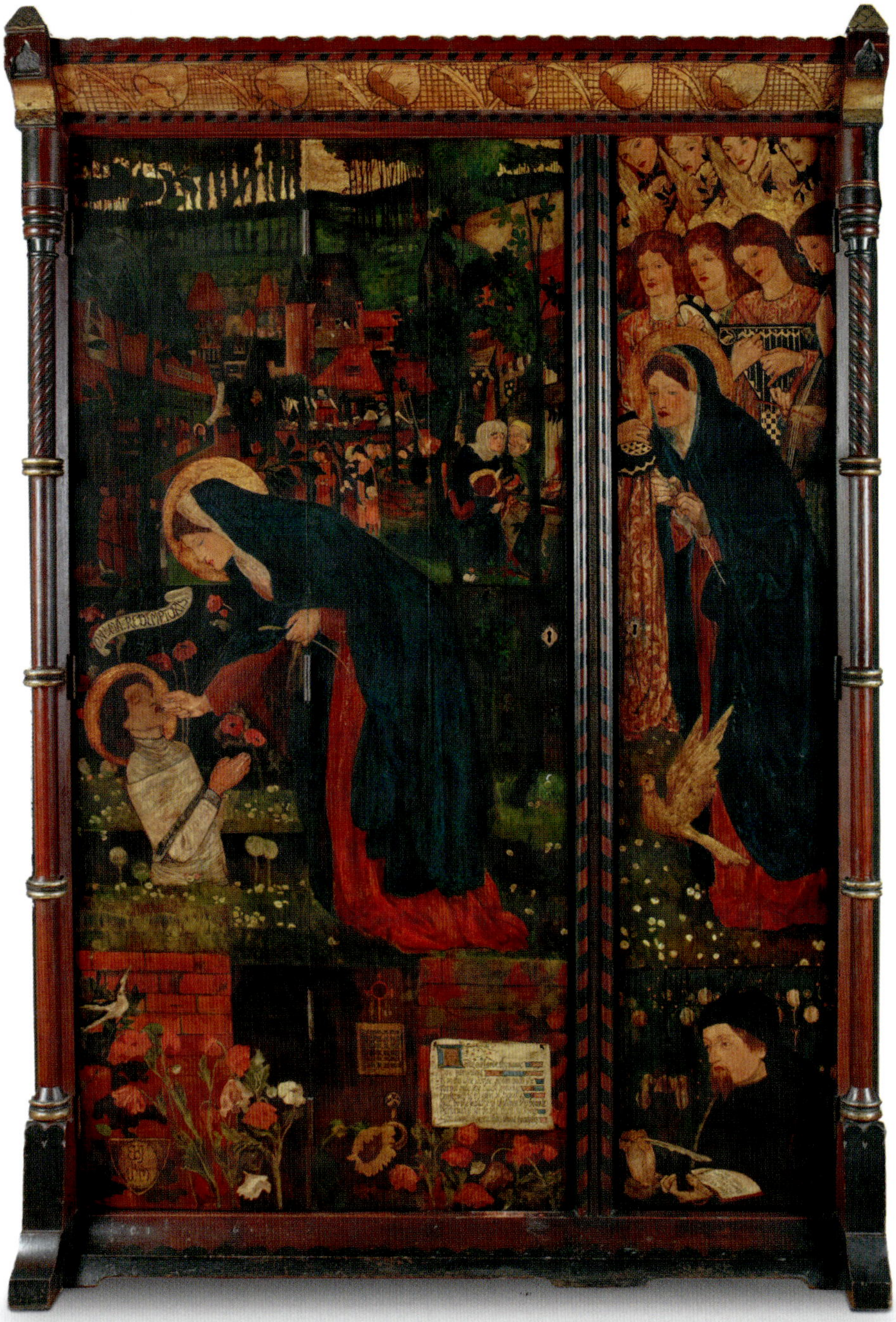

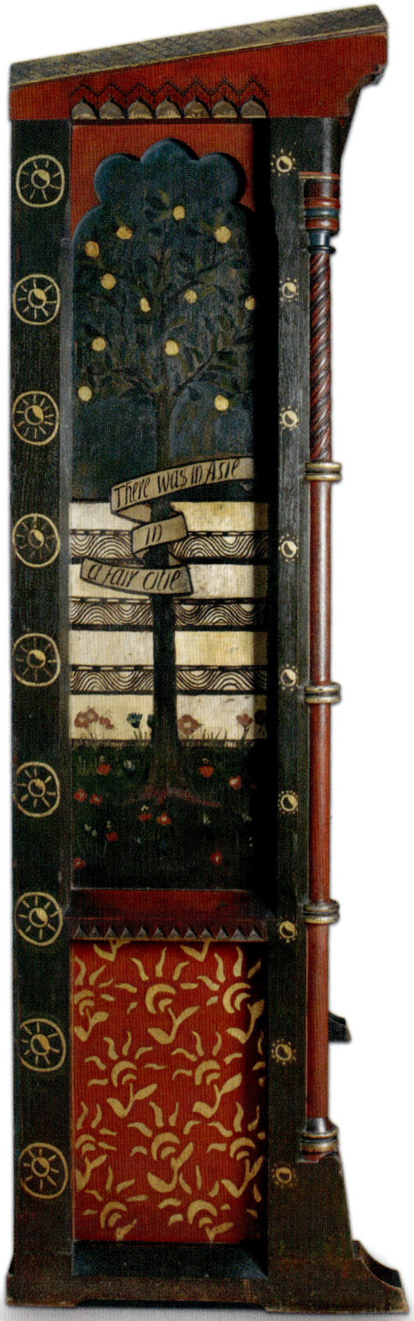

IX.5
The Prioress's Tale **wardrobe**
Philip Webb, Edward Burne-Jones and William Morris, *c.*1858–60
Possibly made by Henry Price, Christopher Street, Hatton Garden
Oil and metal leaf on deal and oak, 219.7 x 157.5 x 53.7 cm
Ashmolean Museum, University of Oxford (WA1939.2)
Bequeathed by May Morris, 1939

This painted wardrobe exemplifies the idea of 'storytelling' furniture. Created as a wedding gift for Morris and Jane, it remained a treasured family possession, used in the master bedroom at Red House and later in the drawing room at Kelmscott House in Hammersmith (fig.15). It is Webb's earliest known design for furniture and, as Tessa Wild has argued, its subtle Gothic detailing provided a 'stylistic lexicon' for Red House. Compare, for example, the crenellated banding along the top of the wardrobe with the dining-room dresser (fig.159).

In the spring of 1858, Burne-Jones began to paint the doors with scenes from Chaucer's 'Prioress's Tale', modelling the figure of the Virgin on Jane. It was his first ambitious painting in oil and Webb's hinged door provided a large canvas for the main narrative.

According to the tale, a Christian boy sings a hymn in praise of Mary each day as he walks through the Jewish quarter, angering the inhabitants who conspire to have him murdered. His body is thrown in a privy pit but is discovered when the Virgin places a grain of corn in his mouth allowing him to sing again.

The most thorough discussion of the iconography and its anti-Semitic associations can be found in Allison Stielau's 'Habits of Encounter' (2009). As argued elsewhere in this volume, the interior doors showing women at their toilette were likely to have been painted by Morris before the wardrobe was assembled (VI.4). As an early collaborative venture, reflecting the friends' interests in literature and merging the fine and decorative arts, the significance of this piece cannot be overstated.

Fig.170 **The side of the wardrobe, the scroll bears the opening lines of the 'Prioress's Tale'. The painted decoration is attributed to Morris and Webb and the fruit tree and patterns were later echoed in the interior decoration of Red House.**

IX.6

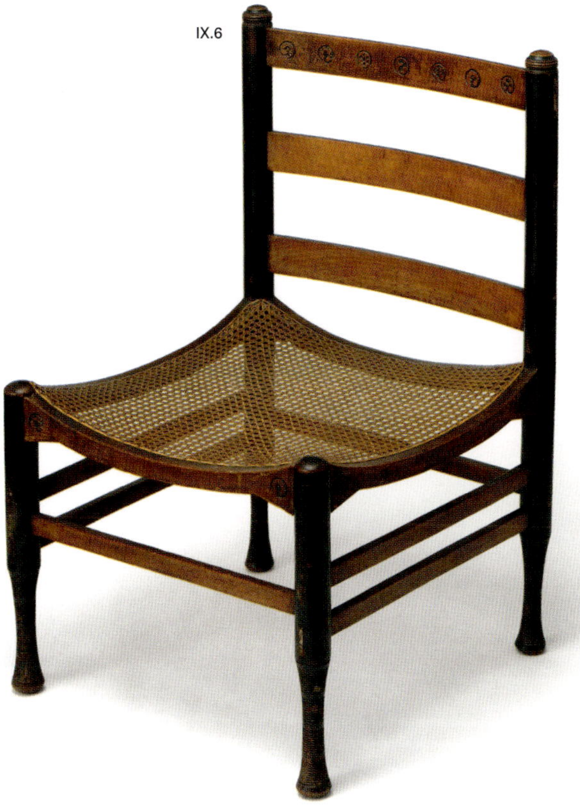

IX.6 **Egyptian chair**
Designed by Ford Madox Brown, *c.*1857–8
Unknown maker
Satinized wood, partly ebonized with cane seat, 84.5 x 55 x 54.5 cm
V&A (W.13–1985)

Other members of Morris's circle were designing furniture for their own use in the late 1850s. In 1856 or 1857 Madox Brown had a medieval-style oak table made by a carpenter to his own design. In December 1857 he visited William Holman Hunt and saw a pair of elaborate inlaid Egyptian-style chairs designed by Hunt and made by the fashionable firm of J.G. Crace (Birmingham Museum and Art Gallery). According to Hunt, Madox Brown 'idolised' these chairs and 'set a carpenter to work to make some of similar proportions.' Hunt's source was an ancient Egyptian stool and other Egyptian furniture at the British Museum.

In his diary for 17 January 1858, Madox Brown recorded that since the previous November he had created four designs for chairs, which probably included this example. He simplified Hunt's design – the chair has the same low curved seat and turned legs but a ladder-back in place of diagonal bars and incised circles instead of inlay. It was one of a pair which both remained in Madox Brown's possession until his death. An article in *The Artist* (May 1898) illustrated the chair, claiming that it was manufactured by Morris, Marshall, Faulkner & Co. To date there is no conclusive evidence that the design was sold commercially but the chair is an interesting precursor to Madox Brown's later designs for the firm (IX.11). MB

IX.7
***Ladies and Animals* sideboard**
Painted by Edward Burne-Jones, 1860
Unknown maker
Oil and gold and silver leaf on deal, 116.8 x 152.4 x 73.7 cm
V&A (W.10–1953)
Given by Margaret Mackail

IX.7

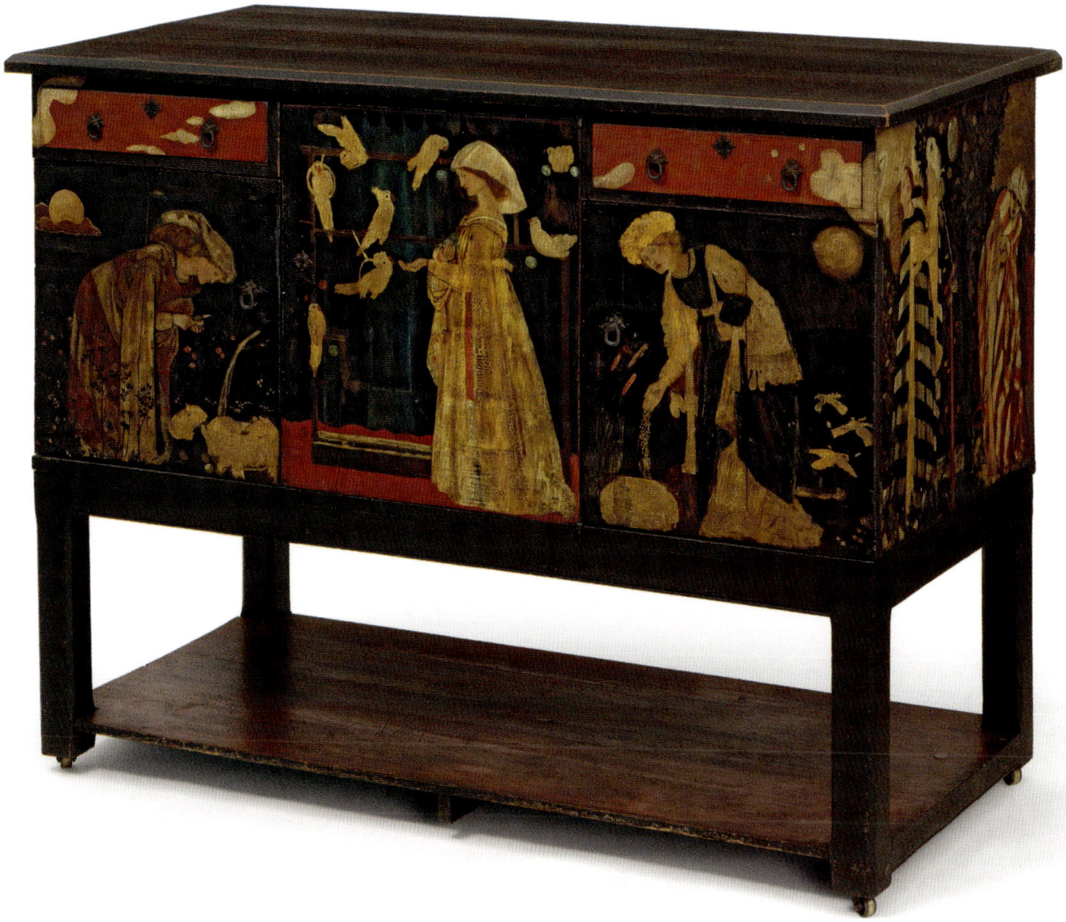

Burne-Jones painted this sideboard, which was already in his possession, to amuse himself in the unsettled week before his marriage in June 1860. He described the subject simply as 'ladies and animals'. The three scenes on the front show 'kind and attentive' ladies feeding pigs, parrots and fish, while the panels on each end depict the cruel treatment of an owl and some goldfish, counterbalanced by an attack of angry bees and a frightening newt. Sketches survive at Birmingham Museum and Art Gallery.

The arrangement of the painted decoration is carefully contained within the structure of the sideboard and the red-brown finish on the top and bottom shelf is similar to that used on the stand of the *St George* cabinet. After the Burne-Joneses moved to Kensington in 1865 the sideboard was varnished and it is shown beneath a low mirror in Thomas Rooke's watercolour of their dining room at The Grange, in Fulham (fig.162). The details were once easier to read but the backgrounds have darkened over time.

IX.8

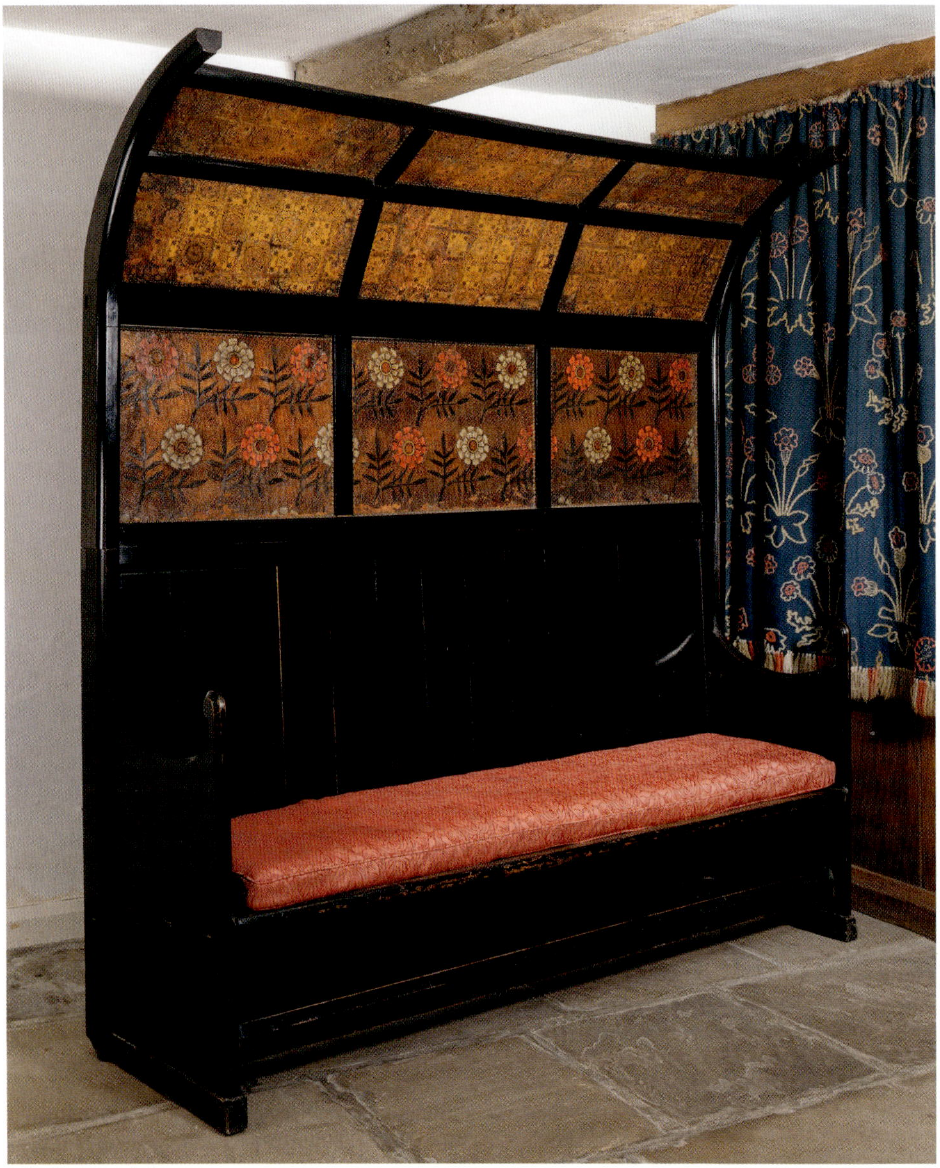

IX.8
Settle
Designed by Philip Webb, *c.*1860
Ebonized oak, embossed leather, painted and gilded, 209 x 194 x 56.5 cm
The Society of Antiquaries of London, Kelmscott Manor (KM034)

This settle was made for Red House where, according to Aymer Vallance, it stood by the fireplace in the dining room, and was later moved to the drawing room at Kelmscott House (fig.15). The design, with its canopied top, drew inspiration from traditional, vernacular settles and also from Morris's high-backed 'medieval' chairs (IX.3). The reverse is decorated with three panels of painted botanical motifs in green and white. Webb's account book for 1862–3 includes designs for painted and lacquered leather panels, indicating a demand for such decoration, and the ebonized finish was also used on the firm's furniture.

Several versions of this settle were made by the firm, some with gilt gesso decoration by Kate Faulkner and others with designs by John Henry Dearle. The firm's catalogue offered settles with embossed leather panels at £35 or undecorated at £30. An oak example, with elaborate gesso work, was supplied for Wickham Flower's drawing room at Old Swan House, Chelsea, and photographs of it *in situ* were reproduced in *The Studio* (September 1893) and Morris & Co.'s *Specimens of Furniture* catalogue (*c.*1911).

IX.9

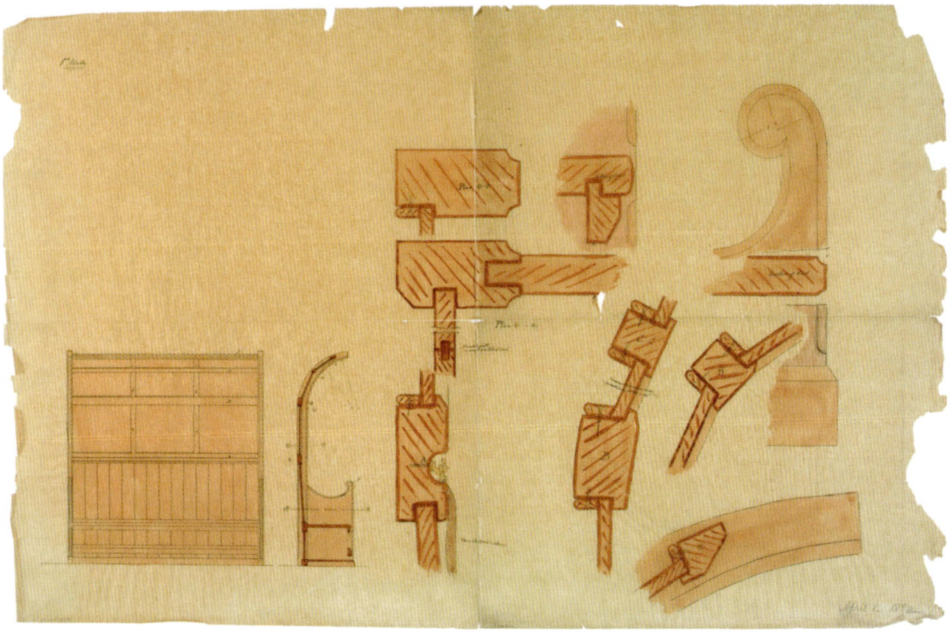

IX.9
Design drawing for settle
Philip Webb, dated 1 April 1882
Pencil, ink and wash on tracing paper, 39 x 50 cm
V&A (E.395:2–2014)
Accepted in lieu of inheritance tax from the estate of John Brandon-Jones, 2014

This drawing shows an elevation of the rear and a section through the side of the settle, as well as details of the joinery. One of the details includes a small hook, designed to hang a 'thin stuffed cushion' from the back of the seat. It is very rare for construction drawings like this to survive for the firm's furniture. The profile of the bench end was echoed in other furniture at Red House, for which the settle was first conceived.

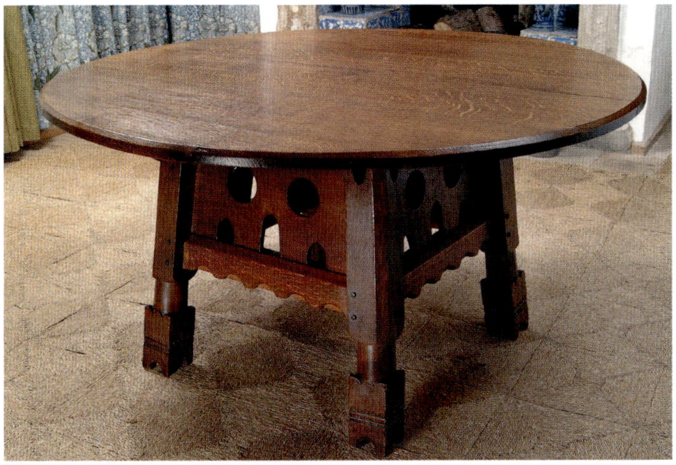

IX.10

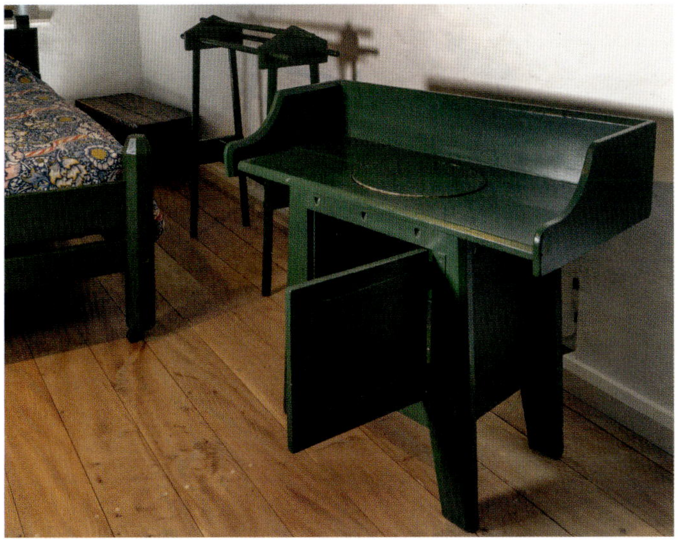

IX.11

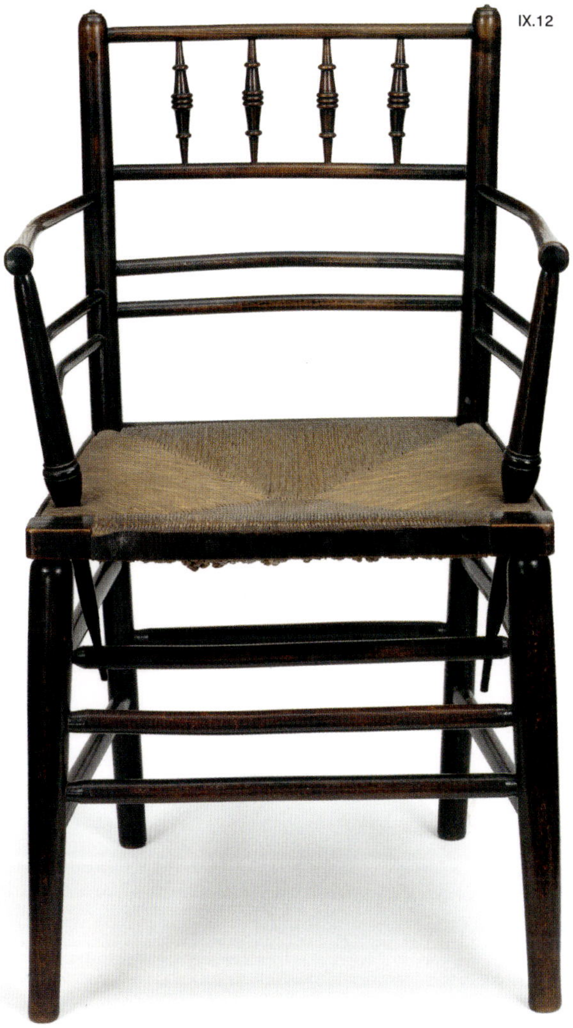

IX.12

IX.10
Round table
Designed by Philip Webb, *c.*1860
Oak, 72 x 142.5 cm
The Society of Antiquaries of London, Kelmscott Manor (KM282)

This table may be the one described in the memorandum attached to May Morris's will as 'Red House the first made' (*The Antiquaries Journal,* 43:1, 1963). It was possibly used in the drawing room, and the design fits into that environment of youthful enthusiasm for the thirteenth and fourteenth centuries that Morris, Webb and their friends embraced. The combination of boarded sides pierced with openings, massive column-like legs with crenellated bases and solid top results in a truly medieval-looking piece.

It illustrates Webb's interest in medieval details, probably taken from architectural sources, particularly church woodwork and stonework, rather than a dependence on Puginian principles of revealed construction. The crenellated bases on the legs were also used on a side table for the Burne-Jones family, probably supplied about 1865 (IX.25).

IX.11
Washstand and towel horse
Designed by Ford Madox Brown, *c.*1860–2
Manufactured by Morris, Marshall, Faulkner & Co.
Painted wood, originally stained, 88 x 93 x 63 cm, 106 x 92.5 x 71 cm
The Society of Antiquaries of London, Kelmscott Manor (KM298, KM304)

May Morris attributed the bed in this photograph to Webb, but the washstand and towel horse were designed by Madox Brown. These examples were probably used at Red House and are now at Kelmscott Manor. The green paint is a later addition; they were originally stained green at Madox Brown's suggestion. In 1865, the firm's business manager Warington Taylor recommended that the practice of staining furniture be discontinued as it was difficult to remove water marks.

Madox Brown's account book with Morris, Marshall, Faulkner & Co., covering the years 1862–75, is preserved in the Violet Hunt Papers at Cornell University. On 4 September 1862, the firm supplied him with '3 toilet horses; 3 toilet tables; 2 washstands' for his own use. It is not clear how many of these designs were put into commercial production. Unpretentiously simple and massive in form, Madox Brown's bedroom furniture was suitable for execution by a joiner rather than a cabinet maker.

IX.12
***Sussex* armchair**
Possibly designed by Philip Webb, early 1860s
Manufactured by Morris, Marshall, Faulkner & Co. and later Morris & Co.
Ebonized beech with rush seat, 85 x 52 x 44 cm
V&A (Circ.288–1960)

One of the most recognizable pieces of furniture associated with Morris and the firm, the *Sussex* armchair in its quirky angularity became an icon of artistic taste and was much copied, notably by Liberty and Heal & Son's. It is based on a Regency prototype, a painted chair or armchair, with turned uprights and imitation bamboo frame. Mackail's comment that the chair was adapted from a country chair found in Sussex suggests the origin of the name, not necessarily that the design was typical for chairs made in that region.

Black or red *Sussex* chairs were used at Red House and Edward and Georgiana Burne-Jones ordered black chairs with rush seats from the Industrial Home for Destitute Boys on Euston Road in 1860. Chosen by Myles Birket Foster for The Hill, Witley in Surrey, they were later recommended by Robert Edis in *Decoration and Furniture of Town Houses* (1881) as excellent, comfortable and artistic, at 9*s.* 9*d.*, although 'somewhat rough in make'. *Sussex* armchairs furnished the studios of Burne-Jones and the sculptor Alfred Gilbert, and one appears in Picasso's 1922 drawing of Bertie Landsberg (Fitzwilliam Museum).

IX.13

***King René's Honeymoon* cabinet**

Designed by John Pollard Seddon, assisted by William Burges, 1861

Manufactured by Thomas Seddon, 1861–2

Oak inlaid with various woods, painted panels and metalwork, 133.4 x 252 x 87 cm

V&A (W.10–1927)

Purchased with Art Fund support

This cabinet, designed in 1861 by Seddon for his architectural office, was made by his father's cabinet-making firm. Seddon also designed the metalwork and inlay but commissioned ten panels depicting the Fine and Applied Arts from the Morris firm (J.P. Seddon, *King René's Honeymoon Cabinet*, 1898). Burges drew the lion rampant for the Seddon coat of arms on the sloping top.

In 1852 Seddon's brother, the painter Thomas Seddon, had written to Madox Brown expressing his admiration for King René of Anjou, a noted artist and patron. Madox Brown later suggested imaginary incidents from the king's life as a suitable theme for the cabinet and designed the left-hand panel representing *Architecture*. *Painting* and *Sculpture* were by Burne-Jones, while Rossetti was responsible for *Music* and also for the smaller panel, *Gardening*. The other small panels were *Embroidery* by Val Prinsep, *Pottery*, *Weaving*, *Ironwork* (showing Morris as a smith) and *Glass Blowing*. Morris designed the decorative backgrounds.

Displayed by Seddon at the 1862 International Exhibition, the cabinet received mixed reviews. However, the South Kensington Museum, recognizing its importance, attempted, unsuccessfully, to purchase it from the exhibition and finally acquired it from Seddon's daughter Margaret Birch in 1927. Several of the firm's designs were adapted for stained glass (VII.13) and worked up into paintings.

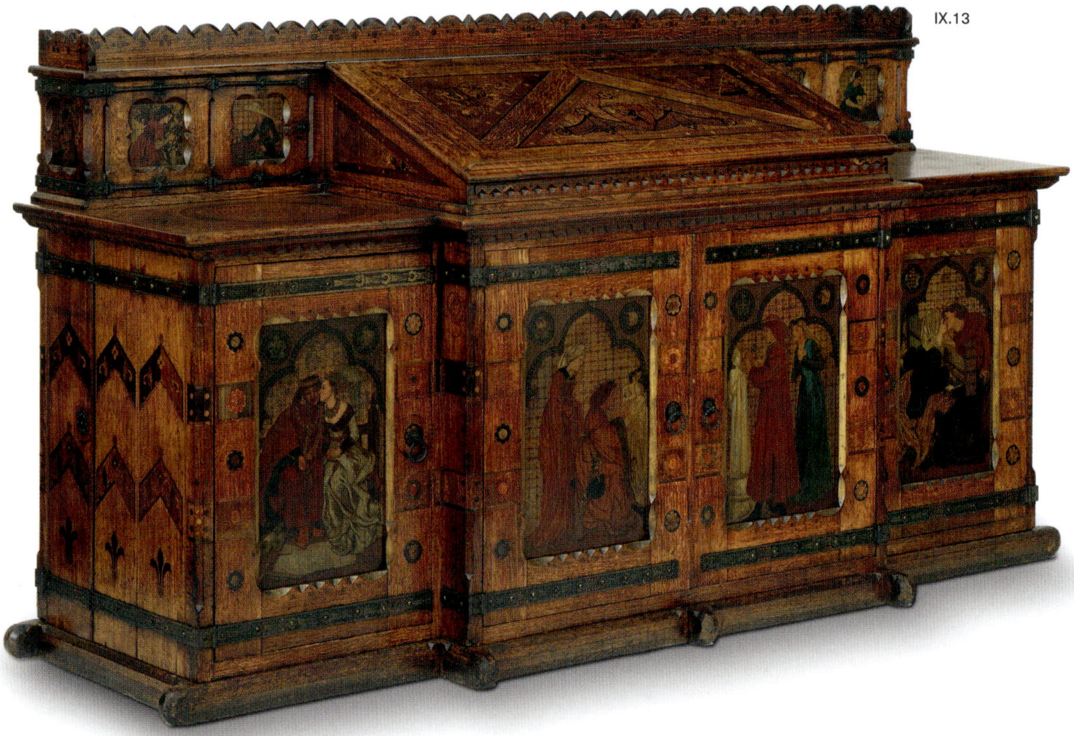

IX.13

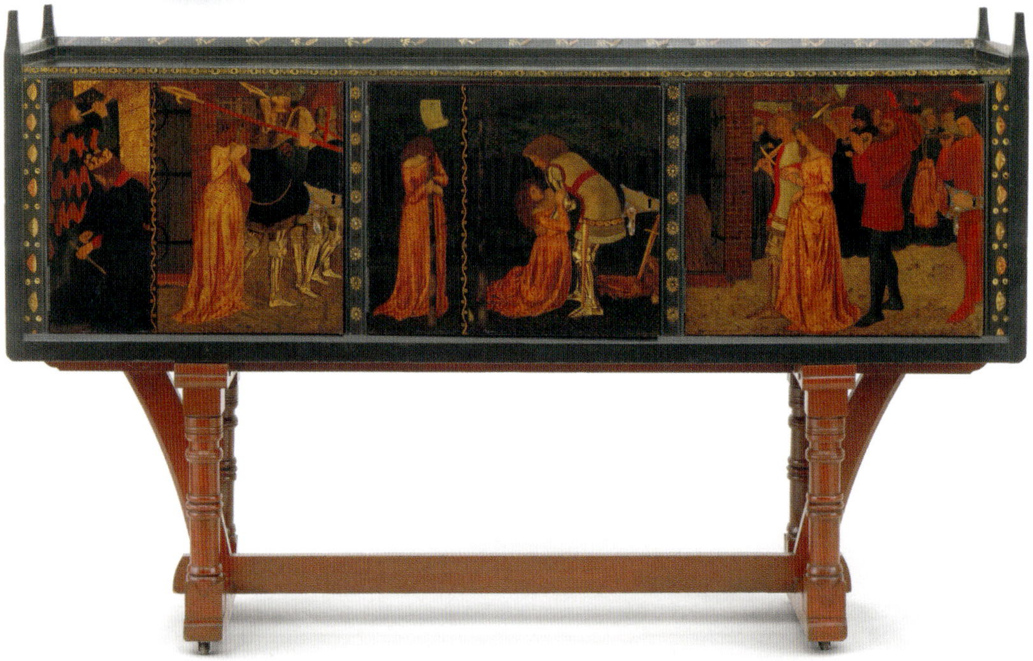

IX.14

IX.14

***St George* cabinet**

Designed by Philip Webb and painted by William Morris

Manufactured by Morris, Marshall, Faulkner & Co., 1861–2

Mahogany, oak and deal, painted and gilded, copper handles, 96 x 178 x 43 cm

V&A (341–1906)

This cabinet was made for the 1862 International Exhibition, the first public showing of the firm's work. Webb charged £1 10*s*. for his design and Morris conceived and executed the decoration (see VI.24). Rossetti described it enthusiastically in a letter to Charles Eliot Norton on 9 January 1862, 'I wish you could see a painted cabinet with the history of St George, and other furniture of great beauty which we have in hand.' It was exhibited with some of Webb's drinking glasses on top and priced at £50.

The Building News (8 August 1862) criticized the lack of co-ordination between the structure and the painted panels: 'This studied affectation of truthfulness, in placing ironwork in the midst of a picture, is one of the many sins which have to be purged from the Mediævalists.' Morris used Burges's revived medieval method of layering tinted varnishes on silver leaf for the decoration inside the cabinet (see fig.229), but did not follow his lead in integrating painted decoration into the overall structure. The cabinet appears in a list of the firm's stock approved at a meeting on 11 February 1863. At a later date it belonged to Laurence Hodson of Compton Hall, near Wolverhampton, an enthusiastic client of the firm and was acquired from his sale (Christie's, 6 July 1906).

IX.15

***The Backgammon Players* cabinet**
Philip Webb and Edward Burne-Jones
Manufactured by Morris, Marshall, Faulkner & Co., 1861–2
Painted and gilded deal, oil on leather and metalwork, 185.4 x 114.3 x 53.3 cm
Metropolitan Museum of Art, New York (26.54)
Rogers Fund, 1926

Webb's accounts of 1861 record a payment of £1 10*s*. for the design of the 'chess players' cabinet. It was displayed at the 1862 International Exhibition and purchased by the politician Henry Labouchère, Baron Taunton, for Quantock Lodge in Somerset. A letter from the firm in the Metropolitan Museum archives (11 December 1862) records that it had to be repaired after minor damage in transit to and from the exhibition.

Burne-Jones painted the leather panels with a scene of a couple playing backgammon in a garden setting. Often said to recall the atmosphere of the garden at Red House with its trellised enclosures, the subject also appears in medieval manuscripts. He executed several works on this theme, including an exquisite large-scale pencil drawing of similar dimensions to the cabinet doors (1861, Fitzwilliam Museum). When it came to painting the cabinet, he simplified the detail, especially the background, but added patterns to the costumes.

The extensive patterning on both the exterior and interior (fig.171) has all the hallmarks of Webb's design, though an entry in Burne-Jones's account book for the period January–April 1862 ('Gold cabinet woodwork 5£ painting 10£') suggests he may have had a hand in its execution. Compared to the painted patterns on other furniture produced by the firm, including the *St George* cabinet, it is extremely refined and carefully applied.

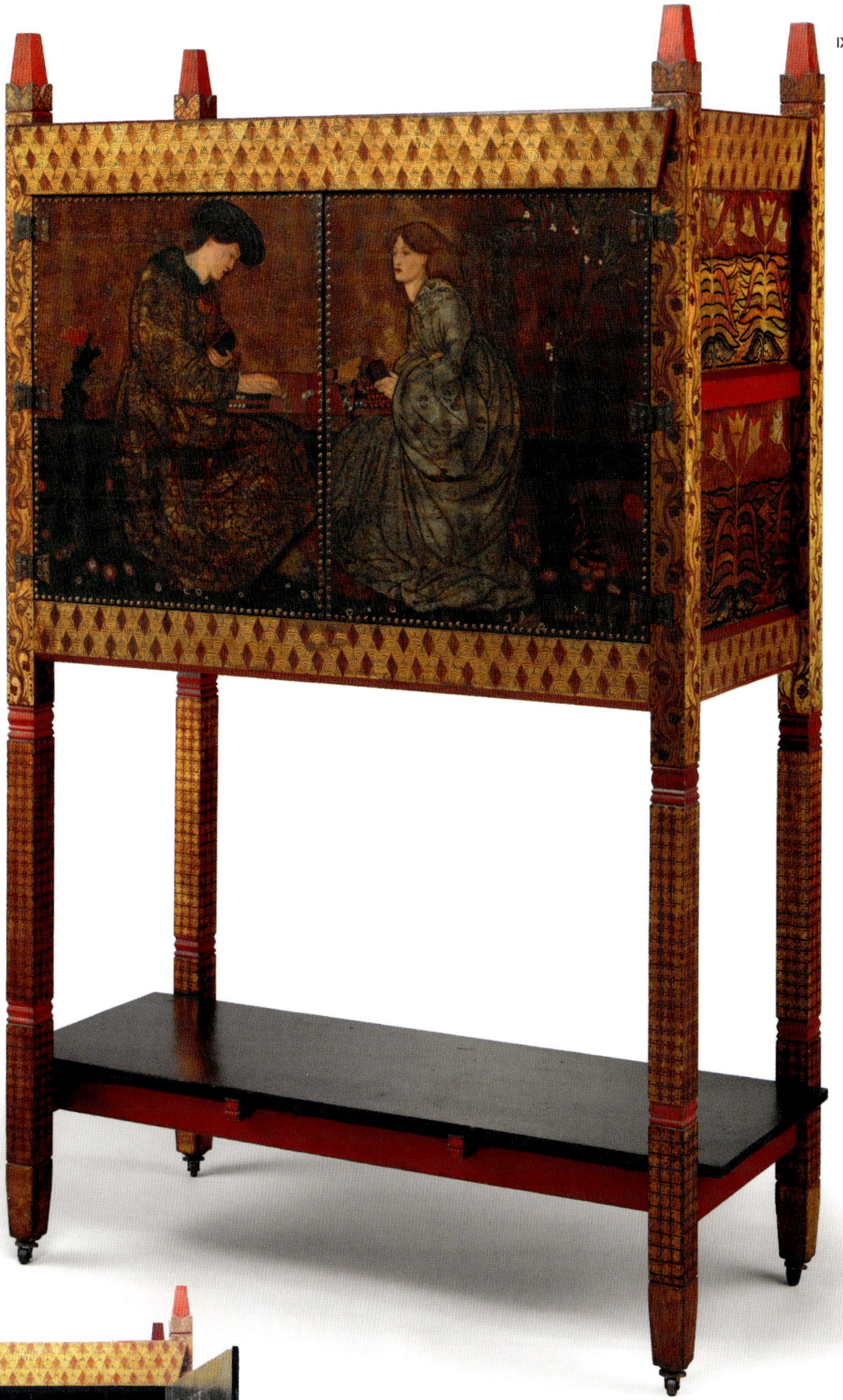

IX.15

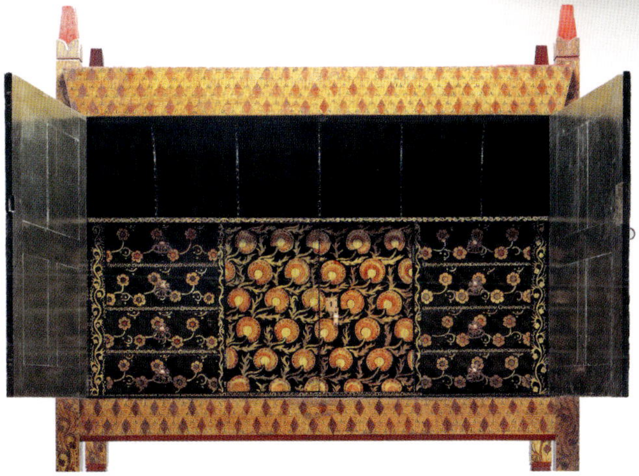

Fig.171 **Interior of *The Backgammon Players* cabinet, suggesting the influence of Japanese lacquerware.**

IX.16

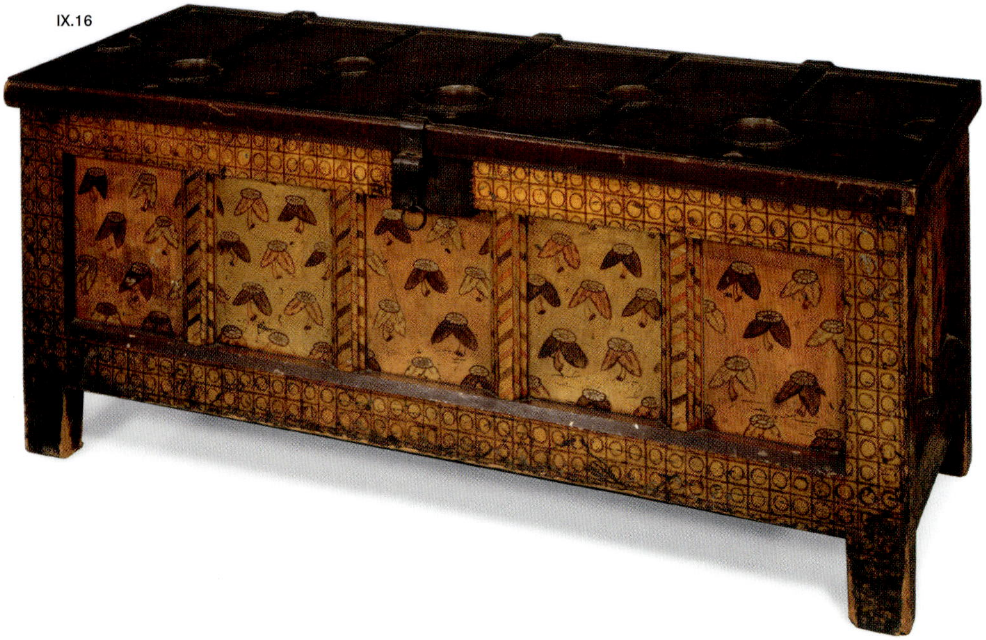

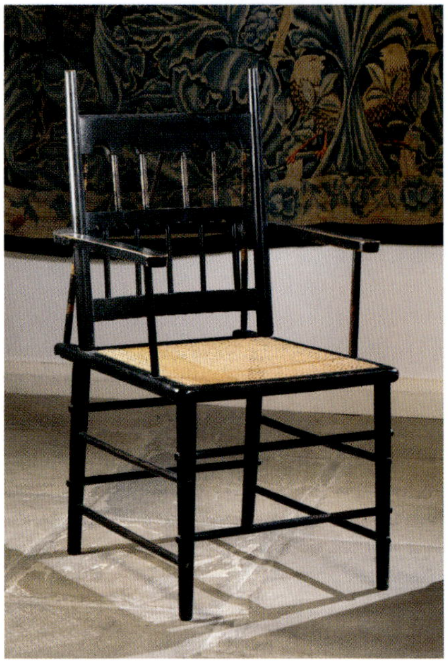

IX.17

IX.16
Chest
Designed by Philip Webb
Manufactured by Morris, Marshall, Faulkner & Co., 1862
Probably deal, covered with silver leaf, glazed and painted with tinted varnishes, iron mounts,
53.3 x 132 x 51.2 cm
V&A (W.35–1978)

Although without provenance, the Gothic form, painted design and decorative technique suggest that this was the chest shown by the firm in the Medieval Court at the 1862 International Exhibition. Webb's 1862 accounts include the design of a chest with ironwork, at £1 10*s*. *The Parthenon*'s review of the firm's furniture (4 October 1862) mentioned 'a lacquered chest' described as having 'diaper flower-decorations'. Morris used patterns of formalized daisies in many of his early designs and he may have had a hand in the decoration.

The design was created using silver leaf, glazes and tinted varnishes, the medieval technique revived by Burges for his *Yatman* cabinet of 1858 and also found on the interior of the *St George* cabinet. Indian red, a popular paint colour for medieval enthusiasts, was used on the inside of the chest, and also on Burne-Jones's sideboard of 1860 (IX.7) and on the stand for the *St George* cabinet (IX.14).

IX.17
Armchair
Designed by Philip Webb, 1861–2
Manufactured by Morris, Marshall, Faulkner & Co.
Ebonized wood with gilded bands,
99 x 41 x 43 cm
The Society of Antiquaries of London, Kelmscott Manor (KM075)

This distinctive design by Webb was one of two different 'stained and gilded drawing-room chairs' noted by the designer Christopher Dresser at the 1862 International Exhibition (*Development of Ornamental Art in the International Exhibition*, 1862). He commented approvingly on the structural design, achieved by the unusual combination of extended side rails on the seat joining diagonal struts from the back, a feature found in his own furniture. Although praised by the *Illustrated London News* (18 October 1862), the chair was perhaps too unconventional for general approval and remained in Morris's possession. It is depicted in May Morris's watercolour of the drawing room at Kelmscott House (William Morris Gallery).

Webb's account book includes a simple sketch, possibly the same chair, the design priced at 10*s*. The combination of ebonized finish and gilded bands is reminiscent of Egyptian design and of Rossetti's sofa (IX.18). However, it could also be an example of the firm's interest in eighteenth-century sources as mentioned by Warington Taylor.

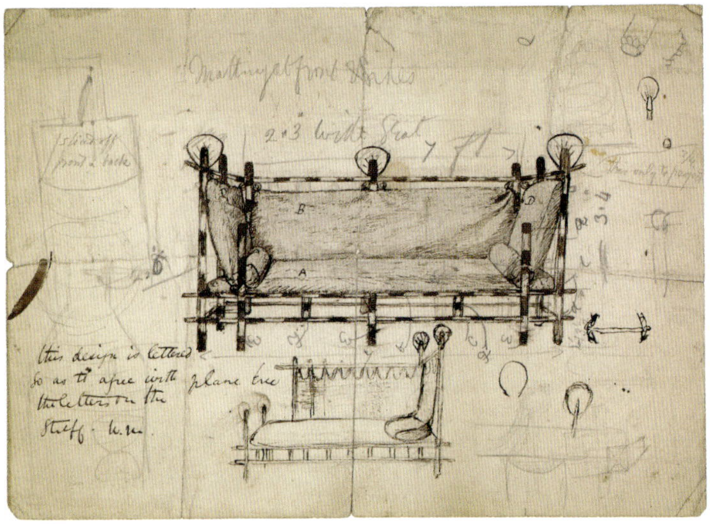

IX.18

IX.18
Two sofa designs
Dante Gabriel Rossetti for Morris, Marshall, Faulkner & Co., 1861–2
Pencil, pen and black ink,
25.3 x 35.2 cm
Inscribed: the lower left-hand annotations are by Morris
Birmingham Museums Trust (1904P471)
Presented by Subscribers

The top design for an Egyptian-style sofa was made of ebonized and white wood for the firm's display at the 1862 International Exhibition. It had covers of red serge decorated with lines and crotchets in imitation of bars of music and was priced at £30. Ridiculed by various critics including Charles Dickens in *All the Year Round* (30 August 1862) for its uncomfortable rectangular construction, the sofa was praised by *The Athenaeum* (27 September 1862) for the ingenious upholstery and for the admirable colour scheme, which apparently contrasted with the firm's embroidered green serge hangings nearby.

Rossetti's 1860 drawing of *Joseph before Potiphar* (also in Birmingham Museum and Art Gallery) depicts a similar sofa and an illustration of his Chelsea dining room shows a dresser with the same palmette finials. Madox Brown's account book with the firm records a payment of £1 for 'Rossetti Sofa' but it is not clear what his contribution was. Although its present whereabouts are unknown, in 1900 the sofa belonged to Harold Rathbone and was illustrated in *The Furnisher* (November 1900) with the caption 'Cane couch designed by Dante Gabriel Rossetti for Ford Madox Brown'.

IX.19

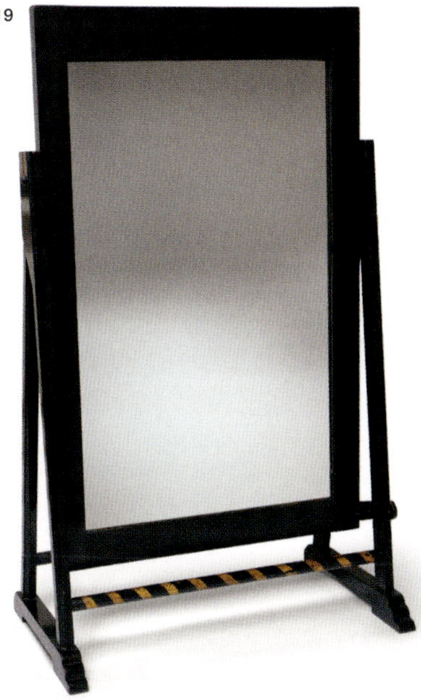

IX.19
Mirror
Designed by Philip Webb, *c.*1862
Manufactured by Morris, Marshall, Faulkner & Co.
Ebonized wood with gilt decoration, 90 x 49 x 33 cm
The Society of Antiquaries of London, Kelmscott Manor (KM323)

There are two mirrors of this design at Kelmscott Manor, either of which could be the one May Morris listed as from Red House in the memorandum attached to her will. The ebonized finish and gilded decoration relate to other pieces of furniture made in the 1860s, particularly for the International Exhibition, and a letter Rossetti wrote to Jane on 7 May 1868 suggests that he ordered an ebony chimney glass and shelf from the firm.

The design is an interesting reminder of the firm's more practical furniture. Originally it incorporated a pin that allowed the angle of the mirror to be adjusted (a feature also used by Ford Madox Brown for a similar mirror), and at least one oak version survives. Another example, with candleholders, was supplied for Red Barns, Coatham, Redcar, the house designed by Webb in 1868 for Hugh Bell.

IX.20

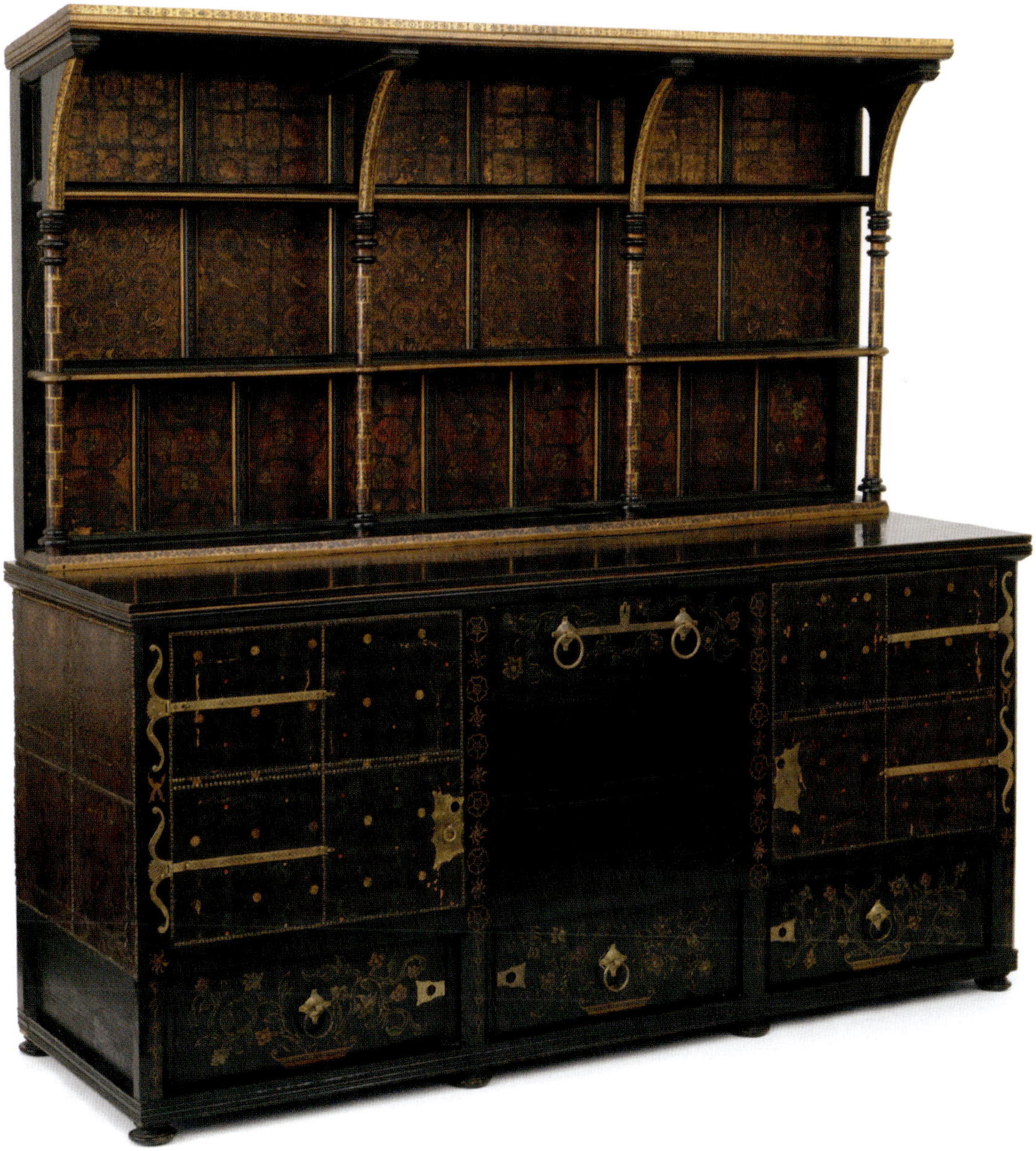

IX.20
Sideboard
Designed by Philip Webb, *c.*1862
Manufactured by Morris, Marshall, Faulkner & Co.
Ebonized wood with painted decoration and panels of stamped leather, 195.7 x 198.2 x 66 cm
V&A (Circ.540–1963)
Given by Ben Weinreb

Webb's account book records designs for three sideboards in 1862–3, and work on painted and lacquered leather panels, some of which were intended for a sideboard. This may represent one of these early commissions. The base was originally open but has been altered and is now filled with drawers. The leather panels, with birds and flowers in roundels, and stiff meandering floral trails, are very similar to those on a sideboard illustrated in the firm's catalogue, *Specimens of Furniture*, described as being made 'in the earliest days of the firm at Red Lion Square (*c.*1862)'. The pattern in the uppermost row is identical to that on the canopy of the Red House settle (IX.8).

Frederick Leyland, an important patron of both Rossetti and Whistler and a client of the firm, owned a similar sideboard, photographed in the 'Peacock Room', his famous dining room at 49 Prince's Gate, London, in 1892. He may have acquired it either for this house, which he bought in 1874, or for his earlier house at 23 Queen's Gate furnished from 1867. Both this and another example, now in the Musée d'Orsay, are of similar form to the V&A's sideboard, but their leather panels have a large-scale scrolling pattern, more reminiscent of seventeenth-century Dutch or Spanish leather.

IX.21
Mirror
Philip Webb and Edward Burne-Jones, 1862
Manufactured by Morris, Marshall, Faulkner & Co.
Gesso, oil and gilding on walnut with brass fittings, 83.8 x 73.7 x 21 cm
Los Angeles County Museum of Art (M.2001.19.1)
Purchased with funds provided by Mr and Mrs Russell McKinnon and other donors

Webb's account book with the firm lists the design of a 'looking glass for Taylor' on the 10 September 1862, priced at 10*s*. Later that year, he created two designs for the side panels at a cost of £1 each. Both illustrate incidents from Aesop's Fables. The story of the peacock and the jackdaw warns of the dangers of vanity and on the other side the tale of the fox and the crow cautions against listening to flattery. Playful subjects for a mirror, the client was Warington Taylor, later the firm's business manager (1865–70). Taylor commissioned other bespoke furniture around the same time, including an ebonized bookcase designed by William Burges and decorated with panels attributed to Rossetti (The Higgins Bedford).

Burne-Jones designed the figures on the front of the mirror's compartment doors. The blindfolded woman represents Fortune, and Love is shown holding his bow, standing on a flowery mound. The same designs were used for painted tiles at The Hill, Witley, and for stained-glass panels in the ground-floor passage at Red House.

IX.22
***Sussex* round-seated chair**
Possibly designed by Ford Madox Brown, early 1860s
Manufactured by Morris, Marshall, Faulkner & Co. and later Morris & Co.
Ebonized wood with rush seat, 83 x 41.9 x 43 cm
The Society of Antiquaries of London, Kelmscott Manor (KM307)

The design of this chair was attributed to Ford Madox Brown by E.M. Tait in *The Furnisher* (November 1900). The *Sussex* range was popular with members of the firm and Burne-Jones is known to have purchased round-seated chairs in 1878 for The Grange, Fulham. Described by Robert Edis as a bedroom chair and recommended for its cheapness and serviceability (*Decoration and Furniture of Town Houses*, 1881), this model was available for 10*s*. 6*d*. according to Morris & Co.'s later catalogue (fig.167).

IX.23
***Rossetti* armchair**
Possibly designed by Dante Gabriel Rossetti, *c.*1863
Manufactured by Morris, Marshall, Faulkner & Co. and later Morris & Co.
Ebonized beech with red painted decoration and rush seat, 88.9 x 49.5 x 47 cm
V&A (Circ.304–1961)
Acquired from Barbara Morris

This chair, based on early nineteenth-century French country chairs, was traditionally known as the *Rossetti* armchair although no evidence identifying him as the designer has yet been found. He was clearly involved with the firm's furniture and a letter to Webb on 20 May 1866 referred to his advice on 'rush-bottoms and ascetic glutaei'. An 1863 photograph of Rossetti with John Ruskin and the artist William Bell Scott in his garden at 16 Cheyne Walk, Chelsea, shows an almost identical chair (fig.7). This may be an early product of the firm or one of Rossetti's second-hand pieces. An example, possibly the same one, appears in Henry Treffry Dunn's 1882 watercolour of Rossetti's ground-floor parlour (National Portrait Gallery).

IX.21
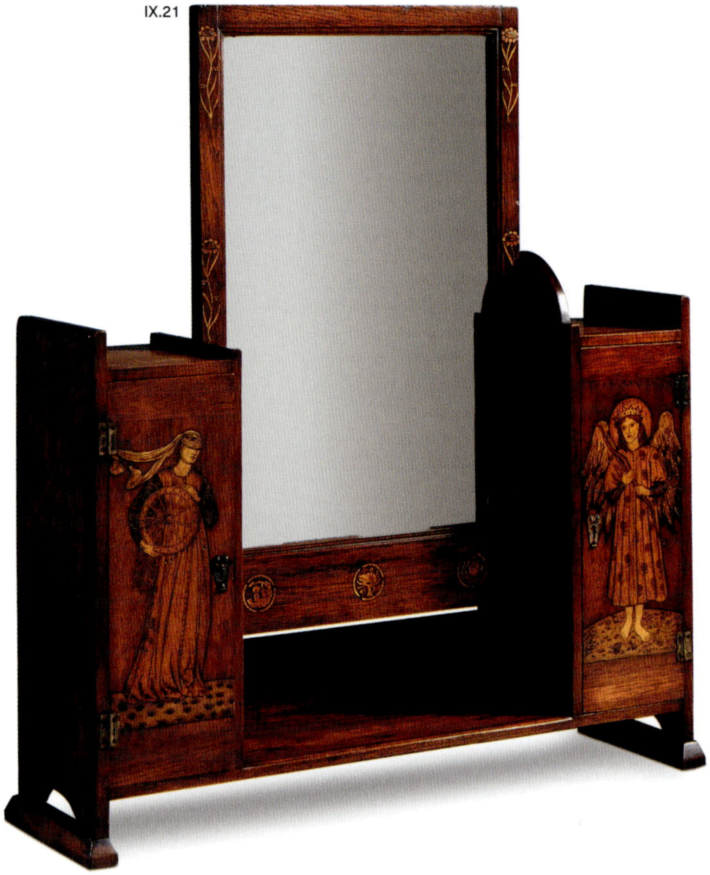

IX.22
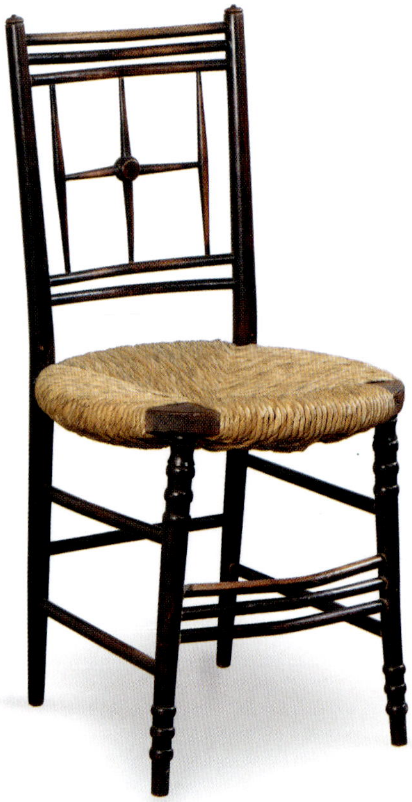

IX.23
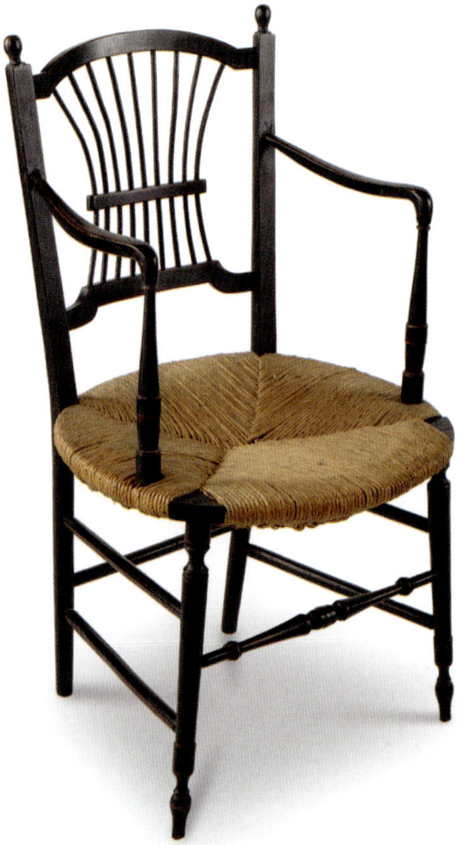

IX.24
Centre table
Designed by Philip Webb, *c.*1865
Manufactured by Morris, Marshall, Faulkner & Co. and later Morris & Co.
Mahogany, 72.5 x 144 x 125.5 cm
National Trust, Standen (NT1213993)

Several pieces of furniture designed by Webb in the 1860s combined turned stretchers and abstract structures, probably derived from a mixture of vernacular and Japanese sources. This table was a popular design and walnut and oak examples are also known. The top is oval but was more commonly circular. Examples were used at Owens College, Manchester, designed by Alfred Waterhouse and Wickham Flower's London residence, Old Swan House, Chelsea.

Webb also designed a round table with a flat circular stretcher and turned legs that was used in Georgiana Burne-Jones's sitting room at The Grange. Other versions of this table include one with six legs described by Warington Taylor in a letter to E.R. Robson in the early 1860s (Burne-Jones Papers, Fitzwilliam), and one supplied for the sitting room at Great Tangley Manor in Surrey, Wickham Flower's country house.

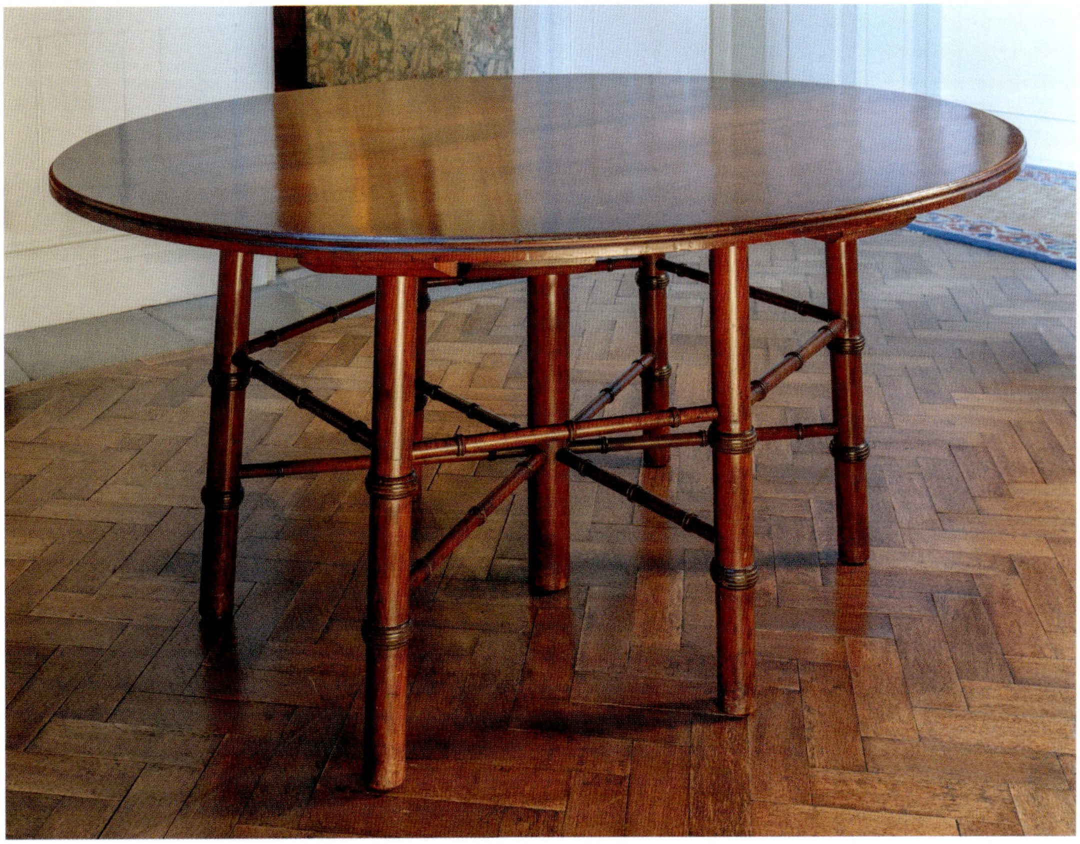

IX.24

IX.25
Side table
Designed by Philip Webb, *c.*1865
Manufactured by Morris, Marshall, Faulkner & Co.
Oak, 73.7 x 165 x 59.8 cm
V&A (W.45–1926)
Purchased from Margaret Mackail

The design of this table epitomizes Webb's subtle use of medieval details and is one of the most successful pieces of Reformed Gothic furniture. Some of Webb's most interesting furniture was designed for the Burne-Jones family, including a trestle dining table (fig.162), a round table with a flat circular stretcher and this side table.

According to Margaret Mackail (Burne-Jones's daughter), the side table was acquired later than the 1860 dining table. It was probably the table, costing £6 6*s*., ordered by Burne-Jones from the firm in 1865 for his new home in Kensington Square. Originally plain oak, it was apparently stained green by Burne-Jones in the 1880s. The London barrister Vernon Lushington, who also moved to Kensington Square in 1865, ordered a version with ebonized finish and gilt details. This was sold by the Lushington family at Sotheby's in 1983.

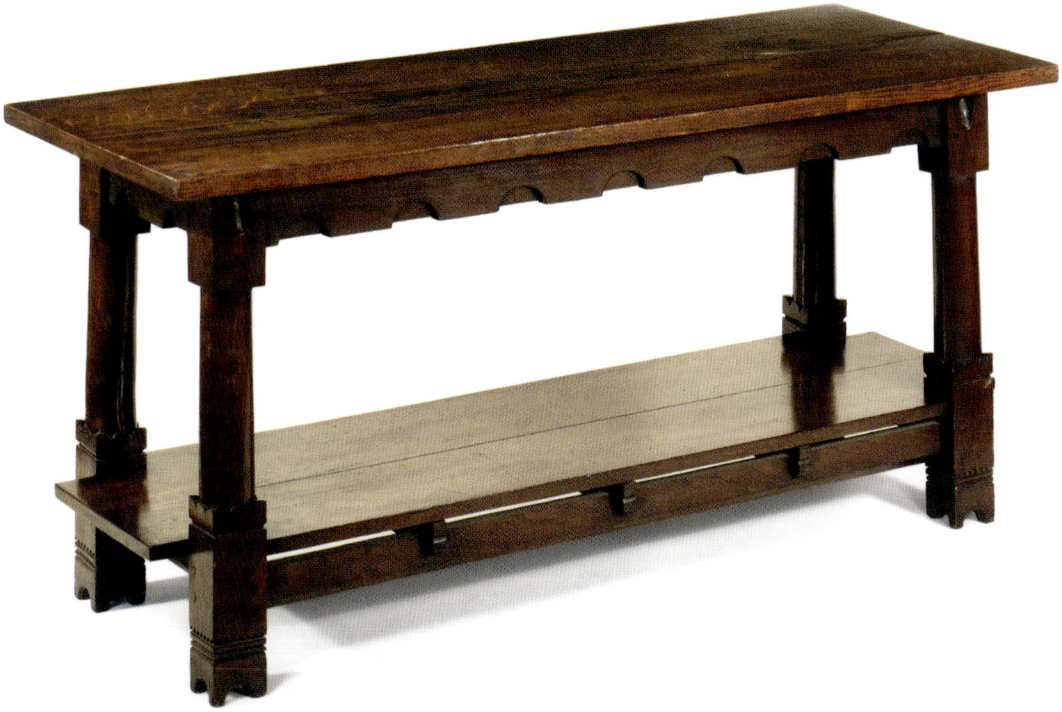

IX.25

IX.26

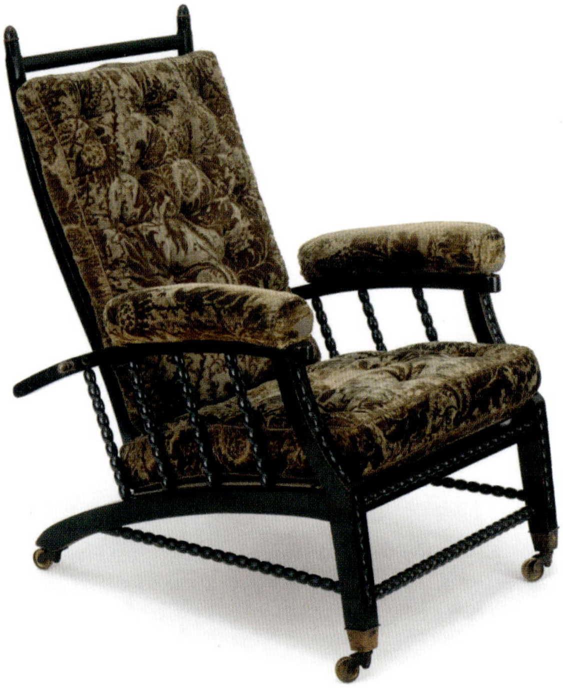

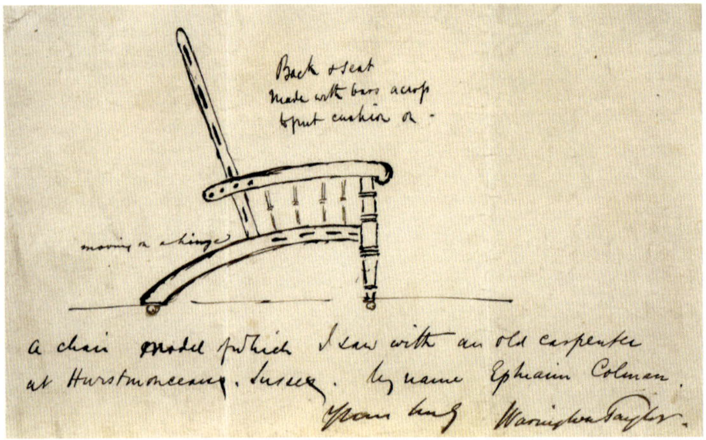
Back & seat
made with bars across
to put cushion on -
moving on a hinge
a chair model of which I saw with an old carpenter
at Hurstmonceaux. Sussex. by name Ephraim Colman.
Yours truly Warington Taylor.

IX.27

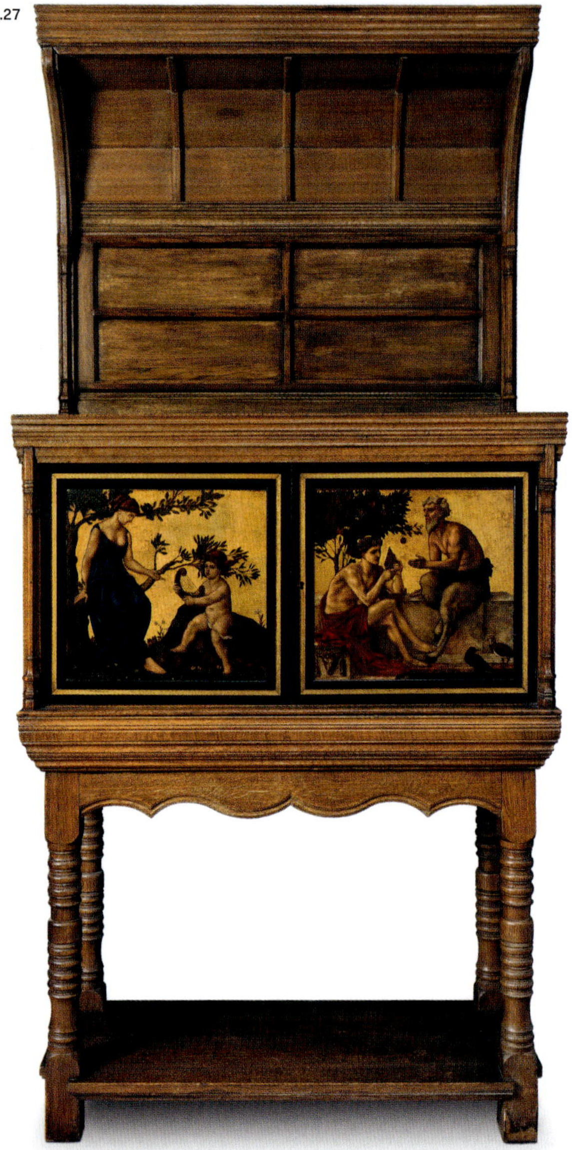

IX.26
Adjustable-back chair
Warington Taylor and Philip Webb, 1866
Manufactured by Morris, Marshall, Faulkner & Co. and later Morris & Co.
Ebonized wood with *Utrecht Velvet* upholstery, 99 x 63 x 79 cm
V&A (Circ.250–1961)
Given by J.G. Carruthers

Warington Taylor sketched the model for this chair in a letter to Philip Webb in 1866, having seen it in the workshop of Ephraim Colman, a carpenter in Herstmonceux, Sussex. Webb reworked the original conventional reclining chair, retaining the bars in the seat but substituting bobbin turning. This traditional technique and the ebonized finish were used on other seat furniture produced by the firm, including a day bed from the dining room at Kelmscott House, now at Kelmscott Manor.

Morris and Burne-Jones both furnished their own homes with adjustable-back chairs (figs 15 and 200). The design, also available in mahogany, was a commercial success and widely imitated by British and American firms, including Liberty and Gustav Stickley's workshops in America. The earliest examples were upholstered in *Utrecht Velvet* (XII.33), though less costly printed cotton covers were later available as an alternative. The donor was the son of John Carruthers, a friend of Morris and his companion on his final journey to Norway in 1896.

Fig.172 **Warington Taylor's sketch in a letter to Philip Webb, 1866.**
National Art Library, V&A (MSL/1958/691)

IX.27
Cabinet
Designed by Philip Webb and painted by William De Morgan, *c.*1870s
Manufactured by Morris, Marshall, Faulkner & Co.
Oil and gilding on oak, 241.3 x 115 x 49.5 cm
William Morris Gallery, London Borough of Waltham Forest (G25)

The canopy on this painted cabinet recalls Webb's settle and sideboard designs (IX.8 and 20). It was a bespoke item made for Isabel Olga Lucas (née d'Avigdor), wife of the artist Horatio Joseph Lucas who died in 1873. The couple lived at 5 Westbourne Terrace, Hyde Park, and were friends of William De Morgan. The back of the cabinet was originally covered with a stamped and embossed leather paper. De Morgan painted a second cabinet for Isabel depicting St George and the dragon, now in the collection of the De Morgan Foundation.

The execution and classical subject matter of the painted decoration is very different from the firm's early medieval-style pieces. De Morgan trained as a fine artist in the Royal Academy Schools and designed for stained glass and furniture in the 1860s before he turned to ceramics. On the left, a young Hermes wearing a winged helmet (*petasus*) holds a lyre, an instrument he invented, accompanied by Maia, or possibly the muse Erato. On the right Silenus teaches Dionysus to play the pipes.

In 1934 Morris & Co. resold the cabinet to Etta May Gubbins who replaced the leather paper with lustre tiles by De Morgan (since removed but also in the William Morris Gallery's collection).

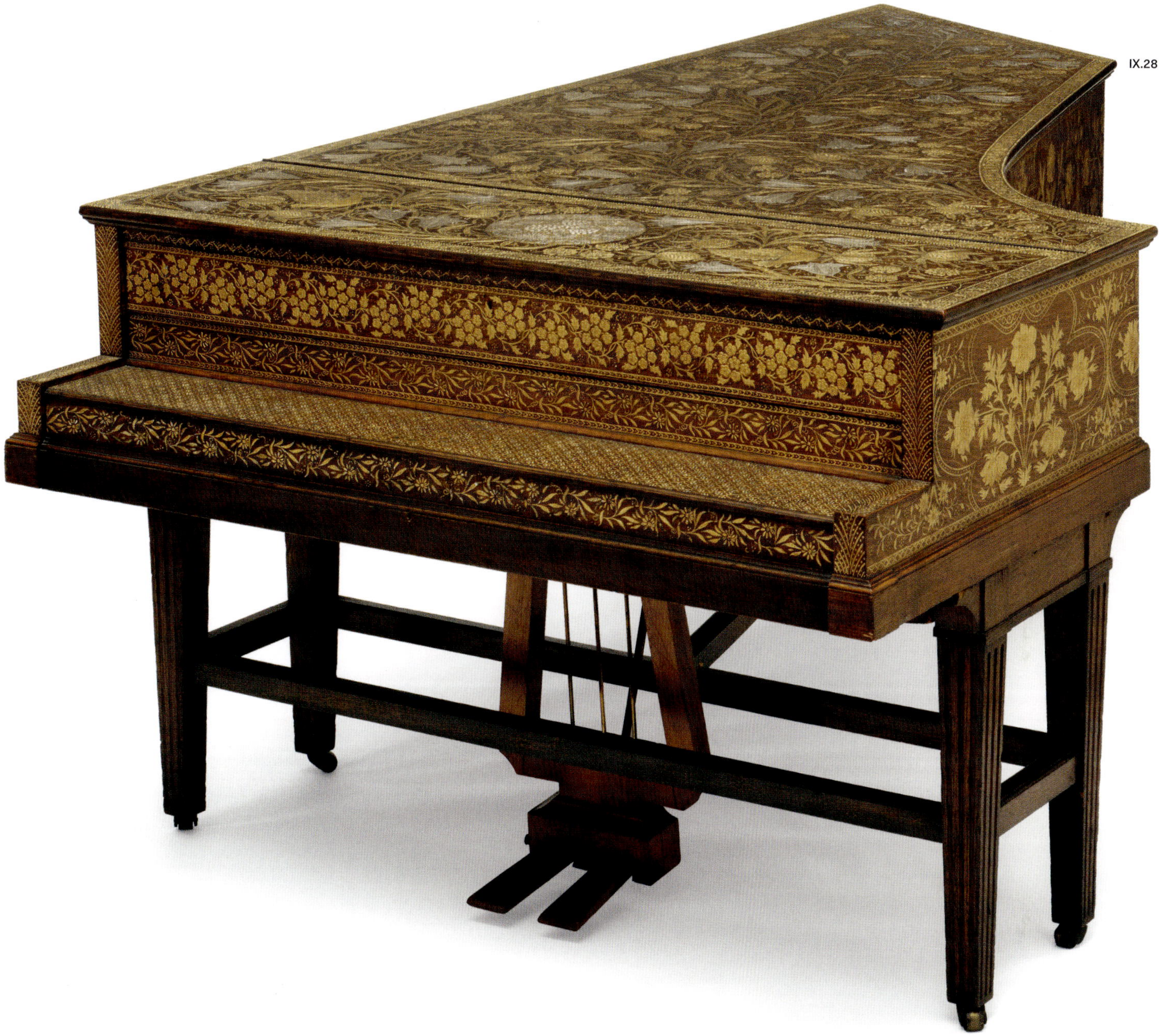

IX.28

IX.28
Grand piano
Edward Burne-Jones and
Kate Faulkner
Manufactured by John Broadwood & Sons, 1883
Oak, stained and decorated with gold and silver gesso, 96.5 x 259 x 141 cm
V&A (W.23–1927)
Given by Mrs A.C. Ionides

Aleco Ionides commissioned this piano for the second drawing room of 1 Holland Park (fig.42). The case and stand reveal the influence of Burne-Jones who, assisted by W.A.S. Benson, had already designed a number of innovative pianos inspired by the form of eighteenth-century harpsichords. The intricate gesso work was conceived and executed by Kate Faulkner in 1884–5. It was a time-consuming project and Philip Webb, a close friend, wrote in March 1885, 'I did *not* smile when you told me the piano was not yet gone, as I felt quite serious over your wish to make it as perfect as you could – all art-work shd be done in that spirit.' The delicate all-over pattern of scrolling leaves, fruit and flowers on the lid recalls the dish painted by Faulkner a few years earlier (X.24).

Ionides loaned the piano to the first show organized by the Arts and Crafts Exhibition Society in 1888 and the catalogue listed the ten craftsmen involved in making the case and movement. Reviews in *The Builder* (6 October 1888) and *The British Architect* (23 November 1888) both admired the gesso decoration, although the former noted that its rich and striking effect was 'rather overdone; at all events it would certainly require the whole apartment to be designed up to it.' This was certainly true of the opulent interiors of 1 Holland Park. Faulkner received other commissions for decorated piano cases. Correspondence between Morris and Webb in 1892–3 records how her declining health made it difficult for her to complete one of these projects. The Holland Park piano was loaned to the exhibition of *British and Irish Decorative Arts* held at the Louvre in 1914.

IX.29
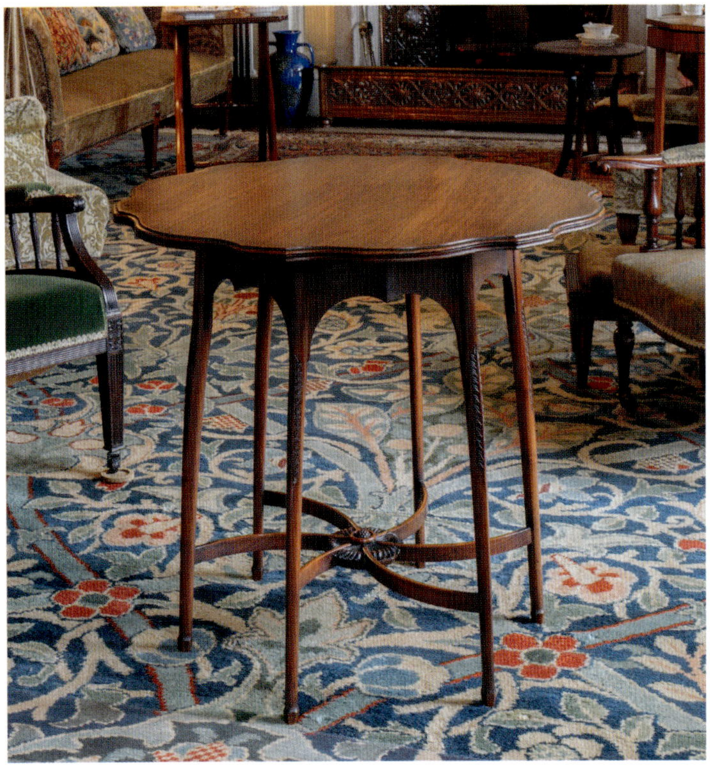

IX.29
Occasional table
Designed by George Jack, *c.*1889
Manufactured by Morris & Co.
Walnut, 68.5 x 76 cm
Stamped: MORRIS & CO 449
OXFORD STREET W 1000
National Trust, Standen (NT1214006)

Morris & Co. exhibited a mahogany version of this table at the 1889 Arts and Crafts Exhibition. The slender legs are each carved with a stylized branch of leaves and terminate in pointed hexagonal toes. The stretchers, shaped as curved spokes, join a central carved sunflower motif. Bedford Lemere's photographs of William Knox D'Arcy's Stanmore Hall show examples of this table furnishing the drawing room and so-called octagonal room. It was a popular design and remained in production into the twentieth century. A plainer and less costly version, without the carved details, was also available. This table was purchased by the National Trust in 1983. Examples can also be found in the collections of the Saint Louis Art Museum and Los Angeles County Museum of Art.

IX.30
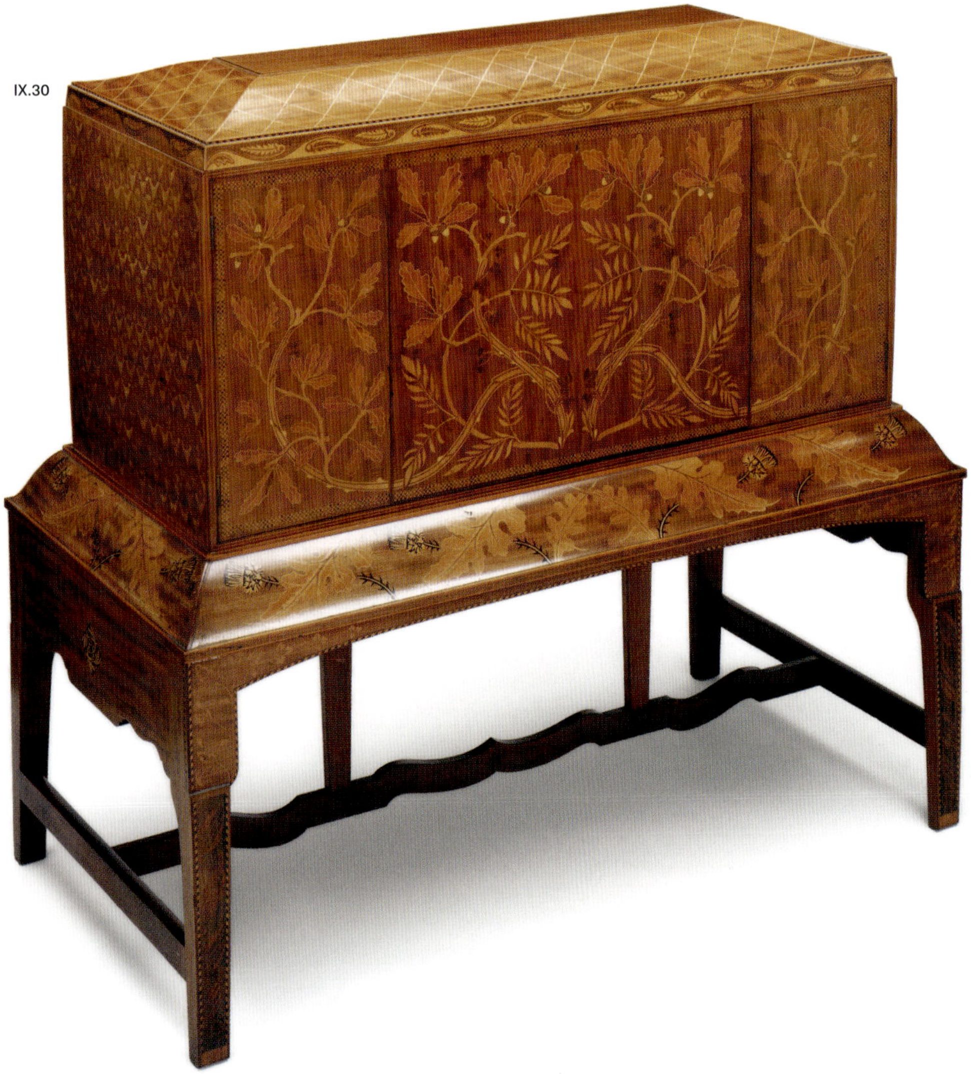

IX.30
Secretaire
Designed by George Jack, *c.*1889
Manufactured by Morris & Co.
Mahogany with marquetry of sycamore and other woods,
131 x 141 x 68.5 cm
Stamped: MORRIS & CO. 449
OXFORD S. W. 1147
V&A (Circ.40–1953)
Acquired from the Trustees of the Middlemore Estates, London

This secretaire reflects Jack's knowledge of eighteenth-century furniture in its singular appearance and revival of marquetry. The motifs include thistle, ash and oak leaves and the arrangement of the branches recalls the design of Morris & Co. embroideries. Inside the shaped top is a velvet-lined compartment and the central panel opens to reveal a writing desk and pigeonholes. An example was first shown at the 1889 Arts and Crafts Exhibition (described as an 'inlaid cabinet') and was generally praised for the design of the marquetry, choice of materials and quality of workmanship, although *The Cabinet Maker and Art Furnisher* (1 November 1889) described it as 'an exaggerated inlaid tea-caddy on a clumsy stand'.

Used by the Middlemore family at Melsetter House, Orkney, other examples with variations in the design of the marquetry furnished Stanmore Hall, Compton Hall, Tapeley Park (two still *in situ*) and Ickworth. One was acquired by Ralph Radcliffe Whitehead for his American Arts and Crafts community (now Philadelphia Museum of Art) and three others, with unknown provenances, also survive. Normally the firm's stamp on the fall front included a number, suggesting a production sequence. Versions with decorated inlay cost £98, plain alternatives 'inlaid with lines' cost £60.

IX.31

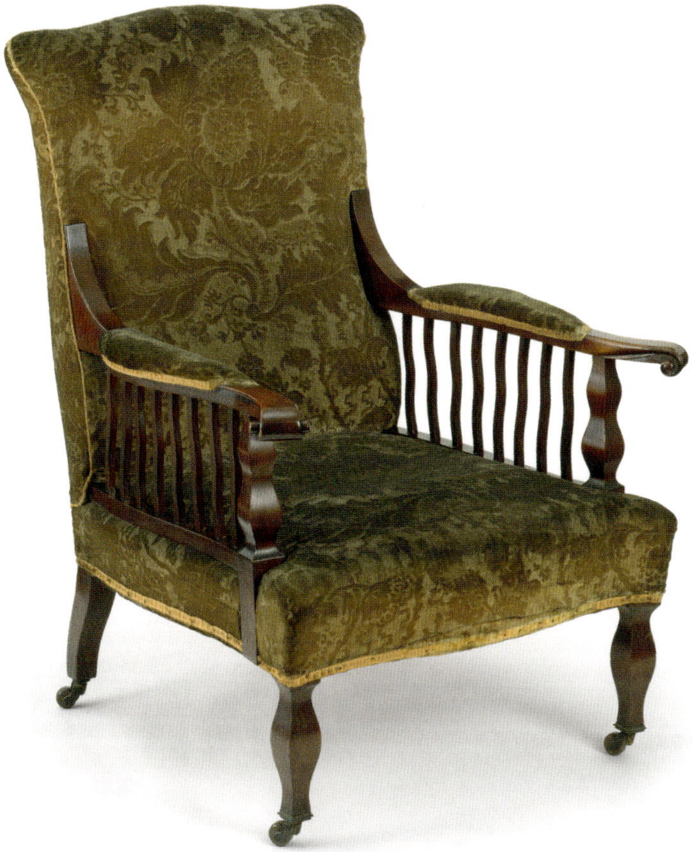

IX.31
***Saville* armchair**
Design attributed to George Jack, *c.*1890
Manufactured by Morris & Co.
Mahogany upholstered in *Utrecht Velvet*, 96.5 x 61 x 76.2 cm
V&A (Circ.401–1960)
Given by Frances Jane Lefroy

George Jack probably designed this armchair although it is not listed in his account book of work executed for Morris & Co., preserved at the William Morris Gallery. The wavy outlines of the vertical rails under the arms are reminiscent of details on his sideboard shown by the firm at the Manchester Jubilee Exhibition in 1887 (fig.168) and illustrated in *The Cabinet Maker and Art Furnisher*, 1 July 1887. The *Utrecht Velvet* on this chair has faded from its original olive green. In Morris & Co.'s *Upholstered Furniture* catalogue (*c.*1911) the chair was offered with *Cherwell* velvet at £7 5*s*. or with chintz for £6 5*s*.

Frances Lefroy, the donor, was the niece of Wickham Flower, whose country house, Great Tangley Manor, was furnished with *Saville* armchairs in the sitting room and one of the bedrooms (fig.152).

IX.32

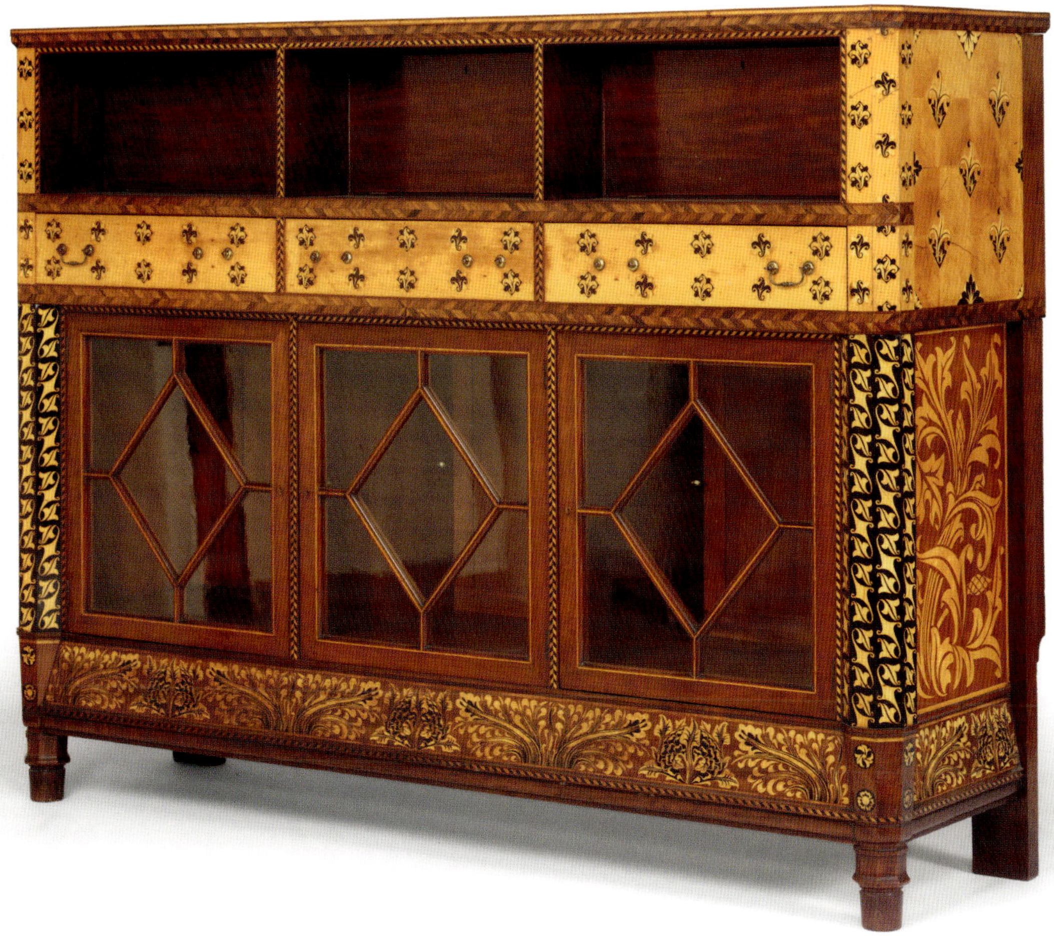

IX.32
Cabinet
Designed by George Jack, *c.*1890–1
Manufactured by Morris & Co.
Mahogany inlaid with sycamore, ebony and other woods, 152.5 x 206 x 61 cm
Stamped: MORRIS & CO. 449 OXFORD STREET 612
V&A (W.42–1929)
Given by Doris Thorne

This cabinet was designed for the staging of Henry Arthur Jones's play *The Crusaders*, which opened at the Avenue Theatre on 2 November 1891. The playwright was a close friend of Emery Walker, who introduced him to Morris. The firm was commissioned to supply the furniture and draperies and the programme requested the 'indulgence of the audience ... between the acts, as the stage is small and the scenery is rather elaborate.' The play – a satire about a group of people trying to reform London – was a failure but the sets were well received. There were two settings, a Mayfair drawing room and a country cottage near Wimbledon. This sophisticated piece, combining narrow bands of geometric designs with foliate motifs, presumably furnished the former.

Jones retained the cabinet and used it to store his manuscripts and Kelmscott Press books. In 1902 he purchased Morris & Co.'s tapestry version of Botticelli's *Primavera* and loaned this, together with an inlaid screen, to the *British and Irish Decorative Arts* exhibition at the Louvre in 1914. A similar cabinet, with a different upper section, is in the collection of Paul Reeves.

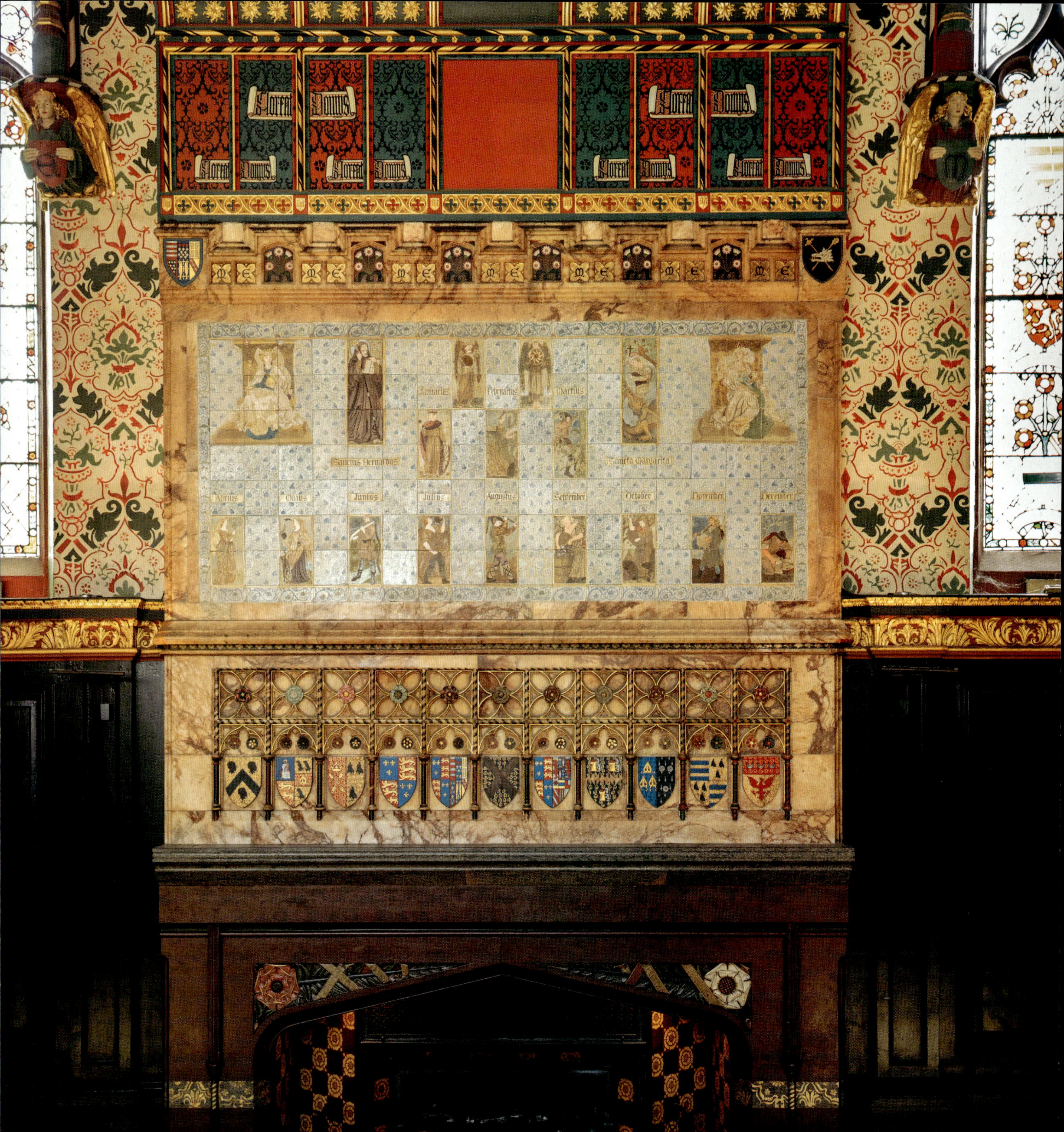

Floreat
Domus
Januarius
Februarius
Martius
Sanctus Bernardus
Sancta Margarita
Aprilis
Maius
Junius
Julius
Augustus
September
October
November
December

X

TILES AND TABLEWARE

Jennifer Hawkins Opie

'I should say that the making of ugly pottery was one of the most remarkable inventions of our civilisation.'

William Morris, 'The Lesser Arts of Life', 1882

Hand-painted tiles were among the first products offered by Morris, Marshall, Faulkner & Co. and in the 1860s the firm received a number of important tile commissions for both domestic and church settings. Morris, Edward Burne-Jones and Philip Webb contributed the majority of designs, although Dante Gabriel Rossetti and Ford Madox Brown were also involved, and there was a great deal of overlap with designs for other media, especially stained glass. As well as medieval-inspired patterned tiles, the firm created a distinctive range of figurative and narrative designs on subjects including Chaucer's *Legend of Good Women*, Greek mythology and traditional fairytales. Morris never manufactured his own tiles or glassware, but he chose his collaborators carefully in order to achieve the effects he desired. As the retail side of the business expanded, especially after the opening of the Oxford Street showroom in 1877, he also sold ceramics and metalwork by makers whom he admired, most notably William De Morgan and later W.A.S. Benson.

Morris's earliest tile designs were created for Red House. In the garden porch, usually known as 'Pilgrim's Rest', a sturdy oak bench has a tiled backrest with three patterns illustrating his interest in heraldry – Morris's motto 'Si je puis' entwined around an oak sapling, the medieval symbol of the rose in splendour and the coat of arms adopted by his father in 1843 (fig.174). The only other tiles that remain *in situ* from the Morris family's occupancy can be found in the fireplace surrounds of the two west-facing bedrooms. Morris or Webb designed the simple pattern of 'leaves and berries' (fig.175). Burne-Jones later recorded that he had also designed tiles for Red House; these are likely to have been figurative compositions in which he specialized.

By May 1862, the firm was confident enough to advertise itself by purchasing space in the Medieval Court of the International Exhibition held in South Kensington. According to John William Mackail, tiles designed by Rossetti, Burne-Jones, Webb and Morris were exhibited, although few details are known. One panel, decorated with verses by Morris, was discreetly removed after being criticized by William Burges, chairman of the hanging committee. Richard and Hilary Myers have suggested that this was *The Judgment of Paris* now at Kelmscott Manor, which is decorated with an inscription in black on a dark blue ground making it difficult to read. Despite this setback, the exhibition led to valuable new commissions, including a series of fairytale tiles for The Hill at

Fig.173 **Tiled overmantel in the Hall at Queens' College, Cambridge, executed in two phases, 1862–4 and the mid-1870s (see X.7).**

Witley in Surrey, home of the painter Myles Birket Foster. By the end of the year the firm's minute book records the importance of the sale of tiles and table glass, retailed from the showroom in Red Lion Square.

For the decoration of much of the firm's early production, Morris and his colleagues drew inspiration from the medieval period of many different countries. In Britain, from the thirteenth century onwards, sturdy, practical tiles were made for floors in red and white clays with honey-coloured lead glazing. Morris firmly rejected these, perhaps because from the 1830s reproductions had been made by the hugely successful Staffordshire and Shropshire pottery industries. This overwhelming commerce combined with the stiffly formal, Gothic patterns was doubly unappealing – heraldry without chivalry. Instead, Morris's tiles were developed either as decorative panels for fireplaces and furniture or – in much the same spirit as were the embroidered hangings and the papers – as wall decoration. Patterns or images were often derived from the same sources. In 1863 Morris himself, in a draft letter to prospective clients, claimed to have been 'particularly successful in the revival (as we think we may call it) of the art of painting on china tiles for walls similar in manner to the ancient maiolica', and called 'attention to the suitability of these tiles for the decoration both internal & external of churches and public buildings' (British Library Add. MS 45336). By this date the collections in the South Kensington Museum, a favourite haunt of both Morris and Webb, were already rich in Renaissance Italian ceramics. Clearly Morris was well aware of the technique as well as drawn to the appearance of this colourful, attractive ware.

As stated above, Morris never made his own tiles. Instead he turned to an outside source for the production of the tile blank and for several reasons he went to the Netherlands, for which he had a well-developed affection. Until at least the 1880s tile production there still used traditional methods, in a hand-based but streamlined technique that allowed mass-production and inexpensive prices. Handmade and hand-cut blanks were covered with a tin-based lead glaze (which when fired turned to a warm, softly glossy white) and then painted. Glaze and decoration were fired in one operation so that the colour was 'absorbed', giving the typically soft-edged appearance of 'in-glaze' decoration.

Nineteenth-century Dutch patterns, too, were a continuing tradition, developed from the

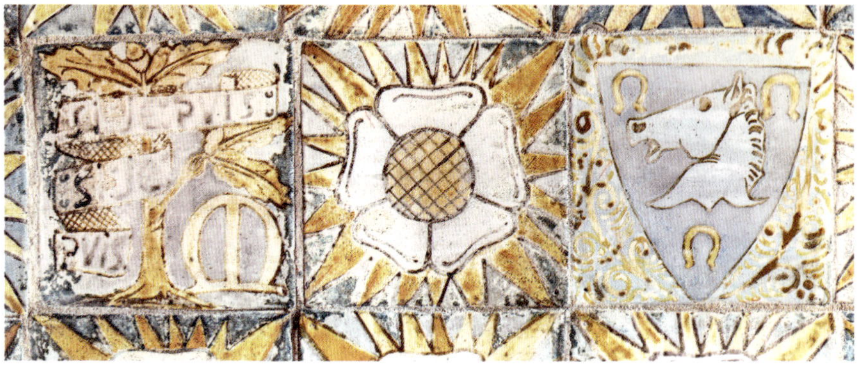

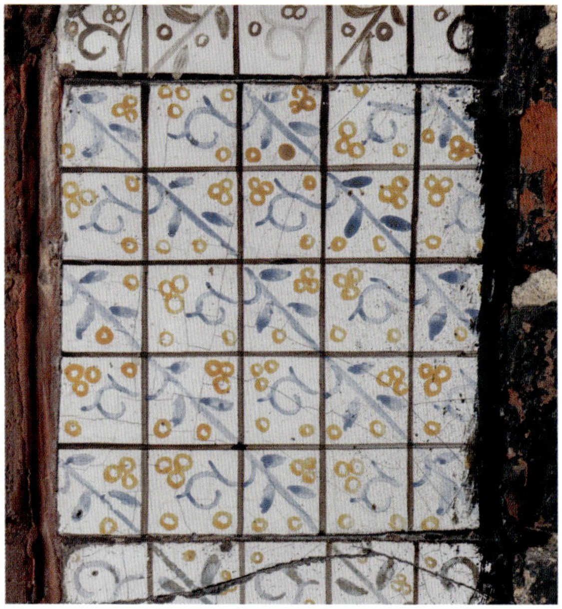

Fig.174 **Detail of the garden porch tiles at Red House, designed by William Morris, made *c.*1861.**
National Trust, Red House

Fig.175 **'Leaves and berries' tiles in one of the bedrooms at Red House, designed by William Morris or Philip Webb, made *c.*1861.**
National Trust, Red House

seventeenth and eighteenth centuries on tiles as well as dishes and other wares. Hand-painted decoration was of simple scenes and patterns, often flowers, reduced to stylized folk elements, sometimes in bright colours, but most particularly in a distinctive blue on the white tin-glazed background. These are the type known as 'Dutch Delft'. Similar ceramics were also made in the mid-eighteenth century in Britain as Lambeth, Bristol or Liverpool 'Delft'. For Morris these, together with illuminated manuscripts, herbals and 'millefleur' tapestries, spoke more than anything of a simple medieval domesticity, which he loved.

Morris may have had a ready-made contact with tileries in the Netherlands through the London-based Dutch dealer Murray Marks, introduced to the circle by Rossetti. It is also possible that Webb was an important source of information, both on suppliers of imported Dutch blanks and on the traditional patterns. In one of his notebooks from the early 1860s

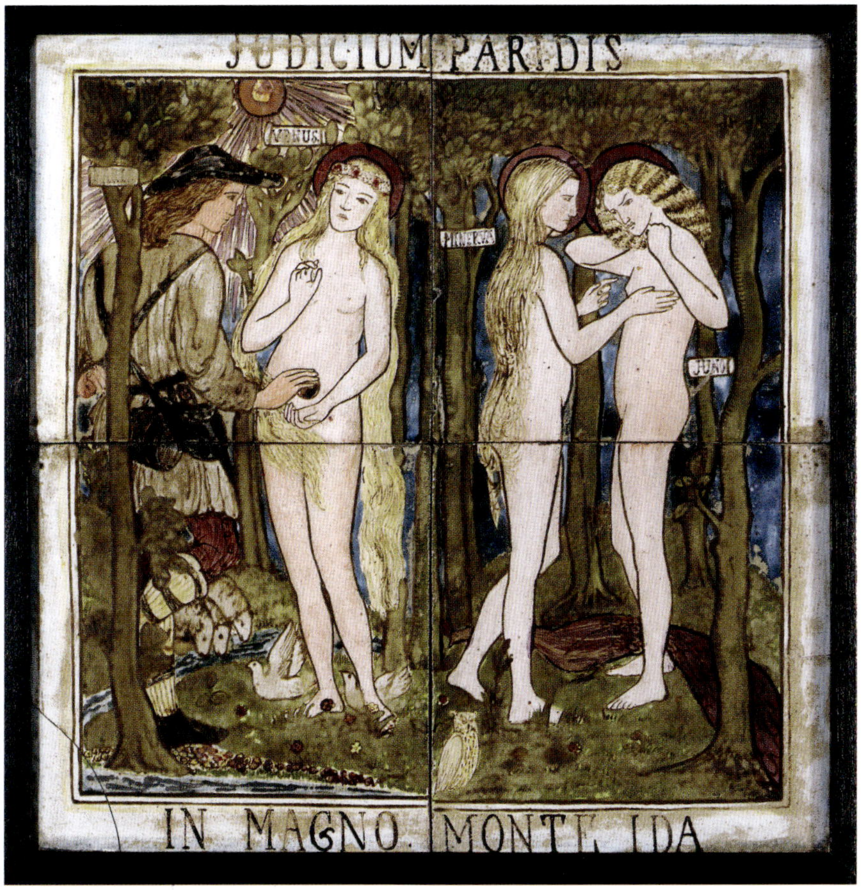

Fig.176 ***The Judgment of Paris*** **tile panel, designed by Edward Burne-Jones, early 1860s.**
William Morris Gallery

he listed Rosher & Company in Blackfriars Road, Southwark, London, as stockists of imported Dutch tiles. He later described 'Dutch Delft' as the ware 'I am so fondly inclined to' and several of his designs for the firm are in this idiom, including a group of bird tiles (*Raven*, *Hare* and *Cock*) from the late 1860s. The latter were made and decorated for the firm in the Netherlands. It is possible that this was Webb's intention from the start, however, correspondence between Webb and the Portuguese-born dealer Charles Augustus Howell in October 1868 suggests that they explored the possibility of having them made in Lisbon. It is not known what, if anything, came of these discussions.

Although documentary evidence is lacking, it is accepted that white, undecorated tiles ordered from Dutch manufacturers arrived at the Morris works in London ready-glazed and fired. These were then painted by the firm. Of necessity this was done in enamel colours and this 'on-glaze' decoration was fired (a second firing for the tin-glaze) alongside the enamel-decorated stained glass in the firm's own kilns in the basement of Red Lion Square. Aymer Vallance records that in 1862,

> Morris, Faulkner and others set about experimenting with various glazes, enamels, &c., until the desired results were obtained ... An iron muffle with iron shelves carried the glass in the middle part, while the tiles were so placed as to be exposed to the greatest heat, at the top and bottom. A small wind-furnace was employed for slips and for colour-testing experiments.

Such 'on-glaze' decoration is not as sturdy as the 'in-glaze' type (see X.2). Combined with the attendant complications of firing in a kiln shared with, and built for stained glass, the tiles were often less than successful. A second and sometimes a third firing risked dull, bubbled or even lost colours.

Most of the firm's partners provided designs for tiles but only rarely did they carry out the decoration themselves. Tile painting, along with embroidery, was an area where women made an important contribution. Lucy Jane Faulkner, sister of Charles Faulkner, one of the partners, specialized in painting figurative tiles. She often signed her work with her monogram, 'LJF' or later 'LF', and the execution of many of the firm's most important pictorial tiles can be assigned to her (X.4 and X.7–10). As Emma Ferry's research has shown, Lucy's change of name following her marriage in 1870 to Harvey Orrinsmith has obscured the significant role that she played in the 1860s. Both Lucy and her younger sister Kate Faulkner, who also painted tiles, worked for Morris in a freelance capacity and according to May Morris carried out some of the work in their own home, 35 Queen Square, Bloomsbury, close to the firm's headquarters. Mackail records that Georgiana Burne-Jones painted 'figured tiles' in the early days although sadly no examples have yet been identified. As orders and commissions increased, tile decoration was also carried out by the stained-glass painters under the foreman George Campfield, first at Red Lion Square and from 1865 at Queen Square.

Burne-Jones supplied the majority of figurative designs, for which panels of two or more tiles were combined to create 'canvases' for painting on. In January 1862 his accounts list nine tile designs with subjects from Greek mythology, of which *The Judgment of Paris* is the only one known to have been executed. Two versions survive, one at Kelmscott Manor referred to above, and a second, almost certainly later example, at the William Morris Gallery without the decorative verses (fig.176). Showing figures in a sylvan landscape, the tiles reflect Morris and Burne-Jones's lifelong fascination with medieval depictions of the Trojan War and its origins. The Latin inscription translates 'The Judgment of Paris on great Mount Ida'. The goddesses Venus, Minerva and Juno are identified by inscribed banners and accompanied by doves, an owl and a peacock respectively. The Greek subjects were followed by a series based on Chaucer's *Legend of Good Women*, most probably designed in the summer of 1862 (X.5–6) and later adapted for embroidery and stained glass. Some versions of these tiles show figures against tiled backgrounds, a flat-pattern device used in medieval manuscripts and also reminiscent of the interior in Rossetti's watercolour *The Blue Closet* (1856–7, Tate). Sometimes, the firm's own tile patterns are suggested (X.5).

The most distinctive and inventive of all Burne-Jones's designs for tiles were undoubtedly the fairytale series, originally conceived for The Hill, one of the earliest houses with extensive decorations by the firm (X.8–10). The village of Witley was popular with artists and one of Birket Foster's neighbours was Henry Cole, first director of the South Kensington Museum. Georgiana Burne-Jones described how the commission proved a welcome outlet for her husband's 'abounding humour'. The Hill was demolished in the early 1950s but fortunately the tiles were rescued, and photographs survive showing them *in situ* (fig.177). The designs were repeated a number of times. In 1865 Lucy Faulkner presented a set of *Beauty and the Beast* tiles to Alice and John Lockwood Kipling (parents of Rudyard) as a marriage gift, shortly before their departure for India. This set has not been traced and, as Barbara Bryant has suggested, it is possible that they are still in Mumbai or Lahore. Fairytale tiles were also used by the writers William and Mary Howitt at The Orchard, Claygate, in Surrey, where they moved in 1867.

As well as domestic commissions, the firm carried out a small number of prestigious tile schemes in public buildings. In 1862 the architect George Frederick Bodley commissioned a tiled overmantel for the Hall at Queens' College, Cambridge (fig.173). Set against a background of Morris's *Swan* tiles, the figurative designs were a collaborative effort with contributions from Burne-Jones, Madox Brown, Rossetti, Webb and Morris (see also X.7). They depict the Labours of the Months, Saint Bernard, Saint Margaret and the Angels of Night and Day. Panels with the college's founders, Margaret of Anjou and Elizabeth Woodville, executed to designs made by Madox Brown in 1873, were inserted during a second

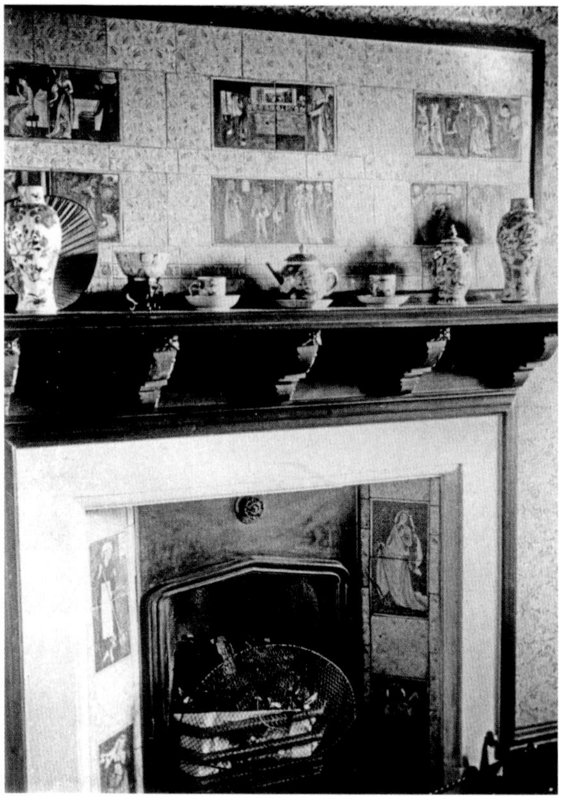

Fig.177 ***Cinderella* tiles in one of the bedrooms at The Hill, Witley, Surrey, photographed by William Foster in the 1880s.**
William Morris Gallery

phase of works in the mid-1870s. Several possible sources for the iconography of the *Labours* have been suggested, including sculpted representations on the portals of French Gothic cathedrals and twelfth-century floor mosaics at Aosta Cathedral, Italy. While these may well have inspired Morris, Michaela Braesel has demonstrated that his principal source was the calendar miniatures in medieval Books of Hours in the British Museum, which he studied and made notes on (British Library Add. MS 45305). The firm later supplied tiles for the Hall and Combination Room at Peterhouse, Cambridge.

Ambitious large-scale tile panels were also designed for churches. In 1864 George Edmund Street, Morris and Webb's former employer, commissioned six panels with biblical scenes and processing angels for the chancel walls of St Peter's in Bournemouth. Morris's bold cartoons for the latter survive in Birmingham Museum and Art Gallery and are related to his designs for the nave ceiling at Jesus College Chapel, Cambridge. Unfortunately, the tile decoration deteriorated quickly and they were finally removed in 1899. Such issues with production explain the reluctance of the firm's business manager, Warington Taylor, to take on further commissions. When the firm

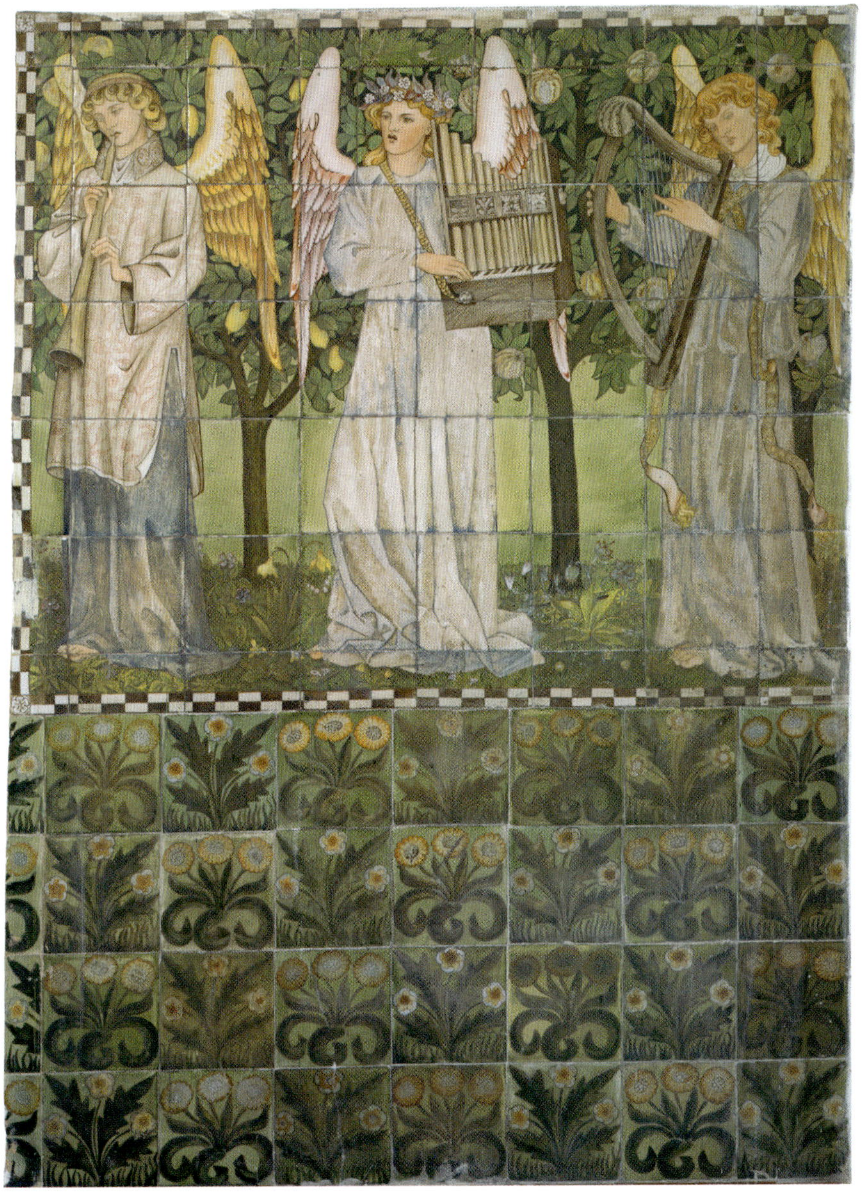

Fig.178 ***Minstrel Angels*** **at St John the Baptist, Findon, West Sussex, designed by William Morris, *c.*1867–8.**

was approached to supply tiles for St John the Baptist at Findon in West Sussex, Taylor sent one of his fearsome letter-memos to Webb, 'About this Findon tile reredos – we cannot do it – *see this settled at once.* must write Lady Bath saying circumstances have compelled us to discontinue the manufacture. Bournemouth was a disgrace – & only half done now. *see this letter written to Lady Bath*'. Thankfully Taylor was overruled as the tiles at Findon are one of the firm's most splendid achievements and have survived in remarkable condition (fig.178). Even more technically accomplished was a tiled reredos with four archangels designed by Morris and installed at the Church of the Blessed Virgin Mary in the neighbouring Sussex parish of Clapham around 1873–4 (fig.179). George Gilbert Scott Junior seems to have overseen the restoration of both churches.

At some point, probably around 1870, Morris decided to transfer production of the firm's most popular repeating patterns to the Netherlands, presumably to those makers who had hitherto supplied the blanks for London decoration. The Dutch tiles were made using the more durable 'in-glaze' technique. It is not known to which factory he gave the commission and Morris-patterned tiles appear in the catalogues of several firms (some certainly unauthorized). The Myers suggest that the most likely candidate was the Ravesteijn tileworks in Utrecht, probably also Morris's chief suppliers of tin-glazed blanks. Dutch-decorated versions of the firm's *Swan*, *Artichoke* and *Sunflower* patterns can be found in the fireplace of the Green Room at Kelmscott Manor, Morris's country home from 1871. The date of installation is unrecorded, but they were certainly there during Morris's lifetime as they appear in a photograph taken by Frederick Evans just before his death in 1896 (the *Sunflower* tiles were probably added in the 1960s when the fireplace was repaired). Dutch-decorated *Sunflower* tiles were also used in Morris's study at Kelmscott House in London.

Alongside its own designs, the firm also sold traditional Dutch tiles. In a letter to Webb dated 4 August – and most probably from 1871 – Jane Morris ordered 6 dozen 5-inch tiles from the firm's stock for the dining-room fireplace at Kelmscott Manor. She did not specify the pattern, indeed she asked for Webb's guidance, but she did insist that they 'must be blue'. The tiles are no longer *in situ* but from photographic evidence the Myers have identified the pattern as a traditional Dutch design with tulips and carnations. In October 1873 Burne-Jones's account book with the firm records that he ordered a large quantity of 5-inch bird tiles for his own use. These were also likely to have been Dutch and were possibly those that were used to decorate the garden bench that appears in photographs of the Burne-Jones and Morris families at The Grange, Fulham, in 1874 (fig.13).

Morris was not the only British retailer to stock traditional Dutch patterns, or to commission the production of new 'artistic' designs in the Netherlands. As noted earlier he may well have had assistance or advice from Murray Marks. By the early 1860s, Marks was working at his father's furniture and decorative-goods shop in Oxford Street. He took a particular interest in

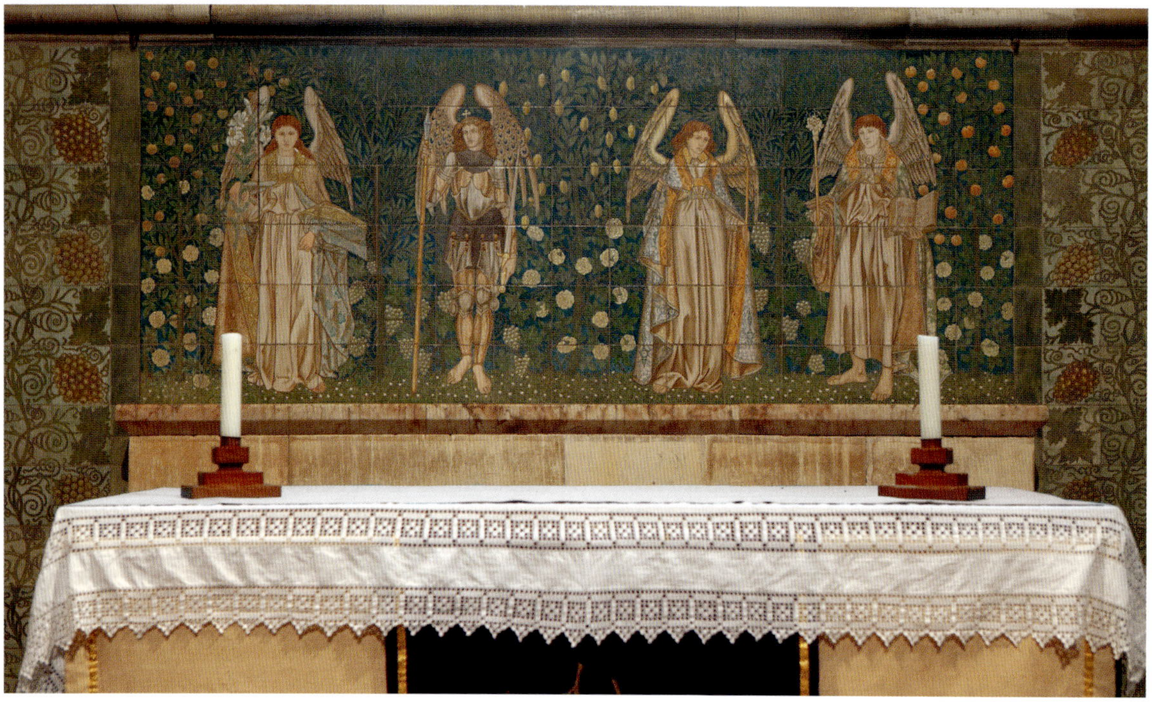

Fig.179 **Tiled reredos at the Church of the Blessed Virgin Mary, Clapham, West Sussex, designed by William Morris, *c.*1873–4.**

ceramics and supplied the painters James McNeill Whistler and Rossetti with Chinese seventeenth- and eighteenth-century blue-and-white porcelain, fanning their competitive and obsessive collecting. Aymer Vallance records in *The Easter Art Annual* of 1900 that, in about 1868, Burne-Jones made two designs for tiles for Marks who 'intended to have them made in Holland; but they never were actually executed.' Marks later went into business with the Durlacher brothers, importing a range of Dutch tiles, and sometime between 1885 and 1887 they transferred the tile rights to Thomas Elsley's Portland Metal Works. Among the designs commissioned by Marks or Elsley are two patterns copied directly from sixteenth-century Turkish Iznik tiles. One of these designs, the so-called *Persian Flower* (fig.180), was used in the Tapestry Room at Kelmscott Manor and appears in Frederick Evans's photograph of 1896. This has sometimes led to a misattribution to Morris, but it is now clear that he had no hand in their production or retail.

The firm's new designs in the 1870s were mainly for patterned tiles, most often used to decorate fireplaces. In 1877 Lucy Orrinsmith (née Faulkner) recommended the firm's products in *The Drawing-Room: Its Decorations and Furniture*. This was her contribution to a series of advice manuals published by Macmillan & Co. and aimed at a growing middle-class audience interested in interior decoration. Although Morris & Co. are not named in the text, the following passage refers explicitly to the firm's designs:

> At present hand-painted over-glazed tiles in blue and white, or yellow and white, may be purchased at certain well-known London houses, at prices varying from one shilling to two shillings each. A tile called the 'Longden' pattern can be recommended for surrounding borders or slanting sides of grates or hearths ... Others, such as the swan, sunflower or bough patterns, differ but slightly in price and are all suitable.

As Emma Ferry has argued, *The Drawing-Room* drew on expertise that Orrinsmith had acquired through her work for Morris, Marshall, Faulkner & Co. in the 1860s. It also records her admiration for 'Persian and old Dutch tile paintings' in the South Kensington Museum, a resource that she must have called upon to inform her own work.

Some of the new tile patterns in the 1870s were designed by Kate Faulkner, who also designed wallpapers and printed cottons for the firm, though she is best known for her superb gesso work (IX.28, X.22–4, XI.18–19, XII.40 and 66). In a letter of February 1885, Webb referred to using Faulkner's patterned tiles of a 'pleasant quiet kind' for the fireplaces of the best bedrooms at Clouds, the country house near Salisbury that he built for Percy and Madeline Wyndham. The context suggests that by this date Faulkner was independently supplying tiles on her own account.

As well as subcontracting work to a Dutch firm, Morris turned to one of his most skilful and inventive collaborators, William De Morgan. They first met in 1863, introduced by the stained-glass artist Henry Holiday. De Morgan trained as a fine artist but in the 1860s, and probably with Morris's encouragement, switched to the decorative arts, initially focusing on stained glass and furniture (IX.27). By the end of the decade, he was totally absorbed in the decoration of tiles and ceramics, setting up a makeshift kiln at his home in Fitzroy Square and attempting to revive the 'lost' technique of lustreware. In 1872 he moved to Chelsea and it was probably here that he successfully produced lustre tiles for the first time.

The intermeshing of Morris and De Morgan tile design, production and sales is immensely complicated. Vallance claimed that De Morgan supplied Morris with enamels but this is an isolated reference and should probably be read with caution. It is more likely that he advised Morris, rather than supplied materials. Both designed for each other, both imported blanks from the Netherlands and production of the same design by both companies overlapped (X.17–18). The firm sold both its own production and, increasingly, that of De Morgan; by the 1880s De Morgan was the main supplier to the Morris shop. Both the firm and De Morgan's tiles were sold by other dealers and by manufacturers of cast-iron fireplaces such as Barnard, Bishop & Barnards and Thomas Elsley of the Portland Metal Works. In addition, De Morgan produced designs that are variations on those of Morris. What is certain, however, is that Morris deeply admired his friend's artistic and technical skills and felt that his ceramics complemented the firm's 'house style'. Among the best examples of their fruitful collaboration are the ambitious and superbly executed tile panels created for Membland Hall in Devon (X.21).

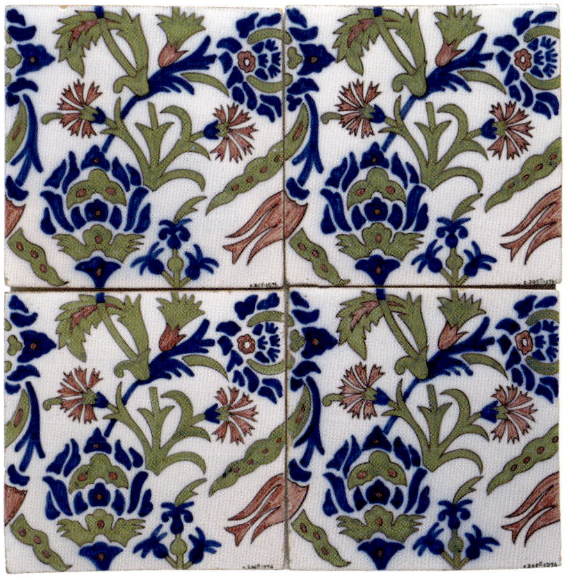

Fig.180 ***Persian Flower*** **tiles, copied from a sixteenth-century pattern and probably made by J.W. Mijnlieff, Utrecht, *c.*1880s–1930s. Tiles of this design in blue and yellow were used by the Morris family at Kelmscott Manor.**
V&A (C.205–1976)

To add a further layer of complexity, even after outsourcing production to the Netherlands and De Morgan, the firm continued to decorate some of its own tiles using the 'on-glaze' technique. All of these interrelated permutations and the enormous number of variations between glowing success (see X.2a) and outright failure (see X.13) of the firm's own production make the precise identification of tiles often difficult.

Morris was famously a bon viveur and surely chose his tablewares with as much pleasure and care as he chose and enjoyed his food and wine. According to Mackail, 'blue china or delft for vessels of household use' were among the few ready-made items that Morris bought when he furnished Red House. Photographs of the interiors at Kelmscott House, the family's London home from 1878, suggest that his (and presumably Jane's) taste in ceramics was wide-ranging and eclectic (see, for example, VIII.16 and fig.212). This is borne out by the varied collection that survives at Kelmscott Manor including blue and white porcelain, Iznik wares of the sixteenth and seventeenth centuries, blue-decorated Persian ceramics, sixteenth- and seventeenth-century Hispano-Moresque lustred wares, nineteenth-century Swiss and Italian painted wares and what Morris and his contemporaries called 'Grès de Flandres'. Caution is needed as the provenance of these items is complex – some pieces belonged to Rossetti, others were acquired by May Morris and the collection was also added to by later occupants (this apparently applies, for example, to the Iznik wares). However, it is clear, particularly from the photographs of the dining room and drawing room at Kelmscott House, that richly decorated and patterned ceramics, including lustreware, were carefully arranged and played an important role in the overall aesthetic of these spaces. It is difficult to appreciate the impact from black-and-white images but May left an evocative description of how the 'lustre plates above the chimneypiece suggested flushed sunsets and dim moonlit nights beyond the elms'.

Gillian Chitty and David Stocker's research into the large collection of 'Grès de Flandres' at Kelmscott Manor offers important insights into Morris's long-held interest in this type of ceramic. This attractive, salt-glazed stoneware was produced in the Westerwald region of Germany from the seventeenth century onwards. Twenty-nine pieces remain at the Manor and the majority can confidently be said to have belonged to Morris. His early interest is evidenced by the inclusion of an eighteenth-century Westerwald pitcher in his painting *La Belle Iseult* (VI.12), begun in 1858, and May's description of some of the pieces having been used at Red House. The largest group at the Manor dates from the mid-nineteenth century and the pieces appear to have been used, rather than just displayed. Chitty and Stocker have convincingly argued that Morris was drawn to these wares because they were still being manufactured in small, family-run workshops in the Rhineland, continuing a long tradition of wheel-thrown and hand-decorated pottery using local clays. Morris may have visited these workshops on his travels in Europe, possibly on his honeymoon or his trip to Bad Ems in 1869. He was no doubt aware that the future of these small craft-based workshops was being threatened by new factories geared up for mass production. As well as acquiring pieces for his own use, according to Mackail, the firm also sold 'Grès de Flandres' and helped to popularize its use in 'artistic' interiors.

Morris's collection of other types of ceramics deserves further study. He certainly owned some porcelain and according to Henry Treffry Dunn's memoirs he was present – with Whistler, Rossetti, George Howard, Burne-Jones, two of the Ionides brothers and others – at a famous dinner party given by Charles Augustus Howell to show off a dish of the 'choicest Nankin ... a veritable piece of Imperial ware', with which Howell wanted to excite Rossetti's envy. It seems an unexpected setting for the distinctly unrarified Morris. Perhaps the best sense of his tastes can be gleaned from a passage in *News from Nowhere*, where he describes the tableware used by the inhabitants of his imagined utopia:

> The glass, crockery, and plate were very beautiful to my eyes, used to the study of mediæval art; but a nineteenth-century club-haunter would, I daresay, have found them rough, and lacking in finish; the crockery being lead-glazed pot-ware, though beautifully ornamented; the only porcelain being here and there a piece of old oriental ware. The glass again, though elegant and quaint, and very varied in form, was somewhat bubbled and hornier in texture than the commercial articles of the nineteenth century.

Glasswares, too, were investigated on his travels. May Morris recalled the family's visit to a glasshouse in Murano in 1878 when the glassmaker quickly produced 'a simple little glass of slightly coloured, bubbly metal', following an outline that Morris had sketched on the workshop floor with his stick. Morris failed to convince him that he wanted to place a serious order for the Oxford Street shop. Perhaps he was less than convinced himself. After all, the Whitefriars glassworks was in London and reliable.

He certainly had views on the design and some knowledge of glassmaking. In his lecture 'The Lesser Arts of Life' (1882) he said, 'In the hands of a good workman the metal is positively alive, and is, you may say, coaxing him to make something pretty. Nothing but commercial enterprise capturing an unlucky man and setting him down in the glass-maker's chair with his pattern beside him ... could turn out ugly glasses.'

The glass intended for his own use was that designed by Webb specifically for Red House (see X.26). This range was largely Germanic in taste, with overtones of Venice in its forms and its enamel decoration. It is unmistakably identifiable with the beginnings of emerging mid-nineteenth-century glass historicism. Webb was a regular visitor to the South Kensington Museum from the later 1850s, where he could have studied such Venetian and Northern European glass.

This personal tableware was to be made by James Powell & Sons' Whitefriars glassworks. Webb, as an architect, very likely had well-established contacts with the stained-glass department. On Rossetti's recommendation, both Burne-Jones and Madox Brown designed stained glass for Powell's during the late 1850s. The fact that only one example of this Red House range is known – and that is one of the unpainted goblets (fig.185) – suggests that little was made. The degree of time-consuming skill and the multiple processes necessary for enamelling and gilding glass and consequent expense may be one reason. It may also be that Morris himself preferred unpainted glass as more in keeping with Ruskinian principles. Webb soon produced designs for a

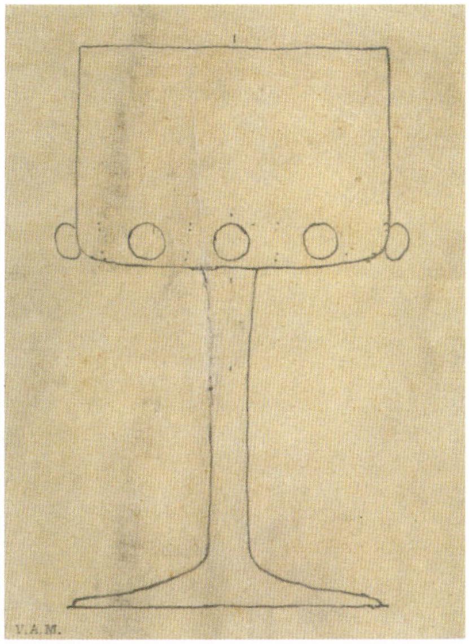

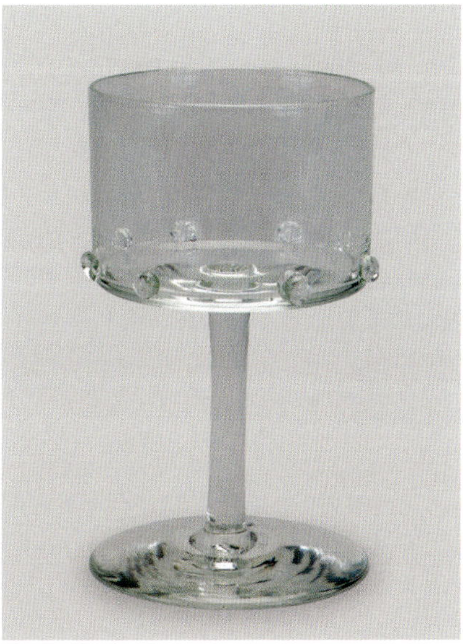

Fig.181 (above left) **Design for a claret glass, Philip Webb for James Powell & Sons, early 1860s.**
V&A (E.330–1944)
Given by Dorothy Walker

Fig.182 (above right) **Claret glass, designed by Philip Webb for James Powell & Sons.**
Birmingham Museums Trust

much larger, plainer range for sale through the firm (figs 181–2 and X.28). Its deceptively simple undecorated shapes formed by highly skilled hand-blowing are now seen as pioneeringly uncluttered and modernistic although it, too, has its design roots in seventeenth- and eighteenth-century Venetian and Northern European glass. This sold well at first but, curiously, from 1873 to some time after 1900 there is no record of table glass made to Webb's design and supplied by Powell's to the firm. A brochure produced in the 1880s makes no mention of table glass in an otherwise detailed list of stock. The firm was in financial difficulties in the mid-1870s and was reconstituted as Morris & Co. in 1875; this may be part of the explanation.

As the designs developed and moved further away from Webb's originals, his name and that of Morris were both embedded in the increasingly mythic association. Powell's themselves capitalized on this. After initial caution, as the Webb glass began to be sold successfully through Morris, Marshall, Faulkner & Co., Powell's commissioned further designs in similar taste from the architect Thomas Graham Jackson. They also evolved 'in-house' a range for standard glasshouse production of both Webb and Jackson-style glass. After 1900 parts of the 1862 range were re-introduced into production by Powell's.

There is no evidence that Morris ever designed any glass for the firm, though he may have occasionally taken an interest in its production. The painter William Blake Richmond and his wife Clara lived near to the Morrises in Hammersmith and the families were close friends. Many years later their son Sir Arthur Richmond recalled that when he was boy, around 1887, Morris called at the house, 'in a blue blouse with untidy trousers and disordered hair and beard ... In each hand he carried a large glass goblet he had just had made and now presented to my mother ... he pointed out their noble proportions, each capable of containing nearly a bottle of champagne – goblets, as he declared, fit for Vikings to drink from.' The two glasses (in a private collection) survive and are surely the work of a skilled glassmaker. They are in the form of a Dutch or German *Berkemeyer* (beaker) of around 1600 – generous but not over-sized. Were they made at Powell & Sons perhaps? There, James Crofts Powell was responsible for designs inspired by glassware in paintings seen in Dutch museums in the 1880s. If so, it is possible that Morris, who may well have been one of the many visitors to the glassworks, had some say in the detail and size of glasses presented to him on such an occasion.

In 1866 Warington Taylor wrote to Webb of Morris: 'How is he looking – I trust well & rosy with good wine.' A year or two later, censorious of the expense of Morris's good living and the state of the firm's finances he appealed to Morris directly: 'You must reduce your wine consumption down to 2½ bottles a day – this at 1/6 is somewhere about £68 a year.' Webb and Burne-Jones's account books with the firm also record substantial wine orders including Burgundy, White Burgundy, Bordeaux, Geisenheimer, Sparkling Burgundy and Claret.
It seems possible that the sizeable consumption resulted in the need for regular replacements of the glassware. In both account books there are references to the firm's tiles and glassware being purchased or taken in payment from stock at regular intervals for their own use. In the 1860s and early 1870s, the circle of Morris's own family, friends and followers all used Powell's glass tableware. Today it continues to be much sought-after by museums and collectors.

X.1

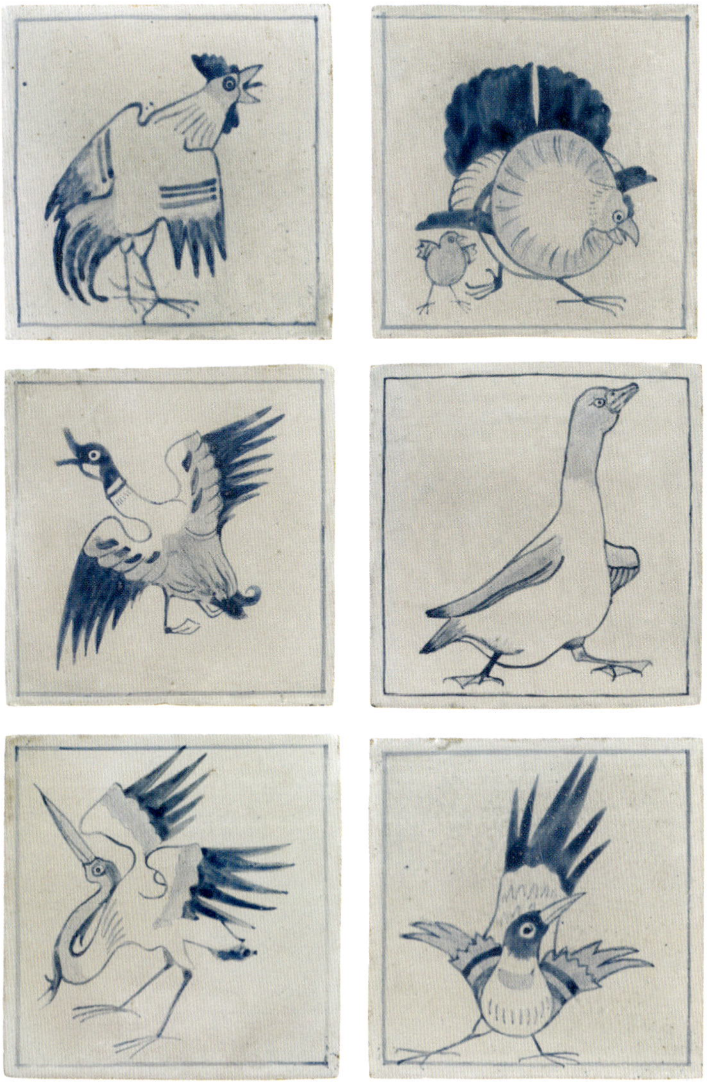

X.2a

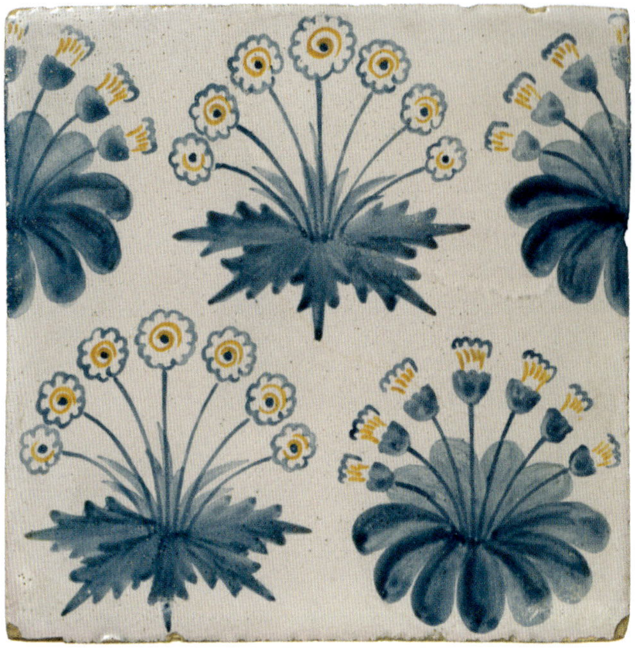

X.2b

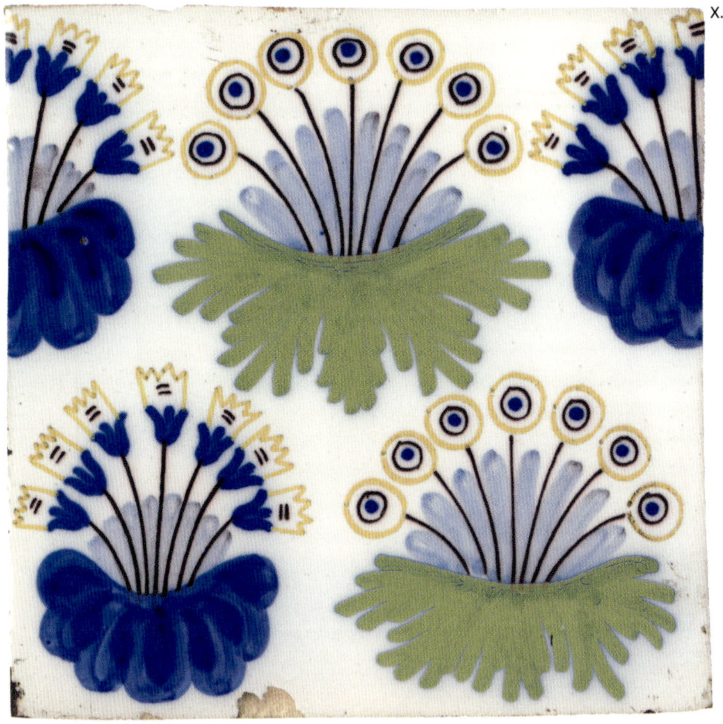

X.1
Six bird tiles
Designed by Philip Webb, *c.*1859–60
Decorated by Morris, Marshall, Faulkner & Co., 1860s
Hand-painted in blue on tin-glazed earthenware Dutch blanks, 15.2 x 15.2 cm each
V&A (C.72–77–2005)

These animated tiles, featuring a cock, hen and chick, duck, goose, heron and magpie, come from the fireplace of a house in Cambridge, where they were set among examples of the 'leaves and berries' pattern (fig.175). The designs were first used for stained-glass quarries at Red House (see VII.5) and at Sandroyd, near Cobham in Surrey, built by Webb for the painter John Roddam Spencer Stanhope between 1860 and 1861.

The bird motifs were inspired by medieval prototypes. Richard and Hilary Myers have identified stained-glass precedents at Wells Cathedral and The Commandery in Worcester. The William Morris Gallery owns five examples of these bird tiles, three of which once belonged to Lucy Orrinsmith (née Faulkner) and were probably painted by her or by her sister Kate. Produced in small batches, the details and shading differ slightly. Some, like these examples, have a simple line border while others have grass or wave motifs beneath the birds.

X.2
***Daisy* tiles**
Designed by William Morris, *c.*1862

a Decorated by Morris, Marshall, Faulkner & Co., *c.*1870s
Hand-painted in blue and yellow on tin-glazed earthenware Dutch blank, 13 x 13 cm
Mark: '108' (painted)
V&A (C.58–1931)
Bequeathed by James Richardson Holliday

b Probably made by Ravesteijn tileworks, Utrecht, *c.*1890–1914
Tin-glazed earthenware hand-painted with in-glaze colours, 15 x 15 cm
Hans van Lemmen

This design was inspired by patterned wall hangings depicted in a fifteenth-century illuminated manuscript (fig.205), as were early embroideries and wallpaper (XII.3 and XI.1). The tile decorated by the firm was painted on a Dutch blank (X.2a). These were made by rolling out damp clay and cutting it to size by hand using a template and cutter. The lead glaze contains tin, giving it an opaque white appearance when fired. The firm's painters applied the blue and yellow on top of the already fired Dutch glaze. The tile was then fired again at a lower temperature, 700–800°C. The glaze therefore barely softened and consequently the colour sits on top of the background and is not fully fused into it.

Daisy was a very popular pattern and was copied in England (the Staffordshire firm of Minton Hollins produced a transfer-printed version) and Holland from the late 1880s. Hand-painted in-glaze versions were produced by both Ravesteijn of Utrecht (pattern no. 438) and Tjallingii of Harlingen (pattern no. 492).

Myles Birket Foster owned a washstand with an early version of the *Daisy* tiles, possibly acquired at the 1862 International Exhibition or soon after.

X.3
***Primrose* tile**
Designed by William Morris, *c.*1862–5
Decorated by Morris, Marshall, Faulkner & Co.
Hand-painted in blue on tin-glazed earthenware Dutch blank, 13 x 13 cm
Mark: '102' (painted)
V&A (C.59–1931)
Bequeathed by James Richardson Holliday

Morris's inspiration for this type of simple flower design, used on both tiles and embroideries, came from illuminated manuscripts, herbals and the eighteenth-century Dutch and English tradition of flower-painted tin-glazed tiles. No official name for this pattern has been recorded.

X.4
Pomegranate tree and shield
Designed by William Morris, *c.*1862
Probably painted by Lucy Faulkner for Morris, Marshall, Faulkner & Co.
Hand-painted in various colours on tin-glazed earthenware Dutch blanks, 12.7 x 12.7 cm each
William Morris Gallery, London Borough of Waltham Forest (C214)
Six tiles purchased with the assistance of the MGC/V&A Purchase Grant Fund, 1995; the seventh presented by Richard and Hilary Myers, 1996 (not illustrated)

These tiles formed the central motif of the hall fireplace at Sandroyd, home of John Roddam Spencer Stanhope whose initials appear on the shield. A photograph of the fireplace before the removal of the tiles (reproduced in Myers 1996) shows that the decoration included figures of *Adam* and *Eve*, flanking a Latin inscription from the Book of Genesis. Below this was the pomegranate tree, with figures from Chaucer's *Legend of Good Women* on either side – *Alceste*, *Cleopatra*, *Philomela* and *Thisbe*. The use of a built-up layer of enamel to create a relief effect can be seen in the leaves and fruit of the tree. A note in a copy of Aymer Vallance's *William Morris: His Art, His Writings and His Public Life* that once belonged to Lucy Orrinsmith (née Faulkner), suggests that she painted the Sandroyd overmantel, or at least the figurative tiles (William Morris Gallery, K330a).

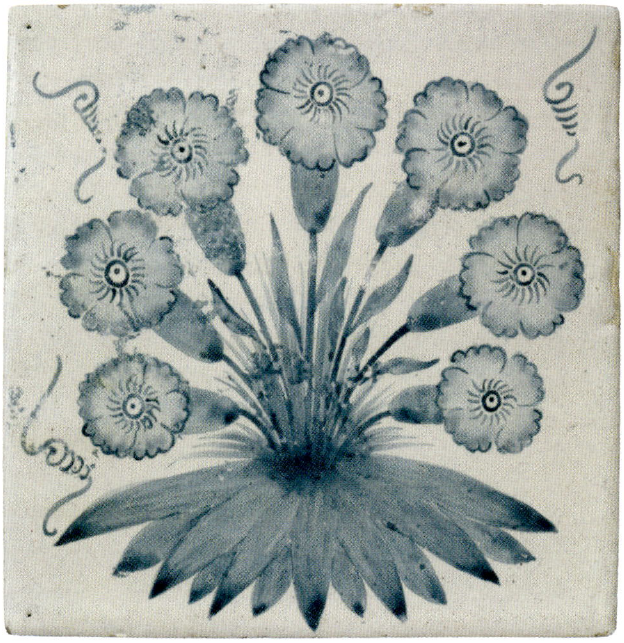
X.3

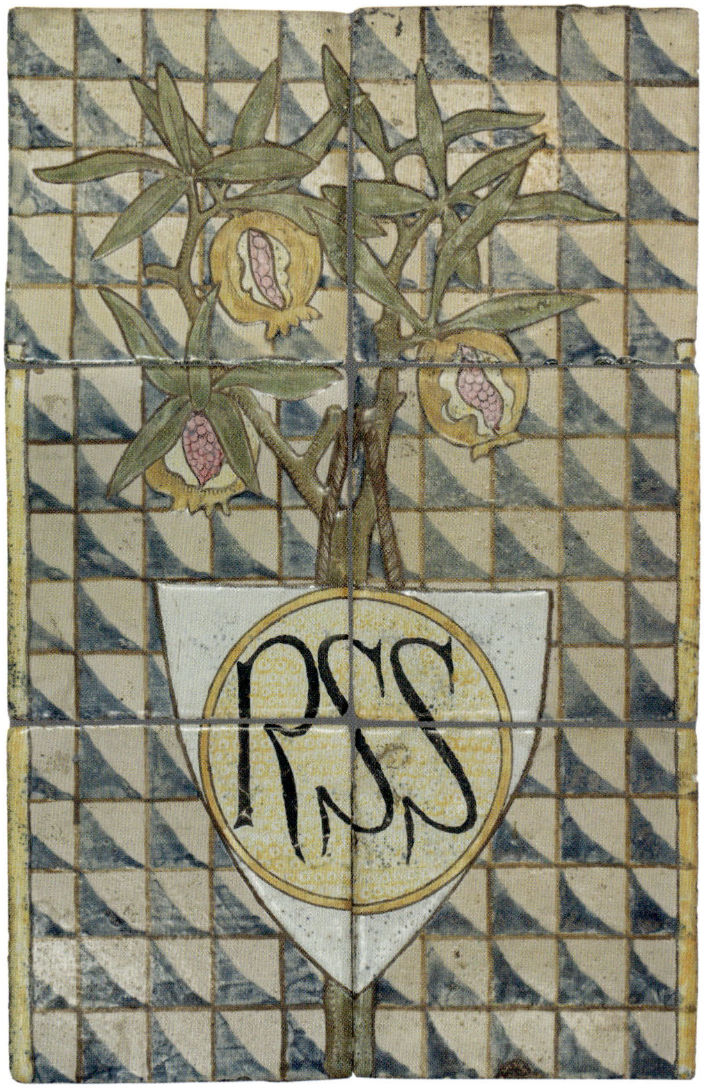

X.4

X.5

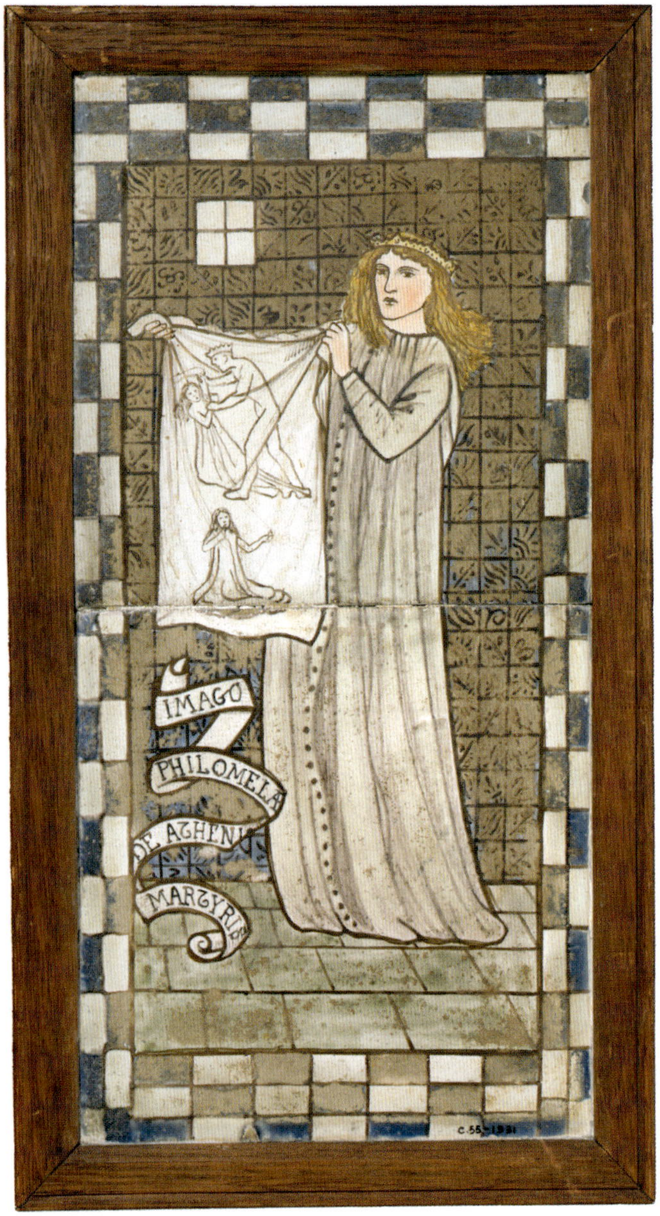

X.6

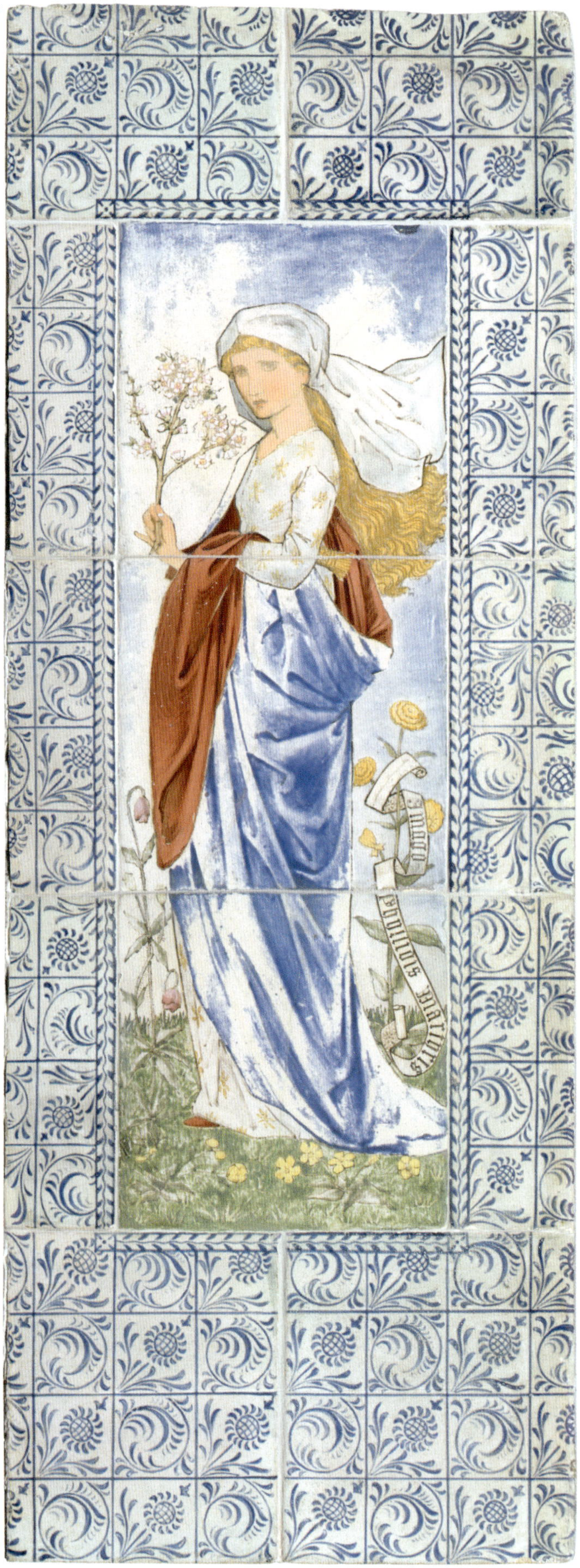

X.5
Imago Philomela de Atheni Martyris
Designed by Edward Burne-Jones, 1862
Decorated by Morris, Marshall, Faulkner & Co., 1860s or early 1870s
Hand-painted in various colours on tin-glazed earthenware Dutch blanks, 30.5 x 15.3 cm
V&A (C.55–1931)
Bequeathed by James Richardson Holliday

In the summer of 1862 Burne-Jones's account book lists a payment of £3 for 'Tiles 12 single figures'. This almost certainly refers to a series of designs based on Chaucer's *Legend of Good Women*. The Athenian princess Philomela first appeared in the tiled fireplace at Sandroyd (see X.4). Kidnapped and raped by her brother-in-law Tereus, who cut out her tongue, she revealed his crime by weaving a tapestry. The painted tile background includes an approximation of the *Swan* pattern (X.12) and a fleur-de-lis.

For the brightest result, different colours can be fired at different temperatures, depending on the metallic oxides and fluxes composing them. This is a time-consuming and expensive practice and here Morris followed the more usual route of applying and firing all the colours in a single process, which can present a number of problems. On this panel, the blue has been painted on to the tin-glaze first, followed by the brown details. Although cobalt blue is a colour that can survive very high temperatures (hence its use in blue and white porcelain) here much of it is lost.

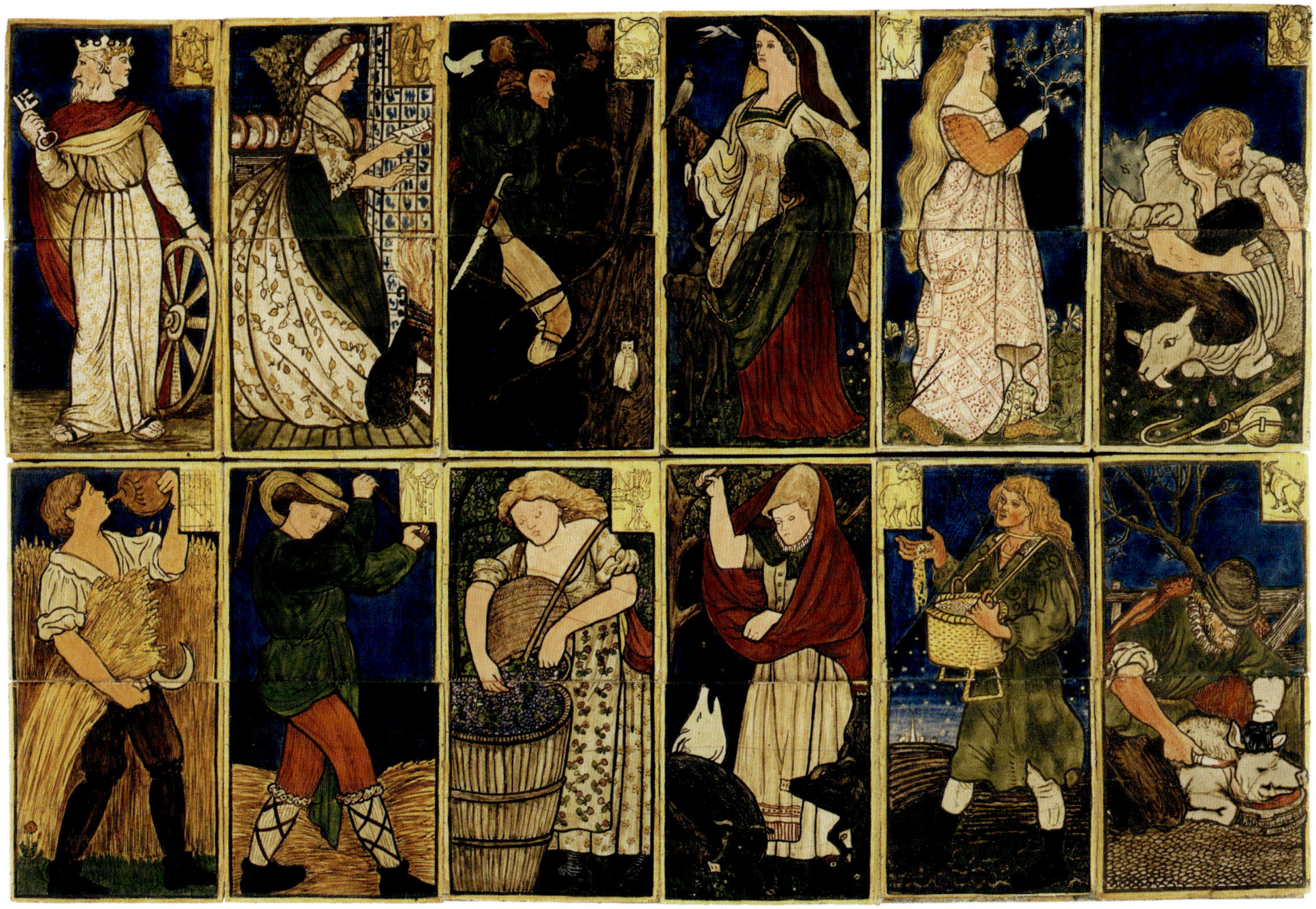

X.7

X.6

Imago Phyllidis Martyris
with *Scroll* border
Designed by Edward Burne-Jones and William Morris, 1864 and *c.*1870 respectively
Decorated by Morris, Marshall, Faulkner & Co., *c.*1870
Hand-painted in various colours on tin-glazed earthenware Dutch blanks, 77.2 x 30.2 cm
V&A (Circ.530–1962)
Given by the Crown Estate Commissioners

This panel is one of two acquired from a fireplace at 1 Palace Green, the London house of George Howard, later Earl of Carlisle. Phyllis, daughter of the King of Thrace, holds a sprig of almond blossom. In classical mythology, abandoned by her lover Demophoön, she commits suicide. The gods transform her body into a tree that blossoms on her lover's return. The story is treated in Chaucer's *Legend of Good Women*, as is that of Ariadne, the subject of the second Palace Green panel (Circ.531–1962).

Both figures are versions of those designed in 1864 for stained glass at Birket Foster's house, The Hill, Witley (VII.20). The figure of Phyllis has suffered some of the technical problems that Morris encountered in the firing of his tiles. The skilfully decorated *Scroll* tiles, with a special border added for the Palace Green commission, are the only known examples painted by the firm (there is another single tile from the same batch in the V&A's collection, C.25–1995). All other examples of the pattern, and many variations, are Dutch-made and decorated.

X.7

Labours of the Months
Designed by William Morris, Dante Gabriel Rossetti, Edward Burne-Jones, Ford Madox Brown and Philip Webb, *c.*1862
Painted by Lucy Faulkner for Morris, Marshall, Faulkner & Co.
Hand-painted in various colours on tin-glazed earthenware Dutch blanks, 12.7 x 12.7 cm each
William Morris Gallery, London Borough of Waltham Forest (C216)
Purchased with the assistance of the MGC/V&A Purchase Grant Fund, National Heritage Memorial Fund, Friends of the William Morris Gallery and Walthamstow Historical Society, 1995

This series illustrating the 12 months of the year was also used for the overmantel at Queens' College, Cambridge (fig.173), although there are differences in the colours, choice of subjects and size of the tiles. Ten of the panels in this set have the addition of zodiac symbols, designed by Webb (Aquarius bearing a strong likeness to Morris). Lucy Faulkner, who painted the tiles from the partners' designs, added her monogram to the borders of February and December.

The tiles appear to have been framed by Morris & Co. in the early twentieth century, when April (flower-bearer) and May (falconry) were set in the incorrect sequence. In 1916 they were loaned to the Arts and Crafts Exhibition at the Royal Academy. Nothing is known of their earlier history. A third complete set, produced for the house of Lord Justice and Lady White in Unthank Road, Norwich, remains in a private collection and three figures from the series were used for a tiled fireplace at Cavendish Rectory, Suffolk. Several of the designs were also made in stained glass for Onecote Vicarage in Staffordshire and The Hill at Witley.

X.8

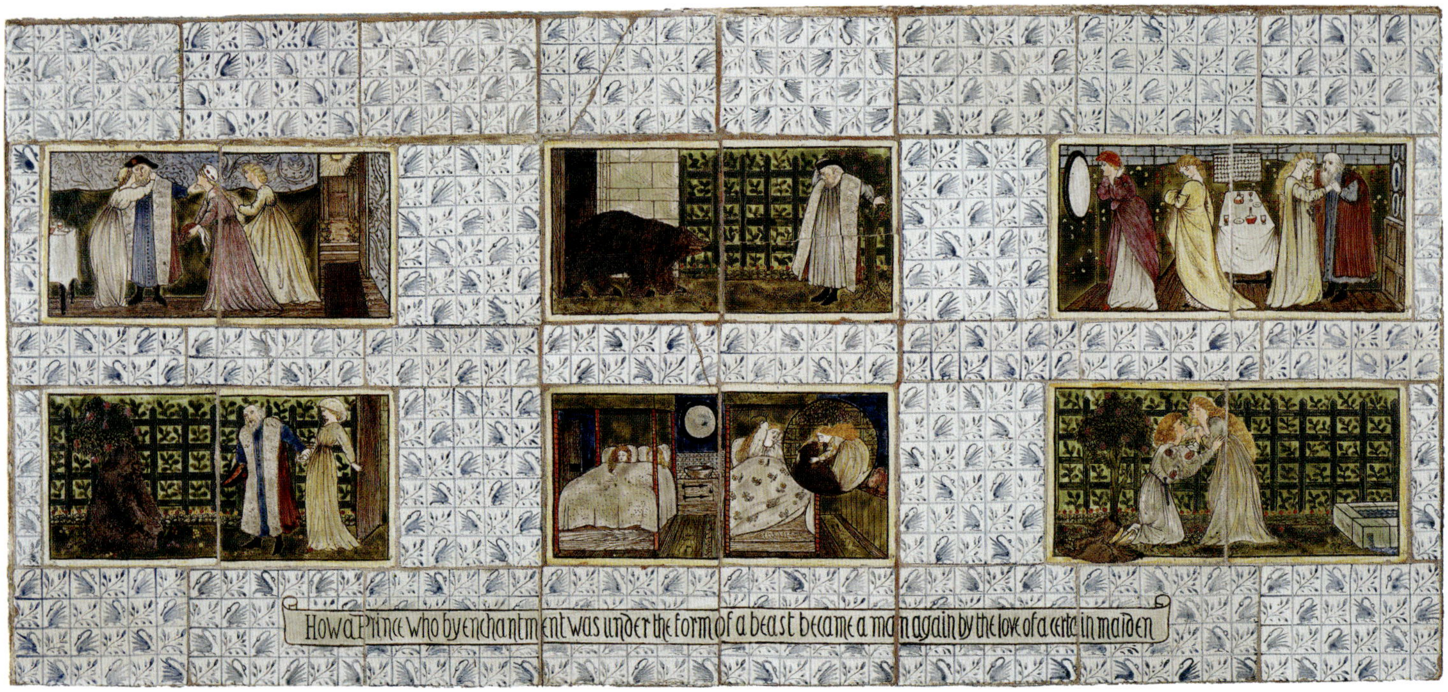

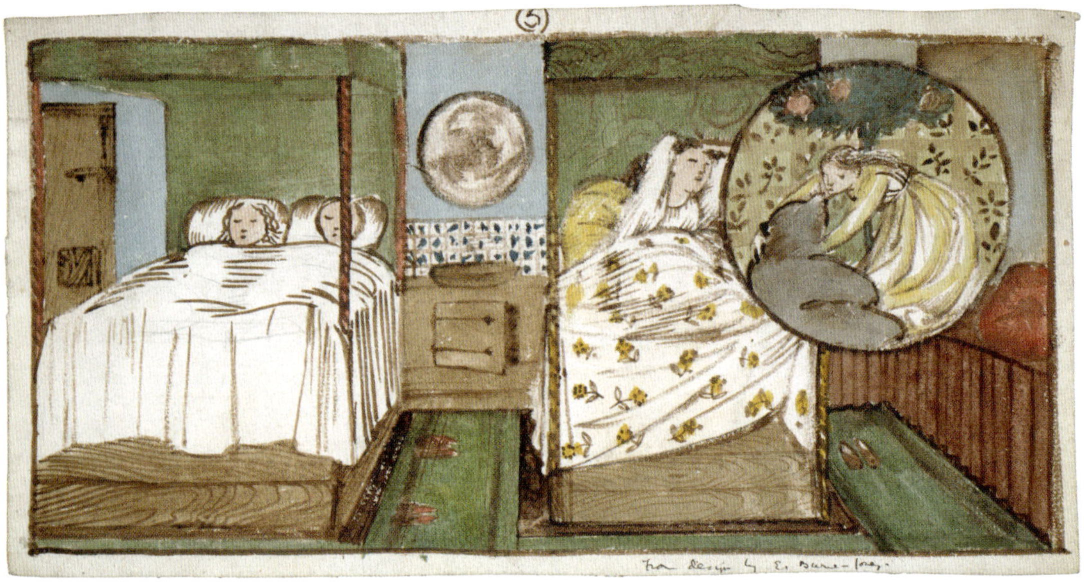

Fig.183 **Beauty dreams of kissing the Beast, drawing after Burne-Jones's original design, possibly by Charles Fairfax Murray.**
V&A (E.1297–1931)

X.8
Beauty and the Beast
Designed by Edward Burne-Jones, 1863
Painted by Lucy Faulkner for Morris, Marshall, Faulkner & Co., *c.*1863–4
Hand-painted in various colours on tin-glazed earthenware Dutch blanks, 60.5 x 127 cm
William Morris Gallery, London Borough of Waltham Forest (C75)

This is one of three fairytale panels ordered by the painter Myles Birket Foster to go above bedroom fireplaces in his new house, The Hill, at Witley. Burne-Jones designed the six narrative scenes and noted in his account book with the firm a payment of £6 for 'Set of subjects for Tiles "Beauty & Beast"' in July 1863. A further payment of £2 the same month was probably for the separate designs of *The Prince* and *Beauty* (or *The Merchant's Daughter*) that decorated the splays of the fireplace below and were later adapted for stained glass (VII.22). Morris designed the blue and white *Swan* pattern (X.12) and Lucy Faulkner painted the tiles, signing the border of each scene with her initials 'LJF'. The scroll below is inscribed: 'How a Prince who by enchantment was under the form of a beast became a man again by the love of a certain maiden'.

Preliminary sketches by Burne-Jones are in the Tate (A00107) and the V&A (E.2890–1927). The V&A also has a series of drawings made after the originals, possibly by Charles Fairfax Murray. These were annotated by Burne-Jones's son Philip in 1921 (who mistakenly claimed they were made about 1861). The *Beauty and the Beast* designs were repeated, with variations, for later commissions including an overmantel for Tromode House, Isle of Man, made around 1870 (sold at Christie's, June 1993). Two tiles depicting the third scene were bequeathed to the V&A by James Richardson Holliday in 1931 and were probably acquired directly from Morris & Co. (C.54–1931).

X.9

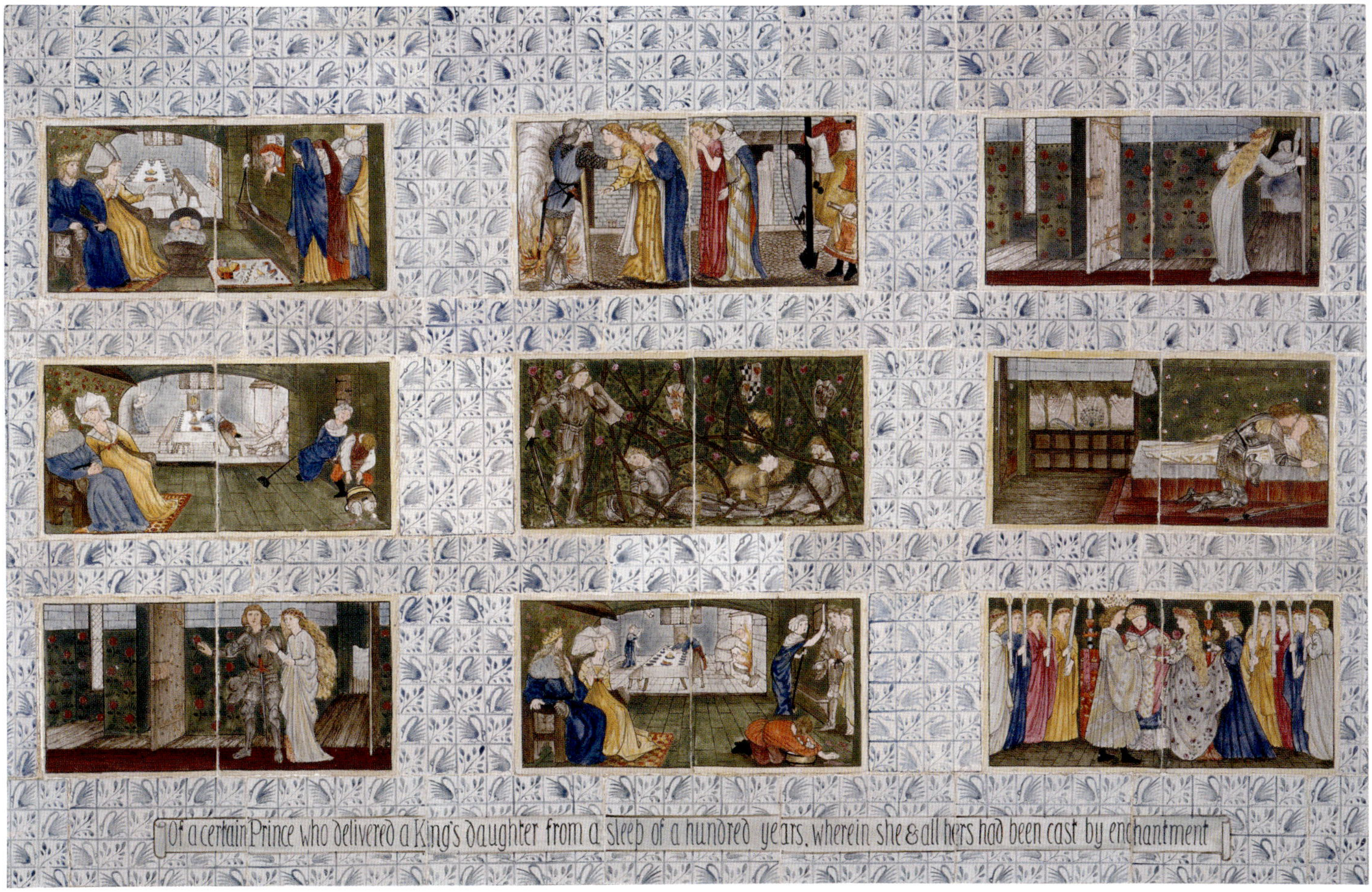

X.9
Sleeping Beauty
Designed by Edward Burne-Jones, 1864
Painted by Lucy Faulkner for Morris, Marshall, Faulkner & Co., *c.*1864–5
Hand-painted in various colours on tin-glazed earthenware Dutch blanks, 76.2 x 120.6 cm
V&A (Circ.520–1953)

This is the third fairytale overmantel that Burne-Jones designed for The Hill, illustrating the legend of Sleeping Beauty from her birth to her wedding. In January 1864 his account book with the firm noted (with a degree of humour): 'To 10 designs of Sleeping Beauty at the mean & unremunerative price of 30/– ea[ch]'. This came to a total of £15, more than he had received for the *Beauty and the Beast* series the previous year. As the panel only includes nine scenes it is not clear what the tenth design related to.

The inscription reads: 'Of a certain Prince who delivered a King's daughter from a sleep of a hundred years, wherein she & all hers had been cast by enchantment'. As Emma Ferry first identified, Lucy Faulkner's monogram can be found on the third scene showing Beauty and the wicked fairy. The medieval-style interiors of the castle, including the king and queen's canopied settle and the walls of the princess's bedchamber, recall the decoration of Red House.

The panel was purchased by the V&A following its loan to the exhibition of *Victorian and Edwardian Decorative Arts* held in 1952. The lender had acquired the tiles, along with the William Morris Gallery's *Beauty and the Beast* panel, from the last owner of The Hill. *Sleeping Beauty* tiles were also used in the drawing room of Heath Old Hall, near Wakefield in Yorkshire, and another set is in the Ashmolean Museum, signed by Lucy Faulkner.

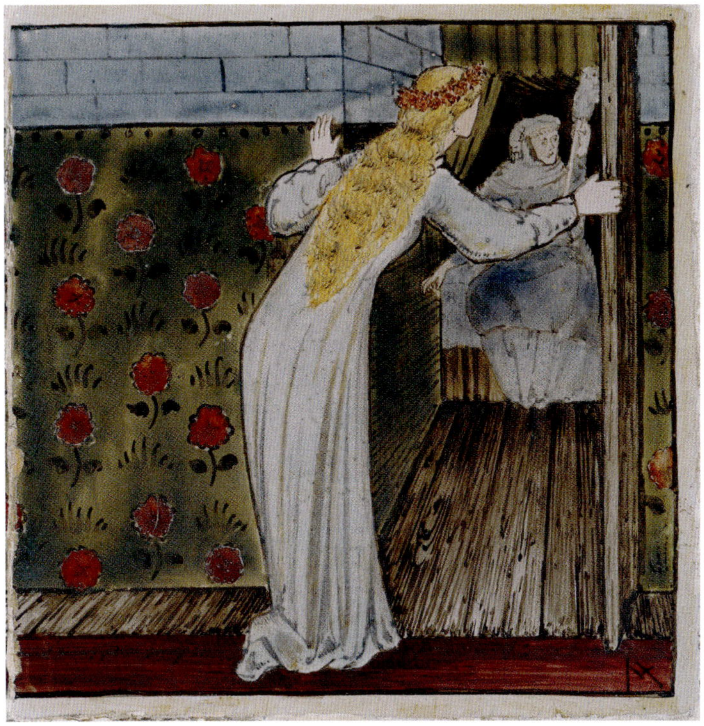

Fig.184 **Detail of *Sleeping Beauty*, with Lucy Faulkner's monogram in lower right corner.**

X.10

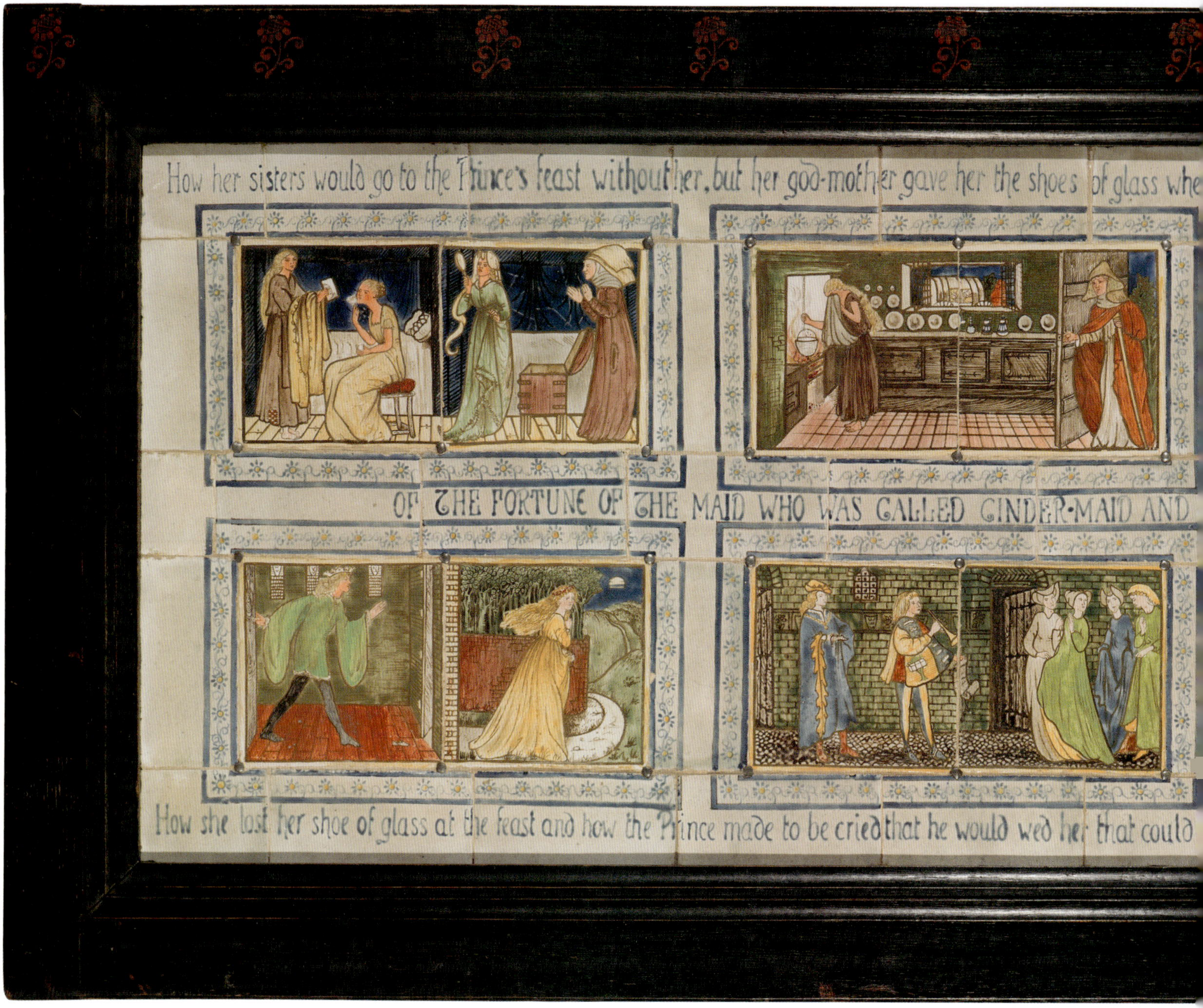

X.10
Cinderella
Designed by Edward Burne-Jones, 1862
Painted by Lucy Faulkner for Morris, Marshall, Faulkner & Co., before 1870
Hand-painted in various colours on tin-glazed earthenware Dutch blanks, 71.8 x 141.6 cm
The Huntington Library, Art Museum and Botanical Gardens (2000.5.1872)

Cinderella was the first fairytale tile series that Burne-Jones designed for The Hill and is recorded in his account book in September 1862 for a fee of £7 10*s*. The original panel is in the Walker Art Gallery, Liverpool, and a photograph shows it *in situ* (fig.177). This is a later version, without the *Swan*-patterned background, produced for an unknown client. Each narrative scene is surrounded with a border of daisies and the descriptive captions are more extensive than in Birket Foster's example. The ebonized oak frame is also decorated with a row of daisies. The panel is signed with Lucy Faulkner's monogram and therefore presumably pre-dates her marriage in 1870.

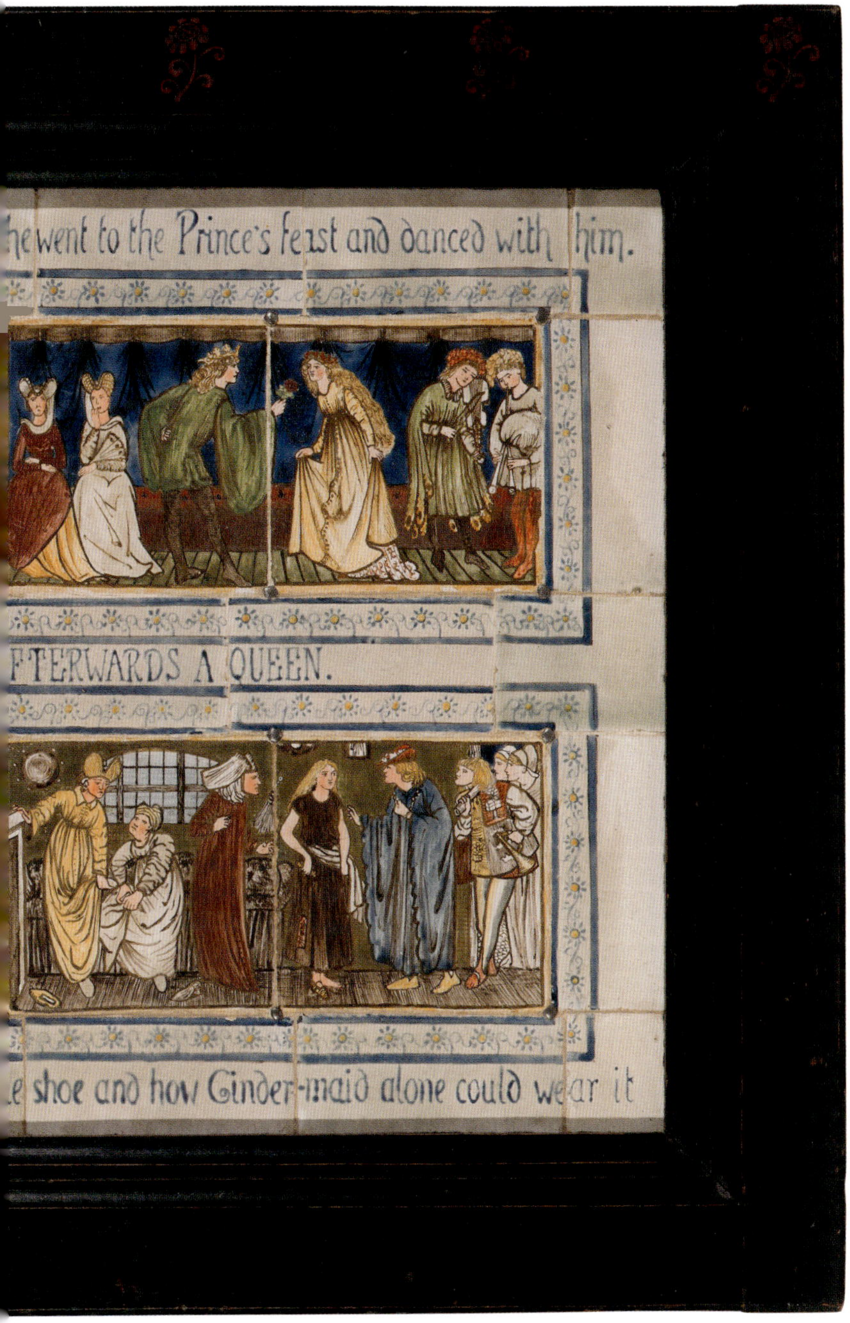

X.11

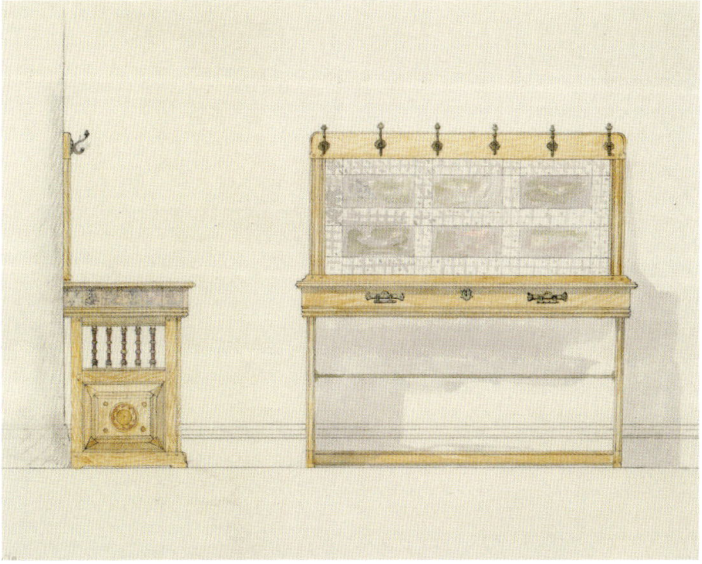

X.12

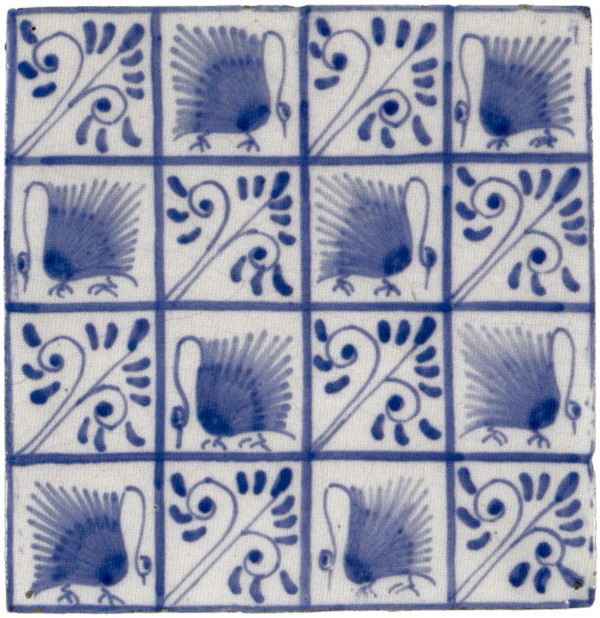

X.11
Design for hall table
John Pollard Seddon, undated
Pencil, ink and watercolour,
34.4 x 49.5 cm
Inscribed: 'Seddon & Co.
70 Grosvenor St., J.P.S.'
V&A (D.1804–1896)
Presented by Margaret Birch

As the Myers first noted, the V&A's collection of designs for furniture and decorative fittings by the architect John Pollard Seddon includes several that feature the firm's tiles. Beneath the hat pegs on this hall table, for example, appears to be a fairytale series and the 'flower clump' designs on the side elevation may be attributable to Morris. The collection also includes a single sheet showing the layout of three tiled fireplaces (*Beauty and the Beast*, *Cinderella* and the *Heads of Chaucer, Saint Cecilia* and *Penelope*) and a tiled panel that includes the *Labours of the Months* (D.2050–1896). Seddon was close to the Morris circle in the early 1860s, famously commissioning painted panels for *King René's Honeymoon* cabinet (IX.13), and his use of the firm's tiles warrants further investigation.

X.12
***Swan* tile**
Originally designed by William Morris, *c.*1862
Possibly made by Ravesteijn tileworks, Utrecht, 1870s or later
Tin-glazed earthenware hand-painted with in-glaze blue,
15.6 x 15.5 cm
British Museum (1994,0512.1)

This design was attributed to Morris by Aymer Vallance and by May Morris in the catalogue of the V&A's 1934 exhibition on the centenary of Morris's birth. It was used for the backgrounds of the overmantels at The Hill and Queens' College, Cambridge (fig.173). These early iterations were decorated by the firm using the 'on-glaze' technique. Around 1870, Morris transferred the production of some of the firm's most popular repeating patterns to the Netherlands. This tile is entirely Dutch-made and decorated using the more durable 'in-glaze' technique. Dutch versions like this can be found in the Green Room fireplace at Kelmscott Manor and were photographed *in situ* in 1896.

X.13
The Seasons
Originally designed by Edward Burne-Jones, *c.*1863–4
Decorated by Morris, Marshall, Faulkner & Co., *c.*1870s
Hand-painted in blue on tin-glazed earthenware Dutch blanks, 15.2 x 15.2 cm each
William Morris Gallery, London Borough of Waltham Forest (C213)

One of the bedroom fireplaces at The Hill, Witley, featured an earlier set of *The Seasons*, with a surround of *Swan* tiles. The scene with women seated around a well is closely related to Burne-Jones's watercolour *Green Summer* (1864) and the Myers have argued that the series was possibly inspired by an unpublished romance by Morris with the same title. The tiles illustrated here were painted after Burne-Jones's designs had been redrawn around 1870, probably by Charles Fairfax Murray. They were acquired from the collection of G.K. Beaulah.

Blue seems to have been painted over the Dutch tin-glaze, without any further glazing, and has flaked off leaving behind only the residual effects of the colour. Perhaps this problem was caused by an inappropriate kiln (the tiles were fired with stained glass in the enamelling kilns) and insufficient control over temperature, atmosphere and rates of heating. Such flaking could occur during firing or very soon afterwards. Insufficiently glazed tiles, fixed where they were subjected to daily wear or to extreme temperatures or smoke, would quickly deteriorate.

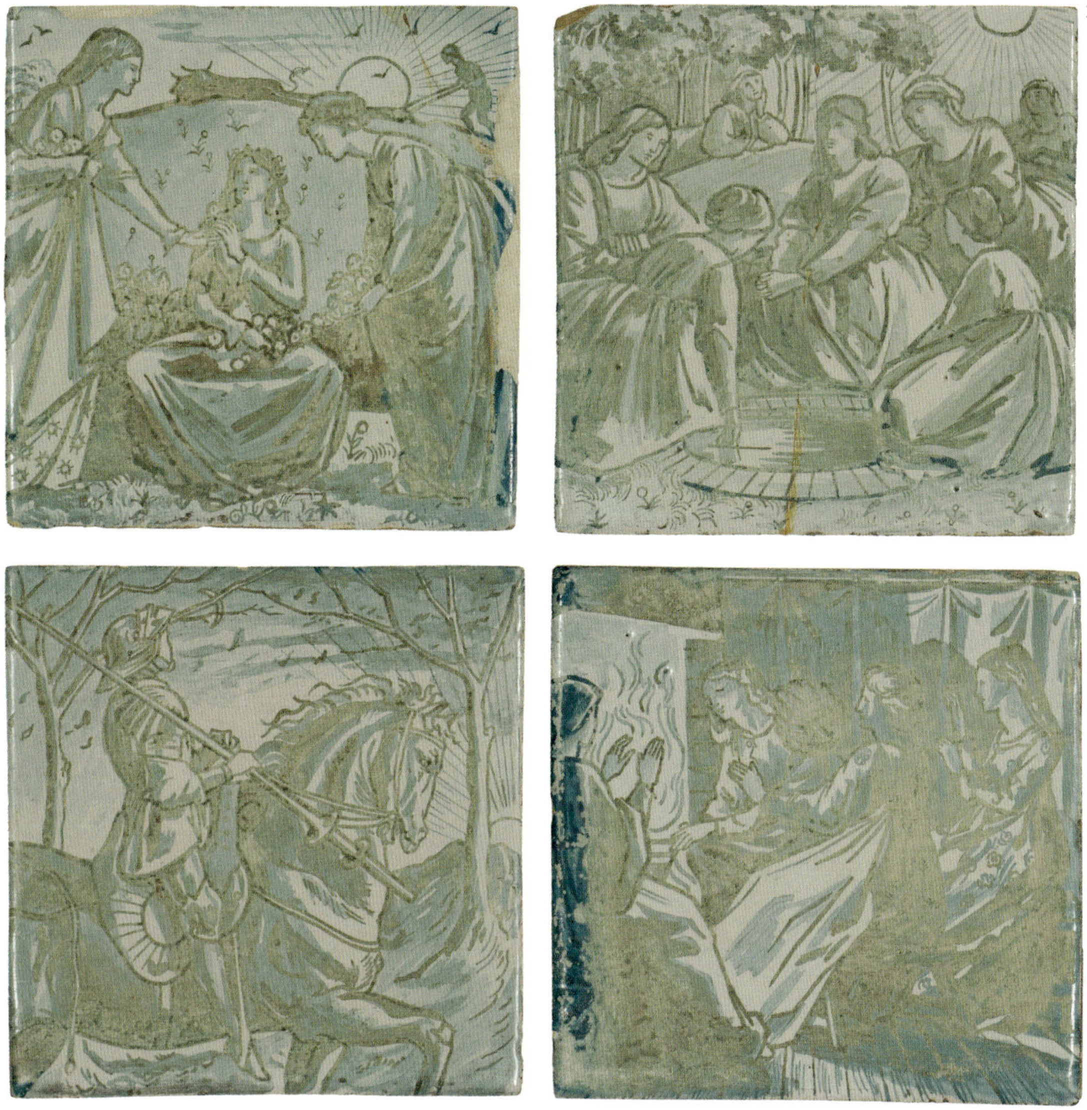
X.13

X.14
Geoffrey Chaucer
Designed by Edward Burne-Jones, 1863
Painted by William Morris for Morris, Marshall, Faulkner & Co., 1864
Hand-painted in various colours on tin-glazed earthenware Dutch blank, 15.3 x 15.3 cm
V&A (C.61–1979)

The frame has a handwritten inscription on the reverse: 'Enamelled by W. Morris, 1864. Very few of the tiles subsequently issued by Morris & Co. appear to have been painted by Morris himself but rather by draughtsmen employed in his works. Mr Morris told me with respect to this tile that he painted it himself. Arthur Church.' Sir Arthur Church was a chemist and ceramics expert who wrote the handbooks on *English Pottery* (1884) and *English Porcelain* (1885) for the South Kensington Museum. In 1895 he advised Morris on methods for bleaching ink-stained paper at the Kelmscott Press.

The model for Chaucer is believed to have been Rossetti. It was one of a number of roundel heads first designed for stained glass at Onecote Vicarage, Staffordshire (1863). The tile was acquired from an untraced source via the Fine Art Society.

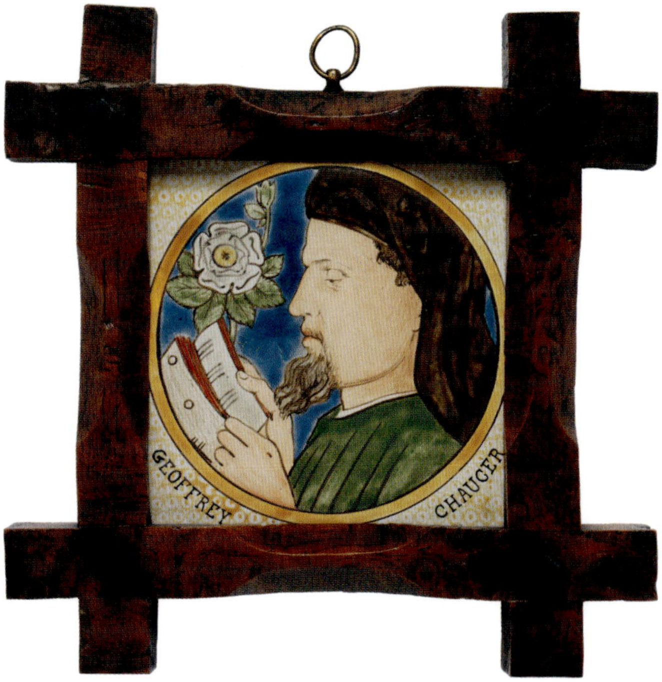

X.14

X.15
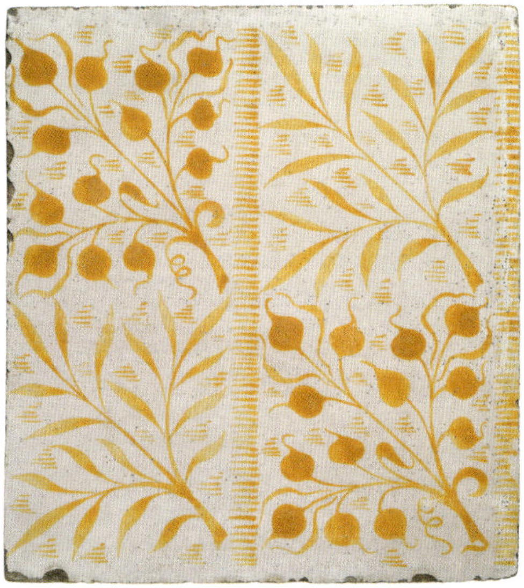

X.17a
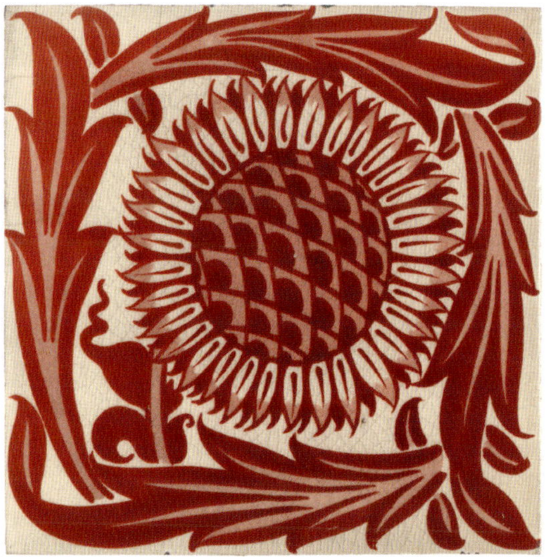

X.16
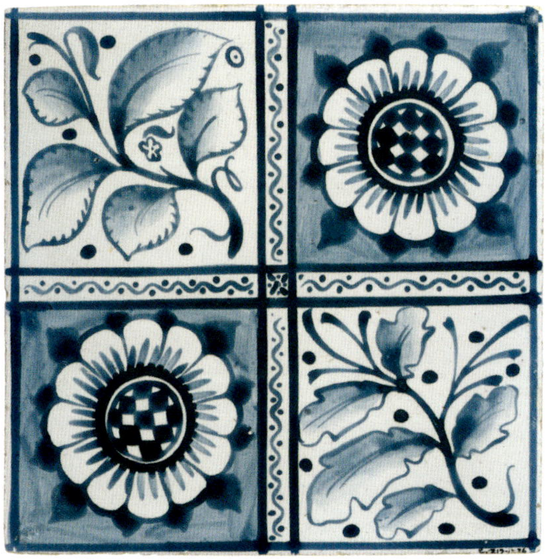

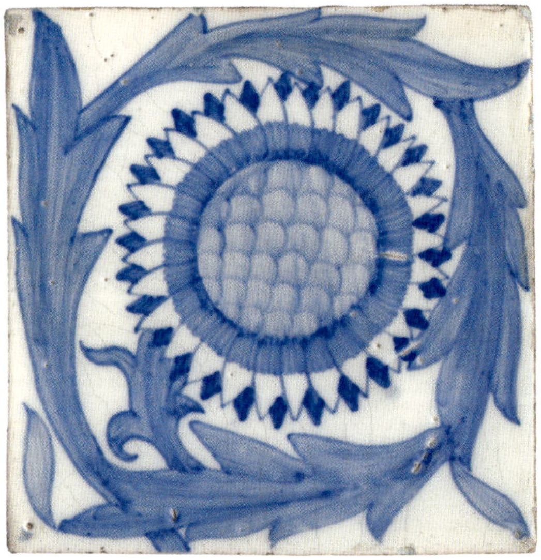
X.17b

X.17
***Sunflower* tiles**
Designed by William Morris
or William De Morgan, *c.*1870

a Decorated by William De Morgan, *c.*1870s
Stencilled, red lustre on earthenware
English blank, 15.3 x 15.3 cm
Hans van Lemmen

b Made by Ravesteijn tileworks, Utrecht, *c.*1890
Tin-glazed earthenware hand-painted with in-glaze blue, 15.3 x 15.3 cm
Hans van Lemmen

The design for *Sunflower* was lent by Morris & Co. to the centenary exhibition held at the V&A in 1934. Although it was credited to Morris in the catalogue (no. 196) – overseen by May Morris – William De Morgan's involvement cannot be ruled out. He made a number of variations of the design in both coloured and, as here, in lustre glazes. The English tile is a dust-pressed glazed blank. The decoration was stencilled onto the already fired glaze. The metallic finish was created by introducing smoke into the kiln during the lustre firing.

The Dutch tile was tin-glazed and decorated and then fired in one operation. The blue decoration has therefore fused into the glaze. The pattern was transferred from a paper tracing probably by 'pouncing': minute holes delineate the outline of the pattern and this outline is transferred by dabbing powdered colour through the holes onto the tile. Of the Dutch tile makers, Ravesteijn is the only one where *Sunflower* has been identified in its catalogues.

X.15
***Bough* tile**
Designed by William Morris, *c.*1870
Decorated by Morris, Marshall Faulkner & Co., early 1870s
Hand-painted in yellow on tin-glazed earthenware Dutch blank,
15.3 x 14 cm
Private collection

The pattern has echoes of Morris's *Fruit* wallpaper (XI.3) and Webb's gesso decoration for the Green Dining Room at the South Kensington Museum (VIII.5). It was also available in blue (e.g. V&A C.57–1931). By the 1880s, versions were produced by the Dutch tile companies Ravesteijn of Utrecht (probably with Morris's approval) and Tjallingii of Harlingen in 5-inch and 6-inch sizes. A related sixteen-square design was made in both Morris and William De Morgan's workshops; the latter called it *Small B.*

X.16
Tile, probably *Longden* design
Probably designed by Philip Webb
Decorated by Morris, Marshall, Faulkner & Co., *c.*1870
Hand-painted in blue on tin-glazed Dutch earthenware blank, 15 x 15 cm
V&A (C.219–1976)

This tile demonstrates how successful the firm could be with ceramic firing. Much depends on temperature and this example was presumably fired in a reasonably hot part of the kiln. Under a microscope, the blue clearly sits on top of the tin glaze. This dispels any doubt that this is a Dutch-made tile decorated in London. Interestingly, no further glaze layer over the painting is visible. The pits or holes are probably stilt-marks. Tiles are normally fired in stacks of about six, each supported one on top of the other by tiny unglazed clay props known as 'stilts'. The confidently painted cobalt blue includes a form of gum to help it to adhere and has been thinned, possibly with water, to make possible the washed, shaded areas.

An entry in Philip Webb's accounts for 1 January 1870 – a year in which he records designing at least five other tile patterns – notes a payment of 10*s.* for 'Design. Longden, tile'. Named after the iron-founders Longden of Sheffield, it is thought to be this oak, bayleaf and sunflower pattern. One of the firm's most popular designs, it was also available in yellow and was sold by Barnard, Bishop & Barnards of Norwich as side panels to their cast-iron fireplace surrounds. Ravesteijn of Utrecht also made a version of this pattern.

A *Longden* tile decorated by the firm in a private collection is marked with a printed stamp '449 Oxford Street Morris London W'.

X.20

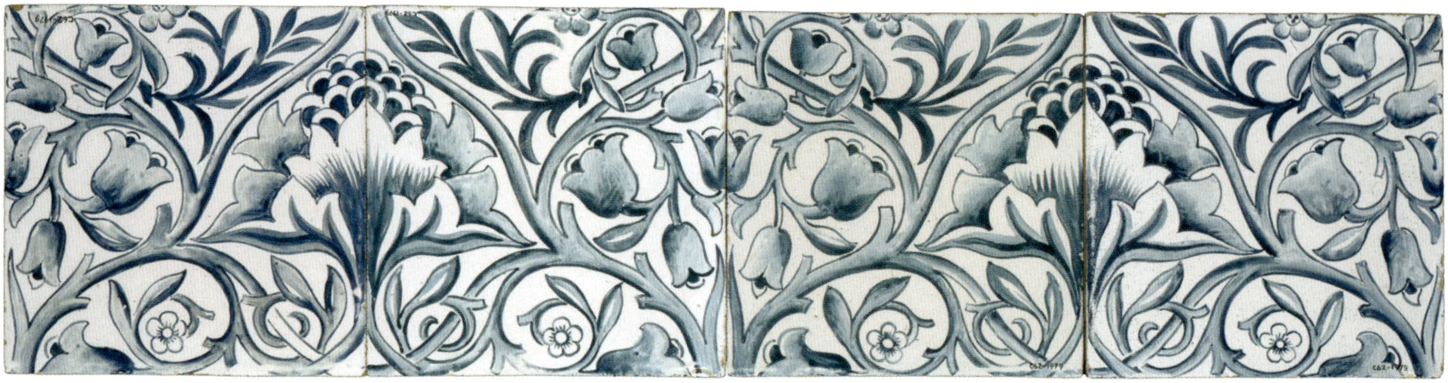

X.18

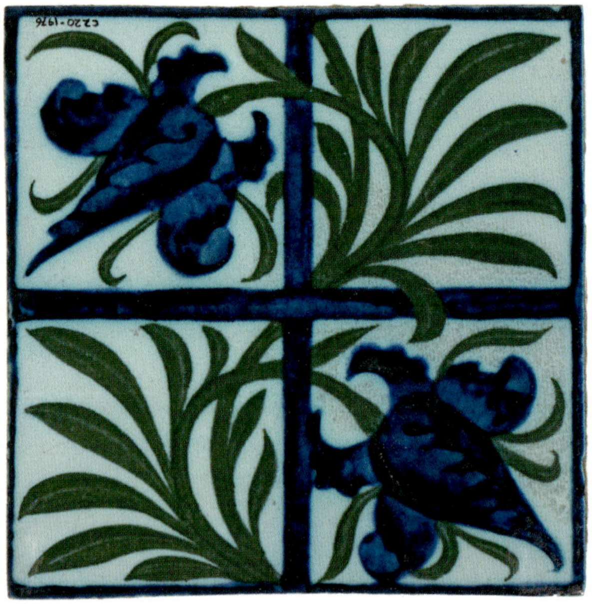

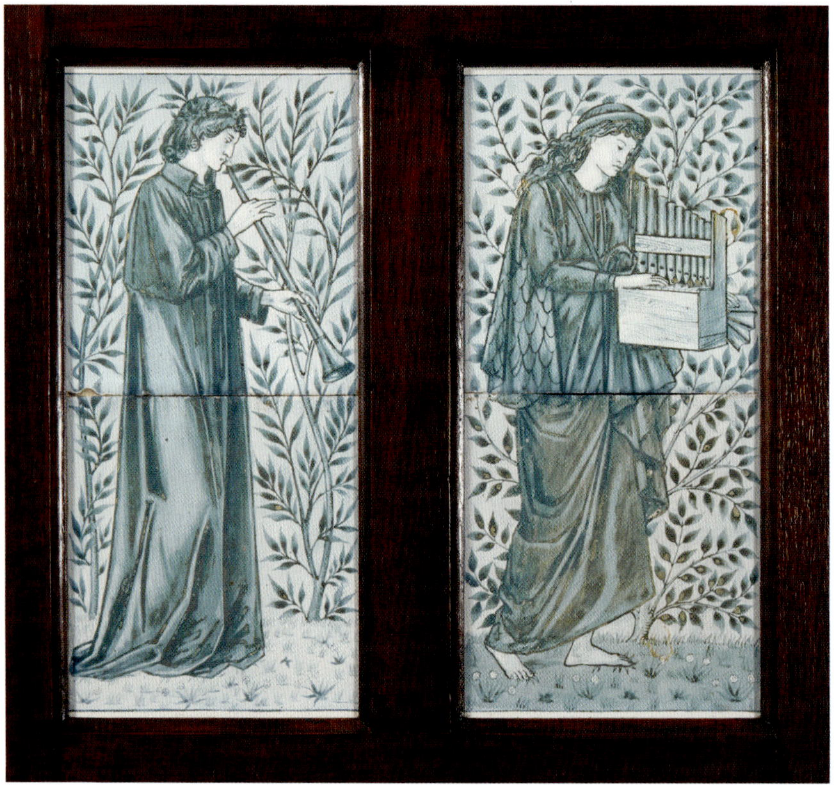

X.19

X.18
***Tulip and Trellis* tile**
Designed by William Morris, *c.*1872
Decorated by William De Morgan
Hand-painted in blue and green on tin-glazed earthenware Dutch blank, 15.5 x 15.5 cm
V&A (C.220–1976)

William De Morgan's sister-in-law, Wilhelmina Stirling, recalled that he said, 'Morris never made but three designs for my execution, the *Trellis and Tulip*, the *Poppy* and another – I forget the name. I never could work except by myself and in my own manner' (*William De Morgan and his Wife*, 1922). More commonly called *Tulip and Trellis*, Morris probably created the design around the time De Morgan set up his pottery in Chelsea in 1872. For some years it was made both by De Morgan (in colours) and by the firm (in blue). An example of the latter is in the William Morris Gallery (C268).

X.19
Two minstrel figures
From designs by Charles Fairfax Murray after William Morris
Decorated by Morris, Marshall, Faulkner & Co., *c.*1872
Hand-painted in blue-green on tin-glazed earthenware Dutch blanks, frame size 41.9 x 44.5 cm
V&A (Circ.104–1965)
Given by Novello & Co. Ltd

These tiles are from a series of minstrels supplied to decorate the premises of the music publishers Novello & Co. at 1 Berners Street in London, around 1872. Three other examples, believed to have the same provenance and formerly in the Handley-Read collection, are at The Higgins Bedford (C.1204–6). These figurative tiles, like the reredos at Clapham (fig.179), were painted after Lucy Faulkner's marriage in 1870 when she stopped working for the firm, so clearly other painters were employed on figure painting.

The earliest minstrels and minstrel angels were designed for stained glass and church tiles by William Morris and were a much repeated and reworked series. The figure with the long flared pipe was used at Findon and the minstrel with the organ appears on the firm's painted organ case at St Mary's, Beddington, in Surrey. Charles Fairfax Murray adapted Morris's designs for tiles and his drawing of the minstrel with the organ is in the Ashmolean Museum (WA1940.61). It was acquired directly from Morris & Co.

X.20
Four tiles
Probably designed by William Morris for Morris & Co., *c.*1875
Hand-painted in blue on tin-glazed earthenware Dutch blanks, 15.2 x 60.8 cm
V&A (C.62 & A-C–1979)

This design has not been identified so far, nor are any other examples known. Technically the tiles are typical of Morris, Marshall, Faulkner & Co. and there is no doubt that they are by the firm. They are well painted and stylistically compare with those for the Membland Hall commission of *c.*1876, which were painted at William De Morgan's pottery (see X.21). Presumably dating from about 1875, they appear to be among the earliest of Morris & Co.'s production, following the reorganization of the company in that year.

X.21a

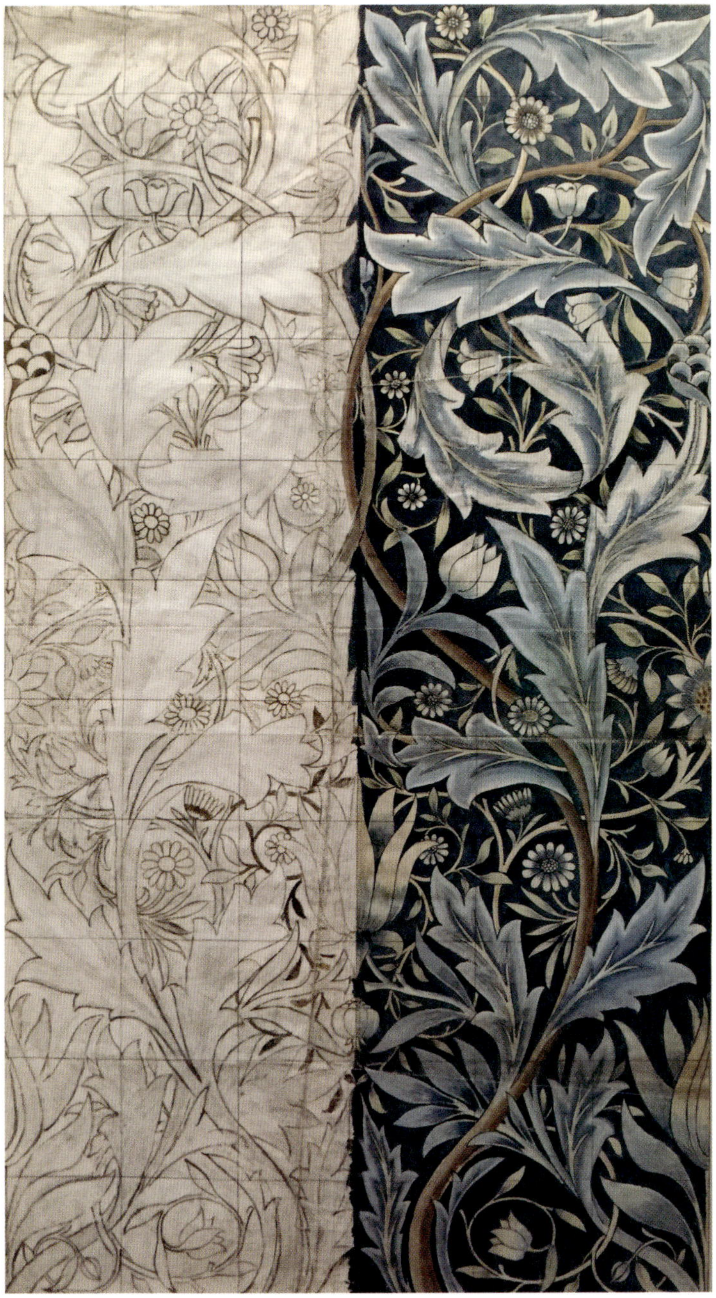

X.21b

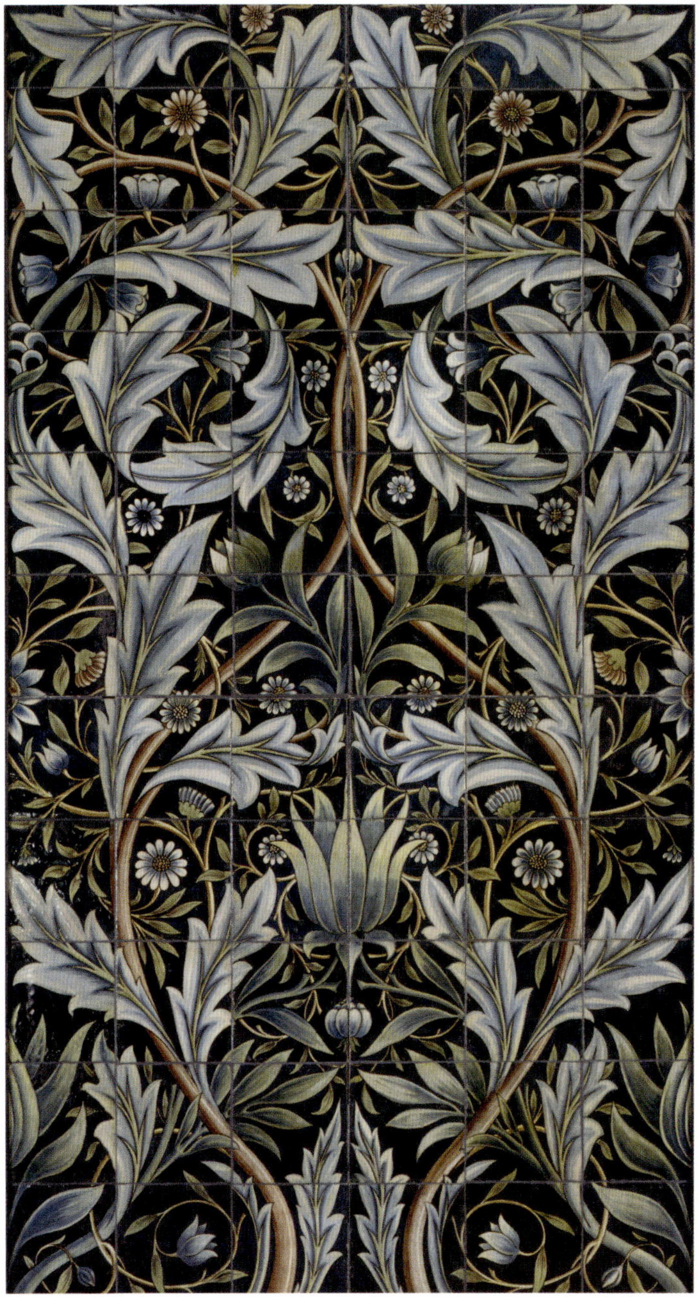

X.21
Membland Hall tiles

a Design
William Morris, *c.*1876
Pencil, watercolour and sepia,
164.3 x 91.4 cm
William Morris Gallery, London Borough of Waltham Forest (A31)
Purchased from Morris & Co.

b Tile panel
Decorated by William De Morgan, *c.*1876
Slip-covered and hand-painted in various colours and glazed on earthenware blanks made by the Architectural Pottery, Poole, Dorset,
160 x 91.5 cm
V&A (C.36–1972)
Given by Charles and Lavinia Handley-Read

This panel is one of six surviving from Membland Hall, near Plymouth. Morris & Co. was involved in the decoration of this property, remodelled and extended in the late 1870s by George Devey, architect to the banker Edward Charles Baring, Baron Revelstoke. Little is known about the extent of this commission. Mackail quotes from the diary of a Morris & Co. employee in 1877, 'G.W. [George Wardle] and W.M. talked over Mrs Baring's house in Devonshire: the work we have proposed to do will certainly take two or three years before all completed: we have to get our Lyons silk-weaver at work for one thing.' The house was demolished in 1928.

These tiles were one of the most successful collaborations between Morris and De Morgan. The execution of Morris's design of scrolling acanthus leaves against a background of interwoven daisy sprays relied on De Morgan's technical skills, especially given the scale (each panel is made up of 66 tiles) and the need to produce a matching set. The squared-up design is inscribed 'Tiles for bathroom Membland', although it appears likely that they were never installed. Other panels from the set are at the William Morris Gallery and the Museum of Applied Arts, Cologne. An identical panel is illustrated in Lewis F. Day's *The Art of William Morris* (1899) where it is dated 1876. The design remained on Morris & Co.'s stocklists until *c.*1912–13 and a number of panels, other than the Membland six, are known to have been made. At least one uses De Morgan's own Fulham Pottery tiles.

X.22

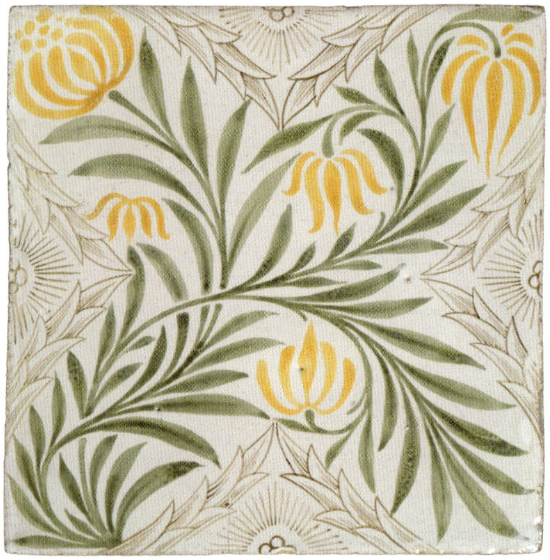

X.23

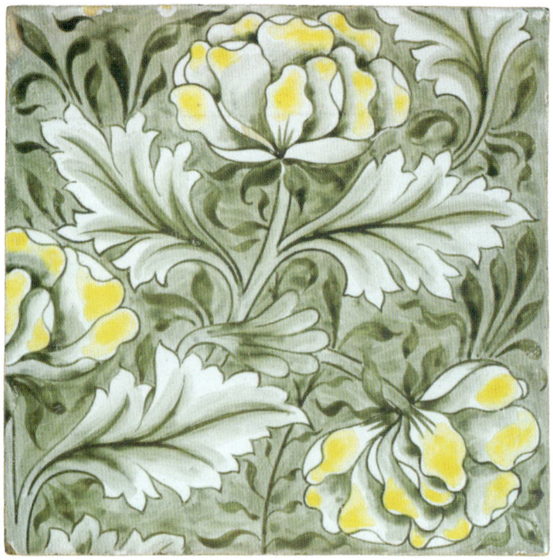

X.24

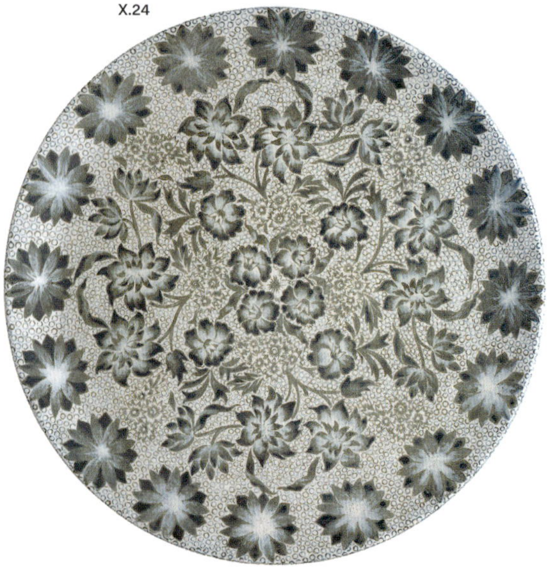

X.22
Tile
Design attributed to Kate Faulkner, *c.*1876
Decorated by Morris & Co.
Hand-painted in green, brown and yellow on tin-glazed earthenware Dutch blank, 15.3 x 15.3 cm
Marks: '5A', '711' or '144' (painted)
V&A (C.56–1931)
Bequeathed by James Richardson Holliday

Philip Webb used tiles of this pattern in one of a pair of semi-detached houses he designed on Redington Road, Hampstead, in 1876. They later featured in one of the fireplaces at Stanmore Hall, Middlesex, an extensive scheme carried out by the firm in the 1890s. The pattern, using brown in place of yellow, was also made by the Dutch pottery, Tjallingii of Harlingen, who marketed it in the 1890s (pattern no. 537). The pattern has some affinities with Kate Faulkner's gesso decoration on furniture.

X.23
***Peony* tile**
Designed by Kate Faulkner, *c.*1877
Decorated by Morris & Co., *c.*1880
Hand-painted in greens and yellow on tin-glazed earthenware Dutch blank, 15.3 x 15.3 cm
V&A (Circ.614–1954)
Given by Miss E. Wilkinson

Kate Faulkner's *Peony* pattern for printed cotton was registered on 22 June 1877. In the textile the flowers are open to reveal their stamens and the leafy background is more formal. However, while not identical, the similarities are close enough to suggest that the design for the tile was probably made at around the same time. Very few tiles of this pattern survive. One showing the matching repeat is in the William Morris Gallery.

X.24
***Star Flower* dish**
Designed and decorated by Kate Faulkner for Morris & Co., 1880
Hand-painted on-glaze in blue on earthenware blank made by Pinder, Bourne & Co., Burslem, Stoke-on-Trent, 45 cm diameter
Marks: 'Pinder, Bourne & Co.' (impressed), 'KF 1880' (painted)
V&A (C.324–1930)

Purchased from Morris & Co. in 1930, no further information came with the dish at the time of its acquisition. Possibly 'in stock' from the 1880s it was described as being 'painted by the late Miss Kate Faulkner'. The blank was made by Pinder, Bourne & Co. of Nile Street, Burslem, a company founded in 1849 that had undergone several changes of name and which was finally purchased by Doulton in 1878. The name was retained until 1882. The rimless form was made by many commercial factories and was thought especially suitable as an uninterrupted surface for painted decoration. No other versions of this pattern are known on either tiles or textiles. Painted over a commercial lead-glaze and re-fired without further glazing, the decoration has consequently been subject to some colour loss.

X.25
***Pink and Hawthorn* tiles**
Possibly designed by William Morris, mid-1870s
Decorated by William De Morgan
Slip-covered and hand-painted in colours and glazed on earthenware blanks made by the Architectural Pottery, Poole, Dorset,
15.5 x 15 cm each
Mark: 'Architectural Pottery Poole Dorset'
V&A (C.39 & A–C–1975)

Evelyn De Morgan, William De Morgan's widow, gave a large collection of De Morgan's designs and other papers to the V&A in 1917. Three stocklists mention Morris's name, including an entry of *c.*1887 that lists 'Pink & Hawthorn'. It is not clear from this document if the design was by Morris or simply a pattern done for Morris & Co. Like others (X.21), they are painted on blanks made by the Architectural Pottery. Morris & Co. also decorated tiles with this pattern. Webb used a monochrome version for one of the fireplaces at Smeaton Manor, Yorkshire, designed in 1876.

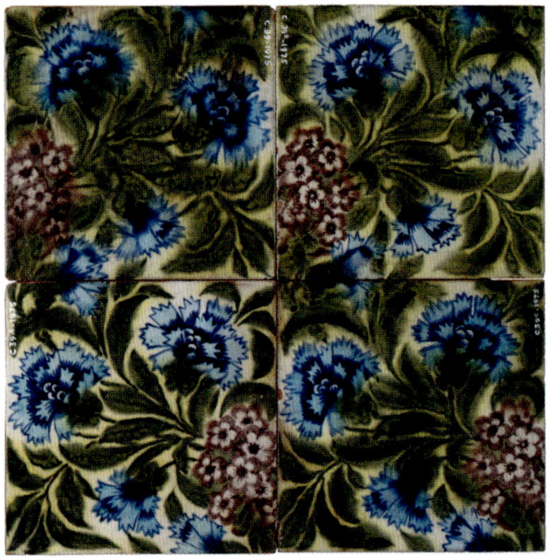

X.25

X.26

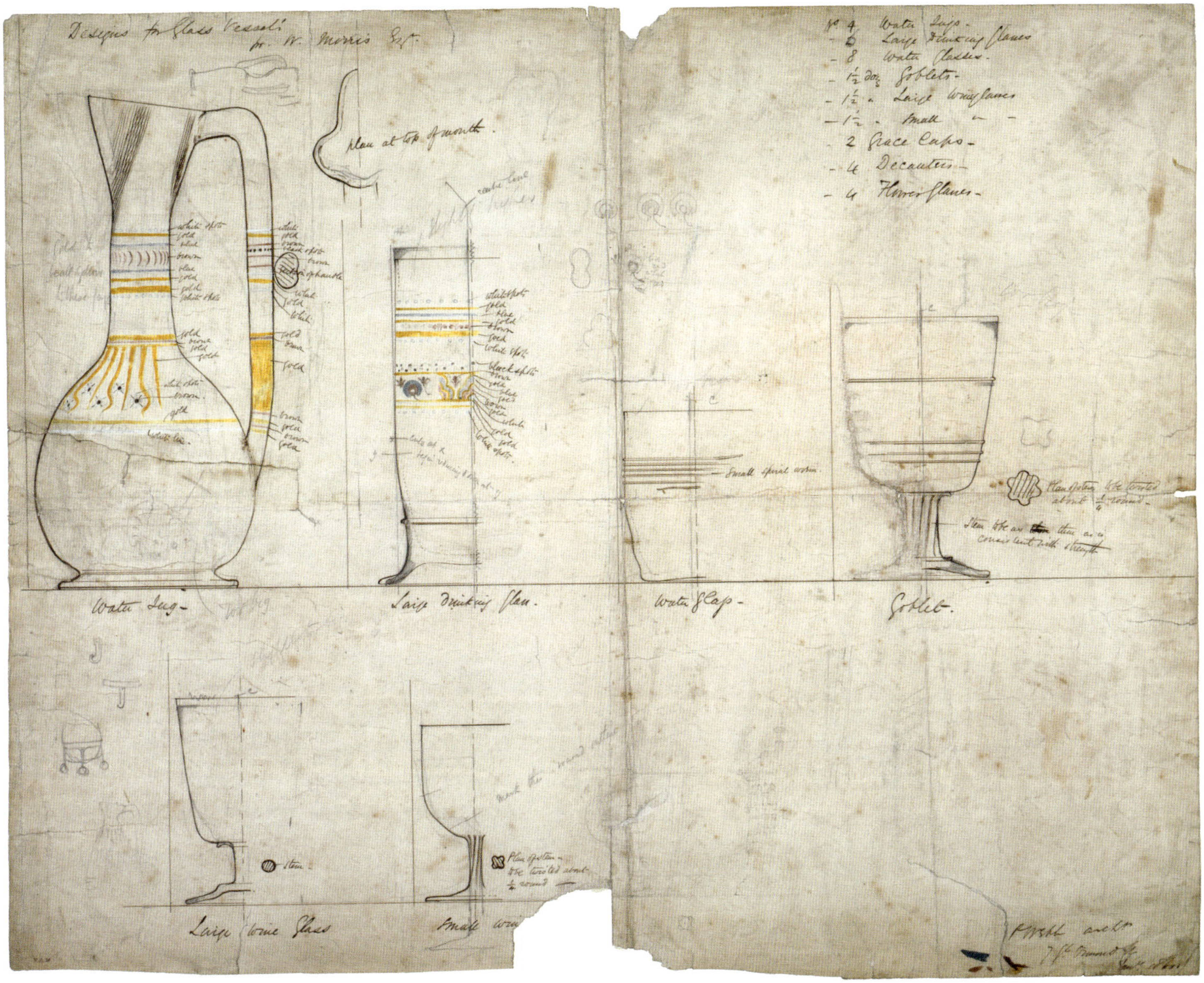

X.26
Designs for table glass for Red House
Philip Webb, dated January 1860
Pencil, pen and wash, 53 x 66 cm
Inscribed: 'Designs for Glass Vessels for W. Morris Esq' and other notes
V&A (E.340–1944)
Given by Dorothy Walker

In January 1860 Webb designed a set of table glass for Morris's personal use at Red House, to be made by James Powell & Sons, Whitefriars glassworks. The historicism of these designs was relatively avant-garde for its time. Fully developed historicism appeared in glass some two or three years later and then was largely Italian-based. Historic influences here range from Roman, in the use of thinly trailed lines of hot glass, to seventeenth-century German and eighteenth-century English in the shapes. Painted enamel decoration makes an unexpected appearance and may have been derived from either Venetian or German examples, which Webb – and Morris – could have seen in the South Kensington Museum. They were both frequent visitors and by the late 1850s the museum had over 350 glass vessels – many of them as part of the Bernal and Soulages collections – of which the majority were Venetian and North European. Enamelled decoration may have appealed to Morris for its affinity with medieval illuminations in its minutely jewel-like gilding and preciousness, although it was in direct confrontation with Ruskin's influential principle of allowing undecorated glass to speak for itself. Only one example of table glass is known that precisely matches the Red House designs, a goblet bequeathed by May Morris to Birmingham Museum and Art Gallery (fig.185).

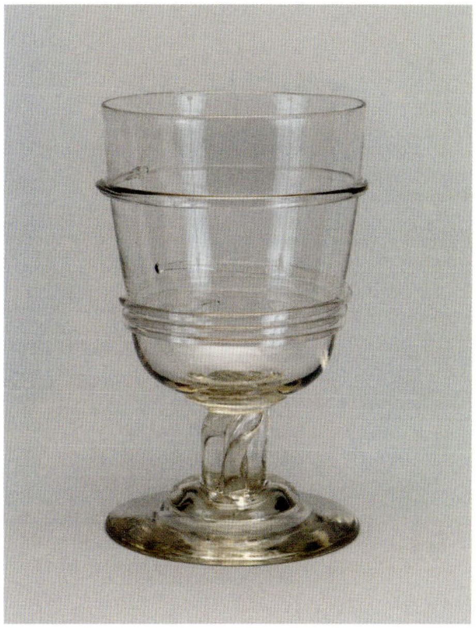

Fig.185 **Goblet, designed by Philip Webb in 1860 and made by James Powell & Sons.**
Birmingham Museums Trust

X.28

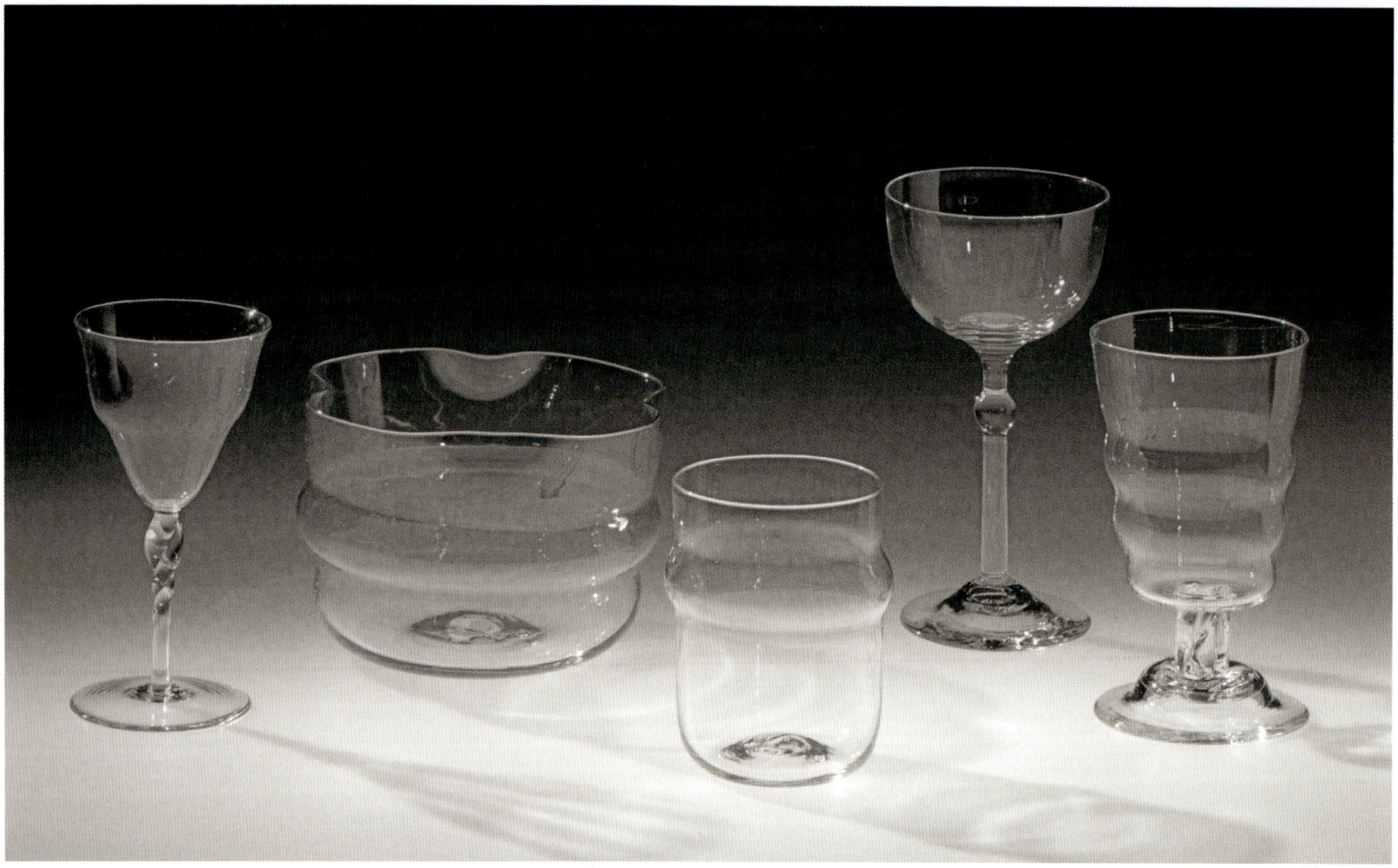

X.27

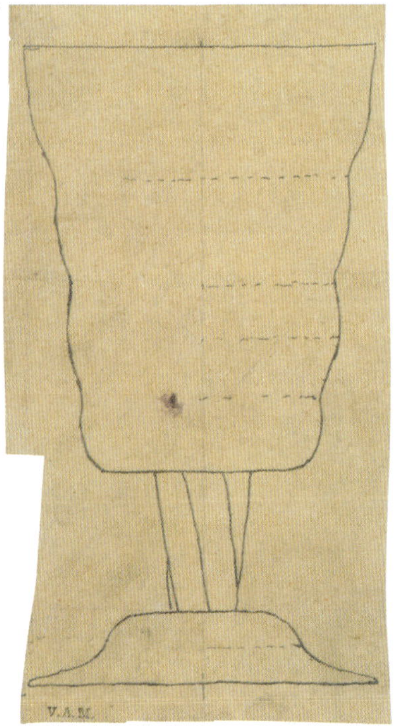

X.27
Design for goblet
Philip Webb for James Powell & Sons, *c.*1860–2
Pen and ink, 14.8 x 8.1 cm
V&A (E.333–1944)
Given by Dorothy Walker

By 1862 Webb was converting the more elaborate, enamelled designs for Red House (see X.26) into a plainer range, which relied for its decorative effect on hot-worked glass. This line drawing is from a group of fourteen designs, which includes a claret glass (fig.181). A version of the goblet is in the V&A's collection (X.28e). Webb's account book with the firm includes sketches of the table glass he ordered for his own use (fig.34). Both the goblet and the claret glass appear, one version of the latter annotated 'with green spots'. The range was popular with the firm's partners, who presumably ordered pieces at cost price.

X.28
Five items of table glass
Designed by Philip Webb, early 1860s
James Powell & Sons, Whitefriars
Hand-blown and part mould-blown

a White wine glass
13 x 7 cm
V&A (C.81–1939)
Bequeathed by May Morris

b Finger bowl
9 x 14 cm
V&A (C.79–1939)
Bequeathed by May Morris

c Tumbler
9.3 x 7.8 cm
V&A (C.261–1926)
Given by Margaret Mackail

d Champagne glass
15.5 x 8.2 cm
V&A (C.80A–1939)
Bequeathed by May Morris

e Goblet
12.8 x 7.5 cm
V&A (C.263–1926)
Given by Margaret Mackail

By December 1862, when glassware featured significantly in Morris, Marshall, Faulkner & Co.'s balance sheets, Webb had extended and amended the Red House designs (X.26) to form a much plainer range for sale by the firm, for whom they were made exclusively by Powell's. Despite its importance in the firm's accounts, very little of this range has survived. Examples were shown on top of the *St George* cabinet at the International Exhibition of 1862.

The champagne glass corresponds to a sketch in Webb's account book with the firm (fig.34), *c.*1861–2 (he also designed fluted versions). The goblet, in six different sizes, was exhibited by Powell's in their Wigmore Street showroom in 1927 and illustrated in an article in *The Studio.* The white wine glass, finger bowl and tumbler are all distantly related to the known Webb designs.

All of these pieces were acquired from either Margaret Mackail (Burne-Jones's daughter) or May Morris and may have been chosen and used by their parents.

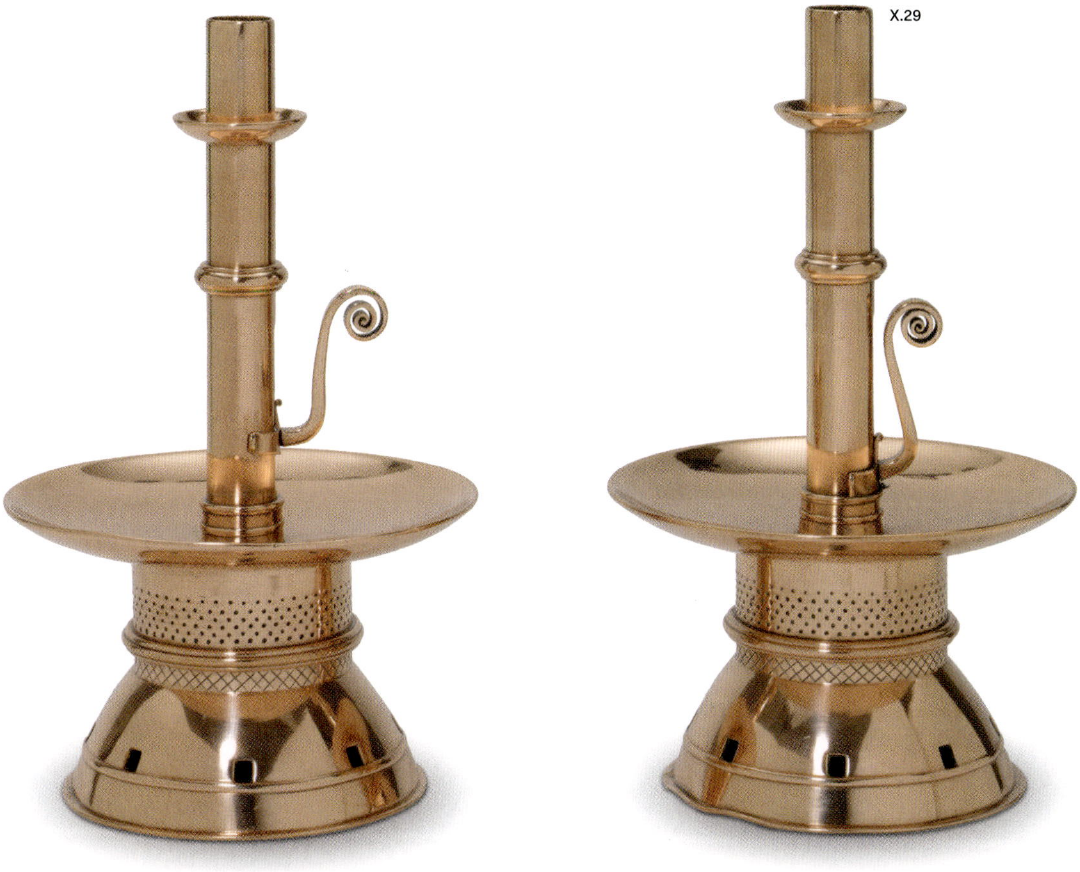
X.29

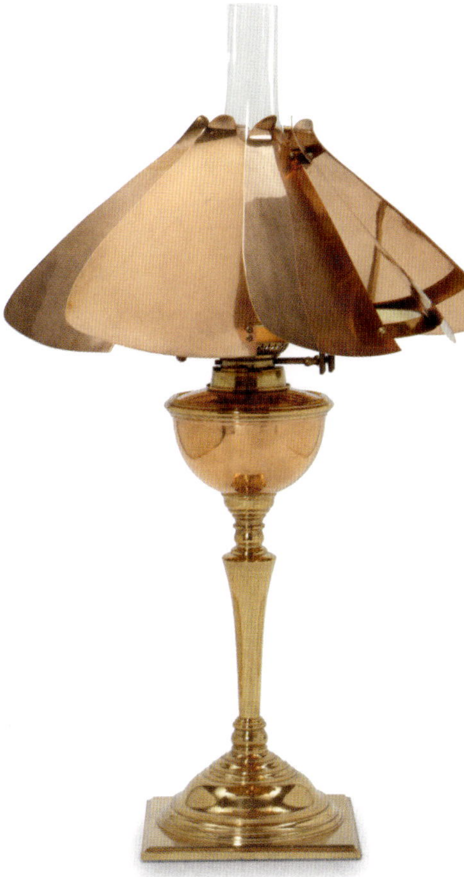
X.30

X.29
Pair of candlesticks
Designed by Philip Webb, *c.*1860
Morris, Marshall, Faulkner & Co.
Copper, 26.7 x 17.8 cm diameter
V&A (M.1130 & A–1926)
Purchased from John William Mackail

Although 'Metal Work in all its branches, including Jewellery' was one of the five categories advertised by Morris, Marshall, Faulkner & Co. in its 1861 prospectus, these candlesticks are a rarity. Problems with technique or in finding a suitable manufacturer willing to undertake small-scale production may have been the cause. However, they were popular with the partners. Designed originally for Red House, this pair was purchased from the firm by Burne-Jones. Both copper and brass examples survive at Kelmscott Manor and in the collection of the William Morris Gallery. In the summer of 1863, Webb charged the firm £1 10*s.* for a 'Design for Candlesticks' but this is likely to be a different, later design. ET/LP

X.30
Table lamp
Designed and manufactured by W.A.S. Benson, *c.*1890
Originally retailed by Morris & Co.
Brass and copper, 68.5 x 40 x 40 cm
V&A (Circ.21–1961)
Given by Helen Mary Beale

W.A.S. Benson initially trained as an architect in the office of Basil Champneys. It was through his friendship with Burne-Jones that he met Morris and they both encouraged him to set up his own workshop in 1880. The firm prospered and survived until his retirement in 1920. Benson designed his goods almost exclusively for mechanical production and had been interested in engineering since boyhood. In 1905, when Morris & Co. became a limited company, Benson was appointed Chairman and served on the board until 1917.

Benson's fittings became an integral part of many Morris & Co. interiors – either bought directly from the Morris & Co. shop or simply seen as a congenial accessory. Many important houses owned such fittings and this example was part of the 1890s furnishing of Standen, East Grinstead. ET

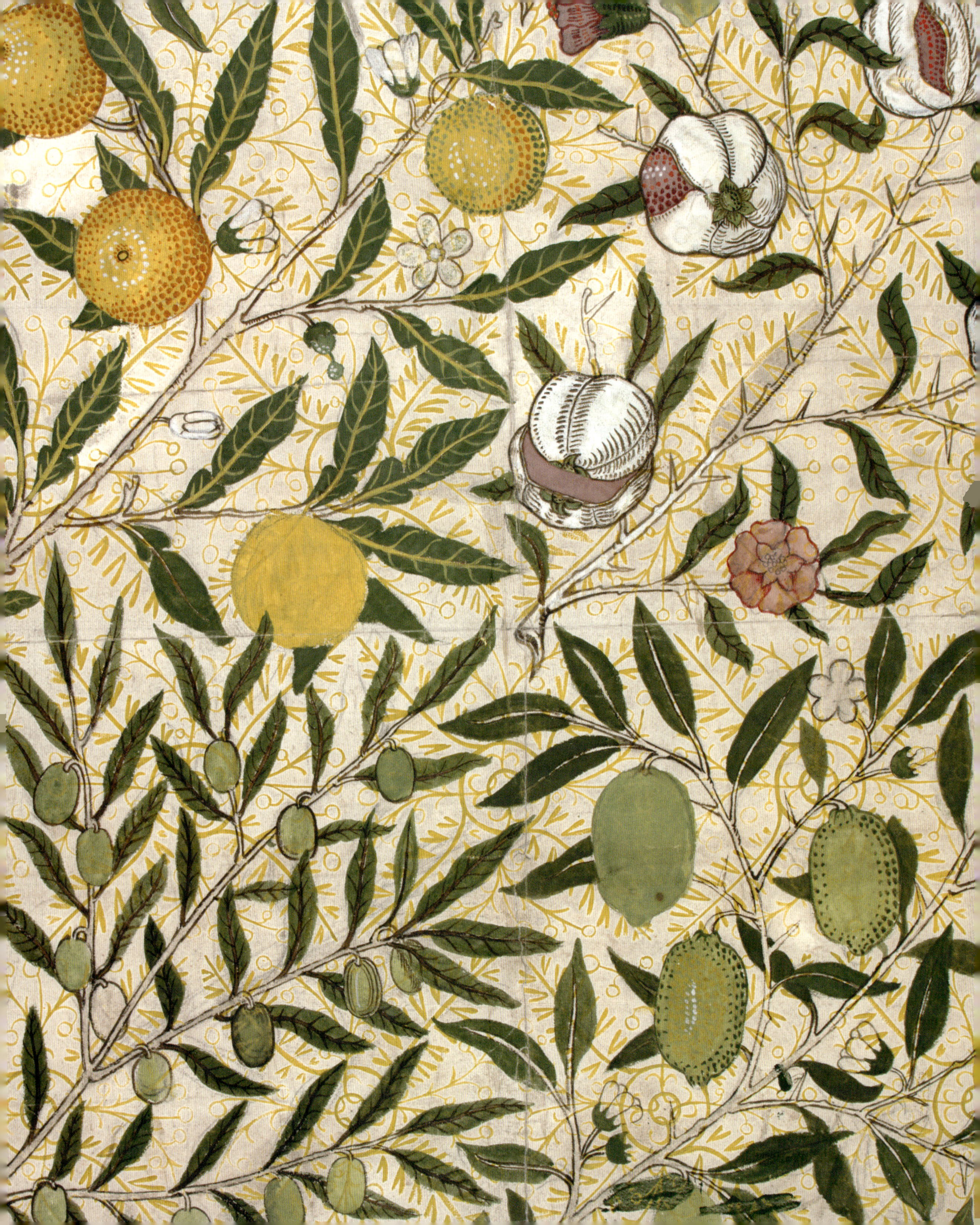

XI
WALLPAPER

Lesley Hoskins

'Whatever you have in your rooms think first of the walls, for they are that which makes your house and home ...'
William Morris, 'The Lesser Arts of Life', 1882

Fig.186 **Design for *Fruit*, also known as *Pomegranate*, wallpaper, William Morris, *c.*1866 (see XI.3).**
V&A (E.299–2009)
Purchased with Art Fund support

By the 1860s wallpapers – known at that time as paper-hangings – were in widespread use. Technical developments and fiscal changes helped British output to soar from 1.2 million rolls a year in 1834 to 32 million in 1874, feeding a growing consumer market. In this context Morris, Marshall, Faulkner & Co. decided in 1862 to introduce wallpaper into its range as an item of off-the-peg serial production, second after its glass tableware. It was in wallpaper that Morris first achieved his mastery of flat repeating pattern, despite later stating in his lecture 'The Lesser Arts of Life' that 'printing patterns on paper for wall hangings' was only a 'quite modern and very humble, but, as things go, useful art'. While most specialist wallpaper companies produced large ranges every couple of years, the firm only ever added a few new patterns a year. Nonetheless, wallpapers were an important component of its output, especially from the 1870s onwards when William Morris was developing the firm as a successful retail concern with a coherent style. It offered paper-hangings in a broad range of prices, which customers could use to achieve the Morris & Co. 'look' relatively easily.

The patterns

During Morris's lifetime approximately 70 wallpaper patterns in numerous colourways and finishes were produced. Morris himself designed some 50 of these patterns and about 16 were by other designers working for the firm. Four were adapted from eighteenth-century examples. In a few cases there is some uncertainty about authorship partly because, at that period, the designers were not publicly credited but also because, with Morris taking overall responsibility for the output, the designs mostly followed his idiom. Morris & Co. continued to introduce new patterns after Morris's death in 1896 and around 1909 issued a brochure, *Morris Wall-Papers*, which listed all the designs that were for sale. A revised edition of about 1912 gave the names of the designers. This edition now comprises the main source for discussing authorship, but attribution also considers stylistic clues, contemporary textual references and comparisons with other media, especially printed textiles. There is likewise some uncertainty around dating. However, a reliable source for some of the designs is a series of copyright records now held at The National Archives, Kew. A law of 1839 introduced protection against piracy for designs that were officially registered. In order to acquire this copyright a company had to pay a fee and deposit a sample of the pattern immediately before it went into production. Both Morris, Marshall, Faulkner

& Co. and Morris & Co. registered some of their wallpapers, which can thereby be securely dated.

After some initial technical difficulties, the firm's first two wallpaper patterns – *Daisy* (XI.1) and *Trellis* (fig.187 and XI.2) – were issued in early 1864. According to John William Mackail, Morris had begun working on the design for *Trellis* in November 1862; *Daisy* was designed later but, again according to Mackail, came out first. Both reflected the ambience at Red House and the informal medievalism of the early days of the firm. Derek Baker has suggested that *Trellis* draws on Martin Schongauer's *The Madonna of the Rose Bower* altarpiece of 1473 at St Martin's Church in Colmar, Alsace, which Morris may have seen on his honeymoon. Mackail also relates it to the 'wattled rose-trellises inclosing [*sic*] richly-flowered square garden plots' at Red House. Flower trellises appear frequently in the work of Morris and his associates, for example in the 1862 stained glass for St Helen's, Darley Dale (VII.6). The source for *Daisy*, a simple pattern of freestanding clumps of meadow flowers on a grass-like ground, can be seen in a wall hanging illustrated in a fifteenth-century manuscript of Jean Froissart's Chronicles (fig.205). The hangings embroidered for the master bedroom at Red House in the early 1860s used similar flower groups though on a larger scale (XII.3). Both *Trellis* and *Daisy* were registered, indicating the firm's desire to protect its designs and its commitment to a business-like approach. *Fruit*, also known as *Pomegranate* (fig.186 and XI.3), followed in about 1866. This pattern is built of four rectangular elements in a tile arrangement, each 'tile' showing the fruits, flowers and foliage of pomegranates, lemons, oranges or peaches. There are strong resemblances between *Fruit* and the painted panels that form part of the dado decoration of the Green Dining Room at the South Kensington Museum, begun in 1866 (fig.147).

These three patterns form a coherent and distinctive group within Morris's wallpaper designs. They were markedly different from wallpapers at a similar level of the market that were available from other producers at the time and which were generally either 'French' or 'reformed' in style. The former included highly realistic floral bunches or trails and imitation textiles – moirés, watered silks, ribbon trellises and upholstery trimming borders. They were pretty, sugary confections on pale satinized grounds. Many were French imports but some very creditable attempts at the genre were made by such English companies as William Woollams (fig.188). In economic, aesthetic and moral opposition to these were the English patterns issuing from the Design Reform movement. With their abhorrence of realism, insistence on the conventionalization of natural forms and respect for the flatness of the wall, they are exemplified by the work of Owen Jones (fig.189), who had been designing wallpapers since about 1840, both for decorative commissions and for general sale. As Peter Floud argued, the fruit and flowers of *Trellis*, *Daisy* and *Fruit* had something in common with the 'naturalistic' type, but they were also akin to 'reformed' patterns by virtue of their strong colouring and conventionalization of nature.

Five patterns of a very different type were added in the late 1860s or early 1870s, despite opposition from the firm's business manager Warington Taylor, who warned in a memorandum that sales were

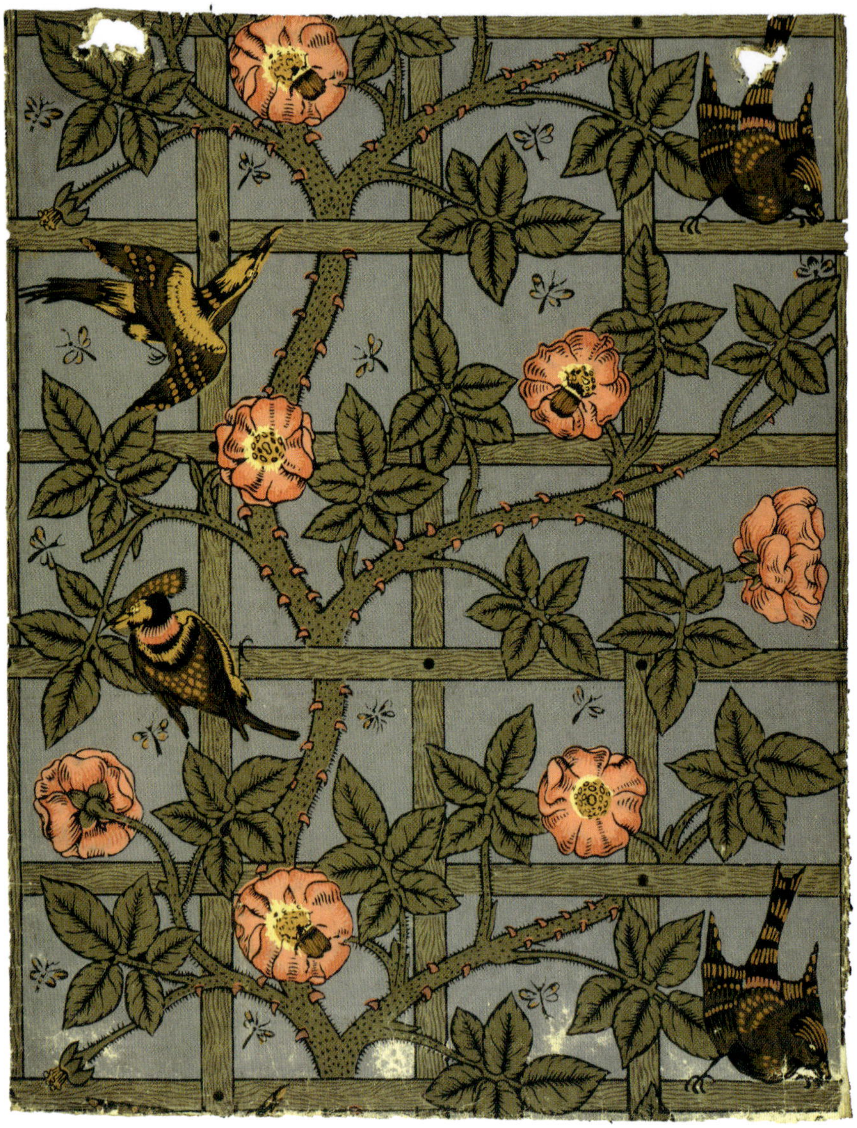

Fig.187 ***Trellis* wallpaper, colourway 9, designed by William Morris and Philip Webb in 1862 and registered 30 March 1864. Block-printed in distemper colours, repeat h. 52.7 cm.**
V&A (E.452–1919)
Given by Morris & Co.

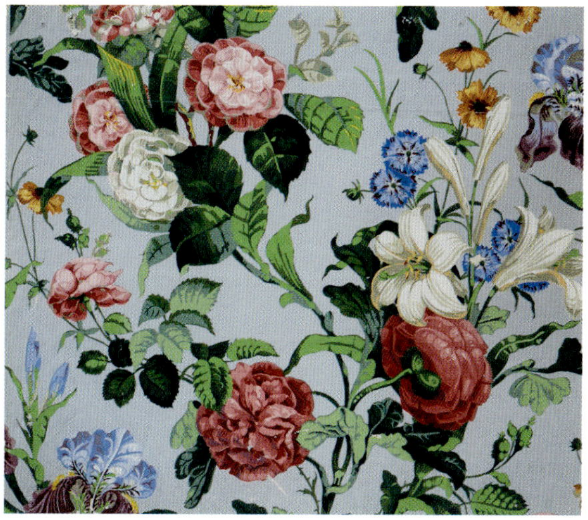

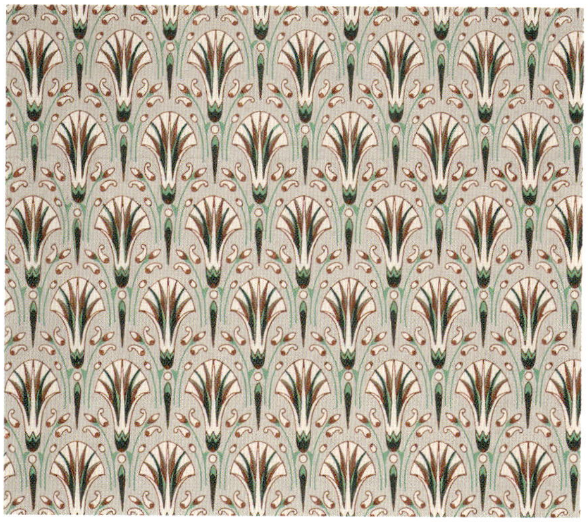

Fig.188 (right) **'French' style floral wallpaper, William Woollams & Co., London, 1849.**
Sanderson Design Group Archive

Fig.189 (far right) ***Lotus* wallpaper with a highly stylized 'reformed' pattern, Owen Jones, 1858.**
V&A (8342:41)
Given by Catherine Jones

small and it was expensive to hold stock. *Diaper* (XI.4), probably designed by Philip Webb, is a small-scale, two-colour, non-directional tile pattern, useful as a companion paper or on its own. *Queen Anne*, *Indian* (XI.5), *Venetian* and *Spray* are adaptations of eighteenth-century patterns. At least some of these were provided by architects associated with George Frederick Bodley, who commissioned stained glass from the firm and later set up his own decorating business, Watts & Co. This group of papers used only one or two light fresh colours each and were considerably cheaper than the earlier designs and less challenging to use. William Richard Lethaby later said that they were an early manifestation of the Queen Anne decorative style, which was much influenced by Morris's use of white paint in his drawing room at 26 Queen Square, Bloomsbury (*Philip Webb and his Work*, 1935).

It was in the 1870s that Morris definitively mastered designing for wallpaper and the firm widened its range of patterns and prices to attract a variety of customers. By the end of the decade there were an additional 23 designs in a variety of colourways as well as new colourings of the older patterns. Early in this period Morris developed a pattern structure that he was to use a great deal at that time and occasionally thereafter. The design is built up in two layers – an all-over background of foliage is overlaid with scrolling stems whose curling offshoots bear flowers or fruit. It appears at its best in *Jasmine* of 1872 (fig.190) where the background of hawthorn leaves, blossoms and branches on a disguised vertical meander is overlaid with a scrolling tracery of jasmine, delicately but clearly defined. The two layers are so well integrated that, from a distance, the paper gives an effect of subtle broken colour. Morris also used this structure for printed textiles (for example *Tulip and Willow* of 1873, XII.34), but it is particularly suited for wallpaper – a flat and unforgiving medium. *Vine* (XI.7), designed in about 1873, employs this structure, where the background and foreground are sufficiently interwoven to provide a complex all-over pattern with a shallow depth.

At the same time, several simpler patterns were introduced. *Lily* (XI.8) and *Powdered*, both of 1874, return to the sprightly freshness of *Daisy*. *Willow*, 1874 (seen in XI.9), is a simpler stylized all-over foliage pattern, very similar to the backprint of *Vine*. *Larkspur*, 1872, and *Marigold* (XI.11), of about 1875 were single-colour designs, which are necessarily less susceptible to the layered approach. The printing logbook for the mid-1870s (XI.9) reveals the introduction of a new more 'Aesthetic' palette – pale terracottas and greeny-blues for example – both for new patterns and for additional versions of old ones. It also documents the firm's attempts to issue some designs in transparent watercolour wash.

Acanthus, produced in 1875, marks the start of a period of large repeats and rich dense effects (XI.10, figs 191 and 192). Because of its size, this design required 30 blocks to complete the pattern, making it one of the firm's most expensive 'ordinary' papers. Here and in *Pimpernel* (XI.12), *Wreath* (both of 1876) and in the 1877 patterns, *Rose* and *Chrysanthemum* (XI.13), are vigorous scrolls of foliage and flowers; the colours are deep and sombre; hatching and veining give three-dimensionality.

Metal grounds, lacquering and embossing were introduced around this time. *Vine* on a gold lacquer ground (XI.7b) was added to the stock range in 1875. *Sunflower* (XI.14) and *Acorn*, two new, rather rigid and upright, single-colour patterns of 1879, were issued from the very beginning as gold-ground papers as well as distemper prints. Morris & Co. used gold-ground versions of *Sunflower* in its extensive decorative work for George Howard, later Earl of Carlisle, and his wife, Rosalind, at their London house, 1 Palace Green, Kensington, and at Castle Howard, Yorkshire, in the late 1870s and early 1880s. William Morris's letters to them reveal that there were problems with the colours. It is not known whether the gold-ground versions were specially developed for the Howards and then put into the range or vice versa. Although the gold, glimpsed through the deep colours of the printed patterns, shows traces of the firm's early medievalism, these finishes probably owed more to the growing fashion for papers imitating embossed and gilded leather. Excellent examples had been available from a French company, Balin, since the mid-1860s but by the later 1870s they were also produced by several English firms, including Jeffrey & Co., who printed Morris's wallpapers. *Chrysanthemum*, stamped, lacquered and gilded to imitate embossed leather (XI.13b and fig.203), first appears in the logbook in 1878, a year after its introduction as an ordinary paper and other designs were subsequently treated in this manner (see XI.25). Such effects were very expensive. The brochures of about 1909 and 1912 quoted the gold or embossed patterns as costing 25*s*. to 40*s*. a roll, whereas *Sunflower* as an ordinary print cost between 4*s*. 6*d*. and 5*s*. 9*d*.

Another very expensive paper, originally designed as part of a decorative commission but subsequently available for purchase was the *St James's* (XI.15) with its accompanying *St James's Ceiling* (XI.16). Morris & Co. undertook extensive decoration at St James's Palace in 1880–1 including a specially designed paper for the Grand Staircase. A fully worked scheme for the paper was approved by Queen Victoria. As befitting the grandeur and size of the space, *St James's* is a very large and formal pattern of acanthus leaves and flower heads, offset by a more domestic treatment of the roses and the leaves and small flowers in the underlay. Sixty-eight blocks were needed to print the pattern. The cutting and printing must have been a gigantic task, carried out at speed, since only four months separated the approval of the plan and its completion. The pattern was also used on the Queen's Staircase and the Ambassadors' Staircase; on the latter and on the Grand Staircase it was teamed with imitation leather papers designed by Bruce Talbert and Walter Crane respectively. *St James's* was listed in the 1912 brochure as costing 32*s*. 6*d*. a roll; it doubtless had to be specially ordered and printed. It is known to have been used elsewhere, for example in the drawing room of businessman and art collector Henry F. Makins at 180 Queen's Gate, South Kensington.

While these rich effects were a feature of the late 1870s and early 1880s, the firm also expanded its wallpaper range with the addition of less expensive patterns. *Apple* of 1877 is a light and airy design of simplified acanthus leaves, apples and willow leaves on a pale ground (fig.193). Soon afterwards the company introduced a single colour, non-directional, densely patterned paper (XI.17), specifically intended for use on ceilings, despite Morris's declared opposition to papered ceilings in his 1879 lecture 'Making the Best of It': 'a room papered all over would be like a box to live in.' By this time Morris was willing to relax his personal hold a little and of the eight new patterns after *Chrysanthemum*, three – *Loop Trail* of 1877 (XI.18) and *Mallow* and *Bramble* of 1879 – were designed by Kate Faulkner, youngest sister of Charles Faulkner, one of the partners in the original firm. As well as working for Morris

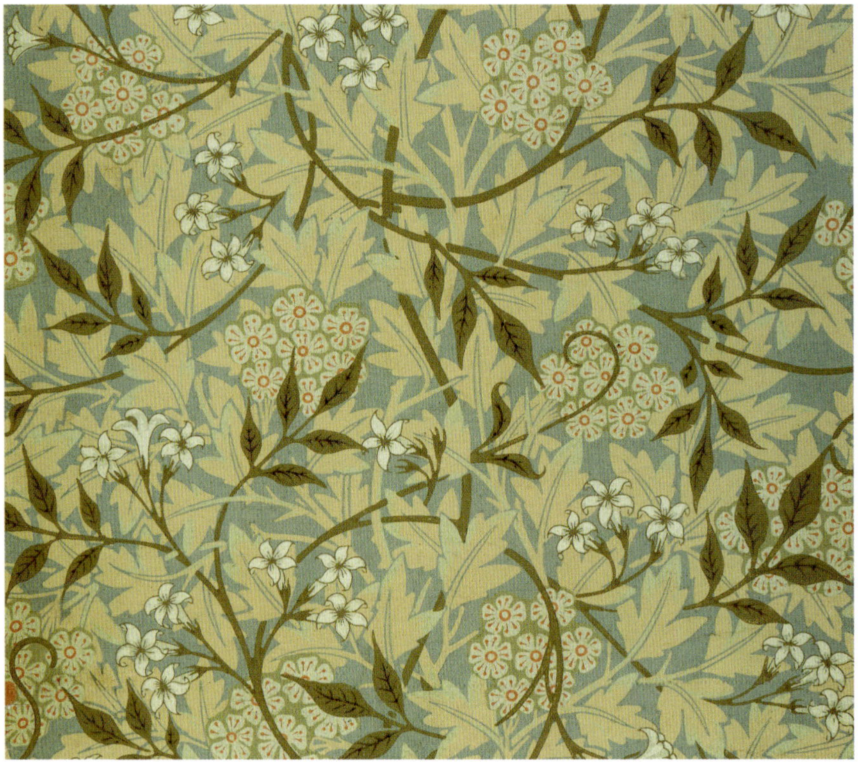

Fig.190 ***Jasmine* wallpaper, colourway 31, designed by William Morris *c.*1872 and first issued in that year. Block-printed in distemper colours, repeat h. 70.5 cm.**
V&A (E.475–1919)
Given by Morris & Co.

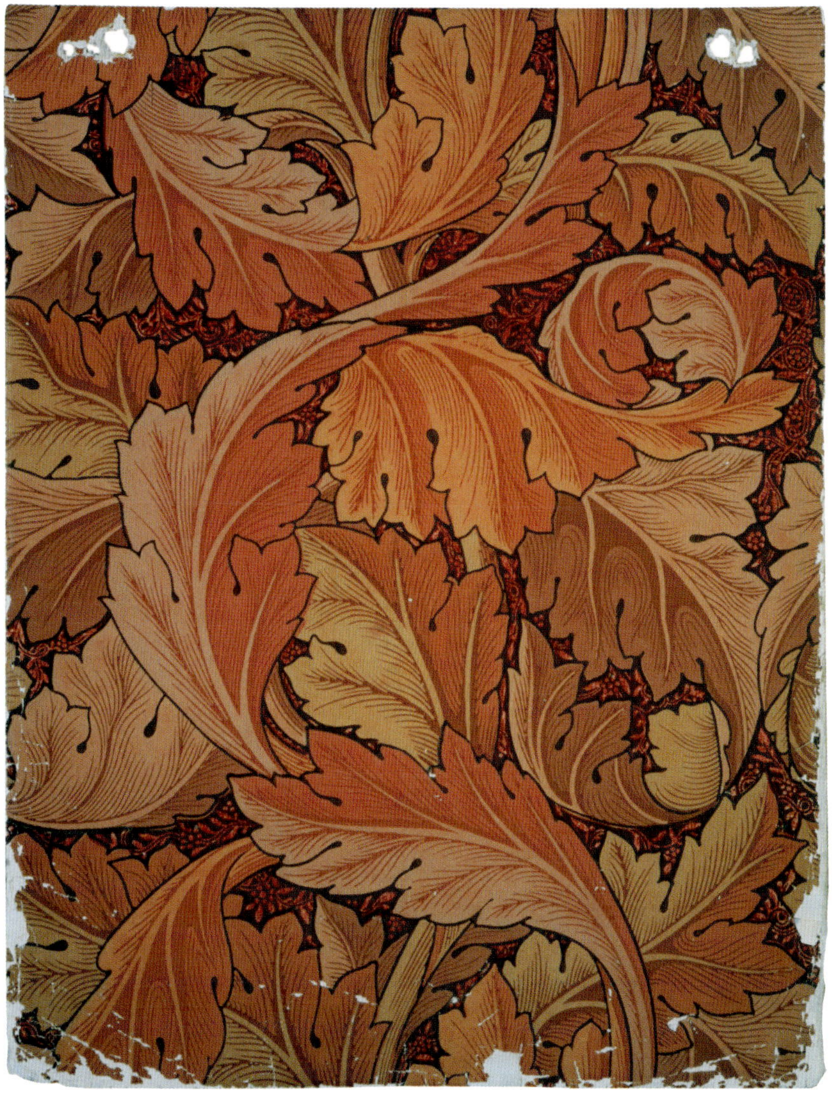

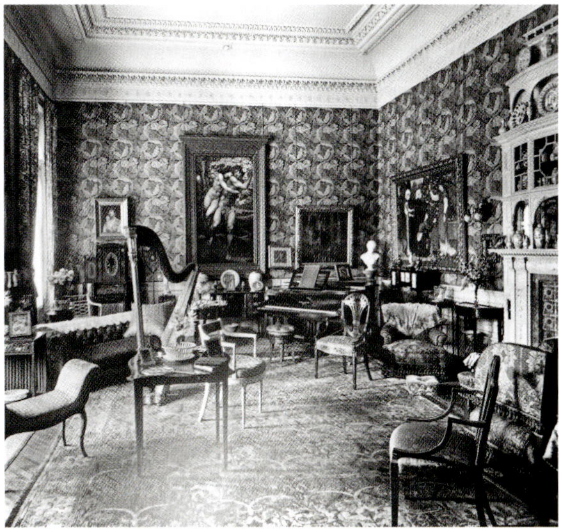

Fig.191 *Acanthus* wallpaper, colourway 79, designed by William Morris and registered 22 July 1875. Block-printed in distemper colours, repeat h. 65.2 cm.
V&A (E.494–1919)

Fig.192 William Imrie's drawing or music room at Holmstead, 51 North Mossley Road, Liverpool, photographed in 1901 by Bedford Lemere & Co. Even in such a large room the *Acanthus* wallpaper is striking but it was obviously considered a good background for paintings, including Edward Burne-Jones's *The Tree of Forgiveness*.
Historic England Archive

& Co. in other media, she designed wallpapers on her own account. Several of her patterns were issued by Jeffrey & Co. in the early 1880s. *Mallow* and *Bramble* are simple all-over flower-and-leaf designs. *Mallow* and *Loop Trail* are reminiscent of the firm's earlier Queen Anne style. *Carnation* of 1880 (XI.19), also by Faulkner, marks a further innovation – perhaps against Morris's aesthetic better judgment – as it was printed by machine rather than by hand. This meant that it was much less expensive but, as was the case with that technology, the colours were thin and there was some blurring. It is possible that Morris himself was contemplating designing for machine at about this time, as two versions of the design for *Poppy* (both held at the William Morris Society) are marked 'Machine Wall Paper' (XI.20a). However, in the end, the pattern, also known as *Pink and Poppy*, was hand-printed (XI.20b) and only one other machine print was issued during his lifetime. The cheaper papers that fleshed out the range at the Oxford Street showroom were the work of other manufacturers, as Morris confirmed in a letter to Catherine Holiday in September 1885, 'we find it desirable for our customer's convenience to keep a book of cheap papers in case they want something for some inferior room ... of course these are not my designs, nor sold with my definite approval as designs.'

Between 1882 and 1896 the firm issued a further 35 new patterns in a variety of types and prices. By this time wallpapers were no longer Morris's main concern and tend to reflect his other designing interests. *Bird and Anemone* of 1882 (XI.21), for example, was the same as the textile of that name although larger in scale. From 1884 onwards many of the papers, like the printed textiles, showed a structure based on diagonally meandering stems. Layering was reduced in favour of backgrounds dotted or covered with tiny stylized flowers and trails. *Wild Tulip* of 1884 (XI.23) was the first. With its mass of pin-dotting, it appears to be a simple design but it uses many subtly different colours and 18 blocks were needed to complete the pattern. May Morris later wrote in the first volume of *Artist, Writer, Socialist*, that 'The character of this delicate design is all "Kelmscott" to me: the peony and wild tulip are two of the richest blossomings of the spring garden at the Manor'. *Norwich* and *Double Bough* of 1889 and 1891 use a similar structure, while the pin-dots of *Wallflower*, *c.*1890 (XI.28), complicate a simple airy pattern, as in the earlier *Apple*.

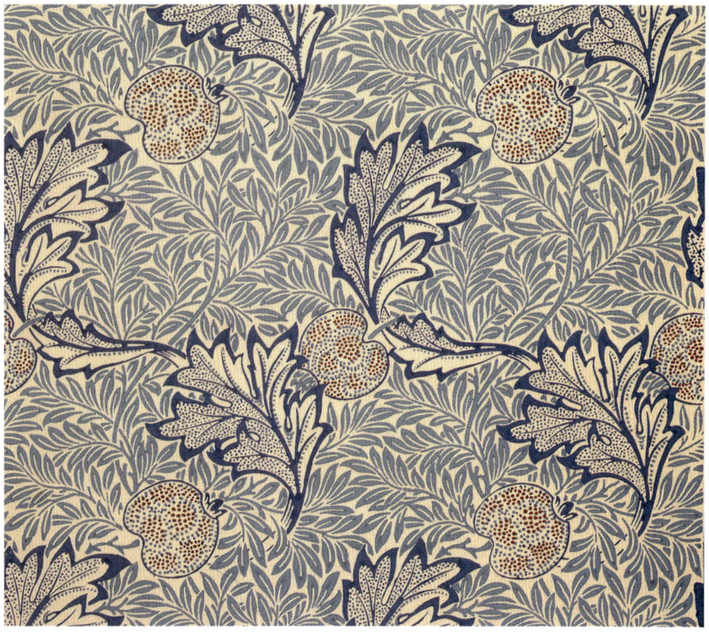

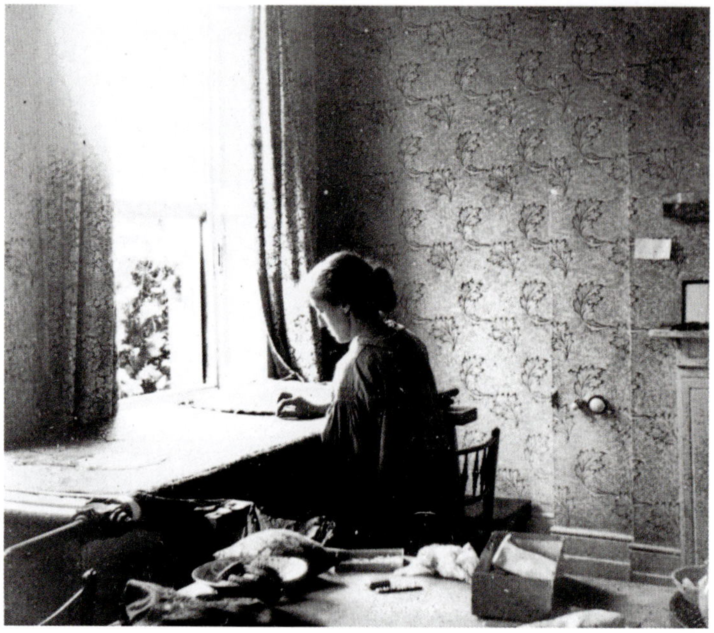

Fig.193 ***Apple* wallpaper, colourway 97, designed by William Morris in 1877. Block-printed in distemper colours, repeat h. 31 cm.**
William Morris Gallery

Fig.194 **May Morris photographed at her home, 8 Hammersmith Terrace, in the early 1890s; *Apple* wallpaper behind her.**
William Morris Gallery

Other designers were involved in these years. Faulkner produced *Blossom*, a pretty and naturalistic floral pattern, in 1885 and *Merton* in 1888. The latter was the second, and last, machine print to be issued during Morris's lifetime and was similar to her earlier *Loop Trail* (XI.18). May Morris designed *Horn Poppy* (1885) and *Arcadia* (about 1886), which both use her father's diagonal structure, the latter being very similar to his *Fritillary* of the same year. Although there is some debate over the attribution, she is now thought to be responsible for *Honeysuckle*, 1883 (XI.22), an all-over tangle of flowers, stems and leaves in a similarly naturalistic style to William's *Willow Boughs* pattern of 1887 (XI.24). John Henry Dearle, who was increasingly in charge of the production side of the business, also began to provide designs. His first known wallpaper pattern is *Iris* (XI.26) of about 1887; thereafter his contribution increased considerably, although his emulation of Morris's style makes attribution difficult.

A curious development of 1887–8 was the introduction of a powdered mica (silicate of magnesia) ground, which gave a sparkly effect. This was employed on new versions of *Venetian* and on *Bruges*, a large, formal, textile-based design of 1888 (XI.27). Flocking was introduced at the same time. This technique had originated in about 1700 to simulate wall hangings of cut velvet or silk damask. Morris & Co. first used it for *Ceiling* (as seen in the printing log, XI.25) and soon afterwards for the textile-based patterns, *Indian*, *Venetian*, *Bruges*, and for *Grafton*, first issued in 1883 (XI.31), and *Autumn Flowers* of 1888, a rather rigid, non-naturalistic design. Sometimes, flocking was used together with a mica ground. It is hard to imagine these innovations as Morris's own. He was at this time actively involved in politics and a letter of February 1887 to his wife suggests that his heart was far from the day-to-day development of the range: 'Smith [one of the company's business managers] is insisting on paper-hangings so I must do one at least, besides those I have in hand.' Morris's diary, however, shows that he was still designing wallpaper in 1895.

After Morris's death, the firm continued to offer the old patterns, going to great lengths to standardize colourings to the original versions. Initially, any additional new designs and colourings were much in Morris's own style but, within a few years, the wallpapers began to reflect changes in fashionable taste. Morris & Co. produced in total about 108 patterns in numerous colours and finishes. The last of all though, *Bird and Pomegranate* issued in 1927, was, as the name suggests, a return to the very earliest imagery.

Production

The firm's minute book records that in 1862 the partners intended to print *Trellis*, their first wallpaper pattern, in the workshop at 8 Red Lion Square, using etched zinc plates and oil-based inks, perhaps with the aim of producing transparent washes of colour. However, according to Aymer Vallance this technique proved slow and laborious. Nor was the following attempt using wood blocks cut by Barrett's of Bethnal Green, satisfactory, perhaps because Morris hoped to use transparent pigments, which were then not in general use. The manufacture of wallpapers was thereafter transferred wholesale – the contracting of block or roller cutting as well as the printing – to Jeffrey & Co., a London wallpaper producer, then of Kent and Essex Yard, Whitechapel, later of 64 Essex Road, Islington. Jeffrey & Co.'s papers were largely at the upper end of the market and Jeffrey's was one of about 15 English paper-hanging manufacturers that showed at the International Exhibition of 1862. The company had been printing Owen Jones's patterns for him since the beginning of the 1860s and was therefore already experienced in dealing with this type of 'private' work.

Jeffrey's working practices of 1862 (not long before Morris, Marshall, Faulkner & Co. gave them the contract) were described in a report of a Parliamentary Commission into children's employment in factories. At that date the company employed 75 workers: 36 adults; 25 young persons, aged 13 to 18; and 14 children, most of whom were over ten. Several of the workmen interviewed said that they had been paper stainers all their working lives and that their sons were now working with them. The boys, who applied the colour to the blocks, hung the paper to dry and made it into rolls, were employed and paid by the block printers and earned something like 1*s.* 6*d.* to 5*s.* 6*d.* a week depending on their usefulness. The usual hours were from 8am to 8pm, with one and a half hours for breaks. Subsequent legislation gradually improved conditions for young workers. By 1895 the minimum age of employment was 12, with a shorter working week and half-time school attendance for those under 14. The enquiry of 1862 also demonstrates the considerable concern, which had increased in the 1850s, about some of the chemicals used in making wallpapers, particularly white lead and arsenic. The latter intensified colours and was most often, but not only, used in printing the 'emerald green' that was very popular in wallpapers from the 1820s. It was known that printers working with white lead could develop paralysed 'drop hands' and that contact with arsenic could result in sores and lesions but many of the printers at Jeffrey's disclaimed any serious ill-effects. Clearly, Jeffrey & Co. was no working paradise but, although the days were long and pay was low, block printers and their young assistants worked at their own pace and, for the boys, the work was not heavy or dangerous.

P.W.J. Bartrip has described the fears, too, from the 1850s onwards, that wallpapers printed with arsenical colours were a health risk for their users. Numerous reports in the press of illness and death, supposed to be from this source, greatly alarmed the public, leading wallpaper manufacturers to change their processes and adopt the slogan 'free from arsenic' in marketing their wares. Three letters of 1885 from Morris to Thomas Wardle, the textile dyer and printer of Leek, show that Morris himself (who had been a Director of the Devon Great Consols mine, a major supplier of arsenic in the 1850s and 1860s) thought that too much was made of the danger to the consumer. But while tests by Andy Meharg have shown that some early Morris & Co. wallpaper contained arsenic, by 1883 at the latest the company's publicity material was claiming that its papers were entirely free from the substance.

The reported smoothness of the relationship between the two firms owed much to Metford Warner, who joined Jeffrey's as a junior partner in 1866 and was sole proprietor by 1871. Warner was an enthusiast for good new design and saw its commercial potential, making his company the most highly regarded wallpaper manufacturer of the last quarter of the nineteenth century. He later recalled Morris as characteristically forceful: 'tell them "not to improve my colourings" was a message I had to convey to the factory from the master in blue blouse – bare feet in slippers and hands blue from the dye vat' (National Art Library MSL/1971/185). In May 1898 *The Journal of the Society of Arts* published his testimony that Morris took the greatest personal interest in production and allowed nothing to pass until he was quite satisfied that it was right both in colour and design. He remembered a case where Morris had an entire set of expensive blocks put aside because he was not satisfied with the design. Some of the artwork (for example XI.8) bears very detailed instructions for the printer. But there are indications of collaboration too. In the early 1870s Jeffrey's did experimental wash printing on Morris's behalf, with some success, while in the late 1870s Morris adopted the imitation leathers that Jeffrey's had perfected.

Jeffrey & Co., although taken over by the giant Wall Paper Manufacturers Ltd in 1924, continued to print Morris & Co.'s papers until 1927, when Arthur Sanderson & Sons Ltd took on the work.

Details of the arrangement between Morris and Jeffrey & Co. are not known, but it seems from Taylor's memorandum mentioned above (p.238) that, in the late 1860s, the firm would take an initial 100 rolls of a new pattern or colourway for stock. This was a sizeable amount and, as Taylor pointed out, expensive. Once there were enough patterns to warrant it, Jeffrey's maintained special logbooks recording all the Morris & Co. patterns and colourways, each with their own number. These logs, now held in the Sanderson Design Group Archive, are a valuable source of information, indicating, for example, that by the mid-1870s, the standard stock order was for 75 rolls of a particular 'way'. However, it is not wise to rely on these records too heavily for dating the earliest papers, as the books were probably not instigated until the 1870s.

During Morris's lifetime, the majority of the company's designs were printed by the traditional wood-block process that was widely used to produce high-quality papers (see XI.30). Each colour in the final pattern was printed from a separate block, usually about 25 inches square and 3 inches thick. The blocks were made of a triple sandwich of wood: the bottom two layers deal; the topmost a hard and fine-grained fruit wood. The outlines of each colour were transferred to a separate block and the unwanted portions cut away, leaving 'islands' of wood as the printing surface. Dots or lines were produced by hammering strips or pins of metal into the printing block. Much depended on the cutter's skill in accurately and sympathetically tracing the original design. George Wardle in his 'Memorials of William Morris' recalled that the block cutter's tracing of the pattern was always submitted to Morris before it could be 'rubbed off', while Morris himself in a letter of 19 December 1882 mentioned 'Mr. Barret [*sic*] the Wood-Cutter come to see about cutting the design I made'. A letter, probably of 1867, from Warington Taylor shows that getting the blocks made was an expensive business – the cost of cutting 12 blocks for a design (which must have been *Fruit*) was £15, plus £1 10*s*. for trial proofs.

To print the pattern, the blocks were charged with printing colour and then pressed face-down on to the paper. Each colour was applied along the full length of the paper and left to dry before the next was applied, and so on in the same way, until the pattern was completed (fig.195). This was a necessarily slow process, requiring skill and training. The colours used were mostly distemper – pigment carried in a water-based medium of size or whiting, which produces a somewhat thick and chalky surface. In a design with many distemper colours, it is possible to see and feel the crisp build-up of the colours (see, for example, XI.3). In machine printing all the colours were printed in one pass, before those below had dried. In order to speed drying, the colours were made thinner but, even so, there was inevitably blurring (see XI.19) – an effect that William Morris did not like and which he only rarely employed. Moreover, while block printers had some freedom to manage their own work and time, machine printers were tied to the demands of the non-stop production process.

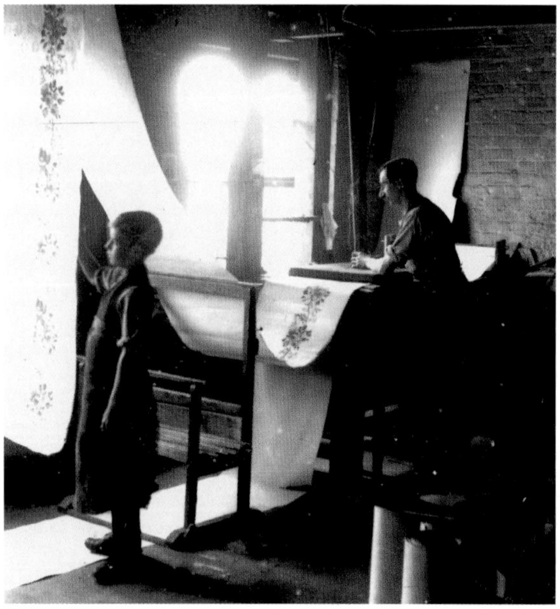

Fig.195 **Jeffrey & Co. photographed in the early twentieth century. Hanging the paper to dry before printing the next block.**
Temple Newsam House, Leeds

The market for Morris wallpapers

In the 1860s, with a small range of patterns and colourways, the customers for the wallpapers seem to have been few. Warington Taylor wrote to Webb about the 'limited sale of our papers'. At this time the company's showroom was at 26 Queen Square, Bloomsbury, which was not a shopping area. Mackail describes 'visits made to Queen Square in its first days by purchasers who had *accidently* [my italics] seen some of his [Morris's] wall-papers', indicating that they made a special trip there. The marketing was at that stage personal. Dante Gabriel Rossetti's contacts were most useful, as an anecdote related by Lady Mount Temple in her *Memorials* suggests. She describes the French-style decoration of her London house in about 1865: 'watered paper on the walls, garlands of roses tied with blue bows! Glazed chintzes with bunches

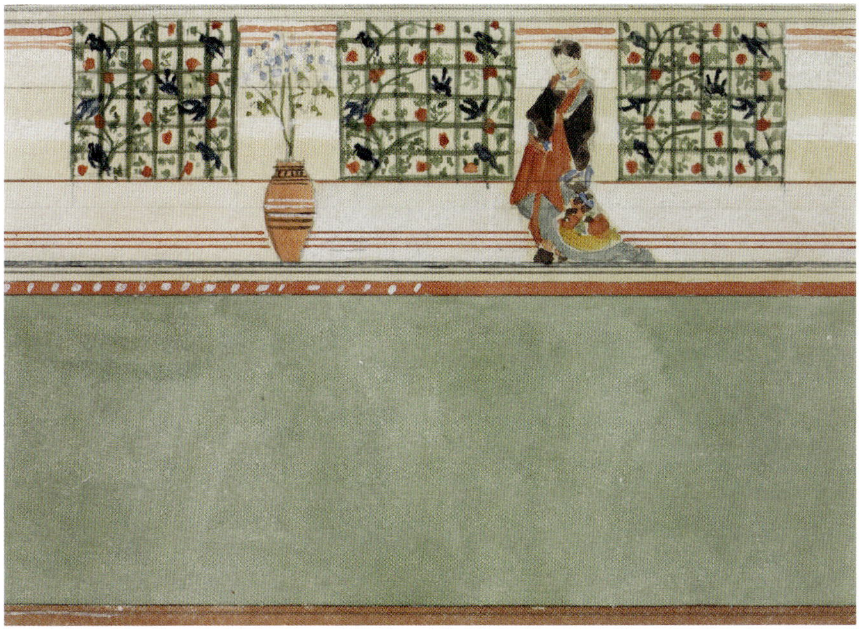

Fig.196 **Design for Japanese-style wall decoration, incorporating *Trellis* wallpaper, for Dromore Castle, County Limerick, Ireland, by E.W. Godwin, *c.*1869.**
V&A (E.491–1963)
Given by Mr Edward Godwin

of roses'. Rossetti came to dinner and was asked his opinion. '"Well," he said frankly, "I should begin by burning everything you have got!".' Shortly afterwards, she wrote, when the staircase needed renovation, the firm did it up with a Morris paper on the walls and Burne-Jones stained glass in the window. Lady Mount Temple goes on to say: 'Now our taste was attacked on the other side, and all our candid relations and friends intimated that they thought we had made our pretty little house hideous!' The record books (held by the V&A) of Cowtan & Sons, a London-based decorating company that catered to the wealthy and the elite, bear this out, showing that the Mount Temples installed Morris's grey *Daisy* pattern in one of their attic rooms in September 1865 – but that this was a completely isolated example among their clients at the time.

A more likely milieu for Morris papers in the early days was the sort offered by Frederick Leyland, the Liverpool shipping magnate and patron of the arts, who had close connections with Rossetti. *Daisy*, *Trellis* and *Fruit* were used at Speke Hall, his house near Liverpool, in about 1867. Morris papers were also used for his famously decorated London houses in the late 1860s and 1870s. Similarly, E.W. Godwin's designs for a wall decoration for Dromore Castle, County Limerick, of about 1869, which use the *Trellis* pattern, also locate the patterns in artistic circles (fig.196). But, even by 1869, the papers were beginning to gain wider attention. Charles Eastlake's *Hints on Household Taste* was the first of a new genre of books on how to furnish and decorate, aimed at the growing middle classes. It was very successful, going into at least four editions. The first, of 1868, showed only rigid diaper patterns of the 'reformed' sort but the second edition, of 1869, singled out Messrs. Morris, Marshall & Co. as providing wallpapers 'not only luxurious in effect, but of high artistic excellence.'

In the 1870s Morris developed the firm's marketing strategies and significantly expanded the wallpaper range. At the new showroom in London's Oxford Street, opened in 1877, decorators, customers and window shoppers could see the wallpapers displayed to good effect, alongside other goods in the Morris style. The printing logbooks show that, by 1879, there were 32 patterns in 125 different colourings or effects on offer. The *Morris Wall-Papers* brochures of about 1909 and 1912 give prices, which are likely to have been similar to those of 1890. The cheapest machine-printed paper cost 2*s.* 6*d.* a roll; the ordinary hand-prints ran from 3*s.* to 16*s.* while a gold-ground or embossed paper could cost as much as 40*s.* It has been suggested that Morris & Co.'s goods were expensive. While its papers were certainly at the upper end of the market, they were in the same sort of range as Sanderson's which, in the 1870s, was distributing French hand-printed papers for between 4*s.* 6*d.* and 16*s.* a roll and which, around 1880, was selling its own single-colour block-prints for 3*s.* or 3*s.* 6*d.*

The wallpapers and other items could also be seen elsewhere. Morris & Co. made a brief foray into running a shop in Manchester in 1883–4. Subsequently, its goods were available through Kendal, Milne & Co. In the Midlands, Chamberlain, King & Jones of Birmingham were the sole agents in about 1900. As early as 1871 J.F. Bumstead & Co. of Boston, USA, was the agent for Morris, Marshall, Faulkner & Co. By 1882 Elliot & Goodwin of New York (afterwards Elliot & Bulkley, then A.E. Bulkley) was Morris & Co.'s American agent, selling through outlets in the major cities of the East Coast and the Midwest. Participation in exhibitions, both at home and abroad, increased exposure. Morris wallpapers were shown at the Centennial International Exhibition of 1876 in Philadelphia in the display put on by Jeffrey & Co. and more exposure was gained at the 1883 Boston Foreign Fair, where Morris & Co. had its own large stand. On a smaller scale, the company contributed furnishings for two model rooms of a 'small house' in the new Art Gallery in Queen's Park, Manchester, in 1884. *Daisy* – costing at least 6*s.* 6*d.* a roll – was used in the sitting room (fig.149) and *Willow* in the bedroom. The cost of both was prohibitive for a working-class artisan and Morris's correspondence reveals his frustration with this state of affairs and initial reluctance to take part in the project.

By now, Morris & Co.'s papers were featuring in other how-to-decorate books. Lucy Orrinsmith – Kate Faulkner's sister – in *The Drawing-Room: Its Decorations and Furniture* of 1877 recommended using a 'calm and suggestive decorative floral pattern' on the walls. Her only wallpaper illustrations were three (unattributed) Morris & Co. designs: *Jessamine* (*Jasmine*), *Vine* and *Rose*. Robert Edis noted the 'general artistic excellence' of Morris & Co.'s papers in his *Decoration and Furniture of Town Houses* (1881). His own London drawing room, papered with *Fruit* (fig.198), is illustrated as the frontispiece of the book. The type of consumer to whom the papers appealed is perhaps typified by the 'artistic' occupants of the new Queen Anne suburb, Bedford Park, in west London. In his essay on the suburb, published in 1882 as part of *Travels in South Kensington*, Moncure Conway noted that:

> Those who purchase or lease houses at Bedford Park are allowed the choice where their wall-papers shall be purchased, what designs shall be selected, and what colors shall be used on the wood-work ... As a matter of fact, a majority of the residents have used the wallpapers and designs of Morris ... This natural selection of the Morris designs by so many families, independently of each other, could hardly have occurred a few years ago, or, if it had occurred, would have been a misfortune of monotony; but recently these designs have been sufficiently varied, and the new patterns, which may be had in divers colors and shades, are now so numerous that it is quite possible for all to be satisfied without a calamitous sameness.

Morris's paper-hangings were commercially successful but, perhaps more importantly, they played a significant part in raising the status of the English product to a position of international pre-eminence in the last quarter of the nineteenth century. Morris had been among the first to take wallpaper design out of anonymity and it was possibly his example that encouraged Metford

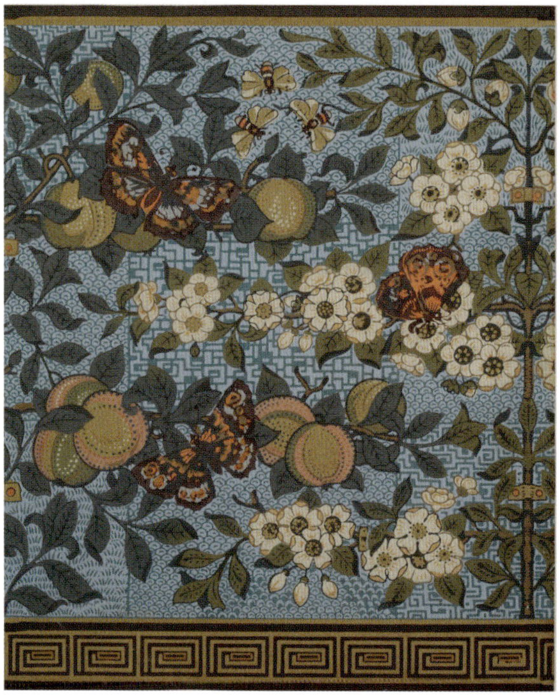

Fig.197 **Wallpaper frieze, designed by Bruce Talbert, made by Jeffrey & Co., 1877.**
V&A (E.1855–1934)
Given by the Wall Paper Manufacturers Ltd

Warner to commission patterns from important architects and designers. From 1871 onwards the Jeffrey & Co. logbooks show an increasing number of 'art' patterns (Arts and Crafts, Gothic, Japanesque) which, by about 1875, had completely ousted the previously dominant 'French' styles. Some of these were clearly influenced by Morris's designs (especially the first three). Notable examples are Bruce Talbert's *Fruit* frieze, 1877 (fig.197), Charles Eastlake's *Solanum* (which he illustrated in the 1878 edition of *Hints on Household Taste*) and Walter Crane's *La Margarete*, which won a prize at the Philadelphia Centennial Exhibition in 1876. Other companies followed suit. Mass manufacturers took up the Arts and Crafts style – by 1884 'Morrisonian' had become a recognizable term throughout the trade, press coverage increased and paper-hangings had a heyday.

Although Morris contributed to the spate of 'art' wallpapers, he remained unconvinced by the 'artistic' fashion of using different patterns for dado, filling, frieze, ceiling and borders. His views on the appropriate use of paper are given in his lecture 'Making the Best of It' and, in great detail, in George Wardle's brochure for the firm's display at the Boston Foreign Fair in 1883. He suggested that, unless a room was very high, the division of the wall into two – either with a dado of about 4 ft 6 in. or with a narrow frieze – was quite

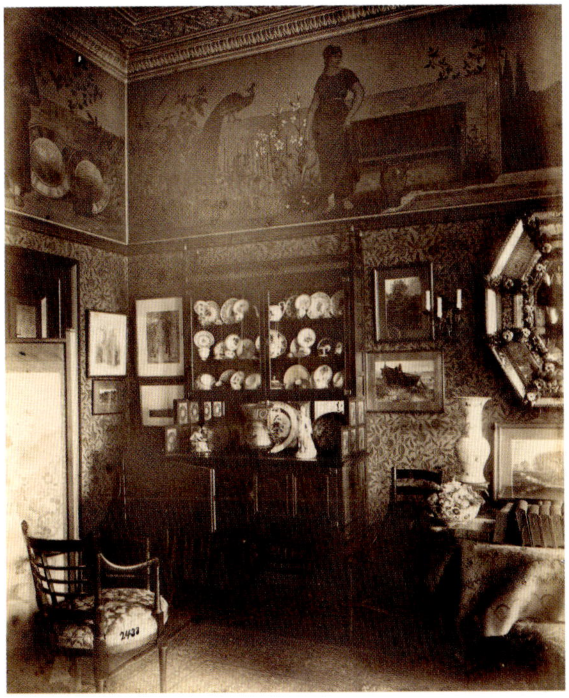

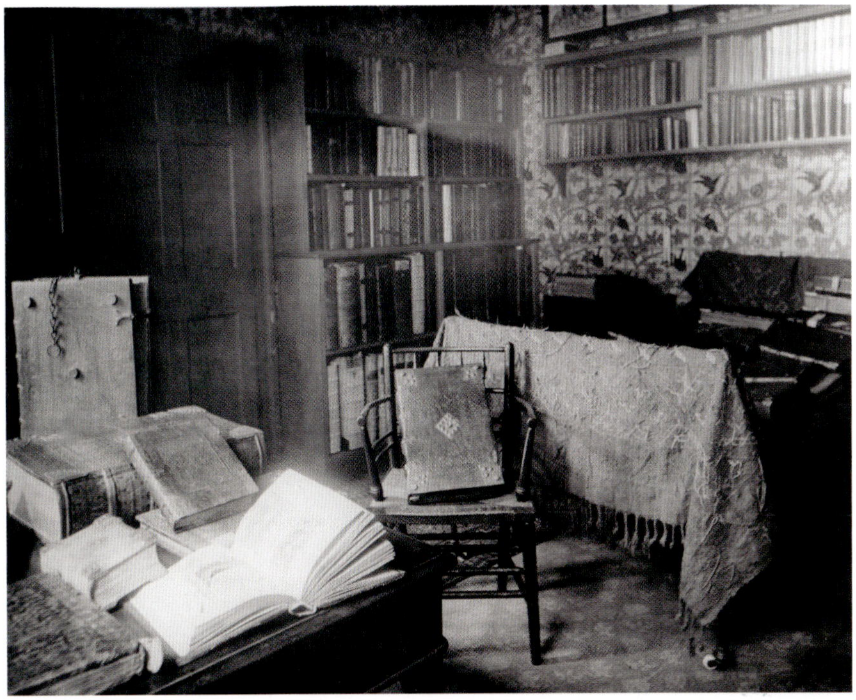

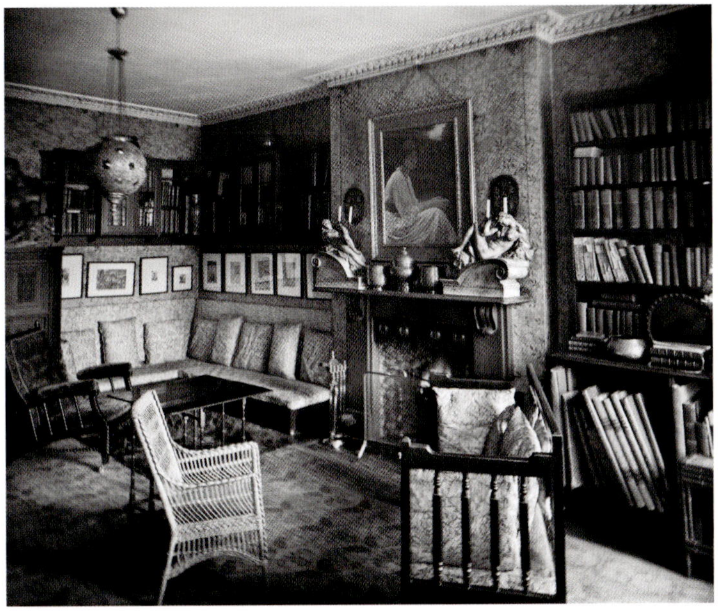

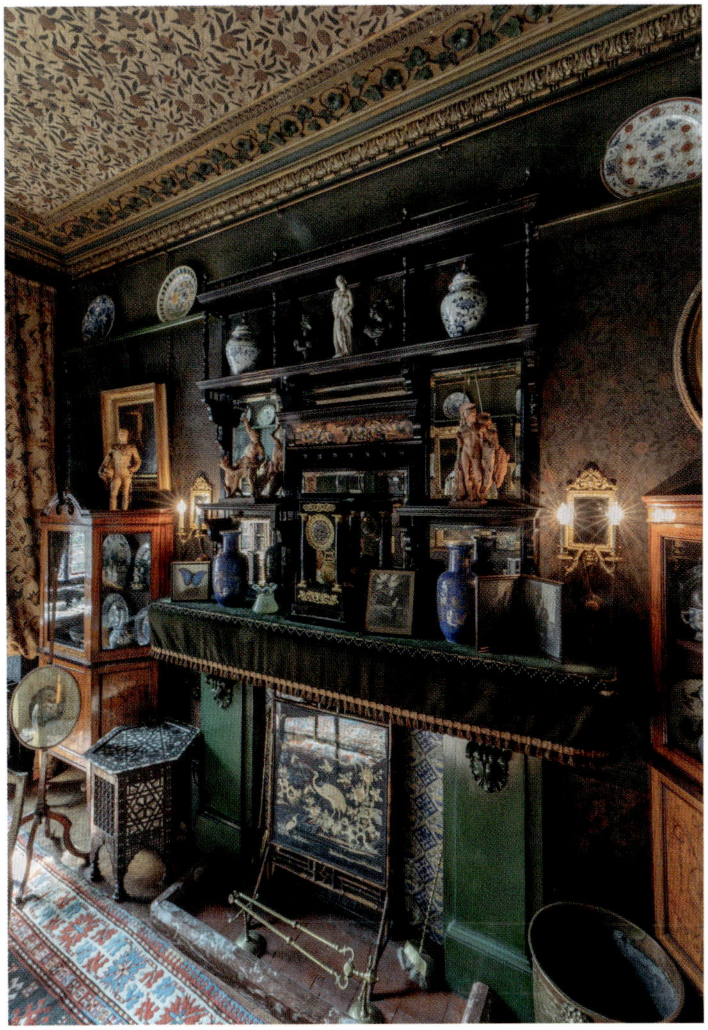

Fig.198 (top left) **Robert Edis's drawing room, designed 1871, photographed by Bedford Lemere & Co., *c.*1880. The lower part of the wall is papered with *Fruit*.**
RIBA

Fig.200 (above) **The Burne-Joneses' drawing room at The Grange, Fulham, with *Jasmine* wallpaper and Morris & Co. furnishings, probably photographed by Frederick Hollyer, 1887.**
Historic England Archive

Fig.199 (top right) **William Morris's bedroom at Kelmscott House with *Trellis* paper on the wall, photographed *c.*1896.**
Hammersmith & Fulham Local Studies and Archives Centre

Fig.201 (right) **The morning room at 18 Stafford Terrace with *Fruit* on the wall and ceiling and *Diaper* as the frieze, installed 1875 and re-papered 1912.**

enough. 'Never stoop to the ignominy of the paper dado'; 'Our wallpapers ... are simple fillings: they imitate no architectural features, neither dados, friezes, nor angles'; 'I have seen a good deal of the practice of putting pattern over pattern in paperhanging, and it seems to me a very unsatisfactory one.' According to Morris, only one pattern should be used in a room. A second one was just permissible if it merely broke the surface colour. He disliked papered ceilings. But, in the face of fashionable usage, the firm compromised to an extent, offering several special ceiling papers and suggesting the use of some of the single colour patterns, such as *Diaper*, *Venetian*, *Mallow* and *Bird and Anemone*. The yellow and pale-green ways were said to be the most suitable. Similarly, although during Morris's lifetime the firm never issued any frieze designs, it was proposed that *Daisy*, *Fruit*, *Larkspur*, *Apple* and *Sunflower* could be adapted for this purpose. The Boston brochure also made suggestions for complementary paint colours.

William Morris's own approach to using wallpaper can be seen in photographs of his and his friends' houses. He often hung the earlier naturalistic patterns, especially in bedrooms or the less public rooms of a house. *Lily* was on his bedroom walls at Kelmscott Manor and in Margaret Burne-Jones's bedroom at The Grange in Fulham, where *Jasmine* was used in the drawing room (fig.200). A photograph of about 1896 shows that Morris had *Trellis* in his bedroom at Kelmscott House (fig.199). May Morris used *Apple* in her house in Hammersmith (fig.194) as well as *Willow Boughs* to recall 'pleasant river scenes' at Kelmscott Manor. In these schemes the paper is hung, as Morris recommended, very simply, running from floor to ceiling. Even in his dining room at Kelmscott House, where the dense, rich *Pimpernel* is used, there is no frieze or ceiling paper; instead the papered wall provides a background for the magnificent Persian carpet hanging against it (VIII.16). Linda Parry's discussion of the commissioned interiors in Chapter VIII describes some richer effects, while in the houses of ordinary customers there was nothing to prevent the papers being used in complex and elaborate 'artistic' schemes. A fine example that remains *in situ* and can be visited is at 18 Stafford Terrace, London, home of the *Punch* cartoonist Linley Sambourne. Morris wallpapers were used throughout in 1875. The walls and ceiling of the morning room were hung with *Fruit*, and *Diaper* was used for the frieze (fig.201). The room was re-papered with the same patterns in 1912. W.A.S. Benson, whose lamps were retailed by Morris & Co. and who designed at least one wallpaper for the firm, had *Daisy* on the walls of his drawing room in a characteristically 'Morris' arrangement (fig.202). *Daisy* was one of the most consistently popular of the firm's papers, still selling well, according to the brochure of about 1912, nearly 50 years after it was first issued.

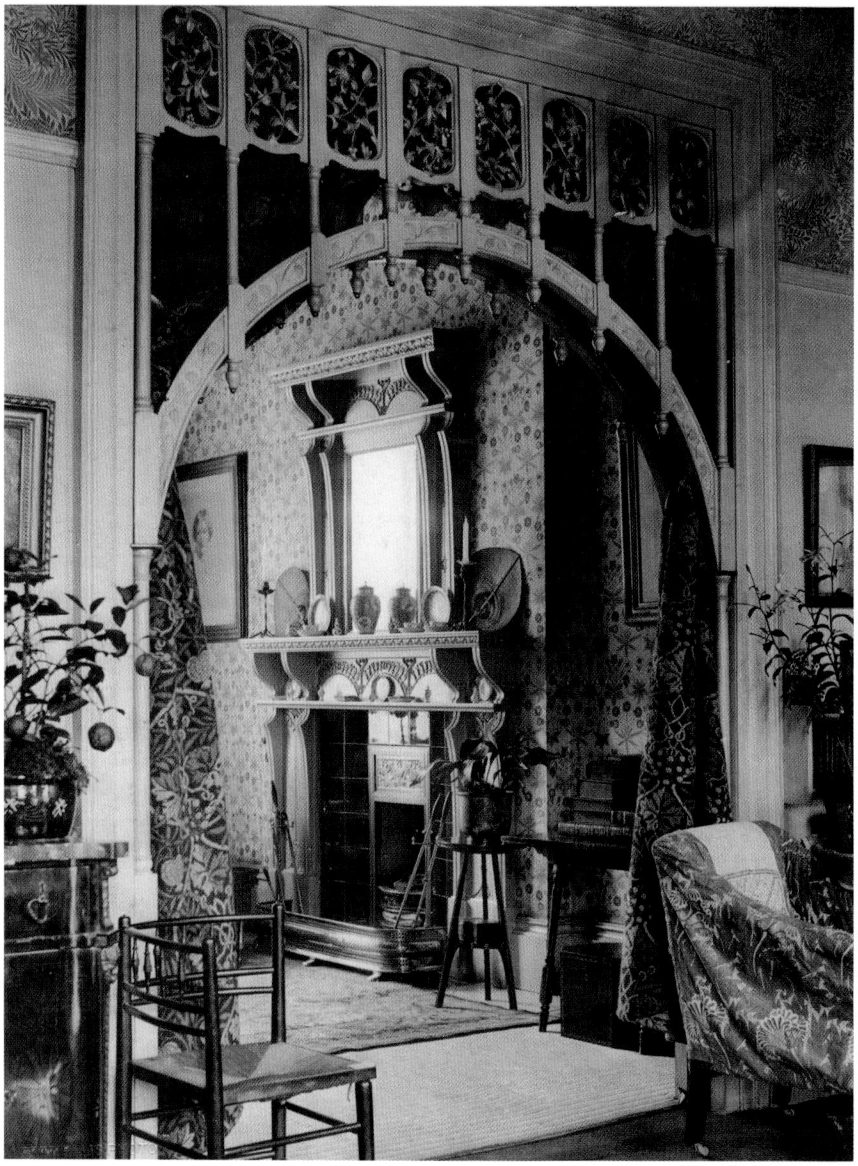

Fig.202 **W.A.S. Benson's drawing room at 39 Montagu Square, with *Daisy* on the wall, *Larkspur* used as a frieze, combined with other Morris & Co. furnishings, *c.*1898.**
Collection of Michael and Mariko Whiteway

XI.1
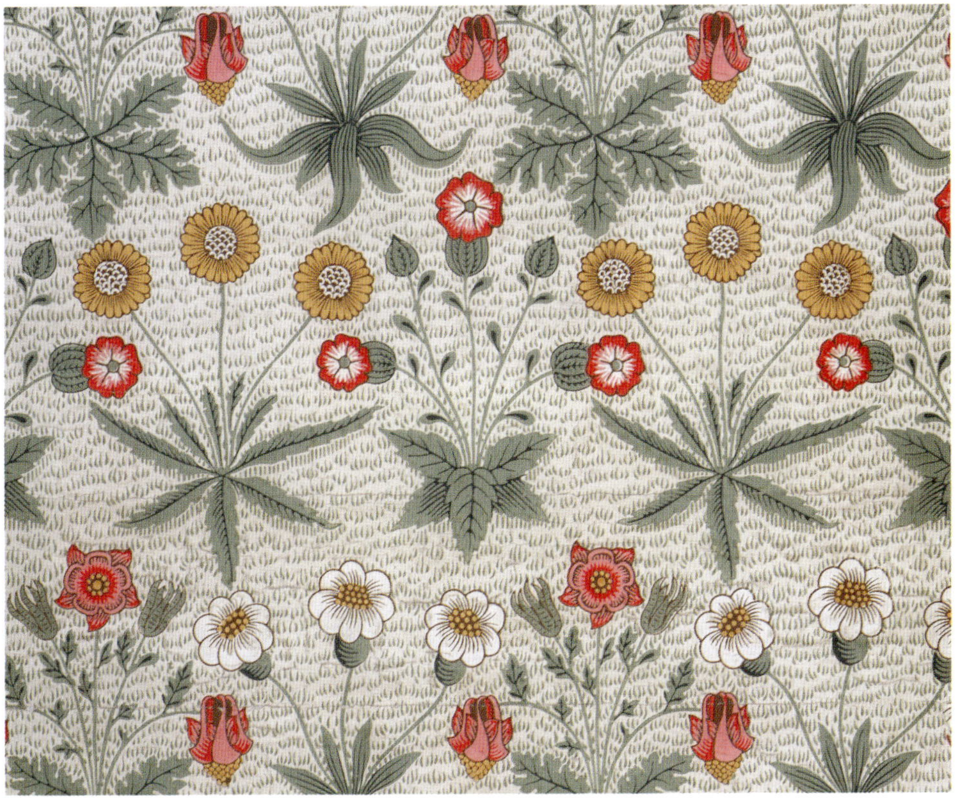

XI.2
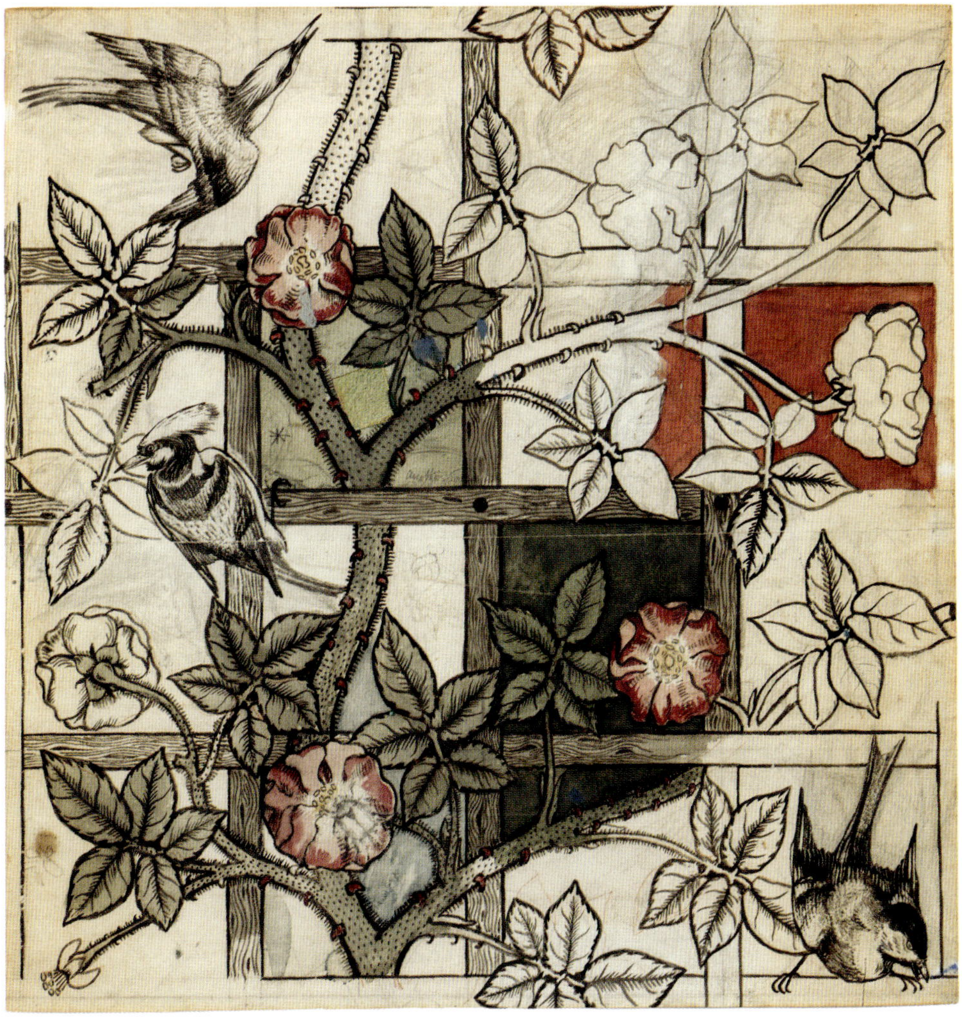

All wallpapers were made by Jeffrey & Co. The number in brackets after the pattern name denotes the 'way' – the combination of pattern and colour or finish. These numbers were stamped on the back of the papers in the customers' pattern books. They also appear in the logbooks that Jeffrey & Co. kept for the Morris wallpapers and tend to reflect the order in which the ways were issued. Most of the wallpapers were produced in rolls or 'pieces' 12 yards (about 10 metres) long and were approximately 21 inches (52 cm) wide plus the selvedge. To indicate the scale of the pattern the approximate vertical height of the repeating design element is given.

XI.1
Wallpaper, *Daisy (2)*
Designed by William Morris, registered 1 February 1864
Block-printed in distemper colours, repeat h. 35.3 cm
V&A (E.442–1919)
Given by Morris & Co.

Daisy was the first wallpaper to be issued. The first three patterns – *Daisy*, *Trellis* and *Fruit* – were all, from an early date, offered on a light, medium and dark ground. Further colourings were added later. This colourway was called *Light Daisy*.

XI.2
Design for *Trellis* wallpaper
William Morris, birds drawn by Philip Webb, November 1862
Pencil and watercolour, 66 x 61 cm
William Morris Gallery, London Borough of Waltham Forest (BLA472)

The precise date of this, Morris's first wallpaper design, is given by Mackail. The layout is complete but additional detailing would have been necessary for etching or block cutting. As in the other early patterns, there is some depth in the drawing but no integration between the motifs and the ground. Four different background colours are sketched in. Only three colourways were issued initially.

XI.3

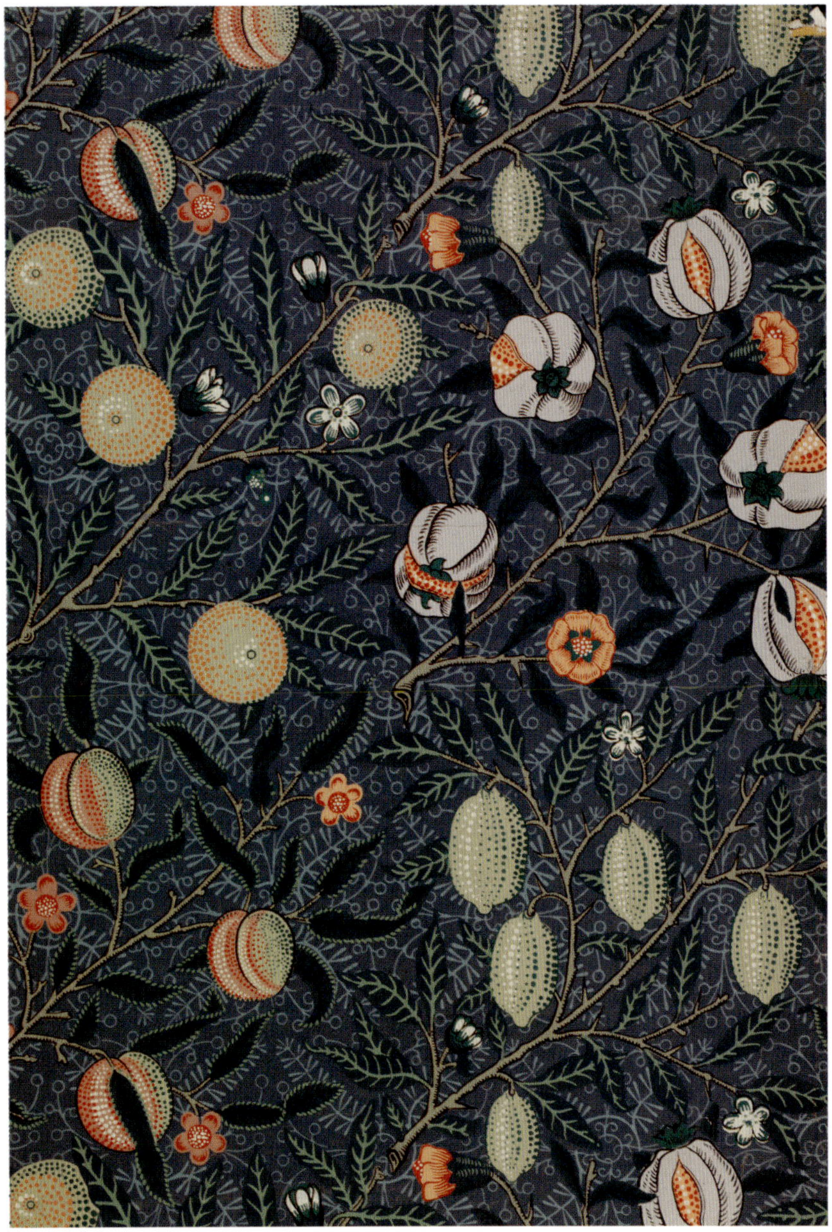

XI.4

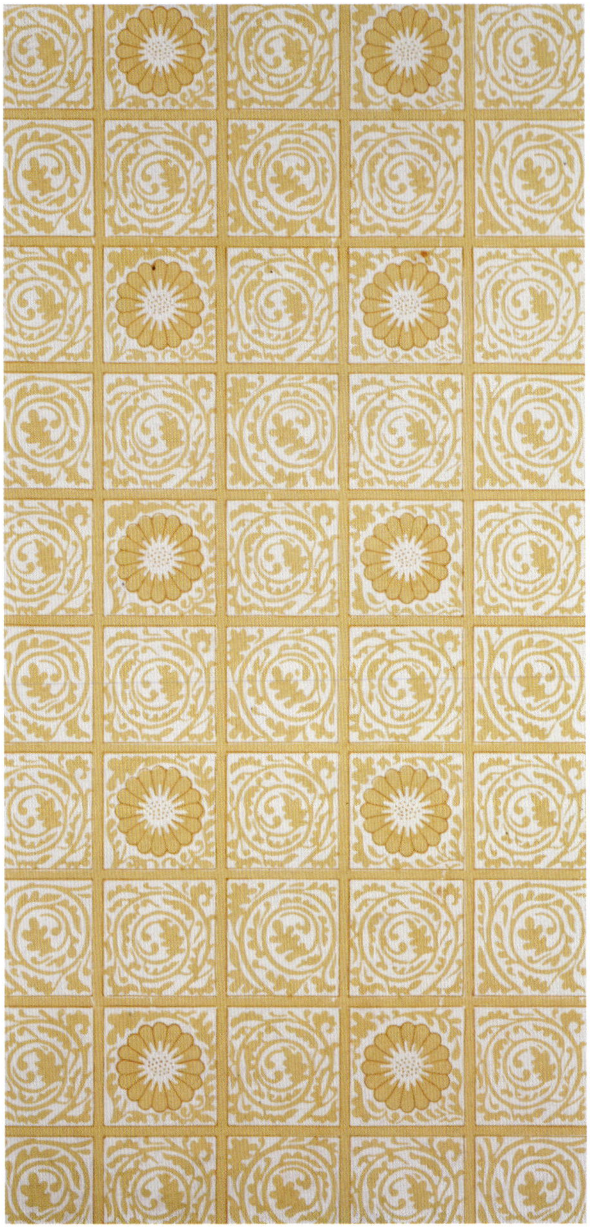

XI.3
Wallpaper, *Fruit*, also known as *Pomegranate*, *(Dark Fruit)*
Designed by William Morris, first issued *c.*1866
Block-printed in distemper colours, repeat h. 53.5 cm
V&A (E.3710–1927)
Bequeathed by James Richardson Holliday

This pattern is usually given an earlier date because the serial numbering in the printing log places it between *Daisy* and *Trellis*. Mackail, however, states that Morris was seen at Queen Square working on the design for *Pomegranate* in 1866. Mackail's notes also show that George Campfield, the firm's foreman, recollected the design being made at Queen Square (i.e. no earlier than 1865). A letter from Warington Taylor, probably of 1867, calls it 'our last new paper'.

Two versions of the design are known. That illustrated on p. 236 (fig.186) is an earlier iteration; its olive branches, leaves and fruits are replaced in a later design (private collection; illustrated in the sale catalogue published by Thomson, Roddick and Medcalf, 2002) and in the issued wallpaper by peaches.

XI.4
Wallpaper, *Diaper (18)*
Probably designed by Philip Webb, first issued 1868–70
Block-printed in distemper colours, repeat h. 13.2 cm
V&A (E.458–1919)
Given by Morris & Co.

Although an original design, *Diaper* sits happily with the group of adapted patterns of similar date. A letter from Warington Taylor shows that it was issued before *Indian* and *Queen Anne*.

The brochure *Morris Wall-Papers* of about 1912 credits William Morris with the design, however Richard and Hilary Myers have pointed out that a surviving tile uses the same motif as the wallpaper. Entries in Webb's account book for 1870 log several tile designs including a 'diaper pattern'. The wallpaper is stylistically much more akin to Webb's work in various media at this time than it is to Morris's.

Initially produced in two colourways, yellow and olive, another seven were added in the 1870s. In most cases the printed colours were only slightly deeper than the ground. Morris disapproved of using more than one paper in a room but, if a second was required, he recommended using a pattern like this. A non-directional design, it was also suitable for use as a ceiling paper.

XI.5

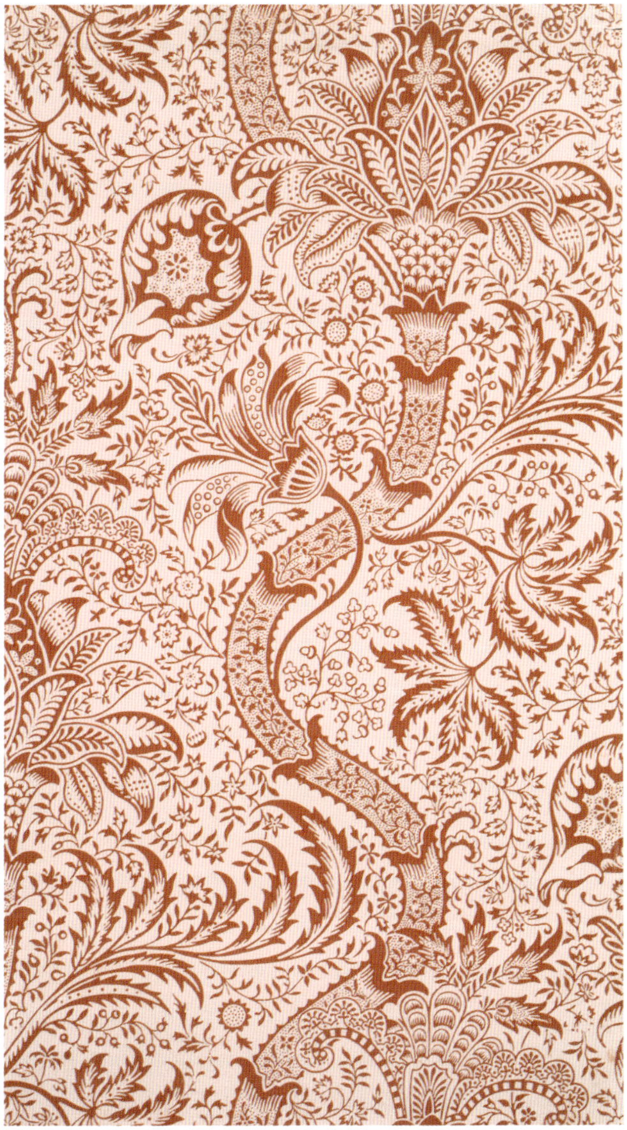

XI.6

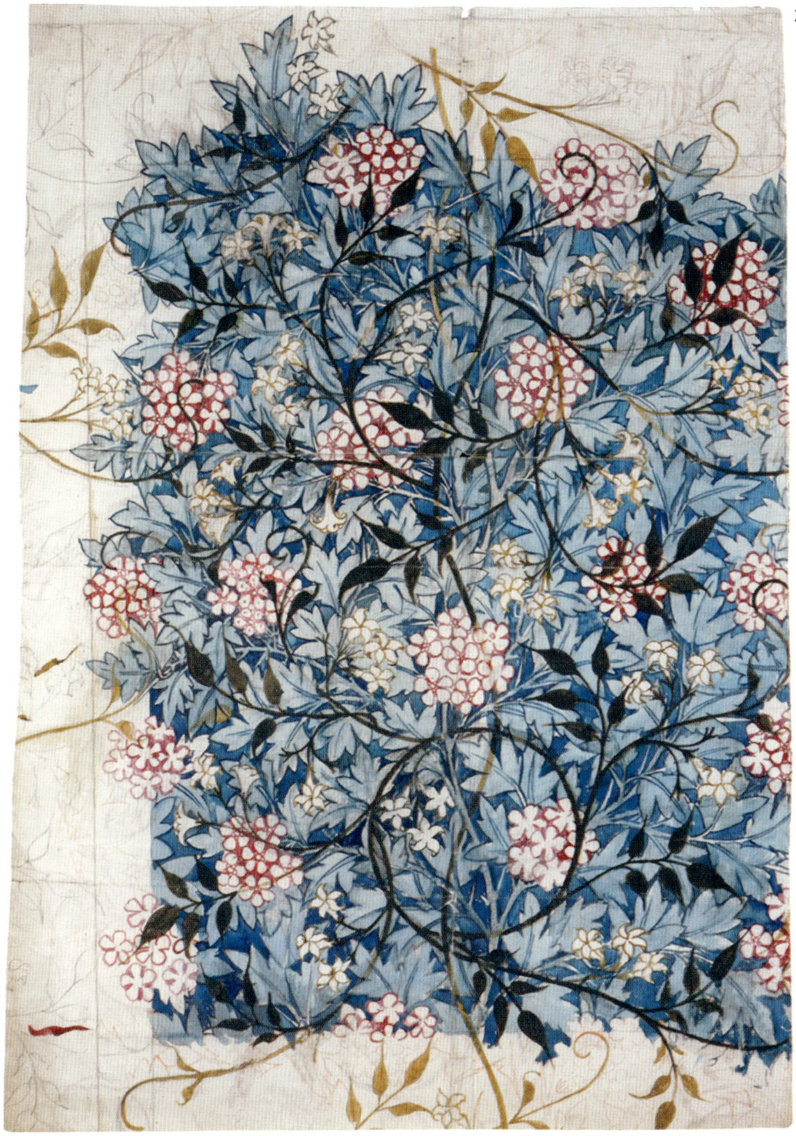

XI.5

Wallpaper, *Indian (Red Indian)*
Possibly designed by George Gilbert Scott Junior, first issued 1868–70
Block-printed in distemper colours, repeat h. 71.7 cm
V&A (E.3706–1927)
Bequeathed by James Richardson Holliday

'Mural Decoration' in *The Encyclopaedia Britannica*, XVII, 1884, by Morris and John Henry Middleton, illustrates the source of this pattern, describing it as an 'Early 18th-century wall-paper ... apparently copied from an Indian chintz'. It is one of a group of four designs (the others are *Queen Anne*, *Spray* and *Venetian*), adapted from earlier examples, which were possibly designed by the architect G.F. Bodley and his associates.

Similarities between these patterns and the early papers of Watts & Co., founded in 1874 by Bodley, George Gilbert Scott Junior and Thomas Garner, tend to support the connection and a generally accurate account of Bodley's career states that he had designed one or two of William Morris's early wallpapers (E. Warren, 'The Life and Work of George Frederick Bodley', *Journal of the RIBA,* 3rd series, 17, 1910). Warington Taylor refers to a wallpaper as 'Scott's "Indian"', which perhaps suggests that Scott Junior was the designer in this case.

XI.6

Design for *Jasmine*
William Morris, *c.*1872
Pencil and watercolour, 90.3 x 64.1 cm
William Morris Society, Kelmscott House, London (D3)

There are three other known drawings for this wallpaper, at different stages of completion: one is at Birmingham Museum and Art Gallery and two sketches are in the Huntington Art Museum, California.

The many deletions and substitutions in the printing logbook indicate initial difficulties with the pattern and it appears that the number of blocks used for its production was reduced from 20 to 11. Attempts made in 1874 to print it in wash colours seem to have been unsuccessful.

XI.7a

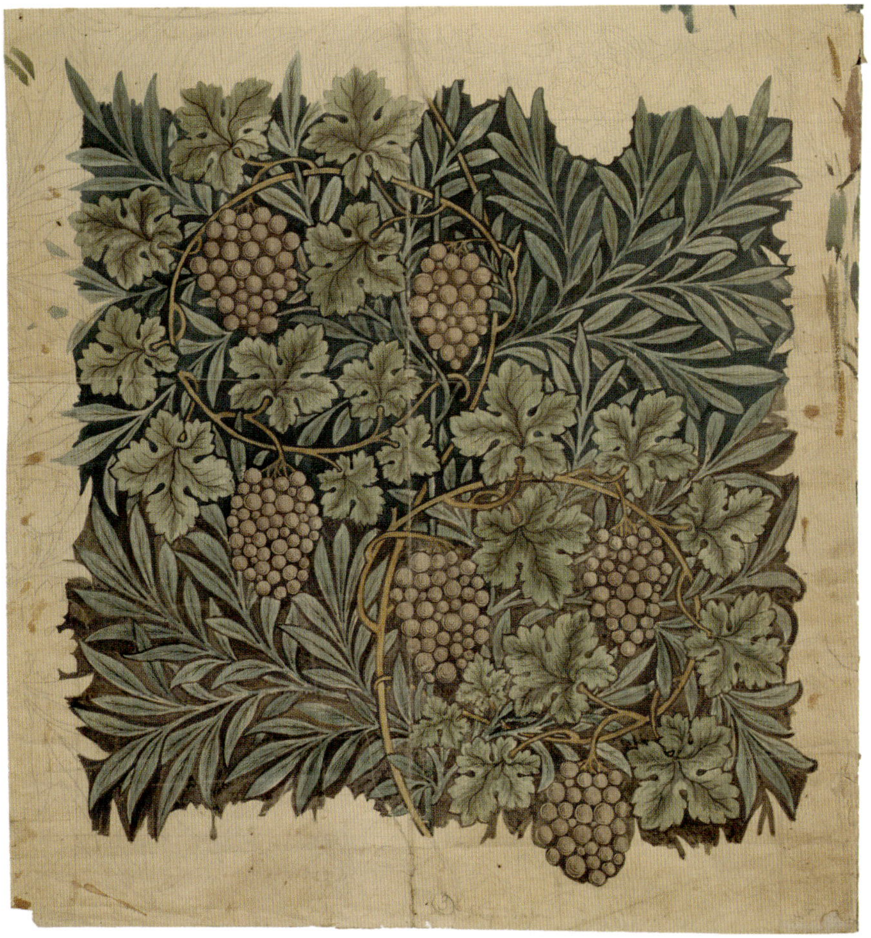

XI.7b

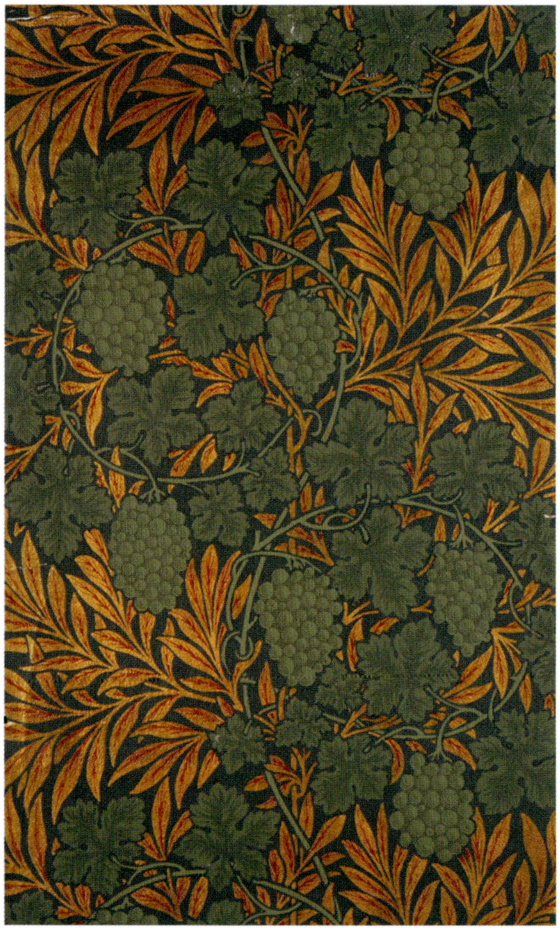

XI.8

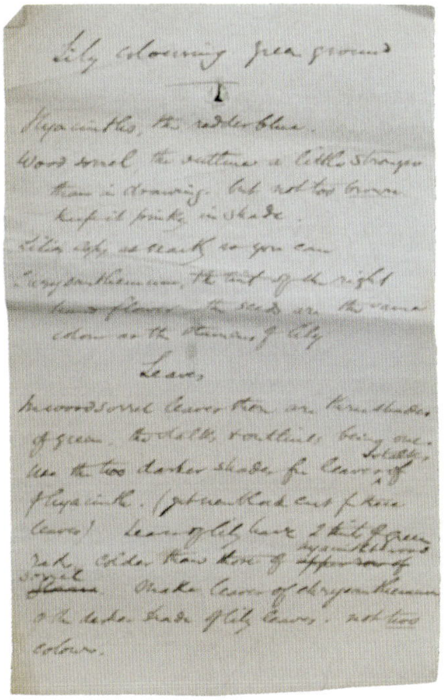

Lily colouring green ground

I

Hyacinths, the redder blue.
Wood sorrel, the outline a little stronger than in drawing but not too brown keep it pinky in shade.
Lilies [illegible] as [illegible] as you can
Chrysanthemum, the tint of the right hand flower, the seeds are the same colour as the stamens of lily

Leaves

the wood sorrel leaves there are three shades of green, the stalks & outlines being one. Use the two darker shades for leaves of hyacinth. (just within the cut of those leaves) leaves of lily have 2 tints of green rather colder than those of hyacinth and sorrel. Make leaves of chrysanthemum of the darker shade of lily leaves: not too colour.

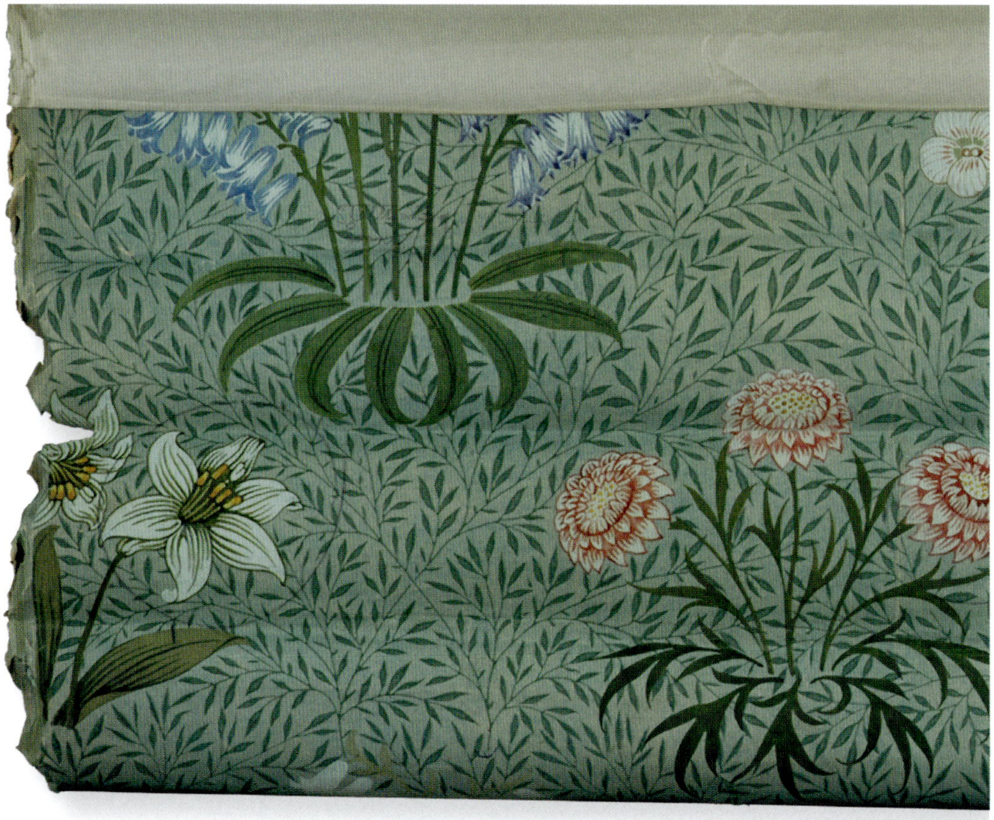

XI.9

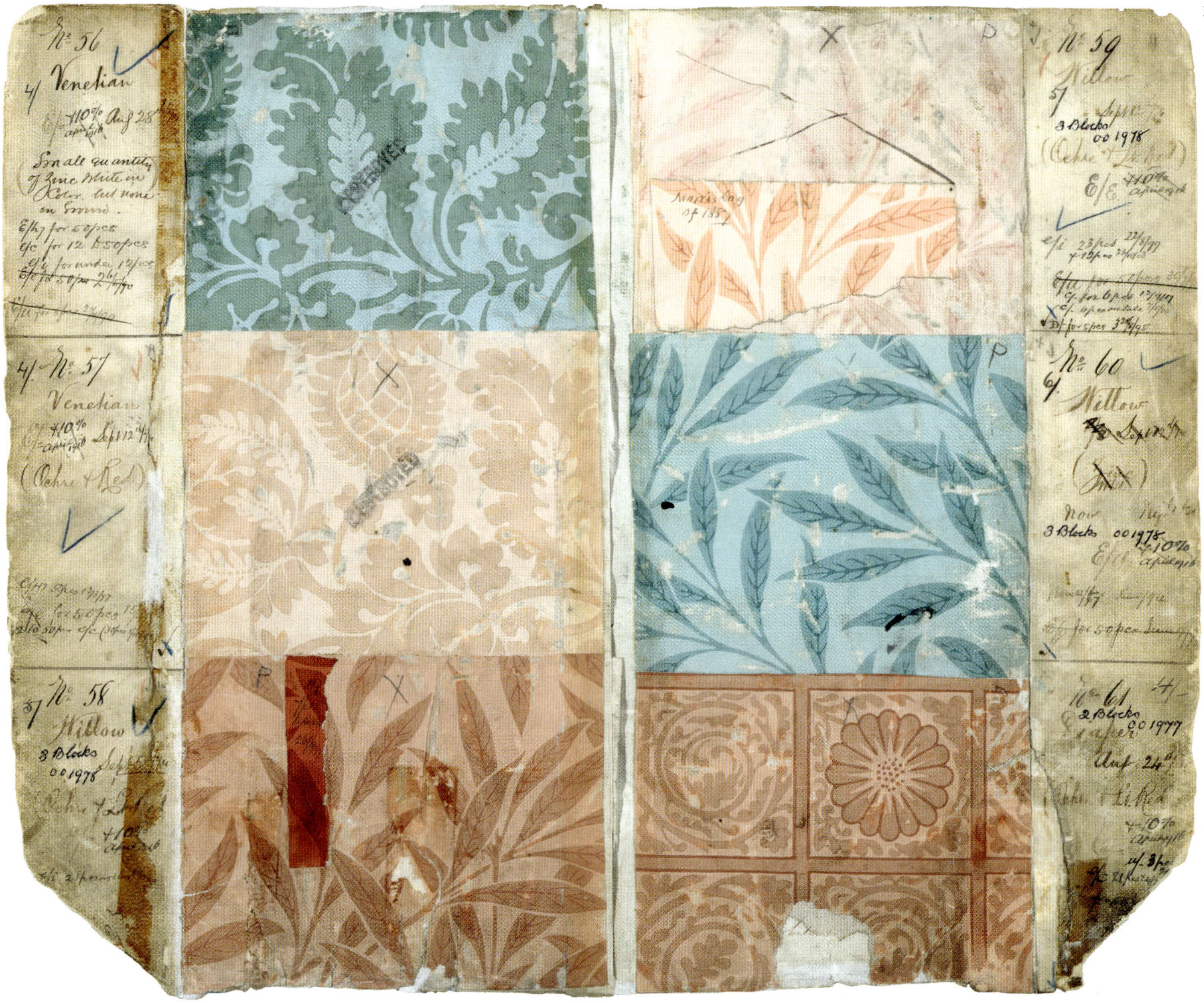

XI.7
Vine

a Design, William Morris, *c.*1873
Pencil and watercolour, 81.5 x 65.2 cm
V&A (E.1074–1988)

b Wallpaper, *Vine (80)*
First issued 1874, this colourway 1875
Block-printed in distemper and oil colours on foiled, crape-embossed and lacquered paper, repeat h. 53.4 cm
William Morris Society, Kelmscott House, London (WMS-WP-V11)

The central portion of the design, a complete repeat, is fully worked and coloured and the beginnings of the adjoining repeats are clearly traced in. Notes, in Morris's hand, give instructions on the order of printing from the blocks. *Willow*, issued in the same year, is a simple pattern similar to the backprint of *Vine*.

XI.8
Wallpaper, *Lily*
Designed by William Morris, *c.*1874
Printed, partially painted in watercolour, attached working notes for printer, 40 x 55 cm
Sanderson Design Group Archive

This example gives a valuable insight into the design and production process. Worked on a wash ground, it is at an intermediate stage. Some of the colours are printed but others have been painted on as a guide. The accompanying note with its very precise colour details includes an instruction to get a new block cut. There appear to have been considerable problems with printing *Lily* as the logbook shows several deleted versions.

XI.9
Wallpaper logbook, open to show ways *56–61*, *c.*1874
Maintained by Jeffrey & Co. for Morris & Co., *c.*1870–81
Wallpaper samples, pasted into an old account book, with pattern names, numbers and annotations in the margins, 39.7 x 41 x 6 cm
Sanderson Design Group Archive (Logbook 1a)

Jeffrey & Co. kept a log of the firm's papers. A sample of each published colouring of a pattern, annotated with name and number, was entered as a permanent record. New ways were often added some time after a pattern was initially brought out. The book is open to show *Venetian* and *Diaper*, both first issued in about 1870, and *Willow*, first issued 1874. When *Venetian* first appeared it was in soft bright colours on a white ground; the ways shown here are more 'Aesthetic'. A similar palette was frequently used for different patterns.

Number 59 in the book is an unsatisfactory attempt at a wash effect. Morris's original intent in 1862 was to make papers with transparent colours, and the printing log for 1874 and 1875 shows a return to this aim. Although success was eventually achieved there were problems in perfecting the process. Rosalind Howard had obviously found such a paper unsatisfactory for, in July 1875, Morris wrote to her, 'I am very vexed but not at all surprised, knowing, as I told you, what a risky thing that transparent colour was: I don't believe it to be the paperhanger's fault.' The wash patterns were printed on special paper, either supplied by Morris & Co. or acquired on its behalf, and the logs often specify the colours required.

XI.10

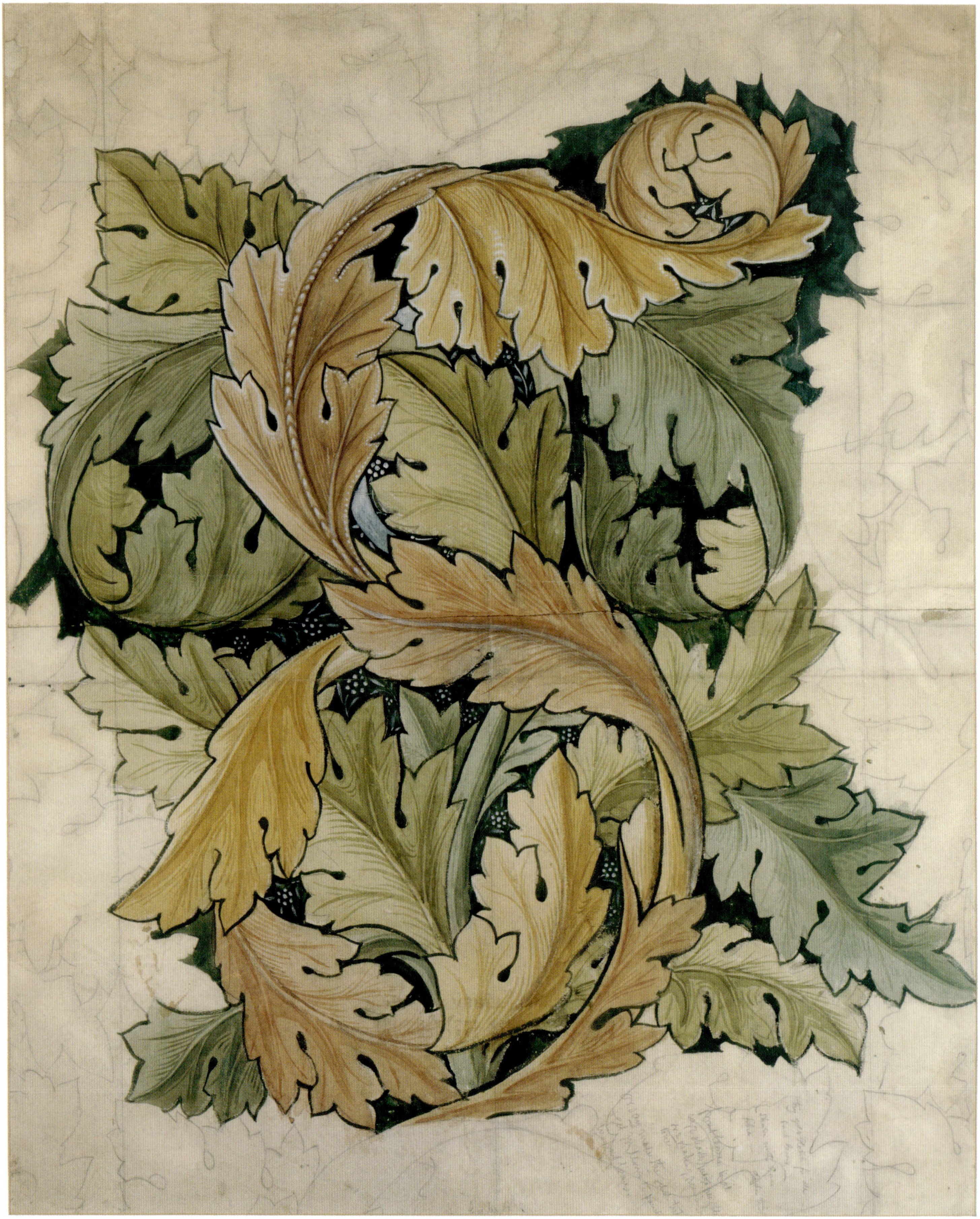

XI.10
Design for *Acanthus* wallpaper
William Morris, 1874
Pencil, watercolour and bodycolour, 81.5 x 65.2 cm
V&A (Circ.297–1955)

The two layers in this design are given equal weight. A very similar conjunction of tiny background motif and scrolling leaves also appears in Morris's calligraphic and illuminated manuscripts.

The design is largely worked in watercolour and the printer would have had to interpret this in distemper – hence the colour notes on the front. The comment 'get Mr. Morris to paint in front leaves' is probably a request from Jeffrey & Co. Notes on the back include 'The property of Mr. Morris 15/12/74'. Another version of the design, in different colours, is in Birmingham Museum and Art Gallery.

XI.11
Wallpaper, *Marigold (42)*
Designed by William Morris, registered 4 February 1875
Block-printed in distemper colours, repeat h. 27 cm
William Morris Gallery, London Borough of Waltham Forest (B91)

This design was well under way by late October 1874 as Rossetti then wrote to Morris, 'I have been making a pattern for a new colouring of the marigold paper and will send it with remarks.'

Although printed in only one colour, the design achieves complexity by overlaying a lightly meandering vertical stem carrying curving sprays of foliage and flowers on a densely patterned background. A similar format had been used for *Scroll*, *c*.1871, and *Light Larkspur*, *c*.1872. *Marigold* was registered as a fabric in April the same year (XII.38).

XI.12
Wallpaper, *Pimpernel (82)*
Designed by William Morris, registered 29 February 1876
Block-printed in distemper colours, repeat h. 42.4 cm
V&A (E.497–1919)
Given by Morris & Co.

In general effect and colouring, *Pimpernel* is similar to *Acanthus*. However, the pattern is more like the mirror repeat of the *African Marigold* printed textile, registered in October 1876.

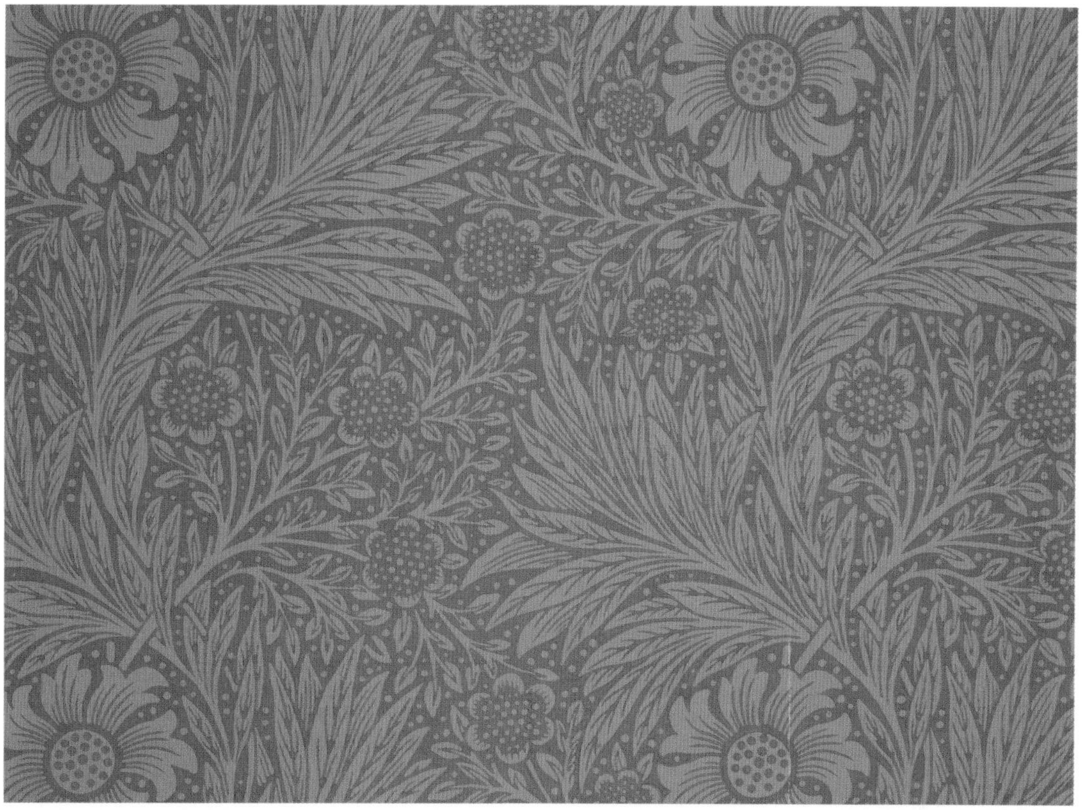
XI.11

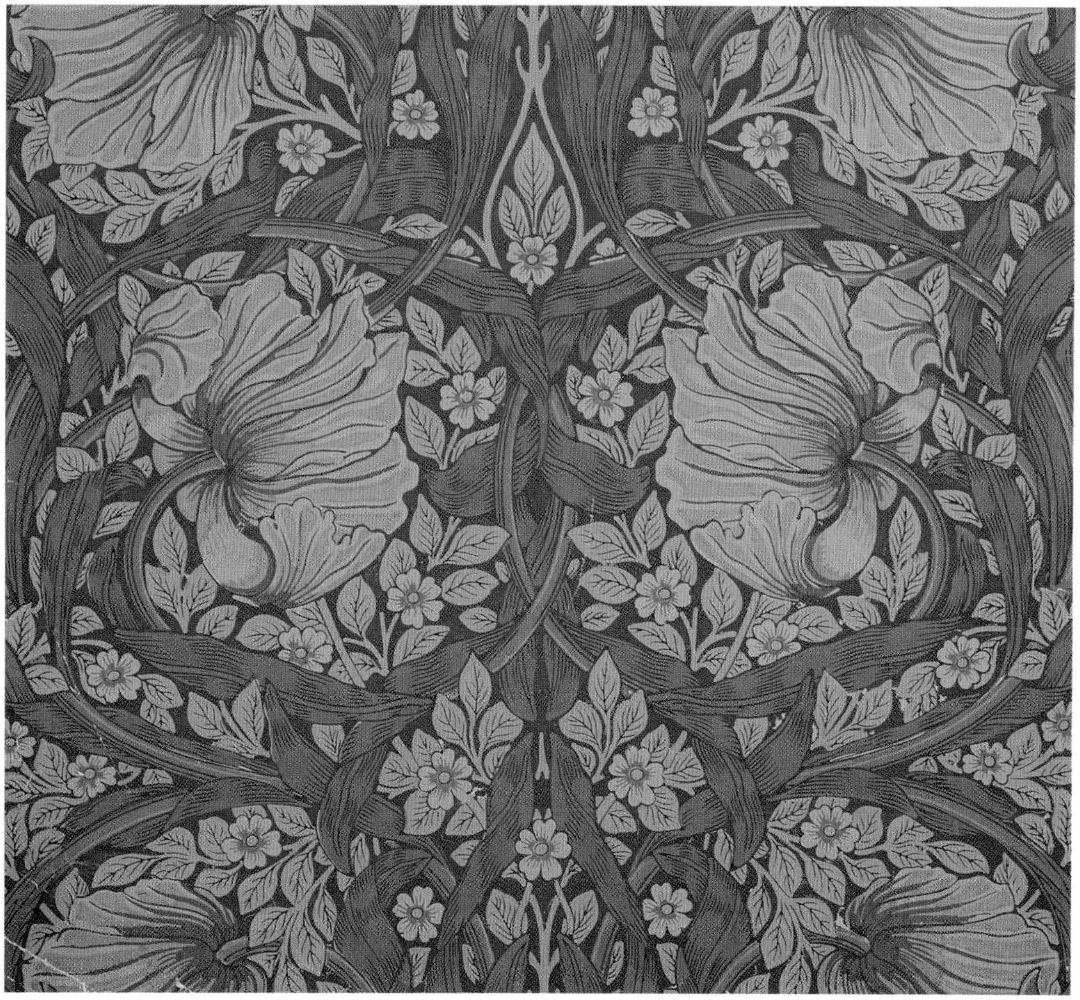
XI.12

XI.13a

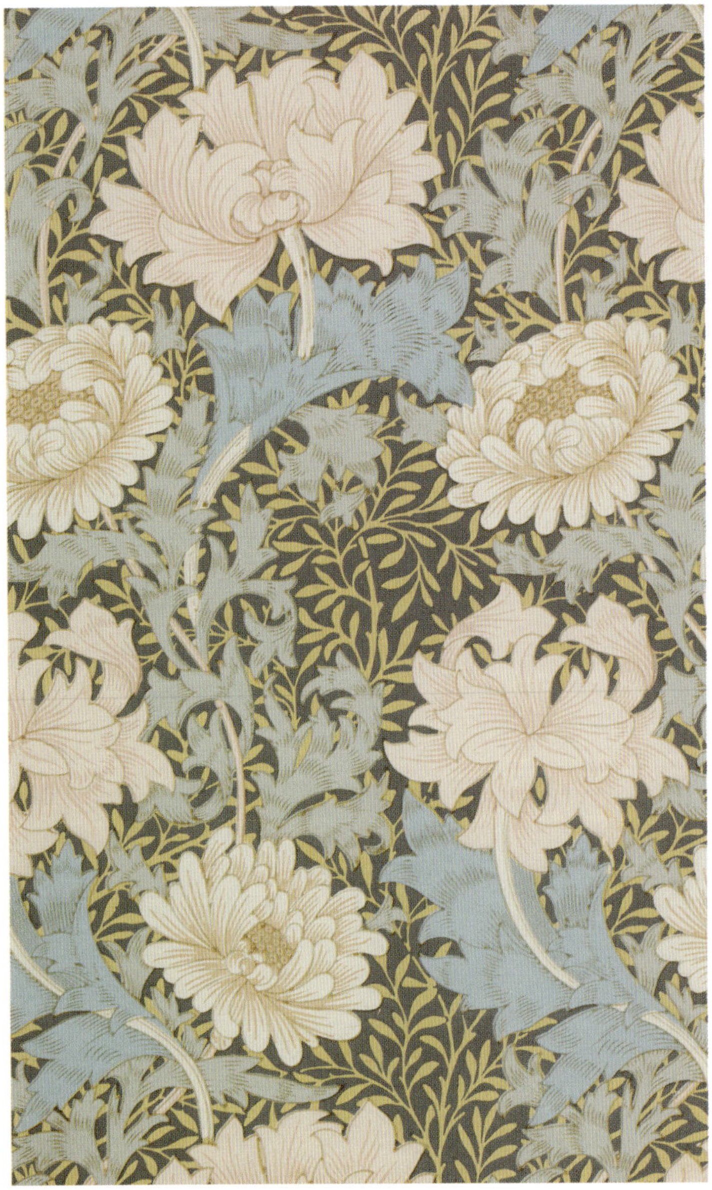

XI.13b

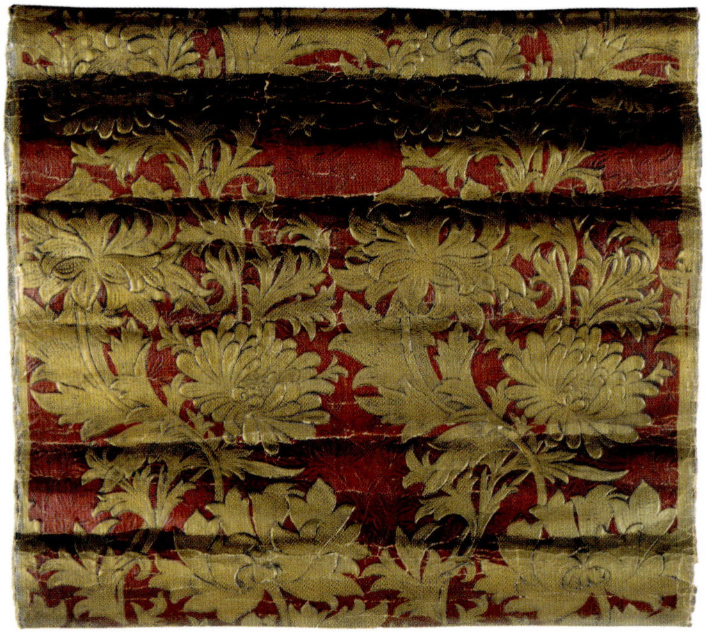

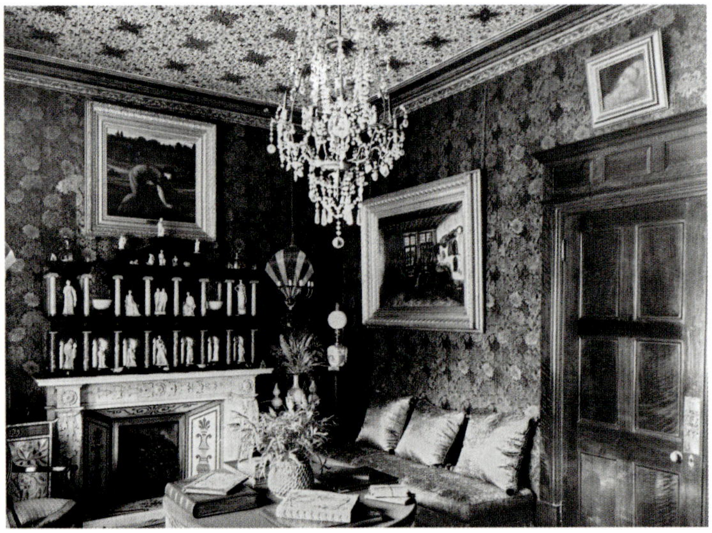

XI.13
Chrysanthemum

a Wallpaper, *Chrysanthemum (92)*
Designed by William Morris, registered 25 January 1877
Block-printed in distemper colours, repeat h. 52.9 cm
V&A (E.802–1915)
Given by Allan F. Vigers

b Wallpaper, *Chrysanthemum*
This version probably issued *c.*1886
Foiled paper, stamped, lacquered and stencilled in oil colour, 53.3 x 57 cm
Sanderson Design Group Archive

A fully worked design for the printed version of *Chrysanthemum* is at the William Morris Gallery.

Paper imitations of embossed and gilded leather hangings were very fashionable from the 1870s to the 1890s. Jeffrey & Co. was one of the English manufacturers to perfect a technique for their production, winning a medal at the Paris Exposition Universelle of 1878 for a 'leather' version of *Peacocks and Amorini*, designed by Walter Crane (the process is described in *The Building and Engineering Times*, 6 September 1884).

Morris, Marshall, Faulkner & Co. had always, as mentioned in its circular of about 1861, offered real embossed leather and first adopted imitations in 1878. Unlike the earlier gold-ground papers, the patterns of the imitation leathers were stamped rather than printed. Morris commended imitation leathers in his 1884 *Encyclopaedia Britannica* essay on mural decoration. This example probably dates from about 1886. Another version, installed by Morris & Co. in the first drawing room at 1 Holland Park for Alexander Ionides, was described in *The Art Journal*, 1893, as 'lacquered in transparent colour over silver; the leafage is of bright bronze green, the background of deep madder, the flowers in lighter and brighter tints'.

Fig.203 **An embossed and lacquered version of *Chrysanthemum* in the first drawing room at 1 Holland Park. Photographed by Bedford Lemere & Co., *c.*1889.**
Historic England Archive

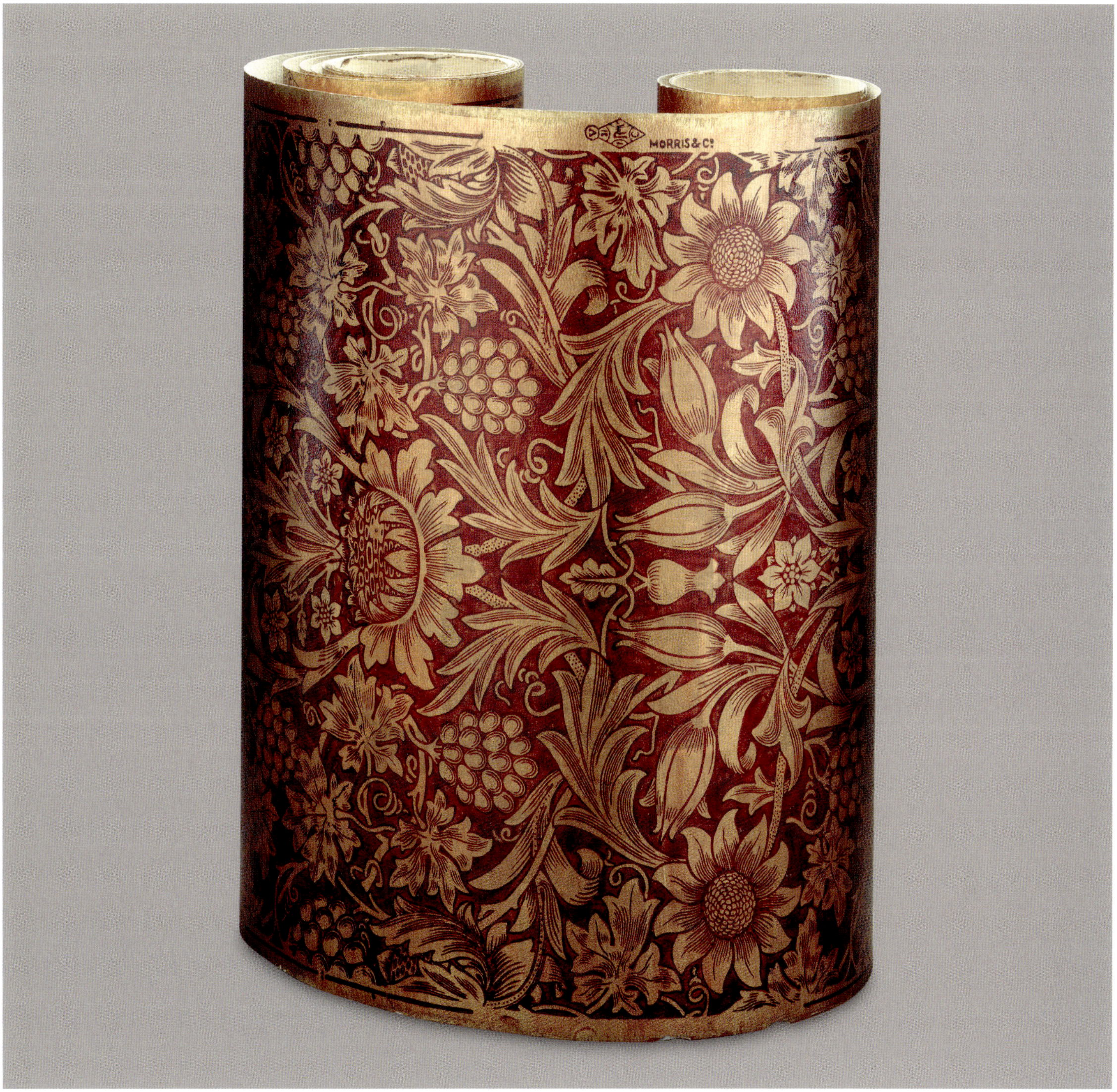

XI.14
Wallpaper, partial roll, *Sunflower (132)*
Designed by William Morris, registered 21 January 1879, this version first issued *c.*1881
Block-printed in oil colour on a foiled, crape-embossed and lacquered ground, width 57.1 cm
University of Victoria Legacy Art Galleries, Canada
Gift of Edmund Parker

This is a very straightforward design compared with many patterns of the earlier 1870s. It uses the turn-over structure associated with woven fabrics and hand-knotted carpets. There is no attempt to mask the obvious horizontal and vertical repeats and there is no backprint to draw attention from the main pattern. The use of line on the flowers, leaves and fruit gives only the slightest sense of depth.

Sunflower, Acorn and *Mallow* (the last designed by Kate Faulkner) were registered as a group. They are all simple, single-colour patterns, issued, for the most part, as ordinary distemper prints in soft, pale tones with blues and yellows predominating. The cheapness of these patterns (4*s*. 6*d*. to 5*s*. 6*d*. per roll) was intended to balance the range against papers such as *Chrysanthemum*, which cost 11*s*. However, also in 1879, an extremely expensive version was published. *Sunflower (108)* was printed in greenish-black oil colour on a gold crape-embossed ground and cost 30*s*. a roll. Morris wrote in December of the same year to the Howards about a gold *Sunflower* paper which upon inspection 'to our grief ... would not do'.

The version shown here, printed in red on a gold ground, was entered in the printing log in about 1881. In November that year Morris was writing to Rosalind Howard: 'The gold & red sunflower is on my board at Queen Square: & I will do my best to hit the due colour.' Further correspondence confirms that the gold-ground papers tended to look too bright on the wall.

XI.15a

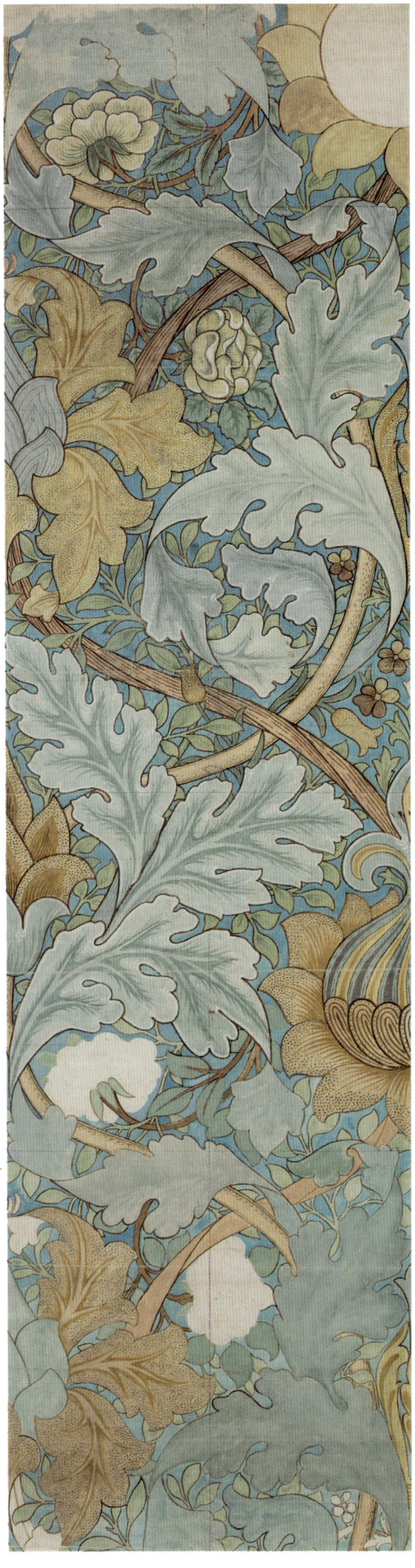

XI.15b

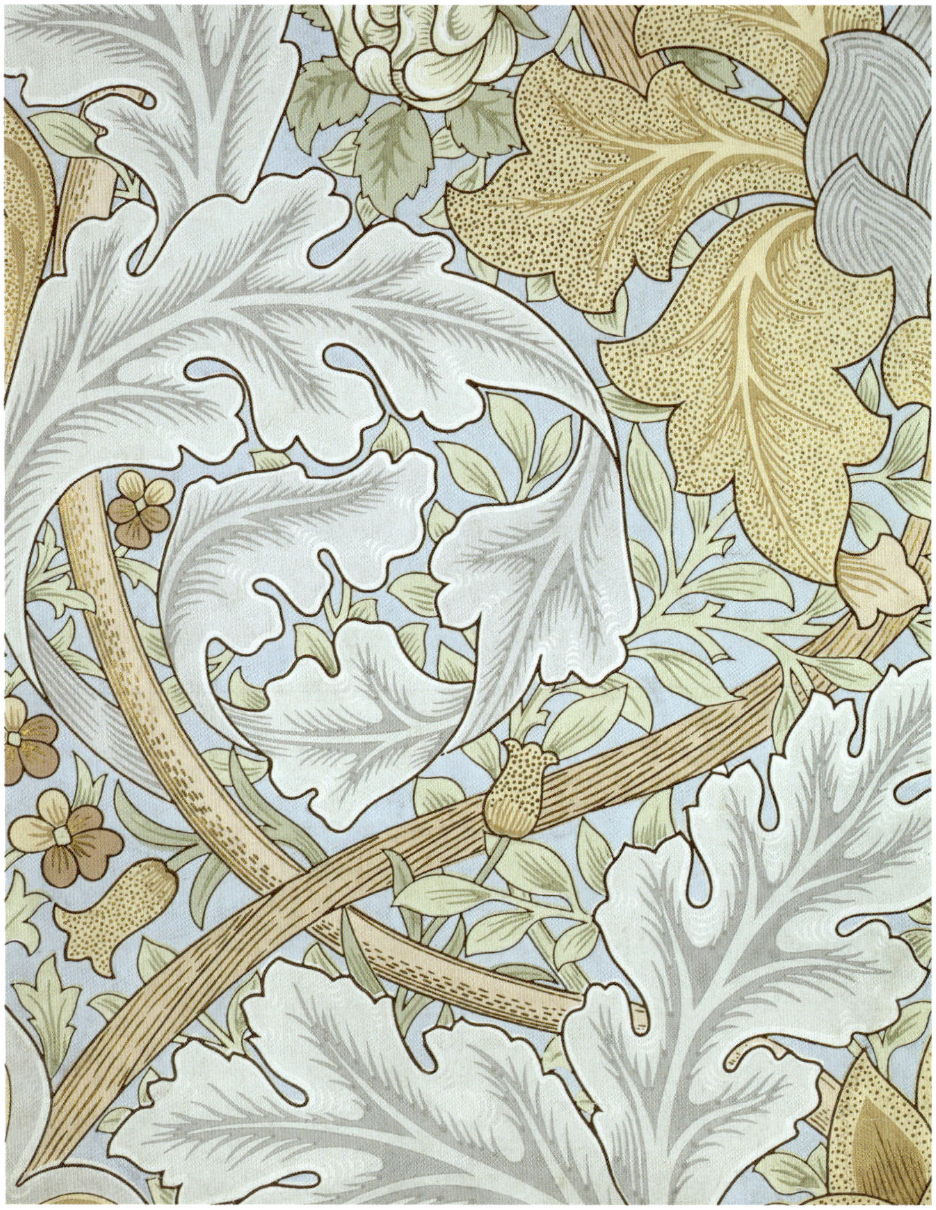

XI.15
St James's

a Design, William Morris, 1880
Pencil, pen and sepia ink, watercolour, 194.2 x 52.6 cm
William Morris Gallery, London Borough of Waltham Forest (A40a)

b Wallpaper, *St James's (126)*
First issued 1881
Block-printed in distemper colours and silver and gold, repeat h. 119.4 cm
V&A (E.528–1919)
Given by Morris & Co.

On 16 July 1880, Morris met with representatives of the Board of Works concerning the redecoration of St James's Palace. A scheme including this fully worked and coloured design for the Grand Staircase wallpaper was submitted on 24 October 1880 and approved by Queen Victoria on 2 November.

An earlier, monochrome, version of the design, also at the William Morris Gallery (A40), shows a great deal of working, particularly on the central motif, the upright stem meander. In his 1879 lecture 'Making the Best of It', Morris said 'no amount of delicacy is too great in drawing the curves of a pattern, no amount of care in getting the leading lines right from the first, can be thrown away, for beauty of detail cannot afterwards cure any shortcoming in this.'

The successful completion of the decoration of the entrances was followed by a commission for the main suite of State Apartments, including the Banqueting or Waterloo Room. This was hung with a red re-colouring of *St James's*, varnished, as on the staircases.

XI.16

XI.17

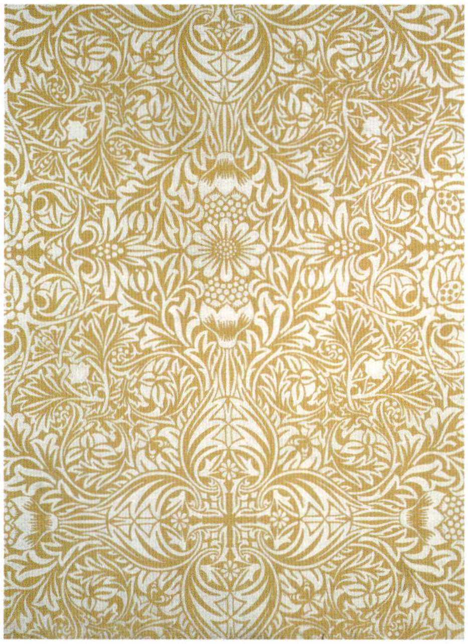

XI.18

XI.19

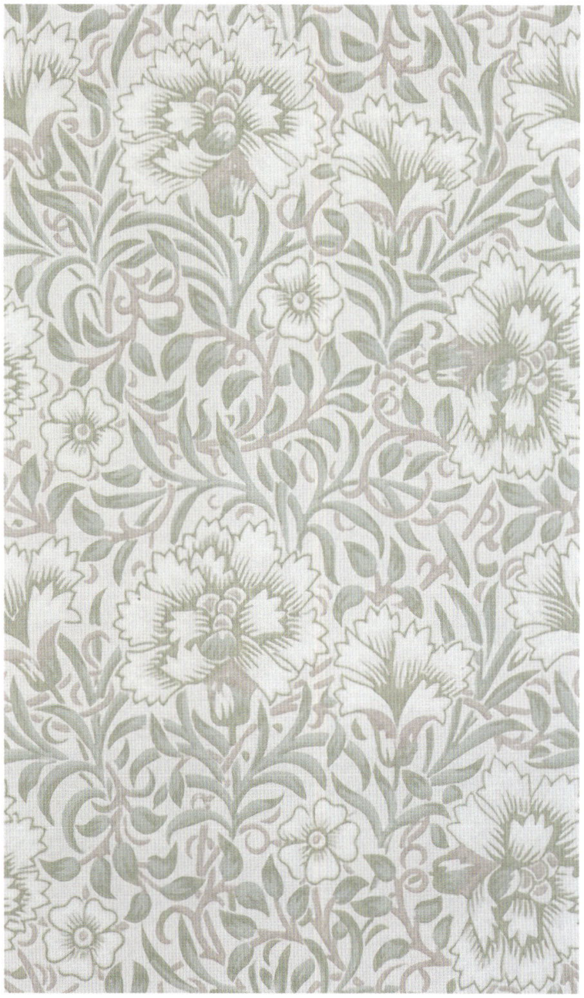

XI.16
Wallpaper, *St James's Ceiling (293)*
Designed by William Morris, 1881
Block-printed in distemper colours, repeat h. 108 cm
V&A (E.594–1919)
Given by Morris & Co.

A large ceiling pattern designed to be hung with the red *St James's* in the Banqueting Room at the Palace. Morris's diary records that he was working on the design in late August and early September 1881. Like the *St James's* wallpaper, this too entered the standard range. It can be seen *in situ* at Newark Park, Gloucestershire.

XI.17
Wallpaper, *Ceiling (101)*
Designed by William Morris, registered 22 November 1877
Block-printed in distemper colour, repeat h. 53.7 cm
V&A (E.510–1919)
Given by Morris & Co.

Morris disliked papered ceilings. This reticent monochrome pattern – with a flat treatment of the leaf, fruit and flower forms – repeats vertically and horizontally on a rectangular scheme. This initial colourway was followed by several others, all employing pale colours and light grounds. It was issued as a flock in 1887.

XI.18
Wallpaper, *Loop Trail (169)*
Designed by Kate Faulkner, registered 12 May 1877
Block-printed in distemper colours, repeat h. 33 cm
William Morris Society, Kelmscott House, London (WMS-WP-L23)

Loop Trail is the first of the firm's papers, apart from the four adaptions of about 1868–70, by a designer other than Morris. He had by now mastered the medium, production was running smoothly and, absorbed in textile printing and dyeing, he was able to delegate.

With its small floral trails, more akin to the Queen Anne style, the paper is not immediately recognizable as 'Morris & Co.'. This was perhaps an advantage in widening the range.

XI.19
Wallpaper, *Carnation (125)*
Designed by Kate Faulkner, first issued 1880
Machine printed by surface roller in distemper colours, repeat h. 22.8 cm
William Morris Society, Kelmscott House, London (WMS-WP-C1)

The firm issued only two machine-printed papers during Morris's lifetime. This and *Merton*, 1888, were designed by Faulkner. *Carnation* is a respectable example of a roller print and, at only 2*s*. 6*d*. a roll for a four-colour pattern, it was considerably cheaper than even a single-colour hand print. However, the thin, smeary colours show why Morris preferred block-prints.

XI.20a

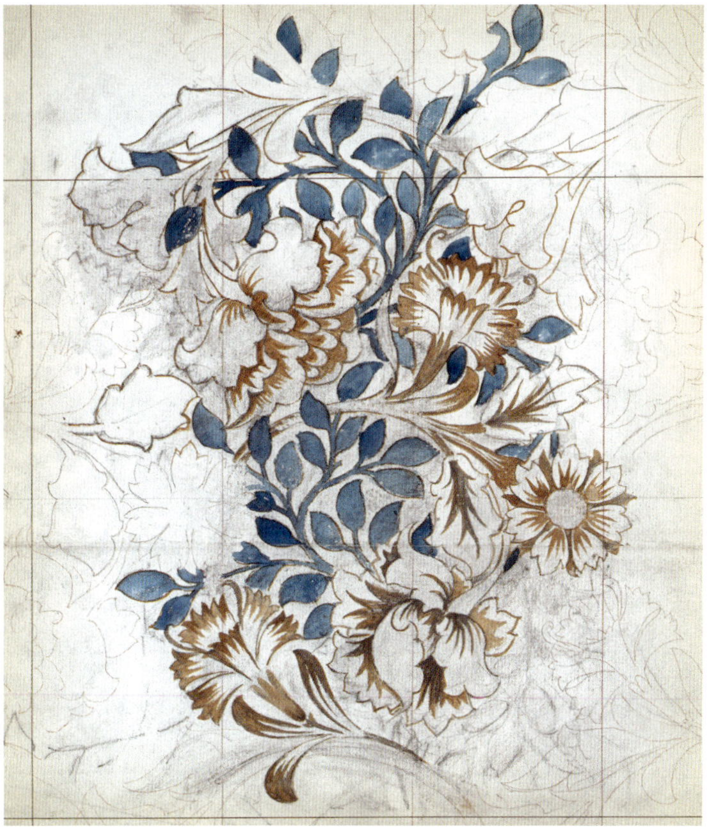

XI.20b

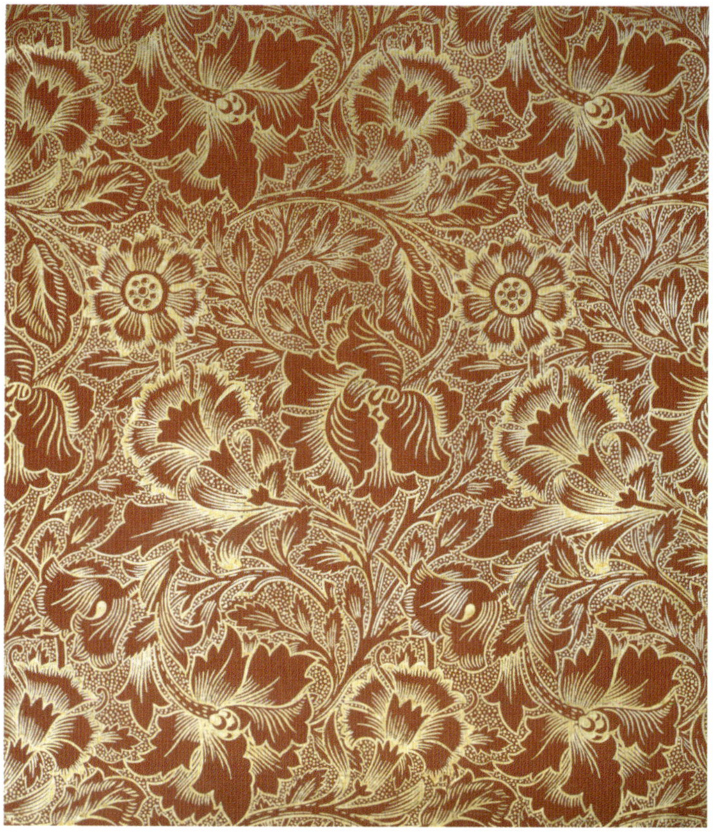

XI.21

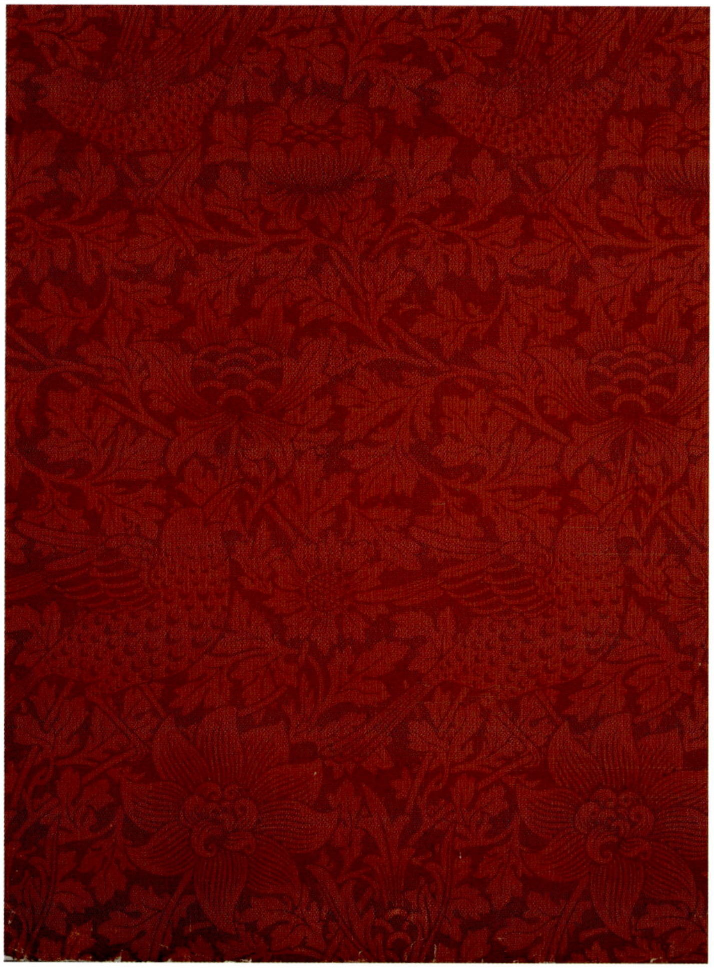

XI.20
***Poppy*, also known as**
Pink and Poppy

a Design, William Morris, April 1880
Pen, pencil and watercolour,
107.8 x 68.8 cm
William Morris Society, Kelmscott House, London (D6)

b Wallpaper, *Poppy (123)*
Block-printed in silver paint and lacquer, repeat h. 43.8 cm
V&A (E.521–1919)
Given by Morris & Co.

Veining and dotting (printed by pins hammered into the blocks) give movement to wallpaper patterns. Speaking about designing paper-hangings in his 1882 lecture 'The Lesser Arts of Life', Morris said 'Here is the place, if anywhere, for dots and lines and hatchings: mechanical enrichment is of the first necessity in it.'

There is another version of this design, also held at the William Morris Society. Both are inscribed 'April 1880' and both are marked 'Machine Wall Paper'. In the event, however, the published paper was block-printed and the ways that used gold or silver were both expensive (21*s*. a roll) and rich looking. Ten colourways were issued between 1880 and 1882. A Morris & Co. bill of October 1888 for 1 Holland Park refers to 'providing and hanging Gold Poppy Paper'.

XI.21
Wallpaper, *Bird and Anemone (143)*
Designed by William Morris, first issued 1882
Block-printed in distemper colours, repeat h. 65.4 cm
V&A (E.530–1919)
Given by Morris & Co.

Morris was perhaps referring to this design in his diary for 17 May 1881: 'Working on paper hanging tulip & anemone'. According to the wallpaper logbook, Jeffrey & Co. dispatched the first consignment on 15 June 1882. A printed fabric of the same name and design was registered on 17 June. A comparison of paper and textile reveals differences that are partly due to technique, but which also indicate that straight matching was not intended. The wallpaper pattern is larger; the crispness, solidity and distinctness of the colours in the paper are far removed from the unevenness and slight blurring seen in the cottons, especially those printed by the discharge process. The paper version has the same colour balance as the fabric (i.e. the pattern shows light on a darker ground). Although not always used, this was Morris's preferred method of dealing with one-colour prints.

XI.22a

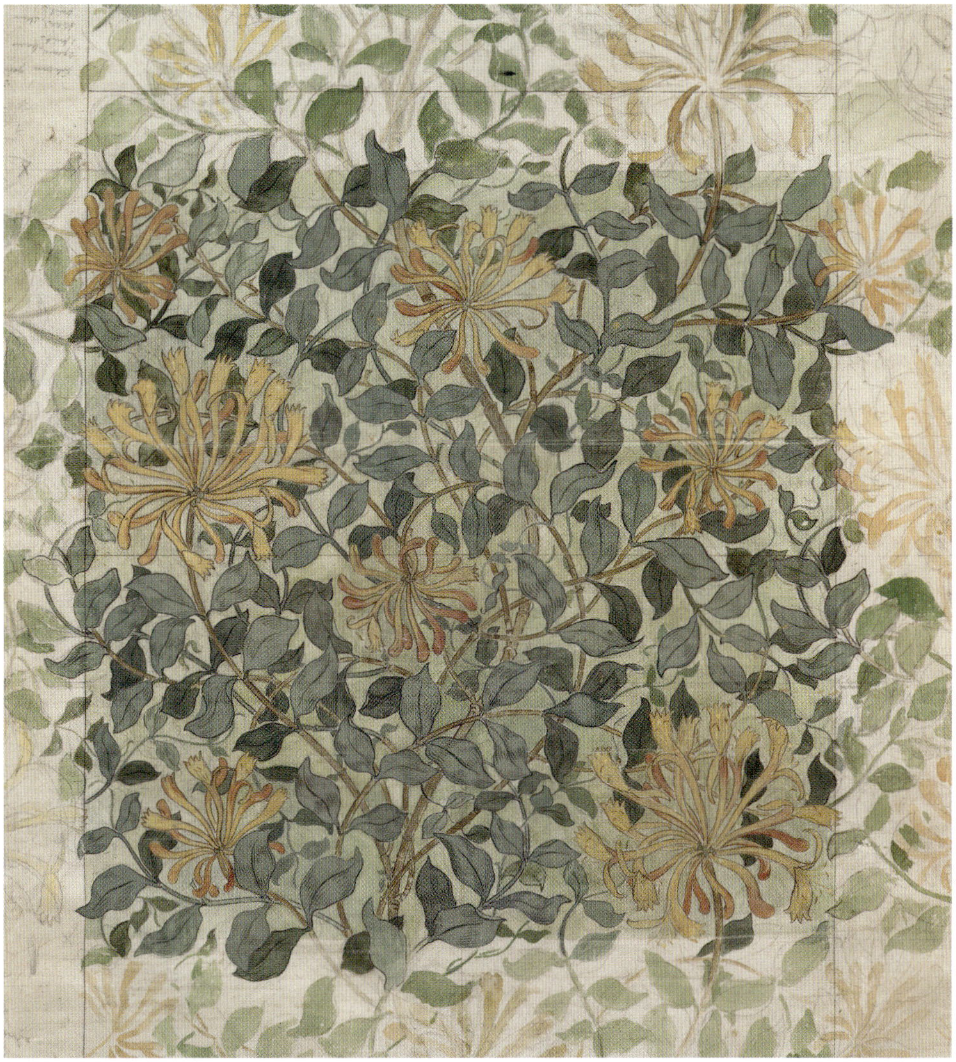

XI.22b

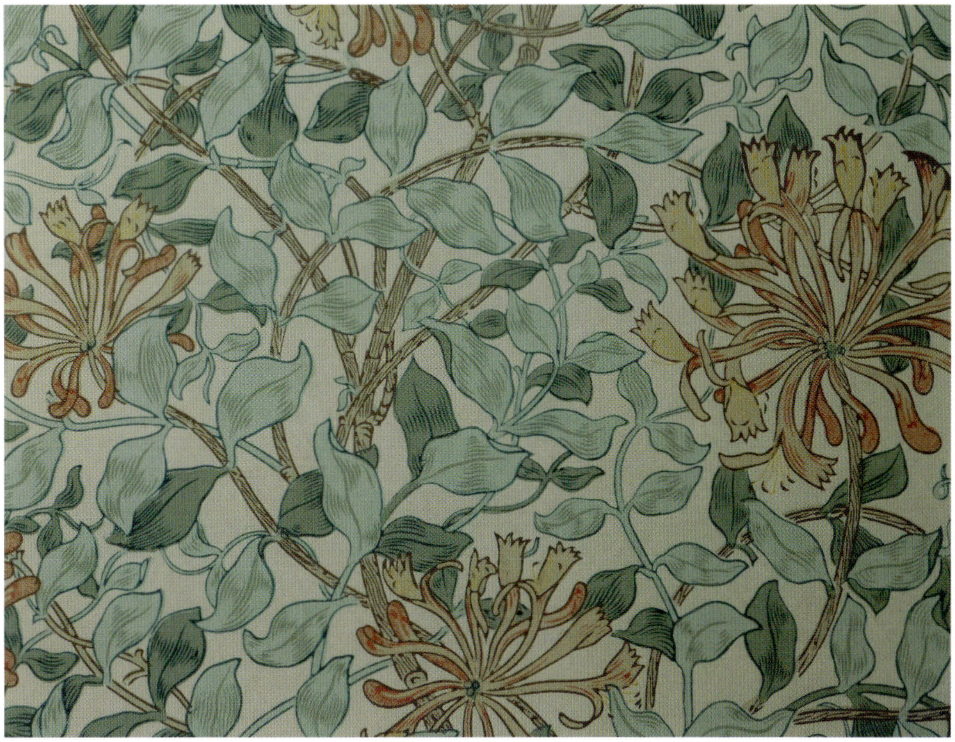

XI.22
***Honeysuckle* wallpaper**

a Design, attributed to May Morris, *c.*1879–83
Pencil and watercolour, 99.6 x 68.6 cm
Inscription on front includes: 'Machine [deleted] Wallpaper 8 blocks No. 6575'
William Morris Society, Kelmscott House, London (D7)

b Wallpaper, *Honeysuckle (147)*
Registered 28 April 1883
Block-printed in distemper colours, repeat h. 53.5 cm
William Morris Society, Kelmscott House, London (WMS-WP-H3)

There has been some debate as to whether William or May Morris designed *Honeysuckle*. A letter from Morris to his mother on 23 May 1883 claims that May 'has been doing some very pretty things lately & made a good design for a paper'; this could be *Honeysuckle*. The brochure, *Morris Wall-Papers,* of about 1912 attributes it to May Morris and she does *not* include it in the list of her father's 40 most successful wallpaper designs in Volume I of *Artist, Writer, Socialist.* But an article about May Morris in *Woman's World*, published in 1890, gave the designer as William Morris. Monk and Gooch, in their 1978 study of designs owned by the William Morris Society, additionally used stylistic arguments for attributing it to William Morris. The soft naturalism of this design is similar to that of William Morris's *Willow Boughs* pattern of 1887 (XI.24).

XI.23

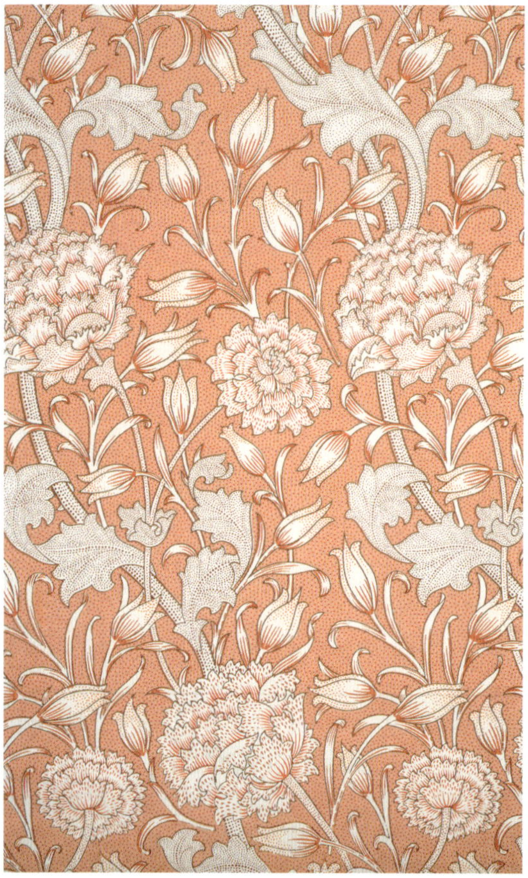

XI.24

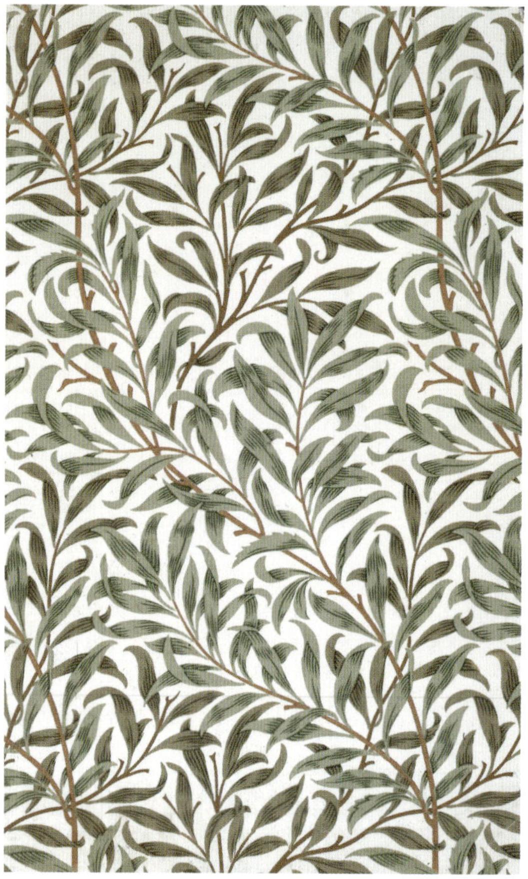

XI.25

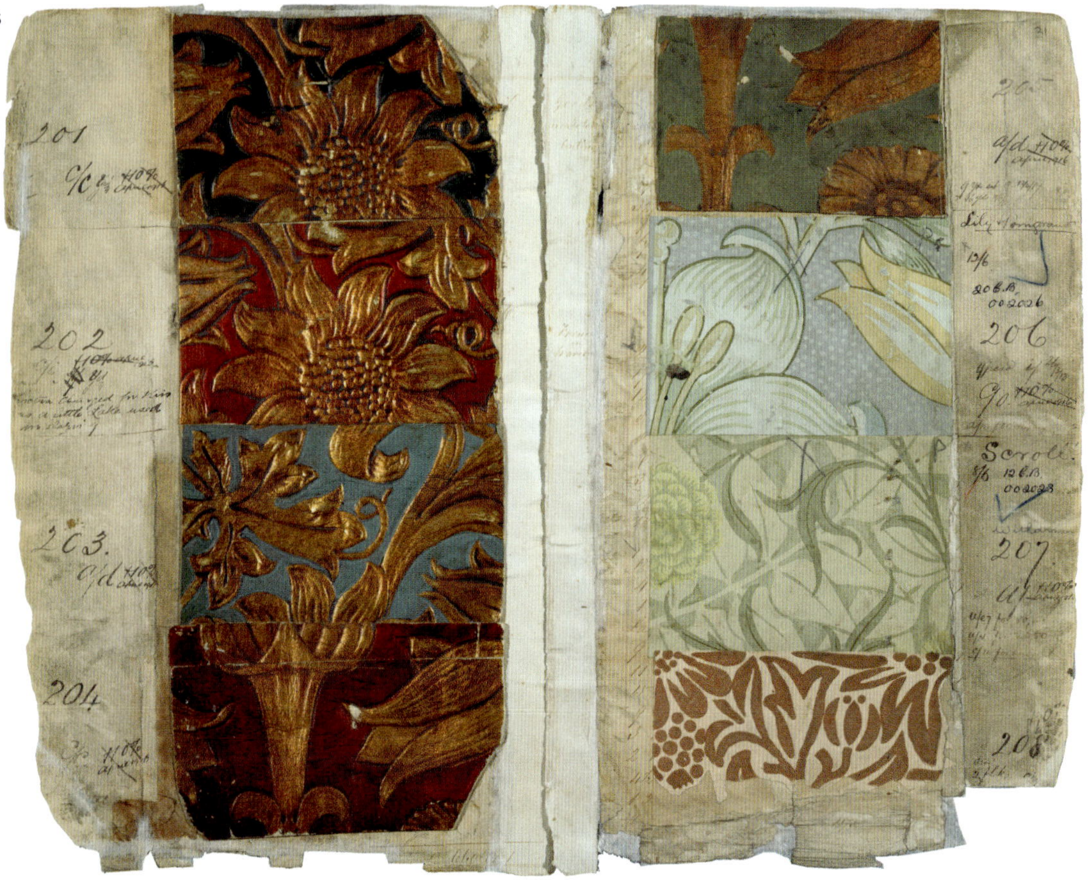

XI.23
Wallpaper, *Wild Tulip (162)*
Designed by William Morris,
registered 21 November 1884
Block-printed in distemper colours,
repeat h. 64.8 cm
V&A (E.538–1919)
Given by Morris & Co.

Wild Tulip is similar to the *Cray* printed textile (XII.61) of the same date and was the first wallpaper to show the diagonal meander that characterizes many of Morris's designs thereafter. It was issued initially in eight ways; some expensive variants employed gold or silver spot grounds. An original design is at Birmingham Museum and Art Gallery.

XI.24
Wallpaper, *Willow Boughs (210)*
Designed by William Morris,
first issued 1887
Block-printed in distemper colours,
repeat h. 45.3 cm
V&A (E.557–1919)
Given by Morris & Co.

A naturalistic treatment of one of Morris's favourite themes. May Morris wrote in Volume I of *Artist, Writer, Socialist*: 'We were walking one day [at Kelmscott Manor] by our little stream that runs into the Thames, and my Father pointed out the detail and variety in the leaf-forms, and soon afterwards this paper was done, a keenly-observed rendering of our willows that has embowered many a London living-room.' An original design is at The Whitworth, University of Manchester.

XI.25
Wallpaper logbook, open to show ways *201–8*, *c.*1886
Maintained by Jeffrey & Co. for
Morris & Co., *c.*1881–93
Wallpaper samples, pasted into an old account book, with pattern names, numbers and annotations in the margins, 39.6 x 41 x 5.5 cm
Sanderson Design Group Archive (Logbook 1b)

The opening shows three imitation leather variants of *Sunflower*, two 'leather' and one distemper-printed version of *Lily and Pomegranate* (1886), *Scroll* and a flocked version of *Ceiling*. *Lily and Pomegranate* is the only new design. The others are additional versions of existing patterns.

XI.26

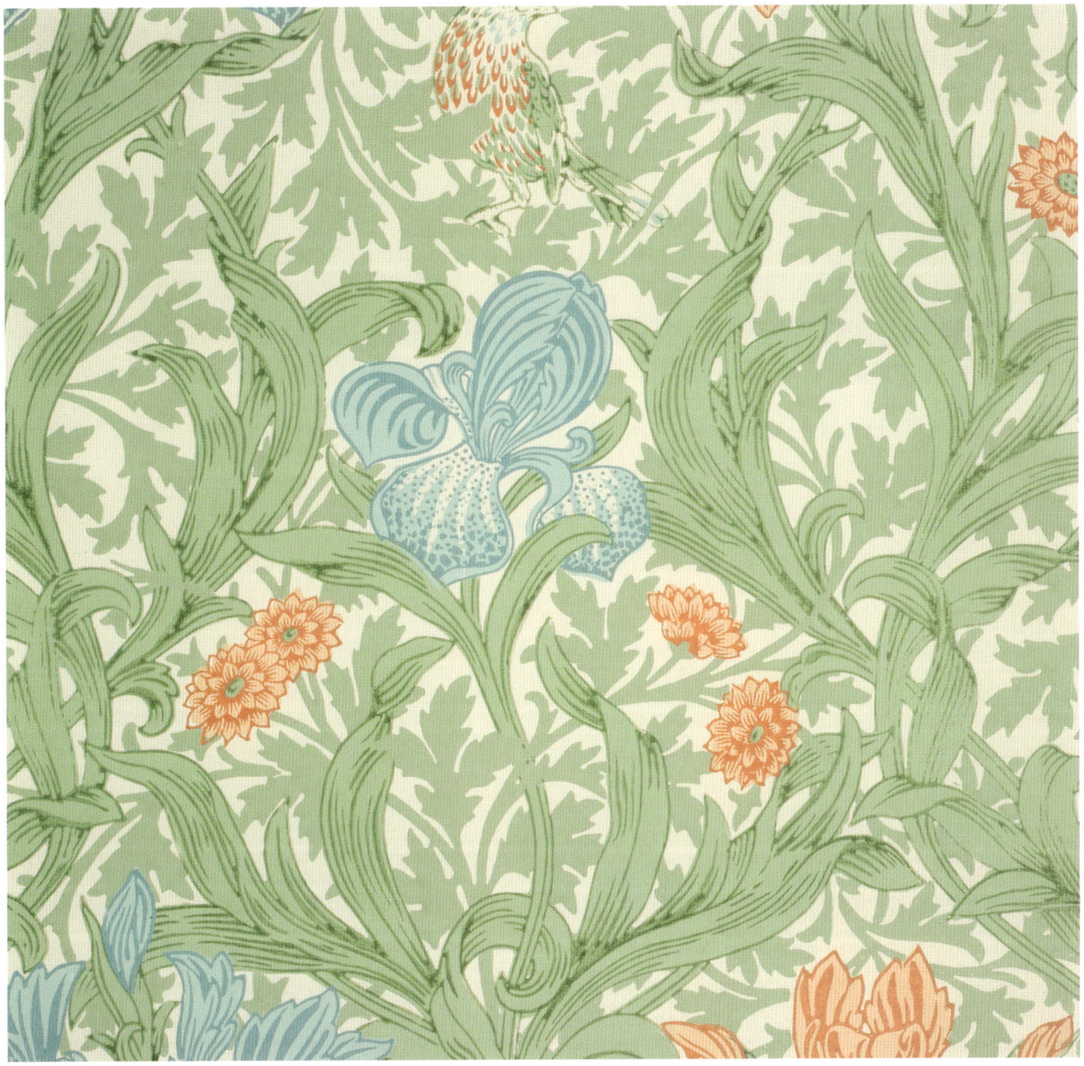

XI.27

XI.28

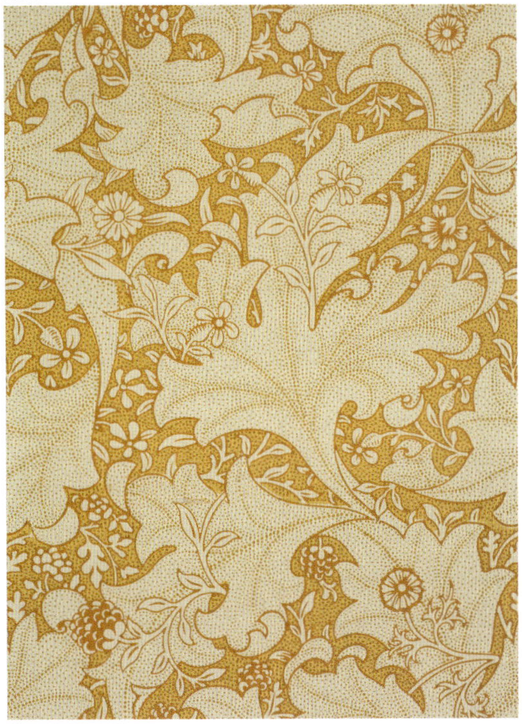

XI.26
Wallpaper, *Iris (224)*
Designed by John Henry Dearle, first issued *c.*1887
Block-printed in distemper colours, repeat h. 44.1 cm
William Morris Gallery, London Borough of Waltham Forest (B90)

According to the brochure *Morris Wall-Papers* of about 1912, this is the first wallpaper designed by John Henry Dearle. The treatment of the flowers is somewhat naturalistic but the stylized birds and backprint are reminiscent of Morris's *Bird and Anemone* of 1882 (XI.21).

XI.27
Wallpaper, *Bruges (237)*
Designed by William Morris, first issued 1888
Block-printed in distemper colour on mica ground, repeat h. 61.3 cm
V&A (E.561–1919)
Given by Morris & Co.

A large, formal textile-based pattern. The logbook shows that *Bruges* was issued in ten ways at this time. Some were distemper printed, some flocked, some (as in this example) on a mica ground to give a sparkling effect, and some were in a combination of these techniques. It was available in either one or two colours. The mica-ground version was more expensive than the ordinary distemper print.

XI.28
Wallpaper, *Wallflower (268)*
Designed by William Morris, first issued *c.*1890
Block-printed in distemper colours, repeat h. 36 cm
William Morris Gallery, London Borough of Waltham Forest (B91)

A light and easy pattern that, with its pin-dots and curving acanthus leaves, achieves a similar effect to *Apple* of 1877 (see fig.193).

XI.29

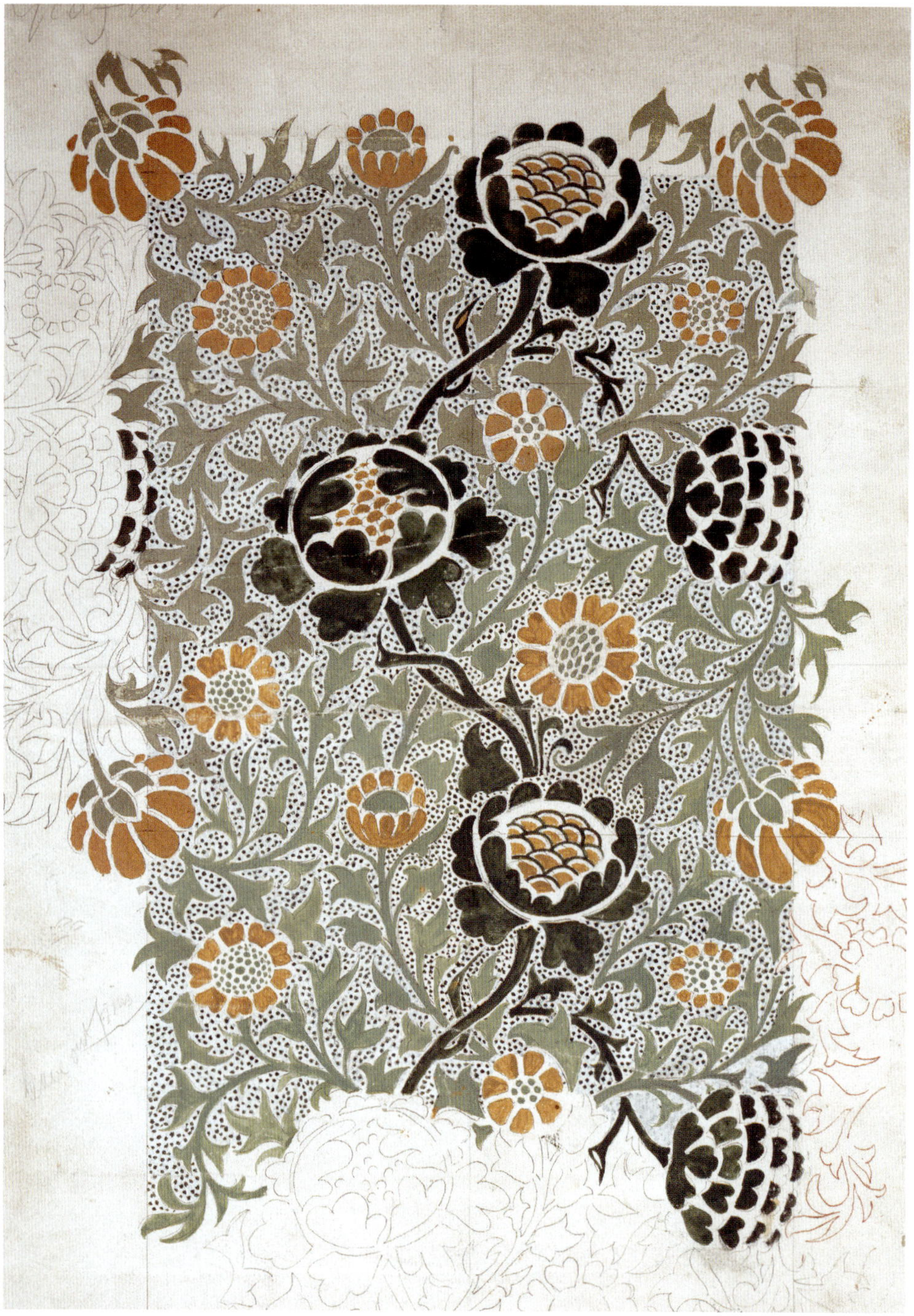

XI.30

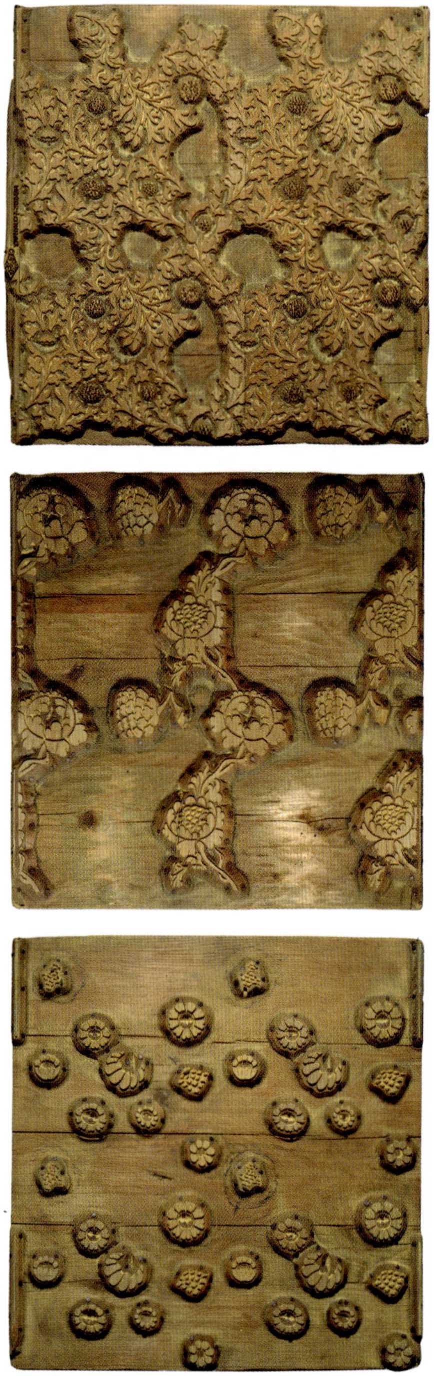

XI.29
Design for *Grafton* wallpaper
William Morris, *c.*1883
Pencil, watercolour and bodycolour, 68.8 x 43.5 cm
William Morris Society, Kelmscott House, London (D5)

A fully worked and coloured design ready for the block cutter and printer. It is marked 'leave out pins' and the paper was issued without the dotted ground. The pattern has been traced out in pencil and horizontal and vertical guidelines are visible. The repeating element is small, appearing twice within the 21-inch square format. The central portion has been coloured, somewhat roughly, and a list of blocks is given: 'Pale Green 1; Yellow 2; 2nd green 3'.

Without dotting, hatching, veining, outline or under-print, this is a two-dimensional, non-naturalistic pattern. The use of the ground to separate individual elements in the flowers and stems is reminiscent of stencilling, where the natural qualities of the process result in the same effect. Another less neatly worked version of this design, without the pin-dots, is in the V&A.

XI.30
Three wallpaper printing blocks for *Grafton* pattern
Carved deal and fruit wood, approx. 56 x 51 x 5 cm each
Sanderson Design Group Archive

The blocks are composed of a triple sandwich of wood. The bottom two layers are deal, the topmost is a hard and fine-grained fruit wood. Those areas that are not required to print have been cut away. *Grafton* is built up of flat fields of colour, without lines or dots, and the blocks do not feature any of the metal strips or pins that would be necessary for fine detail. During the course of normal use, blocks sometimes have to be repaired or recut. These examples, however, are the original set and one of the blocks still bears the 1883 registration mark at the edge.

XI.31

XI.32

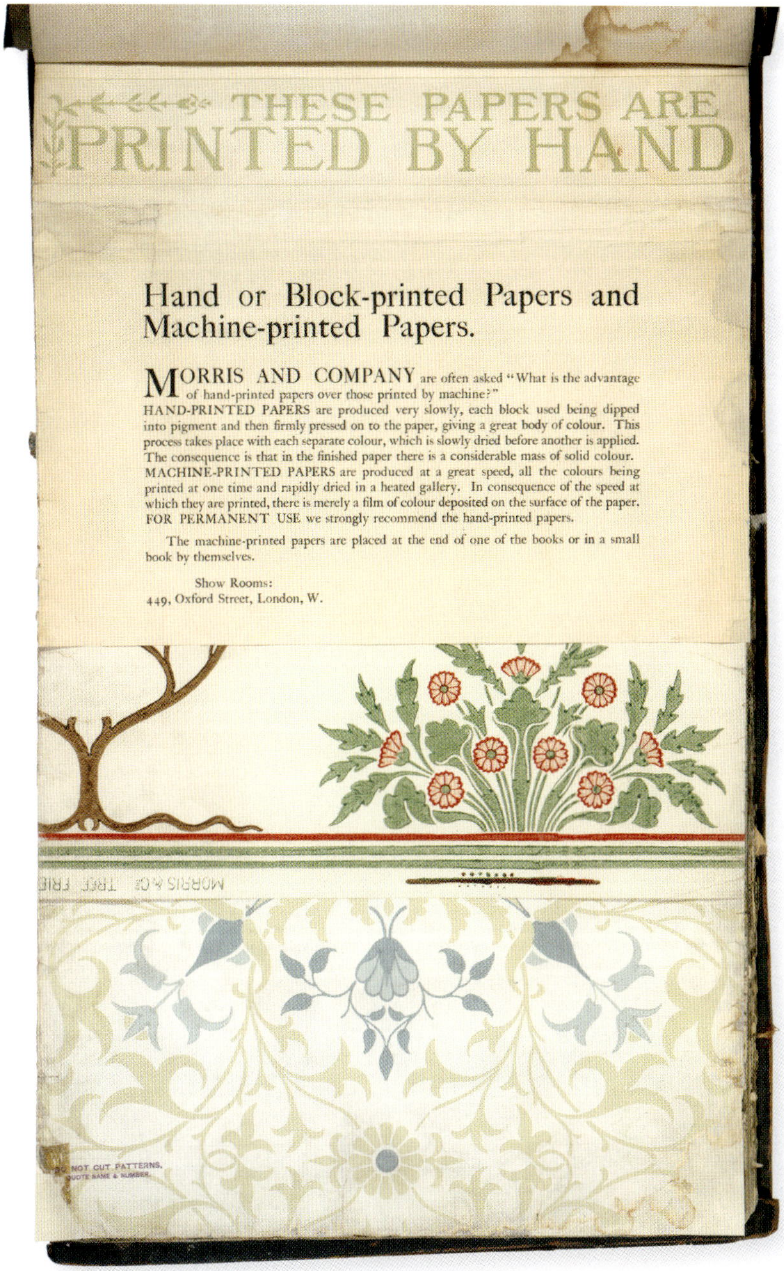

XI.31
Wallpaper match piece, *Grafton (235)*
Designed by William Morris, pattern registered 29 June 1883, match piece made *c.*1950
Printed by Arthur Sanderson & Sons Ltd
Block-printed in distemper colours, 1,000 x 56 cm
Sanderson Design Group Archive

A match piece is the printer's template. It shows the colours to be used and the order of printing. Three blocks (XI.30) were used to print *Grafton*, which was available as both a two- and three-colour pattern. In this example two blocks print the same shade of yellow.

XI.32
Wallpaper stand-book
Morris & Co. from 449 Oxford Street, *c.*1905
Wooden easel stand, wallpaper samples, leatherette cover, 89 x 53 x 9 cm
V&A (E.2734 to 2866–1980)
Given by Shand Kydd Ltd

A display book from the Oxford Street showroom containing 132 specimens, each marked on the back with pattern name, way number and price. No machine prints are included. It is big enough to show a full repeat of all but the very largest patterns. Smaller 'table books' were also available, probably for loan to customers. It is pointed out on the cover that the papers are 'free from arsenic'.

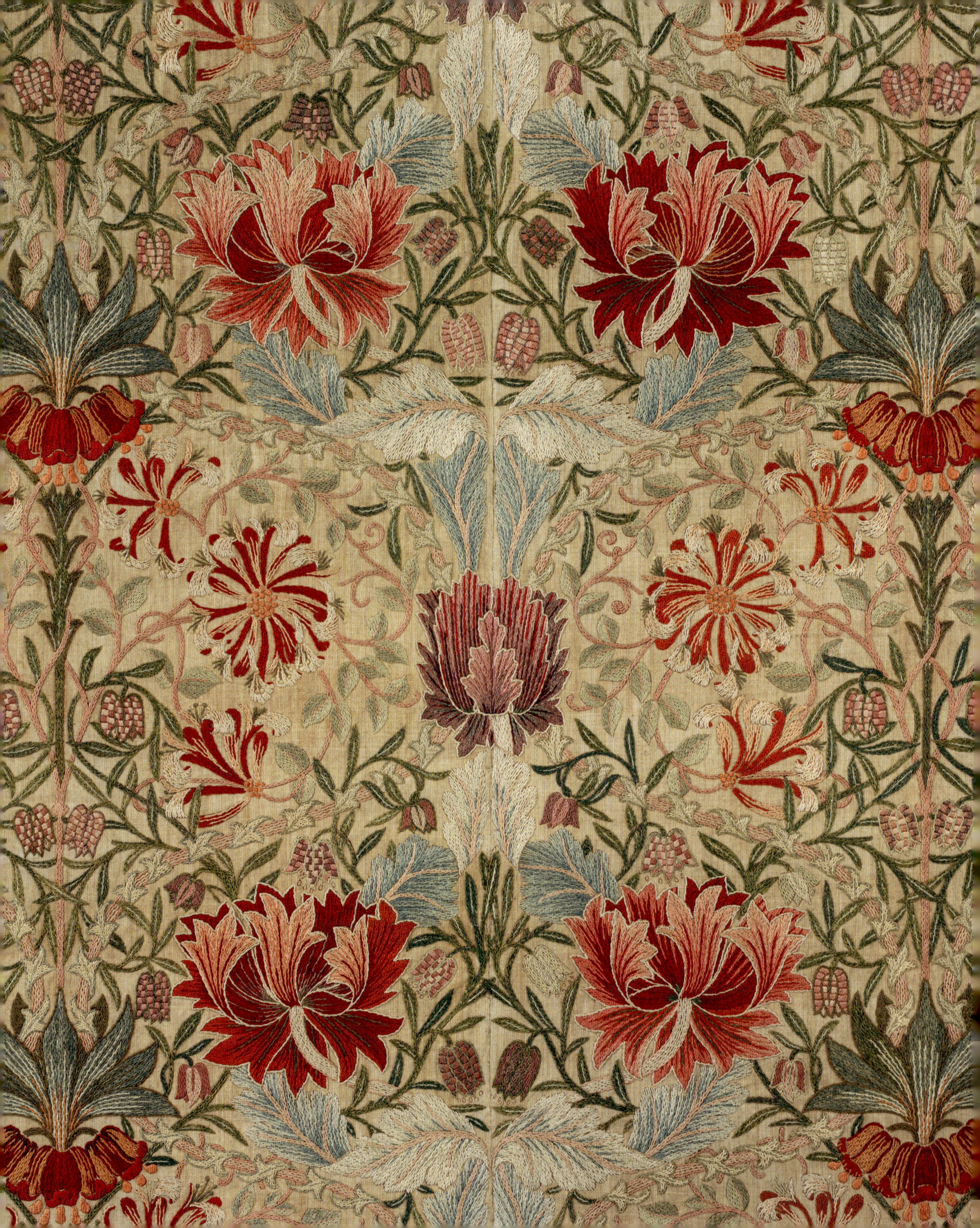

XII
TEXTILES

Linda Parry

'I think it of capital importance that a pattern-designer should know all about the craft for which he has to draw.'
William Morris, 'Some Hints on Pattern-Designing', 1881

Morris remained fascinated with textiles throughout his life. His first interests were purely aesthetic, developed through a natural love of pattern and texture. In an attempt to produce the effects he most admired, this was followed by a preoccupation with the complexities of technique. Visual and practical aspects became equally important to him, and his ability to balance and harmonize these two vital elements in his own work, a rare quality for a textile designer of any age, is the single most important reason for his success.

Designing and making textiles helped Morris to solve a number of problems. Having failed in his early ambition to be a painter, they provided the means of creating figurative art on a grand scale. More modestly, they improved the appearance of his own homes and of those he furnished and decorated for others. Furthermore, by undertaking the complex preparations and often hard physical labour involved in manufacture, his intellectual and manual needs were exercised and frequently fulfilled.

His career as a designer both began and ended with the design and production of textiles, and this chapter shows how this activity outpaced his involvement with any other form of the visual arts. His earliest crudely worked panels, embroidered from about 1856, were attempts to reproduce medieval-looking hangings. His last examples, tapestries woven shortly before he died, finally achieved this dream. What developed between was a long and complex search for perfect patterns, colours, textures and effects for the home. Because such interests tend to be associated with women rather than men, and as Morris is seen to have succeeded in these activities with apparent ease, this side of his achievements is frequently underestimated, depreciated or simply misunderstood. Yet a study of his textile career, because of the length of time and consistency of his interest, provides a fascinating analogy for his life as a whole.

Morris's childhood brought him into contact with good quality yet conventional textile furnishings. Although his family lived in considerable middle-class comfort, original art and avant-garde design were absent from the home. As an adult he remembered only one textile item, a crewel-work embroidered picture of Abraham and Isaac. In describing the subject and technique he added nothing of its history. For someone who was to become one of the great textile historians of his generation this is strange but shows how, in his formative years, aesthetic judgments preceded intellectual curiosity.

Fig.204 ***Honeysuckle*** **curtain or hanging, designed by William Morris, 1876 (see XII.15)**
William Morris Gallery

History and romance soon took a firm hold, nurtured by childhood wanderings and through the family's library at Woodford Hall. As well as popular adventure novels, he introduced himself to John Gerard's *Herball or Generall Historie of Plants* (1597), an encyclopaedic study with careful drawings of plants, which was to remain a favourite reference book throughout his life. His first sight of historic textiles used as decorative furnishings was tapestries of leaf and plant design, hung in the upper room of a hunting lodge, built originally for Henry VIII, in neighbouring Epping Forest. He later recalled in his lecture 'The Lesser Arts of Life' the impact of the 'faded greenery … and the impression of romance that it made', which was, no doubt, heightened by entering the house itself, his first tangible experience of early British domestic life and one he spent his first years as a decorator attempting to recreate.

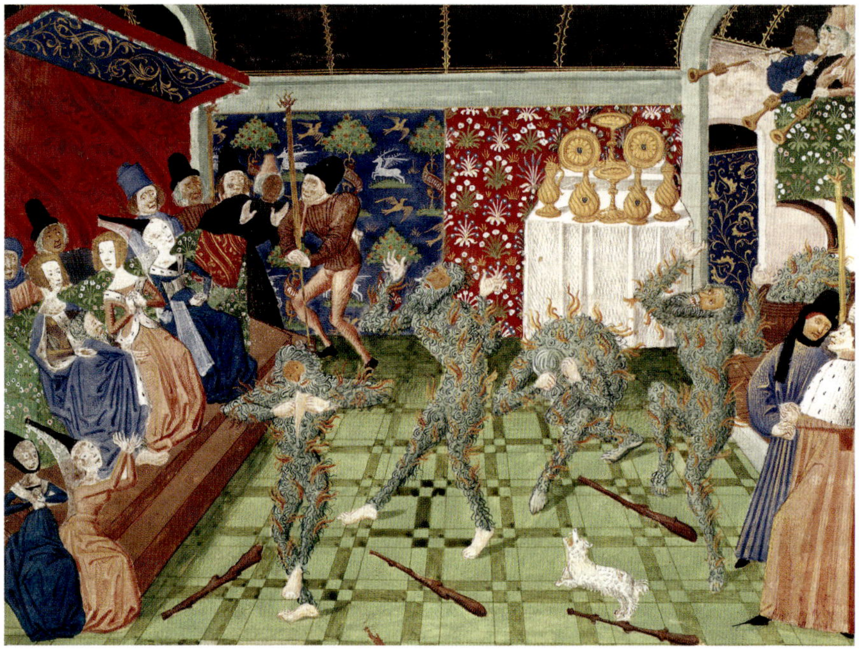

Fig.205 **'The Dance of the Wodewoses', from Jean Froissart's Chronicles, Bruges, *c*.1470–72.**
British Library

From such early experiences Morris realized that textiles were an essential part of the decoration and comfort of a home, so it is not surprising that they were included in his first attempts at house furnishing; the rooms rented with Edward Burne-Jones from August 1856 in Upper Gordon Street and soon afterwards at 17 Red Lion Square in Bloomsbury. Morris's first hangings were attempts to reproduce the effect of medieval tapestries, but the results were unconventional and must have looked incongruous in the Georgian architecture of the rented rooms (XII.1). With neither experience nor skills he used the only means available, stitching in a haphazard way with darning needles and thick wools on to a coarse linen ground. For the design of the embroideries, Morris chose as his source wall hangings depicting a repeating pattern of trees, birds and animals shown in court scenes from a fifteenth-century illuminated manuscript of Froissart's Chronicles (fig.205) that he had studied either in the British Museum or through Henry Noel Humphreys's 1844 edited volume. Morris's design was similar but included what was to be the first use of his boyish motto 'If I can'. The form of these wall hangings remained at the back of Morris's mind for some time. He included a similar panel in the decorative detailing in his 1858 textile-strewn painting of Jane as *La Belle Iseult* (VI.12) and other examples were made in the first years of commercial production by Morris, Marshall, Faulkner & Co. (XII.2).

The naive appearance and structure of this early work is surprising when it is realized that Morris had, by the time he settled in London, already spent seven months apprenticed to the notable neo-Gothic architect George Edmund Street. One of the most influential and experienced church textile designers of the nineteenth century, Street's embroidery had already attracted 'widespread notice and imitation' when shown at the Great Exhibition of 1851, five years before Morris entered his office. Whereas Morris's first amateur attempts can be seen as the results of his own tentative experiments, they may also suggest a reaction against the socially acceptable, very high standards of Street's professional church embroidery.

However, although Morris continued to develop his own quite individual style for domestic textiles and particularly those made for his own use, Street's work did provide the inspiration for Morris, Marshall, Faulkner & Co.'s early ecclesiastical textile furnishings. Morris and Philip Webb shared these projects and it is difficult to separate their work. They had met in Street's office and were aware of daily practice and procedure there, Webb more so than Morris, being chief assistant at the time. The first documented textile produced by the firm, and now the only known example from the first three important decorative schemes commissioned by George Frederick Bodley for churches in Brighton, Selsley and Scarborough, is an embroidered frontal for St Martin's, Scarborough. This shows a 'powdered' design of floral sprigs worked in silks and then cut out and applied to a velvet ground (XII.8), echoing the late medieval *opus anglicanum* technique employed by Street in his own work and advocated by him in lectures. In one of Webb's surviving notebooks, used during his early years in Street's office, he authoritatively describes a technical variation in the gold embroidery of a thirteenth-century cloth. The notebook also lists Street's thread suppliers, and, alongside a note 'wd give info', the name and address of Agnes Blencowe, one of the most competent and celebrated professional embroiderers of her day and an expert on medieval work. Webb, like Morris, had begun to build up historic references for later use.

It is not recorded when Morris started to collect examples of early textiles. He recognized from an early age the importance of colour and texture that furnishings created in an interior, so it was a natural progression to amass examples of types that appealed to him. By close study and, occasionally, unpicking sections of the cloth he was able to discover why they looked the way they did and by doing so identified various ancient weaving and embroidery techniques. He was as fascinated by traditional European craft textiles, as those from the commercial manufacturing centres of Italy, Turkey and the Middle East and this is reflected in his own collection (XII.11). In time, Morris's interest in, and knowledge of, historic textiles grew and his reputation as an expert in the field became widely recognized.

Embroidery continued to provide the only practical means of decorating textiles for the first years of the firm's existence. Work was sewn in the home by Jane Morris, her sister Elizabeth (Bessie) Burden and friends. John William Mackail claimed that several women worked under the supervision of Jane and Bessie, including Eliza Fanny Campfield (née Beal), the wife of the foreman of the stained-glass painters. However, no payments to embroiderers appear in the accounts for the firm's first years of production (which include wages for George Campfield, among others) and few embroidery orders are mentioned in the discussion of business at each meeting (fig.33). This suggests that most of the work undertaken was for personal use and that of friends. This lack of a professional framework may account for only a brief mention of textiles in the firm's first prospectus sent out in 1861, as quoted by Mackail. However, following success at the 1862 International Exhibition, the partners decided, at their meeting on 14 January 1863, to circulate an updated list of the firm's work to prospective clients. An accompanying letter was drafted, which included the information that they were 'ready to supply all kinds of embroidered hangings both for domestic and ecclesiastical purposes in linen, cotton, woollen, silk or velvet from the simplest line embroidery to elaborate needlework tapestry of figures and subjects' (British Library Add. MS 45336).

Morris, Marshall, Faulkner & Co. had occupied two stands at the 1862 exhibition for which they were awarded two medals with the judges' commendation that 'the general form of the furniture, the arrangement of the tapestry, and the character of the details are satisfying to the archaeologist for the exactness of the imitation, at the same time that the general effect is excellent'. With no details in the official exhibition catalogue (it is probable that the firm refused to pay), it is difficult to discover what they exhibited. It is likely that all embroideries produced to date were shown, although only the Scarborough frontal (XII.8) can be identified positively. Contemporary newspaper and magazine accounts hint tantalizingly at the rest. Both *The Ecclesiologist*'s reference to 'most antique-looking tapestry-hangings, which are effective in colour, but of rude manufacture' and *The Clerical Journal*'s description of items unsuitable for church use because of their 'homliness', probably refer to examples of the *If I Can* design (XII.1).

The unusual nature of the firm's exhibits was further emphasized by Christopher Dresser, himself one of the most inventive designers of the period, who wrote of 'a series of quaint fabrics that have the pattern wrought upon them in thick worsted threads of many colours which is sewn to the surface'. The hangings that caught his attention were likely to include those made for Morris's first home, Red House (XII.3). For these Morris, yet again, derived the design, of brightly coloured daisy clumps, from Froissart. He was to use this pattern repeatedly throughout his career and it appears on painted furniture, stained glass, tiles, wallpaper, calligraphy, machine-woven carpeting and tapestry weaving. The Red House hangings were embroidered in outline with couched wools on a dark blue woollen ground, a technique characteristically belittled by Dante Gabriel Rossetti with the comment, 'Top has taken to worsted work'. It is likely that this simple yet effective stitching was actually suggested by Jane, a skilful practitioner who by then had become the busy mother of two babies with little time to devote to the firm's work. It proved to be the most practical and successful to date and was also used for another contemporary hanging of sunflower design, which is now housed at Kelmscott Manor.

Not nearly so successful were Morris's plans for a set of figurative panels to be hung around the walls of the dining room at Red House. Despite careful planning and design, the scheme, loosely based on one of Morris's favourite medieval romances, Chaucer's *The Legend of Good Women*, and depicting a number of classical, biblical and Arthurian heroines, was over ambitious. He had overestimated the enthusiasm and expertise of his resident workforce. Choosing the complex appliqué technique first used for the Scarborough altar frontal, the design of draped figures proved far more testing, requiring a level of skill that only Jane and Bessie possessed. With Jane preoccupied, the scheme was never fully realized, although a number of panels in various stages of completion survive. The most finished is the figure of *St Catherine* worked by Jane, which shows one of the decorative trees that were part of the intended composition (fig.206). Three figures embroidered by Bessie Burden were retained by her following the move from Red House and later incorporated into a screen for George Howard (XII.4).

The firm's range of commercial textile goods was expanded following the move of headquarters in 1865 from 8 Red Lion Square to 26 Queen Square. The Morris family now also occupied these premises and, while living over the shop, William became engrossed in the dyeing of embroidery threads and plain fabrics. By using natural dyestuffs he hoped to reproduce the colours and tones that he most admired in historic textiles. Despite turning to historic sources for reference, Morris was surprisingly scientific in application, combining ancient recipes (often requiring translation) with modern technology (XII.37).

Morris remained responsible for the firm's production of textiles, but other partners also contributed designs. Both Webb and Burne-Jones's account books dealing with the firm list embroideries. Ford Madox Brown's household accounts mention designs for two worsted bell ropes (see XII.9) and he is also said to have created designs for embroideries, stamped velvets and silks although, sadly, none of these are identifiable today. Though exaggerated, the opinion that 'as a designer for tiles and textiles Ford Madox Brown was probably unequalled' (E.M. Tait, *The Furnisher*, November 1900) suggests he was a more significant contributor than has been recognized. From the early 1870s, a hard-wearing woollen velvet with an impressed design provided an alternative furnishing to the plain blue and green woollen serges that the firm had sold from its beginnings and was used as upholstery on a number of early chairs (XII.33). Probably supplied by the Manchester decorating firm of John Aldam Heaton and based on a Flemish seventeenth-century type, this is possibly one of the stamped velvets said to have been designed by Madox Brown.

Having achieved his aims with embroidery, Morris's next textile furnishings were a series of

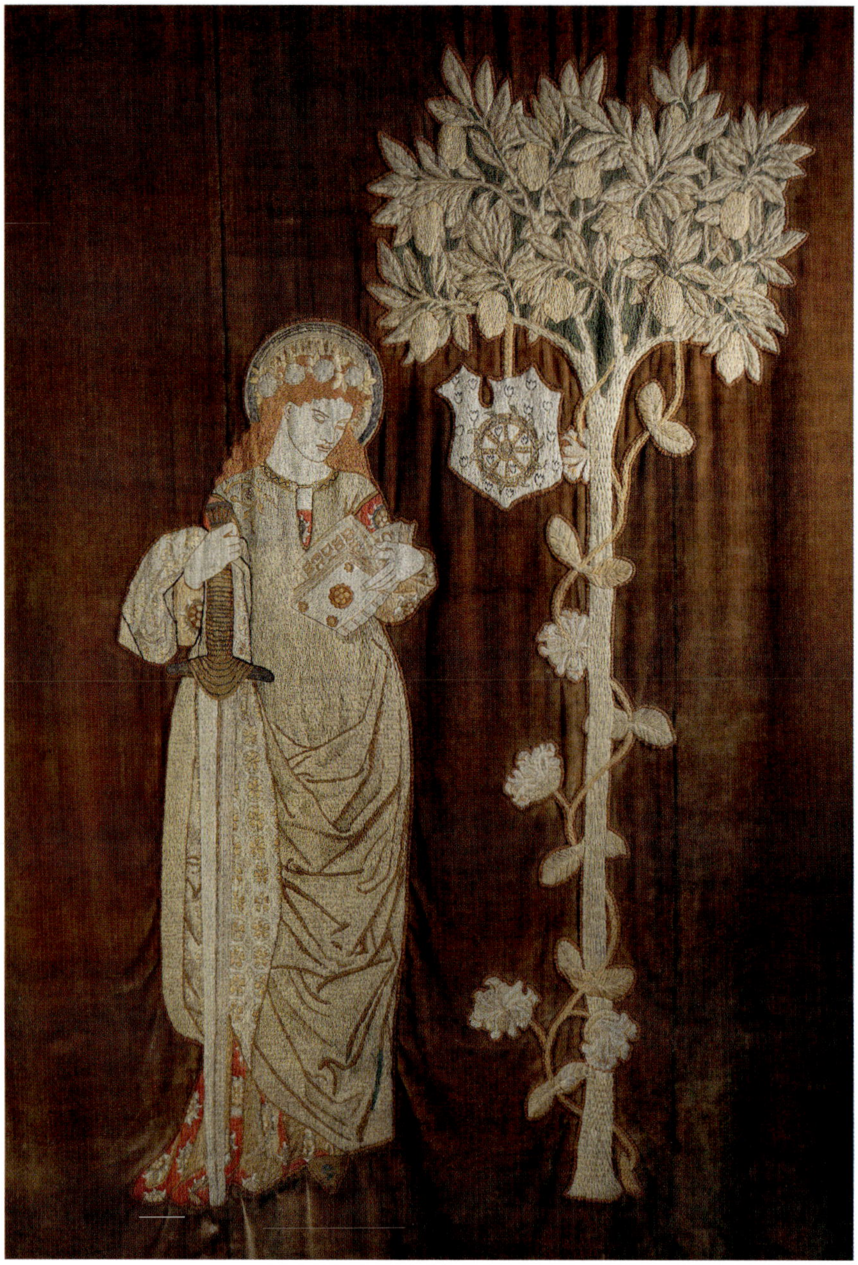

Fig.206 ***St Catherine* embroidery, worked by Jane Morris for Red House, early 1860s.**
The Society of Antiquaries of London, Kelmscott Manor

reproduction designs, block-printed on to fine woollen grounds at his request by a leading Lancashire firm (XII.31). These copies of 1830s patterns were very popular throughout the life of the firm and, ironically, contributed to Morris's reputation as the major British designer of naturalistic floral 'chintz' patterns.

By the early 1870s Morris finally accepted that his talents lay not with the figurative forms of the fine artist but as a practical designer of applied repeating pattern. This had been demonstrated by the popularity of his commercial work so far, his wallpapers and painted decoration for interiors in particular, and by the increasingly decorative quality of his book illumination. Following what proved a lifetime's habit of studying and perfecting one technique at a time, Morris devoted the next decade to becoming a successful designer, manufacturer and retailer of printed and woven textiles, machine-made and hand-knotted carpets and tapestries.

Initial dyeing, block-printing and weaving experiments took place at the firm's headquarters in Queen Square and the adjacent Great Ormond Yard. These complex and time-consuming procedures, and Morris's subsequent search for suitable outside firms capable of manufacturing his designs in the form he desired, are documented through specific examples in this chapter. What is not evident simply by studying individual designs is the vital part played by others in helping Morris achieve his aims. Reading the extensive correspondence between Morris and Thomas Wardle of Leek in Staffordshire, for instance, gives insight into the tortuous path this frequently took. Not only is Wardle's enormous contribution as Morris's main early printer and dyer evident, but the letters also demonstrate how this was often completed under the most challenging conditions. Why Wardle should have continued to co-operate in an undertaking with such a difficult client and for which he suffered personal financial loss is debatable. Morris's forceful yet charismatic personality can only have been part of the reason. More likely was Wardle's realization that Morris's work was of considerable aesthetic and technical significance.

While emphasizing the importance of Morris's strong management to the success of early textile

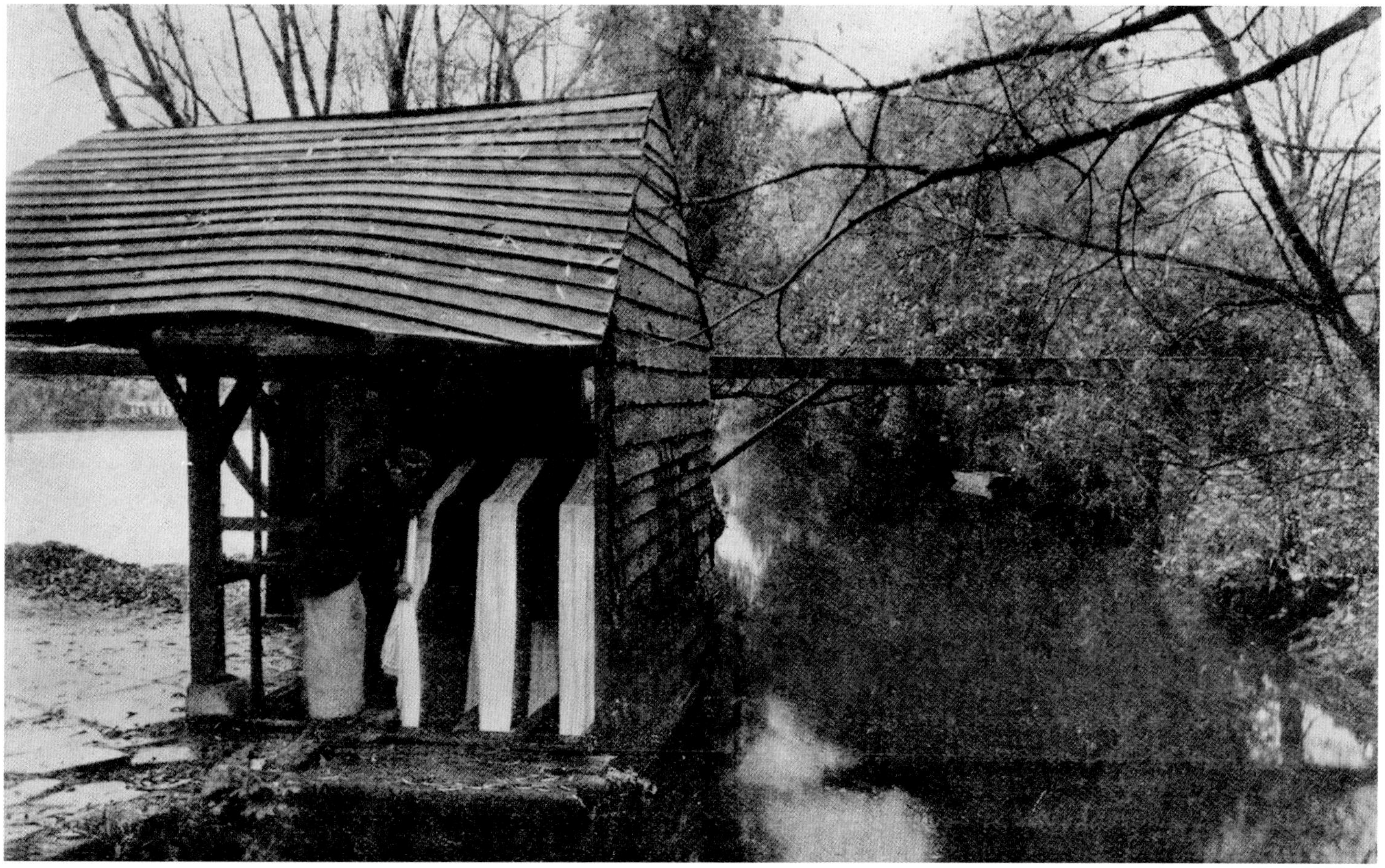

Fig.207 **Washing cotton in the river Wandle at Merton Abbey to remove impurities and prepare the cloth for printing. Published in Lewis F. Day's *The Art of William Morris*, 1899.**
V&A

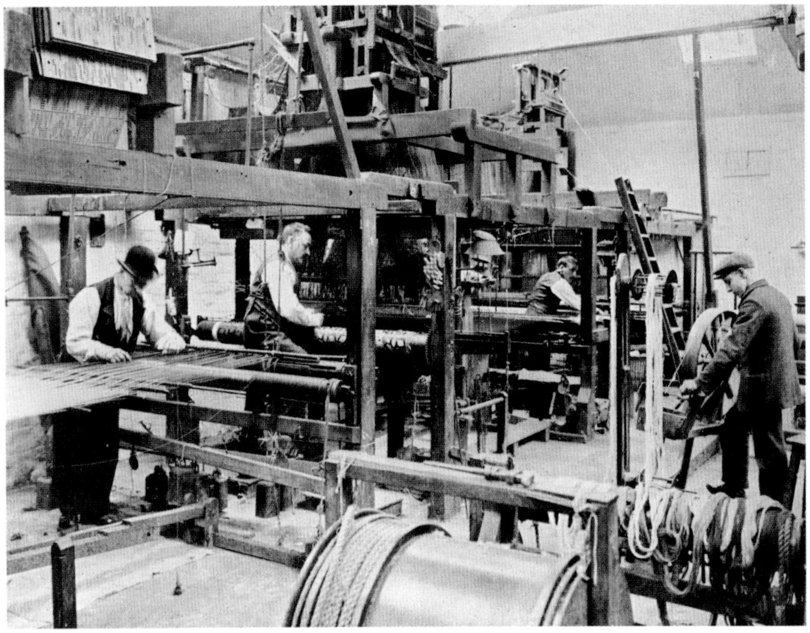

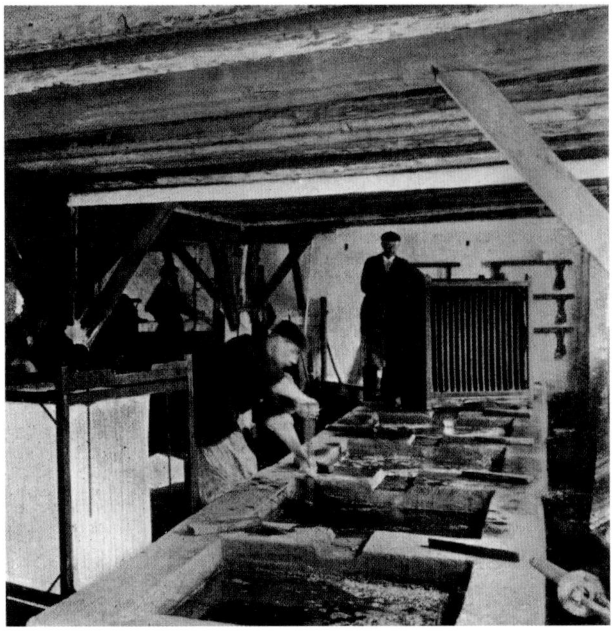

production, it must not be forgotten that he too contributed considerable physical and mental effort. He believed, rightly, that successful design could not be achieved without a sound understanding of 'all about the ware ... and its relation to similar wares', as he described it in his lecture 'Making the Best of It' in 1879. Yet this did not always come easily to him despite his considerable natural abilities as a designer, a talent referred to by his daughter May as his 'heaven sent gift'. This is demonstrated by his first heavy-handed attempts at embroidery, the months spent working the dye vats at Leek (when his blue hands often illustrated the most successful results) and the 516½ hours spent weaving his first tapestry in his bedroom at Kelmscott House (XII.105). Such tenacity proved of major importance to his eventual success and added to the enjoyment of his participation. Writing to Georgiana Burne-Jones from Leek in 1877, he excused his shaky handwriting caused by 'doing journeyman's work the last few days: delightful work, hard for the body and easy for the mind.'

It is understandable that, of all the textile techniques Morris used, he left weaving to the last. Not only did mastering the working of the various looms for furnishings, carpet weaving and tapestry present the greatest number of technical difficulties, but he also demanded a great deal of the craft. His appreciation of texture, particularly the natural qualities of wool, silk, cotton and linen, was of paramount importance to him as a designer and manufacturer. His greatest wish, and one that would cause him the greatest trouble, was to master traditional structures such as damasks, brocatelles and double and triple cloths, types he had studied carefully for a number of years in the collection of the South Kensington Museum.

Despite his love of historic pattern and early woven techniques, Morris used these as the inspiration for new effects by including traditional motifs in many of his patterns and by mixing fibres and colour in a totally unique way. He never underestimated the intricacies of the loom and despite the great commercial success of his woven fabrics, preparation did not always go well. The time spent building a loom for gold brocading was commercially unsound, yet Morris had to prove it was possible (XII.76). Even as late as 1888, the year he drew his last designs for repeating textile patterns, he was still struggling to overcome weaving problems which, in a letter to his daughter Jenny, he described as 'not so simple as the world in general seems to think.'

Morris had taught himself the various textile techniques he wished to use in cramped and unsuitable conditions and for a number of years he relied, frustratingly, on outside contractors to produce the commercial quantities of his textiles needed for the shop. His search, in 1881, for a factory in which he could undertake this work for himself was conditioned by the need to find the facilities necessary for textile production, even though other forms of the firm's manufacture were

Fig.208 (above left) **The fabric-weaving sheds at Merton Abbey, showing hand-activated jacquard looms in use. Published in Morris & Co.'s *Silk and Wool Tapestries, Brocades etc.* brochure, *c.*1912.**

Fig.209 (above right) **Indigo-discharge printing at Merton Abbey. Once dyed blue in these deep vats, the cloth was printed with a bleaching agent, which drew dye out of the patterned areas. Published in Morris & Co.'s *Printed Linens and Cottons* brochure, *c.*1912.**

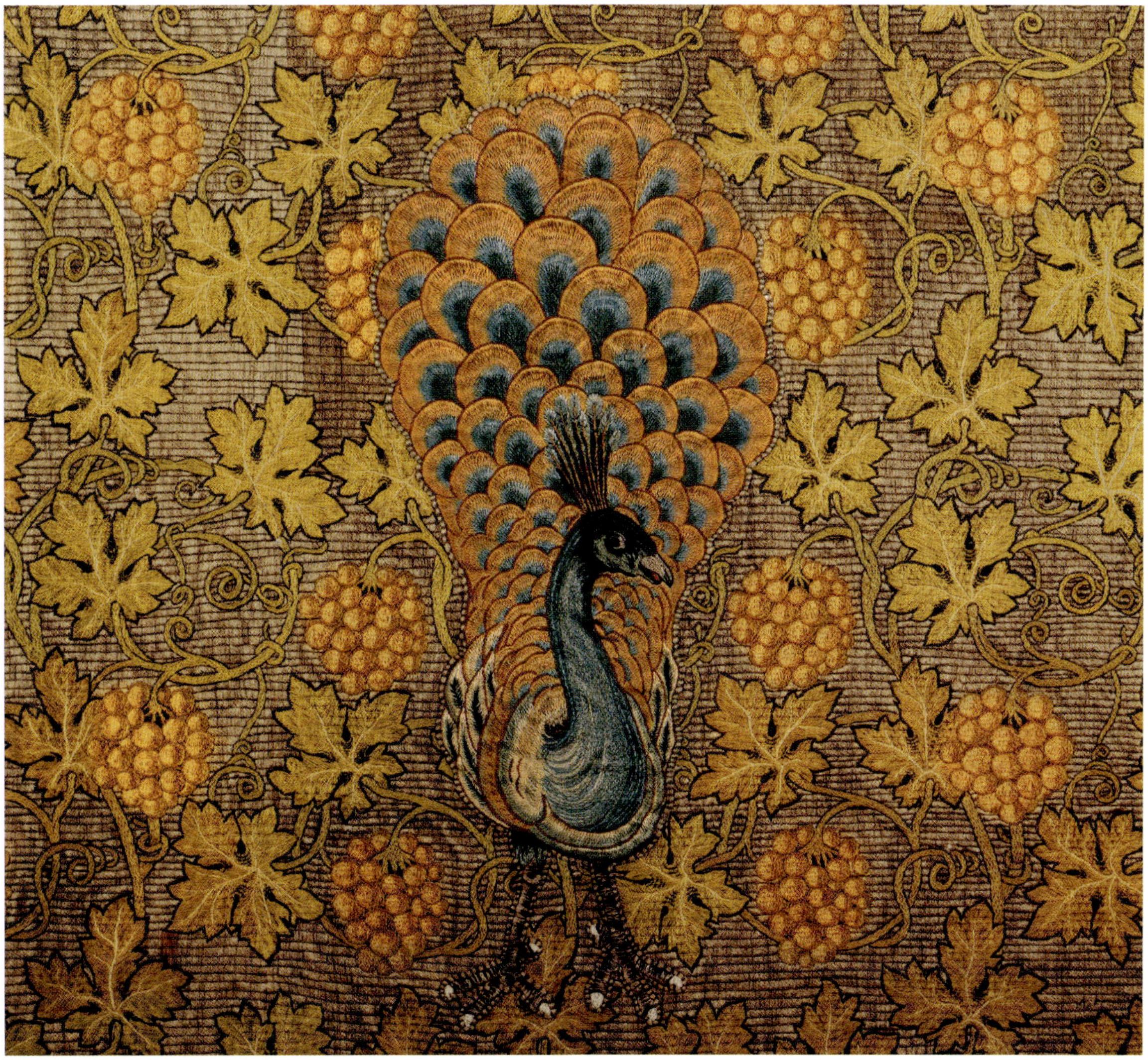

Fig.210 **Detail of *Peacock and Vine* embroidery, designed by Morris and Philip Webb, displayed at the Philadelphia Centennial Exhibition in 1876.**
William Morris Gallery

also to be moved there. Merton Abbey, an old textile-printing works near Wimbledon, was chosen because the river Wandle, which ran alongside the workshops, provided limitless supplies of soft water. This, and the acres of grounds surrounding the site, allowed for the necessary washing and drying of cloth before and after production (fig.207). The existing, many-windowed buildings provided both light and space for the printing and weaving of furnishings (figs 25 and 208) and the large-scale manufacture of tapestries and carpets (fig.38). Within a short time of moving there Morris had also built indigo vats (fig.209) in order to produce the blue dye so important to his work and which had so far eluded him. At last he was able to establish himself as a comprehensive manufacturer of textiles and no other London decorator or retailer could boast of producing such a wide and varied range of fabrics under one roof.

The sale of printed and woven textiles, machine-woven carpets and embroideries became an important side of the business from the time the firm's shop moved from Queen Square to Oxford Street in 1877. Embroidery was then worked by a small band of professionals under the direction of Bessie Burden and later, from 1885, by May Morris who had learnt skills from both parents. Whereas important commissions such as the Rounton Grange or Smeaton Manor schemes (XII.12 and XII.17) occasionally enticed Morris back to his drawing board, an endless stream of designs for cushion covers, screens, portières and bedcovers was needed to provide the shop with the staple commercial stock demanded by clients. Initially these items were designed by Morris and later by May and John Henry Dearle, Morris's assistant. Although 'Morris' embroideries (as they all became known, irrespective of who had designed them)

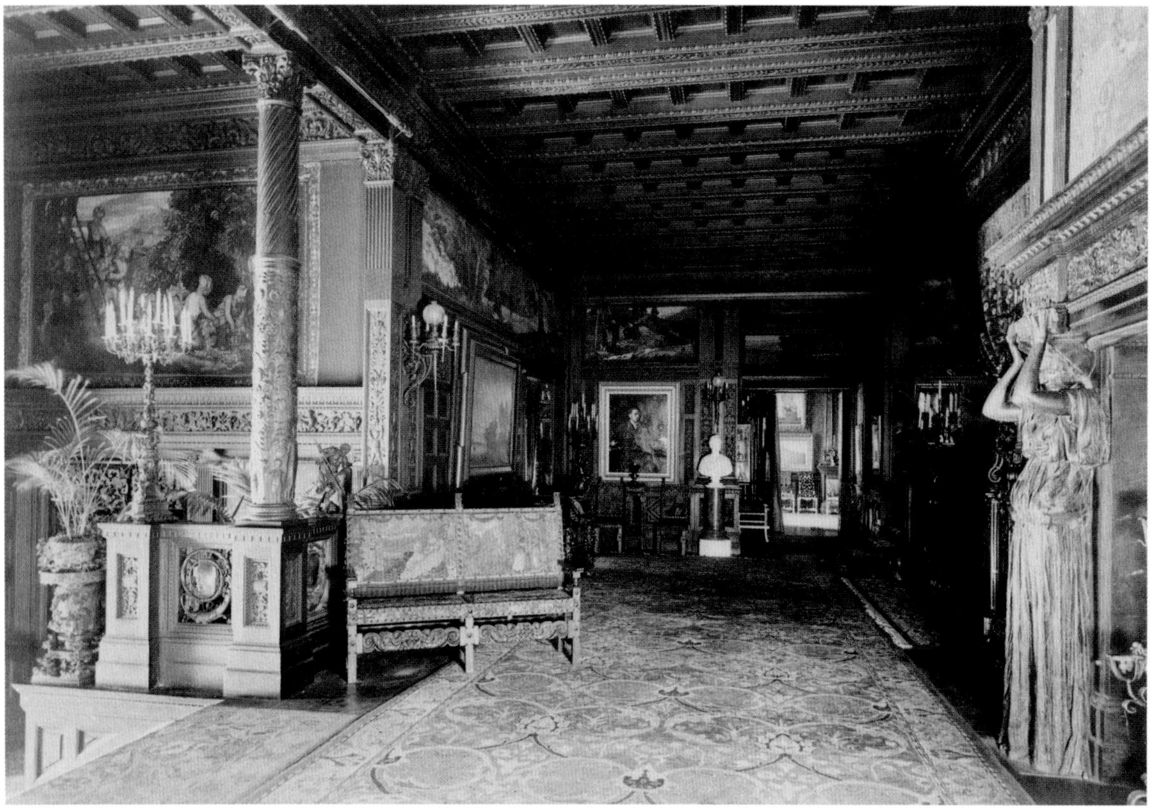

Fig.211 (left) **Morris & Co. hand-knotted carpets furnishing the entrance hall of Cornelius Vanderbilt II's New York residence, 1882.**
George B. Post Collection, The New-York Historical Society

Fig.212 (below left) **One end of the drawing room at Kelmscott House, Hammersmith, showing *Bird* woven cloth on the walls and *Peacock and Dragon* curtains, *c.*1896.**
St Bride Foundation

Fig.213 (below right) **The drawing room at Buller's Wood, Chislehurst, Kent, a house decorated by Morris & Co. from 1889.**
Private collection

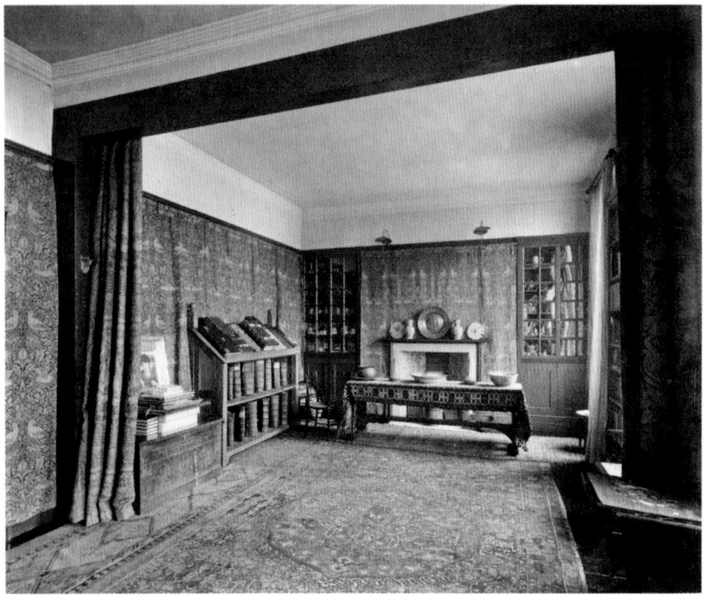

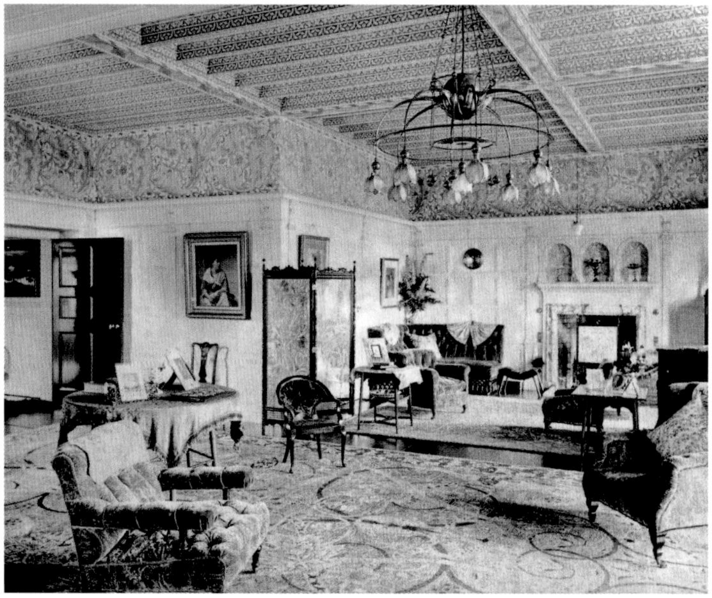

were one of the popular forms of 'art needlework', competition was rife. Morris's work was not exclusive to Morris & Co. and a number of designs were produced by Morris and Burne-Jones for the Royal School of Needlework in the 1870s (XII.14–15). Examples were shown in important international exhibitions such as the Philadelphia Centennial Exhibition of 1876 (fig.210) and this greatly helped in advertising Morris's work outside Britain before he actively pursued this himself.

Despite some early reluctance to sell abroad on its own account, Morris & Co. produced a stand of six compartments for the Boston Foreign Fair of 1883. However, even before this the firm had done work for an influential American client. Morris's diary for July to December 1881 mentions

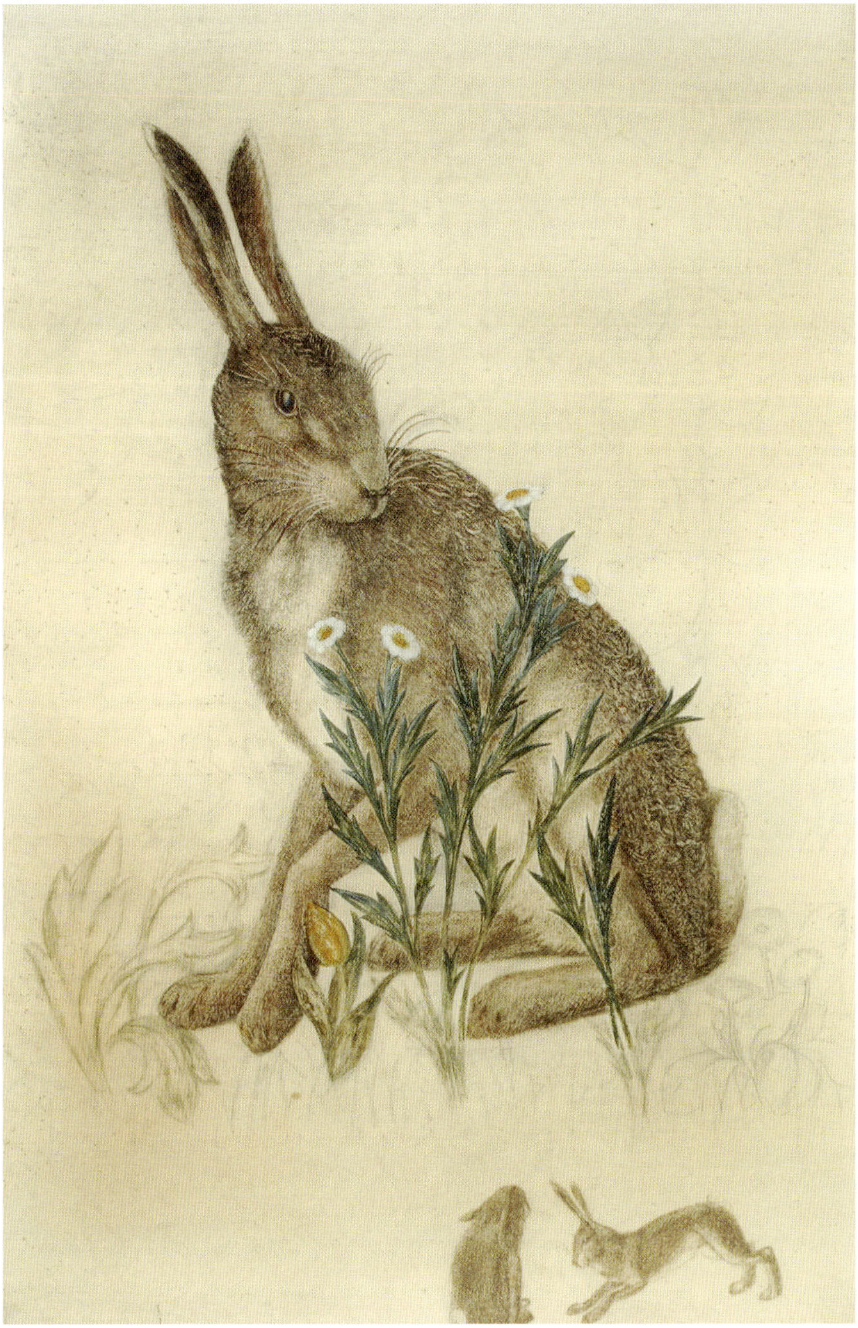

Fig.214 **Drawing of a hare for *The Forest* tapestry which hung at 1 Holland Park, by Philip Webb, 1886 (see XII.110).**
National Trust, Wightwick Manor

designing carpets for 'Vanderbilt' and several splendid hand-knotted examples can be traced to Cornelius Vanderbilt II's mansion on Fifth Avenue and West 57th Street, New York (fig.211). The success of this commission may well have encouraged Morris to exhibit the company's wares at Boston (XII.95–6).

The brochure accompanying the Morris & Co. exhibit at the Boston Fair, written by the firm's general manager George Wardle, is important not only in listing the range of goods available during its most commercially successful period but also in its recommendations concerning house decoration and how Morris products should be used in the home. As the only existing account of the firm's practice, this is vital study for anyone attempting to assess Morris's role as a designer as, for him, appropriateness of use was as vital a component in controlling the way he drew his patterns as choosing the correct technique for manufacture. Wardle's introduction recommends, among other items, printed wools for bed and window curtains and unlined cotton damasks 'for portières in summer cottages, or for window-curtains'. He also gives specific details of the firm's most original use of fabrics – draped or stretched on walls around the room. This method was first used by Morris in the drawing room of his London home, Kelmscott House, where *Bird* woven cloth hung 'to within two feet of the ceiling' (fig.212). 'The cloth is hooked up, to the top rail,' Wardle continues, 'and is but slightly plaited – only enough modulation of the surface being allowed to just break the pattern here and there.' The second method involved attaching fabrics to 'thin laths or batons first nailed to the margins of the wall – that is, above the dado, under the cornice or frieze, and around doors and windows.' From these instructions a very clear picture emerges of the importance, and occasional dominance, of textiles in the ideal 'Morris' interior.

Despite Wardle's very specific advice in the 1883 brochure, the firm's use of textiles in its decorative design schemes was extremely varied, controlled as much by the client and architecture of the building as by the firm itself. A comparison of the interiors of two houses, 1 Holland Park and Buller's Wood, both decorated by Morris & Co., shows how different these could look. The decoration of Holland Park is opulent and cluttered, designed to show to advantage the Ionides family's treasured possessions (fig.42 and VIII.15), whereas the decoration of the drawing room in Buller's Wood, a house near Chislehurst in Kent (fig.213), centres on the specially designed hand-knotted carpets made for the house.

Original furnishings such as the *Redcar*, *Rounton Grange*, *Carbrook*, *Holland Park* and *Bullerswood* carpets provided additional individuality in the furnishing of many houses. More pragmatically, such commissions allowed Morris to explore new sources of design and manufacture at the expense of his wealthy clients. He had begun his career designing special embroideries for his own use at Red House; his last years were devoted to designing

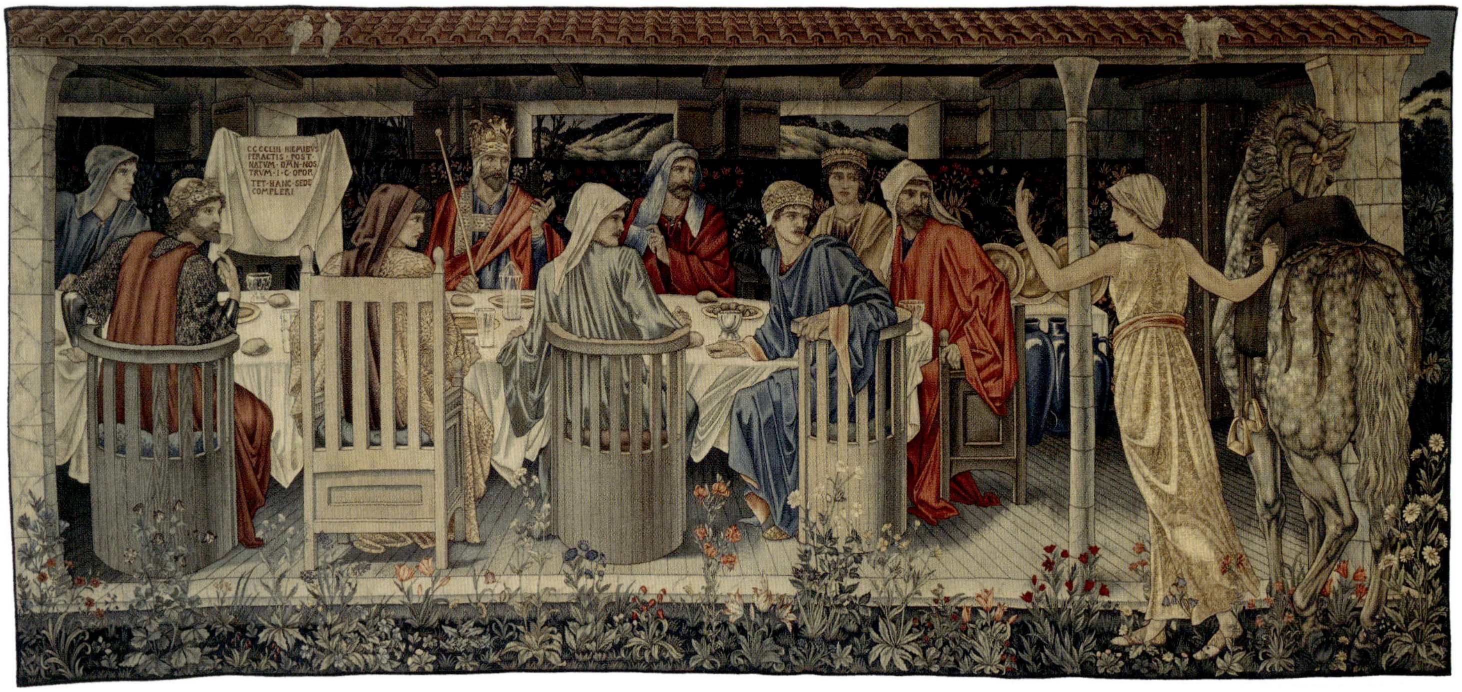

individual carpets and tapestries for the homes of others. These late labours represent many of his most original designs and are now judged as his most prized artefacts.

Since 1879 Morris had been responsible for producing a number of tapestry panels of various subjects designed chiefly by Burne-Jones but also by himself and others (fig.214). However, it was not until 1890 with the decoration of Stanmore Hall, Middlesex, the last commission he worked on, that Morris was able to achieve his most important ambition, the production of a set of narrative tapestries in the medieval manner, the 'bright dream' he had nurtured since childhood (XII.120). Even the choice of subject for the tapestries, the Quest for the Holy Grail, provided an appropriately romantic ending to his career (fig.215). By accomplishing this scheme shortly before his death, Morris finally completed a full circle as designer, manufacturer and retailer of textiles. Whereas his initial ambitions to produce cloth, which was attractive and useful, were modest, his final achievements in the scale and range of activities went far beyond this, unequalled in his own or any other age.

Fig.215 ***The Summons*** **tapestry from the *Holy Grail* series, woven for George McCulloch, 1898–9.**
Birmingham Museums Trust

XII.1

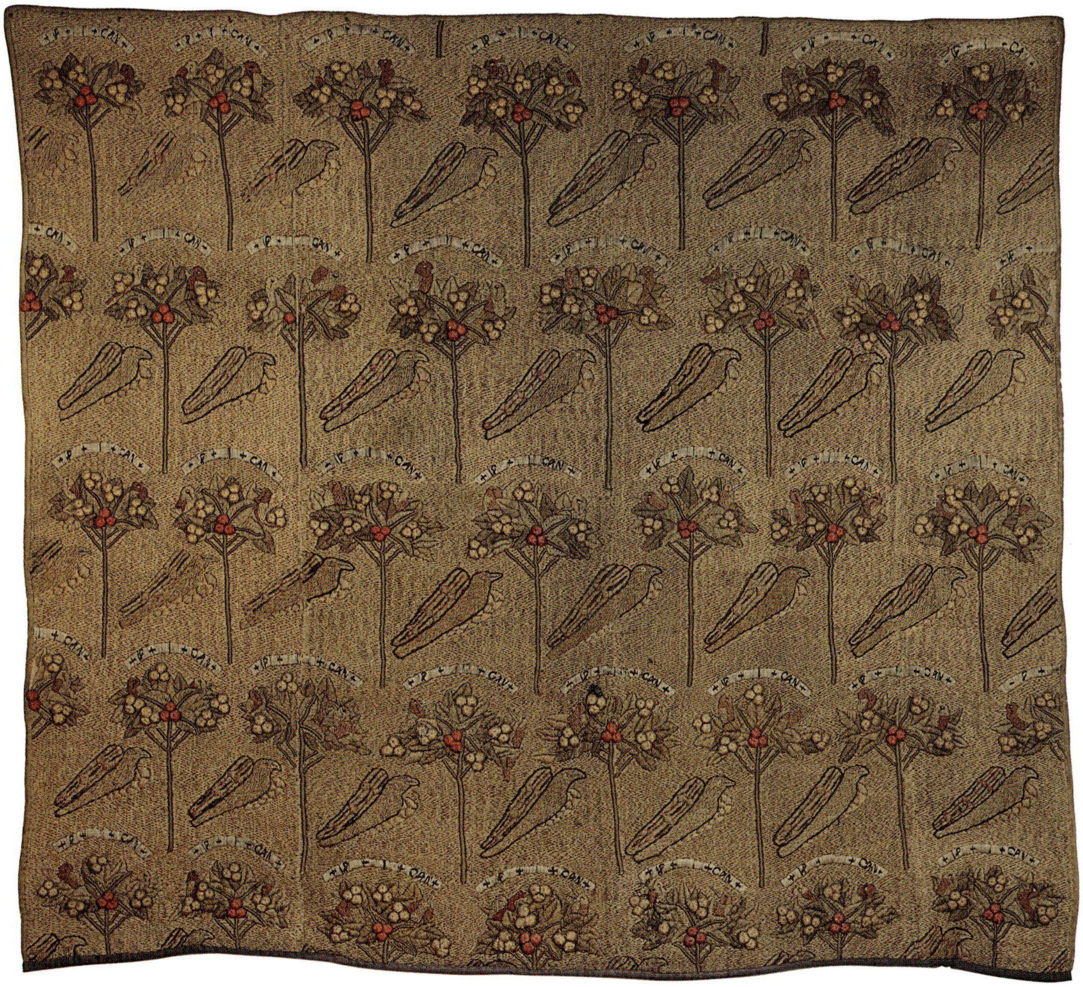

XII.2

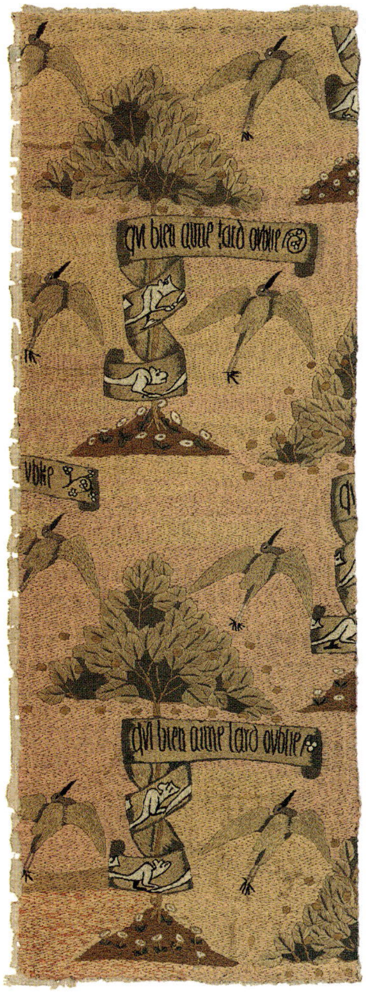

EMBROIDERY

XII.1
If I Can **hanging**
Designed and worked by
William Morris, *c.*1856–7
Linen ground embroidered with wools in unorthodox flat and padded stitches, 168.5 x 187 cm
The Society of Antiquaries of London, Kelmscott Manor (KM141)

This is the remaining example of Morris's first textile scheme made for his rooms at Red Lion Square. 'He started experiments [in embroidery] before he knew me,' wrote Jane, 'got frames made, had worsted dyed to his taste by an old French couple, and began a piece of work with his own hands.' The pattern of repeating fruit trees with birds in flight is adapted from an illumination in Froissart's Chronicles (fig.205). Morris adopted and anglicized Jan van Eyck's motto 'Als ich can' following his trip to the Low Countries in 1856. Despite the naivety of technique, there is a suggestion, in the rendition of leaves and fruit, of a more experienced hand, possibly Mary Nicholson, who worked as the maid at Red Lion Square. A hanging of a similar design appears in the background of the painting *La Belle Iseult* (VI.12). The colours were once more vibrant and have almost completely faded.

XII.2
Qui bien aime tard oublie **hanging**
Designed by William Morris, early 1860s
Worked by more than one hand
Linen ground embroidered with wools in random embroidery stitches, 185.5 x 66.3 cm
William Morris Gallery, London Borough of Waltham Forest (F390ii)

The inscription roughly translates as 'who loves best loves longest' and comes from Chaucer's fourteenth-century poem *The Parliament of Fowls*, in which birds gather to choose their mates on St Valentine's Day. It is one of four hangings of the same design from Penkill Castle, Ayrshire, the home of Alice Boyd, mistress of William Bell Scott, a close friend of Rossetti's who Morris first met in the late 1850s. The same inscription was used in the painted wall decoration of the drawing room at Red House, where it appeared on scrolls around repeating auricula stems (fig.145). The design is similar to the *If I Can* panel and shows the same naive technique. However, dye analysis has detected a synthetic violet dye not available until the early 1860s. Could the hangings have been originally intended for Red House, continuing the house's theme of love? The design was inspired by the background decoration of two illuminations in Froissart's Chronicles, the same source used for the blue serge hangings in the master bedroom (XII.3).

When and how they arrived in Scotland is unknown, although Rossetti refers to 'the Topsaic tapestries' being at Penkill in a letter to Boyd dated 17 November 1868. The panels show the work of at least three embroiderers, one far more competent than the others. These are likely to be the type of hangings exhibited at the 1862 International Exhibition. Such 'tapestries' were priced at £3 per square yard on the firm's stand.

XII.3

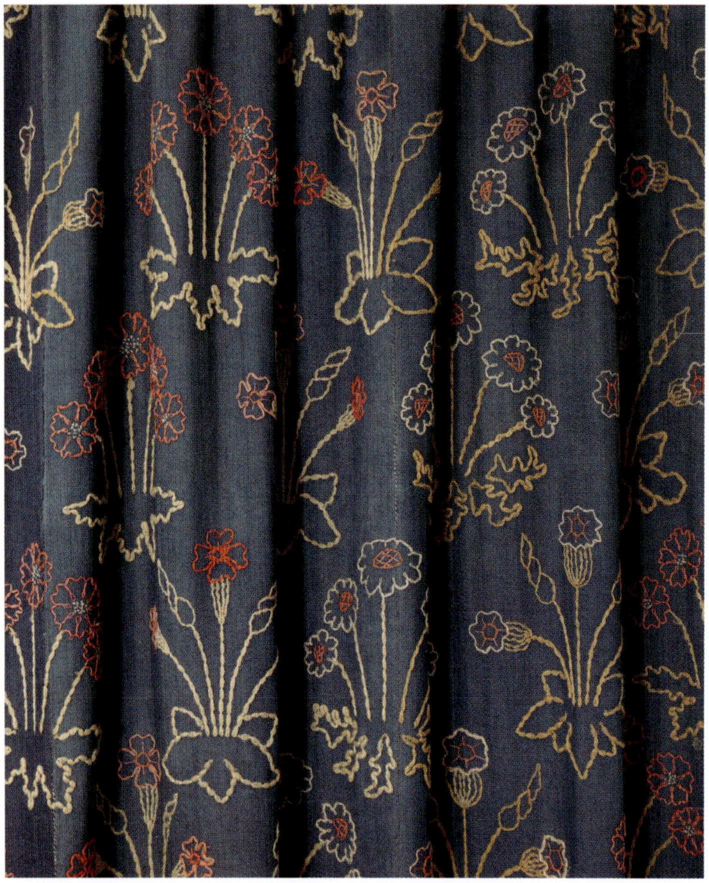

XII.3
***Daisy* hanging**
Designed by William Morris, early 1860s
Worked by Jane Morris, Bessie Burden and others
Woollen ground embroidered with wools in couched stitches, 167 x 299 cm
The Society of Antiquaries of London, Kelmscott Manor (KM033)

Five hangings survive from this scheme for the master bedroom at Red House. The daisy, one of Morris's most enduring motifs, features in the prologue to Chaucer's *The Legend of Good Women*, the inspiration for the dining-room embroideries, so there is a literary link between the two schemes worked for the house (see XII.4–6). Like most of Morris's early domestic embroideries, the design is inspired by an illumination in Froissart's Chronicles (fig.205).

Jane Morris noted that 'The first stuff I got to embroider on was a piece of indigo dyed blue serge I found by chance in a London shop ... I took it home and he was delighted with it, and set to work at once designing flowers – these we worked in bright colours in a simple rough way – the work went quickly'. Jane's discovery was significant, and wool soon became the favoured ground for embroidery. 'Serge hangings' exhibited by the firm at the 1862 International Exhibition cost 12*s*. a square yard. This blue cloth, dyed with indigo and sulphuric acid, was very popular in the nineteenth century despite being prone to fading. The red embroidery threads were produced with synthetic dyes.

Angela Thirkell, granddaughter of Edward Burne-Jones recalled that the *Daisy* embroideries later hung at North End House, the Burne-Joneses' home in Rottingdean (*Three Houses*, 1931). Another set of five 'blue serge curtains ... embroidered by Miss Burden from Morris's design' were made in 1871 for the dining room at 1 Palace Green, the home of George and Rosalind Howard. They cost £53, of which £40 was charged for the embroidery.

XII.4

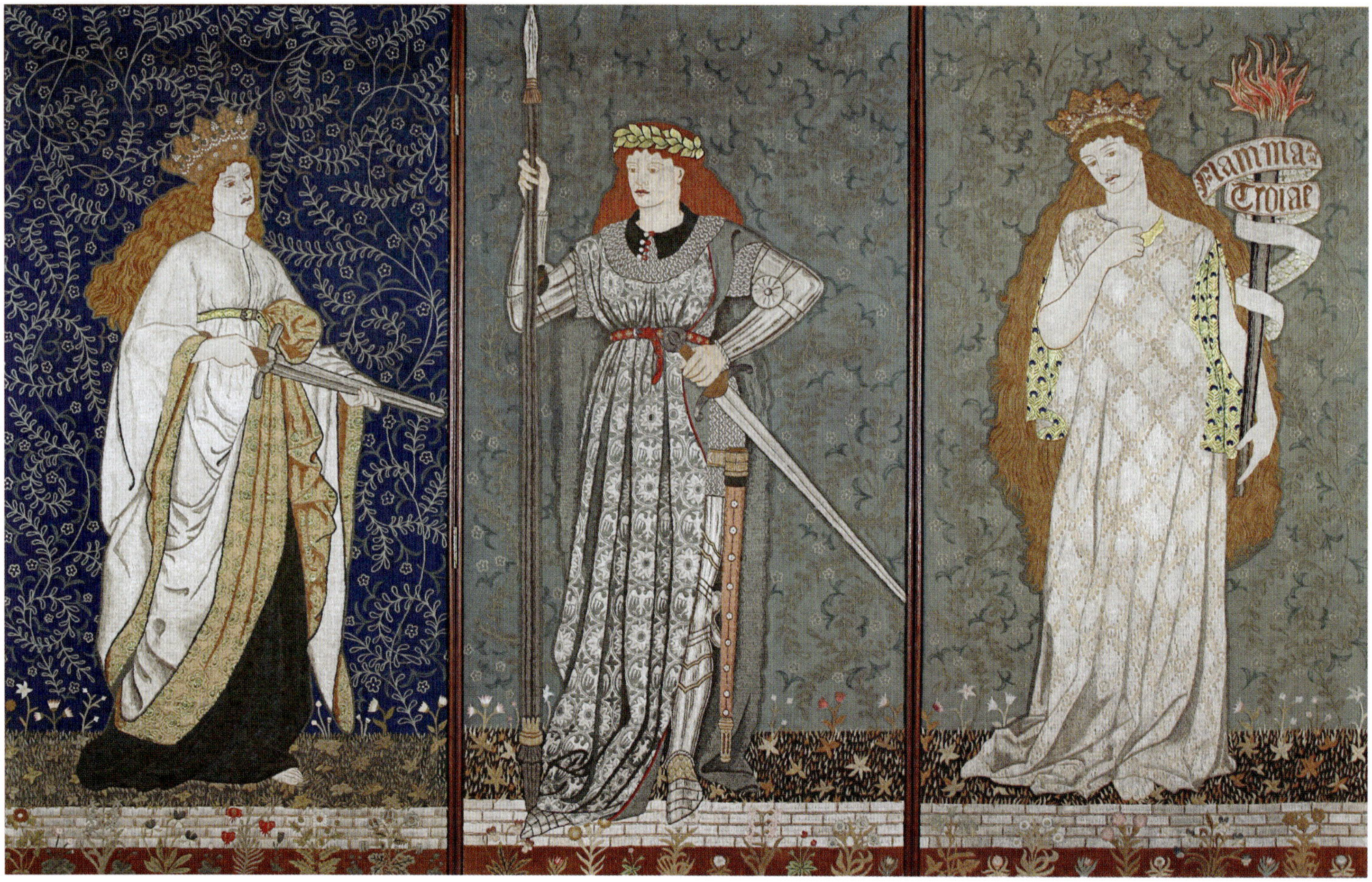

XII.4

Screen with embroidered panels depicting heroines

Designed by William Morris, *c.*1860
Worked by Bessie Burden, made into a screen in 1889
Woollen and linen grounds embroidered with wools and silks in chain, long and short, brick and darning stitches with gold couched threads, 171.5 x 73.6 cm each panel
Castle Howard Collection (TX120)

These panels were part of an ambitious decorative scheme planned to hang around the dining-room walls at Red House. A notebook in the British Library includes preliminary sketches for the composition (Add. MS 45336). In his design Morris followed the concept of Chaucer's late fourteenth-century poem *The Legend of Good Women* but selected his own group of heroines. His subjects, chosen from classical, religious and medieval sources, reflected the house's overriding theme of love in its many forms.

Jane Morris recorded that the frieze consisted of 12 large figures 'with a tree between each two, flowers at the feet and a pattern all over the background'. Seven were completed. This screen depicts Lucretia (with a sword), Hippolyte (with sword and lance) and Helen of Troy (with a flaming torch). Three hangings showing St Catherine, Penelope and Guenevere are on display at Kelmscott Manor and Aphrodite was acquired by the National Trust in 2007 (fig.144). Various designs survive for the project (VI.18–21), however, not all 12 subjects have been identified.

It was intended that the panels would be worked in a traditional late medieval technique with each figure embroidered in wool and silk onto a linen ground, then cut out and applied to woollen serge. The scheme was never finished and when the Morris family moved out of Red House in 1865 the panels were dispersed among the various embroiderers, who included Jane Morris, Bessie Burden and Georgiana Burne-Jones.

Bessie Burden exhibited three panels at the 1888 Arts and Crafts Exhibition, catalogued as Penelope, Hippolyte and Helen. On 8 February 1889 George Howard sent a cheque for £80 'in payment for the three needlework figures which you have sent to Messrs Morris to be framed'.

XII.5

Unfinished panel depicting a pomegranate tree (detail)

Designed by William Morris, *c.*1860
Linen ground embroidered with wools in brick, stem, satin, long and short and couching stitches, 160.5 x 69.8 cm
V&A (T.124–1985)

This embroidery was intended to form part of the Red House dining-room scheme. Two other embroidered trees related to the project survive. An appliquéd lemon tree, the trunk entwined with honeysuckle, was later made into a curtain with the figure of St Catherine (fig.206) and is now at Kelmscott Manor. For many years it was in the Burne-Jones household and can be seen in Thomas Matthews Rooke's watercolour of the dining room at The Grange, Fulham (fig.162).

An embroidered orange tree worked in silks, and now at Bateman's, Rudyard Kipling's house in Sussex, is clearly related to Morris's original design for the Red House scheme. The similarity between these stylized trees and images in early Coptic tapestry weaving is proof of Morris's early interest in historic textiles.

XII.6

Phyllis

Designed by William Morris or Edward Burne-Jones, *c.*1860–3
Probably worked by Georgiana Burne-Jones
Linen ground, partially painted, embroidered with wools in brick, stem and long and short stitches, 129 x 81.2 cm
V&A (T.122–1985)

It has been suggested that this unfinished panel belonged to a second series of heroines, designed in 1863 by Burne-Jones to be embroidered for John Ruskin by the girls of Winnington Hall School in Cheshire. The figure is similar to the existing sketch plan for the Winnington scheme and identical to the Burne-Jones stained-glass design for the Phyllis subject, both of which are in Birmingham Museum and Art Gallery.

However, the style, dimensions and technique of the embroidery strongly compare with the earlier Red House scheme, albeit not of such good workmanship as examples worked by Jane Morris and Bessie Burden. Furthermore, Georgiana Burne-Jones in the *Memorials*, the only source of information for the Winnington scheme apart from the sketch plan, and the person in charge of the work, states that only 'one ... (Hypsipyle) was actually begun'.

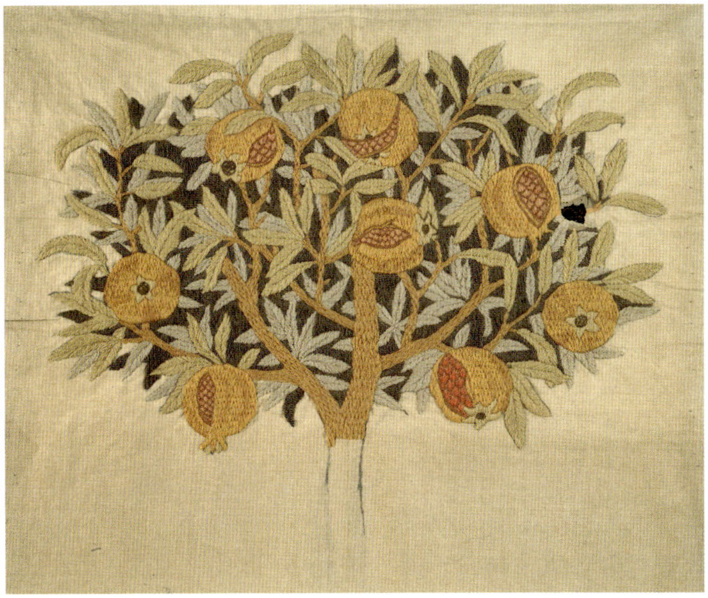
XII.5

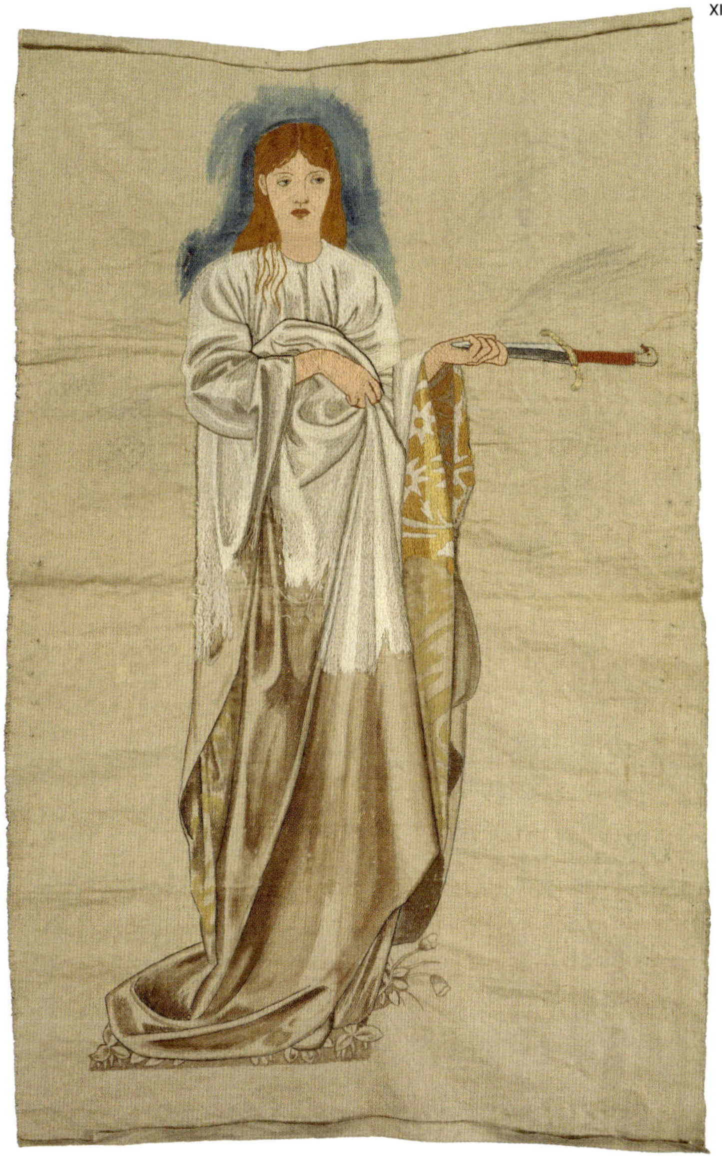
XII.6

XII.8

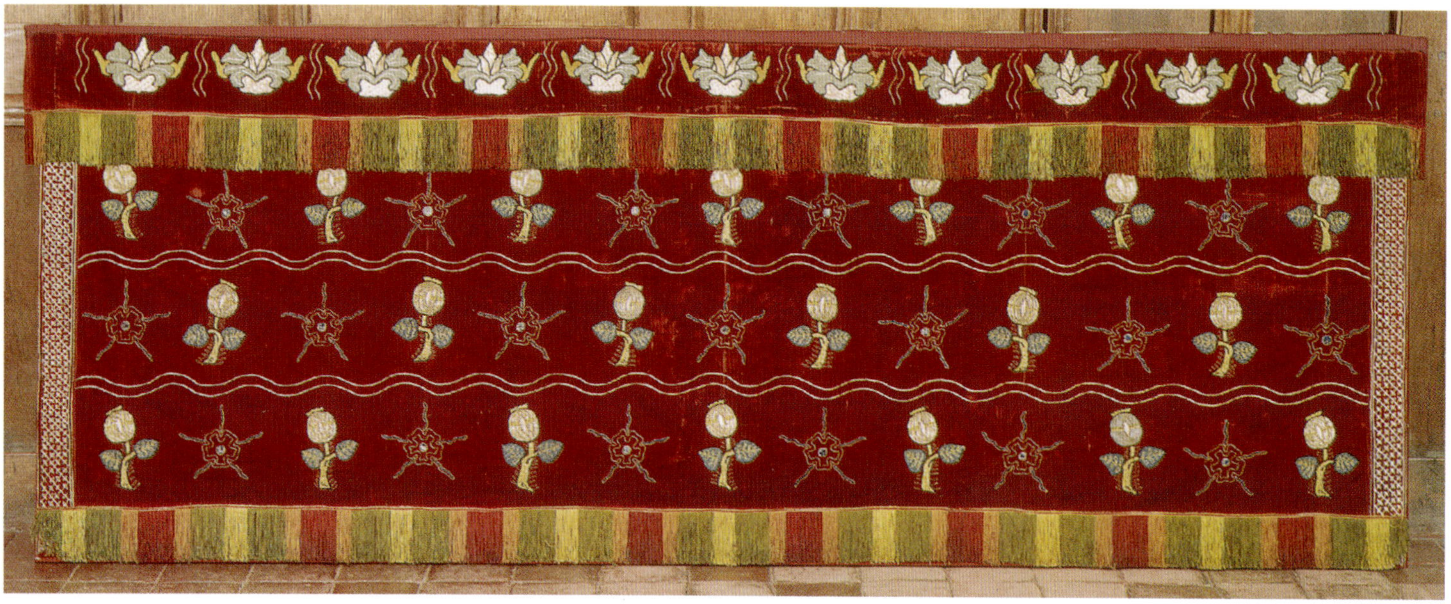

XII.7

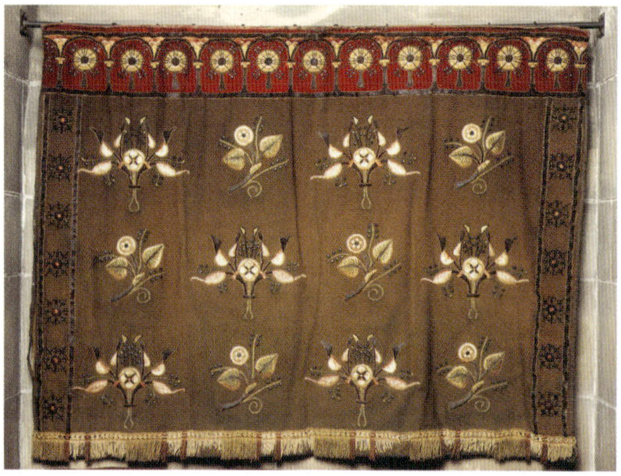

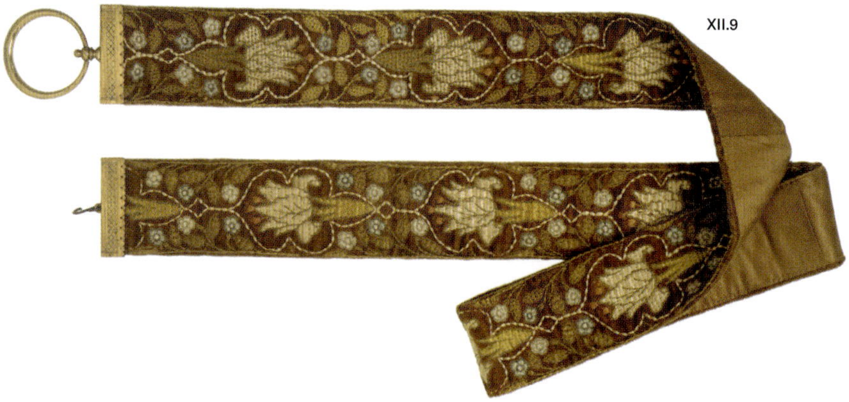

XII.9

XII.7
Sedilia hanging
Designed by George Edmund Street
Worked by Miss Hutchinson of Checkley, Staffordshire, *c*.1859–61
Felted woollen ground embroidered with silks and applied motifs, gilt metal thread and spangles in long and short, stem and couching stitches, 84 x 111 cm
Vicar and Church Wardens of the Church of St John, Hollington

The hanging shows 'powdered' floral motifs influenced by late fifteenth-century English work, known as *opus anglicanum*, a style much favoured by the architect. Having seen such designs in Street's office, some of Morris's earliest patterns take this form, including the dresser cover in his painting *La Belle Iseult* (VI.12) and decorative detailing on the *St George* cabinet (IX.14). A similar dispersed design was used on the firm's earliest church embroidery, a frontal made for St Martin-on-the-Hill, Scarborough (XII.8). From 1854 many of Street's designs were carried out by the Ladies Ecclesiastical Embroidery Society set up by his sister, Mary Ann Street, and Agnes Blencowe, the latter's work was well known to and admired by Webb.

XII.8
Altar frontal
Designed by William Morris
Embroidered by Morris, Marshall, Faulkner & Co., 1862
Velvet ground laid and couched with silks and gold threads, 96.5 x 246.4 cm (super-frontal 25.4 cm high)
Vicar and Church Wardens of the Parish of St Martin-on-the-Hill, Scarborough

Part of the Bodley commission to decorate St Martin's Church, consecrated in July 1863. Although Webb was heavily involved in the project there is no mention of the frontal in his account book with the firm, which lists similar work in the same period (for example, drawings for 'Clapham Altar cloth'). Morris was most likely responsible for the design, which is strongly influenced by both English late medieval embroideries and Street's commercial church textiles. The repeating pomegranate motif was modelled on an illustration in Charles Hartshorne's *English Medieval Embroidery* (1848). The frontal appears listed under 'Stock' in the end-of-year statement recorded on 11 February 1863. It is likely that it was finished specifically to be exhibited in the 1862 International Exhibition. By 20 May 1863 the debt of £28 had increased to £42 9*s*. for 'Scarborough altar cloth and hangings'.

XII.9
Bell pull
Designed by William Morris or, possibly, Ford Madox Brown, *c*.1865
Manufactured by Morris, Marshall, Faulkner & Co., *c*.1870s
Velvet embroidered with silks in stem, satin stitches and couching, 257.3 x 10.7 cm
V&A (T.5–1919)

An early example of a practical domestic object. In an article in *The Artist* for May 1898, a list of Madox Brown's work for the firm includes 'embroideries, stamped velvets ... and silk'. His household account book mentions 'two sets of worsted bell ropes' designed for the firm. No examples have been positively identified. The donor of this bell pull, Annette Wormald, a friend of Jane Morris's, lived in Woodcote Hall, a house in Carshalton, Surrey. According to S. & S. Dunn's records, Morris & Co. undertook some work on the house in 1876. Another surviving version was bought from the Oxford Street shop in the 1920s by Etta May Gubbins.

XII.10
Bedcover
Thorbjörg Magnúsdóttir, Icelandic, late seventeenth century
Woollen ground embroidered with wools in cross-stitch and diagonal eye stitch, 172.7 x 134.6 cm
V&A (8–1884)

Morris recommended the acquisition of this hanging to the South Kensington Museum in 1884. It was part of a small group of textiles bought for £80 from Sigrídr, the wife of Eiríkr Magnússon, with whom he translated the Icelandic sagas. The Magnússons travelled with Morris on his first trip to Iceland in 1871 and their common interest in the country led to a long friendship. In 1882 Mrs Magnússon recruited Morris to her Mansion House Relief Committee set up to help relieve famine in her native land. The proceeds of the sale of these textiles were to be used for this purpose.

The hanging shows a traditional northern European composition based, Morris believed, on a thirteenth-century design illustrating 'the abiding influence of Byzantine Art in Iceland'. The subject is religious and the hanging is said to have hung formerly in a church. However, its original use was domestic, part of the inscription translating 'This coverlet is owned by Thorbjorg'. It has been identified as the work of Thorbjörg Magnúsdóttir (1667–1737), a noted Icelandic embroiderer.

XII.11
Fragment of embroidery
Cyclades Islands, Greece, eighteenth century
Linen embroidered with silks in satin, darning and herringbone stitches, 19 x 36.8 cm
V&A (T.121–1939)
Bequeathed by May Morris

This small embroidered band belonged to Morris and is likely to have come from the hem or sleeve of a garment, although it has also been suggested it was originally part of a bed valance from the island of Pholegandros. It may have been acquired at the same time as two faded pieces of Cretan embroidery brought back 'by the English Consul' that Morris sent to Thomas Wardle in April 1876 stating, 'Mrs Wardle will find some stitches in them worth looking at.' The patterns were also worth noting as 'there are strong marks of Italian influence in many of the designs I have seen.'

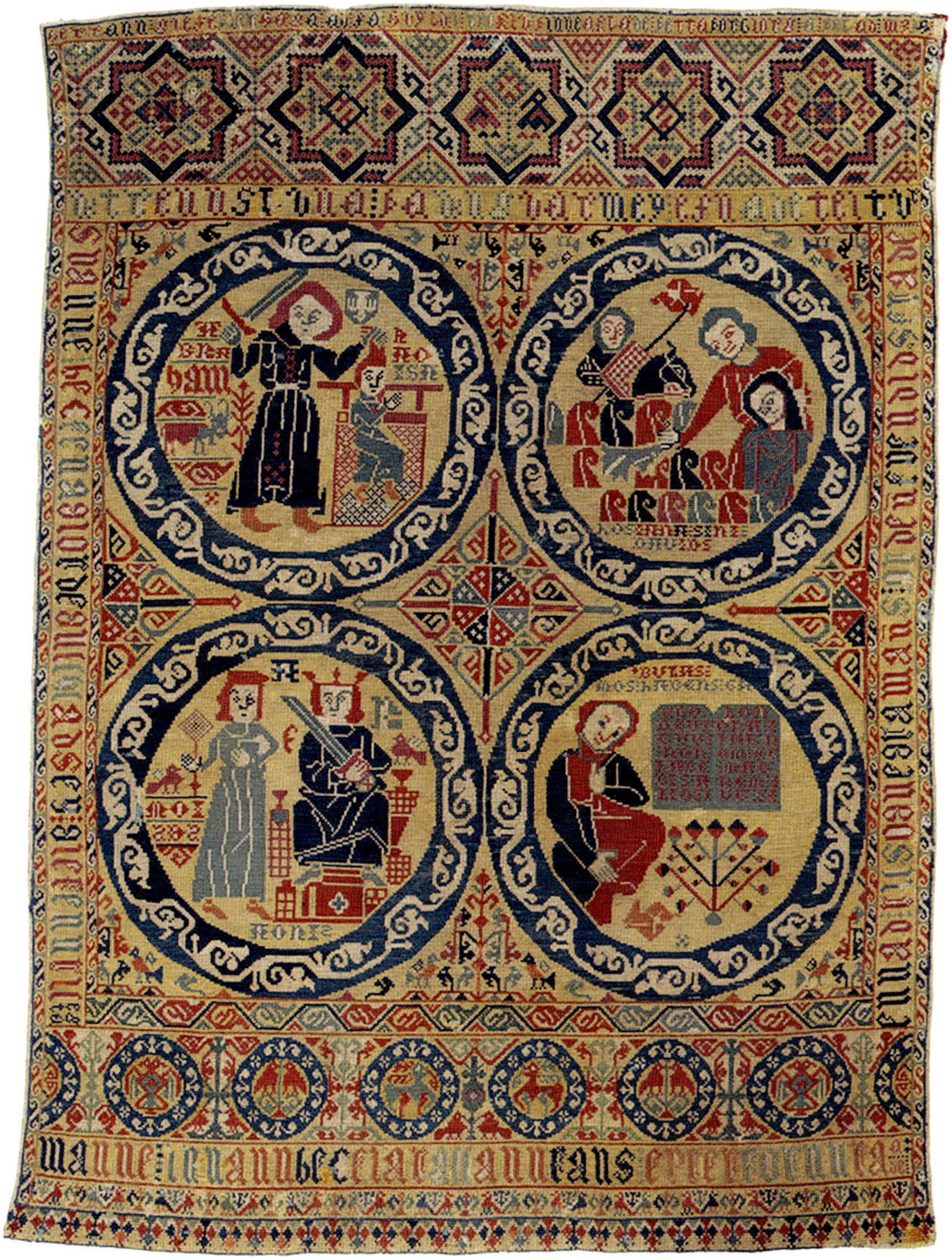
XII.10

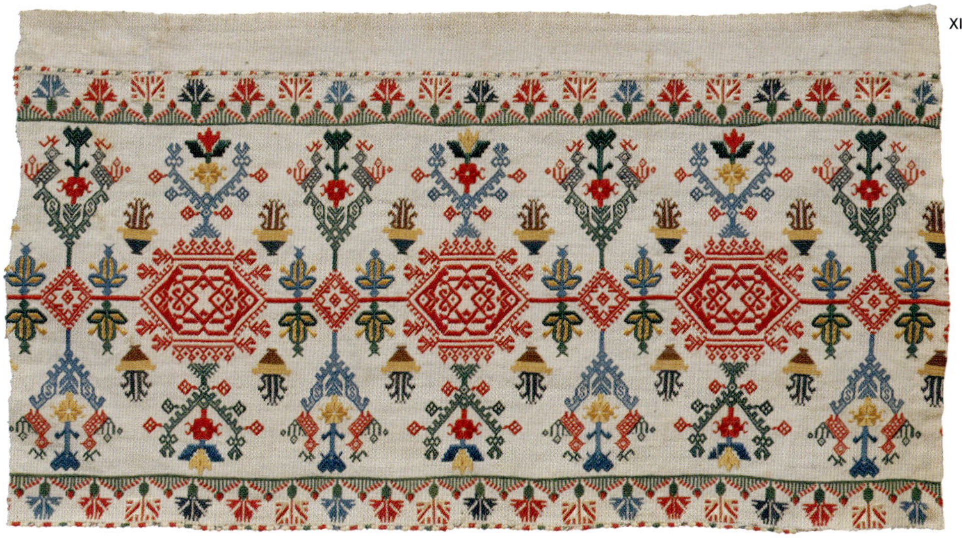
XII.11

XII.12

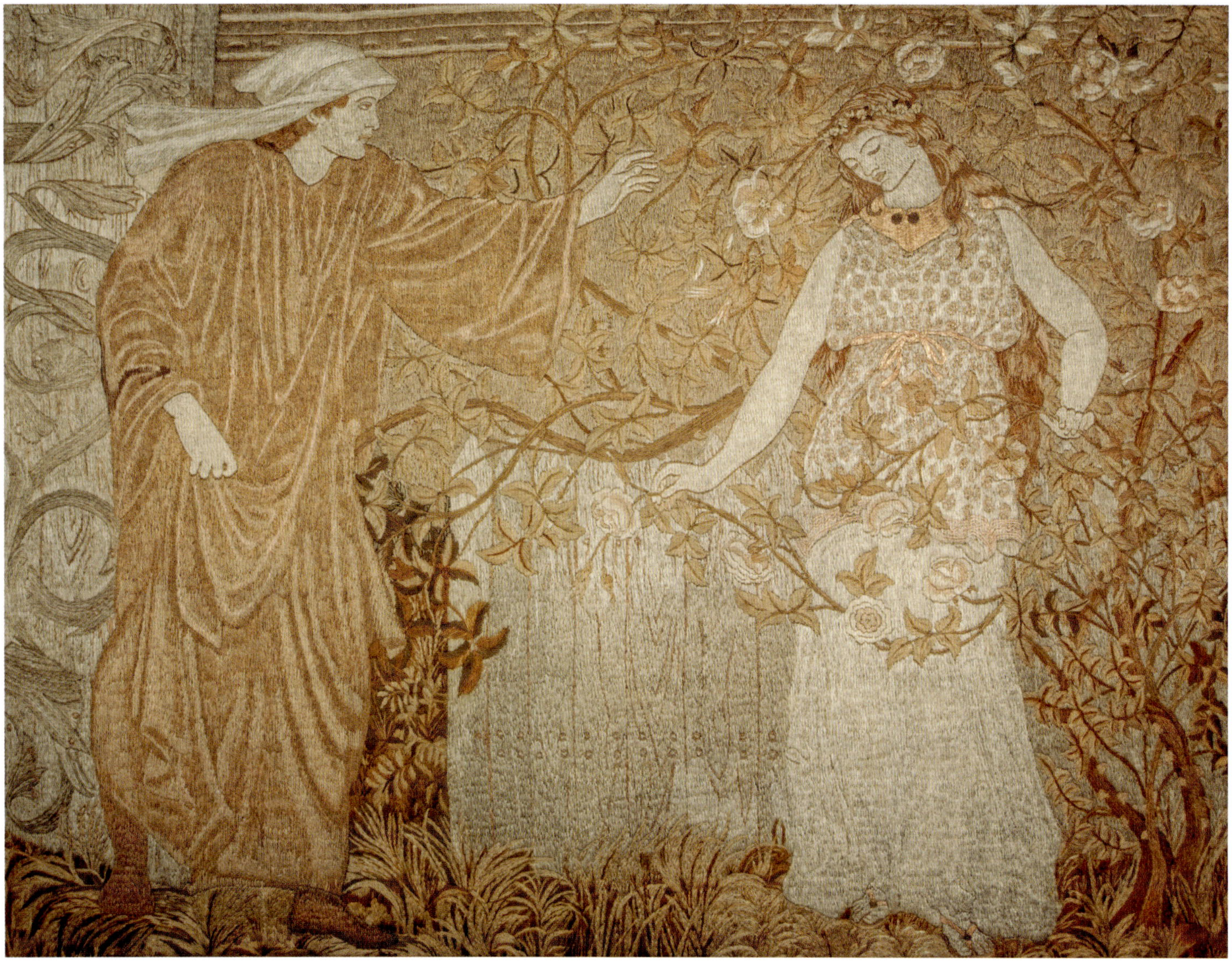

XII.12

Scene from *The Romance of the Rose* embroidered frieze

Designed by Edward Burne-Jones and William Morris, 1874–6

Worked by Margaret Bell and her daughters Florence and Ada, 1874–82

Linen embroidered with coloured silks, wools and couched gold thread in long and short, split, stem, satin and other stitches, 92.7 x 115.5 cm (this panel)

William Morris Gallery, London Borough of Waltham Forest (F140e)

This panel is from a series of five wall hangings made for the dining room of Rounton Grange, Northallerton, a house built by Webb for the northern industrialist Sir Isaac Lowthian Bell and his wife Margaret. They were the first of a number of collaborative embroidery designs with Burne-Jones supplying the general figurative composition and Morris adding decorative details.

The literary source for this scheme was *The Romaunt of the Rose*, a poem by Chaucer based on an early medieval French original. The design was devised in three sections, for the south, north and west walls of the room. Emblematic figures representing the Vices and Virtues hung opposite each other (on the south and north walls respectively) while on the west wall, between them, the Pilgrim was led by Love through a thicket of briar roses. This panel, *The Pilgrim at the Heart of the Rose*, depicts the climax of the tale. Its original location within the dining room scheme is unclear from the surviving evidence. The subject was later adapted for tapestries worked at Merton Abbey in the 1890s.

The frieze featured early in plans for the furnishing of the house and a note in Webb's account book for 1873 mentions 'Arrangement for Mr Bell's Tapestry ... Not charged'. An 1874 entry in Burne-Jones's accounts lists £40 for '1st panel of the Romance of the Rose for tapestry'. Four further entries from November 1874 until 1876 give a total cost of £340 for designs. Whether the firm made additional charges for transcribing Burne-Jones's designs into working drawings is not recorded. A letter from Burne-Jones to Bessie Burden (Huntington Library) urging her to hurry George Wardle with some drawings for the project suggests this process occasionally held up work.

Margaret Bell and her daughters Florence and Ada were very experienced and accomplished embroiderers (see XII.17 and XII.19). They took eight years to complete this frieze. Morris admired their efforts and must have mentioned the project to his mother, Emma. She expressed a desire to see part of the completed work when it was in London. In a letter of 13 July 1877 he welcomes a visit 'but I am afraid that Mrs Bell's work will be gone in two or three days.' Two working drawings are in the V&A (E.63, 64–1940).

XII.13

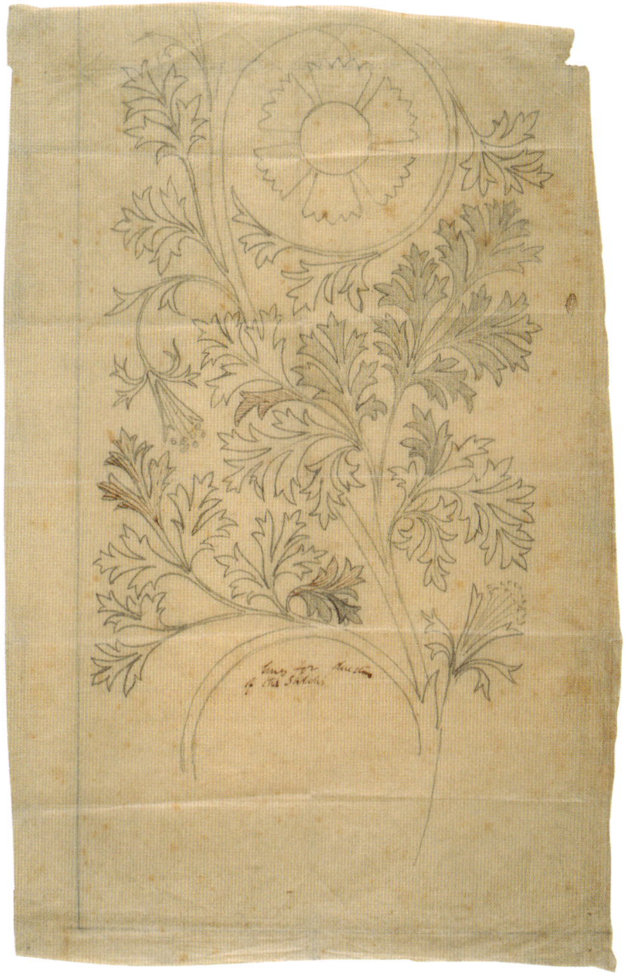

XII.14

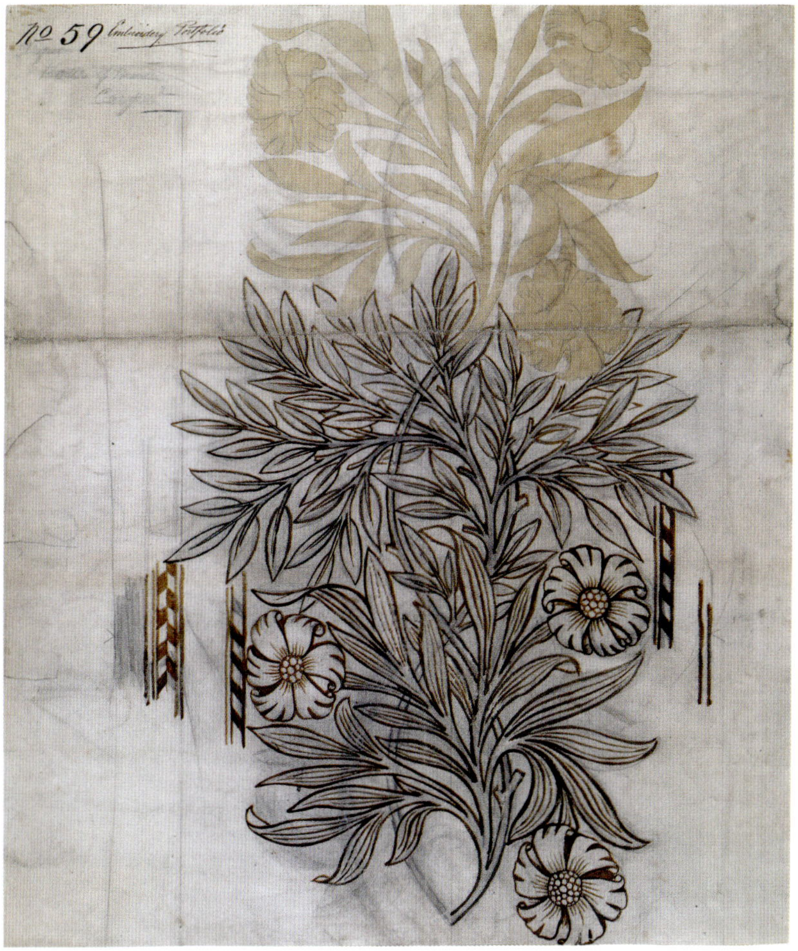

XII.13
Design for embroidery
William Morris, *c.*1865–70
Pencil and ink, 36.2 x 23.5 cm
The Huntington Library, Art Museum and Botanical Gardens (2000.5.91)

This drawing probably dates from the early period of the firm, when Morris personally instructed the embroiderers. The paper has been folded to fit an envelope so is likely to have been sent to one of the firm's freelance workers. Inscribed 'lines for direction of the stitches', Morris's instructions are interesting for two reasons. The lines suggested conventionally emphasize the growth of the plant by following the veins of the leaves but also show a sophisticated laying of stitches across leaves, a much more difficult result to achieve. A border may be suggested as the design is intended to repeat, but no sideways matching has been attempted.

The sunflower was a favourite early Morris motif, as it was for many contemporary designers. It can be seen in other 1860s work, including the inside of the *St George* cabinet (fig.229) and an embroidered hanging made for Red House and now at Kelmscott Manor. It was also the subject of a later embroidery worked by Catherine Holiday around 1876 (XII.16).

XII.14
Embroidery design
William Morris, *c.*1875
Pencil, pen and ink and watercolour, 71.7 x 67.3 cm
V&A (E.41–1940)
Bequeathed by May Morris

Similar to *Marigold*, registered in April 1875 (XII.38), this is one of a small series of designs made for the Royal School of Needlework. In December 1872, the year of the School's foundation, it approached the Morris firm offering embroidery services, but this was refused. In March 1875 the School decided to collaborate with established artists and in July Morris met with Madeline Wyndham, a founder member, and agreed to supply designs.

Morris's sister-in-law, Bessie Burden, taught at the School soon after its inception and, following an acrimonious break, returned in 1875 on the advice of Madeline Wyndham who believed she was the only person skilful enough to supervise the designs recently commissioned from Burne-Jones and Morris. Burden organized the School's highly influential stand at the Philadelphia Centennial Exhibition of 1876 on which some Morris embroideries featured including the *Peacock and Vine* dado frieze (fig.210).

A fuller repeating version of this popular design, described as 'Design for a Sofa-Back Cover', is illustrated in Letitia Higgin's *Handbook of Embroidery* (1880). Linen chair-back covers are listed in the book as costing between 7*s*. 6*d*. and £1 1*s*. for 'prepared work and materials'.

XII.15

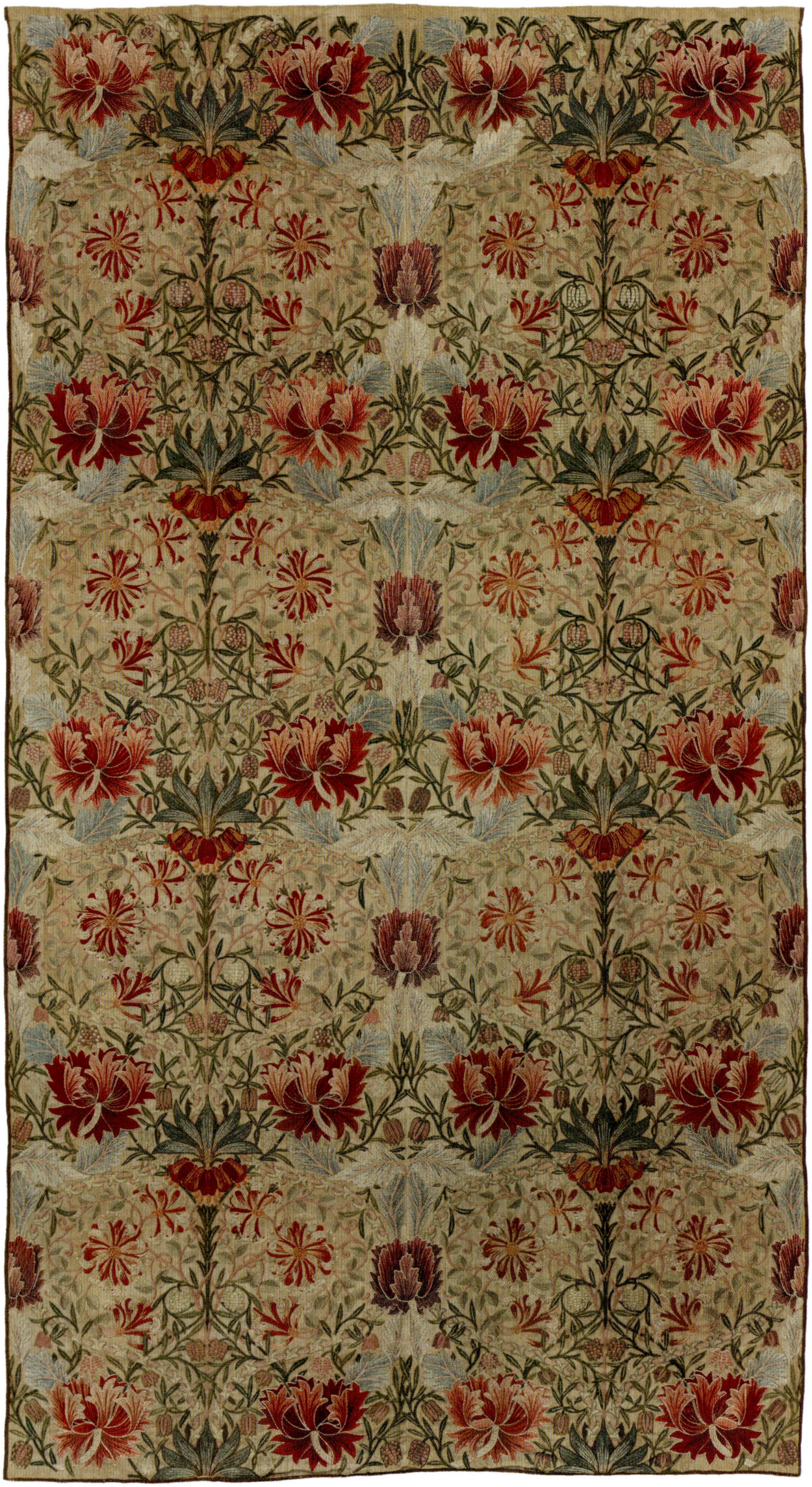

XII.15

***Honeysuckle* curtain or hanging**
Designed by William Morris, 1876
Worked by Jane and Jenny Morris
Linen embroidered with silks in long and short, stem and satin stitches, 266.7 x 144.7 cm

William Morris Gallery, London Borough of Waltham Forest (F434)

Registered by Morris & Co. as a printed textile in 1876, this pattern was also sold through the Royal School of Needlework (see *Handbook of Embroidery*, 1880). This hanging is one of the few existing embroideries known to have been worked by Jane and her daughter Jenny, both experienced and talented embroiderers. May described this as 'one of the finest of all Morris embroideries' (V&A correspondence). It was exhibited at the first Arts and Crafts Exhibition in 1888 and sent by May to the Louvre exhibition of *British and Irish Decorative Arts* in 1914. The panel was purchased from the Kelmscott Manor sale in 1939 and remained in the Hodson family until 2013.

XII.16

***Sunflower* coverlet or hanging**
Designed by William Morris, *c.*1876
Worked by Catherine Holiday
Linen embroidered with silks in various stitches including long and short, stem and satin, 190.5 x 166.4 cm

V&A (Circ.196–1961)

A rare identifiable Morris design by his favourite embroiderer, Catherine Holiday, made for the Earl of Southampton. A very experienced professional worker with a strong, individual style, she is now best known for work embroidered from designs by her artist husband, Henry. Holiday worked for Morris & Co. on a freelance basis. The firm supplied her with materials and kept ten per cent of the proceeds from any work sold through the shop. She was very ambitious for her work and wished to export to the United States before Morris was ready. He was also worried that she would price herself out of the market by overcharging. Sending a cheque for £60 on 6 December 1877 'on account of the coverlit [*sic*]', he explained 'I must ask you to wait to see what I can sell it for ... I am afraid we are hardly likely to get £120 for it ... this opens up the difficulty in a commercial way of the whole industry'.

A series of letters from Morris to Holiday concerning specific orders (Huntington Library) emphasizes not only his vast experience and knowledge of embroidery technique but also his great admiration for her work. Henry Holiday claimed that Morris thought her 'the only person he has ever met whose work is as good as the old.'

XII.16

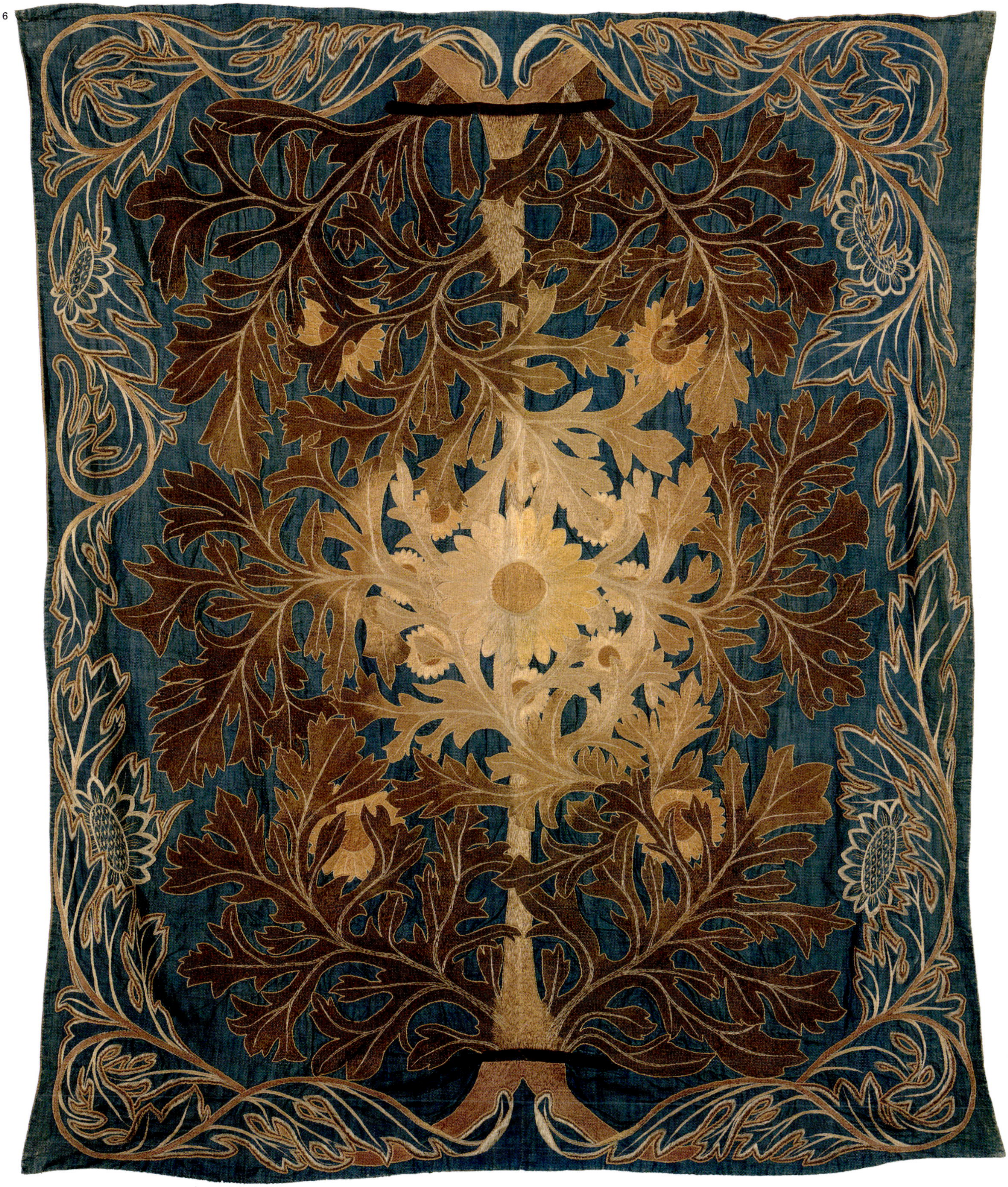

XII.17

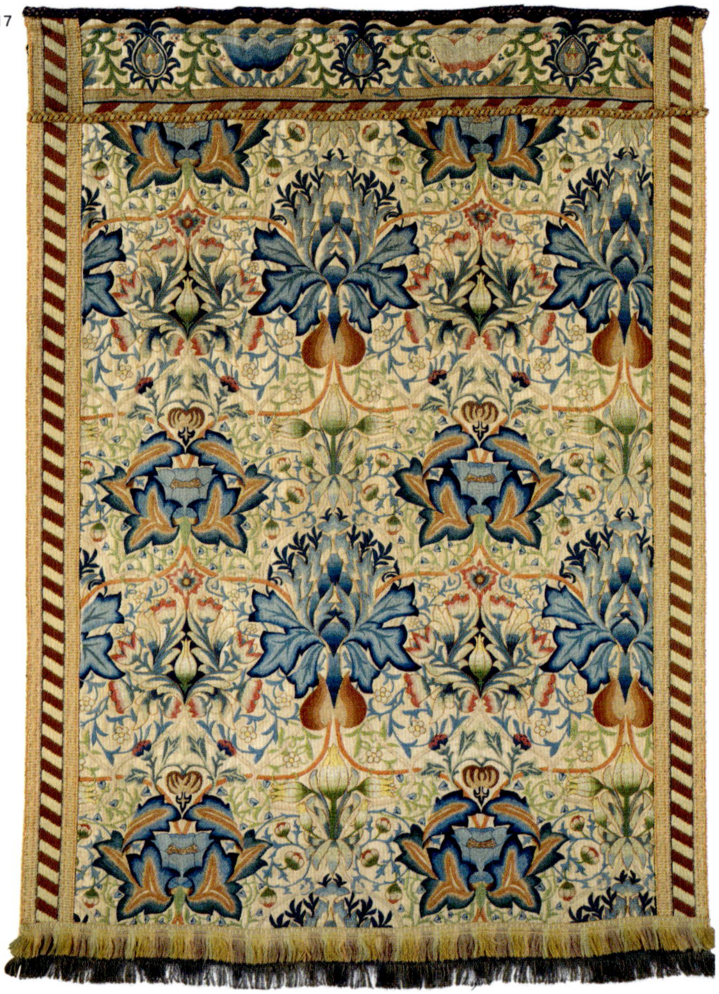

XII.18

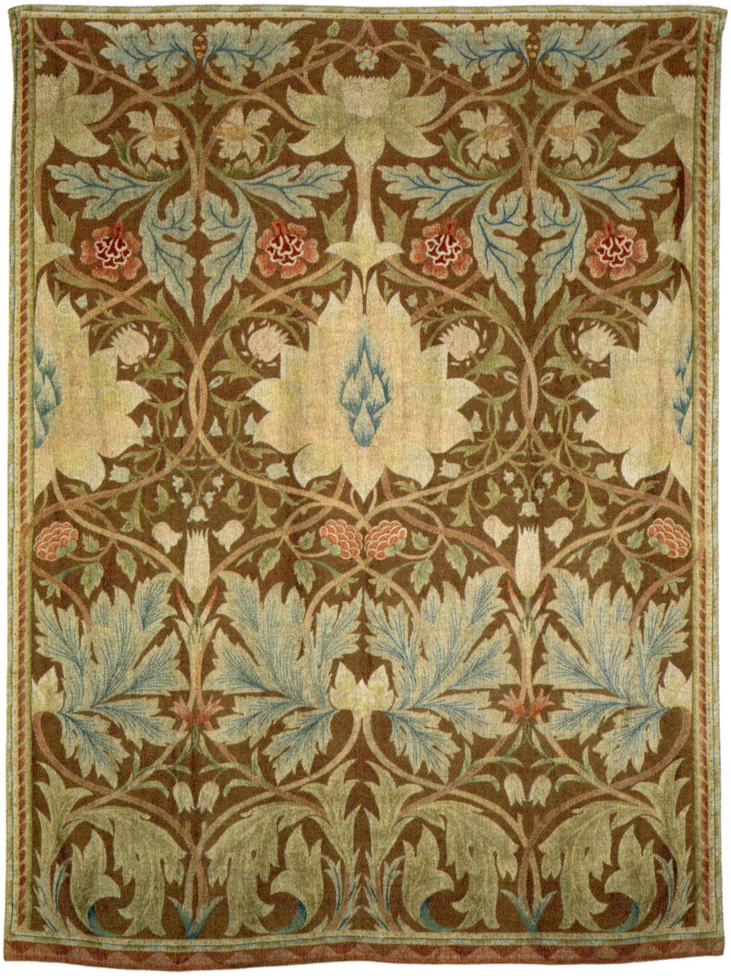

XII.17
***Artichoke* hanging**
Designed by William Morris, 1877
Worked by Ada Phoebe Godman, 1877–1900
Linen embroidered with wools in long and short, stem and satin stitches and French knots, 213 x 150 cm
V&A (T.166–1978)

Repeating patterns of large traditional motifs are characteristic of Morris's embroidery designs in the late 1870s and 1880s, indicating a preoccupation with Turkish, Middle Eastern and Italian woven silks and velvets, which he studied at the South Kensington Museum.

The design was delivered to Smeaton Manor, Northallerton in North Yorkshire on 31 August 1877. The client, Ada Godman, a daughter of Margaret and Isaac Lowthian Bell (see XII.12), spent many years embroidering the pattern onto a number of hangings for the drawing-room walls of her Philip Webb designed house. A drawing by Frank Bramley shows Ada still at work on the project in 1900. Other panels from the series are now in the Fitzwilliam Museum and the William Morris Gallery.

The V&A acquired the original design in 1898 before the Smeaton panels were finished. It did not remain exclusive to the client. Margaret Beale and her daughters worked a pair of hangings of the same pattern for their home, Standen, West Sussex.

XII.18
***Lotus* hanging**
Designed by William Morris, *c.*1875–80
Worked by Margaret Beale, *c.*1880s
Canvas embroidered with silks in various techniques including long and short, brick, satin and darning stitches, 241 x 188 cm
V&A (T.192–1953)
Given by Mr G. Beale from the estate of the late Mrs Kate Beale

Stylistically this repeating design dates from the 1870s, before Morris's large designs show quartered mirror images, a direct influence of his interest in hand-knotted carpet manufacture. Margaret Beale embroidered the hanging when living at 32 Holland Park, London, before the family built their country home, Standen, in the 1890s. It is likely that the Beales were introduced to the work of Morris & Co. by their near neighbours in Holland Park, the Ionides family.

The work is extremely accomplished, both in technique and rendition of the design, and it is possible that it was partially executed in the Morris & Co. workshops. A working drawing is in the V&A (E.32–1940).

XII.19

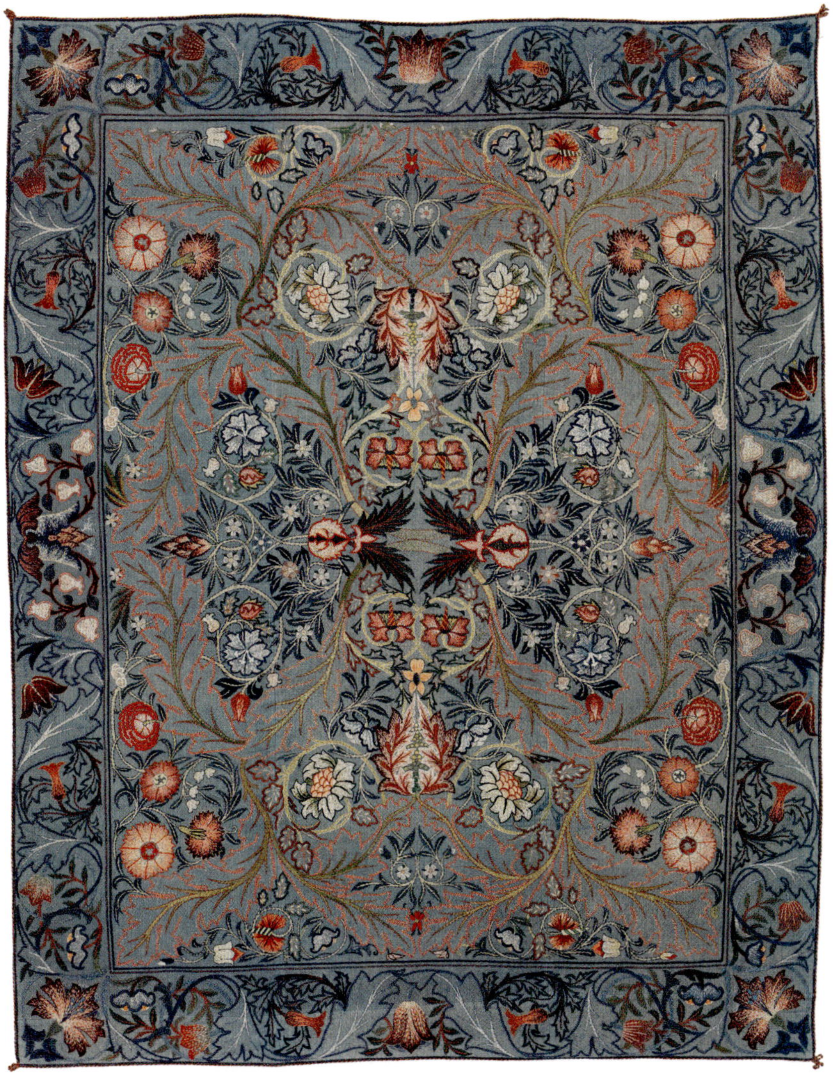

XII.20

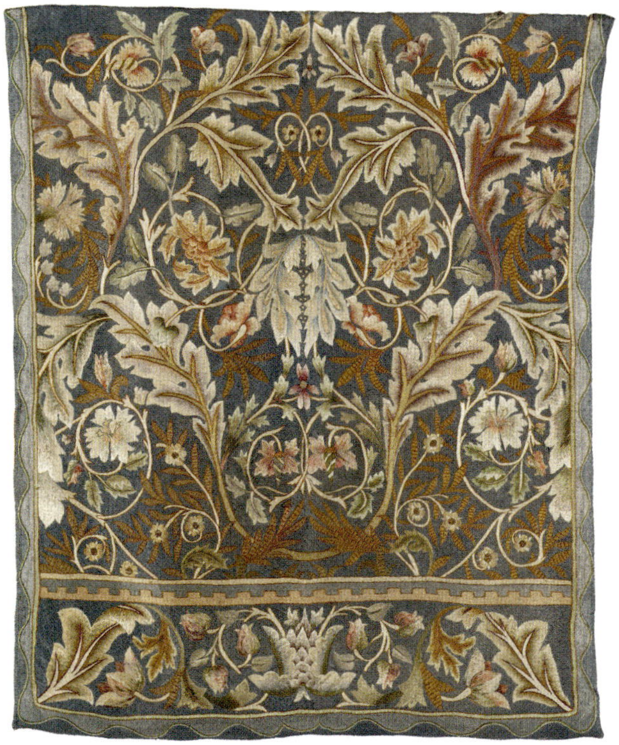

XII.20
***Acanthus* sample hanging**
Designed by William Morris, *c.*1880
Worked in the Morris & Co. workshops, *c.*1890–1900
Cotton embroidered with silks in vertical flame, long and short and satin stitches with laid and couched work and French knots, 129.5 x 108 cm
V&A (T.153–1979)

This shows a truncated version of the upper half of the *Acanthus* design (XII.19) with part of the original side border and other geometric alternatives. It was probably used in Morris & Co.'s Oxford Street shop to show to potential clients.

XII.19
***Acanthus* bedcover or hanging**
Designed by William Morris, *c.*1880
Worked by May Morris and others, *c.*1900–10
Felted woollen cloth embroidered with silks in stem, satin and darning stitches with laid and couched work and speckling, 248.8 x 200.6 cm
V&A (T.66–1939)
Bequeathed by May Morris

This quartered design reflects the form of hand-knotted carpets, a subject that preoccupied Morris from the late 1870s. It was one of Morris & Co.'s most popular embroidery compositions. May recorded 28 orders for *Acanthus* in the firm's Embroidery Day Book before 1896 (though some of these were for smaller panels and variations of the design). The V&A owns three examples including one, possibly the first produced, worked in wools on linen about 1880 by Margaret Bell and her daughters for Rounton Grange, Northallerton (Circ.524–1953). A fourth version is in the collection of the National Museum of Wales. The unusual background to this example suggests May embroidered it for her own use and it shows her great skills as a colourist and an interpreter of her father's designs. A working drawing is in the V&A (E.55–1940).

XII.21

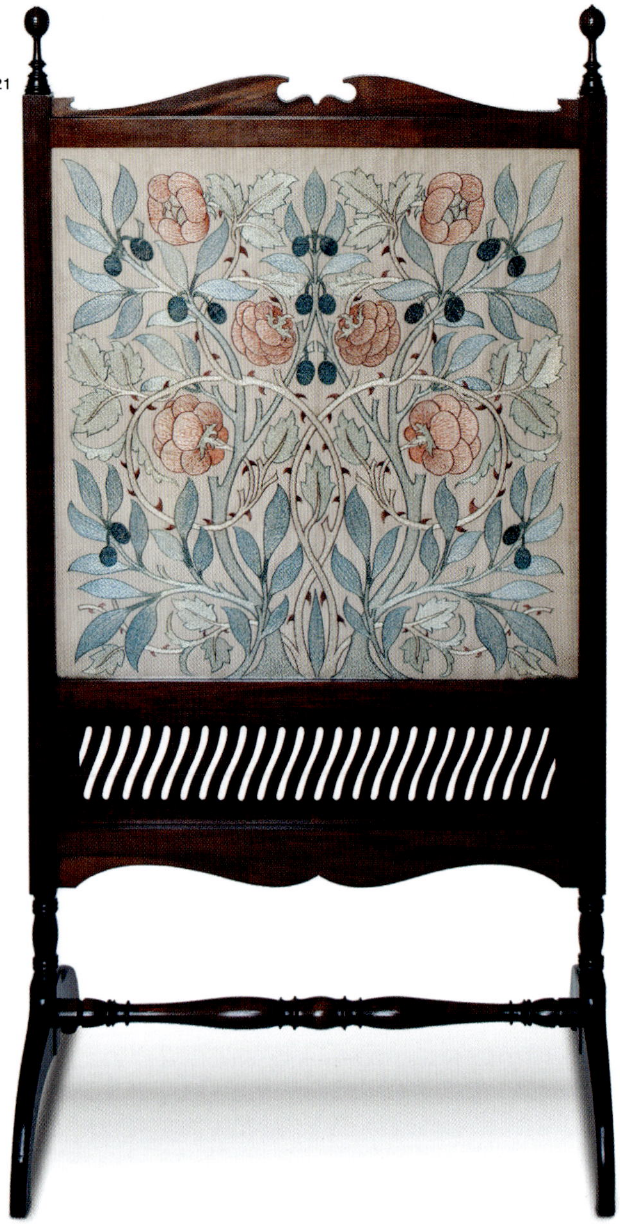

XII.22

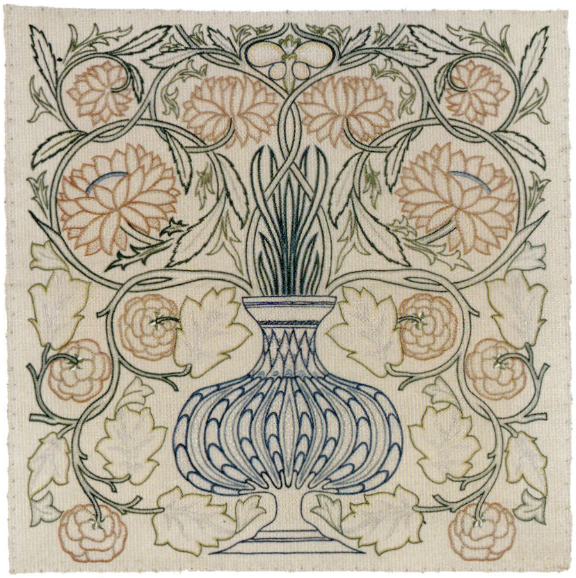

XII.23

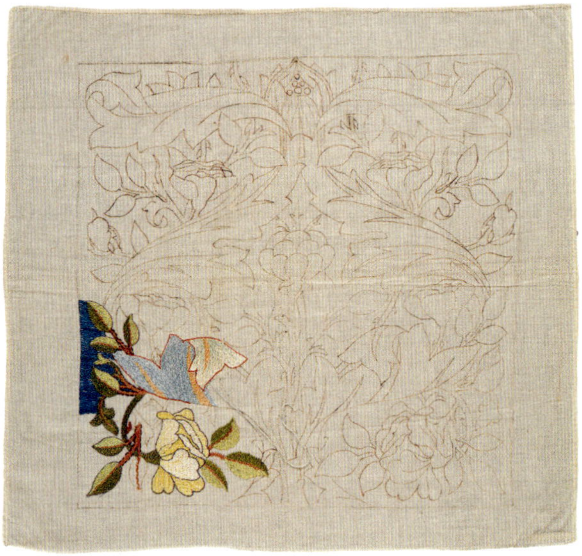

XII.21
***Olive and Rose* fire screen**
Designed by William Morris, *c.*1880
Probably worked in the Morris & Co. embroidery workshop, *c.*1890–1910
Coloured silks on silk embroidered in stem, satin and darning stitches, glazed mahogany frame 119 x 64 x 32 cm, embroidery 56.5 x 57.6 cm
Frame stamped: MORRIS & CO (4)49 OXFORD ST W 1221
Private collection

One of the most commercially popular Morris & Co. designs, this example retains its original mahogany fire screen. The embroidery is illustrated in the firm's catalogue *Embroidery Work* (*c.*1912), both as a panel and a fire screen where it is priced at £4 10*s*. This included 'stretching and mounting customers' own embroidery under glass'. A partially worked kit of this design is in the V&A (Circ.300–1960).

The design was listed 13 times between 1892 and 1896 in the firm's Embroidery Day Book, mostly as kits for the Oxford Street shop. A number of versions survive, produced both within the firm's workshop and at home, the latter of varying quality. They include examples worked in monochrome and outline stitches as well as ones in which the ground is completely covered in darning stitches.

XII.22
***Flowerpot* panel**
Designed by William Morris, *c.*1876
Worked by May Morris, *c.*1890s
Wool embroidered with silks in chain, satin and stem stitches and speckling, 54.6 x 54.6 cm
V&A (T.68–1939)
Bequeathed by May Morris

One of a number of small square designs produced for cushions or mounted fire screens. Many of these were sold from the late 1870s onwards and provided an inexpensive means of acquiring an example of Morris design. They could be purchased as completed embroideries or in kit form to be completed at home (see XII.21 and XII.23).

This design is likely to be one of Morris's last patterns for embroidery and is based on two square, Italian seventeenth-century lacis-work panels acquired by the South Kensington Museum in 1875. The pattern starts from the central lower edge (in this case the base of the pot) billowing upwards and outwards from this point to fill the upper space. A number of amateur and professional versions survive in a variety of techniques. This example and one at the William Morris Gallery are both thought to have been worked by May Morris and show different interpretations of the design. A working drawing is in the William Morris Gallery (A1061).

XII.23
***Rose Bush* embroidery kit**
Designed by May Morris, *c.*1890
Cotton ground with ink tracing, partially worked with silks in stem and darning stitches, 62.6 x 66 cm
V&A (Circ.301–1960)
Given by Miss Vere Roberts

This is an unworked kit bought from Morris & Co. around 1900. The firm sold embroideries in various levels of completion: as finished work, as kits with marked ground and silks and, more popularly, in this form with a small corner completed so that the recommended technique could be seen and followed at home. A design on paper is in the collection of the William Morris Society and a version inked onto glazed cotton ready for transferring on to a suitable ground for embroidery was bequeathed to the V&A by May Morris (AAD/190/6).

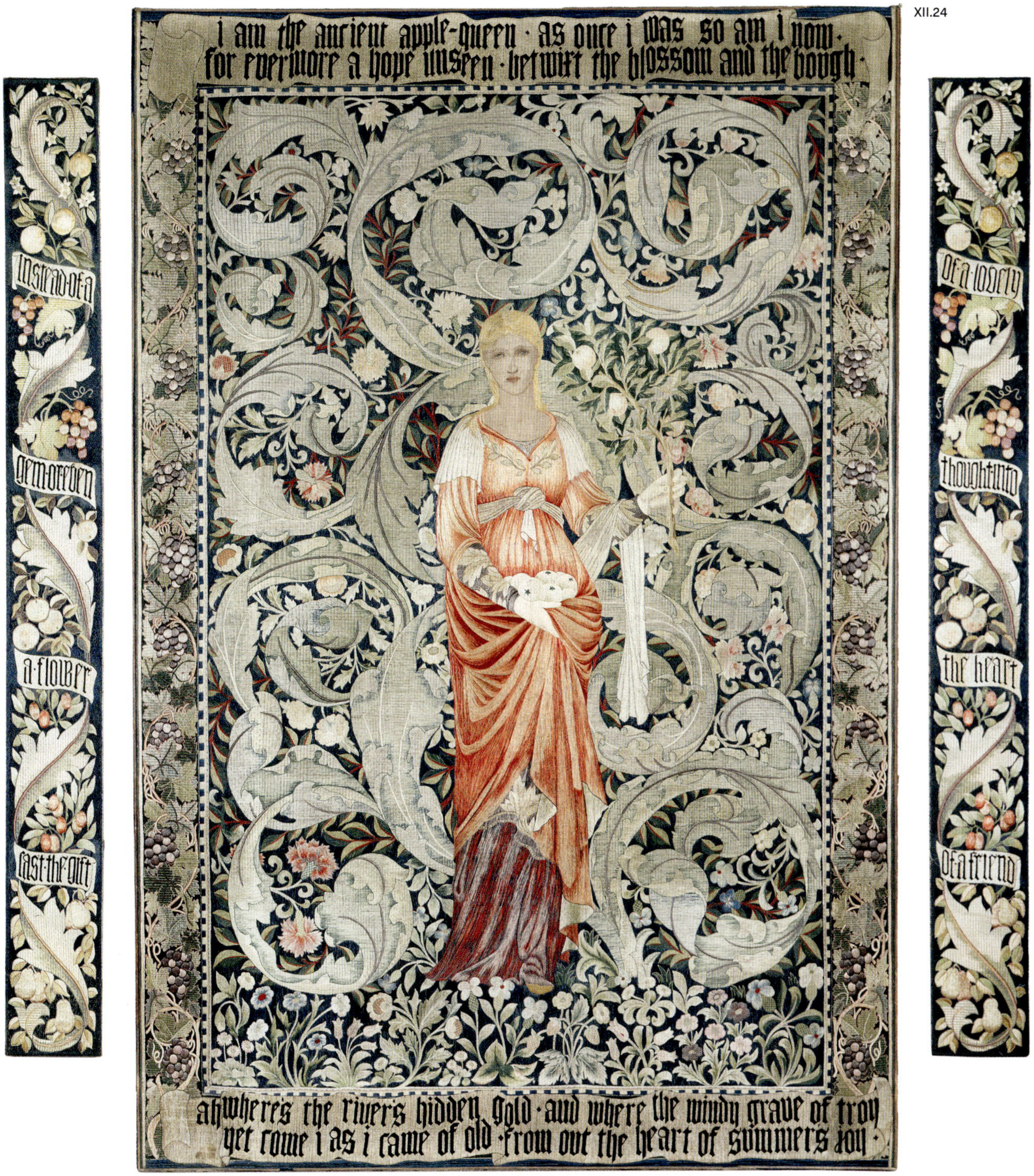

XII.24

XII.24
Pomona embroidered panel
Designed by Edward Burne-Jones and William Morris, *c.*1883–5
Embroidered at the Royal School of Needlework under the direction of May Morris and Miss Barker, 1891
Silks on linen in a variety of embroidery techniques including long and short stitches and laid and couched work, 321 x 281.5 cm
Private collection

Burne-Jones and Morris produced a group of designs for the Royal School of Needlework (RSN) depicting female figures representing allegorical subjects such as *Musica* and *Poesis*. These were available either in complex multi-coloured silk versions or worked in monochrome wools in outline. Burne-Jones designed the figures with Morris providing all other decorative details including background, foreground and borders.

Pomona is a copy of the Morris & Co. tapestry woven in 1885 now in The Whitworth, University of Manchester (see XII.114), depicting the Roman goddess of fruit and orchards, whose tale appears in Ovid's *Metamorphoses*. More than one embroidered version is known. This example is probably the first produced and has two additional decorative borders designed by Morris, intended to hang either side of the larger panel. The inscription is taken from a poem by Morris, which was later published in *Poems by the Way* (1891). A smaller version was embroidered by RSN-trained Lady Jane Cory in 1907 and forms part of a collection of embroideries she worked to the designs of Burne-Jones, Morris and others in Te Papa Tongarewa Museum, New Zealand. The RSN also produced embroidered versions of works in other media, including a vast copy of Burne-Jones's painting *The Mill*, now at Wightwick Manor.

XII.25

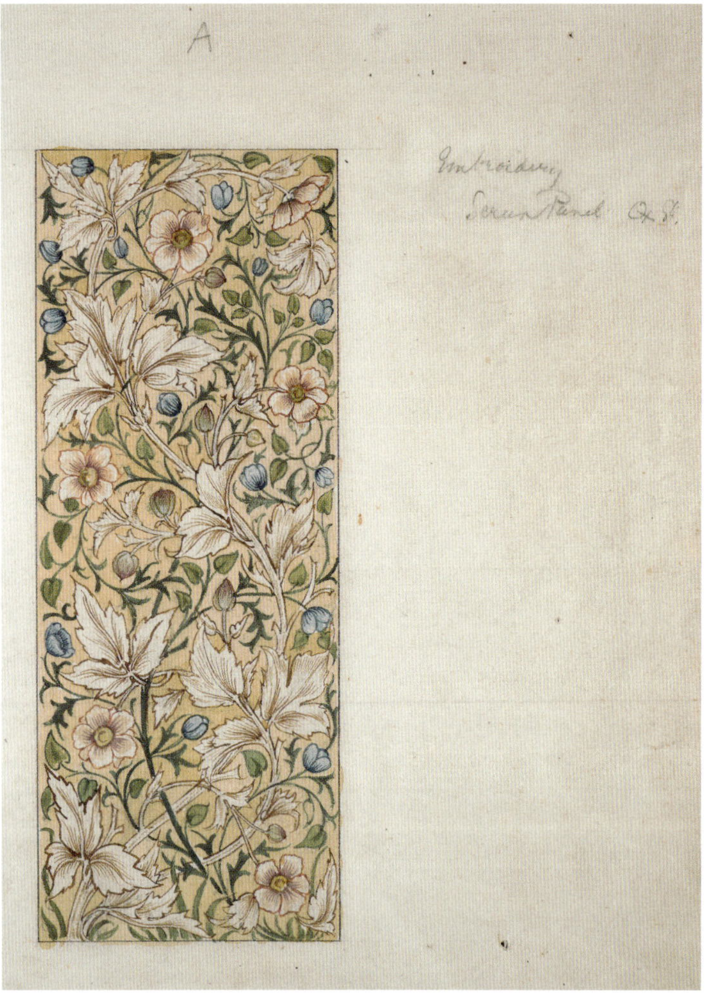

XII.25
Design for *Anemone* screen panel (detail)
John Henry Dearle, *c.*1885–90
Pencil, ink and watercolour, 31.8 x 34.3 cm
The Huntington Library, Art Museum and Botanical Gardens (2000.5.116)

Although May Morris designed most of Morris & Co.'s embroidery from the mid-1880s, John Henry Dearle also produced a number of single panels for wall hangings and screens, available as completed works or in kit form (XII.26–8).

May was responsible for overseeing the completion of all the firm's embroideries and her spirited interpretation of Dearle's designs has led to confusion over authorship. However, Dearle's style was quite different, often using designs centred on single meandering trees and leaves, whereas May Morris's work was more complex in detail.

Dearle's panel designs were very popular and occasionally the same subject reoccurs. On the reverse of this drawing is a *Peony* panel marked 'B' with May Morris's comment 'This is likely to be most suited as "A" is rather too like "Anemone" panel already worked'. Embroidered versions of both designs are illustrated in the firm's catalogue *Embroidery Work*. They also appear, identified as Dearle's work, in Lewis F. Day's 'A Disciple of William Morris' (*The Art Journal*, 1905), one of the few articles on the work of Morris's underrated assistant who became artistic director of Morris & Co. on Morris's death.

XII.26
Design for *Apple Tree*, *Vine*, *Pomegranate* and *Plum* panels
John Henry Dearle, *c.*1905
Pencil and wash, 52.4 x 78.6 cm
The Huntington Library, Art Museum and Botanical Gardens (2000.5.446)

These four designs are from a series based on fruit trees, a variation of the bird panels designed a few years earlier (XII.28). The paper is watermarked 'J WHATMAN 1905'. Many of these tree panels were sold separately as wall hangings rather than mounted into wooden screens. A set of six, worked between 1919 and 1923 by Helen, Lady Lucas-Tooth, now at the William Morris Gallery, includes the *Apple Tree*. However, in these later examples, the strongly characteristic Morris motif of a trailing acanthus leaf is omitted, an indication of how fashions had changed.

XII.26

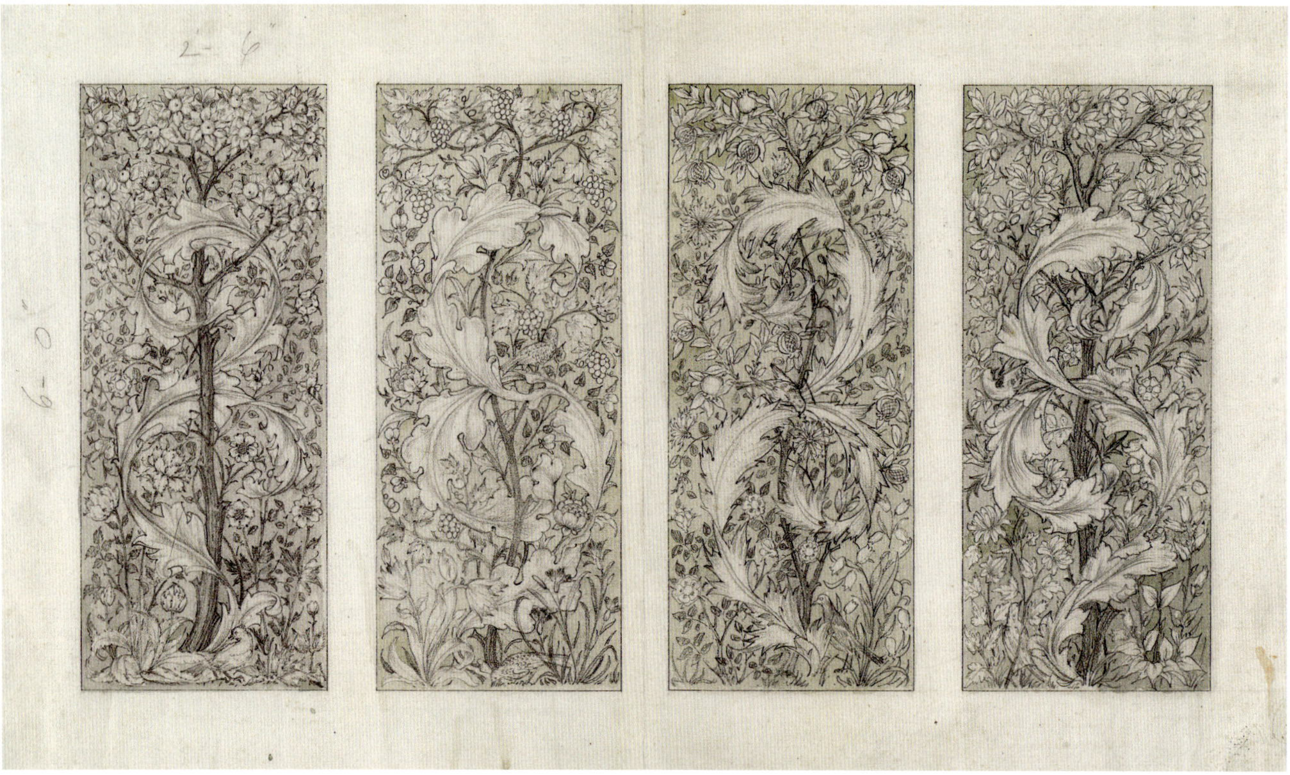

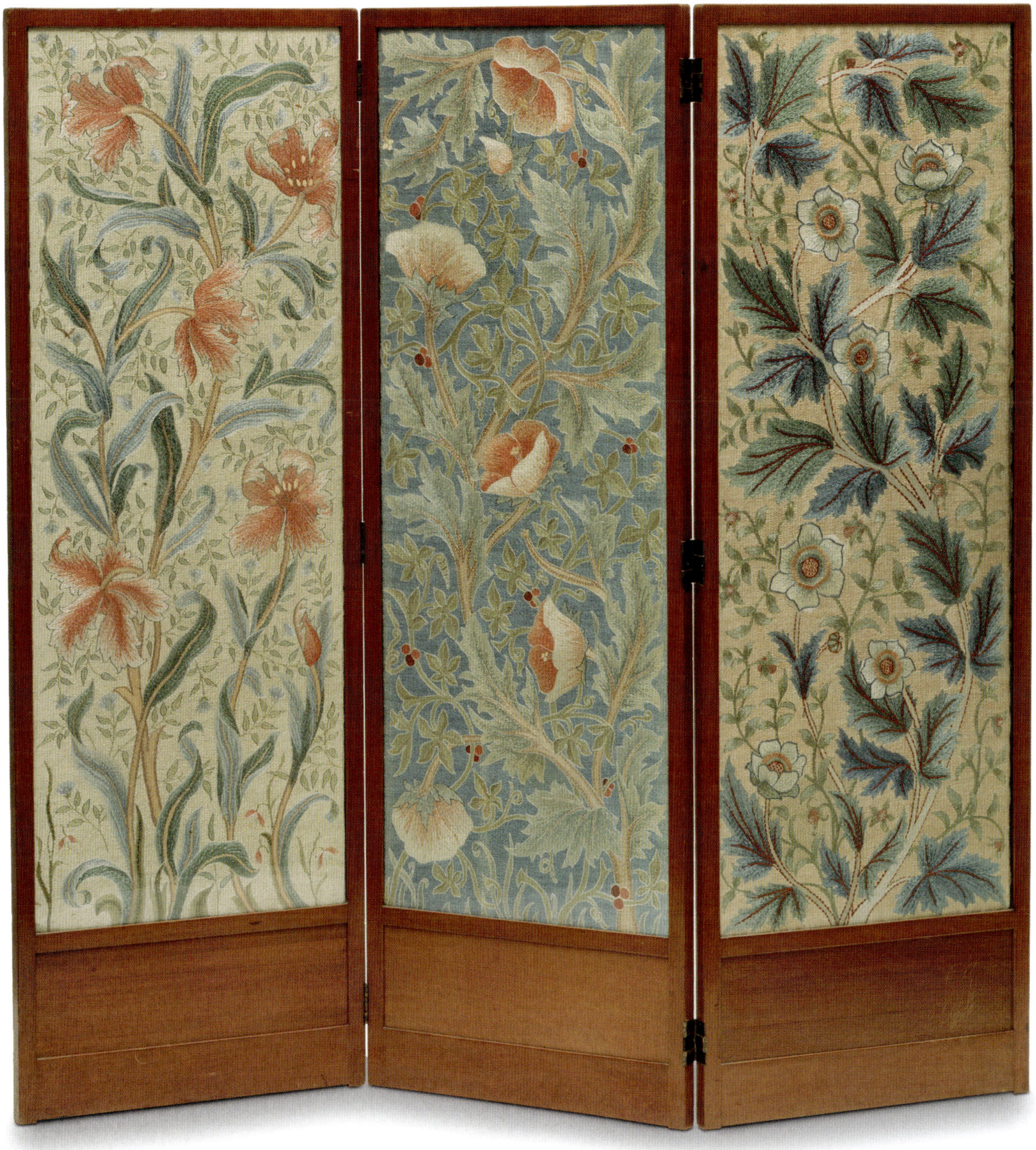

XII.27
Screen with *Parrot Tulip*, *Large Horned Poppy* and *Anemone* panels
Designed by John Henry Dearle, *c.*1885–90
Canvas embroidered with silks in darning, stem and satin stitches in glazed mahogany frame, 155 x 49.5 cm each panel
V&A (Circ.848–1956)
Given by Miss J. Constant

This shows three of Dearle's panel designs, including the first version of *Anemone* (see XII.25). An identical three-fold screen with reversible hinges and with panels of *Large Horned Poppy* and *Anemone* is illustrated in Morris & Co.'s *Embroidery Work*, where it is priced at £17 10*s*. Photographs of Morris & Co. interiors show that a number of clients, including the Sanderson, D'Arcy and Barr Smith families, all found these screens essential furnishing for the drawing room.

XII.28

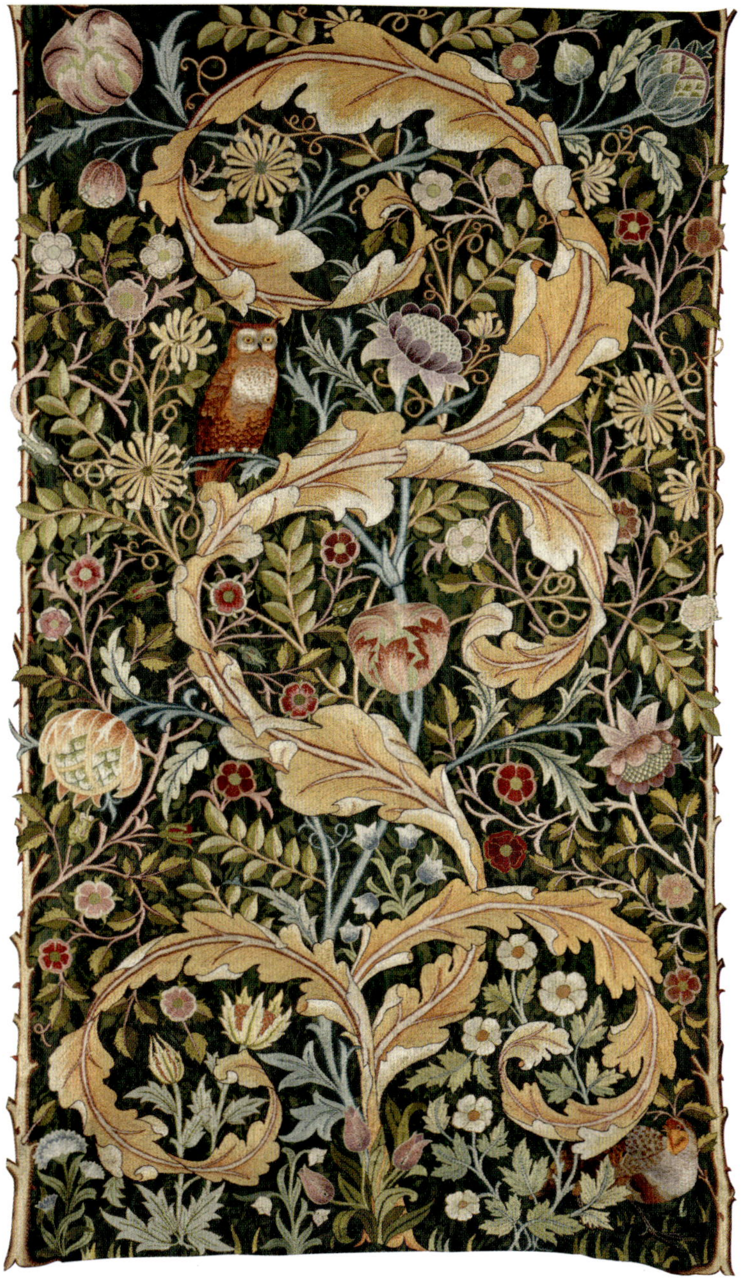

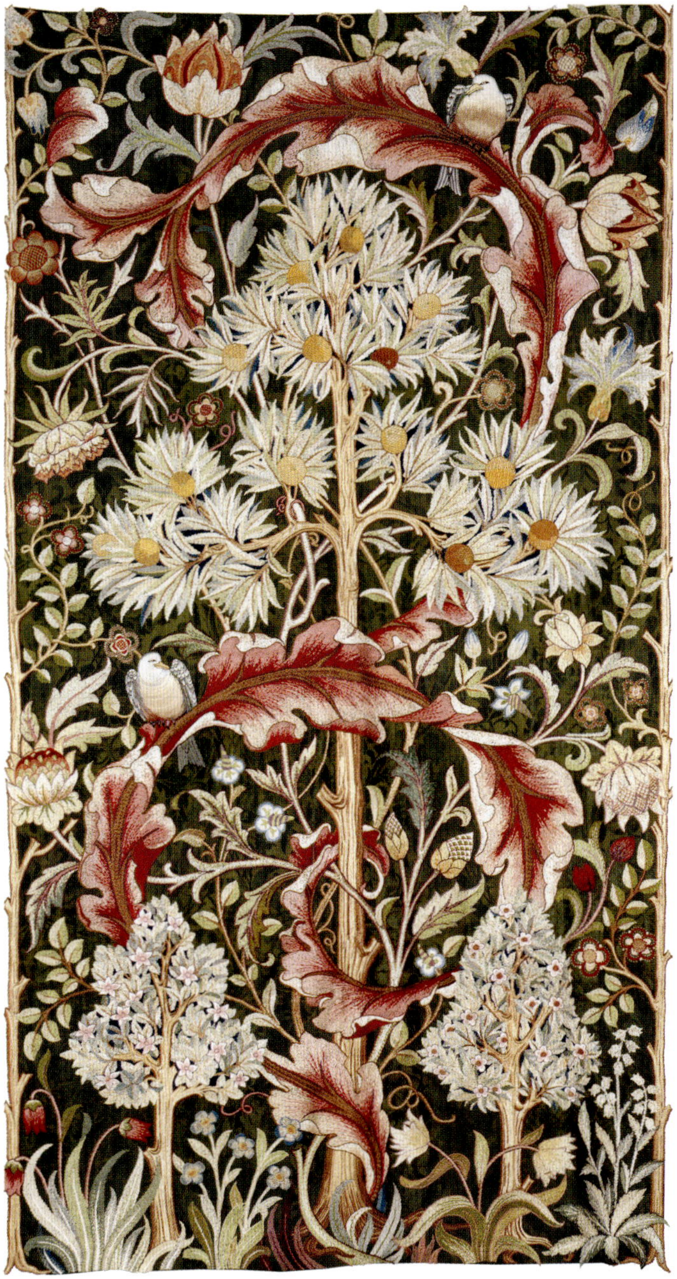

XII.28
***Owl* and *Pigeon* wall hangings or portières**
Designed by John Henry Dearle, *c.*1895
Worked by Frances Battye, from 1898
Oak silk damask embroidered in silks in satin, stem and darning stitches, 189 x 161 cm and 315 x 232 cm
V&A (T.369 & A–1982)
Given by Misses Audrey and Norah Battye

Bought from Morris & Co. as kits, these panels were very ambitious projects. The finely worked results show the high standard of amateur needlework among middle-class women at the time. Frances Battye was a good client. A panel incorporating the arms of the Battye family, drawn in the Morris workshops and worked by her, is now at the William Morris Gallery.

Dearle designed three bird hangings, all larger and more complex than the tree screen panels. *Owl* is a variation of the third design, *Partridge*, which was illustrated in *The Art Journal* in 1905. A number of versions survive. One, bought in 1904 by Mrs Cunliffe of Eaton Square, London, is now in a private collection in Canada, another, with an embroidered inscription was sold at Christie's in 1991.

XII.29

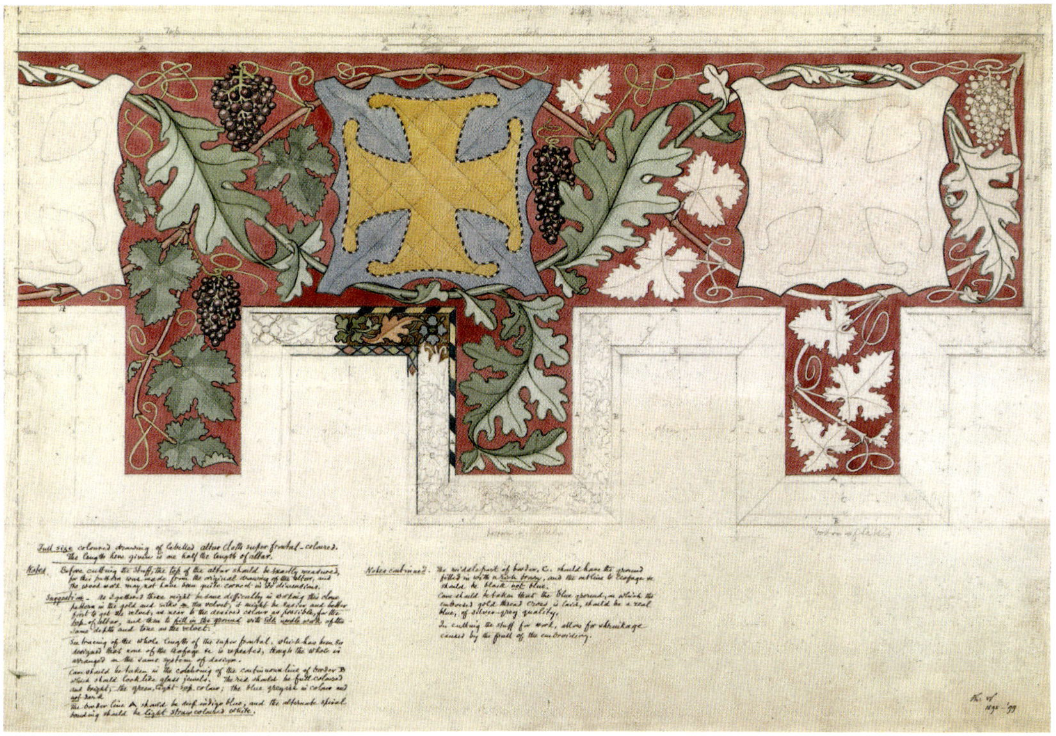

XII.30

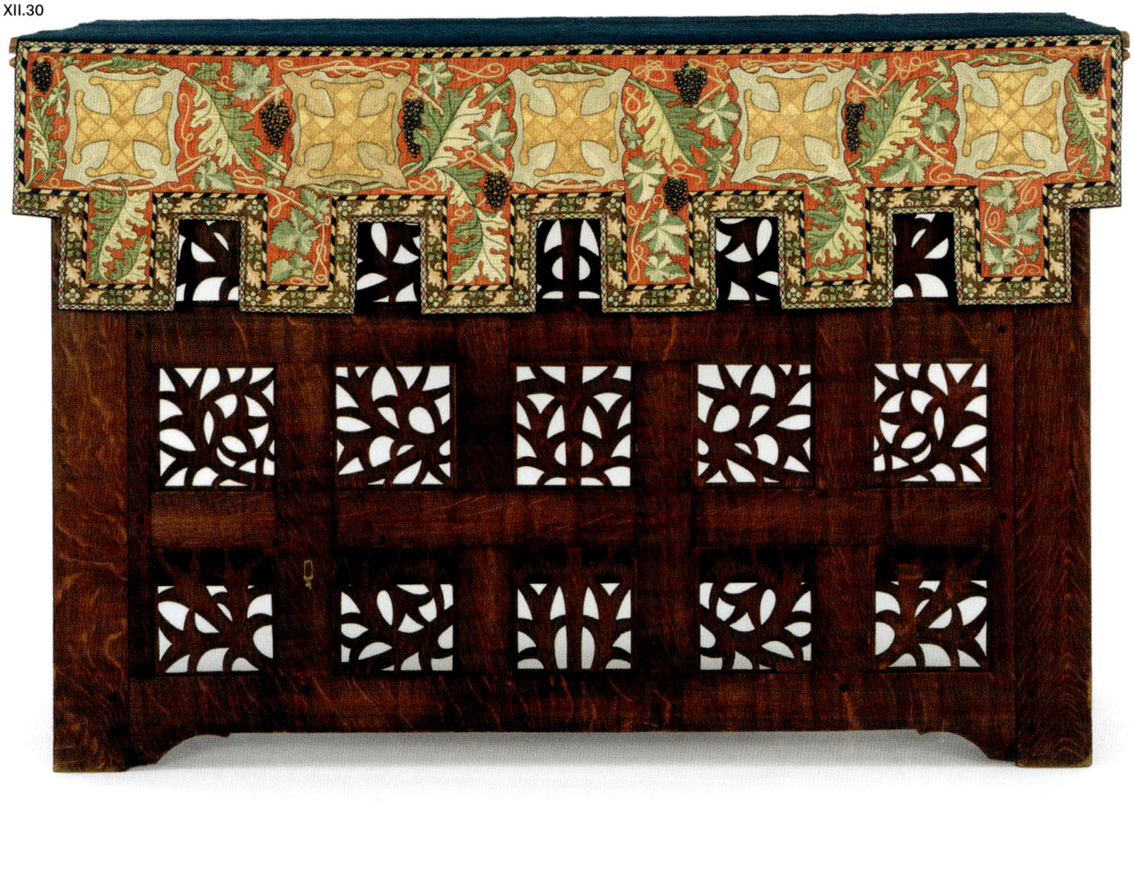

XII.29
Design for a super-frontal for an altar
Philip Webb, 1898–9
Pencil, ink and watercolour, 51.4 x 76.3 cm
V&A (E.58–1940)
Bequeathed by May Morris

This piece was ordered by Morris's sister Isabella Gilmore, who ran the Rochester and Southwark Diocesan Deaconess House, an Anglican community in Clapham, London. Webb designed the chapel, its altar table and furnishings including this super-frontal, an altar cross, candlesticks and lectern, all of which are now in the V&A collection. The drawing is full of meticulous detail; however, he does not underestimate the talents and abilities of the embroiderer, May Morris, and whereas some effects he hopes to achieve, such as jewel-like colours, are suggested, much is left for her interpretation.

XII.30
Festival super-frontal
Designed by Philip Webb, 1898–9
Worked by May Morris
Linen embroidered with silks and gold thread in stem, long and short, satin and split stitches with French knots and laid and couched work, 34.9 x 145.4 cm (embroidered area)
V&A (T.379–1970)
Given by the Rochester and Southwark Diocesan Deaconess House

From 1896, when she gave up management of Morris & Co.'s embroidery department, May Morris concentrated on private commissions. This work, which is quite different from her commercial production, shows her great abilities, both in the sensitivity of her interpretation of Webb's design and in her superb craftsmanship.

Used on special feast days, this super-frontal was never intended to have a matching frontal as in conventional church arrangements but provided a decorative upper border to the front of the Webb-designed altar table, its distinctive shape and rich colour complementing the pierced and carved oak. A plain indigo-dyed panel (called a 'dowla mensa') is attached to the top of the embroidery and was designed to anchor the frontal to the table and provide a cover onto which the cross and candlesticks were placed.

Like her father before her, May advocated the revival of traditional techniques to regain the skills of the past. Here she used a range of traditional stitchery in a lively and modern interpretation of the design. As a well-known practitioner, teacher and writer on the subject, she has probably been of far greater influence over following generations of British embroiderers.

XII.31

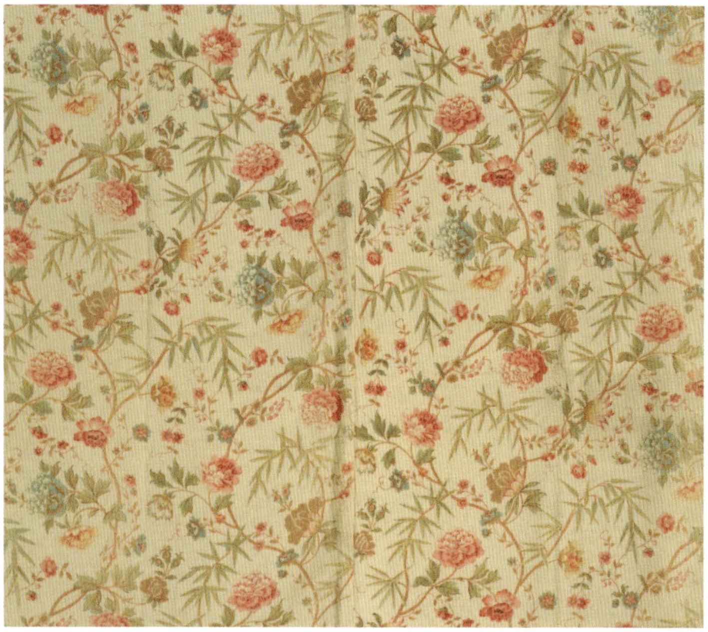

XII.33

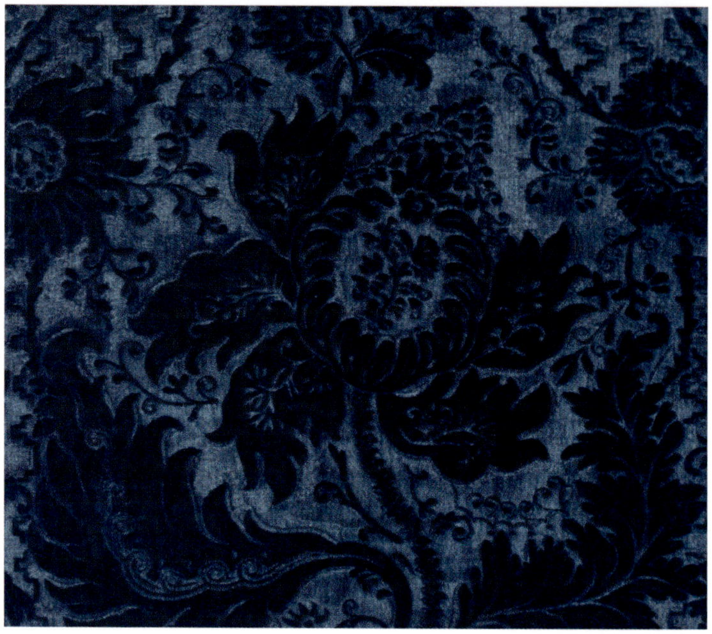

XII.32

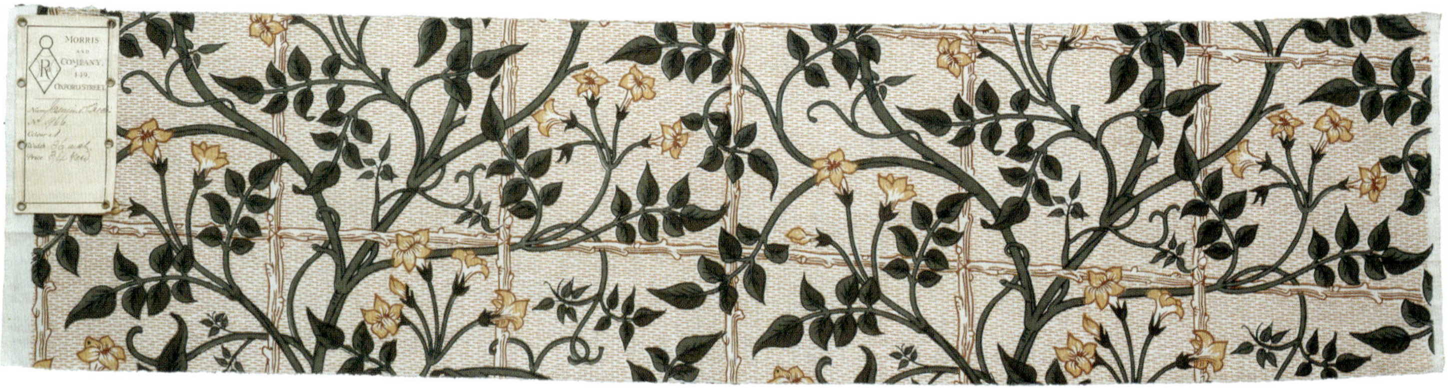

PRINTED TEXTILES

XII.31
Small Stem
Adapted from an 1830s British design
Sold by Morris, Marshall, Faulkner & Co. from *c*.1868
Block-printed wool, 254 x 175 cm, repeat 89.5 x 91.5 cm
V&A (T.37–1979)
Given by Mr and Mrs M. Woodall

After organizing the firm's production of wallpapers, Morris turned his attention to furnishing textiles and approached Thomas Clarkson of Bannister Hall, the leading Lancashire cotton printer. As Clarkson's production centred on roller printing, the results of which Morris disliked, a compromise was found, and his first textiles printed by Clarkson's were from 1830s blocks selected from the store at the Lancashire factory. This woollen example was one of the first and bears the early Queen Square selvedge mark. Three other designs printed at that time were *Large Stem*, *Jasmine Twill* and *Coiling Trail*. A revival of interest in these patterns in the early twentieth century followed the fashion for traditional chintz designs on white grounds.

XII.32
Jasmine Trellis
Designed by William Morris, *c*.1868–70
Manufactured by Thomas Clarkson and later by Thomas Wardle
Block-printed cotton, 22.9 x 94 cm, repeat 45 x 45.5 cm
V&A (T.70–1953)
Given by Mrs Winifred Nicholson

Satisfied with the early results from Clarkson, Morris commissioned the firm to print this, his first design for furnishing textiles. It is not as original as the earlier *Trellis* wallpaper (fig.187), and the simplification of pattern and colouring, which suited Clarkson's commercial, mostly chemical, palette of dyes may be the result of Morris designing a pattern that he knew could be produced successfully.

It is the closest he ever came to attempting an 'Aesthetic' design, the style most fashionable in London at that time. There are similarities to commercial patterns by Christopher Dresser and Bruce Talbert, and Morris may have been influenced by their work. However, the firm's products did not go unnoticed in these circles and E.W. Godwin, one of the most original Aesthetic architects and designers, used *Trellis* wallpaper in his influential interior scheme at Dromore Castle, Ireland (fig.196).

XII.33
Utrecht Velvet
Sold by Morris, Marshall, Faulkner & Co. from *c*.1871
Stamped woollen mohair plush, 46.4 x 62.2 cm, repeat 66 x 61 cm
V&A (T.210–1953)
Given by Etta May Gubbins

This fabric was not manufactured by the firm but was selected as a suitable textile to use as upholstery on furniture (IX.26 and IX.31) and to sell by the yard under its own label. George Wardle claimed that a Manchester firm, Heaton & Co., supplied them with woollen serges and Heaton's later used this textile to furnish cabins on the *Titanic*, so it is probable that it was one of their products. A practical and hard-wearing fabric, it imitates and takes its name from stamped velvets first produced in the Low Countries in the seventeenth century.

In a letter to Thomas Wardle dated 10 September 1875, Morris refers to the dyeing of 'woollen velvet ... done ... in any colours that are possible', so it is likely that he tried to manufacture similar cloth himself or had these dyed at Leek. The fabric, which continued to be commercially successful throughout the nineteenth century, was available in at least 14 colours. After Morris's death the firm sold a second design, *Acorn*.

XII.34

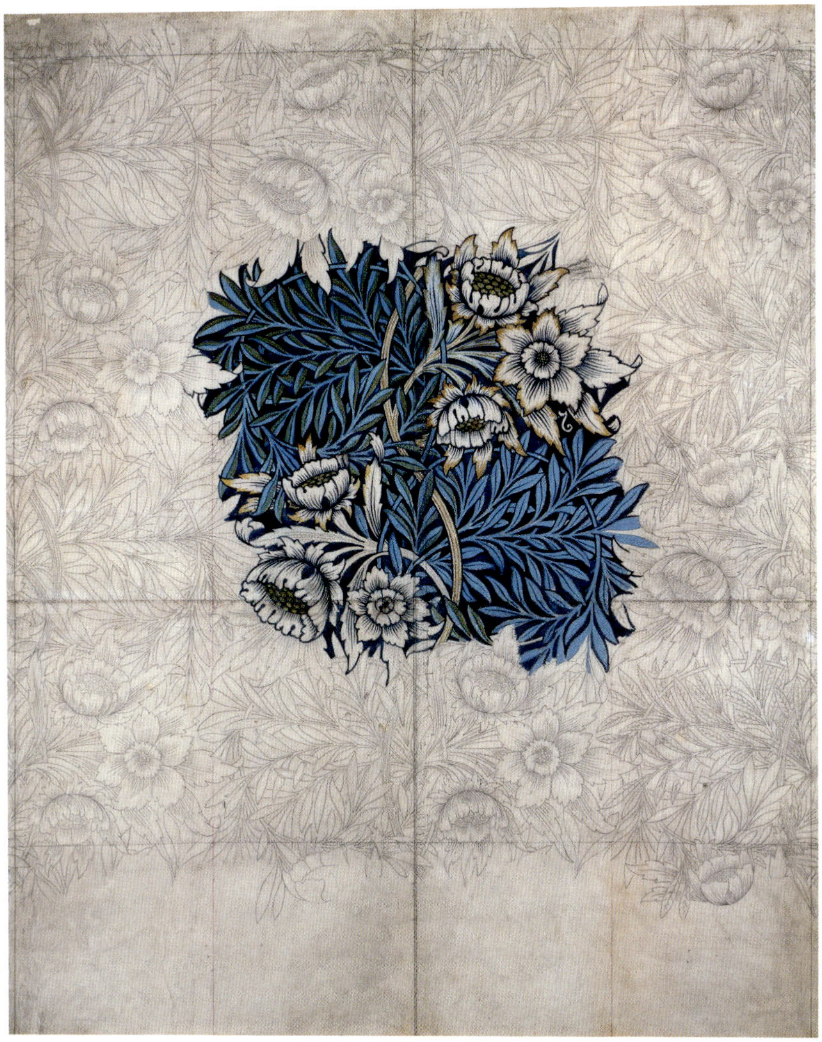

XII.35

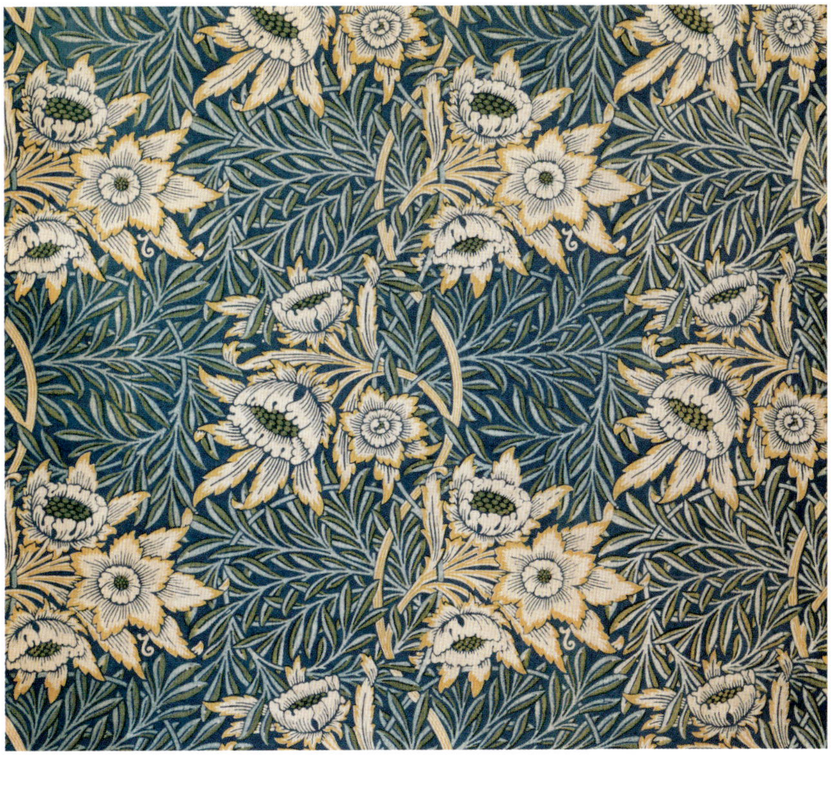

XII.34
Design for *Tulip and Willow* printed textile
William Morris, 1873
Pencil, watercolour and body colour, 114.3 x 94 cm
Birmingham Museums Trust (1941P393)

Morris's second printed textile design, this was manufactured initially by Clarkson's and later at Merton Abbey. This is the first of a number of patterns with a dense background of willow leaves, a form seen in many of his textile designs throughout the 1870s and 1880s. It was purchased from Morris & Co. by the Friends of Birmingham Museum and Art Gallery.

XII.35
Tulip and Willow
Designed by William Morris, 1873
Printed at Merton Abbey from 1883
Block-printed and indigo-discharged linen, 137.2 x 88.9 cm, repeat 44 x 44 cm
V&A (Circ.91–1933)
Given by London County Council

A sample of *Tulip and Willow* was submitted to the Design Registry in Thomas Clarkson's name on 30 December 1873 and shows the crude effect of Prussian blue dye, causing Morris to abandon the pattern until 1883 when he was finally able to achieve the result he required with indigo-discharge printing. This, the final version, was printed successfully ten years after it was designed.

After moving to Merton Abbey in 1881 Morris set about constructing an indigo vat. His first discharge prints were monochrome patterns: *Brother Rabbit* (XII.46), *Bird and Anemone* and *Rose and Thistle* (XII.47). This design, which used only two colours, tones of blue (indigo), yellow (weld) and mixtures of these, is likely to have followed them into production. The printing blocks are owned by the William Morris Gallery.

XII.36

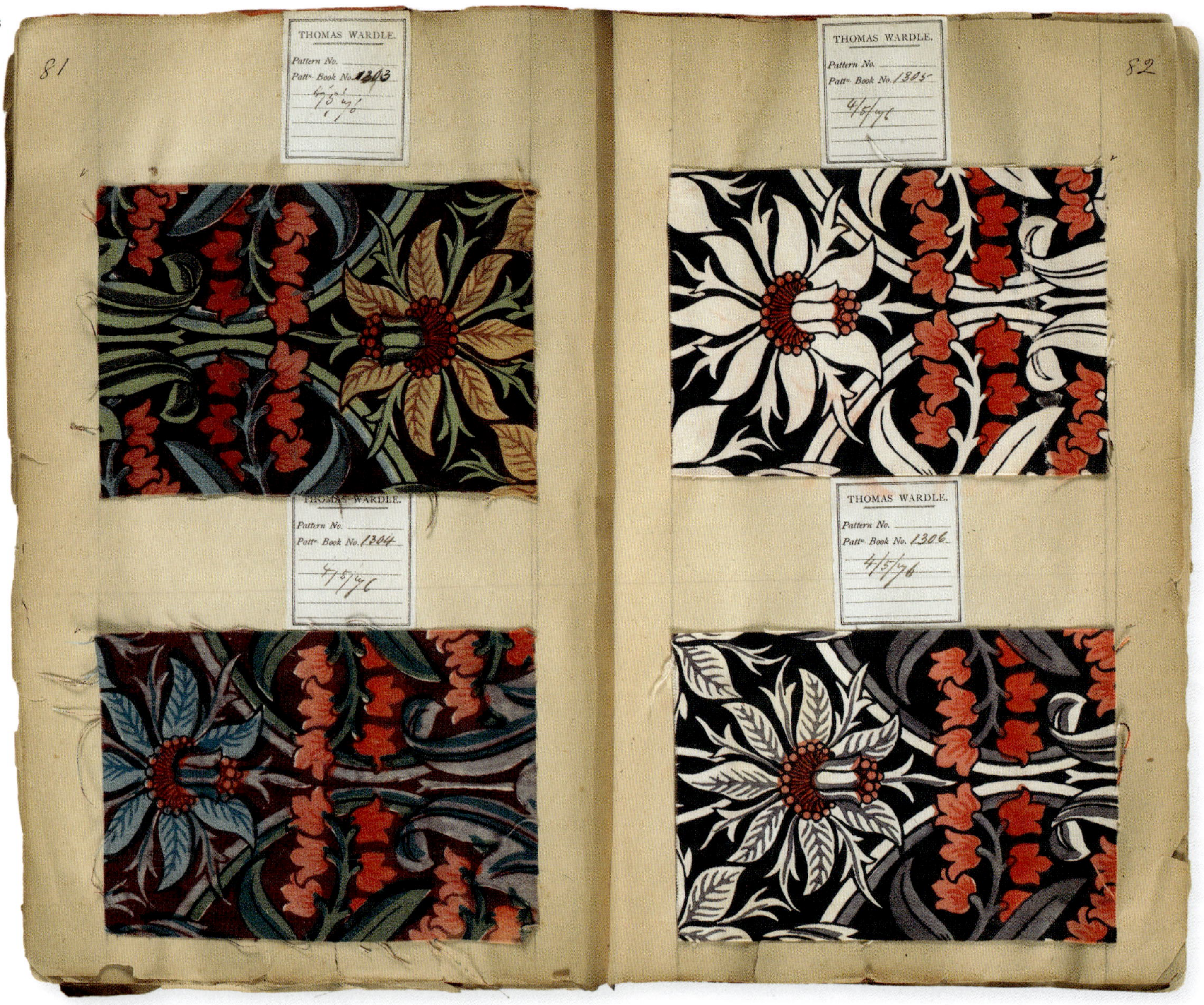

XII.36
Sample book of block-print trials
Thomas Wardle, November 1875–May 1876
Block-printed cottons, printed labels, pencil and ink notes, 33 x 43 x 3 cm (open)
The Whitworth, University of Manchester (T.14003)

This is a record book of printed textiles manufactured at Thomas Wardle's Hencroft Works in Leek, Staffordshire. Unhappy with Clarkson's printing of *Tulip and Willow*, Morris approached Thomas Wardle, the brother-in-law of George Wardle, the firm's manager, who had recently set up his own dye works. Keen to re-establish the use of natural dyestuffs, Morris and Wardle worked in Leek throughout July 1875 combining old recipes with new techniques, including steam setting and chemical mordants. A long correspondence and further visits followed.

All of Morris's printed textiles designed between 1875 and 1878 were printed at Leek and this is the earliest of five surviving volumes documenting Wardle's work for Morris & Co. Included are samples of all the colour trials attempted, a number of which were not put into commercial production. By 1878 Wardle was printing 15 patterns for Morris & Co., as well as dyeing lining fabrics. This collaboration lasted throughout the nineteenth century and these patterns continued to be produced at Leek despite the move to Merton Abbey in 1881.

XII.37
Printers' Notes
Morris & Co., *c*.1880–5
Ink and pencil, 26.6 x 18.2 cm (closed)
National Art Library, V&A (MSL/2000/13)

This is a unique record of the firm's early printing practices. Although the only discernible date is 1883, Morris may have started making notes in the book (early entries are in his hand) before the move to Merton Abbey in 1881 to record details he wished to follow when he became a commercial printer of his own designs.

Information includes a reference list of dyeing manuals, covering volumes published between 1760 and 1877, and a comparison of recipes for indigo dyeing from such publications as Jean-François Persoz's *L'Impression des Tissus* (Paris, 1846) and James Napier's *A Manual of the Art of Dyeing* (London, 1853), with more contemporary findings studied in the Manchester *Textile Colourist* magazine (1876–7). Morris's ability to read and select from these publications shows an extraordinary comprehension of the technological and chemical components of the craft.

Other entries include details of the temperature needed for acquiring specific effects on cloth and hints on how to keep the printing shed warm and humid: 'some boil a kettle in the shop to keep the air moist; some hang up damp clothes; this last is best'.

XII.37

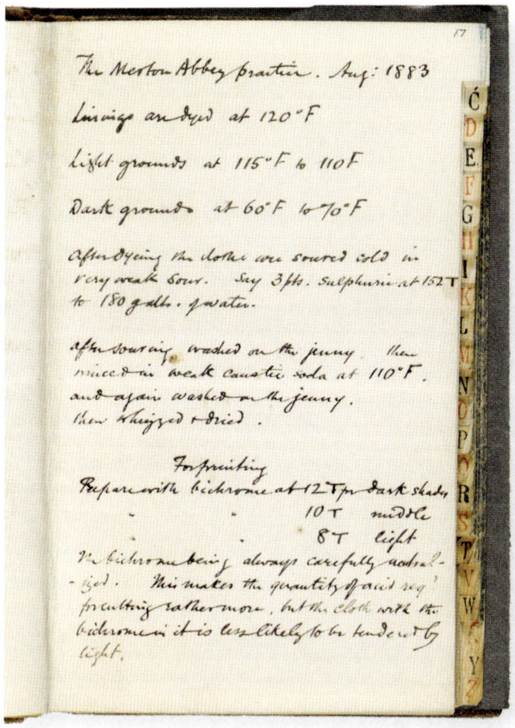
The Merton Abbey practice. Aug: 1883

Linings are dyed at 120°F

Light grounds at 115°F to 110F

Dark grounds at 60°F to 70°F

After dyeing the cloths are soured cold in very weak sour. Say 3 pts. sulphuric at 152T to 180 galls. of water.

After souring washed on the jenny. then rinsed in weak caustic soda at 110°F. and again washed on the jenny. then whizzed & dried.

For printing
Prepare with bichrome at 12T for dark shades
" " 10T middle
" " 8T light

The bichrome being always carefully neutralized. This makes the quantity of acid req'd for cutting rather more, but the cloth with the bichrome in it is less likely to be tendered by light.

XII.38

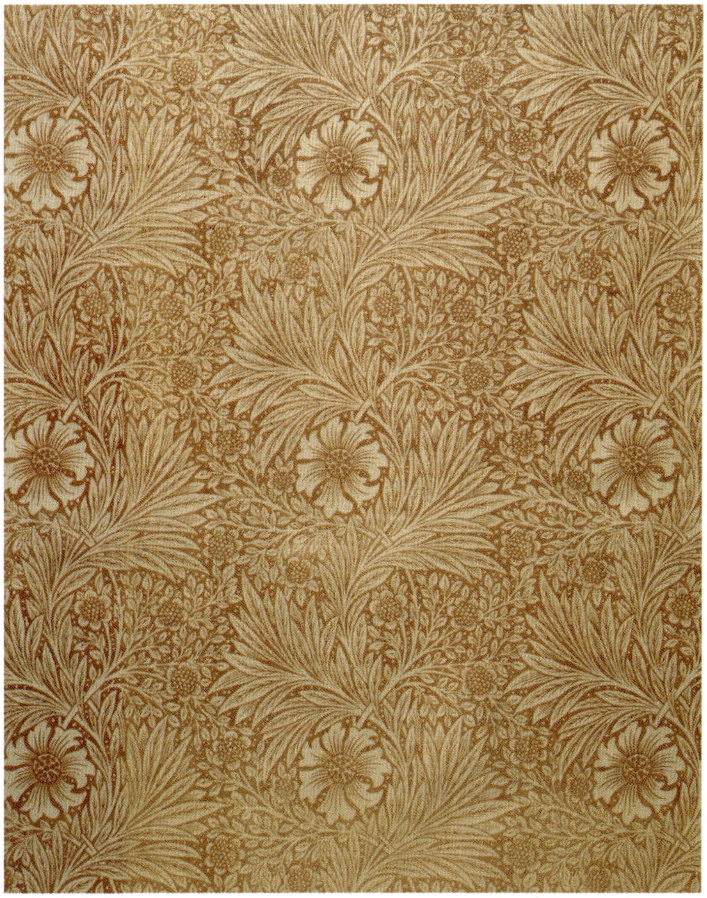

XII.39

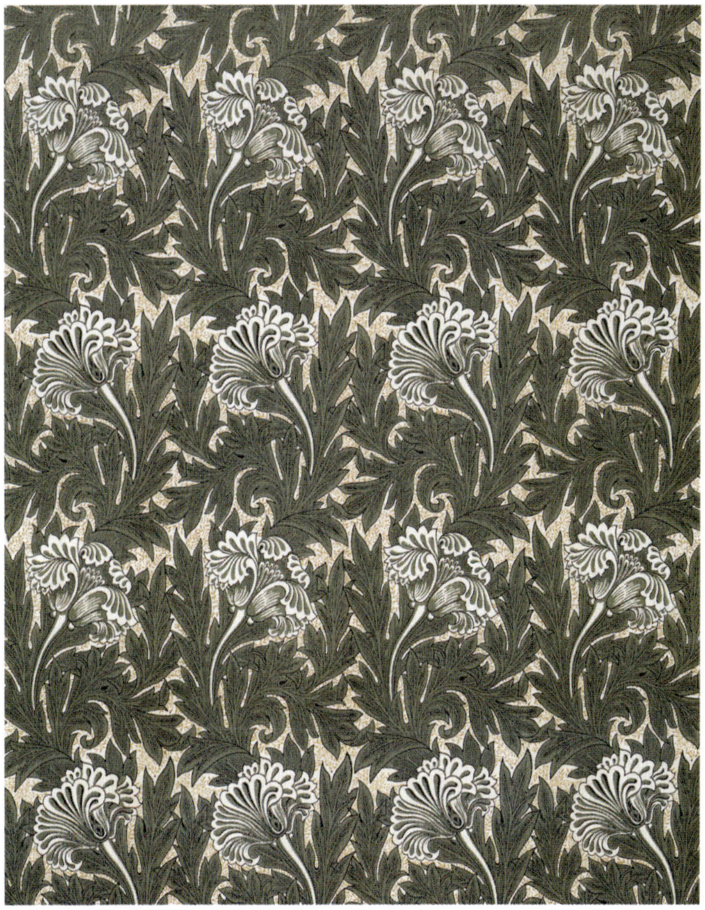

XII.38
Marigold
Designed by William Morris, registered as a textile 15 April 1875
Manufactured by Thomas Wardle, Leek
Block-printed silk, 97.5 x 55 cm, repeat 23 x 23 cm
V&A (Circ.496–1965)

This is likely to have been the first of Morris's patterns to be printed by Wardle at Leek, although the earliest surviving evidence of colour experiments for this design are dated 25 November 1875 (XII.36). *Marigold* is one of only two designs, with *Larkspur*, approved by Morris for use as both wallpaper and furnishing textile (XI.11).

This sample was one of a small group of Morris designs on printed silk exhibited by Thomas Wardle at the Paris Exposition Universelle of 1878. Included in the British India Section (presumably because of their imported ground) they were acquired by the V&A soon afterwards and lay undiscovered as British work until the 1960s. Morris refers to an earlier display of silk examples when writing to Wardle on 23 November 1875. 'You are quite welcome to send the prints to the India house ... As to our using them the only drawback seems to be that they are made awkward widths for our present blocks ... By the way I think the Carnation would look well on the Tussore.'

Wardle was particularly interested in silk. He spent a number of years experimenting with sericulture and perfecting the dyeing and printing of tussah, the ground for this example. He was a founder member and President of the influential Silk Association and published books and articles on the subject.

XII.39
Tulip
Designed by William Morris, registered 15 April 1875
Manufactured by Thomas Wardle, Leek
Block-printed cotton, 167 x 92 cm, repeat 54.5 x 23 cm
V&A (Circ.410–1953)
Given by Etta May Gubbins

Morris drew five textile designs in 1875, this is one of three (with *Marigold* and *Larkspur*) registered on the same day. All three are densely floriated with a repeating zigzag of wavy leaves and show Morris's preoccupation with wallpaper design at this time. Despite the simplicity of the pattern, many colour trials were undertaken and a letter as early as 3 September 1875 refers to the 'dark outline of the tulip'.

This example is a late nineteenth- or early twentieth-century printing of the design. It was bought in the 1930s by one of the firm's most prolific patrons, Etta May Gubbins, for her large home at 55 Blackwater Road in Eastbourne. The original design (BLA500) and 12 printing blocks are at the William Morris Gallery.

XII.40

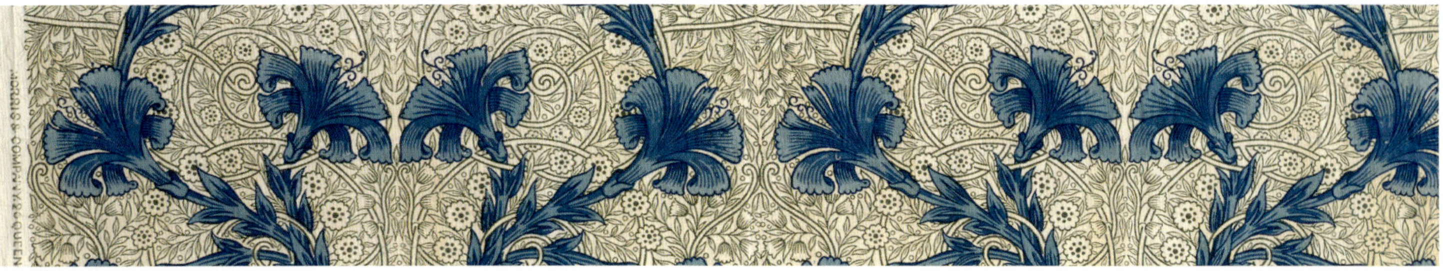

XII.41

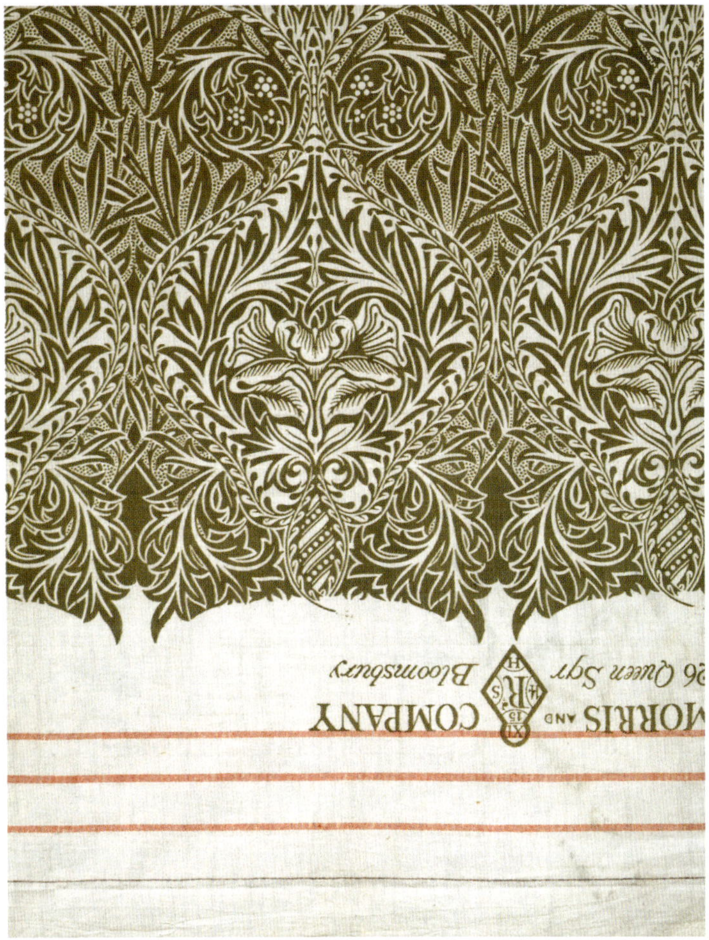

XII.42

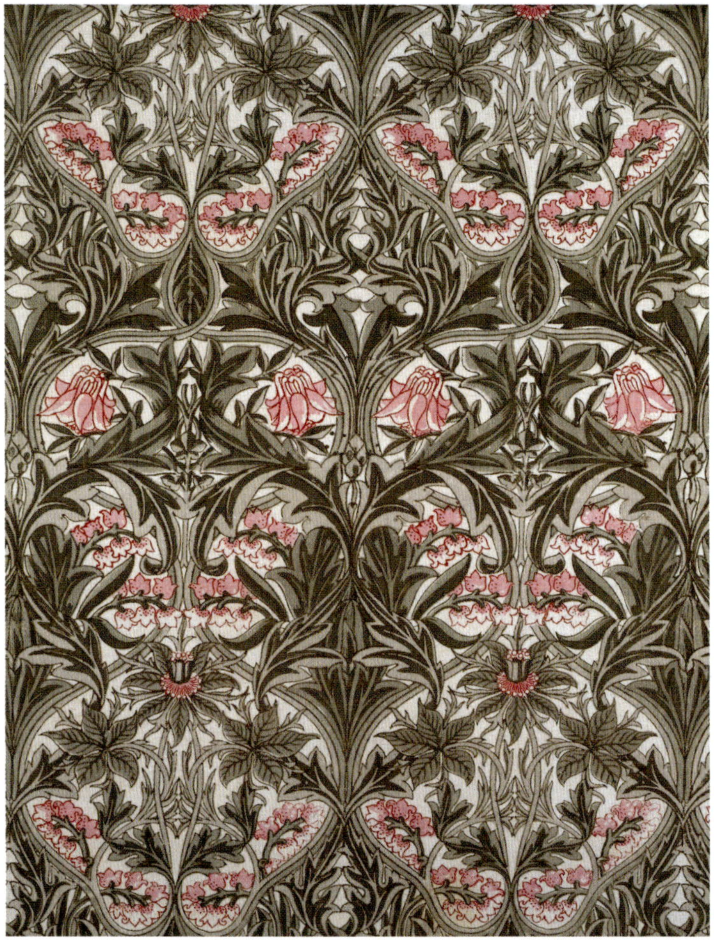

XII.40
Carnation
Probably designed by Kate Faulkner, registered 15 October 1875
Manufactured by Thomas Wardle, Leek
Block-printed cotton, 16.6 x 93 cm, repeat 24 x 46.5 cm
V&A (T.248–1984)
Given by Miss Sue Tarran

One of the few existing early examples of Morris printed textiles in pristine condition, this shows Wardle's use of Prussian blue dye, which Morris believed 'a terrible disappointment'. The pattern is first mentioned in a letter from Morris to Wardle on 8 September 1875. This sample, which has a selvedge mark for 26 Queen Square, was printed before April 1877.

Although previously recorded as a William Morris design, Henry Currie Marillier, Managing Director of Morris & Co., claimed it was not by him when offering cotton samples to the V&A in 1919. On stylistic grounds it is likely that this pattern was drawn by Kate Faulkner, who produced tile and wallpaper designs and undertook gesso decoration for Morris & Co. This sample was taken from inside the lining of curtains used at Belton House, Lincolnshire, where it had been utilized as interfacing.

XII.41
Trial printing of *Iris*
Designed by William Morris, registered 25 April 1876
Manufactured by Thomas Wardle, Leek
Block-printed cotton, 59 x 45 cm, repeat 49 x 23 cm
V&A (T.45–1919)
Given by Morris & Co.

Morris called the pattern by the little-used ancient title of 'Flower de Luce' when discussing a madder red printing trial in a letter to Wardle on 24 December 1875. This olive-green colouring may well be earlier in date.

The structure of both *Iris* and *Bluebell* (XII.42) was inspired by a block-printed linen in the South Kensington Museum, thought at the time to be of fifteenth-century Rhenish origin but exposed in 1962 as a fake.

The original design for *Iris*, now in the Huntington Art Museum, is inscribed by Morris, 'The block must have square ends. That is it must not follow the shape of the pattern.' This trial shows that the blocks were cut exactly to Morris's instructions. The printed diamond registration mark on this sample is incorrect and gives the date when *Tulip*, *Marigold* and *Larkspur* were registered.

XII.42
Trial printing for *Bluebell* or *Columbine*
Designed by William Morris, 1876
Manufactured by Thomas Wardle, Leek
Block-printed cotton, 99 x 88.9 cm, repeat 45.5 x 24 cm
V&A (Circ.44–1956)
Given by B. Wardle & Co.

Wardle's first printing trials for this design are dated 4 May 1876 (XII.36). This later trial shows the initials of the block-printer plus 'No. 1', suggesting that this may be the first attempt at this particular colouring. Other printed references on the sample include 'Registered' (although no registration has been found) and the name and address of the Oxford Street shop.

Morris was very critical of Wardle's dyers and printers. He referred to a number of them by name in various letters, demanding from them efficiency and economy for his work. On 23 November 1875 he suggested that rather than needing more staff to undertake a new technique (pencilling with indigo), children could be used, 'Our boys at 5/6 a week would be quite up to it.'

XII.43
Honeysuckle
Designed by William Morris, registered 11 October 1876
Manufactured by Thomas Wardle, Leek
Block-printed silk, 49.5 x 99 cm, repeat 76 x 91.5 cm
V&A (Circ.491–1965)

This is one of Morris's most complex patterns with a large-scale turnover repeat. It shows his increasing interest in designing for the loom, where this type of design is best suited. Trial printing of the pattern started about June 1876 and Morris continued to check the results sent to him by Wardle until 29 November, when he claimed the sample sent 'is not right yet, but it is hopeful'.

This experimental silk shows only half the pattern width, but the translucence of colour created by the subtly shimmering surface of the silk is very effective. As with the illustrated example of *Marigold* (XII.38), this sample was acquired by the South Kensington Museum directly from the 1878 Paris Exposition Universelle.

The original design is at Birmingham Museum and Art Gallery (1941P401) and the pattern was also used for embroidery (XII.15).

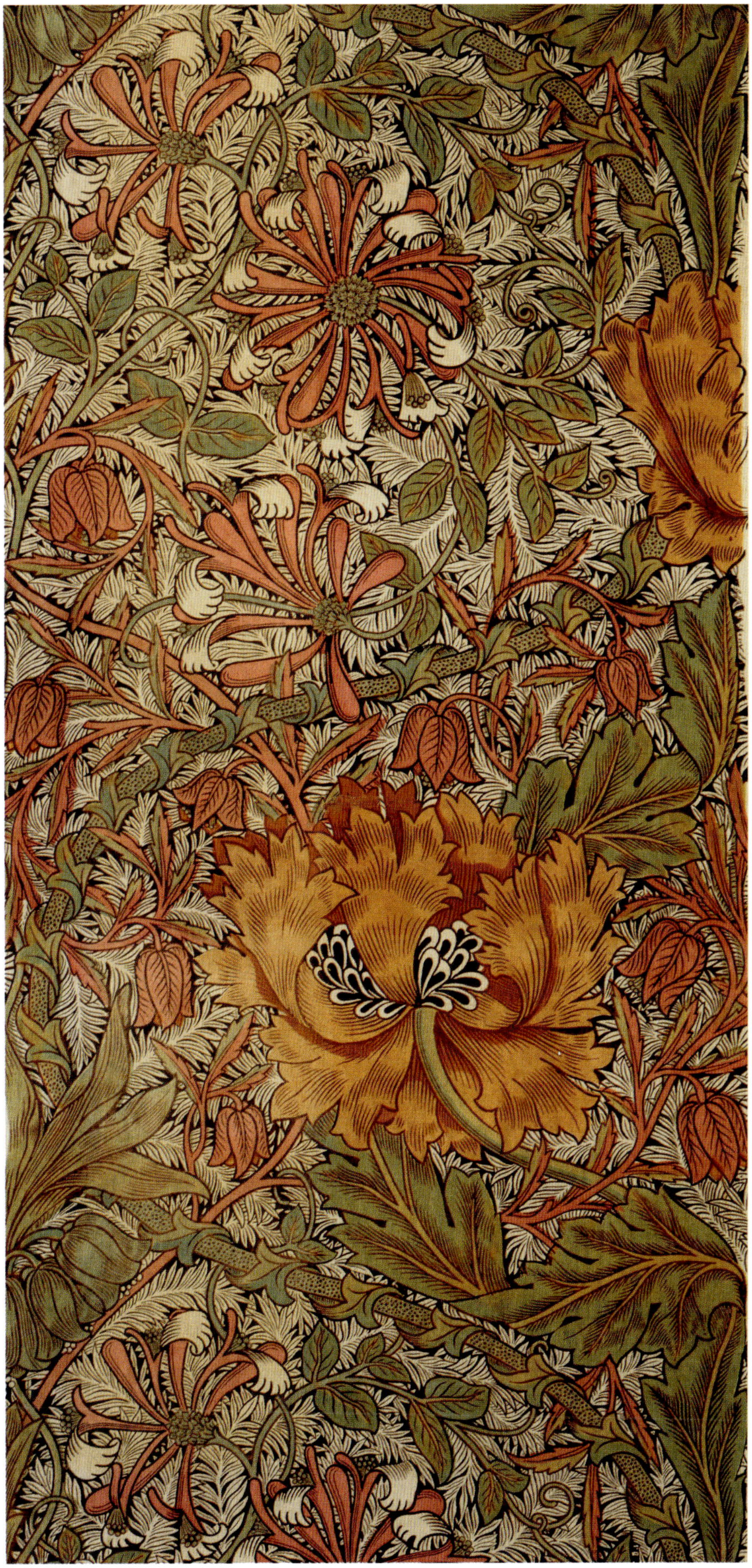
XII.43

XII.44

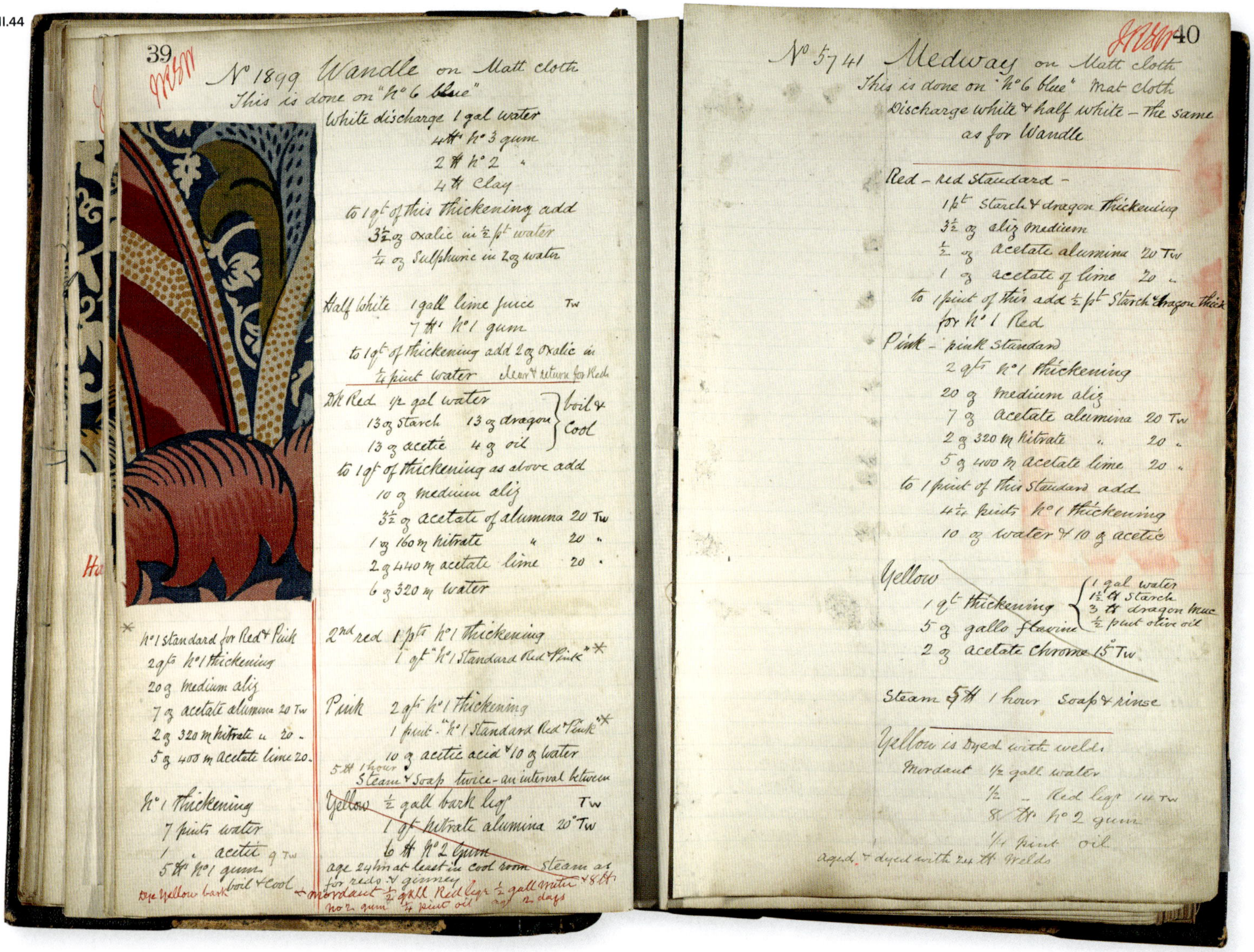

XII.44

Merton Abbey dye book
Morris & Co., 1882–91
Printed fabrics glued to paper, notes in ink, 34 x 22.7 x 6.5 cm
The Huntington Library, Art Museum and Botanical Gardens (2000.5.3387)

This handwritten ledger is a working record of printed cottons manufactured at Merton Abbey between 1882 and 1891. Each page lists recipes used for printing identified and numbered patterns, many of which are illustrated with samples of cloth. Pages 1 to 72 are initialled 'JREW' and pages 73 to 111 'JHD' (for John Henry Dearle). Later amendments show changes in recipes and processing. As Morris's early printed fabric designs continued to be printed at Thomas Wardle's factory at Leek, this book itemizes patterns designed and printed after 1881. Only *Honeysuckle* (in red) and *Peony* (in brown) appear to have been printed in both places.

Recipes are arranged according to colour, beginning with reds from madder, then yellows and buffs from weld, indigo-discharged blues, greens and mixed colours. The left page illustrated shows the dye recipe for *Wandle*, and on the right for *Medway*.

XII.45

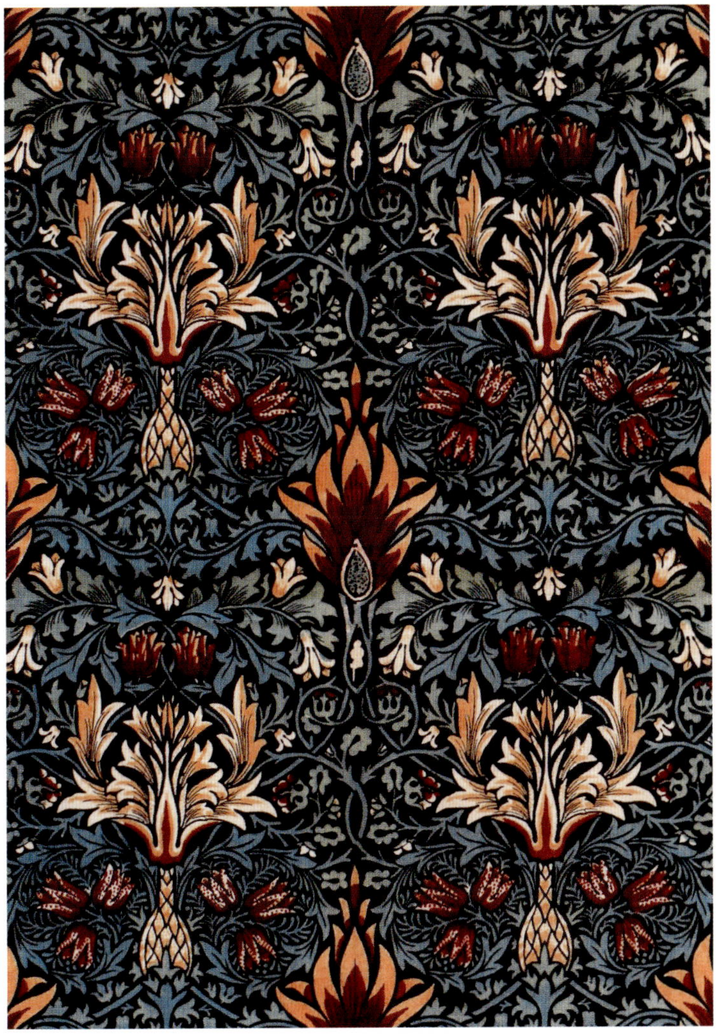

XII.46

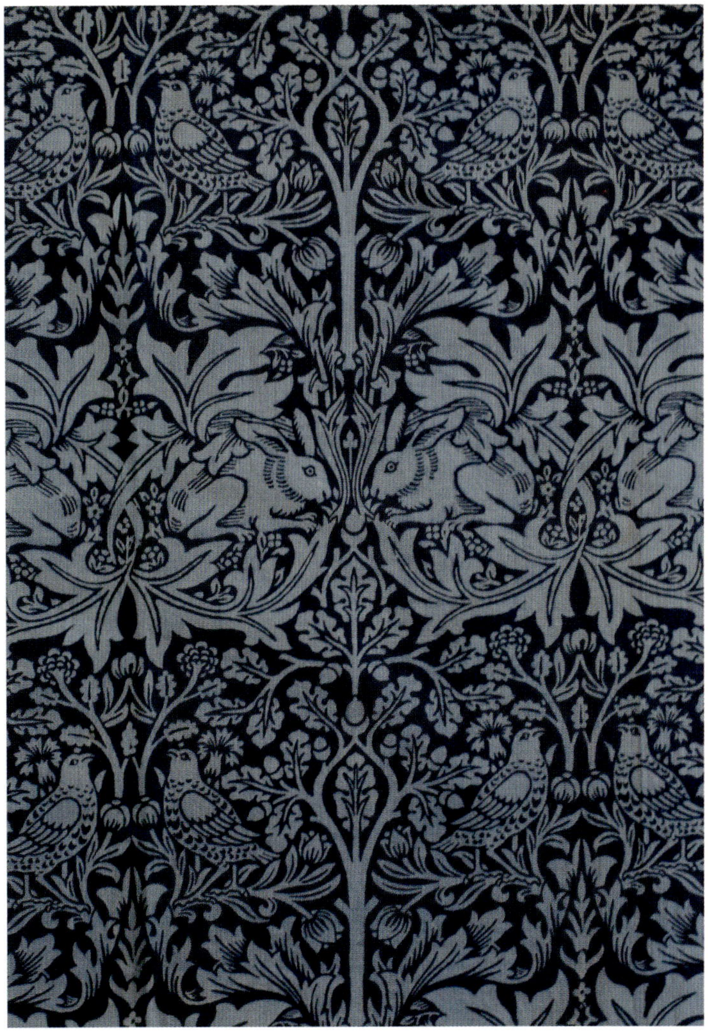

XII.45
Snakeshead
Designed by William Morris, 1876
Manufactured by Thomas Wardle, Leek
Block-printed cotton, 123 x 93 cm, repeat 29.5 x 23 cm
V&A (T.37–1919)
Given by Morris & Co.

Between late 1875 and 1877 Morris produced a small group of designs influenced by the colouring and patterns of Indian textiles. At this time Wardle was importing Indian silks and dyeing and overprinting these for Liberty's. Morris may well have seen examples during his visits to Leek.

This pattern first appears in the Wardle pattern books for January 1877 and trials continued until March. Printed onto a pre-dyed dark ground, it shows Morris's increasing interest in gaining depth of pattern through the overprinting of primary colours. He was finally to achieve this effect with indigo-discharge printing. The original design is at Birmingham Museum and Art Gallery (1941P397) and four printing blocks at the William Morris Gallery.

XII.46
Brother Rabbit
Designed by William Morris, before June 1881
Manufactured at Merton Abbey
Indigo-discharged and block-printed cotton, 64.7 x 93.9 cm, repeat 33.5 x 23 cm
V&A (T.647–1919)

In January 1878 Morris registered his last design to be printed at Leek. Unhappy with Wardle's general standard of printing and inability to undertake indigo dyeing successfully, it was not until 1881, when he had found Merton Abbey and set up the indigo vat, that he returned to designing for this technique. This is one of three patterns, along with *Bird and Anemone* and *Rose and Thistle*, drawn before June 1881 and designed specifically for this method. However, its registration was delayed until May 1882 and, as Morris noted in a letter to his daughter Jenny, printing was not perfected until December 1882.

The pattern, also called *Brer Rabbit*, is named after one of the characters in Joel Chandler Harris's collection of African American folktales, *Uncle Remus, His Songs and His Sayings*, published in the US in 1880, which was being read by the Morris family at this time. It was first displayed at the Boston Foreign Fair in 1883, possibly to attract the American audience. Webb has been credited with drawing the birds and animals for this design (*William Morris and Kelmscott*, 1981). The textile was also available in reds and yellows and the printing blocks are owned by the William Morris Gallery.

XII.47

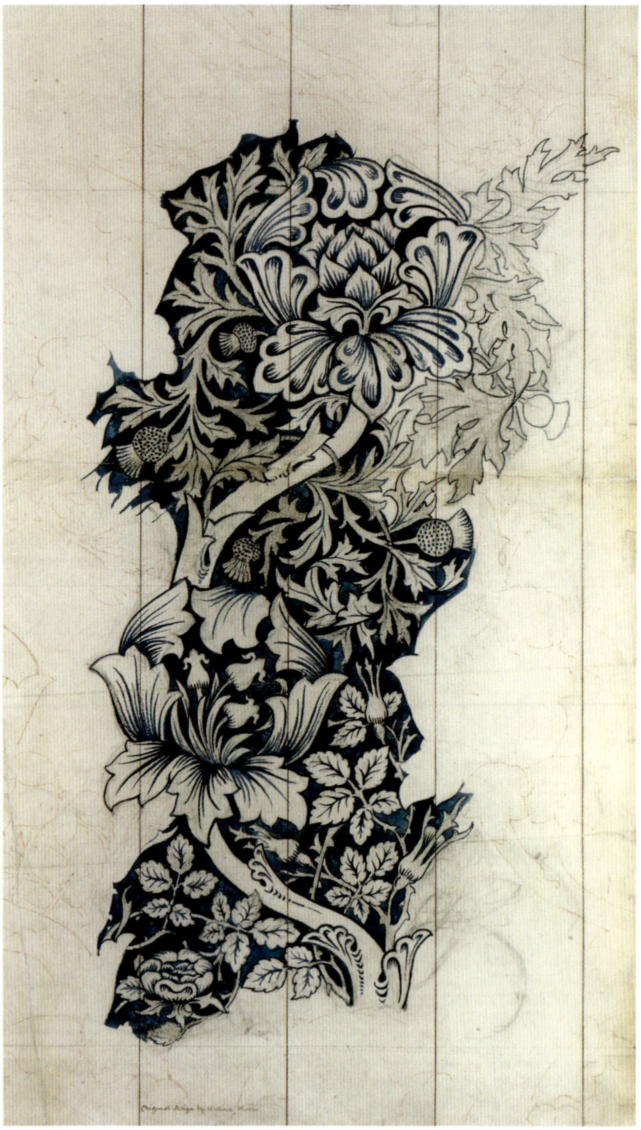

XII.48

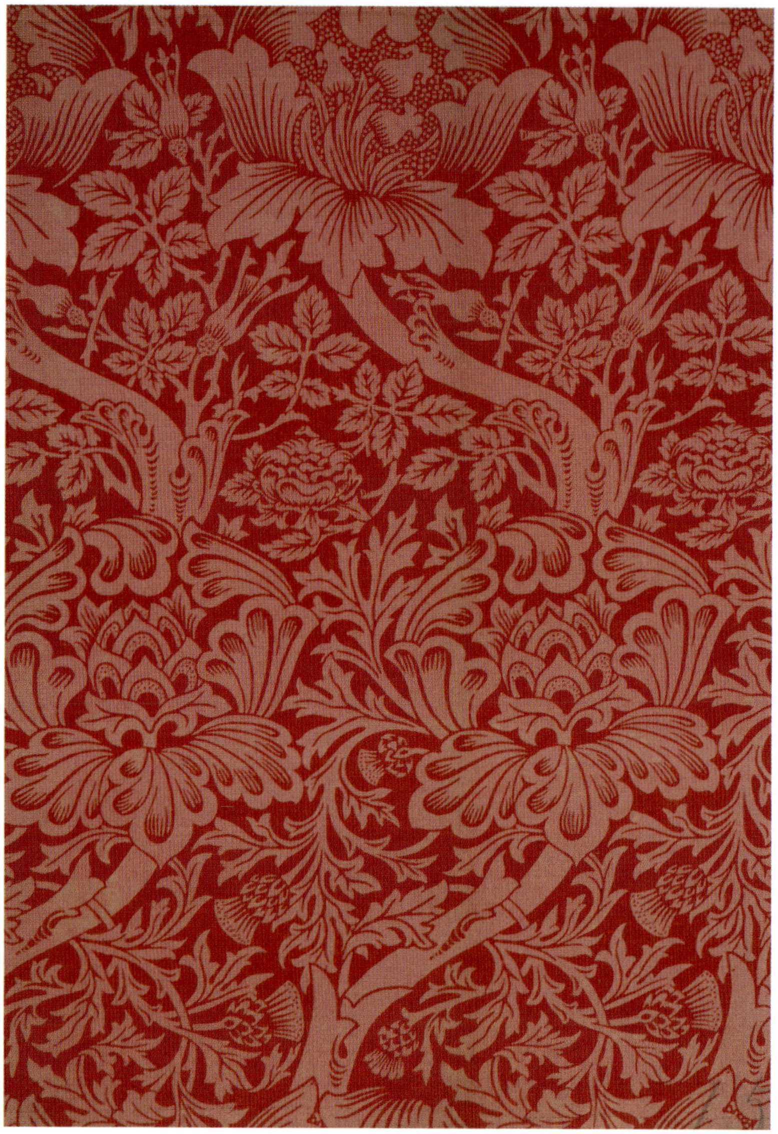

XII.47
Design for *Rose and Thistle* printed textile
William Morris, before June 1881
Pencil, pen and ink, coloured chalk and watercolour, 103 x 68.2 cm
V&A (E.293–1939)
Bequeathed by May Morris

The design is marked '26 Queen Square', confirming that it was drawn before the move to Merton Abbey in June 1881 when Morris was experimenting with the indigo-discharge process at Queen Square. It is one of three patterns designed by Morris especially for the technique, a fact emphasized by the dark blue colour used. This is the first of Morris's printed designs in which a meandering or, as he called it, 'branch' repeat is used, and marks a transition from the symmetrical 'net' patterns characterized in his printed fabrics before 1880.

XII.48
Rose and Thistle
Designed by William Morris, 1881
Manufactured at Merton Abbey
Madder-discharged and block-printed cotton, 64.7 x 97.1 cm, repeat 60.5 x 23 cm
V&A (T.637–1919)
Given by Morris & Co.

Designed specially for the discharge technique, this example is dyed with madder and shows a half discharge of the colour (dye) in the lighter areas. This is one of four examples of this design with madder and indigo discharge given to the V&A by Morris & Co. in 1919, although printed much earlier. The four printing blocks are owned by the William Morris Gallery.

XII.49

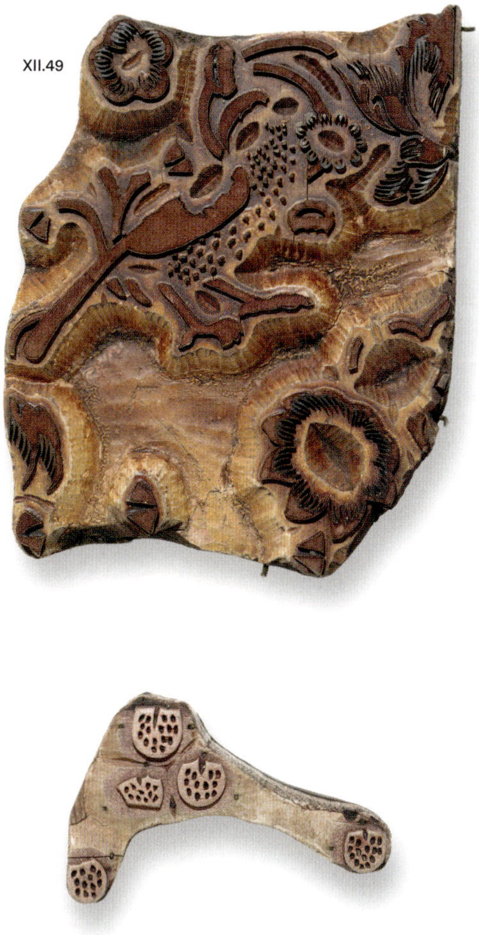

XII.50

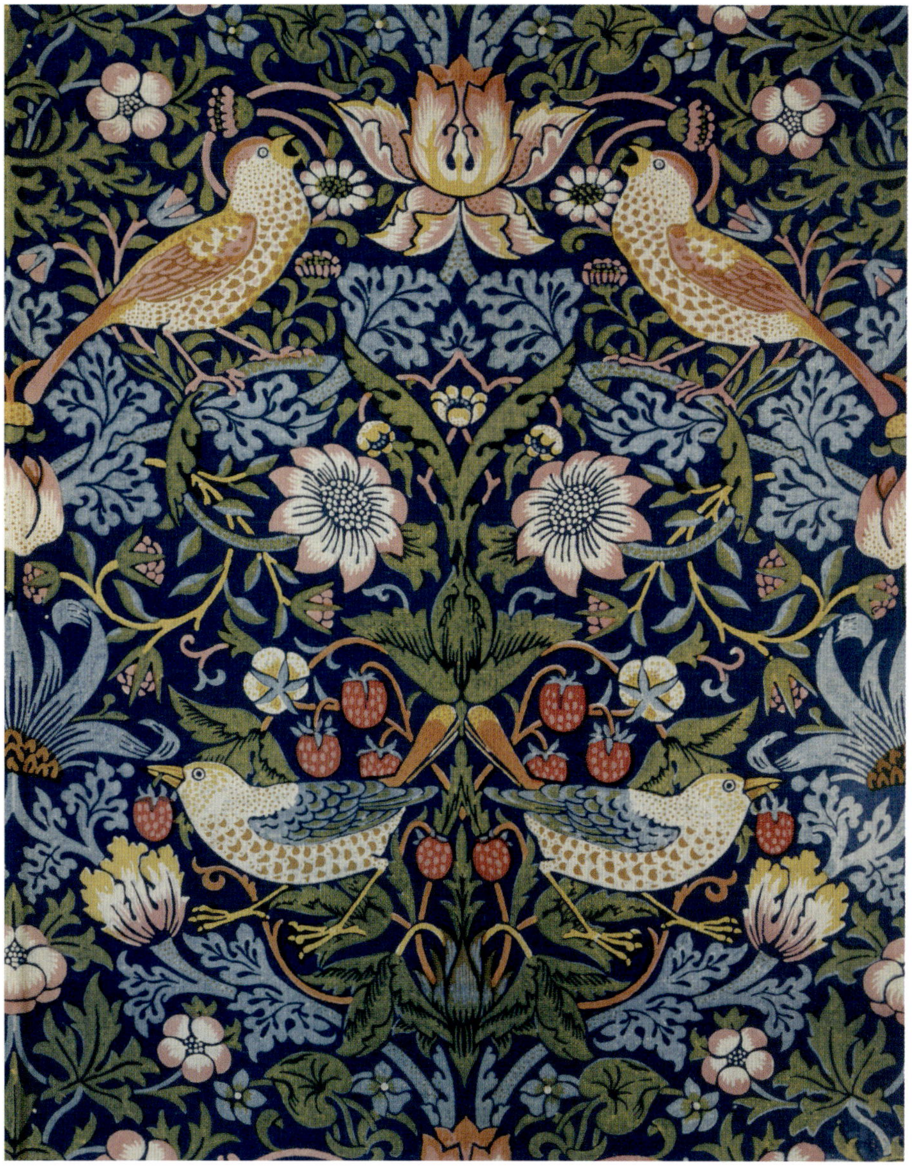

XII.49
Printing blocks for *Strawberry Thief*
Made by Barrett's, London, 1883
Pear wood with metal, felt inlay, various sizes
V&A (T.125 & A–1980)
Given by Stead McAlpin & Co.

Morris had personal experience of cutting printing blocks having taught himself the craft in 1865 while preparing illustrations for his aborted publication of *The Earthly Paradise* (fig.221). However, there is no evidence to suggest that he cut any of his own fabric blocks. Examples used for printing early Morris textiles are likely to have been made at Bannister Hall (Thomas Clarkson) and at Leek (Thomas Wardle) and once the firm moved to Merton Abbey, instead of employing a block cutter at the works, Morris sent his designs to Barrett's, a family firm in Bethnal Green. He was probably introduced to their work through Metford Warner of Jeffrey and Co.

This design was originally printed by the indigo-discharge method and the main pattern blocks cut in negative so that, when printed with a bleaching agent on the solid indigo-dyed ground and washed a number of times, a white, or lightly coloured image was produced on the cotton ground. Some of these blocks were later re-cut for surface printing (applying the colours directly rather than using a bleaching agent). Illustrated here are two blocks from a set of 24.

XII.50
Strawberry Thief
Designed by William Morris, registered 11 May 1883
Manufactured at Merton Abbey
Indigo-discharge and block-printed cotton, 60 x 95.2 cm, repeat 52 x 44.5 cm
V&A (T.586–1919)
Given by Morris & Co.

On Whit Monday, only three days after registration of this design, Morris wrote to Jenny, 'I was a great deal at Merton last week ... anxiously superintending the first printing of the Strawberry thief, which I think we shall manage this time'. As this was his first indigo-discharged design to include red (in this case alizarin) and yellow (weld), Morris's anxiety is understandable. The Merton Abbey dye book (XII.44) states that the design 'comes three times on table' and lists the order that colour should be applied with blue, red and then yellow, each being dyed, printed and cleared (washed) in turn. This entire process would have taken a number of days to complete and, consequently, this is one of the firm's most expensive cottons. Clients were not put off and it proved to be one of Morris's most commercially popular patterns.

XII.51

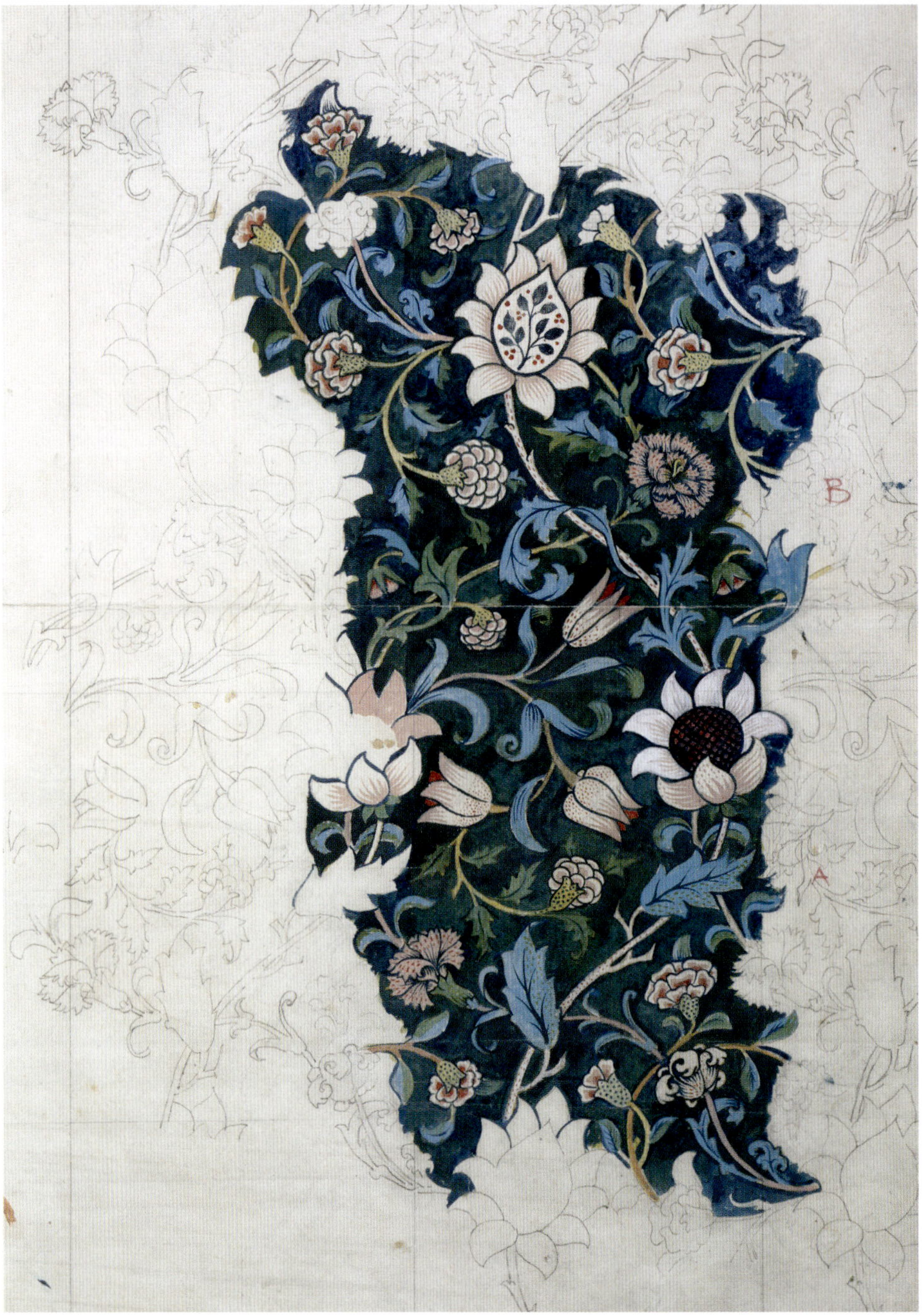

XII.52

XII.51
Brocaded velvet
Genoa, Italy, seventeenth century
Cut and uncut silk velvet with ground brocaded with gold thread, 163 x 53.3 cm
V&A (442A–1883)

Peter Floud's seminal article 'Dating Morris Patterns' in *The Architectural Review* of July 1959 cites this velvet as the single greatest influence on Morris's later pattern-making. The repeating format of diagonally meandering stems was used for a number of designs drawn after 1883, the year that the South Kensington Museum acquired this piece. At the time Morris was advising the museum on the acquisition of textiles. Patterns of this type include *Evenlode*, *Wey*, *Kennet*, *Windrush*, *Wandle*, *Cray* and *Medway*. As if to emphasize the natural flow of these designs, they are named after tributaries of the Thames. Although this velvet clearly influenced Morris, it is worth noting that a similar structure is seen in two earlier patterns, *Rose and Thistle* (XII.47), a printed fabric and the woven *Madras Muslin* (XII.74), both designed by 1881.

XII.52
Design for *Evenlode* printed textile
William Morris, registered 2 September 1883
Pencil, pen and ink, black chalk, watercolour and body colour, 99.9 x 62.9 cm
V&A (E.543–1939)

A complex pattern designed for the indigo-discharge technique, originally printed with a dark green ground, produced by printing yellow (weld) over blue (indigo). This is the first of Morris's designs called after tributaries of the Thames. He drew the pattern at Kelmscott House while suffering from gout and found some difficulty in naming it. In a letter to May on 3 March 1883 he wrote 'I have been at work pretty hard & have made a new pattern which in honour of the occasion I ought to call "Colchicum": only as Colchicum is nothing less than a crocus & I have stupidly omitted to put a crocus in, to avoid questions being asked I must fall back on a river and call it Evenlode.'

In 1906 Morris & Co. produced the pattern on a white-discharged ground in line with current fashions. The 33 blocks used to print this design are at the William Morris Gallery.

XII.53

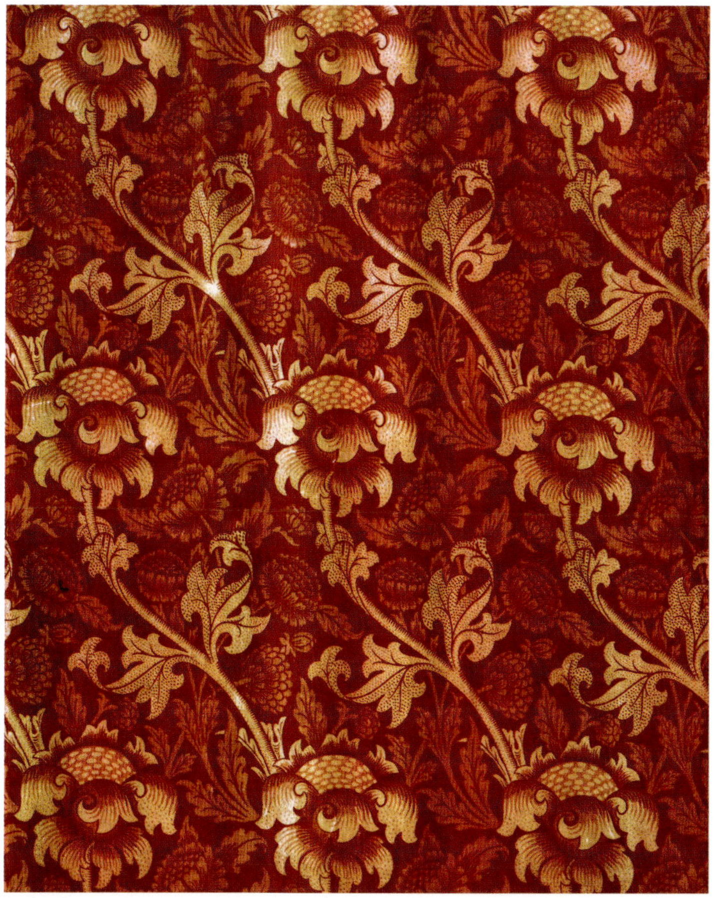

XII.53
***Wey* curtain**
Designed by William Morris, *c.*1883
Manufactured at Merton Abbey
Block-printed cotton velveteen, 231 x 396 cm, repeat 23.5 x 30.5 cm
V&A (T.87A–1980)
Given by Forest Gate Unitarian Church

The pattern was originally designed to be printed as an indigo-discharged cotton but was also produced in this form, as a printed cotton velveteen. This curtain is one of a pair, part of the Morris & Co. decoration of Forest Gate Unitarian Church, London. The estimate, dated 28 October 1901, quotes to make a 'curtain 14ft x 7ft 9ins ... if in cotton velvet £10.10.0 (ten guineas) ... if in 3-ply tapestry without lining £10.15.0'. This shows that the technique of block printing on velveteen was almost as time consuming and costly as weaving. The original design is at Birmingham Museum and Art Gallery (1941P395).

XII.54
Kennet
Designed by William Morris, registered 18 October 1883
Manufactured at Merton Abbey
Block-printed and indigo-discharged cotton, 68 x 96.5 cm, repeat 70 x 22 cm
V&A (T.48–1912)
Given by Morris & Co.

This has a very strong diagonal pattern designed especially for indigo discharge. Although also available as a surface print (colours printed directly onto the cloth), the design is shown at its best when discharged in full but with areas of half discharge when a weaker solution of bleaching agent is used producing a lighter colour. Here weld yellow was used for the flower heads and over-printed to produce a part green leaf. The Merton Abbey dye book gives recipes for both discharge (indigo) and Prussian blue (surface) versions.

The design was also produced at the end of the nineteenth century as a woven silk (XII.79) and printed velveteen. Alexander Morton & Co.'s records show that the firm wove a muslin of a similar design. Whether this was produced for Morris & Co. is not known. A preparatory drawing is at Birmingham Museum and Art Gallery (1941P404) and the original printing blocks are at the William Morris Gallery.

XII.54

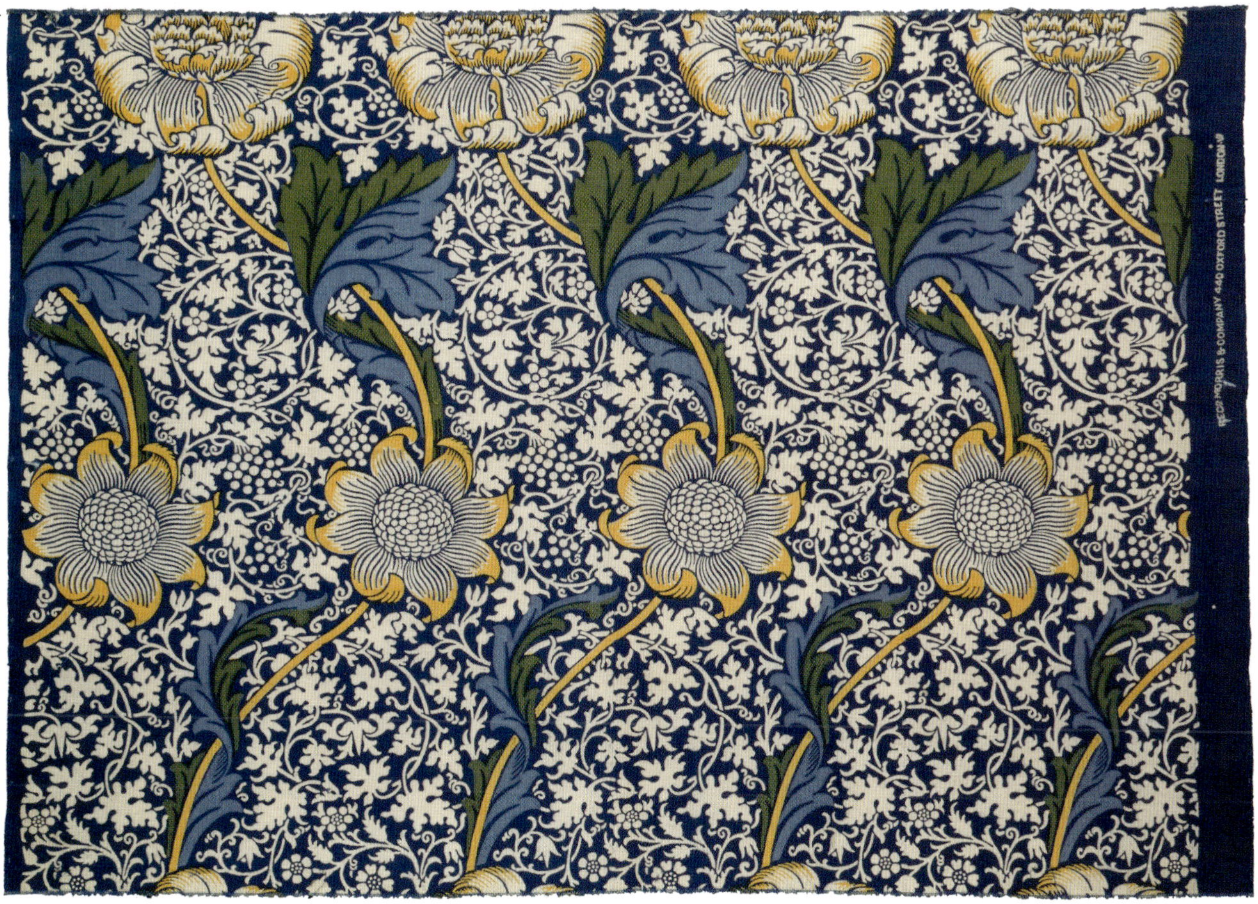

XII.55

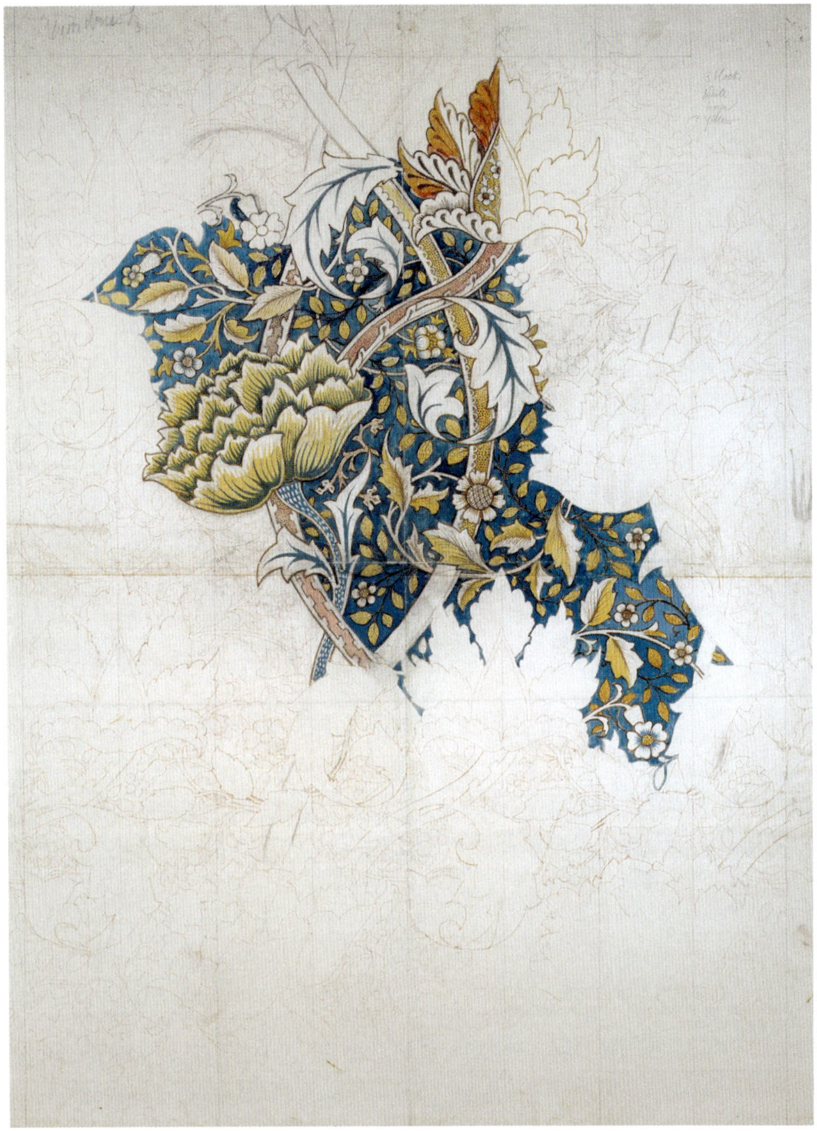

XII.56

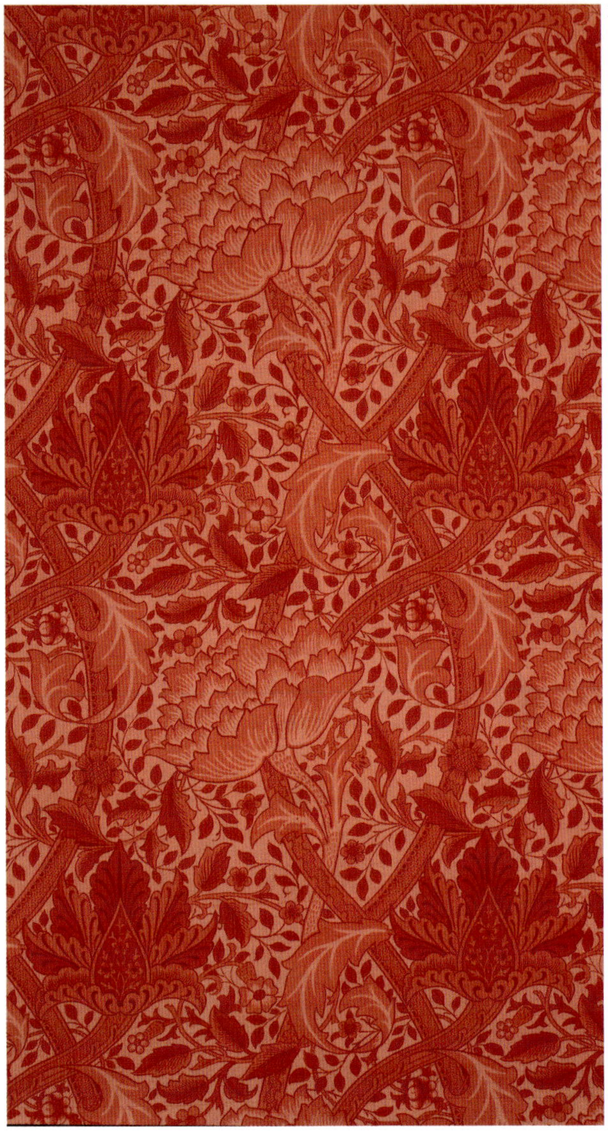

XII.55
Design for *Windrush* printed textile
William Morris, c.1881–3
Pencil, pen and ink, and watercolour, 131.5 x 99.6 cm
William Morris Society, Kelmscott House, London (D32)

Morris's designs became more and more impressionistic and although gridlines are shown in this example, he has included only enough of the pattern to make it clear to the block cutter how it works as a repeat. The design moves one stage further from the simple meandering stem seen in earlier patterns and here a second stem cuts across, providing complicated figures of eight. It also contains a more formal decoration within the open flower heads, a device Morris described as 'the inhabited leaf'. His source for this was the Persian and Turkish carpets he was studying at this time. The blue ground is surprisingly bright for Morris's natural dye palette and the pattern was usually surface printed to reproduce this effect. The paper is watermarked 'J WHATMAN 1881'.

XII.56
Windrush
Designed by William Morris, registered 18 October 1883
Manufactured at Merton Abbey
Block-printed cotton, 206 x 98 cm, repeat 52 x 44.5 cm
V&A (Circ.424–1953)
Given by Etta May Gubbins

Printed onto cotton and linen, both discharged and surface-printing techniques were used for this design although the latter is most commonly seen in surviving samples. It was, almost certainly, the discharged version that Morris promised Jane to hang in the drawing room at Kelmscott House 'as a summer change' in January 1884.

This example is not madder discharge, as expected from a design showing vast areas of the same colour, but is a late surface print. Manufactured after 1917, it shows an attempt to neutralize Morris's multi-coloured design for the twentieth-century market.

XII.57
Design for *Flowerpot* printed textile
William Morris, 1883
Pencil, ink and watercolour, 43 x 39 cm
Birmingham Museums Trust (1941P417)

Registered on 18 October 1883, this is one of four small-scale designs drawn by Morris for curtain linings. These patterns were also used as dress fabrics. On 6 January 1883 Morris wrote to May referring to an earlier example, 'there is a new block come in for the printed dresses, and we can dye piece cotton goods for such like things famously so, give your orders ladies, as even the humble can indulge in these simple articles'.

Morris's design, which is very similar to contemporary embroidered panels, shows only half of the turnover pattern. As it is one of the few discharged designs to use all of his primary and secondary colour palettes of red, blue and yellow with overprinted greens and oranges his notes are very specific.

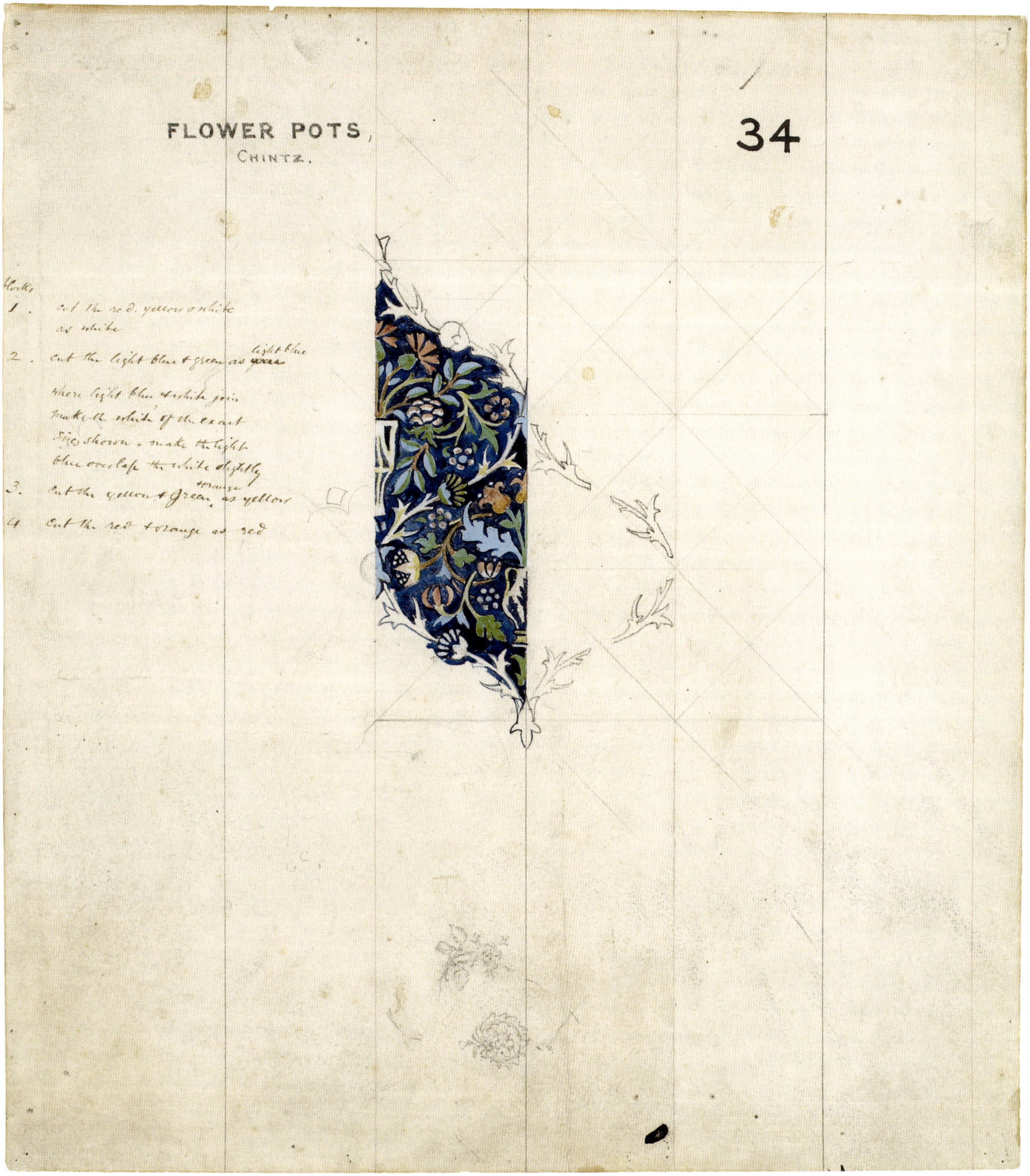
FLOWER POTS,
CHINTZ.
34
Blocks
1. Cut the red. yellow & white as white
2. Cut the light blue & green as light blue
where light blue & white join make the white of the exact size shown. make the light blue overlap the white slightly
3. Cut the yellow & green & orange as yellow
4 Cut the red & orange as red

XII.58

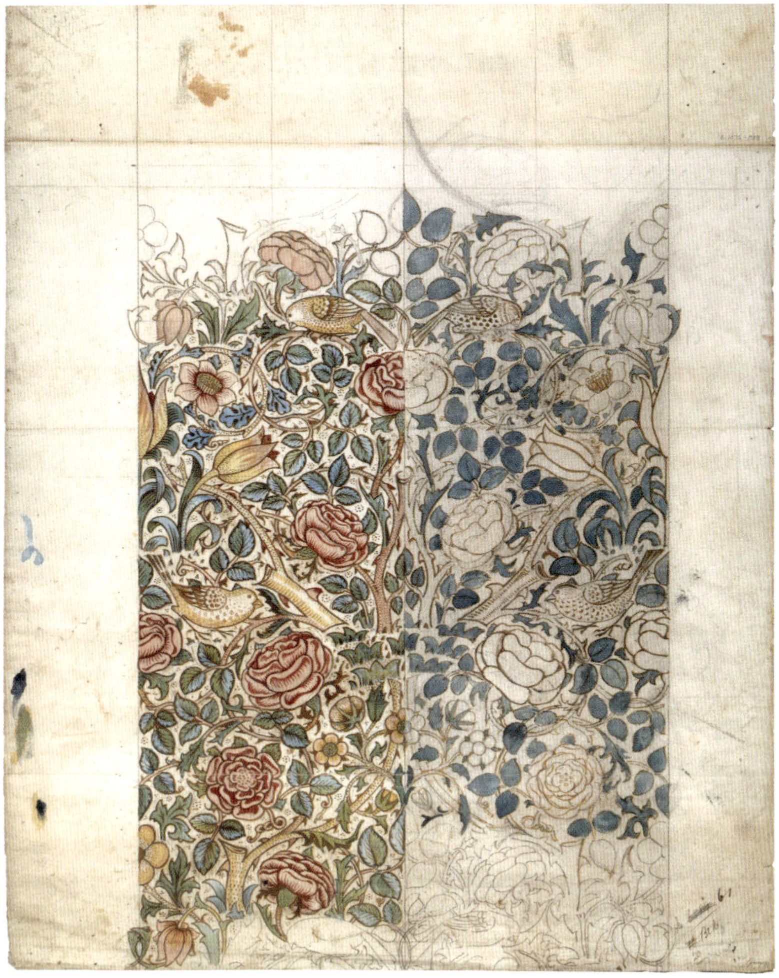

XII.59

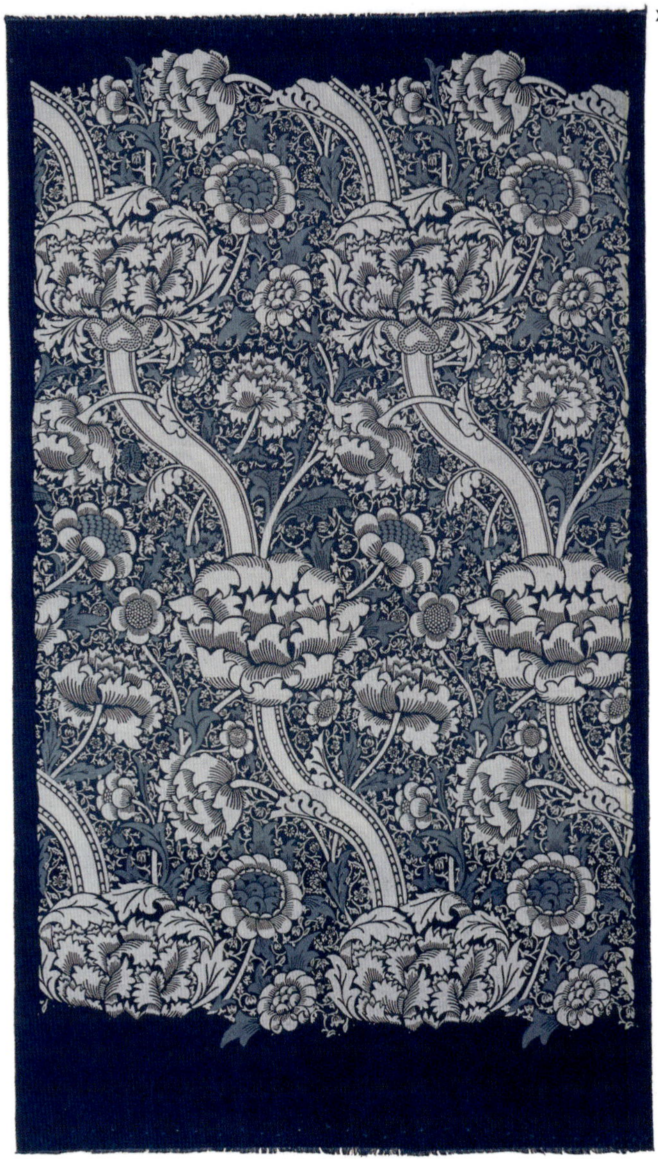

XII.58
Design for *Rose* printed textile
William Morris, 1883
Pencil, pen and ink, watercolour, 90.6 x 66.3 cm
V&A (E.1075–1988)
Purchased with Art Fund support and assistance of the National Heritage Memorial Fund and the Friends of the V&A

Registered on 8 December 1883, this is one of only four printed textile patterns in which Morris depicted birds (along with *Brother Rabbit*, *Strawberry Thief* and *Bird and Anemone*). He announced in a letter to Thomas Wardle of 25 March 1877 that he was studying birds to put in his next design, so it is probable that he drew these himself. Morris insisted on printing this complex pattern by the indigo-discharge process, despite this involving the bleaching and clearing of most of the white ground. The design was once owned by the architect Arthur Halcrow Verstage.

XII.59
Trial sample of *Wandle*
Designed by William Morris, registered 28 July 1884
Manufactured at Merton Abbey
Indigo-discharged and block-printed cotton, 160 x 96.5 cm
V&A (Circ.427–1953)
Given by Etta May Gubbins

This is a trial piece left unfinished at the indigo-discharge stage. The fabric has been dipped and dyed in the indigo vat, then soaped and washed until the dye was set. It was then block-printed with two sets of blocks, one having a strong bleaching agent to clear all of the blue from the ground leaving the white areas of the pattern, the other a weaker solution so that only part of the blue was discharged, resulting in a pale blue. The edge of the cloth shows the pin marks made when securing the cotton in the vat.

XII.60

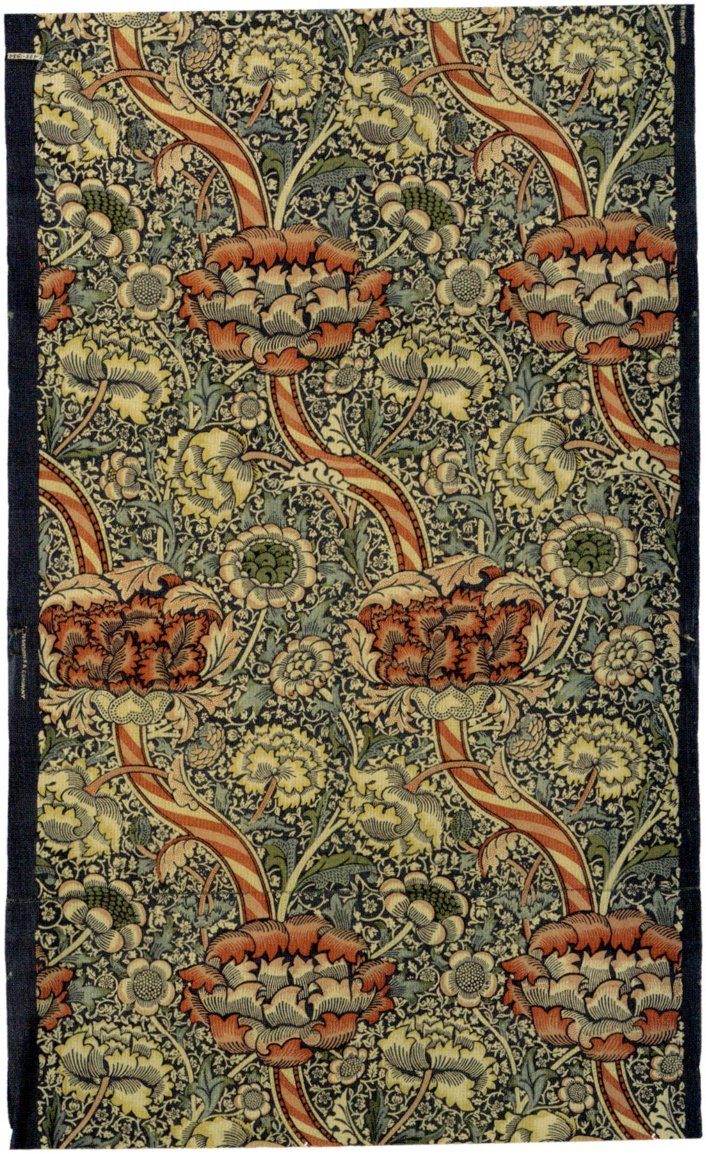

XII.61

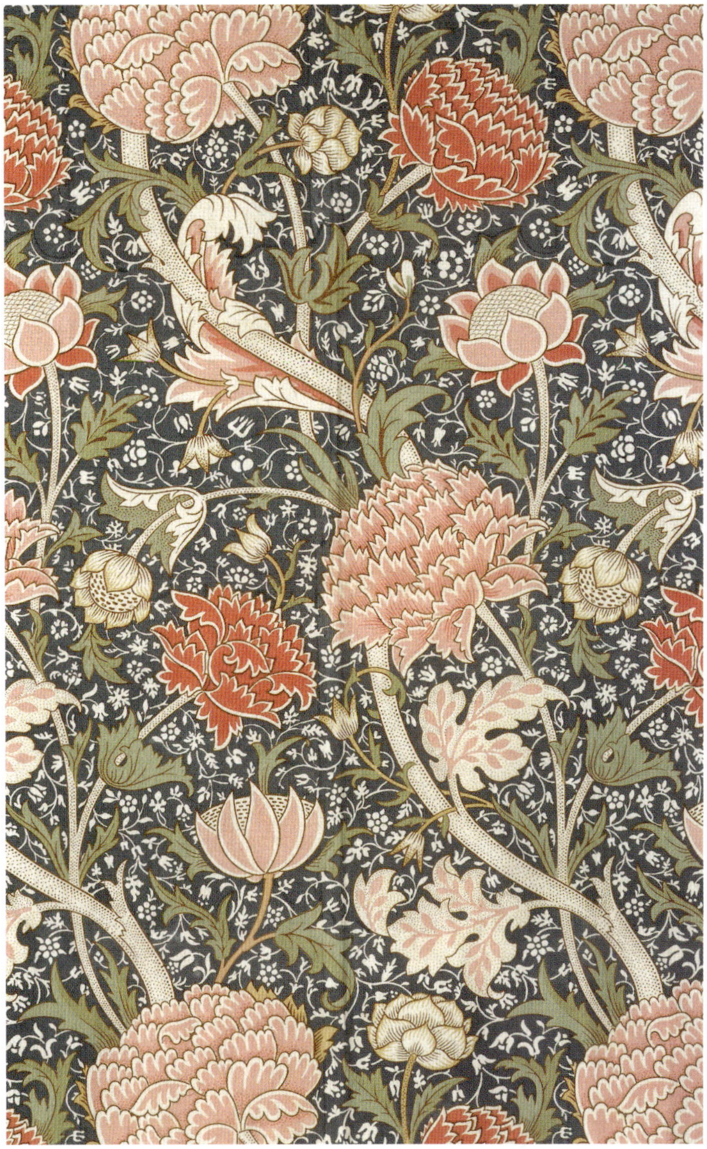

XII.60
Wandle
Designed by William Morris, registered 28 July 1884
Manufactured at Merton Abbey
Indigo-discharged and block-printed cotton, 165 x 92 cm, repeat 98.5 x 44.5 cm
V&A (T.425–1934)
Given by the British Institute of Industrial Art

This large-scale design took some time to develop and was named after the river that ran through the Merton Abbey site. Drawing began in 1883 and Morris wrote to Jenny on 4 September saying 'if it succeeds I shall call it Wandle: the connection may not seem obvious to you as the wet Wandle is not big but small, but you see it will have to be very elaborate & splendid and so I want to honour our helpful stream.' Fents were not struck (trial printings made) until 18 March 1884, when Morris expressed his view that 'it will be very grand' in a letter to Jane, and it was not registered for another four months.

The repeat is the largest attempted by Morris, and the striped barber's-pole effect echoes medieval motifs. After *Cray* it was the most expensive cotton furnishing produced by Morris & Co. A simplified version of this design was woven as a muslin by Alexander Morton. The original printing blocks are at the William Morris Gallery.

XII.61
Cray
Designed by William Morris, 1884
Manufactured at Merton Abbey
Block-printed cotton, 96.5 x 107.9 cm, repeat 92 x 45 cm
V&A (Circ. 82–1953)
Given by Mrs Winifred Nicholson

Thirty-four blocks were needed to print this complicated large pattern, consequently this was the most expensive printed textile produced by Morris & Co. Despite this it became very popular and was available in a number of different colourways on dark and light grounds in cotton or in linen. The pattern adapted to changing fashions and a number of early twentieth-century printings have survived showing pale colours on a white ground. It was one of Morris's last designs for printed textiles. He was already preoccupied with complex weaving techniques and for the next four years concentrated on designing for the loom. A few more printed patterns were drawn but none has the scale, breadth of design or depth of colouring of *Cray* or *Wandle*. The printing blocks are at the William Morris Gallery.

XII.62

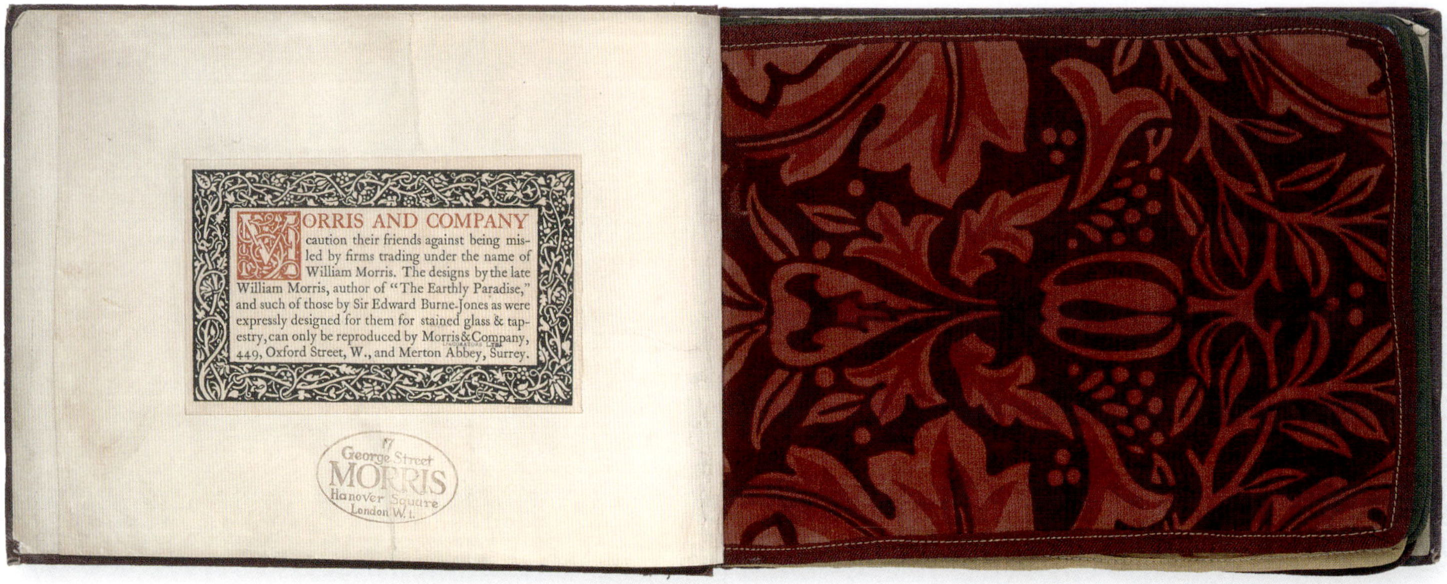

XII.63

XII.62
Sample book of printed velveteens
Morris & Co., 1890s
Block-printed velveteen,
21 x 54.5 x 2 cm (open)
V&A (T.660–1919)
Given by Morris & Co.

A sample book of ten printed velveteens manufactured by Morris & Co., including three colourways of *Acanthus* (shown), two of *Cherwell* and *Florence* and single samples of *Wey*, *Severn* and *Mole*. Printed velveteens became very fashionable in the 1870s and provided one of the most recognizable artistic furnishings of the period. In February 1877 Morris wrote to Wardle, 'we could have a trade in velvets & serges if we could get the colours good and fast'. Examples were exhibited by Morris & Co. at the first Arts and Crafts Exhibition in 1888 and the patterns included in this book were designed by Morris and Dearle over a long period from 1876 (*Acanthus*, registered on 25 April) to *Mole*, designed after 1892. *Acanthus*, *Florence* and *Mole* were only used as velveteens, whereas *Cherwell* and *Wey* were also available on cotton.

The velveteen, which was printed on a narrow 27-inch (68.5 cm) ground, was used for curtains and upholstery. It went out of fashion some years before this book was offered to the V&A in February 1919. Marillier wrote 'I have found you after a long hunt an ancient pattern book of Morris's printed cotton velvets, which had a great vogue in their day. They are beautiful materials and I can't imagine why they ever lost popularity but they did.'

XII.63
Sample book of printed cottons
Morris & Co., 1925–40
Manufactured at Merton Abbey
Printed cotton samples with printed labels, 21 x 58 x 2.8 cm (open)
V&A (T.34–1982)

This book contains 58 printed cottons showing the range of patterns and colourways available for sale from Morris & Co. These swatches were used both in the shop at George Street, Hanover Square, and loaned to customers. Similar examples are in the collections of the Cooper Hewitt Museum, New York, and the Art Gallery of South Australia, Adelaide, sent to prospective clients in these cities. Included are some of the firm's earliest designs (*Small Stem*, *Large Stem* and *Coiling Trail*) plus 17 well-known Morris patterns, six Dearle designs (*Daffodil*, *Yare*, *Compton*, *Bourne*, *Eden*, *Briar*) and two adapted Morris wallpaper patterns (*Willow* and *Powdered*). *Tangley*, *Haddon* and *Holkam* are early nineteenth-century designs adapted for the early twentieth-century fashion for revival patterns. Prices range from 3*s*. a yard for *Bird and Anemone* in madder-discharged cotton, to 10*s*. 6*d*. for a wider example (137 cm) of *Large Stem* on linen.

XII.64

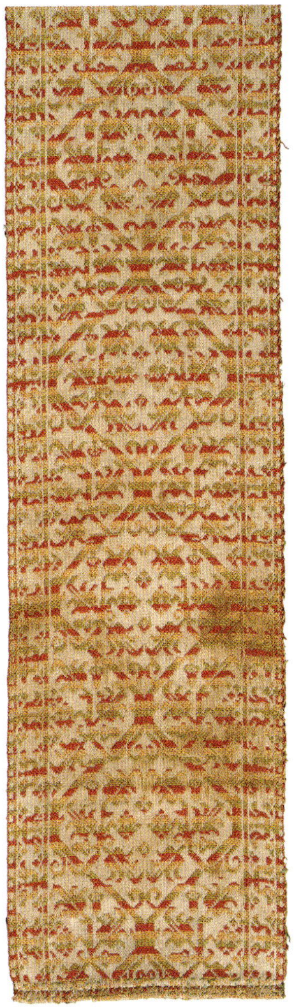

XII.65

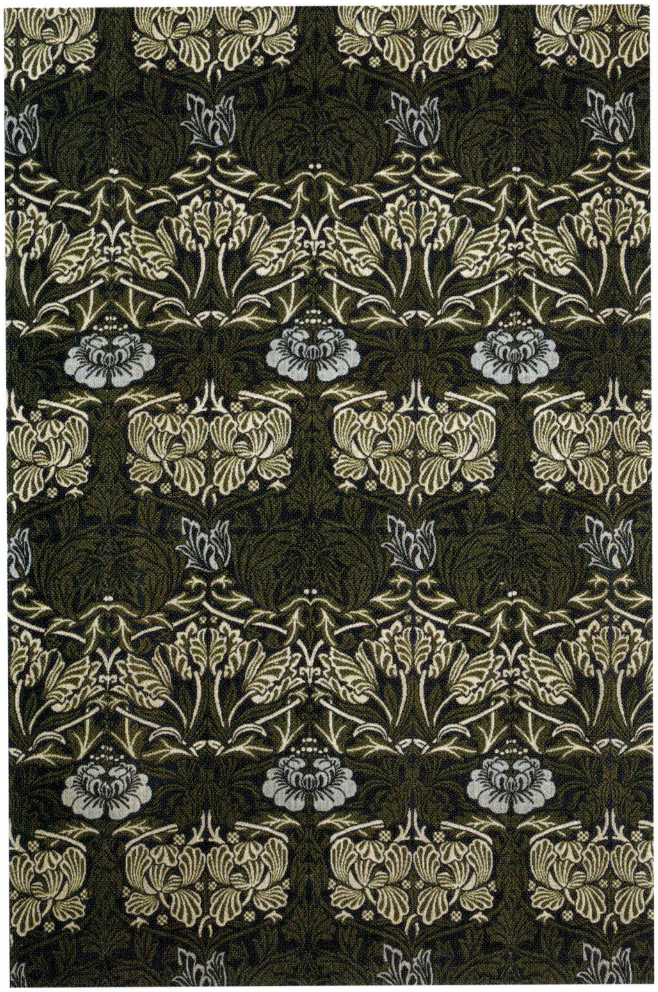

XII.66

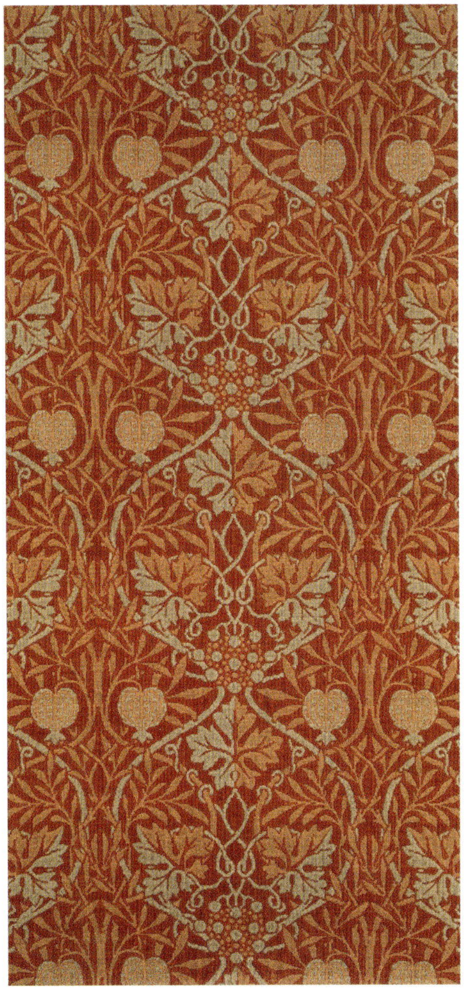

WOVEN TEXTILES

XII.64
Woven band
Italian or German, first half of the seventeenth century
Silk and linen double cloth, 38.1 x 11.4 cm
V&A (T.123–1939)
Bequeathed by May Morris

This Italian or Italian-influenced German weaving is from Morris's own collection, acquired for technical rather than pattern reference although the design of repeating ogee shapes was frequently seen in his work (XII.65–6).

Morris designed a number of woollen double cloths and one example, *Dove and Rose*, was woven in silk and wool. His understanding and appreciation of the tactile quality of fibres and interest in how they react when woven together is evident in many of his woven textiles. He was particularly fond of using linen, although the firm's first commercial silk and linen fabric, *Golden Bough* (designed about 1888), was one of Morris's last designs for the technique.

XII.65
***Tulip and Rose* curtain**
Designed by William Morris, registered 20 January 1876
Manufactured by Heckmondwike Manufacturing Company, Yorkshire
Woven woollen triple cloth, 297 x 171 cm, repeat 89 x 43 cm
V&A (Circ.390A–1970)
Bequeathed by Mrs G.M. Spear

This pattern is the first datable design by Morris for woven furnishing textiles, though he had been considering adding these to the firm's range for some time. In a letter of November 1875 Morris mentioned the Macclesfield silk weaver Joshua Oldfield Nicholson, suggesting that having no facilities to weave commercially he was planning to approach outside contractors to produce this work for the firm.

The Heckmondwike Manufacturing Company had already been commissioned to produce triple cloths as Kidderminster-type carpeting (XII.84). *Tulip and Rose* was one of a series of fabrics of the same structure registered as furnishing textiles rather than floor coverings, though probably used for both purposes. Later it was also available as power-loom woven silk and linen, and silk and cotton mixtures. The all-wool version was recommended for upholstery.

XII.66
Vine and Pomegranate
Designed by William Morris or Kate Faulkner, *c.*1877
Manufactured by Heckmondwike Manufacturing Company, Yorkshire
Woven woollen triple cloth, 221 x 183 cm, repeat 40.5 x 41 cm
V&A (Circ.383–1962)
Given by Mr and Mrs Michael Waterhouse

Morris & Co. often referred to two- and three-ply woven textiles as 'tapestries', to differentiate them from the Kidderminster carpeting of the same technique and to suggest the effect of the fabric's draping qualities. This technically incorrect term, which was never used by Morris, has led to considerable confusion with the firm's actual production of tapestry.

Designed at a period when Kate Faulkner was working for Morris & Co., it has been suggested that this may be one of a small group of her designs. A particularly bold pattern using the traditional repeating device of intersecting ogees, the influence of early Italian, Turkish and Middle Eastern woven silks and velvets is plain to see, although the trailing grape and willow leaf would have given the pattern a modern appearance in its time. Morris recommended the red colourway to George Howard in January 1882 for Brampton Church, Cumbria. This textile was given to the V&A by the grandson of Alfred Waterhouse, the architect, and originally used in the furnishing of Yattendon Court, near Newbury, Berkshire.

XII.67

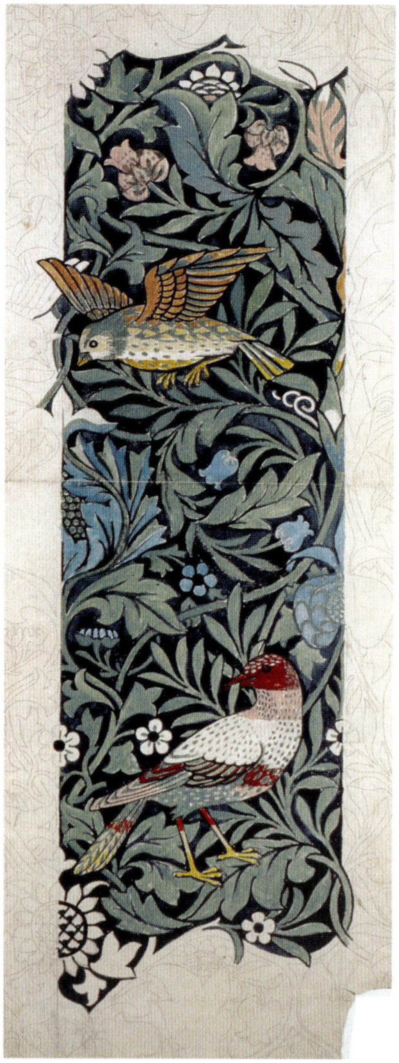

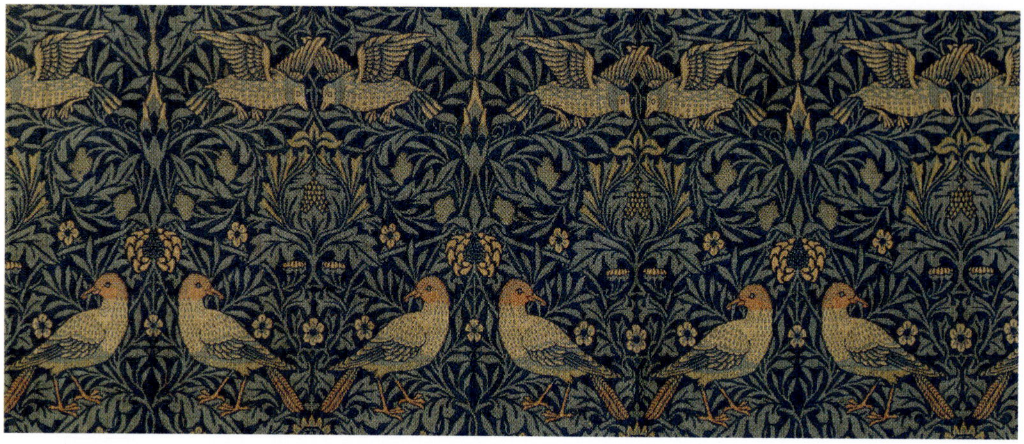

XII.68

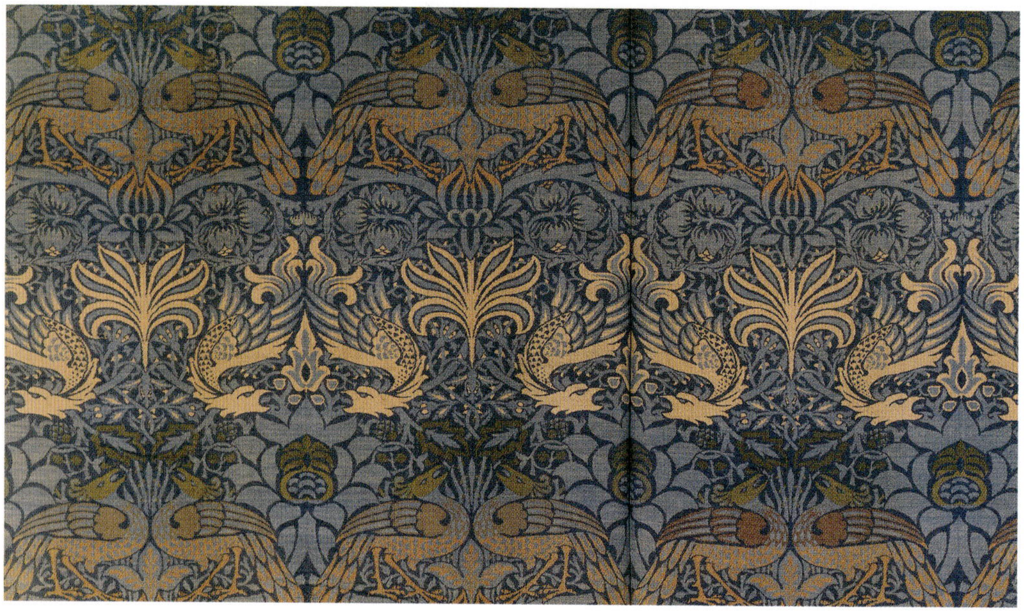

XII.69

XII.67
Design for *Bird* woven textile
William Morris, 1878
Pencil and watercolour, 101.6 x 68.2 cm
William Morris Society, Kelmscott House, London (D31)

On 25 March 1877 Morris wrote to Thomas Wardle, 'I am studying birds now to see if I can't get some of them into my next design'. This is the first of a group of designs showing pairs of facing birds, perched and in flight. Morris was inspired by sixteenth- and seventeenth-century Italian woven silks from Lucca and Sicily in the collection of the South Kensington Museum. In December 1882, he described studying examples offered to the museum by Canon Bock, among them 'a noble piece of Sicilian woven stuff of a pattern I havn't [*sic*] seen before'. In his 1884 lecture 'Textile Fabrics', he claimed these textiles provided the perfect balance between 'the wild fancy and luxurious intricacy of the East with the straight-forward story-telling imagination ... of medieval Europe'.

XII.68
***Bird* curtain**
Designed by William Morris, 1878
Manufactured at Queen Square and later at Merton Abbey
Handloom jacquard-woven woollen double cloth, 304 x 182 cm, repeat 72.5 x 47 cm
V&A (Circ.501a–1962)
Given by Mrs J. Laughton

In 1877 Morris decided to attempt weaving at Queen Square initially focusing on brocade weaving, and Thomas Wardle assisted Morris in finding a French silk weaver by the name of Bazin, who arrived with his loom in June 1877. After some initial difficulties, most of Morris's woven textiles were produced at Queen Square until the move to Merton Abbey. Contractors were employed only when the technique demanded additional equipment or for large quantities of cloth.

Bird was draped around the walls of the first-floor drawing room at Kelmscott House. May Morris believed the pattern 'intimate and friendly ... the most adaptable to the needs of ordinary life. It suggests not the wealth of the millionaire but the modest competence of a middle-class merchant who lives ... with the few beautiful things he has collected slowly and carefully.'

This curtain belonged to Sydney Cockerell, Morris's secretary and one of his executors. The V&A also owns *Bird* curtains presented by May Morris, which are almost certainly from Kelmscott House. Other examples from the house were given to Emery Walker and are part of the furnishings at 7 Hammersmith Terrace, Walker's home from 1903.

XII.69
***Peacock and Dragon* curtain**
Designed by William Morris, 1878
Manufactured at Queen Square and later at Merton Abbey
Handloom jacquard-woven woollen twill, 396 x 353 cm, repeat 109 x 90 cm
V&A (T.64–1933)

Morris's increasing study of early woven textiles is particularly noticeable in his woven patterns of the late 1870s and 1880s. A visit to Vincent Robinson's shop in March 1878 to see a complete room from Damascus 'all vermillion & gold & ultramarine very beautiful and is just like going into the Arabian Nights', probably influenced the colouring of this example and the alternative red version. Although based on Sicilian weavings of the fifteenth and sixteenth centuries, Morris's finished designs are quite different with a much larger repeat than is seen in these early pieces. Furthermore, the fabric was woven in wool rather than silk to produce the effect of a medieval hanging.

Used in a number of houses, including the drawing room at Kelmscott House, this proved one of Morris's most popular textiles, particularly with international clients. This curtain is from a set of four used in the hall at Clouds, Percy and Madeline Wyndham's country house near Salisbury.

XII.70

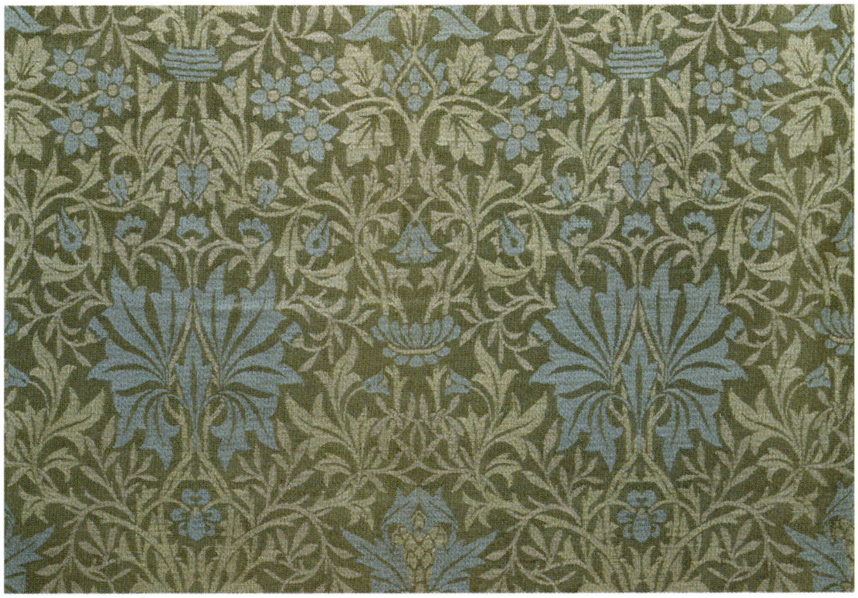

XII.71

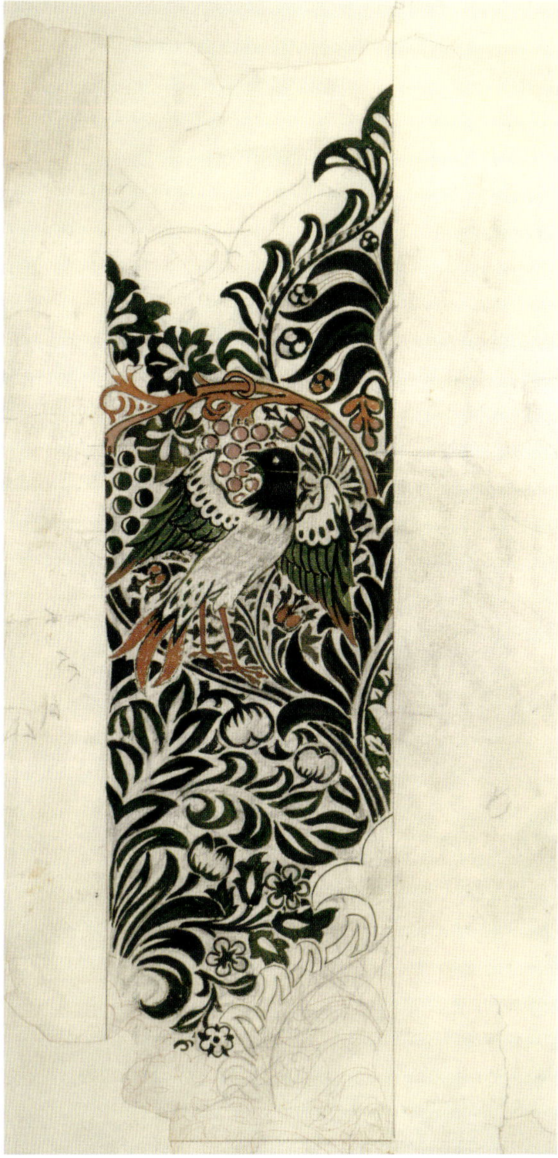

XII.72

XII.70
***Flower Garden* curtain**
Designed by William Morris, 1879
Manufactured at Queen Square
and later at Merton Abbey
Handloom jacquard-woven silk
and wool, 231.6 x 271 cm,
repeat 48 x 34.5 cm
V&A (Circ.80a–1966)
Given by Mrs John Webster and
Mrs Claude Coombe

In March 1879 Morris wrote to Georgiana Burne-Jones, 'I am writing in a whirlwind of dyeing and weaving, and even as to the latter rather excited by a new piece just out of the loom, which looks beautiful, like a flower garden.' Morris claimed to have chosen the colours to 'suggest the beauties of inlaid metal' influenced, no doubt, by items from Damascus he had studied in Vincent Robinson's shop in March 1878.

The pattern type, of formal repeating flower heads in cross-section was used by Morris in the background of *Bird* (XII.68) and for large embroidered hangings being produced at this time, particularly *Artichoke* designed for Ada Godman in 1877 (XII.17).

Flower Garden was used in a number of Morris & Co. decorative commissions, including Rounton Grange, 1 Holland Park and Stanmore Hall. This is one of a pair of curtains from Holland Park, given to the V&A by descendants of Aleco Ionides.

XII.71
Preparatory design for *Bird and Vine* woven textile
William Morris, 1879
Pencil, pen and ink, coloured chalks, watercolour and body colour,
101.5 x 68.4 cm
V&A (E.40–1940)
Bequeathed by May Morris

Comparing this design with the finished woven textile a number of differences can be seen. In the fabric vine leaves replace the more complex arrangement of flowers and leaves in the lower cartouches and the bunches of grapes are positioned differently. The dark, rather crude colouring of the design suggests that Morris originally intended this textile to be a multi-coloured pattern and consequently a complex and costly fabric. The final woven version was produced in restrained, two-tone colouring.

XII.72
Bird and Vine
Designed by William Morris,
registered 15 May 1879
Manufactured at Queen Square
and later at Merton Abbey
Handloom jacquard-woven wool,
60 x 90.5 cm, repeat 68.5 x 38.5 cm
V&A (T.14–1919)
Given by Morris & Co.

One of a series of designs by Morris depicting pairs of birds within a traditional ogee repeat pattern of stylized leaves and flower forms. This fabric proved very popular for churches because of the symbolic use of grapes and dove-like birds in its design.

It was available in 11 different colourings, four of which were given to the V&A following the move of Morris & Co.'s shop from Oxford Street to George Street, Hanover Square in 1917.

XII.73

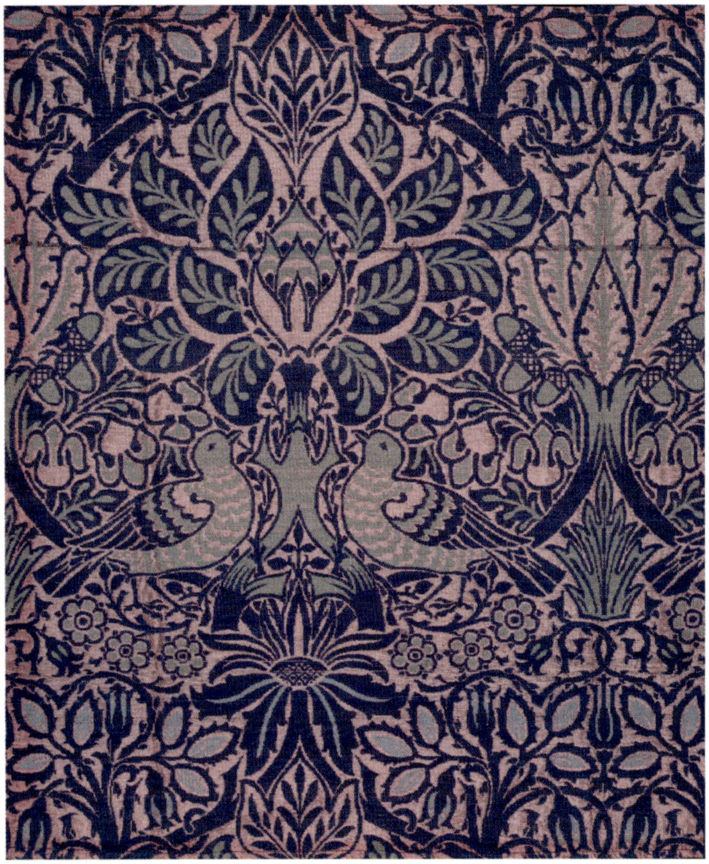

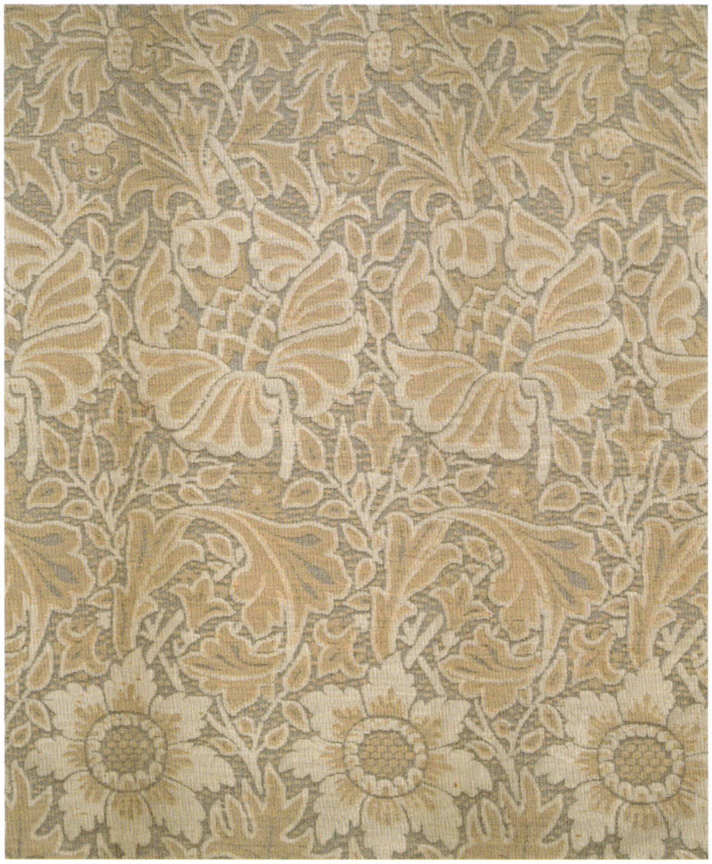

XII.74

XII.73
Dove and Rose
Designed by William Morris, 1879
Manufactured by Alexander Morton & Co., Darvel, Scotland, and later at Merton Abbey
Handloom jacquard-woven silk and wool double cloth, metal thread, 63.5 x 53 cm, repeat 52 x 45.5 cm
V&A (Circ.126–1953)
Given by Christabel Marillier

This is very similar pattern to *Bird and Vine*, however, the different weaving structure provides a different effect. This cloth was woven with two separate warps of wool and silk. The pattern is made by varying the lifting of threads in weaving, producing areas of solid wool, silk or mixtures of the two. It was first woven for Morris & Co. by Alexander Morton, the Scottish manufacturer. The delicate structure of the fabric was designed for curtains and hangings rather than upholstery (although Morris covered a chair at home and found it worked better than expected).

Morris was pleased with the subtle colourings available, even though the dyes used were not always fast, a common problem with contractors' work. On recommending a red version of the fabric to Rosalind Howard on 24 November 1881 he declared, 'it will last as long as need be since the cloth is really very strong. I can't answer so decidedly as to the colour; but the colours in it when looked at by themselves you will find rather full than not; 'tis the mixture that makes them look delicate'.

The pattern was available in different sizes during Morris's lifetime. Two samples in the V&A collection, one shot with gold thread, were trials not put into commercial production. This version proved the most popular. The design is at Birmingham Museum and Art Gallery (1941P399) and a point paper is at the William Morris Gallery (A451).

XII.74
Madras Muslin
Designed by William Morris, 1880
Manufactured by Alexander Morton & Co., Darvel, Scotland
Woven cotton and silk leno (gauze), 60.9 x 173.9 cm, repeat 57 x 17 cm
V&A (T.657–1919)
Given by Morris & Co.

This cloth provided the perfect alternative to roller blinds or machine-made Nottingham lace curtains, which Morris disliked. The use of silk in the weave provides a contrasting sheen to the cotton. As specialized looms were needed, it is probable that Alexander Morton and Co. was the sole manufacturer. Highly experienced in supplying such goods, the firm had been set up in the 1860s to take advantage of the impoverished local muslin industry in Darvel, Scotland.

Morris & Co. were supplying gauzes by March 1880, as the first bill for decorations at 1 Holland Park included muslin curtains for both the dining room and the Antiquities Room. Unfortunately, the designs used are not named nor are they identifiable from contemporary photographs.

This pattern, with its meandering repeat, is similar to a number of printed textile designs, *Kennet* in particular (XII.54). The name underlines the fact that it was influenced by fine contemporary Indian imports of similar cloth. Although rare, other Morris designs were woven as muslins. A second example appears in the firm's twentieth-century pattern book (XII.81) and Morton & Co. produced versions of *Cherwell* and *Cray* under its own name.

XII.75

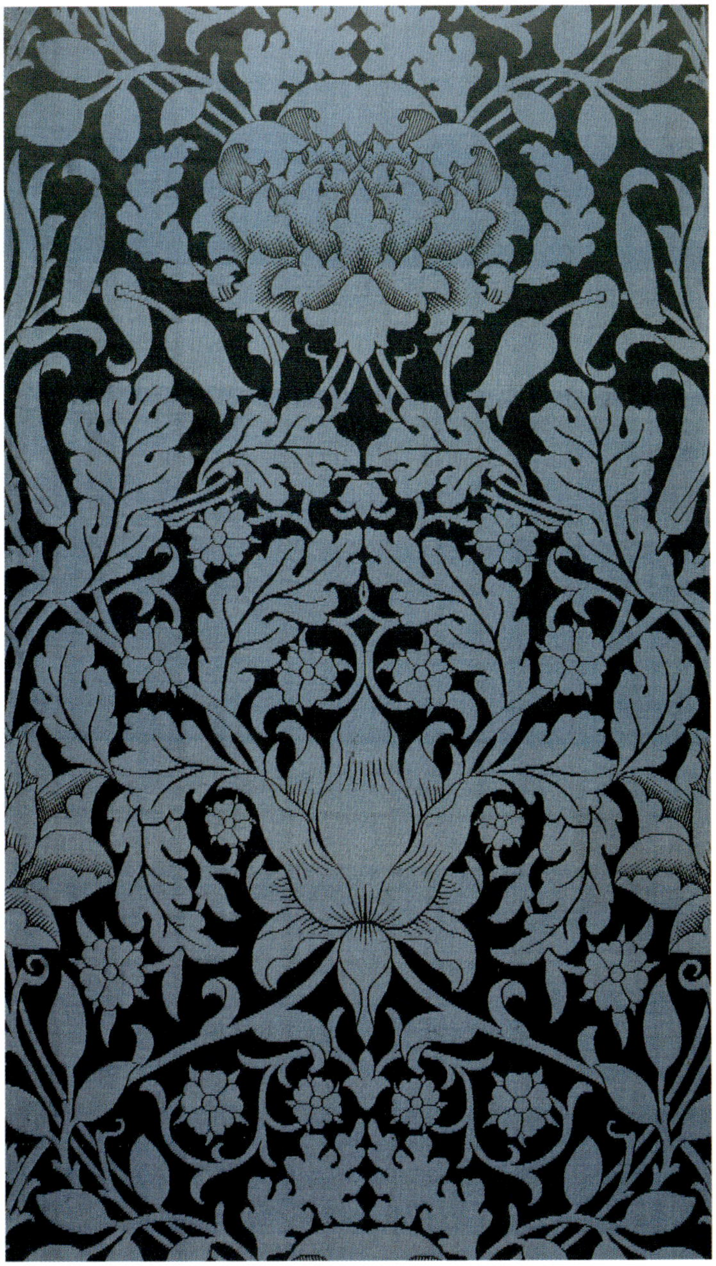

XII.76

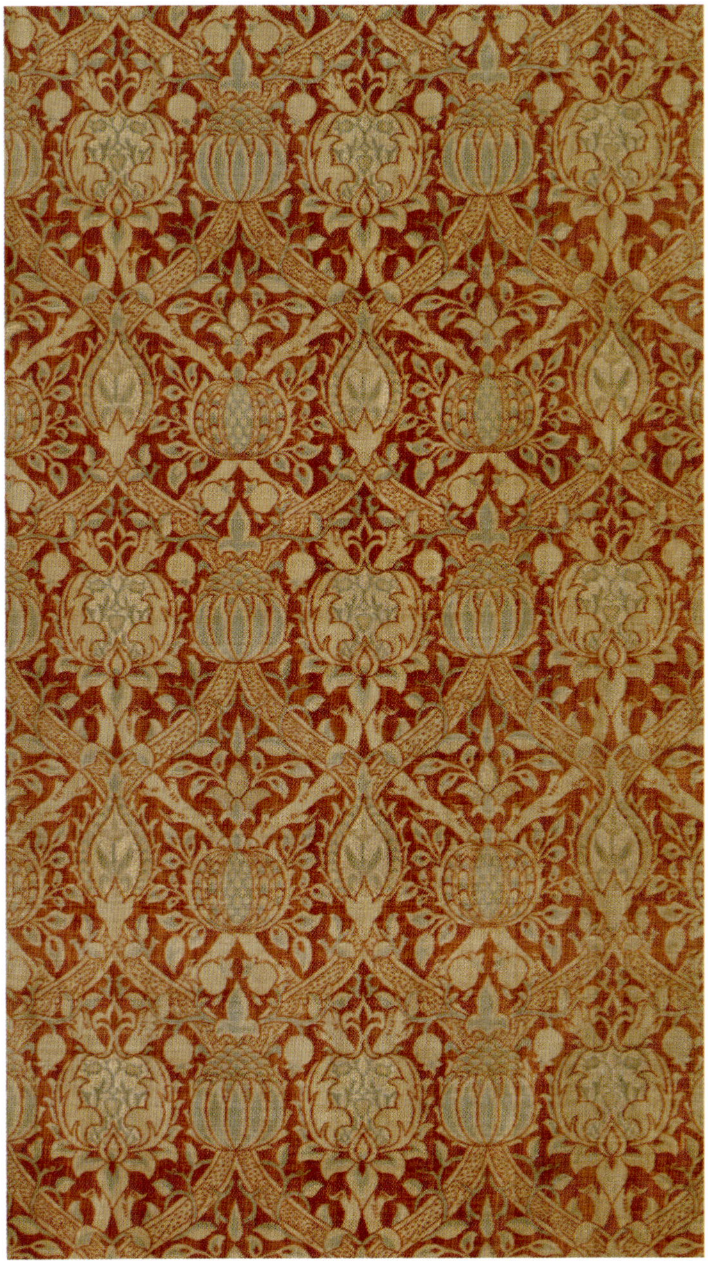

XII.75
Oak
Designed by William Morris, 1881
Manufactured by Joshua Oldfield Nicholson, Macclesfield, and later at Merton Abbey
Hand- and power-loom jacquard-woven silk damask, 270.5 x 53.3 cm, repeat 81.5 x 52 cm
V&A (T.74–1919)
Given by May Morris

One of two designs for silk damasks made for the decoration of the Throne Room and Blue Room at St James's Palace. None of the existing photographs of the Morris & Co. scheme show this pattern, so it may have been offered initially as an alternative to the *St James*, which was used stretched and battened to the walls and for curtains and valances. Although the commission for curtains at the palace was not received until December 1881, Morris was busy designing the silks in September of that year.

This design was very popular and used extensively by Morris & Co. for furnishings and as the background for embroidered hangings (XII.28). It was available in a large number of colourways, both with plain and 'shot' (iridescent) silks. In writing about the *St James* silk to Rosalind Howard in November 1881 Morris declared, 'what would you say to dullish pink shot with amber; like some of those chrysanthemums we see just now?'

XII.76
Granada
Designed by William Morris, 1884
Manufactured at Merton Abbey
Woven silk velvet brocaded with gilt thread (gilt paper round a silk core), 194.9 x 67.3 cm, repeat 40 x 22 cm
V&A (T.4–1919)
Given by Morris & Co.

Morris's interest in the technical aspects of weaving increased and some of his last designs attempt to reproduce complex historic structures. He began to weave this, his only velvet, in March 1884 on a specially constructed loom. The blue areas were block-printed. Although he was successful, the process was so time consuming and expensive that the fabric was not put into commercial production. Only 20 yards (18.3 metres) were woven and the price was prohibitive at £10 a yard. *The Art Journal* for 1891 claimed it to be 'the only English velvet that bears any comparison to the old Flemish velvets'.

XII.77

XII.78

XII.77
Brocatel
Designed by William Morris, *c.*1888
Manufactured at Merton Abbey
Handloom jacquard-woven silk and wool, 76 x 68 cm, repeat 72.5 x 45.5 cm
V&A (Circ.125–1953)
Given by Christabel Marillier

This was a valiant attempt by Morris to reproduce the effect of a traditional brocatelle in which the raised pattern, often using metal threads, shows through a ribbed surface. Using the nineteenth-century invention of jacquard weaving and gold coloured silks he was able to suggest the sumptuous stiffness of the original. To match the effect of the early textile, he produced a pattern strongly influenced by Middle Eastern design.

This tightly woven fabric proved ideal for upholstery and, with its large repeat, for hangings stretched and battened to walls. Exhibited at the 1888 Arts and Crafts Exhibition, this could be one of the designs that Morris's partners, the Smith brothers, were pressing him to finish earlier in the year. It is likely to be one of his last repeating patterns. It is often confused with the later, similar Dearle design *Persian Brocatel*.

XII.78
Tulip and Net
Designed by William Morris or John Henry Dearle, *c.*1888–9
Manufactured at Merton Abbey
Handloom jacquard-woven wool, 193 x 178 cm, repeat 66 x 44 cm
V&A (T.57–1934)

Morris's last datable textile patterns were drawn in 1888. With his increasing interest in tapestry weaving, book printing and political activity, it was around this time that John Henry Dearle took over the role of textile designer for the firm. This pattern has strong similarities with Morris's *Brocatel* (XII.77) but is also close in style to Dearle's *Persian Brocatel* drawn soon afterwards. Could both men have been involved, with Morris providing the main structure leaving Dearle to provide pattern details?

Dearle had worked alongside Morris since entering the firm as a young man in 1878. His patterns tend to be stiffer and more stylized than Morris's, though they often include such familiar devices as curling acanthus leaves. Many of his designs, like this one, show the influence of Persian textiles and, like Morris, he frequently studied the collections at the South Kensington Museum.

XII.79
Kennet
Designed by William Morris as a printed cotton, 1883
Manufactured at Merton Abbey or by an outside contractor
Handloom jacquard-woven silk, 69.8 x 70.4 cm, repeat 70 x 22 cm
V&A (T.69–1919)
Given by Morris & Co.

This is the only example of a Morris design used as both a printed (XII.54) and woven textile. It is not known when it was first woven, although the pattern is reversed, suggesting that the original printed cotton design was used after Morris's time for cutting the jacquard cards for the loom.

The design was exhibited at the 1899 Arts and Crafts Exhibition, described as a pattern for 'silk hanging', indicating that this form was more popular by this date. It also appears in the Morris & Co. *Printed Linens and Cottons* catalogue published about 1912, where it is inadvertently described as a 'figured silk brocade' at the high cost of 19*s*. 6*d*. per yard.

XII.80
***Cross Twigs* sample weaving**
Designed by John Henry Dearle, *c.*1893
Manufactured at Merton Abbey
Handloom jacquard-woven silk and linen, 88.9 x 139.7 cm, repeat 68 x 45.5 cm
V&A (T.20–1919)

This trial sample, which shows two different colourings of the design, was probably kept for reference. The earliest recorded use of the fabric is as luxurious hangings on a state bed purchased for the visit of the Prince of Wales to Penrhyn Castle, Bangor, North Wales, in 1894 where they were lined with gold coloured silk and finished with tassels and fringes. A pair of *Cross Twigs* hangings has also been discovered in a collection formerly belonging to the Glessner family of Chicago who were important patrons of the firm in the late nineteenth century.

XII.79

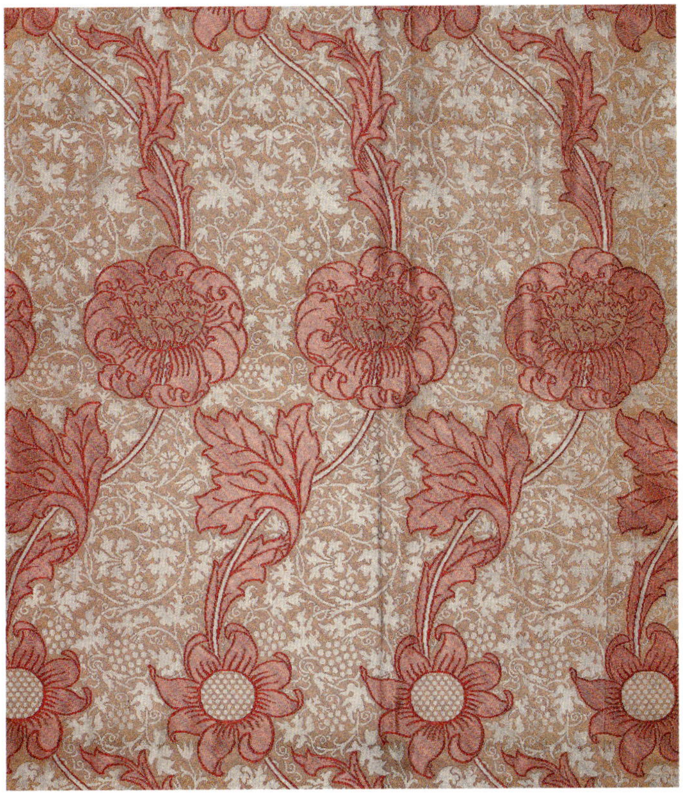

XII.80

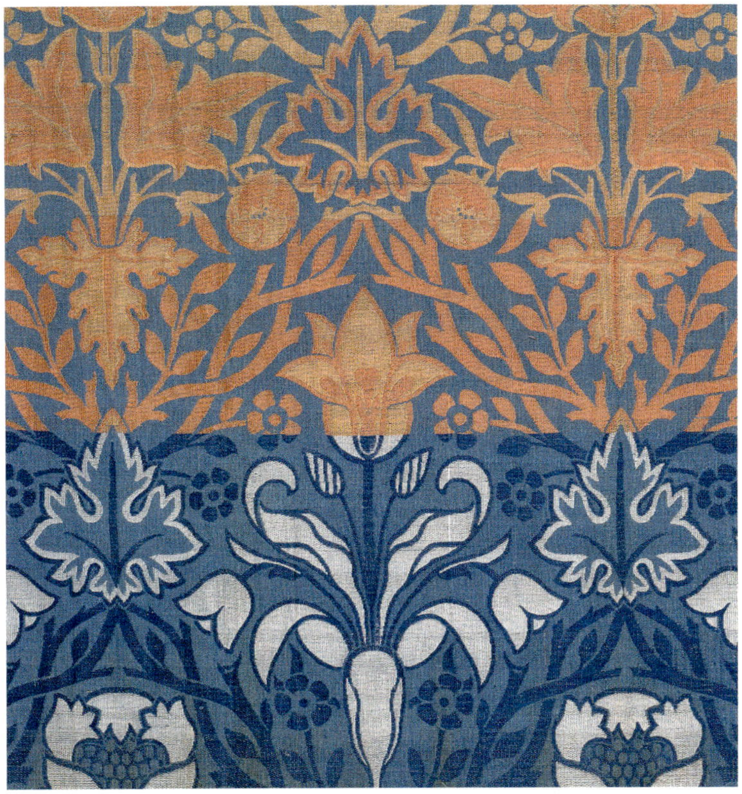

XII.81

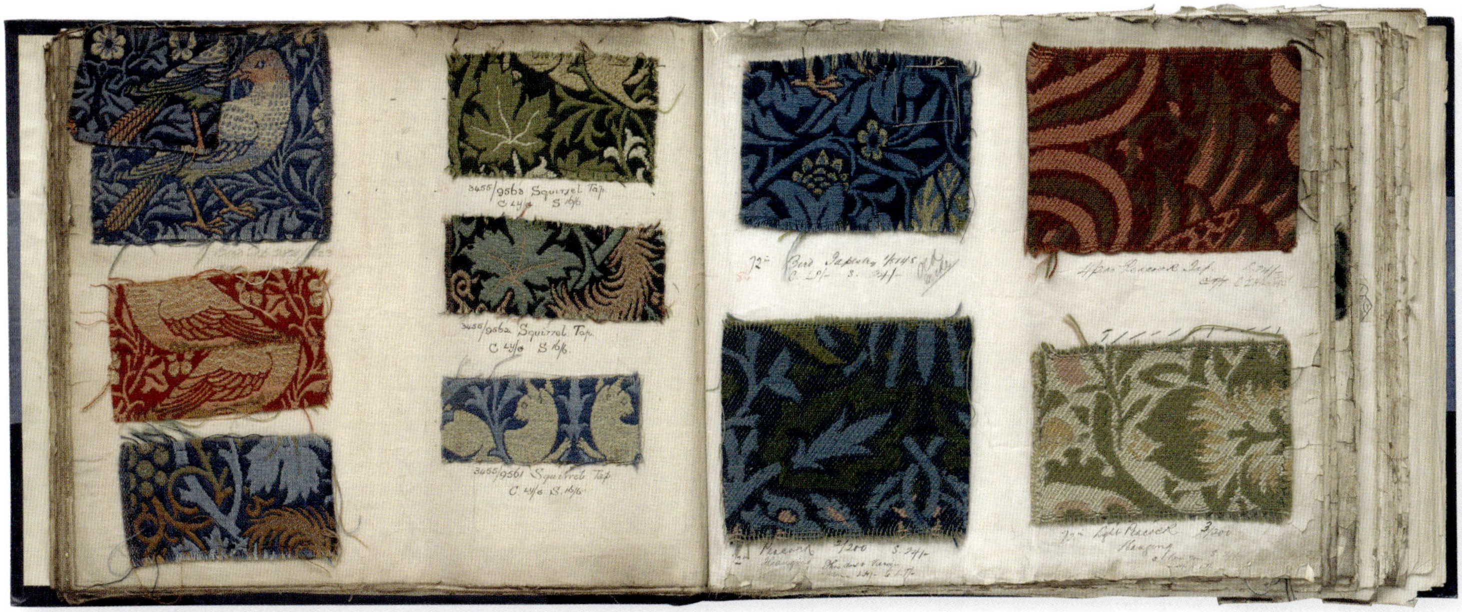

XII.81
Working pattern book
Morris & Co., twentieth century
Linen and paper with woven and printed samples, 52 x 125 x 12.5 cm (open)
V&A (T.30–1940)

This undated pattern book is a record of many of the Morris & Co. textiles available in the twentieth century. It includes swatches of woven and printed fabrics, as well as printed velveteens and embossed velvets. The inscriptions record pattern numbers and prices and a few are prefaced with 'sell ...' and a price suggesting that this was a guide used by staff in the shop at Oxford Street, and later at George Street, Hanover Square. The pattern numbers would also have been useful when sending orders to Merton Abbey or one of Morris & Co.'s contractors.

Many of Morris's most popular designs are represented, often in new colourways and with altered pattern sizes. It is an interesting gauge of early twentieth-century fashions and how Morris's patterns were used in the years following his death. This book also provides the only source of various late designs by John Henry Dearle. It was presented to the V&A in July 1940, two months after the firm was placed in the hands of the Receiver.

XII.82

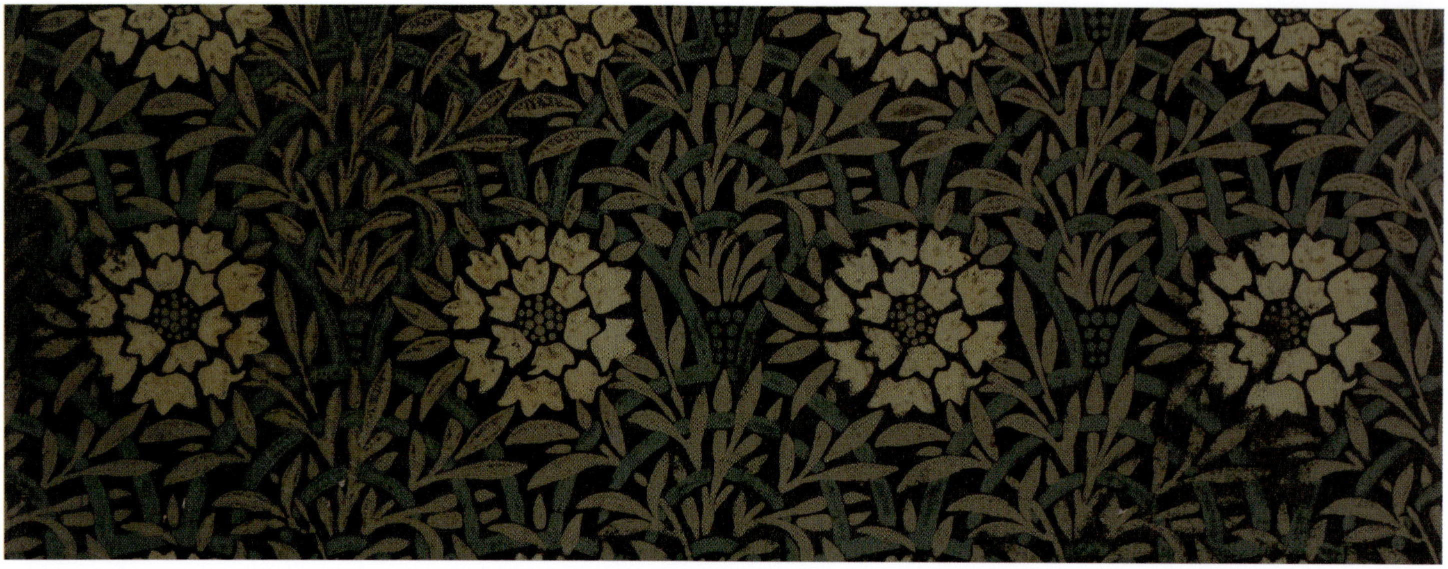

XII.83

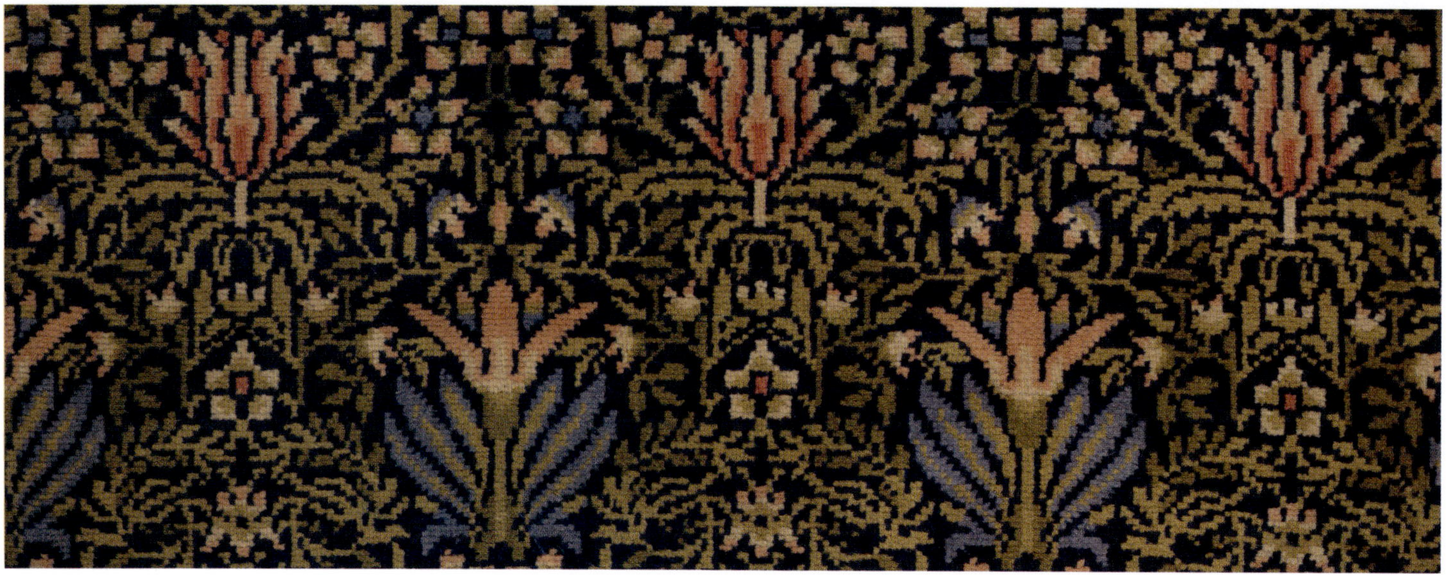

FLOOR COVERINGS

XII.82
Linoleum
Designed by William Morris, registered 7 June 1875
Manufactured for Morris & Co. by an outside contractor
Printed corticine (ground cork and India rubber), 40.6 x 60.9 cm
V&A (Circ.527–1953)
Given by Miss H.M. Beale

This was Morris's first design for a floor covering. As a significant new manufacturing venture, it warranted registration with the Patent Office. It was possibly made by Nairn's of Kirkcaldy in Scotland, the most prolific manufacturers of linoleum at this time, whose own designs show a marked similarity to Morris's work.

Lino was as popular as machine-woven carpeting from the 1860s, although only used selectively. Morris's pragmatic advocacy of the use of both in the home helped these cheaper forms of floor coverings become more respectable. Despite its popularity with clients, only one linoleum design has been traced. This was available in 72-inch widths (183 cm) in two colourways and cost 3*s*. 10*d*. per square yard.

The design of marigolds against an arched trellis shows Morris's preoccupation at this time with the manufacture of other furnishings. His *Marigold* design for wallpaper and printed textiles (XI.11 and XII.38) was registered just two months earlier and the square repeat is similar to that used on tiles.

XII.83
***Lily* machine-woven carpeting**
Designed by William Morris, *c*.1874
Manufactured by Yates & Co., Wilton, Wiltshire (later Wilton Royal Carpet Factory Ltd)
Wilton-type carpeting with woollen pile on jute, 66 x 43.2 cm, repeat 24 x 22 cm
V&A (Circ.65B–1959)

At Christmas 1875 Morris & Co. registered two carpet designs, both of which were woven at Wilton. Morris believed 'Wilton carpets must be classed as the best kind of machine-woven carpets ... If well made the material is very durable, and by skilful treatment in the designing, the restrictions as to color are not noticeable' (Boston Foreign Fair brochure, 1883). The carpet has a soft velvety texture (woven at 50–150 tufts to the inch) and the pattern is formed on the surface by different coloured warp thread loops, which are later cut, on a strong woven foundation.

Lily was one of 24 Wilton carpet designs available through Morris & Co. and this type of floor covering proved the most commercially successful of all those sold by the firm. Available in four widths, from 18 to 36 inches, they cost 10*s*. 6*d*. per yard. 'Saxony-Wilton' or 'Velvet carpet', a more luxurious pile carpet, was available at 12*s*. 6*d*. per yard. Patterned borders were popular, and the firm sold complete Wilton bordered carpets. This sample was part of a larger carpet used in a house in Lowndes Square, London.

XII.84

XII.85

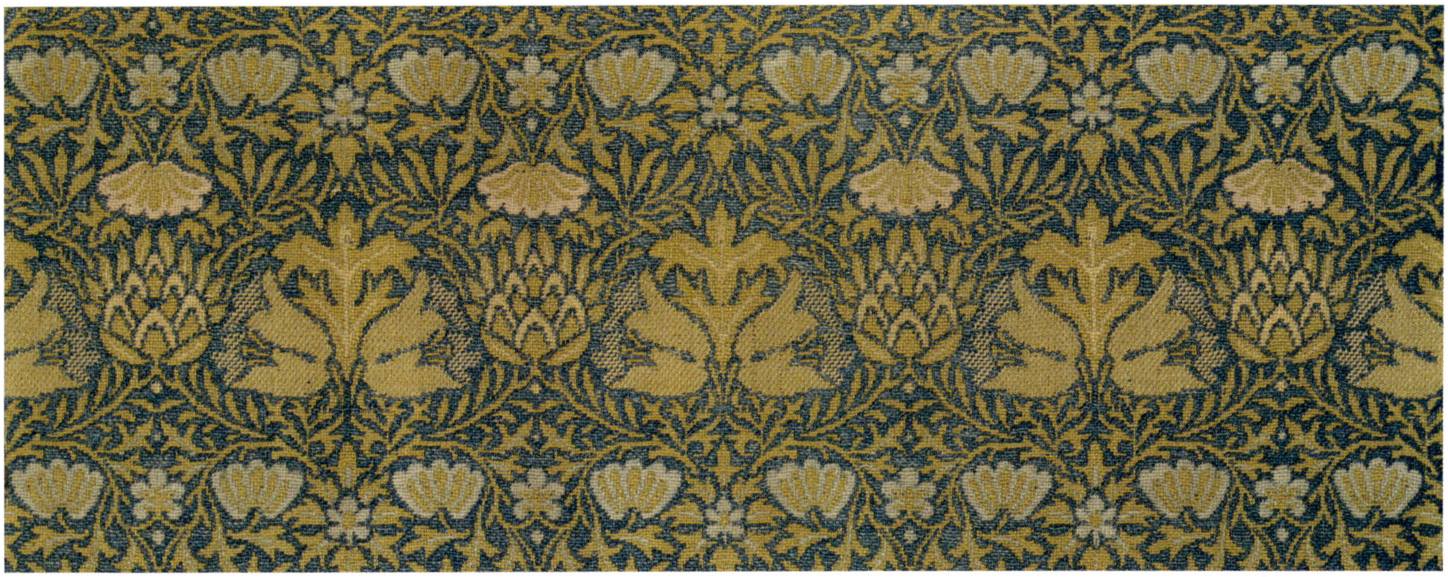

XII.84
***Tulip and Lily* machine-woven carpeting**
Designed by William Morris, *c.*1876–7, registered 27 December 1878
Manufactured by Heckmondwike Manufacturing Company, Yorkshire
Three-ply woollen Kidderminster-type carpeting, 58.4 x 85.2 cm, repeat 35.5 x 23 cm
V&A (T.101–1953)
Given by Dorothy Walker

In May 1875 Morris was already designing carpets and 'trying to get the manufacturers to do them'. It was probably Kidderminster carpet (a flat weave also known as 'Scotch' or 'inlaid') that he first attempted and the 'Heck-people', as he referred to them later, were a newly incorporated company when first approached by Morris.

The initial process of transferring Morris's designs to point papers for the loom did not go well. The manufacturer blamed this on the simplicity of the design and Morris on the work of the Yorkshire draughtsmen. From then on Morris & Co. supplied its own point papers. Unhappy with the colours produced in early samples, Morris also provided all the wools needed for manufacture, having them dyed to his specification by Thomas Wardle at Leek, and a trial weaving of this carpet was delivered to Queen Square on 25 June 1877. Morris soon realized that the Heckmondwike firm was registering and selling carpets of very similar design to his own, which may have forced him to register the design over a year after its first weaving.

This sample was given to the V&A by the daughter of Emery Walker and was used in their house at 7 Hammersmith Terrace. It was also used in the drawing room at Kelmscott House with eastern rugs laid over the top.

XII.85
***Artichoke* machine-woven carpeting**
Designed by William Morris, *c.*1875–80
Manufactured by Heckmondwike Manufacturing Company, Yorkshire
Three-ply woollen Kidderminster-type carpeting, 113 x 89.5 cm, repeat 27.5 x 22 cm
V&A (T.188–1984)
Given by S. Franses Ltd

Kidderminster carpets were woven in two qualities of double and triple thickness (two- and three-ply) and in three widths: 22 and 27 inches to use in single runs for stairs and corridors and 36 inches for rooms. These last were then seamed to make full-size carpets. The prices ranged from 4*s.* 5*d.* to 7*s.* per square yard. Plain colours with patterned borders were also available, as was fringing for which the firm charged 9*d.* per yard.

Morris & Co. catalogues mention seven Kidderminster designs. The identification of patterns is challenging as a number of two-ply weaves were used for curtaining and it is impossible to know which designs were recommended for walls and which for floors.

Morris helped to popularize this type of cheaper carpeting, which before his time tended to be used only for service corridors and secondary rooms. In the 1870s and 1880s the firm received a number of orders from clients living in large town and country houses, including Aleco Ionides who ordered a Kidderminster carpet of seamed lengths of thirteen yards of material with fringed edging for 1 Holland Park in 1884. A design for this pattern is at the William Morris Gallery (BLA449).

XII.86

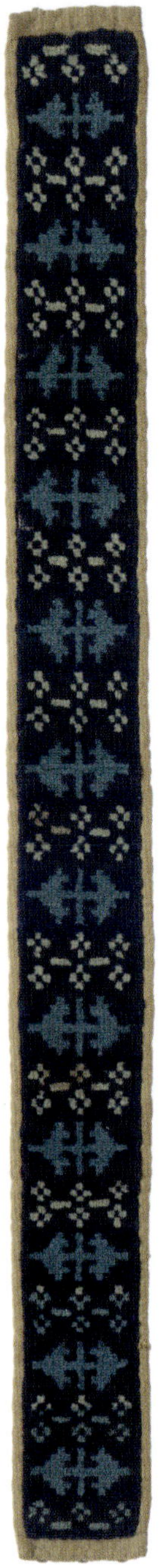

XII.87

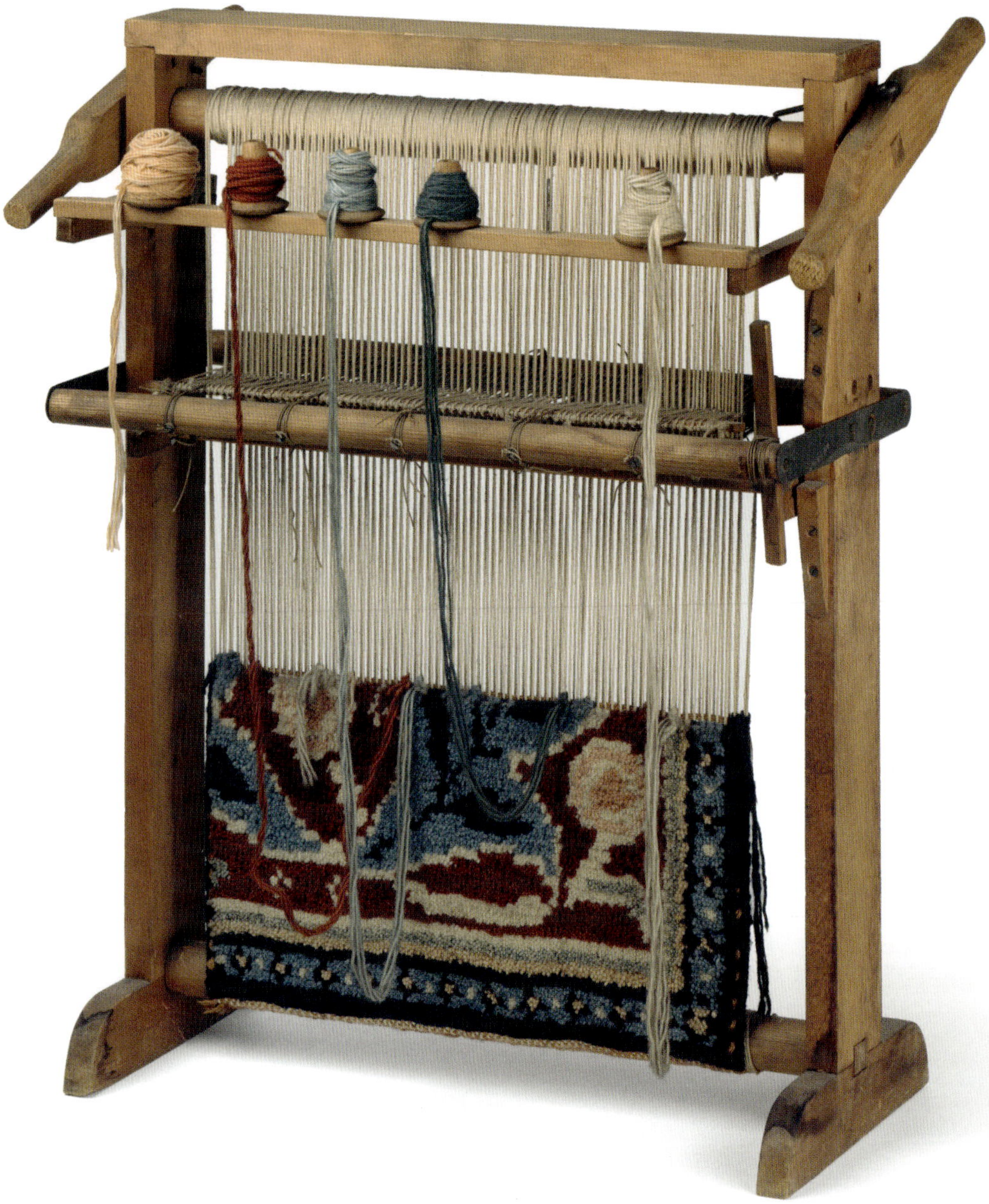

XII.86
Fotaband
Icelandic, eighteenth or nineteenth century
Knotted woollen pile, 81.2 x 7.6 cm
V&A (T.122–1939)
Bequeathed by May Morris

This is from William Morris's own collection. Fotabands were used in Iceland for tying skirts below the knee when riding side-saddle. A label attached to the band is inscribed 'Icelandic Fine Carpet pile – given by Mrs Magnússon 8/5/78'. The wording of the label emphasizes its technical interest to Morris. Sigrídr Magnússon and her husband were in frequent contact with Morris throughout the 1870s so she probably gave Morris the band knowing of his preoccupation with hand-knotted carpeting at this time. It was acquired only a short while after his first experiments with the technique and the same year that he produced his first commercial hand-woven rug.

XII.87
Miniature carpet loom
Made at Merton Abbey, late nineteenth century
Wood with metal fittings, 68 x 56 x 29.5 cm
V&A (293–1893)
Given by William Morris

Used for the instruction of carpet weavers, the loom holds a small sample of work in progress. This is a simplified version of the full-sized looms constructed by Morris, initially in the coach house at Kelmscott House and later at Merton Abbey.

Morris & Co. hand-knotted carpets were woven at a thickness of 25 knots to the square inch (when beaten down closer to 28 knots to the inch). At first carpets were woven on a mohair or worsted warp, but this proved impractical, so later samples used cotton, which was stronger and less expensive. Morris chose the Turkish (Ghiordes) knot over the more complex Persian (Senna) knot and created broad designs that suited this technique and his newly trained workforce.

Unlike tapestry, carpets were knotted with the weavers sitting in front of the work (see fig.38). At Merton Abbey the looms faced the windows for maximum light. The point paper, drawn from the design and indicating the colour of each knot, was pinned as a guide to the top of the loom. All of the carpet weavers at Merton Abbey were women and a number of sisters were employed.

XII.88

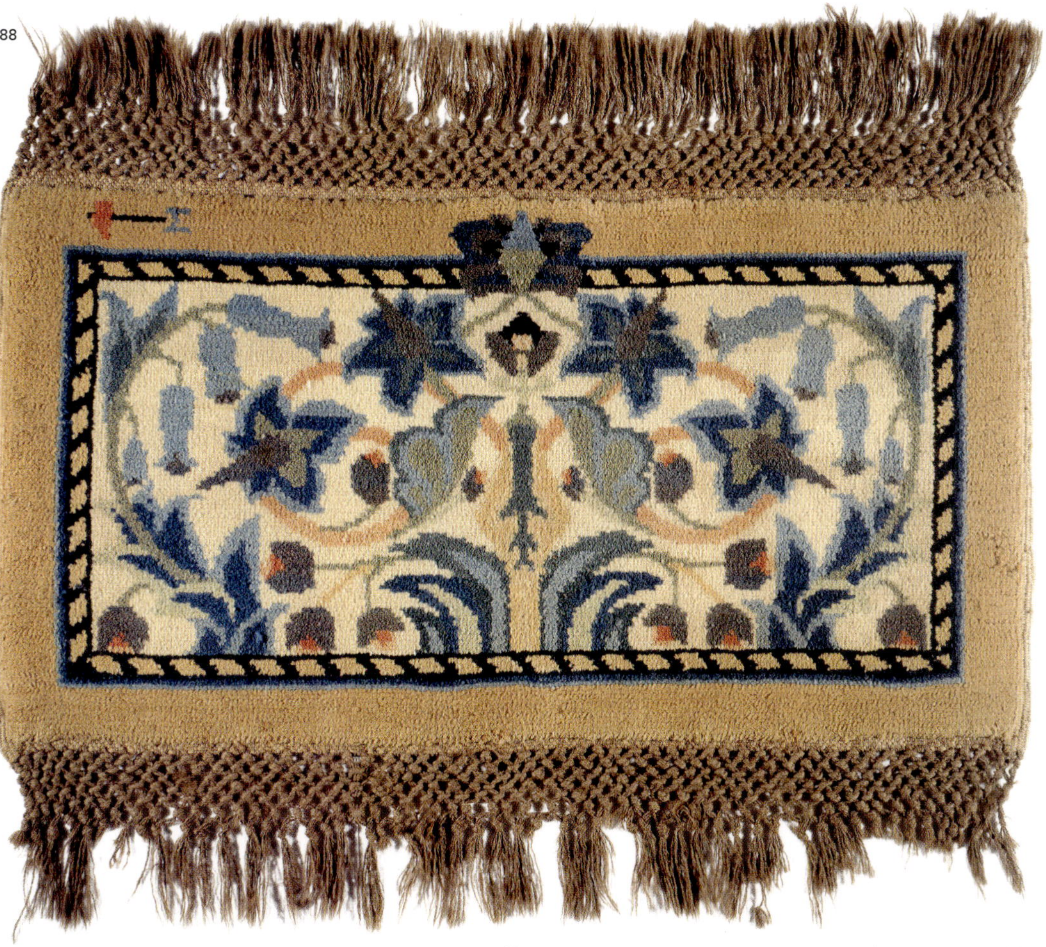

XII.89

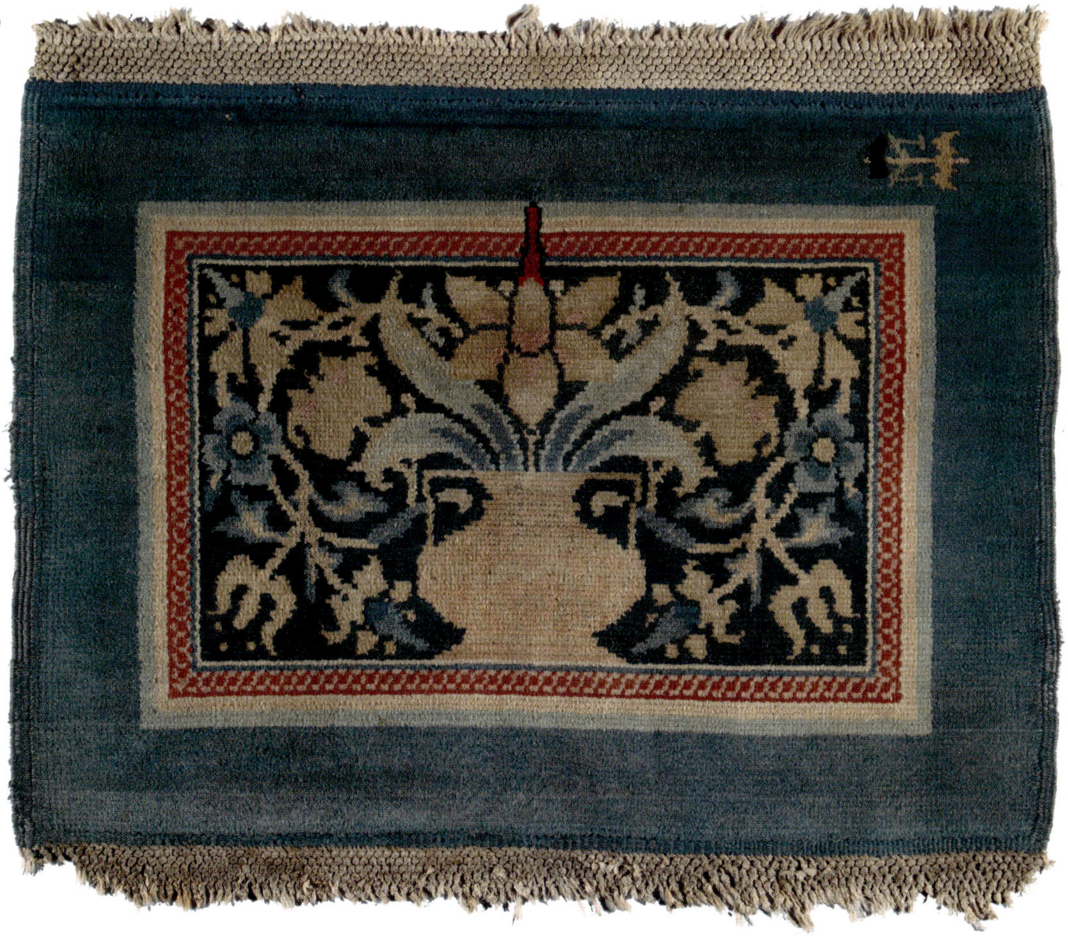

XII.88
Small rug
Designed by William Morris, *c.*1878–9
Made at Kelmscott House, Hammersmith
Hand-knotted woollen pile on a worsted warp, 95 x 110 cm
Castle Howard Collection (TX066)

On 13 April 1877 Morris wrote to Thomas Wardle that he was unwilling to undertake other new work 'till I get my carpets going'. By 1 January 1878 he was more confident: 'I want my Iceland wool tried on a rug: I will take the greatest pains in designing one when the frame is ready.' The frame is likely to have been a simple loom used for these small early wall rugs and it was not until 1879 that the coach house and adjoining stable at Kelmscott House were converted for large-scale carpet manufacture.

A number of small rugs survive that may have been woven as trials and novelties for clients and friends. This, an early example, has a worsted warp, a technique quickly abandoned as impractical. It is one of several made for the Howard family who used them on the floor in guest bedrooms.

The rug has an early Hammersmith mark of a hammer and the letter 'M', denoting that it was made at Kelmscott House. The term 'Hammersmith' continued to be used for Morris hand-knotted carpets after production moved to Merton Abbey. Later carpets bear no identification marks.

XII.89
Small rug
Designed and possibly made by William Morris, *c.*1878–81
Made at Kelmscott House, Hammersmith
Hand-knotted woollen pile on a cotton warp with jute binding wefts, 94 x 108 cm
Crab Tree Farm, Lake Bluff, Illinois (ACA.193.95)

The flowerpot design is very close to a series of embroidered fire-screen panels and cushion covers designed by Morris around the same time (XII.21–2). This rug shows another form of the early Hammersmith mark in which stylized waves are added to the hammer and letter 'M', signifying that it was woven in the coach house at Kelmscott House. It is not known whether these small-format rugs were put into regular commercial production.

Between 1884 and 1888, Morris & Co. produced a series of similar small rugs for the Century Guild using designs by Arthur Heygate Mackmurdo or Herbert Horne. These were sold through the Morris shop and advertised in the Guild's magazine *Hobby Horse*.

XII.90

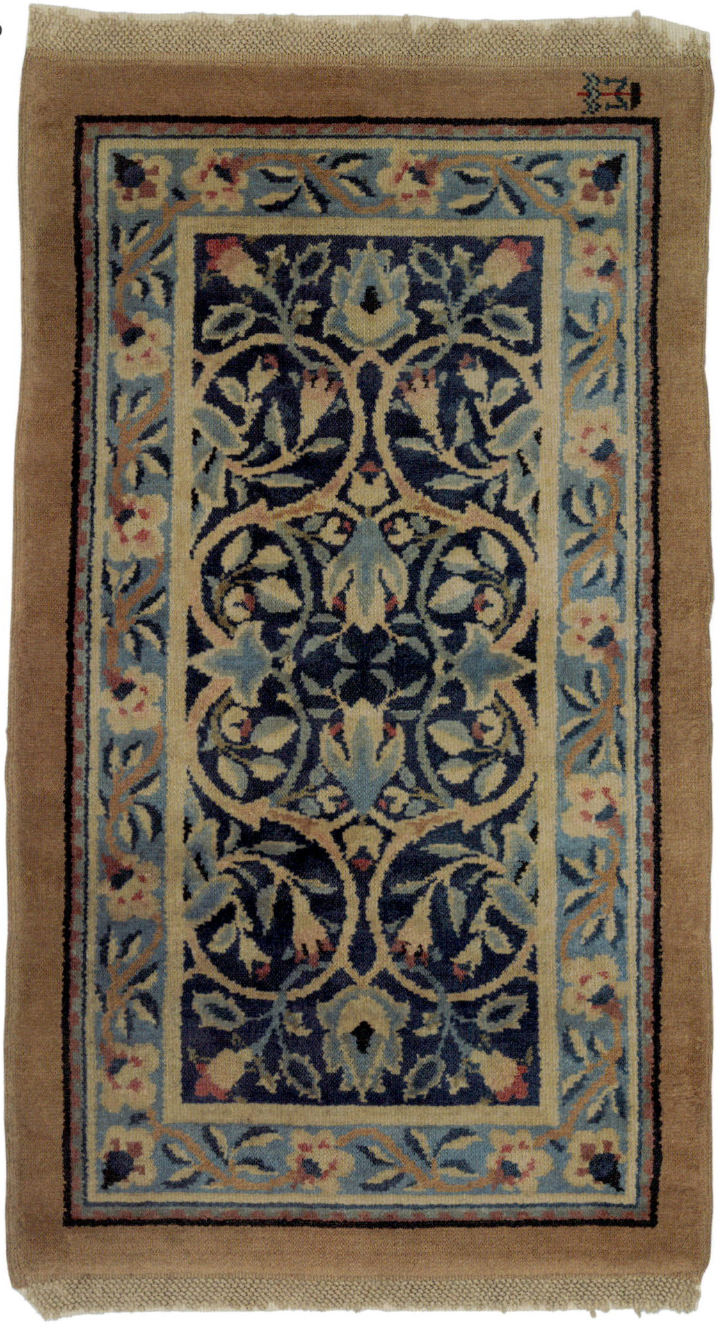

XII.91

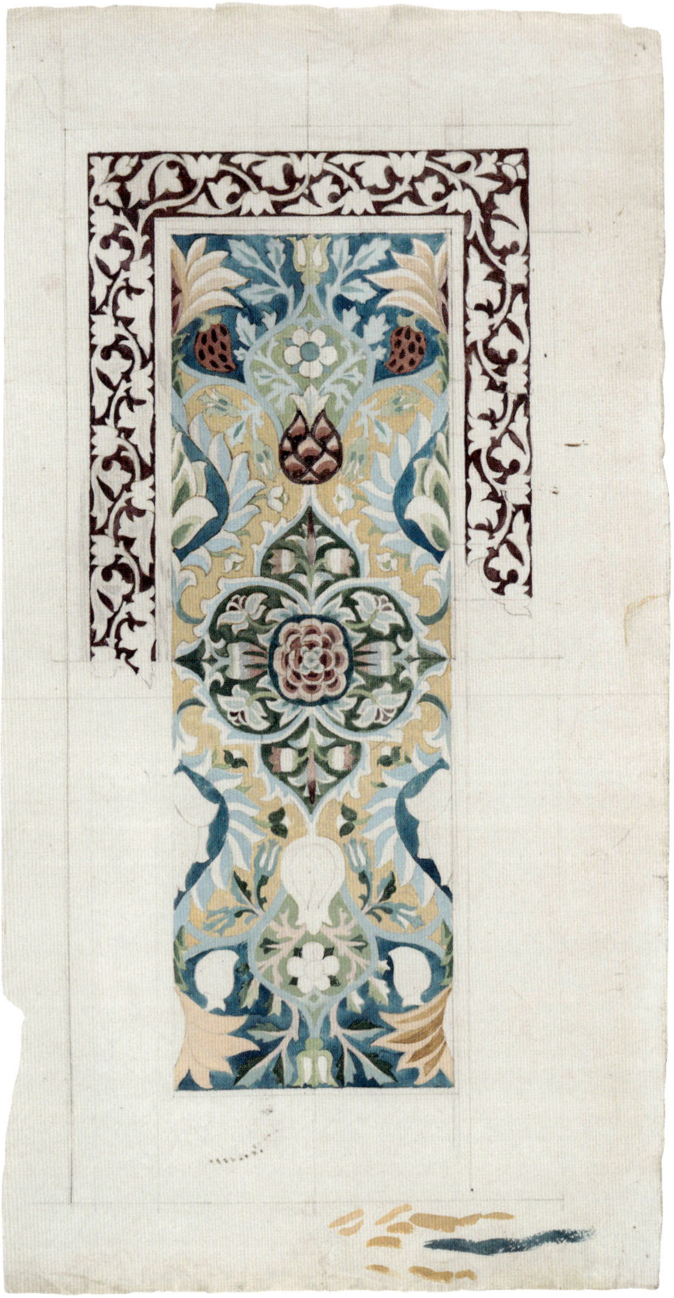

XII.90
Rug
Designed by William Morris, *c.*1880
Hand-knotted woollen pile on a cotton warp, 249 x 136 cm
V&A (T.104–1953)

This rug was a wedding present to Margaret, daughter of Edward and Georgiana Burne-Jones, on her marriage to John William Mackail in September 1888. On 21 August Morris wrote, 'I have bidden our Mr Smith to send you an "article" called a Hammersmith Rug (made at Merton Abbey) which Janey and I ask you to take as a small and unimportant addition to your "hards".'

Morris's description 'made at Merton Abbey' is confusing as the rug has an early Hammersmith mark, thought to signify that it was woven in the coach house at Kelmscott House. However, Mr Smith may well have selected it from stock, choosing an old weaving rather than undertaking a new one. When acquired by the V&A, through Clare Mackail, the couple's daughter, the rug was said to have been 'produced at Hammersmith'.

The design, with pale camel colouring, tightly curving leaves and profiled flower heads shows Chinese influence, especially in the pastel colours and peony motifs of the inner border. This was one of Morris's most popular small rug designs and a number were woven. An example given by Morris to his sister Henrietta was displayed at the V&A in 1952.

XII.91
Design for a Hammersmith carpet
William Morris, *c.*1880
Pencil, watercolour and body colour, 67.7 x 35.7 cm
V&A (E.298–1939)
Bequeathed by May Morris

The colouring of this design, almost certainly intended for a rug rather than a larger carpet, is the same as a number of the small rugs first woven in the coach house at Kelmscott House, Hammersmith (see XII.88–9). The combination of pale blues, pinks and camel colours comes directly from Chinese carpets and shows Morris's interest in this work at the time.

XII.92

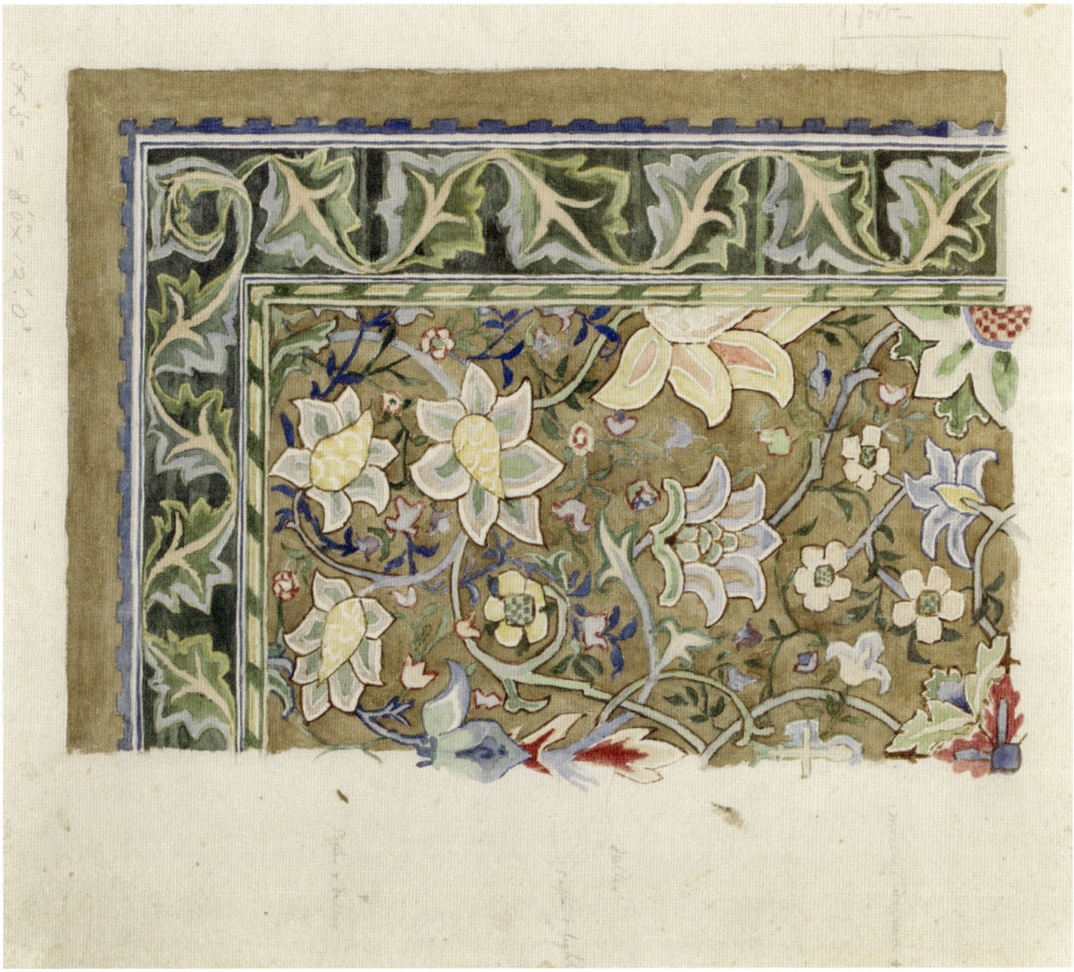

XII.93

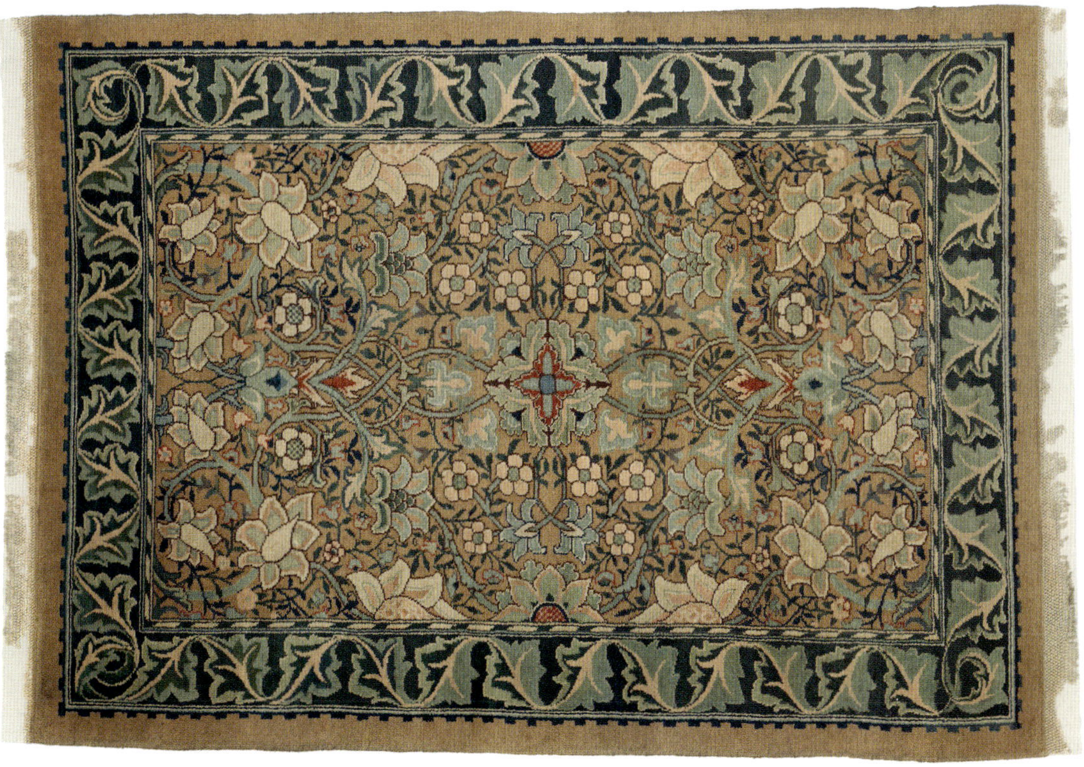

XII.92
Design for *Redcar* carpet
William Morris, 1881
Pencil, watercolour, body colour and Chinese white, 34.5 x 48.5 cm
V&A (E.144–1919)
Given by Morris & Co.

The original carpet was commissioned by Hugh Bell, son of Margaret and Isaac Lowthian Bell, for the drawing room in a new extension to his Yorkshire home – Red Barns in Coatham near Redcar. The design (one-sixth full size) was used by Morris & Co. to show to prospective clients and various inscribed notes, such as 'softer & lighter' and 'softer & duller', suggest requests from clients rather than instructions from the designer. When it was given to the V&A in 1919, the firm asked if it could be loaned back should they receive further orders.

XII.93
***Redcar* carpet**
Designed by William Morris, 1881
Woven early twentieth century
Hand-knotted cotton warp with mohair, camel hair and woollen pile with jute binding wefts, 243.8 x 304.8 cm
V&A (T.3–1919)
Given by Thomas Glass

The original version of this carpet, made for Hugh Bell and still in a private collection, has the early Hammersmith mark, confirming that it was woven in the coach house at Kelmscott House. On 17 February 1881 Morris wrote to Jane, 'Bell's carpet is well on, & I believe if it were not really dark today it would look well'.

A number of versions of the carpet were made, including this later example. It was bought from Morris & Co. and presented to the V&A by Thomas Glass, who was associated with the Templeton carpet factory in Glasgow. In a letter from Morris & Co. to the museum, it was described as showing 'the original colours rather better than a carpet which has had about twenty five years wear', presumably referring to Bell's original.

The pale colouring with camel ground and pastel detailing is the same as some early wall rugs (see XII.88) and may have been Morris's first chosen colour scheme for carpets. Although this was repeated in a few later commissions, most of his mature work woven at Merton Abbey relied on his characteristic combination of indigo blue and madder red.

XII.94

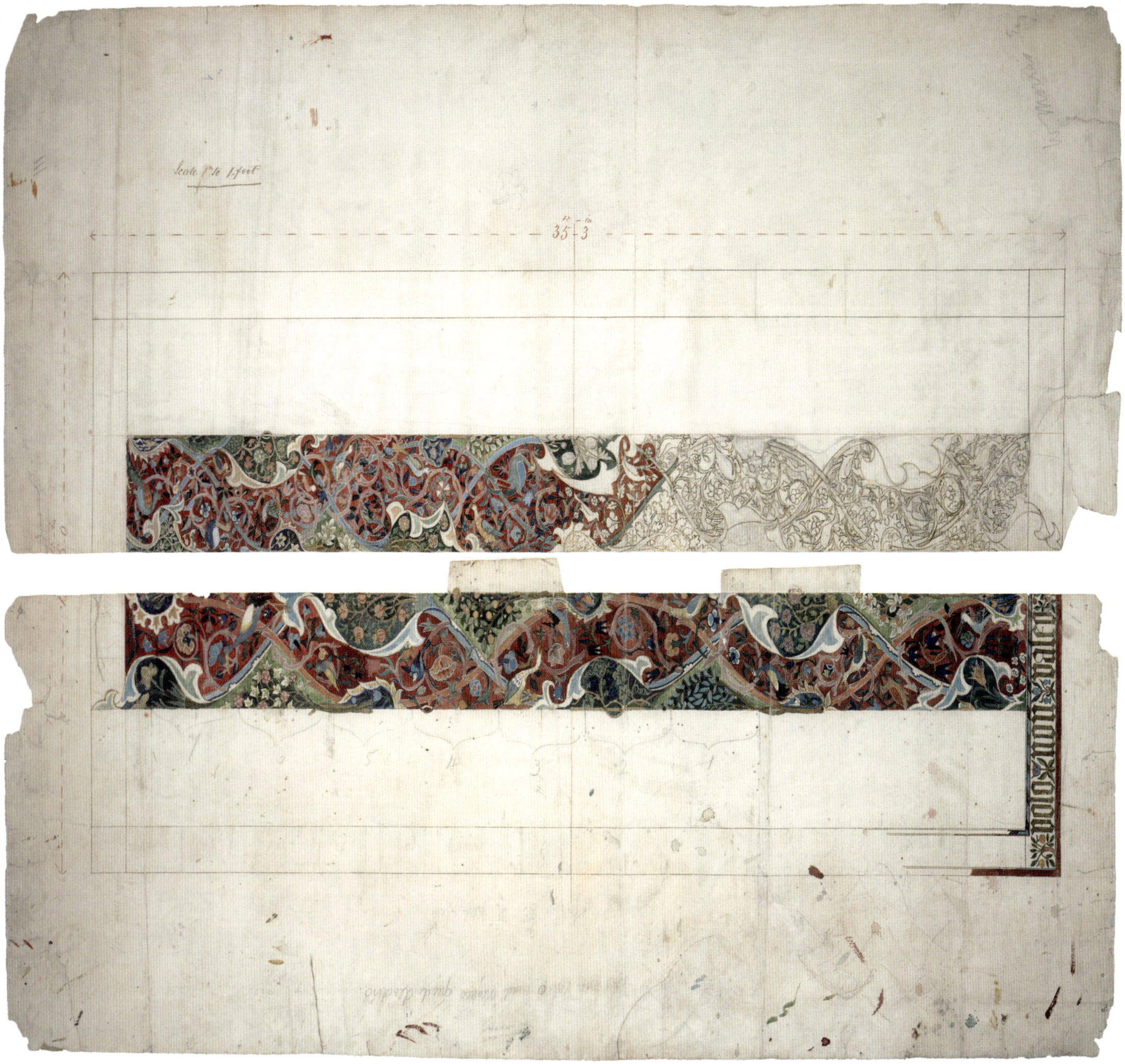

XII.94
Two designs for a carpet for Naworth Castle
William Morris, 1881
Pencil, body colour and watercolour, 31 x 101 cm, 36.5 x 101 cm
V&A (E.47, 48–1940)
Bequeathed by May Morris

These designs were prepared for the commission of a carpet for the library at Naworth Castle, Cumbria, one of the homes of George Howard, Earl of Carlisle. Morris's diary for 20 February 1881 notes, 'Began a sketch of Howard's carpet'. Three days later he wrote to Jane, 'I am starting designing the long carpet for Naworth ... 'tis rather a difficult job, & I am puffing and blowing over it rather'. The letter suggests this may well have been Morris's first large, complicated carpet commission. It also includes his first mention of looking for new premises. The projects were possibly linked, as the weaving of the *Naworth* carpet was delayed until the move to Merton Abbey, the finished size (9.5 x 4.6 m) being too large for the looms at Hammersmith.

These drawings show two alternative designs for the central infill, both busy and complicated patterns that include unusual motifs such as seagulls, wading birds, palms and naturalistic fruit trees. On one version Morris has incorporated the Howard family motto '*volo non valeo*' ('I am willing but not able'). These were the most ambitious and eclectic of all Morris's carpet designs until the *Bullerswood* in 1889 (XII.100). The V&A owns a third alternative design for the project, a more conventional pattern of birds and scrolling branches (E.287–1939), which was probably the version selected by the Howards.

Although the painting of point papers took a month, the weaving was speedy. The move to Merton took place in June 1881, yet on 3 November Morris wrote to Howard 'your carpet has been finished for a week or two: I have been keeping it back to try for a fine day to spread it on our lawn; so that I may see it all at once ... it looks very well I think & seems to be satisfactory as to manufacture ... I shall have to send someone down to Naworth to get it into its place: it weighs about a ton I fancy.' It cost £200 and the purchase appears in the Howards' accounts for 1882. The carpet was sold in 1947 and was later used in the Hotel Ambassador, Bournemouth. Its present whereabouts are unknown.

XII.95

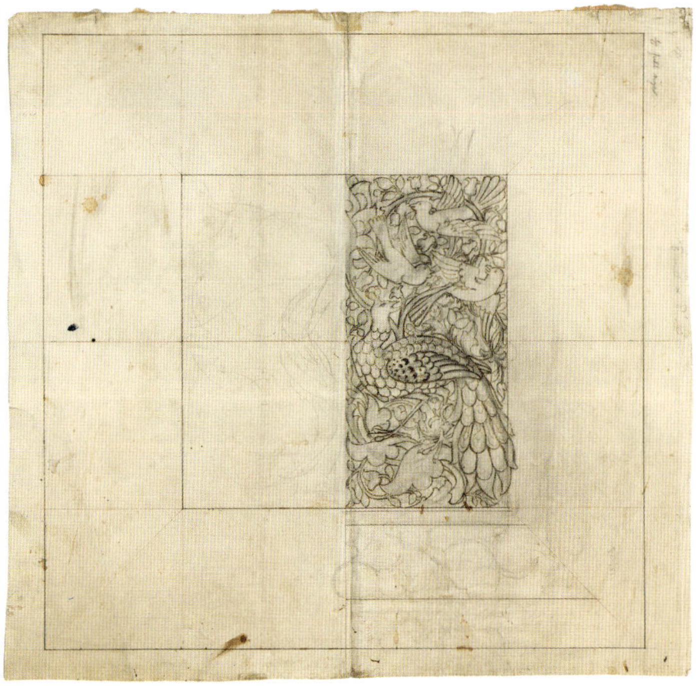

XII.95

Design for carpet

Designed by William Morris, 1881
Sepia wash and pencil, 66 x 69.2 cm

William Morris Gallery, London Borough of Waltham Forest (A43)

The drawing was purchased from Morris & Co. in 1940 when the company went into liquidation. Until the rediscovery of the 'Vanderbilt' carpet in America in 2013 (XII.96), it was assumed that it never went into production. It shows Morris's usual habit of producing only a section of the design, in this instance half of the mirror repeat. It is likely that further drawings were made to include the colour scheme and border design. References in Morris's diary for December 1881 suggest that Kate Faulkner helped prepare the point paper for the border. The composition, designed to be viewed from one direction only, is unusual among Morris's carpet designs.

XII.96

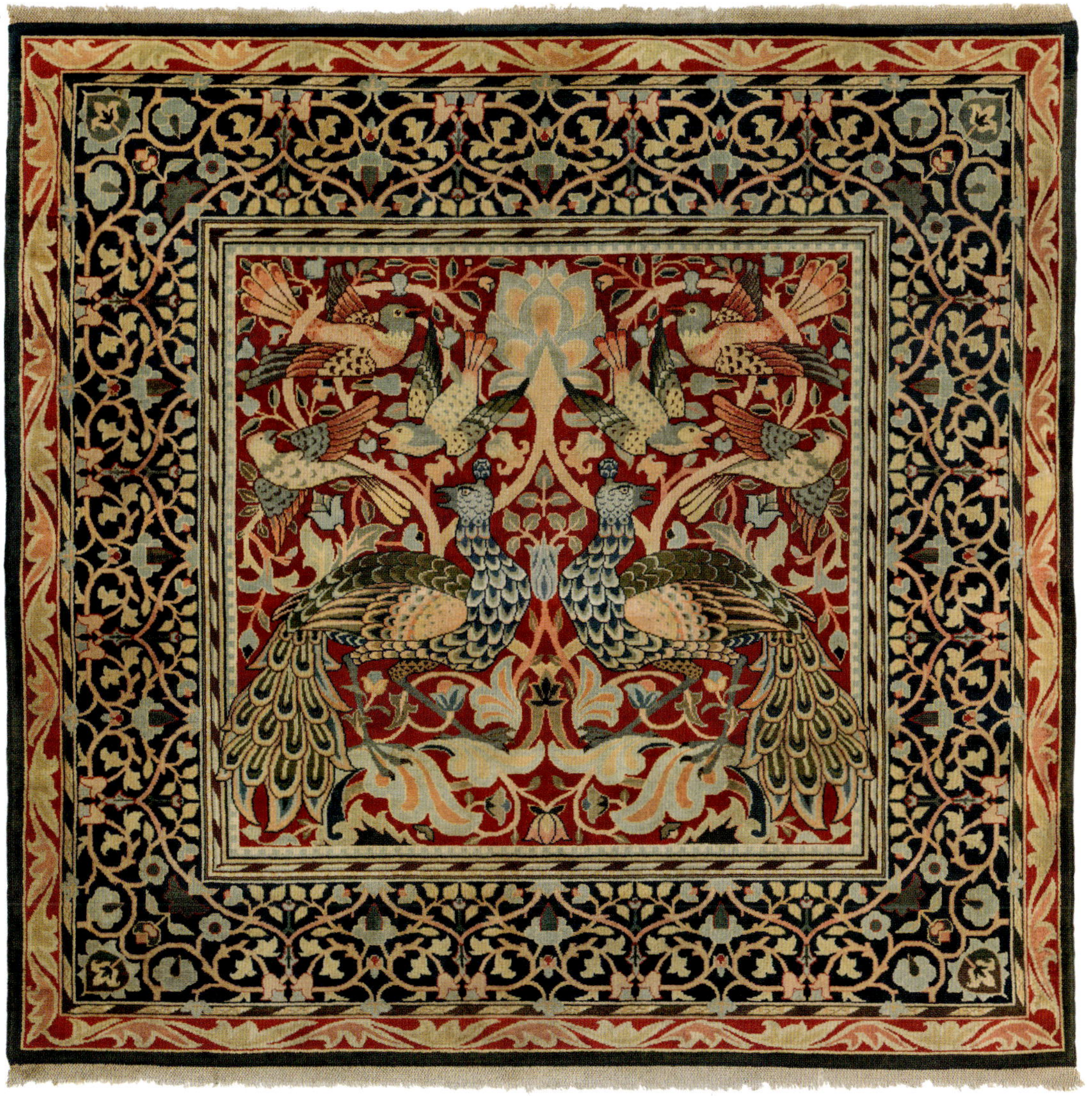

XII.96

Carpet with design of peacocks and birds

Designed by William Morris, 1881
Woven at Merton Abbey in 1882
Hand-knotted woollen pile on a cotton warp, 410 x 410 cm

William Morris Gallery, London Borough of Waltham Forest (N17)
Gift of The Monument Trust, 2010

There is strong circumstantial evidence that this unusual square carpet was made for Cornelius Vanderbilt II, the American socialite and railroad magnate. References to designing carpets for 'Vanderbilt' appear in Morris's diary from 21 July to 29 December 1881 and an entry for Christmas Eve includes 'did work on Vanderbilt Peacock'. At least four carpets were made for Vanderbilt, described by Morris as two large, a square and a narrow example (a runner). Three of these can be identified in photographs of the entrance hall in Cornelius Vanderbilt's vast newly built New York mansion on Fifth Avenue and West 57th Street in 1882 (fig.211). When the building was remodelled in the 1890s, Morris & Co. carpets furnished the billiard room. As this is the only square Morris carpet known to exist, and the only one depicting peacocks as the principal motif, it is likely that it formed part of this important early American commission. The mansion was demolished in 1927 but Morris & Co. hand-knotted runners survive at Cornelius's summer residence, The Breakers, in Newport, Rhode Island.

XII.97

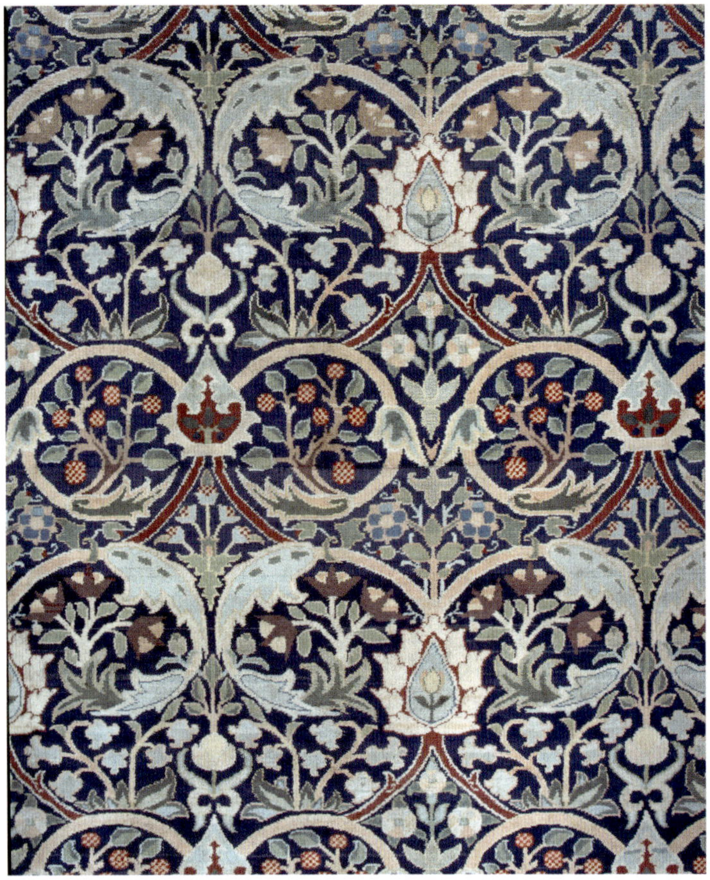

XII.98

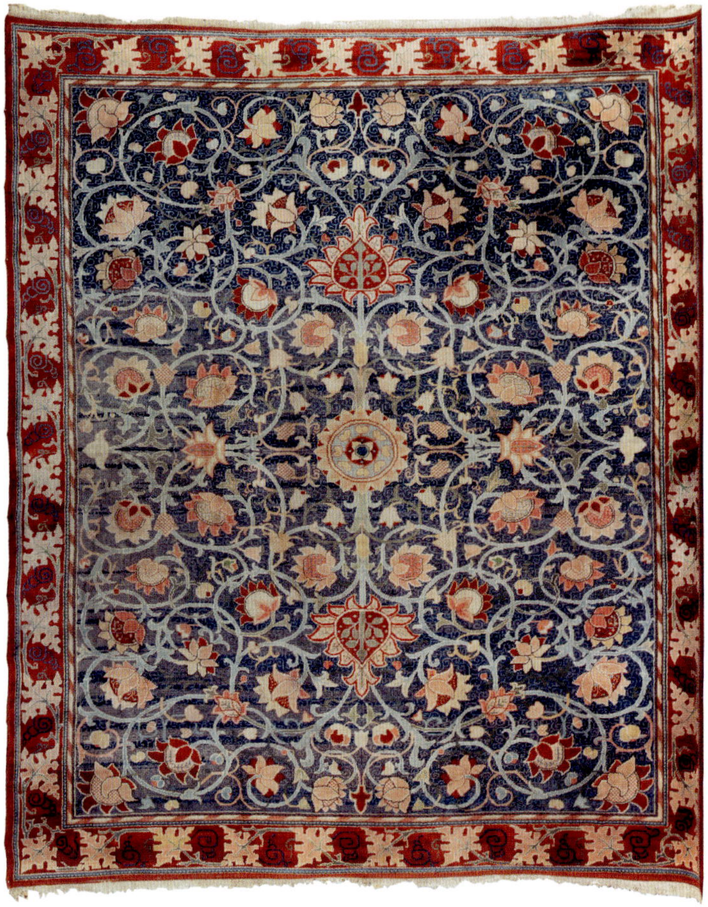

XII.97
***Rounton Grange* carpet (detail)**
Designed by William Morris and woven at Merton Abbey, *c*.1881–2
Hand-knotted woollen pile on a cotton warp with jute binding threads, 678 x 441 cm
Private collection

Morris produced two hand-knotted carpets for the Bell family, *Redcar* (see XII.93), and this larger example, designed for Rounton Grange in Northallerton, Yorkshire, the home of Margaret and Isaac Lowthian Bell. The design depicts curving branches filled with fruit and garden flowers on a deep blue ground with a madder red border. It was most likely woven in 1882, as it was not until 27 December 1881 that Morris set up a 13-foot loom at Merton Abbey and therefore had the equipment to weave designs on this scale. A second version was woven for Cornelius Vanderbilt II in the same year (see fig.211). Morris seems to have welcomed the technical challenges involved in producing these vast and complex pieces. Another example was *Hurstbourne*, an enormous curved carpet with inscriptions and heraldic devices, woven for Lord Portsmouth around 1885 and now in a private collection.

XII.98
***Holland Park* carpet**
Designed by William Morris and woven at Merton Abbey in 1883
Hand-knotted woollen pile on a cotton warp with jute binding threads, 528 x 398 cm
Private collection

This carpet was designed specially for the second drawing room of 1 Holland Park, home of Aleco Ionides. It cost £113 and was one of four Hammersmith carpets made for the house (see also XII.99).

It was Morris's most popular carpet design and at least eight examples have been traced. Five of these are in this, Morris's most widely used colour scheme, an indigo-blue field with a madder-red border. Two others have apricot coloured grounds and another cream with details in pale blues and pinks. This example is probably the original carpet although, when purchased from Morris & Co. in the 1920s, it was said to have come from Clouds, Percy Wyndham's house near Salisbury. However, the version made for Clouds (1889) is most likely that sold at Sotheby's in 1986 by a descendant of the Wyndham family.

Gleeson White in his *Studio* magazine article on 1 Holland Park (1898) described the carpet as displaying features that Morris had made his own: 'robust generous curves blossoming into flower-like patterns, and with a sense of space'. While it does retain these characteristic elements, this carpet presents a turning point in Morris's style. Its format is far more traditional than had been seen before and from this time his designs tend to show quartered patterns based around a central medallion. This change was affected by Morris's increasing interest in historic carpets. In February 1883 he was asked to advise the South Kensington Museum on the acquisition of a group of Persian carpets offered by a Bond Street dealer. Although Morris had collected eastern carpets for many years and knew a great deal about them, the coincidence of this visit and this new departure in pattern is significant. Two versions of the carpet were exhibited at the Arts and Crafts Exhibitions in 1888 and 1899.

XII.99

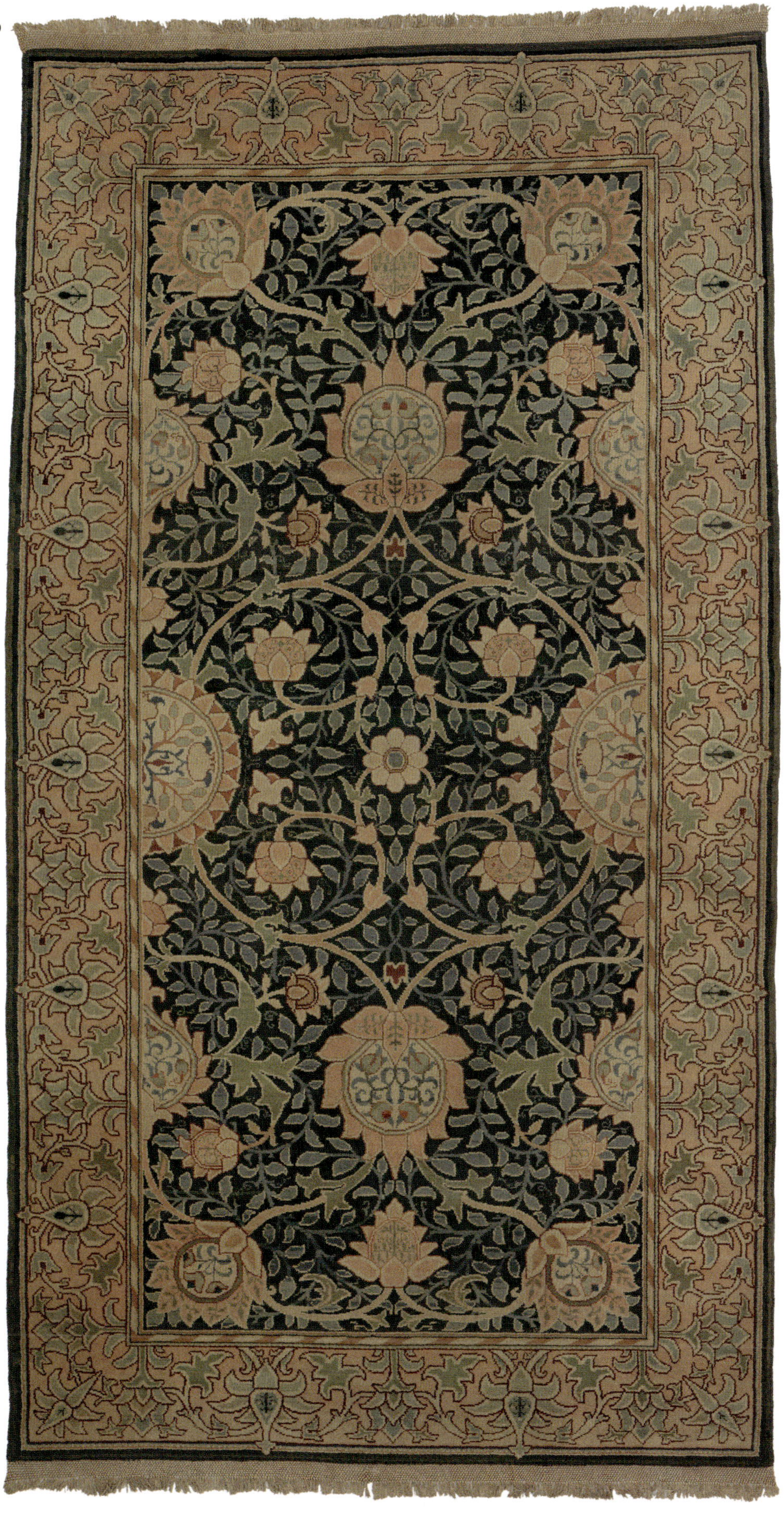

XII.99
***Carbrook* carpet**
Designed by William Morris, *c*.1880–3
Woven at Merton Abbey in 1884
Hand-knotted woollen pile on a cotton warp and with jute binding threads, 541 x 292 cm
V&A (Circ.458–1965)
Bequeathed by Miss Aglaia Ionides

Around 1879–80 Morris & Co. was commissioned to decorate Carbrook House, near Larbert in Stirlingshire, the home of Joseph Cheney Bolton, a partner in a Glasgow firm of East India merchants and, from 1880, the MP for Stirlingshire. An inscription on a drawing for St James's Palace (VIII.12) suggests that work was being prepared for Carbrook at the same time, and the William Morris Society also owns a ceiling design for the Carbrook scheme. According to the diary of David Parr, an employee of Frederick Leach whose company was subcontracted by the Morris firm, he worked on the house between May and September 1883, so the commission was extensive.

This, the second weaving of the design, was made for the Antiquities Room (also known as the first drawing room) of Aleco Ionides' house at 1 Holland Park. In 1883 the carpet was estimated at £82 and billed (and presumably woven) the following year (VIII.14). It is an uncharacteristically formal composition for this early date. The overall network of trailing leaves, Morris's most identifiable style, is subsidiary, the main interest of the pattern lies in the repeat of large traditional medallions and palmettes. In C.E.C. Tattersall's *History of British Carpets* (1934) the carpet is described as having a blue field and red border, which was probably the original colouring. This lighter version was chosen to match the exotic surroundings of the room, which had a Morris silver lacquer paper on the walls and displayed Ionides' collection of Tanagra statues.

XII.100

***Bullerswood* carpet**

Designed by William Morris with John Henry Dearle and woven 1889
Hand-knotted with woollen pile on a cotton warp, 765 x 399 cm

V&A (T.31–1923)

Given by J. Sanderson

In 1889 John Sanderson, a wool trader, commissioned Morris & Co. to decorate his house, Buller's Wood in Chislehurst, Kent. Built in 1866 it had been subject to recent alterations by Ernest Newton, possibly to accommodate the nine Sanderson children. Three Hammersmith carpets were ordered for the house; one for the hall and two for the drawing room. V&A records from 1921 state, 'it appears that the Drawing Room was decorated by William Morris under his personal supervision and nothing was allowed to be placed in it in addition to objects executed by himself except such as met with his approval.' If accurate, then clearly the clients were very accommodating.

This carpet is an extraordinarily exuberant amalgamation of almost every motif devised by Morris for the technique. It is reminiscent of the early sampler designs prepared for Naworth Castle (XII.94) but it also shows later, more formal design elements characteristic of Dearle's work. There is a strong possibility, therefore, that the carpet was a collaborative project.

It was exhibited at the 1893 Arts and Crafts Exhibition. Despite the size and complicated design three versions are known. One formed part of the Henderson bequest to Bath City Council in 1954 and the other is in a private collection in Australia.

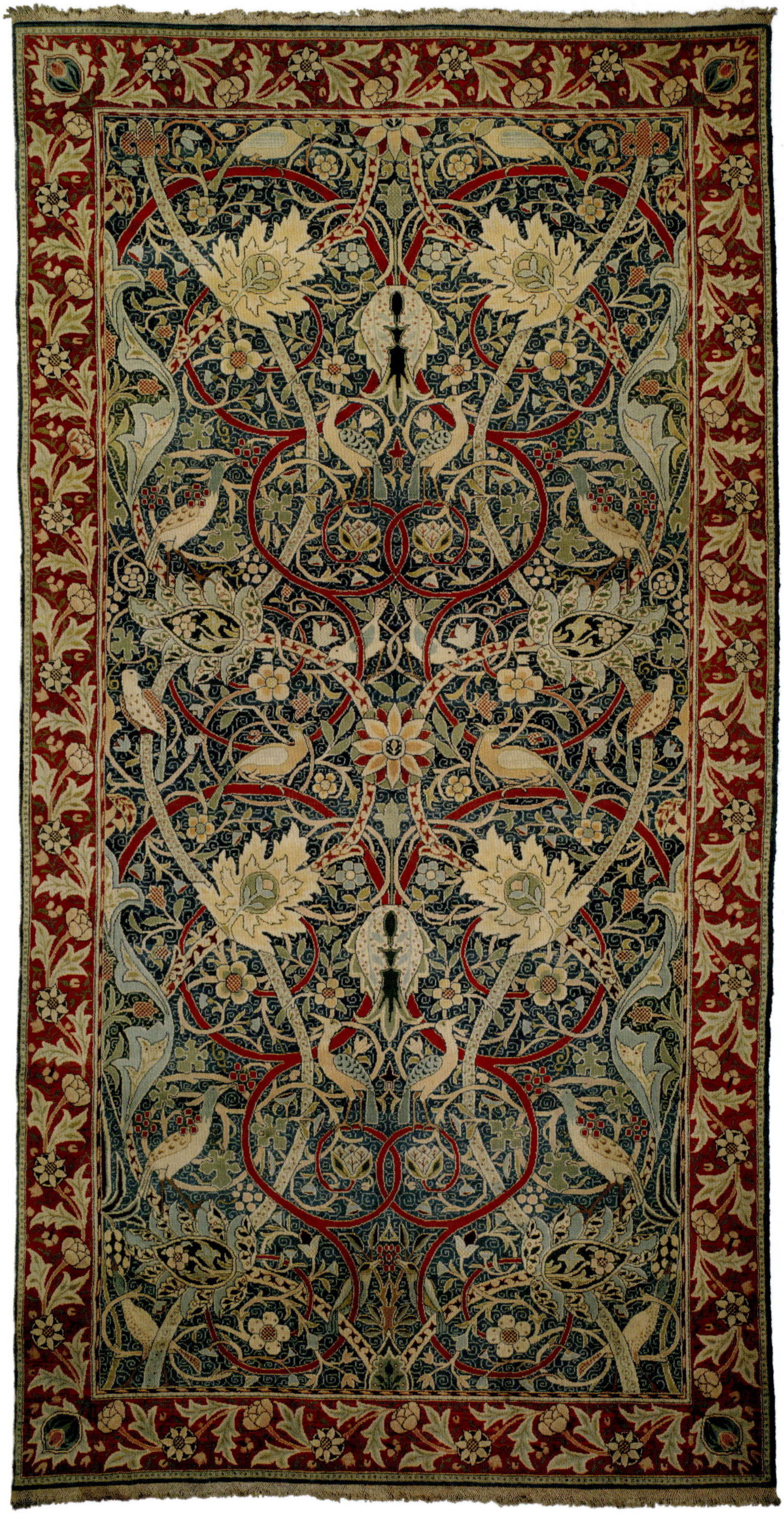

XII.100

XII.101

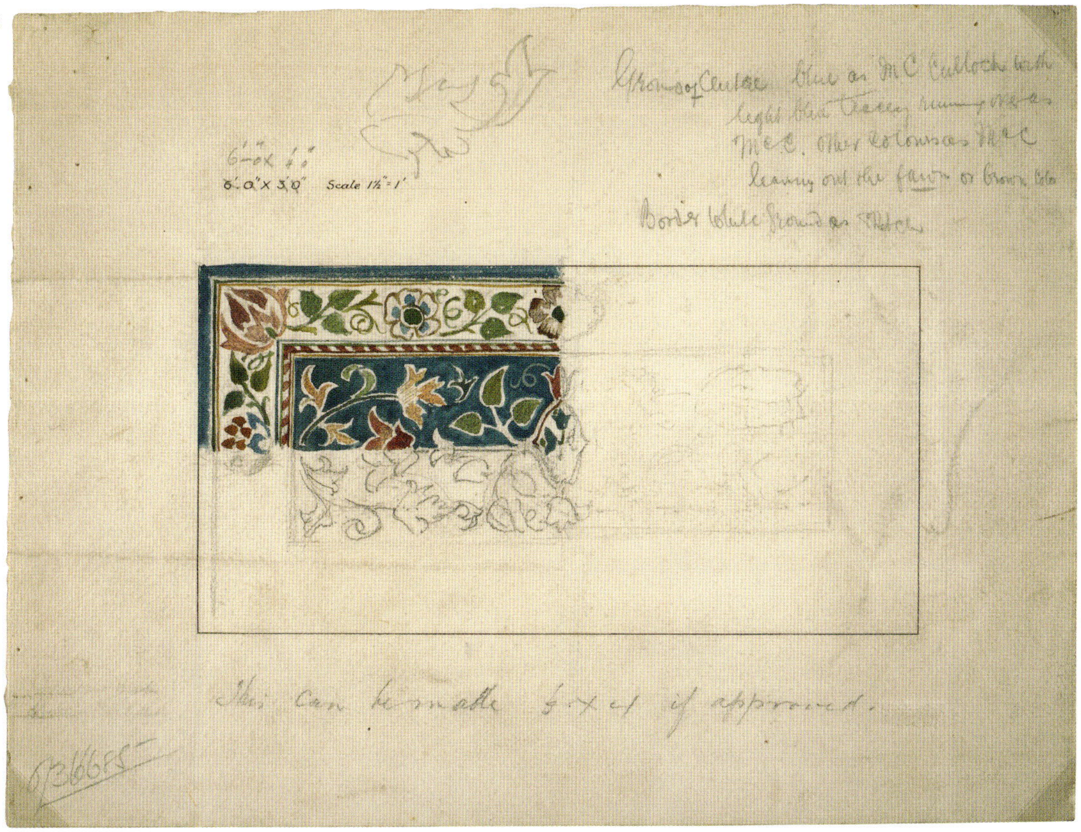

XII.101
Design for a hand-knotted runner
John Henry Dearle, *c.*1898–1902
Pencil, ink and watercolour,
25.4 x 34 cm
The Huntington Library, Art Museum and Botanical Gardens (2000.5.88)

The inscription suggests that this rug was a later copy of a design originally prepared for George McCulloch, a good client of Morris & Co. who ordered a partial set of *Holy Grail* tapestries in 1898 and a special Hammersmith carpet (known as *McCulloch*). A Scottish-born businessman with mining interests in Australia, McCulloch lived at 184 Queen's Gate in London and was probably introduced to the work of the firm through his friend William Knox D'Arcy of Stanmore Hall, Middlesex.

Dearle's drawing shows one quarter of the design and the notes suggest variations in colours from the original. It also illustrates Dearle's brighter more varied palette than earlier Morris examples. The inscribed size suggests it was intended as a carpet runner, possibly for a hall or landing.

XII.102

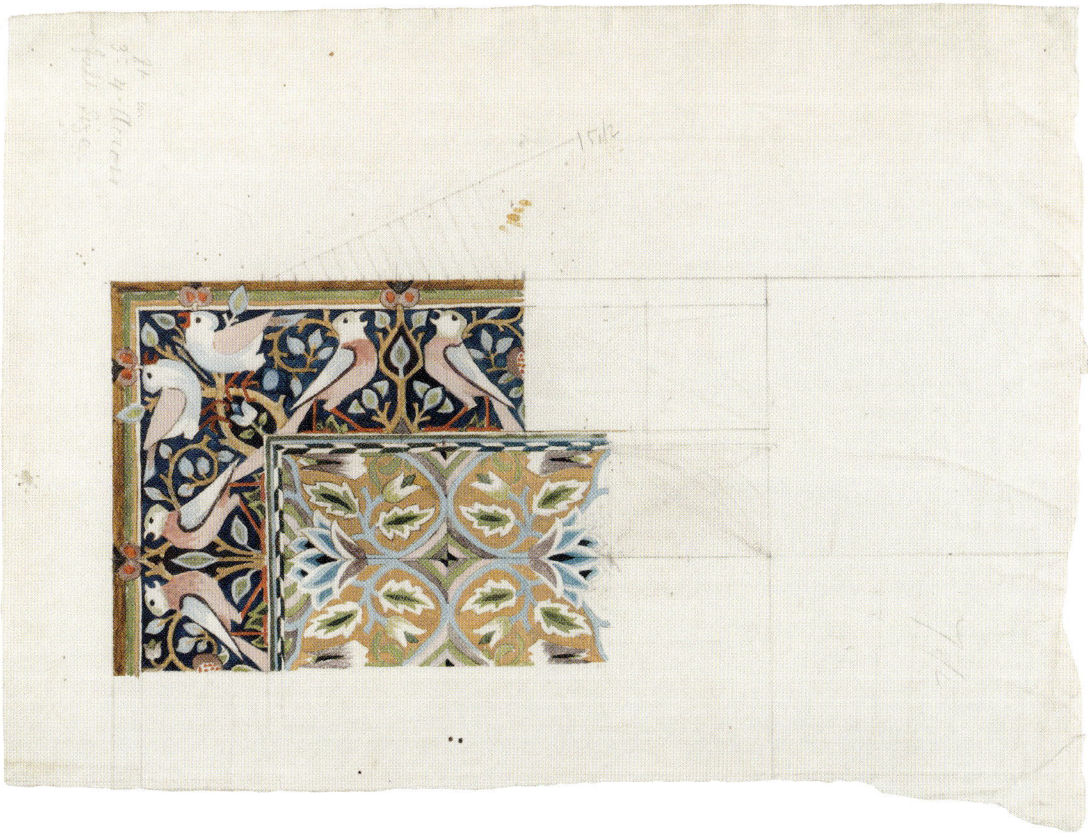

XII.102
Design for hand-knotted rug
Morris & Co., late nineteenth century
Pencil, body colour and Chinese white, 37.7 x 50.3 cm
V&A (E.301–1939)
Bequeathed by May Morris

This bold, colourful drawing was probably painted in the Morris & Co. workshop to show to potential clients. It is one of a group in the V&A's collection that includes a range of patterns, from Morris's earliest small rugs to Dearle's late repeating patterns. The bird border on this design was used on a plain carpet now in the chapel of Peterhouse, Cambridge. It has strong similarities with embroidery designs drawn by May Morris in the 1890s and may point to her involvement in this side of the firm's work.

TAPESTRY

XII.103
Design for *Acanthus and Vine* tapestry
William Morris, 1879
Pencil, pen and ink, black chalk, watercolour and body colour, 49.5 x 68.2 cm
V&A (E.45–1940)
Bequeathed by May Morris

This is Morris's first design for a woven tapestry. It shows half of the mirror-imaged composition with the left-hand section faintly suggested in pencil. There are splashes of colour on one side and the drawing has a sharp fold down the centre.

The structure of the design, with plant growth emanating from the centre of the lower border, is one Morris used frequently when designing for square and rectangular formats in the late 1870s and early 1880s, especially wall rugs and embroidered cushion covers and screen panels.

XII.104
Cartoon for *Acanthus and Vine* tapestry
Probably Morris & Co. studio after a design by William Morris, 1879
Pencil and watercolour, 179.5 x 135.6 cm
V&A (E.3472–1932)

This is likely to be the working cartoon for Morris's first tapestry. Tapestry cartoons need to be the same size as the finished work. They are used at the loom to mark sections of the warp in readiness for weaving and as a general guide to the composition. Morris's inexperience as a weaver at this time accounts for a slight discrepancy in size between this and the finished tapestry. As with the original design, only half of the composition has been drawn in detail. In later years the firm's tapestry (and stained-glass) cartoons were made from photographic enlargements of the original design (XII.118).

Whereas the design and finished tapestry remained with the Morris family, the cartoon, which was probably drawn in the Morris & Co. studio, possibly by George Campfield under Morris's supervision, remained the property of the firm until purchased by the V&A in 1932.

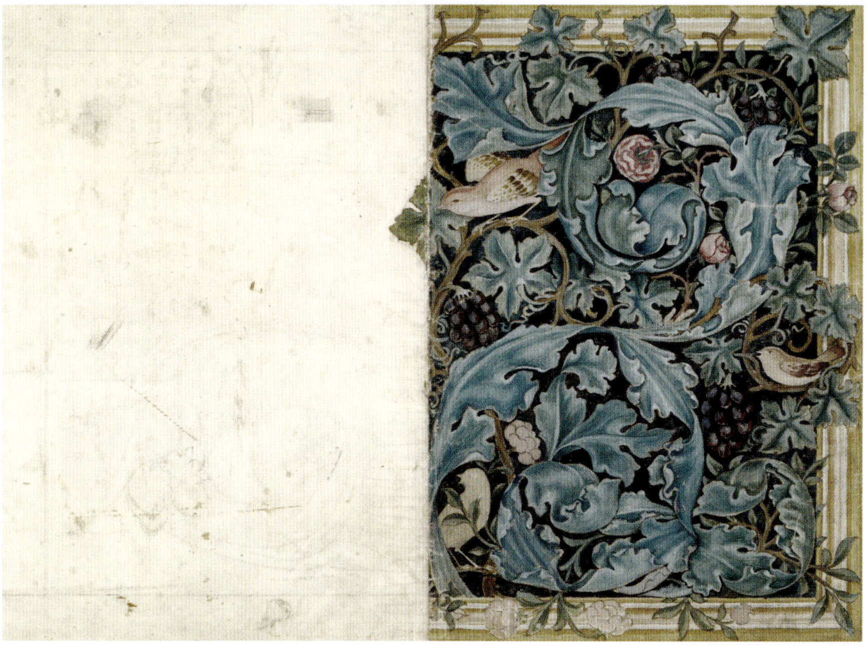

XII.103

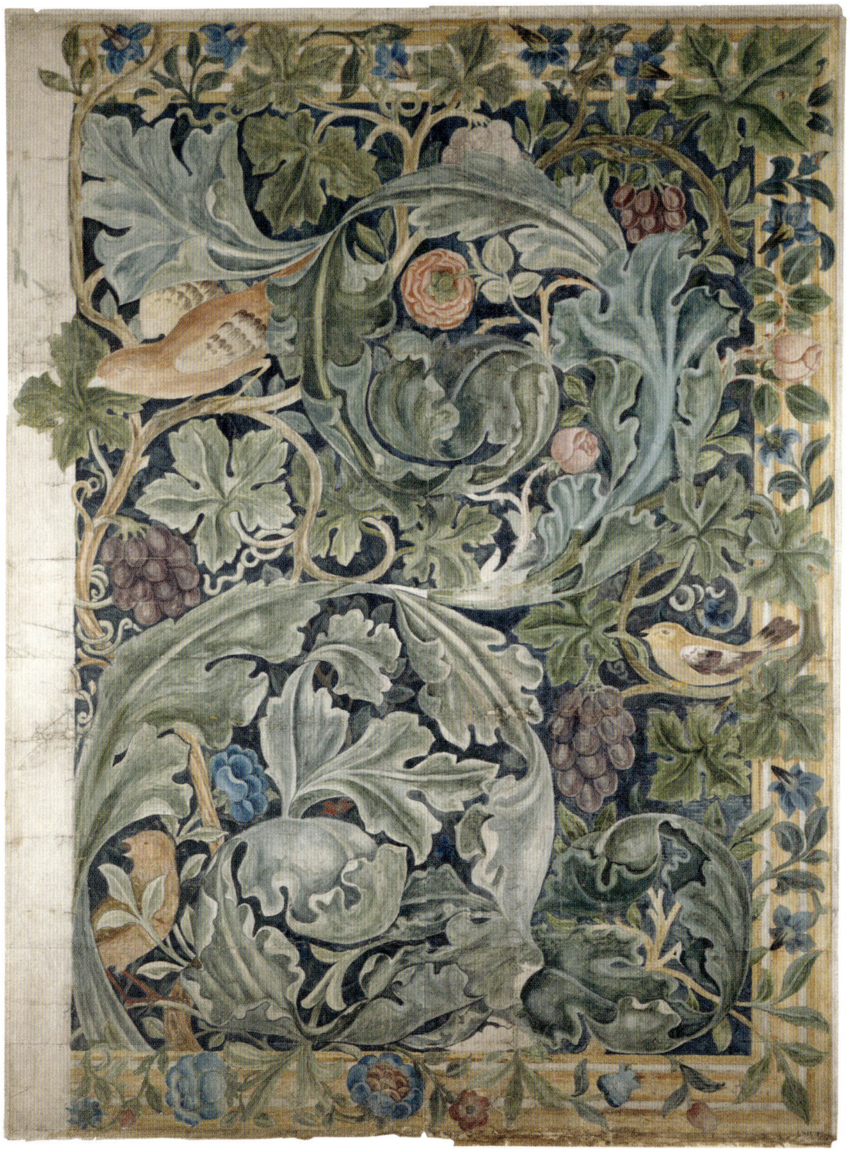

XII.104

XII.105

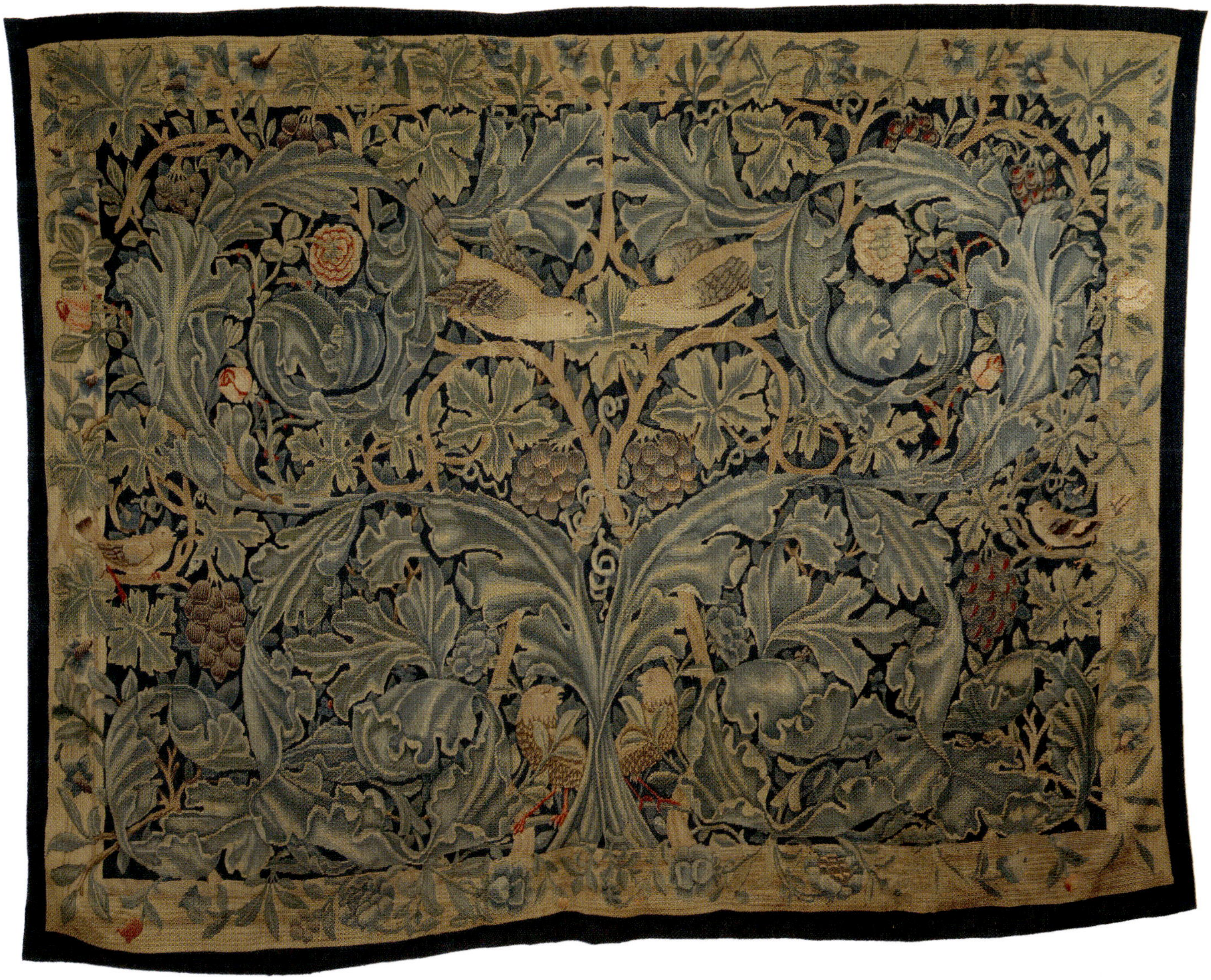

XII.106

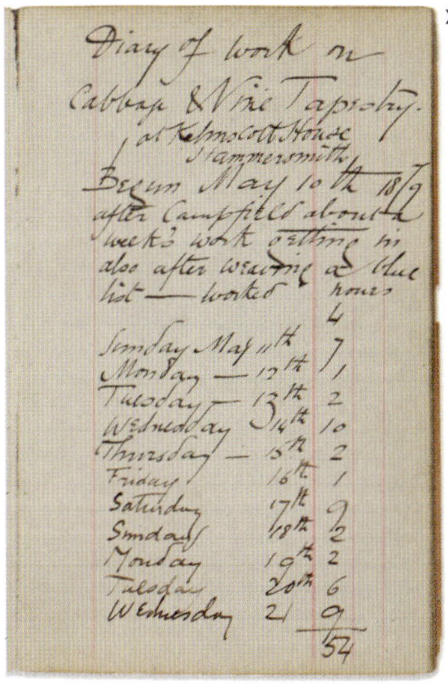

Diary of work on
Cabbage & Vine Tapestry.
at Kelmscott House
Hammersmith
Begun May 10th 1879
after Campfield about a
week's work setting in
also after weaving a blue
list — worked hours
4
Sunday May 11th 7
Monday — 12th 1
Tuesday — 13th 2
Wednesday 14th 10
Thursday — 15th 2
Friday 16th 1
Saturday 17th 9
Sunday 18th 2
Monday 19th 2
Tuesday 20th 6
Wednesday 21 9
54

XII.105
***Acanthus and Vine* tapestry**
Designed and woven by William Morris at Kelmscott House, 1879
Tapestry woven wool, with some silk, on a cotton warp, 191 x 234 cm
The Society of Antiquaries of London, Kelmscott Manor (KM032)

This is Morris's first attempt at tapestry weaving, which May Morris described as 'W.M's own piece'. He first set up a tapestry loom in 1877 and it is likely that experimental work preceded this. 'I used to get up at daylight to puzzle out the tricks of the loom for myself' was how he described this later (*Daily Chronicle*, 9 October 1893).

Morris prepared the project in the traditional manner with a design and full-scale cartoon (XII.103–4). He began weaving on 10 May 1879 in his bedroom at Kelmscott House, snatching hours between other commercial duties. The tapestry took 516½ hours and was finished on 17 September. Coarsely woven at seven to ten warp threads to the inch, distortion is due to this variation in weave and uneven loom tension.

The choice of large curving leaves in the design and the use of faded colours in the weaving is significant. Morris's inspiration was 'large-leaf' verdure tapestries woven in France and Flanders in the sixteenth century. It is likely that examples of these were the 'faded greenery' that made a significant impression on him as a young boy visiting Queen Elizabeth's Hunting Lodge in Epping Forest. The tapestry remained the property of the Morris family and was affectionately referred to as *Cabbage and Vine.*

XII.106
Notebook
William Morris, 1879
Handwritten in pencil, 18 x 23 cm (open)
V&A (NAL MSL/1939/2637)

Morris kept a personal record of the time spent weaving the *Acanthus and Vine* tapestry. The book is inscribed 'Diary of work on Cabbage & Vine Tapestry at Kelmscott House, Hammersmith. Begun May 10th 1879 after Campfield about a week's work vetting in also after weaving a blue list [*sic*]'. This suggests that George Campfield spent a week preparing the cartoon and Morris started weaving the tapestry with a plain blue selvedge (border) before timekeeping began.

The hours devoted to the work each day are noted line by line and the last entry, for three hours, is on Wednesday 17 September. During this four-month period Morris spent 516½ hours working on the panel. How he found time for this non-commercial venture with Morris & Co. experiencing one of its busiest periods is difficult to comprehend. At the back of the notebook is a list of historic textile fragments, either owned by Morris or more likely examined by him on behalf of the South Kensington Museum.

XII.107

Design for a tapestry depicting acanthus, birds and peacocks

William Morris, *c.*1879–81

Pencil, pen and ink, watercolour and body colour, 56.5 x 39 cm

V&A (E.620–1939)

Bequeathed by May Morris

Similarities in colouring, composition and style, including swirling acanthus leaves, suggest this tapestry design was made around the same time as *Acanthus and Vine* (XII.105). The date palm and exotic birds appear in other designs from this period, including the peacock embroidered frieze exhibited at Philadelphia in 1876 (fig.210), *Peacock and Dragon* woven furnishing of 1878 (XII.69), preliminary designs for the *Naworth* carpet in 1881 (XII.94), and the peacock carpet woven for the Vanderbilt family in 1882 (XII.96). Highly finished in detail and colour, it may have been worked up in the studio from a Morris design.

The drawing has been remounted and an uncharacteristic tree and scroll border added. It is likely this was done in the latter years of Morris & Co. when the firm was attempting to adapt early designs for the modern market. It is inscribed 'original design by William Morris' in the hand of Sydney Cockerell, one of his executors.

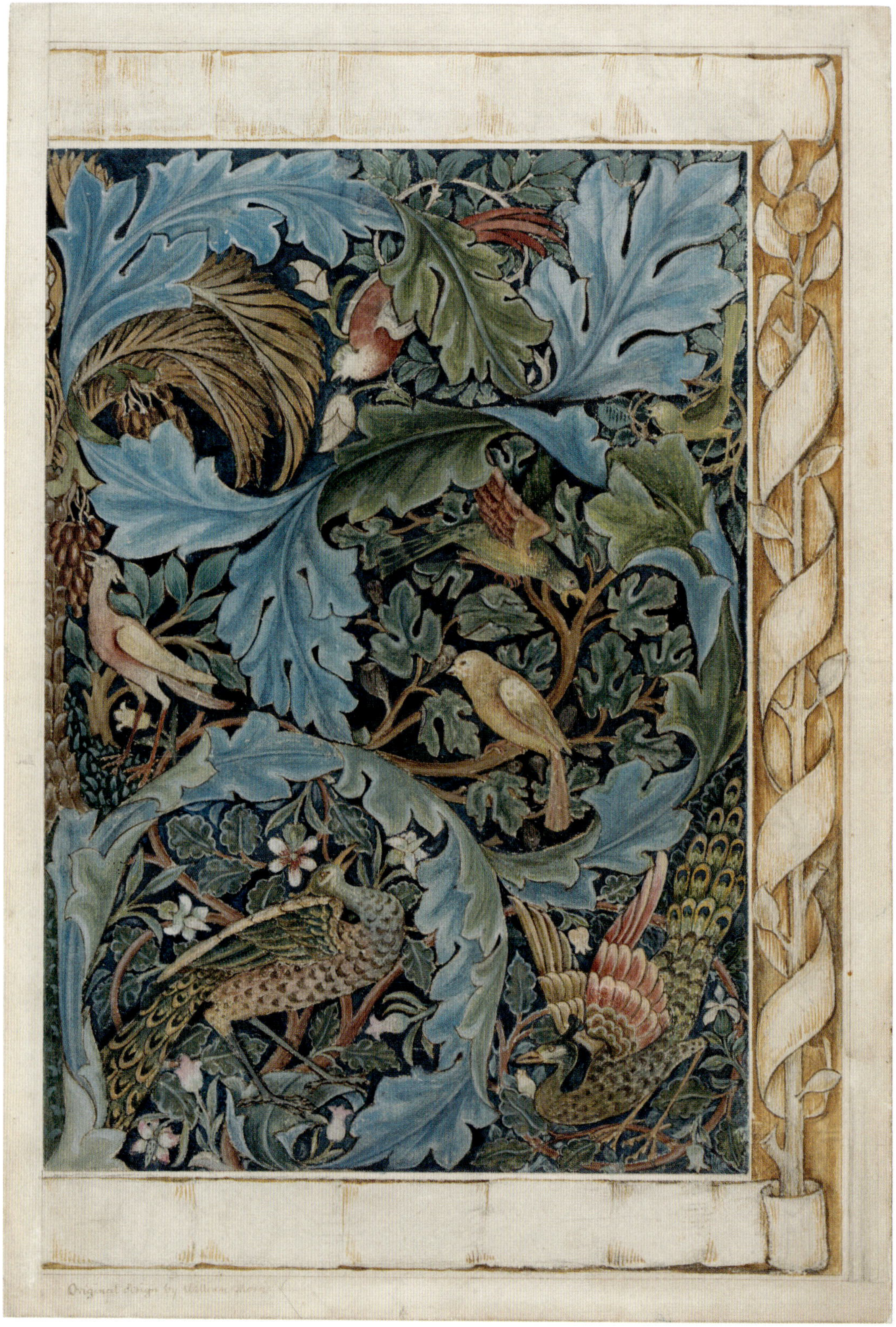

XII.107

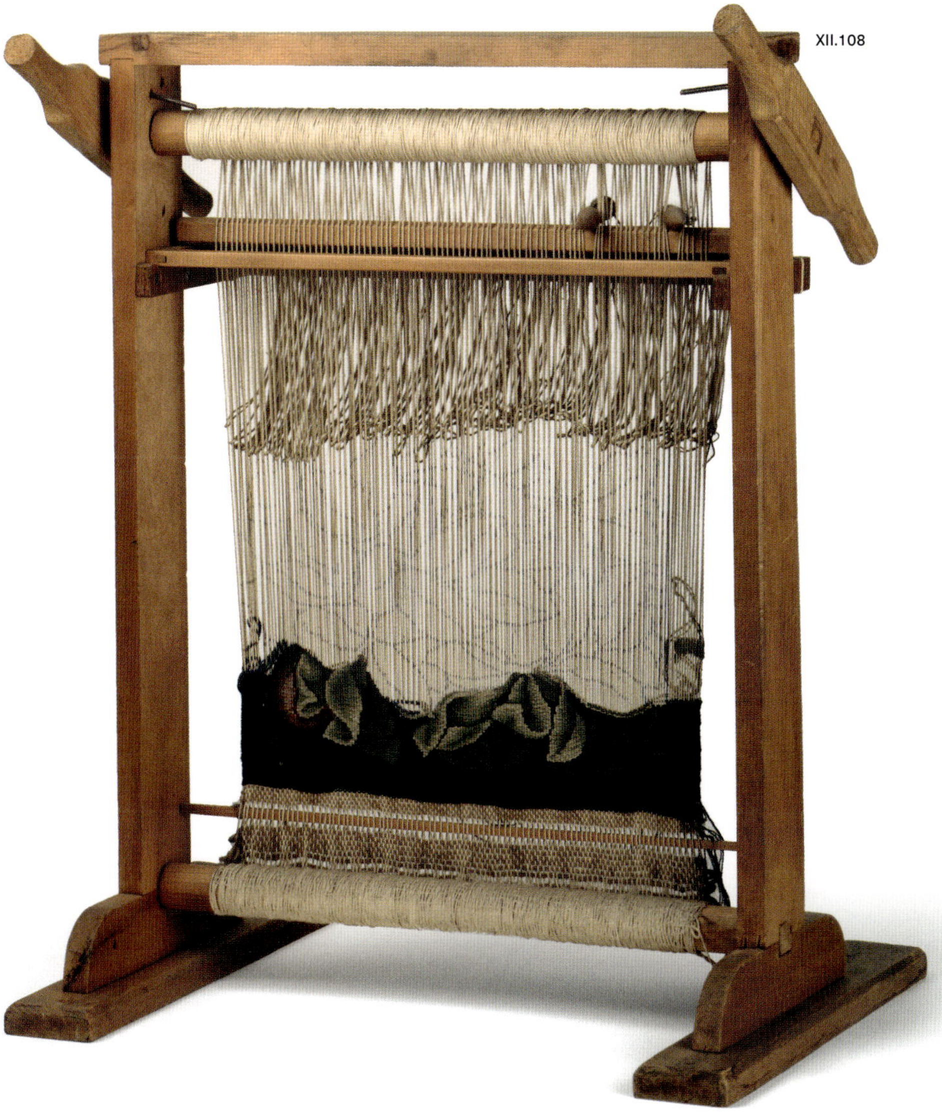

XII.108

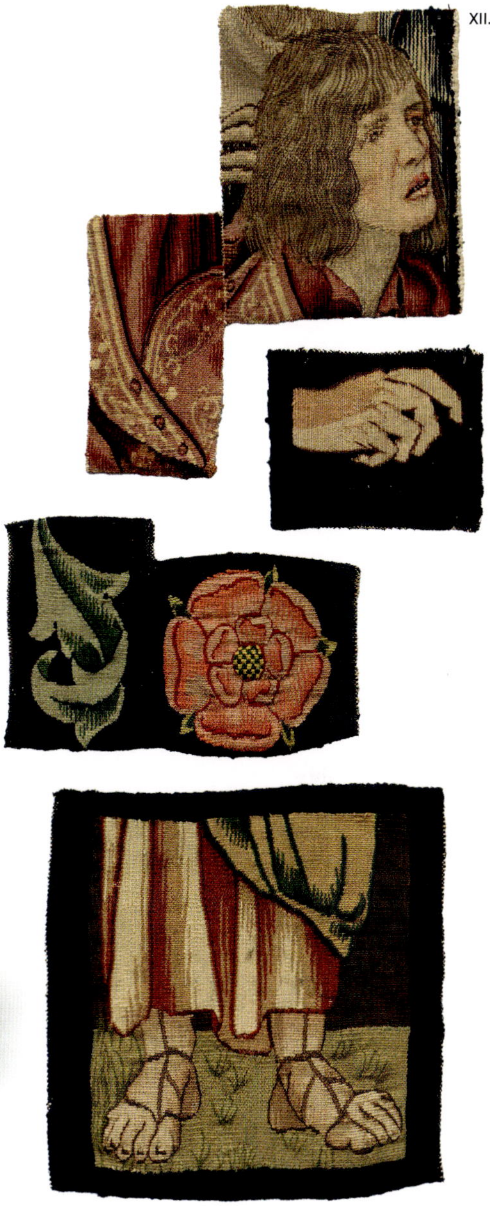

XII.109

XII.108
Miniature tapestry loom
Merton Abbey, late nineteenth century
Wood with metal fittings, 71.5 x 55.2 x 38.7 cm
V&A (156–1893)
Given by William Morris

This loom was used to instruct apprentice tapestry weavers at Merton Abbey and retains the partially worked warp and bobbins. Morris chose to use the *haute lisse* or upright tapestry loom in preference to the horizontally worked *basse lisse*. This was the technique used by medieval weavers and gave the effects that he most admired. Using this type of loom, weavers work from the back of the weaving tracing their progress by looking through the vertical warp threads to a mirror that hangs in front of the work. Because of the limits of the widths of the loom, designs are usually worked sideways.

Morris visited the Gobelins factory in Paris in his Oxford vacation of 1854. This was the only commercial tapestry manufactory using the upright loom at that time. Although he disliked the work, later arguing that it reduced the art to a mere 'upholsterer's toy', the visit provided an opportunity for him to see tapestry production on a large scale.

Morris's equipment was uncluttered and practical and did not follow the romantic, symbolic and decorative vision of weaving represented in a number of Pre-Raphaelite works of art.

XII.109
Sample weavings by a tapestry apprentice
Woven by Douglas Griffiths at Merton Abbey, *c.*1935–9
Tapestry woven wool and silk on a cotton warp, various sizes (max 34 x 30 cm)
William Morris Gallery, London Borough of Waltham Forest (F275)

These samples are from a group of exercises woven by an apprentice at Merton Abbey in the twentieth century. The method of training is likely to have changed little since Morris transferred Dearle from the glass-painters' shop to become his first tapestry apprentice at Queen Square in 1879. Morris believed that young boys were the best recruits as tapestry 'involves little muscular effort and is best carried out by small flexible fingers'. They were given a weekly stipend, board and lodgings and were looked after by a housekeeper in a house on the Merton Abbey site.

Weaving exercises included copying both historic and contemporary patterns. Geometric border designs were followed by more complex floral forms with hands, feet and finally heads being given to the more experienced weavers. One of these examples is a copy of a head from the Brussels sixteenth-century tapestry *Pity Restraining Justice*, which Morris had advised the South Kensington Museum to buy in 1890.

XII.110

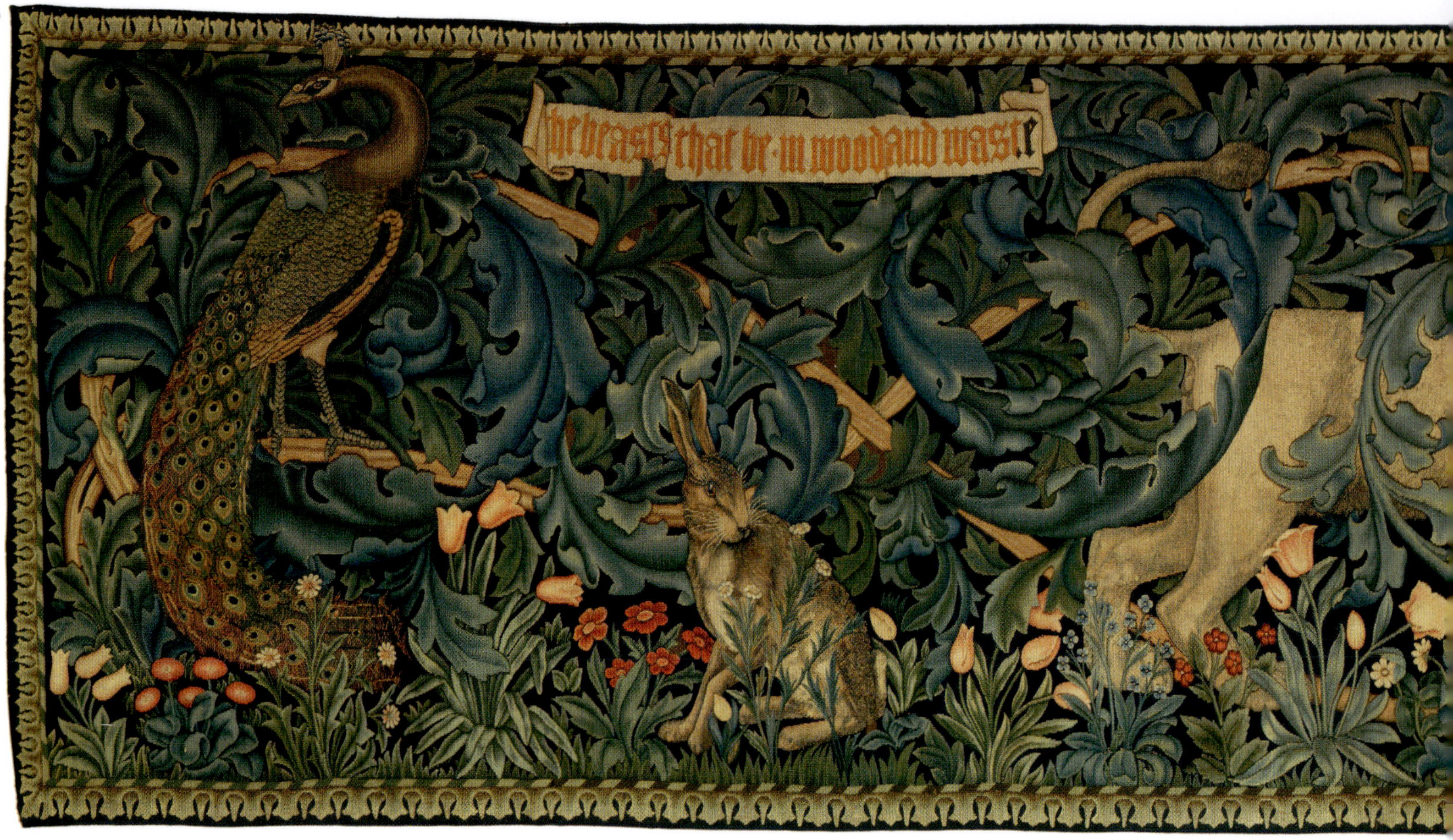

XII.110
***The Forest* tapestry**
Designed by William Morris, Philip Webb and John Henry Dearle
Woven at Merton Abbey by William Knight, John Martin and William Sleath, 1887
Tapestry woven wool and silk on a cotton warp, 122 x 452 cm
V&A (T.111–1926)
Purchased with Art Fund support

Morris's use of birds and animals in early tapestries is a direct development from his later carpet patterns. This design, one of his most successful compositions, uses a dense cover of trailing acanthus leaves, as seen in his first tapestry *Acanthus and Vine* (XII.105), into which have been placed Philip Webb's five studies of animals and birds (fig.214). It is likely that Dearle supplied foreground floral details, although these are also suggested in Webb's preparatory drawings. The verse, 'the beasts that be in wood and waste, now sit and see nor ride nor haste,' was later published under the title 'The Lion' in Morris's *Poems by the Way* (1891).

The tapestry was woven by Morris & Co.'s three most senior weavers 'under the superintendence of William Morris', according to the 1890 Arts and Crafts Exhibition catalogue. Purchased by Aleco Ionides for 1 Holland Park, it hung in the study together with an acanthus-leaf panel (see VIII.15). The V&A purchased the tapestry in 1926 for £500 from Morris & Co. acting on behalf of George Ionides. Four of Webb's exquisite preparatory drawings were bought by Laurence Hodson of Wolverhampton and are now in the collection of Wightwick Manor.

XII.111
Tapestry of a scrolling acanthus leaf
Designed by William Morris or John Henry Dearle
Woven at Merton Abbey, *c.*1890
Tapestry woven wool on a cotton warp, 55 x 156 cm
V&A (T.111–1986)

This panel is similar in design to a tapestry owned by Aleco Ionides, which hung above the study door alongside *The Forest* at 1 Holland Park. This example is unfinished and without a border and may have been woven at Merton Abbey as a pattern trial.

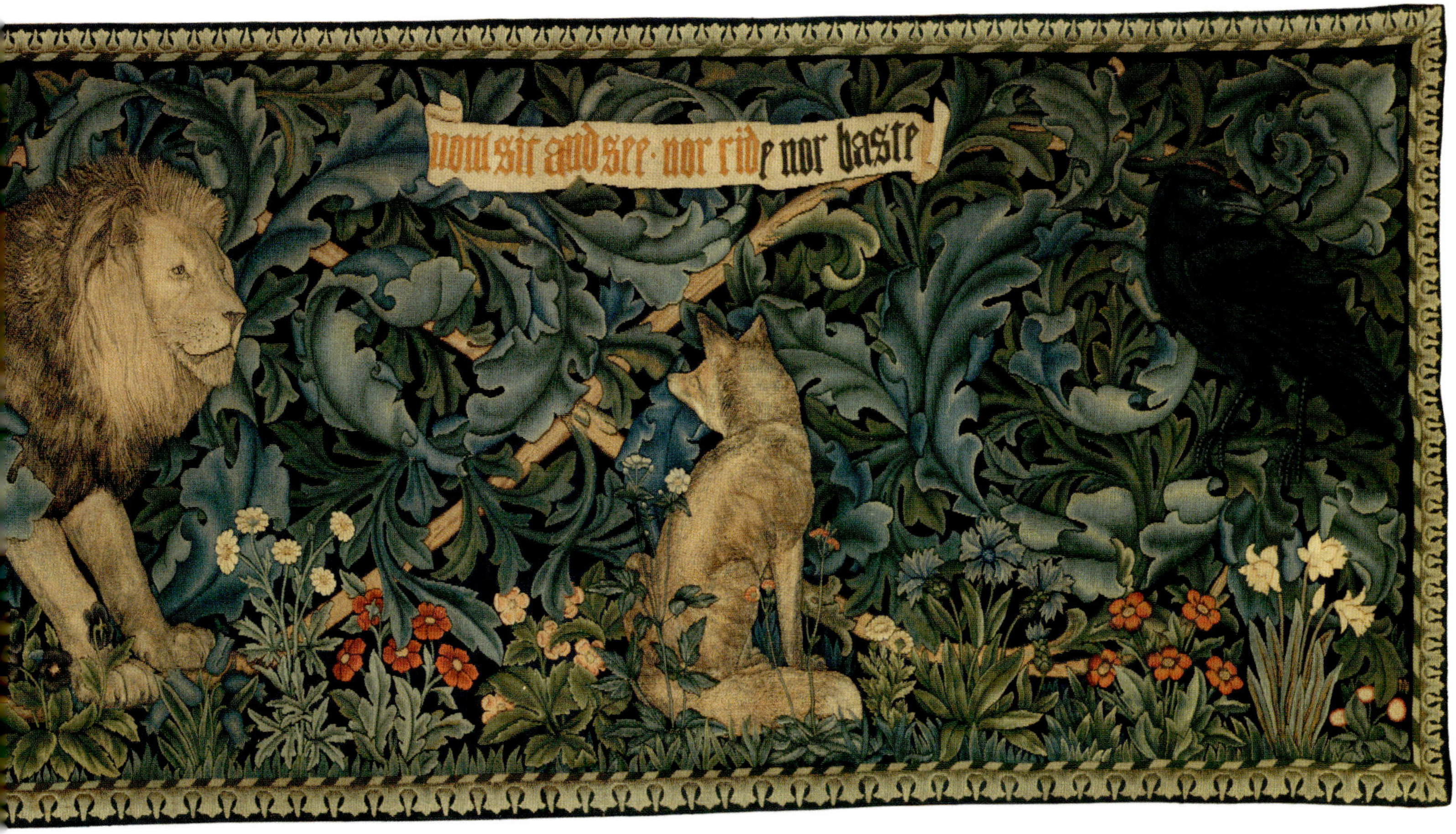

XII.111

XII.112

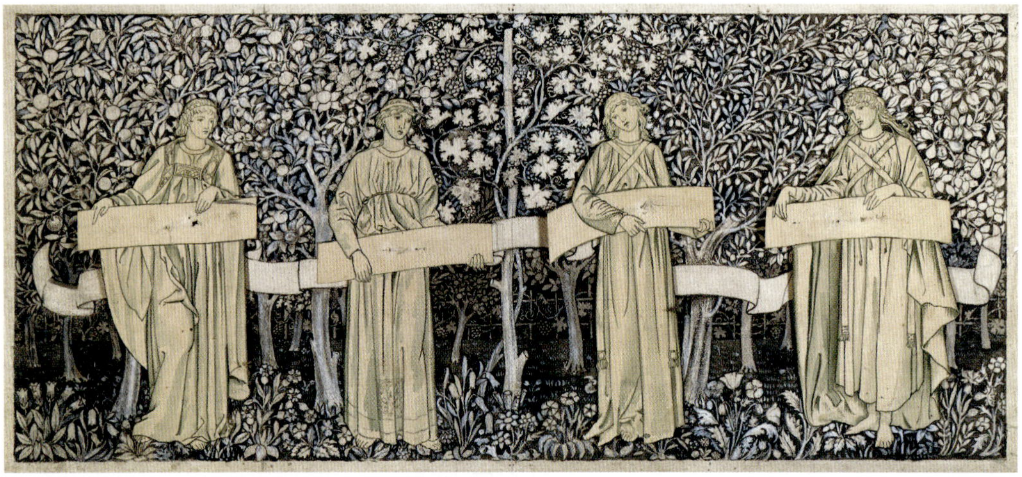

XII.113

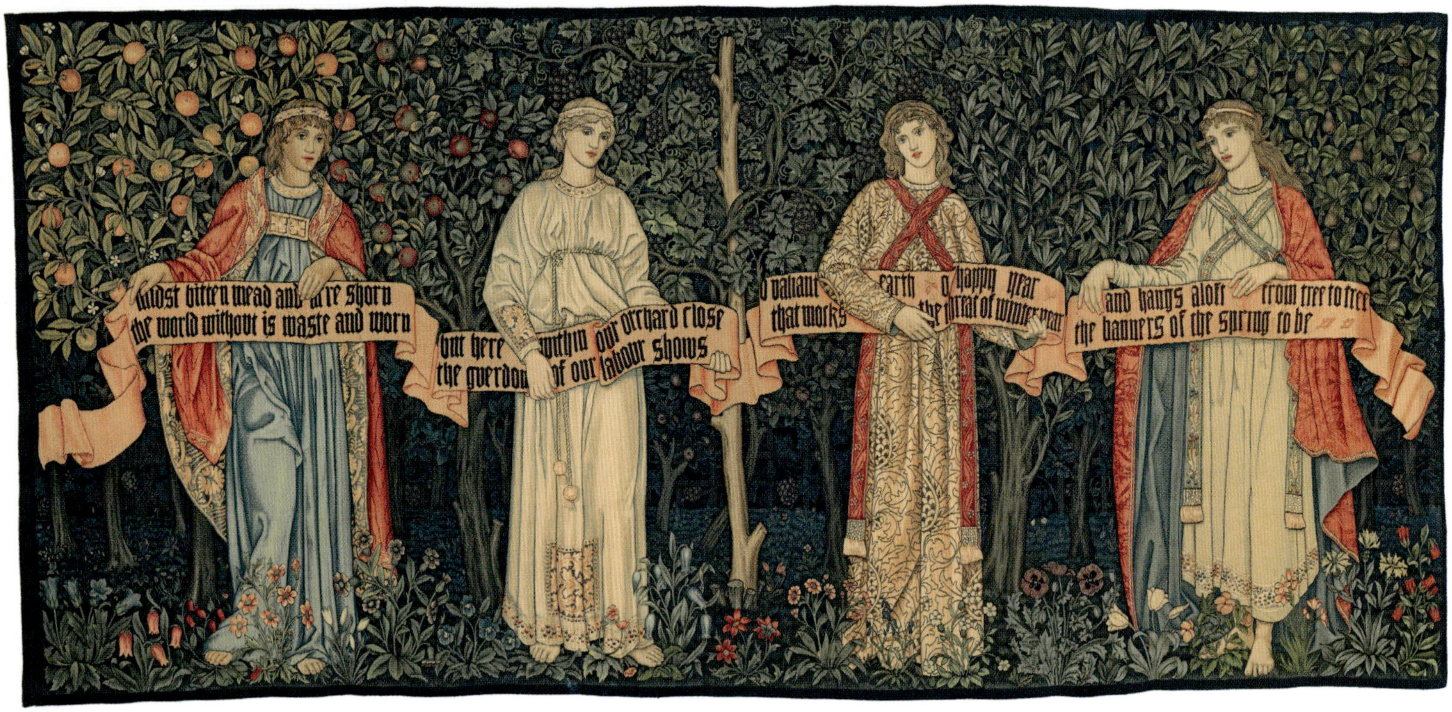

XII.112
Design for *The Orchard* or *The Seasons* tapestry
Morris & Co. after William Morris, *c.*1890
Pencil, pen and ink, watercolour, Chinese white and body colour, 49.4 x 68.2 cm
V&A (E.544–1939)

Morris first drew these figures for the decoration of the nave ceiling in Jesus College Chapel, Cambridge, in 1866 (figs 126–7). In the original, the angels hold scrolls inscribed with the medieval hymn *Vexilla Regis prodeunt*. The idea to adapt the ceiling angels as allegorical figures in a tapestry was Morris's but this scale design was drawn in the Morris & Co. workshop. The background of fruit trees and trellis fence is the work of Dearle, although in the Morris tradition. The figures, copied from the originals in the firm's studio, are probably by George Wardle. Drawn on re-used paper, they are detachable and have been partially stuck over the top of the floral background.

XII.113
***The Orchard* or *The Seasons* tapestry**
Designed by William Morris and John Henry Dearle
Woven at Merton Abbey by William Knight, William Sleath and John Martin, 1890
Tapestry woven wool, silk and mohair on a cotton warp, 221 x 472 cm
V&A (154–1898)

By 1890, with a decade's production behind the firm, Merton Abbey tapestries were becoming increasingly popular with rich clients who wished to own unique works of art by Morris & Co. Figurative designs, in particular, were sought after and a number by Burne-Jones had already been woven (see XII.114). This panel was Morris's first attempt to include figures in one of his own tapestry designs. He had not drawn from a model since the first half of the 1870s so it was to an earlier project that he turned. The Jesus College Chapel commission provided him not only with successful figures but also scrolls for inscriptions, an essential part of Morris's tapestry designs at the time. These he updated by using his own poem 'The Orchard', composed especially and later published in *Poems by the Way* (1891).

The tapestry was woven under the close supervision of Dearle who reported to the V&A when it was acquired that, 'The colouring as well as the general design are by Mr Morris and parts of the figures have been woven by his own hand'. Sleath and Knight were the first tapestry apprentices taken on after Dearle and were trained by him. John Martin eventually became the first tapestry restorer employed by the V&A.

The design was woven only once and the panel did not find a private buyer, indicating that Burne-Jones's figure designs (and by now he was a much sought-after artist) were far more popular. The tapestry was sent on approval to Clouds, Percy Wyndham's country house near Salisbury, and an existing photograph shows it hanging in the hall. However, Dearle's *Greenery* tapestry was eventually purchased.

XII.114
***Pomona* tapestry**
Designed by Edward Burne-Jones and John Henry Dearle
Woven at Merton Abbey, *c.*1900
Tapestry woven wool and silk on a cotton warp, 168 x 109 cm
V&A (T.33–1981)

Burne-Jones's account book shows that he was paid £25 by Morris & Co. in December 1882 for the figure of *Pomona*, his first design specifically for tapestry. A letter from Morris to Jenny on 28 February 1883 states, 'Uncle Ned has done me two lovely figures for tapestry, but I have got to design a background for them: I shall probably bring them down [to Kelmscott Manor] next time I come for my holiday task'. The original tapestry with Morris's background and border design was woven with its pair, *Flora*, at Merton Abbey between 1884 and 1885. Both panels are now in The Whitworth, University of Manchester.

This is one of seven later versions approximately half the size of the original, with a background design by Dearle. Reducing the size and adding a millefleurs ground proved to be commercially expedient. In his 1927 publication, *History of the Merton Abbey Tapestry Works*, Henry Currie Marillier recorded six examples woven between 1898 and 1920. Apart from this panel, others have been traced to Exeter College, Oxford, the Harris Art Gallery, Preston, Pannet Art Gallery, Whitby, and the Art Institute of Chicago. The 1920 version woven for James Fleming of Aldwick Grange, West Sussex, is now in the de Young museum, San Francisco, and yet another version, with a slightly altered ground, was woven in 1936 as part of the planned celebrations for the coronation of Edward VIII. This was sold at Christie's South Kensington on 3 October 1989.

Eleven small-scale *Flora* tapestries are recorded. Two have the same border design as this panel. One, which shows similar weaving interpretations to this example and may be contemporary, was sold at Sotheby's, 4 December 1985, the other, a later version, is in a private collection in Australia. A design with an alternative background design inscribed 'Baroda Museum' is in the collection of the William Morris Gallery (BLA484), and a watercolour design, probably painted in the Morris workshops, is at Wightwick Manor.

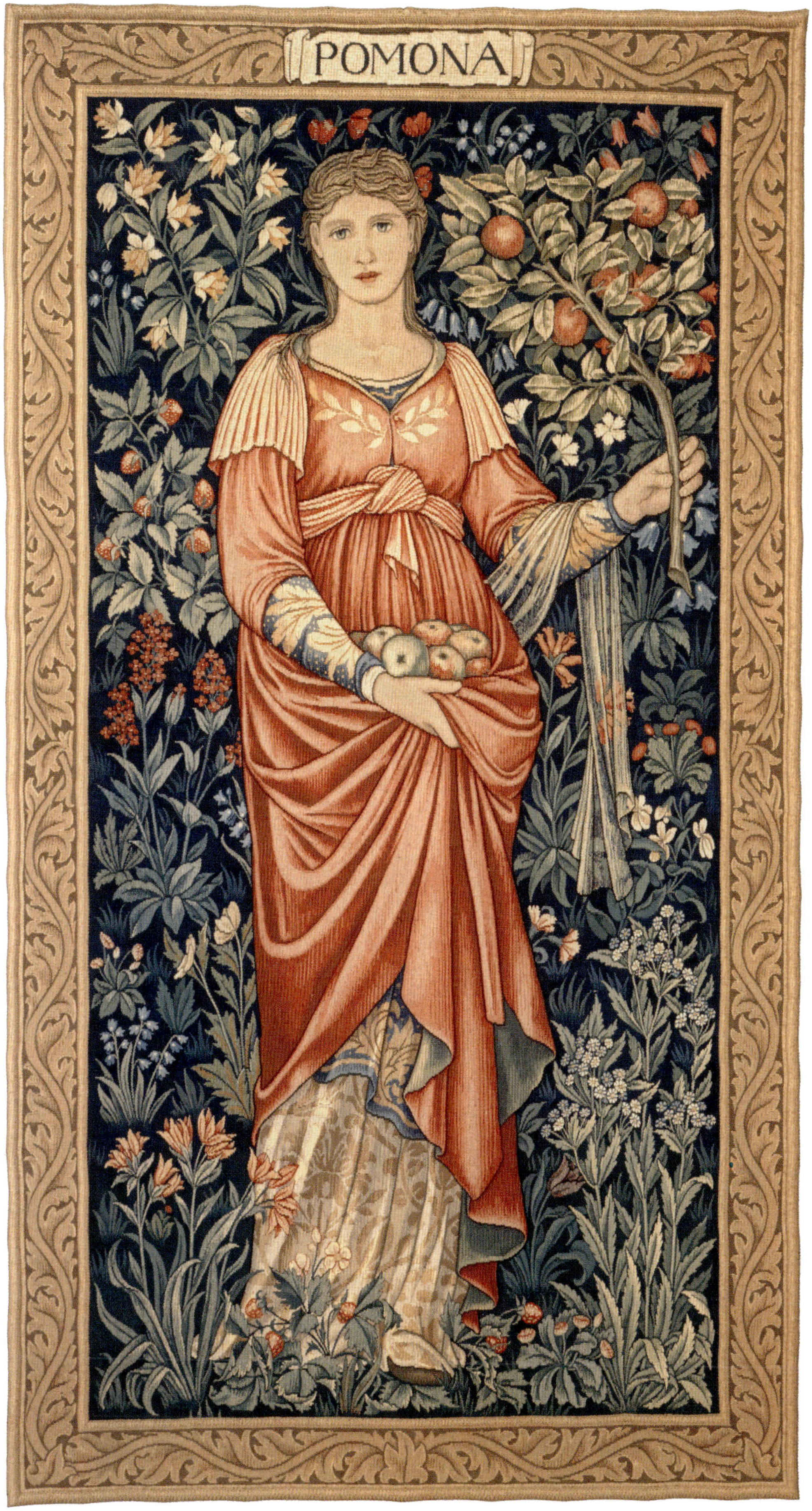

XII.114

XII.115

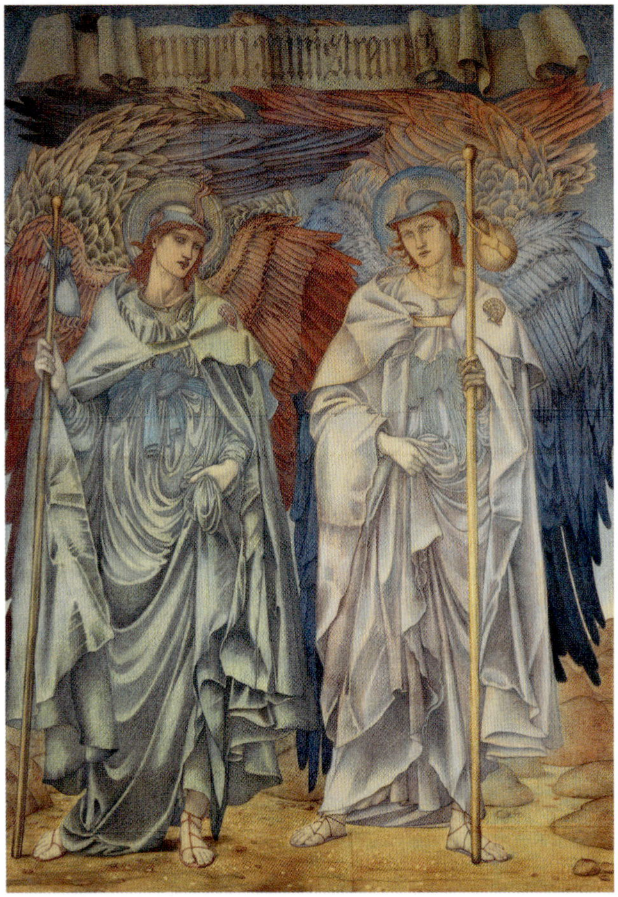

XII.116

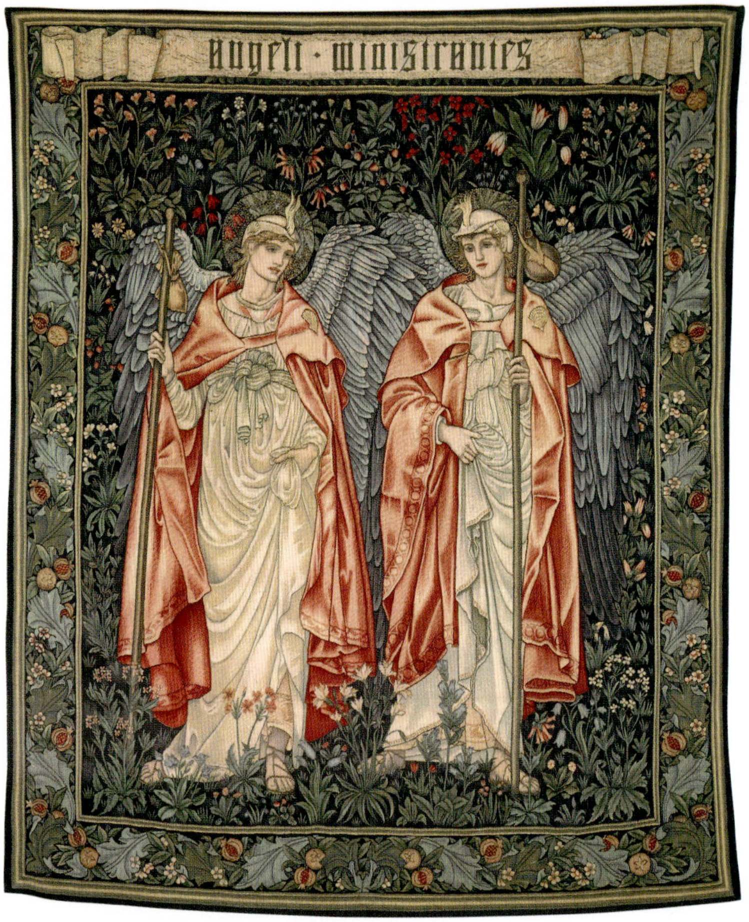

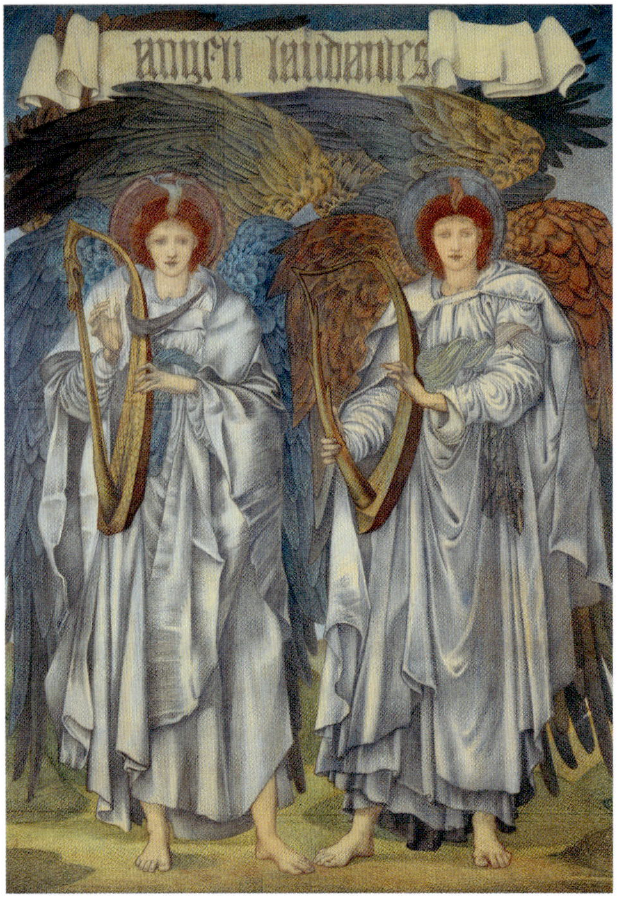

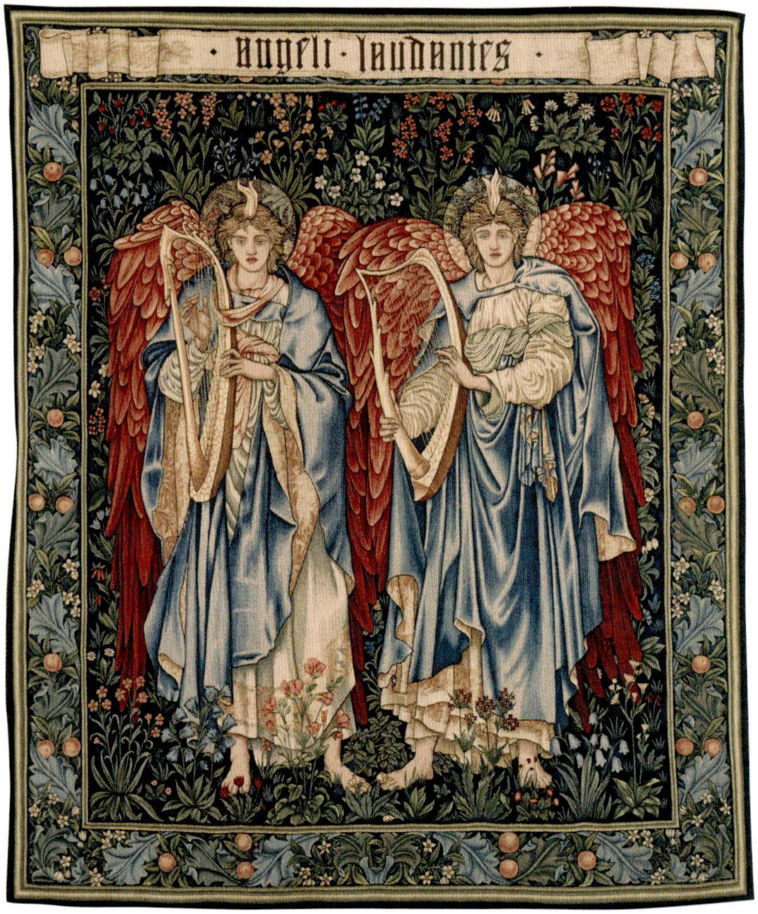

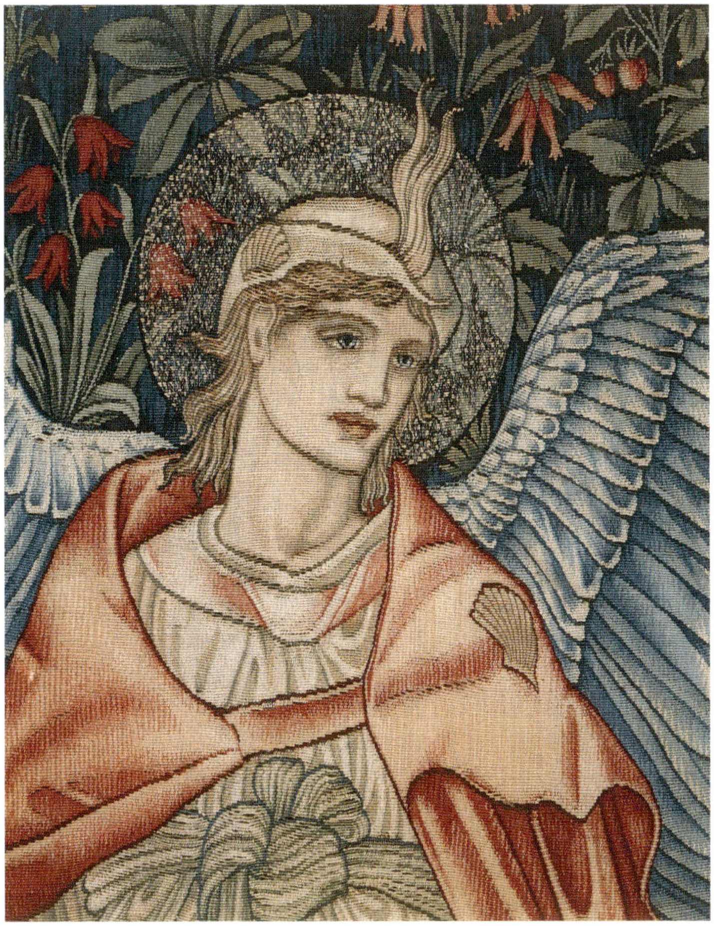

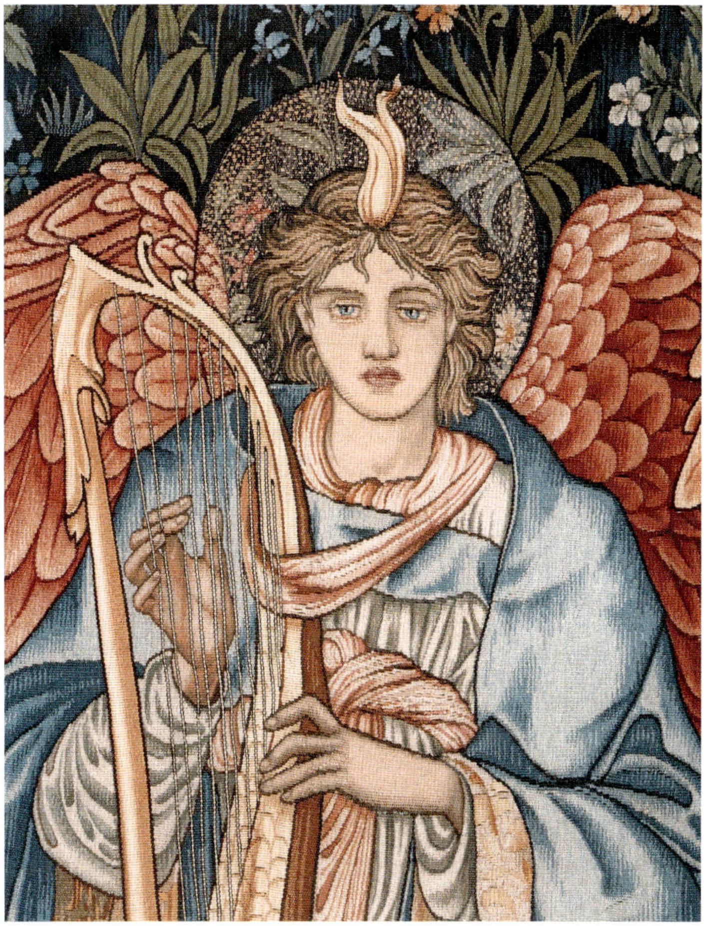

XII.115

***Angeli Ministrantes* and *Angeli Laudantes* designs**

Edward Burne-Jones, 1877–8

Coloured chalks on paper on canvas, 212.3 x 150.5 cm, 212.8 x 154.3 cm

Fitzwilliam Museum, University of Cambridge (699.1-2)

Originally drawn by Burne-Jones for stained-glass windows in the south choir aisle of Salisbury Cathedral (fig.129), these designs were later adapted for tapestries woven at Merton Abbey. An entry between March and August 1878 in Burne-Jones's account book listed '4 colossal and sublime figures of Angels £20 ea[ch]'. The figures are the same size as the original finished tapestries and these drawings may have been used at the loom (before they were coloured with chalks), although it is likely that the cartoons took the form of photographic copies onto which foreground, background and border details were added by hand.

A label on the back of *Angeli Ministrantes* is inscribed in Georgiana Burne-Jones's hand, 'Design made for a window in Salisbury Cathedral by E. Burne-Jones December 6th 1887 [or 9]. Lent to the South London Free Library for 3 months'. It was subsequently given by Burne-Jones to William Rossiter, founder of the South London Art Gallery, in memory of his wife Elizabeth. Both drawings were presented to the Fitzwilliam Museum by Charles Fairfax Murray in 1910.

XII.116

***Angeli Ministrantes* and *Angeli Laudantes* tapestries**

Designed by John Henry Dearle with figures by Edward Burne-Jones

Woven at Merton Abbey by John Martin, William Haines and John George Eleman, 1894

Tapestry woven wool, silk and mohair on a cotton warp, 242 x 200 cm, 238 x 202 cm

V&A (T.459–1993)

Purchased with Art Fund support and the National Heritage Memorial Fund

V&A (153–1898)

Burne-Jones's angel figures were adapted for tapestry with millefleurs grounds and matching pomegranate and orange borders designed by Dearle. Manufactured at Merton Abbey in 1894 by the firm's most experienced weavers at that time, they were woven at 15 warp threads to the inch, the average pitch of the firm's tapestries throughout production.

In 1898 the South Kensington Museum purchased the *Laudantes* panel from Morris & Co. for £225 on the recommendation of the artist John Hungerford Pollen and the Earl of Carlisle. The *Ministrantes* tapestry was bought by Edwin Waterhouse of Feldemore in Surrey. It subsequently formed part of the Handley-Read Collection and was purchased by the V&A in 1993.

A number of later variations of these tapestries were woven, including a *Laudantes* panel in 1898 for Major Charles Sydney Goldman (Metropolitan Museum of Art, New York) and a single angel with a harp inscribed 'Alleluia' in 1904 (Harris Art Gallery, Preston). The designs proved particularly appropriate for church use, and in 1902 a pair of single angels was woven for All Saints, Brockhampton, Herefordshire, in memory of the parents of Ebenezer Jordan. These were repeated in 1904 for a private memorial and in 1905 both panels were adapted for Eton College Chapel. Woven in memory of former students killed in the Boer War, they have an inscription and a lower verdure border of shields. An embroidered interpretation of *Laudantes* with additional medieval figures worked by Lady Catherine Milnes Gaskell is now in Much Wenlock parish church, Shropshire.

Fig.216 **Details from *Angeli Ministrantes* (left) and *Angeli Laudantes* (right) tapestries.**

XII.117

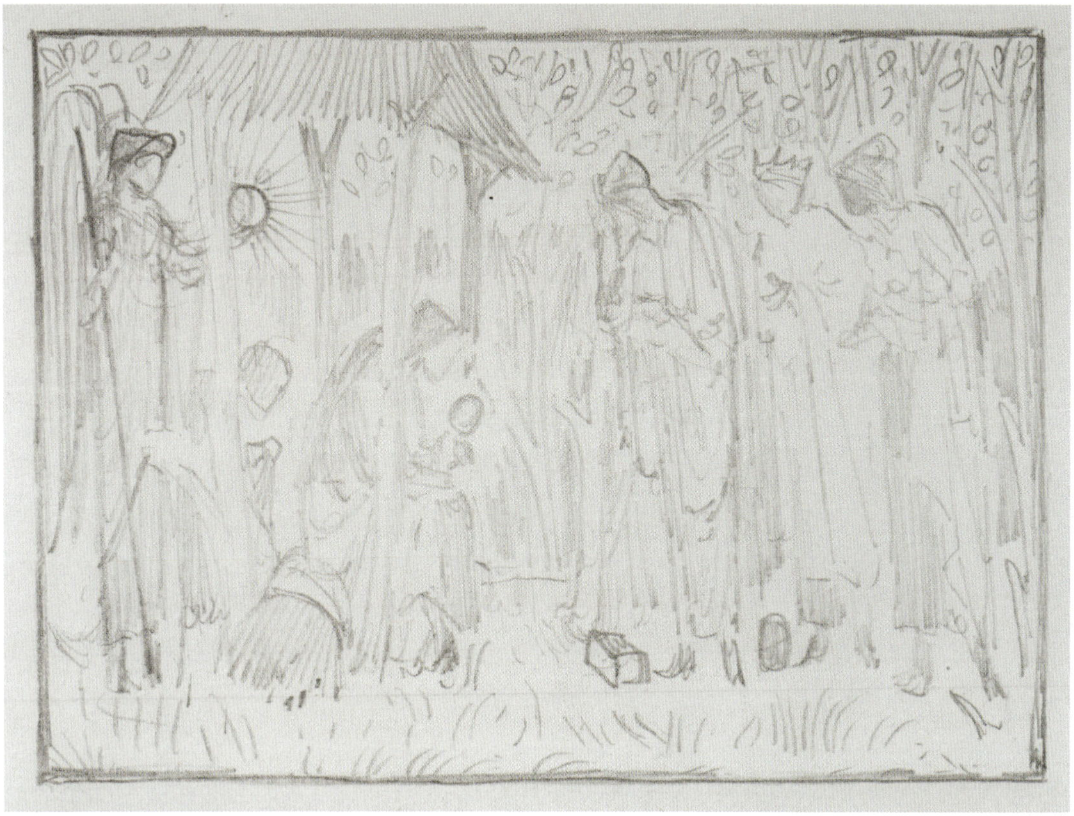

XII.117
Sketchbook
Edward Burne-Jones, 1880s
Pencil, 10.2 x 17.2 x 2 cm (closed)
V&A (E.9–1955)
Given by Dr W.L. Hildburgh

This sketchbook includes various studies for paintings, stained glass, mural decoration and the peacock used in the design of Laura Lyttelton's memorial tablet in the church of St Andrew in Mells, Somerset. It also shows a number of preliminary drawings for *The Adoration* tapestry, including one page inscribed: '8 x 6 x 12.9 figures near life size'.

Burne-Jones's finished watercolour design for this tapestry was exhibited at the Burlington Fine Arts Club in 1899 and at the Fine Arts Society in 1979; it remains in a private collection.

XII.118

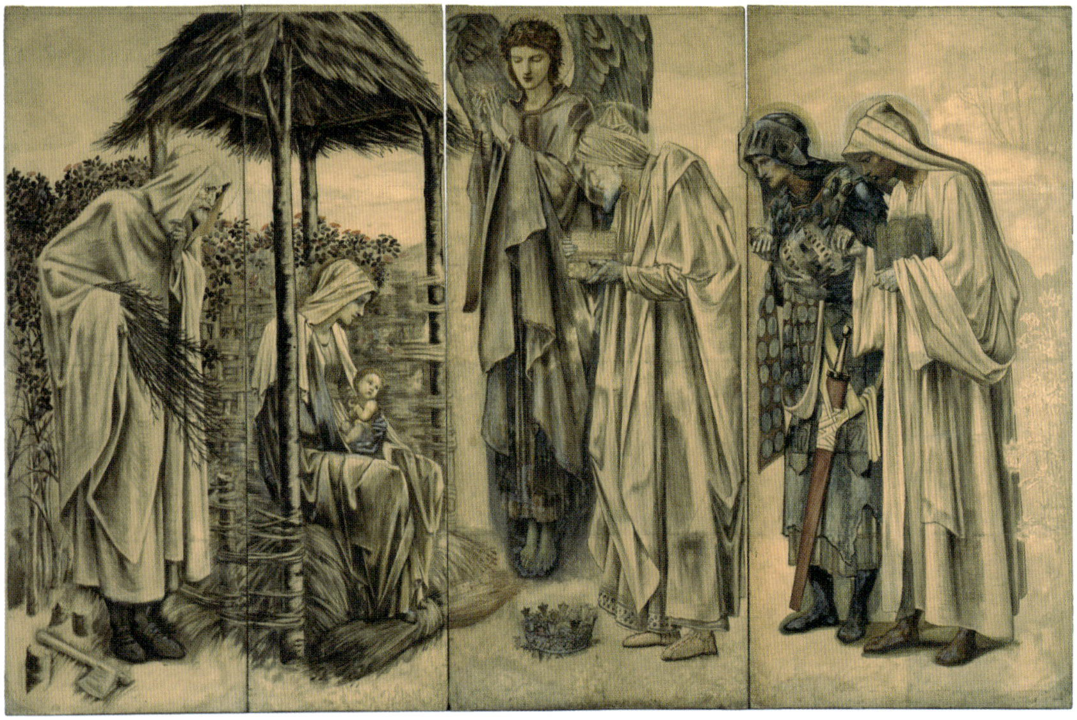

XII.118
Cartoon for *The Adoration* tapestry
After Edward Burne-Jones with details added by the artist, 1888
Photographic paper heightened with watercolour and body colour, 240 x 376 cm
V&A (E.5012–1919)

This photographic tapestry cartoon is in four parts. The process used by Morris & Co. for transferring tapestry designs to the loom is described in A.B. Bence-Jones's unpublished manuscript 'The Holy Grail Tapestries' (National Art Library, V&A). Burne-Jones's watercolour designs, which were never more than 15 inches high, were photographed and then enlarged to the desired finished size of the tapestry by the firm of Walker & Boutall of Fleet Street in London.

The photographs were then sent to Burne-Jones for any necessary adjustments to his figures and general composition and then to Morris or Dearle for the addition of background and foreground decoration and clothing patterns. Once approved by the three men, they were delivered to the weavers at Merton Abbey and the design marked on the warp in sections.

XII.119

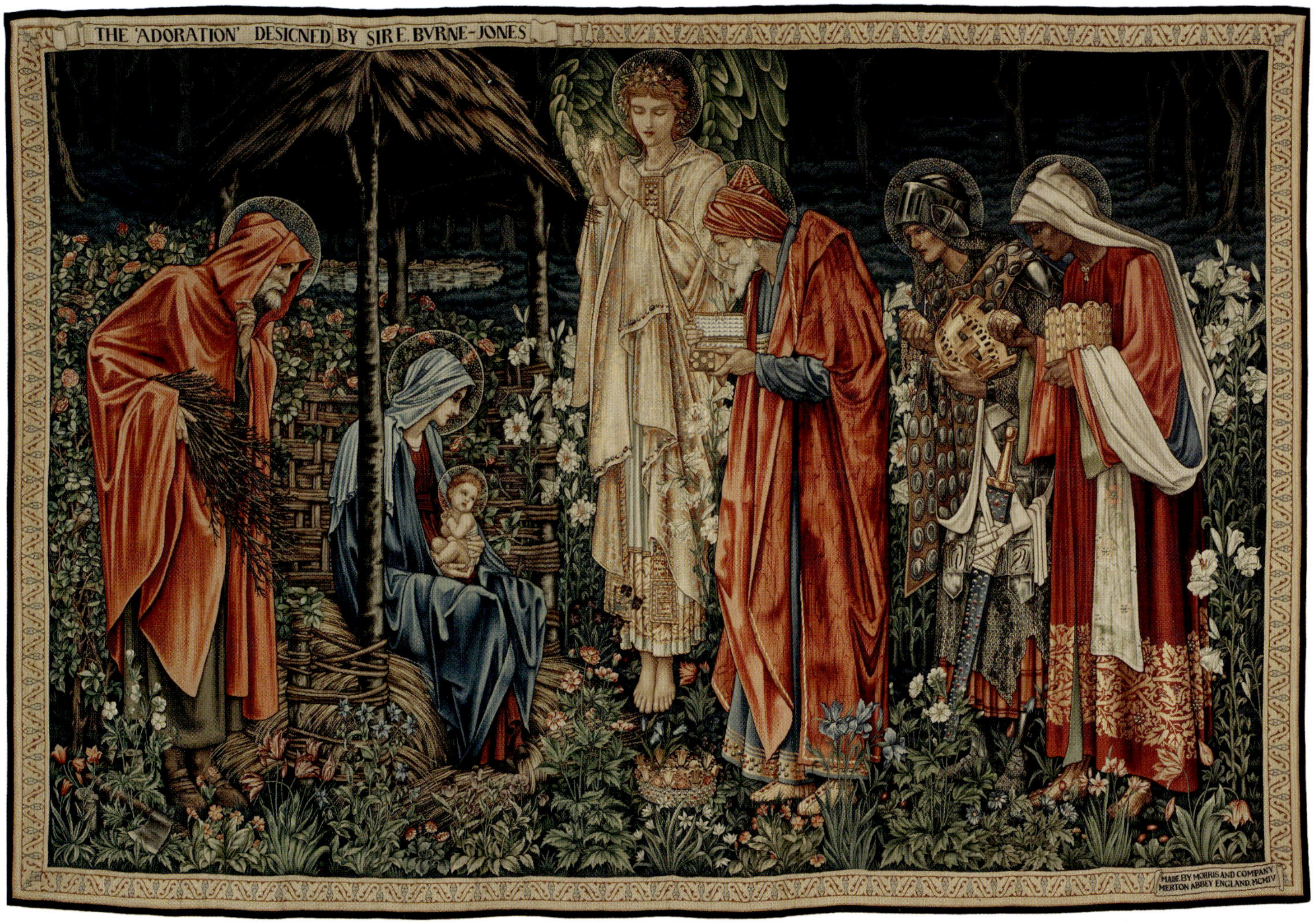

XII.119
***The Adoration* tapestry**
Designed by Edward Burne-Jones, William Morris and John Henry Dearle, 1888
Woven at Merton Abbey, 1904
Tapestry woven wool, silk and mohair on a cotton warp, 258 x 377.5 cm
Musée d'Orsay, Paris (OAO 1786)

This tapestry was first commissioned in 1886 for the chapel of Exeter College, Oxford, where Morris and Burne-Jones had both studied. The College Rector, John Prideaux Lightfoot, suggested the nativity subject, which Morris approved of as suiting 'the genius of tapestry completely' (4 September 1886). A few days later Morris viewed the proposed site. Colour, he believed, was particularly important and needed to be 'both harmonious & powerful, so that it would not be overpowered by the stained glass'.

The commission took four years to realize, including two years with three weavers at the loom. Morris applied his usual eye for detail and visited Hampton Court on 1 September 1888, 'to have a good look at the tapestries as we [are] about beginning the figure of the Virgin in our big tapestry.' It was finally finished in February 1890 and exhibited in the Oxford Street shop (see fig.39). With hyperbolic approval, *The Queen* reported, 'The outlines of the design only are Mr Burne-Jones's, the colouring and the ornamentation being Mr Morris's, and very beautiful are all three – so perfect, indeed, in every detail, that there is nothing left to desire' (26 April 1890).

In April 1893 Morris described the tapestry as 'the most important piece I have yet done' and ten versions were woven for both church and domestic settings. The second weaving was made for the poet Wilfrid Scawen Blunt between 1890–94 and cost £525, the same price as the original commission. Other orders followed: Manchester Corporation (1894); Eton College (1895); the Museum für Kunst und Gewerbe, Hamburg (1900); Sir George Brookman (1901), now in the Art Gallery of South Australia, Adelaide; the Russian art collector Sergei Shchukin (1902), now in the Hermitage, St Petersburg; the Colman family of Carrow Abbey, Norwich (1906), now in Norwich Castle Museum, and finally St Andrew's Church, Roker, Sunderland (1907).

This version was woven in 1904 for Guillaume Mallet, who came from a French banking family, and his heiress wife, Marie-Adélaïde, for their Edwin Lutyens house, Le Bois des Moutiers, near Dieppe in France. The tapestry was hidden during the Second World War when the house was occupied by the Nazis. It later belonged to Yves Saint Laurent and Pierre Bergé and was donated by the latter to the Musée d'Orsay in 2009.

XII.120a

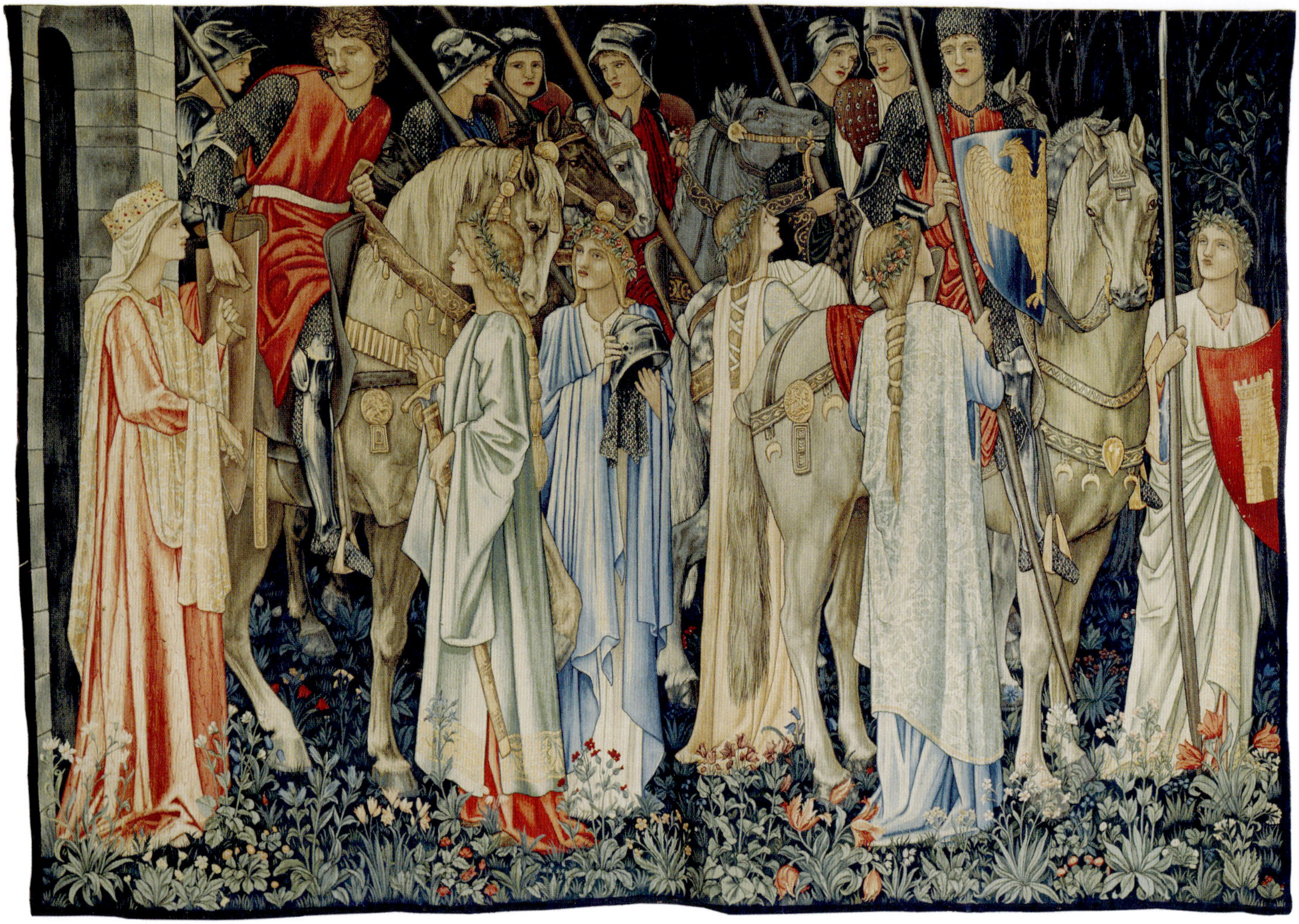

XII.120b

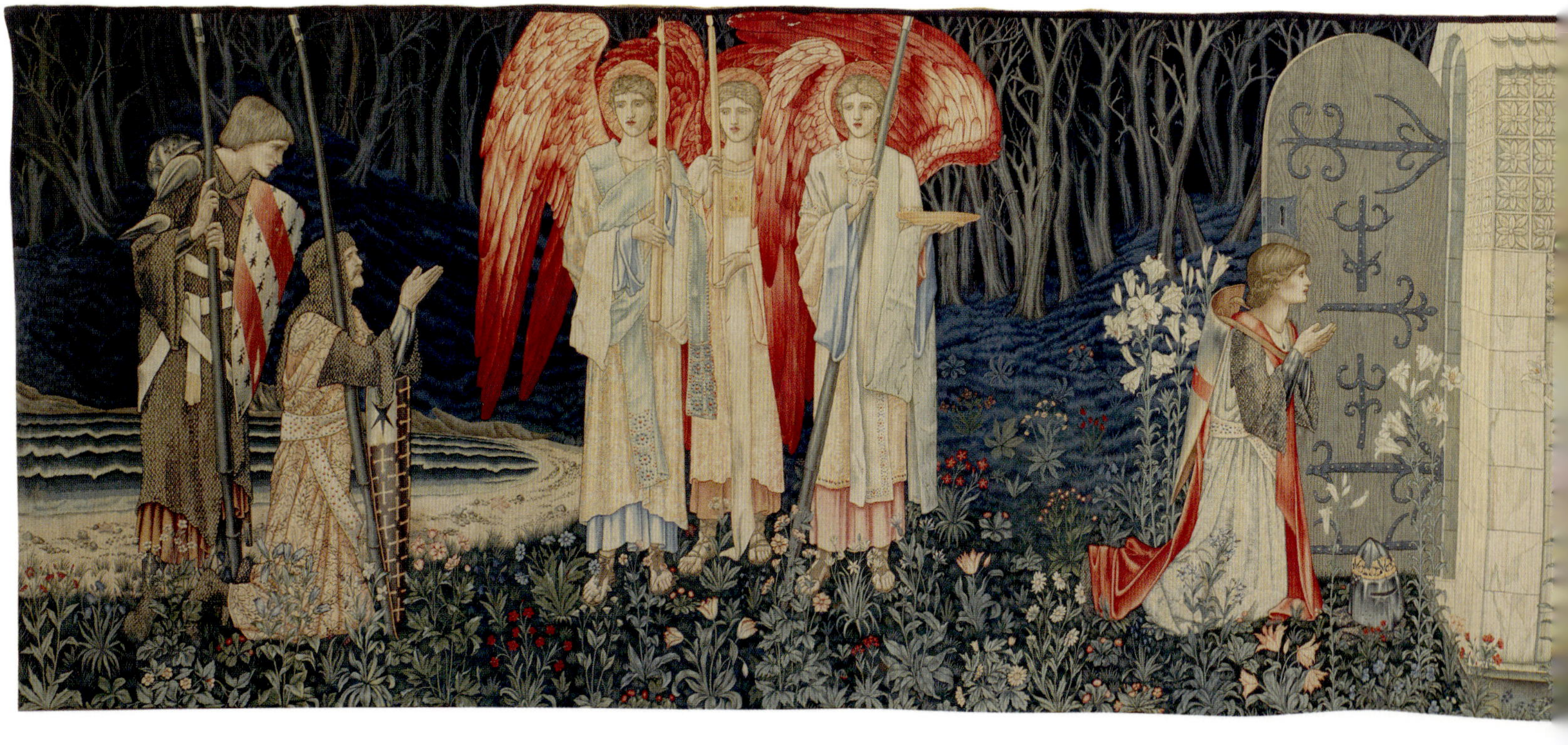

XII.120
Two tapestries from the *Holy Grail* series
Designed by Edward Burne-Jones, William Morris and John Henry Dearle, from 1890
Woven at Merton Abbey by John Martin, Walter Taylor, William Sleath, Robert Ellis, William Knight and Jesse Keech, 1890–94
Tapestry woven wool and silk on a cotton warp
Collection Jimmy Page/courtesy Paul Reeves London

a *The Arming and Departure of the Knights of the Round Table on the Quest for the Holy Grail*
240 x 347 cm

b *The Attainment: The Vision of the Holy Grail to Sir Galahad, Sir Bors and Sir Perceval*
239 x 749 cm

Morris first visited Stanmore Hall, Middlesex, the home of William Knox D'Arcy, on 22 December 1888, to discuss an extensive scheme of decoration. This included specially designed furnishings, the most important of which was a set of tapestries for the dining room. D'Arcy, whose considerable wealth was earned from interests in mining and oil, seemed content to finance Morris's dream commission, allowing him considerable freedom in the design and arrangement of the tapestries.

The tapestries were not part of the initial commission, as early photographs of the dining room show the walls hung with *Acanthus* wallpaper. The first detailed mention is in a letter of 23 December 1890 from Burne-Jones to his friend Lady Leighton of Tapley Hall in Knutsford, Cheshire, in which he described working on designs 'for tapestry to go round a big room ... not in an ancient room, such bliss isn't for me – in some newfangled place but there, there. The subjects are five in number – with life size figures'.

D'Arcy employed A.B. Bence-Jones, a financial journalist, to document the project through interviews with Morris, Burne-Jones and Dearle. This typescript, now in the National Art Library, provides one of the most enlightening accounts of the late workings of Morris & Co. The choice of subject was simple for Morris and Burne-Jones, who had been smitten with the Arthurian romances since their Oxford days. Morris believed the Quest for the Holy Grail was 'the most beautiful and complete episode of the legends' and 'in itself a series of pictures'. Five narrative scenes were eventually chosen and a narrow panel depicting a ship was added to indicate travel and the passage of time. The subjects selected were: *The Summons* (also known as *The Beckoning*), *The Arming and Departure of the Knights*, *The Failure of Sir Gawaine*, *The Failure of Sir Lancelot*, *The Ship* and *The Attainment*. One further scene dropped before weaving was *The Death of Galahad amid the Host in the City of Sarras*. To explain the narrative, six smaller verdure panels with inscriptions were designed by Dearle to hang below five of the figurative tapestries. These showed woodland scenes of deer with shields of the knights hung from trees.

The series took four years to weave and it is likely that designing and weaving, with Morris and Dearle supervising, occurred simultaneously. The final cost of the tapestries was a considerable £3,500, of which Burne-Jones was paid £1,000 for his designs.

The Attainment was exhibited at the 1893 Arts and Crafts Exhibition and noted, with mixed feelings, in the artistic press. *The Artist* (4 November 1893) believing that the panel 'is so befogged with detail, and overloaded with foreground that we envy not the mansion destined to receive it'. In sharp contrast, the *Daily News* observed that the scene was reproduced 'in a manner that would have been incredible in the most sanguine hopes for textiles a short time ago'.

After D'Arcy's death, the original tapestries were sold at Sotheby's on 16 July 1920 and bought by Henry Grosvenor, 2nd Duke of Westminster, for 3,400 guineas. These two panels, together with *The Failure of Gawaine*, were sold again at Sotheby's in April 1978 for a total price of £104,000. Numerous Burne-Jones drawings for the series are known and some of the photographic cartoons are at the William Morris Gallery.

Three further partial sets were woven from these designs. In 1895–6 the second, fourth and sixth panels were woven for Laurence Hodson of Compton Hall and are now in Birmingham Museum and Art Gallery. In 1898–9 the full set of narrative scenes plus one verdure was woven for George McCulloch, an associate of D'Arcy's. These were exhibited at the Paris Exposition Universelle of 1900 and at the British Empire Exhibition, Wembley, of 1925. Briefly on loan to the V&A, in 1927 Lord Lee of Fareham purchased them for 880 guineas. By 1953, when they were sold abroad, the price had dropped to 370 guineas, reflecting how unfashionable Morris's work had become. *The Summons* was brought back to England and sold to Birmingham Museum and Art Gallery in 1980. The remaining four McCulloch narrative panels (cut into six pieces) were purchased by Lord Lloyd Webber in 1994 and have since been restored to their original form.

From 1929 to 1932, *The Summons* and *The Attainment* were repeated for Henry Beecham of Lympne Castle, Kent. *The Summons* is in the Stadtmuseum, Munich, and *The Attainment* was sold at Sotheby's in 1987. Single re-weavings included *The Ship* panel plus one verdure for the Middlemore family (now in Birmingham Museum and Art Gallery) and a verdure panel without shields for John Edward Ellis of Wrea Head, Scalby, Scarborough (now Wrea Head Hall Hotel).

The elegance of the finished designs and exceptional quality of the weaving combined to create what is now considered the most important tapestry series woven in the nineteenth century. They influenced the work of a number of younger European artists and designers, particularly through their display in Paris in 1900. After Morris and Burne-Jones died, the tapestry department never worked on such original designs again, but it continued to flourish well into the twentieth century.

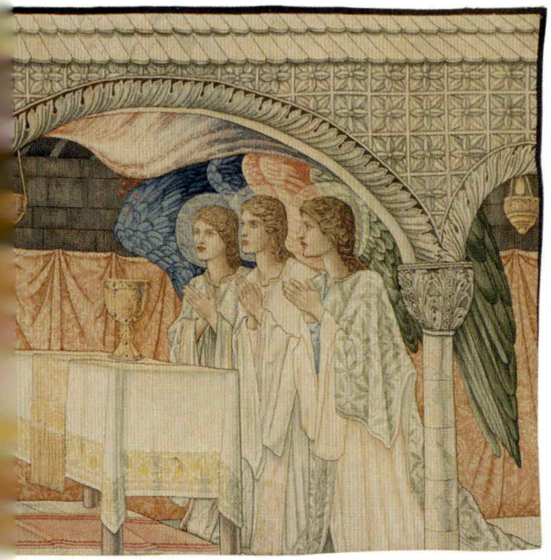

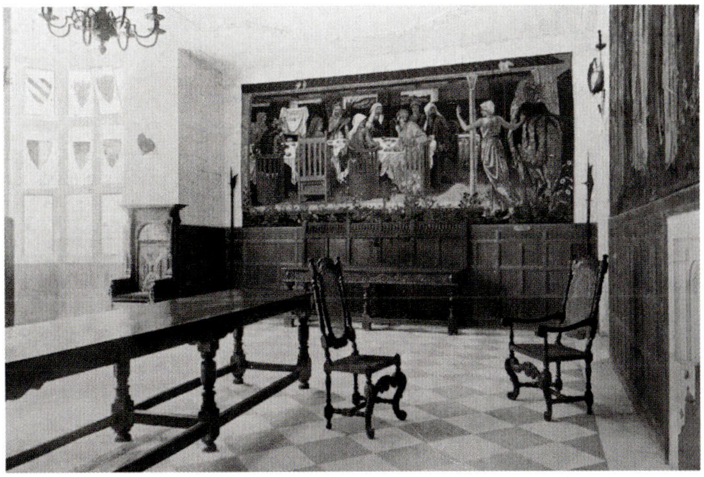

Fig.217 **Section of the British Pavilion, Paris Exposition Universelle, 1900, showing two of the *Holy Grail* tapestries woven for George McCulloch.**
V&A

G

Ah Moon of my delight who knowest no wane,
The Moon of Heaven is rising once again:
How oft hereafter rising shall she look
Through this same garden after me — in vain.

75

And when Thyself with shining foot shall pass
Among the guests star-scattered on the grass,
And in thy joyous errand reach the spot
Where I made one — turn down an empty glass!

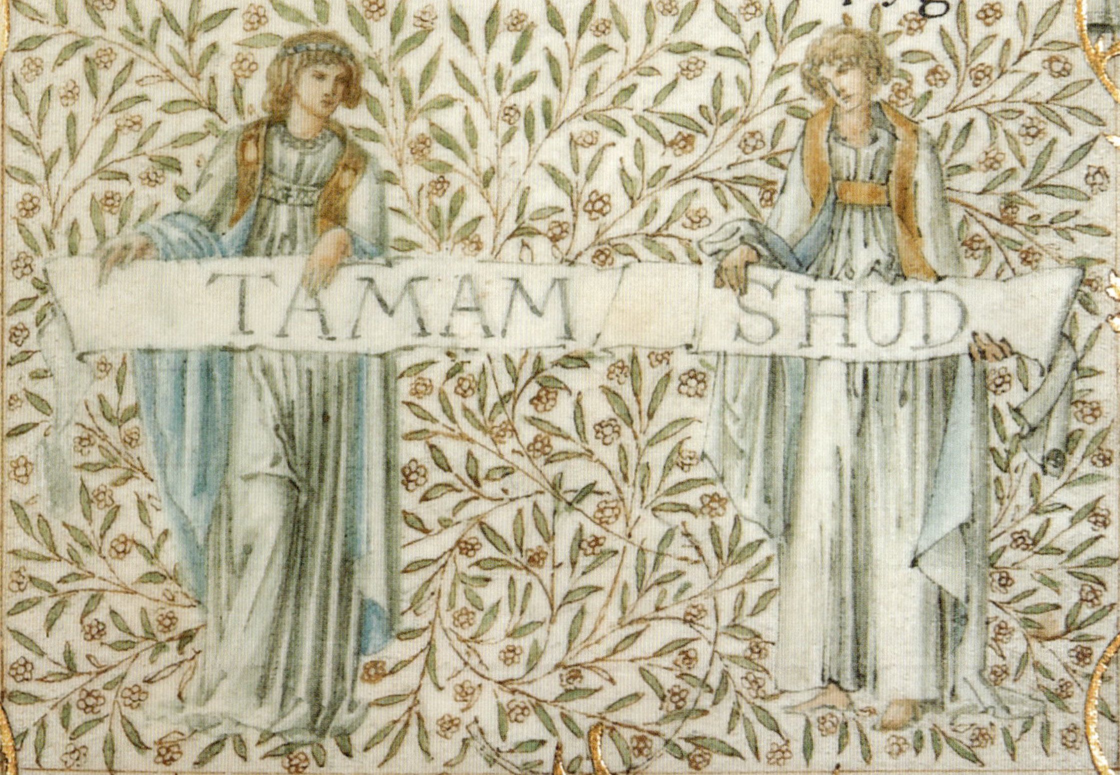

XIII
CALLIGRAPHY

John Nash

'As to what I am doing in my Scribe's capacity ... I am very keen on the thing just now, & really enjoy my Sundays very much at it ...'
William Morris to Charles Fairfax Murray, March 1874

Between 1869 and 1875 William Morris planned, wrote out and (in whole or in part) illuminated some 21 manuscript books. Of these only three could be said to be complete, and of others only fragments and trial pages survive, but it says something for Morris's prodigious energy that these works, usually delicate and exacting to an excruciating degree, were carried out at the same time as running a thriving business, moving house, travelling to Iceland, studying Icelandic and translating Icelandic sagas, and (not least) coping with great emotional pain caused by the relationship between his wife Jane and the painter Dante Gabriel Rossetti.

Morris's energy, however, is well known and well documented. What is less well known is the extent of his achievement during this period, not only in the way he developed medieval and Renaissance illuminated page design to his own idiom (which was to manifest itself much later in the design of the Kelmscott Press books) but also in his research into gilding techniques, and most particularly in his instinctive rediscovery of the basic principles underlying the beautiful, clear writing of the early manuscripts that he had so much admired as a student at Oxford, and would later prize as a collector. Some 35 years later the calligrapher and designer of lettering Edward Johnston was to show, in print and in the classroom, that the beauty of the writing in Carolingian, medieval and Renaissance manuscripts was as important as the illumination, and in most cases more so. Manuscripts shown to him by the collector and expert Sydney Cockerell influenced him greatly, and among these was the work of Morris. In his notes for the first class he taught in 1898 Johnston wrote, 'Morris ... has shown us how in every case the *method* is to be sought in our old work.'

By the beginning of the Victorian period the disciplines that produced the handsome writing of the past had been forgotten. From the early eighteenth century, the pointed steel nib increasingly superseded the cut quill; the result was the dominance of copperplate scripts, with their thicks and thins entirely produced by varying pressure. In the nineteenth century palaeography developed rapidly as a historical discipline, but the scholars who dissected the great scripts had next to no idea of the practical disciplines that lay behind these, and (in general) no particular interest in finding out. The Gothic Revival brought a great upsurge of interest in illuminated manuscripts, especially those of the thirteenth and fourteenth centuries whose complicated historiated decoration offered

Fig.218 **Detail from the 'Rubáiyát of Omar Khayyám', William Morris, Edward Burne-Jones and Charles Fairfax Murray, finished 16 October 1872 (see XIII.7).**
British Library

glimpses of medieval life. Aided by the invention of chromolithography, popularizers such as Henry Shaw, Owen Jones and Henry Noel Humphreys were able to produce a succession of books, some very elaborate, which brought the colourful details of Gothic ornament and illumination within reach of the general public. The steady stream of lesser handbooks that followed in their wake (bearing such titles as *The Art of Illuminating: What it was – What it should be – And how it may be practised*) resulted in a great vogue for 'illuminated gift books', both printed and handmade, decorated to look as 'medieval' as possible, and setting forth texts that were usually biblical and inspiring, and always written in ornate 'textura' Gothic – or rather not written, as the letter forms tended to be drawn in minute outline and more or less neatly filled in.

According to Morris, the formative impression made on him as a boy by Canterbury Cathedral, and by his first sight of illuminated manuscripts, was crucial: 'These first pleasures which I discovered for myself were stronger than anything else I have had in life.' While at Oxford, from 1853 to 1855, he was a constant visitor to the Bodleian, as can be seen from the Visitors' Book (his favourite manuscript being the thoroughly Gothic Douce Apocalypse, *c.*1265–70), and in later life he was to become so familiar with the manuscripts in the British Museum that, as his daughter May remarked, he liked to consider them his. Given his absorption in things medieval as an antidote to the ugliness of the capitalist and industrialist world around him, it was only to be expected that by 1856 and 1857, when first sharing lodgings with Edward Burne-Jones in London and studying painting under Rossetti's influence, he had already been trying his own hand at illumination. Rossetti claimed at the time that, 'In all illumination and work of that kind he is quite unrivalled by anything modern that I know'. Three examples survive from this period, all executed on single sheets of vellum and presented to friends as gifts. The first, an excerpt from Robert Browning's *Paracelsus*, is now in the Huntington Library, and this was likely followed by 'Guendolen', a passage from one of Morris's poems, which he presented to Georgiana Macdonald (later Burne-Jones). His third experimental attempt was a rendering of a tale from the Brothers Grimm, 'Der Eisenhans' or 'The Iron Man' (XIII.1).

Morris could not have been oblivious to the Victorian illumination fad that was then gaining momentum (Jones and Humphreys's

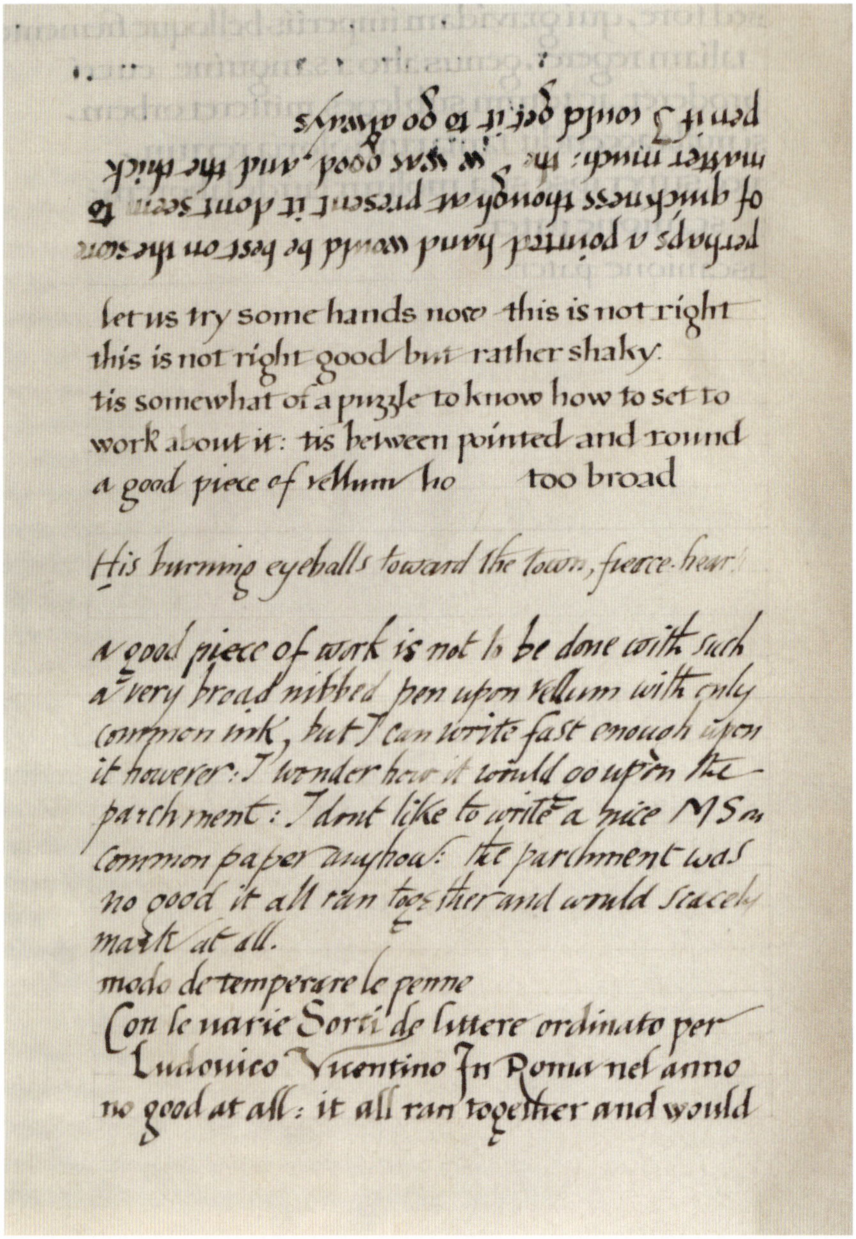
let us try some hands now this is not right
this is not right good but rather shaky.
tis somewhat of a puzzle to know how to set to
work about it: tis between pointed and round
a good piece of vellum ho too broad

His burning eyeballs toward the town, fierce hear

a good piece of work is not to be done with such
a very broad nibbed pen upon vellum with only
common ink, but I can write fast enough upon
it however: I wonder how it would do upon the
parchment: I dont like to write a nice MS on
common paper anyhow: the parchment was
no good it all ran together and would scarcely
mark at all.
modo de temperare le penne
Con le uarie Sorti de littere ordinato per
Ludouico Vicentino In Roma nel anno
no good at all: it all ran together and would

Fig.219 **Page of writing trials by Morris, *c.*1875. At the bottom is proof that he was experimenting with an italic directly based on his own copy of Arrighi.**
The Morgan Library and Museum, New York

The Illuminated Books of the Middle Ages had been published seven years before in 1849) and the influence shows in his ornate and somewhat eccentric illumination scheme, and his heavy-footed Gothic. William Whitla states categorically that Morris owned copies of works by Henry Shaw and Owen Jones and read them attentively. However, it is noticeable that in none of these early efforts does he imitate his contemporaries in going to the Bible for his texts, and the illumination, drawn probably from fourteenth-century sources, seems much too lively to have been copied from any pattern book. Joseph Dunlap, in his definitive study 'The Road to Kelmscott' (1972), quotes Morris's friend

Burne-Jones: 'all his life, he hated the copying of ancient work as unfair to the old and stupid for the present, only good for inspiration and hope.'

Then, without warning, the source of his inspiration seems to have changed. In a list of the books in his library drawn up in (or about) 1876 there appears a bound volume containing four sixteenth-century Italian Renaissance writing manuals (XIII.2): Ludovico Vicentino degli Arrighi's *La Operina* and *Il Modo de Temperare le Penne*, Giovanni Antonio Tagliente's *Lo presente libro* and Ugo da Carpi's *Thesauro de Scrittori*. The date of purchase of these books remains uncertain, but in 1864 Morris became friends with Frederick Startridge Ellis, publisher and rare-book dealer, and it is more than possible that the writing books were bought at around that time, a sign of a veering of Morris's interest away from Gothic towards Renaissance. He certainly studied them and kept returning to them. At the bottom of a sheet of writing trials a clear reference to Arrighi appears – in fact, after roughly writing out 'modo de temperare le penne' (the title of Arrighi's second manual) Morris produced a fair imitation of the last two lines of Arrighi's title-page, complete with elaborately flourished *V* and *I*, which implies he had the original in front of him, or at least close to hand (fig.219). It is immensely frustrating to think that this scrap of vellum may be the only one remaining of all those trials which (as Burne-Jones recalled) littered the floor of Morris's workroom. Few of these throwaway sheets, however, would have been of such importance, showing as it does something of what was going through Morris's mind as he grappled with recalcitrant vellum and badly cut nibs.

In the 1860s he was working on his long poem sequence *The Earthly Paradise*, filling page after trial page with his rapid scrawl and doodling in the margins either as he did so or shortly thereafter. As 1870 approached, flower and vine designs began to give way to sketches for illuminated initials, and to trials of letters and sentence fragments. In a draft of 'Bellerophon in Lycia' (fig.31 and XIII.3) we see flowers in the margin of the verso page and, on the recto, the beginnings of the small rounded italic script, furnished with many extraneous hairlines, of which Morris was to make great use; this, along with a scattering of rather awkward capitals, is definitely written with an edged pen, producing natural thicks and thins.

As *The Earthly Paradise* was nearing completion, Morris had become intensely interested in the literature of the Icelandic sagas, which he began reading and translating with Eiríkr Magnússon in 1868. He naturally used these translations as texts for most of the manuscripts that he now began to work on, developing as he did so a repertoire of five scripts – two based on Renaissance humanist (now called 'roman') minuscule, three on humanist cursive, or 'italic'. In his first manuscript from this period, 'The Story of the Dwellers at Eyr' (XIII.4), three of these scripts are in use – rounded, rather laboured roman minuscule (perhaps influenced by 'antica tonda' models to be found in Arrighi and Tagliente) used for the running heads, descriptive chapter headings in the rounded italic already referred to, and (for much of the text) a larger, more cursive and lighter weight italic with connecting strokes and curved ascenders that are definitely Renaissance-based. Capitals, both in the title at the top of the opening page (following the Renaissance model) and in the decorated initials that form almost the only illumination, are what one would expect from a beginner – amateurish in the extreme; those used in the text are laboriously formed and generally over-tall, one of the many mannerisms of which Morris was never to rid himself.

In Morris's second manuscript, 'The Story of the Volsungs and Niblungs' (XIII.5), there is a marked improvement in written quality both of capitals and of the text hand: rounded italic with diagonal hair-strokes to *m*, *n* and *h*, curved descenders to *f* and *y*, curved ascenders generally, straight descender to *p*, and earless *g* with a sharpened flourish.

Watching the weary spindle fly

This is also the text hand of Morris's next effort, one of only three books in which both writing and illumination were fully carried out – 'A Book of Verse' (XIII.6), dated 1870. Like all Morris's more ambitious calligraphic projects, it was a collaborative venture – Morris did the writing and involved himself heavily in the gilding and decoration, but he had little confidence in his abilities as draughtsman or painter and brought in Burne-Jones and the painter and illustrator Charles Fairfax Murray to contribute illustrations and historiated initials. A second version of 'The Story of the Dwellers at Eyr' (Birmingham Museum and Art Gallery) bore a proud colophon, dated 19 April 1871, in which Morris noted that he carried out all the work himself, except for the gilding.

For his next project – 'The Rubáiyát of Omar Khayyám' (fig.218 and XIII.7) – Morris thought at least fleetingly along italic lines, as trial versions show; but the completed manuscript of 1872 is in tiny, formal, almost monoline roman minuscule, with straight *y*, cut-off *f*, *g* with rounded flourish and sticking up ear, and tall ascenders with minute tick serifs.

this Universe, and why not knowing

As with other aspects of Morris's work, it is most engaging to imagine this burly, vastly impatient man, subject to famous rages, carrying out the most minute and exacting tasks, such as writing microscopically with a crow quill. His determination to use the best materials available was just as evident in this craft as any other he practised. Some of his manuscripts are on paper but for the most ambitious projects Morris sourced vellum from Rome, with the assistance of Murray. In their correspondence Morris urged him to locate the same quality and hardness used in medieval books. Gilding was another ancient technique that he learnt to embellish his manuscripts. May's description of Morris at work captures the delicacy of the task, 'there was pale gold in shells, and gold-leaf in books, which we were shown standing in ceremonial attitude of respect and drawing in our breath, lest the fragile glitter should break asunder ... and my father would pass the broad badger-hair brush ... through his forest of thick curls in the orthodox way, before laying it gently on the leaf of gold.'

In the 'Rubáiyát', as in his other four major manuscripts, he was able to discipline himself to remain consistent in his writing, but it must be stressed that this was usually far from the case. Warington Taylor, business manager of Morris, Marshall, Faulkner & Co., wrote in 1868 of his work habits: 'Morris will start half a dozen jobs; he has designs for perhaps half of them, and therefore in a week or two they have to be given up. They are put away, bits get lost, have to be done over again; hence great loss of time and money.' It is highly likely that this was also the approach Morris took to his manuscript work. In the first version of 'The Dwellers at Eyr' the open, lightweight, rather tentative italic of the opening pages changes, after around page 40, to the blacker and more angular italic that characterizes 'The Volsungs and Niblungs'. In other words, Morris either developed a different script as he wrote, or (as Dr Dunlap suggests) wrote the second part of 'The Dwellers', 'after he had succumbed to the diagonals', or the persistent hairlines that plague that particular script. In the period 1873–4 at least 10 or 11 of his Icelandic translations were produced calligraphically in the form of incomplete versions or trial pages; few of those that extended beyond four or five pages are written in the same script throughout. The italic of 'King Hafbur and King Siward' (XIII.9) is fundamentally that of 'The Volsungs and Niblungs', but *w* has acquired a Gothic look, *f* has acquired a strange hairline flourish to its top, ascenders tend to end suddenly in a slashing diagonal stroke, and the ornate capitals are definitely Gothic inspired.

In swift words nowise light

'The Story of Hen-Thorir' and 'The Story of the Banded Men' (XIII.11–12) were probably written at around the same time, and each employs basically the same script (small, rounded formal italic with flourished *f* and 'sharpened' *g*), but the former manuscript supplies this italic with the famous diagonal hair-strokes, which then die out after page 10, and the latter changes script markedly after page 28, the rather squat *g* becoming narrower and more graceful, *e* and *a* taking on uncial forms and the descender of flourished *f* becoming straight.

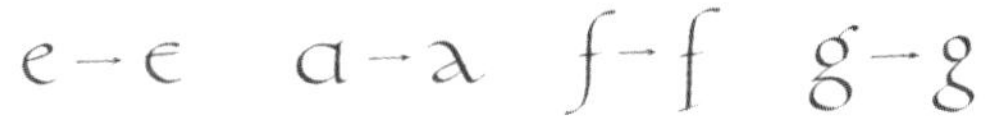

In the manuscript of 'The Story of Gunnlaug the Worm-Tongue' (XIII.10), after 32 pages of neat 'Rubáiyát' roman, Morris breaks off at the bottom of the page with 'arma virumque cano' written in an excellent, straightforward emulation of humanist cursive. Whatever the reason (had he simply become fed up with 'Gunnlaug'?), this shows that he had studied and gained from original Renaissance humanist manuscripts, apart from the wood-engraved models in his Renaissance writing books, and that the idea of writing out all or part of the *Aeneid* was already in his mind. His work throughout this period, finally, demonstrates more than simply his restless nature; it shows that his main preoccupation was with the writing. Where manuscripts remain unfinished, it is almost invariably the illumination that remains incomplete; and most of the manuscripts just named have either a minimum of gilding and illumination, or none at all.

The two manuscripts with which Morris ended his six years of concentrated calligraphic activity – the 'Odes' of Horace and Virgil's 'Aeneid' (XIII.13–14), both in their original Latin – also represent, respectively, the culmination of his efforts at developing an italic and roman minuscule as formal book-hands, faithful as possible to the range of Renaissance models that he kept always in mind and attempting to reach a standard that might be worthy of those models. It is uncanny how far he succeeded. Consciously or unconsciously he expressed in practice what Johnston was later to express in words: that the secret of recreating the beauty and clarity of the best of ancient scripts lay not in simply copying *styles*, but in analysing and following the best scribal *methods*, in order to acquire deeper understanding. It must be admitted that the italic of the Horace and the roman of the Virgil are not entirely free from irritating mannerisms. The *f*'s of the italic retain the little hairline flourish that Morris found so unaccountably delightful; in the roman, the tops of *v* and *u* are closed off by overlong serifs (interfering with legibility), and straight descenders (as on *p* and *q*) sprout obtrusively long diagonal finishing strokes. But the consistency and quality of each is, in the end, most remarkable. Morris, though intensely self-critical at all times, was proud of himself ('I have much improved by the way both in my ornament and my writing', he wrote to Murray in February of 1874), and he had reason to be. Working only on Sundays and at odd moments snatched from an overpoweringly busy life, he had not only reached a remarkably high personal standard, but had also laid the groundwork for Johnston's discoveries and for a clearer understanding of the principles of Western writing, which was to benefit scholars and teachers to come.

Morris was to produce no more extended calligraphic manuscripts. His involvement with the 'Aeneid' had led him, with his usual enthusiasm, to set himself the immense task of translating the work himself; this project, not unnaturally, began to occupy all his spare time. Also, he now reorganized both the firm and his private life by buying out his partners and ending the joint lease with Rossetti at Kelmscott Manor; and he began increasingly to participate in public campaigns leading to his involvement with socialism. In effect, a new period in his life was beginning. But his interest in calligraphy did not die. The doodlings in the margins of his rough drafts and socialist lecture notes continued to include letter forms; the last page of his 1881 journal contains various letters and words in upright and sloping roman, and (curiously) a carefully written roman minuscule alphabet similar in weight and characteristics not so much to the 'Aeneid' hand as to the 'antica tonda' shown in rather crude, wood-engraved form in his copy of Arrighi's *Il Modo*. Around 1890 (according to Sydney Cockerell's well-informed guess) – the same year as the appearance of the Golden type and the designing of the first Kelmscott Press book – he returned to his rounded, somewhat angular italic to write out a short catalogue of manuscripts and books then owned by him, in a carefully planned, wholly Renaissance-inspired layout on vellum (Mark Samuels Lasner Collection, University of Delaware Library, Museums and Press).

A letter written in November 1894 to an enthusiastic amateur who had sent him an example of calligraphy for his opinion produced some pointed comments, including (ironically enough), 'there are too many "flicks" in it'. It is curious to note that, while he sends his correspondent to look at books written or printed before the sixteenth century to find the best models for page layout, he cites only manuscripts 'written about 1120 or even earlier' as providing the best models for writing – no mention of the Renaissance scribes by whom he had once set such store. Two years later he was dead – as his doctor put it, simply from being William Morris and cramming into one life several lifetimes' achievements, of which his venture into calligraphy was by no means the least.

XIII.1

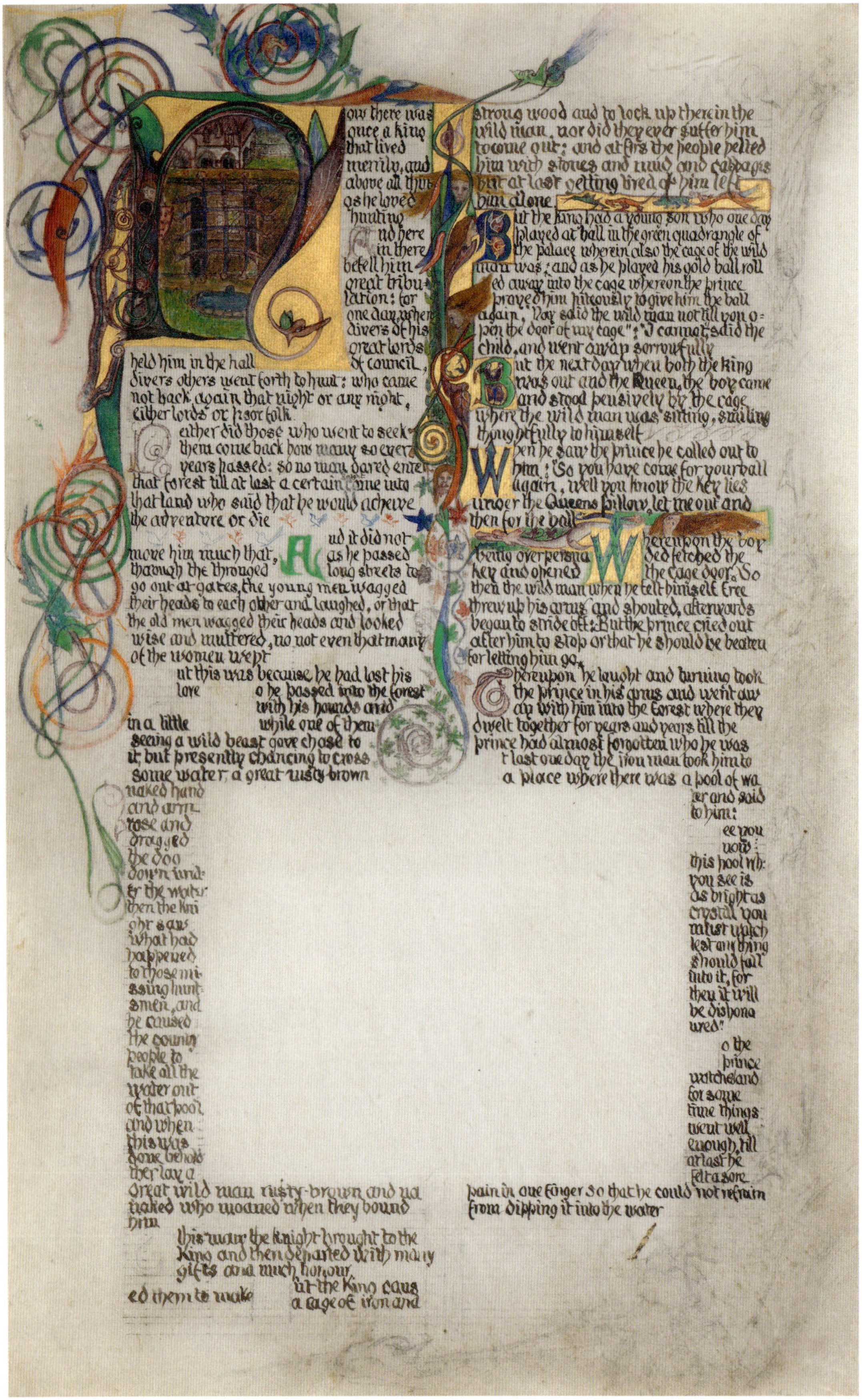

XIII.1
'Der Eisenhans' (The Iron Man) by the Brothers Grimm
William Morris, *c.*1857
One leaf, watercolour and gold paint on vellum, 37 x 23.5 cm
The Wormsley Library

By 1857 Morris was established with Burne-Jones in their rooms at Red Lion Square, and had already tried his hand at various pursuits, including (as was the Victorian fashion at the time) manuscript illumination. Three of his attempts from this period are known to have survived, of which this, an incomplete transcription of his own retelling of a Grimm Brothers tale, was given to Louisa, younger sister of Georgiana Macdonald (later Burne-Jones). Morris was later to dismiss this as his 'first attempt at illumination' (although this was almost certainly not the case); and it is not difficult to see why. Leaving the drawing, colour and decoration aside, the writing is so formless as to look brush-written, though it is most likely that a soft, badly cut quill was to blame. Morris himself was undoubtedly conscious of the failings of the piece, as can be witnessed in the unfinished decorative elements, the badly smudged erasures down the right-hand margin and the perverse breaking off of the story at a particularly dramatic point. However, it remains valuable for two principal reasons: it demonstrates the heavy Gothic influence from which Morris's later manuscript work was to free itself, and it shows what a very long way he had to go.

XIII.2

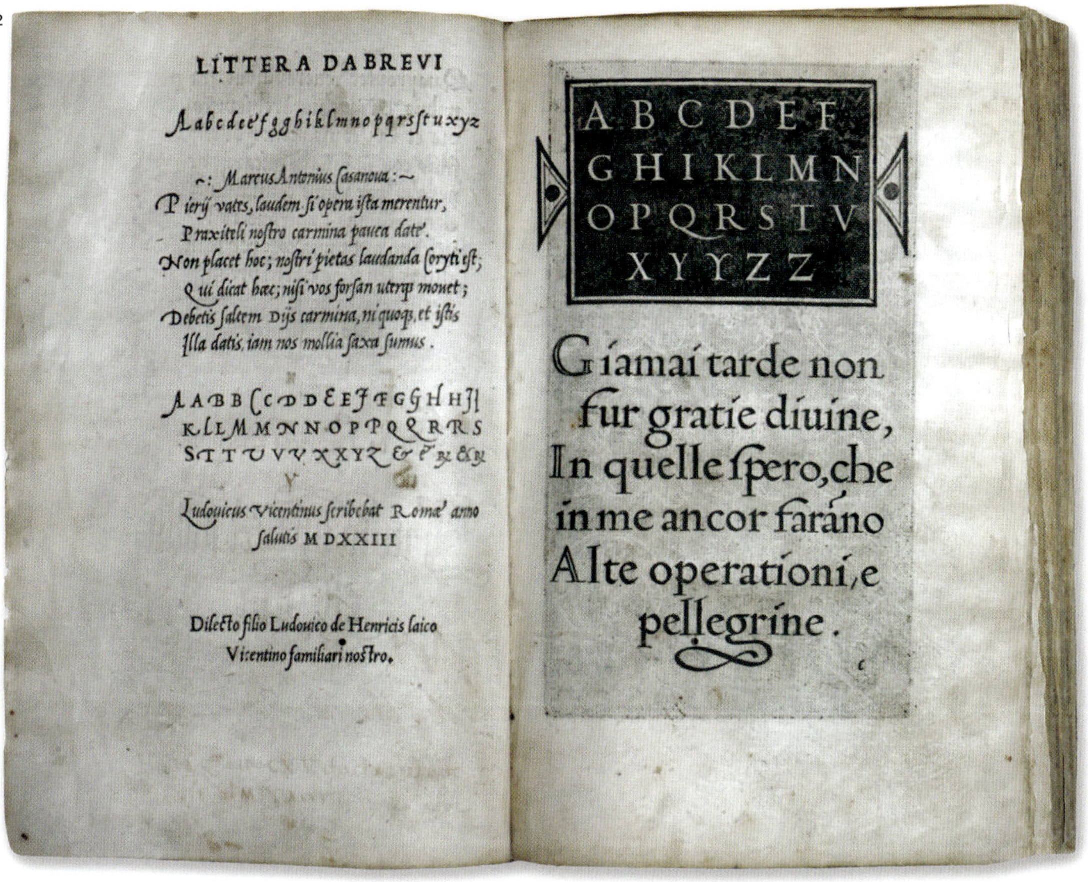

XIII.3

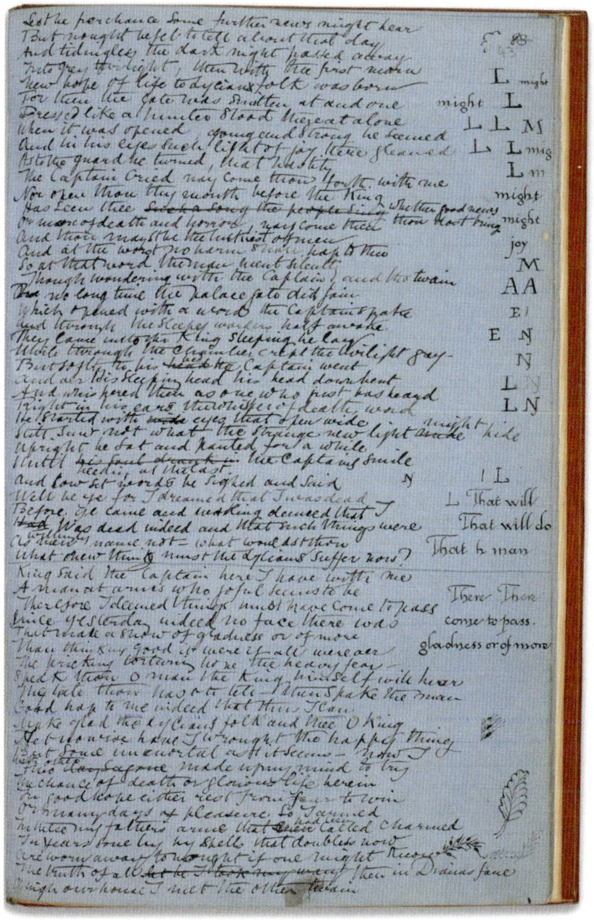

XIII.2

Four writing books by Ludovico Vicentino degli Arrighi, Giovanni Antonio Tagliente and Ugo da Carpi

Italian, sixteenth century, bound in the eighteenth century, 20.9 x 13.5 cm leaf

The Society of Antiquaries of London (141.166.167.159)

By 1876, and probably considerably before that, Morris had acquired at least four Renaissance writing manuals: Arrighi's *La Operina* (in the edition printed by Ugo da Carpi in 1525 after his quarrel with Arrighi) and *Il Modo de Temperare le Penne* (*c.*1526), Tagliente's *Lo presente libro* (1525) and da Carpi's *Thesauro de Scrittori* (1525–6). Arrighi's *Operina* is concerned only with the 'cancelleresca corsiva' (chancery cursive) but his *Il Modo*, as well as illustrating different stages in quill cutting, offers models of commercial hands, inscriptional capitals and decorative alphabets.

The pages shown demonstrate, on the left, another version of italic ('littera da brevi'), and on the right, capitals in small size and a bold version of roman minuscule ('antica tonda'), which undoubtedly had an influence on Morris (see A.S. Osley, 'The Kelmscott Manor Volume of Italian Writing-Books', *The Antiquaries Journal*, 64:2, 1984). After Morris's death, Emery Walker purchased the volume from the sale of his books at Sotheby's and presented it to May Morris.

XIII.3

Draft of 'Bellerophon in Lycia', from *The Earthly Paradise* by William Morris

Autograph copy by Morris with marginalia, 1869

Ink on paper, 33 x 21 cm

British Library (Add. MS 45301, fol. 43r)

As he produced rough drafts of the poems that would go to make up *The Earthly Paradise*, mostly written in his everyday hand, Morris's customary marginal doodles – flower and vine designs to begin with – demonstrate more and more that his mind was turning to lettering and calligraphy. Drafts of 'Rhodope' (1869, BL Add. MS 45304) and 'Orpheus and Eurydice' (*c.* late 1869, BL Add. MS 45307) show trials of capitals and designs for ornamented initials. This draft of 'Bellerophon' shows extensive trials of flourished ('swash') capitals and of the rounded italic with diagonal hair-strokes to *m, n,* and *h*, of which he was to make extensive use, already well developed. In the pages shown (see also fig.31), Morris switches, from one page to the next, from sketches of floral designs to lettering trials in which his use of the edged pen is already clear.

XIII.4

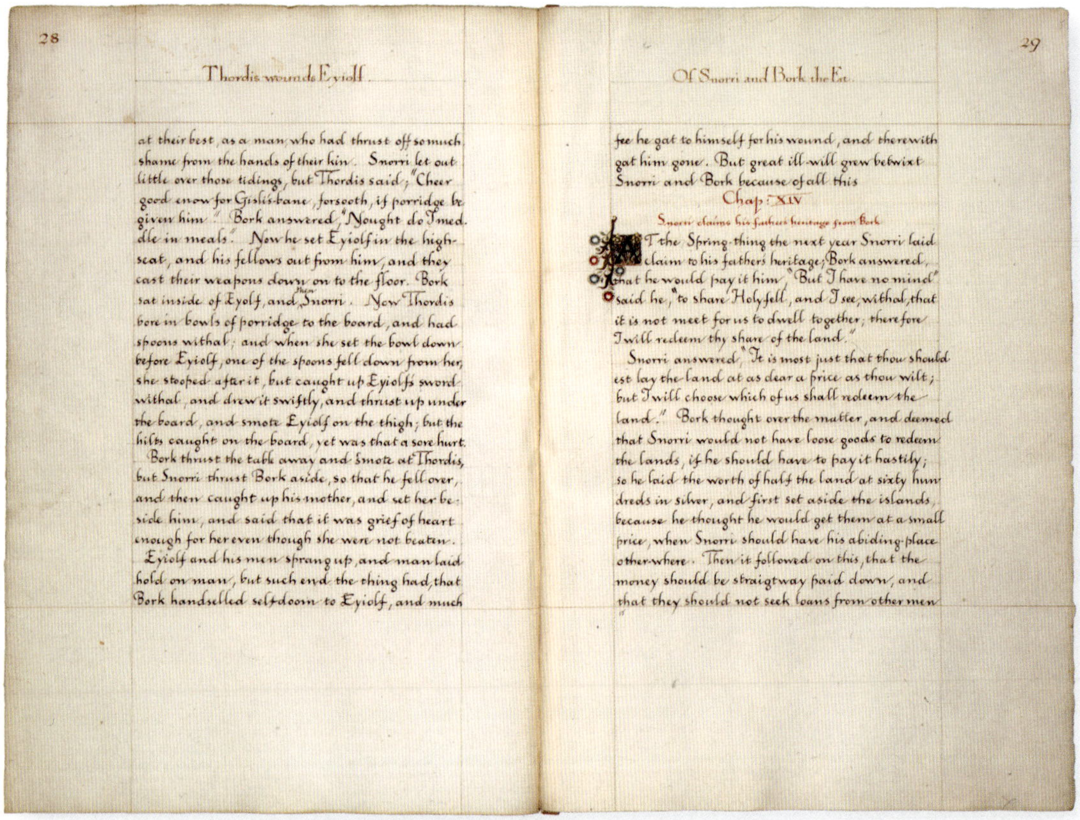
28

Thordis wounds Eyiolf

at their best, as a man who had thrust off so much shame from the hands of their kin. Snorri let out little over those tidings, but Thordis said; "Cheer good enow for Gislis-bane, forsooth, if porridge be given him." Bork answered, "Nought do I meddle in meals." Now he set Eyiolf in the high-seat, and his fellows out from him, and they cast their weapons down on to the floor. Bork sat inside of Eyolf, and then Snorri. Now Thordis bore in bowls of porridge to the board, and had spoons withal; and when she set the bowl down before Eyiolf, one of the spoons fell down from her; she stooped after it, but caught up Eyiolf's sword withal, and drew it swiftly, and thrust it up under the board, and smote Eyiolf on the thigh; but the hilts caught on the board, yet was that a sore hurt. Bork thrust the table away and smote at Thordis, but Snorri thrust Bork aside, so that he fell over, and then caught up his mother, and set her beside him, and said that it was grief of heart enough for her even though she were not beaten. Eyiolf and his men sprang up, and man laid hold on man, but such end the thing had, that Bork handselled selfdoom to Eyiolf, and much

29

Of Snorri and Bork the Fat

fee he gat to himself for his wound, and therewith gat him gone. But great ill-will grew betwixt Snorri and Bork because of all this

Chap: XIV

Snorri claims his father's heritage from Bork

At the Spring-thing the next year Snorri laid claim to his fathers heritage; Bork answered, that he would pay it him. "But I have no mind" said he, "to share Holyfell, and I see, withal, that it is not meet for us to dwell together; therefore I will redeem thy share of the land."

Snorri answered, "It is most just that thou shouldest lay the land at as dear a price as thou wilt; but I will choose which of us shall redeem the land." Bork thought over the matter, and deemed that Snorri would not have loose goods to redeem the lands, if he should have to pay it hastily; so he laid the worth of half the land at sixty hundreds in silver, and first set aside the islands, because he thought he would get them at a small price, when Snorri should have his abiding-place otherwhere. Then it followed on this, that the money should be straightway paid down, and that they should not seek loans from other men

XIII.4
'The Story of the Dwellers at Eyr', translated by William Morris and Eiríkr Magnússon
William Morris, 1869–70
Ink and watercolour on paper, 36.5 x 25.5 x 1.3 cm (closed)
Bodleian Library (MS. Eng. misc. c. 265, fols. 28v–29r)

This is generally accepted as Morris's first manuscript from his second phase of calligraphy. As such, the capitals of the title at the beginning and the italic of the text are both amateurish and tentative, and the illuminated initials, both in quality and design, are nothing short of dismal. In the pages shown, however, it can be seen that the roman minuscule of the running heads (somewhat reminiscent of the 'antica tonda' of Arrighi's *Il Modo*) and the weightier italic of the chapter headings are already done with confidence. A second version of the story, incorporating some pages from this earlier endeavour, was written and ornamented as a gift for Georgiana Burne-Jones in 1871 (Birmingham Museum and Art Gallery).

XIII.5

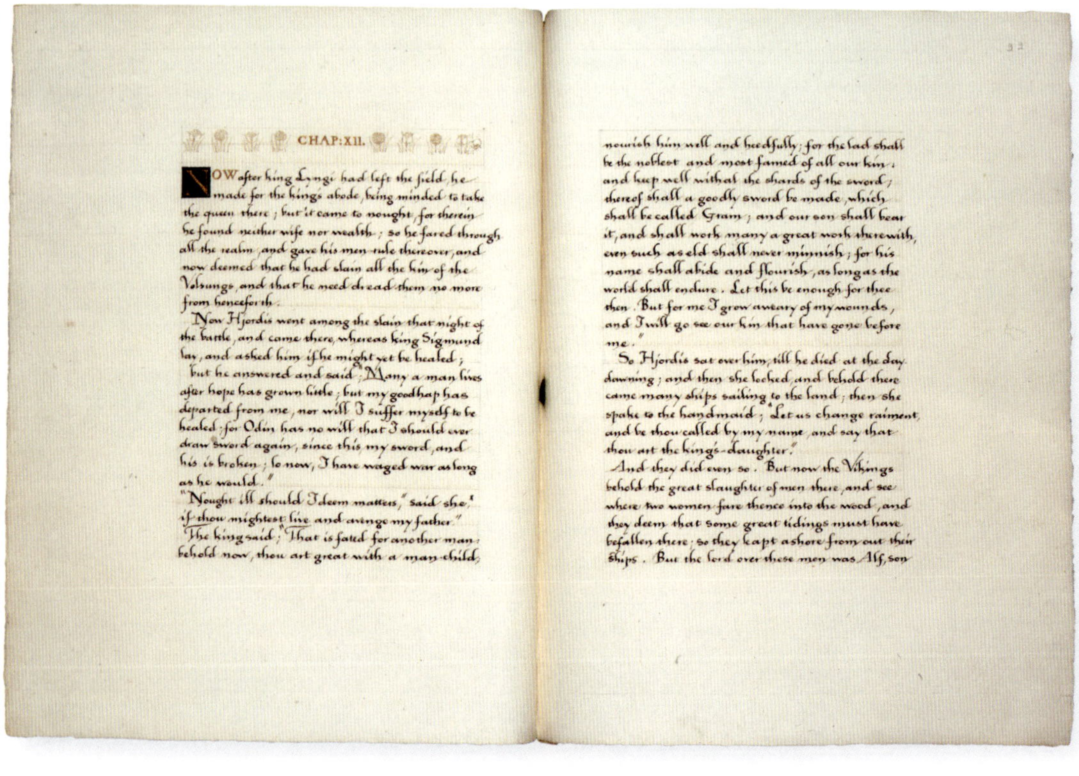
CHAP: XII.

NOW after king Lyngi had left the field, he made for the kings abode, being minded to take the queen there; but it came to nought, for therein he found neither wife nor wealth; so he fared through all the realm, and gave his men rule thereover, and now deemed that he had slain all the kin of the Volsungs, and that he need dread them no more from henceforth.

Now Hjordis went among the slain that night of the battle, and came there, whereas king Sigmund lay, and asked him if he might yet be healed; but he answered and said, "Many a man lives after hope has grown little; but my good-hap has departed from me, nor will I suffer myself to be healed; for Odin has no will that I should ever draw sword again, since this my sword, and his is broken; lo now, I have waged war as long as he would."

"Nought ill should I deem matters," said she, "if thou mightest live and avenge my father."

The king said, "That is fated for another man; behold now, thou art great with a man-child;

nourish him well and heedfully; for the lad shall be the noblest and most famed of all our kin; and keep well withal the shards of the sword; thereof shall a goodly sword be made, which shall be called Gram; and our son shall bear it, and shall work many a great work therewith, even such as eld shall never minish; for his name shall abide and flourish as long as the world shall endure. Let this be enough for thee then. But for me I grow aweary of my wounds, and I will go see our kin that have gone before me."

So Hjordis sat over him, till he died at the day-dawning; and then she looked, and behold there came many ships sailing to the land; then she spake to the handmaid; "Let us change raiment, and be thou called by my name, and say that thou art the king's daughter."

And they did even so. But now the Vikings behold the great slaughter of men there, and see where two women fare thence into the wood, and they deem that some great tidings must have befallen there; so they leapt ashore from out their ships. But the lord over these men was Alf, son

XIII.5
'The Story of the Volsungs and Niblungs', translated by William Morris and Eiríkr Magnússon
William Morris, Charles Fairfax Murray and George Wardle, 1870
Ink, pencil and watercolour on paper, 29 x 23 x 2.3 cm (closed)
Bodleian Library (MS. Eng. misc. d. 268, fols. 21v–22r)

This manuscript, of which 73 leaves were completed, is roughly contemporary with the heavily illuminated 'A Book of Verse'. However, it is almost without illumination itself, except for a beautiful opening page with eight musicians lightly sketched with pencil (one painted) and an historiated initial, executed by Murray, of Sigurd seated on the body of the dragon Fafnir. It is noticeable that the initial capitals of the beginnings of the chapters have improved greatly in quality. Assuming they are Morris's work, he must have been practising hard.

XIII.6

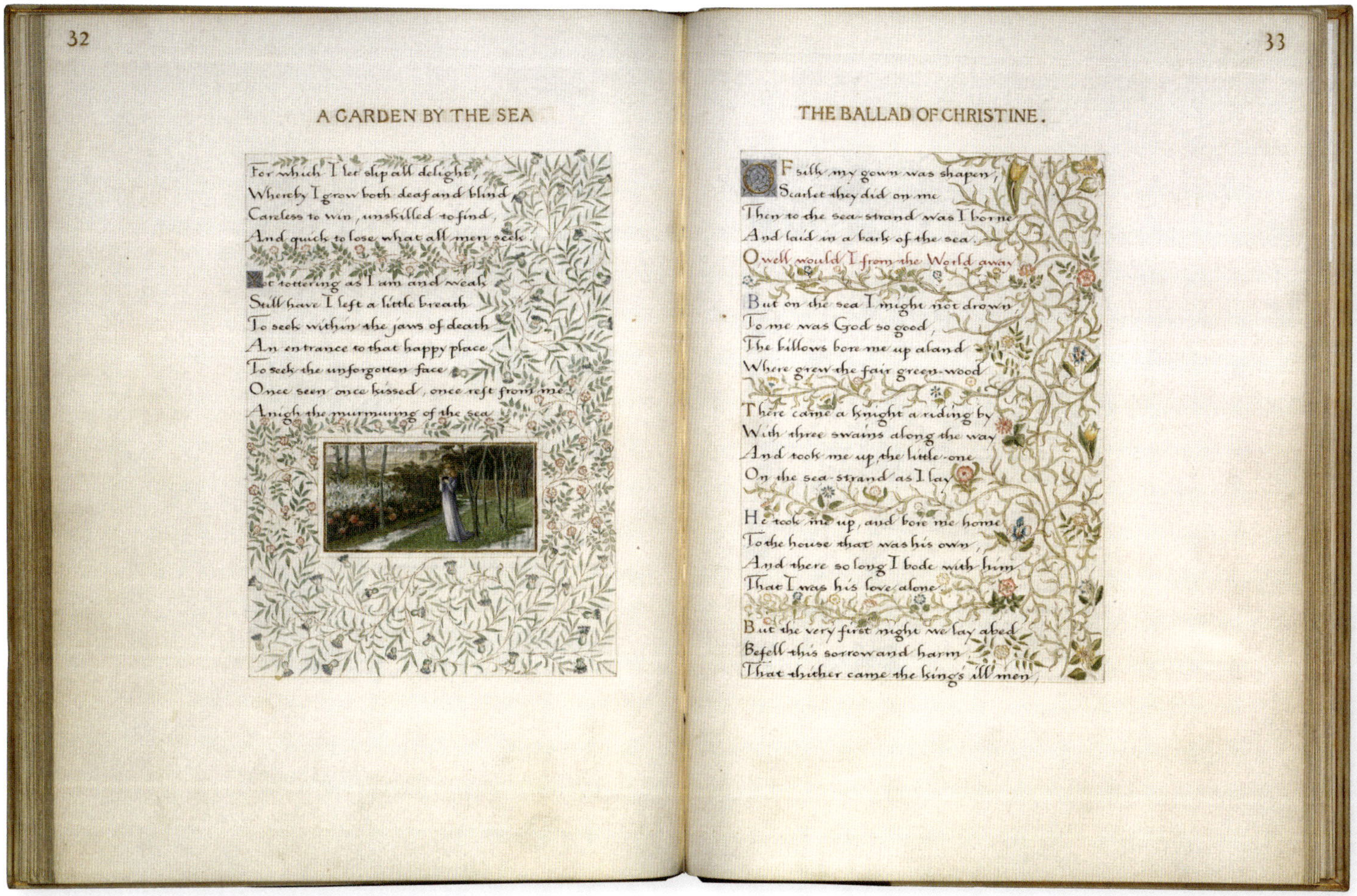
32

A GARDEN BY THE SEA

For which I let slip all delight,
Whereby I grow both deaf and blind,
Careless to win, unskilled to find,
And quick to lose what all men seek.

Yet tottering as I am and weak,
Still have I left a little breath
To seek within the jaws of death
An entrance to that happy place,
To seek the unforgotten face
Once seen, once kissed, once reft from me
Anigh the murmuring of the sea.

33

THE BALLAD OF CHRISTINE.

Of silk my gown was shapen,
Scarlet they did on me
Then to the sea-strand was I borne
And laid in a bark of the sea.
O well would I from the World away.

But on the sea I might not drown
To me was God so good;
The billows bore me up aland
Where grew the fair green-wood.

There came a knight a riding by
With three swains along the way
And took me up, the little-one,
On the sea-strand as I lay.

He took me up, and bore me home
To the house that was his own,
And there so long I bode with him
That I was his love alone.

But the very first night we lay abed
Befell this sorrow and harm
That thither came the king's ill men,

XIII.6
'A Book of Verse'
William Morris, Charles Fairfax Murray, Edward Burne-Jones and George Wardle
Ink, watercolour and gilding on paper, 27.9 x 21.6 cm leaf
Inscribed: 'August 26th 1870'
National Art Library, V&A (MSL/1953/131)
Purchased with assistance from the National Art Collections Fund and Friends of the National Libraries

A collection of Morris's poetry, with two additional poems translated from the Icelandic, this was the first manuscript book gifted to Georgiana Burne-Jones. The title was probably inspired by a stanza in Edward Fitzgerald's translation of the *Rubáiyát*, a text the friends held in great affection (see XIII.7).

One of Morris's few completed manuscripts, it was a collaborative effort, somewhat in the medieval tradition. As Morris explained in the colophon, Burne-Jones did one illustration at the beginning, Murray painted the remaining pictures (some based on Morris's designs), as well as the famous portrait of Morris on the title-page, done from a photograph. George Wardle helped with the ornamentation and did the coloured initials and Morris himself did all the writing and finished the ornament.

There is a shift in the style of decoration as the book unfolds. The first ten pages are characterized by 'powdered' designs of regularly placed rows of blossoms and sprays. Thereafter, the forms are more organic, with scrolling branches arranged to envelop the text. This was one of four manuscripts loaned by Georgiana to the 1888 Arts and Crafts Exhibition, a rare opportunity for those outside Morris's immediate circle to encounter his 'painted books'.

XIII.7

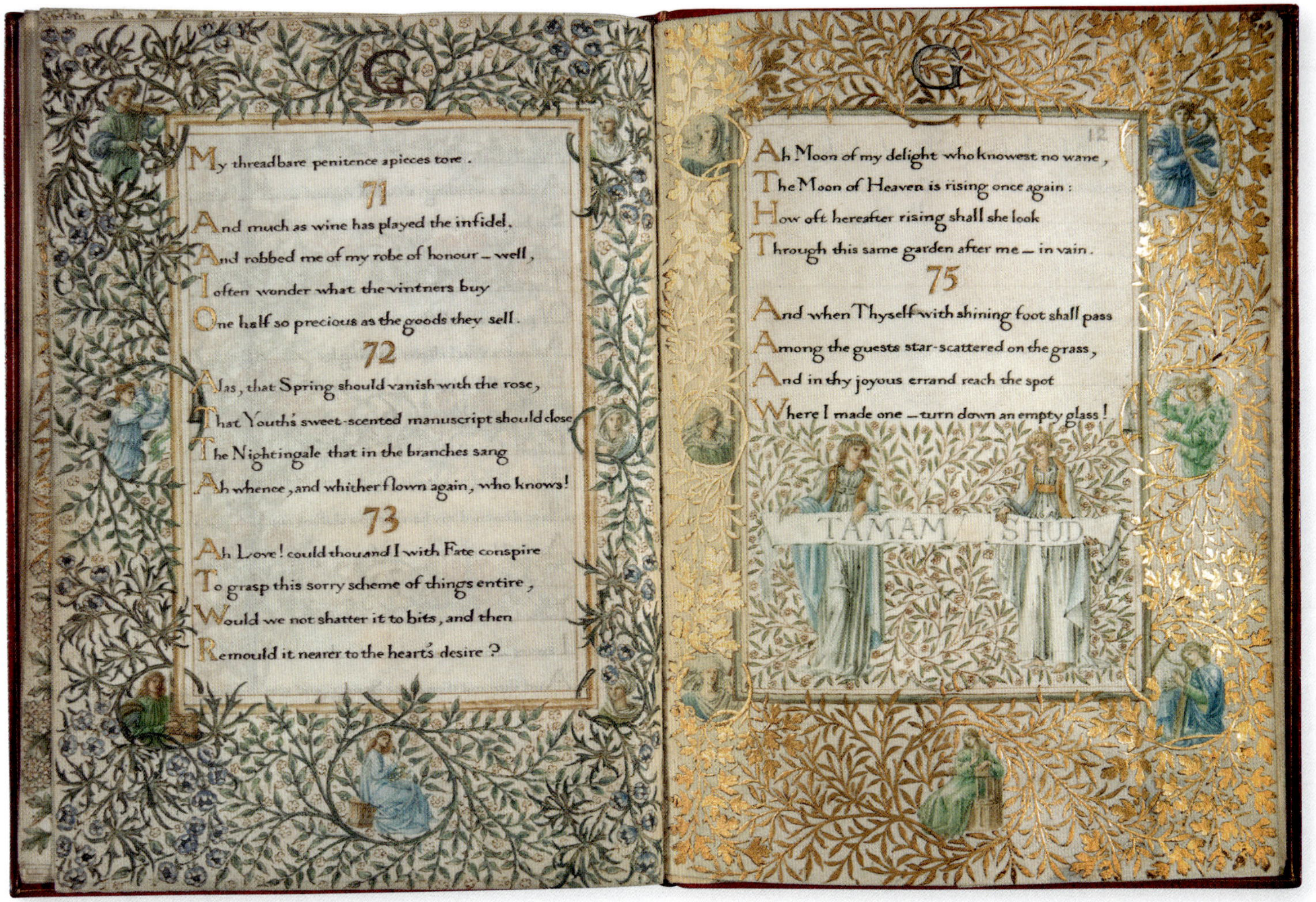

XIII.7
'Rubáiyát of Omar Khayyám', translated by Edward Fitzgerald
William Morris, Edward Burne-Jones and Charles Fairfax Murray, finished 16 October 1872
Ink, watercolour and gilding on vellum, 15 x 23 cm (open)
British Library (Add. MS 37832, fols. 11v–12r)

This small-format book, another gift for Georgiana Burne-Jones, was one of four versions of the *Rubáiyát* written out by Morris. Here he opted for an entirely different script – a tiny roman minuscule, probably written with a crow-quill. The letter *G* in the decorated border stands for 'Georgiana'.

As well as the calligraphy, Morris designed all the ornamentation including spiralling foliage in delicate shades of gold and green. The ending, illustrated here, gives a good idea of the quality and profusion of the illumination on the most richly decorated pages. The figures, some playing instruments and others with turban-like headdresses, were painted by Murray to designs by Morris and Burne-Jones. Michaela Braesel has demonstrated how these designs relate to the firm's earlier work, especially stained glass, and how the extensive use of gold, luxuriant foliage, and allusions to music were used to convey the mood of the poem.

In the introduction to Volume IX of *The Collected Works*, May Morris claimed that each flower used in this 'jewel-like' manuscript was identifiable, describing the project as 'a flower-garden turned into a book'. A note added by Georgiana Burne-Jones in 1908 before she gifted the manuscript to the British Museum, claims Morris executed the work 'in order to do honour to the poem and its English translator, Edward Fitzgerald, whose name he did not then know.'

XIII.8
'The Story of Frithiof the Bold', translated by William Morris and Eiríkr Magnússon
William Morris and Charles Fairfax Murray, *c.*1873, completed by Louise Powell and Graily Hewitt, 1907
Watercolour and gilding on paper, 40.1 x 26.5 cm leaf
The Wormsley Library

Although Morris completed little of the decoration and illumination of this 22-page manuscript himself, he worked the design out so carefully that Murray (doing the two historiated initials), Louise Powell (completing the floral decoration) and Graily Hewitt (completing the gilded running heads, chapter headings and initials) were eventually able to carry out his intentions very faithfully – even more so, perhaps, than in the 'Aeneid'. Hewitt's trained hand is evident in the beautiful and precise gilded capitals of the initials – something Morris never quite mastered – and in the running heads, where, although he cannot help improving on Morris's capitals, he is careful to preserve the Master's somewhat haphazard spacing.

Morris did, however, complete the writing – another indication that this was the facet of his manuscript work in which he was most involved. It is perhaps the single most consistent and beautifully sustained example of his compressed formal roman minuscule, which would seem to indicate that it was done towards the end of his 'manuscript period'. The book was given or sold by Morris to Murray. The binding, by Thomas James Cobden-Sanderson, is in turquoise straight-grain morocco.

CHAP. XIII

NOW weareth away the mid-winter, and when spring cometh, the weather groweth fair, the wood bloometh, the grass groweth, and ships may glide betwixt land and land.

So on a day the king says to his folk: "I will that ye come with us for our disport out into the woods, that we may look upon the fairness of the earth."

So did they, and went flock-meal with the king into the woods: but so it befell, that the king and Frithiof were gotten alone together afar from other men, and the king said he was heavy, and would fain sleep: then said Thief: "Get thee home, then, lord, for it better beseemeth men of high estate to lie at home than abroad."

"Nay" said the king "so will I not do." And he laid him down therewith, and slept fast, snoring loud. Thief sat close by him, and presently drew his sword from his sheath, & cast it far away from him.

A little while after the king woke up, and said: "Was it not so, Frithiof, that a many things came into thy mind een now? but well hast thou dealt with them, and great honour shalt thou have of me. Lo now, I knew thee straightway, that first evening thou camest into our hall: now nowise speedily shalt thou depart from us, and somewhat great abideth thee."

39

Said Frithiof: "Lord king, thou hast done to me well, and in friendly wise; but yet must I get me gone soon, because my company cometh speedily to meet me, as I have given them charge to do."

So then they rode home from the wood, and the king's folk came flocking to him, and home they fared to the hall and drank joyously: and it was made known to all folk that Frithiof the Bold had been abiding there through the winter-tide.

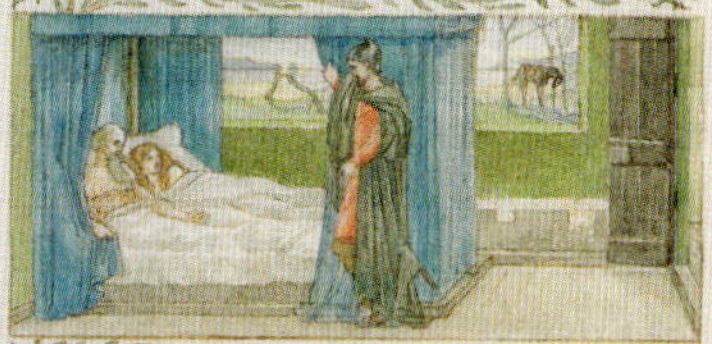

CHAP. XIV

EARLY of a morning-tide one smote on the door of that hall, wherein slept the king and queen, and many others: then the king asked who it was that called at the hall door; and so he who was without said: "Here am I, Frithiof; and I am arrayed for my departure."

Then was the door opened, and Frithiof came in, and sang a stave:

Have great thanks for the guesting
Thou gavest with all bounty;
Dight fully for departure
Is the eagles' feeder now;
But Ingibiorg I mind thee
While yet on earth I dwell;
Live gloriously! I give thee
This gift for many kisses.

40

XIII.9

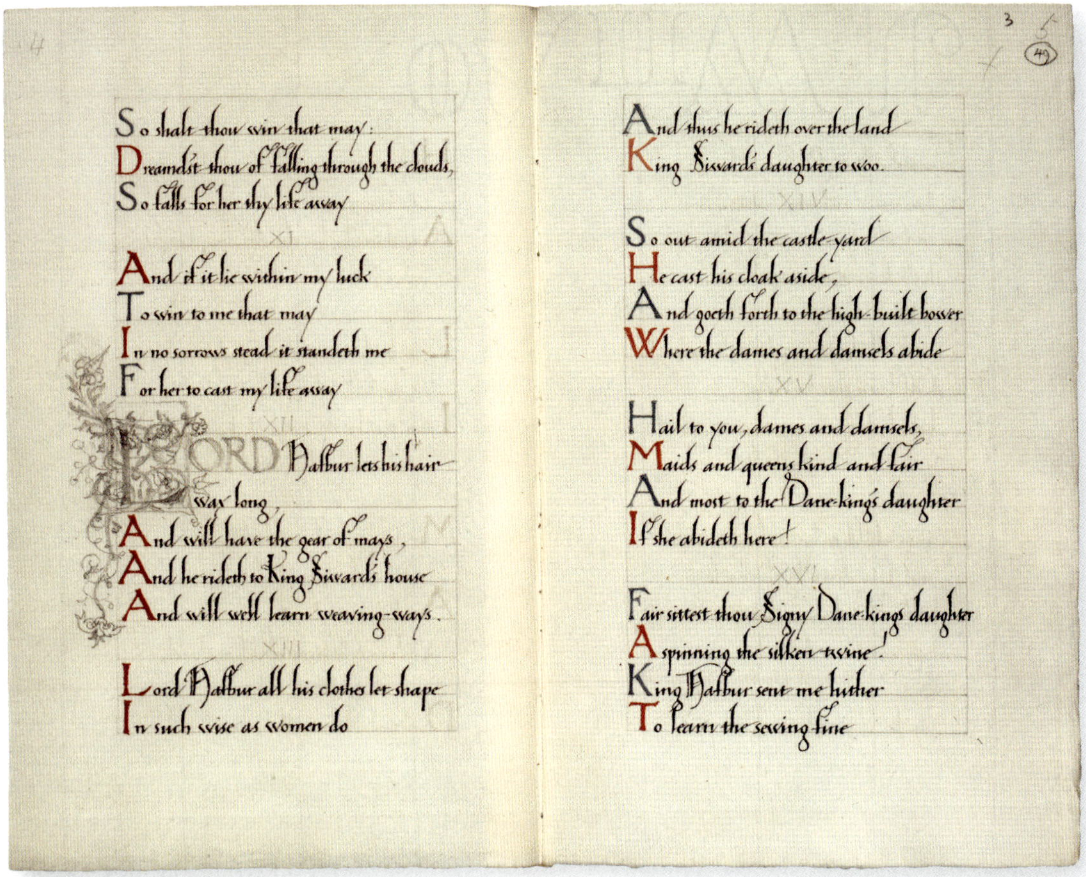

XIII.9
'King Hafbur and King Siward', translated by William Morris
William Morris, *c.*1873
Ink, watercolour and gilding on paper, 20.8 x 13.5 cm leaf
Bodleian Library (MS. Eng. misc. e. 233/2, fols. 2v–3r)

Of this translation Morris wrote 56 quatrains out of 90 before abandoning the work. It marks the appearance of a new, angular, more upright italic with a somewhat Gothic look (especially where *w* and capitals are concerned). As can be seen, the illumination is merely a pencilled design.

XIII.10

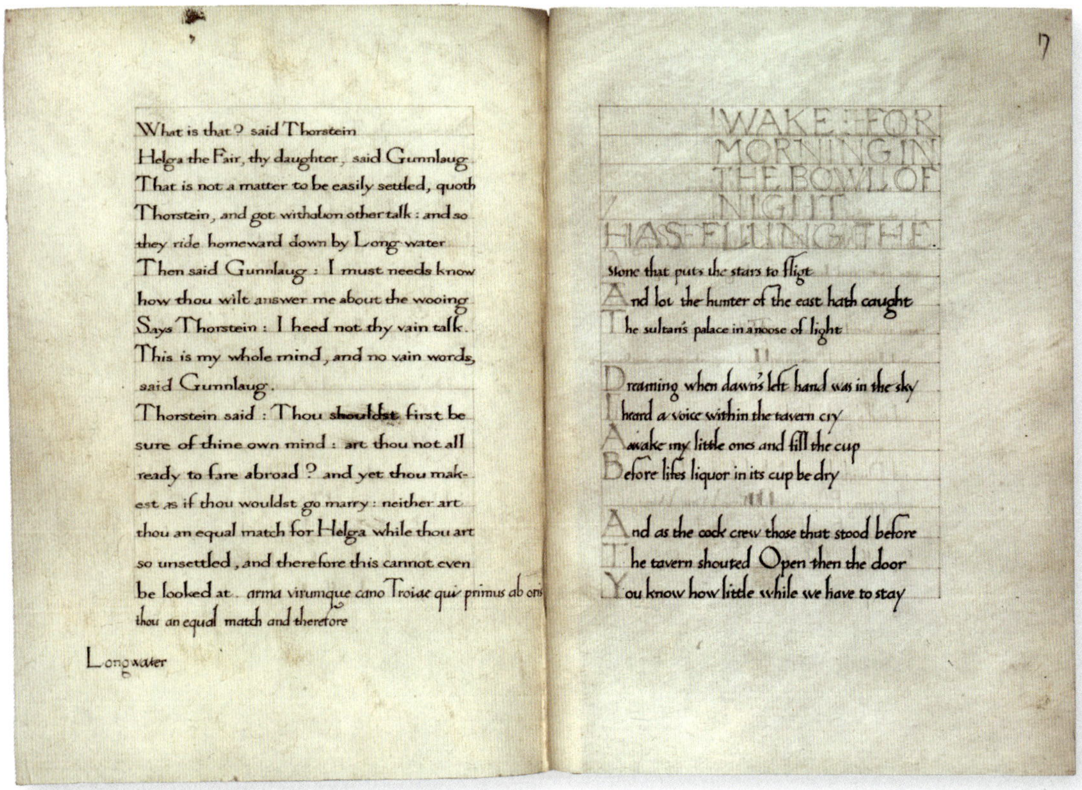

XIII.10
'The Story of Gunnlaug the Worm-Tongue', translated by William Morris and Eiríkr Magnússon
William Morris, *c.*1874
Ink on vellum, 15.2 x 10.8 cm leaf
Bodleian Library (MS. Eng. misc. e. 233/1, fols. 16v–17r)

After writing out more than 30 pages of his translation in the fine roman minuscule seen, for example, in the 'Rubáiyát' (XIII.7), Morris's attention began to wander. On folio 16 he strayed at three points into a very competent emulation of humanist cursive, free of mannerisms; on the following page (seen here on the left) he abandons Gunnlaug altogether at the bottom with the opening words from the *Aeneid*, written in this same cursive – the script of the Horace. He therefore had both his final projects already firmly in mind. Note the isolated name 'Longwater' in the bottom left corner – half in roman, half in italic.

XIII.11

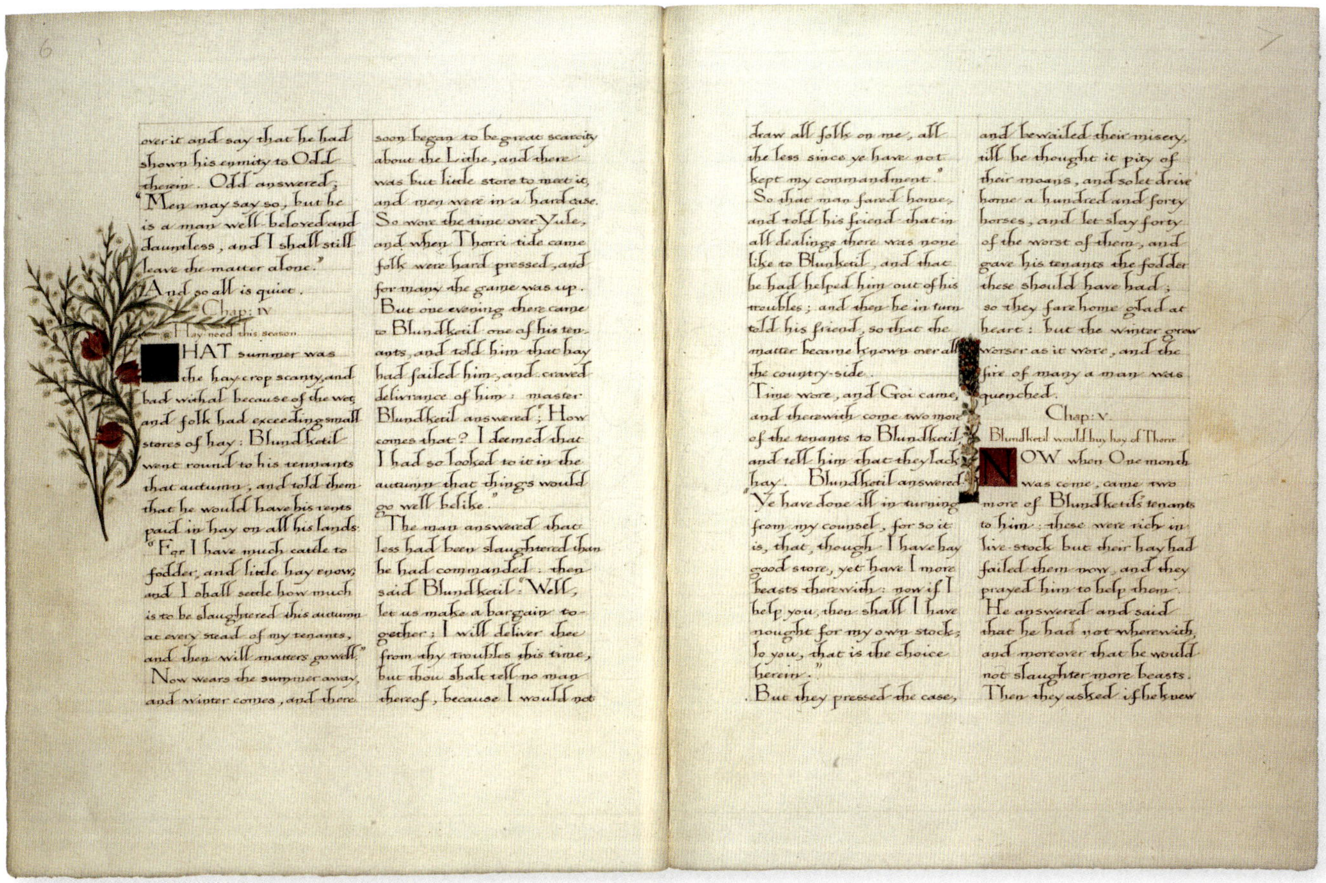
over it and say that he had
shown his enmity to Odd
therein. Odd answered;
"Men may say so, but he
is a man well beloved and
dauntless, and I shall still
leave the matter alone."
And so all is quiet.
Chap: IV
Hay need this season.
[redacted]HAT summer was
the hay crop scanty, and
bad withal because of the wet,
and folk had exceeding small
stores of hay: Blundketil
went round to his tenants
that autumn, and told them
that he would have his rents
paid in hay on all his lands:
"For I have much cattle to
fodder, and little hay enow;
and I shall settle how much
is to be slaughtered this autumn
at every stead of my tenants,
and then will matters go well."
Now wears the summer away,
and winter comes, and there
soon began to be great scarcity
about the Lithe, and there
was but little store to meet it,
and men were in a hard case.
So wore the time over Yule,
and when Thorri tide came
folk were hard pressed, and
for many the game was up.
But one evening there came
to Blundketil one of his ten-
ants, and told him that hay
had failed him, and craved
deliverance of him: master
Blundketil answered; "How
comes that? I deemed that
I had so looked to it in the
autumn that things would
go well belike."
The man answered that
less had been slaughtered than
he had commanded: then
said Blundketil: "Well,
let us make a bargain to-
gether; I will deliver thee
from thy troubles this time,
but thou shalt tell no man
thereof, because I would not
draw all folk on me, all
the less since ye have not
kept my commandment."
So that man fared home,
and told his friend that in
all dealings there was none
like to Blunketil, and that
he had helped him out of his
troubles; and then he in turn
told his friend, so that the
matter became known over all
the country-side.
Time wore, and Goi came,
and therewith come two more
of the tenants to Blundketil,
and tell him that they lack
hay. Blundketil answered:
"Ye have done ill in turning
from my counsel, for so it
is, that, though I have hay
good store, yet have I more
beasts therewith: now if I
help you, then shall I have
nought for my own stock;
lo you, that is the choice
herein."
But they pressed the case,
and bewailed their misery,
till he thought it pity of
their moans, and so let drive
home a hundred and forty
horses, and let slay forty
of the worst of them, and
gave his tenants the fodder
these should have had;
so they fare home glad at
heart: but the winter grew
worser as it wore, and the
fire of many a man was
quenched.
Chap: V.
Blundketil would buy hay of Thorir.
NOW when One month
was come, came two
more of Blundketil's tenants
to him: these were rich in
live-stock but their hay had
failed them now, and they
prayed him to help them.
He answered and said
that he had not wherewith,
and moreover that he would
not slaughter more beasts.
Then they asked if he knew

XIII.12

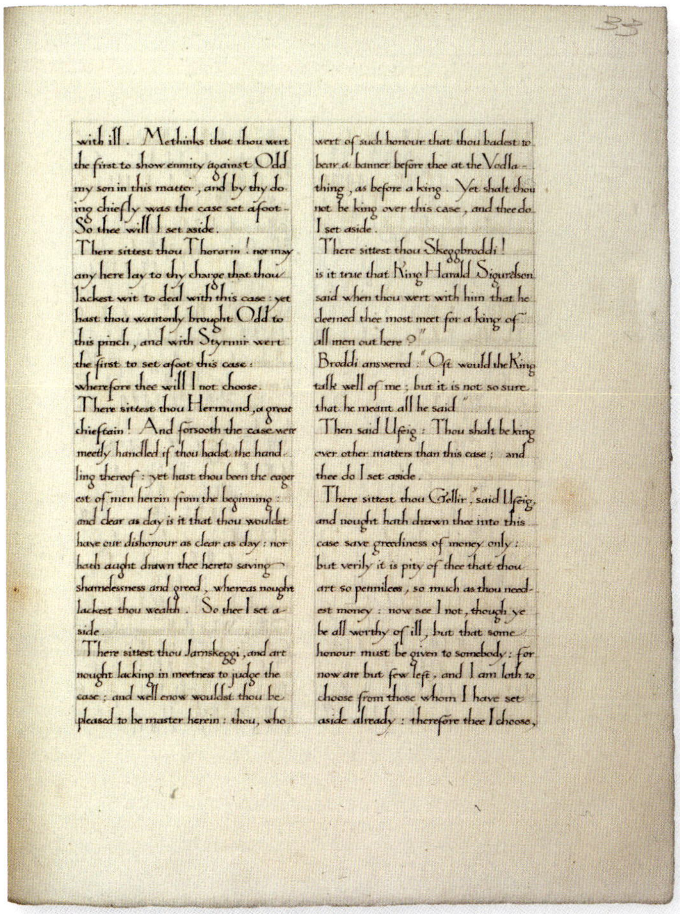
with ill. Methinks that thou wert
the first to show enmity against Odd
my son in this matter, and by thy do-
ing chiefly was the case set afoot.
So thee will I set aside.
There sittest thou Thorarin! nor may
any here lay to thy charge that thou
lackest wit to deal with this case: yet
hast thou wantonly brought Odd to
this pinch, and with Styrmir wert
the first to set afoot this case:
wherefore thee will I not choose.
There sittest thou Hermund, a great
chieftain! And forsooth the case were
meetly handled if thou hadst the hand-
ling thereof: yet hast thou been the eager-
est of men herein from the beginning:
and clear as day is it that thou wouldst
have our dishonour as clear as day: nor
hath aught drawn thee hereto saving
shamelessness and greed, whereas nought
lackest thou wealth. So thee I set a-
side.
There sittest thou Jarnskeggi, and art
nought lacking in meetness to judge the
case; and well enow wouldst thou be
pleased to be master herein: thou, who
wert of such honour that thou badest to
bear a banner before thee at the Vodla-
thing, as before a king. Yet shalt thou
not be king over this case, and thee do
I set aside.
There sittest thou Skeggbroddi!
is it true that King Harald Sigurdson
said when thou wert with him that he
deemed thee most meet for a king of
all men out here?"
Broddi answered: "Oft would the King
talk well of me; but it is not so sure
that he meant all he said."
Then said Ufeig: Thou shalt be king
over other matters than this case; and
thee do I set aside.
There sittest thou Gellir," said Ufeig,
and nought hath drawn thee into this
case save greediness of money only:
but verily it is pity of thee that thou
art so penniless, so much as thou need-
est money: now see I not, though ye
be all worthy of ill, but that some
honour must be given to somebody: for
now are but few left, and I am loth to
choose from those whom I have set
aside already: therefore thee I choose,

XIII.11
'The Story of Hen-Thorir', translated by William Morris and Eiríkr Magnússon
William Morris, *c.*1873
Ink and watercolour on paper, 29 x 22.5 x 1.3 cm (closed)
Bodleian Library (MS. Eng. misc. d. 266, fols. 6v–7r)

Morris's inventiveness seemed endless – no two of his designs were alike. The quality and colour of his decorated versal capitals had, by the time of this manuscript, improved enormously (compare with 'The Story of the Dwellers at Eyr' (XIII.4)).

XIII.12
'The Story of the Banded Men', translated by William Morris and Eiríkr Magnússon
William Morris, *c.*1874
Ink on paper, 29 x 11.3 cm leaf
Bodleian Library (MS. Eng. misc. d. 267, fol. 33r)

Close examination reveals a distinct improvement in sharpness, form and legibility of writing halfway down the page, changing from a stiff, monoline 'typographical' italic, which almost looks roman, to a more natural script that looks forward to the Horace.

XIII.13

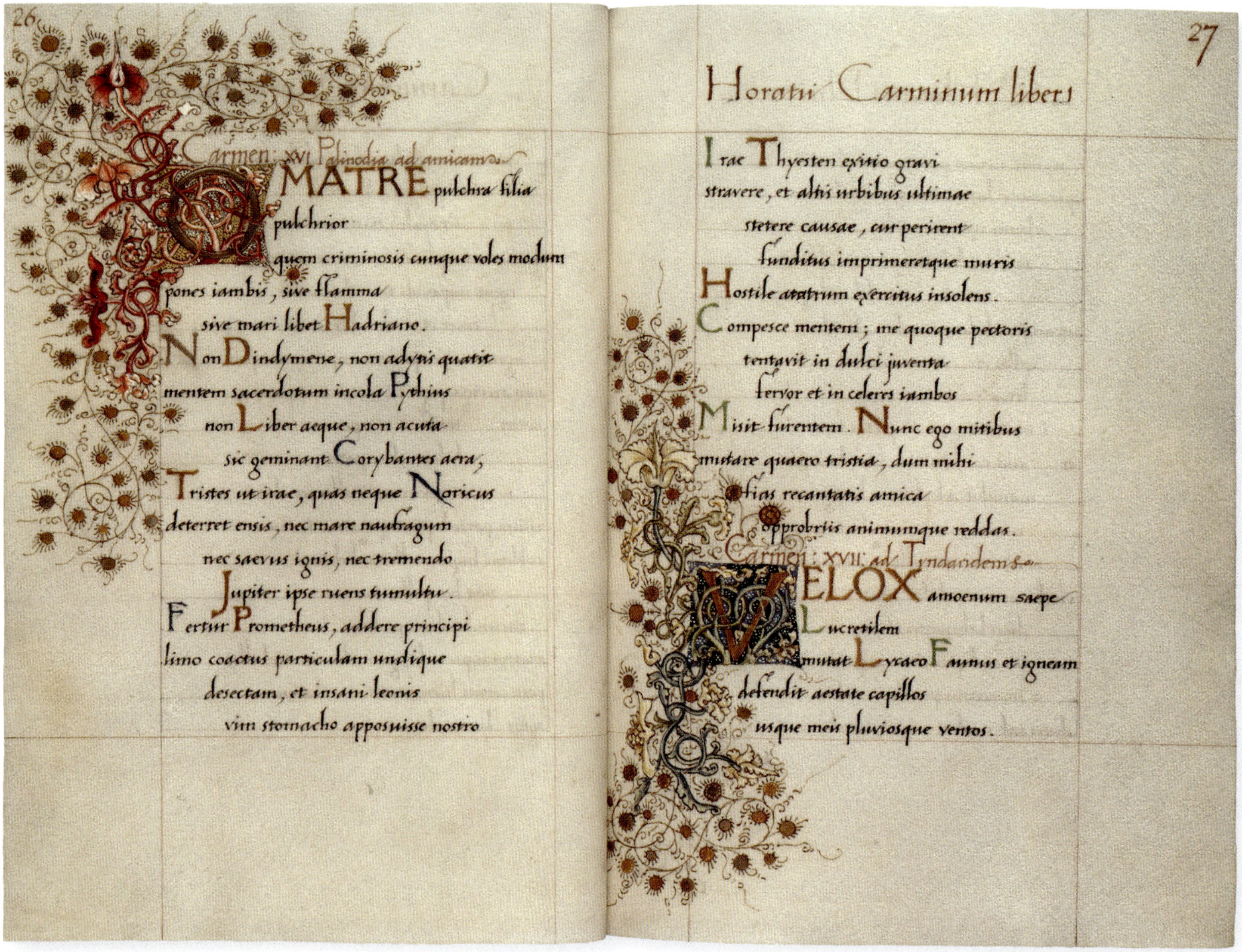

XIII.13
The 'Odes' of Horace
William Morris, Edward Burne-Jones and Charles Fairfax Murray, 1874
Ink, watercolour and gilding on vellum, 16.8 x 11.7 cm leaf
Bodleian Library (MS. Lat. class. e. 38, fols. 26v–27r)

This tiny volume was the culmination of Morris's italic, showing how far his study of Renaissance hands had borne fruit – the only irritating mannerism remaining is the hairline curlicue on *f*. Although he finished the writing of all four books, on 183 pages, he never completely finished the decoration; this did not prevent a few of the pages (principally the openings of three of the books) from being, with Burne-Jones and Murray's help, among the most elaborate illumination schemes he ever carried out.

XIII.14
'The Aeneid' of Virgil
William Morris, Edward Burne-Jones and Charles Fairfax Murray, 1874–5, Louise Powell and Graily Hewitt, *c.*1904–10
Ink, pencil, watercolour and gilding on vellum, 35 x 22.3 cm leaf
Private collection

The culmination of Morris's roman minuscule. Graily Hewitt identified the writing as being modelled specifically on a fifteenth-century manuscript of the works of St Jerome (BL MS Harley 3109), but Alfred Fairbank disagreed, and indeed it seems much more likely that the beautiful clear script, marred by one or two strange traits, was the result of Morris's study and experimentation over several years rather than the conscious copying of one hand. The miniature illustrated shows Juno and her peacock-driven chariot, standing before the city of Carthage. Although Morris ended the writing at 177 pages (he later sold the manuscript to Murray, who commissioned Hewitt and Louise Powell to complete the writing and illumination) it represents a magnificent sustained effort, and is, as he planned it to be, his calligraphic masterpiece.

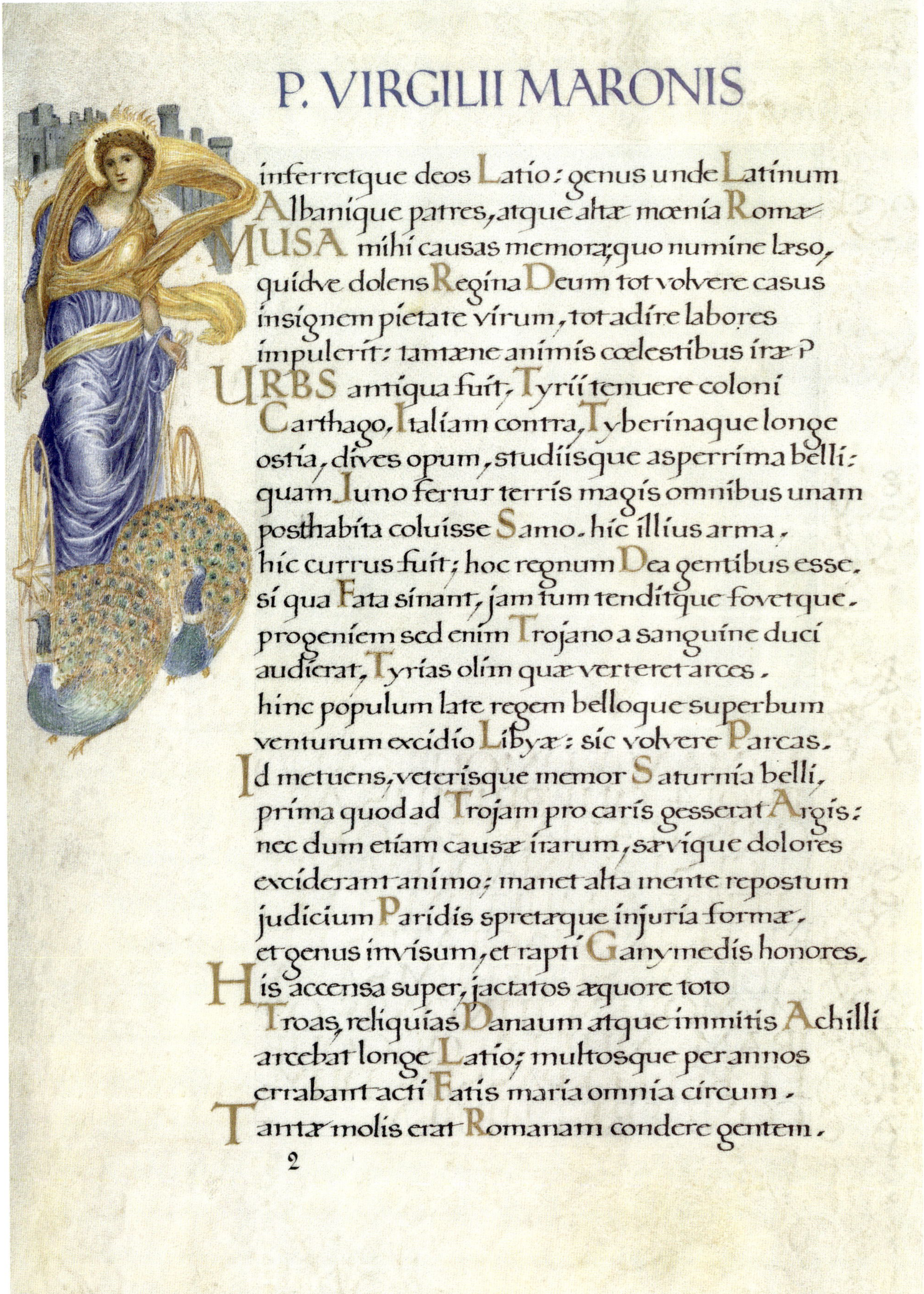

P. VIRGILII MARONIS

inferretque deos Latio: genus unde Latinum
Albanique patres, atque altæ mœnia Romæ.
MUSA mihi causas memora; quo numine læso,
quidve dolens Regina Deum tot volvere casus
insignem pietate virum, tot adire labores
impulerit: tantæne animis cœlestibus iræ?
URBS antiqua fuit, Tyrii tenuere coloni
Carthago, Italiam contra, Tyberinaque longe
ostia, dives opum, studiisque asperrima belli:
quam Juno fertur terris magis omnibus unam
posthabita coluisse Samo. hic illius arma,
hic currus fuit; hoc regnum Dea gentibus esse,
si qua Fata sinant, jam tum tenditque fovetque.
progeniem sed enim Trojano a sanguine duci
audierat, Tyrias olim quæ verteret arces.
hinc populum late regem belloque superbum
venturum excidio Libyæ: sic volvere Parcas.
Id metuens, veterisque memor Saturnia belli,
prima quod ad Trojam pro caris gesserat Argis:
nec dum etiam causæ irarum, sævique dolores
exciderant animo; manet alta mente repostum
judicium Paridis spretæque injuria formæ,
et genus invisum, et rapti Ganymedis honores.
His accensa super, jactatos æquore toto
Troas, reliquias Danaum atque immitis Achilli
arcebat longe Latio; multosque per annos
errabant acti Fatis maria omnia circum.
Tantæ molis erat Romanam condere gentem.

2

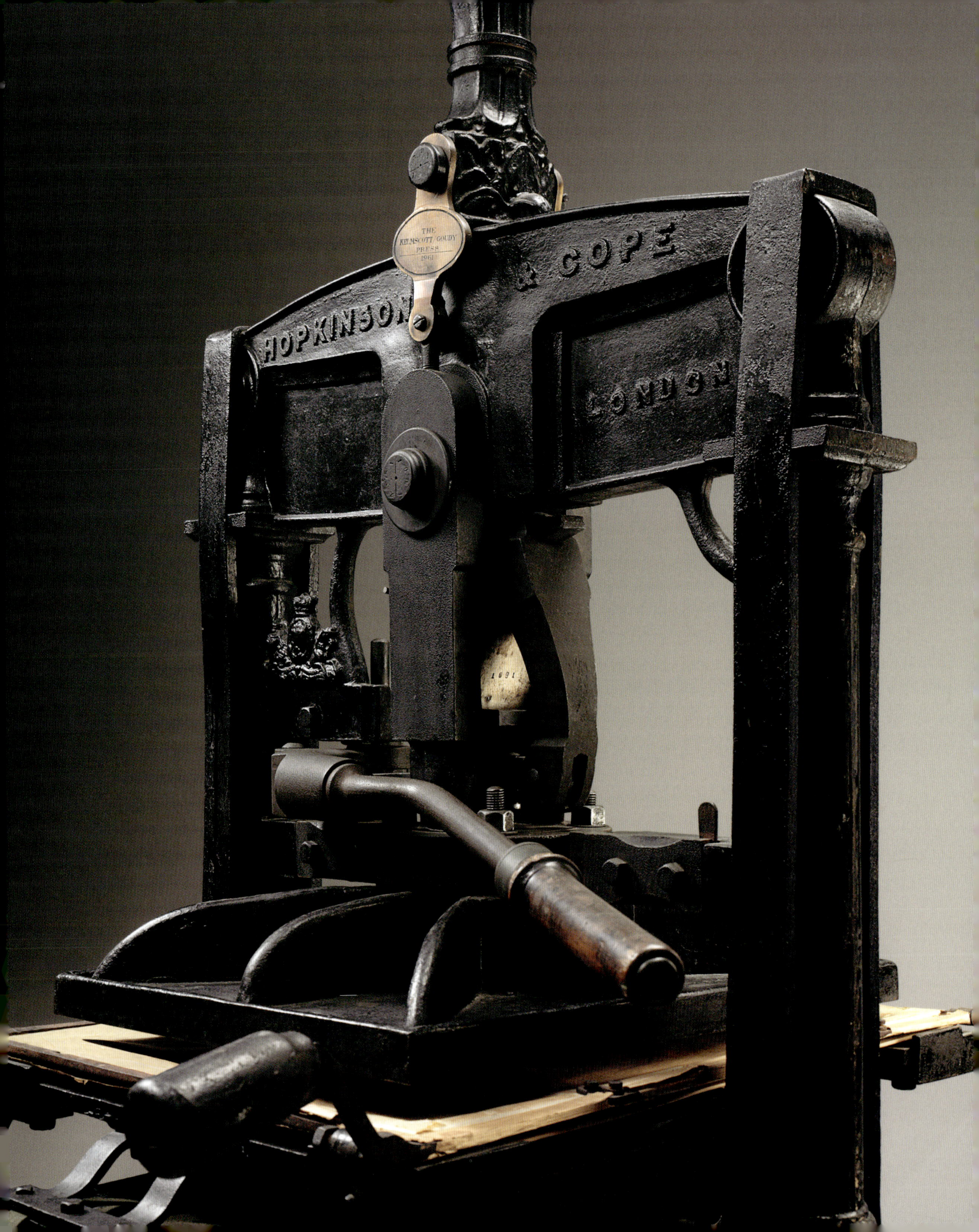
THE
KELMSCOTT/GOUDY
PRESS
1961
HOPKINSON & COPE
LONDON

XIV

THE KELMSCOTT PRESS

John Dreyfus

'I felt that for the books I loved and cared for there might be attempted a presentation ... which should be worthy of one's feelings.'

William Morris in an interview published in *Bookselling*, Christmas 1895

Fig.220 **Albion Press no. 6551, made by Hopkinson & Cope in 1891. Purchased by Morris in 1894 and used to print the Kelmscott Chaucer.**
Cary Graphic Arts Collection, Rochester Institute of Technology, New York

All through his adult life, Morris persistently wrote, designed, collected and produced numerous books and manuscripts. Why then did he reach his mid-fifties before deciding to become a printer and publisher with his own private press?

In part it was because a host of other commitments left him too little time; but there was also a technical obstacle. To design his own type would have involved a great deal of intricate work on a very small scale, which Morris found uncongenial. Then it suddenly struck him that he could in fact design his types on a conveniently large scale. The idea came to him in November 1888 when his Hammersmith friend and neighbour Emery Walker projected greatly enlarged photographic images of fifteenth-century types during a lecture on printing given to the Arts and Crafts Exhibition Society in London.

Walker had wide experience of the printing trade and ran his own photo-engraving business. Some of Walker's slides had been made in his studio from books lent by Morris, who realized that if Walker were to supply enlarged photographic prints of the types projected during the lecture, he could study them in detail. Next, he could draw his own types on the same enlarged scale, relying on Walker to reduce them to the size in which they would be needed. More than once before the lecture, Morris had remarked casually to Walker that he would like 'to have a shot' at type-designing but the event was the impetus. According to May Morris, as they returned to Hammersmith that evening, he said to Walker, 'Let's make a new fount of type.'

By 1888 Morris was well qualified to become a great producer of books. Much skill and invention had gone into the volumes written by hand in a variety of beautiful scripts, which John Nash describes in this publication. The experience of making these calligraphical masterpieces taught Morris a great deal about the shapes of letters as well as the decoration and illustration of text pages. Moreover, he had learnt the secrets of how to use space and how to control margins to enhance the effect of what was placed upon the page. His extensive library of books and manuscripts was another source from which he built up his typographic skill. He loved to spend hours examining and discussing works in his library with his close friends Walker and Sydney Cockerell (who became the second Secretary of the Kelmscott Press). Morris had a particularly high regard for the books illustrated with woodcuts printed during the 1460s in Augsburg.

He had also acquired a practical knowledge of contemporary printing from his early twenties. Editing the first number of *The Oxford and Cambridge Magazine* in 1856 had brought him into contact with one of the best book printers of that time, Charles Whittingham of the Chiswick Press. Several of Morris's own books were later printed at the Chiswick Press, which had played a leading role in bringing back into favour William Caslon's eighteenth-century types. It also owned some unique types and ornaments made for its exclusive use. Nearer to the time when Morris decided to start his own press, he gained some managerial experience of printing when he became editor and publisher of *Commonweal*. This was the official journal of the Socialist League. Its foreman printer was Thomas Binning, of whom Morris wrote to a fellow socialist in July 1885, 'He is to be my man you understand, & I am to be the capitalist printer: this he insisted on.' A few years later, Binning became father of the chapel (the printers' equivalent of shop steward and the workers' representative) at the Kelmscott Press.

The formation of the Arts and Crafts Exhibition Society in 1887 brought Morris into more frequent contact with bookish founder members, such as Walter Crane and the bookbinder Thomas James Cobden-Sanderson who later worked in close association with the Kelmscott Press. The newly formed Society's first exhibition catalogue was printed at the Chiswick Press, whose books were well represented in the 1888 display. In the same year work started at the Chiswick Press on Morris's book *The House of the Wolfings*, his first long prose romance. While writing it, his daughter May recalled, 'his taste of younger days for early printed books had been developing into a practical interest in all the details of fine printing'. Proof of this can be found in *The Roots of the Mountains*, his next book printed at the Chiswick Press (XIV.2). Morris admitted he was 'so pleased with my book – typography, binding, and must I say it, literary matter – that I am any day to be seen huggling it up, and am become a spectacle to Gods and men because of it.' Even deeper pleasure was soon to follow from printing his own works in his own types and on his own presses.

By the late 1880s he had shed or reduced many of his commercial and political commitments. Aware that his health might deteriorate further, he relished the prospect of setting up his press within two-minutes walk of Kelmscott House. There he could count on frequent visits and help from Walker, who lived and worked nearby. With such competent help, Morris was able to write and translate more than a third of the works printed at the Kelmscott Press. He also designed every Kelmscott edition published in his lifetime, and drew, according to Cockerell's 'A Short History and Description of the Kelmscott Press' (1898), 644 initials, borders, ornaments, frames for illustrations, title-pages, large initial words and printer's marks.

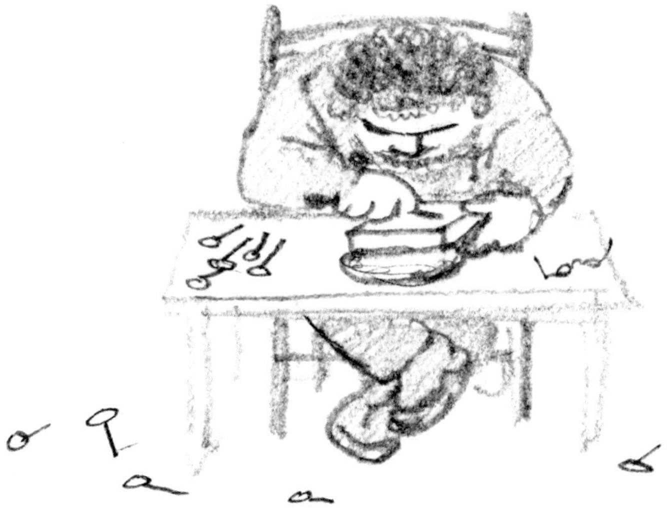

Fig.221 **Morris cutting a wood block, caricature by Edward Burne-Jones, *c*.1866.**
British Museum

Morris set out to print books hoping that some would, as he put it, 'have a definite claim to beauty'. Admitting that it was only natural for him to try to ornament his books suitably because he was a decorator by profession, he nevertheless tried to keep in mind the need for decoration to be made part of the page of type. He believed a book without ornament could look positively beautiful, not merely un-ugly, provided that it was architecturally good. By this he meant that pages needed to be clear and easy to read. This they could not be unless the type was well designed, and therefore easy to read; never should it be troublesome to the mind because of any eccentricity in the letter forms. To present-day readers the types Morris designed for his press may look rather eccentric, if only a few lines are seen in reproduction. Their effect is quite different when used in Kelmscott books, accompanied by woodcut ornament and illustration, and printed on fine handmade paper or vellum with dense black ink, occasionally relieved by brightly coloured inks.

Morris sought to recreate the rich Gothic texture he admired in books printed in the third quarter of the fifteenth century. He began by designing a Roman type named Golden because he meant it to be seen for the first time in the Kelmscott edition of *The Golden Legend*. Such difficulties arose in producing this lengthy text in three volumes that publication was delayed until 1892. So the Golden type's debut was in his own work, *The Story of the Glittering Plain*, when the first Kelmscott edition appeared on 8 May 1891. Designing this type proved to be the most troublesome task Morris ever undertook. Although we speak of designing a type in the singular, it actually involves making a set of drawings for upwards of 80 characters, merely to produce a fount that includes capitals, lower-case, numerals, punctuation marks and tied letters such as Æ and ff. Trial proofs always show up a few awkward letter combinations, which can be overcome only by altering the original designs. The first stage in creating metal type is to cut punches in steel (XIV.9a). Morris brooded for hours over his punchcutter's proofs, which he carried around in matchboxes stuffed into his pockets. At Walker's suggestion, all the punches for the Kelmscott Press types were made by Edward Prince, an extremely competent punchcutter who had previously done some work for Walker.

Morris chose to base his design for a Roman type on enlarged photographs of types used at Venice in 1476 by Nicholas Jenson and Jacobus Rubeus (XIV.3); but he decided to make his own type much stronger in colour. In this way its weight would match the woodcut lines of the decorations and illustrations that he intended to make such a feature of Kelmscott books; moreover, these woodcuts could be placed alongside the type on the bed of the hand press used for printing his books. His type turned out to be a hybrid. Walter Crane reacted in a way that delighted Morris: 'Crane when he saw it beside Jenson thought it more Gothic-looking; this is a fact and a cheerful one to me.'

Morris was even happier with his second type, a Gothic letter named Troy because it was intended for setting his edition of *The Recuyell of the Historyes of Troye* (1892). In designing Troy, he set himself the task of redeeming Gothic type from the 'charge of unreadableness' commonly brought against it. He felt that charge could not be reasonably levelled at the types used by Peter Schoeffer at Mainz for his Bible of 1462, nor against Günther Zainer for his editions of *The Golden Legend* printed at Augsburg between 1471 and 1475. Morris believed his Troy type to be 'as readable as a Roman one, and to say the truth I prefer it to the Roman.' He called his design a semi-Gothic, designed with a special regard to legibility. Two sizes of Troy were used in *The Recuyell*, an 18-point for the text and a 12-point for the table of contents and glossary. Later, the smaller size was used in double column for the great folio Chaucer and became known as the Chaucer type.

From his pre-Kelmscott experience of printing, Morris knew that type looked at its best only if it was most carefully spaced. Too much space between letters and between words tends to make a page harder to read. Morris disliked wide gaps between lines, although he sometimes added a little extra space between lines set in his own types. His experience of writing formal manuscripts had strengthened his conviction that words needed to be set close together to prevent vertical shafts of white from disrupting the solid texture he wanted to maintain in a page of type. He insisted that the unit to be considered in book design was the pair of facing pages that form an 'opening' (on the grounds that they are always seen together by the reader). Victorian printers tended to centre text on the page. Instead, Morris advocated the practice established in medieval times of having all four margins around the type area differ – the inner margin narrowest, the top wider, the outer edge wider again, with the bottom margin widest of all.

Morris had very clear ideas about the paper he wanted for his Kelmscott books. Realizing that it 'would be a very false economy to stint in the quality of the paper as to price', he opted for a paper with the same characteristics that he admired in books printed during the 1470s in Venice and Bologna. He owned a book printed in Venice by Johannes de Colonia and Johannes Manthen in 1475, with a text by Alexander of Hales, *Summa universae theologiae* (now in the collection of the Society of Antiquaries). Inside this copy, a note by Cockerell records that Morris took it to discuss with Joseph Batchelor, a hand papermaker at Little Chart in Kent. This mill had been recommended by Walker, who went down with Morris to place the order in October 1890. They obtained an excellent making of pure linen paper, well sized, very tough, and ideally suited for printing on a hand press. Like the early Italian paper that Morris admired, the paper made by Batchelor had narrowly spaced wire-lines, without unduly prominent chain-lines (created by the impression of the wire mesh used in the paper mould). Morris drew three watermarks – flower, perch and apple – for the different sizes in which his paper was supplied.

As he disapproved of large paper editions because of their badly proportioned margins,

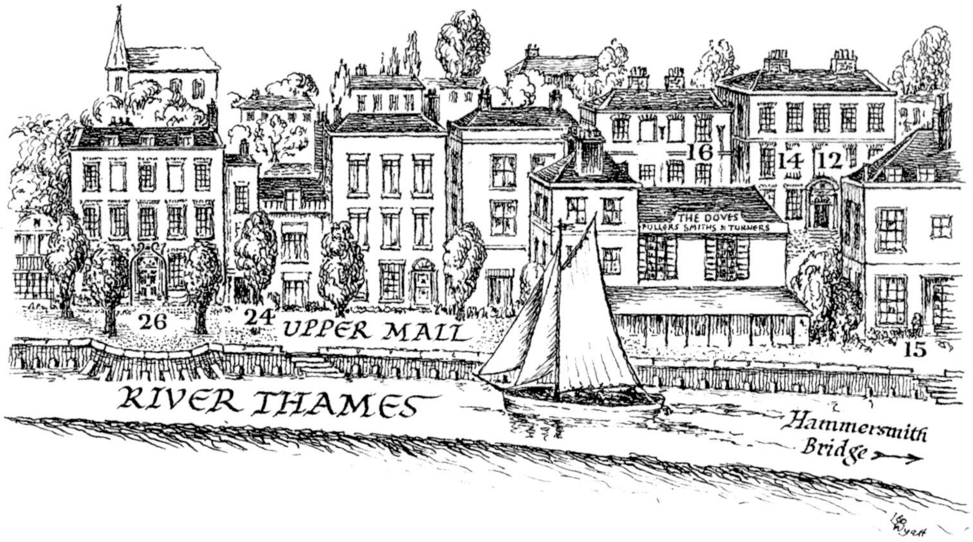

Fig.222 **Bird's-eye view of the Upper Mall, from a drawing by Leo Wyatt.**

Key:
12. Sussex House, Emery Walker's Works, established 1886
14. Sussex Cottage, Kelmscott Press, 1891–8
15. Doves Bindery, established 1893
16. Kelmscott Press, January–May 1891
24. River House, Thomas Cobden-Sanderson, 1903–9
26. Kelmscott House, William Morris, 1878–96

he decided to print copies on vellum for his richer customers, just as Gutenberg had done with the first printed book in 1456. Morris persuaded a dealer in vellum and parchment, Henry Band of Brentford in Middlesex, to experiment with skins chosen from calves less than six weeks old. Eventually Kelmscott vellum was made specially thin and its fine surface was untainted by white lead. When larger quantities were needed than Band could deliver, vellum was also supplied by William J. Turney of Stourbridge in Worcestershire.

Morris realized that the full effect of his own types upon his specially made paper and vellum would depend to a great extent upon the quality of his ink. After many trials, samples were sent to him by inkmakers in England and America. Neither was perfect because of red or blue undertones; but neither maker was willing to meet Morris's criticisms. So once again Walker was consulted. He recommended an excellent ink made in Hanover by the firm of Jänecke. Its colour was good, without any distracting undertone. It never clogged the type nor spoiled the impression. But it had one drawback. According to a letter Walker wrote in 1931 to John Johnson, the University Printer at Oxford, the ink was tremendously stiff and very hard work for the pressmen. It provoked something close to a strike when it was introduced at the Kelmscott Press, whereupon Morris,

> rather weakly gave in and used the best ink he could get in England. This turned out to be unsatisfactory, so Morris read the riot act and said if they wouldn't use the German ink he could close the Press. As his pressmen were very well paid they naturally didn't want to lose their jobs and gave way. However, they took it out of [*sic*] Morris another way and the number of sheets turned out per day was extraordinarily small.

It was probably in 1893 that Morris briefly used the German ink, reverting to ink supplied by Shackell, Edwards and Co., a London manufacturer, until, in 1895, alarming yellow stains appeared on sheets of the Chaucer and he insisted that from then on only the Jänecke ink would be used.

When the Press reached full production, about 10 or 12 compositors and pressmen were employed. Printing began in January 1891 at its premises on Upper Mall, a few doors away from Kelmscott House (fig.222). As output increased, Morris leased the adjacent Sussex Cottage, attached to Sussex House where some of Walker's staff worked. In 1893, soon after Cobden-Sanderson set up his Doves Bindery opposite Sussex House, Morris was able to rent upstairs rooms there for his proofreaders, who stayed until the summer of 1894. Additional premises were taken on 1 January 1895 to house a third Albion press (fig.220), which had been specially reinforced to take the great pressure needed to do full justice to the woodcuts in the folio Chaucer, on which work had fallen seriously behind schedule. The new premises were next to the Doves Inn, even closer to Kelmscott House.

Walker declined to become a partner in the Press, but he constantly gave advice to Morris on typographical questions. For help in various matters, Morris turned to his son-in-law and fellow socialist, Henry Halliday Sparling, and gave him the title Secretary of the Kelmscott Press (fig.223). Sparling had previously worked alongside Morris as sub-editor of *Commonweal*. He edited three long Kelmscott editions published in 1892–3 but resigned his position in July 1894 after his marriage to May Morris collapsed. Many years later, just before his death in 1924, he published *The Kelmscott Press and William Morris Master-Craftsman,* which provides much useful information.

Cockerell succeeded Sparling and became a far more effective Secretary, and a much closer

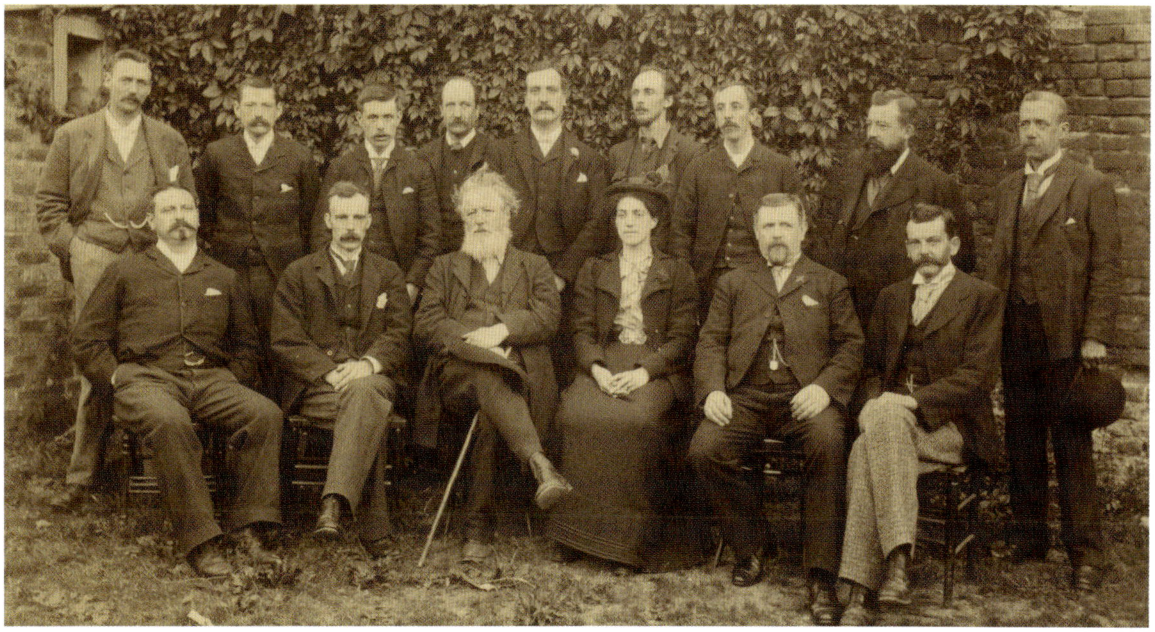

Fig.223 **William and May Morris and the staff of the Kelmscott Press, photographed *c.*1893.**

Front row, from left: Stephen Mowlem (pressman), William Henry Bowden (pressman), William Morris, May Morris, W. Collins (pressman), W.L. Tasker (printer). Back row, from left: H. Howes (printer), Carpenter (printer), F. Collins (printer), Emery Walker (friend and adviser), R. Eatley (printer), Henry Halliday Sparling (Secretary until July 1894), John Tippet (printer), Thomas Binning (printer and father of the chapel), G. Heath (printer). (The word printer has been used where an individual is known to have worked at the Press, but where it is uncertain whether he worked as a compositor, pressman or proofreader.)

V&A (1819–1939)

friend of Morris. He was a deft administrator whose sound judgment and devotion to detail brought great benefits to the Press. He also helped to improve the accuracy of its texts. Further help with proofreading and editing came from Frederick Startridge Ellis, a retired bookseller who had previously been Morris's publisher (*The Earthly Paradise*, 1868–70, had appeared over his imprint). Cockerell and Ellis gave invaluable help and attention to Morris in his final years. As trustees they ran the Press for about 18 months after his death and completed several of his unfinished projects, with some assistance from May Morris.

Apart from receiving administrative help in running the Press, Morris relied on other artists to design illustrations for Kelmscott books. The major contribution came from his old friend Edward Burne-Jones, who had sketched over 100 illustrations for a planned illustrated edition of Morris's *Earthly Paradise* in the 1860s before this scheme was abandoned (see XIV.1). The two friends collaborated again with dazzling success in the Kelmscott Chaucer, completed shortly before Morris died. His decorative designs for that work and Burne-Jones's drawings for illustrations were all photographed on to wood, and then cut by skilled trade engravers. Before Burne-Jones's delicate pencil drawings were engraved, every line and dot was strengthened or adjusted by Robert Catterson-Smith, artist and later Headmaster of Birmingham School of Art. He developed a set of consistent linear abbreviations to provide marks which the engraver, William Harcourt Hooper, could follow and which were approved by Burne-Jones (see XIV.27).

Other illustrators of Kelmscott books included Walter Crane and two artists from the Birmingham School, Charles March Gere and Arthur Joseph Gaskin. Of these three artists, Gaskin's work has attracted particular praise, partly because it brought, as Colin Franklin remarked in his 1969 study, *The Private Presses*, 'a strictness of form and composition none of the others provided'. However, the mass of decorations, ornaments, borders and lettering supplied by Morris have such strength and consistency that most readers are more impressed by his contribution to Kelmscott books than they are by the illustrations designed by other artists. An exception must be made of the Kelmscott Chaucer, where the text, illustrations and ornament combine to create a single harmonious work of art.

Because that massive folio has been displayed and reproduced so often, it is frequently forgotten that Morris used seven different formats at his Press. His three translations of thirteenth-century French romances (*The Tale of King Florus and the Fair Jehane*, *Of the Friendship of Amis and Amile* and *The Tale of King Coustans*) appeared in an elegant little 16mo format (14.3 × 10.4 cm), which had been used in 1893 with great success for his essay on *Gothic Architecture*. Various other formats were appropriately chosen to print his other texts.

Morris's previous experience of manufacture and marketing led him to take a keen interest in the way his Kelmscott books were financed and sold. Profit earned him the freedom to work as he wished, both as an author and as a designer. The 52 titles Morris chose to publish (in 66 volumes) fell broadly into three categories – his own literary works, medieval texts and standard classics of English literature. He published poetry by his friends and collaborators, including Algernon Swinburne, Dante Gabriel Rossetti and Wilfrid Scawen Blunt. In the early years these books were sold either by Reeves & Turner, who ran a bookshop on the Strand with a small publishing department, or by the antiquarian bookseller and publisher Bernard Quaritch. From May 1893 Morris published the majority of Kelmscott books himself. These became so well known to collectors and librarians that most editions were subscribed in advance. By becoming his own publisher, Morris increased his profits. The most ambitious and time-consuming projects, such as the Chaucer, were subsidized by the smaller Kelmscott books that had healthy profit margins. From October 1895 announcements of new titles were only circulated if the edition was not almost sold out by the time that sheets were sent to the binder.

Two standard Kelmscott bindings were devised by Morris and both were executed in London by the firm of John & James Leighton. Distrusting the quality of goat and calf skins available through leather suppliers, Morris decided to use limp vellum with coloured silk ties dyed by his own firm. His alternative was a quarter linen binding with a printed label on the spine, and with sides of blue-grey laid paper. The latter style was regarded by Morris as a satisfactory temporary binding; but most surviving Kelmscott books have never been rebound. Occasionally the Doves Bindery produced leather bindings for individual Kelmscott customers. While Douglas Cockerell (Sydney's younger brother) was working at the Doves Bindery he carried out 48 special bindings in blind-stamped pigskin with silver clasps for the Kelmscott Chaucer, to a design devised by Morris (see XIV.32).

Other private presses soon copied the two standard binding styles devised by Morris for his Kelmscott books. So powerful and inventive were his designs for every aspect of bookwork that it was hard to escape his influence. The outcome was sometimes sadly inept; a style so well suited to Morris's medieval taste was inappropriate for texts of an entirely different character. Far happier results came about when other designers paid attention to the principles that led to the development of his style. These principles were clearly set out in Morris's essays and lectures on the 'Ideal Book', under which title they were published in 1982 by the University of California Press, most capably edited and introduced by William S. Peterson.

Morris had a healthy influence on those who never mimicked his mannerisms but applied his principles to books produced by twentieth-century production methods. Brilliant artificers of the book, such as Bruce Rogers in the United States and Francis Meynell in Britain, placed as much importance as Morris on fine papers, carefully designed and spaced type with suitable ornament, and high standards of presswork. Unlike Morris, they accepted modern methods for making paper by machine, as well as mechanical typesetting and power-driven presses. Rogers and Meynell found fresh ways of applying decoration to the printed page and used new types (or good revivals of old types made for mechanical typesetting machines), which resulted in books that differed greatly in style from those printed at the Kelmscott Press. Nevertheless, Morris's insistence on matters such as tight spacing of words, decent margins, and the need to integrate illustrations with text, all had their effect on later typographers who had looked closely at the way Morris's books reflected his clearly stated ideals. Kelmscott books were real eye-openers – and they opened minds.

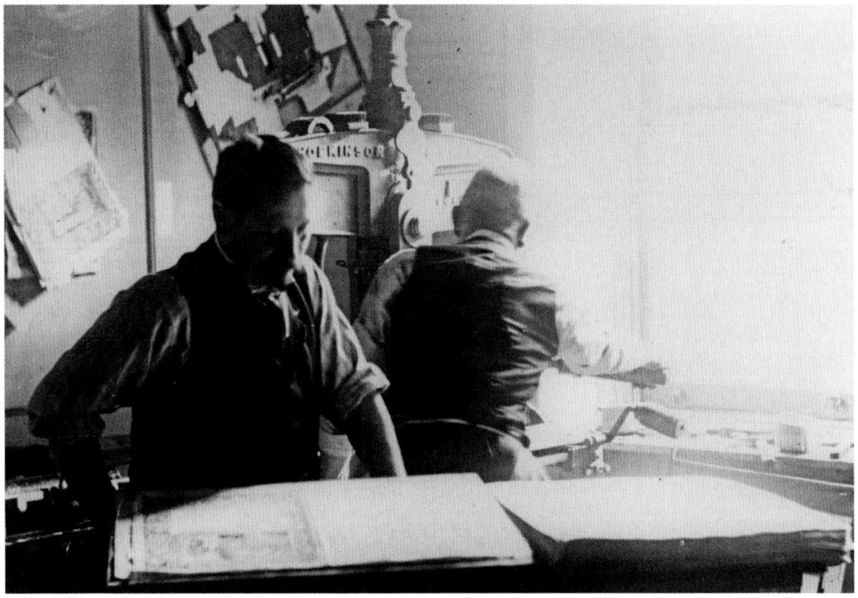

Fig.224 **The Press Room, with William H. Bowden and W. Collins at work on the Chaucer.**
St Bride Foundation

XIV.1a

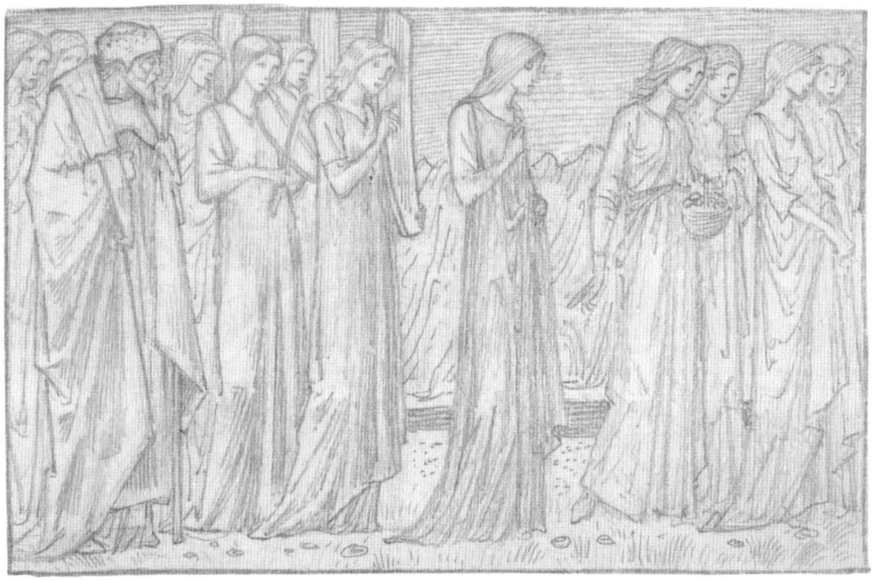

XIV.1b

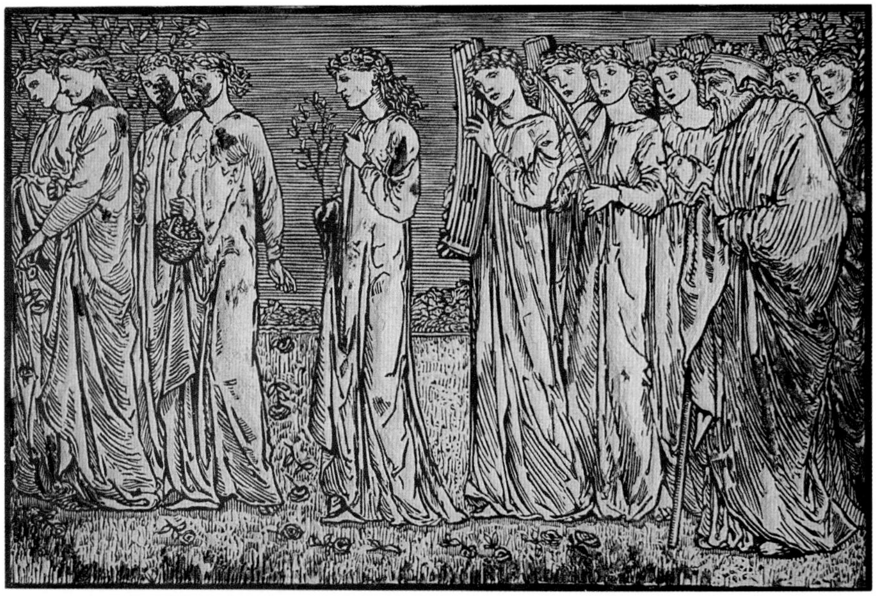

XIV.1c

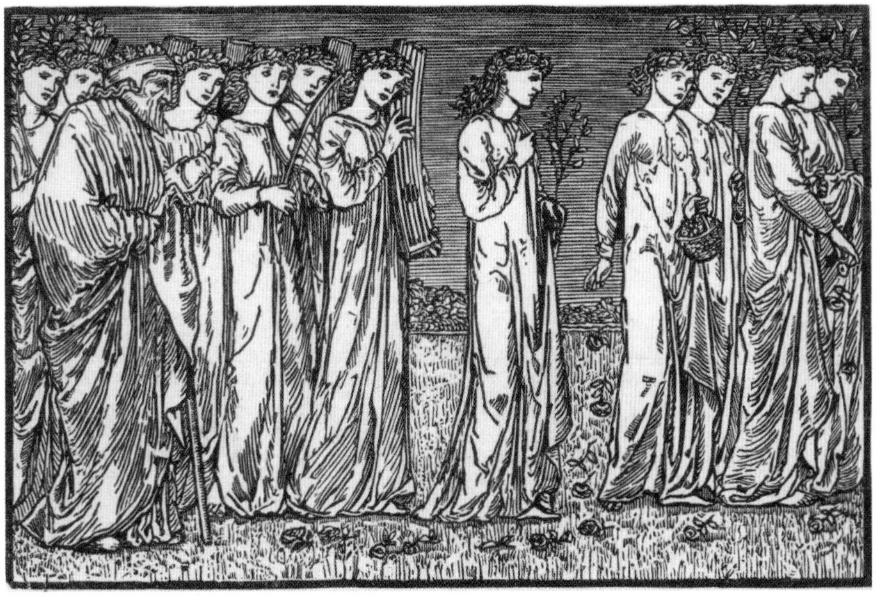

XIV.1

***The Procession to the Hill* from 'The Story of Cupid and Psyche'**

a Drawing
Edward Burne-Jones, *c.*1866
Pencil, 9.8 x 15.2 cm (image size)
V&A (E.30–1955)

b Wood block
Possibly cut by William Morris, *c.*1866
10.3 x 15.7 x 2.4 cm
The Society of Antiquaries of London (934.52)

c Proof
10 x 15.3 cm (image size)
V&A (E.1814–1920)

'Cupid and Psyche' was one of 24 stories in Morris's *Earthly Paradise* (1868–70). He intended to publish the work at his own expense with over 300 woodcut illustrations by Burne-Jones. Work on these began in earnest in the summer of 1866, and over a hundred designs were executed, the majority for 'Cupid and Psyche'.

Considerable sensitivity was needed to transfer Burne-Jones's delicate drawings onto the wood blocks, a task undertaken by George Wardle, who later became the firm's general manager. Wardle, George Campfield, Lucy Faulkner and Bessie Burden all cut blocks for the project, but Morris executed the majority himself. According to Wardle, he became possessed by the idea, 'If I could do it, why not he? and he took them all in hand ... not without some lively scenes in Queen Square ... He cut with great ardour and with much knowledge of the forms certainly, but the work did not always go to his mind. It was necessarily slow & he was constitutionally quick. There were then quarrels between them.'

Burne-Jones's caricature (fig.221) reflects Wardle's account. In his impatience Morris has sent nearly as many graving tools flying to the floor as remain on his work table. May recalled how her father 'would work with bright cutting tools on a little block of wood, which sat on a plump leather cushion.' Despite his temperamental difficulties with such a slow and exacting process, Morris mastered the craft admirably.

Work on the illustrations continued until *c.*1867. After trial prints were made the project was abandoned because Morris was unable to devise a satisfactory typographical setting to match the quality of the wood-engraved illustrations. In 1974 the original 'Cupid and Psyche' blocks were printed with Morris's text composed in his own Troy type.

May Morris bequeathed 44 blocks to the Society of Antiquaries. Burne-Jones's drawings are in the V&A, Birmingham Museum and Art Gallery, Ashmolean Museum, Oxford, and The Morgan Library and Museum, New York.

XIV.2

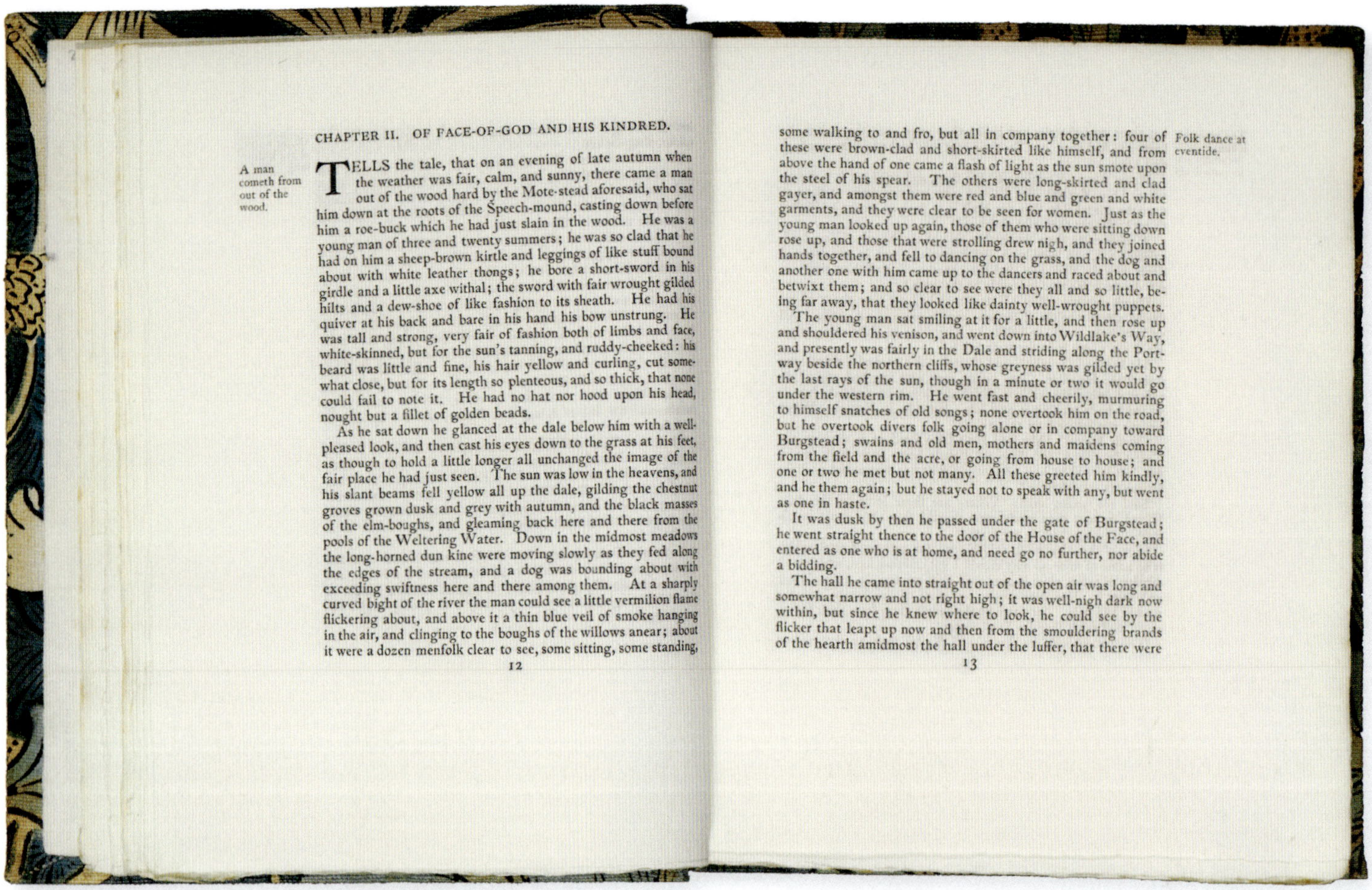

CHAPTER II. OF FACE-OF-GOD AND HIS KINDRED.

A man cometh from out of the wood.

TELLS the tale, that on an evening of late autumn when the weather was fair, calm, and sunny, there came a man out of the wood hard by the Mote-stead aforesaid, who sat him down at the roots of the Speech-mound, casting down before him a roe-buck which he had just slain in the wood. He was a young man of three and twenty summers; he was so clad that he had on him a sheep-brown kirtle and leggings of like stuff bound about with white leather thongs; he bore a short-sword in his girdle and a little axe withal; the sword with fair wrought gilded hilts and a dew-shoe of like fashion to its sheath. He had his quiver at his back and bare in his hand his bow unstrung. He was tall and strong, very fair of fashion both of limbs and face, white-skinned, but for the sun's tanning, and ruddy-cheeked: his beard was little and fine, his hair yellow and curling, cut somewhat close, but for its length so plenteous, and so thick, that none could fail to note it. He had no hat nor hood upon his head, nought but a fillet of golden beads.

As he sat down he glanced at the dale below him with a well-pleased look, and then cast his eyes down to the grass at his feet, as though to hold a little longer all unchanged the image of the fair place he had just seen. The sun was low in the heavens, and his slant beams fell yellow all up the dale, gilding the chestnut groves grown dusk and grey with autumn, and the black masses of the elm-boughs, and gleaming back here and there from the pools of the Weltering Water. Down in the midmost meadows the long-horned dun kine were moving slowly as they fed along the edges of the stream, and a dog was bounding about with exceeding swiftness here and there among them. At a sharply curved bight of the river the man could see a little vermilion flame flickering about, and above it a thin blue veil of smoke hanging in the air, and clinging to the boughs of the willows anear; about it were a dozen menfolk clear to see, some sitting, some standing,

12

Folk dance at eventide.

some walking to and fro, but all in company together: four of these were brown-clad and short-skirted like himself, and from above the hand of one came a flash of light as the sun smote upon the steel of his spear. The others were long-skirted and clad gayer, and amongst them were red and blue and green and white garments, and they were clear to be seen for women. Just as the young man looked up again, those of them who were sitting down rose up, and those that were strolling drew nigh, and they joined hands together, and fell to dancing on the grass, and the dog and another one with him came up to the dancers and raced about and betwixt them; and so clear to see were they all and so little, being far away, that they looked like dainty well-wrought puppets.

The young man sat smiling at it for a little, and then rose up and shouldered his venison, and went down into Wildlake's Way, and presently was fairly in the Dale and striding along the Portway beside the northern cliffs, whose greyness was gilded yet by the last rays of the sun, though in a minute or two it would go under the western rim. He went fast and cheerily, murmuring to himself snatches of old songs; none overtook him on the road, but he overtook divers folk going alone or in company toward Burgstead; swains and old men, mothers and maidens coming from the field and the acre, or going from house to house; and one or two he met but not many. All these greeted him kindly, and he them again; but he stayed not to speak with any, but went as one in haste.

It was dusk by then he passed under the gate of Burgstead; he went straight thence to the door of the House of the Face, and entered as one who is at home, and need go no further, nor abide a bidding.

The hall he came into straight out of the open air was long and somewhat narrow and not right high; it was well-nigh dark now within, but since he knew where to look, he could see by the flicker that leapt up now and then from the smouldering brands of the hearth amidmost the hall under the luffer, that there were

13

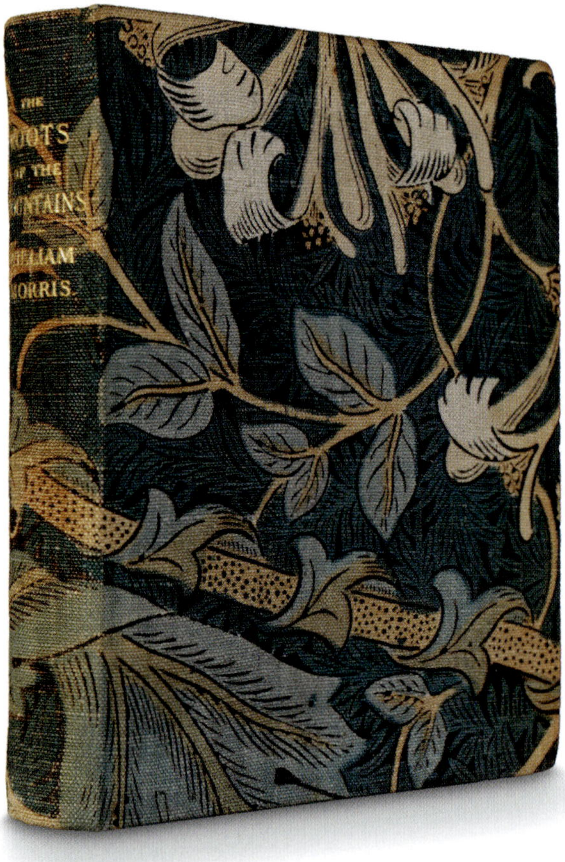

XIV.2
***The Roots of the Mountains* by William Morris**
London, Reeves & Turner, 1889
19.5 x 16 cm leaf
National Art Library, V&A (Museum no.38041019040955)

This was the second experimental volume printed by the Chiswick Press shortly before Morris founded his own press. It was issued in November 1889 (though dated 1890) and Jane Morris's correspondence confirms that it was 'selling well'. Morris chose the Basle type, based on a fount used by Johann Froben in Switzerland in the early sixteenth century. It was created for the exclusive use of the Chiswick Press and Morris had earlier employed it for some specimen pages of *The Earthly Paradise* in the 1860s.

Though similar in design to *The House of the Wolfings* issued the previous year, Morris improved several features. Margins are better proportioned. Spacing between words is generally tighter. Instead of page headings, shoulder notes are set at the top of both outer margins. (Walker remarked while lecturing in 1890 that many early books had no headlines, which he believed often destroyed the effect of unity in a page.) Morris worked out a better way to compose and display his chapter titles. The Basle type was also improved by replacing the 'e' with a new cutting in which the distracting oblique cross-bar was made horizontal. According to Cockerell, Morris considered it to be the best-looking book issued since the seventeenth century.

This example is from the superior edition of 250 copies printed on slightly larger Whatman paper and bound in Merton Abbey block-printed linens designed by Morris – either *Honeysuckle*, as here, or *Little Chintz*. The Chiswick Press exhibited this edition at the 1890 Arts and Crafts Exhibition and Morris commissioned the Swiss artist Edmond Reuter to embellish his own copy with illuminations, six sheets of which were also exhibited.

XIV.3

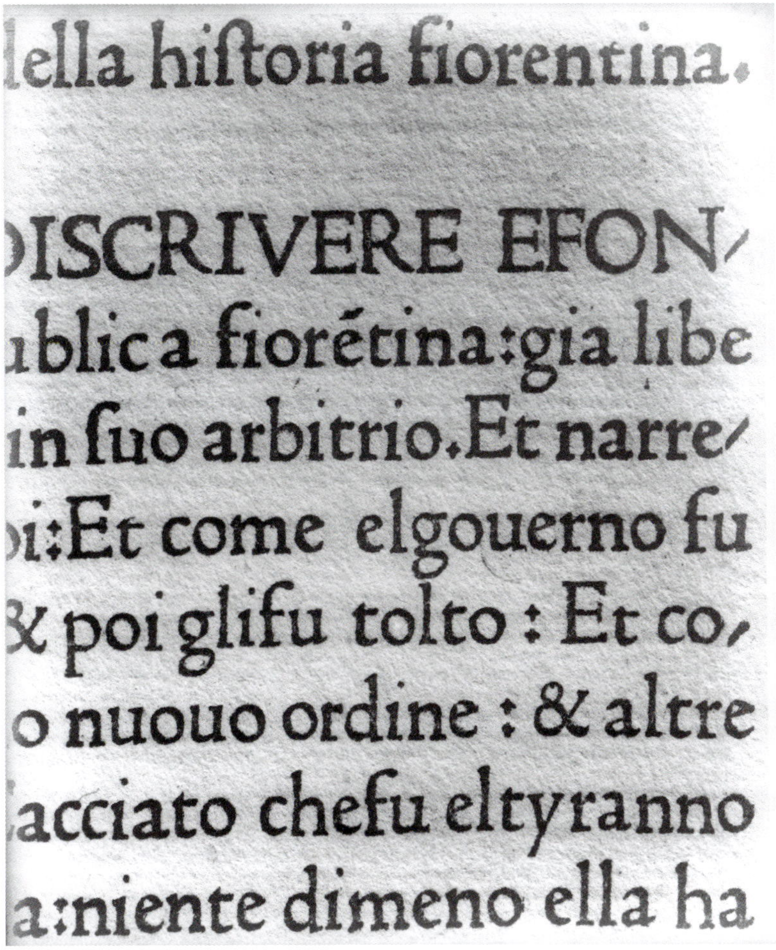
ella hiſtoria fiorentina.
ISCRIVERE EFON/
ublica fiorẽtina:gia libe
in ſuo arbitrio.Et narre/
i:Et come elgouerno fu
& poi glifu tolto : Et co/
o nuouo ordine : & altre
acciato chefu eltyranno
a:niente dimeno ella ha

XIV.4

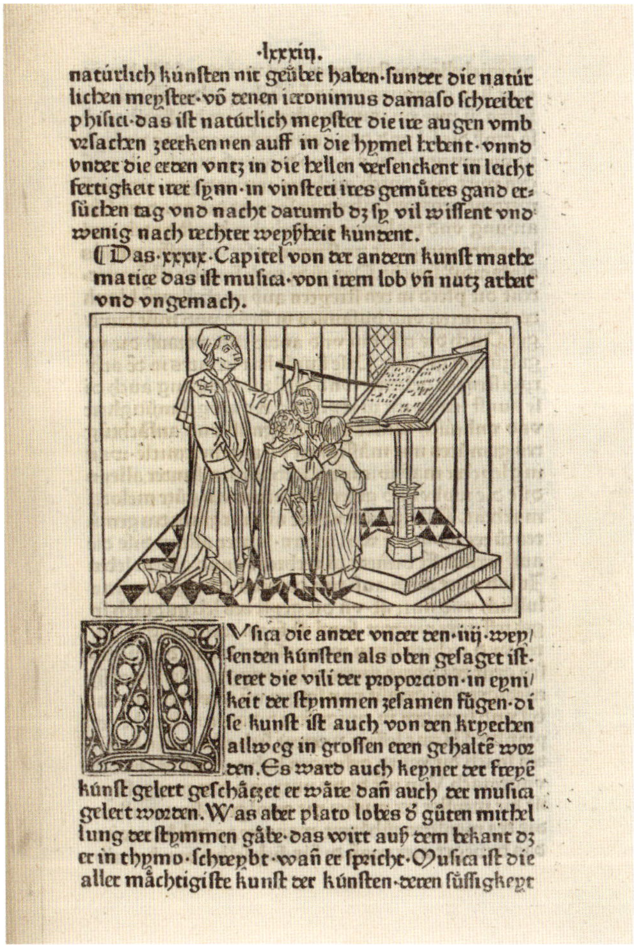
·lxxxiij.
natúrlich künſten nit geübet haben·ſunder die natúr
lichen meyſter·võ denen ieronimus damaſo ſchreibet
phiſica·das iſt natúrlich meyſter die irē augen vmb
vrſachen zeerkennen auff in die hymel kebent·vnnd
vnder die erden vntz in die hellen verſenckent in leicht
fertigkeit irer ſynn·in vinſterī ires gemútes gand er
ſúchen tag vnd nacht darumb dz ſy vil wiſſent vnd
wenig nach rechter weyßheit künnent.
¶ Das·xxxix·Capitel von der anderen kunſt mathe
matice das iſt muſica·von irem lob vñ nutz arbeit
vnd vngemach.

Vſica die ander vnder den·iiij·wey/
ſen künſten als oben geſaget iſt·
leret die vili der propoꝛcion·in eyni/
keit der ſtymmen zeſamen fügen·di
ſe kunſt iſt auch von den kriechen
allweg in groſſen eren gehaltẽ woꝛ
den.Es ward auch keyner der freyē
künſt gelert geſchätzet er wäre dañ auch der muſica
gelert worden.Was aber plato lobes ð güten mitel
lung der ſtymmen gäbe·das wirt auß dem bekant dz
er in thymo·ſchreybt·wañ er ſpricht·Muſica iſt die
aller mächtigiſte kunſt der künſten·deren ſüſſigkeyt

XIV.3
Bound volume of photographic enlargements of fifteenth-century types
Made by Emery Walker, given by William Morris to Talbot Baines Reed in 1891
38.2 x 66 cm open
St Bride Foundation, London

Morris was greatly excited in 1888 by seeing photographic enlargements of early types projected during Emery Walker's lecture on printing to the Arts and Crafts Exhibition Society. He realized that large-scale prints of Walker's slides would simplify his own detailed study of types he admired and would also allow him to draw his types on the same conveniently large scale, reduced afterwards to the sizes in which they would be cast.

Walker made enlarged prints at his photo-engraving business. A collection of these enlargements survives in an album bequeathed to the National Library of Wales by May Morris's companion, Mary Lobb (BP240). These are probably the original set used by Morris and appear alongside reproductions of medieval manuscripts, early printed books and woodcut illustrations. A duplicate set of the enlargements was made up into this album owned by Talbot Baines Reed, head of the family type foundry where the Kelmscott types were cast. Reed noted that the album contained 'enlarged photos of early Roman and Gothic type collected and presented to me by William Morris, 1891', and that the prints included 'the models of the founts designed for use in the Kelmscott books'.

The photograph illustrated shows a detail from an edition of Leonardus Brunus Aretinus's *Historiae Florentini populi* printed by Jacobus Rubeus in Venice in 1476, enlarged to five times the original size. This was one of the models that Morris used to design his Golden type.

XIV.4
***Spiegel des menschlichen lebens* [*Speculum vitae humanae*] by Rodericus Zamorensis**
Published by Günther Zainer of Augsburg, *c.*1476
Original blind-stamped pigskin binding, 32.5 x 21 cm
The Morgan Library and Museum, New York (PML 139)
Purchased with the Bennett collection, 1902

Morris purchased this book in the summer of 1890. He had a particularly high regard for the artistic qualities of woodcut books printed at Ulm and Augsburg in the fifteenth century. His essay on this subject published in 1895 asserted that the most distinguished were those printed by Günther Zainer of Augsburg and by his kinsman Johann Zainer of Ulm.

An insertion describes Morris's feelings for it: 'A vernacular edition of one of the most popular of mediaeval books ... I should call this the best of the Augsburg picture books ... These cuts together with the beautiful Augsburg "Blooming-letters", and Gunther Zainer's bold and handsome second Gothic type make up as good ornamental pages as are to be found in all typography.'

The decorated initials and woodcut illustrations in this book clearly influenced the style of woodcuts that Morris commissioned for his Press, as well as the decorated initials he designed in tribute to Zainer's sturdy, blooming letters.

XIV.5

Early designs for Troy type

William Morris, 1891

Pencil and ink, 35.6 x 39.4 cm

The Huntington Library, Art Museum and Botanical Gardens

An insight into Morris's methods of type design can be gained from this sheet of early designs for his Troy type. At the left he has traced letters from a photographic enlargement supplied by Walker. Fragments of words in ten successive lines are inked-in tracings from an edition of St Augustine's *De civitate Dei* printed at Subiaco near Rome by Conradus Sweynheym and Arnoldus Pannartz in 1467. Morris later abandoned the idea of basing his own type on this interesting pattern.

To the right of the Subiaco letters are four different versions of a lower-case alphabet (one incomplete), and a sketch for a set of capitals. None of these was based on a single specific model. The final design of Troy type differed greatly from many of the letters on this sheet, but there are nevertheless similarities in the weight and proportions shown here.

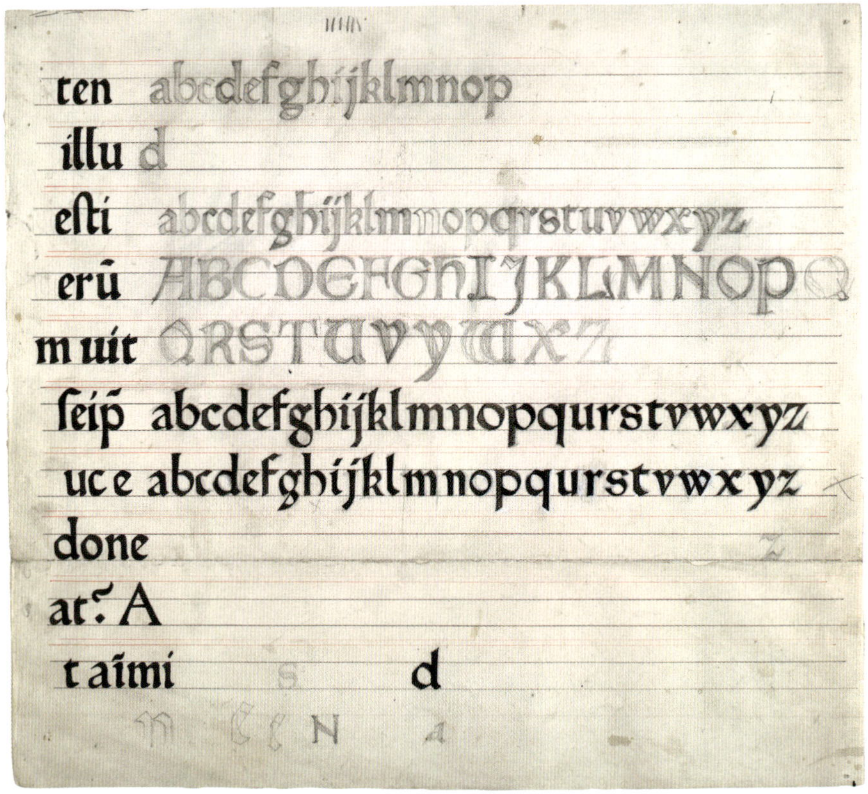

XIV.5

XIV.6

Experimental model of Troy type

William Morris, 1891

37.8 x 29.7 cm

The Wilson Art Gallery and Museum, Cheltenham (1991.1016.940)

This paste-up was made so that Morris could judge how one of his designs for an alphabet of type would look when individual letters were combined to form words. By using a paste-up, Morris was able to make a judgment without going to the expense, or through the delay, of cutting trial punches and casting an experimental fount.

It was probably assembled by draughtsmen employed by Emery Walker; his note at the foot of this sheet describes it as a 'model of "Troy" type designed by William Morris for the Kelmscott Press'. Another line in Walker's handwriting instructs that the paste-up is to be reduced with the greatest care to one fifth of its original size; the reduced print was then used to make a line-engraving, from which two or more proofs were printed, thus creating a realistic impression of how the type might look if made from the experimental model. The complete alphabet of letters used in this paste-up is seen in the last full line of XIV.5.

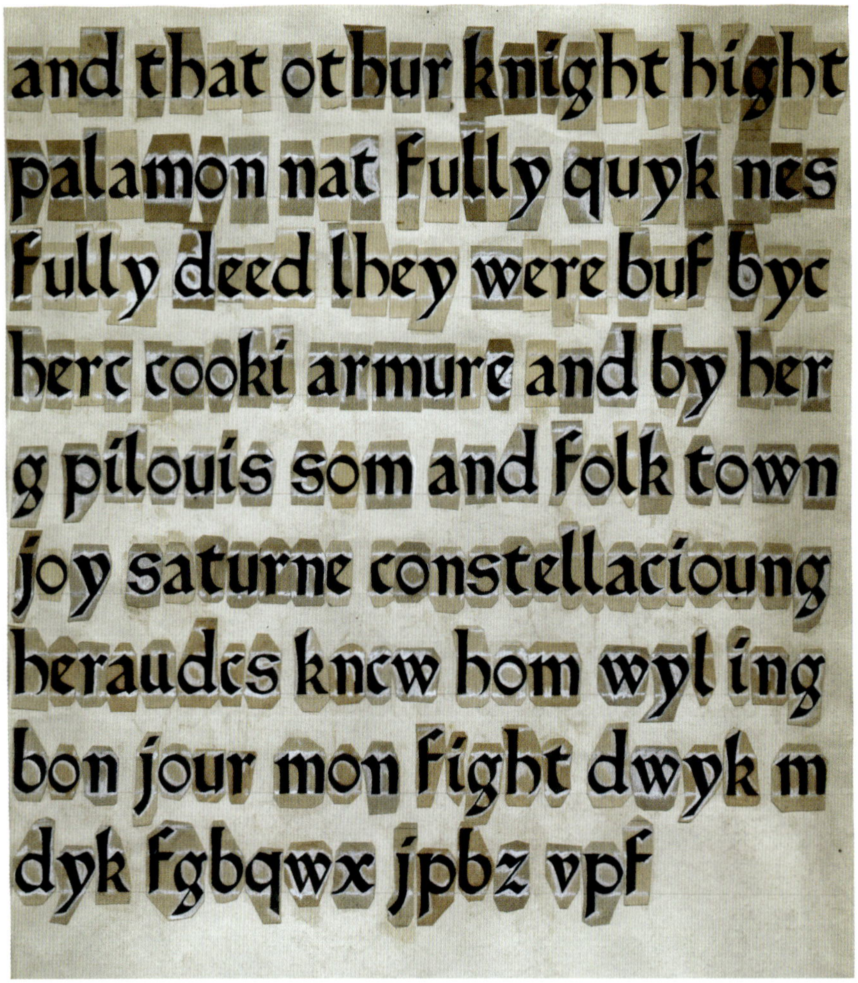

XIV.6

XIV.7

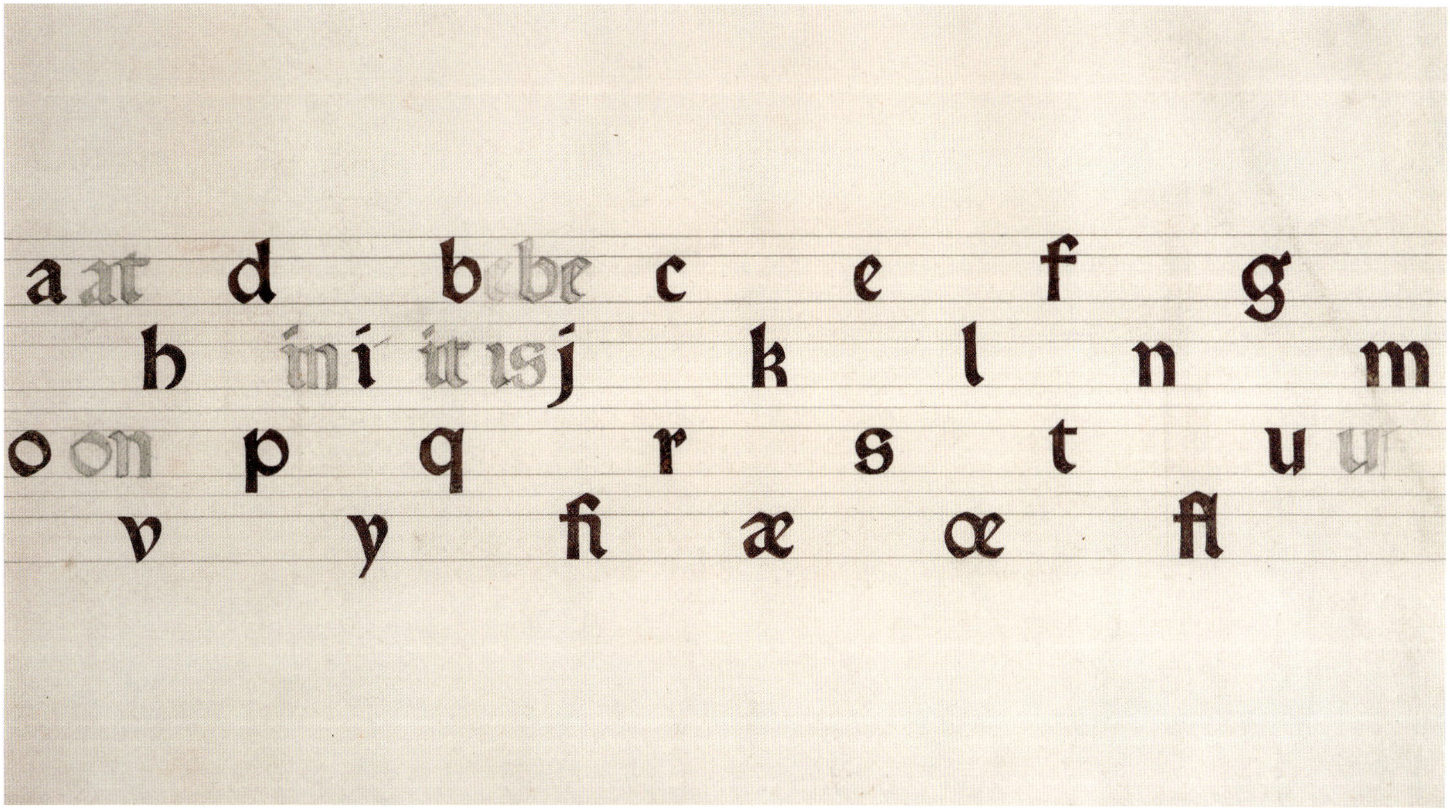

XIV.8

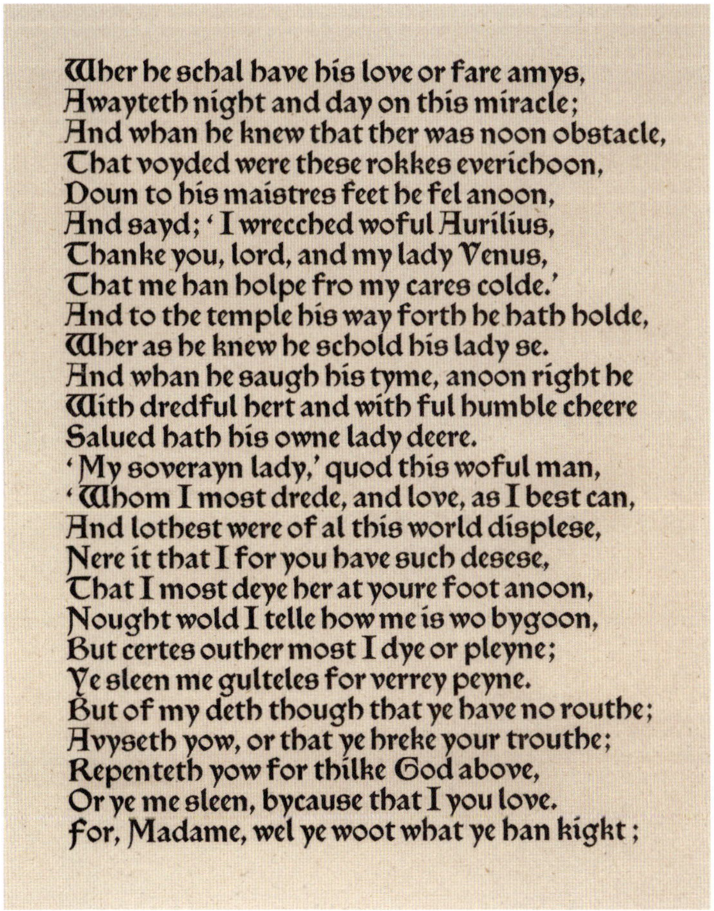

Wher he schal have his love or fare amys,
Awayteth night and day on this miracle;
And whan he knew that ther was noon obstacle,
That voyded were these rokkes everichoon,
Doun to his maistres feet he fel anoon,
And sayd; 'I wrecched woful Aurilius,
Thanke you, lord, and my lady Venus,
That me han holpe fro my cares colde.'
And to the temple his way forth he hath holde,
Wher as he knew he schold his lady se.
And whan he saugh his tyme, anoon right he
With dredful hert and with ful humble cheere
Salued hath his owne lady deere.
'My soverayn lady,' quod this woful man,
'Whom I most drede, and love, as I best can,
And lothest were of al this world displese,
Nere it that I for you have such desese,
That I most deye her at youre foot anoon,
Nought wold I telle how me is wo bygoon,
But certes outher most I dye or pleyne;
Ye sleen me gulteles for verrey peyne.
But of my deth though that ye have no routhe;
Avyseth yow, or that ye breke your trouthe;
Repenteth yow for thilke God above,
Or ye me sleen, bycause that I you love.
For, Madame, wel ye woot what ye han hight;

XIV.7
Final designs for lower-case Troy type
William Morris, 1891
Pencil and ink, 26.6 x 42 cm
The Huntington Library, Art Museum and Botanical Gardens

The letters inked-in on this sheet by Morris are very close to the shapes cut by Edward Prince for the Troy type. In a few cases Morris pencilled sketches next to an inked-in letter to indicate how it might look when adjacent to a letter of different structure.

Troy lower-case has a character of its own, even though several letters show similarities to letters found in books printed by Günther Zainer (notably g and s) and Peter Schoeffer (where similar shapes are found of a, d, e, f, m, n, o, p, r and t).

Illness prevented Morris from handing over his designs until late in the summer of 1891. Punchcutting was completed by the end of the year and a full fount cast early in 1892. On balance, the small alterations introduced by Prince during punchcutting made Morris's designs work better as cast type and Morris paid tribute to his 'intelligence and skill'.

XIV.8
Specimen of Troy type
Designed by William Morris, 1891
29 x 20.4 cm
The Huntington Library, Art Museum and Botanical Gardens

The text of this specimen is taken from 'The Franklin's Tale' by Chaucer. It is one of several specimens set in Troy type late in 1891, all using passages from the same tale. This indicates that, as soon as he could, Morris began to test Troy's suitability for his ambitious plan to print Chaucer's works. However, for such a lengthy text it proved impractical to use a type as large as Troy, so a smaller 12-point size of the same design was cut between February and May 1892 and was named Chaucer. Production of the Chaucer type was preceded by trial photographic reductions; these were sensitively interpreted by Prince when he cut the smaller version.

The capital I in this specimen looks as if it had crept in from a Roman fount. Morris replaced it by a more Gothic form with swirling, asymmetrical serifs (final strokes at the top and bottom of the letter), taking further an idea that he had sketched in pencil (see XIV.5).

XIV.9

Punches, matrices and type (resting on matrix) for the Kelmscott Press

Various sizes

The Syndics of Cambridge University Library

Morris's drawings for his types were reduced photographically to the sizes in which they were needed. These reduced prints were then used by Edward Prince as a model for the letters he cut on steel punches. Before steel is hardened (by exposure to great heat followed at once by immersion in cold water), it is relatively easy to file and cut; but the punchcutter's task requires exceptional co-ordination of eye and hand, and a deep understanding of the factors that make a set of types combine into evenly spaced and perfectly aligned words.

Punches (XIV.9a) are needed for each letter and sign in order to strike a reverse impression into a matrix made of softer metal. Matrices (XIV.9b) are then attached to a casting machine. This produces founts of type (XIV.9c) in a mixture of lead, antimony and other ingredients, strong enough to withstand the pressure of a hand press.

After Prince cut the Kelmscott Press types, he was engaged to cut punches for other prominent private presses in England, Germany, the Netherlands and the USA – notably for the Doves, Vale, Ashendene, Essex House, Cranach, Zilverdistel and Merrymount presses.

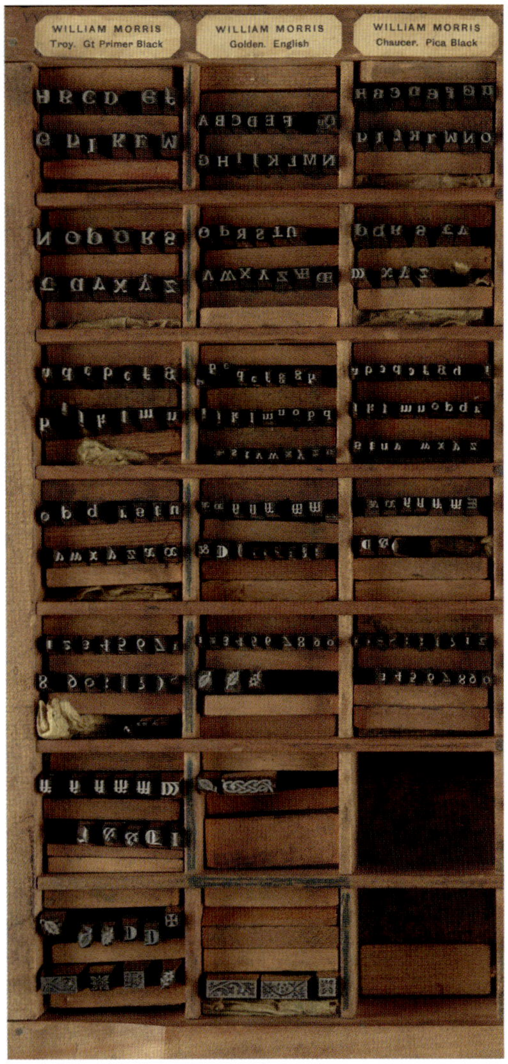

XIV.9a

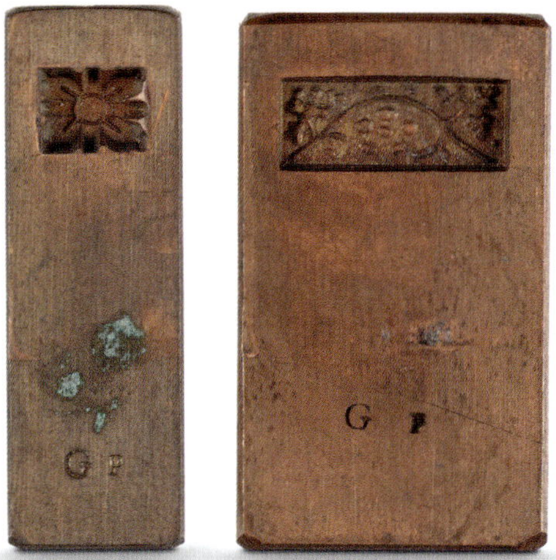

XIV.9b

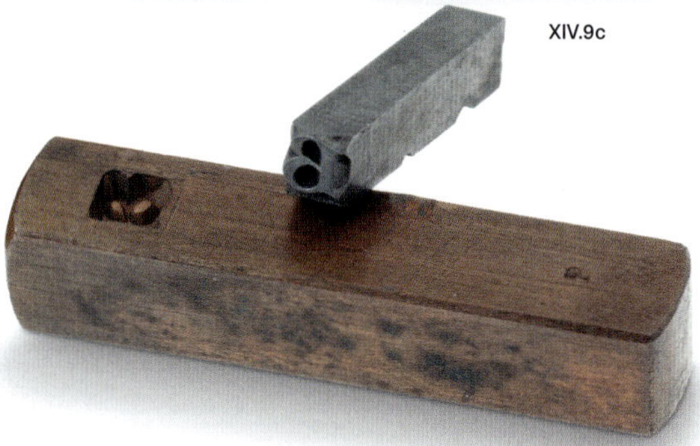

XIV.9c

XIV.10

***The Story of the Glittering Plain* by William Morris**

Kelmscott Press, issued 8 May 1891

Paper, 19.9 x 14 cm leaf

National Art Library, V&A (L.1620–1893)

Purchased for £6 10s. from John & James Leighton

This was the first book issued by the Kelmscott Press. In the autumn of 1890 Morris planned to print this story with illustrations by Walter Crane. After serious problems delayed publication of *The Golden Legend* (XIV.12), which Morris had intended to be the first Kelmscott book and the first use of his Golden type, he decided to publish his story without waiting for Crane's illustrations; these were published in a later edition (XIV.19).

Morris created an inviting and restful page with his Golden type. Ornamentation was restricted to one border and some six- and ten-line initials, which he designed. Six copies were printed on vellum imported from Rome about 20 years earlier for his calligraphic experiments.

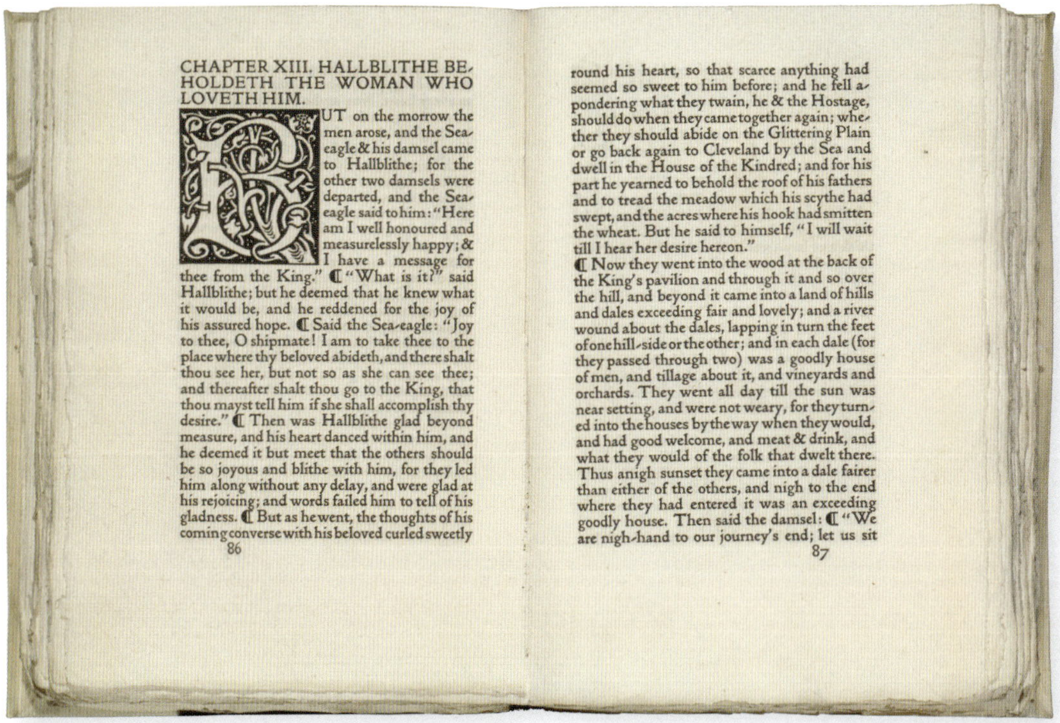

CHAPTER XIII. HALLBLITHE BEHOLDETH THE WOMAN WHO LOVETH HIM.

BUT on the morrow the men arose, and the Sea-eagle & his damsel came to Hallblithe; for the other two damsels were departed, and the Sea-eagle said to him: "Here am I well honoured and measurelessly happy; & I have a message for thee from the King." ¶ "What is it?" said Hallblithe; but he deemed that he knew what it would be, and he reddened for the joy of his assured hope. ¶ Said the Sea-eagle: "Joy to thee, O shipmate! I am to take thee to the place where thy beloved abideth, and there shalt thou see her, but not so as she can see thee; and thereafter shalt thou go to the King, that thou mayst tell him if she shall accomplish thy desire." ¶ Then was Hallblithe glad beyond measure, and his heart danced within him, and he deemed it but meet that the others should be so joyous and blithe with him, for they led him along without any delay, and were glad at his rejoicing; and words failed him to tell of his gladness. ¶ But as he went, the thoughts of his coming converse with his beloved curled sweetly

86

round his heart, so that scarce anything had seemed so sweet to him before; and he fell a-pondering what they twain, he & the Hostage, should do when they came together again; whether they should abide on the Glittering Plain or go back again to Cleveland by the Sea and dwell in the House of the Kindred; and for his part he yearned to behold the roof of his fathers and to tread the meadow which his scythe had swept, and the acres where his hook had smitten the wheat. But he said to himself, "I will wait till I hear her desire hereon."

¶ Now they went into the wood at the back of the King's pavilion and through it and so over the hill, and beyond it came into a land of hills and dales exceeding fair and lovely; and a river wound about the dales, lapping in turn the feet of one hill-side or the other; and in each dale (for they passed through two) was a goodly house of men, and tillage about it, and vineyards and orchards. They went all day till the sun was near setting, and were not weary, for they turned into the houses by the way when they would, and had good welcome, and meat & drink, and what they would of the folk that dwelt there. Thus anigh sunset they came into a dale fairer than either of the others, and nigh to the end where they had entered it was an exceeding goodly house. Then said the damsel: ¶ "We are nigh-hand to our journey's end; let us sit

87

XIV.10

XIV.11

The Love-Lyrics* & *Songs of Proteus
by Wilfrid Scawen Blunt
Kelmscott Press, issued 27 February 1892
Paper, 20.5 x 14.2 cm leaf
National Art Library, V&A (L.888–1893)
Purchased for £2 12*s.* from John & James Leighton

The poet Wilfrid Scawen Blunt was a friend of the Morris family. It is not known whether Morris was aware that his wife was having an affair with Blunt when he agreed to print these poems. Jane read and criticized both manuscript and proofs. Blunt had visited the Kelmscott Press while its second publication, Morris's *Poems by the Way*, was being printed in red and black; he remarked in his diary, 'most beautiful they are with their rubrics'.

On 19 November 1890, Morris informed Blunt, 'I shall of course be very pleased to print your book, if I may have my own way about the get up – which, I take it is what you want.' In fact, Blunt persuaded Morris against his better judgment to print the large initials in red. When Morris saw the finished book, he commented that it looked very gay and pretty with its red letters, but he never again used red in this way.

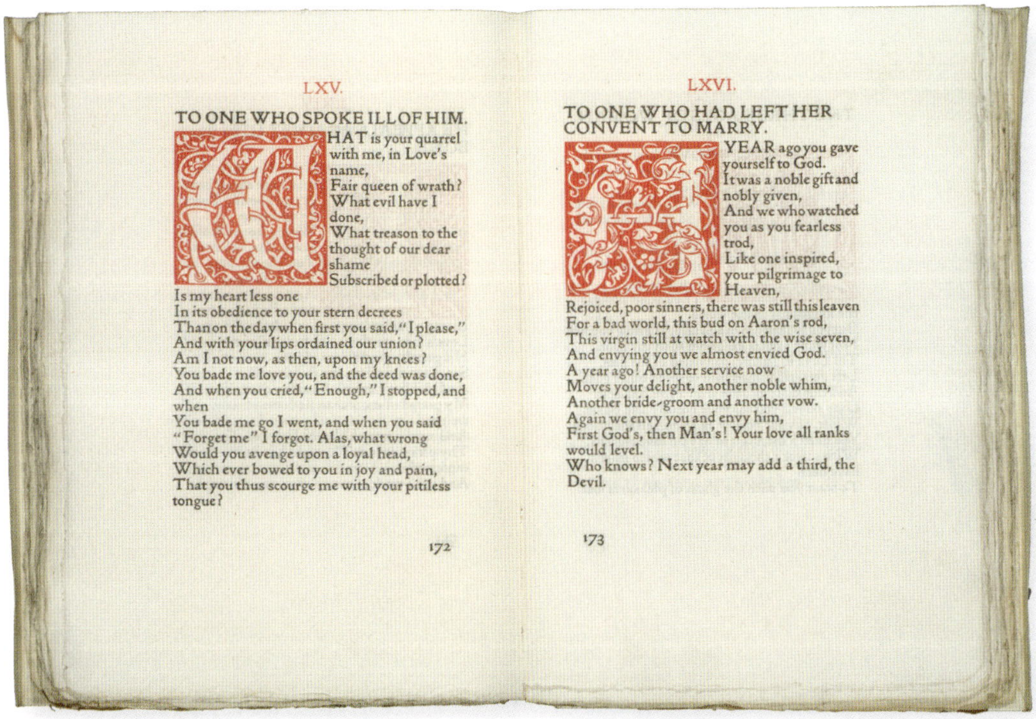

XIV.11

XIV.12a

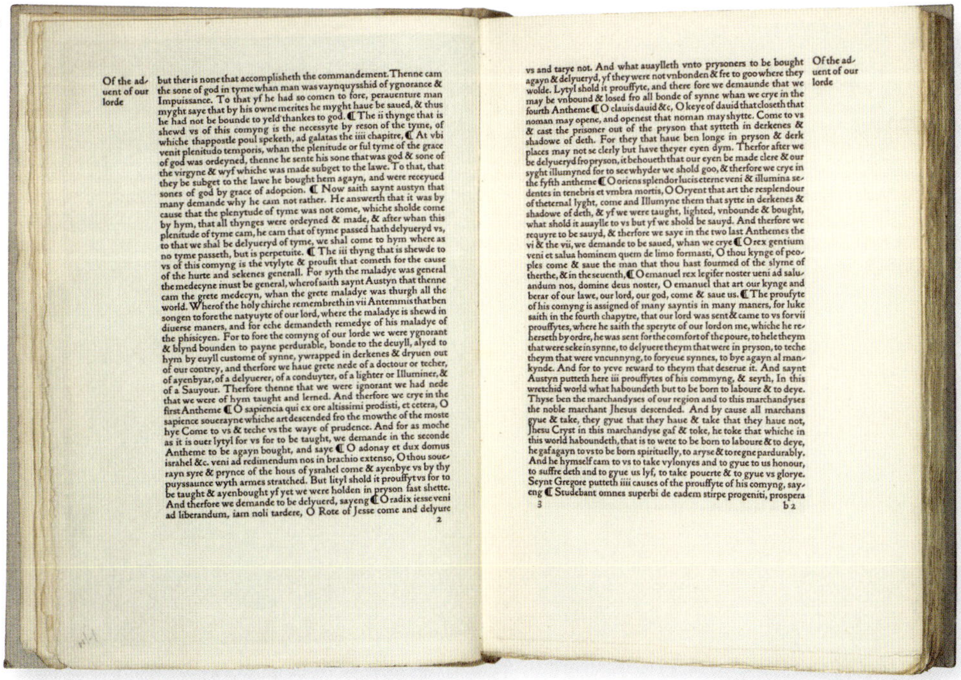

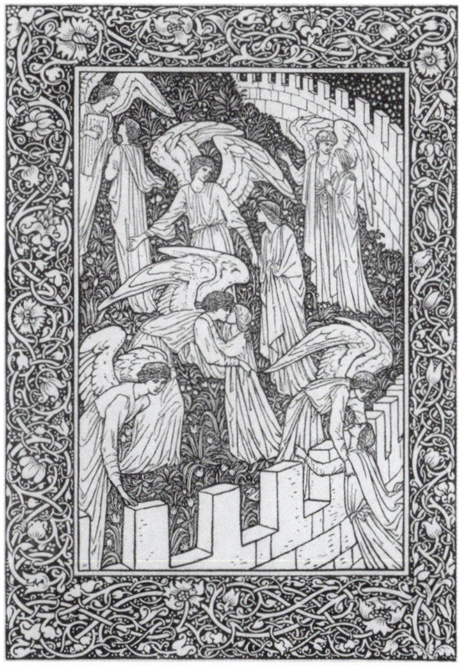

XIV.12b

XIV.12

***The Golden Legend* by Jacobus de Voragine, translated by William Caxton, Volume I**

a Kelmscott Press, issued 3 November 1892
Paper, 28.7 x 20.5 cm leaf
William Morris Gallery, London Borough of Waltham Forest (K17a)

b Trial proof sheet
Paper, 31 x 24.8 cm
V&A (E.1784–1920)

'The most superbly beautiful book that ever, I should think, came from any press', was the opinion of the poet Algernon Swinburne. This medieval collection of saints' lives had been intended as the first publication of the Press and was the reason why Morris named his first type Golden. But the immense task of transcribing the text from Caxton's 1483 edition, preparing it for publication and creating the decorations and illustrations could not be rushed. Two illustrations by Burne-Jones were his first contributions to the Kelmscott Press. The edition also contained the first woodcut title designed by Morris.

This was the first Kelmscott edition to be sold by Bernard Quaritch. His contract with Morris and Frederick Ellis (who edited the text and whose daughter, Phyllis, made the transcription) specified: 'Mr Morris to have absolute and sole control over choice of paper, choice of type, size of the reprint and selection of the printer.' Unfortunately the publication of this work gave rise to several misunderstandings between Morris and Quaritch, which soured their dealings.

XIV.13

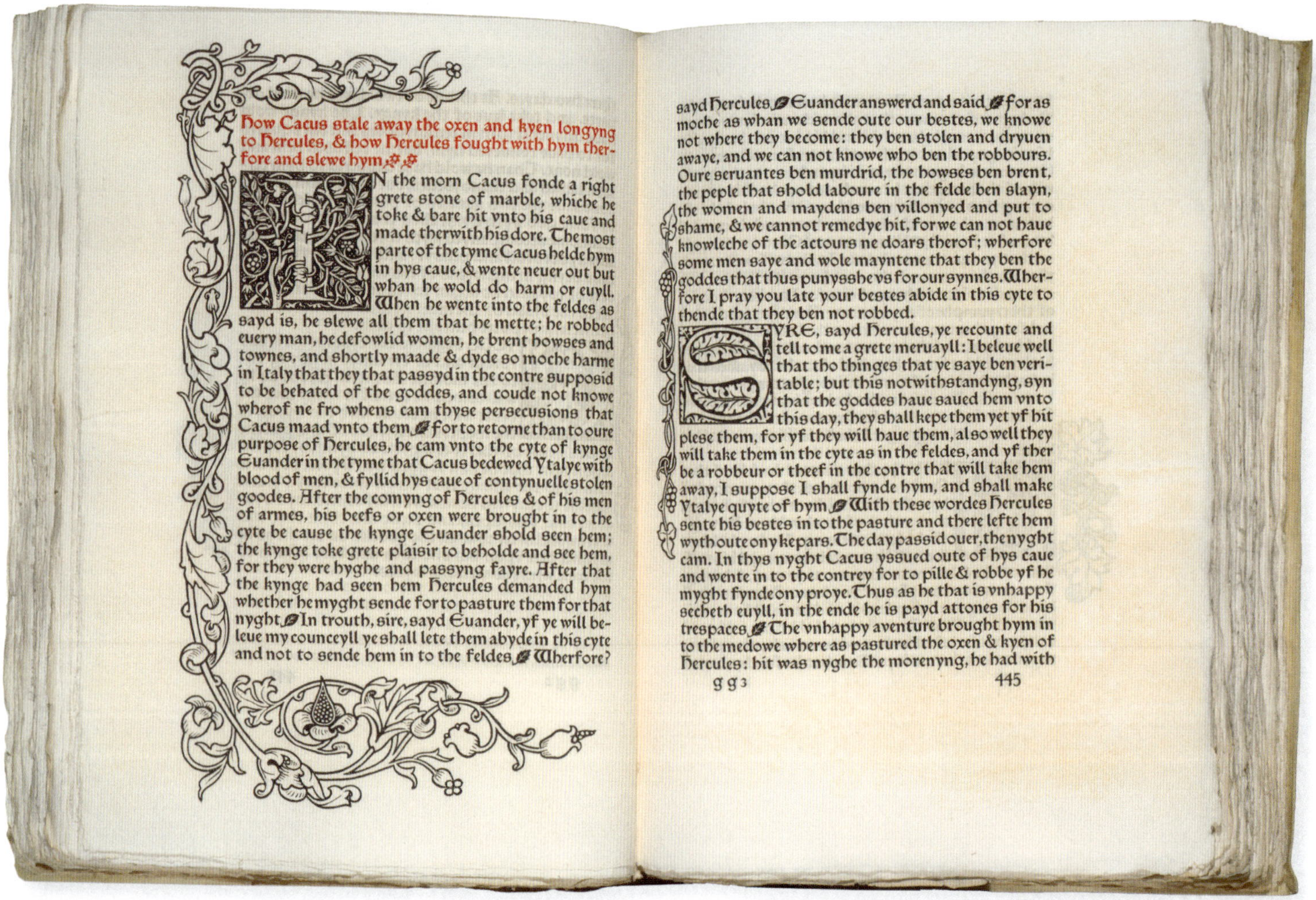

How Cacus stale away the oxen and kyen longyng to Hercules, & how Hercules fought with hym therfore and slewe hym

IN the morn Cacus fonde a right grete stone of marble, whiche he toke & bare hit vnto his caue and made therwith his dore. The most parte of the tyme Cacus helde hym in hys caue, & wente neuer out but whan he wold do harm or euyll. When he wente into the feldes as sayd is, he slewe all them that he mette; he robbed euery man, he defowlid women, he brent howses and townes, and shortly maade & dyde so moche harme in Italy that they that passyd in the contre supposid to be behated of the goddes, and coude not knowe wherof ne fro whens cam thyse persecusions that Cacus maad vnto them. For to retorne than to oure purpose of Hercules, he cam vnto the cyte of kynge Euander in the tyme that Cacus bedewed Ytalye with blood of men, & fyllid hys caue of contynuelle stolen goodes. After the comyng of Hercules & of his men of armes, his beefs or oxen were brought in to the cyte be cause the kynge Euander shold seen hem; the kynge toke grete plaisir to beholde and see hem, for they were hyghe and passyng fayre. After that the kynge had seen hem Hercules demanded hym whether he myght sende for to pasture them for that nyght. In trouth, sire, sayd Euander, yf ye will beleue my counceyll ye shall lete them abyde in this cyte and not to sende hem in to the feldes. Wherfore? sayd Hercules. Euander answerd and said, for as moche as whan we sende oute our bestes, we knowe not where they become: they ben stolen and dryuen awaye, and we can not knowe who ben the robbours. Oure seruantes ben murdrid, the howses ben brent, the peple that shold laboure in the felde ben slayn, the women and maydens ben villonyed and put to shame, & we cannot remedye hit, for we can not haue knowleche of the actours ne doars therof; wherfore some men saye and wole mayntene that they ben the goddes that thus punysshe vs for our synnes. Wherfore I pray you late your bestes abide in this cyte to thende that they ben not robbed.

SYRE, sayd Hercules, ye recounte and tell to me a grete meruayll: I beleue well that tho thinges that ye saye ben veritable; but this notwithstandyng, syn that the goddes haue saued hem vnto this day, they shall kepe them yet yf hit plese them, for yf they will haue them, also well they will take them in the cyte as in the feldes, and yf ther be a robbeur or theef in the contre that will take hem away, I suppose I shall fynde hym, and shall make Ytalye quyte of hym. With these wordes Hercules sente his bestes in to the pasture and there lefte hem wythoute ony kepars. The day passid ouer, the nyght cam. In thys nyght Cacus yssued oute of hys caue and wente in to the contrey for to pille & robbe yf he myght fynde ony proye. Thus as he that is vnhappy secheth euyll, in the ende he is payd attones for his trespaces. The vnhappy aventure brought hym in to the medowe where as pastured the oxen & kyen of Hercules: hit was nyghe the morenyng, he had with

gg3 445

XIV.13

***The Recuyell of the Historyes of Troye* by Raoul Lefèvre, translated by William Caxton, Volume II**

Kelmscott Press, issued 24 November 1892

Paper, 28.7 x 20.5 cm leaf

National Art Library, V&A (L.894–1893)

Purchased for £9 9*s*. from John & James Leighton

Three weeks after *The Golden Legend* (XIV.12) was published, Morris issued the first book set in his second type – Troy, so named because it had been planned from the outset to make its first appearance in this title. As well as using Troy for the text, the smaller size of the same design (named Chaucer) was used in the table of contents and glossary.

The beauty of the edition is entirely the result of Morris's typographical and decorative gifts. There are no illustrations, but Morris makes superb use of corner and marginal decorations, inspired by Johann Zainer's woodcuts of 1473.

Commending the text to Quaritch's customers, Morris wrote that it made a 'thoroughly amusing story, instinct with mediæval thought and manners. For though written at the end of the Middle Ages and dealing with classical mythology, it has in it no token of the coming "Renaissance" but is purely mediæval ... Surely this is well worth reading, if only as a piece of undiluted Mediævalism.'

XIV.14

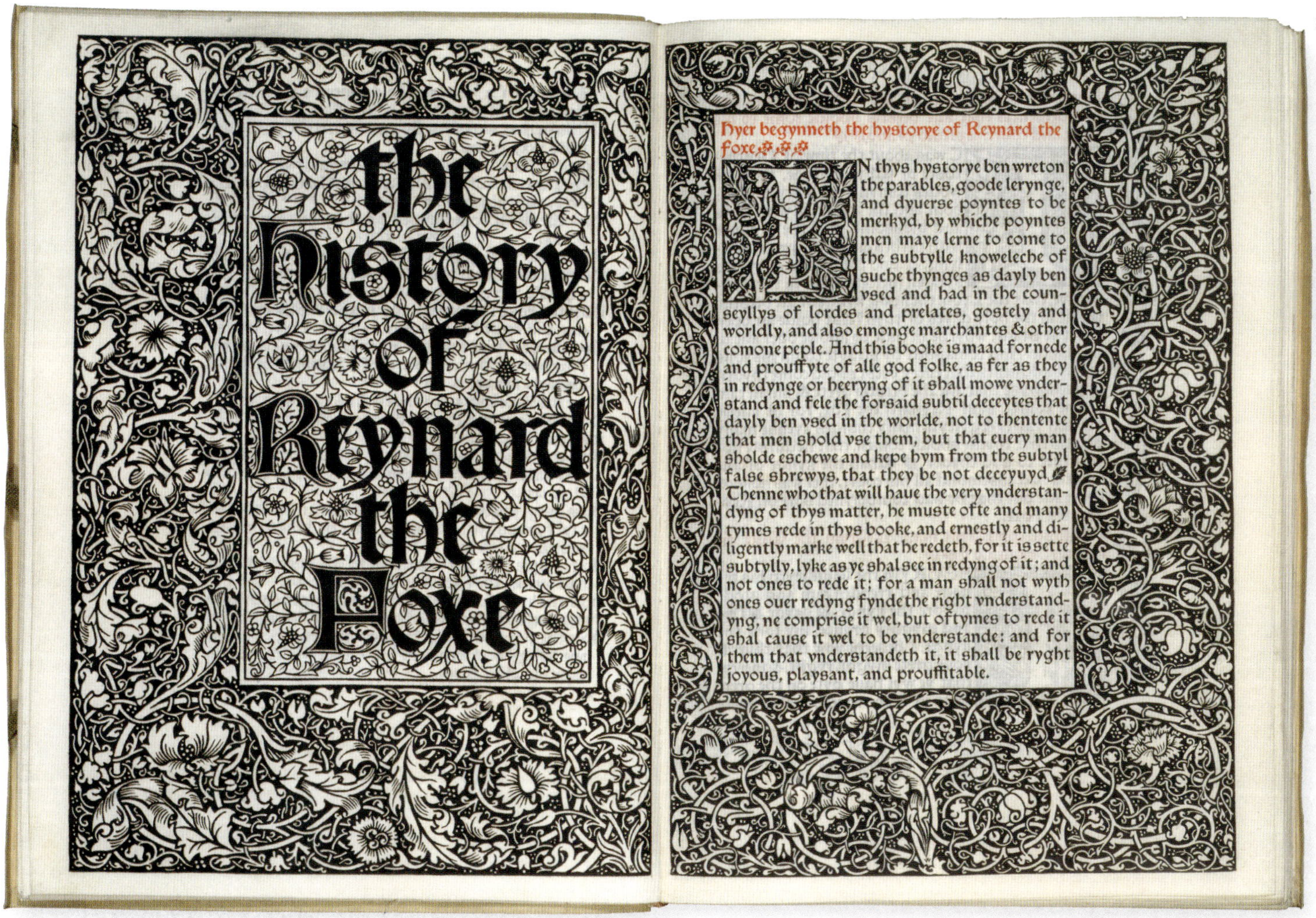

XIV.14

***The History of Reynard the Foxe*, translated by William Caxton**
Kelmscott Press, issued 25 January 1893
Vellum, 28.7 x 20.5 cm leaf
National Art Library, V&A (L.1134–1893)
Purchased for £16 10*s*. from John & James Leighton

This was the third Caxton edition to be reprinted by Morris, who published it in the same format as *The Golden Legend* and *The Historyes of Troye*. His approach to editing Caxton's texts was explained by his son-in-law, Henry Halliday Sparling, who is mentioned in the colophon as having corrected this book for press. Caxton's texts were to be taken as a basis but were not to be looked upon as 'archaeologically sacrosanct'. Mistranslations were to be put right and omissions filled in, taking care to preserve Caxton's style and flavour.

Ten copies were printed on vellum, twice as many as were produced for *The Historyes of Troye*, although 300 copies of each were printed on paper.

XIV.15

Proof of title-page for *The History of Reynard the Foxe*
Designed by William Morris, 1893
Paper, 41.3 x 27.3 cm
The Huntington Library, Art Museum and Botanical Gardens

This is the only Kelmscott Press title-page to have been proofed in colour. It is not clear why this design was proofed in red, but as another proof in red has survived with the inner lettered panel cut away, the purpose may have been to simulate the effect of a red frame surrounding the lettered panel printed in black. Apparently, Morris decided that the effect was too strident for his taste. (For his reluctance to print large initials in red, see XIV.11.)

XIV.15

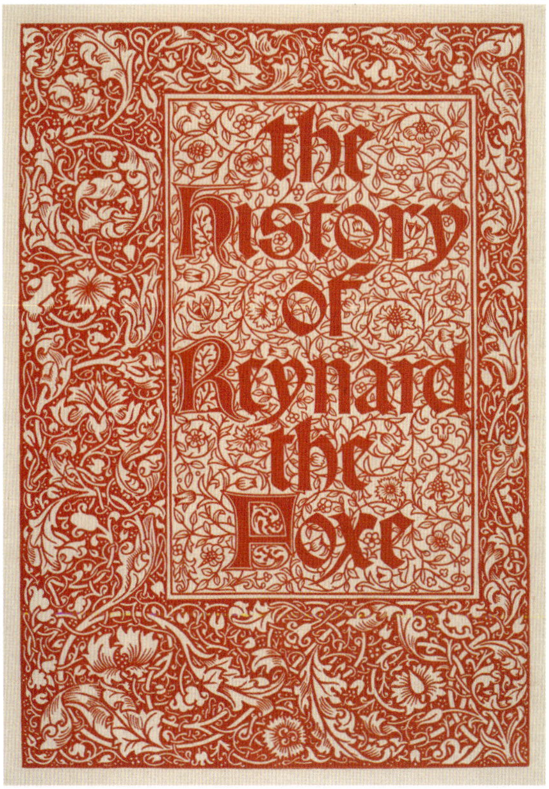

XIV.16a

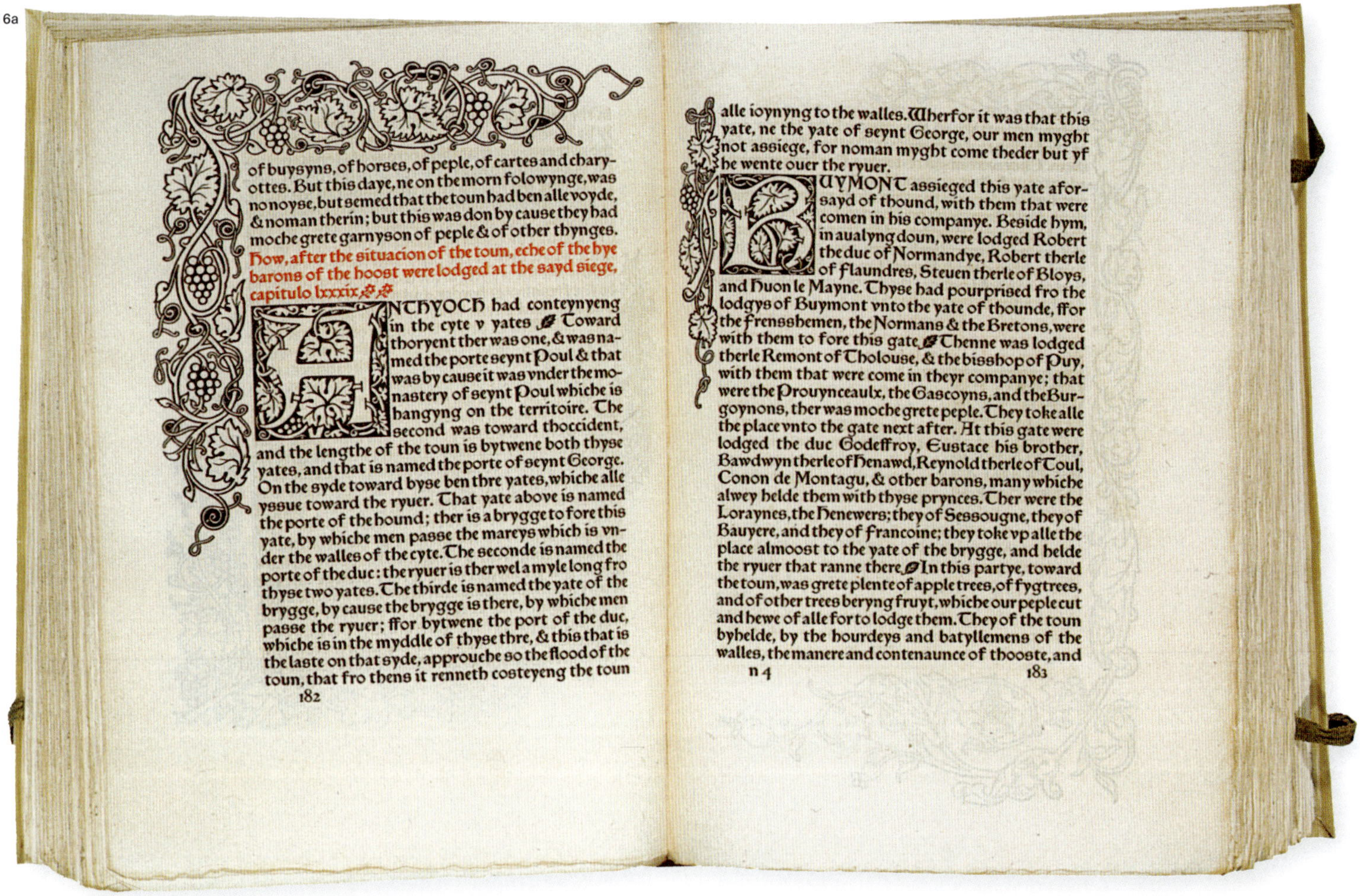

of buysyns, of horses, of peple, of cartes and chary-
ottes. But this daye, ne on the morn folowynge, was
no noyse, but semed that the toun had ben alle voyde,
& noman therin; but this was don by cause they had
moche grete garnyson of peple & of other thynges.
How, after the situacion of the toun, eche of the hye
barons of the hoost were lodged at the sayd siege,
capitulo lxxxix.
ANTHYOCH had conteynyeng
in the cyte v yates. Toward
thoryent ther was one, & was na-
med the porte seynt Poul & that
was by cause it was vnder the mo-
nastery of seynt Poul whiche is
hangyng on the territoire. The
second was toward thoccident,
and the lengthe of the toun is bytwene both thyse
yates, and that is named the porte of seynt George.
On the syde toward hyse ben thre yates, whiche alle
yssue toward the ryuer. That yate above is named
the porte of the hound; ther is a brygge to fore this
yate, by whiche men passe the mareys which is vn-
der the walles of the cyte. The seconde is named the
porte of the duc: the ryuer is ther wel a myle long fro
thyse two yates. The thirde is named the yate of the
brygge, by cause the brygge is there, by whiche men
passe the ryuer; ffor bytwene the port of the duc,
whiche is in the myddle of thyse thre, & this that is
the laste on that syde, approuche so the flood of the
toun, that fro thens it renneth costeyeng the toun
182

alle ioynyng to the walles. Wherfor it was that this
yate, ne the yate of seynt George, our men myght
not assiege, for noman myght come theder but yf
he wente ouer the ryuer.
BUYMONT assieged this yate afor-
sayd of thound, with them that were
comen in his companye. Beside hym,
in aualyng doun, were lodged Robert
the duc of Normandye, Robert therle
of flaundres, Steuen therle of Bloys,
and Huon le Mayne. Thyse had pourprised fro the
lodgys of Buymont vnto the yate of thounde, ffor
the frensshemen, the Normans & the Bretons, were
with them to fore this gate. Thenne was lodged
therle Remont of Tholouse, & the bisshop of Puy,
with them that were come in theyr companye; that
were the Prouynceaulx, the Gascoyns, and the Bur-
goynons, ther was moche grete peple. They toke alle
the place vnto the gate next after. At this gate were
lodged the duc Godeffroy, Eustace his brother,
Bawdwyn therle of Henawd, Reynold therle of Toul,
Conon de Montagu, & other barons, many whiche
alwey helde them with thyse prynces. Ther were the
Loraynes, the Henewers; they of Sessougne, they of
Bauyere, and they of francoine; they toke vp alle the
place almoost to the yate of the brygge, and helde
the ryuer that ranne there. In this partye, toward
the toun, was grete plente of apple trees, of fygtrees,
and of other trees beryng fruyt, whiche our peple cut
and hewe of alle for to lodge them. They of the toun
byhelde, by the hourdeys and batyllemens of the
walles, the manere and contenaunce of thooste, and
n 4 183

XIV.16
The History of Godefrey of Boloyne **by Guilelmus, Archbishop of Tyre, translated by William Caxton**

a Kelmscott Press, issued 24 May 1893
Paper, 28.7 x 20.5 cm leaf
National Art Library, V&A (L.897–1893)
Purchased for £6 6s. from John & James Leighton

b Three border designs
William Morris
Ink and Chinese white, 22.7 x 24.6 cm
V&A (D.1558 to 1560–1907)
Purchased from Sydney Carlyle Cockerell

Once again Morris chose a Caxton text, arguing that this one 'must from a literary point of view be considered one of Caxton's most important works'. He did not regard it as a romance, as it had been called by others, but a very serious piece of history. He found Caxton's style vigorous and agreeable and altogether 'a delightful book to read'. It also inspired him to design a profusion of new ornaments. The decorative scheme was similar to that used in his previous two quartos (XIV.13–14).

He designed an intricate title-page, numerous borders varying in size from side and corner units to half- and three-quarter borders. In addition, he drew six- and eight-line initials, most of them with floral or vine patterns. His second printer's mark made its first appearance in this book.

The total effect may have been too powerful for some Kelmscott subscribers; or perhaps too few of them shared Morris's delight in the text. For whatever reason, the edition never sold out, and in June 1897 Jane Morris gave the overstock to British public libraries.

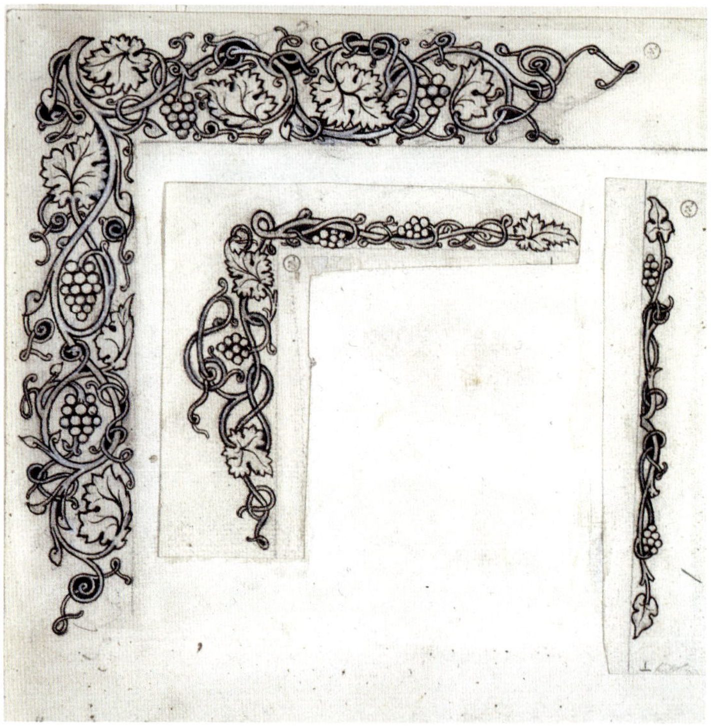

XIV.16b

XIV.17

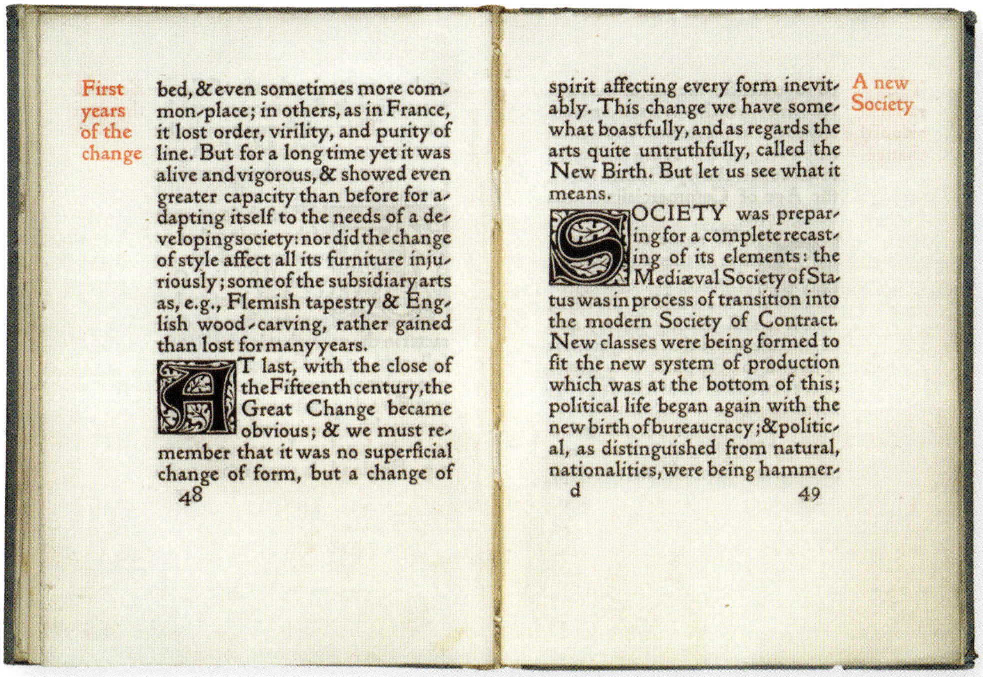

First years of the change

bed, & even sometimes more common-place; in others, as in France, it lost order, virility, and purity of line. But for a long time yet it was alive and vigorous, & showed even greater capacity than before for adapting itself to the needs of a developing society: nor did the change of style affect all its furniture injuriously; some of the subsidiary arts as, e.g., Flemish tapestry & English wood-carving, rather gained than lost for many years.

AT last, with the close of the Fifteenth century, the Great Change became obvious; & we must remember that it was no superficial change of form, but a change of

48

spirit affecting every form inevitably. This change we have somewhat boastfully, and as regards the arts quite untruthfully, called the New Birth. But let us see what it means.

A new Society

SOCIETY was preparing for a complete recasting of its elements: the Mediæval Society of Status was in process of transition into the modern Society of Contract. New classes were being formed to fit the new system of production which was at the bottom of this; political life began again with the new birth of bureaucracy; & political, as distinguished from natural, nationalities, were being hammer-

d 49

XIV.18

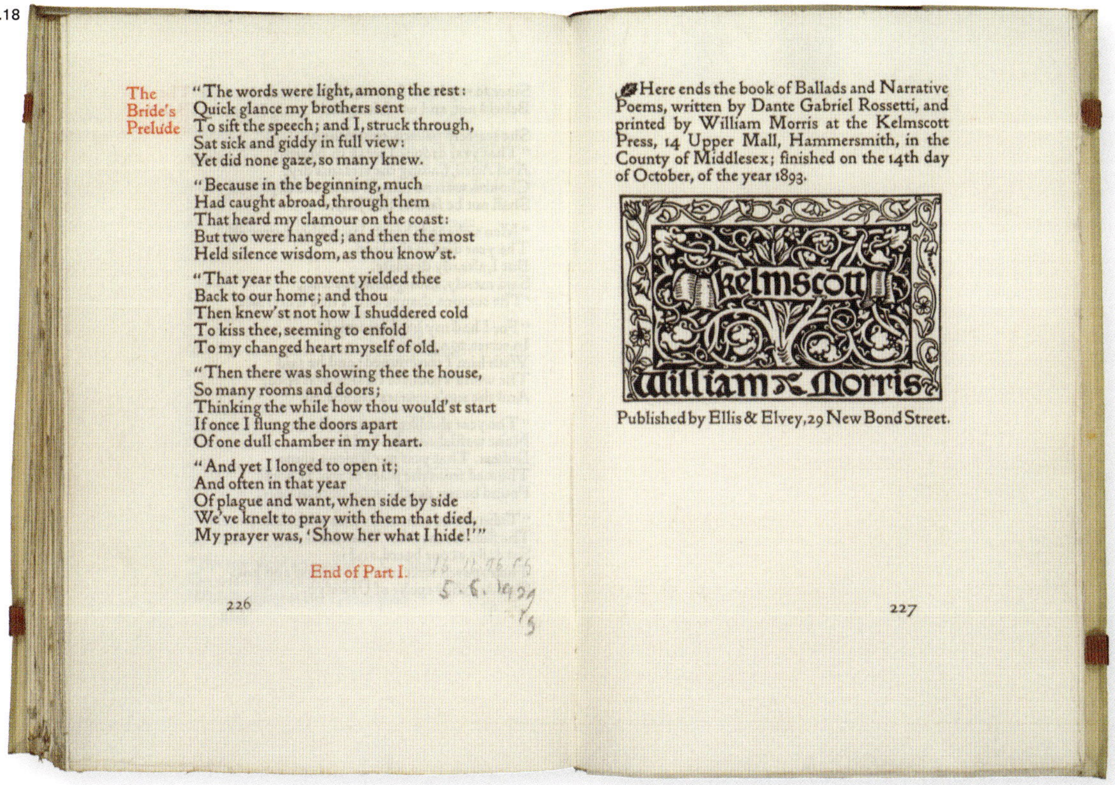

The Bride's Prelude

"The words were light, among the rest:
Quick glance my brothers sent
To sift the speech; and I, struck through,
Sat sick and giddy in full view:
Yet did none gaze, so many knew.

"Because in the beginning, much
Had caught abroad, through them
That heard my clamour on the coast:
But two were hanged; and then the most
Held silence wisdom, as thou know'st.

"That year the convent yielded thee
Back to our home; and thou
Then knew'st not how I shuddered cold
To kiss thee, seeming to enfold
To my changed heart myself of old.

"Then there was showing thee the house,
So many rooms and doors;
Thinking the while how thou would'st start
If once I flung the doors apart
Of one dull chamber in my heart.

"And yet I longed to open it;
And often in that year
Of plague and want, when side by side
We've knelt to pray with them that died,
My prayer was, 'Show her what I hide!'"

End of Part I.

226

Here ends the book of Ballads and Narrative Poems, written by Dante Gabriel Rossetti, and printed by William Morris at the Kelmscott Press, 14 Upper Mall, Hammersmith, in the County of Middlesex; finished on the 14th day of October, of the year 1893.

Published by Ellis & Elvey, 29 New Bond Street.

227

XIV.17
Gothic Architecture
by William Morris
Kelmscott Press, issued
21 October 1893
Paper, 14.3 x 10.4 cm leaf
National Art Library, V&A (L.169–1893)
Purchased for *2s. 6d.* from the Kelmscott Press

This was the first of six Kelmscott books produced in this small but elegant format. It was later used for four other texts written or translated by Morris.

He had given this lecture for the Arts and Crafts Exhibition Society in 1889. Unusually, this edition was not printed on the premises of the Kelmscott Press. Instead, one of the Kelmscott Albion presses was set up at the New Gallery, Regent Street, while the Arts and Crafts Exhibition Society held its show during October and November 1893. According to Sparling, the crowds surrounding the pressman W. Collins were so enthusiastic that they imposed a severe strain on his Celtic modesty.

It seems that three editions of about 500 copies each were printed at the New Gallery. This was an exceptionally high figure for a Kelmscott edition; the separate printings made it possible to correct some of the misprints that occurred all too often in Kelmscott books. The Golden type was used after a trial setting in Chaucer type (used for most of the later books in this format).

XIV.18
Ballads and Narrative Poems
by Dante Gabriel Rossetti
Kelmscott Press, issued
November 1893
Paper, 20.5 x 14 cm leaf
William Morris Gallery, London Borough of Waltham Forest (K446)

Early in July 1893, Morris agreed to print two volumes of poems by Rossetti, who had died in 1882, for the London publishers Ellis & Elvey. This volume was followed five months later by *Sonnets and Lyrical Poems*. Both were printed in the same format, set in Golden type and decorated with borders as well as six- and ten-line initials.

Proofs of the texts were read by the poet's younger brother, William Michael Rossetti, who supervised the books with great care. The pages illustrated include the first of three pressmarks designed by Morris for his Kelmscott editions.

XIV.19a

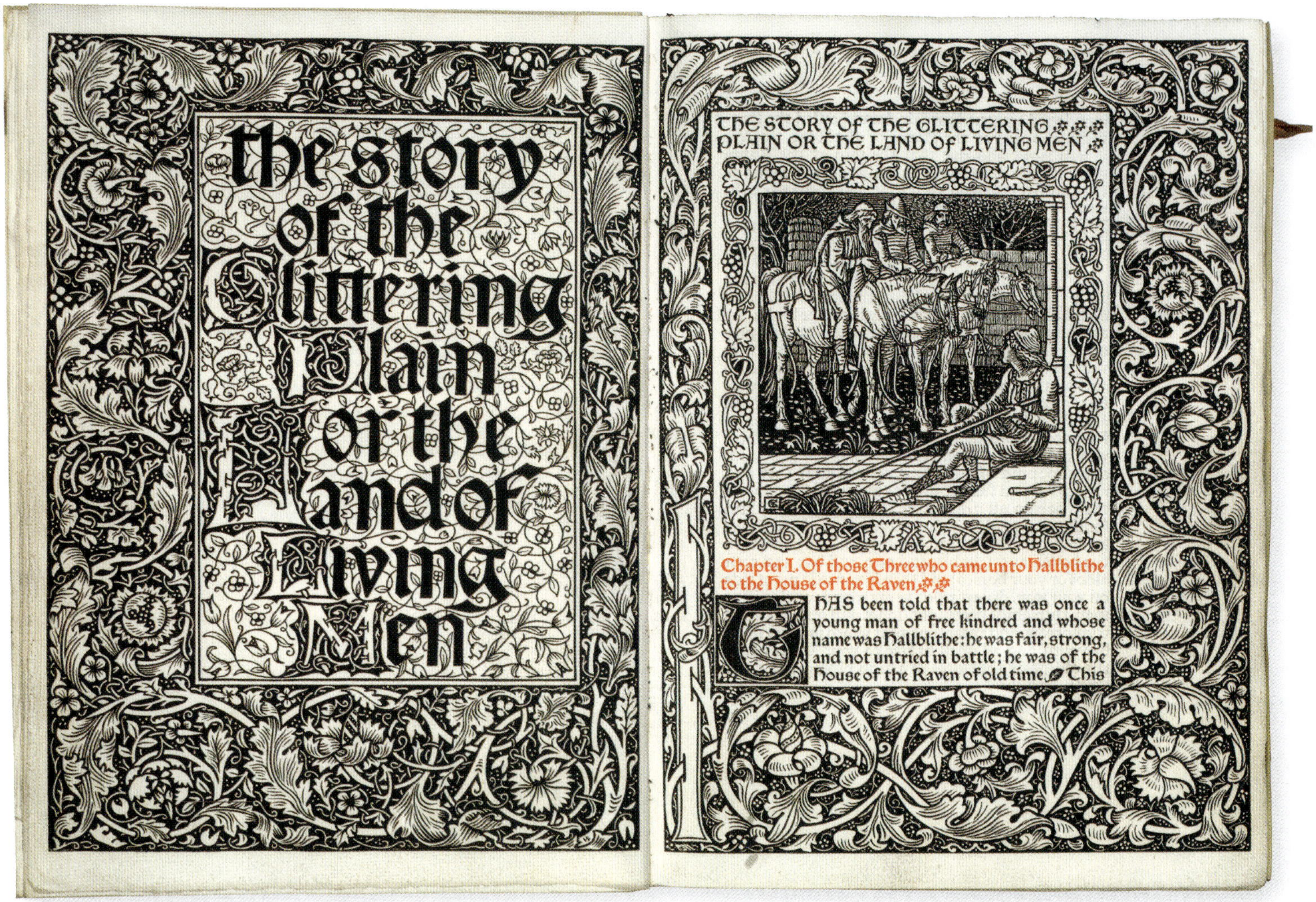

XIV.19b

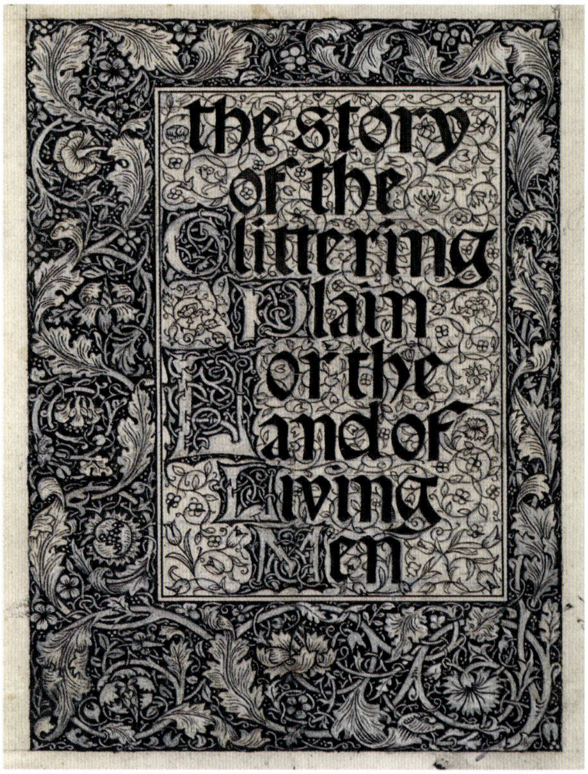

XIV.19

***The Story of the Glittering Plain* by William Morris**

a Kelmscott Press, issued
17 February 1894
Paper, 29.1 x 21 cm leaf
National Art Library, V&A (L.579–1894)
Purchased for £5 5*s*. from the Kelmscott Press

b Design for title-page
William Morris, 1894
Graphite, ink and Chinese white, 35.6 x 25.4 cm
Inscribed: 'Reduce 1/16 in width'
The Huntington Library, Art Museum and Botanical Gardens

This was the only text published in two separate editions by the Kelmscott Press. Morris was so impatient to get the first edition into print that he proceeded without the planned illustrations from Walter Crane (XIV.10). In February 1894 this second version was published in a larger format, set in his Troy type with 23 illustrations drawn by Crane and engraved on wood by Arthur Leverett.

As the sizes of type that Morris installed at his Press were restricted to those suitable for text composition, they were not large enough for displayed lines; so he produced title-page designs in which he combined his talents as a decorator with his gift for designing larger letter forms. In the fourth, fifth and sixth lines of the design for the title-page, Morris was disturbed to find a distracting vertical stress in the words 'Plain', 'the' and 'Land', created by the stems of the letters i, h and d falling so closely beneath each other. When his design was cut on wood, the three words were staggered to avoid this.

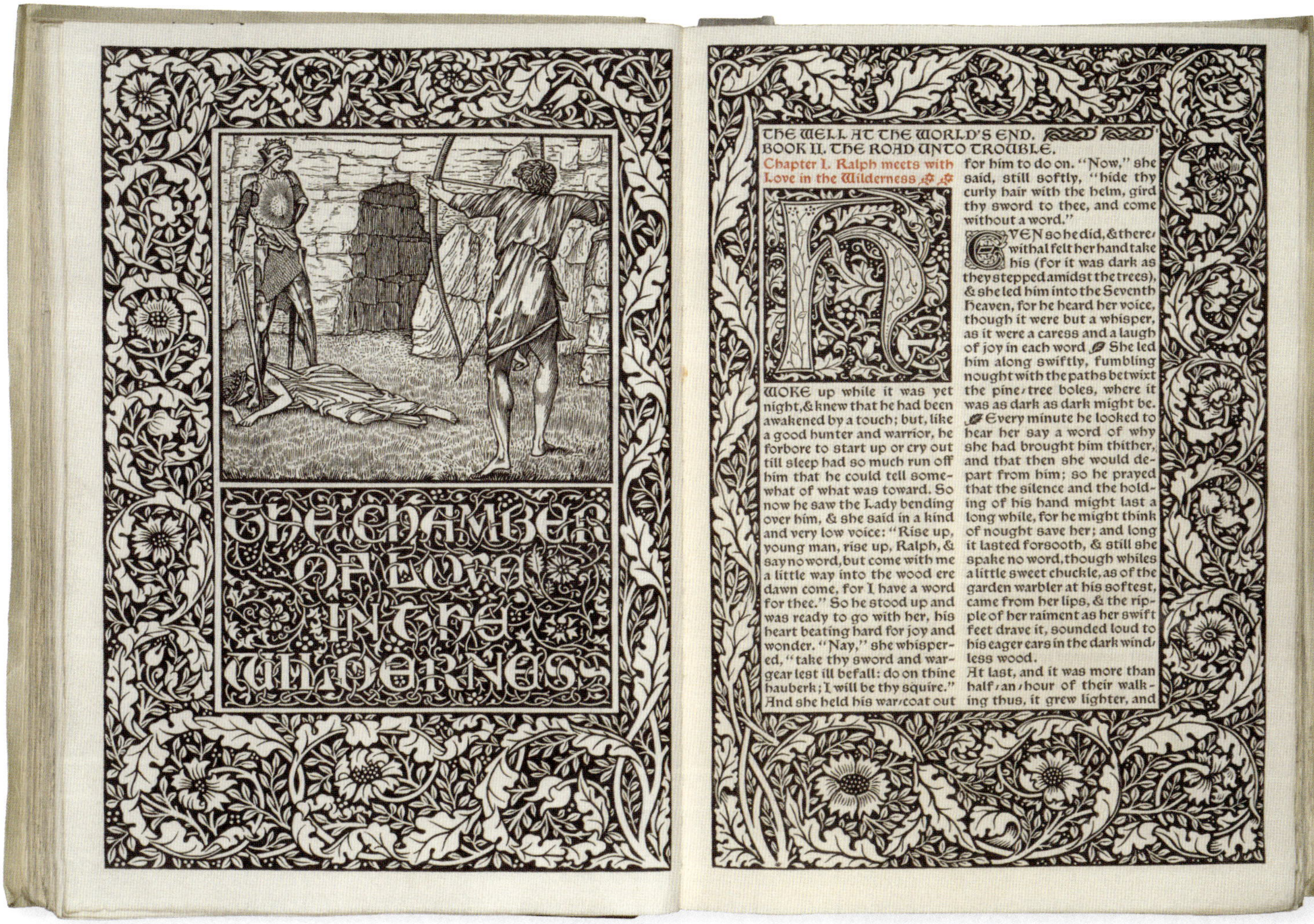

THE CHAMBER OF LOVE IN THE WILDERNESS

THE WELL AT THE WORLD'S END.
BOOK II. THE ROAD UNTO TROUBLE.
Chapter I. Ralph meets with Love in the Wilderness

HE WOKE up while it was yet night, & knew that he had been awakened by a touch; but, like a good hunter and warrior, he forbore to start up or cry out till sleep had so much run off him that he could tell somewhat of what was toward. So now he saw the Lady bending over him, & she said in a kind and very low voice: "Rise up, young man, rise up, Ralph, & say no word, but come with me a little way into the wood ere dawn come, for I have a word for thee." So he stood up and was ready to go with her, his heart beating hard for joy and wonder. "Nay," she whispered, "take thy sword and wargear lest ill befall: do on thine hauberk; I will be thy squire." And she held his war-coat out for him to do on. "Now," she said, still softly, "hide thy curly hair with the helm, gird thy sword to thee, and come without a word."

EVEN so he did, & therewithal felt her hand take his (for it was dark as they stepped amidst the trees), & she led him into the Seventh Heaven, for he heard her voice, though it were but a whisper, as it were a caress and a laugh of joy in each word. She led him along swiftly, fumbling nought with the paths betwixt the pine-tree boles, where it was as dark as dark might be. Every minute he looked to hear her say a word of why she had brought him thither, and that then she would depart from him; so he prayed that the silence and the holding of his hand might last a long while, for he might think of nought save her; and long it lasted forsooth, & still she spake no word, though whiles a little sweet chuckle, as of the garden warbler at his softest, came from her lips, & the ripple of her raiment as her swift feet drave it, sounded loud to his eager ears in the dark windless wood.

At last, and it was more than half-an-hour of their walking thus, it grew lighter, and

XIV.20

The Well at the World's End
by William Morris
Kelmscott Press, issued 4 June 1896
Paper, 28.5 x 20.4 cm leaf
National Art Library, V&A (L.688–1896)
Purchased for £4 9*s*. 3*d*. from the Kelmscott Press

This work was longer in production than any other Kelmscott book. Cockerell saw proofs in April 1892, and by October of that year Morris was busy on the borders. The main reason for the delay was the trouble Morris experienced in finding an acceptable set of illustrations for his text. Charles Fairfax Murray was named as his choice before he commissioned Arthur Gaskin, an artist of the Birmingham School and a most talented illustrator. He visited Kelmscott House in 1892 with samples of his work, which Morris admired. An extensively illustrated edition was planned, for which Gaskin received £250.

Unhappily, the outcome did not please Morris, who eventually settled for only four illustrations by Burne-Jones; that shown here is 'The Chamber of Love in the Wilderness'. These were used at the head of each 'book' with the title below lettered by Morris, who also provided a great variety of borders, initials and a 14-line initial word. The text was set in Chaucer type from Longman's trade edition, which was printed at the Chiswick Press while the Kelmscott edition was in production.

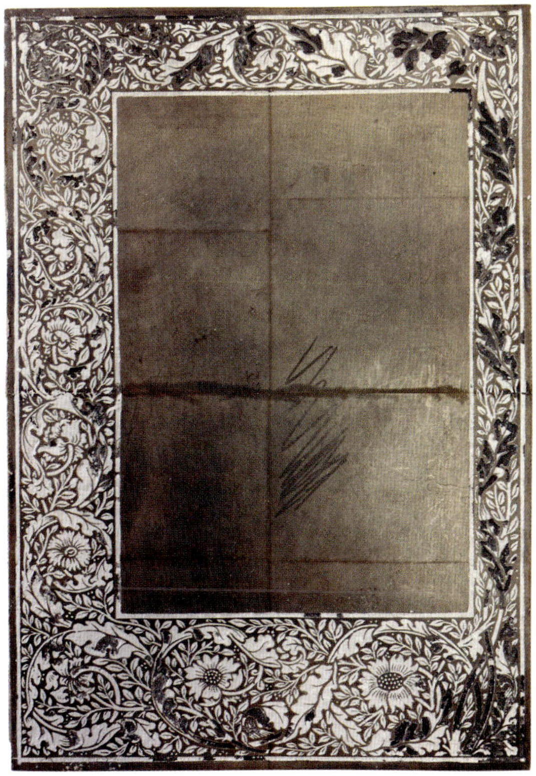

XIV.21

Wood block for *The Well at the World's End* by William Morris
27.8 x 19.5 x 2.5 cm
British Museum (1897,1228.17)

Wood block engraved with a Morris border and used for the right-hand page above. Powdered chalk has been applied to engraved portions of the border so that the design can be 'read' in black and white, much as it would appear. The block is marked 'Border 7' and the top edge is stamped with the name of its maker or supplier: 'J. SCOTT WHITEFRIARS ST EC'.

XIV.22

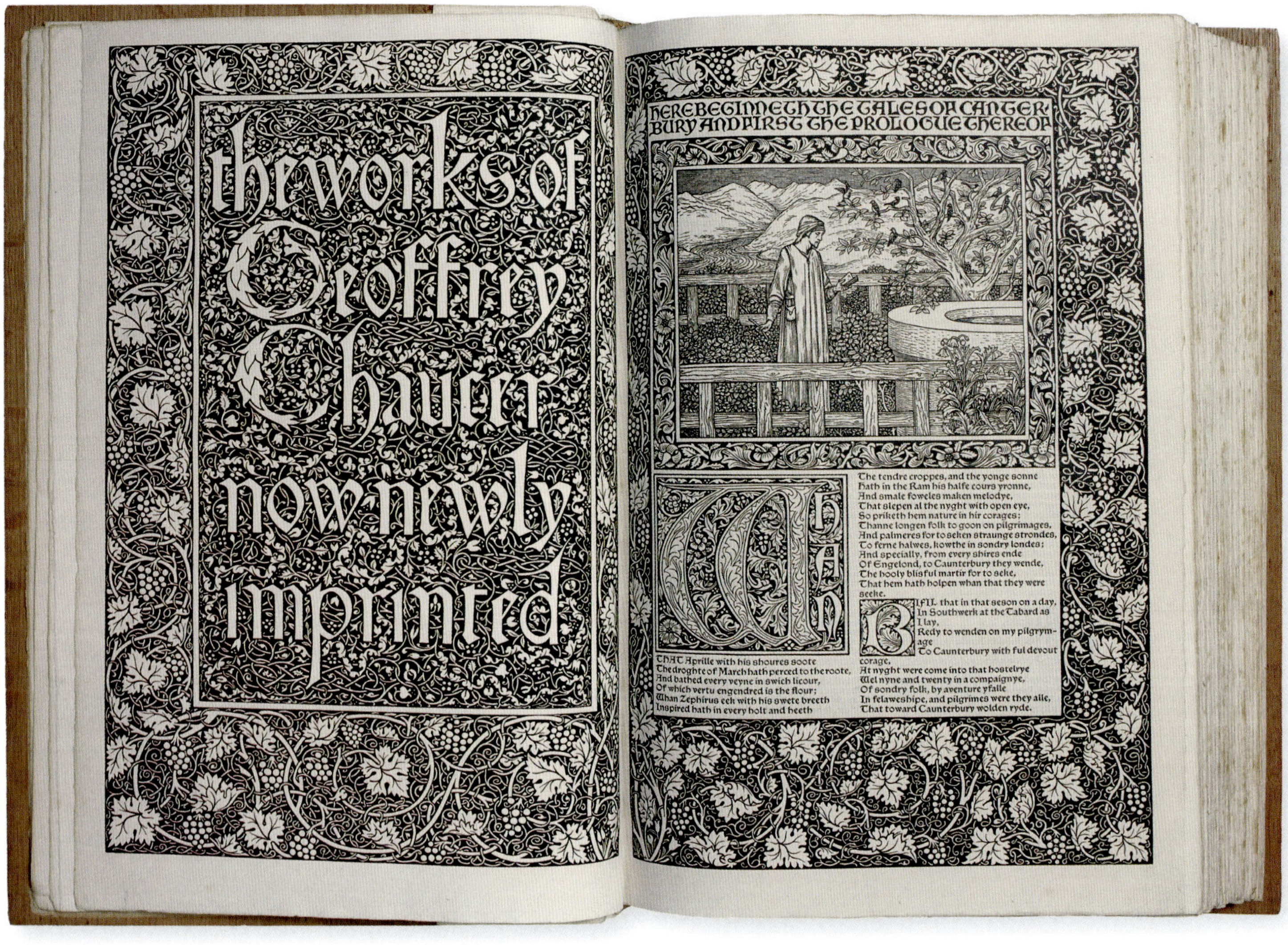

The Works of Geoffrey Chaucer
Kelmscott Press, 1896

This was the crowning Kelmscott Press achievement of Morris's collaboration with Burne-Jones. As undergraduates at Oxford they had counted Chaucer as one of their great discoveries. Later their admiration for him steadily grew.

Scenes from 'The Prioress's Tale' were painted by Burne-Jones on the wardrobe that he gave Morris as a wedding present. Embroideries, stained glass and tile designs were based on *The Legend of Good Women*, and Morris showed his veneration of Chaucer in his poem *The Life and Death of Jason* (1867) by calling him his master. The creation of the Chaucer Society in 1868 raised interest in his works and in 1878 Morris was asked to write an introduction to an edition of Chaucer's writings, but refused because only a small selection was planned. His heart was set on producing a complete edition from a carefully restored text, and with a wealth of illustrations by Burne-Jones. Eventually permission was obtained to use a text that the Reverend Walter W. Skeat had prepared for Oxford University Press.

At the outset, around 60 illustrations were envisaged. Their number rose to 87 (for which 85 pencil drawings survive at the Fitzwilliam Museum, Cambridge). Before these were cut on wood, their lines were considerably strengthened with great skill and sensitivity by Robert Catterson-Smith (see XIV.27). Morris's ornaments were also cut on wood by highly competent craftsmen, so the work of both friends was made more homogeneous, and better suited to the weight of line given to the Chaucer type used for the densely set double-column text.

Morris's typography was much enhanced by the large quantity of decorative designs and lettering that he drew for this edition. He supplied the title-page, 26 large initial words, scores of decorated initials – many of them used in earlier Kelmscott books – as well as 14 large outer borders and 18 frames for illustrations. This setting delighted Burne-Jones who loved

> to be snugly cased in the borders and buttressed up by the vast initials – and once or twice when I have no letter under me, I feel tottery and weak; if you drag me out of my encasings it will be like tearing a statue out of its niche and putting it into a museum – indeed when the book is done, if we live to finish it, it will be like a pocket cathedral.

The two friends had the greatest mutual admiration for each other's part in the production. Morris called the illustrations 'magnificent and inimitable' and saw them as 'the most harmonious decoration possible'. Burne-Jones regarded Morris as simply 'the greatest master of ornament in the world'. Both enjoyed immersing themselves in antiquity. As they sat together on Sundays while the illustrations were being drawn – or re-drawn, as so many were – Burne-Jones recalled 'we never got to speak of anyone later than the ninth century'.

Burne-Jones was too prim to illustrate the bawdier passages in some of Chaucer's tales, as Morris hoped he would. Despite this limitation, the artist showed himself capable of entering wholeheartedly into Morris's scheme, and painstaking in trying to interpret Chaucer accurately, though he sometimes failed. He preferred to deal with the more chivalric and courtly elements in the text. His greatest strengths were in the composition of his drawings and in his handling of figures against intricate backgrounds.

The Kelmscott Chaucer captured the public's imagination from the moment it was first announced. It remains the best-known Kelmscott edition and the most highly prized. Although it was rapidly sold out, it failed narrowly to cover its costs and was in effect subsidized by healthy profits made on smaller Kelmscott books.

XIV.23

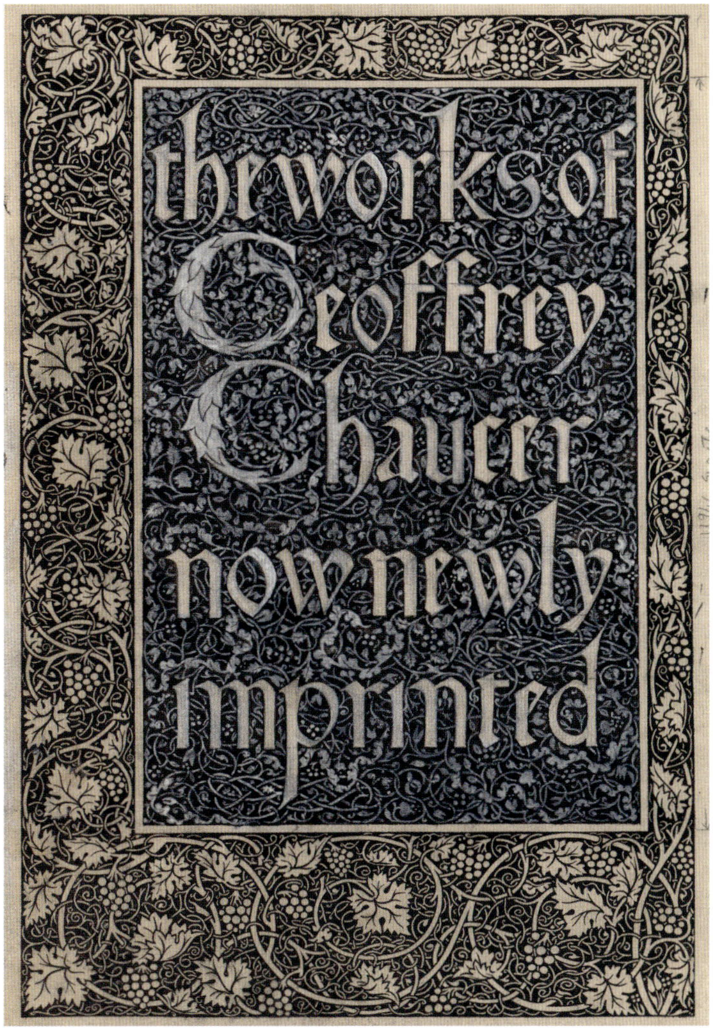

XIV.24

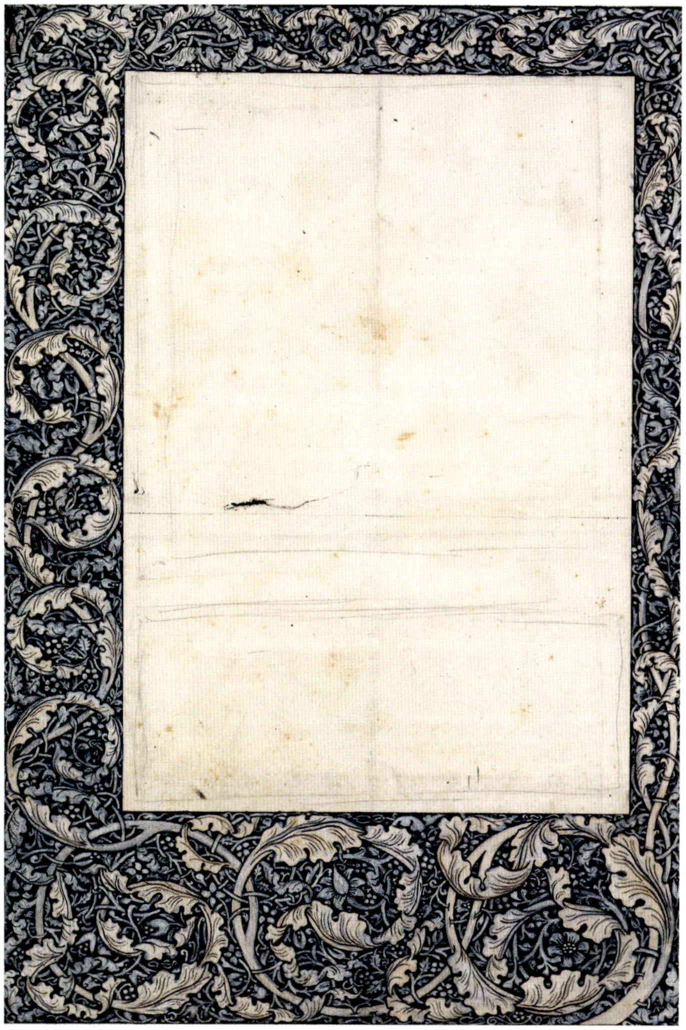

XIV.22
The Works of Geoffrey Chaucer
Kelmscott Press, issued 26 June 1896
Paper, 42.5 x 29.2 cm leaf
The Wilson Art Gallery and Museum, Cheltenham (1991.1016.996.G1)

This copy was given to Emery Walker by William Morris. Apart from the illustration engraved on wood after a design by Burne-Jones, all the decoration, lettering and type on these pages are the work of Morris.

XIV.23
Design for title-page of *The Works of Geoffrey Chaucer*
William Morris, February–May 1896
Graphite, ink and Chinese white, 42.2 x 29 cm
The Morgan Library and Museum, New York (PML 76923.4)
Gift of John M. Crawford Jr.

This was Morris's last design for the Chaucer. He began it on 19 February 1896 after Burne-Jones (whose illustrations were completed in December 1895) expressed his anxiety over the delay. Morris finished this design at the end of March; after some retouching in May, the title-page was printed when the final sheet went through the press.

XIV.24
Design for a large border for *The Works of Geoffrey Chaucer*
William Morris, 1896
Graphite, ink and Chinese white, 41.8 x 32.2 cm
V&A (D.1552–1907)

One of Morris's 14 designs for large borders drawn in ink and Chinese white. This example appears on page 470. Long experience of designing wallpapers and textiles helped him to resolve the transitions from broad to narrow spaces in the four segments of the design. W.R. Lethaby saw Morris at work creating his borders:

He would have two saucers, one of Indian ink, the other of Chinese white. Then, making the slightest indications of the main stems of the pattern he had in mind, with pencil, he would begin at once his finished final ornament by covering a length of ground with one brush and painting the pattern with the other. If a part did not satisfy him, the other brush covered it up again, and again he set to to put in his finished ornament ... The actual drawing with the brush was an agreeable sensation to him; the forms were led along and bent over and rounded at the edges with definite pleasure; they were stroked into place, as it were, with a sensation like that of smoothing a cat ... It was to express this sensuous pleasure that he used to say that all good designing was felt in the stomach.

XIV.25

Wood block for a frame for *The Works of Geoffrey Chaucer*

16 x 20 x 2.5 cm

Inscribed: 'Chaucer no.19', 'Reason'

British Museum (1897,1228.73)

Because the same borders, frames and decorated letters were used repeatedly throughout the Chaucer, they were printed from copies known as electrotypes. These were made from the wood blocks engraved by William Harcourt Hooper after Morris's designs.

This block could not have been used for printing because the space within the border has not been cleared. Consequently, the entire surface would have been covered by ink when the rollers went over it. In fact, the surface of the block still has some remains of the graphite with which it was covered before an electrotype copy was made.

Electrotypes were produced from a wax mould of the surface of the wood block. Graphite prevented the surface of the block from sticking to the beeswax-based compound used for making the mould. Copper was deposited on the moulds through electricity developed by magnetism – a method known as galvanism.

Morris feared a loss of quality by using electrotype copies. Walker won him over by proofing on one sheet of paper two rows of the same decorated letters. One row was printed from the wood blocks, the other from electrotypes. In fact, Morris managed to put his finger on the electrotypes, but admitted he had done so almost by chance – and agreed to use electrotypes.

XIV.26

Wood block for Edward Burne-Jones's illustration for 'The Legend of Goode Wimmen' for *The Works of Geoffrey Chaucer*

12.6 x 16.5 x 2.5 cm

Inscribed: 'Chaucer no.62, p.431'

British Museum (1897,1117.96)

This block was used to print the illustration on page 431. It shows Medea and Hypsipyle in the foreground with the *Argos* in the background. The edges of the block have cardboard wedges, which were used to keep the block in place within its electrotype frame. A further advantage of using electrotypes to assemble the more elaborately decorated pages in the Chaucer was that a metal electrotype mounted on a wooden base had great strength, and could withstand considerable pressure when blocks, type and other typographical elements were wedged within it.

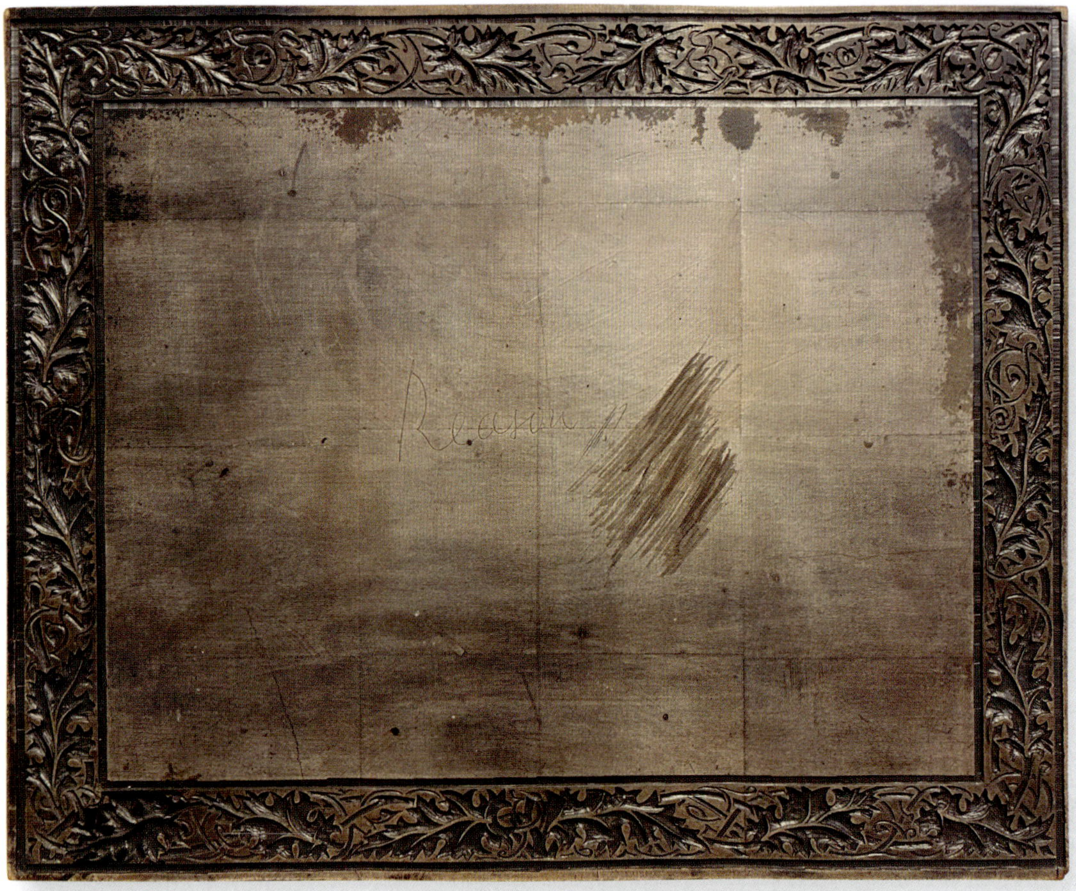

XIV.25

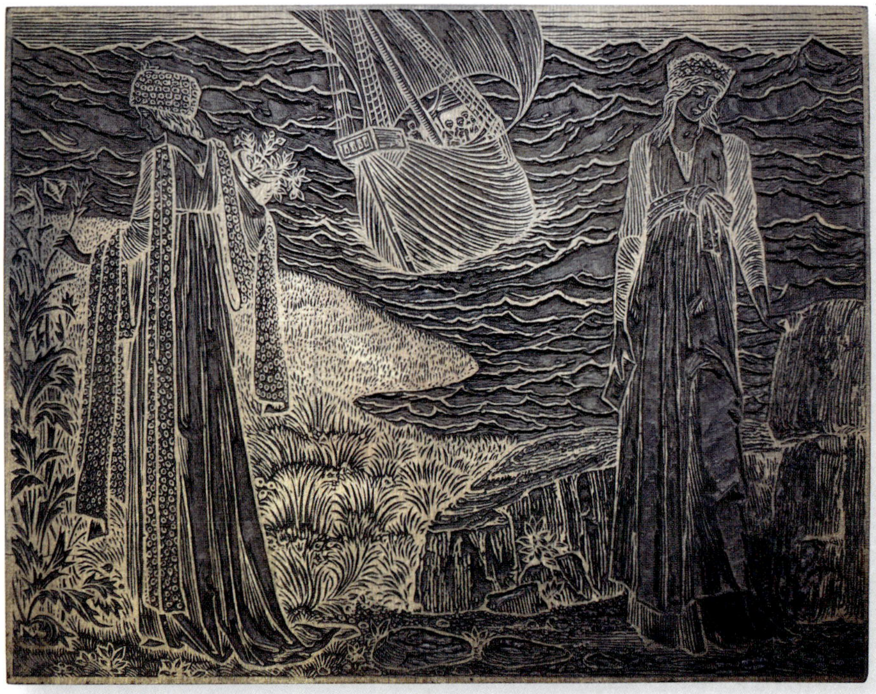

XIV.26

XIV.27

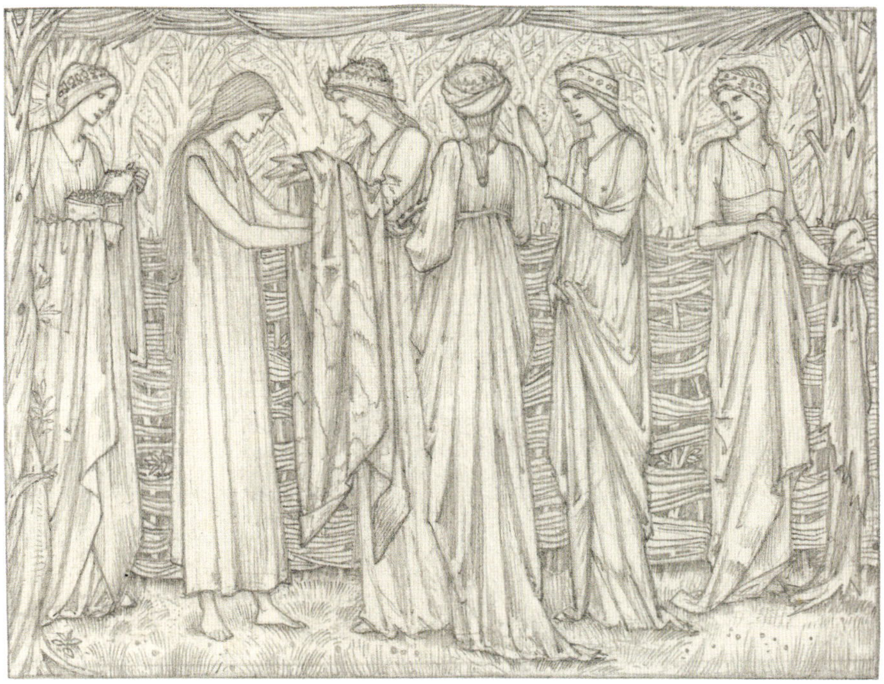

XIV.28

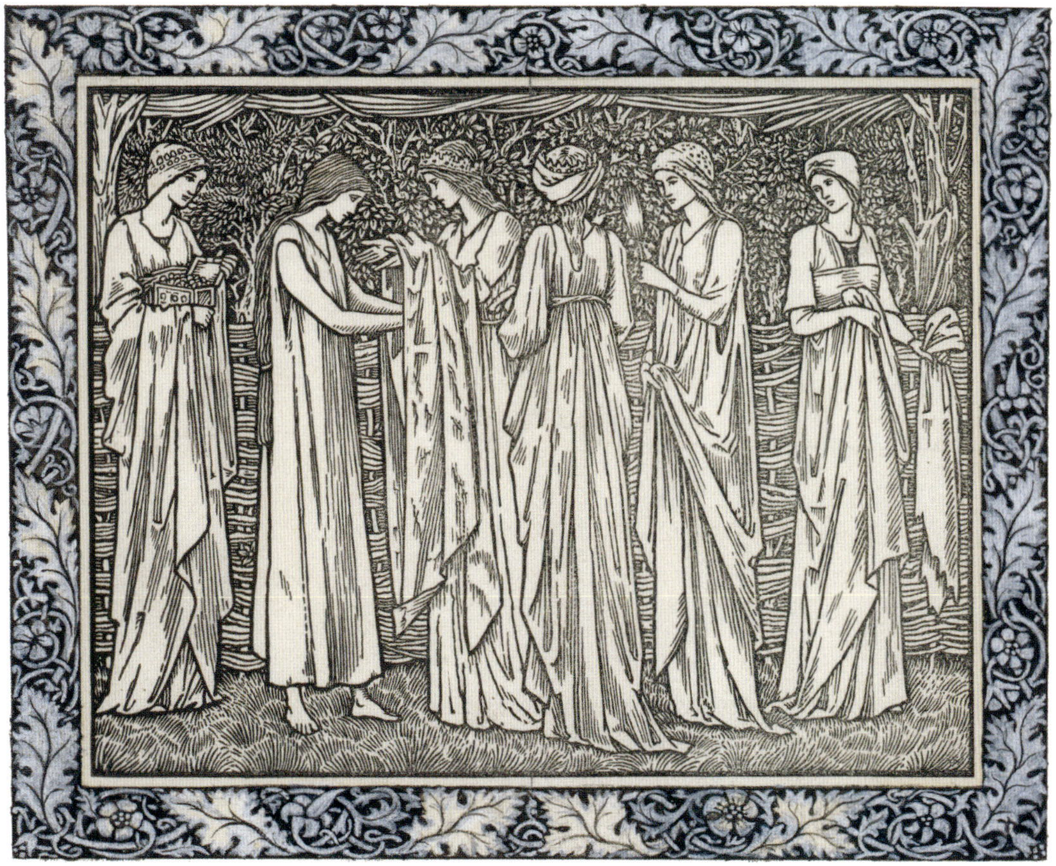

XIV.27

Design for 'The Tale of the Clerk of Oxenford' for *The Works of Geoffrey Chaucer*

Edward Burne-Jones, *c.*1895

Pencil, 13 x 17 cm

Fitzwilliam Museum, University of Cambridge (1050.15)

Given by Stanley Baldwin Esq.

The illustration shows Griselda, the heroine of the Clerk's tale. A pivotal part in translating Burne-Jones's drawings onto woodcuts was played by Robert Catterson-Smith. Here is an extract from his explanation of the intermediary stages:

> Emery Walker made a very pale print of a photograph (a platino) from Sir E.B.J.'s pencil drawing – the exact size of the drawing – I then stuck the print down on stout card board, and, in order to avoid the expansion of the paper I put the paste on the card board first and then applied the paper print very quickly, so quickly that it had no time to absorb moisture and so expand, then I immediately ran a hot smoothing iron over it which at once dried the paste. Next I gave the print a thin even wash of Chinese white with a little size in it. The result was to get rid of everything but the essential lines. Next I went over the pale lines with a very sharp pencil, copying and translating from the B-J. drawing which was in front of me ... When the pencil drawing was finished all trace of the photograph had disappeared. Next came the inking over, which was done with a fine round sable brush and very black Chinese ink which I bought in bottles. By putting a little size in the Chinese white, as above mentioned, the ink was not absorbed by the white and so remained jet black – otherwise it would have become grey ... When difficulties arose in the treatment of passages, I consulted B-J. Sometimes work by Albert Durer was consulted to see how he had dealt with passages. Some of the drawings were done over several times ... Finally E. Walker made a photograph on the woodblock and [W.H.] Hooper cut it.

XIV.28

Proof with original border design for *The Works of Geoffrey Chaucer*

Border by William Morris, 1896, proof from illustration by Edward Burne-Jones

Graphite, Indian ink and Chinese white, 22.2 x 27.7 cm

V&A (D.1554–1907)

Purchased from Sydney Carlyle Cockerell

One of 18 frames designed by Morris; this example was used on page 129 to encase Burne-Jones's illustration in the second part of 'The Tale of the Clerk of Oxenford' (see XIV.27).

XIV.29a

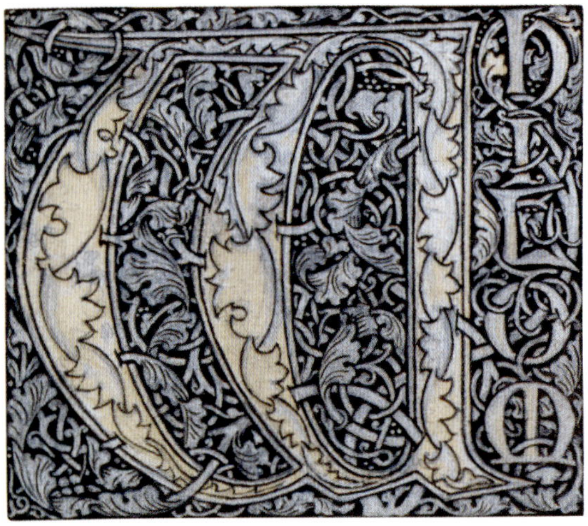

XIV.30

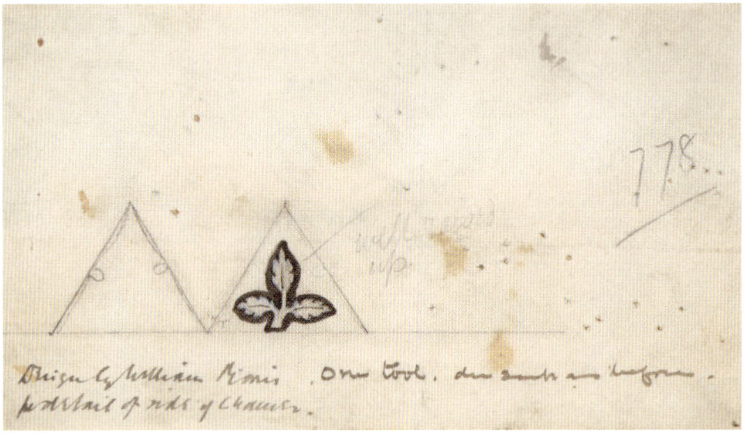

XIV.29b

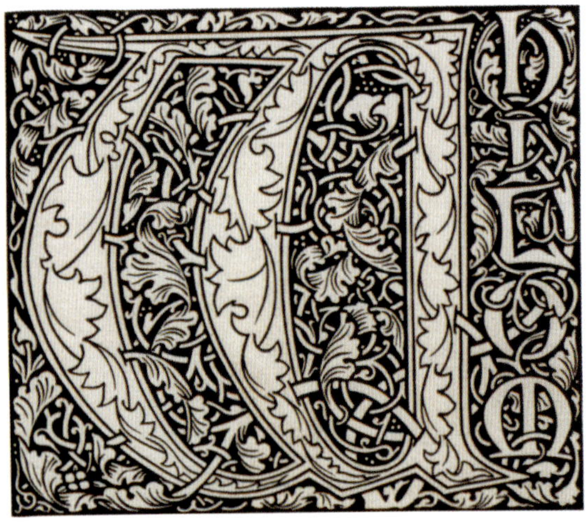

XIV.31

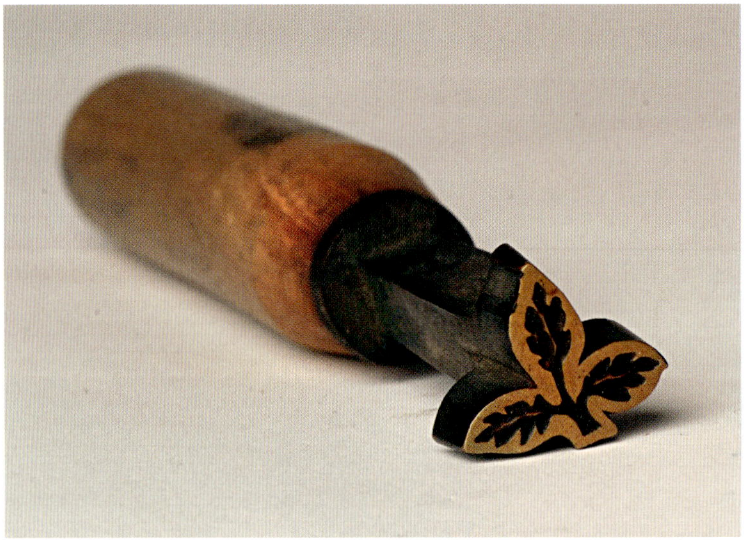

XIV.29
Initial word 'Whilom' for *The Works of Geoffrey Chaucer*

a Design
William Morris, 1896
Graphite, ink and Chinese white, 14.4 x 21.5 cm
Inscribed by Emery Walker: 'Big letter for Chaucer', 'this width exactly'
V&A (D.1553–1907)

b Proof
From a wood block engraved by William Harcourt Hooper
10.5 x 13 cm
V&A (D.1553a–1907)

One of 26 large initial words drawn by Morris in ink and Chinese white. His design was subsequently redrawn by Robert Catterson-Smith and the wood block was cut after the design had been photographically transferred on to its surface. The proof shows how sensitively Catterson-Smith and Hooper interpreted Morris's design.

XIV.30
Design for a binding tool for *The Works of Geoffrey Chaucer*
William Morris, *c.*1896
Pencil and watercolour, 9 x 16.1 cm
Inscribed: 'Well raised up' and other notes
V&A (E.195–1955)

One of a set of designs by Morris for tooling the pigskin Chaucer bindings. This example is endorsed in the handwriting of the bookbinder Thomas James Cobden-Sanderson: 'Design by William Morris for detail of side of Chaucer.' Another hand has added: 'One tool die sunk as before.'

XIV.31
Metal tool for binding of *The Works of Geoffrey Chaucer*
19.5 cm long, 2.5 cm wide
The Society of Antiquaries of London (933.20)

Tool cut from original design (XIV.30) used for the pigskin binding of the Kelmscott Chaucer.

XIV.32
The Works of Geoffrey Chaucer
Kelmscott Press, issued 26 June 1896
Vellum, special stamped pigskin binding, 42.5 x 29.2 cm leaf
The Syndics of Cambridge University Library (Sel.1.16)

In February 1896, the Kelmscott Press announced that it would accept orders for supplying the Chaucer in four varieties of special bindings. Two were to be executed to Morris's design by Thomas James Cobden-Sanderson, either in full white tooled pigskin, or in half pigskin over oak boards; the other two were to be carried out by John & James Leighton to a different design by Morris, in either full or half pigskin over boards.

Because his health was failing, Morris only finished one of these binding designs between December 1895 and January 1896 (in the collection of the Society of Antiquaries), although he made a start on a second. He regarded white pigskin as a 'beautiful material for wearing and showing designs'. Forty-eight copies were bound to his design at the Doves Bindery. The majority were tooled by Douglas Cockerell with variations in quality, both in the exactness with which the design was followed, and in the strength with which the tools were impressed into the pigskin bindings over the oak boards.

Morris took his inspiration for this design from a binding in his library by Ulrich Schreier of Salzburg (1478) on a copy of a large Koberger Bible, close in size to the Kelmscott Chaucer.

On the upper (front) cover, the grape-vine border is related to his own design for the title-page and the facing text-page. The lower (back) cover relates more closely to the Schreier binding, with its diagonal bands forming large lozenges enclosing stylized oak leaves. Many of Schreier's bindings combined cut-leather work and tooling. The cut leather often had a criblée background, which seems to have inspired the small dots on Morris's grape-vine border. His small tools in the centre panel of the upper cover are also related to those on Schreier's binding. Despite noting these similarities, Dr Paul Needham regards Morris's binding for the Chaucer as 'a work of art in its own right, the lower cover especially having a clarity and simplicity that excels its model.'

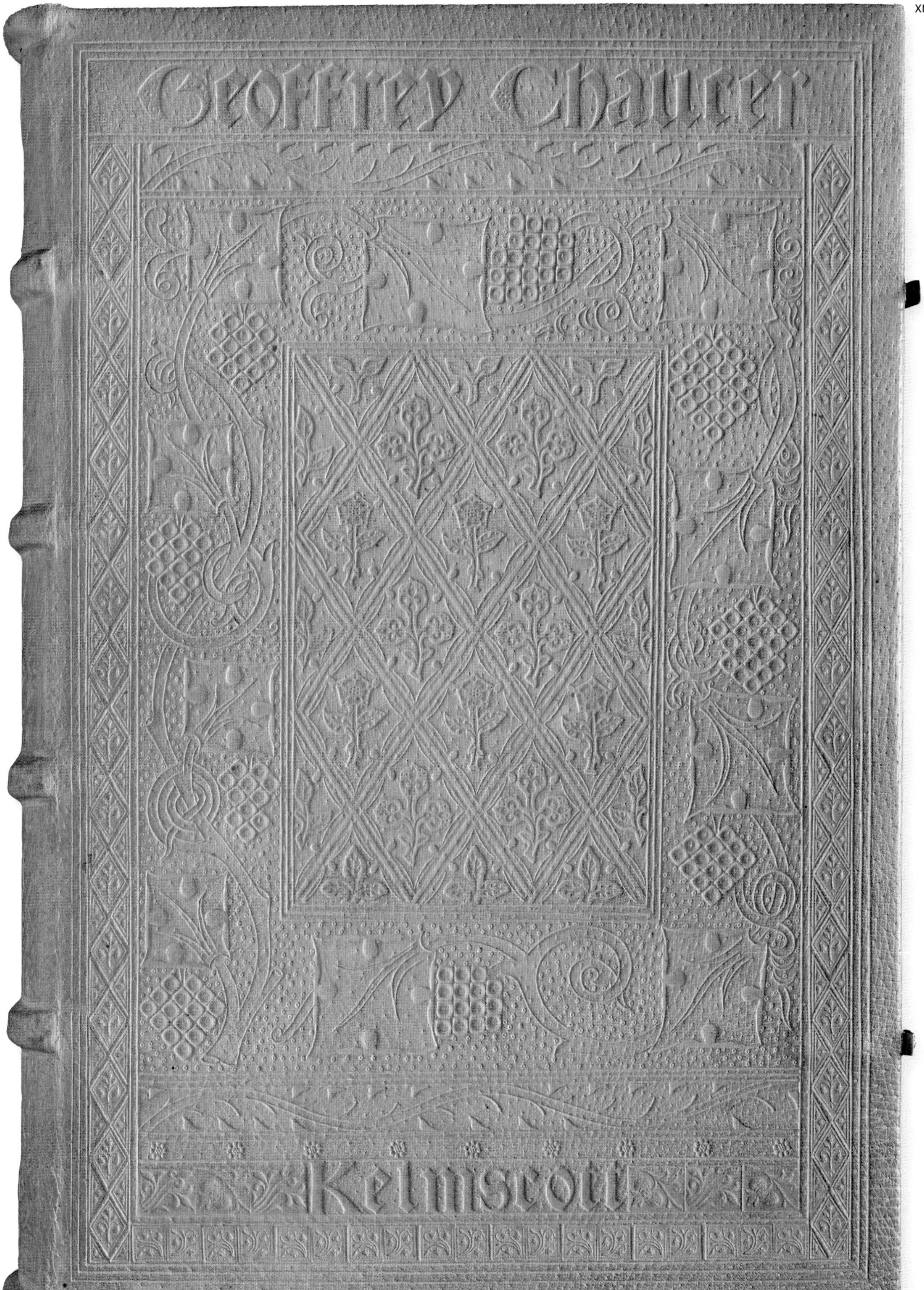
Geoffrey Chaucer
Kelmscott

XIV.33

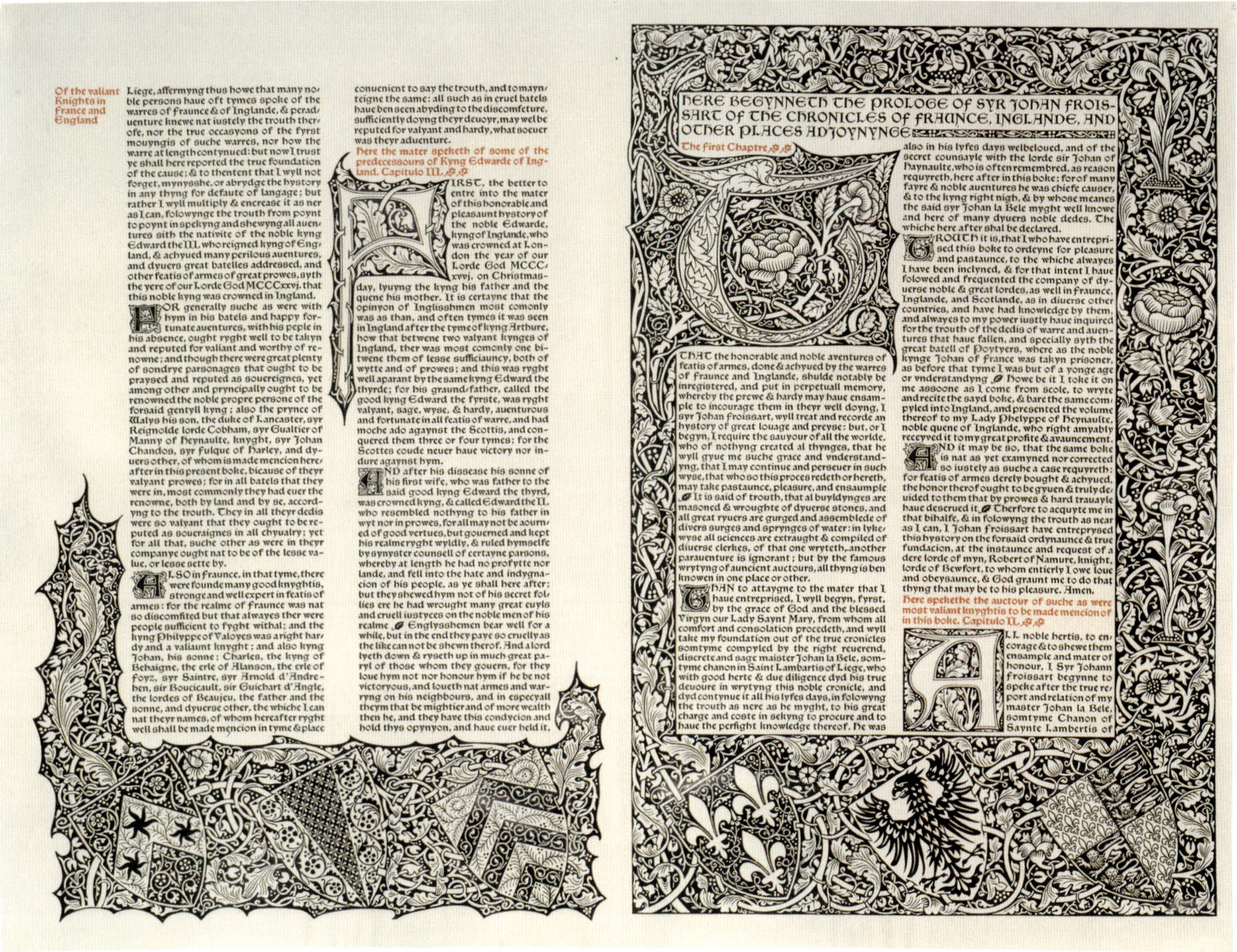

Froissart's *Chronicles*
Kelmscott Press, 1897

Since university, Morris had retained a great enthusiasm for Lord Berners' translation of the Chronicles of Jean Froissart, a fourteenth-century account of the Hundred Years' War. As soon as his Troy type was delivered in January 1892, he had a single-column trial page of Froissart set up. Early in 1893 further trial pages were set in double-column using his Chaucer type. In March he showed some new initials for Froissart to his friends.

In October 1893 Burne-Jones offered to provide an illustration of St George for the frontispiece of Volume I and some shields of arms. A drawing of Fame was intended for Volume II, but if this offer had been accepted, it might have delayed completion of his promised frontispiece and illustration for *The Life and Death of Jason*, which appeared in July 1895.

So Morris devoted some of his own energy and imagination to working on the decoration of specimen pages for a Kelmscott edition of Froissart. An interview given in 1895 reported Morris as saying:

> no book I could do would give me half the pleasure I am getting from the Froissart. I am simply revelling in it. It's such a noble and glorious work, and every page [proof] as it leaves the press delights me more than I can say. I am taking great pains with it, and doing all I can to realise what I have long wished.

Unfortunately, the venture had to be held in abeyance while the Chaucer absorbed the greater part of his presses' capacity.

Before he was able to carry out his plans, Morris died. A formal announcement that Froissart's *Chronicles* would not be published was made in November 1896. By then about 34 pages of the work had been set up in type, but no sheets had been printed. His executors decided to print 16 pages in an edition of 32 copies for distribution to his friends. In addition, 160 copies of a two-leaf specimen were printed on vellum for sale (XIV.33).

The three objects illustrated here give a tantalizing impression of the manner in which Morris might have produced his edition of Froissart's Chronicles, had he lived to complete it.

XIV.33
Two specimen pages of Froissart's *Chronicles*
William Morris, issued 7 October 1897
Vellum, 42.1 x 56.4 cm
V&A (E.504–1903)

These pages show Morris experimenting with a new decorative style. Having proved his ability to work within the constraints of rectilinear shapes, he now had the audacity to explore more exuberant forms of borders and initials, which captured the pageantry of Froissart's text.

The profile of the initial T on the right page is cusped and is most skilfully integrated with the border immediately to its left. The cusping echoes the profile of the heraldic decoration at the foot of the left page and is also visible in the initial F above. Two other cusped initials were designed for the Froissart: though they were never used, they were shown in the final Kelmscott book printed in 1898, *A Note by William Morris on his Aims in Founding the Kelmscott Press*.

XIV.34

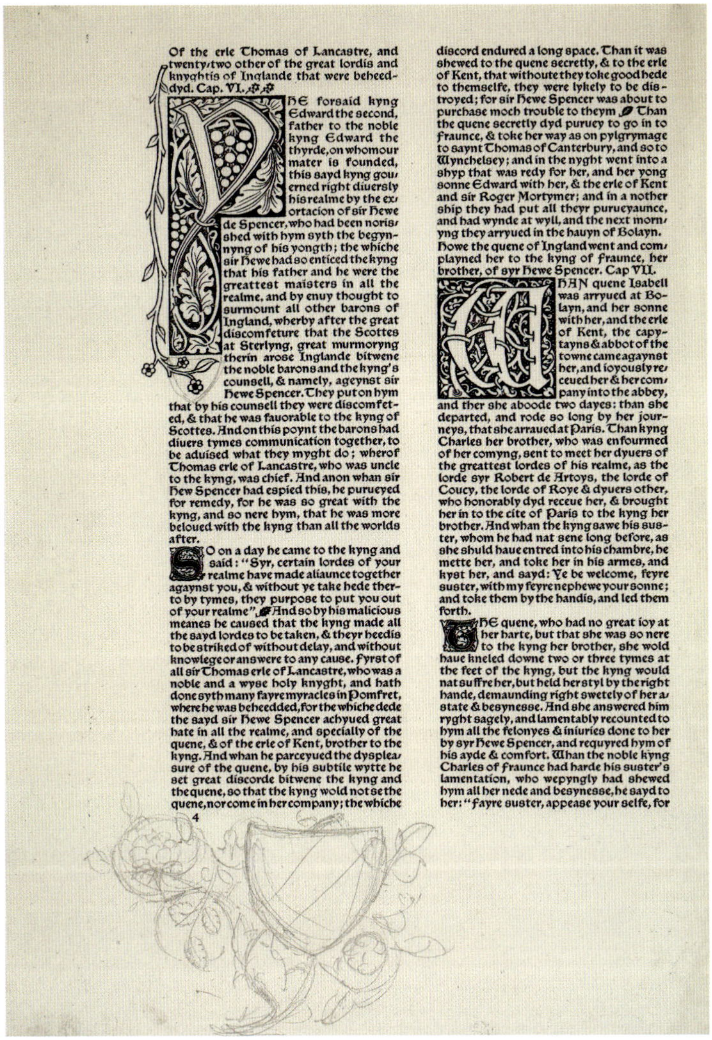

Of the erle Thomas of Lancastre, and twenty-two other of the great lordis and knyghtis of Inglande that were beheeddyd. Cap. VI.

THE forsaid kyng Edward the second, father to the noble kyng Edward the thyrde, on whom our mater is founded, this sayd kyng gouerned right diuersly his realme by the exortacion of sir Hewe de Spencer, who had been norisshed with hym syth the begynnyng of his yongth; the whiche sir Hewe had so enticed the kyng that his father and he were the greattest maisters in all the realme, and by enuy thought to surmount all other barons of Ingland, wherby after the great discomfeture that the Scottes at Sterlyng, great murmoryng therin arose Inglande bitwene the noble barons and the kyng's counsell, & namely, ageynst sir Hewe Spencer. They put on hym that by his counsell they were discomfeted, & that he was fauorable to the kyng of Scottes. And on this poynt the barons had diuers tymes communication together, to be aduised what they myght do; wherof Thomas erle of Lancastre, who was uncle to the kyng, was chief. And anon whan sir Hew Spencer had espied this, he purueyed for remedy, for he was so great with the kyng, and so nere hym, that he was more beloued with the kyng than all the worlds after.

SO on a day he came to the kyng and said: "Syr, certain lordes of your realme have made aliaunce together agaynst you, & without ye take hede therto by tymes, they purpose to put you out of your realme". And so by his malicious meanes he caused that the kyng made all the sayd lordes to be taken, & theyr heedis to be striked of without delay, and without knowlege or answere to any cause. Fyrst of all sir Thomas erle of Lancastre, who was a noble and a wyse holy knyght, and hath done syth many fayre myracles in Pomfret, where he was beheedded, for the whiche dede the sayd sir Hewe Spencer achyued great hate in all the realme, and specially of the quene, & of the erle of Kent, brother to the kyng. And whan he parceyued the dyspleasure of the quene, by his subtile wytte he set great discorde bitwene the kyng and the quene, so that the kyng wold not se the quene, nor come in her company; the whiche

4

discord endured a long space. Than it was shewed to the quene secretly, & to the erle of Kent, that withoute they toke good hede to themselfe, they were lykely to be distroyed; for sir Hewe Spencer was about to purchase moch trouble to theym. Than the quene secretly dyd puruey to go in to Fraunce, & toke her way as on pylgrymage to saynt Thomas of Canterbury, and so to Wynchelsey; and in the nyght went into a shyp that was redy for her, and her yong sonne Edward with her, & the erle of Kent and sir Roger Mortymer; and in a nother ship they had put all theyr purueyaunce, and had wynde at wyll, and the next mornyng they arryued in the hauyn of Bolayn.

Howe the quene of Ingland went and complayned her to the kyng of Fraunce, her brother, of syr Hewe Spencer. Cap VII.

WHAN quene Isabell was arryued at Bolayn, and her sonne with her, and the erle of Kent, the capytayns & abbot of the towne came agaynst her, and ioyously receued her & her company into the abbey, and ther she aboode two dayes: than she departed, and rode so long by her journeys, that she arraued at Paris. Than kyng Charles her brother, who was enfourmed of her comyng, sent to meet her dyuers of the greattest lordes of his realme, as the lorde syr Robert de Artoys, the lorde of Coucy, the lorde of Roye & dyuers other, who honorably dyd receue her, & brought her in to the cite of Paris to the kyng her brother. And whan the kyng sawe his suster, whom he had nat sene long before, as she shuld haue entred into his chambre, he mette her, and toke her in his armes, and kyst her, and sayd: Ye be welcome, feyre suster, with my feyre nephewe your sonne; and toke them by the handis, and led them forth.

THE quene, who had no great ioy at her harte, but that she was so nere to the kyng her brother, she wold haue kneled downe two or three tymes at the feet of the kyng, but the kyng would nat suffre her, but held her styl by the right hande, demaunding right swetely of her astate & besynesse. And she answered him ryght sagely, and lamentably recounted to hym all the felonyes & iniuries done to her by syr Hewe Spencer, and requyred hym of his ayde & comfort. Whan the noble kyng Charles of Fraunce had harde his suster's lamentation, who wepyngly had shewed hym all her nede and besynesse, he sayd to her: "Fayre suster, appease your selfe, for

XIV.35

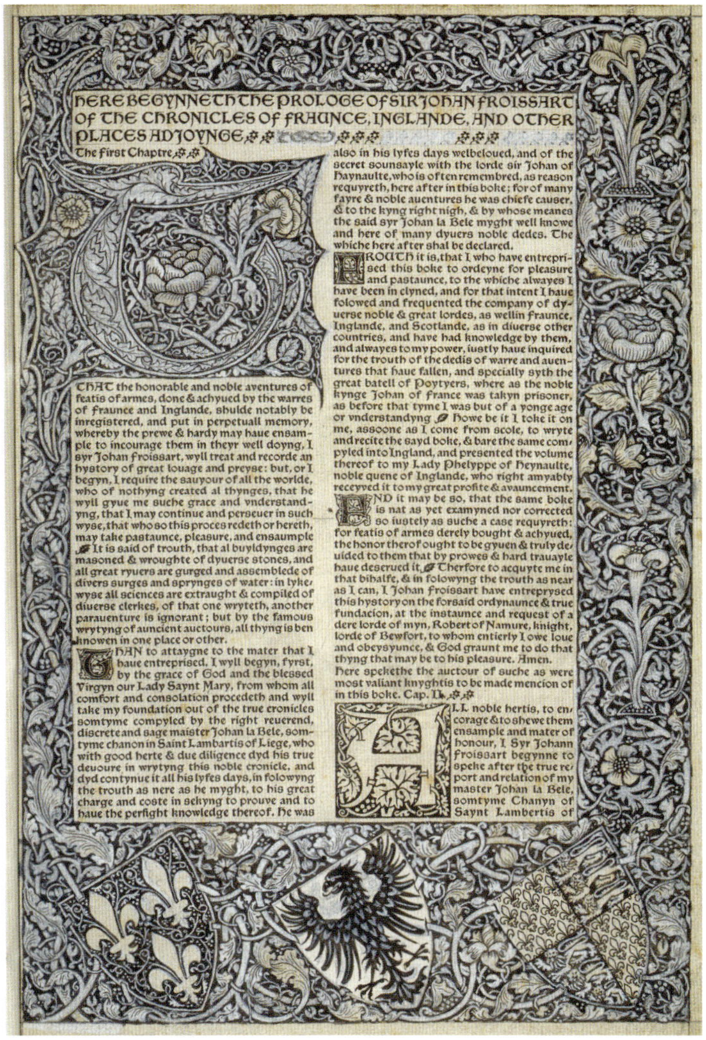

HERE BEGYNNETH THE PROLOGE OF SIR JOHAN FROISSART OF THE CHRONICLES OF FRAUNCE, INGLANDE, AND OTHER PLACES ADJOYNGE

The first Chaptre

THAT the honorable and noble aventures of featis of armes, done & achyued by the warres of Fraunce and Inglande, shulde notably be inregistered, and put in perpetuall memory, whereby the prewe & hardy may haue ensample to incourage them in theyr well doyng, I syr Johan Froissart, wyll treat and recorde an hystory of great louage and preyse: but, or I begyn, I require the sauyour of all the worlde, who of nothyng created al thynges, that he wyll gyue me suche grace and vnderstandyng, that I may continue and perseuer in such wyse, that who so this proces redeth or hereth, may take pastaunce, pleasure, and ensaumple. It is said of trouth, that al buyldynges are masoned & wroughte of dyuerse stones, and all great ryuers are gurged and assemblede of divers surges and sprynges of water: in lykewyse all sciences are extraught & compiled of diuerse clerkes, of that one wryteth, another parauenture is ignorant; but by the famous wrytyng of auncient auctours, all thyng is ben knowen in one place or other.

THAN to attaygne to the mater that I haue entreprised, I wyll begyn, fyrst, by the grace of God and the blessed Virgyn our Lady Saynt Mary, from whom all comfort and consolation procedeth and wyll take my foundation out of the true cronicles somtyme compyled by the right reuerend, discrete and sage maister Johan la Bele, somtyme chanon in Saint Lambartis of Liege, who with good herte & due diligence dyd his true deuoure in wrytyng this noble cronicle, and dyd contynue it all his lyfes days, in folowyng the trouth as nere as he myght, to his great charge and coste in sekyng to prouve and to haue the perfight knowledge thereof. He was also in his lyfes days welbeloued, and of the secret sounsayle with the lorde sir Johan of Haynaulte, who is often remembred, as reason requyreth, here after in this boke; for of many fayre & noble auentures he was chiefe causer, & to the kyng right nigh, & by whose meanes the said syr Johan la Bele myght well knowe and here of many dyuers noble dedes. The whiche here after shal be declared.

TROUTH it is, that I who have entreprised this boke to ordeyne for pleasure and pastaunce, to the whiche alwayes I have been in clyned, and for that intent I haue folowed and frequented the company of dyuerse noble & great lordes, as well in Fraunce, Inglande, and Scotlande, as in diuerse other countries, and have had knowledge by them, and alwayes to my power, iustly haue inquired for the trouth of the dedis of warre and auentures that haue fallen, and specially syth the great batell of Poytyers, where as the noble kynge Johan of France was takyn prisoner, as before that tyme I was but of a yonge age or vnderstandyng. Howe be it I toke it on me, assoone as I come from scole, to wryte and recite the sayd boke, & bare the same compyled into Ingland, and presented the volume thereof to my Lady Phelyppe of Heynaulte, noble quene of Inglande, who right amyably receyved it to my great profite & avauncement.

AND it may be so, that the same boke is nat as yet examyned nor corrected so iustely as suche a case requyreth: for featis of armes derely bought & achyued, the honor therof ought to be gyuen & truly deuided to them that by prowes & hard trauayle haue deserued it. Therfore to acquyte me in that bihalfe, & in folowyng the trouth as near as I can, I Johan Froissart have entreprysed this hystory on the forsaid ordynaunce & true fundacion, at the instaunce and request of a dere lorde of myn, Robert of Namure, knight, lorde of Bewfort, to whom entierly I owe loue and obeysyunce, & God graunt me to do that thyng that may be to his pleasure. Amen.

Here spekethe the auctour of suche as were most valiant knyghtis to be made mencion of in this boke. Cap. II.

ALL noble hertis, to encorage & to shewe them ensample and mater of honour, I Syr Johann Froissart begynne to speke after the true report and relation of my master Johan la Bele, somtyme Chanyn of Saynt Lambertis of

XIV.34
Proof for Froissart's *Chronicles* with sketch by William Morris, *c.*1895
Paper, 41.9 x 28.6 cm
The Huntington Library, Art Museum and Botanical Gardens

The large initial Y was illustrated in *A Note by William Morris on his Aims in Founding the Kelmscott Press* (1898) and described by Cockerell as having been 'designed for the Froissart, but never used'. Morris experimented here with a scheme to place a single heraldic shield beneath the left column. It shows the style of decoration he intended to support the single stumpy shield (later replaced by a row of three shields).

XIV.35
Album of designs and trial pages for Froissart's *Chronicles*, compiled *c.*1897
Paper, some vellum; various sizes, image shown 42.4 x 28.5 cm
National Art Library, V&A (1995056850)
Bequeathed by Mrs Alan Thomas

This album was assembled and annotated by Sydney Cockerell. As Secretary of the Kelmscott Press and later as one of Morris's executors, he had a close knowledge of the project and knew the individuals connected with it. The leaf illustrated shows Morris's border design surrounding a printed proof of the text.

Supporting the evidence visible in Morris's splendid design for the opening page with its magnificent heraldic border, the album also contains a list of coats of arms, followed by Emery Walker's notes on the arms and their tinctures. Wood blocks for the Froissart borders are in the collection of the British Museum.

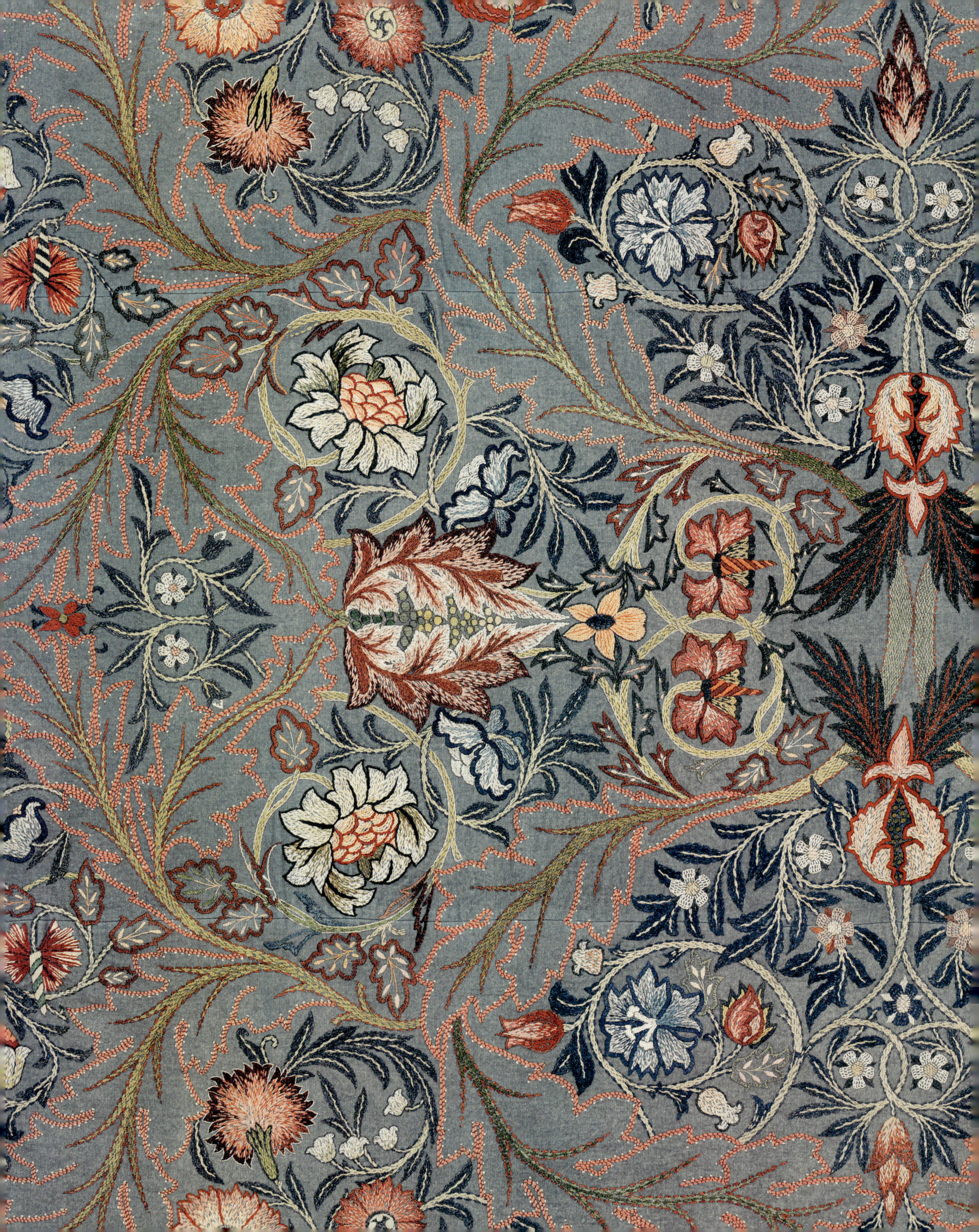

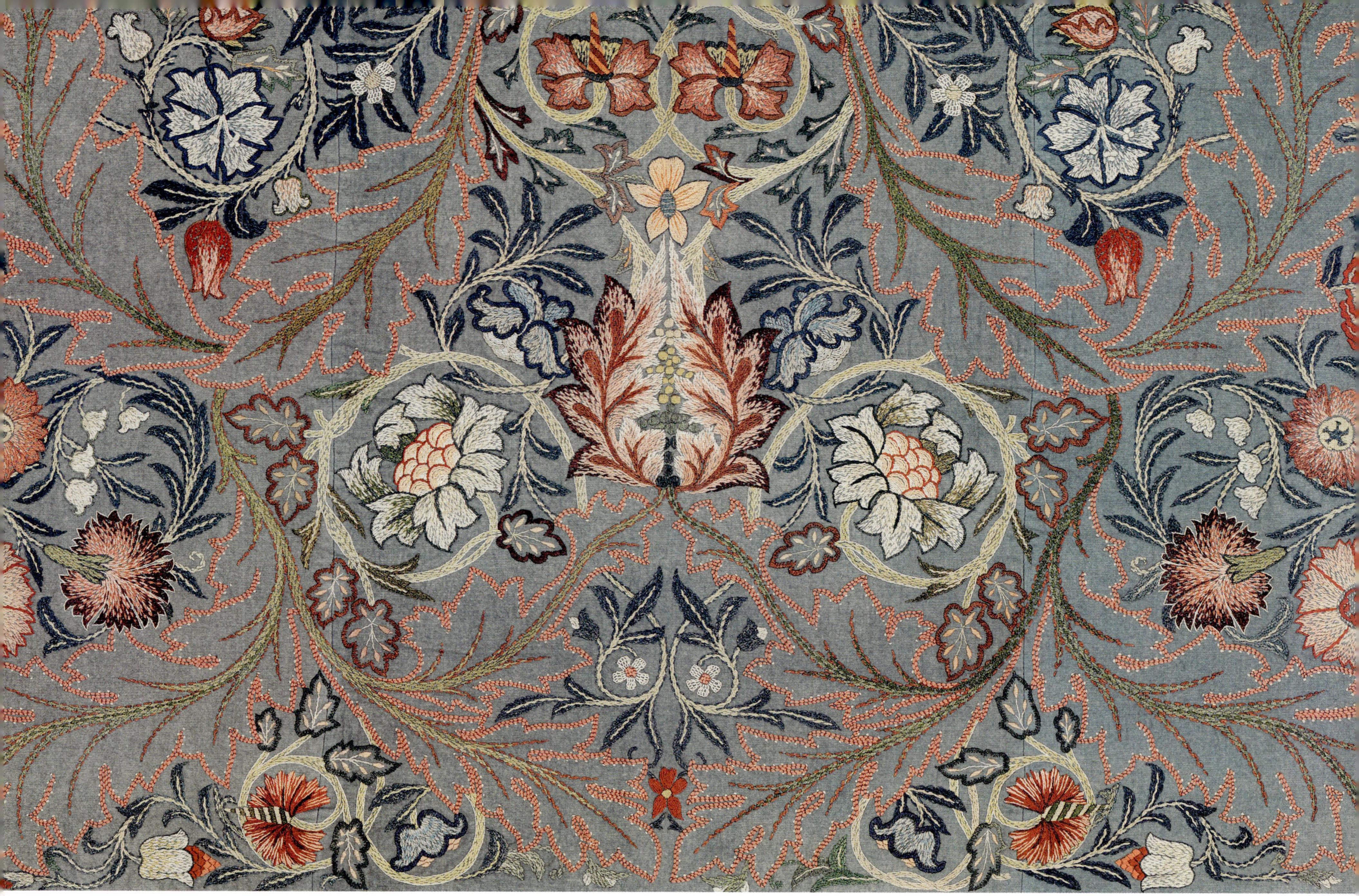

THE LEGACY

XV

WILLIAM MORRIS AND THE V&A

Tristram Hunt

'I do not want art for a few, any more than education for a few, or freedom for a few.'

William Morris, 'The Lesser Arts', 1877

William Morris was a defining thinker, activist and aesthete in the story of British socialism, one of the most important designers in our modern canon and a pioneer of modern craft practice. He was also a founding figure in the history of the Victoria and Albert Museum, or the South Kensington Museum, as it was then known. As designer and manufacturer, Morris frequently turned to South Kensington for inspiration: 'No doubt many of you, like me ... have wandered ... through the galleries of the admirable museum of South Kensington, and, like me, have been filled with wonder and gratitude at the beauty which has been born from the brain of man.'

In turn, Morris's resulting artistic *oeuvre* – appreciated most prominently through the Arts and Crafts Movement – has directly shaped the V&A's collections and interiors. From the café to the exhibition halls, and from the permanent galleries to the museum architecture, Morris's visual legacy suffuses South Kensington.

Before visitors even step into the V&A, Morris's likeness can be glimpsed on the external façade. Located on the Aston Webb building on Exhibition Road, his full-size statue surveys the crowds below (fig.226). His imagined figure stands in the company of other great, albeit all male, British craftsmen, artists and architects – a shop window celebrating British creativity – all prominently sculpted onto the 1909 façade: John Flaxman, William Hogarth, Thomas Chippendale and Josiah Wedgwood, to name a few.

Inside the museum, visitors can discover Morris's work within numerous settings, most prominently in the British Galleries, as well as in the famous 'Morris Room' of the V&A café. It is a remarkable fact that many of his best-loved designs for repeating patterns have remained in almost continuous production since his death – it is difficult to think of another designer whose work has proved so enduring (incidentally *Strawberry Thief* (see XII.50) consistently tops the list for the most searched-for object on the V&A's website). Interpreted in different colours and treatments for each generation, for use in the home but also for fashion and a vast array of merchandise, this ubiquitousness and sense of 'familiarity' can mask just how radical his art and his ideas were, how strange and complex he seemed to many of his contemporaries.

Morris's relationship with the V&A extends far beyond his visual presence or design aesthetic. The depth of Morris's partnership with South Kensington sprang equally from his philosophy of ethical socialism. His ideas about the

Fig.225 **William Morris, photographed by Frederick Hollyer, 1886.**
V&A (7715–1938)

Fig.226 ***William Morris*, sculpted by Arthur George Walker, 1905–6. Exhibition Road façade, V&A.**

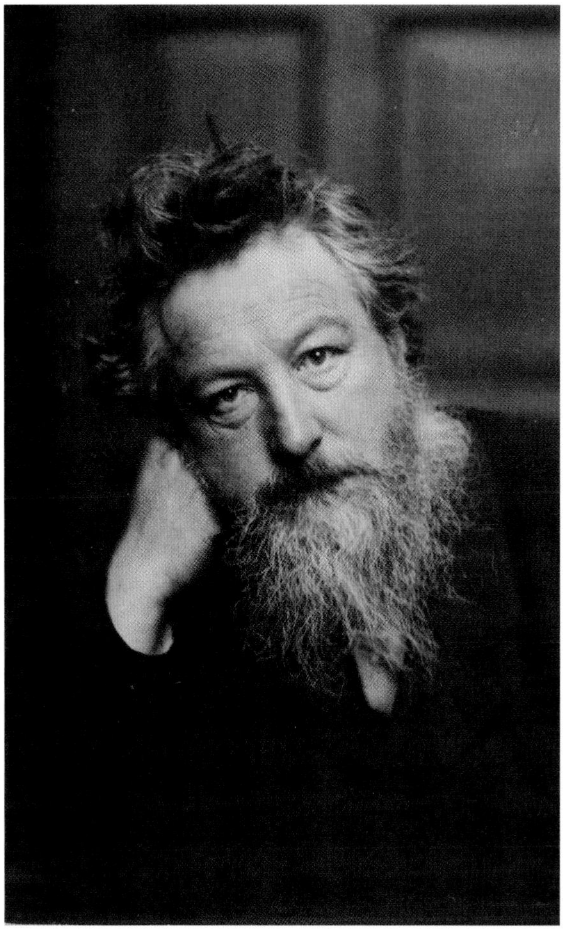

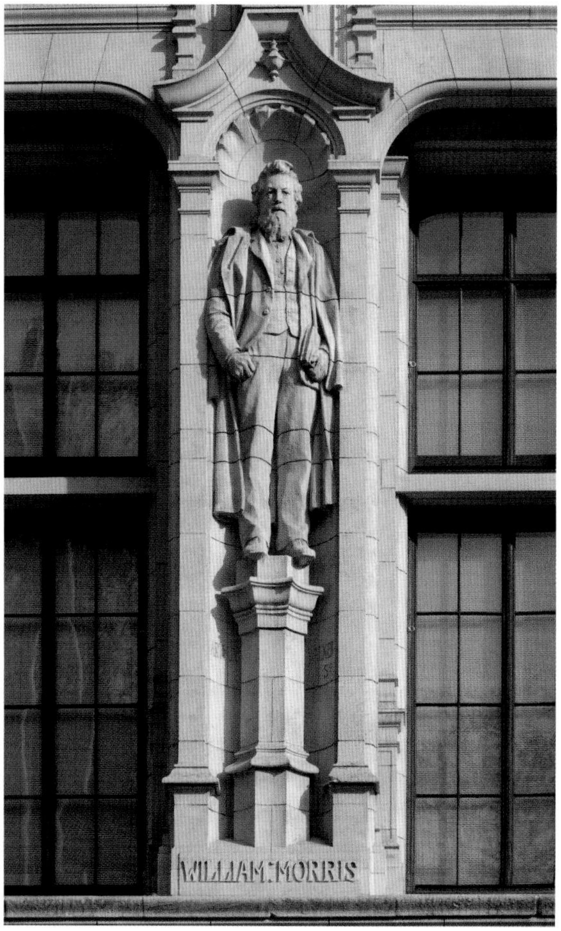

relationship between art and society, his passion for democratizing art, his love of history and his respect for the anonymous craftworkers, from many different periods and cultures, who created works of imaginative brilliance and technical skill, can all be explored by examining his relationship with the museum, its founding principles and its ongoing mission today.

Morris's concept of art was broad, encompassing the built environment as well as the objects that furnished it. From 1877, through founding and campaigning for the Society for the Protection of Ancient Buildings, Morris made the powerful and, for his time, radical argument that everyone, including future generations, had a stake in historic buildings and that protecting their integrity should come before the whims of private owners. As we shall see, and alongside the efforts of other designers and artists of his generation, Morris's role in shaping the South Kensington Museum's growing collections was an extension of the same idea, bringing exemplary design and craftsmanship into the public realm.

From the very beginning, education for the designer and manufacturer was at the heart of the museum's founding mission – a parallel undertaking that Morris enthusiastically supported. His passion for improving the state of British art and design mirrored the South Kensington Museum's dedication 'to elevate the Art-Education of the whole people', in the words of its first director Henry Cole (1808–1882). Like Cole, Morris believed in the universal need for creative education: 'Everybody ought to be taught to draw just as much as everybody be taught to read and write', he argued in 1882. Cole sought to demonstrate the everyday importance of good design, just as Morris worked tirelessly to bring beautifully designed products into daily life. For him, beauty was 'a positive necessity', not a luxury but essential to human happiness. The beauty of humanity and the soul of society should be expressed through the joy of designing and making. Today, the V&A remains true to these egalitarian aims, and the civic principles that Morris first helped to codify still resonate throughout the museum.

Morris as designer

In 1851 William Morris and his family visited the famed Great Exhibition in London's Hyde Park – the first truly international gathering of design and manufacture – and, though not yet a designer, the 17-year-old Morris refused to go inside. He condemned the 'wonderfully ugly' British objects on display and rejected the modern spectacle of Joseph Paxton's steel-and-glass building encasing them. The Great Exhibition, a triumph of consumerism, industry and progress, would come to exemplify the sort of exploitative Victorian materialism that Morris fought against throughout his life. In his considered disregard for the capitalist precepts of mid-nineteenth-century Britain, Morris instead advocated recasting the present on the model of the past.

It is perhaps interesting then that Morris's fledgling firm, Morris, Marshall, Faulkner & Co., would first come to prominence at the Great Exhibition's successor, the 1862 International Exhibition in London. Like its predecessor, the International Exhibition was an exemplar of technological progress, and the firm's display of furniture, stained glass and embroideries in the Medieval Court met with mixed reviews. '[T]hey are no more adapted to the wants of living men than mediaeval armour would be to modern warfare', wrote one contemporary in *The Building News*. But the Exhibition Jury also praised the works and even awarded medals of commendation. It was not long before Morris's medieval-inspired aesthetic began to capture the attention of the nascent South Kensington Museum, with the first acquisition in 1864: four panels of stained glass, purchased at a total cost of £19 10*s*. Three of these panels came from a series based on Geoffrey Chaucer's *Legend of Good Women*, a dream-like poem composed around 1385–6, which became a favourite source for Morris and his circle (fig.227).

Morris's medieval aesthetic sprang partly from his revulsion toward contemporary machine-age goods. 'What is there in modern life for the man who seeks beauty? Nothing', he once lamented. 'The age is ugly – to find anything beautiful we must look "before and after"'. By 1851, the census had revealed England to be the first industrialized urban nation with over 50 per cent of its population resident in towns or cities. For Morris, this industrialized Britain was a world where 'the automatic machine ... supersedes hand-labour, and turns the workman who was once a handicraftsman helped by tools, and next a part of a machine, into a tender of machines.' Morris was concerned not only with the wellbeing of the workforce, but also with the impact of mass-production on the quality of the end product. For him these two things were inextricable – the bland uniformity (and often poor quality) of a machine-made object represented only dehumanization, the subjugation of workers denied the right to be creatively occupied in their work.

Morris clearly concurred with the critique that Karl Marx and Friedrich Engels had developed in *The Communist Manifesto* (1848) on the psychological effects of industrialization on the worker: 'Owing to the extensive use of machinery, and to the division of labour, the work of the proletarians has lost all individual character, and, consequently, all charm for the workman.' Morris looked to the past for alternatives and championed the revival of traditional techniques and handcraftsmanship. He longed for 'the face of medieval England', where communities of artisans could express their creative individuality with dignity, free from the exploitations of factory labour and the destructive competitiveness of modern society. Morris was certainly not oblivious to some of the less appealing realities of medieval life, in his article 'The Revival of Handicraft'

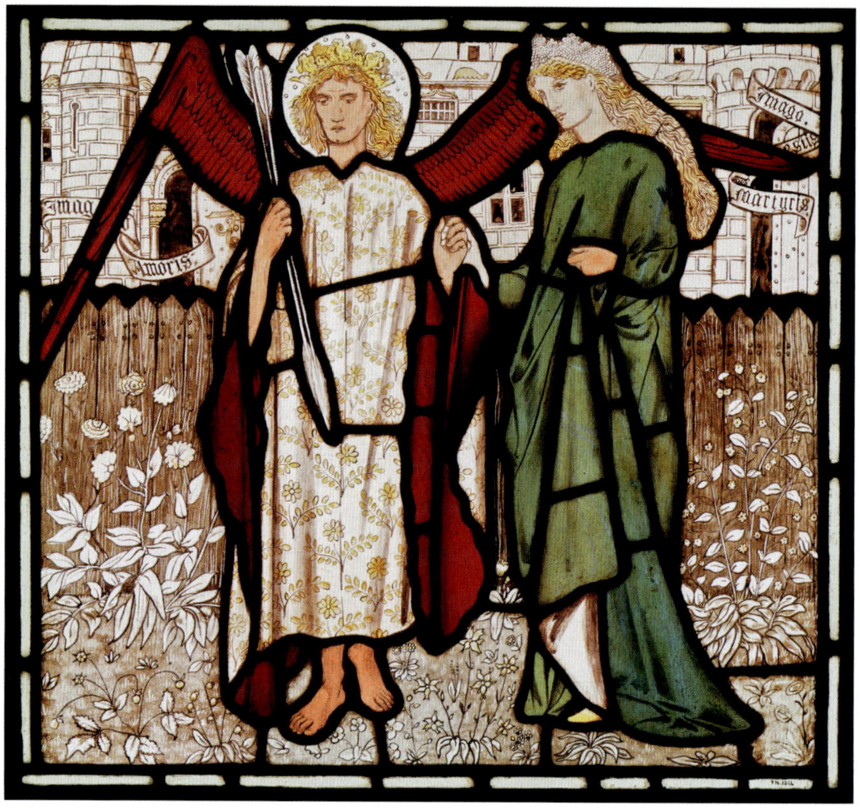

Fig.227 ***The God of Love and Alceste*, one of the South Kensington Museum's earliest purchases from Morris's firm (see VII.20).**
V&A (776–1864)

(1888) he acknowledged that it was also a time of 'war and turmoil and uncertainty of life', yet, he argued, the opportunity to participate in intelligent handicraft made life tolerable and worth living.

For Morris, like his friend and intellectual mentor, John Ruskin, progress meant, in fact, spurning mass production and specialization, rejecting excessive reliance on machinery and the modern institutions of the state, and turning back, in Ruskin's words, to 'the subtlest of all machines, which is the human hand.' Art and work should be indivisible, with all work, artistic or otherwise, of equal moral merit; artistic value could even be measured by the labour involved. These principles, including truth to nature and moral emphasis, were encouraged and championed by Ruskin, helping Morris to articulate and nurture his new artistic culture. Morris was always quick to make known his debt, as in his preface to the 1892 Kelmscott Press edition of Ruskin's 'The Nature of Gothic':

> To some of us when we first read it ... it seemed to point out a new road on which the world should travel ... For the lesson that Ruskin here teaches us is that art is the expression of man's pleasure in labour; that it is possible for man to rejoice in his work...

This convergence of opinion stopped with the South Kensington Museum (fig.228). Unlike Morris, Ruskin thought the museum to be confused, vulgar and fundamentally antagonistic to his aesthetic principles. More than that, he was adamantly opposed to the 'modern art-teaching, centralized by Kensington'. But perhaps the greatest affront to Ruskin was the sheer richness of the collections. He thought the museum 'full of precious and instructive things, but they are surrounded by the vilest, and the very aspect of these, even if not chosen for imitation, prevents the qualities of the good ones from being felt.' In Ruskin's view, this abundance prevented the student or workman from gaining a higher level of intellectual or artistic understanding from the displays. Evidently this was not so for Morris, who rejoiced at the unceasing inspiration he could harvest from South Kensington's galleries, 'perhaps I have used it as much as any man living.'

Morris's focus on medieval techniques was one way in which their shared philosophies could be ratified in an age of capitalist ephemera. Among other notable works from the 1862 International Exhibition, the most famous is the *St George* cabinet (see IX.14) – designed by Philip Webb and painted by Morris with scenes from the legend of the patron saint of England. Critics praised its 'true medieval spirit'. Morris had – in his figurative scheme – attempted to emulate the narrative qualities of late medieval Italian marriage chests. What is more, the cabinet borrowed a medieval technique for layering tinted varnishes on a ground of silver leaf (fig.229), a method revived by the designer William Burges. Also on display at the International Exhibition was *King René's Honeymoon* cabinet (see IX.13), designed by the architect John Pollard Seddon and decorated by Morris's firm with panels representing the Fine and Applied Arts. The panel illustrating ironwork features a loose portrait of Morris himself as a smith (fig.230). Both cabinets are totally unique, as Allison Stielau has written, 'the allure of the stridently one-of-a-kind piece in the midst of an age still reeling from the effects of the industrial revolution must have been powerful. And it may explain the bold asymmetries of Morris's and Webb's early furniture ... Like medieval armoires and sideboards, this furniture was not reproducible.' If to many contemporaries the furniture looked eccentric, this was deliberate. It was an opportunity to stir things up, to get noticed.

The firm's experiments with painted furniture were short-lived – soon giving way to Webb's more restrained (and practical) furniture – however, medieval art continued to influence and fascinate Morris in equal measure. As Linda Parry's research has shown, Morris's revival of lost or vanishing

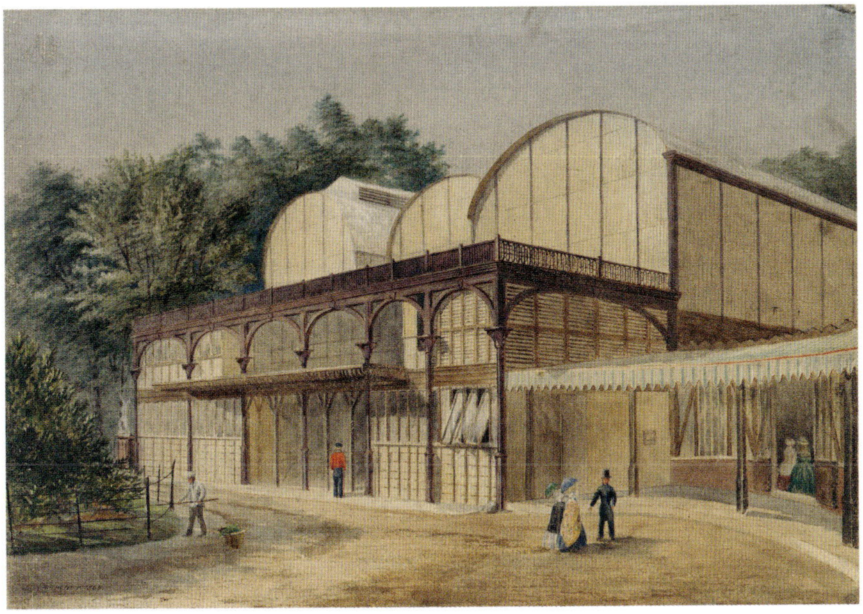

Fig.228 ***The South Kensington Museum* by J.C. Lanchenick, 1863.**
V&A (D.11–1903)

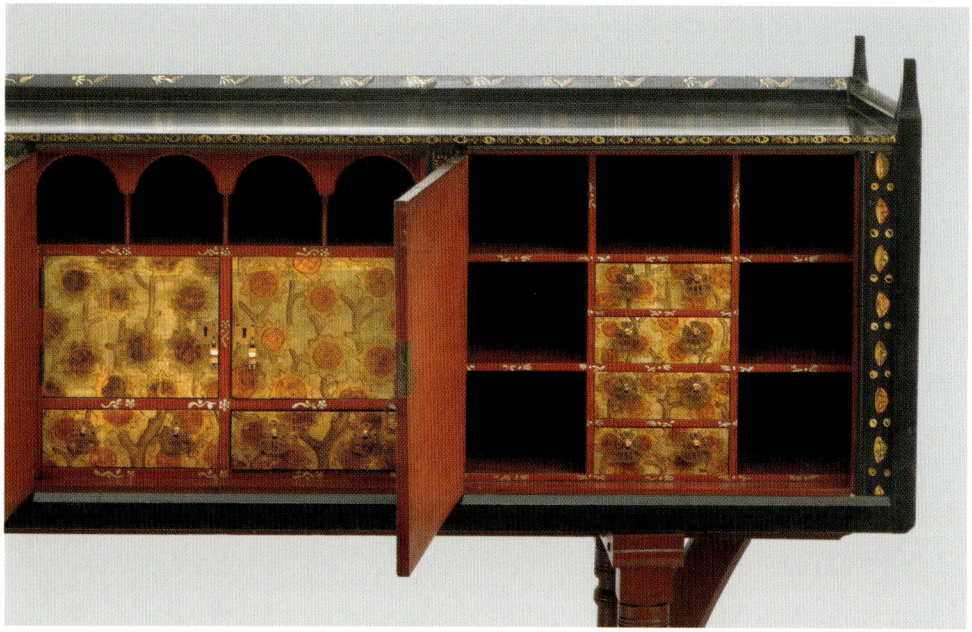

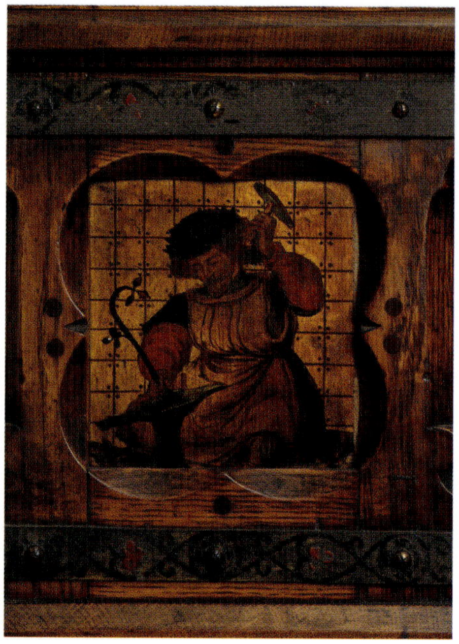

Fig.229 **Detail of the interior of the *St George* cabinet, decorated using a medieval technique (see IX.14).**
V&A (341–1906)

Fig.230 **Morris as a smith, detail from *King René's Honeymoon* cabinet (see IX.13).**
V&A (W.10–1927)

craft techniques was physically and intellectually extremely demanding, and often an expensive process of trial and error. It was an extraordinary achievement that Morris was able not only to attain such high standards of craftsmanship but also to make his products commercially viable in the nineteenth century. His revival of tapestry weaving was perhaps one of his greatest triumphs; just a few short years after he began to experiment with the technique, the firm's tapestries had become desirable high-status artworks (not since the seventeenth century had this been the case in England). The tapestries in the South Kensington Museum's collection were an important source of inspiration. Morris singled out one of his favourite examples, an early sixteenth-century Flemish work, *The Three Fates* (fig.231), in his lecture 'Textile Fabrics' delivered at the South Kensington Museum in 1884: 'This beautiful piece is a representative of a particularly pleasing kind of decoration, where figures are introduced on a background of conventional flowers'.

In further testament to his appreciation for the work, Morris even asked the museum's then-Director for Art, Thomas Armstrong, if he could borrow the tapestry as a prop to illustrate his 'Textiles' lecture delivered in November 1888 – part of a series sponsored by the Arts and Crafts Exhibition Society. Armstrong deeply admired Morris's work, believing him to be 'a man who has done more than any other in our times to raise and ennoble the position of the decorative artist'. Though it is not clear if Armstrong agreed to lend the tapestry, this remains a strong demonstration of how Morris repeatedly used the museum collections to assist and promote his creative purpose. Among the earliest works acquired by the museum after Morris's death was the exquisite *Orchard* tapestry (see XII.113), purchased on the recommendation of the artist John Hungerford Pollen and Morris's close friend, George Howard, Earl of Carlisle, and illustrating his homage to medieval precedents.

Alongside such museum exhibits, Morris's influence extended into the very fabric of the building. Cole commissioned Morris's nascent firm to design one of the museum's three new refreshment rooms in 1865, just a year after first acquiring examples of the designer's work. These rooms were an innovation – the first purpose-built museum refreshment rooms in the world – designed for comfort and pleasure, while attracting new visitors. 'A bridge between pleasing the public and offering instruction', as described by Giles Waterfield in his seminal book, *The People's Galleries* (2015). Cole had learnt about visitors' practical requirements while managing the Great Exhibition and his vision, which twinned education with leisure, often stressed the provision of refreshment. Most other museums did not invest in catering until the twentieth century.

The 'Western Refreshment Room' was one of the firm's first important secular commissions (fig.140). In October 1867 plans were approved

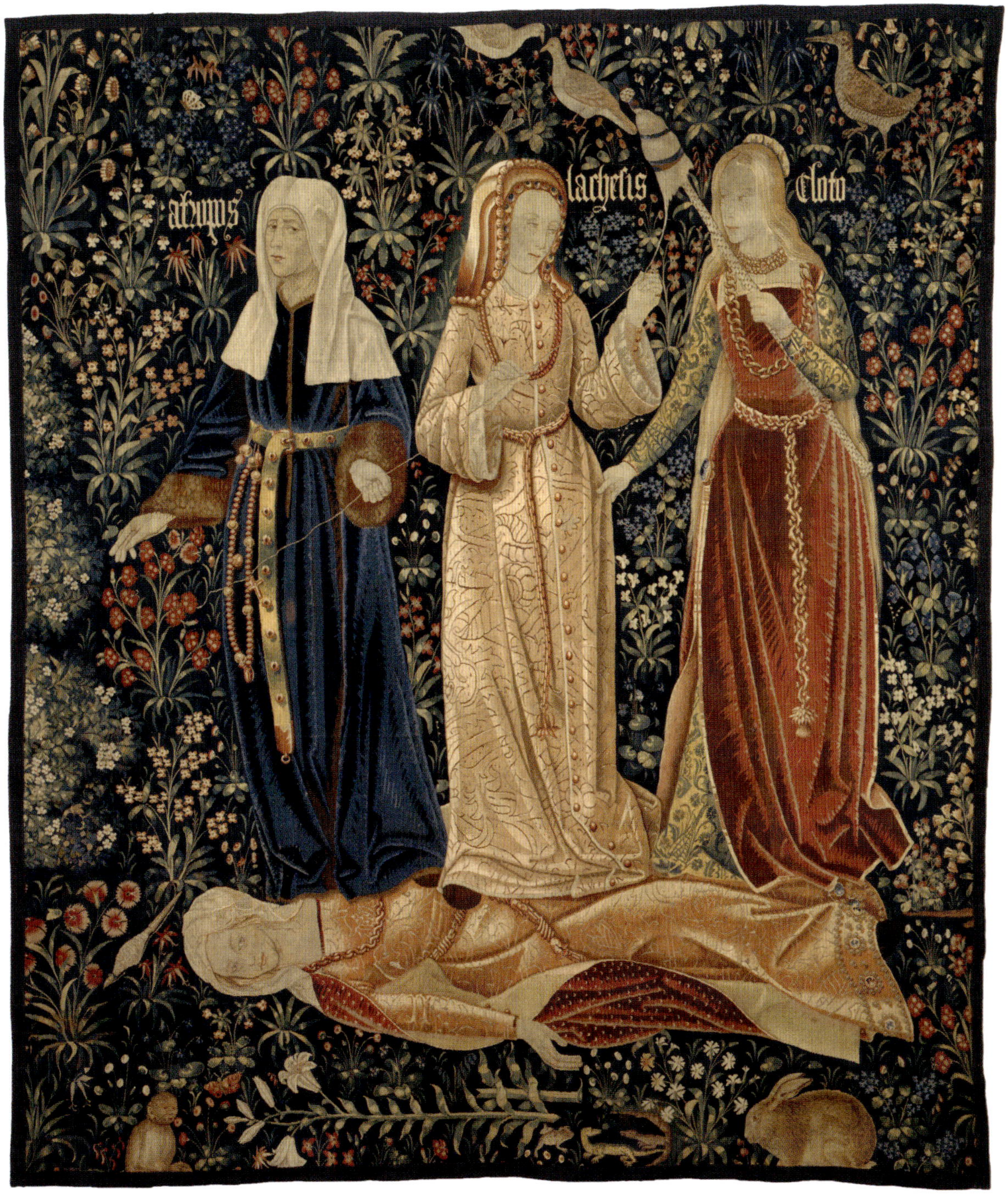

Fig.231 ***The Three Fates*** **tapestry, Flemish, *c.*1510–20.**
V&A (65 & A–1866)

and Morris, Webb and Edward Burne-Jones began collaborating on the room's richly decorated panelling and plasterwork. Painted panels depicted the signs of the zodiac, fruits and foliage, and stained-glass windows showed women tending to or adorned with flowers. The ceiling featured floral arabesques and geometric patterns transferred from paper cartoons. The room became a popular meeting place for artists and writers, including J.M. Whistler, Edward Poynter and George du Maurier.

The 'Green Dining Room', as it came to be known thanks to its distinctive colour scheme, is the only Morris decoration within the V&A to have remained intact. Today, the space – still in use within the museum café and little changed – is named in the designer's honour. Yet many visitors remain unaware of the radical nature

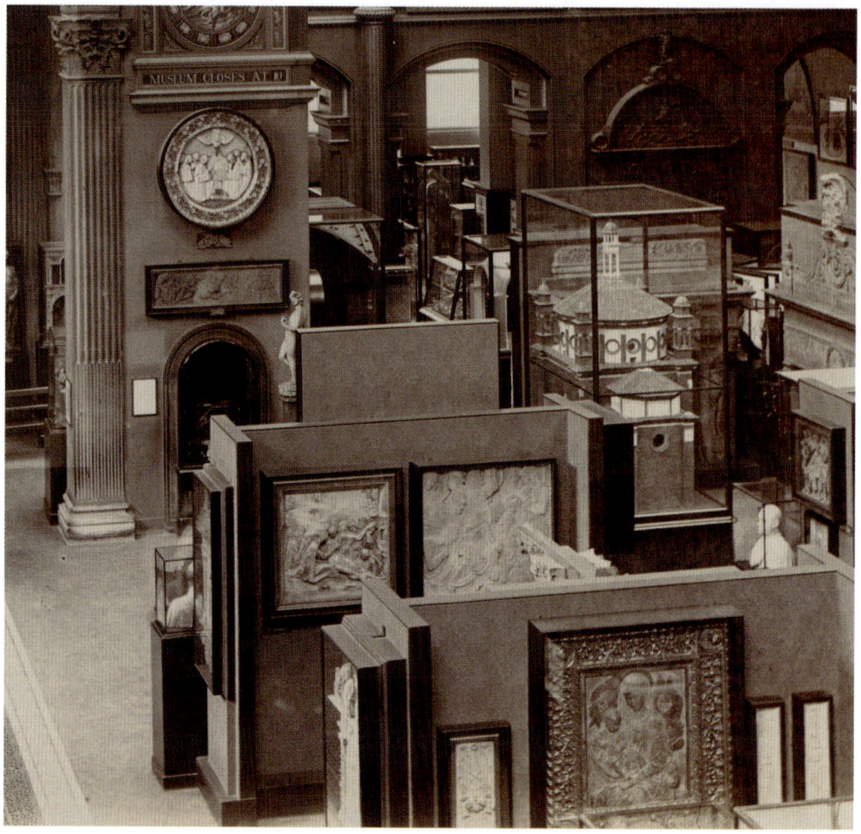

Fig.232 **The North Court in the late nineteenth century, showing display stands decorated with Morris & Co.'s *Marigold* wallpaper.** V&A (E.1101–1989)

of its design at the time of its creation, what Sally-Anne Huxtable has called a 'political manifesto writ large'. With the room's idyllic pastoral scenes – the interjection of the countryside into South Kensington – city dwellers could escape to Arcadia. The Victorian city held no place in Morris's pursuit of beauty. The artists' anti-urban vision for society, carried out in the spirit of medieval revival, also reflected the museum's own democratic aspirations. This was a communal setting that everyone, the working classes included, could utilize and enjoy. Cole was deeply attentive to his visitors' experiences, and with his pioneering restaurant, all were welcome to admire the beautiful surroundings. For Morris, who strove to make art omnipresent in everyday life, this egalitarian setting must have been a welcome development.

Later on, in his lecture 'The Lesser Arts' published in *Hopes and Fears for Art* (1882), Morris would further express his support for this type of unrestricted approach. He spoke of his desire for London's museums to be open seven days a week (instead of six), to enable an 'ordinarily busy man' to be able to visit. Cole, too, wanted the museum to be open on Sundays, and in pushing for its realization, Sunday opening was finally achieved for London's national museums in 1896.

Further Morris contributions to the museum's interior design have not survived – most notably wallpapers that once adorned the walls of the Sheepshanks painting galleries and display stands in the North Court (fig.232). One of these was the *Marigold* pattern, first produced in 1875. Interestingly, Thomas Armstrong, thinking it 'desirable to have a pattern on the walls on which the pictures are hung', commented that the paper's colour was 'a little too bright'. In response, Jeffrey & Co. of Islington, Morris & Co.'s wallpaper printers, produced a bespoke colourway in 'ochres only and ochres distressed with Vandyke Brown' and presented the alternative for Armstrong's approval in November 1893. Just as Armstrong deeply admired Morris's work, Morris too appeared to mutually respect Armstrong's judgment.

The refreshment room commission raised the firm's profile and the business flourished in its mission to promote beautiful domestic design. 'If you want a golden rule that will fit everybody, this is it: have nothing in your houses that you do not know to be useful, or believe to be beautiful,' as Morris memorably put it. Through Morris's design brilliance and business marketing gift, alongside a growing middle class keen to clad their houses in the most edifying designs, he helped to change the late Victorian aesthetic. As Aymer Vallance wrote in his 1897 study, Morris had:

> brought Art, through the medium of the handicrafts, within reach of thousands who could never hope to obtain but a transitory view of Pre-Raphaelite pictures; his distinction, by decorating the less pretending but not less necessary articles of household furnishing, to have done more than any man in the present century to beautify the plain, everyday, home-life of the people.

Morris as Art Referee

Morris and the South Kensington Museum continued to develop a relationship based on mutual respect and support. Even before his official appointment to the museum's remunerated Committee of Art Referees in 1884 – on which he served until his death – he was consulted on prospective museum acquisitions, especially on important carpets and tapestries, and asked to make recommendations (or otherwise) on objects that were being considered by the museum for purchase. With this appointment, Morris had

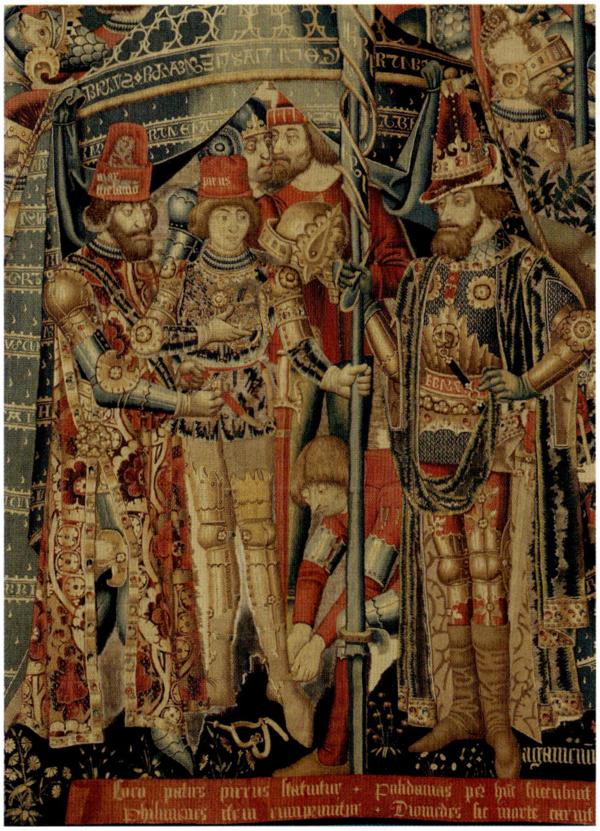

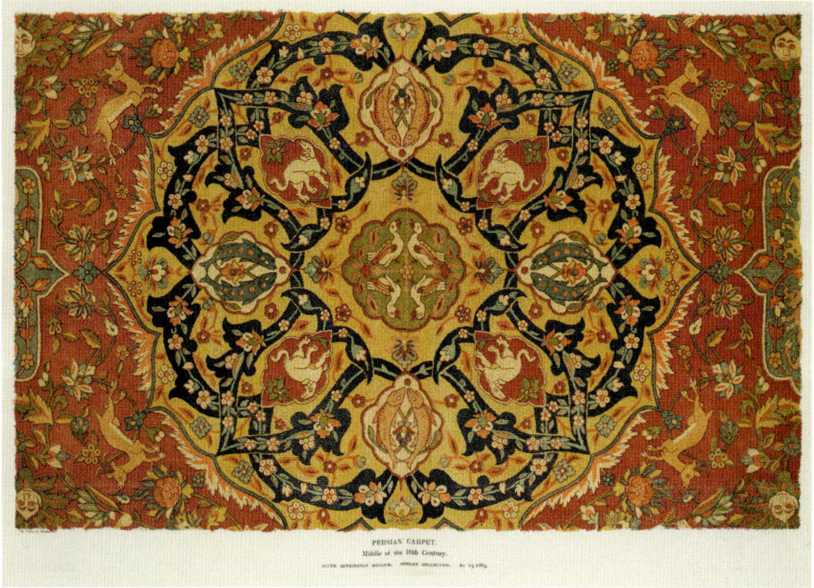

Fig.233 **Detail of the Trojan War tapestry with scenes inspired by medieval retellings of the classical legend, Tournai, late fifteenth century.**
V&A (6–1887)

Fig.234 **Medallion carpet, Iran, sixteenth century. Recommended by Morris and published in the South Kensington Museum's *Portfolio of Persian Art*, 1884.**
V&A (23–1883)

acquired another means to enhance public access to great works of design.

Morris's referee reports brim with passion and excitement for the objects he advised on. In 1886 he wrote a letter of support for the acquisition of a medieval tapestry from Tournai in northern France (modern-day Belgium) depicting scenes from the Trojan War (fig.233). It was made as one of a set of lavish large-scale tapestries (together measuring over 100m), illustrating the classical myth retold as a medieval romance. Both Morris and Burne-Jones agreed 'there is not in existence such another piece of romance as this tapestry. It represents the later middle ages in the limit', Morris adding, 'I should be in despair if you let such a Chance slip.' The legend of Troy had fascinated Morris since his twenties, featuring in his early poetry and considered for one of the decorative schemes at Red House. It is easy to see why this tapestry meant so much to him, combining his love of storytelling with exquisite technical skill and meticulously observed details, not least the luxurious patterned damasks. The museum did indeed acquire the tapestry, and he later wrote in his 'Socialist Diary': 'Went to SKM yesterday with Jenny to look at the Troy tapestry again since they have bought it for £1250: I chuckled to think that properly speaking it was bought for me, since scarcely anybody will care a damn for it.' Today it is regarded as one of the most significant and well-documented survivals from the period.

Perhaps the most famous acquisition that Morris was to consult on was the Ardabil Carpet (fig.235). This vast and complex object was made in Iran in the early sixteenth century, originally one of a pair though this was not publicly known when it came on the market in London. The world's oldest dated carpet, it is considered a masterpiece of Safavid design. Knotted by hand, it was produced for the ancestral shrine of the Safavid shahs, though for Morris its principal significance was its design quality rather than its historical associations. As a carpet manufacturer himself, he would have been in awe of the exceptionally dense knot count, which allowed for very precise rendering of details. His deep personal admiration for the object is palpable in his letters: 'It would be a crime to let it go. I never saw such a design in my life.' He was adamant in his conviction: 'the design is of singular perfection; defensible on all points, logically and consistently beautiful, with no oddities or grotesqueries which might

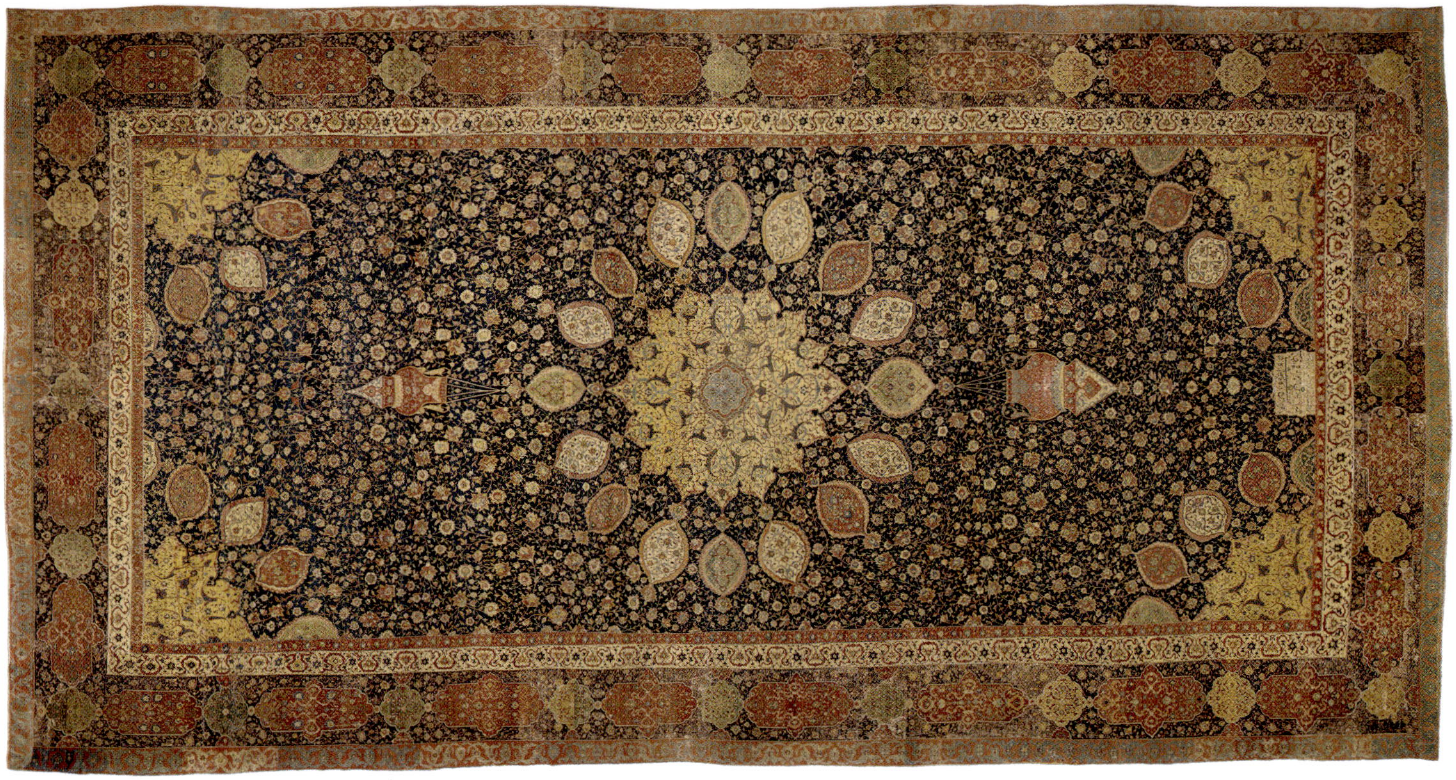

Fig.235 **The Ardabil Carpet, signed and dated 946H (1539–40), Iran.**
V&A (272–1893)

need an apology, and therefore most especially valuable for a Museum, the special aim of which is the education of the public in Art.' Morris was instrumental in persuading the museum to raise, with the aid of public subscription, the vast sum required to purchase the carpet in 1893. But his comments also reflect his instinctive support of the museum's educational mission: 'there was nothing more suited to further the ends for which your Museum and your Schools exist than the constant sight of a work of such exceptionally high merit and beauty'.

This insistence on the educational importance of historic Iranian carpets had been evident in his correspondence with the museum for many years. As early as 1883, before his formal appointment as Art Referee, Morris had enthusiastically supported the purchase of another sixteenth-century medallion carpet: 'I have no hesitation in classing the carpet amongst the most excellent of the *ancient* examples of the art ... there is no chance of meeting with a similar one'. He described it as 'most valuable from an artistic and educational point of view ... I beg to remark that at present the Museum possesses *no* fine example of carpet weaving, a very serious deficiency in such a collection.' Accepting Morris's verdict, the museum purchased the carpet for £308 (fig.234).

Morris would likely have been thrilled by the V&A's extensive and renowned collections from the Islamic Middle East today, particularly the twelve centuries of Persian and Iranian art. For Morris, the fluid plant forms, rich colour palettes and traditional techniques of Persian design registered perfectly with his own creative philosophy. He admired the way that patterns combined the suggestion of natural growth with a high degree of abstraction, remaining essentially two-dimensional. 'To us pattern-designers, Persia has become a holy land, for there in the process of time our art was perfected', Morris enthused in 1879. Morris's great ardour for non-European art – a passion that he shared with other contemporaries including Owen Jones (1809–1874), Christopher Dresser (1834–1904) and Henry Cole – brought the influence of Islamic art into many of his own designs.

By the time the Ardabil Carpet came onto the market in the 1890s, Morris was one voice among many supporters, but his appreciation for these historic carpets was, at first, not often shared. Speaking at the Kidderminster Chamber of Commerce in 1880, one leading manufacturer referred to 'oriental' carpets as 'atrocities ... worn threadbare, almost filthy'. They have become popular, he declared, because 'Mr Morris and some other upholstering poets have sung their praises'. At the V&A, we can be thankful for Morris's foresight, particularly when increasingly competitive prices were later placing many historic carpets out of reach of meagre museum budgets. It is only through Morris's energy and resolve that we can view many of these spectacular works in the museum today.

Morris as educator

By improving the quality of British museum collections, Morris sought to enrich the sourcebook of inspiration available to artists and designers. Of course, the South Kensington Museum – with its particular remit around creative and technical learning – was an obvious ally to Morris's own ambitions for art education. Its place within the Government Schools of Design and the Department of Science and Art gave it a dedicated mission as a vehicle for improvement and knowledge transfer. Wishing to reform British design training, the Government Schools were established with a commercial mission, to improve national design standards in order to compete in international markets. Initially, the South Kensington Museum was envisaged as a teaching aide for the design schools, with acquisitions considered for their didactic benefit and value for study. To assist this educational cause, Morris agreed to serve as an examiner for the South Kensington School of Design from the late 1870s. Morris's own daughter, May, would enroll at the School in 1878, where she focused on embroidery, an aspect of her father's business that she would take on responsibility for in 1885.

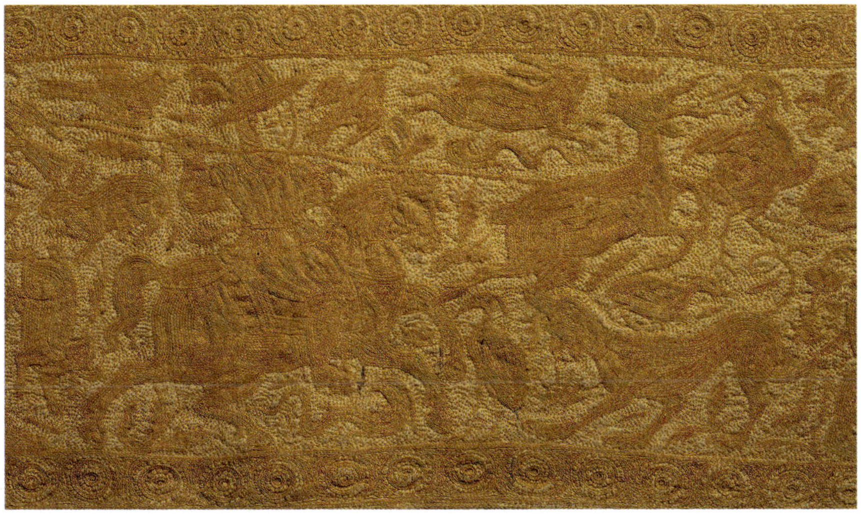

Fig.236 **Detail of embroidered quilt from Morris's collection, Bengal, early seventeenth century.**
V&A (616–1886)

When the Royal Commission on Technical Instruction gathered at the museum in 1882 to examine the British education system in response to international competition, Morris was called as an expert witness. In echoes of the 1835 Select Committee on Arts and Manufactures, which famously resulted in the creation of the Government Schools of Design, the Commission acknowledged the poor standards of design and lack of professional opportunity. Unsurprisingly, Morris argued that design standards could be improved with a greater knowledge of the manufacturing processes: 'I think it essential that a designer should learn the practical way of carrying out the work for which he designs'. This opposition to the division of labour was a philosophy shared by many of his socialist contemporaries.

Just as Morris supported the system of regional design schools around the country, he also championed the educational role of museums in manufacturing centres outside of London. For Morris, who had benefited so much from the collections at South Kensington, believed this type of resource essential for any designer. Much like Ruskin, he argued that: 'A museum, to be of any great use to those who are studying in it as artists or as designers, must be arranged in a permanent manner, so that one can come day after day to see the same thing'. Though the idea of static displays might seem unappealing to a contemporary audience, it does show how intensely Morris used the collections, returning again and again for inspiration. Though it took some time, it was partly through Morris's influence on leading artist–educators such as Walter Crane, Robert Catterson-Smith and William Richard Lethaby that the teaching of craft skills was flourishing in art schools around the country by the turn of the twentieth century.

Morris also contributed to the museum's collections himself. In 1893 he donated miniature carpet and tapestry looms – previously used to instruct weavers at Morris & Co.'s Merton Abbey workshops (see XII.87 and XII.108). Both hold small samples of work in progress to help visitors visualize the making process. In addition, Morris lent items from his personal collection for exhibition, most significantly in 1896, when he loaned five illuminated manuscripts, including the Worksop Bestiary, the Huntingfield Psalter and the Grey or Clifford Hours. Other works were sold to the museum, offered at fair prices, such as an early seventeenth-century embroidered quilt (fig.236), described by Morris as 'Goa embroidery done for a European', and acquired in 1886 for £120. After Morris's death, and presumably with his wishes in mind, Jane Morris sold the museum the fine Iranian carpet that once decorated their dining room in Hammersmith (VIII.16) and now hangs in the Jameel Gallery.

Morris as socialist

With its café, gas lighting for evening visits, Sunday openings and conscious ethos of accessibility, the museum actively invited working-class audiences. Between 1857 and 1883, more than 6.5 million of the total 15 million visits were made during the evenings when the working-class population could attend. The museum's purpose was to serve, in the words of Henry Cole, as a 'Schoolroom for Everyone'. Its focus on public access and the support of national design education, was a natural fit for Morris, not only in his role as designer, but also as political thinker, activist and social reformer.

Morris's passion for art and design was inherently tied to his ethical socialism and during the course of the late nineteenth century he steadily took his design thinking in a more avowedly left-wing direction. Morris had always felt uneasy about the disparity between his comfortable lifestyle and the conditions endured by the British working classes, and he deeply regretted that his products were so expensive. He was under no illusion that he was providing beautiful things for the 'swinish luxury of the rich', as he described the clientele of his firm. His own experiences as a manufacturer had taught him that 'art cannot have a real life and growth under the present system of commercialism and profit-mongering.'

Morris joined Henry Hyndman's Democratic Federation in 1883 – the first organization in Britain to publicize and advocate Marx's ideas clearly – but was never a fully-fledged scholar of Marxian political economy. According to the Scottish socialist John Bruce Glasier, Morris once exclaimed at a public meeting;

> To speak quite frankly, I do not know what Marx's theory of value is, and I'm damned if I want to know ... It is enough political economy for me to know that the idle class is rich and the working class is poor, and that the rich are rich because they rob the poor.

After falling out with Hyndman, he joined key figures such as Edward Aveling and Eleanor Marx in establishing the Socialist League in 1884, with its beautifully designed journal *Commonweal* launching the following year.

Unsurprisingly, Friedrich Engels was wont initially to dismiss Morris as 'a very rich but politically inept art lover', but after the split from the Social Democratic Federation and the discovery of a shared interest in Old Norse mythology the friendship warmed. Not for long: as soon as the ill-disciplined Morris started to flirt with anarchism, Engels excommunicated him as 'a sentimental dreamer pure and simple'.

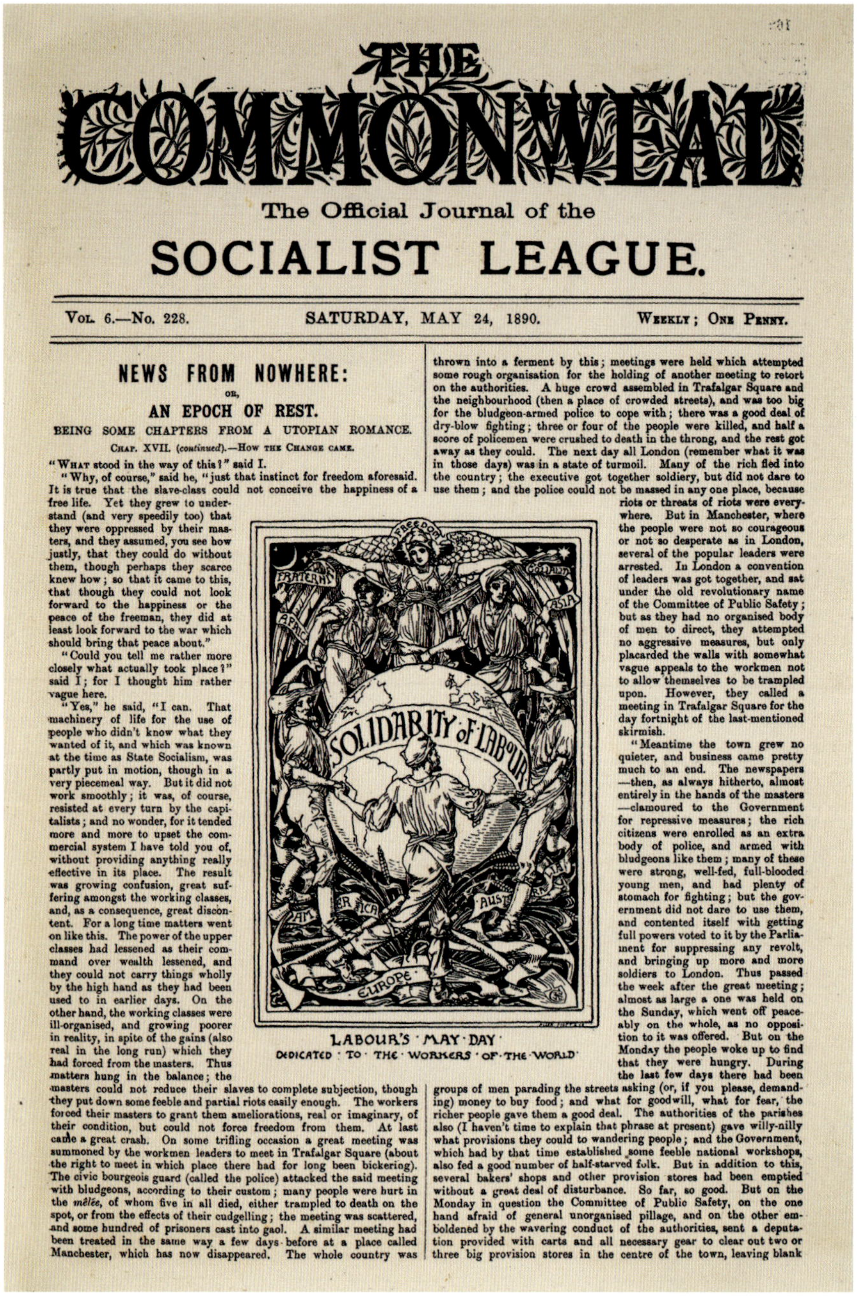

THE COMMONWEAL

The Official Journal of the

SOCIALIST LEAGUE.

VOL. 6.—No. 228. SATURDAY, MAY 24, 1890. WEEKLY; ONE PENNY.

NEWS FROM NOWHERE:

OR,

AN EPOCH OF REST.

BEING SOME CHAPTERS FROM A UTOPIAN ROMANCE.

CHAP. XVII. (*continued*).—HOW THE CHANGE CAME.

"WHAT stood in the way of this?" said I.

"Why, of course," said he, "just that instinct for freedom aforesaid. It is true that the slave-class could not conceive the happiness of a free life. Yet they grew to understand (and very speedily too) that they were oppressed by their masters, and they assumed, you see how justly, that they could do without them, though perhaps they scarce knew how; so that it came to this, that though they could not look forward to the happiness or the peace of the freeman, they did at least look forward to the war which should bring that peace about."

"Could you tell me rather more closely what actually took place?" said I; for I thought him rather vague here.

"Yes," he said, "I can. That machinery of life for the use of people who didn't know what they wanted of it, and which was known at the time as State Socialism, was partly put in motion, though in a very piecemeal way. But it did not work smoothly; it was, of course, resisted at every turn by the capitalists; and no wonder, for it tended more and more to upset the commercial system I have told you of, without providing anything really effective in its place. The result was growing confusion, great suffering amongst the working classes, and, as a consequence, great discontent. For a long time matters went on like this. The power of the upper classes had lessened as their command over wealth lessened, and they could not carry things wholly by the high hand as they had been used to in earlier days. On the other hand, the working classes were ill-organised, and growing poorer in reality, in spite of the gains (also real in the long run) which they had forced from the masters. Thus matters hung in the balance; the masters could not reduce their slaves to complete subjection, though they put down some feeble and partial riots easily enough. The workers forced their masters to grant them ameliorations, real or imaginary, of their condition, but could not force freedom from them. At last came a great crash. On some trifling occasion a great meeting was summoned by the workmen leaders to meet in Trafalgar Square (about the right to meet in which place there had for long been bickering). The civic bourgeois guard (called the police) attacked the said meeting with bludgeons, according to their custom; many people were hurt in the *mêlée*, of whom five in all died, either trampled to death on the spot, or from the effects of their cudgelling; the meeting was scattered, and some hundred of prisoners cast into gaol. A similar meeting had been treated in the same way a few days before at a place called Manchester, which has now disappeared. The whole country was thrown into a ferment by this; meetings were held which attempted some rough organisation for the holding of another meeting to retort on the authorities. A huge crowd assembled in Trafalgar Square and the neighbourhood (then a place of crowded streets), and was too big for the bludgeon-armed police to cope with; there was a good deal of dry-blow fighting; three or four of the people were killed, and half a score of policemen were crushed to death in the throng, and the rest got away as they could. The next day all London (remember what it was in those days) was in a state of turmoil. Many of the rich fled into the country; the executive got together soldiery, but did not dare to use them; and the police could not be massed in any one place, because riots or threats of riots were everywhere. But in Manchester, where the people were not so courageous or not so desperate as in London, several of the popular leaders were arrested. In London a convention of leaders was got together, and sat under the old revolutionary name of the Committee of Public Safety; but as they had no organised body of men to direct, they attempted no aggressive measures, but only placarded the walls with somewhat vague appeals to the workmen not to allow themselves to be trampled upon. However, they called a meeting in Trafalgar Square for the day fortnight of the last-mentioned skirmish.

"Meantime the town grew no quieter, and business came pretty much to an end. The newspapers —then, as always hitherto, almost entirely in the hands of the masters —clamoured to the Government for repressive measures; the rich citizens were enrolled as an extra body of police, and armed with bludgeons like them; many of these were strong, well-fed, full-blooded young men, and had plenty of stomach for fighting; but the government did not dare to use them, and contented itself with getting full powers voted to it by the Parliament for suppressing any revolt, and bringing up more and more soldiers to London. Thus passed the week after the great meeting; almost as large a one was held on the Sunday, which went off peaceably on the whole, as no opposition to it was offered. But on the Monday the people woke up to find that they were hungry. During the last few days there had been groups of men parading the streets asking (or, if you please, demanding) money to buy food; and what for goodwill, what for fear, the richer people gave them a good deal. The authorities of the parishes also (I haven't time to explain that phrase at present) gave willy-nilly what provisions they could to wandering people; and the Government, which had by that time established some feeble national workshops, also fed a good number of half-starved folk. But in addition to this, several bakers' shops and other provision stores had been emptied without a great deal of disturbance. So far, so good. But on the Monday in question the Committee of Public Safety, on the one hand afraid of general unorganised pillage, and on the other emboldened by the wavering conduct of the authorities, sent a deputation provided with carts and all necessary gear to clear out two or three big provision stores in the centre of the town, leaving blank

LABOUR'S · MAY · DAY ·
DEDICATED · TO · THE · WORKERS · OF · THE · WORLD ·

Fig.237 **Front page of the 24 May 1890 edition of *Commonweal*, showing one of the weekly instalments of *News from Nowhere* and a cartoon by Morris's socialist comrade, Walter Crane.**
Labadie Collection, University of Michigan

Engels feared it would take an exhaustive course of bi-weekly seminars to teach Morris anything credible about socialism, 'but who has the time to do it, and if you drop him for a month, he is sure to lose himself again. And is he worth all that trouble even if one had the time?' And so Engels whimsically and short-sightedly turned his back on potentially the most inspiring and magnetic figure within the British socialist pantheon.

Despite Engels's disregard, Morris continued to meditate on the nature of socialism. Perhaps the clearest account of his socialist philosophy was his utopian fiction, *News from Nowhere* (1890), first published in serial form in *Commonweal* (fig.237) and later revised and printed by his own Kelmscott Press (see fig.67). Set in the London of the future, Morris depicted a society where capitalism and parliamentary governance had been overthrown by violent revolution.

> 'Tell me one thing if you can,' said I. 'Did the change ... come peacefully?'
>
> 'Peacefully?' said he; 'what peace was there amongst those poor confused wretches of the nineteenth century? It was war from beginning to end: bitter war, till hope and pleasure put an end to it.'

Standing in place of London – 'the heart of the Empire' – was a rural Elysium where artisans (in fourteenth-century dress) lived in small communes and worked in self-governing craft guilds, where the Houses of Parliament had been converted into a giant dung heap, and factories and suburbs had been replaced by forests and meadows.

The Thames landscape was a very different place. 'The soap-works with their smoke-vomiting chimneys were gone; the engineer's works gone; the lead-works gone; and no sound of riveting and hammering came down the west wind.' Morris depicted an epoch of rest after the socialist revolution; a land of beauty and art that would teach a desire for a better life. The nineteenth century urban-industrial world was recast as a symbol of greed and misery. There could be no more attempts at gradual reform; it had to be destroyed and reborn as a different society.

Morris was motivated by the perception that industrial capitalism separates people from their true humanity by diverting individual longing into 'sham wants'. The citizens of 'Nowhere', by contrast, have 'cast away riches and attained to wealth'. Social revolution restored to mankind those things which were the gifts of nature. And at the heart of it was a notion of beauty and the importance of beauty in everyday life. This was the Morris vision, and his rebellion against the modernity and manufacturing of the nineteenth century ironically enough found a warm welcome at the South Kensington Museum: a museum born of the Great Exhibition, committed to the advancement of British manufacture, and a public – as consumer – that could invigorate a capitalist society. Unlike the museum, which was educating designers and manufacturers in preparation for modern industry, Morris instead sought to rescue them from it, inspired by the noble world of the past to imagine a new kind of future.

Beneath this apparent paradox, there lay a profound accord, and not just because the museum had given Morris's firm one of its first significant commissions. In the nineteenth-century concept of the educational museum, South Kensington and its system of design schools was the archetype – a model replicated by museums worldwide. Just as Morris's firm recognized the commercial importance of originality and beauty, so, too, the South Kensington Museum asserted its duty to trade and industry through collecting and displaying instances of remarkable design. Both were committed to the educational pursuit of design reform and above all, both insisted upon the strength of the museum's collections for these purposes. Morris's unshakeable faith in the usefulness of the museum as reference collection would ultimately overcome any residual reservations about the legacy of 1851 and its tarnished, commercial foundations.

Legacy

Though a few examples of Morris's work were purchased by the South Kensington Museum during his lifetime, most designs in the collection were acquired posthumously. Morris characteristically showed little regard for his own memorialization and made no bequests to museums or galleries. His superb library and collection of manuscripts were sold off after his death and many of his finest works of decorative art were still in private hands, furnishing the homes of his illustrious clients. His firm, Morris & Co., continued in business until 1940. The original designs of the founding partners were highly prized and valuable assets, often continuing to serve a practical function in the workshop. Given these commercial sensitivities, it is not surprising that it took some time and determination to build up the V&A's Morris collection.

After Morris's death in 1896, Jane and May Morris began their careful work shaping and preserving his legacy. With her passion and talent for embroidery as an art form, May lectured widely on the subject, continuing her father's educational mission and upholding the philosophy and design ideals of the Arts and Crafts Movement. She took on the formidable task of editing his literary work; the 24 volumes of *The Collected Works* were published between 1910 and 1915 with new biographical introductions. Though she had no formal role in Morris & Co. after her father's death, it seems May continued to undertake some freelance embroidery work for the firm and tried, wherever possible, to encourage them to uphold her father's exacting standards of craftsmanship.

May also developed a long relationship with the V&A. She shared Morris's passion for the museum and the collections, especially of medieval English embroidery, which strongly influenced her own design practice. After co-founding the Women's Guild of Arts in 1907, to offer mutual support and encouragement for women working professionally in the arts, she used her connections with museum staff to support the Guild's activities. In 1911, for example, she took Guild members to view the V&A's collection of Persian pottery. Over time she helped develop the Morris collection, often acting as a valuable intermediary between the firm and the museum. In 1919 she wrote to the Keeper of Textiles, A.F. Kendrick, 'Morris & Co ... have piles of designs ... they really ought to be considered museum things now.' A steady campaign of correspondence, and the promise of future bequests, were used to encourage the creation of a permanent 'Morris Room' exhibit. Though this display did not fully materialize in her lifetime, May's determination culminated in the V&A's high-profile *William Morris Centenary Exhibition* in 1934 (fig.239). From more than 350 works on display, May loaned over eighty family possessions, temporarily stripping the interiors of her inherited home, Kelmscott Manor. More than that, May – in an unofficial curatorial role – was instrumental in co-writing the catalogue and advising on the selection and display of the objects. 'Completely successful', wrote *The Times,* 'it brings home the enormous range, versatility, and fertility of Morris'.

On her death in 1938, May bequeathed to the V&A a sizeable collection of her father's work. The gift included joint endeavours such as the *Acanthus* bedcover or hanging (see XII.19), designed by Morris and worked by May, as well as designs for wallpaper, textiles and embroidery. Other personal possessions were included in the bequest, for example a collection of jewels belonging to her late mother. Some of these were given to Jane Morris by Dante Gabriel Rossetti after serving as props in his paintings; this heart-shaped brooch for example was worn by the model Fanny Cornforth in *The Blue Bower* of 1865 (fig.238). It is largely thanks to May's determined efforts as custodian of her father's legacy that the V&A holds such a prominent and expansive collection relating to Morris's life.

Morris remained an important figure to the V&A throughout the twentieth century, and further exhibitions were staged to commemorate his diverse contributions. In 1952 the largest section of the V&A's *Victorian and Edwardian Decorative Arts* was devoted to the work of Morris and his associates. This groundbreaking show, widely recognized as a turning point in the appreciation and study of Victorian art, was conceived by Peter Floud (1911–1960), the charismatic Keeper of the Department of Circulation. Under Floud's leadership this branch of the museum developed a new scholarly expertise on the decorative arts of the nineteenth and twentieth centuries. His colleagues included Barbara Morris, Shirley Bury and Elizabeth Aslin, all art-school trained, who would go on to make major contributions to research in this field. The timing of the exhibition was important; in the early 1950s many of Morris's clients and business contacts were still alive and correspondence shows that Floud and his team determinedly followed these leads, capturing information that would otherwise have been lost. Though the literature on Morris is now an industry in its own right, serious study of his decorative work had not yet begun when they undertook this endeavour. The show was unexpectedly popular with the public and helped to inspire a new generation of collectors, dealers and art historians.

The major *William Morris* exhibition held at the V&A in 1996 to mark the centenary of the designer's death, and subsequently touring to Japan, introduced Morris to a new generation. Curated by Linda Parry, it combined a wealth of new research with a wider focus on the full range of Morris's activities as a designer, maker and campaigner. In particular, the detailed attention to process and the way that Morris

Fig.238 **Heart-shaped brooch gifted to Jane Morris by Dante Gabriel Rossetti.**
V&A (M.40–1939)

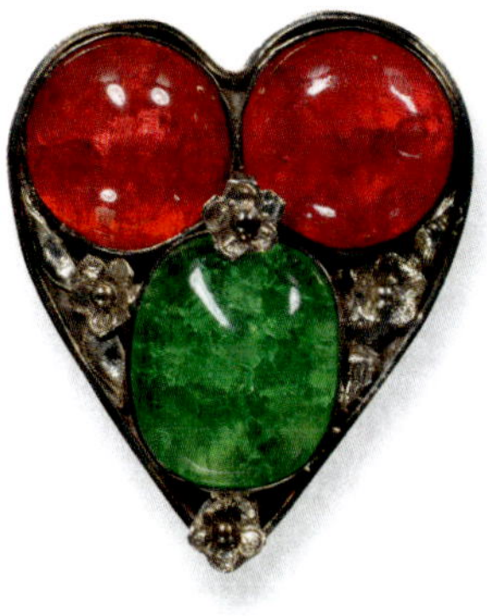

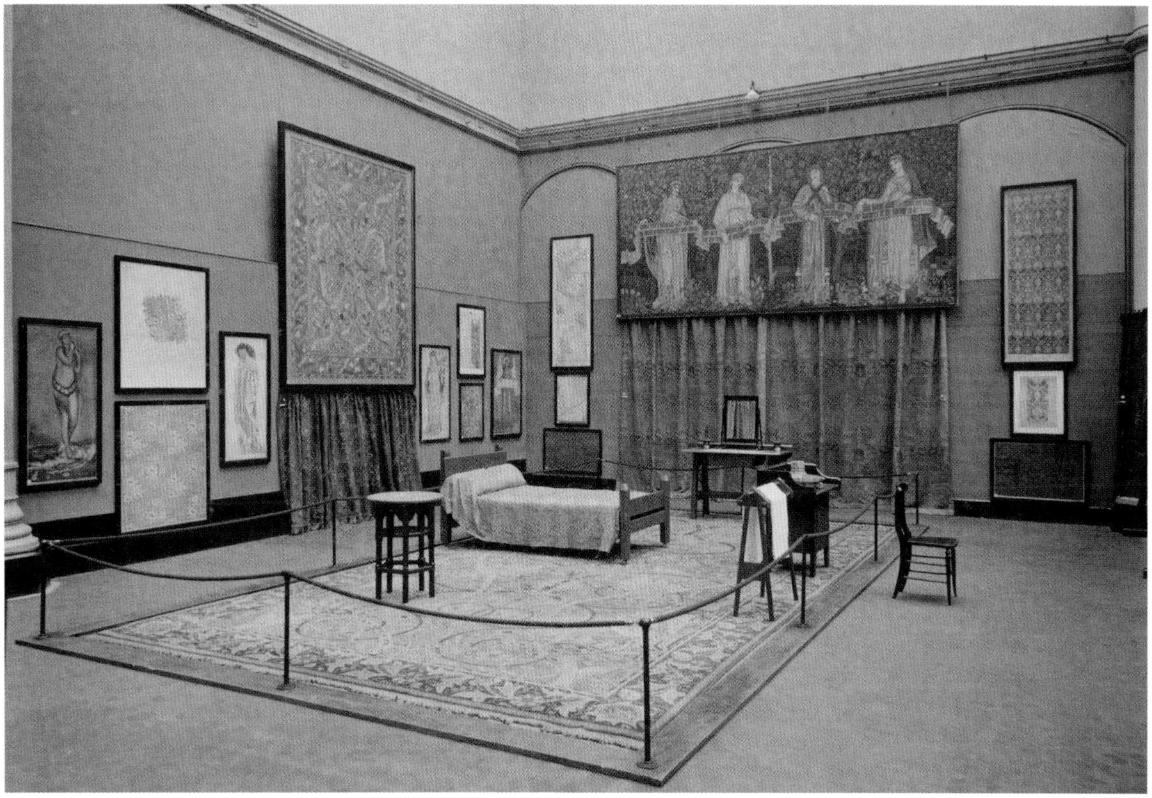

Fig.239 **View of the *William Morris Centenary Exhibition* held at the V&A in 1934.**
V&A (MA/32/231)

and his collaborators conceived and made their products, dispelled forever the myth that Morris's return to handiwork was a comfortable, nostalgic exercise. As Julie Codell has written in *Teaching William Morris* (2019), 'For Morris, craft tradition was not a fixed language or determined by unchanging technological practices and motifs to be repeated or imitated over and over, but was fluid, ever-changing'. Morris did not simply revive, he adapted and reinvigorated crafts practices to create something new for the world in which he lived and the future that he longed to see.

When we reflect on Morris's legacy and his enduring role at the V&A today, perhaps it is his educational mission that is most compelling. In recent years, we have renewed and reaffirmed our commitment to the nation's creative industries, looking to our roots in the design school movement of the 1840s – and to that same spirit of democratization and 'education for all' that drove Morris – to reinvest in young people's creative futures. At a time when access to culture is increasingly the preserve of the socio-economic elite, we are working hard to ensure that the V&A is once again a national incubator for creativity and a setting where the next generation of creative leaders, designers, makers, innovators and entrepreneurs can come to be inspired.

Our contemporary view of Morris should not be one of unquestionable advocacy; nor should we accept Morris's sweeping condemnations of modern industry without enquiry. But with his insistence on originality, artistry and craftsmanship, Morris helped revolutionize the late-Victorian interior, and today leaves a legacy of beauty and social conviction that remains compelling and relevant for the museum and design school he did so much to support in his lifetime. By continually updating the meaning of this museum as a contemporary force for democratizing access to art, culture and, above all, beauty for all, I hope we are honouring his memory with honesty and conviction.

XVI

BRITAIN AND BEYOND: MORRIS AND THE ARTS AND CRAFTS MOVEMENT

Karen Livingstone

By the end of his life, William Morris's legacy was secured and advanced through the development of the Arts and Crafts Movement in Britain, and beyond. His example as a skilled maker and designer, and the principles he applied to understanding materials, techniques and processes of making, provided inspiration and an important model for the architects, designers and makers of the next generation. As a reviewer of the Arts and Crafts Exhibition Society's fifth exhibition – which had been due to open on 3 October 1896 but was postponed following news of Morris's death that same day – wrote in *The Studio*:

> it was a splendid moment for a hero to die. The battle had been long, and the victory for many years by no means assured. Thus at the very hour – officially – when the new Arts and Crafts Exhibition opened its doors, when, instead of being a parochial or a national arena, it had assumed a cosmopolitan interest, the work he had done had received the laurels of success. True that the personal sadness of each member of the society imparted a gloom to the event; yet looking at the beautiful objects which his enterprise had made possible, one felt that although the master had been taken, the principles he had established were so firmly rooted, that the legend of William Morris would be the creed of the new movement, and loyal adherence to his teaching would rank more than ever as its watchword.

Morris was the main inspiration for the Arts and Crafts Movement; he was its spiritual father. Thanks to him and his followers, it became the dominant movement in craft and design in Britain from 1880 until about 1910 (sometimes persisting well into the twentieth century). The sympathetic ideals and practices of Arts and Crafts that flowed from Morris, and the example he set, quickly spread throughout North America and Europe and even further afield, including Japan.

The Arts and Crafts Movement brought about long-lasting changes to the way we appreciate crafts and how we think about the way things are made, how we live, and what we own. It ensured the survival of craft techniques and changed the way design and crafts were taught. Thanks to new organizations and new models for individual and workshop production, many more people started practising crafts and made them the focus of their lives and livelihoods. From the outset the Movement also had strong links with

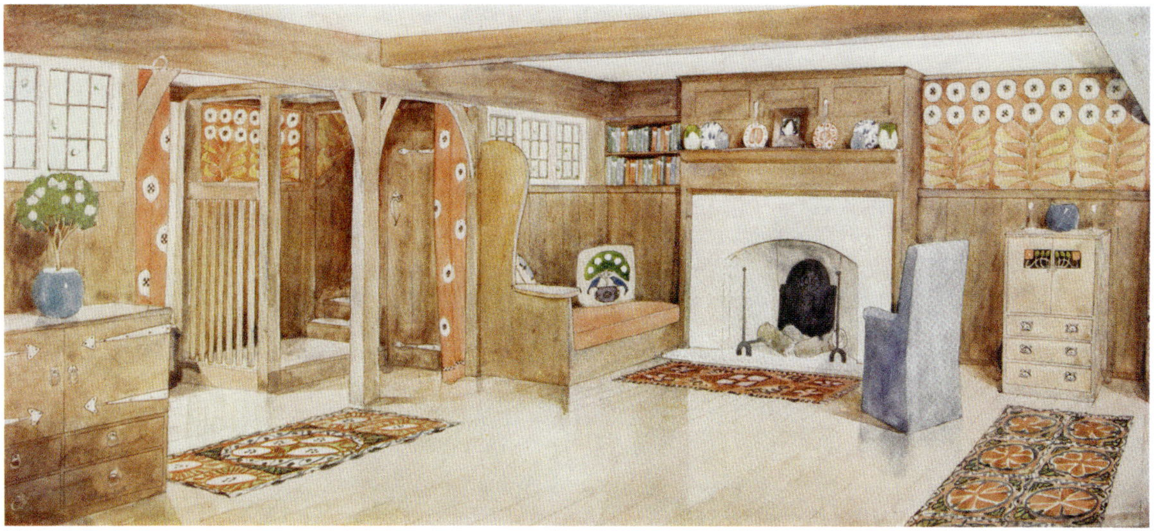

Fig.240 **Dining Room, Falkewood, designed by M.H. Baillie Scott. Published in *Houses and Gardens*, 1906.**
National Art Library, V&A (1515–1906)

commercial manufacturers and retailers. Through commissions and collaborations, Arts and Crafts designers helped to steer some manufacturers away from novelty and cheap production techniques towards a more considered approach to design and manufacture, allowing the quality of materials to be appreciated. Arts and Crafts designs were exhibited and sold by retailers not just in Britain, but in Europe and America too, reaching a much wider audience as a result.

There was both a sophisticated urban dimension and a radical rural faction to the Arts and Crafts Movement. It developed and flourished in large cities, such as London, Birmingham, Liverpool and Edinburgh, but the promise of a simpler life led others to leave the city to pursue new ways of living and working in the countryside, in locations as far apart as the Lake District, Surrey, Cornwall and the Cotswolds.

The new movement took its name from the Arts and Crafts Exhibition Society, which had been founded in London in 1887. The Society's purpose was to raise the status of the decorative arts and of the individual craftsman, and to influence the quality of industrial design. Morris himself created designs for machine production, and many Arts and Crafts designers specialized in designing rather than making. They were not opposed to the use of a machine if it served as an instrument for producing a well-designed and high-quality product.

The origins of the Arts and Crafts Movement, and the importance it placed on the home, began with how Morris furnished his own interiors and the central role that the design and manufacture of items for domestic decoration played in the success of Morris & Co. In Morris's own homes, first at Red House in Bexleyheath, then at Kelmscott Manor in the Cotswolds and Kelmscott House in Hammersmith, he showed how a home could represent a way of life and a set of beliefs. It was in these radical and eclectic interiors that the many Morris seekers who had the opportunity to meet him at home would have been received. With these spaces he established a model for how art could be part of everyday life through the use of beautiful but functional things.

The new movement gave rise to a generation of original thinkers, many of them architects who also designed furniture, wallpapers, textiles, tiles, metalwork and other furnishings, as well as buildings. Not everyone shared Morris's political persuasions, but most were aligned with his ideas about fellowship, community, nature and the environment, and the home. The new generation shared the belief that the quality of peoples' lives could be improved through access to good design for the home.

Arts and Crafts buildings and interiors ranged from simple cottages to grand architectural statements. A single item could be made, purchased at an exhibition or shop, or a whole building and its furnishings commissioned from an architect and an army of craftworkers. This, as Walter Crane wrote in 1911, is the 'great advantage and charm of the Morrisian method … it lends itself to either simplicity or to splendour.'

The architect and designer M.H. Baillie Scott (1865–1945) was one of many who took his lead from Morris and set out his ideas in his 1906 publication *Houses and Gardens* – a sort of 'how to' manual for planning an Arts and Crafts home. Two chapters begin with quotes from Morris's *A Dream of John Ball* in which the character narrated what he saw as he entered interiors 'so strange and beautiful', the descriptions evocative of the interiors designed by Baillie Scott. According to Baillie Scott the dining room, for example, was to be a flexible, open-plan and multi-purpose space to create efficiency and avoid the need for separately heated spaces (fig.240). The room illustrated has the characteristic features of an inglenook, low beams and elongated staircase spindles and plain wooden chests with long metal strap hinges. The colour, pattern and texture come from the rugs and repeating pattern of the wall decoration; the curtains are ready to be drawn to screen the entrance hall when the (possibly vegetarian) meal is served. This was a radical but practical new way of designing for living.

The work of Arts and Crafts designers was published and reviewed in newspapers and frequently featured in the new artistic journals and magazines such as *The Studio*, *Art Quarterly* and their international equivalents. Arts and Crafts practitioners were also fiercely engaged themselves in writing and lecturing, publishing technical manuals, debating and discussing their ideas. This legacy of published work, summarised in an anthology by Mary Greensted, gives voice to the Movement today and was an important medium for the dissemination of ideas around the world at the time.

Britain 1880–1914

There was no single manifesto for the Arts and Crafts Movement, which was born of ideals and broad and varied in expression. It encompassed a wide range of like-minded societies, workshops and manufacturers. As well as the Arts and Crafts Exhibition Society, two other groups that were influential in its development were the Century Guild, which was active *c.*1882–92, and the Art Workers' Guild, established in 1884 and still in existence. The idea of a 'Guild' remained a popular notion for its evocation of the pre-industrial world and links to the Guild of St George, founded by Ruskin in 1871 as a utopian endeavour to provide education in art and crafts, and support for the rural economy. It still operates as a charitable foundation today.

The Century Guild, set up by the young architect Arthur Heygate Mackmurdo (1851–1942), with Herbert Horne (1864–1916) and Selwyn Image (1849–1930), was a collective of designers who wanted to find a way to make good design available to a wider audience. They published the *Hobby Horse*, a journal first issued in 1884, which marked the beginning of a generation of art and design publications that were considered objects in their own right. The Art Workers' Guild was formed to bring together 'Handicraftsmen and Designers in the Arts' and to provide a forum for social and professional exchange. Its members included painters and sculptors, as well as architects, decorative artists, designers, manufacturers and craftsmen. The connections between members led to commissions and collaborative projects that produced many great Arts and Crafts works.

Morris was a member of both the Art Workers' Guild and the Arts and Crafts Exhibition Society, treating them with scepticism and enthusiasm in equal measure, and regarded these essentially small non-political organizations as ineffectual in furthering the socialist agenda. He was not party to the plans to form the Arts and Crafts Exhibition Society and in a letter to W.A.S. Benson on 31 December 1887, expressed some doubt about its viability, sure that 'the general public don't care one damn about the arts and crafts'. Morris did nonetheless become fully engaged as an exhibitor and served as its President from 1890 until his death. He gave lectures and technical demonstrations, and it was after attending a lecture by Emery Walker at the 1888 exhibition that he was moved to establish the Kelmscott Press.

The success of the Arts and Crafts exhibitions in London stimulated a new era of societies and exhibitions, which were formed around similar ideals and principles. In *History of Design* (2013), Pat Kirkham and Susan Weber estimate that, between 1888 and 1914, over 360 Arts and Crafts workshops and organizations were active across the length and breadth of Britain and Ireland and this number will continue to grow as new research emerges, for example, on the Arts and Crafts Movement in Scotland. These societies hosted exhibitions, lectures and demonstrations, and created places to exhibit and sell work in many different media and from a broad range of designers and makers, evidence of a stimulus in the teaching and support of people with crafts skills. They pioneered and excelled in the development or revival of many different craft techniques, including jewellery, embroidery, furniture, ceramics, lettering, calligraphy, illumination, bookbinding, printing, sgraffito, gesso and plasterwork, mural decoration, tempera painting, enamelling and stained glass.

Evidence of a handcraft revival and some formal endeavours to encourage and promote traditional crafts beyond the metropolitan centres, can be found around the United Kingdom even before the formation of the Arts and Crafts Exhibition Society. The case for rural craft industries had long been made by John Ruskin. His writings on craftsmanship, nature and the importance of art 'in which the hand, the head, and the heart of man go together' were, for many, as influential as Morris's.

Ruskin found great inspiration in the Lake District and eventually made it his home. As Sara E. Haslam has written, the 'Lakeland Arts Movement' saw a rich return of traditional skills, craft workshops and teaching, including the Langdale Linen Industry and the Keswick School of Industrial Arts. The woodworker Arthur W. Simpson (1857–1922) established a workshop in 1885 and ran woodcarving classes. With a library full of Arts and Crafts texts, including by Morris, he gave lectures on his belief that 'everyone was capable, with a little training, of producing some art work more or less valuable, for the beautifying of the home.'

Reformers and followers of Ruskin and Morris ran initiatives in England, Wales, Scotland and Ireland and there was often interaction between them and the Arts and Crafts schools and societies. These organizations represented an alternative thread in the development of the Arts and Crafts Movement. The Home Arts and Industries Association was established in 1884 to provide training, keep traditional craft skills alive, and create income for rural communities, including many women, through the exhibition and sale of work. As explained in Janice Helland's book, similar in organization and intent were the Irish Industries Association (1886), the Scottish Home Arts and Industries Association (1888) and the Welsh Industries Association (1898), the latter with London and Cardiff offices, and branches in almost every county in Wales.

Women were at the centre of the Arts and Crafts Movement from the outset, as designers, artists, makers, writers and patrons. Both in the way they raised their daughters and through their own collaborations, Jane and William Morris demonstrated a more enlightened attitude to women in the realm of crafts than some of their Arts and Crafts fellows. The Art Workers' Guild did not permit women as members, so those who wanted to create a space for the growing number of professional women in the arts and crafts set up their own societies. The Women's Guild of Arts was founded in 1907 by a group of leading female artists and craftswomen, with May Morris as a co-founder. Also on the founding committee were the stained-glass artist Mary Lowndes (1856–1929), sculptor Feodora Gleichen (1861–1922), and artist Mary Sargant Florence (1857–1954). Their activities, accounted for in depth by Zoë Thomas, in many ways mirrored those of the Art Workers' Guild, with meetings and lectures, and they participated in exhibitions.

May Morris, the younger of the Morrises' two daughters, was a dynamic and influential force, creating a lasting legacy in her own right. She was a highly skilled and original embroiderer, a designer, author, editor and teacher (see, for example, XI.22, XII.19 and XII.30). Her accomplishments, only now being re-examined and given due credit, were the result of being encouraged by her parents to develop skills and take a lead. After attending the National Art Training School in South Kensington she became head of the embroidery section of Morris and Co. She was a visible and active participant in Arts and Crafts, political and women's rights circles, and used her energy and contacts to write, teach and travel, including to America in 1909–10.

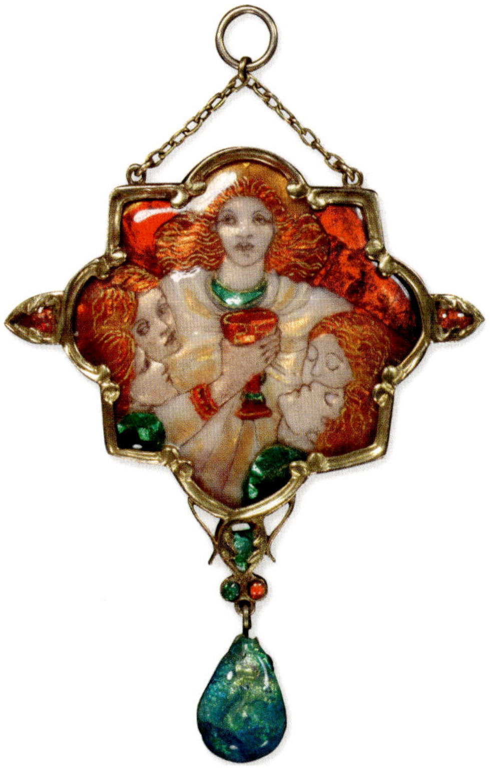

Fig.241 ***The Love Cup*, enamel and gold pendant, designed and made by Phoebe Anna Traquair, 1907.**
V&A (M.194–1976)
Given by Mrs H.V. Bartholomew

Irish-born Phoebe Anna Traquair (1852–1936) was an artist at the centre of the Arts and Crafts Movement in Scotland, and the first woman to be elected a member of the Royal Scottish Academy. Based in Edinburgh, she produced extraordinary works in a range of materials, including embroidery, enamel, manuscript illumination, mural decoration and painting (fig.241). Her circle included Patrick Geddes (1854–1932), a founder of the Edinburgh Social Union, a connection that led her to commissions for public art murals in Edinburgh, including the Mortuary Chapel at the Royal Hospital for Sick Children (1885–6), and Mansfield Place Church (1904–5). The Dun Emer Guild was a collaborative for women craftworkers established in Dublin in 1902 by Evelyn Gleeson (1855–1944) and sisters Lily (1866–1949) and Elizabeth (Lolly) Yeats (1868–1940). The Yeats family were associates of the Morrises, and Lily worked under May Morris in the embroidery department at Morris & Co. for six years, where she contributed to the hangings for Morris's bed at Kelmscott Manor. The three women were skilled in weaving, embroidery and printing. They themselves trained other young women in these crafts, to make banners, lace, linen and carpets with motifs drawn from Celtic sources (fig.242).

In London, Christopher Whall (1849–1924) was a leading figure in a new generation of stained-glass artists who transformed the art by bringing design and craftsmanship back together. His insistence that the craftsman should undertake both design and execution was a development from Morris & Co., where these roles were separate. His series of stained-glass windows, produced for Gloucester Cathedral between 1899 and 1913, are among the finest modern glass works in an ancient setting. Whall set up his own studio and was an influential teacher, at the Central School of Arts and Crafts and the Royal College of Art. He wrote the manual on *Stained Glass Work* (1905) and set a path for a new style of stained glass undertaken by the likes of Veronica Whall (1887–1967) and Wilhelmina Geddes (1887–1955) (fig.243).

Of those who came after Morris, the most ardent of his disciples translated his vision in to their own missions, lives and ways of working, while also forging innovative and inspiring paths which in turn had far reaching and lasting impact.

The Guild of Handicraft, founded in 1888 by the architect and designer Charles Robert Ashbee (1863–1942), was one of the most remarkable examples of Morris's ideals in action. It was housed next to Toynbee Hall, a settlement for easing poverty in East London, and set out to train craftsmen in the skills of furniture making, metalwork and later enamelling and jewellery. In 1898 Ashbee also set up the Essex House Press, after taking on the printing presses and many of the printers employed at the Kelmscott Press following Morris's death. The Guild produced individual hand-crafted pieces, restrained in design to emphasize the materials and marks of making (fig.244). Ashbee believed that to 'train up little children or fine craftsmen in London is a cruelty unmentionable' and that 'the proper place for the Arts and Crafts is in the country'. At first, the Guild supported country retreats until, in 1902, around 150 guildsmen and their families relocated to Chipping Campden in Gloucestershire. The promised simple life in the countryside was not without its hardships and difficulties, but Ashbee's Guild experiment left a long legacy that persists to this day. Ashbee was not just a disciple but became an inspiration and model, at home and internationally, for how to put Morris's ideas in to practical application.

Ernest Gimson (1864–1919) was an architect, designer and furniture-maker who was set on his path through the direct and personal impact of Morris. According to his brother Sydney, 'he always felt that he owed his great opportunity to the visits of William Morris to

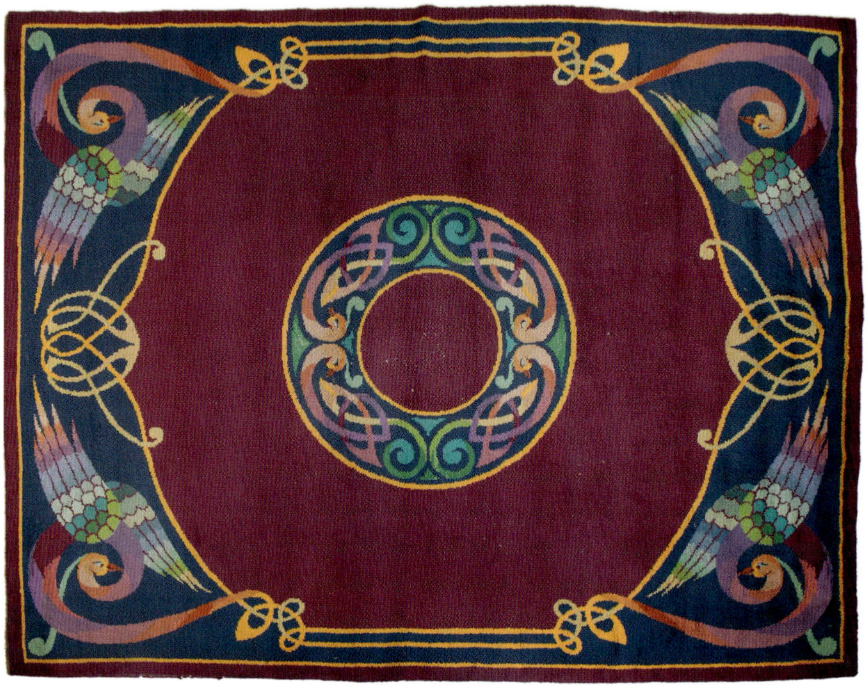

Fig.242 **Hand-knotted carpet, designed by Evelyn Gleeson for the Dun Emer Guild, 1902.**
Private collection

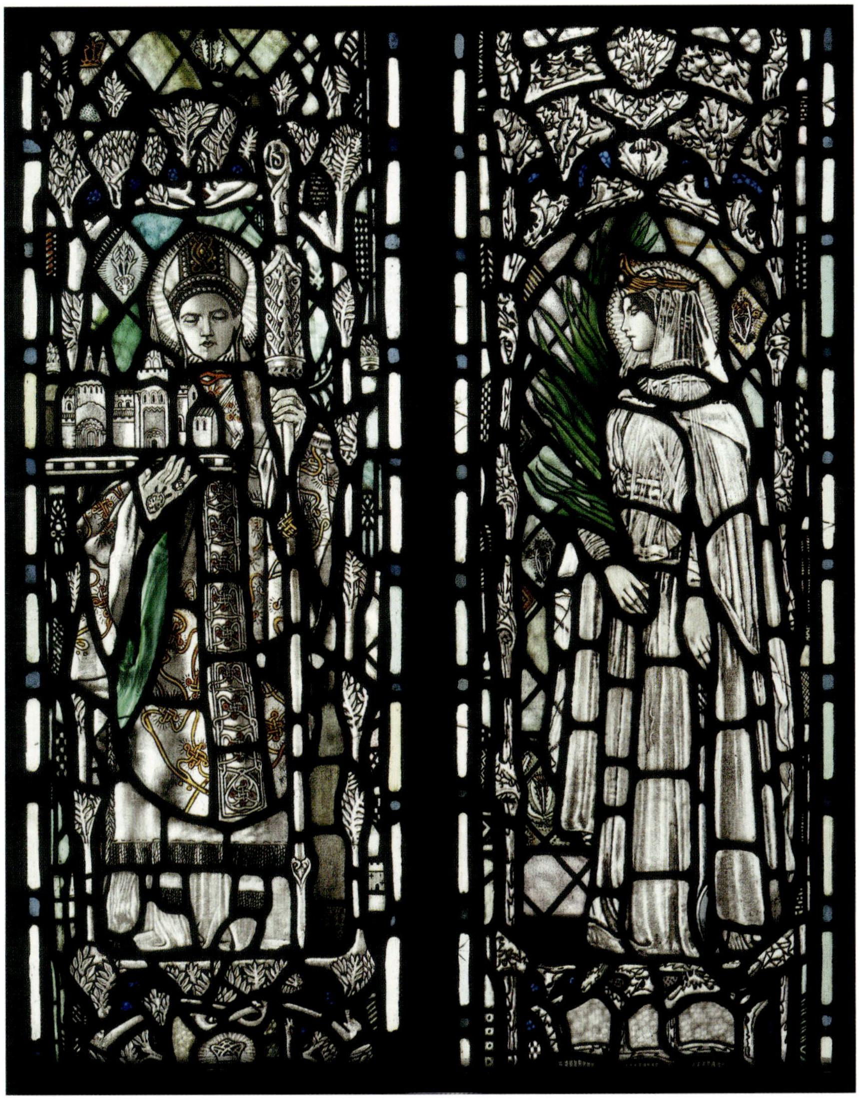

Fig.243 ***St Chad*** **and** ***St Agatha*****, smaller versions of stained-glass windows designed as part of a large window illustrating the** ***Childhood of the Blessed Virgin Mary*****, by Christopher Whall for the Lady Chapel, Gloucester Cathedral, 1899–1913.**
V&A (C.87 and C.88–1978)

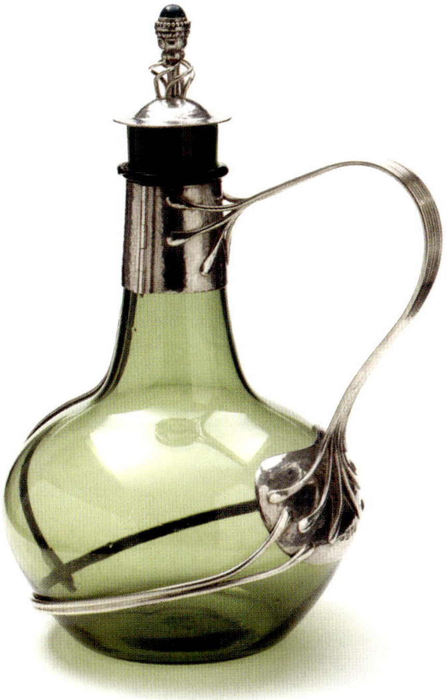

Fig.244 **Decanter with silver mounts and a chrysoprase set in the finial, designed by Charles Robert Ashbee. Glass bottle made by James Powell & Sons, Whitefriars, London. Mounts made by the Guild of Handicraft Ltd, Chipping Campden, 1904–5.**
V&A (M.121–1966)

Leicester.' The monograph on Gimson by Annette Carruthers, Mary Greensted and Barley Roscoe (2019) describes in detail the relationship and its benefits. Gimson's family had hosted Morris at their home in Leicester in 1884, when he came to deliver his lecture on 'Art and Socialism'. Gimson's absorption of Morris's ideas about finding enjoyment in work, understanding materials, learning from old work, and taking inspiration from nature underpinned everything he went on to achieve. He travelled in England studying ancient buildings and took with him everywhere he went large pieces of Morris-designed chintz so he always had something beautiful to look at. Morris secured Gimson a place in the office of architect John Dando Sedding, and when in London Gimson enjoyed the fellowship of the Arts and Crafts circles. He visited Morris's workshops at Merton Abbey, and watched his master hold court at Gatti's restaurant in London after the meetings of the Society for the Protection of Ancient Buildings (SPAB). Gimson's following of Morris led him to become one of the purest proponents of an Arts and Crafts life. In 1893 he pioneered a move to the Cotswolds in Gloucestershire, where he learned how to make furniture (fig.245) and set up his own furniture workshop and later blacksmith's forge. Gimson was a friend of May Morris, and worked with her at Kelmscott to design some cottages and a village hall in memory of her parents.

A different kind of Arts and Crafts figure, but no less of a direct successor of Morris, was C.F.A. Voysey (1857–1941), one of the most influential, original, principled and innovative architects and designers of his age. Voysey's vision was to remove 'ugliness' from the world and to

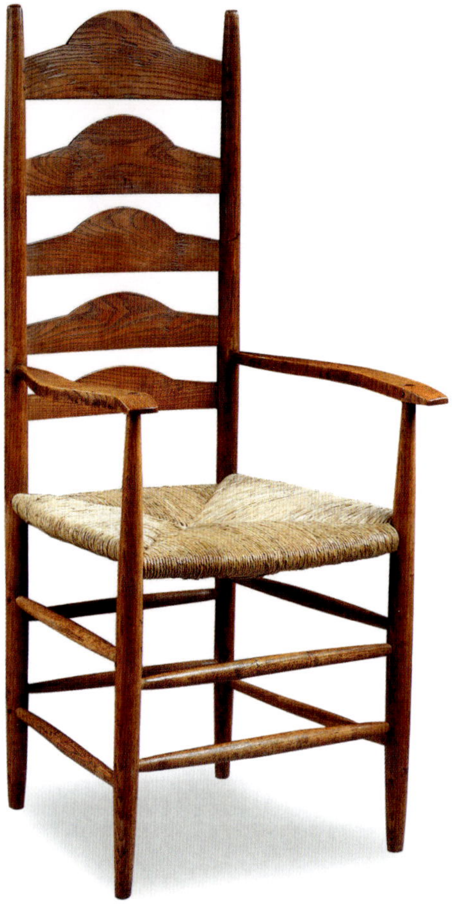

achieve a higher purpose through a life shaped by art and lived close to nature. As a designer of pattern he achieved great recognition. In *The Studio* in 1896 a 'Voysey wallpaper' was claimed to be as familiar to customers as a 'Morris chintz'. In his unpublished autobiography Voysey acknowledged Morris as his greatest influence and said that 'Morris had prepared the public mind and educated it'. He was also wary of becoming too immersed and wanted to preserve his own originality and vision, recalling that, as a young man, he was too afraid to enter the Morris & Co. shop for fear of being overly influenced by what he saw there. The differences in vision included politics. Voysey steered himself by his own moral compass, putting people-before-profit and always opting for the most economical and practical solution. There was a contrast with Morris, too, in his approach to flat pattern, in his abstraction of nature, and in the use to which his patterns were deployed (fig.246). A highly skilled and talented architect, artist and draughtsman, but not a hands-on craftsman, Voysey excelled as a designer for manufacturing and his most successful collaborations were with artistically minded manufacturers such as Jeffrey and Co. and Essex and Co., who produced his wallpapers, and Alexander Morton and Co., the textile manufacturers. Voysey knew and understood production and making, but it was not unusual to see the same pattern reproduced both as a wallpaper and a furnishing fabric, something Morris would sanction only in rare exceptions.

Morris and Philip Webb forged a new appreciation of old buildings, and the quality of materials and craftsmanship to be found in them. This led the next generation of architects such as Edward Schroder Prior (1852–1932), a founding member of the Art Workers' Guild, to develop a style of architecture that combined tradition and innovation in the use of vernacular materials, pattern and building techniques. Prior was an authority on English Gothic architecture and was Slade Professor of Fine Art and one of the founders of the School of Architecture at Cambridge University. One of his outstanding achievements was the Church of St Andrew, Roker, in County Durham, notable for its scale and structure, and which is also filled with stained-glass windows by Henry Payne (1868–1940), a cross, candlesticks and furniture by Gimson, a Morris & Co. tapestry designed by Burne-Jones and a foundation stone with lettering by Eric Gill (1882–1940).

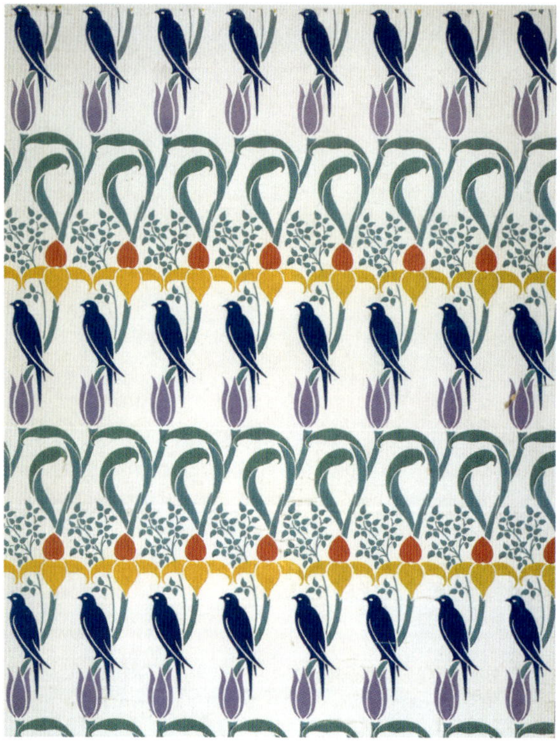

Fig.245 **Ladder-back armchair, designed and possibly made by Ernest Gimson, *c.*1895.**
V&A (Circ.232–1960)

Fig.246 ***Minto* wallpaper, designed by C.F.A. Voysey and manufactured by Essex & Co., 1901.**
V&A (E.311–1974)
Given by Courtaulds Ltd

Fig.247 **'Gloria in Altissimis Deo', illuminated manuscript by Louise Lessore (later Powell), 1905.**
National Art Library, V&A (MSL/1959/4396)

Fig.248 **Chair, designed by Charles Rennie Mackintosh, c.1897–1900.**
V&A (Circ.130–1958) Given by the Glasgow School of Art

The architect, designer, writer and educator William Richard Lethaby (1857–1931) did as much as any of Morris's followers to find practical ways to pass on crafts skills and to take a leading role in ensuring an appreciation of older buildings. A co-founder of the Art Workers' Guild, he was active and influential in the SPAB and became Surveyor of Westminster Abbey. He designed furniture, for a short while in collaboration with Gimson, and in his architecture he pushed the boundaries of traditional and modern building techniques, such as at All Saints, Brockhampton (1902).

Lethaby became co-Principal of the progressive Central School of Arts and Crafts when it was founded in London in 1896. Through his approach to practical training, he led a transformation in art-school education, which set the direction for design education in Europe in the early twentieth century. The tutors were all skilled practitioners and among some of the most well-known and influential were May Morris, sculptor and enameller Alexander Fisher (1864–1936) and Edward Johnston (1872–1944), who taught calligraphy. One of his earliest and most talented pupils was Louise Lessore (later Powell, 1882–1956), who evolved her own richly decorative style of illumination (fig.247), as well as working on some of Morris's incomplete illuminations after his death.

New art schools were founded across the United Kingdom, devoted to the practical training of professional designers and craftworkers. From the schools in Aberdeen, Birmingham, Dublin, Edinburgh, Glasgow, Liverpool, London, Manchester and elsewhere, talented designers and makers emerged, forming their own groups and identities and often heavily influenced by the teaching staff and by visiting lecturers.

The teachers and students at Glasgow School of Art produced a unique and influential style through multiple media. The school became well known for its embroidery teaching, under Jessie Newbery (1864–1948), and acclaimed for the work of a group of students that included Charles Rennie Mackintosh (1868–1928). Their extraordinary and modern style was particularly celebrated in Europe, but the work still had echoes of traditional forms and an emphasis on craftsmanship, such as this chair based by Mackintosh on a traditional Scottish model but exaggerating the height of its plain, tapering back (fig.248).

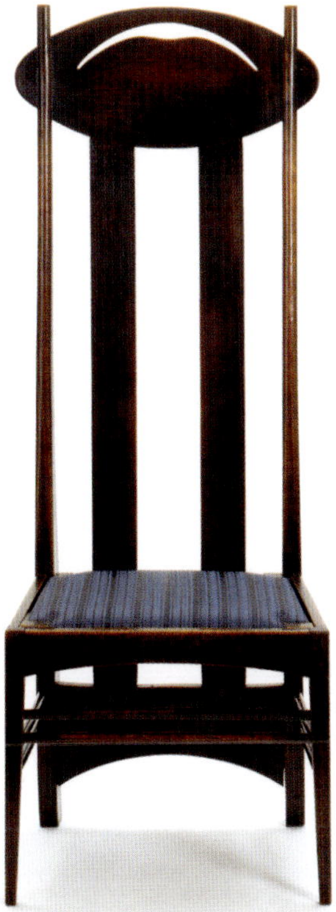

On rare occasions Morris himself would visit the art schools to lecture, for example at Birmingham Municipal School of Art in 1894.

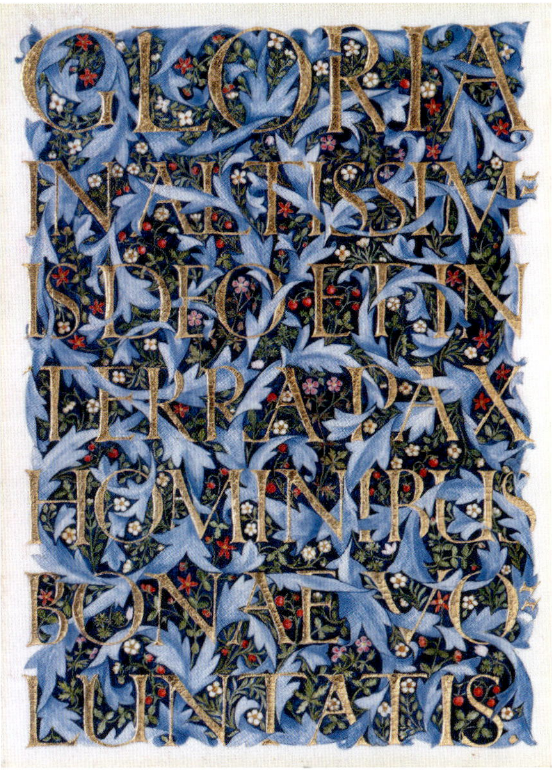

Lethaby also visited Birmingham in 1901 to give a talk on 'Morris as Work-Master' in which he outlined Morris's achievements, including the 'full force' of his patterns that 'bring into our rooms some reminder of the beauty and freshness of nature, some message from Earth Mother.' May Morris taught for three years at Birmingham, where she had been invited to become Special Teacher of Needlework in 1899, using the opportunity to try and raise technical and design standards. Mary Newill (1860–1947) was first a student and then a teacher of embroidery (fig.249). An accomplished illustrator and a designer of stained glass too, she was a central figure in overlapping memberships of the Bromsgrove Guild, the Birmingham Guild of Handicraft, and the Birmingham Group, coalitions of designers and makers who made, published and exhibited together.

The immense scale and richness of Arts and Crafts activity can only be suggested here. The widespread translation of Morris's writings, the exhibition and publication of Arts and Crafts work and ideas, and the rising profile of the next generation beyond Britain, secured not only Morris's legacy but established the Arts and Crafts Movement as the most radical social-design movement to have emerged from Britain in modern times, with a reach and impact far beyond its island shores.

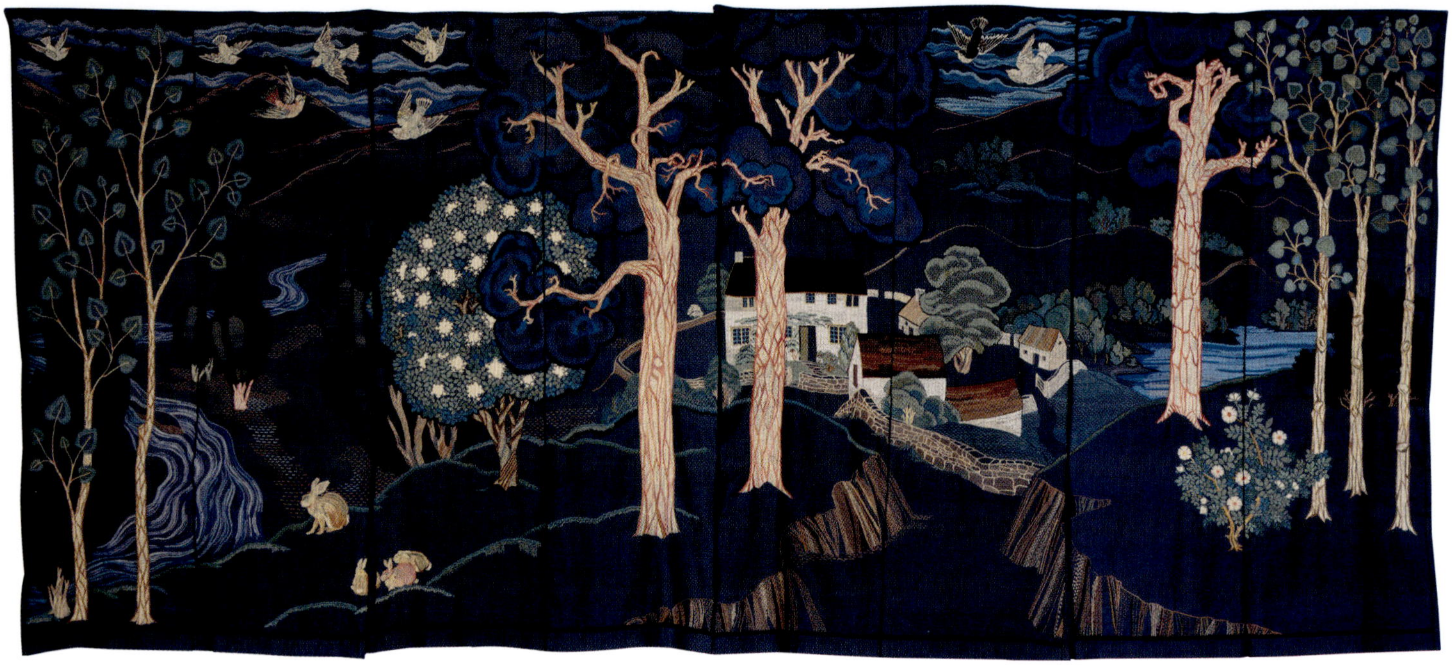

North America

Morris resisted America, according to his biographer Fiona MacCarthy, but his reputation and status had a strong impact and direct influence on the development of an American Arts and Crafts Movement. British Arts and Crafts leaders, such as Crane and Ashbee, were also well known and travelled to the United States, as did May Morris who saw initiatives such as Hull House in Chicago during her tour of 1909–10. Similarly, Americans interested in the Arts and Crafts Movement visited Britain, to meet architects and designers, see the exhibitions and shops, and in some cases to be received by Morris himself. The poet Emma Lazarus made a trip to England in 1883, meeting Morris on more than one occasion and recording her visit to Merton Abbey as 'A Day in Surrey with William Morris' published in *The Century* in 1886, and which she described as a 'noble and successful solution' to industrialization.

As in Britain and Europe, magazines and journals were important conduits for the dissemination of Morris's message of reform to the American population. The most widely circulated popular magazines to feature Morris and the Arts and Crafts Movement on the same pages as the work of emerging American architects such as Frank Lloyd Wright (1867–1959), were *House Beautiful* and *The Ladies' Home Journal*. Readers were encouraged by the magazine editors to consume less but better, to enjoy nature and craftsmanship, and to do good work. There was a much more commercial approach to Arts and Crafts in America, along with a strong sense of national identity.

As Edward R. Bosley has explored, Morris, Marshall, Faulkner & Co. goods first became available for sale in Boston in 1871 and achieved more widespread attention and reach when displayed at the Centennial Exhibition in Philadelphia in 1876, and the Boston Foreign Fair in 1883. Prominent and fashionable figures had Morris furnishings in their homes, and some commissions came directly from clients, for stained glass and textiles. Arts and Crafts societies in America helped provide some structure and coalition to an otherwise broad and dispersed movement. The first societies were formed in Minneapolis (1896), Boston and Chicago (both 1897), with hundreds more springing up across the country and Canada. Morris's status as a hero figure was evident in the way that the Hull House social settlement was established in 1889 and run by its founders Ellen Gates Starr (1859–1940) and Jane Addams (1860–1935), who had portraits of Morris and Ruskin on the walls, overseeing them as they worked to address poverty by teaching handicrafts to the local community. Ellen Gates Starr had been to England to study bookbinding under Thomas Cobden-Sanderson and sought to bring something similar to Chicago. The founding member of Canada's Arts and Crafts Society, Mabel

Fig.249 **Set of curtains, embroidered linen with wools, designed and executed by Mary Newill, 1906.**
V&A (T.170–1953)
Given by E. Newill and Charles Gere

Cawthra Adamson (1871–1943), spent time in England with the Guild of Handicraft, and others paid homage by adopting Morris-like mottos for their societies.

Morris's example came to influence American architecture and the reform of a range of craft skills and materials including embroidered textiles, stained glass, typography and printing, metalwork and furniture. The emphasis was on raising the status from craft to art and preserving the legacy of traditional techniques, while also creating something new and distinctively American.

Glessner House in Chicago (1885–7) was designed on Arts and Crafts principles, a collaboration between architect and client to create a simple and comfortable family home, which was filled with Morris & Co. furnishings. The architect was Henry Hobson Richardson (1838–1886) who had visited Morris in England in 1882 and who Morris later described as 'one of the few modern architects anywhere who have produced a distinctly original style.' The Californian architects Greene & Greene also declared themselves to be sympathetic with Morris, among other influences. Charles Sumner Greene (1868–1957) and Henry Mather Greene (1870–1954) designed furniture and interiors for their houses such as the Blacker House in Pasadena, including a reclining armchair or 'Morris' chair inspired by the adjustable-back armchair designed by Webb for Morris & Co. (IX.26). In Chicago Frank Lloyd Wright developed a style of Arts and Crafts architecture in response to the low-lying Prairie landscape and conceived of the interiors and furnishings as completely as the exteriors.

Fig.250 **'Craftsman House Number X, Series of 1904: The Living Room', *The Craftsman*, October 1904.**
National Art Library, V&A (140295)

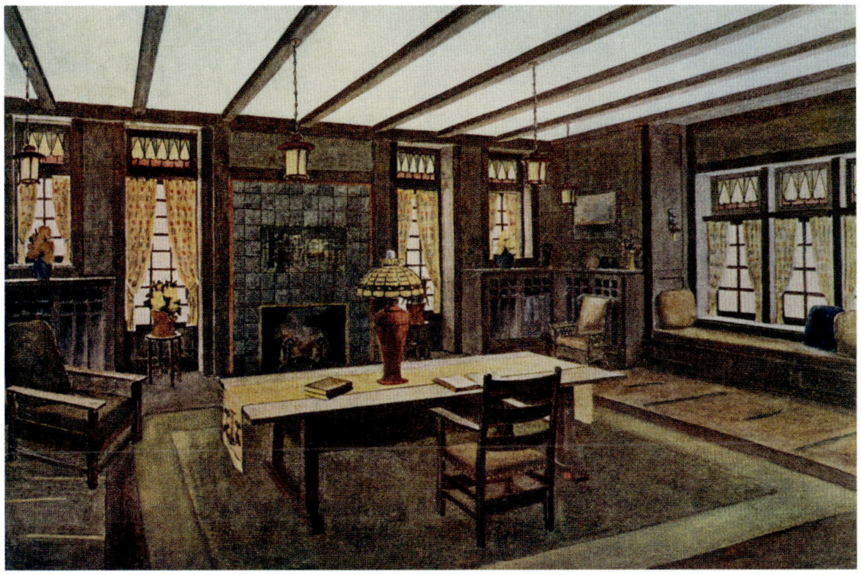

At the forefront of the American craft revival was Candace Wheeler (1827–1923), a designer of textiles, wallpapers and interiors, teacher and author who led a new movement in the design, teaching, techniques and making of embroidered art textiles, inspired by the work of the Royal School of Needlework that she saw at the Centennial Exhibition. Her mission was also one of reform in women's rights – she founded the Society of Decorative Art in New York in 1877, and later the Woman's Exchange, to teach needlework skills to women to enable them to earn a living. She was one of the first women to design for manufacturing and trained many more through her women-only textile firm, Associated Artists, which she established in 1883.

American stained glass of the late nineteenth and early twentieth century, was designed and produced by the firm of Cram, Goodhue and Ferguson in Boston, whose directors claimed the influence of Morris and Burne-Jones, and later Whall, in their company's endeavours to move on from the 'decadent and old fashioned' opalescent glass of previous decades. The arts of typography and printing were transformed by the example of the Kelmscott Press and the impression it made on the new American generation of craftsmen, with interpretations of this fresh approach found in the work of, for example, the Roycroft Printing Shop, founded by Elbert Hubbard (1856–1915) in East Aurora, New York, in 1895.

The entrepreneur, designer and furniture maker Gustav Stickley (1858–1942) was, according to Bosley, the anointed 'American William Morris' for his adoption and widespread translation of Arts and Crafts ideals into America. Perhaps more than anyone else, Stickley defined the Arts and Crafts Movement as it evolved in the United States. Although he fully subscribed to Arts and Crafts ideals, and had made a pilgrimage to England in 1898, his approach was more commercially aware. Stickley sought economic viability as well as moral satisfaction. In 1898 he founded the United Crafts (later Craftsman Workshops) in Syracuse, New York, for the production of furniture, metalwork and textiles, adopting the Morrisian motto 'Als Ik Kan' and the spirit of fellowship and good work when he established his community.

From 1901 to 1916 he published *The Craftsman*, an influential magazine in which he illustrated his own work as well as that from

Britain, mainland Europe and other parts of America. Both Ruskin and Morris were featured heavily in the magazine, with the first issue dedicated to Morris and the second to Ruskin. From 1904 it featured a series of 'Craftsman' homes that had been designed and built by Stickley's Craftsman Workshops. Craftsman homes illustrated an ideal of honesty, simplicity and usefulness. Stickley believed that the living room was the heart of the home, a place to nurture family life and a sanctuary for the working man. Its furniture should be simple and harmonize with the woodwork in colour and finish (fig.250).

Stickley's great 'back to the land' experiment was Craftsman Farms, New Jersey, which he established in 1908 as a centre for young people to be taught handicrafts and learn about farming the land. He is quoted by David E. Shi to have remarked that 'Just as I said that everyone should live in the country at least part of the year ... so I saw that every boy should receive part of his education on a farm.'

Stickley was not alone in his experiments to form idealistic communities based on the joys of nature, fellowship and work in the Morris tradition and inspired by Ashbee's experiment at Chipping Campden. The Byrdcliffe Art Colony at Woodstock, New York, was one of the Arts and Crafts communities in America to be based directly on the principles of Ruskin and Morris. Its founder Ralph Radcliffe Whitehead (1854–1929) was a Yorkshireman who had studied at Oxford under Ruskin, and who had married an American. He purchased some land to set up an artists' community, with workshops for pottery, metalworking and furniture-making, as well as houses and a library for the craftspeople who settled there. Rose Valley community in Philadelphia was founded in 1901, inspired by the utopian society described in *News from Nowhere*. It too provided workshops and housing, and a saleroom, for craftworkers making furniture, pottery and bookbinding.

Among all this, the clarion call of Morris's socialism was often quietly forgotten and was not a strong thread in a country that viewed progress and industry as essential to its core. So much so that Herbert Langford Warren, president of the Boston Society of Arts and Crafts, quoted by Shi, deemed it 'not only futile but wrong to attempt to carry on a crusade against those great systems [of production] which have made the best that there is in the modern world.'

Europe

National versions of the Arts and Crafts Movement developed in Germany, Austria, Holland, Sweden, Norway, Finland, Denmark, Hungary, Poland, the Czech region and Russia. Other countries including Belgium, France and Spain also had versions of a 'new art', in part inspired by Morris and the Arts and Crafts Movement, but the broader socio-political contexts created different responses. A common thread was the revival of traditional crafts in the face of increased industrialization. The political and social context in each country also created a need to build a stronger sense of national identity, unity and purpose. The design and making of useful and beautiful objects and homes became the means through which to improve everyday life, and to claim a more familiar but progressive national identity and future.

New British design was well known throughout Europe. Magazines and publications featured the work of Morris and the leading figures of the Arts and Crafts Movement, including the British *Studio*, the French *Art et Décoration*, and the German and Austrian magazines *Der Moderne Stil*, *Dekorative Kunst* and *Kunst und Kunsthandwerk*. British Arts and Crafts work was exhibited and retailed internationally, museums such as the National Museum in Oslo, Norway, collected examples of Arts and Crafts design, and leading figures such as Crane, Ashbee and Baillie Scott travelled or undertook commissions in Europe, including in Darmstadt, Germany, spreading the word further.

Artists, designers and architects drew on indigenous and vernacular techniques, styles and traditions to define a mode of living and working that reflected the desire for increased autonomy and political independence, but which in turn were also to have an influential impact on design in the twentieth century. Norwegian textile artist Frida

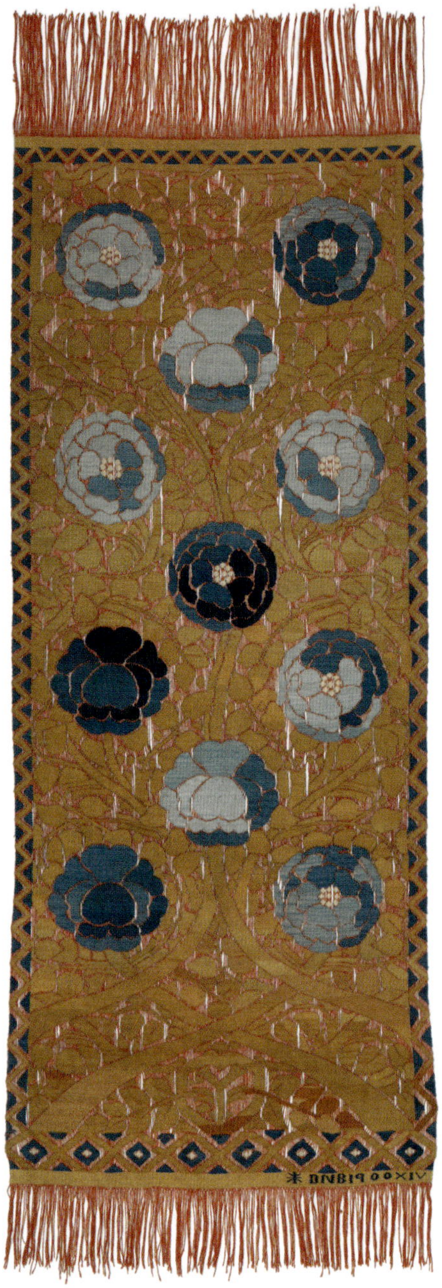

Fig.251 **Tapestry woven in hand-spun and hand-dyed wools, designed by Frida Hansen for the Norwegian Weaving Society, 1900.**
V&A (1683–1900)

Fig.252 **Wall cabinet, designed by Elena Polenova for the Abramtsevo workshop, *c.*1885–90.**
V&A (W.4–2004)
Bought with the aid of a bequest from Mrs Mowbray Garden

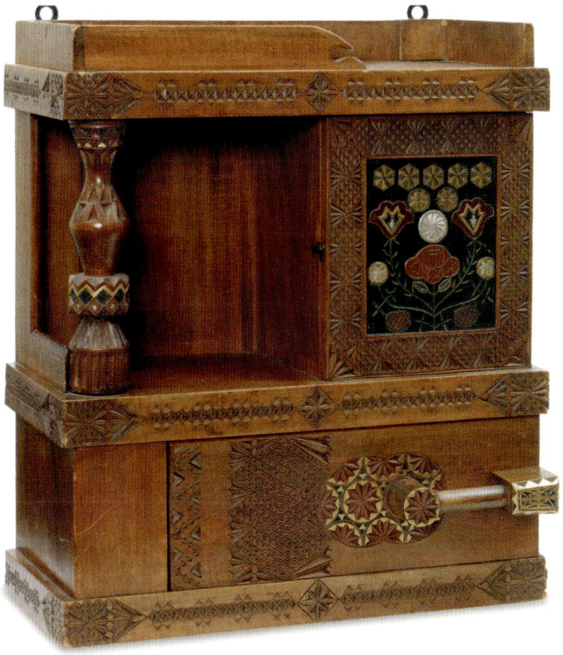

Hansen (1855–1931) travelled around Norway learning about yarns and dyes and weaving traditions, adopting ancient and specifically Nordic techniques into her work (fig.251). She set up her own weaving studios in Oslo, including the Studio for Handwoven Tapestries in 1890. She combined her knowledge of modern art and design developments, and the influence of nature and ancient mythology, using unique colour combinations to create works that were both ageless and innovative.

By the 1860s economic and social development in Russia was beginning to undermine rural communities. As in other countries, Arts and Crafts reformers founded artistic ventures with the aim of reviving and developing the local craft industries. The most notable were the Abramtsevo artists' colony, founded in 1874 by the young industrialist Savva Mamontov (1841–1918), and the workshops at Talashkino founded by Princess Maria Tenisheva (1858–1928) in 1898 (fig.252). Similarly, in Hungary, Aladár Körösfői-Kriesch (1863–1920) and Sándor Nagy (1869–1950) founded the Gödöllő Artists' Colony in 1902, with the belief that making and using handcrafted objects, living with nature and following a vegetarian diet, would help in reforming society. In Poland the Young Poland movement (1890–1918), the subject of a book by Julia Griffin and Andrzej Szczerski, worked to define a new national identity and abolish hierarchies in art by looking to vernacular buildings and folk art, and the Arts and Crafts Movement in Britain, for its models. Organizations such as the Kraków Workshops association exhibited and published the work of artists, architects, craftsmen and designers, as well as examples of traditional crafts. Their aim was to improve the quality of handicraft production using folk craft techniques and materials.

An alternative model, where artists and designers work more closely and collaboratively with established manufacturing also bore fruit in Denmark and Germany, for example. Thorvald Bindesbøll (1846–1908) was a Danish architect who designed for ceramics and silver wares, embroidery, books and graphic arts (fig.253). Long-lasting effects were also seen in Germany, where the British attitude was felt to be too anti-industrial and designers found that technology combined with traditional materials and design could support innovation and economic stability. The centres of reform included Darmstadt, Dresden, Munich and Weimar. Here, it was considered legitimate to use technology so long as standards in materials and quality were maintained in the end product. The architect and designer Richard Riemerschmid (1868–1957), for example, was at the heart of the Arts and Crafts Movement in Munich. Highly versatile, he designed an innovative range of stoneware based on a traditional ware from the Westerwald region of Germany. He created solid

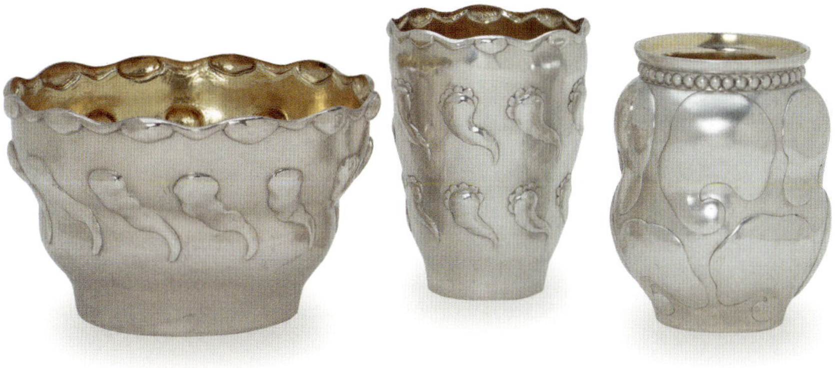

Fig.253 **Silver bowl and beakers, designed by Thorvald Bindesbøll and made by A. Michelsen, 1900.**
V&A (1612 to 1614–1900)

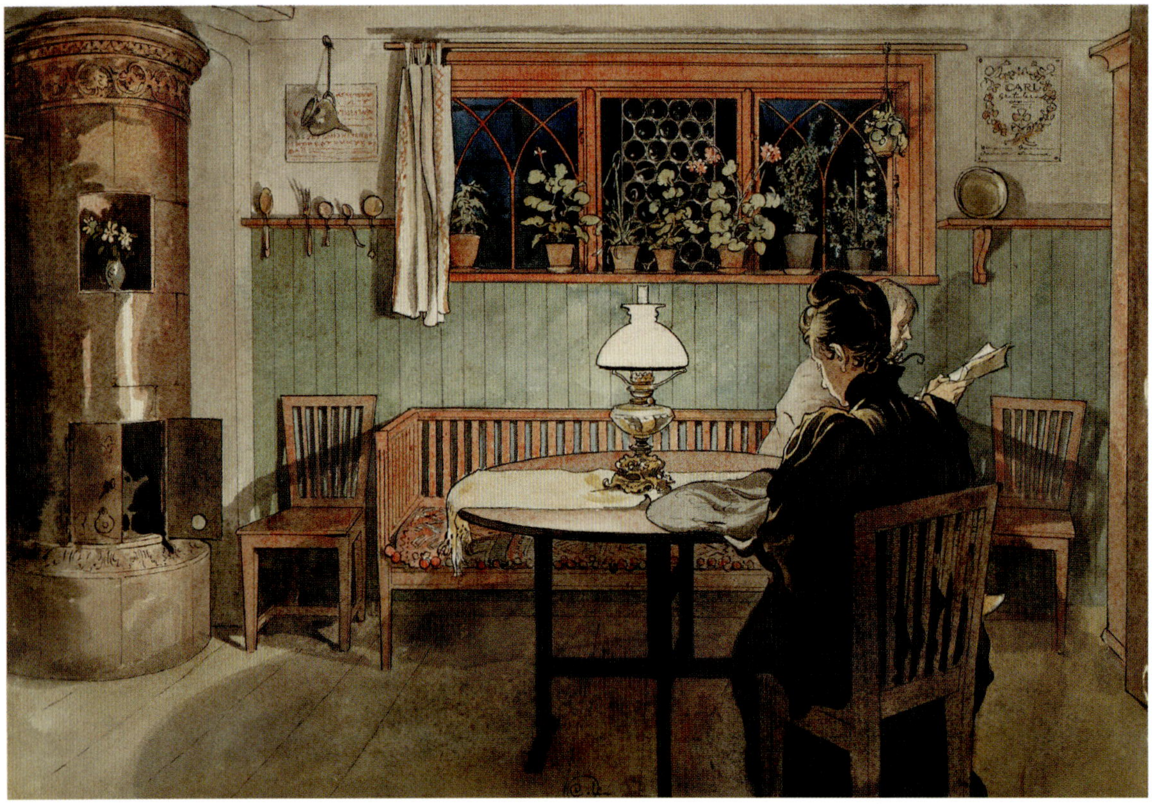

Fig.254 **'When the Children Have Gone to Bed', by Carl Larsson, from a series published in *Ett Hem* ('A Home'), 1899.**
Nationalmuseum, Stockholm

stoneware shapes and decorated them with abstract patterns in time-honoured colours (fig.255).

The emphasis on the home and quality of life persisted in all manifestations of the Arts and Crafts Movement in Europe. The idea of a domestic space that could reflect personal and national identity was seen in the homes designed and built by artists and architects for their own use, or for display at exhibitions, to demonstrate a life lived simply, surrounded by art. In Sweden, for example, the artists Carl and Karin Larsson made a family home together, Lilla Hyttnäs, which they filled with their own art and creations, publishing the results in a series of illustrated books that served as a new model for living (fig.254).

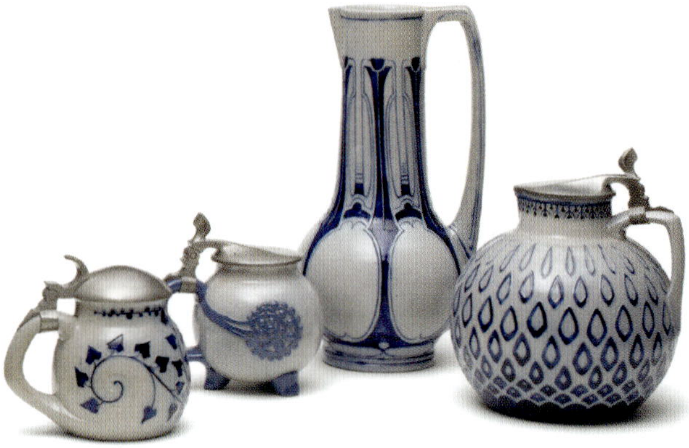

Fig.255 **Stoneware vessels, designed by Richard Riemerschmid and Peter Behrens (tall jug) and made by Hohr-Grenzhausen, Westerwald, Germany, 1903.**
V&A (C.32 to 34–1990, C.88–1997)

Japan

In Japan the ideas of European designers and theorists, especially Ruskin and Morris, also played a significant role in the evolution of a radical new modern craft movement, the Mingei (Folk Crafts) movement. This championed the work of individual artist–craftsmen and sought to preserve and raise the standards of traditional artisanal craft production threatened by industrialization. The movement was led by the philosopher and critic Yanagi Sōetsu (1889–1961), described by Yuko Kikuchi as the 'Japanese William Morris'. It was officially established in 1926 and maintained momentum until 1945, a period of time when increasing westernization was causing Japanese society to look to its past for guidance.

Yanagi's associates in the movement were a new generation of Japanese potters: Hamada Shōji (1894–1978), Tomimoto Kenkichi (1886–1963), Kawai Kanjirō (1890–1966) and the English artist and potter Bernard Leach (1887–1979). Together their aim was to preserve and revitalize rural folk crafts, and through them establish a new brand of

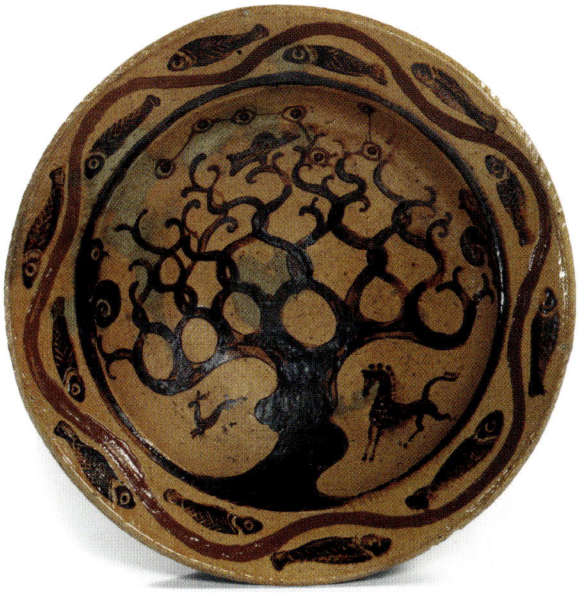

Fig.256 ***Tree of Life* dish, made by Bernard Leach, 1923.**
V&A (Circ.1278–1923)

modern crafts. They collected historical folk crafts for inspiration, published books and journals, organized exhibitions and founded museums. They lived in homes that they designed to reflect their intellectual artistic lives, adapting vernacular architecture and creating interiors that mixed historical crafts with contemporary pieces.

Japan's introduction to Morris was in 1891, when his work as a poet was first featured in a few magazines and a select few scholars, including Lafcadio Hearn (1850–1904) began to study and lecture on his poetry. *News from Nowhere* was published in translation in 1904 and soon artists also began to study and write about Morris's work, translating his ideas and making them relevant for themselves and for Japan. They were also aware of, and inspired by, other European Arts and Crafts activities, and the work of artists, designers and craftsmen in Britain, Sweden, Austria and Germany.

One of the most remarkable of Morris's disciples in Japan was Tomimoto Kenkichi. As Chiaki Ajioka has described, he visited London in 1908–10 and was able to study Morris's wallpaper and textile designs and probably read his lectures. He spent time at the V&A, where he saw textiles and paintings hanging together, impressing on him that art and craft could have the same value. When he returned to Japan, he took up weaving, established a design office, and experimented with making ceramics, driven by a 'desire to make craft which can be used by anyone for everyday life, at the lowest price possible.'

Two other important figures at the heart of the Mingei movement were the potters Hamada Shōji and Bernard Leach, who consolidated the connections between Britain and Japan, and bring this narrative full circle. Leach had spent the first four years of his life in Japan, but it was when he returned there in 1909, intending to teach the art of etching, that he met Yanagi and began the next chapter of his life as a potter.

In 1918 Hamada and Leach met in Tokyo and, as quoted by Rupert Faulkner, struck up an immediate friendship. In 1920 they came to England together, as Leach had been invited to set up a pottery in St Ives, Cornwall. Together they discovered the English slipware tradition, and they began to make their own versions and abstracted recreations of slipware in what have been described as the first efforts of the studio pottery movement, which dominated the next decades of the twentieth century (fig.256).

In 1921 they made a memorable visit to the Arts and Crafts community in Ditchling, Sussex, an experience of craftsmanship and life in the English countryside that inspired Hamada to move to the traditional pottery village of Mashiko when he returned to Japan. Leach remained in St Ives and established a life and tradition of making simple and utilitarian pottery. His work, teaching and writing had a lasting and iconic influence, representing, as Tanya Harrod has described, both an ending and a beginning in the story of crafts in Britain and beyond.

This rich, deep and far-reaching story comes to life through the individual endeavours and skills of the many hundreds, or thousands, of individuals who committed to making the world a better place, and to a life made better through art and good work. Morris's extraordinary vision inspired a new generation, and, when addressing art students in Birmingham in 1894, he encouraged those who came after him to do the same: 'so that the next after you may need no encouragement save what they will get from their own work, the pleasure of creating beautiful things, which is the greatest pleasure in the world.'

WILLIAM MORRIS CHRONOLOGY

1834
Born 24 March at Elm House, Walthamstow, Essex, eldest surviving son of city broker William Morris Senior and Emma Shelton Morris.

1840
Family moves to Woodford Hall, a Georgian mansion on the edge of Epping Forest. As a child, enraptured by the novels of Sir Walter Scott.

1847
William Morris Senior dies unexpectedly.

1848
Enrolls at Marlborough College, Wiltshire. Explores the surrounding countryside including Savernake Forest and prehistoric sites at Avebury and Silbury Hill. Family moves to Water House in Walthamstow (now the William Morris Gallery). Pre-Raphaelite Brotherhood is formed.

1851
Refuses to visit the Great Exhibition in Hyde Park. Withdrawn from Marlborough College.

1853
Enters Exeter College, Oxford, where he befriends Edward Burne-Jones and his circle of friends from Birmingham. Reads Ruskin's 'The Nature of Gothic'.

1854
First visit to northern France and Belgium with his sister Henrietta.

1855
Turns 21 and comes into his inheritance. During a trip to northern France with Burne-Jones, the friends decide to dedicate their lives to art. Returns to Oxford to take his degree in the autumn.

1856
Signs articles with the Gothic Revival architect George Edmund Street, in whose office he meets Philip Webb. Launches *The Oxford and Cambridge Magazine*. Takes up carving, clay modelling, embroidery, calligraphy and wood engraving. Begins to paint under the influence of Dante Gabriel Rossetti and gives up architecture by the end of the year. Leases unfurnished lodgings at 17 Red Lion Square, Bloomsbury, with Burne-Jones.

1857
Together with Rossetti, Burne-Jones and others, decorates the debating chamber of the Oxford Union with Arthurian murals. In the autumn, meets his future wife, Jane Burden, when she is persuaded to model for the artists.

1858
Publishes his first volume of poetry, *The Defence of Guenevere and Other Poems*. Morris and Jane become engaged in the spring; starts to paint *La Belle Iseult*. Tours France exploring medieval art and architecture with Webb and Charles Faulkner; during this trip Webb makes his first sketch for Red House.

1859
Marries Jane Burden on 26 April at St Michael's Church, Oxford; they embark on a six-week honeymoon in Belgium, the Rhineland and France. Webb finalizes his designs for Red House and construction begins. Morris joins the Corps of Artist Volunteers.

1860
The Morrises move into Red House in June and collaborate with their circle of friends to decorate the interiors.

1861
Birth of first daughter Jane Alice (Jenny) Morris on 17 January. Morris, Marshall, Faulkner & Co. ('the firm') is founded by Morris and six partners in April. They lease premises at 8 Red Lion Square and recruit apprentices from the nearby Industrial Home for Destitute Boys.

1862
Birth of second daughter Mary (May) Morris on 25 March. The firm makes its debut at the International Exhibition in South Kensington. Receives two medals of commendation. Morris's contribution includes the decoration of the *St George* cabinet. Designs his first wallpaper in November.

1865
The firm leases larger premises at 26 Queen Square, Bloomsbury. In November, Morris and his family leave Red House to live above the showroom.

1866
Commissions underway to decorate one of the new refreshment rooms at the South Kensington Museum (now the V&A), later known as the Green Dining Room, and the Armoury and Tapestry Rooms at St James's Palace. Morris sells Red House.

1867
Publishes *The Life and Death of Jason* to great acclaim. The Burne-Joneses move to The Grange, North End Road, Fulham.

1868
The first volume of *The Earthly Paradise* secures Morris's reputation as a leading poet. Begins studying Icelandic with Eiríkr Magnússon.

1869
Visits the spa town of Bad Ems on account of Jane's health. Resumes his interest in calligraphy. Publishes his first Icelandic saga translations with Magnússon.

1870
The final volume of *The Earthly Paradise* appears. Sits (reluctantly) to have his portrait painted by George Frederic Watts. Presents Georgiana Burne-Jones with 'A Book of Verse' for her birthday.

1871
Leases Kelmscott Manor in Oxfordshire, signing a joint tenancy with Rossetti. Jane, Rossetti and the children spend the summer there while Morris makes his first journey to Iceland. Joins the Board of Devon Great Consols, the copper and arsenic mine that made his family's fortune.

1872
Publishes his poem *Love is Enough*. The firm's decoration of 1 Palace Green underway.

1873
Moves to Horrington House, Chiswick (the firm continues at Queen Square). Makes his first journey to Italy with Burne-Jones in April; returns to Iceland in the summer.

1874
Rossetti gives up his share of the lease of Kelmscott Manor. Morris signs a petition against the replacement of the tower at Hampstead Church.

1875
The firm is reconstituted as Morris & Co. under Morris's sole direction. Resigns from the Board of Devon Great Consols. Agrees to supply designs for the Royal School of Needlework. Begins vegetable dyeing experiments with Thomas Wardle of Leek. Publishes his translations of Virgil's *Aeneid* and *Three Northern Love Stories*.

1876
First involvement with politics; joins the Eastern Question Association (EQA). The firm's wallpapers and textiles shown at the Philadelphia Centennial Exhibition. Visits Paris with Thomas Wardle in search of ancient dyeing manuals. Publishes his epic poem, *The Story of Sigurd the Volsung and the Fall of the Niblungs*. Jenny suffers her first epileptic attack.

1877
Together with Webb, founds the Society for the Protection of Ancient Buildings (SPAB). Issues his first political manifesto, *Unjust War*. Morris & Co. opens a new showroom on Oxford Street. Starts producing woven textiles at Queen Square with the assistance of a French silk weaver. Delivers his first public lecture, 'The Decorative Arts' (later published as 'The Lesser Arts').

1878
Begins experiments with hand-knotted rugs at Queen Square. Witnesses medieval mosaics being stripped from St Mark's in Venice. Moves to Kelmscott House in Hammersmith, named in honour of his country home. Designs decorations for Westminster Hospital on behalf of the Kyrle Society.

1879
Weaves his first tapestry *Acanthus and Vine* (nicknamed *Cabbage and Vine*). The SPAB initiates a campaign against the proposed restoration of St Mark's.

1880
Work begins on the decoration of 1 Holland Park for the Ionides family. Exhibition of hand-knotted rugs at Oxford Street. Submits proposals for second phase of decoration at St James's Palace.

1881
Morris & Co. workshops move from Queen Square to larger premises at Merton Abbey, Surrey.

1882
Publishes *Hopes and Fears for Art*. Gives evidence before the Royal Commission on Technical Instruction at the South Kensington Museum. Supports the Iceland Famine Relief Fund.

1883
Crosses the 'river of fire' and becomes a revolutionary socialist; joins the Democratic Federation. Registers design for *Strawberry Thief* printed cotton. Morris & Co. exhibits at the Boston Foreign Fair.

1884
Delivers some of his most famous socialist lectures including 'Useful Work versus Useless Toil' and 'How We Live and How We Might Live'. Splits from the Social Democratic Federation to found the Socialist League in December. Becomes an official Art Referee for the South Kensington Museum.

1885
Launches, edits and finances *Commonweal*, the journal of the Socialist League. Designs the *Woodpecker* tapestry.

1886
A Dream of John Ball starts to appear in installments in *Commonweal*.

1887
Keeps short-lived 'Socialist Diary' (January–April). Performs in his socialist play *The Tables Turned; or Nupkins Awakened*. Takes part in free speech demonstration in Trafalgar Square on 13 November, later known as 'Bloody Sunday'. Publishes his translation of Homer's *Odyssey*. Morris & Co. exhibits at the Manchester Jubilee Exhibition.

1888
Publishes *Signs of Change*, a collection of his socialist lectures, and the first of his prose romances, *A Tale of the House of the Wolfings*. Participates in the inaugural exhibition of the Arts and Crafts Exhibition Society at the New Gallery, Regent Street. Attends Emery Walker's lecture on letterpress printing and inspired to design his own type.

1889
Morris and Dearle collaborate on the *Bullerswood* carpet.

1890
Exhibits *The Adoration* tapestry for Exeter College in the Oxford Street showroom. *News from Nowhere* serialized in *Commonweal*. Leaves the Socialist League and forms the Hammersmith Socialist Society.

1891
Kelmscott Press begins printing. Morris and Jenny tour the cathedrals of northern France. Publishes *Poems by the Way*. Morris & Co. designs furniture and draperies for Henry Arthur Jones's play *The Crusaders*.

1892
Considered for the Poet Laureate following the death of Tennyson. Ruskin's 'The Nature of Gothic' printed by the Kelmscott Press with a preface by Morris.

1893
Contributes to *The Manifesto of English Socialists*. Supports the South Kensington Museum's acquisition of the Ardabil Carpet.

1894
Morris & Co. completes weaving of the first set of *Holy Grail* tapestries for Stanmore Hall.

1895
Protests against tree-felling in Epping Forest. Publishes translation of *Beowulf* with A.J. Wyatt. Speaks at the funeral of Sergius Stepniak.

1896
Kelmscott Press Chaucer completed. On 3 October Morris dies at Kelmscott House, Hammersmith, aged 62. Buried at St George's Church in Kelmscott village three days later. The following year Webb designs his simple tombstone, which he describes as like that of 'one of his old northern heroes in his cairn'.

SELECT BIBLIOGRAPHY

ABBREVIATIONS

JDAS *Journal of the Decorative Arts Society*
JPRS *Journal of Pre-Raphaelite Studies*
JWMS *Journal of the William Morris Society; since 2002 Journal of William Morris Studies*
WMSM *William Morris Society Magazine*

NOTE ON MANUSCRIPT SOURCES

Important collections of the papers of Morris and his circle are held at Birmingham Museum and Art Gallery; British Library, London; Fitzwilliam Museum, Cambridge; Huntington Library, California; International Institute of Social History (IISH), Amsterdam; Society for the Protection of Ancient Buildings, London; Archive of Art and Design, V&A; National Art Library, V&A; William Morris Gallery, London; William Morris Society, London and The Wilson Art Gallery and Museum, Cheltenham.

WORKS BY WILLIAM MORRIS

Boos, Florence S. (ed.), *William Morris's Socialist Diary*, 2nd edn, Nottingham, 2018
Faulkner, Peter (ed.), *William Morris: Selected Poems*, Manchester, 1992
Fitzgerald, Penelope (ed.), *The Novel on Blue Paper*, London, 1982
LeMire, Eugene D. (ed.), *The Unpublished Lectures of William Morris*, Detroit, 1969
Miele, Chris (ed.), *William Morris on Architecture*, Sheffield, 1996
Morris, May (ed.), *The Collected Works of William Morris*, 24 vols, London, 1910–15
—(ed.), *William Morris: Artist, Writer, Socialist*, 2 vols, Oxford, 1936
Morris, William, *Icelandic Journals*, introduction by Magnus Magnusson, London, 1996
—, *News From Nowhere*, Kelmscott Press facsimile edn, introduction by Rowan Williams, London, 2017
Peterson, William S. (ed.), *The Ideal Book: Essays and Lectures on the Arts of the Book*, Berkeley and London, 1982
Pinkney, Tony (ed.), *We Met Morris: Interviews with William Morris, 1885–96*, Reading, 2005
Poulson, Christine (ed.), *William Morris on Art and Design*, Sheffield, 1996
Salmon, Nicholas (ed.), *William Morris: Political Writings: Contributions to Justice and Commonweal, 1883–1890*, Bristol, 1994
—(ed.), *William Morris: Journalism: Contributions to Commonweal, 1885–1890*, Bristol, 1996
—, *William Morris on History*, Sheffield, 1996
Wilmer, Clive (ed.), *William Morris: News from Nowhere and Other Writings*, London, 1993

PUBLISHED CORRESPONDENCE

Aplin, John (ed.), *The Letters of Philip Webb*, 4 vols, New York and Abingdon, 2016
Fredeman, William E. (ed.), *The Correspondence of Dante Gabriel Rossetti*, 10 vols, Cambridge, 2002–15
Kelvin, Norman (ed.), *The Collected Letters of William Morris*, 4 vols, Princeton, 1984–96
Sharp, Frank C. and Jan Marsh (eds), *The Collected Letters of Jane Morris*, Woodbridge, 2012

BOOKS ON MORRIS AND HIS CIRCLE

Anon., *Arts Décoratifs de Grande-Bretagne et d'Irlande: Exposition organisée par le Gouvernement Britannique, Palais du Louvre, Pavillon de Marsan, Avril–Octobre 1914*, London, n.d. [1914]
Arscott, Caroline, *William Morris & Edward Burne-Jones: Interlacings*, New Haven and London, 2008
Banham, Joanna and Jennifer Harris (eds), *William Morris and the Middle Ages*, exh. cat., Manchester, 1984
Barringer, Tim, Jason Rosenfeld and Alison Smith, *Pre-Raphaelites: Victorian Avant-Garde*, exh. cat., London, 2012
Bennett, Mary, *Ford Madox Brown: A Catalogue Raisonné*, 2 vols, New Haven and London, 2010
Bennett, Phillippa and Rosie Miles (eds), *William Morris in the Twenty-First Century*, Oxford, 2010
Bliss, Anthony and Margaretta Lovell, *William Morris: The Sanford and Helen Berger Collection*, exh. cat., Berkeley, 1984
Boos, Florence S. (ed.), *The Routledge Companion to William Morris*, New York and Abingdon, 2021
Burman, Peter, '"A Stern Thinker and Most Able Constructor": Philip Webb, Architect', *Architectural History*, 42 (1999), pp. 1–23
Burne-Jones, Georgiana, *Memorials of Edward Burne-Jones*, 2 vols, London, 1904
Calloway, Stephen and Lynn Federle Orr (eds), *The Cult of Beauty: The Aesthetic Movement 1860–1900*, exh. cat., London, 2011
Crane, Walter, *William Morris to Whistler*, London, 1911
Crossley, Alan, Tom Hassall and Peter Salway (eds), *William Morris's Kelmscott: Landscape and History*, Bollington, 2007
Crow, Gerald H., *William Morris Designer*, London, 1934
Day, Lewis F., 'The Art of William Morris', *Easter Art Annual, Art Journal Extra Number*, London, 1899
Elliott, David B., *Charles Fairfax Murray: The Unknown Pre-Raphaelite*, Lewes, 2000
Faulkner, Peter, *Against the Age: An Introduction to William Morris*, London, 1980
— and Peter Preston (eds), *William Morris: Centenary Essays*, Exeter, 1999
Fitzgerald, Penelope, *Edward Burne-Jones: A Biography*, London, 1975
Gere, Charlotte, *Nineteenth-Century Decoration: The Art of the Interior*, London, 1989
—, *Artistic Circles: Design & Decoration in the Aesthetic Movement*, London, 2010
— and Michael Whiteway, *Nineteenth-Century Design: From Pugin to Mackintosh*, London, 1993
Gibeling, Keith E., 'Peter Paul Marshall: The Forgotten Member of the Morris Firm', *JWMS*, 12:1 (Autumn 1996), pp. 8–16
Goodwin, K.L., *A Preliminary Handlist of Manuscripts and Documents of William Morris*, London, 1983
Harrison, Martin and Bill Waters, *Burne-Jones*, 2nd edn, London, 1989
Hartley, Eeyan, 'Morris & Co. in a Baroque Setting', *JWMS*, 11:2 (Spring 1995), pp. 5–9
Harvey, Charles and Jon Press, *William Morris: Design and Enterprise in Victorian Britain*, Manchester, 1991
—, *Art, Enterprise and Ethics: The Life and Works of William Morris*, London, 1996
Henderson, Philip, *William Morris: His Life, Work and Friends*, London, 1967
Horner, Frances, *Time Remembered*, London, 1933
Hulse, Lynn (ed.), *May Morris Art & Life: New Perspectives*, London, 2017
Hunt, William Holman, *Pre-Raphaelitism and the Pre-Raphaelite Brotherhood*, 2 vols, London, 1905
Institute of Contemporary Arts, *William Morris Today*, exh. cat., London, 1984
Kirk, Sheila, *Philip Webb: Pioneer of Arts & Crafts Architecture*, Chichester, 2005
Lethaby, William Richard, *Philip Webb and His Work*, Oxford, 1935; reprint with additional material, introduction by Godfrey Rubens, London, 1979
Lochnan, Katherine A., Douglas E. Schoenherr and Carole Silver (eds), *The Earthly Paradise: Arts and Crafts by William Morris and His Circle from Canadian Collections*, exh. cat., Toronto, 1993
MacCarthy, Fiona, *William Morris: A Life for Our Time*, London, 1994
—, *The Last Pre-Raphaelite: Edward Burne-Jones and the Victorian Imagination*, London, 2011
—, *Anarchy & Beauty: William Morris and His Legacy 1860–1960*, exh. cat., London, 2014
Mackail, John William, *The Life of William Morris*, 2 vols, London, 1899
Marsh, Jan, *Jane and May Morris: A Biographical Story 1839–1938*, London, 1986
—, *William Morris and Red House*, London, 2005
—(ed.), *Pre-Raphaelite Sisters*, exh. cat., London, 2019
Menz, Christopher, *Morris & Company: Pre-Raphaelites and the Arts and Crafts Movement in South Australia*, exh. cat., Adelaide, 1994
—, *Morris & Co.*, exh. cat., Adelaide, 2002
Monk, George and Walter Gooch, 'A Study and Catalog of Morris and Company Designs in the Collection of the William Morris Center, London [now William Morris Society]', unpublished typescript, 1978
Morris, May, *The Introductions to The Collected Works of William Morris*, Joseph R. Dunlap (ed.), 2 vols, New York, 1973
Naylor, Gillian (ed.), *William Morris by Himself: Designs and Writings*, London, 1988
Newman, Teresa and Ray Watkinson, *Ford Madox Brown and the Pre-Raphaelite Circle*, London, 1991
Parkins, Wendy (ed.), *William Morris and the Art of Everyday Life*, Newcastle, 2010
Parry, Linda (ed.), *William Morris*, exh. cat., London, 1996
—(ed.), *William Morris: Art and Kelmscott*, London, 1996
Pinkney, Tony, *William Morris in Oxford: The Campaigning Years, 1879–1895*, Grosmont, 2007
Robertson, Michael, *The Last Utopians: Four Late Nineteenth-Century Visionaries and Their Legacy*, Princeton and Oxford, 2018
Robinson, Duncan and Stephen Wildman, *Morris & Company in Cambridge*, exh. cat., Cambridge, 1980
Roe, Dinah, 'Naturally Artificial: The Pre-Raphaelite Garden Enclosed', *Victorian Poetry*, 57:1 (Spring 2019), pp. 131–53
Rose, Fiona, 'Retelling the Tale of Taylor: A New Look at the Life of Warington Taylor', *JWMS*, 23:1 (2018), pp. 69–95
Royal Academy of Arts, *Pre-Raphaelite and Other Masters: The Andrew Lloyd Webber Collection*, exh. cat., London, 2003
Salmon, Nicholas with Derek Baker, *The William Morris Chronology*, Bristol, 1996
Salmon, Nicholas and David Taylor, 'Morris & Co. in Manchester', *JWMS*, 12:3 (Autumn 1997), pp. 17–19
Saxby, David, *William Morris at Merton*, London, 1995
Schoenherr, Douglas E., 'Edward Burne-Jones's Account Books with Morris &

Company (1861–1900): An Annotated Edition', *Journal of Stained Glass*, 35 (2011), pp. 78–241
Smith, Alison (ed.), *Edward Burne-Jones*, exh. cat., London, 2018
Staley, Allen, *The New Painting of the 1860s: Between the Pre-Raphaelites and the Aesthetic Movement*, New Haven and London, 2011
Stanford University Art Gallery, *Morris & Co.*, exh. cat., Stanford, 1975
Stansky, Peter, *Redesigning the World: William Morris, the 1880s, and the Arts and Crafts Movement*, Princeton, 1985
Stoppani, Leonard et al. (eds), *William Morris and Kelmscott*, exh. cat., Farnham/London, 1981
Surtees, Virginia (ed.), *The Diaries of George Price Boyce*, Norwich, 1980
—(ed.), *The Diary of Ford Madox Brown*, New Haven and London, 1981
Thompson, E.P., *William Morris: Romantic to Revolutionary*, revised edn, London, 1977
Thompson, Paul, *The Work of William Morris*, revised edn, Oxford, 1991
Treuherz, Julian, *Ford Madox Brown: Pre-Raphaelite Pioneer*, exh. cat., London, 2011
V&A, *William Morris Centenary Exhibition*, exh. cat., London, 1934
—, *Victorian and Edwardian Decorative Arts*, exh. cat., London, 1952
—, *Morris & Co. Centenary Exhibition*, exh. cat., London, 1961
Vallance, Aymer, *William Morris: His Art, His Writings and His Public Life*, London, 1897
Waggoner, Diane (ed.), *The Beauty of Life: William Morris & The Art of Design*, exh. cat., London, 2003
Wardle, George, *The Morris Exhibit at the Foreign Fair*, Boston, 1883
—, 'Memorials of William Morris', in Harvey and Press (1996), pp. 83–115
Watkinson, Ray, *William Morris as Designer*, London, 1967
Whittaker, Esmé, *William Morris: Story, Memory, Myth*, exh. cat., London, 2011
Wild, Tessa, *William Morris and His Palace of Art: Architecture, Interiors & Design at Red House*, London and New York, 2018
Wildman, Stephen and John Christian, *Edward Burne-Jones: Victorian Artist-Dreamer*, exh. cat., New York, 1998

LITERATURE

Bennett, Phillippa, *Wonderlands: The Last Romances of William Morris*, Oxford, 2015
Boos, Florence S., *History and Poetics in the Early Writings of William Morris, 1855–1870*, Columbus, 2015
Faulkner, Peter (ed.), *William Morris: The Critical Heritage*, London, 1973
Hanson, Ingrid, *William Morris and the Uses of Violence, 1856–1890*, London, 2013
Helsinger, Elizabeth K., *Poetry and the Pre-Raphaelite Arts: Dante Gabriel Rossetti and William Morris*, New Haven and London, 2008
—, *Poetry and the Thought of Song in Nineteenth-Century Britain*, Charlottesville and London, 2015
Sasso, Eleonora, *How the Writings of William Morris Shaped the Literary Style of Tennyson, Swinburne, Gissing, and Yeats*, Lampeter, 2011
Sharp, Frank C., 'William Morris and the Search for Poet Laureate, 1892', *JPRS*, 5 (Spring 1996), pp. 71–80
Vaninskaya, Anna, *William Morris and the Idea of Community: Romance, History and Propaganda, 1880–1914*, Edinburgh, 2010
Waithe, Marcus, *William Morris's Utopia of Strangers: Victorian Medievalism and the Ideal of Hospitality*, Cambridge, 2006

POLITICS

Boos, Florence S. and Patrick O'Sullivan, 'Morris and Devon Great Consols', *JWMS*, 19:4 (Summer 2012), pp. 11–39
Kinna, Ruth, *William Morris: The Art of Socialism*, Cardiff, 2000
Miller, Elizabeth Carolyn, *Slow Print: Literary Radicalism and Late Victorian Print Culture*, Stanford, 2013
Morris, William, *Poems of Protest*, introduction by Michael Rosen, London, 2013
Salmon, Nicholas, '"The Down-Trodden Radical": William Morris's Pre-Socialist Ideology', *JWMS*, 13:3 (Autumn 1999), pp. 26–43
—, 'A Reassessment of *A Dream of John Ball*', *JWMS*, 14:2 (Spring 2001), pp. 29–38
—, 'The Communist Poet-Laureate: William Morris's *Chants for Socialists*', *JWMS*, 14:3 (Winter 2001), pp. 31–40
—, 'William Morris: The Final Socialist Years', *JWMS*, 14:4 (Summer 2002), pp. 12–24
Stott, Martin, '"A garden party at Kelmscott house... would be pleasant"... the story of the 1888 photograph of the Hammersmith Socialist League', *WMSM* (Spring 2017), pp. 10–15
Taylor, Rosemary, '"The City of Dreadful Delight" William Morris in the East End of London', *JWMS*, 18:3 (Winter 2009), pp. 9–28

ARCHITECTURE AND CONSERVATION

Brownlee, David B., *The Law Courts: The Architecture of George Edmund Street*, Cambridge, MA, and London, 1984
Crawford, Alan, 'Supper at Gatti's: The SPAB and the Arts and Crafts Movement', in Miele (2005), pp. 101–27
Donovan, Andrea Elizabeth, *William Morris and the Society for the Protection of Ancient Buildings*, New York and Abingdon, 2008
Drury, Michael, *Wandering Architects: In Pursuit of an Arts and Crafts Ideal*, revised edn, Donington, 2016
Miele, Chris, '"Their Interest and Habit": Professionalism and the Restoration of Medieval Churches, 1837–77', in Chris Brooks and Andrew Saint (eds), *The Victorian Church: Architecture and Society*, Manchester, 1995, pp. 151–72
—, '"A Small Knot of Cultivated People": William Morris and Ideologies of Protection', *Art Journal*, 54:2 (Summer 1995), pp. 73–9
—, 'The Battle for Westminster Hall', *Architectural History*, 41 (1998), pp. 220–44
—(ed.), *From William Morris: Building Conservation and the Arts and Crafts Cult of Authenticity, 1877–1939*, New Haven and London, 2005
—, 'Morris and Architecture', in Boos (2021), pp. 169–87
Sharp, Frank C., 'A Lesson in International Relations: Morris and the SPAB', *JWMS*, 10:2 (Spring 1993), pp. 9–15
—, 'Exporting the Revolution: The Work of the SPAB outside Britain 1878–1914', in Miele (2005), pp. 187–212
Stamp, Gavin, *An Architect of Promise: George Gilbert Scott Junior (1839–1897) and the Late Gothic Revival*, Donington, 2002
Swenson, Astrid, *The Rise of Heritage: Preserving the Past in France, Germany and England, 1789–1914*, Cambridge, 2013
Whyte, William, *Unlocking the Church: The Lost Secrets of Victorian Sacred Space*, Oxford, 2017

PAINTING AND DRAWING

Anon., 'William Morris, Poet and Artist', *Quarterly Review*, 190 (July–October 1899), pp. 487–512
Cherry, Deborah, 'The Hogarth Club: 1858–1861', *Burlington Magazine*, 122:925 (April 1980), pp. 237–44
Cruise, Colin, *Pre-Raphaelite Drawing*, exh. cat., London, 2011
Del Re, Sonia (ed.), *Beauty's Awakening: Drawings by the Pre-Raphaelites and Their Contemporaries from the Lanigan Collection*, exh. cat., Ottawa, 2015
Doughty, Oswald, *A Victorian Romantic: Dante Gabriel Rossetti*, London, 1949
Dowding, Helen, 'An Investigation into the Original Decoration and Possible Treatment of a Painted Settle in William Morris's Red House', Courtauld Institute of Art, unpublished report, 2005
Dudkiewicz, Julia, 'Kelmscott Manor *Venus* and Morris's idea for a "House of Love" at Red House', *Useful & Beautiful, Newsletter of the William Morris Society in the United States*, 1 (Winter 2016), pp. 3–18
Faulkner, Peter, 'Morris and Pre-Raphaelitism', *JWMS*, 19:4 (Summer 2012), pp. 40–62
Faxon, Alicia Craig, *Dante Gabriel Rossetti*, New York, 1989
Glab, Tracee, '"More Than Pictures": Dante Gabriel Rossetti and The Oxford Union Mural Project', *Wayne State University Theses*, Paper 56, 2010
Goodwin, K.L., 'William Morris's "New and Lighter Design"', *JWMS*, 2:3 (Winter 1968), pp. 24–31
Hart, Imogen, 'The designs of William Morris', in Elizabeth Prettejohn (ed.), *The Cambridge Companion to the Pre-Raphaelites*, Cambridge, 2012, pp. 211–22
McEvansoneya, Philip, 'Edward Burne-Jones, William Morris, Dante Gabriel Rossetti, Harry Ward and Illuminated Manuscripts', *Burlington Magazine*, 157:1350 (September 2015), pp. 599–601
Malory, Thomas, *Le Morte d'Arthur*, introduction by Helen Moore, Ware, 1996
Marsh, Jan, 'William Morris's Painting and Drawing', *Burlington Magazine*, 128:1001 (August 1986), pp. 569–77
—, 'La Belle Iseult', *JWMS*, 19:2 (Summer 2011), pp. 9–19
Prettejohn, Elizabeth, *Modern Painters, Old Masters: The Art of Imitation from the Pre-Raphaelites to the First World War*, New Haven and London, 2017
Prinsep, Val C., 'A Chapter from a Painter's Reminiscence. The Oxford Circle: Rossetti, Burne-Jones, and William Morris', *Magazine of Art*, 2 (1904), pp. 167–72
—, 'A Chapter from a Painter's Reminiscences. Part II. Dante Gabriel Rossetti', *Magazine of Art*, 2 (1904), pp. 281–6
Renton, John D., *The Oxford Union Murals*, 3rd edn, Oxford, 1996
Schoenherr, Douglas E., 'Drawings', in Lochnan, Schoenherr and Silver (1993), pp. 37–97
Smith, Alison (ed.), *Reflections: Van Eyck and the Pre-Raphaelites*, London, 2017
Street, George Edmund, 'On the Future of Art in England', *The Ecclesiologist*, 19:127 (August 1858), pp. 232–40
Surtees, Virginia, *The Paintings and Drawings of Dante Gabriel Rossetti (1828–1882): A Catalogue Raisonné*, 2 vols, Oxford, 1971
Thistlewood, Jevon, 'Early Paintings by William Morris Inside the Prioress's Tale Wardrobe', *William Morris Society Newsletter* (Summer 2015), pp. 14–17
Treuherz, Julian, Elizabeth Prettejohn and Edwin Becker, *Dante Gabriel Rossetti*, exh. cat., London, 2003
Watkinson, Ray, *Pre-Raphaelite Art and Design*, London, 1970
—, 'Red House Decorated', *JWMS*, 7:4 (Spring 1988), pp. 10–15
—, 'Painting', in Parry (1996), pp. 90–105

STAINED GLASS AND CHURCH DECORATION

Cheshire, Jim, *Stained Glass and the Victorian Gothic Revival*, Manchester, 2004
—, 'William Morris and Stained Glass', in Boos (2021), pp. 188–206
Coley, Sandra (ed.), 'Burne-Jones Special Issue', *Journal of Stained Glass*, 35 (2011)
Galicki, Marta, *Victorian & Edwardian Stained Glass: The Work of Five London Studios 1855–1910*, Bristol, 2001
Hall, Michael, *George Frederick Bodley and the Later Gothic Revival in Britain and America*, New Haven and London, 2014
Harrison, Martin, *Victorian Stained Glass*, London, 1980
Morris, William, 'Glass, Painted or Stained', in D. Patrick (ed.), *Chambers's Encyclopaedia: A Dictionary of Universal Knowledge*, Edinburgh, 1890, pp. 246–8
Schoenherr, Douglas E., 'The "Cartoon Book" and Morris & Company's Sale of Burne-Jones's Cartoons in 1901–1904', *Journal of Stained Glass*, 29 (2005), pp. 82–134
Sewter, A.C., *The Stained Glass of William Morris and his Circle*, 2 vols, New Haven and London, 1974–5

Waggoner, Diane, 'Stained Glass & Church Decoration', in Waggoner (2003), pp. 64–75
Waters, William and Alastair Carew-Cox, *Edward Burne-Jones: Pre-Raphaelite Glass in Birmingham*, Abbots Morton, 2009
—, *Angels & Icons: Pre-Raphaelite Stained Glass 1850–1870*, Abbots Morton, 2012
—, *Damozels & Deities: Pre-Raphaelite Stained Glass 1870–1898*, Abbots Morton, 2017
—, *Saints & Symbols: Pre-Raphaelite Stained Glass*, Abbots Morton, 2021

INTERIOR DECORATION

Anon., 'Decorations at the Westminster Hospital', *The Builder*, 11 January 1879, p. 51
—, 'The Kyrle Society', *Magazine of Art*, 3 (1880), pp. 210–12
Dakers, Caroline, *Clouds: The Biography of a Country House*, New Haven and London, 1993
Dunn, S. & S., records, unpublished typescript of work undertaken for Morris & Co. (William Morris Gallery)
Edwards, Jason and Imogen Hart (eds), *Rethinking the Interior, c.1867–1896: Aestheticism and Arts and Crafts*, Farnham, 2010
Elletson, Helen, *A History of Kelmscott House*, London, 2009
Frederick, Margaretta S., 'William Morris and Interior Design', in Boos (2021), pp. 207–26
Hart, Imogen, *Arts and Crafts Objects*, Manchester and New York, 2010
Harvey, Charles and Jon Press, 'The Ionides Family and 1 Holland Park', *JDAS*, 18 (1994), pp. 2–14
Kirk, Sheila and Rosemary J. Curry, *Philip Webb in the North*, exh. cat., Middlesbrough, 1984
MacDonald, Sally, 'For "Swine of Discretion": Design for Living: 1884', *Museums Journal*, 86:3 (December 1986), pp. 123–9
Mitchell, Charles, 'William Morris at St James's Palace', *Architectural Review*, 42 (January 1947), pp. 37–9
Norman, Anna, *The David Parr House: Life and Art in a Worker's Home*, London, 2019
Parry, Linda, 'William Morris and The Green Dining Room', *The Magazine Antiques*, 150:2 (August 1996), pp. 198–205
Ridgway, Christopher, 'A Privileged Insider: George Howard and Edward Burne-Jones', *The British Art Journal*, 3:3 (Autumn 2002), pp. 4–18
—, 'If he puts up with me we shall jog along alright', *WMSM* (Spring 2018), pp. 6–11
Rubens, Godfrey, 'The Small House', *WMSM* (Summer 2018), pp. 6–8
Weaver, Lawrence, 'Rounton Grange, Yorkshire', *Country Life*, 26 June 1915, pp. 906–12
Whelan, Robert, '"The poor, as well as the rich, need something more than meat and drink": the vision and work of the Kyrle Society', in Elizabeth Baigent and Ben Cowell (eds), *Octavia Hill: Social Activism and the Remaking of British Society*, London, 2016, pp. 91–117

FURNITURE

Acker, Paul, 'Elizabeth Siddal's Jewelry Box for Jane Morris', *William Morris Society in the United States Newsletter* (January 2013), pp. 5–6
Andrews, John, *Arts and Crafts Furniture*, 2nd edn, Woodbridge, 2015
Anon., 'Madox Brown's Designs for Furniture', *The Artist*, 22:1 (May 1898), pp. 44–51
Boram, John, 'Thirteenth Century Painted Church Furniture and its Later Influence', *Regional Furniture*, 21 (2007), pp. 207–20
Carruthers, Annette, '"... like Incubi and Succubi": A Table by Webb or Morris', *Craft History*, 2 (April 1989), pp. 55–61
— and Mary Greensted, *Good Citizen's Furniture: The Arts and Crafts Collections at Cheltenham*, London, 1994
Clarke, Amy, 'George Jack, Master Woodcarver of the Arts and Crafts Movement', *JDAS*, 28 (2004), pp. 82–107
Donnelly, Max, '"Rapture and Ridicule": Furniture in the 1862 Medieval Court', *JDAS*, 38 (2014), pp. 106–31
—, 'The "Mediæval" Furniture of John Pollard Seddon', in Handelingen: Neostijlen in het interieur, 1850–1900, *Stichting Ebenist*, Amsterdam, 10 (2014), pp. 5–16
—, 'Rossetti, Poynter and two bookcases commissioned by John Jones at the Victoria and Albert Museum', *Burlington Magazine*, 158 (October 2016), pp. 803–11
Dufty, A.R., *Kelmscott: Exoticism and a Philip Webb Chair*, London, 1986
Dumas, F.G. (ed.), *The Franco-British Exhibition: Illustrated Review*, London, 1908
Ellwood, Giles, 'Three Tables by Philip Webb', *Furniture History*, 32 (1996), pp. 127–40
Esposito, Donato, 'From Ancient Egypt to Victorian London: the impact of ancient Egyptian furniture on British art and design 1850–1900', *JDAS*, 27 (2003), pp. 80–93
Gaimster, Amy, *George Jack 1855–1931: Architect and Designer Craftsman*, exh. cat., London, 2006
Grieve, Alastair, 'The Content and Form of Furniture in Rossetti's Art of 1848–58', *JPRS*, 8 (Fall 1999), pp. 9–28
Jervis, Simon, '"Sussex" Chairs in 1820', *Furniture History*, 10 (1974), p. 99
Jones, Doris Arthur, *The Life and Letters of Henry Arthur Jones*, London, 1930
Kirkham, Pat, 'William Morris's Early Furniture', *JWMS*, 4:3 (Summer 1981), pp. 25–8
Kisluk-Grosheide, Daniëlle O., Wolfram Koeppe and William Rieder, *European Furniture in the Metropolitan Museum of Art*, New Haven and London, 2006
Marsh, Jan, 'The Red Lion Square Chairs: Chronology and Iconography', *JPRS*, 8 (Fall 1999), pp. 28–48
Ormond, Richard, 'Holman Hunt's Egyptian Chairs', *Apollo*, 41 (July 1965), pp. 55–8
Pevsner, Nikolaus, 'Colonel Gillum and the Pre-Raphaelites', *Burlington Magazine*, 95:600 (March 1953), pp. 76, 78–9, 81
Seddon, John Pollard, *King René's Honeymoon Cabinet*, London, 1898
Stielau, Allison, 'Habits of Encounter: The Prioress's Tale Cabinet', MA thesis, Bard Graduate Center, New York, 2009
Tait, E.M., 'The Pioneer of Art Furniture: Madox Brown's Furniture Designs', *The Furnisher*, 3 (November 1900), pp. 61–3
Wildman, Stephen (ed.), *Waking Dreams: The Art of the Pre-Raphaelites from the Delaware Art Museum*, Alexandria, VA, 2004
Wilson, Arnold, 'More from Morris and Company', *Apollo*, 29 (July 1964), pp. 57–9

TILES AND TABLEWARE

Braesel, Michaela, 'The Tile Decoration by Morris & Co. for Queens' College, Cambridge: The Inspiration of Illuminated Manuscripts', *Apollo*, 443 (January 1999), pp. 25–33
Bryant, Barbara, 'Alice Kipling: Pre-Raphaelite Sister of the Raj', in Julius Bryant and Susan Weber (eds), *John Lockwood Kipling: Arts & Crafts in the Punjab and London*, New Haven and London, 2017, pp. 329–60
Catleugh, Jon, *William De Morgan Tiles*, London, 1983
Chitty, Gillian and David Stocker, 'Westerwald Stoneware at Kelmscott Manor: Morris, Pottery and the Politics of Production', *The Antiquaries Journal*, 99 (2019), pp. 363–97
Cormack, Peter, *Morris & Company Tiles*, exh. cat., London, 1996
Dunn, Henry Treffry, *Recollections of Dante Gabriel Rossetti and His Circle*, London, 1904
Ferry, Emma, 'Lucy Faulkner and the "Ghastly Grin"', *JWMS*, 18:1 (Winter 2008), pp. 65–84
—, '"The Other Miss Faulkner": Lucy Orrinsmith and the "Art at Home Series"', *JWMS*, 19:2 (Summer 2011), pp. 47–64
Hamerton, Ian (ed.), *W.A.S. Benson: Arts and Crafts Luminary and Pioneer of Modern Design*, Woodbridge, 2005
Jackson, Lesley (ed.), *Whitefriars Glass: The Art of James Powell & Sons*, Shepton Beauchamp, 1996
Kelly, Tessa, 'The Morris Reredoses at St John the Baptist Church, Findon, and The Church of The Blessed Virgin Mary, Clapham, West Sussex', *JWMS*, 13:4 (Spring 2000), pp. 30–4
van Lemmen, Hans, 'Nineteenth-Century Dutch Tiles', *Journal of the Tiles and Architectural Ceramics Society*, 1 (1982), pp. 1–7
Morris, Barbara, *Victorian Table Glass and Ornaments*, London, 1978
Myers, Richard and Hilary, *William Morris Tiles: The Tile Designs of Morris and his Fellow-Workers*, Shepton Beauchamp, 1996
—, 'Addenda & Corrigenda to *William Morris Tiles*', unpublished typescript, 2014 (William Morris Gallery)
Richmond, Arthur, *Twenty-Six Years 1879–1905*, London, 1961
Rudoe, Judy and Howard Coutts, 'The Tableglass Designs of Philip Webb and T.G. Jackson for James Powell & Sons, Whitefriars Glassworks', *JDAS*, 16 (1992), pp. 24–41
Vallance, Aymer, 'The Decorative Art of Sir Edward Burne-Jones, Baronet', *Easter Art Annual, Art Journal Extra Number*, London, 1900
Williamson, George C., *Murray Marks and his Friends*, London, 1919

WALLPAPER

Baker, Derek, *The Flowers of William Morris*, London, 1996
Bartrip, P.W.J., 'How Green Was My Valance? Environmental Arsenic Poisoning and the Victorian Domestic Ideal', *English Historical Review*, 109:433 (September 1994), pp. 891–913
Burke, Doreen Bolger et al., *In Pursuit of Beauty: Americans and the Aesthetic Movement*, exh. cat., New York, 1986
Clark, Fiona, *William Morris: Wallpapers and Chintzes*, London, 1973
Conway, Moncure, *Travels in South Kensington*, London, 1882
Cowper-Temple, Georgina, *Memorials [of William Francis Cowper-Temple, Baron Mount Temple]*, London, 1890
Ellis, Frederick S., 'The Life-Work of William Morris', *Journal of the Society of Arts*, 46:2375 (27 May 1898), pp. 618–30
Floud, Peter, 'The Wallpaper Designs of William Morris', *The Penrose Annual*, 54 (1960), pp. 41–5
Hoskins, Lesley (ed.), *The Papered Wall: The History, Patterns and Techniques of Wallpaper*, revised edn, London, 2005
Meharg, Andy, 'The Arsenic Green', *Nature*, 423 (12 June 2003), p. 688
Sanderson & Sons Ltd, Arthur, *Catalogue of Block-printed Wallpapers*, London, 1993
Schoeser, Mary, *Sanderson: The Essence of English Decoration*, London, 2010
Sugden, Alan Victor and John Ludlam Edmondson, *A History of English Wallpaper, 1509–1914*, London, 1926
Thorndycraft, Dawn, 'A Royal Commission: Morris & Co. at St James's Palace', MA thesis, Royal Holloway College, London, 1993
Tibbles, Tony, 'Speke Hall and Frederick Leyland: Antiquarian Refinements', *Apollo*, 387 (May 1994), pp. 34–7
Wells-Cole, Anthony and Barbara Walker, *Wallpapers at Temple Newsam 1635 to the Present*, Leeds, 2017

TEXTILES

Craven, Wayne, *Gilded Mansions: Grand Architecture and High Society*, New York and London, 2009
Dufty, A.R., *Morris Embroideries: The Prototypes*, London, 1985
Floud, Peter, 'Dating Morris Patterns', *Architectural Review*, July 1959, pp. 15–20
Higgin, Letitia, *Handbook of Embroidery 1880*, introduction by Lynn Hulse, London, 2010
Hulse, Lynn, 'Elizabeth Burden and the Royal School of Needlework', *JWMS*, 21:1 (Winter 2014), pp. 22–34
King, Brenda M., *The Wardle Family and Its Circle: Textile Production in the Arts and Crafts Era*, Woodbridge, 2019
Marsh, Jan, 'The Topsaic Tapestries and Penkill Castle', *JWMS*, 13:4 (Spring 2000), pp. 35–40
Parry, Linda, *Textiles of the Arts and Crafts Movement*, London, 1988
—, *William Morris Textiles*, revised edn, London, 2013
— and David Cathers, *Arts and Crafts*

Rugs for Craftsman Interiors: The Crab Tree Farm Collection, New York, 2010
Saxby, David, 'The San Graal Tapestry Weavers at Merton Abbey', *WMSM* (Spring 2016), pp. 10–15
—, 'From Merton Abbey to Dovecot: Weaving Scotland's First Tapestry', *WMSM* (Spring 2017), pp. 2–5
—, 'From *The Arming of the King* to *Nativity*', *WMSM* (Autumn 2018), pp. 6–10
—, 'The Carpet Knotting Girls', *WMSM* (Autumn 2019), pp. 14–16
Sharp, Frank C., 'Isabella Morris Gilmore', *JWMS*, 11:4 (Spring 1996), pp. 31–8

CALLIGRAPHY AND THE KELMSCOTT PRESS

Blunt, Wilfrid Scawen, *My Diaries: Being a Personal Narrative of Events, 1888–1914*, 2 vols, New York, 1980
Braesel, Michaela, 'Text and Image in William Morris's "A Book of Verse"', *Apollo*, 471 (May 2001), pp. 41–58
—, 'William Morris, Edward Burne-Jones and "The Rubáiyát of Omar Khayyám"', *Apollo*, 504 (February 2004), pp. 47–56
Dreyfus, John, *Morris and the Printed Book*, London, 1989
Dunlap, Joseph R., *The Book That Never Was*, New York, 1971
—, 'The Road to Kelmscott', PhD thesis, Columbia University, New York, 1972
—, 'Morris and the Book Arts Before the Kelmscott Press', *Victorian Poetry*, 13:3/4 (1975), pp. 141–57
Fairbank, Alfred, 'A Note on the Manuscript Work of William Morris', in William Morris and Eiríkr Magnússon, *The Story of Kormak*, introduction by Grace J. Calder, London, 1970, pp. 53–72
Morris, William, *A Book of Verse*, facsimile edition, introduction by Roy Strong and Joyce Irene Whalley, London, 1980
—, *The William Morris Manuscript of The Odes of Horace*, with commentary by Clive Wilmer, London, 2014
Needham, Paul (ed.), *William Morris and the Art of the Book*, exh. cat., New York, 1976
Peterson, William S., *A Bibliography of the Kelmscott Press*, Oxford, 1984
—, *The Kelmscott Press: A History of William Morris's Typographical Adventure*, Oxford, 1991
— and Sylvia Holton Peterson, *The Kelmscott Chaucer: A Census*, New Castle, DE, 2011
Sparling, Henry Halliday, *The Kelmscott Press and William Morris Master-Craftsman*, London, 1924
Whitla, William, '"Sympathetic Translation" and the "Scribe's Capacity": Morris's Calligraphy and the Icelandic Sagas', *JPRS*, 10 (Fall 2001), pp. 27–108

WILLIAM MORRIS AND THE V&A

Bryant, Julius, *Designing the V&A: The Museum as a Work of Art (1857–1909)*, London, 2017
Campbell, Thomas P., *Tapestry in the Renaissance: Art and Magnificence*, New York, 2002
Carey, Moya, *Persian Art: Collecting the Arts of Iran for the V&A*, London, 2017
Codell, Julie, 'William Morris and the Intersection of the Histories of Art and Design', in Jason D. Martinek and Elizabeth Carolyn Miller (eds), *Teaching William Morris*, Vancouver, 2019, pp. 235–48
Dudkiewicz, Julia, 'Memorialising her father's legacy: May Morris as curator and gatekeeper of William Morris's estate and the role of Kelmscott', in Hulse (2017), pp. 209–35
Harvey, Charles and Jon Press, 'William Morris and the Royal Commission on Technical Instruction, 1881–84', *JWMS*, 11:1 (Autumn 1994), pp. 31–44
Huxtable, Sally-Anne, 'Re-reading the Green Dining Room', in Edwards and Hart (2010), pp. 25–40
Morris, Barbara, 'William Morris and the South Kensington Museum', *Victorian Poetry*, 13:3/4 (1975), pp. 159–75
—, *William Morris and the South Kensington Museum*, London, 1987
—, 'The 1952 Exhibition of Victorian and Edwardian Decorative Arts at the Victoria and Albert Museum: A Personal Recollection', *JDAS*, 25 (2001), pp. 11–24
Parry, Linda, 'Morris and Company in the Twentieth Century', *JWMS*, 6:4 (Winter 1985–6), pp. 11–16
Sutton, James, 'It's a cover up! Interior design at the South Kensington Museum', V&A blog, 16 July 2014, vam.ac.uk/blog/caring-for-our-collections/its-a-cover-up-interior-design-at-the-south-kensington-museum
Waterfield, Giles, *The People's Galleries: Art Museums and Exhibitions in Britain 1800–1914*, New Haven and London, 2015

BRITAIN AND BEYOND

Ajioka, Chiaki, 'A Revaluation of Morris's Influence in Japan', *JWMS*, 12:4 (Spring 1998), pp. 21–8
Anon., 'The Arts and Crafts Exhibition', *The Studio*, 9:43 (October 1896), pp. 54–5
Backemeyer, Sylvia and Theresa Gronberg (eds), *W.R. Lethaby 1857–1931: Architecture, Design and Education*, London, 1984
Barter, Judith A. (ed.), *Apostles of Beauty: Arts and Crafts from Britain to Chicago*, New Haven and London, 2009
Blakesley, Rosalind P., *The Arts and Crafts Movement*, London, 2009
Bosley, Edward R., *Greene & Greene*, London, 2000
—, 'Two Sides of the River: Morris and American Arts & Crafts', in Waggoner (2003), pp. 134–67
Carruthers, Annette, *The Arts and Crafts Movement in Scotland: A History*, New Haven and London, 2013
— and Mary Greensted (eds), *Simplicity or Splendour: Arts and Crafts Living: Objects from the Cheltenham Collections*, London, 1999
—, Mary Greensted and Barley Roscoe, *Ernest Gimson: Arts & Crafts Designer and Architect*, New Haven and London, 2019
Cook, Martin Godfrey, *Edward Prior: Arts and Crafts Architect*, Ramsbury, 2015
Cormack, Peter, *Arts & Crafts Stained Glass*, New Haven and London, 2015
Crawford, Alan, *C.R. Ashbee: Architect, Designer & Romantic Socialist*, New Haven and London, 2005
Cumming, Elizabeth and Wendy Kaplan, *The Arts and Crafts Movement*, London, 1991
E.B.S., 'Some Recent Designs by Mr. C.F.A. Voysey', *The Studio*, 7:38 (May 1896), pp. 209–18
Evans, Stuart and Jean Liddiard, *Arts and Crafts Pioneers: The Hobby Horse Men and their Century Guild*, London, 2021
Faulkner, Rupert, *Japanese Studio Crafts: Tradition and the Avant-Garde*, London, 1995
Fontán del Junco, Manuel and María Zozaya Álvarez (eds), *William Morris y compañía: el movimiento Arts & Crafts en Gran Bretaña*, exh. cat., Madrid, 2017
Gordon Bowe, Nicola and Elizabeth Cumming, *The Arts and Crafts Movements in Dublin & Edinburgh, 1885–1925*, Dublin, 1998
Greensted, Mary (ed.), *An Anthology of the Arts and Crafts Movement: Writings by Ashbee, Lethaby, Gimson and their Contemporaries*, Aldershot, 2005
Griffin, Julia and Andrzej Szczerski (eds), *Young Poland: The Polish Arts and Crafts Movement 1890–1918*, London, 2020
Harrod, Tanya, *The Crafts in Britain in the 20th Century*, New Haven and London, 1999
Haslam, Sara. E., *John Ruskin and the Lakeland Arts Revival, 1880–1920*, Cardiff, 2004
Helland, Janice, *British and Irish Home Arts and Industries, 1880–1914*, Dublin, 2007
Kaplan, Wendy, *'The Art that is Life': The Arts and Crafts Movement in America, 1875–1925*, Boston, 1987
Kikuchi, Yuko, 'A Japanese William Morris: Yanagi Sôetsu and *Mingei* Theory', *JWMS*, 12:2 (Spring 1997), pp. 39–45
— and Toshio Watanabe, *Ruskin in Japan 1890–1940: Nature for Art, Art for Life*, Tokyo, 1997
Kirkham, Pat and Susan Weber (eds), *History of Design: Decorative Arts and Material Culture, 1400–2000*, New York, 2013
Livingstone, Karen and Linda Parry (eds), *International Arts and Crafts*, exh. cat., London, 2005
Livingstone, Karen with Max Donnelly and Linda Parry, *C.F.A. Voysey: Arts & Crafts Designer*, London, 2016
Mason, Anna, Jan Marsh, Jenny Lister, Rowan Bain and Hanne Faurby, *May Morris: Arts & Crafts Designer*, London, 2017
Nakayama, Shuichi, 'The Impact of William Morris in Japan, 1 904 to the Present', *Journal of Design History*, 9:4 (1996), pp. 273–83
Peck, Amelia and Carol Irish, *Candace Wheeler: The Art and Enterprise of American Design 1875–1900*, New York, 2001
Shi, David E., *The Simple Life: Plain Living and High Thinking in American Culture*, New York and Oxford, 1985
Snodin, Michael and Elisabet Stavenow-Hidemark, *Carl and Karin Larsson: Creators of the Swedish Style*, London, 1997
Stickley, Gustav, *Craftsman Homes: Architecture and Furnishings of the American Arts and Crafts Movement*, New York, 1909; reprinted by Dover Publications, 1979
Thomas, Zoë, *Women Art Workers and the Arts and Crafts Movement*, Manchester, 2020
Ueland, Hanne Bate (ed.), *Frida Hansen – Art Nouveau i Full Blomst (Frida Hansen: Art Nouveau in Full Bloom)*, Stavanger, 2015
Voysey, C.F.A., 'The Value of Hidden Influences as Disclosed in the Life of One Ordinary Man', unpublished typescript, RIBA VoC/4/6, 1931
de Waal, Edmund, *Bernard Leach*, London, 1997

ONLINE RESOURCES

Burne-Jones Catalogue Raisonné, eb-j.org
The William Morris Internet Archive, marxists.org/archive/morris
Boos, Florence S. (ed.), *William Morris Archive*, morrisarchive.lib.uiowa.edu
McGann, Jerome (ed.), *The Rossetti Archive. The Complete Writings and Pictures of Dante Gabriel Rossetti*, rossettiarchive.org
Peterson, William S. and Sylvia Holton Peterson (eds), *The Kelmscott Chaucer*, kelmscottchaucer.wordpress.com
— (eds), *The Library of William Morris. A Catalogue*, williammorrislibrary.wordpress.com

NOTES ON AUTHORS

Stephen Astley previously worked in the Designs section of the Collection of Prints, Drawings and Paintings at the V&A and was subsequently Curator of Drawings at the Sir John Soane's Museum.

Mary Bennett was formerly Keeper of British Art at the Walker Art Gallery, Liverpool, having begun her career at the William Morris Gallery. She originated three ground-breaking exhibitions in the 1960s on Ford Madox Brown, John Everett Millais and William Holman Hunt. Her publications include *Ford Madox Brown: A Catalogue Raisonné* (2010).

Frances Collard was formerly Curator of British nineteenth-century objects in the Furniture and Woodwork Collections at the V&A. She has published on various aspects of nineteenth-century furniture design, including *Regency Furniture* (1985).

John Dreyfus (1918–2002) was a typographer and printing historian. He was Typographical Adviser to Cambridge University Press and the Monotype Corporation. His appointments included President of the Printing Historical Society and he published widely, including *Into Print* (1994).

Peter Faulkner taught English at Fircroft College, Birmingham, the University of Durham, and the University of Exeter until his retirement in 1998. He is a former editor of *The Journal of William Morris Studies* and a former Honorary Secretary of the William Morris Society.

Julia Griffin is a Courtauld-trained art historian and curator specializing in Victorian art and design. She is a contributor to *The Routledge Companion to William Morris* (2021), co-editor of *Young Poland: The Polish Arts and Crafts Movement 1890–1918* (2020) and co-curator of the accompanying exhibition at the William Morris Gallery (2021).

Martin Harrison FSA writes and lectures widely on stained glass and twentieth-century art. He has published *Victorian Stained Glass* (1980) and *Francis Bacon: Catalogue Raisonné* (2016). He is Editor-in-Chief of the Estate of Francis Bacon Publishing and was guest editor of *The Journal of Stained Glass*, 'Medievalism: Special Issue' (2019).

Charles Harvey is Professor of Business History and Management and Director of the Centre for Research on Entrepreneurship, Wealth and Philanthropy at Newcastle University. **Jon Press** is the Managing Director of Grange Park Consulting. He was formerly Professor of Business Entrepreneurship and Registrar at Falmouth University. Together they are the authors of numerous publications including *William Morris: Design and Enterprise in Victorian Britain* (1991) and *Art, Enterprise and Ethics: The Life and Works of William Morris* (1996).

Lesley Hoskins specializes in the material culture of British homes and institutions in the nineteenth and twentieth centuries. She edited *The Papered Wall* (2005) and has been curator of several collections relating to domestic interiors, including Sanderson's archive.

Tristram Hunt has been Director of the V&A since 2017. Prior to joining the V&A, Dr Hunt was Labour MP for Stoke-on-Trent Central and Shadow Secretary of State for Education. He has a doctorate in Victorian history from Cambridge University.

Karen Livingstone is a Deputy Director at the Fitzwilliam Museum, University of Cambridge, previously holding senior roles at the Science Museum Group and the V&A. Her publications include *International Arts and Crafts* (with Linda Parry, 2005) and *C.F.A Voysey: Arts & Crafts Designer* (with Linda Parry and Max Donnelly, 2016).

Fiona MacCarthy (1940–2020) was a biographer and critic who wrote extensively on nineteenth- and twentieth-century design. Her publications included *Eric Gill* (1989), *William Morris* (1994), *The Last Pre-Raphaelite* (2011) and *Walter Gropius* (2019). In 2014 she curated *Anarchy & Beauty*, an exhibition on Morris's legacy at the National Portrait Gallery.

Anna Mason is former curator and manager of the William Morris Gallery and has worked for the National Trust at Red House, Bexleyheath. She contributed to *May Morris: Arts & Crafts Designer* (2017) and is currently co-editing the correspondence of May Morris.

Chris Miele is a chartered planner and senior partner at Montagu Evans, a London-based property consultancy. He trained as an architectural historian (PhD) and continues to maintain that profile through publications, lectures and affiliations with the University of Leicester and the University of Glasgow, where he is an Honorary Professor.

John Nash has studied and taught calligraphy and lettering since 1968 and was the first American chairman of the Society of Scribes and Illuminators. He is the co-author of *Practical Calligraphy* (with Gerald Fleuss, 1992).

Jennifer Hawkins Opie was former Head of Ceramics and Glass Collections at the V&A and specializes in nineteenth- and twentieth-century studies. She contributed to and was responsible for many V&A exhibitions and publications, including *Minton, 1798–1910* (1976); *Art and Design in Europe and America, 1800–1900* (1987); *Art Nouveau, 1890–1914* (2000) and *Art Deco, 1910–1939* (2003).

Linda Parry MBE FSA is former Deputy Keeper of the Department of Furniture, Textiles and Fashion at the V&A, where she worked for over thirty years. Her publications include *Textiles of the Arts and Crafts Movement* (1988), *William Morris* (1996) and *William Morris Textiles* (2013). She curated the landmark centenary exhibition *William Morris* at the V&A in 1996. She is past President of the William Morris Society, was Honorary Curator at Kelmscott Manor and is a patron of Red House.

Nicholas Salmon (1957–2002) was a Morris scholar. He edited and introduced two volumes of Morris's socialist writings: *Political Writings* (1994) and *Journalism* (1996). Other publications included *William Morris on History* (1996), *The William Morris Chronology* (with Derek Baker, 1996) and many articles. He was editor of *The Journal of the William Morris Society* (1996–2001) and co-founded 'The William Morris Internet Archive'.

Eric Turner was previously a curator in the Metalwork Department of the V&A for 44 years. He has published and lectured extensively, nationally and internationally, on nineteenth- and twentieth-century metalwork subjects.

ACKNOWLEDGMENTS

First and foremost our thanks go to Linda Parry for her inspiring scholarship, for which her fellow contributors pay especial tribute.

We are very grateful to the many librarians, archivists, curators and individuals who have enriched this book in numerous ways and given so generously of their time and expertise. Current and former colleagues at the William Morris Gallery, Walthamstow, have been unfailingly supportive and this endeavour owes much to their knowledge and collaboration; special thanks go to Rowan Bain, Roisin Inglesby, Carien Kremer and Ainsley Vinall. During the extraordinary circumstances of 2020, Ainsley's commitment to facilitating remote access to the collections and archive has been hugely appreciated. Florence S. Boos and Kimberly Maher (University of Iowa) have answered endless enquiries with great patience and kindness and the resources and scholarship they have made freely accessible through the William Morris Archive have been invaluable. Peter Cormack, Max Donnelly (Curator of Nineteenth-Century Furniture, V&A), Hans van Lemmen, Jan Marsh, Bridget Salmon, David Saxby, Frank C. Sharp, Jevon Thistlewood (Ashmolean Museum) and Tessa Wild have provided critical help and expertise. We also wish to thank Anna Norman for allowing us to read and quote from the diary of her great-great-grandfather David Parr and Tatjana LeBoff for bringing the letter from Constance, Lady Leconfield, in the archive at Petworth to our attention.

A catalogue of names fails to do justice to the many ways the following individuals have provided inspiration and assistance but we thank them all warmly. Ming Aguilar (Huntington Library, Art Museum and Botanical Gardens), Leif Anderson (Stanford University), John Aplin, Elly Bagnall (Red House, National Trust), Kate Bagnall (Society of Antiquaries), Helen Bratt-Wyton (Wightwick Manor, National Trust), Eleanor Brooke-Peat (Castle Howard), Helena Buqué (St John the Baptist, Findon), Jordan Busson, Alastair Carew-Cox, Moya Carey, Annette Carruthers, David and Angela Chalmers, Hugo Chapman (British Museum), Jim Cheshire (University of Lincoln), Brian Clarke, Jane Cohen, Helena Collett (National Trust), Caroline Corbeau-Parsons (Tate), Tom Corrick (Oxford Union Society), Alan Crawford, Colin Cruise (Aberystwyth University), Vanya and Viggo Dickens, Yvette Dickerson (London Library), Anna and Piotr Dudkiewicz, Jane Eade (National Trust), Helen Elletson (William Morris Society and Emery Walker's House), Donato Esposito, Simon Evans (The National Library of Wales), Emma Ferry (Nottingham Trent University), Margaretta Frederick (Delaware Art Museum), Melanie Gardner (Tullie House Museum and Art Gallery), Tracee J. Glab (Flint Institute of Arts), Maggie Goodall (Society for the Protection of Ancient Buildings), Ted Griffin, Emma Hardy, Sarah Hardy (The De Morgan Foundation), Clara Harrow (The Baring Archive), Kirsty Hartsiotis (The Wilson Art Gallery and Museum, Cheltenham), Kathy Haslam (Kelmscott Manor, Society of Antiquaries), Mallory Horrill (Emery Walker's House), Roger Huddle (Friends of the William Morris Gallery), Lynn Hulse, Sally-Anne Huxtable (National Trust), James Joll, Brenda M. King, Karin Kyburz (Courtauld Institute of Art), Dennis T. Lanigan, Mark Samuels Lasner (University of Delaware Library, Museums and Press), Ayla Lepine, Martin Levy, Bryan Maggs (The Wormsley Library), Heidi L. Meyer (Lord Leycester Hospital), María Isabel Molestina (The Morgan Library & Museum), Stephanie Moser (University of Southampton), Dru Muskovin (Crab Tree Farm), Hilary Myers and the late Richard Myers, Peter Nahum (The Leicester Galleries), Shirley Nicholson (18 Stafford Terrace), Patricia O'Connor, Jimmy Page, Caroline Palmer (Ashmolean Museum), Domniki Papadimitriou (Cambridge University Library), Don Parry, Victoria Partridge (The Higgins Bedford), Nicole Perry (Red House, National Trust), William S. Peterson and Sylvia Holton Peterson, Lorraine Price Bowsher, Keren Protheroe (Sanderson Design Group Archive), Paul Reeves, Jill Reichenbach (New-York Historical Society), Bob Richardson (St Bride Foundation), Caroline Riedel (University of Victoria Legacy Art Galleries), George Roberts (National Trust), Michael Robertson (The College of New Jersey), Fiona Rose, Chris Rowlin (National Trust), Douglas E. Schoenherr, Kath Shawcross (Hammersmith & Fulham Archives), Paul A. Shutler, Liam Sims (Cambridge University Library), Martin Stott, Dawn Thorndycraft, Sarah Vowles (British Museum), Frank Waterton (Society of Antiquaries), Victoria West (Society for the Protection of Ancient Buildings), Michael and Mariko Whiteway, Stephen Wildman (University of Lancaster), Stuart Williams (Bradfield College), Matthew Winterbottom (Ashmolean Museum) and Victoria Witty (Standen, National Trust).

The kind assistance of V&A colleagues has been crucial, especially Claire Allen-Johnstone, Keiron Boyle, Zorian Clayton, Richard Davies, Joanne Dodd, Eloise Donnelly, Sarah Duncan, Catriona Gourlay, Joanne Hackett, Ruth Hibbard, Alexandra Jones, Peter Kelleher, Jenny Lister, Christopher Marsden, Nika Narkeviciute, Paul Robins, Suzanne Smith, Florence Tyler, Melanie Vandenbrouck and Catherine Yvard.

At the V&A Publishing team it has been a pleasure to work with Jane Ace, Coralie Hepburn, Andrew Tullis and Tom Windross. Lucy Macmillan provided expert and meticulous assistance with picture research. Development Editor Hannah Newell deserves special mention for her professionalism, input and support – we could not have done it without her. At Thames & Hudson, thanks go to Julian Honer, Susannah Lawson and Avni Patel as well as to Senior Editor Julia MacKenzie for the great care and sensitivity with which she has overseen this project. We would also like to thank the designer, Ocky Murray, for all his efforts.

The editor extends her warmest appreciation to all the contributors and dedicates her part in this endeavour to Roger and Helen Mason, and in loving memory of Carol Birch (1950–2014).

PICTURE CREDITS

All images are © Victoria and Albert Museum, London, unless otherwise stated.

Adam's Auctioneers fig.242; Art Gallery of South Australia, Adelaide, Mrs Mary Overton Gift Fund 1999, 996F2 fig.163; © Ashmolean Museum, University of Oxford figs 113, 166, 170, VI.4, IX.5; Gertrude Bell Archive, Newcastle University (PERS_U_046) fig.148; Photo Birmingham Museums Trust, licensed under CC0 Acquired with Art Fund support (with a contribution from The Wolfson Foundation) and with the assistance of the V&A Purchase Grant Fund, The John Feeney Charitable Trust and the Public Picture Gallery Fund, 2016 VII.1b; Photo Birmingham Museums Trust, licensed under CC0 figs 180, 185, 215, VI.13, VII.6, XII.34, IX.18, XII.57; © Bodleian Library, University of Oxford 2021 XIII.4, XIII.6, XIII.9–13; St Bride Foundation figs 212, 224, XIV.3; Photo Bridwell Library Special Collections, SMU fig.17; © British Library Board, All Rights Reserved/Bridgeman Images figs 31, 55, 56, 106, 205, 218, XIII.3, XIII.7; © The Trustees of the British Museum figs 8, 12, 221, VI.9, X.12, XIV.21, XIV.25–6; Courtesy of Bullers Wood School fig.213; By permission of the Syndics of Cambridge University Library XIV.9, XIV.32; Photo © Alastair Carew-Cox, Seraphim Press Ltd figs 115, 117, 121–4, 128, 131–3, 136, 138–9; David Chalmers Photography fig.120; The Cheltenham Trust and Cheltenham Borough Council/Bridgeman Images fig.63, IX.2, XIV.6, XIV.22; Jim Cheshire fig.116; © Christie's Images Limited fig.220, IX.3 (detail); Photo Chronicle/Alamy Stock Photo fig.60; The Brian Clarke Collection of Stained Glass VII.16; Photo © Country Life/Future Publishing Limited fig.164; Photo The Courtauld Institute of Art, London fig.94; Crab Tree Farm, Illinois XII.89; Delaware Art Museum/Bridgeman Images fig.20, IX.3 (reverse); Delaware Art Museum, Wilmington, FV DuPont Acquisition Fund 1985 fig.135; Mark Samuels Lasner Collection, University of Delaware Library, Museums and Press fig.156; Kevin Eaves/Alamy Stock Photo fig.74; Published with permission of the Rector and Scholars of Exeter College, Oxford VII.17; © The Fitzwilliam Museum, Cambridge figs 45, 101, VII.10, XII.115, XIV.27; Photo Helmut Gernsheim/Warburg Institute, Source: Historic England Archive fig.146; Photo Getty Images fig.3; Collection of the Guild of St George, Museums Sheffield fig.91; Guildhall Art Gallery, City of London fig.88; Hammersmith & Fulham Archives fig.199; Photo Martin Harrison figs 125, 130; © Historic England Archive figs 35, 68, 134, 150–2, 154, 192, 200, 203; Mark Horn/Getty Images fig.75; Reproduced by kind permission of the Howard Family XII.4, XII.88; Photo Hulton Archive/Getty Images figs 7, 77; © Courtesy of the Huntington Art Museum, San Marino, California figs 33, 39, 99, VI.3a, VI.3b, VI.3c, VI.21, VII.19, X.10, XII.13, XII.25–6, XII.44, XII.101, XIV.5, XIV.8, XIV.7, XIV.19b, XIV.15; International Institute of Social History, Amsterdam figs 53, 59, 62; Photo Dennis Jeffrey fig.70; Jesus College, Cambridge, photo Chris Loades figs 126–7; Kelmscott Manor, Oxfordshire, UK/Bridgeman Images fig.160; Photo Peter Kelleher fig.81; Labadie Collection, University of Michigan fig.237; www.lacma.org IX.21; © The Bernard Leach Family. All rights reserved, DACS 2021 fig.256; Leeds Museums and Art Galleries (Temple Newsam House) UK/Bridgeman Images fig.195; Hans van Lemmen X.17a–b; Courtesy of the Patron, Governors and Master of the Lord Leycester Hospital, Warwick VII.26; © Manchester Metropolitan University Special Collections Museum fig.61; Photo Lucy Macmillan fig.179; Marx Memorial Library & Workers' School, London, photo Prudence Cummings Associates fig.64; The Metropolitan Museum of Art, New York, Rogers Fund, 1926 Acc. No. 2654 fig.171, IX.15; The Morgan Library & Museum, New York, MA 4011, Gift of Norman Strouse, 1975 fig.219; The Morgan Library & Museum, New York, PML 139, Purchased with the Bennett collection, 1902 XIV.4; The Morgan Library & Museum, New York, PML 769234, Gift of John M. Crawford, Jr, 1975 XIV.23; © William Morris Gallery, London Borough of Waltham Forest endpapers, figs 1, 2, 11, 28, 32, 40, 44, 47, 50–1, 54, 58, 66, 114, 176, 177, 193, 194, 210, VI.14, VII.31, X.4, X.7, X.8, X.13, X.21a, XI.11, XI.26, XI.28, XII.2, XII.12, XIV.12a, XIV.18; William Morris Gallery, London Borough of Waltham Forest, photo © Paul Tucker figs 27, 108, 111–12, 204, VI.10, VII.7, VII.18, IX.4, IX.27, X.12, XI.15a, XII.15, XII.95–6, XII.109; © The William Morris Society frontispiece, figs 22, 29, 48, VIII.10–13, XI.6, XI.7b, XI.18–XI.20a, XI.22a–b, XI.29, XII.55, XII.67; © Musée d'Orsay Dist RMN-Grand Palais, photo Patrice Schmidt XII.119; Courtesy The Dennis T. Lanigan Collection, National Gallery of Canada VI.11; National Galleries of Scotland, Purchased with assistance from the Art Fund 1999 fig.69; By kind permission of The National Library of Wales figs 87, 93; © National Portrait Gallery, London figs 14, 16, 65; © National Gallery, London fig.107; © National Trust Images/Andrew Butler fig.6; © National Trust Images/James Breslin fig.144; © National Trust Images/Andreas von Einsiedel figs 141–3, 145, 162; © National Trust Images/Sophia Farley and Claire Reeves VI.23; © National Trust Images/Paul Highnam fig.214; Reproduced by kind permission of the National Trust, photo Peter Kelleher figs 159, 174–5, VI.8, VI.15, IX.24, IX.29; © New-York Historical Society fig.211; Courtesy The Oxford Union Society, photo Peter Kelleher figs 21, 23, 109, VI.6–7; Collection Jimmy Page, courtesy Paul Reeves, London XII.120a–b; Private collection/Bridgeman Images XII.24; Private collection/© Christie's Images/Bridgeman Images XIII.14; By permission of Queens' College Cambridge, photo Robin D.H. Walker, 2020 fig.173; RIBA Collections fig.198; Photo © RMN-Grand Palais (Musée d'Orsay)/Hervé Lewandowski fig.165; Courtesy Royal Borough of Kensington and Chelsea, photo Peter Kelleher fig.201; Reproduced by kind permission of Salisbury Cathedral fig.129; Courtesy of Sanderson Design Group fig.188, XI.8–9, XI.13b, XI.24, XI.30–1; Suzy Covey Comic Book Collection, Special and Area Studies Collections, George A. Smathers Libraries, University of Florida, Gainesville, FL, USA fig.83; © The Society of Antiquaries of London fig.97, XIV.1b, XIV.31; © The Society of Antiquaries of London (Kelmscott Manor) fig.10, VI.17, IX.10, IX.19, XIII.2; Courtesy The Society of Antiquaries of London (Kelmscott Manor), photo Peter Kelleher fig.206, IX.8, IX.11, IX.17, IX.23, XI.I3, XII.1, XII.105; Courtesy of the Society for the Protection of Ancient Buildings (SPAB) figs 82, 85–6, 90, 96; Courtesy of the Society for the Protection of Ancient Buildings (SPAB)/William Morris Gallery, London Borough of Waltham Forest © Paul Tucker fig.95; Courtesy of Sotheby's XII.98; State Library of South Australia/PRG 733/438 fig.153; Photo © Tate, London, 2021 figs 103–5, VI.12, VI.19, VII.4, VII.9, VIII.1; Nicholas Temple-Fry/Alamy Stock Photo fig.79; From the collections at Tullie House Museum, Carlisle VI.20; © Tyne & Wear Archives & Museums/Bridgeman Images fig.137; Colin Underhill/Alamy Stock Photo fig.89; Courtesy University of Victoria Legacy Art Galleries, Canada Gift of Edmund Parker Image © Art Gallery of Ontario, Photo Robert Keziere XI.14; Courtesy Michael and Mariko Whiteway fig.202; © The Whitworth, University of Manchester 2021 XII.36; © The Trustees of the Wormsley Fund fig.49, XIII.1, XIII.8; © Estate of Leo Wyatt fig.222.

INDEX

The various aspects of Morris's work and interests are listed directly under their names, for example, embroidery, stained glass, writings, etc. Page numbers in *italic* refer to the illustrations.